THEOLOGY AND CONVERSATION

BIBLIOTHECA EPHEMERIDUM THEOLOGICARUM LOVANIENSIUM

CLXXII

THEOLOGY AND CONVERSATION

TOWARDS A RELATIONAL THEOLOGY

EDITED BY

J. HAERS & P. DE MEY

LEUVEN
UNIVERSITY PRESS

UITGEVERIJ PEETERS
LEUVEN

2003

ISBN 90 5867 338 3 (Leuven University Press)
D/2003/1869/63
ISBN 90-429-1388-6 (Peeters Leuven)
D/2003/0602/140

Library of Congress Cataloging-in-Publication Data

Theology and conversation : towards a relational theology / edited by J. Haers & P. De Mey.
    p.cm -- (Bibliotheca Ephemeridum theologicarum Lovaniensium ; 172)
    Includes bibliographical references.
    ISBN 90-429-1388-6 (alk. paper)
    1. Theology--Methodology--Congresses. 2. Catholic Church--Doctrines--Congresses.
    3. Religious pluralism--Catholic Church--Congresses. 4. Dialogue--Religious aspects--
Catholic Church--Congresses. I. Haers, Jacques. II. De Mey, P. III. Series.

BX1751.3.T48 2003
230--dc22
                                                                            2003062385

Leuven University Press / Presses Universitaires de Louvain
Universitaire Pers Leuven
Blijde-Inkomststraat 5, B-3000 Leuven (Belgium)

© 2003 – Peeters, Bondgenotenlaan 153, B-3000 Leuven (Belgium)

PREFACE

This collection of articles presents the main contributions to the third LEST (Louvain Encounters in Systematic Theology) conference, held at the K.U.Leuven's Faculty of Theology, November 2001. Its theme, *Theology and Conversation: Towards a Relational Theology*, continues the explorations in contemporary theology as set out in the 1997 LEST I conference on *The Myriad Christ* (BETL 152) and in the 1999 LEST II conference on *Sacramental Presence in a Postmodern Context* (BETL 160). In LEST III also, the plurality and diversity of theological approaches play a major role and the question is raised whether the contemporary theological endeavour in a global world contains in itself the tools to respectfully and constructively approach this diversity. The ideas of relation and conversation, as found in the theologies of the Trinity and of creation, as presupposed in ecclesial praxis, and as articulated in reflections that take their bearings from spiritual experience, provide a powerful means for renewed theological reflection capable of confronting plurality and diversity.

The keynote lectures and some of the papers presented at the congress have, therefore, been collected under three headings. In the first part, *Reflecting on God and Creation: Conversation and Trinity*, the reader will find fundamental reflections on biblical and methodological issues, relational approaches to creation and eschatology, and contributions to contemporary theology of the Trinity. The second part, *Reflecting on the Church and the World: Conversation and Ecclesiology*, analyses the multifaceted reality of conversation as an ecclesial praxis. Some papers touch issues of conversation in the Roman Catholic Church. Others emphasize the dialogue between churches and religions in a plural world. Still other contributions touch on very specific situations in which ecclesial conversation has played or still plays an important role. The third part, *Reflecting on Theology and Spirituality: Conversation as a Paradigm for Theology*, suggests a renewed theological methodology, drawing from the historically complex relationships between theology and spirituality as well as from theological aesthetics understood as a conversation between theology and the arts, more particularly literature and music.

We hope that all of these contributions will challenge theologians into re-thinking and re-articulating their concepts from a relational and conversational perspective. In that sense, this book offers the basic outline for a worldwide theological research project.

We want to express our gratitude towards the many people who have cooperated both in the success of the conference itself and in the realization of this publication. The LEST conferences constitute a bi-annual initiative of the Research Department of Dogmatic Theology of the Faculty of Theology, K.U.Leuven. Without the active support and cooperation of all the professors, assistants, researchers and collaborators of this department, LEST conferences do not come about. Our gratitude goes to all of them and most particularly to Drs. Johan Ardui, who deserves to be named in particular, as he has been taking care of the complex practical arrangements of the conference. Prof. Dr. Mathijs Lamberigts, Dean of the Faculty of Theology, together with many other benefactors made possible the acquisition of an African piece of Sango art, *Spiritual Trio* by Chituwa Jemali, which is now on permanent display in our Theological Library. We also thank the staff of the Secretariat and of the Library of the Faculty of Theology: their generous commitment and patient assistance has represented an invaluable support. Many doctoral students helped out at the conference secretariat and a group of our Flemish students provided the necessary support for the many coffee breaks during the conference.

In the preparation of these proceedings, apart from the main editors, several devoted collaborators have been involved: Johan Ardui, Krista Carreel, Arni Clamor, Paul Da Ponte, Edmund Guzman, Denis Robinson and Joeri Schrijvers. This book would not have seen the light of day without their work.

We would also like to express our gratitude to the Fund for Scientific Research (F.W.O.-Vlaanderen), the Research Council (Onderzoeksraad) of the K.U.Leuven, and the Netherlands School for Advanced Studies in Theology and Religion (NOSTER) for their generous financial support.

We are grateful to Prof. Dr. Gilbert Van Belle, general editor of BETL, and Peeters Publishers for the opportunity to publish this book in the prestigious BETL series.

Apart from this collection of contributions, a separate Dutch-language publication is dedicated to the conversation between theology and spirituality[1]. We wish the readers a pleasant journey through the various contributions and we challenge all of them to pursue the conversational endeavour of theology.

Jacques HAERS
Peter DE MEY

1. P. DE MEY – J. HAERS (eds.), *Theologie en spiritualiteit. Het gesprek heropend*, Leuven, Acco, 2004.

CONTENTS

II

REFLECTING ON THE CHURCH AND THE WORLD
CONVERSATION AND ECCLESIOLOGY

III

REFLECTING ON THEOLOGY AND SPIRITUALITY CONVERSATION AS A PARADIGM FOR THEOLOGY

DEFENSOR VINCULI ET CONVERSATIONIS

CONNECTEDNESS AND CONVERSATION
AS A CHALLENGE TO THEOLOGY

I. INTRODUCTION

The fact that so many of you have come to participate in this gathering and, more so, have volunteered contributions, reflects the importance of the theme of this third of the Louvain Encounters in Systematic Theology. I think it results from what I would describe negatively as a feeling of uneasiness, frustration or dissatisfaction with theologies that seem to have lost their touch with reality while failing to respond to a lot of the questions and problems of our contemporary world suffering from the clash of identities and the desires for global control. The hermeneutical circle between theology and reality as construed by some of our "classic" approaches, does not seem to fit in well with what one may expect from theology as a stimulating articulation of reality, that allows to formulate creative and responsible answers to real life challenges. Of course, this frustration can be restated in a more positive way, as precisely the desire for such responsive, committed and responsible theologies. And even more than a desire, there seems to be an intuition that theological reflection building on key or root metaphors as "relation", "encounter", "connectedness" and "conversation", may well prove to be a good candidate for a renewed and fruitful interaction with reality. This conference constitutes an attempt at exploring and researching this intuition of a fresh theological style, understood here as a research programme, in the sense proposed by Imre Lakatos[1]. By preferring the expression "research programme" over the more common idea of

---

1. I. LAKATOS, *Falsification and the Methodology of Scientific Research Programmes*, in ID. – A. MUSGRAVE (eds.), *Criticism and the Growth of Knowledge: Proceedings of the International Colloquium in the Philosophy of Sciences*, London, 1965, Vol. 4, London, Cambridge University Press, 1976 [1970], 91-196. See also, particularly with regard to Paul Feyerabend's criticism of the very idea of "method": I. LAKATOS – P. FEYERABEND, *For and Against Method: Including Lakatos's Lectures on Scientific Method and the Lakatos-Feyerabend Correspondence*, Edited and with an Introduction by M. MOTTERLINI, Chicago, IL – London, The University of Chicago Press, 1999.

paradigm change, I want to indicate, among other things, that the word "fresh", as used above, does not mean "radically new". In fact, we are following the footsteps of a respectful theological tradition as will show our references to two of its main representatives, Origen of Alexandria at the onset of Christianity and Karl Rahner in the course of the twentieth century. The negative heuristics of this research programme continue to point to the untouchable core of Christian theology, the saving and healing Creator God encountered in Jesus Christ, while its positive heuristics, using the root metaphors of encounter, relation and conversation, facilitate the interaction with our contemporary world and, in so doing, suggest a renewed exploration and articulation of the inalienable core of the research programme.

While preparing this conference, choices had to be made. So, in the coming days, we will explore the proposed research programme mainly from three perspectives, God, creation, the church and the world in which we live. What is the impact of our root metaphors on these fundamental theological themes? Moreover, could the use of these metaphors shed new light on the troubled history of the relations between theology and spirituality, and open the door for a new covenant between both, also in the form of a renewed theology of religious life and a spirituality of friendship? All of these are important issues debated between theologians today; taken together they cover many of the challenges posed by the new worldviews of postmodernity and globalization, by the stormy waters of interreligious dialogue and plural cultures, and by the search for an empowering and holistic approach to life capable, in a more or less satisfactory way, to tackle the multifacetted and unsettling suffering caused by worldwide poverty, insecurity, environmental degradation and injustice. The goal of our conference is also, through the detailed study of these particular perspectives, to reach a better description and articulation of the research programme itself, to clarify the meaning of our root metaphors, and to solidify our intuitions to the extent that the very research programme become a subject of conversation and exchange, without, however, grinding to the standstill of a hegemonic and static frame of thought. To facilitate this process, I attempt at the onset of this conference to formulate the research programme as a hypothesis by stating what seem to me to be two of its main features: (1) the root metaphors of relation, encounter, connectedness and conversation, provide a solid basis for a creative and fruitful re-articulation of theological ideas and methods today, and (2) this re-articulation, if and only if it takes into account the preferential option for the poor, offers the possibility to confront the main challenges posed today in our globalized world, allowing to formulate clearly these challenges and to discover thought and action provoking avenues into them. As a consequence, to take on the role of *defensor vinculi ac conversationis*, of a defender of the bond and the conversation, is not only an interesting theoretical position; it represents as well an urgently needed and effective existential commitment to our world.

Among the contemporary challenges, we find the need to "warm up" our theologies by reaffirming and strengthening their connection with spirituality as had already been done with regard to ethics and praxis, and we also find the call to open up to a conversation between religions taking into account the complexities of a plural world and recognizing the encounters with the others as a holy ground on which also God is encountered. However, the most important and most urgent challenge seems to me to consist in a commitment to those multitudes of people suffering the apalling worldwide injustices of war, conflict, poverty and degradation of the environment. Of course, all of these challenges are interconnected as Hans Küng and Leonardo Boff have pointed out[2]. Such commitment will be honest, creative and effective only if reflecting a preferential option for the poor[3], meaning the desire, the will and the ability to struggle in close connectedness with the suffering people against the evil that causes pain and exclusion. It calls for a theology that reflects connectedness as one of its most intimate core characteristics[4]. Theologians will have to be particularly attentive for their thinking, however well intentioned it may be, not to continue and intensify the very suffering they want to fight. They will, therefore, attempt to put at the centre of their thought something which they will never be able to fully integrate or to control: compassion and the wound resulting from

2. H. KÜNG, *Global Responsibility: In Search of a New World Ethic*, London, SCM, 1991; L. BOFF, *Cry of the Earth, Cry of the Poor*, Maryknoll, NY, Orbis Books, 1997.

3. E.g. G. GUTIÉRREZ, *The Power of the Poor in History*, Maryknoll, NY, Orbis Books, 1984; ID., *Essential Writings*, edited with an Introduction by J.B. NICKOLOFF, London, SCM, 1996; ID., *Option pour les pauvres: bilan et enjeux*, in *Alternatives Sud* 7 (2000/1) 27-37; J. O'BRIEN, *Theology and the Option for the Poor* (Theology and Life Series, 22), Collegeville, MN, Liturgical Press, 1992; D. DORR, *Option for the Poor: A Hundred Years of Catholic Social Teaching*, Maryknoll, NY, Orbis Books, 1992; ID., *Option for the Poor Re-Visited*, in J.S. BOSWELL – F.P. MCHUGH – J. VERSTRAETEN (eds.), *Catholic Social Thought: Twilight or Renaissance?* (BETL, 157), Leuven, University Press – Peeters, 2000, 249-262; J. SOBRINO, *Theology from amidst the Victims*, in M. VOLF – C. KRIEG – T. KUCHARZ (eds.), *The Future of Theology: Essays in Honor of Jürgen Moltmann*, Grand Rapids, MI – Cambridge, U.K., William B. Eerdmans, 1996, 164-175; N.F. LOHFINK, *Option for the Poor: The Basic Principle of Liberation Theology in the Light of the Bible* (Berkeley Lecture Series, 1), Berkeley, CA, Bibal Press, 1987.

4. E.g. SOBRINO, *Bearing with One Another in Faith*, in ID. – J. HERNANDEZ PICO, *Theology of Christian Solidarity*, Maryknoll, NY, Orbis Books, 1985, 1-42.

the impact of the cry of the voiceless[5]. They will then, hopefully, come to trust the creativity that arises in the midst of poverty as the surest sign of God's presence. I am convinced that theologies shaped by our root metaphors – relation, encounter, connectedness, and conversation – offer the best chances to be truthful to this most urgent of challenges. Of course, one will have to remain critical: speaking about fulfilling relations may disguise profound egoism. The focus should, therefore, always also be, by including them in our relational webs or by paying due attention to their webs, on those who do not participate in our webs of connectedness, those we exclude and by whose exclusion we perversely attempt to construe our selfish togetherness[6]. Given this critical awareness, I will stress that the use of our root metaphors proves fruitful not only for theology, but also for any other committed analysis of reality: re-evaluating our models of analysis from the perspective of relation, encounter, connectedness and conversation will provide new insights that may very well lead to creative new modes of action.

I will not here present an overview of what will be offered over the coming days. Suffice it to say that the elaboration of the proposed research programma will have to be a team effort, an adventure of encounters and conversations. We will criticize and correct one another, even during this congress. All the better so. What I intend to do now, is to present you with a fundamental reflection on the concepts of encounter, connectedness and conversation, as they are in need of clarification and as their impact has to be gauged when they become key metaphors in our theological approaches. I could avoid these tricky issues of clarification by claiming that these ideas, precisely as starting points and root metaphors, should be intuitively understood and that their clarification will result from the thought structures that evolve out of them, but that would be a cheap escape out of what is the need for a fundamental reflection on the research programme itself. I then move to the idea of the

---

5. See SOBRINO, *El principio-misericordia. Bajar de la cruz a los pueblos crucificados* (Presencia teológica, 67), Santander, Sal Terrae, 1992; L. PÉREZ AGUIRRE, *La opción entrañable ante los despojados de sus derechos* (Colección Alcance, 44), Santander, Sal Terrae, 1992. Compassion refers to the capacity to be moved by the cry of the suffering people and it arises from a deep sense of connectedness, not only as the effort to move towards the suffering and to listen to them, but also as the grace of being accepted by them in the common struggle against what causes their suffering. In that connectedness, the people who suffer are never isolated: the suffering of one of us is the suffering of us all. The suffering people become the beating heart of reality, the knots that structure the web of connected reality.

6. Unfortunately, indeed, community building and exclusion mechanisms often, in daily life, reinforce one another.

preferential option for the poor, which I consider to be, particularly in the context of our globalized world, an essential part of this research programme, as I am convinced that it critically forces us into even more precision with regard to the understanding of the key metaphors. In my conclusion I will attempt to formulate some of the tasks ahead for those who desire to be involved in this research programme[7].

II. A FUNDAMENTAL REFLECTION ON THE CONCEPTS OF ENCOUNTER, CONNECTEDNESS AND CONVERSATION

In a challenging book, *Le Dieu commun*, the French theologian Guy Lafon[8] insists on the fact that the name of God can never be separated from the human conversations[9] in which it is uttered. Moreover, human

---

7. This presentation reflects research that I have been publishing over the past years in a series of books and articles. It reflects a personal trajectory and the argumentation in favour of the formulated hypothesis is, therefore, a narrative one. I refer to the following: *Kerk: plaats van ontmoetingen, veld van spanningen en ruimte voor onderscheiding*, in R. MICHIELS – J. HAERS (eds.), *Een werkzame dialoog. Oecumenische bijdragen over de kerk 30 jaar na Vaticanum II* (Nikè, 38), Leuven – Amersfoort, Acco, 1997, 187-227; *Close Encounters of the Third "Week": Enkele voorzichtige theologische overwegingen naar aanleiding van een gesprek over strafbemiddeling*, in *Metanoia* 4 (1997) 58-80; *Het avontuur van de traditie*, Averbode, Altiora, 1999; *De vruchtbare dubbelzinnigheid van het woord "menswording"*, in J. HAERS – T. MERRIGAN (eds.), *Christus in veelvoud: pluraliteit en de vraag naar eenheid in de hedendaagse christologie* (Didachè), Leuven – Amersfoort, Acco, 1999; *Le lieu dont on parle*, in J. HAERS – T. MERRIGAN – P. DE MEY (eds.), *"Volk van God en gemeenschap van gelovigen": Pleidooien voor een zorgzame kerkopbouw*, Averbode, Altiora, 1999, 291-314; *Geloften aan de grens*, Averbode, Altiora, 2000; *Kansanderen. Liefhebben vanuit de marge*, Averbode, Altiora, 2000; *Wrede Weefsels / Vrede Weefsels*, Averbode, Altiora, 2001; *La théologie de la libération, un changement de paradigme? Son apport aux diverses disciplines théologiques*, in *Transversalités* 79 (2001) 101-122.

8. Paris, Le Seuil, 1982. One could criticize Lafon for insufficiently, in his anthropocentric understanding of "entretien", taking into account the non human creation. One could even ask whether Lafon really leaves behind the I perspective that we attempt to put into question. Lafon does not, moreover, explicitly mention narrativity, although one feels it particularly in the part on revelation and in the ever newness of the conversation. Ultimately, in our perspective, we find Lafon lacking for not paying attention to the preferential option for the poor.

9. I translate the French word *entretien* as conversation. The word *conversation* also exists in French and Lafon's choice for *entretien* is, of course, a very conscious one: it emphasizes the "in-between" of a conversation. This in-between is the space of the conversation, welding the conversation partners in a common adventure. However, there is an ambiguity: "*entretien*" covers both the encounter and the conversation. The former is indefinite and not necessarily conscious, whereas the latter refers to conscious activities such as talking, or even to the awareness of an encounter going on. Both are meant by Lafon, and he does not draw a clear distinction. I kept the word "conversation" to uphold that ambiguity of Lafon's approach. "*Entretien*" has a much large range of significance

life is unthinkable outside of such conversations between human beings. Conversation is, so to say, a transcendental condition for human life, that may easily pass unnoticed, even if it is always present in the concrete conversations that structure human history[10]. Conversations express finitude and challenge into ethical positions (acceptance or refusal of their existence); they are cut only by death and they reveal the deep connectedness outside of which human beings do not exist, of which the I cannot be isolated. Religion, according to Lafon, consists in the free assent to be part of the conversation, and thus to be part of the game of life and death that binds human beings together[11]. The core of religion, therefore, lies in the welding together of a community in the space of the conversation, the in-between that refers to the absence both of the origins and of the end, an absence that, in the conversation, may be called God[12]. It refers, in fact, to our belonging, in our conversations, to a game of presence and absence to which we refer by God or love (p. 92). If we want to speak about revelation it can only be within the context of our conversations (p. 148).

By stressing the crucial importance of conversation as well as the undeniability of human togetherness, Lafon critically engages the modern and

than the word "conversation". In a way, it is closer to encounter or togetherness or connectedness. The last word, however, I use more to point to the connected web of reality. Therefore, it has also a holistic flavour.

10. "Mais que la paix et la guerre soient toujours entre nous comme une manière de nous lier aux autres, que règne toujours entre nous quelque chose comme un pacte, jusque dans nos conflits, voilà ce qui passe facilement inaperçu, comme la lumière elle-même, sans laquelle nous ne verrions pourtant pas. Ce méconnu, nous l'appellerons ici entretien" (p. 8). There is, according to Lafon, a tension between "conversation" and "conversations".

11. "Il (l'entretien) est reconnu comme ce sans quoi nous sortirions du jeu de la vie et de la mort. Littéralement, ni l'entretien n'est ni l'entretien n'est pas, mais *il est reconnu* dans le consentement que nous donnons au jeu de vivre et de mourir" (p. 61). "Ce consentement se produit chaque fois que les hommes acceptent et continuent d'accepter de vivre ensemble, c'est-à-dire, d'affronter ensemble, dans la paix et dans la guerre, la vie et la mort" (p. 61). "En effet, la réponse libre à l'entretien que constitue notre consentement à rester pris en lui peut, à bon droit, être nommé religion. Mais on conçoit aussi que ce dernier terme n'aura pas la signification qu'on lui donne communément. Le geste religieux sera celui par lequel nous redoublons, dans notre consentement, cet engagement commun dans un entretien où nous advenons ensemble les uns avec les autres. En un tel sens, la société est religion, la religion est société" (p. 64).

12. "(...) la religion interdit la présence de l'origine, en maintenant toujours celle-ci absente dans le passé, dans ce qu'on nomme le commencement et, tout autant, elle nous préserve de la présence de la fin, en la différant toujours dans l'avenir. (...) l'éloignement de l'origine et le délai de la fin sont, en quelque sorte, poussés à bout, étendus infiniment" (p. 78). "(...) ce *nom* de Dieu. Il suffit alors d'accepter ceci: que Dieu désigne ce au nom de quoi les hommes s'allient dans une alliance sûre, imbrisable, et que l'on vise, en employant ce nom, une absence tenue pour irrémédiable, indépassable, indéfiniment poussée à bout" (p. 79).

postmodern emphasis on the autonomous creative subject[13], on the I as the autonomous centre of decisions and worldviews, independently of whether these decisions and worldviews have universal (modernity) or merely local (postmodernity) range. In his view, the I cannot be dissociated from the encounters that constitute it and in which the world is constituted as spoken about[14]. In a way, the connectedness is prior to the constitution of the I, which originates in the web and in the histories of encounters of which it has always been a part.

Indeed, the easiest way to start reflecting about the issues of encounter, connectedness and conversation, is to become aware of the extent to which we have become conditioned by a modern and postmodern understanding of the "I": it has become difficult for us to consider relations, encounters and conversations, as something else than a mere connection between two "I"s or between an "I" and an "other". Relations are considered from the point of view of an already constituted, existing and autonomous "I"[15]. New Age holistic tendencies, such as expressed in Aldous Huxley's *Island*, react against these I-centred or I-oriented approaches but, very often, in christian circles, they enjoy a bad press. I am convinced that now is the time to reconsider the tension between the "I" and what I would call the "foundational connectedness"[16], and maybe in that tension to give some priority to the latter, so as to avoid what for Luther was the main characteristic of sin, the *cor curvatum in se*, and what, in Levinas' thought, has to be overcome in the encounter with the face of the other: the hypostatic I that has gained its identity out of a chaotic *il y a*[17]. The emphasis on the I as always welded in the connectedness of reality, counteracts the I who considers itself the centrepiece of the world, the perspective from which the world receives its structure and significance. The objection that for modernity not the I but

---

13. But not on the creative subject as such, if it is understood in a fundamental perspective of conversation and connectedness.

14. In that sense, the conversations that constitute reality are created and uncreated: "car la question de la création ne porte jamais sur la création de notre entretien lui-même. (...) En d'autres termes, la création ne porte pas sur la genèse de notre entretien, mais sur sa fécondité interne. De ce fait, notre entretien est toujours, par un côté, créé, et, par un autre côté, incréé" (p. 55). It is uncreated as the creativity of the conversations always also reflects their finitude and their incapacity to control themselves (p. 56).

15. This is reflected in set theory (mathematics) where we speak about relations between elements. One could remark, however, that the elements have already been collected in a set and, therefore, are already related.

16. The Dutch word is "lotsverbondenheid" (one shares with others the fate of living in the same world, being connected to these others precisely by sharing the same world).

17. See E. Levinas, *De l'existence à l'existant*, Paris, Vrin, 1993, 140-141.

rather the rational scientific approach is characteristic, is weak, because this "rational scientific approach" is profoundly related to what the I is: those who are not able to display or use it, cannot really be called an I and cannot really be recognized as full individuals or subjects[18]. The same logic is at work in postmodernity, taking into account that here rationality is not anymore considered an all encompassing monolythic narrative.

We prefer, therefore, to start from the fundamental and founding connectedness: an I is defined on the basis of its being involved in encounters and conversations and so, ultimately, connected to the whole out of which it is empowered to become an I, i.e. ever changing and reshapen in its encounters. This means that the I can never be disconnected and that it always underlies the threat to loose its imagined autonomy because of the risk of being reconfigured in the connectedness. This implies a certain unsettling fluidity to the "I", but it foremost dethrones the I's pretensions. Ultimately, this connectedness has to be thought of very radically as all encompassing: it concerns the whole of the universe, the whole of creation, the whole of the world. Although one can separate out a part of this whole to allow an I to become an I out of its immediate relations to its surroundings, ultimately, one will have to consider that such local topology that renders an I possible, can only be conceived of as a holistic topology. If that were not the case, the I and its local surroundings would become a new "I", a new subject, set apart from the rest of reality. If one wants to avoid a metaphysical "coup d'état" of the subject, its connectedness can be no less than holistic[19].

To consider holistic connectedness as one of the grand narratives attacked by postmodernity, is in my opinion a category-mistake. Grand narratives are the result of I-centred thinking. The reference to connectedness aims at destroying and disabling this I-centredness. Postmodern criticism is, of course, acceptable and necessary when this connectedness becomes the prisoner of a systematic thought system and thus vulnerable to abuse and powergames. Indeed, the temptation to overthrow the mystery of the originary connectedness by rational control mechanisms is,

18. This explains that modernity, which focuses on the I understood from the perspective of (scientific) rationality, has run into difficulties with regard to mentally impaired people. The example shows that, indeed, at the core of the debate with modernity, we will find the issue of otherness and absence, but always as defined from the perspective of the I.

19. Of course, this does not mean that the subject disappears in a whole that would have become a new subject, in control of all the relations that constitute it. The very web of relations, in which subjects arise that turn critical even of the whole, does not allow for a masterplan of the whole.

unfortunately, always strong and not always resisted against. There is always the desire to shape the whole and the connectedness in a rational and controlable way, that provides us with a sense of security (sciences, economics, law) and not to allow for the myriad diversities of relations and encounters that never allow for fixation. In that sense, it is interesting to be aware of the fact that Jean-François Lyotard, going beyond his own description of postmodernity as the fierce criticism of the grand narratives[20], focuses on a model of encounter and conversation allowing for open moves that reflect the mysterious, challenging and creative gap between the conversation partners. At least, this is how I interpret the difference he introduces between "litige" and "différend"[21].

All of what has been said does not mean that the I does not have a consistency of its own. What is meant is that the enclosure of this self-definition of the I is conceivable only in the context of its connectedness with the rest of the world. This shows, once more, that there will always be a crucial rest of powerlessness in defining oneself as an I, experienced by the I itself in its need to define itself as "other" from the rest of the world, in its need to separate itself from others and even from itself. It is too one-sided to claim that the connectedness enjoys total ontological priority over the I, but one has to recognize that ontologically there is no I without prior connectedness, a connectedness that precisely appears when the I differentiates itself and becomes differentiated from the non-I to which it is connected[22]. Ultimately, it is not the I that defines the connectedness, nor is it the goal of the connectedness. I do not, therefore, claim an ultimate monism, but a foundational interdependence upon which the I's unfold in such a way that it will offer the possibility to clarify the deeper interdependence.

It will already have become clear that my own technical language will inevitably be somewhat different from Lafon's, as I do not have a close equivalent for the French *entretien*. I have used up to now the word *conversation* as a translation for Lafon's *entretien*, but I would prefer to use this English word *conversation*[23] for a more explicit and conscious unfolding of the situation of ontic weldedness expressed by the word *entretien*. I will, therefore, at this more fundamental level prefer to use

20. J.-F. LYOTARD, *La condition postmoderne. Rapport sur le savoir* (Collection critique), Paris, Éditions de Minuit, 1979.
21. J.-F. LYOTARD, *Le différend* (Collection critique), Paris, Éditions de Minuit, 1983.
22. The original game of reality is that in which fundamental connectedness and I mutually shape one another.
23. The "cum" implied in "conversation" as from "cum versari" already implies the awareness of an I that can claim to be with a you. It is important to remain aware that the connectedness can be part of conversations – it can be talked about – but that it, nevertheless, will never be exhaustively controled by those conversations.

the expression *encounter* in a very wide sense, or *connectedness* when I want to stress the holistic dimension of the idea that reality is constituted of this multiplicity of encounters without which no singularity, subject or object, I or it, is thinkable. So, whenever we claim to speak as an I or about an I, we should realize that this I is always already embedded or welded into a web of encounters that constitute its first ontological structure as connectedness to the whole of reality in which this I comes to exist and acquires its individuality or subjectivity. This means, of course, that it is a mistake to take the I as the center of reality: its being engulfed and ontologically entrapped in encounters which become conversations, shows its profound decentredness[24], which may very well, phenomenologically, be experienced as frustration, brokenness, or finitude.

The criticism voiced here against I-centred thought, should not be confused with the much more ethically understood criticism against the egocentrism of the I. I-centred thought can be egocentric, that means attempting to torture reality into its own service, but it need not be: one can foster a very altruistic I-centred thought, in which the I continues to be the ontological point of departure that enters into relationships, conversations and commitments altruistically, i.e. with a profound interest in the others. Of course, egocentrism illustrates, in a negative way, connectedness, as even the abuse of connectedness or its very denial is always still an articulation of the connectedness itself. But our idea of connectedness has to go beyond ethical argumentations. The discovery that it is in an altruistic tension that the I acquires its real significance and identity – that seems to be what Levinas teaches us –, can most certainly be interpreted as a transcendental pointer of an ethical nature towards the ontological weldedness of the I in the web of relations that constitutes reality, but it does not fully express this ontological reality. The latter would indeed represent a dangerous putsch, an attempt to control the deep connectedness from the perspective of an ethical discourse. It would represent a grand narrative – be it an ethical one – and a perversion of the very connectedness that aims at overthrowing all grand narratives, as it objects to I-centred thought. Of course, and this cannot be denied, the ontological decentredness of the I will result in an ethical stance and responsibility, not only towards the other, but also towards the web of relations that constitutes reality. Even Luther's struggle with the *cor curvatum in se* is not really a taking leave of an I-oriented way of thinking. Neither is Dietrich Bonhoeffer's criticism of the whole philosophical

---

24. One becomes a person by being called to become one: the idea of a "person", therefore, is profoundly relational in its very constitution.

endeavour as a form of idealism, making the point. We have to delve a little bit further into this difference between ontological and ethical levels, as there seems to be a lot of confusion between both. I will do this by reflecting on some of the ideas developped by my colleague of the Higher Institute for Philosophy, Rudi Visker, who in a response to Richard Rorty, clarifies his criticism of Levinas' thought[25].

If I understand Visker correctly – because of the complexity of the matter I fear, however, to give his thought a twist which he would feel ill at ease with –, he criticizes Levinas for glossing over, by moving all too quickly to the ethically understood appeal of the Other as challenging the egoism of the I's *conatus essendi*, the complexity precisely of this *conatus essendi*. A closer analysis of the *conatus essendi* reveals a profound decentring of the subject, prior to any challenge by the face of the Other, although revealed in this challenge. To Visker, interpreting Foucault's theory of dissociation, the unsettling and disturbing contact with the strange Others who use "final vocabularies" (Richard Rorty) different from our own familiar ones, unveils that the subject is always "tied to or attached to something to which it is denied access and from which it cannot break free": there is a "vague debt" at the core of the subject, an unsettling and disturbing threat that is precisely revealed in the contact with the Other, who is not only some ungraspable face but also reflects his strangeness precisely in the forms in which he expresses defensively his indebtedness to that something else that threatens to dethrone him. The decentration of the Other in the ethical appeal of the Other's face, reveals a more originary decentration both in the Other and in the self, and threatens this my own self that can survive only by lacing in, in terms of these final vocabularies, the threat of the vague debt. So, "the true others force my gaze onto that vague debt, unintentionally of course but no less painfully for that". The final vocabulary used by some of us to protect us from that vague debt and the decentredness at the core of our own self, contains those words "God" and "creation". But exactly in the conversation with others who veil their threat in other terms, the whole weight given to these words and the investment expressed in them, become questionable.

I follow Visker's critique of Levinas' too one-sided rediscription of reality in ethical terms through the introduction of the idea of face. I also

25. R. VISKER, *The Core of my Opposition to Levinas: A Clarification for Richard Rorty*, in *Ethical Perspectives* 4 (1997) 154-170. For more details, see his *Truth and Singularity: Taking Foucault into Phenomenology* (Phaenomenologica, 155), Dordrecht – Boston – London, Kluwer Academic Publishers, 1999.

follow him when he points out that there is more to the matter than egoism and ethics. I think, however, that Visker continues to share two features with the Levinas he criticizes and which I would prefer to abandon: (1) they both continue to work in the frame of an I-oriented thought (be it in different ways); (2) in the expressions "il y a" (Levinas) and "vague debt" (Visker), they indicate a sense of "evil" or "threat", which results either from seeing the construction of the I as an egoistic manoeuvre upon a chaotic background, or from perceiving the vague debt as a subversion of the subject affirmation in the subject itself. Both, therefore, display an I-centred thought and attempt, in a second move, to unsettle the I's power. What I appreciate in Levinas is that the movement of unsettling or dethroning of the I happens in the encounter with the Other as Other and, therefore, in the relationship of encounter with the Other. Nevertheless, with Visker, I consider that this Other as Other is viewed merely as face and, as a consequence, remains insufficiently contextualized. I appreciate in Visker's approach, the analysis of the I that points to a vague debt or decentredness of the I and, therefore, to the ultimate untenability of a self-sufficient, autonomous and content I.

But, I continue to find it difficult to follow both Visker and Levinas in their appreciation of the original rootedness as chaotic "il y a" or threatening "vague debt". This, again, is viewed from the perspective of an I, broken in its own autonomy and frustrated right from the beginning. Would the original rootedness not represent something infinitely more positive, i.c. the connectedness to the whole of reality as the basis for the building of a subject or a self? Would not the evil (Levinas) and the threat (Visker) originate not in the connectedness itself, but in its articulation and as a consequence of competitively settled I's? To the understandable objection that my perception of matters might be over-optimistic and, therefore or thereby, cover up the suffering of so many people, I would like to answer using Paul Ricœur's understanding of original sin[26] in its articulation as something that touches the in-between of encounter precisely in the moment of the constitution of the I as oppositional or tensional to the other I, and that, therefore, does not touch the structures of encounter themselves. Nevertheless, encounters will be affected by original sin to the point that we may be misled into linking evil, brokenness, and sin to the connectedness itself. This means: (original) sin is not the last word about reality – the ultimate connectedness itself is not evil nor

---

26. P. Ricœur, Le "péché originel": Étude de signification, in Id., Le conflit des interprétations: Essais d'herméneutique, Paris, Le Seuil, 1969, 265-282. On p. 281 we find Ricœur's emphasis on the quasi-nature of sin.

a threat – but it is a feature of our reality that we will never be able to escape, to the point that it seems to affect our deepest roots in the connectedness of reality. When one thinks from the perspective of the I, it is, therefore, quite natural to speak about reality in terms of threat and evil. The "final vocabulary" of Christianity is more optimistic and more confident in emphasizing the positive features of ultimate connectedness, even if this remains absent as a distant origin (creation) or an unrealized future (Kingdom of God).

This conversation with Levinas, Visker and Ricœur has offered me the opportunity to make once more the point I want to make – reality as connectedness and web of encounters even before any ethical commitment – and to situate the issue in today's extremely complex philosophical discussions, which, in my opinion, will not really advance through postmodern criticisms on modernity, because I fear that, on the point I make, i.e. the critique of I-centred thought, modernity and postmodernity do not really differ. In my opinion, the new worldview of globalization and holism offers much more opportunities to reach out for a new mode of thinking, as one is now compelled to think about connections, webs and networks.

I would like to emphasize once more that the first connectedness of the whole of reality conceived of as a web of encounters, in which the I's or subjects and objects so to say solidify and gain further solidification in the multiple contexts, trajectories and conversations that arise, is not a dangerous and threatening chaos that has to be overcome by identity affirmation. It has, and here I follow the meaning of Lafon's "entretien", the character of an in-between, a gap that welds reality together. In that sense of a gap, it could even be called "nothing", pregnant of new possibilities that arise in the creative encounter[27]. Nevertheless, out of the nothing of the in-between, may very well arise horror: human creativity may attempt to fill up the gap using violence, oppression and egoistic self-closure.

The metaphor of the encounter as an undeniable and irrefutable in-between, characterized as the creative space of a welding gap, articulates the tensions between nearness and distance, similarity and strangeness, sameness and difference, self and other. It is theologically expressed in

---

27. The gap, pointing to an absence, and, therefore, in the sense Albert Camus gave to the word, to absurdity, may provoke feelings of insecurity or frustration, but it is the gap that allows the encounter and can, therefore, also be understood as a kind of invisible link, a connection of a very special type. This idea of gap will return in our later definition of globalization from the perspective of frontiers of encounter, where frontiers also are a kind of in-between, that allows the encounter. That a gap, ultimately, refers to connectedness, opens up the space for what in theology is called grace. We find here, I think, the reason for the interest in the phenomenon of gifts. See, for example A. VANDEVELDE (ed.), *Gifts and Interest* (Morality and the Meaning of Life, 9), Leuven, Peeters, 2000.

the tensional relationship between transcendence and immanence. The tension between those poles arises in the encounter and produces a history of its own. This unfolding of relations may lead to the awareness of the connectedness that surfaces in the game of sameness and difference. Here, respect for the other as the different, means also respect for the relation with the other and thus for the connectedness. The necessary emphasis on the other as other and, therefore, as truly different, does not mean a denial of the connectedness but protects the connectedness from becoming entrapped in an illusion of sameness whereby the other becomes the playtoy of the same (I). The other is then defined as other merely by the same (I) and not also by the difference that is part of the connectedness defined by the tension between same and different. But this emphasis on the other as other other, as real other, should not in its turn indicate a fundamentally dualistic reality where any nearness or proximity, and so also the fundamental connectedness, has become impossible. The strength of the metaphor of encounter, therefore, lies in the fact that it articulates a tension within which the other may be discovered as a challenging other, different and near. This game of tensions and encounters in the connectedness of our existences, in its turn may work as a transcendental pointer towards the ultimate connectedness of reality.

When in conversation the reflection and return on the encounter has become possible and is thematized as an object to be discussed, the question arises how, in the conversation, the tension between same and different will be safeguarded. Indeed, there exists a real danger that in the conversation attempts will be made to control the encounter and to rob it from its priority over the partners in the encounter. The easiest way to do this is by manipulating the otherness of the partner in the encounter. It is here that I like to appropriate creatively Jürgen Habermas' idea of *herrschaftsfreier Dialog*. I take *herrschaftsfrei* to mean the attempt to open up and keep open the space of in-between that is characteristic of the encounter and that guarantees both the otherness and the nearness of, and the distance and proximity between the partners in the encounter. This is done by avoiding the tempting putsch on the relation with the other, turning it into a relation of dependence, whereby the very encounter is denied. The concept of *herrschaftsfrei*, thus interpreted, comes very close to the idea of indifference as presented in Ignatian spirituality, meaning (a) paying the proper attention to what really is at stake, the relationship, and, therefore, also to the other, as well as (b) the will to pay the price for that attention, i.e. the willingness to undo oneself of what renders one blind for the encounter or interconnectedness, particularly to undo oneself not only of egoistic concerns, but also of an I-oriented perception of reality, be it altruistic. The effort to attain indifference, which ultimately also remains a gift born in the relation itself, requires discernment, the ability to perceive the fundamental connectedness. Particularly in situations of conflict, there exists a temptation to deny the connectedness by emphasizing the antagonism. But even the antagonism, in its own twisted way, signals the interconnectedness, in which ultimately rests the opportunity to deal with the conflict. In a conflict, therefore, not only the persons involved have to be considered, but also proper attention has to be given to the space in-between them.

The ideas of encounter and conversation are no strangers to Christian theology. In fact, the metaphor of "encounter" is crucially important in the very concepts of God and creation, as well as in christology[28]. Details will be forthcoming over the next days, as we discuss the self-revelation of God, the Trinity, the tension between transcendence and immanence, the relation between nature and grace, or the incarnation. Some theologies – process theology is a prime example, but we may also refer to ecological theologies[29] – have taken the ideas of encounter, of connectedness and of holism, as the centerpiece of their reflection. They are often connected to the use of new metaphors in the positive sciences where, over the past thirty years, the willingness to use relational and holistic approaches has grown[30]. They seem to generate and to guarantee levels of freedom, complexity and creativity which were lacking in the usual scientific models based on linearity and causality.

Two examples[31] in the history of Christian theology, Origen and Karl Rahner, may suffice to illustrate my point and plea for what I would call a relational theology, a theology that uses as its root metaphors connectedness, encounter and conversation. My first example – and it is important to realize that this example pre-dates the "separation" between theology and spirituality – concerns one of the greatest of the early Christian

28. Some, as Michael J. Buckley, even claim that modern atheism originated in the one sided stress on the subject, whereby the fundamental importance of the encounter with God was downplayed. See M.J. BUCKLEY, *At the Origins of Modern Atheism*, New Haven, CT, Yale University Press, 1987.

29. Particularly interesting are the ecofeminist theologies. E.g., C. DEANE-DRUMMOND, *Creation*, in S. FRANK PARSONS (ed.), *The Cambridge Companion to Feminist Theology*, Cambridge, UK, Cambridge University Press, 2002, 190-205.

30. As illustrated in the work of Ilya Prigogine. See, for example I. PRIGOGINE – I. STENGERS, *La nouvelle alliance. Métamorphose de la science* (Folio, Essais, 26), Paris, Gallimard, 1986.

31. Thomas Aquinas' understanding of creation would provide another worthwhile example. See A.D. SERTILLANGES, *L'idée de création et ses retentissements en philosophie*, Paris, Aubier, 1945.

theologians, Origen of Alexandria. The traditional approach to his understanding of creation, which to a certain extent provoked the condemnations that have rendered access to his works and thoughts very difficult, based itself on philosophical models of a platonic mood with a strong emphasis on cosmology and the unknowability of the transcendent God. Such interpretation of Origen's thought leads to misunderstandings concerning the existence of a sequence of creations, starting with the ideas in the mind of God, followed by the creation of the *noï* or spiritual natures, and ending up in our material world as the result of God's coping with the fall of the spiritual natures, whereby an incredibly complex variety of beings came about. Undoubtedly, the emphasis on Origen's systematical compendium, the *Peri Archôn*, rather than on his more exegetical and homiletical works, favoured such an interpretation[32]. The attention given by authors as Henri De Lubac and Henri Crouzel to Origen's more spiritually oriented writings allows a different perspective, that confirms the hypothesis of our research programme. What is crucial to Origen and, therefore, also crucial to who wants to understand his concerns and his theology, is the dynamism of the relationship with God, a relationship which takes its form concretely in the reality in which we live. The various creations, mentioned above, are not, then, a sequence in a cosmological creation process, but rather do they represent different layers of reality indicating the discovery of the deeper relations of creation with its Creator and of the creatures within creation.

Origen's point of departure is constituted by the tensions people experience in the real world in which they live, tensions which ultimately reflect the conflict that has arisen between the desire for a fulfilling relationship with God and the attraction that exists to turn away from God by stressing one's own identity – it is here that the idea of body is useful in Origen's thought – through attempts at immersion in and control of the world. The deep creational reality of human beings, their rational or spiritual natures, their logos, is their capacity to relate to God. In fact, they are "relationship with God". In that, all the rational natures are the same, here they are profoundly connected. Their individualization, signified by their bodies, unfolds upon this web of connectedness and provides it with its concrete complexities and tensions. So, to Origen, the deep truth about reality lies in the encounter with God and in the

---

32. For more information, see H. CROUZEL, *Origen*, trans. A.S. WORRALL, Edinburgh, T.&T. Clark, 1989, as well as M. RUTTEN, *Om mijn oorsprong vechtend. Origenes ofwel het optimisme van een mysticus* (Mystieke teksten en thema's), Kampen, Kok; Averbode, Altiora, 1992. See also my unpublished doctoral thesis: *Creation Theology in Origen*, Oxford University, 1992.

interconnectedness that arises from that encounter. Therefore, reality is, profoundly, spiritual, i.e. relational. Bodies are signifiers of the individuation within that network of relations, and this means that one should not, in Origen's thought, look for a soul-matter dualism. The fall reflects not a fundamental evil or threat at the heart of creation itself, but rather the temptation and the attempt, in the process of differentiation of the web of interconnectedness, to one-sidedly emphasize and isolate the I and the subject.

Interestingly, this kind of relational or spiritual approach to theology, in which the concern of the theologian is not some abstract notion of a different God or of some law governing reality, but precisely the relationship between God and human beings – and connected with that the interconnectedness of the created universe –, allows for a discourse about God consistent with a self-revealing God. It also explains the profound connections in Origen's thought, between his "allegorical" method, his spirituality of struggle and discernment, and his key theological themes such as freedom and responsibility.

Not surprisingly, Origen's thought exercised its influence on one of the greatest of the 20th century theologians, Karl Rahner. His is a theology that originates in the context of spiritualities that take the concrete and contextually situated relationship between God and human beings, as well as the relationships between human beings, seriously. At the core of Karl Rahner's theology one finds the idea of the self-revelation and self-communication of God[33]. This self-revelation comes to the surface when discussing the transcendental experience and openness to the whole of reality. It lies hidden in the depths of these structures of openness and conversation that constitute the inalienable existential and ontic structure of human beings and that only a reflexive method, in which the human being discovers its true self as intimately related to the whole of reality, renders visible.

The idea of the self-revelation of God, which in the documents of the Second Vatican Council, particularly in *Dei Verbum*, also constitutes the core of revelation itself (not seen primarily as something that is communicated about God, but as the communication of God Himself), is an important insight, and it clarifies some elements of the encounters that are fundamental to our understanding of reality. If somewhere, it is in the conversation about our deep embeddedness and weldedness in the web of connectedness that constitutes reality, that God comes to the surface and can be talked about. It is, therefore, impossible to disconnect God and

---

33. See his *Grundkurs des Glaubens. Einführung in den Begriff des Christentums*, Freiburg – Basel – Wien, Herder, 1977.

our words about God, from the encounters and conversations that constitute reality and in which we are involved. But then, also, we learn something about the structure of these encounters and conversations.
They reveal who we are and who God is. These relations are not merely
instruments to communicate knowledge to us, they are operative in unveil-
ing our existence and in empowering our commitments in the world[34].

I want to make one last and important theological remark. There always
exists a danger to over-individualize the relationship between God and
human beings as a mere private and intimate encounter between God and
the individual. This should be objected to. In Karl Rahner's case, the
anthropological universality of the transcendental experience and the fact
that it also always involves the world in which we live (openness), form
a bulwark against this individualization. Origen also, is careful to take into
account the various levels of complexity of the relationships. E.g., he
interprets one of the core intimacy texts of our tradition, the Song of
Songs, allegorically on several levels[35]. It concerns the relationship of the
individual soul with God – that is probably one of the reasons why one
might be keen to call Origen at least a precursor of mystical thought –,
the intimate relationships between human beings, and also the relationship between the church and God. We would nowadays be tempted to
understand this connectedness from an even larger perspective, taking
into account also the (ecological) interconnectedness of the whole creation, leading to some kind of holistic perspective, which will in the end
prove to be crucial.

Our attempt to develop a theology of relations and encounters, taking
the in-between field very seriously and cultivating it, is not new and can
boast a tradition, which it would be worthwhile to uncover in the cause

---

34. At various levels theologians will emphasize this connectedness between the self-
revelation of God and the unfolding of creational and human reality. Examples are the
connection Karl Rahner makes between the immanent and the economic trinity, the perspective of the double nature of Christ, the insight revealed in the Flemish word for incarnation, *menswording*, that in Christ both who God is and who a human being is, are
revealed. This approach has also philosophical consequences, e.g. on the level of the concept of truth, which becomes understood from a fundamentally relational perspective. This
seems to indicate very interesting viewpoints on the concept of truth in the Christian
sense of the word: when Jesus claims to be the truth, it has become impossible to understand this as the mere communication of something we should know. Rather, it is constituted by the conviction and faith that the encounter with Jesus reveals the deep connectedness with the whole of reality and ultimately with God himself as the truth of our
existence. This is no claim towards a relativism of truth, but it surely states that there is
no possibility to claim a certain knowledge that once and for all would be true in its human
propositional formulation.
35. See *Sources Chrétiennes* 37bis, pp. 375, 376.

of our research programme. The crucial insight is to perceive the importance of encounter and connectedness as a way to analyze human reality and the Christian faith. Therefore, the title of this contribution is: *defensor vinculi ac conversationis*. To do so in theology, it will be important to use appropriate methods and to develop approaches that reflect and enact the object under study, the encounter with God, between human beings and in the whole of reality, as well as the conversations about these. The idea of encounter has to be articulated as a root metaphor.

From a methodological point of view, the focus on encounter and conversation deepens our understanding of the theological approach itself. The methods that are suited to modern and postmodern approaches, based on an unwarranted confidence in the scientific rationality of the positive sciences and on an I-centred perspective, reduce encounter to a powergame and an issue of control. These methods will have to be complemented and in some cases even replaced by more narrative approaches. One has to be careful not to misunderstand the meaning of the word "narrative" in our context. What is not meant here, is that one tells one's own story and that, ultimately, the various stories told enter into conversation with one another. In such conversation, that stresses the "I" of the various stories, the main concern would be the rights of and the respect for each single narrative. Then, the risk to remain trapped in I-centred approaches is very real. Narrativity understood from the perspective of the I – here is my story and my point of view – leads to a difficult and ultimately unsatisfactory relativism. The point will become even clearer later on when I refer to the attempts to frame the interreligious dialogue in terms of exclusivism, inclusivism and pluralism.

Narrativity, in our perspective here, refers to the transmissal of life experiences in a process of creative identification, validated in a community that is at the same time the keeper and the privileged interpretor of the narratives. This community is always renewed as it is constituted by those who enter into the narratives, interpreting them in their own lives, and interpreting their own lives through the narratives. In the context of their Christian communities, Christians transmit their narratives, constantly enriched by their own lives which have been patterned by these very narratives, as an invitation to enter the experience and the faith of the community. The whole process revolves around the ever new appropriation of key texts, particularly of the Gospels, that open up the encounter with Jesus and in Jesus with God through the channel of lived life. Narrativity involves a complex of hermeneutical circles and spirals through which the meaning of the Gospels, one's own life, the encounter with God in Jesus, the life of Jesus and the belonging to a community are enacted, clarified and passed on. The narrations themselves tend to formulate matters and to conceptually fix meaning and understanding, but they are always subverted by their own dynamism of life encounter and life sharing. Undoubtedly, in the process of narrativity knowledge is transmitted, but much more crucially than knowledge, encounters with God are transmitted through a long history of encounters with human beings and communities. When we understand tradition from the perspective of such a narrative logic, we discover it as an adventure, the formulation of which will never dispense us from the effort to discern the encounters that impact on our lives.

Not surprisingly, in this context, a greater attention ought to be paid to prayer, sacramental life, liturgy and symbolic enactments, as sources and resources for theological thought. They reflect the dynamism of a narrativity that allows for the transmissal and enactment of encounters, and should receive proper attention with regard to the development of theological systematisations and formulations.

One last word about narrativity: the logic of narrativity is one of exploration and discernment, a logic that requires the commitment to life and to encounters, a logic that bears close resemblance to the paths covered in spiritual life. It is an approach that also requires a discourse about itself, a reflective move to uncover its truth, not in the first place as propositional truth, but as the truth of an encounter in which the meaning and direction of our lives is unveiled and remodeled. In this sense, Jesus himself is the truth: he reveals, through our relations with him, over and in gaps that require a narrative logic to be explored and bridged, our deep connectedness in a world that is connected to God himself. The discourse about narrativity, necessary to a narrative process, is also part of the effort of discernment: narrative logic, indeed, is a risky business, as narratives remain very vulnerable to what the Germans call *Hineininterpretierung*, and, therefore, always require the awareness of what our egoism or our I-centred thought may do to pervert them.

Let us now move to some other examples, taken from areas other than theology. These examples will help us to further clarify our ideas and also already give us a taste of what will be said when introducing the idea of the preferential option for the poor. The emphasis on encounter and connectedness is really crucial in a lot of areas of human reflection. I can give only some examples and over the coming years research should certainly be conducted so as to explore more of them, as they will help us to redefine new perspectives for analyzing reality and dealing with its conflicts and struggles. I want to begin by stressing cultural and anthropological studies, also because these are important to what Georges De Schrijver has called a paradigm shift in liberation theologies from socio-economic towards socio-cultural mediations[36]. The editors of the book *The Dialogic Emergence of Cultures*, Dennis Tedlock and Bruce Mannheim[37], reflect in their introduction on the dialogical nature of language, taking their bearings from the work of Mikhail Bakhtin, and suggest that "cultures are continuously produced, reproduced, and revised in dialogue among their members", rather than "particular cultural expressions originating from individual actors". This impacts immediately on the anthropological and ethnological sciences, which in their turn will have to work with dialogical methods so as to become aware of the complex conversations in which the researchers themselves are and become involved. The approach advocated by both authors corresponds to the narrative and hermeneutical methods that we suggested before: "the shared worlds that emerge from dialogues are in a continuous state of creation and recreation, negotiation and renegotiation". The concept of emergence indicates that novelty arises from these dialogical encounters, and to our authors it is clear that individuals can never be dissociated from the social and cultural world to which they belong[38].

If Tedlock and Mannheim are correct, then the paradigm shift in liberation theology will also mean a deeper awareness of the profound relational nature of reality. This will enable methods of encounter and conversation to complement the analytical tools of the political, economic and social sciences, classically used as mediations in liberation theology. The dangers of this shift in meditations are that the emphasis on culture would primarily result in an emphasis on the I-centred search for identity. This would then produce new marginalizations and injustices and would render us blind for the poverty of the others who do not enjoy the luxury to define and pursue their own cultural identities. Cultural empowerment, therefore, has to pass the test of holistic connectedness[39]: culture is defined in the conversations between human beings and is betrayed when membership in the conversation is exclusive and I-centred, in the sense of producing and defining a cultural I. Here appears one of the main

36. G. DE SCHRIJVER (ed.), *Liberation Theologies on Shifting Grounds: A Clash of Socio-Economic and Cultural Paradigms* (BETL, 135), Leuven, University Press – Uitgeverij Peeters, 1998.

37. D. TEDLOCK – B. MANNHEIM (eds.), *The Dialogic Emergence of Cultures*, Urbana – Chicago, IL, University of Illinois Press, 1995. The quotes that follow, are taken from pp. 2 and 3.

38. "The shift to a dialogical approach to language does not mean the end of any interest in the individual speaker, but it does mean that any given speaker at any given moment is immediately an actor within a social and cultural world that is always in process" (p. 12).

39. A similar argument can be found in Bart Pattyn's reflection on the idea of "enclave" on the basis of Mary Douglas' thought. See his *Virtuele en politieke enclaves*, in *Ethische Perspectieven* 12 (2002) 78-92.

reasons why our fundamental reflection on relations, encounters and conversations has to be complemented by a reflection on the preferential option for the poor. In fact, the verb "complemented" is too weak: the preferential option for the poor has to be the heart of our explorations into encounter and conversation. The excluded and marginalized poor are those who through their sufferings will keep our conversations from becoming I-centred[40].

In the same book, in an interesting and challenging article *Dialogical Breakthrough: Catalysis and Synthesis in Life-Changing Dialogue*[41], John Attinasi and Paul Friedrich emphasize several important aspects of these cultural dialogues: "Dialogue, unlike discourse in general, is (1) partly corporeal; (2) driven and energized by shades and blends of emotional affinity and of antagonistic feelings; (3) involves some changes in political empowerment; (4) lacks strong typicality but does tend to take place in certain likely venues, which interact with the sometimes exclusive psychological space around the interlocutors; (5) is a matter of boundaries and partial merger, a transient intercommunication between two centers that leads to some overlap or fusion, or toward the destruction of such qualities". We are attracted particularly by the idea of *liminality*, indicating the partical overlap and sharing that takes place in the dialogue, isolating to a certain extent the participants in the dialogue from their respective backgrounds and, so, offering the possibility for effecting profound changes in the participants themselves, by cementing or rupturing relationships. The creative liminal space of dialogue and encounter will prove to be a key concept in our understanding of globalization and we will link it to the kenotic attitude that characterises the Christian faith.

Iris Marion Young, a political scientist reflecting from a feminist perspective[42], also stresses the importance of encounter and conversation. I look here at some of the ideas expressed in her collection of articles

40. This should not be understood as an attempt to situate the suffering people in some kind of overarching dialectic that would explain and justify their suffering. It is merely a statement of fact: if no attention is paid to those who suffer, precisely in a commitment to fight their suffering, there exists a very real danger that I-centred thought will prevail.

41. J. ATTINASI – P. FRIEDRICH, *Dialogical Breakthrough: Catalysis and Synthesis in Life-Changing Dialogue*, in TEDLOCK – MANNHEIM (eds.), *Dialogic* (n. 37), pp. 33-53. For the quote, see p. 36.

42. The feminist perspective is very interesting from our point of view, because the suffering that surfaces here is closely connected to the quality of relations and to the interpretation given to certain relations. Moreover, feminist theologians cannot but develop radical hermeneutical and narrative approaches to Scripture, so as to allow the reference texts or the classics, to empower them in their struggle for liberation and self-affirmation towards adult social relationships – here it becomes clear that identity is defined by sets of encounters in reality's web of relations and with Scripture, which also reflects these relationships – as well as new perceptions of community life. In the area of conflict resolution,

Intersecting Voices: Dilemmas of Gender, Political Philosophy, and Policy[43]. In her article *Asymmetrical Reciprocity: On Moral Respect, Wonder and Enlarged Thought*[44], she criticizes, in a conversation with Seyla Benhabib, Jürgen Habermas and Hannah Arendt, the idea that symmetrical reciprocity would be the ideal for a good conversation. In her eyes, this is impossible given the fact that partners in a conversation always have various histories and contexts, that are ultimately irreducible to one another. Pleading for symmetry would be an attempt to deny the very real differences between people and to cover up the violence and injustice that take place in relationships. Here we feel the concern for the excluded and forgotten people: they remind us that concrete reality does not correspond to our beautiful reflections on conversation and encounter. Her understanding of encounters and conversations emphasizes asymmetrical reciprocity, so that in an encounter, the understanding of someone else's point of view can never be the same as an obsession to "find things in common", but always involves the act of getting out of ourselves, leaving our safe positions and security to creatively discover new possibilities in the encounter with an other who really is other. The same approach is present in another article of the same book, *Communication and the Other: Beyond Deliberative Democracy*[45], where she contrasts deliberative and communicative democracy. For her, differences are a resource that allow us to transform our points of view. The urge to always reach a common understanding and a common overarching rationality entails the risk to smother the creativity involved in conversations. Therefore, she pleads to go beyond Habermas' approach involving critical argument and assuming the possibility of a shared rationality, and to pay attention to such conversational features as greetings, rhetorical moves, and storytelling. Here, we recognize the need for narrative methods and approaches, capable of articulating and enacting encounters and conversations.

Another challenging author to whom I want to draw the attention, is Bernhard Waldenfels. In an article published in 1974, *Der Geistesgeschichtliche Hintergrund: Vom Ich zum Wir*[46], and following up on his

---

women have a crucial role to play, which is often underestimated. By keeping an eye on their children and the future of these children, for whom they suffer anguish and fear out of love, they are keepers of the connectedness that represents the path towards the resolution of conflicts and sustainable peace.

43. I.M. YOUNG, *Intersecting Voices: Dilemmas of Gender, Political Philosophy, and Policy*, Princeton, NJ, Princeton University Press, 1997.

44. *Ibid.*, pp. 38-59.

45. *Ibid.*, pp. 60-74.

46. In C. HEITMANN – H. MÜHLEN (eds.), *Erfahrung und Theologie des Heiligen Geistes*, Hamburg, Agentur des Rauhen Hauses; München, Kösel-Verlag, 1974, 162-175.

important book on dialogue[47], he points to the ambiguous affirmation of the I. It means both "isolation" as refusal of conversation, and "participation" as openness and willingness to enter into conversations and encounters. The We, referring to the dialogue in which human beings are always involved, breaks down the absolutely privileged position of the I, but at the same time recognizes the position of the I as a partner in the dialogue. There is, therefore, a tension between the I and the We that remains, where the I cannot be conceived of as purely egocentric, as it is always already involved in relationality. The emphasis on the I, even in the context of a We, remains nevertheless important: a one-sided stress on the We and on the social structures in which the I is involved, may well become a means to control the I by means of its order and place in the social network. When Waldenfels later reflects on the understanding of the challenge posed by the stranger in intercultural encounters[48], he points to the interwovenness as in a web of the same and the stranger – *Verflechtung von Eigenem und Fremdem* –, but emphasizes the same issue: we are not dealing here with a unity in which differences disappear, but rather with a mixture: "Wenn Eigenes und Fremdes als Kontrast entstehen und wenn sie sich nie völlig voneinander ablösen lassen, so folgt daraus zweierlei. Am Anfang stehen Differenzen, nicht eine Einheit, und am Anfang stehen Mischungen, nicht eine Reinheit. Jeder Einheits- und Reinheitswahn verflüchtigt sich, wenn Eigenes und Fremdes von vornherein ineinander verflochten sind". Here also, one feels the carefulness not to force the I in the mould of an identity with the other. Two attempts are made to unmix – *Entflechtung* – this mix: putting the I over against the stranger who calls and challenges, and developping a third party view in which it is possible to speak about the stranger even when, in this process of distanciation, the difference between the I and the stranger is threatened with destruction. There should therefore, remain a respect for the challenge posed by the stranger[49]. In an interview of

47. *Das Zwischenreich des Dialogs. Sozialphilosophische Untersuchungen in Anschluss an Edmund Husserl* (Phaenomenologica, 41), Den Haag, Martinus Nijhoff, 1971.
48. *Der Anspruch des Fremden in interkultureller Sicht*, in G. RISSE – H. SONNEMANS – B. THESS (eds.), *Wege der Theologie: an der Schwelle zum dritten Jahrtausend, Festschrift für Hans Waldenfels zur Vollendung des 65. Lebensjahres*, Paderborn, Bonifatius, 1996, 325-331. For the quote, see p. 328.
49. "Anschliessend stellt sich die Frage, wie Fremdes zur Sprache kommen und Beachtung finden kann, ohne unter dem Blick eines Drittes seine Fremdheit einzubüssen. Diese Möglichkeit scheint nur gegeben, wenn alles Reden über das Eigene und Fremde, das dieses einander gleichmacht, zurückbezogen bleibt auf einen Anspruch des Fremden, der seine Fremdheit wahrt als das, *worauf* wir antworten, bevor wir uns fragen können, *was* es ist. Die Erfahrung des Fremden gleicht dem Staunen, der Angst und allen ausser-ordentlichen

1999[50], Waldenfels reflects on his own intellectual history. One of his central concerns when thinking about dialogue and conversation appears: the will to avoid metaphysical and political systematisations that produce an order in which human beings become entrapped. He does not deny the essential relatedness of human beings, but at the same time, under the influence of Michel Foucault[51], has become careful not to allow this essential relatedness to be put at the use of totalitarian visions and interests. He pleads, therefore, to safeguard those spaces where the I does not belong to such orders and he certainly wants to avoid to speak of one great world order. Although I share Waldenfels' critical concerns, particularly at a time when the emphasis on cultural identity as an order of belonging is very strong, I am not convinced that he really touches the issue of what I have called the fundamental rootedness in the web of interconnectedness that constitutes reality. Indeed, this connectedness always remains undefinable even if, by the tensions between the different subjects that originate in it, it always receives a concrete shape, which deceptively tempts some of us to use it in an attempt to define and control the web of connectedness. This makes me wonder if, ultimately, Waldenfels is not still reflecting from an I-centred perspective. His reflections, however, will keep us on our guard: there will always be the temptation to fixate and to control the fundamental rootedness, to use it to

---

Ereignissen darin, dass es sich jeder Einordnung entzieht. Ein Antworten, das den normalen Gang der Dinge durchbricht, kommt immer mit einer bestimmten Nachträglichkeit, da das Antworten anderswo beginnt und nicht bei sich selbst. Diese *Diachronie*, die jedes Gleichmass ausschliesst, verbindet sich mit einer unaufhebbaren *Asymmetrie*. Der neutrale Vergleich, der Unvergleichliches auf einen Nenner bringt, setzt eine Kluft zwischen Eigenem und Fremdem immerzu voraus. Die Herausforderung durch das Fremde konvergiert so wenig mit dem eigenen Antworten, wie Schlafen und Wachen, Leben und Tod konvergieren. Zwischen beidem liegt eine Schwelle, die unüberwindlich ist; im Erwachen und Einschlafen überqueren wir eine Schwelle, ohne dass wir auf beiden Seiten zugleich Fuss fassen können. Ein "interkultureller Dialog" der einseitig auf einen Konsens abzielen würde, vergässe – wie im Märchen – das Eigentliche, nämlich das Fremde, das uns erst zu eigenen Antworten provoziert. Fassbar ist dieses nur in seinen Nachwirkungen, da der Einbruch des Fremden und der Einschnitt, den seine Ankunft markiert, sich nicht in vorgeprägter Form vollzieht. Zwischen Eigenem und Fremdem herrscht eine prästabilierte Disharmonie, die stets auch traumatische Effekte zeitigt. Wer den "interkulturellen Austausch" auf Verstehen und Verständigung reduziert, verharmlost, was fern allem Seitenwechsel zwischen Eigenem und Fremden vorfällt" (pp. 330-331). The similarities with Iris Marion Young are striking.

50. Published in M. FISCHER – H.-D. GONDEK – B. LIEBSCH (eds.), *Vernunft im Zeichen des Fremden. Zur Philosophie von Bernhard Waldenfels* (Suhrkamp Taschenbuch Wissenschaft, 1492), Frankfurt am Main, Suhrkamp Verlag, 2001, 409-459.

51. M. FOUCAULT, *L'ordre du discours. Leçon inaugurale au Collège de France prononcée le 2 décembre 1970*, Paris, Gallimard, 1971.

cover an order of power that we want to define by deceptively presenting it as the interconnectedness of reality. Then the otherness and the
excentricity of the I will remind us that we always are at risk to become
the prisoners of a lie about reality.

A last example I would like to draw from a study made by a licentiate student of our Faculty of Law, Department of Criminology.
Luc Robert recently presented a paper on the link between aboriginal justice and aboriginal holistic spirituality in Canada, contrasting it with
classic Western models of justice and conflict resolution. In doing so he
illustrates the workings of a model of restorative justive that takes its
point of departure from the holistic perspective of connectedness of a
community to which belong both the offender and the victim, a community that is also affected by the offense committed. I quote a passage
from his work that illustrates how in the reflection on justice the perspective of connectedness plays an important role: "In contrast, the
Native justice system is based on the philosophy of interconnectedness.
It cannot exclude people. Instead, Native justice processes provide all
participants with a voice. During a circle, "all members of the circle are
equal in terms of the opportunity to talk and the requirement to listen".
Usually, a turn to talk is signified by a feather, a talking stick, or a rock
that circulates during the hearing. "Rather than focusing only on the
offender and the offence, the response to criminal behaviour occurs
within a broader, holistic framework". Through inclusion of the victim,
the offender and people from the community, "healing" can take a
start"[52].

III. THE PREFERENTIAL OPTION FOR THE POOR IN A GLOBALIZED WORLD

The choices made with regard to theological and philosophical articulations have socio-political consequences. Indeed, theologians and
philosophers provide a terminology, a framework and worldviews not
only to analyse reality, but also to explore and state convictions about the
nature of reality and what may reasonably be expected from reality. Moreover, theologians offer perspectives to people and empower people to follow courses of action and commitment in all kinds of situations, ranging

52. Reference is made to D. CAYLEY's *The Expanding Prison: The Crisis in Crime
and Punishment and the Search for Alternatives*, Toronto, House of Anansi Press, 1998,
and C.T. GRIFFITHS – A. CUNNINGHAM's *Canadian Corrections*, Scarborough, Nelson –
Thomson Learning, 2000.

from family life, over sexual attitudes and patterns of social behaviour, to behaviour in situations of violent conflict. Of course, such frameworks, that easily and for various reasons turn into structures and patterns that demand unconditional allegiance, are always in need of correction, particularly by mediations and analyses that are closer descriptions of reality than theology. These corrections become necessary and imperative when theological frameworks threaten to turn a blind eye on injustices and suffering, when our theological articulations show blind spots. B. Waldenfels has already sharpened our critical sense and shown the importance of resistance mechanisms to systems that become oppressive. These mechanisms of resistance reflect the evasiveness and elusiveness of reality, be it in the excentricity and uncontrollable passions of the I, be it in the radical and unexpected otherness of the other. One can also point to the criticism leveled by postmodernity against universalising modern rationality, that found its way in the construction of overarching theological systems. In his *At the Origins of Modern Atheism*, Michael J. Buckley[53] has demonstrated that this modern move represented a betrayal of the core of the Christian message, i.e. the encounter with Christ and with God in Christ. The same conviction that the relationship with God and with Christ constitutes the heart of the Christian faith, has led authors as Thomas Molnar[54] to emphasize the role played in Christian theological articulations by transcendence as radical difference. I would personally prefer to emphasize the structure of connectedness and encounter, in which transcendence and immanence are interwoven, so as to avoid the trap of a God who escapes the encounter because of his radical transcendence, the trap of hypertranscendence, which ultimately leads to a deification of the world itself, to hypo-immanence.

But, and maybe even more than through reflections on the level of the so-called mediations, we also need to correct our theological conceptions and articulations in the direct contact with broken reality[55], as has already become clear in what was said before on the concept of culture as encounter. Here, we touch the core of the notion of the preferential option for the poor. It is in the poor and in the struggle with the poor, as the

---

53. New Haven, CT, Yale University Press, 1987.
54. T. MOLNAR, *The Pagan Temptation*, Grand Rapids, MI, Eerdmans, 1982.
55. Here is the place to also say a word of gratitude towards those many students who keep us theologians in Leuven on track by reminding us, always anew, that there exists a painful reality that professors sometimes forget in their enthusiasm for theological systematisation and formalisation. I particularly think of Elías López Pérez, who wrote a remarkable licentiate thesis on reconciliation in the context of the crisis in the region of the African Great Lakes, and of the many students participating in challenging seminar sessions and encounters at the Forum for Liberation Theologies.

voiceless ones who die before their time[56], that we trust to discover the critical as well as the creative instance that will allow us to develop theological approaches that remain faithful to the root metaphors of connectedness and encounter, further developped as solidarity[57]. This appears powerfully in the context of globalization.

Indeed, probably the most striking feature of our world today is the ongoing process of globalization. Evaluating globalization is a somewhat tricky matter: some recognize a great opportunity in the growth of communication and interdependence, others fear major disasters because of increasing dependencies, the loss of cultural identities and the magnified possibilities of exploitation[58]. Some will stress the novelty of globalization and the totally new challenges posed by it, others will situate it in a long history of which also colonization formed a part. All in all, globalization remains an ambiguous process that provokes a wealth of literature and thought. Depending on one's perspective, one will formulate a description or a definition of the phenomenon. The definition used will betray the feelings with regard to the valuation of the phenomenon itself. Not surprisingly, theologians also have started to reflect about globalization that to some already represents a new worldview after postmodernity. For example, the paradigm changes in liberation theologies, the move from socio-economic and socio-political perspectives to cultural analyses, are profoundly connected to the issue of empowerment in a globalized world[59]. The first point I want to make in what follows is that the very idea of globalization already suggests the use, not only in theology but also in other sciences, of metaphors of encounter and conversation. My second point stresses that we have to develop, if we want to be serious about the preferential option for the poor – and we have to, were it only

---

56. These are the two definitions as given by Gustavo Gutiérrez in a talk in Leuven last year. See G. GUTIÉRREZ, *Poverty as a Theological Challenge*, in J. HAERS – E. GUZMAN – L.F.A. LESIGUES – D.F. PILARIO (eds.), *Mediations in Theology: Georges De Schrijver's Wager and Liberation Theologies* (Annua Nuntia Lovaniensia, 47), Leuven, Peeters, 2003, 173-182. See also GUTIÉRREZ, *Option pour les pauvres* (n. 3).

57. I have avoided to use the word solidarity, as it has a more ethical tone than the word connectedness and as I have attempted to highlight the fact that connectedness, although it has ethical implications, is not exhausted by that ethical dimension. However, solidarity is the word that is being used in many of the official church documents.

58. See, for an introduction in the issues: D. HELD – A. McGREW (eds.), *The Global Transformations Reader: An Introduction to the Globalization Debate*, Cambridge, UK, Polity Press, 2000.

59. Cf. DE SCHRIJVER, *Liberation Theologies on Shifting Grounds* (n. 36). For more general works on the theological impact of globalization: P. BEYER, *Religion and Globalization*, London, Thousand Oaks; New Delhi, Sage Publications, 1994; R.J. SCHREITER, *The New Catholicity: Theology between the Global and the Local*, Maryknoll, NY, Orbis Books, 1997.

to safeguard our faithfulness to reality as a web of interconnectedness –, approaches to the root metaphors of encounter, conversation and connectedness that will be capable of showing the creative space constituted by the suffering people.

Globalization has to do with an awareness of the intricate web of interrelations – economical, political, cultural, etc. – that binds us all together in one world. It refers to the complex interactions, also of power and, exploitation, in a world that has become profoundly interdependent and, therefore, also very vulnerable. This means that we have grown into a kind of holistic and systemic awareness that more and more conditions our modes of thought, and that is to a large extent reflected in that strange structure that is the world wide web on the internet. We are not yet completely used to this new perspective, in which the world has become our village and in which also the idea of fixed geographical centres or nodes of power and decision has been abandoned for the more elusive reality of moving centres of decision and less definable structures of responsibility. This means that the very understanding of what power is, how it can be localized and how responsibilities can be assigned, has changed in a frightening and disturbing way, creating a new feeling of insecurity. Terrorism illustrates this point very well. We have, therefore, to develop a new language to deal with these changed relations of power, one that cannot any longer concentrate solely on the I that exercises power over the I that has no power, as if power were a feature of the I. Power relations cannot be conceived of any longer in the context of mere I-oriented thinking, but should also take into account more elusive structural realities. Power is not a characteristic of an individual but rather a changing and evolving feature of relations. It can only be understood out of the complexities of relations in which all types of interdependencies play and, therefore, its study requires relational approaches and methodologies.

This new perspective on reality as a web with moving and changing connecting nodes, also challenges the place of religions in the whole. This is particularly true in the case of religions claiming to be the keepers of a revealed message that should be passed on. The dream of one religion governing the whole of reality or the trust in one unique and ultimate truth accessible to all of us, have long been shattered and this evolution has also provoked feelings of insecurity. Some of us feel the urge to find a renewed security in a unified, well ordered, and uniform world and they consider it their vocation and task to build up such a world. But their attempts at soothing their feelings of insecurity often generate only more violence. This is the context in which the issues of interreligious dialogue come to be posed, and we have not yet developed satisfactory ways to cope with this challenge. Indeed, we still seem to operate along the lines of I-oriented thought, as appears in our use of the trinome "exclusivism, inclusivism, pluralism" to situate ourselves and others in the context of interreligious dialogue. Religions are seen as well defined identities or subjects, interacting and competing with one another. I would like to suggest an alternative concept, "reciprocal anonimity"[60], that may possibly prove to be of use as it refers to the quality of the relations and allows for differences to enter as a creative factor in the interreligious encounters and conversations. It also offers a means to evaluate conflictive asymmetries and to deal with them using techniques and approaches developed in sciences that deal with conflict management, without immediately forcing the participants in the conversations to have recourse to strong and powerful, but relationally debilitating, theological claims. The concept I suggest builds on Karl Rahner's idea of anonymous Christians. However, I want to change the pointer inherent in the word "anonymous". Rahner's approach is usually understood to be inclusivistic and represents then another example of I-oriented thought, be it a very liberal and open one. But Rahner's main concern was not to judge non-Christians on the basis of Christian values and principles; he wanted to look from the perspective of God, so as to be able to recognize God at work in the other. His concept of the "anonymous Christian" is, therefore, a very relational one[61]. To me an anonymous Christian is a non-Christian whom I will treat in the same way as I would treat a fellow Christian, this means: whom I will include in my dearest web of connectedness, not because I decide to do so, but because my decision corresponds to the deep structure of reality itself and because I recognize God's grace in this other person as an invitation to grow in my own faith and in my own relation with God[62]. My own identity and my own claims exist only within that web of interconnectedness and cannot, as if it were, cordon off areas as non-existent or less connected. In a theological perspective this means that God is foreign to no area of creation. The reciprocal in the expression "reciprocal anonimity" refers both to the hope that the other will also recognize me

60. I am aware, of course, that the introduction of this concept is no solution to the challenge of interreligious encounters. My intention is not to provide a solution, but to make a move that may invite further clarification of the situation and, even more, may open some creative perspectives in the conversations themselves. I do not claim any originality for a concept that originates in an emphasis more on the process of conversation itself than on the contents presented or defended in the conversation.

61. E.g. in K. LEHMANN – A. RAFFELT (eds.), *Rechenschaft des Glaubens. Karl Rahner Lesebuch*, Zürich – Köln, Benziger; Freiburg – Basel – Wien, Herder, 1979, 269-276.

62. An example of such an approach, lived at a mystical level, is E. VAN BROECK-HOVEN, *Dagboek van een vriendschap*. Met verantwoording en aantekeningen bezorgd door G. NEEFS, Brugge, Emmaüs – Desclée de Brouwer, 1971.

as an "anonymous ..." and to the conviction that ultimately only this reciprocity will reflect the interconnectedness of reality. The "reciprocal", of
course, takes the form of a claim on the other, a claim that may very well
be opposed in the ongoing conversations, a claim that may be perceived
as violence exercised by me on the other. The only way, in such conflict,
not to retreat on the entrenched positions of I-oriented thought, consists
in the willingness not to impose the reciprocity and in the trust that non-
reciprocity is no excuse for cancelling anonimity on my side. Here, we
already perceive a glimpse of the kenotic attitude required to remain faithful to reality's interconnectedness.

It seems to many of us that the most powerful and most empowering
feature of globalization is the improvement and universalisation of communication. That is probably right, but as with everything concerning
globalization, even this feature is ambiguous and should not all too easily be left undiscussed. In fact, it requires a profound and delicate criticism. Indeed, improved communication and relational networks also
uncover massive injustices and huge differences and tensions. Moreover, improved communication is very well capable of creating new
tensions and of hightening the degree of explosiveness of existing ones:
roads are also used to move armies and to wage wars. It has therefore
become imperative to think about the kind of communication we desire.
The remarks made by I. Marion Young and B. Waldenfels, pointing to
the necessity of taking into account the asymmetries in relations as
spaces for creativity and change, should be taken very seriously. Variety
to them is a gain; difference a challenge. This is a move in the direction towards an even more radical idea of preferential option for the
poor, that emphasizes not only the situation of the poor, but also
includes the faith that precisely in the discarded fringe spaces inhabited
by the poor, one may find the creativity and energy to cope with the
new challenges and the new injustices. The increased possibilities for
worldwide communication have revealed to an even larger extent than
was the case before, the suffering provoked by globalization and the
mechanisms that preclude the bounties of communication for many people[63]. This is revealed, at least to me, in a most shocking and challenging way in the refugee camps. Here we find people who are
excluded, who die because they belong to a "no men's land", who have

---

63. E.g., in Flanders, one speaks about a new social divide or fault line, between those
people who enjoy the new oportunities and those who cannot and remain, therefore, frustrated. This new fault line is clearly linked to individualism, authoritarianism and opposition to representative democracy. See M. ELCHARDUS – W. SMITS, *Anatomie en oorzaken
van het wantrouwen*, Brussel, VUB Press, 2002, 116-118.

been stripped of their basic human recognition and of all those elements that in their relationships with fellow human beings give them their dignity and selfworth. Can we, as theologians, find the faith to trust that the no-space they occupy is a centre of creativity and that there the work unfolding reality's deep connectedness will, over and over again, begin?

I would now like to turn in a more systematic way to this notion of the "preferential option for the poor". My starting point are some reflections made by Gustavo Gutiérrez in Leuven during a conference on May 9th, 2001[64]. He suggested two possible, and of course deeply related, "definitions" of who the poor are. The first runs like this: the poor are the people who die an early death, who die before their due time because of outside circumstances that structure their lives. The second refers to the poor as the voiceless and marginalized people, those who count for nothing and who are discarded. Both definitions will lead us to some theological insights that will highlight the importance of relational theology and the central role of the preferential option for the poor in such relational theology, i.e. the fact that relational theology will fall prey to I-centred abuse if the preferential option for the poor is not taken into account.

From the perspective of the first definition, the theological issues at stake are very clear: we refer to the issue of life and death. The definition, however, is coloured by the awareness that death may be the consequence of structural injustices, of relations that are manipulated or have been broken because of human involvement, in the form of fear, anger, egoism, craving for power, etc. Here appears very clearly, what is also true on a much wider scale: life and death are never the issue of the lone individual, the life and death of each one of us concerns all of us. The death of a human being, particularly and very painfully when that death is caused by conditions and contexts of which I also am a part, is always also to a certain extent my death. What happens to the least of my brothers and sisters, happens to me. The preferential option for the poor invites us to take this connectedness very seriously and to turn it into an action principle of solidarity in our lives, as we become ever more committed to the life of the others and particularly of those whose lives are haunted by the question whether life is possible before death[65].

64. Cf. n. 56.
65. This question is raised by theologians as Dorothee Sölle and Pedro Trigo, when discussing the concept of creation. See D. SÖLLE – S.A. CLOYES, *To Work and to Love: A Theology of Creation*, Philadelphia, PA, Fortress Press, 1984; P. TRIGO, *Creation and History* (Liberation and Theology, 10), Tunbridge Wells, Burns & Oates, 1992.

The theological discussion surrounding the "resurrection in death" proposal, also illustrates this issue[66]. Although one can understand the position of Lohfink and Greshake as a reaction against the difficulties arising
from the use of Greek metaphysics in the context of eschatology, the
question should be asked whether their position does not reflect an all too
individualized understanding of eschatology and, in that, a very I-oriented thought, unable to hide its modern background. The two tear eschatology, making the difference between the individual and the collective
judgements, may well seem to provoke unwarranted forms of what Karl
Rahner called an apocalyptic perception of eschatology[67], but it highlights the fact that the resurrection will never be complete if it is not the
resurrection of all, precisely because the I cannot be separated from its
connectedness to the whole of reality. This idea has a long tradition, and
we find it already in Origen's thought about the saints and about the
apokatastasis. Maybe it should be reformulated, but it most certainly
would mean a loss if it were to be abandonned. I have difficulty living
– and, from an eschatological perspective: cannot live – when others, to
whom I am inevitably related and connected, do not live. If I desire life
for myself, I will also desire it for others. Those who die an early death
remind me, in their suffering, of a responsibility for their lives, that
reflects my belonging to the whole of an interconnected creation.

Gutiérrez' two definitions of who the poor are, of course also invite a
christological reflection, which focuses on relational issues. The following of Jesus in his compassion for and commitment to the poor, the
excluded, the sick, the sinners, and the suffering, is often, and rightly so,
interpreted as an ethical matter. There is, however, more to it. This
appears as we apply to our dealings with the gospel the narrative methods that we have expounded before. Following Jesus means, through the
thickness of a tradition that transmits encounters by provoking encounters, entering in a relationship with him, that draws us into his relationship with the poor and, so, in his relationship with the Father, as the one
who is committed to the poor. Our solidarity – in the sense of a creational
connectedness – with the poor is, then, revealed as rooted in God's own
solidarity with the poor. What is at stake in this following of Jesus is
who we are and who God Himself is. We become persons as we are

---

66. Cf. the presentation of this debate between Gerhard Lohfink/Gisbert Greshake and
Joseph Ratzinger in an article by W. KASPER, *Individual Salvation and Eschatological
Consummation*, in J.P. GALVIN (ed.), *Faith and the Future: Studies in Christian Escha-
tology*, New York – Mahwah, NJ, Paulist Press, 1994, 7-24.

67. *The Hermeneutics of Eschatological Assertions*, in *Theological Investigations*,
Vol. 4, Baltimore, Helicon, 1966, 323-346.

called into the following of Jesus Christ to become persons, empowered as we are by God's commitment to the world, preferentially in its poor. This is not the mere consequence of our efforts to follow Christ and to build a life committed to the poor from the perspective of the interconnectedness of reality, it is foremost a gift that arises in these complex relationships. God's self-revelation is a grace, as is the fact that the poor recognize and accept our struggle with them as a struggle for them. Waiting or hoping for this gift or grace, shows how delicate and vulnerable this preferential option for the poor is: it may well be a last, perverted way to affirm our I-oriented thought at the expense of the connectedness of reality[68]. Our deepest solidarity with the world is a task and a gift, is dependent upon that connectedness itself, upon the web of encounters that constitute reality[69].

The second definition of who the poor are, as given by Gutiérrez, i.e. the poor as the voiceless who are not considered and are not a part of the conversations and encounters that "count", provides us an occasion to reflect on ecclesiological matters[70]. The voiceless, by way of their cry indicate, as an open wound, the non fulfillment of the ideal and of the dream of the community that is the Church. The message of Jesus Christ is the kindling of the hope and the promise for the Reign of God, which is compared to a festive meal, to the gathering of people enjoying the joy of God. Jesus is, therefore, the founder of the church, not because he officially or by some act instituted it, but because he proclaimed and lived the Reign of God as community: the very fact of gathering people around him is part of his message. Therefore, the church can never be seen as the mere collection of people who wish to follow Jesus or who recognize him formally as the Christ, the Son of the Living God. To build church, community around God because this is what God calls us to[71], is what people do when they follow Jesus, because it is what Jesus did himself. As such, the community born out of God's desire and self-revelation, is

68. Our service to the poor may be I-centred, after all.
69. For the complexities involved in the dynamics of the preferential option for the poor, see I. ELLACURIA, *Hacia una fundamentación del metodo teológico latinoamericano*, in *Estudios Centroamericanos* 30 (1975) 409-425.
70. Cf. SOBRINO, *Bearing with one another in Faith*, in ID. – J. HERNANDEZ PICO, *Theology of Christian Solidarity*, Maryknoll, NY, Orbis, 1985, 1-42; A. PIERIS, *God's Reign for God's Poor: A Return to the Jesus Formula*, Sri Lanka, Tulana Research Centre, 1999.
71. The word "church" comes from the Greek "kuriakos", i.e. what belongs to the Lord, or what pertains to the Lord. The word "église" comes from another Greek expression, "ek-kaleô", to call forth out of a mass or a multitude. Therefore, church means the gathering of those people called forth to build a community around God and by grace of God.

an object of faith and the church, as the effort to build such a community, is the enactment and the expression of our faith. The difficulties with which this enactment is wrought show sufficiently that, indeed, faith and trust in God's promise to bring the Reign about are part of the deal: the building of communities is a tough work. Over and over again we bend them to our own egoïstic needs, over and over again we exclude people as a way to define the identity of our community by the difference between belonging and not-belonging. The poor, as the voiceless, are those who, in their suffering, remind us that our task and our faith is to build community, to articulate and embody the connectedness that is the gift of creation and the dream of God. In a world, in which the church, because of a modern and post-modern focus on the autonomy of the "I" and its consequent critical perception of institutions that may jeopardize this autonomy, is viewed as a threat and an outdated stupidity that is unconnected and not relevant to our reality, it becomes necessary to rediscover the church as a web of relations, as a space for discernment in open conversation and encounter. Of course, this will only be possible if we, indeed, take into account the criticisms levelled against the factual structures that are the result of our efforts to build church and that very often also reflect our anguishes, our frustrations, our egoisms and our insecurities, but we should never forget, because it is the object of our faith, that building church as a community of solidarity, for the better and for the worse, is what we are called to do. Therefore, connectedness is not only a perception of reality that can be philosophically debated, it is also the core of what Christians believe. So, the preferential option for the poor as the voiceless is the enactment of the desire of God himself to build community with his creation and with his people. Again, the profoundly theological character of the preferential option for the poor surfaces.

Not surprisingly, the issue of globalization is connected not only with solidarity but also with the catholicity of the church, i.e. the fact that the church is being built for and with the whole of creation. This emphasis on catholicity, however, has to be coloured and informed by the preferential option for the poor, lest it become a metaphysical superstructure veiling and hiding the suffering of the voiceless, thereby constituting an I-centred community for lack of holistic openness. One could say it as follows: if catholicity is really our concern, then it should first of all allow for space and voice for those who suffer from the attempts to build the catholic church. The heartbeat of the church is the heartbeat of the suffering people, the excluded ones, excluded also, sometimes, by the very people who attempt to enact the church. It is here, I think, that the suggestion of "reciprocal anonimity" takes all its value, as the subversion, over and over again of all our (inevitable) exclusions in the attempt to build a community. The urge for building the church, and the creative means to do it, often expressed in sacraments, liturgy and symbolic actions[72], comes in the encounter with the poor as the voiceless. Life here means: saving from the death of exclusion and worthlessness, saving from being considered as disposable.

My next step, then, is to look, in our globalized world for a language and metaphors to express both this universal connectedness and the fact that its empowering and creative spaces are to be found with those who suffer the non-recognition[73] of the connectedness, who experience its presence as an inhuman absence, and who can rely on nothing more than their confidence and faith in its reality as a promise of God, to keep up their struggle for life. I will allow myself at this point a personal and narrative argumentation, as I want to suggest a metaphor, the full weight of which still remains to be articulated in more scientific terms. Various experiences and encounters are at the origin of the suggestion I would like to make: to consider globalization as the universalisation of liminal spaces or frontiers, i.e. spaces of encounters, where suffering arises as soon as one attempts to remove them (and so reducing the other to the same by an invasion of the space of the other) or to reduce them to a line of separation (a borderline which cuts as a scalpel of exclusion and draws blood). Let me offer some of those markings on the road to this conceptualisation, as they may well provide narrative challenges to my readers. J.M. Coetzee's book *Waiting for the Barbarians*[74] and the movies *Dances with Wolves* and *Dancer in the Dark*, have offered me metaphors for articulating without ever explaining the unsettling experience of a short, but direct contact with Burundese refugees in Tanzania's refugee camps and the continuing contact with people working in the field at the service of disposable people. Conversations with these refugees and the contact with their liturgies have shattered my prejudice that they can be no party in the efforts at solving the conflicts of which they carry the cross. I believe now that one of the keys to the resolution of these conflicts lies with them and that empowering them

---

72. See, for example V. ELIZONDO, *Guadalupe: Mother of the New Creation*, Maryknoll, NY, Orbis, 1997.

73. Several authors consider precisely this dynamism of recognition as crucial for decent human life (cf. Alex Honneth). When people experience the recognition by others, they become empowered to survive and to live. In that sense, forgiveness and reconciliation, as the effort to recognize even the worst of offenders as human beings, offer the best chances for healing the wounds caused by the offences. E.g., R.D. ENRIGHT – J. NORTH (eds.), *Exploring Forgiveness*, Madison, WI, The University of Wisconsin Press, 1998.

74. Harmondsworth, Penguin Books, 1982.

by recognizing concretely their humanity in the efforts done at their service, is helping to bring about a creative space that aims at a human future, not only for them but for the situations of which they are a part. I know that there will be the constant pain of my own egoism and sinfulness in this struggle in which I want to be with them and on their side, but which is all too often "for" them, thereby aggravating their disposability. The direct contact with detainees in a Leuven jail has made me aware of the efforts at communication and reconciliation done by those who advocate restorative justice[75] and who are willing to trust that reconciliation will come about by working on the wounded relations and connectedness, as they are hurt by the offences committed. The development of mestizo theologies[76], where the frontier mixture and the liminality talked about in the already mentioned cultural and ethnographic studies, provides me with another framework or metaphor to discuss reality as a web of encounters and frontiers. Also the reflection I was asked to perform on the significance of the religious vows helped me to discover the concept of liminality and to articulate the paradox of vowing poverty, obedience and celibacy, in the midst of people suffering from poverty, from oppression and from solitude and exclusion. Finally, I also want to mention the work done in the area of conflict resolution[77] and the contacts with people in the field who invest their energies in processes of reconciliation, building on the faith that no conflict can be as horrible as to completely destroy the fundamental connectedness between people. From them I discovered the importance of field-diplomacy and of the so-called third party, the one who stands on the breach to keep and defend the relations and conversations between people, even between conflicting people, by playing out in their own existence the conflict so as to allow the conflictuous parties to discover new avenues towards reconciliation. The reflective articulation that I attempted in all of those cases points towards the description of globalization given above and towards the conviction that the building of the church as the building of communities of encounter is probably the

75. E.g. T. PETERS, *Slachtofferschap, bemiddeling en herstelgerichte praktijken*, in B. RAYMAEKERS – A. VAN DE PUTTE (eds.), *Krachten voor de toekomst. Lessen voor de eenentwintigste eeuw*, Leuven, Universitaire Pers – Davidsfonds, 2000, 332-366.
76. V. ELIZONDO, *The Future is Mestizo: Life where Cultures Meet*, Boulder, CO, University Press of Colorado, 2000; D.G. GROODY, *Border of Death, Valley of Life: An Immigrant Journey of Heart and Spirit*, Lanham, MD – Boulder, CO – New York – Oxford, Rowman & Littlefield, 2002.
77. E.g., L. REYCHLER – T. PAFFENHOLZ (eds.), *Peace-Building: A Field Guide*, Boulder, CO – London, Lynne Rienner, 2001; J.P. LEDERACH, *The Journey towards Reconciliation*, Scottdale, PA – Waterloo, Ontario, Herald Press, 1999.

single most important task for Christians today. It requires faith, incarnated in a kenotic attitude that puts the relations and the encounters between people first and that is willing to run the risk of being frustrated, contradicted and even destroyed.

The work done in all of these fields represents but a small collection of pebble stones on the road of the proposed research programme. Many more fields should be explored, to show that the convergence of ideas and concerns that is already appearing here with regard to the root metaphors of encounter and conversation and with regard to reality as interconnectedness, is real and important.

Our concepts of encounter and conversation have gained clarity in the encounter with concrete situations and challenges. We are discovering also that there where people are hurt and there where people, because of that hurt, suffer, lie creative spaces that cry out for the need to rediscover and re-articulate our connectedness. They remember us of the fact that the I can never be thought of as loosened from its ties and connections, and that those encounters are universal, have a holistic scope. Globalization in that sense may be used as an argument and a defense in favour of the excluded and marginalized, and one should maybe avoid to speak about globalization where greed, fear, oppression and exploitation, lead the dance. Why then not use these latter words, that describe well enough what is happening, instead of sweetening them up by using the ambiguous "globalization" as if it were to blur the awareness of evil.

IV. FURTHER ELEMENTS FOR A RESEARCH PROGRAMME

What we are discovering, attempting to formulate, and will continue to analyze in the coming days, is a research programme which in a very obvious way and by simple means (the introduction of the metaphor of encounter at the center of our theological endeavours), allows us to touch the core of our faith (the message of the Reign of God tentatively anticipated in the construction of church) and at the same time to take a profound stance in today's broken world (globalization as empowerment on the frontiers). I would like to end this presentation by pointing to some of the tasks ahead in developing and unfolding this research programme which, I am convinced, will help us to develop a theology adapted to our times and touching the very core of our human commitments. These are steps in articulating the hypothesis that was at the departure of this presentation.

1. The need for a fundamental reflection in which the concepts of connectedness, relation, encounter and conversation are explored and studied and in which the proper references are looked for that can be of help to this intellectual endeavour. Proper attention should be paid to the methods used in theology.

2. Work on the level of mediations. This implies identifying those issues and challenges that confront us, precisely as challenges towards our connectedness. To this extent we will have to use existing scientific approaches and maybe develop some new ones. This implies also: discovering and exploring as many fields as possible where the metaphors of connectedness, encounter and conversation play a determining role.

3. Resourcing ourselves in our classics and our history. We have to develop methods to read the gospels anew precisely from the perspective of empowering encounters. Feminist theology will be of great help in this endeavour. This means (a) work on the life of Jesus itself, explaining it as a web of encounters, and (b) the study of our own approaches to the bible, where texts really become "classics" in that they produce an impact that can be narratively analyzed.

4. An analysis of the theological vocabulary from the perspective of encounter (that is to a large extent what we are doing in these LEST days) as well as a rediscovery of an ecclesiology that considers the building of the church as an act of faith and hope in the conversation with God through the following of Jesus.

5. Paying a close look at the history of theology, to discover that there is a long tradition of theologians working from this relational perspective.

6. Re-articulating fundamental moral theology from the perspective of encounter and, therefore, from the perspective of discernment.

7. Learning from interreligious and intercultural dialogue and taking seriously the effort of being involved in those.

8. Rediscovering the importance of spirituality for theology as well as the importance of theology for spirituality. Unfolding the elements that empower people to become keepers of the bond and of the covenant.

9. Developing an action programme from the perspective of those who by their suffering and their cry point to the areas where connectedness and compassion have been broken.

10. Consciously become *defensores vinculi*, i.e. being aware of that "supplementary", and hidden, ontological dimension that Christianity aims at uncovering and developing.

I realize that what I have said may provoke very varied reactions and they will undoubtedly surface in the coming days. May they surface in the context of conversations between friends, because that can be the only space in which to work, if we really want to put the metaphors of conversation and encounter at the centre of our theological endeavours.

I thank you for your patience.

Faculteit Godgeleerdheid
K.U. Leuven
St.-Michielsstraat 6
B-3000 Leuven
Belgium

Jacques HAERS, S.J.

I

REFLECTING ON GOD AND CREATION

CONVERSATION AND TRINITY

GOD AS CONVERSATION

REFLECTIONS ON A THEOLOGICAL ONTOLOGY
OF COMMUNICATIVE RELATIONS

I. WHICH RELATIONALITY? WHICH GOD?

Relationality has become one of the major paradigms in theology in recent times. The theories that are developed within this paradigm come from a variety of sources and employ a variety of strategies of interpretation and conceptual tools. From feminist theologies to process thought, from personalist conceptions to a variety of liberationist perspectives, from neo-patristic syntheses to Reformation theologies, relationality has become one of the major foci of current constructive theological thinking[1]. This concentration on modes of relational thought and practice is by no means restricted to theology. From particle physics to popular psychology relationality discourse has become common parlance. On the one hand, this opens up possibilities of intellectual encounter and communicative exchange between theologies and other arts and sciences. On the other hand, the degree to which relational thinking has become popular also implies the danger that relationality discourse becomes inflationary and opaque.

The critical impetus of the different models of relationality is directed against two dominant paradigms of interpreting reality in the Western tradition. The first is the framework of substance metaphysics within which most forms of discourse on reality can be placed until the beginning of modernity. Substance metaphysics interprets the world as an ordered system of substances. What something is can be conceived by asking what underlies the changing attributes of something as their constant bearer. The underlying being which is ultimately independent of the way it is conceived is the substantial core of a given structure of reality, it constitutes the essential order of being. For Aristotle, for instance, the concept of substance denotes both that of which something is predicated

---

1. Cf. such contrasting works as E. JOHNSON, *She Who Is*, New York, 1992; T. PETERS, *God as Trinity. Relationality and Temporality in Divine Life*, Louisville, KY, 1993; D. PRATT, *Relational Deity. Hartshorne and Macquarrie on God*, Lanham, MD, 2002; C. SCHWÖBEL, *Gott in Beziehung. Studien zur Dogmatik*, Tübingen, 2002.

(first substance), and the attributes which are predicated and which are therefore analysed as classification concepts (second substance). If the order of reality is built upon these elements, all relations must be conceived as external relations which ultimately can be analysed as attributes, indicating being in relation to something else. Relationality is neither constitutive of that of which something is predicated, nor of that which is predicated. In this framework, being in its substantial structure determines knowing. However, the relationship of knowing remains external to being.

The second is the framework of theories of subjectivity which replaced the framework of substance metaphysics in the history of Western thought. Here everything is built upon the self-relation of the knowing subject to such an extent that the question of the possibility of how something can be known has priority over the question what something is. The possibilities of knowing what there is are consequently more and more focussed on the self-relation of the knower so that in the more radical idealist theories of subjectivity everything that there is, is constituted in the self-relation of the knowing subject. Being is to be known, and knowing is grounded in the self-knowledge of the knower as a knowing subject. In contrast to the framework of substance metaphysics, the framework of subjectivity is characterised by relationality. However, there exists the constant danger that everything is only insofar as it is internally related to the self-relation of the knowing subject. In such a framework there can be neither genuine otherness nor objectivity.

The attraction of relational views of reality consists in offering an alternative to both frameworks, both of which have been rendered highly problematical in various areas of our engagement with reality, from particle physics to our understanding of social interaction in society. However, while the critical front over against which relational views of reality are developed can be described with relative clarity, it is much less clear what defines relationality constructively. Are the social relations in which we exist the ultimate paradigm for understanding reality or are they themselves only functions of the physical structure of relationality which seems to undergird everything that there is? Which theory and conceptuality of relationality should be taken as normative for the interpretation of reality? Where are we to turn to in order to develop a relational theology?

The question "which relationality?" cannot be answered without first and foremost dealing with the question "which God?". Whichever conceptualities of relationality Christian theology proposes, they must be rooted in the theological understanding of God. Confessing, as Christian faith does, the triune God, Father, Son and Spirit, as the one who relates to the world in creation, reconciliation and consummation, makes all patterns of relationality dependent on God as the ground, meaning and goal of everything there is. Where patterns of relationality do not have their source and norm in God, we are, in fact, dealing with alternative theologies, a-theo-logies and anti-theologies which confess other deities.

In order to make some first steps in developing a relational theology, I shall try to deal with the theme of this conference in a fairly radical manner. My thesis is that conversation is not something external to Christian theology but that all Christian theology ultimately has the character of conversation. It is of necessity engaged not only in internal theological conversation, but also with the "three publics" as David Kelsey has called them: the church, society and the academy[2]. This, however, is rooted in the fact that Christian faith, which is the basis of Christian theology, has the character of conversation, of a conversation in the church and with the world, which is based in the practice of faith as an ongoing conversation about God and with God. The conversation about God and with God is itself rooted in the fact that God engages in conversation with his creation, from creation until the consummation of God's conversations with his creation in the Kingdom of God. Furthermore, that God engages in conversation with his creation is rooted in God's own being as conversation so that the being of the world has its ground in the conversation that God is. This proposal, which is by no means original, is radical in a precise way since it argues for the view that the conversation that God *has* with creation has its roots in the conversations that God *is*, and both of these in their interconnectedness are the roots of a relational theology. While there is a long tradition of understanding theology as conversation, perhaps most famously represented by Augustine[3], the understanding of God as conversation seems, at least at first sight, much more unusual. The American theologian, Robert W. Jenson, has given the notion of conversation a highly significant place both in his treatment of "The Being of the One God" in volume I of his *Systematic Theology* and in his treatment of "The Creation" in volume II[4]. The remarks made

2. D. TRACY, *The Analogical Imagination. Christian Theology and the Culture of Pluralism*, New York, 1981.
3. Cf. R. HERZOG, *Non in sua voce – Augustins Gespräch mit Gott in den Confessiones*, in K. STIERLE – R. WARNING (eds.), *Das Gespräch, Poetik und Hermeneutik XI*, München, 1984, 213-250. This volume of scholarly contributions on the theme of conversation still remains the most valuable source for further engagement with this topic.
4. Cf. R. JENSON, *Systematic Theology, Vol. I: The Triune God*, New York – Oxford, 1997, p. 223, where "conversation" is the fourth and last characteristic of the one being of God, following "event", "person" and "decision". In *Vol. II: The Works of God*, New York – Oxford, 1999, the theme of "conversation" becomes the guide-line for developing

there were the inspiration for these preliminary explorations into the theme of God as conversation, in the course of which, as befits a Lutheran theologian, Luther became the main witness for such a view in the way in which he developed his theology as scriptural reasoning.

II. BACK TO THE ROOTS: SCRIPTURE AS THE RECORD OF THE DIVINE-HUMAN CONVERSATION

Whenever Christian theology is challenged to lay open the resources in which the activity of doing theology is rooted, it will ultimately have to return to Scripture. The system of signs with which Christian theology operates is closely related to the use of signs in Christian worship, and the signifying activities in Christian worship have their unity in all their variety by drawing on the signs of the biblical witnesses. Therefore, if one asks what connects Christian theology in all its variety, it is its relationship to Scripture, which has its own unity in variety[5]. This is, first of all, a descriptive claim, which applies to all kinds of Christian thought throughout the ages. One could neither say what "Christian" is nor what "theology" is without going back to Scripture. The same applies, of course, for Christian faith. The whole range of its forms of expression and the whole scope of its content would not make sense without understanding its roots in the biblical witness. That Scripture is, in the various forms of its uses in Christian worship and in Christian practice, the ultimate authority of all Christian theology shows itself nowhere more clearly than in the way in which different accounts of authority in the Christian church all adduce arguments of Scripture in order to demonstrate their validity. Arguments about the status of authority always tend to become arguments about the uses of Scripture. All reform movements in the Christian church have drawn their justification from Scripture, and all attempts to question the validity of their concerns have turned to Scripture for validation.

If we look at the scriptural witnesses we can see that quite apart from the specific profile of their different theological conceptions they all present communication as a normative paradigm for depicting the God-world-relationship. God speaks and the world comes into being. Humans

---

the relationship between the being of God and the being of creation: "In the context of creation the specification of God's being as conversation is privileged".

5. I have developed this in more detail in the article: *Bibel IV. Dogmatisch*, in H.D. BETZ et al (eds.), *Religion in Geschichte und Gegenwart*, 4. völlig neu bearbeitete Aufl., Bd. 1, Tübingen, 1998, cols. 1426-1432.

are created in the image of God as those creatures who are addressed and enabled to respond to God. The creaturely responsibility lies in hearing and responding to God's address. The history of God's relationship to his people Israel is one where Israel is created by God's promise and has its being in the faithfulness of God to keep his promise. The covenant is established by a divine promise, and the covenantal relationship is maintained through listening to God's commandments and through God addressing his people again where they fail to listen. The views of Israel's history are in their core accounts of God's talking in promise and judgement and of Israel's responding to this address in obedience or rebellion. Israel's identity is rooted in a promise addressed to Israel, and its ongoing life depends on obeying the mandates that are entailed in the promise. Where Israel stops to listen to its God and begins to listen to other voices God does not remain silent but re-addresses his people in the words of the prophets and through the message communicated in Israel's history. Wisdom consists in following God's word as it is inscribed upon the order of reality and expressed in the Torah. The Psalms offer a rich tapestry of humans addressing God in praise, thanksgiving, petition and lament, in directing the whole life of believers, individually and communally, to God's word, by reminding God of his promises and remembering his past speaking as a promise for the future. The deepest crisis of faith – as the story of Job relates – is encountered where God remains silent so that turning to God in lamentation is the only way of dealing with a situation where God's will cannot be read from the way things go in the world – until God speaks. In the contradictory tensions between the experience of the world and faith in God the only ground for hope is God's word and the expectation that God might speak again.

In the New Testament the traditions of depicting the relationship between God and the world as a communicative relationship is continued in a way that maintains the whole history of God's address and Israel's response and sees it as completed and fulfilled in Jesus Christ as the first and last word of God: "In many and various ways God spoke of old to our fathers by the prophets; but in these last days he has spoken to us by a Son, whom he appointed the heir of all things, through whom also he created the world" (Heb 1,1-2). Jesus is understood as God's address which embraces the whole of the communicative relationship between God and the world from first to last, from the proto-logical beginning to the eschatological fulfilment. The whole of history has its meaning as a history of God's speaking. What is distinctive about Jesus is that he speaks God's word, the word that inaugurated the coming of the Kingdom of God, the word of forgiveness that only God can grant, the word

of healing that can only be the word of the creator, the word of judgment
that remains God's prerogative. What later dogmatic formulations call
the "divinity" of Jesus Christ is grounded in his ability to speak the divine
word with the authority of God. But not only that. Jesus also speaks the
word of the obedient creature; his word is also the perfect response to
God, the response that gathers those together who hear Jesus' word as
God's word and who participate in his response to God as the adequate
human response to God's address. He shows himself as the Son of God
by enabling the people who follow him to address God as Father and
through him to participate as God's sons and daughters in Jesus' filial
relationship to God. What later dogmatic formulations call the "humanity" of Jesus is rooted in his response to God as the perfect creature.
In this respect he is the "pioneer and perfecter of our faith" (Heb 12,2).
The drama of Jesus' fate is centred on the question of whether the claim
implicit in his words and deeds is true: Is he the place of encounter
between God and humanity where God's word and the human response
meet? Is he the culmination of Israel's history with God or is he blas-
pheming God by speaking with his authority and denying the God of
Israel by claiming to be the eschatological fulfilment of that history?
The cross is the place where Jesus bears the silence of God in the God-
forsakeness that is the fate of sinners; the resurrection is God's word of
vindication of Jesus' claim to speak God's word and to articulate the adequate human response. Already in the New Testament we see the beginning of reflection which leads to later dogmatic formulations: If Jesus
speaks the word of God, and if God vindicates Jesus' message, then he
must be the word of God from the beginning which has become embodied in Jesus and through which he maintains communion with those who
believe in him.

    If one surveys the biblical witnesses of the Old and New Testaments
it is hard to avoid the conclusion that what is depicted in a pluriform variety is indeed the record of the divine-human conversation, of how God
spoke in "many and various ways" and of how humans are called to
respond in speaking to God and speaking of God. The emphasis on God's
speaking is nearly always accompanied by the role of God's Spirit in giving life to creation and in enabling creation to respond to God, even to
speak prophetically the word of God. If one sees the Bible as the record
of divine-human conversation one must take the Bible's own claim seriously that this conversation does not finish with the completion of the biblical books. Just as the written form of the biblical witnesses is the scriptural echo of God's speech, so this conversation is to be continued in
translating the written form into speech again so that through Scripture

God's address continues to be heard. This process of translation characterises the practice of Christian worship. The written text is the basis for the oral proclamation of the Gospel, and it is orally enacted in the various forms of liturgical interaction so that through the witness of human words the *viva vox Dei* can be heard and finds its response in the spoken utterances of faith. The implicit presupposition of this practice is that God continues to speak through the proclamation of the gospel and continues to listen to the prayer and liturgical invocation of the congregation.

One of the most problematical aspects of twentieth century theology is that it has often perceived the speaking of God and the acting of God in history as a contrast so that theologies of the word of God were pitted against theologies of history and vice versa. If one looks at the biblical witness one can see that theologies of the word of God and theologies of history are never separated but are combined in complex and sophisticated patterns, both in individual traditions and in the canon as a whole. These different conceptions of God's acting and God's speaking have their unity in God since the God of the Bible is a God who does things with words and who makes things that speak. God's speaking and the human response in word and deed constitute a history, and, conversely, history is punctuated by the events of divine speech, which make up its narrative continuity. God's action is communicative action, and God's speech effects what it says. The same contrast recurs in the opposition between historical criticism and literary, especially narrative criticism. In the texts this is not an opposition because history is constituted through the narratives of divine address and human response, and narrative has realistic intention. What has to be avoided is a theology of the word of God which does not give the word a history-constituting and history-shaping dimension and a theology of history which perceives the mighty deeds of God apart from the events of God's speaking. If we see God's interaction with his creation in terms of a conversation, both come together: The events of God's speaking and of the human response take up time; they form a narrative unity whereby earlier occasions of God's speaking can be remembered (or God can be reminded of them) and so form the expectation of a continuing conversation.

The biblical record of the divine-human conversation, which is continued with reference to this record in Christian proclamation and worship today, forms the basis for the work of dogmatic reconstruction. There are many forms of interpreting the biblical witness in a way that is "ontology-neutral". It is then implicitly denied that the biblical expressions have an ontological import. Such attempts start from a given ontology, a given view of reality, and then attempt to make sense of the biblical witness within that framework. This contradicts the explicit intention of the biblical writers. They develop views of reality in which the events they portray, the narratives they relate, the commandments they hand on to future generations, the rules of wisdom they recount define what there is, how it is, why it is, why it is how it is, and what it is for. The theological challenge therefore consists in taking the biblical texts seriously in their ontological claims and in trying to reconstruct an ontology, a conceptual reconstruction of the biblical views of reality, on their basis. The theological challenge for a relational theology therefore is not to impose an already defined framework of relationality on the biblical witness but to try and define relationality from these roots.

III. ESTABLISHING THE CONVERSATION: CREATION AND COVENANT

It has often been remarked that the account of creation offered by the priestly author of Genesis 1 combines two different sources, an account of creation by word and an account of creation by deed[6]. The point that is to be observed, however, is not that two modes of creation form the background of the text as we have it, but that they could be combined in the way in which we read them today. Creating, in the exclusive sense in which it is used in Genesis 1, is precisely to be understood in terms of creative speaking. What both creative speaking and creative action have in common is that they posit a reality that did not exist before. God's speaking is not making declarations about an already given state of affairs. It calls this state of affairs into being. Therefore God's creative speech is not simply the establishment of existence. What is called into existence by the divine word exists in a specifically ordered relationship to God and to other creatures. Created being has its ground in the divine word. Its particular character of contingent being consists in being dependent for its existence on God's word. God's word is the subsistence of created being. All created being therefore consists in a constitutive relationship to God's word. This applies to the whole structure of created being. Particular created beings exist in a relationship to one another because their constitutive relationship is their relationship to God's word. This is a relationship of absolute dependence, since God in his word is the ground of being of all created being. Nevertheless, within this absolute dependence there is

6. Cf. C. LEVIN, *Tatbericht und Wortbericht in der Priesterlichen Schöpfungserzählung*, in *Zeitschrift für Theologie und Kirche* 91 (1994) 115-133.

room for created and even creative interdependence, since God's word can employ the results of divine speaking as instruments of his creativity[7]. The waters and the earth, both created by God's word, are thus turned into created instruments of God's creativity (cf. Gen 1,20.24). Furthermore, the different kinds of being depend for the maintenance of their existence on one another which is both expressed in the *dominium terrae* and in the provision of food for the different kinds of creatures (cf. Gen 1,28-30).

That creation comes into being by God's word has a number of astonishing implications. In an account of reality which takes Genesis 1 seriously there cannot be a division between being and meaning so that being would have to be seen as a meaningless mass of entities unless meaning is imposed upon it. Rather, meaning, the meaning of God's word, is the source of being. Meaning is invested into the created order from the beginning by God's word. Therefore, the truth about the meaning of being is to be found in the correspondence between statements expressing the meaning of being with the meaning invested into being by the word of God. Moreover, one of the ontological implications of the creation of the world by God's word is that, although the world is dependent on God's communicative relationship to it, it has its own relatively independent ontological status. The ontological truth which the doctrine of *creatio ex nihilo* attempted to formulate is that the world is, on the one hand, wholly dependent for its being on God; on the other hand, it has a created, relative independence which constitutes real otherness. It is not made from prior existing matter so that God's creating could be understood as shaping an already given material. God's word is the unconditional ground of existence. Neither is the world to be understood as being made from God's substance so that it would be a semi-divine extension of divine being. The juxtaposition of making and speaking in Genesis 1 makes it clear that the world is the result of God's free sovereign action and of God's deliberate speaking.

The otherness of creation consists not only in its being called into existence by God's word, but also in its being capable of being addressed by God and of being called into communion with God. Insofar as creation is addressed by God its whole being is responsive being, the existential response to the word of the creator. The relational order of created being is thereby characterised by reciprocity in the relationship to the creator. This reciprocity is strictly asymmetrical. In responding to God's address

---

7. Cf. M. WELKER, *What is "Creation"? Rereading Genesis 1 and 2*, in *Theology Today* 48 (1991) 56-71.

the creatures acknowledge their dependence on God's word. This responsive character of creation is focussed in God's human creatures. The doctrine of the *imago Dei* (Gen 1,26-27) has received in the history of interpretation a wide variety of interpretations. A number of points are immediately clear; others remain open to contextual interpretation. It is clear that the privilege of being created in the image of God which in other ancient near eastern cultures is reserved for the king is extended to all humans. Furthermore, this privilege is granted to male and female in their relationship. The mandate to be fruitful and multiply shows that the *imago Dei* is to be exercised socially, in human community, and historically, in the sequence of human generations. The relationship established between God and his creation is a process which is meant to have a future.

The immediately following mandate of the *dominium terrae* which – although not identical with the *imago Dei* – is closely connected to it, makes it clear that humans have the freedom to exercise dominion over the non-human creation. Humans are *imagines libertatis Dei*, images of the freedom of God[8]. However, this freedom is a freedom which is granted to them by God. It is rooted in and limited by God's mandate. If we read Genesis 2, the Yahwist account of creation, as a commentary on Genesis 1, the way in which this freedom is exercised is by listening to God's word and by responding to it in word and action. In humans the responsive being of the whole created order becomes responsibility before God for one another and for the non-human creation. As *imago Dei* the human being is first *homo audiens* and then *homo loquens*. God's mandate, the form in which the images of God exercise their freedom is to name the animals. God's address to humans to eat of every tree in the garden but not from the tree of the knowledge of good and evil (Gen 2,17) is regarded by Luther in the *Lectures on Genesis* as the foundation of the church.

> Here we have the establishment of the church before there was any government of the home and of the state; for Eve was not yet created. Moreover, the church is established without walls and without any pomp, in a very spacious and delightful place. After the church has been established, the household government is also set up, when Eve is added to Adam as his companion[9].

---

8. Cf. C. SCHWÖBEL, *Imago Libertatis. Human and Divine Freedom*, in C.E. GUNTON, *God and Freedom. Essays in Historical and Systematic Theology*, Edinburgh, 1995, 57-81; in German: *Imago Libertatis: Freiheit des Menschen und Freiheit Gottes*, in SCHWÖBEL, *Gott in Beziehung* (n. 1), pp. 227-256.

9. M. LUTHER, *Lectures on Genesis Chapters 1–5*, in J. PELIKAN (ed.), *Luther's Works*, Vol. I, St. Louis, MO, 1958, p. 103.

The church is truly the creature of the word, established by God's address to Adam. It is the conversation between God and humanity which is established when God first addresses a human being. Luther's intention seems to be to make clear that the communion between God and humanity precedes any ordered human community. The aim of creation is the establishment of communion between the creator and his creation in which the response of creation is focussed in God's human creatures. Creation is from the beginning directed towards a covenantal form of life. This communion has the form of an on-going conversation of God with humanity where humans are responsible to God in everything they do. This conversation is the context in which created, finite freedom is to be exercised.

IV. DISRUPTING THE CONVERSATION: SIN

Against this background, the character of sin as it is depicted in Genesis 3 easily becomes clear. When the serpent "more subtle than any other wild creature that the Lord God had made" asks Eve: "Did God say ...?" (Gen 3,1), it questions God's word and God's will expressed in the permission to eat from all trees except the tree of the knowledge of good and evil. Luther again offers an interesting interpretation of the passage: "... the chief temptation was to listen to another word and to depart from the one God had previously spoken". This temptation can occur because the tempter employs the same mode of communication that God employs in addressing humans: "In the first place, Satan imitates God. Just as God had preached to Adam, so he himself also preaches to Eve". Satan's sermon – if we continue in Luther's mode expression – consists in questioning the created status of human freedom as freedom that is dependent on being exercised within the framework of listening to God's word, as freedom which is grounded in and limited by God's word. He does so by offering a different gospel: "You will not die. For God knows that when you eat of it (sc. the fruit of the tree) your eyes will be opened, and you will be like God, knowing good and evil" (Gen 3,4b-5). Following a different promise than that of the creator destroys the trust in God's word. Therefore: "Unbelief is the source of all sins; when Satan brought about this unbelief by driving out or corrupting the Word, the rest was easy for him"[10]. The temptation therefore consists in longing "for a different wisdom, a wisdom apart from the Word"[11]. Wisdom which does not have its

---

10. LUTHER, *Lectures* (n. 9), p. 147.
11. *Ibid.*, p. 161.

orientation in the word of God, which is not grounded in the relationship is wisdom which leads away from God into alienation from God. The serpent offers enlightenment apart from the word of God, outside of the conversation with God. When the enlightenment occurs – "the eyes of both were opened" (Gen 3,7) – all they see is themselves outside the relationship with their creator: naked, eager to blame one another and afraid of God. What the first humans cannot exercise by their own means is "the ability to distinguish between spirits" (1 Cor 12,10). This ability can only be a gift of the Spirit of truth and so they mistake the illusionary illumination of Satan with the light of true knowledge which cannot be kindled by human means, but can only be made to shine in human hearts by the one who said "Let light shine out of darkness" (2 Cor 4,4).

Genesis 3 gives a vivid account of how contradicting God's word by believing the word of the serpent and thereby denying the relationship with God as the formative relationship in the order of relationships of human life spreads into all relationships in which humans exist. The first humans experience their nakedness as shameful, their relationship to themselves as corporeal beings is disturbed. When they hear the sound of God walking in the garden in the cool of the day, the audible sign of God's presence becomes a threat. The creator to whose word and act they owe their existence becomes a threat to their lives. They try to evade the address to which they owe their being. They have become dislocated in the network of relationships. God's question: "Where are you?" discloses this dislocation. Adam's attempt to justify himself by saying that he hid before God because he was naked is interpreted by Luther as evading responsibility by accusing God. He makes God responsible for fleeing from him. The conversation with God has become perverted in the attempt to evade responsibility. The responsive nature of humanity is abused in the attempt at self-justification. When Adam is reminded of his responsibility he avoids confessing his guilt by blaming Eve. "The woman thou gavest to be with me ..." (Gen 3,12). When Eve is questioned, she blames the serpent: "The serpent beguiled me ..." (Gen 3,13). The relationality which is the hallmark of created existence is turned into a network of sin. The conversation with God serves the only aim to avoid responsibility.

What the author of Genesis 3 illustrates so vividly is the inability of humans to restore the relationship to God, to return to obedience to the word of God once they have questioned the truth of God's word. Their attempt at justifying themselves becomes a symptom of their inability to achieve righteousness by their own means. The doctrine of original sin has as its core the insight into the soteriological powerlessness of humans.

They cannot offer themselves the word of forgiveness, because forgiveness can only be granted by the one who has been sinned against. The self-perpetuating character of sin belongs to the very nature of sin.

> Let us learn therefore, that this is the nature of sin; unless God immediately provides a cure and calls the sinner back, he flees endlessly from God and, by excusing his sin with lies heaps sin upon sin until he arrives at blasphemy and despair. Thus sin by its own gravitation always draws with it another sin and brings on eternal destruction, till finally the sinful person would rather accuse God than acknowledge his own sin[12].

This gravitational pull of sin is what is at the core of original sin which is echoed in every actual sin. The conversation with God turns into a monologue of self-justification by accusing others.

In spite of the disruption of sin God does not end his conversation with his alienated creation. The punishment of death, the ultimate silence of God, is not executed. As the story of humanity unfolds, the creator maintains his relationship to his rebellious creatures by restoring the conversation time and again. God's will to establish community with his creatures is upheld over against all human attempts to escape from community with God. God remains faithful to his will to be a God in conversation with his creation. The promise to the Fathers, the Exodus, the establishment of the covenant with Israel and its reestablishment over against human unfaithfulness all witness to the constancy of God's faithfulness. It is this faithfulness to himself which motivates God again and again to restore the conversation with his people. In his relationship to Israel God makes himself available to Israel's address by disclosing his identity in his name and in his actions and thus gives Israel an identity as the people addressed by God and called to respond in obedience to his word. Sin, the disruption of the divine-human conversation from the human side, cannot establish a new order of relationships in creation; it remains a contradiction which God does not leave uncontradicted.

V. RESTORING THE CONVERSATION: THE INCARNATION OF THE WORD

The Christian gospel portrays the coming of Jesus of Nazareth, his words, deeds and destiny, as the incarnation of the divine Word. If one were to look for evidence for the claim that communication and conversation is the paradigm for the divine-human encounter in the biblical writings, this is perhaps the most striking piece of evidence. The incarnation

---

12. *Ibid.*, p. 175.

is, on the one hand, portrayed in continuity with God's conversation with Israel. Jesus is firmly placed in the context of the story of his people which, as God's conversation partner, is God's people. On the other hand, Jesus is confessed by Christians to be the culmination of Israel's story with God precisely through the fact that the whole of humanity is drawn into conversation with God through God's address in Jesus.

The story of Jesus constantly interweaves two stories. The one is the story about God's conversation with humanity which had begun in creation by addressing humans and calling for their response which – in spite of humanity's contradiction against God's word – is continued through the history of the Fathers and of Israel. This story is continued and perfected in Jesus because in him God addresses humanity in and through a human being who speaks God's word with God's authority. In Jesus' speaking of God, God's address is heard. In his words and deeds of forgiveness and healing God's forgiveness is granted and God's healing of the wounds of creation begins. In his words of judgment God's judgment is pronounced. Jesus' words carry the signature of God's speaking in that they effect what they say. Therefore in Jesus' message of the coming of the kingdom of God the reality of the kingdom becomes actual in his person. The kingdom is not a reality divorced from Jesus' message, it begins to become actual in Jesus' words. Jesus therefore is the point of encounter with God's saving word, believing in his word is believing in God's word.

The other story which is inextricably woven into Jesus' story as the address of God to humanity in Jesus is the story of humanity's response to God's word in Jesus. Jesus is not just the one who speaks God's word, he is also the one who first listens to God's address and follows it in perfect obedience. Jesus is the one who sees the heavens opened; he experiences the disclosure of the aim of God's ways with his creation, is empowered by the Spirit and addressed by God as the beloved Son. When the Spirit leads him into the wilderness and the relationship which is established by God's word and sustained by God's Spirit is tested, Jesus does not follow the other voices which address him offering alternative promises. His listening to the voice of God is not disrupted by turning away from God's word, by doubting God's word and putting his trust in other words. The *anakephalaiosis* of Adam's and Eve's story in Jesus' story, the recapitulation of the archetypical story on which Irenaeus placed such enormous weight, therefore, does not end in sin, but becomes the story of faith, of unbroken trust. This is the restoration of the divine-human conversation from the human side.

Jesus' story is the story of the uninterrupted conversation of God with humanity and of humanity with God. Jesus therefore is the *interlocutor* between God and humanity. His word mediates God's address to humanity so that God's word becomes audible in a human voice, and his word mediates the response of humanity to God, uninterrupted by following other voices. The two stories are interwoven in one story, which relates both the way God relates in Jesus to humanity and the way humanity relates in Jesus to God. The incarnation of the word of God is the way in which the divine word takes the form of embodied human discourse so that God's word becomes audible in a human voice. God's word incarnate is at the same time the perfect human response to God's word, the carnal being of humanity turned into the voice answering to God's address. Here as in many places of the biblical traditions God's word is not without God's Spirit. It is God's Spirit who establishes and maintains Jesus' relationship to God the Father as the stories of Jesus' conception, baptism and temptation are keen to stress, and in the Spirit Jesus turns to God the Father.

God's word in Jesus is depicted in the New Testament as God's universal address to humanity which draws all nations into the conversation with God which from the beginning is humanity's destiny and which shapes the history of Israel. By extending Israel's conversation with God to all nations, the whole of humanity is enabled in Christ to respond to God's call by addressing Israel's God as Father and relating to him as God's children. Again it is the Spirit of God who mediates this relationship and who makes Jesus' address to God the Father available for the whole of humanity (cf. Rom 8,11-17).

Jesus can be interpreted both as God's final word (Heb 1,1-2) and as the word who was in the beginning (John 1,1). The culmination of God's conversation with humanity is rooted in the fact that being in conversation belongs to the being of God from the beginning. The first verse of the Gospel of John, where God's final word is depicted as the word that was in the beginning, is interpreted by Luther in the *Sermons on the Gospel of St. John* in the following way:

> St. John thus declares that there was in God a Speech or Word who occupied all of God, that He was God Himself, that He had preceded the existence of all creatures, even of the angels. No one saw or heard him, not even the angels, since at that time they had not yet been created. Thus it must be a word or conversation, not of any angels or of any creatures but of God Himself, Thus we see here the term "the Word", not any ordinary word but a Word that is as great as God Himself. Indeed, the Word is God Himself[13].

---

13. LUTHER, *Sermons on the Gospel of St. John, Chapters 1–4*, in J. PELIKAN (ed.), *Luther's Works* (n. 9), p. 12.

For Luther, the fact "that God, too, has a Word or conversation within Himself"[14] means that the history of salvation begins with a conversation in the divine Trinity. The way in which the divine conversation precedes and initiates the divine-human conversation is expressed nowhere more vividly than in Luther's hymn "Nun freut euch, liebe Christen gemein", translated by Richard Massie as "Dear Christians, One and All, Rejoice"[15]. After exhorting all Christians to rejoice and sing, proclaiming the wonders God has done, the hymn offers a detailed description of the human situation in bondage to sin.

> Fast bound in Satan's chains I lay,
> Death brooded darkly o'er me,
> Sin was my torment night and day ...
> Life had become a living hell ...

From this situation, liberation by human means is impossible, since "my own good works availed me naught" and "[m]y fears increased till sheer despair". Liberation must come from God who "before the world's foundation" perceives the wretchedness of the sinner, turns "his father's heart" to the sinner, seeks the sinner's redemption and so addresses His Son:

> Tis time to have compassion.
> Then go, bright Jewel of My crown,
> And bring to man salvation;
> From sin and sorrow set him free,
> Slay bitter death for him that he
> May live with thee forever.

In obeying the will of the Father, the Son is born: "He came to be my brother". His redemption of the sinner is proclaimed by the incarnate Son to the sinner.

> To me He spake: Hold fast to Me,
> I am Thy Rock and Castle;
> Thy Ransom I Myself will be,
> For thee I strive and wrestle;
> For I am with thee, I am thine,
> And evermore thou shalt be Mine;
> The Foe shall not divide us.

The word of God establishes a union with the sinner in which the "joyous exchange" takes place – "My innocence shall bear thy sin" – which,

14. *Ibid.*, p. 13.
15. *Lutheran Book of Worship*, p. 299. For a concise analysis of this hymn in the context of Luther's trinitarian theology, cf. C. HELMER, *The Trinity and Martin Luther. A Study on the Relationship between Genre, Language and the Trinity in Luther's Works*, Mainz, 1999, pp. 121-188.

when the Son goes back to the Father is continued by the Spirit who continues the address of the Son to the justified sinner.

> He shall in trouble comfort thee,
> Teach thee to know and follow Me,
> And in all truth shall guide thee,
> What I have done and taught, teach thou,
> My ways forsake thou never; ...

The address of the Son is interpreted as establishing a real communion of mutual belonging which is for ever maintained by the teaching of the Spirit.

VI. CONTINUING THE CONVERSATION FOREVER: THE CHURCH AND THE ESCHATON

The way in which Luther construes the on-going relationship of the justified sinner through the Spirit with the Son leads to the continuation of the restored divine-human conversation in the church. According to the view of the Reformation, the church is *creatura verbi divini*, the creature of the word[16]. It is not the extension of the Incarnation, because the extension of the Incarnation is the reign of Christ at the right hand of God. In contrast to the Son, the church is a creature which is called into being by the address of the word of God, so that the church is understood as the ongoing conversation between God and his creatures – if we follow Luther – already begun in the garden of Eden. The content of this conversation is the gospel of Christ, the message that God has restored the relationship to his human creatures in order to bring about the perfected community with his reconciled creation. The form which this conversation takes is the proclamation of the message of Christ in word and sacrament by means of which God creates a community of believers who respond to this message in thanksgiving, praise, petition and lament. The content of the message that God continues his conversation with humanity finds expression precisely in the form that this conversation is indeed continued in the church.

The church is constituted in such a way that God enables and authorises those who have heard God's word to proclaim it and so to continue

---

16. For the interpretation of this formula cf. C. SCHWÖBEL, *The Creature of the Word. Recovering the Ecclesiology of the Reformers*, in C.E. GUNTON – D.W. HARDY (eds.), *On Being the Church. Essays on the Christian Community*, Edinburgh, 1989, pp. 110-155; in German: *Das Geschöpf des Wortes Gottes. Grundeinsichten der reformatorischen Ekklesiologie*, in SCHWÖBEL, *Gott in Beziehung* (n. 1), pp. 345-377.

the divine-human conversation. The address of God to humanity in Christ is continued by God through calling people who have heard and believed this message to be witnesses of God's address to humanity and by using their witness as an instrument for addressing others. The message of God's word is handed on by the means of human communication which God sanctifies by employing it to address others. The instruments of God's address are the proclamation of the word of the gospel and the administration of the visible words of the sacraments. Their instrumentality consists precisely in the fact that these act of witness do not attempt to continue God's communication with humanity by their own means, but that they point away from themselves to God as the Speaker of his word, and so offer themselves as means of his speaking. By distinguishing their voice from the voice of God the witnesses allow God to use their voice to articulate his message in the power of the Spirit. However, God not only calls, enables and authorises witnesses to proclaim his word; he also enables those who listen to the human witness to hear the divine address in their witness by confirming the truth of the message in their hearts. The authentication of the truth of the message of the witnesses about God can only be performed by God himself. In this way God, the Holy Spirit, constitutes faith as the capacity to respond to God's word by trusting in the speaker of this word and expressing this trust in addressing God in the conversation of prayer.

That Christ as the word of God continues to preach to humanity by sending witnesses of his word so that their witness becomes an instrument of Christ's address is an insight which has shaped the Christian community from the very beginning. Paul demonstrates that with impeccable logic. If calling upon God in faith constitutes the actuality of salvation, if the actuality of salvation, we may say, is the divine-human conversation, the crucial question is: how are people enabled to call upon God, to be in conversation with God? The presuppositions of the answer are spelt out by Paul in a series of rhetorical questions: "... how are humans to call upon him in whom they have not believed? And how are they to believe in him of whom they have never heard? And how are they to hear without a preacher? And how are they to preach without being sent?" (Rom 10,14-16). The conclusion seems obvious: "So faith comes from what is heard, and what is heard comes by the preaching of Christ" (Rom 10,17).

If the church as the creature of the word is constituted in this way, it follows that the church must shape its life as a *community of communication*. Through the communication of the gospel God establishes the communion with himself and the community of believers. However, this is only possible if the word that is communicated to create community is indeed the word of God. The church as a community secures its own identity by securing the identity of what is communicated in the community of the church. Therefore the church as a community of communication can only be a community of communicating the gospel if it shapes its life as a *community of interpretation*. Interpreting the biblical witness as the paradigmatic record of the conversation of God with humanity in Israel and in Christ is the way in which the church safeguards its identity by returning again and again to listen to the word of God by interpreting Scripture. However, this act of interpretation does not come to an end in establishing the meaning of the biblical message. If this message is authenticated as truth by God himself the act of interpretation must be continued in acting on the truth of that message in responding to God who addresses humanity, by acting within the relationship that is established through God's word.

If the word of God is the foundation of the church and if, on the basis of that foundation, the church must shape its life as a community of communication which finds its identity in being a community of interpretation, the word of God must also shape the mission of the church. God's conversation with humanity cannot be enclosed within the walls of the church since God's word is from the beginning directed at the whole creation which has its being from the divine word. Therefore the church can only remain true to its foundation if it continually transcends its boundaries to carry God's word into the world. If the whole of creation owes its existence and destiny to the word of God, the world is not a place where the word of God has never been heard so that the church would bring a message to the world that is alien to its being. Rather, the word of God, God's conversation with creation, is inscribed upon the very structure of the world, albeit distorted for our perception by the power of sin, and only needs to be uncovered and disclosed. The church is not the place where God's conversation with his creation comes to a standstill. God's word carries beyond the walls of the church to the end of creation, both in a spatial and in a temporal sense. Therefore God's conversation with creation and creation's conversation with God is not only the way to the *eschaton* but also the eschatological goal. It is a never-ending conversation.

This is most clearly expressed in Luther's redefinition of eternity and immortality through the divine-human conversation: "Where therefore and with whomever God talks, whether he talks in wrath or in grace, must certainly be immortal. The person of the talking God and the Word signify us as being such creatures with whom God wants to talk in all eternity and immortally"[17]. The immortality of humans is portrayed here as following from God's wish to conduct his conversation with creation as a never-ending conversation, and eternity is the "time" it takes God to conduct his conversation. This conversation will be continued through the last judgement in which all falsity, deception and all lies are removed from our conversation with God and where the word by which God justifies those who trust in his word of grace unconditionally will be confirmed. If we follow this line of thought then the *eschaton* will not only be characterised by the *visio beatifica* where we will then see what we have heard and believe; it will also be the *auditio beatifica* where the voice of the triune God and the voices of God's reconciled creation will be united in perfect harmony.

VII. GOD AS CONVERSATION: THE TRINITY

There is no other theological maxim, it seems, which has been quoted in 20th century theology more often than Karl Rahner's dictum that the economic Trinity is the immanent Trinity and *vice versa*[18]. The interpretation which seems most appropriate is to see the economic Trinity as the self-manifestation of the immanent Trinity. Rahner has in this way found a phrase which does not announce a theological programme, but summarises in the briefest possible form a connection between God's being and action in relation to the world and God's being and action in relation to himself. Does the principle also apply to depicting not only the relationship between the triune God and creation as a conversation but also to the immanent relationship between the Father, the Son and the Spirit? Is God only *in* conversation, or *is* God also conversation?

Luther whom we have appealed to throughout as the main witness for our argument certainly seems to have thought so. All God's speaking is trinitarian speaking and it is this trinitarian discourse of God which prescribes the mode of discourse for theology. In one of the table-talks Luther expresses this connection in the following way:

> The Father is in divine things and matter the grammar, because he gives the words and is the source from which flow good, fine and pure words which one should use in talking. The Son is the dialectics, because he provides the

17. *WA* 43, 481, 32-35: "Ubi igitur et cum quocunque loquitur Deus, sive in ira, sive in gratia, loquitur, is certo est immortalis. Persona Dei loquentis et verbum significant nos tales creaturas esse, cum quibus velit loqui Deus usque in aeternum et immortaliter".
18. K. RAHNER, *Der dreifaltige Gott als transzendenter Urgrund der Heilsgeschichte*, in *Mysterium Salutis* 2 (1967) 317-397, here p. 328.

disposition how one should put matters in an orderly fashion one after the other, so that it concludes and follows with certainty. The Holy Spirit, however, is the rhetoric, the orator, who performs it well, breathes and drives it, enlivens and strengthens it so that it impresses and captures the hearts[19].

This is not simply an illustration of what could also be otherwise expressed. The way the triune God converses with creation is rooted in the conversation which God *is*. God's economic conversation is the self-manifestation of the immanent conversation which God is eternally. "Just like the Father is an eternal speaker, so the Son is spoken in eternity, and so the Holy Spirit is from eternity the Listener"[20]. What the Holy Spirit hears, is communicated to believers in the divine Word who in this way listens in on the divine conversation. God relates to humanity in the way in which God is eternally in relation. God is *in* conversation with creation, because God is *as* conversation.

The doctrine of the Trinity can here be understood as an attempt to answer the question: "Who is God if God is as he speaks, is spoken to and is spoken of in the divine-human conversation recorded and carried out in Scripture and continued in the church?". The trinitarian identification of God, summarised in the invocation of the triune name of Father, Son, and Spirit, is expressed in identity-descriptions and in the proper names of Father, Son, and Spirit. It states that God is really as God says and acts in the conversation with Israel, in addressing the whole of humanity in Jesus and in enabling humanity's response in the Spirit. The important point which has to be noted is that Luther's way of understanding the communicative being of God not only satisfies the criteria of trinitarian dogma but also clarifies it. The hypostatic identity of the three persons *(treis hypostaseis)* is constituted by their conversational relations, just like the unity of the divine essence *(mia ousia)* is constituted in this conversational relation. Understanding God as conversation in this way generates a conceptual account of the personal particularity of Father, Son and Spirit and of the unity of the divine essence. Luther also gives a technical explication of the ontological status of relations which corresponds exactly to the way in which he portrays the Trinity as

---

19. *WA.TR* 1, 564, 2-7: "Der Vater ist in göttlichen Dingen und Sachen die Grammatica, denn er gibt die Wort und ist die Bronnquelle, daraus gute, feine, reine Wort, so man reden soll, fließen. Der Sohn ist die Dialectica, denn er gibt die Disposition, wie man ein Ding fein ordentlich nach einander setzen soll, daß man es gewiß schließe und auf einander folge. Der heilige Geist aber ist die Rhetorica, der Redner, so es fein fürtrügt, bläset und treibet, macht lebendig und kräftig, daß es nachdruckt und die Herzen einnimmt".

20. *WA* 46, 60, 4f.

conversation. From a philosophical perspective relations must be understood as external relations between substances, and therefore they have
no subsistence of their own. Because of that their ontological status is
minimal: "Relatio in rebus non efficit rem, ut dicunt, relatio est minimae
entitatis, et not per se subsistens"[21]. With regard to the Trinity which can
only be spoken of within the discourse of faith[22], the relations between
the three divine persons must be understood as internal and constitutive
relations: "In divinis relatio est res, id est, hypostasis et subsistentia"[23].

This has surprising metaphysical implications. If relations between created beings are only external relations which are not internally constitutive
of the terms of the relation, then created beings have their being precisely
because of their relationship to the divine ground of being. If this ground
of being is the trinitarian conversation of God, then created being has being
because it is spoken by God as something other than God. Or as Robert
Jenson puts it: "... to be, as a creature, is to be mentioned in triune moral
conversation, as something other than those who conduct it"[24].

If we take Luther's account of the Trinity as conversation seriously, this
also raises the question of whether it needs to be developed further. In the
debates of trinitarian theology in recent years, one of the most decisive
proposals consists in going beyond the restriction of inner-trinitarian relations as originating relations. The insight is not a novel one because even
the classical descriptions of these relations imply an implicit mutuality.
As Athanasius argued, the Father is not the Father without the Son so that
the being of the Son is implicitly constitutive of the being of the Father[25].
Similar arguments can be developed for the Spirit. Wolfhart Pannenberg
has pointed out that if we reconstruct the inner-trinitarian relations from
the economic relations there appears a mutuality which is absent from
the classical notion of the generation of the Son and the procession of the
Spirit. Pannenberg illustrates that with a discourse of the way in which
the Son receives the rule over heaven and earth from the Father but also
hands it back to him at the end of time (Cf. Matt 28,18 and 1 Cor 15,28)[26].
A similar mutuality can be found in the pattern of glorification which we
find in John's gospel: Just as the Son glorifies not himself, but the Father

21. From the disputation theses for Petrus Hegemon, *WA* 39/II, 340, 1f.
22. *Ibid.*, 12: "... per rationem et philosophiam de rebus maiestatibus nihil, per fidem
vero omnia recte dici et credi possunt".
23. *Ibid.*, 3f.
24. JENSON, *Systematic Theology*, Vol. II. (n. 4), p. 35.
25. *C. Arian.* 1.29.
26. For Pannenberg's whole argument, cf. W. PANNENBERG, *Systematic Theology*,
Vol. I, Edinburgh, 1991, pp. 308-319, here esp. p. 312.

(John 17,4) and manifests himself in this way as the Son, so the Spirit will glorify the Son (John 16,14) and in this way glorifies the Father in the communion of Son and Father. Understanding the Trinity in terms of the conversation which God is, requires a similar mutuality. The Father who is the initiating speaker in the Trinity also becomes the listener and the responsive speaker when the Son who is first the listener becomes the responsive speaker in his relationship to God the Father. If the Son is our *interlocutor* in the Trinity, then the way we, God's creatures, are mentioned in the Trinity includes that we are mentioned by the Son to the Father. If the Spirit, our intercessor when we do not know how to pray (Rom 8,26), is the personal medium of the communion with the Father and the Son, the personal identity of the Spirit in the divine conversation would have to be developed beyond the description of the role of a mere listener. This mutually does not destroy the *taxis* in the Trinity, the order of personal relations whereby the Father generates the Son and not the Son the Father. However, the understanding of God as Trinity requires that we understand the Trinity as a real conversation of real interaction and mutuality. How could it be different if we, God's creatures, are mentioned in the trinitarian conversation and if the triune God engages us in a conversation which – as the cross and resurrection of Christ shows – matters to the divine being in conversation?

VIII. MERE METAPHOR?

We have come to the end of our preliminary exploration of the possibilities of understanding relationality in Christian theology in terms of conversation on the basis of the scriptural witness. The obvious criticism of such an attempt is that "conversation" is a mere metaphor which does not give any real indication of the structures of relationality which a relational theology would have to develop. There are many arguments to the effect that our interaction with the world cannot avoid the employment of metaphorical discourse and that therefore metaphorical discourse does have a cognitive content and a metaphysical import. What is perhaps more important in the context of our reflections is that if we take the understanding of God as conversation and of his interaction with the world in terms of discourse seriously, the distinction between "literal" and "metaphorical" becomes itself problematical. One implication of trying to understand reality in terms of divine-human conversation is that divine discourse which constitutes being becomes a primary metaphysical category. According to such a view, speaking is prior to being, and

the *legomena* of the conversational interaction between God and humanity and between humans acquires priority before the *phainomena* of visual
perception[27]. Whatever appears must first be spoken into being.

This changes our view of the relationship between words and things.
Words can no longer be used as names for antecedently existing things,
but must be seen as the instrument by which things are spoken into existence. How God does things with words becomes the way in which things
are to be understood, and the question of truth no longer is to be raised
in terms of the *adaequatio rei et intellectus* but in terms of the *adaequatio verbi humani ad verbum divinum*. This does not abolish the question
of reality, the *res* remains a pertinent subject for reflection, although the
res is viewed as the result of divine speaking. On such a view, hermeneutics is not a secondary activity of interpretation directed at an antecedently
given reality which is the realm of ontology. Rather, hermeneutics
becomes the access to all ontological questions.

Much of this may at first appear as a rather strange proposal. However,
it should have become clear that, if we are looking for a relational theology, reflecting on that task in terms of conversation has advantage over
the frameworks of substance metaphysics and subjectivity. Substance
metaphysics reduces relationality to the external relations between existing entities and thereby reduces relations to a secondary ontological
category. The framework of subjectivity is bound to be based on the self-
realisation of a lonely subject whose self-referential loneliness postmodernists have tried to disclose as the "empty self", devoid of any relation.
The difficulties which both these frameworks have created for the understanding of God who is reduced to being either a non-relational super-
substance or an equally absolute and abstract hyper-subject should have
made us aware of the limitations of these conceptualities. They seem to
have very little to do with the conversational relationality the biblical witnesses bring to expression when they speak about God. Taking the understanding of God as conversation seriously, implies that God is eventful,
relational, personal, communal. The divine being is understood as freely
communicative speaking so that the world's being is freely communicated and dependently communicative speaking. On such a view, God's
eternity would have to be understood as the "time" God takes in the conversation God *is* for the conversation God *has* with creation so that God's
time brackets the time of creation. God's omnipresence would have to be
understood as the space God *makes* in the conversation God *is* for creation
so that God envelops the spaces of creation. God's omnipotence would

27. Cf. JENSON, *Systematic Theology*, Vol II (n. 4), p. 36.

have to be understood as the power by which God's address is the ultimate disclosure of truth which overcomes and redeems all contradictions of created speakers by having the final word in the divine-human conversation and by sharing it with his reconciled, perfected creation.

These considerations cannot be more than preliminary explorations, soundings to explore the depths of the claim that God is and engages in conversation. However, if there is anything in such discourse, a theology that engages in conversation need not be called *"Zu den Sachen selbst!"* it is already *bei der Sache*.

Theologische Fakultät   Christoph SCHWÖBEL
Ruprecht-Karls-Universität Heidelberg
Hauptstraße 231
D-69117 Heidelberg
Germany

TRINITY AND PASCHAL MYSTERY

DIVINE COMMUNION AND HUMAN CONVERSATION

I. SYNOPSIS

We come to this conference to converse about conversation and theology. The terrifying events of September 11, and of subsequent happenings, make it an even more challenging theme. It is interesting to reflect on the theologies that have been invoked in the ensuing proclamations on both sides of the situation in recent weeks. But no words about conversation from either side! Would that conversation, in any sense, were possible in such troubled and divisive times! On what hope is our desire for conversation based?

Even a brief reflection on the phenomenon of conversation leads one to realise how rare and precious an event it really is. We live in a world that is saturated with information and communication, yet conversation is as rare a phenomenon as ever, perhaps even more so. So let us firstly consider what it is that we mean when we speak of *conversation*? Some biblical texts provide food for thought on the phenomenon of conversation.

Trinitarian theology surely has something to bring to our understanding of conversation and indeed of the essentially conversational nature of the theological enterprise itself. The psychological analogy, the linchpin of traditional trinitarian theology, has been much criticised in recent times for its attention on the individual subject and its acts of intellect and will and, in particular, for its apparent lack of attention to the interpersonal and social dimensions of authentic subjectivity. The shift to a more overtly social key in the explication of trinitarian theology, as exemplified by liberation trinitarian theologies, effectively marks what we can understand, from a methodological perspective, as a shift in the function of trinitarian meaning, to use Bernard Lonergan's terms, from the cognitive to the communicative.

Another relatively recent development in trinitarian theology, whereby the mystery of the Trinity is approached by way of Jesus' Paschal Mystery, as exemplified in the work of Hans Urs von Balthasar but also demonstrated in the work of such scholars as François Durrwell and Ghislain Lafont, takes the connection between Trinity and conversation in a very different direction, effectively moving to a deeper level of exploration, by shifting the focus of attention to the sheer drama of the encounter of God's entry into human history.

In this paper, coming from a Catholic perspective, I will focus on the perspectives on the divine communion, which the Paschal Mystery offers. I will then explore some ramifications for systematic theology and for Christian spirituality. We shall then turn to conversation more generally and its intrinsically paschal character and finally return to the connection between Trinity and conversation.

II. PRELIMINARY REFLECTIONS ON THE PHENOMENON OF CONVERSATION

We live in such a wordy world, a world in which words abound. Burgeoning communication technologies enable us, as never before, to communicate across the globe with unprecedented ease. The world wide web of networks, email, and the myriad chat rooms make it so very easy to communicate with each other. Communication bytes cross the globe in a fraction of a second! Meanwhile, the professional and commercial world in which we live our lives abounds with conferences, lectures, briefings and updates. So many words, so much communication, and yet ... conversation? So much talk, so many words, so much communication, yet, dare I suggest, so little conversation? Remember September 11 – how could we forget! – were we not, at least momentarily, stunned into silence, suddenly lost for words. What a strange and disquieting quiet that was; and then the beginning of many conversations around issues that previously could hardly be named.

Our theme clearly begs the question as to what we mean by *conversation*? The English language offers a number of terms with which to refer to various forms of speech, with subtle variations in their shades of meaning. Interestingly, the ancients seldom used the word "conversatio", but rather terms such as colloquium, symposium, and dialogue. So what do we mean and what do we hope, indeed, long for, when we speak, quite distinctly, of *conversation*? We could probably more easily agree on what conversation is not than on what it is. Conversation, for example, is not counselling or teaching or persuading. It is not discussion, debate or even dialogue. While elements of each of these forms of communication can occur in conversation, none is synonymous with *conversation*.

We could describe the constituent elements and requirements of what we would consider to be genuine conversation[1]: Conversation firstly

1. For a helpful and insightful treatment of the phenomenon of conversation, see D. TRACY, *The Analogical Imagination. Christian Theology and the Culture of Pluralism*,

demands the willingness and ability to say what one means and say it as accurately as possible; to explain, to persuade, to argue, to confront and to endure conflict, if necessary; and indeed to change one's mind if the evidence warrants it. It demands the willingness to expose oneself, as one attempts to render one's understanding of the truth, oneself and one's tradition and heritage. Genuine self-exposure itself demands genuine self respect, a willingness to enter the particularity of one's own situation, experience, history, and tradition, and to render it as faithfully and truthfully as possible. But there is no conversation without a conversation partner, and, in fact, conversation takes place only when the conversants set aside their individual concerns, allow the subject matter to take over, and yield to its logic and demands, its dynamic and rhythm. Conversation demands a willingness to concentrate on the subject matter and to follow the questioning it prompts, wherever it may go. In this sense, conversation challenges any notion of autonomy and independence. More than this, it demands unconditional acceptance of and respect for each conversant, a willingness to listen, and an empathic imagination to receive what the other has to say. It necessarily engages what we might describe as a form of analogical imagination, for we understand one another, if at all, through analogies to our own experience (and, commensurately, we understand ourselves through our analogous understandings of the other). The analogical imagination does not, however, cancel out differences and dissimilarities in its search for ordered relationships and analogies; rather, it clarifies them, even intensifies them, as the particularity of each position-understanding gains in intensity and becomes clearer to itself and to others, in the course of the conversation. Perhaps most critically of all, conversation requires an openness to change, a readiness to be transformed, and for one's understanding to be transfigured and re-membered, as one enters, in conversation with the other, into a fuller range of possibilities and a larger realm of meaning. Ultimately, conversation demands an openness to conversion, an openness to the possibility of radical change in one's understanding of reality and indeed of the reality that is oneself.

What then would we consider to be genuine conversation? Most generally, it is an exchange, an encounter, an engagement, a sharing – a sharing

---

New York, 1986, pp. 446-455, and *Plurality and Ambiguity. Hermeneutics, Religion, Hope*, San Francisco, CA, 1987, esp. pp. 1-30; 82-114. Indeed, in his preface to *Plurality and Ambiguity*, Tracy notes that "the theme of this small book is conversation" (p. IX).

in an exploration, an exploration in the search for truth. It connotes an encounter that is characterized by authenticity and integrity. It takes for granted respect for the other and indeed a welcome of the other. There is also a certain element of play in the "conversation matter", for we address it in such a way that no one is the authority, no one has dominance or power, everyone has a part to play, and all are ruled by a truth or a concern bigger than us all, but involving each one of us in some way. Tracy notes that "[w]e learn to play the game of conversation when we allow questioning to take over"[2]. To that degree, conversation cannot be planned for; the outcome is uncertain; the Spirit blows where it wills, so to speak. No wonder, given its demands, that conversation is a rare phenomenon, that it is indeed an elusive cultural reality today. At its best, it is an event, a happening. Perhaps we might go so far as to see it as a moment of grace?

III. Some Biblical Pointers on the Phenomenon of Conversation

Some biblical texts provide food for thought on the phenomenon of conversation:

Let us think first of the words from Genesis, in the creation story: God said, "It is not good that the man should be alone; I will make him a helper fit for him" (Gen 2,18). Here in the very beginning, in the story of the origins of our being, we find the notion that human life is not meant to be lived in isolation but rather relationship with others, in collaboration, in communication, in conversation with others, as helpers. What does this text say about our topic?

In the Gospels of Luke and Matthew, we find the commandment to love your enemies (Matt 5,15, Luke 6,27), a command that is all the more startling, all the more striking, in the light of September 11 and of subsequent events. Luke's Gospel elaborates: "Do good to those who hate you, bless those who curse you, pray for those who abuse you ... And as you wish that men would do to you, do so to them ... But love your enemies, and do good ... Be merciful ... Judge not ... condemn not ... forgive ... give ...". And more: "First take the log out of your own eye, and then you will see clearly to take out the speck that is in your brother's eye" (Luke 6,27-42).

What does all this say about our topic of conversation? What does it say about the events of September 11 and our response? Soon after September 11, I was in Nagasaki and visited the Atomic Bomb Museum

---

2. Tracy, *Plurality* (n. 1), p. 18.

there, which records the terrible and terrifying events of the dropping of
the bomb in August 1945, with powerful images and even more powerful records of the stories of some of the survivors. It was very sobering
to ponder the events of September 11 from that perspective. Where is
God in all this, I wonder? Where would Jesus be standing? Where should
we be, as Christians and indeed as Christian theologians in all this? Is theology too far from the fray, to far from the really urgent and important
questions of our time?, I wonder.

These texts from Luke and Matthew surely challenge us to enter into
those really difficult conversations, to include even those we consider to
be our enemies in our conversation. No one, no group, none at all is to
be marginalized or excluded from our conversation; none is to be sacrificed to the interests of others; each and every one has a right to participate in the human conversation. Moreover, in the exhortation to attend
firstly to the log in one's own eye, we have the salutary reminder to attend
first of all to the biases, blind spots and errors in our own perceptions and
understanding, before daring to presume to judge or correct the understanding of the other. Notice, too, that Jesus, having just commanded his
disciples to love their enemies, here speaks in terms of one's "brother".
In the all-embracing all-encompassing fatherhood of God, even the one
we thought to be our enemy is our brother. Recall, too, that in John's
Gospel we have: "A new commandment I give to you, that you love one
another ... By this all will know that you are my disciples, if you have
love for one another" (John 13,34-35) and, later in John, "I am ascending to my Father and your Father, my God and your God" (John 20,18).
The God of Jesus Christ is not just *his* Father, but *our* Father, and it is "our
Father" who makes of us not friends and foes but brothers and sisters, all.

Then, in his letter to the Corinthians (1 Cor 13) Paul reiterates the utter
primacy of love, that words, even the most learned or prophetic, without
love are but "speak", of no more value than a noisy gong or a clanging
cymbal: "If I speak in the tongues of men and of angels, but have not
love, I am a noisy gong or a clanging cymbal. And if I have prophetic
powers, and understand all mysteries and all knowledge, and if I have all
faith ... but have not love, I am nothing. ... Love is patient and kind; love
is not jealous or boastful; it is not arrogant or rude. Love does not insist
on its own way; it is not irritable or resentful; it does not rejoice at wrong,
but rejoices in the right. Love bears all things, believes all things, hopes
all things, endures all things. Love never ends. ... (and Paul adds) Make
love your aim". (Might we add, make *conversation* your aim?) Paul's
reflections on the mystery of love prompts an understanding of conversation as an act of love, that indeed, if our talking is not born out of love,

it is mere speak, mere words, mere noise, mere communication bytes, no matter how seemingly erudite. But even more, this text from Paul prompts the realization and the recognition that love is – a conversation!

In the prologue of John's Gospel we have intimations of conversation within the divine communion, a conversation that is love, a love that is conversation, intimations of the very horizon of unbounded love within which all of our conversation takes place. Here too is testimony to the entry of God who is Love into our human conversation, for the incarnation of the Word resoundingly attests to a God who communicates, a God who enters into conversation with us: "In the beginning was the Word, and the Word was with God, and the Word was God. He was in the beginning with God; all things were made through him, and without him was not anything that was made. In him was life, and the life was the light of men. The light shines in the darkness, and the darkness has not overcome it. ... And the Word became flesh and dwelt among us, full of grace and truth" (John 1,1–5,14).

Notice too the very first words of the Incarnate Word, as attested in the Gospel of John: "What are you looking for?" (John 1,38). Here, in the very first utterance of Jesus, as recorded in that Gospel, is not a command, or a statement, a teaching or exhortation, but an invitation to enter into conversation. "What are you looking for?" he asks. Thus it is that God engages with us, enters into conversation with us, and invites us to conversation and indeed communion with God.

Finally, perhaps most tellingly of all, in John's Gospel we have the extraordinary event of the washing of the feet, the enactment of Jesus' new commandment to love one another: "If I then, your Lord and teacher, have washed your feet, you also ought to wash one another's feet. For I have given you an example, that you also should do as I have done to you ... Love one another; as I have loved you" (John 13,13–15,34). The washing of the feet tangibly demonstrates for all who have eyes to see what it is to love one another: it is to attend to, to tend to, not just to eat with, walk with, be with, talk to, but to engage at this deeply personal level. In the washing of the feet is the concrete manifestation of the love that Paul describes – the love that is patient and kind; not jealous or boastful, arrogant or rude; not insisting on its own way; not irritable or resentful; not rejoicing at wrong, but rejoicing in the right. It is the love that bears all things, believes all things, hopes all things, endures all things. It is the love that knows no bounds, that refuses to be anything but self-giving love, that gives itself even to the point of washing dirty feet and ultimately to the point of death, giving up one's life for one's friends.

Perhaps for us in our time, in this very wordy and noisy world of ours, the washing of the feet translates into conversation! Perhaps conversation is as rare and elusive and radical an event in our culture and context as the washing of the feet in Jesus' culture and context. In other words, might conversation not in fact be the most apt expression in our culture for that profound respect, welcome, compassion, empathic imagination, and authentic engagement with the other that is commanded of us in this new dispensation of love? As He, the Word made flesh, has entered into conversation with us, so too should we not enter into conversation with one another? Should indeed *conversation* be our aim?

IV. TRINITARIAN THEOLOGY
AND THE CLASSICAL PSYCHOLOGICAL ANALOGY

Let us move now to a more explicit consideration of the Trinity, that great mystery of the divine communion to which the incarnation of the Word gives witness and offers entry. Our faith in and understanding of the mystery of the divine communion that is the Trinity surely has something to bring to our exploration of conversation. This great mystery of our faith as Christians has for centuries been traditionally explicated in terms of the psychological analogy, whereby the two processions of Word and Love, Son and Spirit, that are immanent within the divine communion, are understood and explained in terms of the dynamics of divine subjectivity, by analogy with dynamics of human subjectivity and the human mind's acts of intellect and will.

The psychological analogy, which has been the linchpin of traditional trinitarian theology for centuries, has however come under considerable fire in recent times. It has admittedly suffered from the limitations of human understanding in its extrapolations from human subjectivity to the divine subjectivity, as in fact does any analogy, as well as a certain degree of distortion of an intellectualist kind, whereby the intellect has been given priority over the will, knowledge over love. The analogy is, after all, based on the adage, *nihil amatum nisi praecognitum,* that nothing is loved that is not first known.

Even stronger and more vehement though are those criticisms of the psychological analogy that base their objections most especially on the analogy's focus on the acts of the *individual* human mind and the analogy's apparent lack of consideration of the inherently interpersonal and social dimension of authentic human existence. Its critics charge that the psychological analogy, as traditionally explicated, seems quite unconcerned for any particular social or even personal existential context and for related questions of praxis, and remote from the real created world, with its social demands, political struggles and moral dilemmas, in which we live our lives.

It is perhaps hardly surprising, in the light of these concerns, that recently emerging trinitarian theologies show a common feature – a very strong emphasis on the personal, relational and social aspect of being, and its ramifications for human being, coupled with the rejection of any hint of an essentialist metaphysics which accords priority to categories of substance over categories of relation. Consider, for example, the emergence and popularity of what we might call social models of the Trinity – the liberation trinitarian theologies[3] – and their determined emphasis on the doctrine of the Trinity as explicit good news for human community. These models of the Trinity emphasise the social and political-economic ramifications and ethical imperatives which necessarily follow from the trinitarian faith we proclaim. In so doing, they seem to meet an urgent contemporary desire to have trinitarian theology motivate us to explicitly social engagement and action for justice in our world.

Now, while it is true, at least at first glance, that the psychological analogy, in its classical form, lacks overt reference to the social and relational aspects of human life, the analogy in fact readily lends itself to being transposed into a more explicitly social key, when its radical implications for interpersonal and social life emerge clearly. This is demonstrated in the work of Bernard Lonergan and, more recently, by such scholars as Anthony Kelly, CSsR. In Kelly's re-working of the analogy[4], for example, the Trinity re-emerges, pregnant with meaning for a trinitarian orthopraxis that motivates and indeed demands contemporary cosmic, ecological, psychological, political and interfaith conversations, engagements and concerns, as is evident in the variety of applications Kelly himself attempts. When re-worked in this kind of way and released from its undoubtedly outmoded metaphysical wrappings, the psychological analogy once again serves an understanding of the triune God who is revealed in Jesus Christ as love, and inspires and, indeed, expressly demands responsible Christian decision and action in the world[5].

---

3. Consider, for example, Latin American liberation trinitarian theology (L. BOFF, *Trinity and Society*, trans. P. BURNS, London, 1988); feminist trinitarian theology (E.A. JOHNSON, *She Who Is. The Mystery of God in Feminist Theological Discourse*, New York, 1992; C. MOWRY LACUGNA, *God for Us. The Trinity and Christian Life*, New York, 1991); ecologically attuned trinitarian theologies (e.g., D. EDWARDS, *Jesus, the Wisdom of God. An Ecological Theology*, Homebush, NSW, 1995).

4. T. KELLY, *The Trinity of Love. A Theology of the Christian God* (New Theology Series, 4), Wilmington, DE, 1989.

5. See also T. KELLY, *An Expanding Theology. Faith in a World of Connections*, Newtown, NSW, 1993, and *The "Horrible Wrappers" of Aquinas' God*, in *Pacifica* 9

In our criticisms of the psychological analogy, it is important, I suggest, that we do not throw the baby out with the bathwater. Throw the bathwater out, yes indeed (those outmoded metaphysical wrappings); but not the baby (the analogy). The analogy serves a perennially valuable role in reminding us that love necessarily expresses itself intelligently in judgments of value and enacts itself in responsible decisions and loving actions and commitments. Love is neither mindless nor unreal! The psychological analogy, while itself accused of an intellectualist bias which accords priority to knowledge over love, precludes the equally dangerous tendency toward a voluntarist kind of distortion which leaves judgements of value and the concrete demands of responsible decision and loving action precariously unrelated to truth and reality and dangerously subject to personal whim.

From a methodological perspective, criticism of the psychological analogy in classical trinitarian theology, in terms of its apparent lack of concern for the social dimension of human life and the desire for more explicit reference to the ramifications of trinitarian faith for Christian orthopraxis and for human interpersonal and social existence, in fact, marks a significant shift of accent, using Lonergan's terms, in the function of meaning that is demanded of our theology. We see a shift from the cognitive function of meaning, wherein meaning is explicated in ways which are first and foremost geared to intellectual demands for clarity and order, consistency and coherence in our meaning-making (and which the classical psychological analogy actually does remarkably well), to the communicative function of meaning, whereby meaning serves a vital community-making role. In this communicative functioning of meaning, the very process of communication of meaning establishes and motivates a community of shared meanings and values and, in doing so, effects the formation of community itself. It is, after all, the achievement of common meanings and shared values that makes a community. Now meanings and values become common through the process of communication; indeed it is in conversation that our meanings and values are gradually clarified, enriched and transformed. As David Tracy has commented so clearly, there is no community, no tradition, that does not ultimately live by the quality of its conversation[6]. Live, or die, indeed! (For communities can disintegrate, can die!) Conversation is, so to speak, the very life blood of community, for it plays a crucial role, not just in meaning-making but

---

(1996) 185-203. Also A. HUNT, *Psychological Analogy and the Paschal Mystery in Trinitarian Theology*, in *Theological Studies* 59 (1998) 197-218.

    6. TRACY, *Plurality* (n. 1), p. IX.

in community-making. There is no community of shared meaning and value, no community of hearts and minds, no community as such, without conversation.

It is perhaps not really surprising then that, in a world afflicted by a sense of alienation and isolation and lack of community, a yearning for community and ultimately for communion expresses itself in terms of a demand for this shift in accent from the cognitive to the communicative function of trinitarian meaning. The shift itself is symptom of this malaise that afflicts our culture; it is also an indication of hope for a more meaningful communication of faith.

V. THE PASCHAL MYSTERY –
AN ALTERNATIVE APPROACH TO THE MYSTERY OF THE TRINITY

While what we might call the social models of the Trinity and the transposition of the classic psychological analogy into a socially explicit key mark a transition in the function of trinitarian meaning from more cognitive to more communicative and serve to highlight the vital role of conversation in formation and sustenance of human community, another relatively recent development in trinitarian theology, whereby the mystery of the Trinity is approached by way of Jesus' Paschal Mystery, takes the connection between Trinity and Conversation in a very different direction, effectively moving to a radically deeper level of conversation, by shifting the focus of attention to the sheer drama of the encounter of God's entry into human history.

This approach to the mystery of the Trinity, that locates its starting point not in human subjectivity but in the divine subjectivity as it has been revealed to us, technically speaking, begins with the economic Trinity and moves, by way of analogy, to the immanent Trinity. Hans Urs von Balthasar, an outstanding proponent of this approach, would have us see that the Paschal Mystery manifestly reveals the mystery of trinitarian divine love that simply is not to be extrapolated from our experience of interiority. He would persuade us that both intrasubjective and intersubjective analogical approaches to the mystery of the Trinity simply pale into insignificance in comparison to the mystery as revealed to us. The revelation of the Trinity in the Paschal Mystery, he argues, reveals that, quite unlike human experience wherein love is one possibility among others, self-giving love, a love that refuses to be anything but self-giving love, is *the* manifestation of divine power, freedom and glory.

Here, in this section of our exploration of the Trinity-Conversation connection, I will focus first on the perspectives on the divine communion which the Paschal Mystery offers and the key themes which emerge. I will then explore the ramifications for systematic theology and for Christian spirituality. We shall then turn to the implications for human conversation more generally and to the intrinsically paschal character of conversation, before finally returning to the connection between Trinity and Conversation.

VI. TRINITY AND PASCHAL MYSTERY –
PERSPECTIVES ON THE DIVINE COMMUNION

For theologians such as Hans Urs von Balthasar, Ghislain Lafont, and François Durrwell, who choose to ground their trinitarian theology in an exploration of Jesus' Paschal Mystery, that option is grounded in the firm conviction that in the death and resurrection of Jesus we have much more than the revelation of the mystery of our redemption[7]. These theologians recognise that the Paschal Mystery has properly theological significance; it is not just redemptive; it is revelatory, indeed pre-eminently so, of God's eternal being and relationality. It discloses the divine persons in relation to each other, their hypostatic characteristics, their proper roles and distinctive missions. They argue that we have, in the Paschal Mystery, what we might rightly describe, in more technical terms, as the iconic expression, in the symbolic language of a human life, of the eternal trinitarian exchange, and that, indeed, it is entry into this eternal trinitarian exchange that constitutes our redemption and salvation. In this exploration of the Paschal Mystery, we shall first focus on what is disclosed there of trinitarian being, the three divine persons, and the relationality of Father, Son and Spirit, drawing on the insights of Hans Urs von Balthasar, François Durrwell and Ghislain Lafont in this necessarily brief overview[8].

---

7. For primary references to these trinitarian theologies which ground their understanding of the Trinity in an exploration of Jesus' Paschal Mystery, see G. LAFONT, *Peut-on connaître Dieu en Jésus Christ?* (Cogitatio Fidei, 44), Paris, 1969; and *God, Time and Being*, trans. L. MALUF, Petersham, MA, 1992; F.X. DURRWELL, *The Resurrection. A Biblical Study*, trans. R. SHEED, London, 1960; H.U. VON BALTHASAR, *Mysterium Paschale. The Mystery of Easter*, trans. with an introduction by A.N., Edinburgh, 1990.

8. For a detailed treatment of the trinitarian theologies of Hans Urs von Balthasar, Ghislain Lafont, and François Durrwell, see A. HUNT, *The Trinity and the Paschal Mystery*, Collegeville, MN, 1997; also *What Are They Saying About the Trinity?*, Mahwah, NJ, 1998, pp. 49-61.

1. *Death on the Cross*

On the cross, the Father hands over his only and beloved Son to bear our sin. The Son, sent by the Father into the God-forsakenness of the cross, freely and out of love takes on himself the sin of the world. The "delivering up" of the Son by the Father is perfectly complemented by the self-surrender of the Son. Neither Father nor Son offers any resistance to the dreadful series of events which unfolds. The Son gives himself without reserve. The cross reveals that it is of the Son's very being to keep nothing for himself but to yield everything to the Father. (Just as the Father keeps nothing for himself but gives everything in self-surrendering love in the generation of a co-equal Son.)

Jesus' experience of abandonment on the cross is nevertheless real. The Son's cry to the Father is met with silence. The Father does not intervene to save the Son from suffering and death. Rather, the Father withdraws without seeming to make the slightest saving gesture on Jesus' behalf. The Son dies. His death expresses a complete and utter surrender to the divine will for our salvation. Not my will but thine, he prays. His whole existence, in life and in death, is characterised by this self-surrendering other-centredness. His death manifests the very opposite of any sense of independence or autonomy of existence, but rather a choice, a preference, an option, at every turn, for communion with God.

In his obedience, he is, and shows himself to be, the Son. His obedience is grounded in his divine personhood and in his eternal relation to Father and Spirit. It expresses his love for the Father and the unity of love between them. It is constitutive of his identity as the Son, expressive of his divine sonship and his divine freedom. No one takes his life from him. His death is the supreme act of his liberty.

The Son's mission, which he fulfils by his obedience, is properly his own. It is not given to the Son accidentally but as a modality of his eternal personal being and as the extension into creation of his procession from the Father. It too is an expression of his person as the Son. To know his mission is to know who he is, from whence he comes, his role, his person and, through him, the other two divine persons, their relations and roles.

The cross reveals not just the self-surrender of the Son; it is an event of triune surrender, of mutual self-giving and self-yielding love. The Father surrenders his Son, the Son surrenders himself, the Spirit is the Spirit of self-surrendering love. In the Son's consistent option for divine communion, in preference to any autonomy of existence that is manifest in Jesus' life and in his death, there is the intimation that the essence and perfection of divine being lies in communion, as distinct from any autonomy or independence of existence[9].

2. *The Descent into Hell*

The scriptures together with the Apostles' Creed attest that the Son died and was buried and descended into hell (1 Pet 3,19; 4,6). Like the centrepiece of an altar triptych, as Balthasar would see it, it stands mysteriously in between cross and resurrection, and as such, he argues, "forms the necessary conclusion to the cross as well as the necessary presupposition of the resurrection"[10]. Despite the relatively scant biblical warrant for an exploration of this mystery, Balthasar would persuade us that the descent is not just the centre of a theology of the Trinity, but the centre of *all* theology.

It is in the descent into hell that Jesus' self-surrender reaches its utmost limit and where his mission reaches its fullness. In the utter defencelessness and vulnerability of love, he enters into the loneliness and desolation of the sinner in hell. In his descent into hell, the Son himself experiences God-forsakenness. Here is the mystery of our salvation, if we are to be persuaded by Balthasar; it is here, in the descent, in this utter loss of glory, that the glory of the Lord is revealed. It is the glory of Love, of Love that refuses to be anything but Love, even in the depths of hell.

On the cross, his death was the act of his liberty; but in the descent, in this passive "being removed", Jesus' surrender is characterised by the utter passivity of being dead. Now his obedience is the obedience of the dead Christ. It is in this way, in the absolute weakness and powerlessness of love, that God descends into hell, in order to accompany – never to overrule – the sinner in his or her choice. God, in the person of the dead Son, comes to the sinner in hell and, as God, enters into the loneliness and hellish desolation of the sinner ("a being-only-for-oneself" as distinct from "a being-for-the-other"). In love, God enters into this solidarity with those who reject all solidarity. In love, God accompanies the sinner in his or her choice. In love, God shares in the sinner's experience of hellish God-forsakenness and loves even when rejected. Love alone is credible, as Balthasar explains.

Balthasar recognises that the divine descent into hell is only possible because God is triune. The Father sends the Son into hell. The Son, *while*

---

9. Lafont in particular stresses this aspect of the Paschal Mystery. See LAFONT, *Peut-on connaître* (n. 7), pp. 248 ff.

10. *The von Balthasar Reader*, ed. M. KEHL – W. LÖSER, trans. R. DALY – F. LAWRENCE, Edinburgh, 1985, p. 404.

remaining God, descends into God-forsakenness, and assumes the condition of sinful humanity and takes upon himself all that is opposed to God. As the God-forsaken Son of God, Jesus accompanies the sinner in the sinner's choice to damn him/herself and to reject God. Throughout, he remains God. Again, herein lies the mystery of our salvation, as Balthasar sees it. The Spirit accompanies the Son throughout and is the bond between Father and Son, uniting them in their separation, and united with them in their trinitarian will for our salvation. Indeed, as Balthasar explains, the abandonment of the Son by the Father is possible only because, at this greatest point of extreme separation, they are united in love by the Holy Spirit. The Son's being, his whole existence, is always *accompanied* by the Father, through the presence of the Holy Spirit. It is because God is triune, with both difference and unity guaranteed by the Holy Spirit, that the inner-trinitarian difference between Father and Son in the unity of the Holy Spirit can accommodate all created differences, including the death and descent.

In the descent, the Son's obedience and self-surrendering love reaches its most extreme limit, when the Son experiences the God-forsakenness of hell. Love alone is credible, as Balthasar reiterates. In the descent into hell, love enters into the realm of death and desolation and gathers our lostness, our disconnectedness, our isolation and alienation, our God-forsakenness, into God's triune self, for, in the descent into hell, God too experiences our lostness, our disconnectedness, our isolation and alienation and our God-forsakenness.

3. *The Resurrection*

But death and descent do not have the final word. Their meaning is ultimately given, and definitively so, in life. It is in Jesus' resurrection that the revelation of the Trinity appears in full light: the Father to whom is attributed the initiative in raising the Son, the Son who appears as the Living (and wounded) One, and the Spirit, Spirit of their love, who is sent forth into the world. The resurrection affirms and manifests the trinitarian identity of Jesus, the Son, true God and true man. It reveals the Father, who responds to the Son's love unto death, raising him to the fullness of glory of divine Sonship. In the resurrection of the Son, the Father speaks a resounding word of life and love, which reverberates through all creation. The resurrection reveals that, even in the moment of their most extreme separation, Father and Son were united in the Holy Spirit in the Trinity's eternal plan for our salvation. The resurrection reveals the Spirit, the Spirit of their mutual love, who is poured out for us at Pentecost.

Here too the self-surrender and obedience of the Son are evident. Jesus is obedient in the resurrection: he allows the Father to raise him from the dead. He assents, through his obedience and receptivity, to his own identity as Son and to the fatherhood of the Father. He is raised to the fullness of the glory and power of the divine Son. Here too, the Son surrenders himself, and entirely. In unreserved and active receptivity, in his openness to all that the other has to give, he receives the fullness of divinity and enters into full communion with the Father.

The Father raises him and, indeed, raises him to visibility proper to the Paschal Mystery, not to the pre-incarnate condition of the invisible Word. The inseparable unity of death and resurrection, the Paschal Mystery itself, is tangibly expressed in the very body of the Risen Lord. Jesus is not healed of his mortal wounds. In this life out of death, in this glorification, the wounds of his self-surrendering love remain. Death and resurrection are in this very tangible way revealed as the essential and complementary dimensions of the one Paschal Mystery. Death emerges as a vital passage, a kind of birth or passover to new life. Utter self-surrender, symbolised in death, is integral to the passage. The creative, life-giving and salvific action of the Spirit culminates in it. It is the necessary passage or passover to life in communion in the triune God. In this sense, death – understood negatively as the negation of any sense of oneself as independent or autonomous in regard to the other, or positively in terms of a preferential option for communion with the other – is revealed as lying at the heart of the divine being and at the heart of the divine plan for all creation.

When the Father shows to the world his risen and glorified Son, he himself is also, albeit implicitly, disclosed, and precisely through the person of the Son. The Father responds in love to the self-surrendering love of the Son. The resurrection is also the revelation of the Spirit, for the resurrection of Jesus is accomplished in the powerful transfiguring action of the Spirit. The gift to the world of the Holy Spirit, the Paraclete, is made possible through the Paschal Mystery: the Spirit is sent, following the return of the Son to the Father. With the gift of their common Spirit into the world, following Jesus' death, descent and resurrection, God is disclosed in the depths of the divine triune mystery. The resurrection thus reveals the self-giving love in which the Father generates his Son, the receptive self-yielding love with which the Son responds to the Father, the inexhaustible love of the Holy Spirit, their mutual love, and their out-reaching redeeming love by which creation is taken up into their trinitarian communion of life and love.

François Durrwell would also persuade us that the resurrection proceeds from and reveals the primordial mystery of the eternal generation of the Son by the Father in the Spirit; in other words that, in the mystery of the resurrection, Jesus, in his humanity, enters into the fullness of the eternal begetting of the divine Son[11]. From this perspective, the resurrection reveals that primordial mystery of the self-yielding, utter-being-for-another, that holding-on-to-nothing-for-oneself character of the divine being, that renunciation of one's autonomy for the sake of communion, whereby the Father begets a co-equal consubstantial other, the Son, in the love of the Holy Spirit.

VII. The Divine Communion – "Being-in-and-for-Another"

An exploration of the Paschal Mystery reveals, at its core, Jesus' utterly unreserved gift of self in a total ecstasis of self, in the freedom of self-giving self-surrendering love, Jesus gives himself without reserve to God, even unto death, even unto descent into hell, and is raised to communion with God. His life and his death are characterised by a surrender of any sense of self-sufficiency or egoism or autonomy, and an essential openness to that which does not come from himself. His whole existence is directed towards the Father and inspired by the Spirit.

Now, because it is the Son of God whose Paschal Mystery we contemplate, this renunciation of autonomy, this unreserved self-surrender and self-gift, this choice of divine communion in preference to any autonomy of existence, which Jesus expresses so tangibly in his Paschal Mystery, signifies something which is eternally lived in God's triune being. The Paschal Mystery expresses the utter being-for-another character not just of the Son, but of the three divine persons, each in his own way. It expresses the ecstatic (out-going) nature of the trinitarian relations, as first and foremost gift of self to the other, the sheer other-directedness and other-centredness of trinitarian personhood and relationality. It discloses the self-dispossession and self-surrender in love for the other, the unreserved gift of self

11. Durrwell writes, for example, of the resurrection: "The Resurrection brought Christ wholly to birth in the life of the Son, extending to his whole being the glory of his eternal generation. And in that birth, there is no 'tomorrow'. Alongside our ancestor Adam, the old man, who continues to decay within us (2 Cor. 4,16), here is the young Adam, the new man, Son of God, in the everlasting newness of his sonship". DURRWELL, *The Resurrection* (n. 7), p. 131. "Then the Father took him to himself, and introducing him totally into the secret of his divine being, into that embrace which confers sonship, he abolished in him the 'condition of a slave' and brought his whole, once mortal, humanity into the eternal origins of the life of sonship, into the instant of divine generation. He generated him as Son of God in his entire being, saying in the act of glorifying him: 'Thou art my Son, this day have I begotten thee'". DURRWELL, *In the Redeeming Christ*, trans. R. SHEED, London, 1963, p. 329.

to the other, the infinite openness to all that the other has to give, that is positively and essentially constitutive of the trinitarian relations. It manifests the infinite openness of the divine persons to what the other has to give, the unreserved gift of oneself to the other, the perfection of that dynamic unceasing exchange wherein nothing is ever appropriated for oneself, but rather that what is received from the other in joy is given back in unceasing love and thanksgiving. In more technical terms, Jesus' death, descent and resurrection are the iconic expression of the eternal trinitarian exchange, traditionally described in terms of "perichoresis" or "circumincession".

We note too that the Paschal Mystery clearly reveals a *differentiated* divine communion, a communion of three distinct ones, traditionally designated as three "persons". But the notion of person, as gleaned through the Paschal Mystery, is of one who opts for communion as distinct from autonomy; not just one possessing faculties of intellect and will (as the classical form of the psychological analogy envisions the person), but one constituted by mission and relation, freedom and love, one who lovingly and in the spirit of self-gift and other-centredness enters into relationship with the other. The divine person, as revealed in the Paschal Mystery, is intrinsically relational. Relationality is clearly intrinsic to and constitutive of the divine person, as much a primordial dimension of reality as substantiality.

We find that, in the Paschal Mystery, each of the divine persons is expressed, not in terms of substantialist or essentialist or even self-subsistent categories, but rather in terms of its essential orientation toward the other, in an unceasing dynamic exchange of gift and response. There is a certain negation implicit in each person, a "non-priority" and, indeed, "non-property" of each person in itself, for the divine person is expressed not in terms of "being-for-oneself", but rather as "being-in-and-for-another", not in any autonomy or independence of self but in communion, a communion that is utterly free of egoism or self-centredness. To be is to be utterly (and freely) given to and for the other. It is death to absolutely any other reality. It is the very antithesis of sinful being, as is revealed in the descent into hell, with the sinner's choice to be "a being-only-for-oneself", with its hellish consequences.

This then is what is revealed in the Paschal Mystery of the dynamism of the divine communion, the divine "conversation", so to speak, that is trinitarian being (though I use the word "conversation" in regard to the divine communion with considerable reservation, and within the carefully qualified terms of analogical discourse, wherein real similarities are articulated and understood in terms of ever greater dissimilarities). The crux of the matter is that God, God who is Trinity, reveals Godself, communicates Godself, in the Paschal Mystery of Jesus, in this dynamic of death, descent and resurrection. We argue then that precisely, indeed paradigmatically, in that particular paschal modality, something of the essential character of trinitarian perichoresis is disclosed for us, that in its essential structure, the Paschal Mystery is the created projection of the eternal trinitarian exchange, which is, moreover, anterior to and indeed grounds the possibility of the events of salvation history. The economic Trinity surely reveals the immanent Trinity; there is no other. The dynamics of the trinitarian exchange in the economy, played out for us in the Paschal Mystery, *ad extra*, correspond to, are a modality of, God's eternal triune being, *ad intra*. From this perspective, the Paschal Mystery serves as analogy, properly speaking, between the immanent Trinity and the economic Trinity. The Trinity *ad intra* is revealed *ad extra* as a dynamic communion of life and self-giving love, wherein the fullness of divine being is entirely and ceaselessly communicated in a continuous interplay of gift and response between the three divine persons, Father, Son, and Spirit, and which expresses itself *ad extra*, in an overflowing gift of itself as goodness, life and love for all creation, which it invites and directs toward its end of transfiguration and entry into its communion.

VIII. Some Ramifications for Theology

1. *Theology and the Element of Negation*

If Jesus' Paschal Mystery truly signifies what is eternally lived in God's triune being, then it follows that negation, symbolised and realised in the death of Jesus, is an essential element in our human language about God. From this perspective, the Paschal Mystery demands a thorough exploration of the resources of negation in our theologising, for it necessarily introduces the "form of death" into our understanding of theology itself. It prompts the realization that systematics, like the mystery it seeks to speak about, has a certain paschal character, and involves a dying to self in its divine other-centredness.

Now this element of negation lies at the very heart of the analogical imagination – with its exploration of real similarities articulated and understood in terms of ever greater dissimilarities. The analogical imagination, in its own way, requires a self-surrender, a self-transcendence, a renunciation of autonomy, a surrender of self-sufficiency and an essential openness to that which does not come from the self. The very principle of analogy implies an act of consent to a certain non-presence to oneself and to an anteriority which one does not found. In this sense, it effectively implies a "form of death" to any temptation to autonomy or absolute self-affirmation. There is an intrinsically self-surrendering, self-denying dynamism perennially at work in the analogical imagination, which never allows us to be content with insights already gained and understandings already achieved, and which understands that the self-communication of God, the sheer excess of givenness in the data of revelation itself, ever eludes our attempts to express it.

The analogical imagination's exploration of real similarities in real differences effectively ensures the engagement of resources of negation in our theologizing, but it is no more than a clever word game were it not itself grounded in the reality of the essential order and the intrinsic relationality of existence. It is a profound faith in the inherently relational character of all existence that ultimately grounds the analogical imagination and its strategies. That same faith in the essential order and the relationality of all reality grounds the intrinsically relational character of theology itself. Theology is relational, because reality is relational, and the relationality is fruitfully explored by means of the analogical imagination[12].

2. Theology as Communal and Conversational

Our exploration of the Paschal Mystery, and in particular Jesus' consistent option for communion rather than an autonomy or independence of existence, also prompts the realisation that our theological discourse is rightly characterised by this notion of communion, as distinct from any notion which connotes autonomy. What does this mean? It means that theology is an inherently communal enterprise. It means that collaboration, cooperation, and conversation is by no means optional but intrinsic to the theological process. The Trinity of self-yielding, self-surrendering, other-centredness, of being in and for the other, as revealed in the Paschal Mystery, surely challenges us to eschew any sense that any one of us, individually or corporately, has ownership or mastery of the meaning of God's revelation.

The collaboration and cooperation that is intrinsic to the theological process is expressed most obviously and most necessarily in conversation.

---

12. Notice that the classical techniques of systematic theology, as stated by Vatican Council I, are all essentially relational: "If human reason, with faith as its guiding light, enquires earnestly, devoutly and circumspectly, it does reach, by God's generosity, some understanding of the mysteries, and that a most profitable one. It does this by analogy with the truths it knows naturally, and also from the interconnection of the mysteries with one another, and in reference to the final end of man". See *Constitution on Divine Revelation* (*Dei Filius*), DS 3019.

It is conversation that serves as the means to a better understanding of and closer approximation to the truth we seek, the truth that sets us free. Conversation is essential at each and every level of the various disciplines that together comprise the theological endeavour. Conversation is demanded among the members of the ecclesial community. Conversation is also demanded at the level of the world religions, in the domain of inter-faith dialogue and indeed with those who espouse views that are very alien, even antagonistic to our own. Recall Jesus' teaching to love our enemies, to enter into even those most difficult of conversations, and to enter them as brothers and sisters, members of the one family of God, indeed to enter those conversations by way of footwashing! That is the utterly radical engagement to which we are called!

Moreover, our experience of human conversation intimates and implicates the very mystery of trinitarian being, wherein, interpersonal relationality is characterised by an "ecstasis" or "decentering" of self in radical other-regarding relationality, a radical renunciation of autonomy, a surrender of egoism, self-sufficiency and autonomy, and an essential openness to that which comes from the other. Indeed, the analogical imagination recognizes human conversation in terms of the divine communion, that our human conversation takes place within the divine communion, within that dynamic indwelling and mutual interpenetration of the three divine persons that the tradition names perichoresis. As Balthasar explains: "It is a case of the play within the play: our play 'plays' in his play"[13]. Human conversation takes place within that "conversation" that is the divine communion. Hence, I suggest, that there is a certain sense of homecoming, of "being at home", indeed of grace, in our experience of conversation and that sense of sacred space and of precious and holy ground in the experience. For truly, our conversation is nothing less than a participation in the divine "conversation", so to speak, that is trinitarian being, a share in and an entry into the one trinitarian consciousness, a participation in that radical "being-for-another" that is the essence of innertrinitarian life and love.

IX. SOME RAMIFICATIONS FOR SPIRITUALITY – THE PASCHAL CHARACTER OF OUR LIVES, THE PASCHAL CHARACTER OF CONVERSATION

We now return to the Paschal Mystery, where there is clearly that aspect of meaning and significance that relates to Jesus' unique divine

13. H.U. VON BALTHASAR, *Theo-Drama. Theological Dramatic Theory*, vol. I, *Prolegomena*, trans. G. HARRISON, San Francisco, CA, 1988, p. 20.

person and which leads us to contemplate the mystery of trinitarian being and relations. But there is also that aspect of the Paschal Mystery which is true for us all and which has meaning and significance for us as human beings *qua* human beings and for Christian life and spirituality.

Much and all as it may disturb and perplex us, Jesus' Paschal Mystery shows that entry into communion with God necessarily passes through a stage of radical renunciation of self and finally physical death[14]. Because it is transfiguring, transforming us from one kind of human existence to another, the gift of God is, in a very real sense, mortifying. It involves, indeed necessitates, a rupture from our immediate existence, a real wrenching, a mortification. The Paschal Mystery shows that this transfiguration of existence requires what seems like a radical renunciation of existence, a total surrender and transcendence of the self. Physical death is the pre-eminent sign in the economy of this self surrender. In our exploration of the Paschal Mystery, death emerges as an event of radical renunciation of autonomy and independence for the sake of communion, and a necessary step to resurrection and new life. It assumes utmost significance as the supreme expression of one's surrender of autonomy and one's gift of self, through which we enter into communion with God.

The Paschal Mystery also shows that the human person is *invited* to this radical gift of self, this radical self-transcendence, to freely given self-surrender in response to God's self-communication and offer of communion. It reveals that the possibility of this total "ecstasis" of self – this "decentering" of self in a radical other-regarding relationality – is our ultimate meaning and vocation: through it, we enter into the life of the trinitarian communion of life and love, that unceasing exchange of life and love, joy and thanksgiving, gift and response that is trinitarian life.

14. The notion of radical renunciation of self may be a disturbing and perplexing notion, particularly from the perspective of liberation theologies. Feminist theology, for example, recognizes that the self-denying self-yielding renunciation of the women in a male dominated society has been a critical factor in the structure and system of oppression that has so abused and demeaned women. Labeled as a feminine, as distinct from a masculine trait, defined as normative for the female gender role, the notion that renunciation and self-surrender (to the male authority and good) is her right and proper role has militated against her, and been used to oppress her and dominate her, hold her in subjection to the authority of others (men), and has served to marginalize and exclude her from decision-making structures. In contrast, the self renunciation or surrender which the Paschal Mystery manifests is freely, actively and authentically given, given with dignity, given with integrity, not yielded unfreely or slavishly or in a spirit of serfdom or subordination or the denial of her dignity, her freedom, and her rights. Certainly, the risk of distortion is here, but so too is the biblical witness, as expressed in the person of Jesus himself. But let it not be misconstrued or misappropriated!

The Paschal Mystery discloses that humanity; the world, indeed all creation, finds its meaning in this radical transfiguration and entry into the
trinitarian exchange. Here is the meaning of our salvation as revealed in
the Paschal Mystery: It is to enter, with and in Christ, into the trinitarian
communion of life and love, the trinitarian perichoresis (or circumincession). Death is the supreme expression of the self-surrender, this radical
renunciation of autonomy, this total ecstasis, gift of self, to God, which
is necessary in order to enter into this trinitarian communion.

Now this radical surrender of self, this renunciation of autonomy of
existence that is necessary if we are to respond to the gift of God's self-
communication and enter into the divine communion, is not confined to
the moment of death at the end of our lives. The paschal dynamic pervades every moment and level of our existence. We are called to die
every day in all kinds of little ways, in order to live more fully in the
Trinitarian life. Though we refer to death as if it were merely the final
moment at the end of our lives, in truth, dying is a life long process. (I am
often intrigued by the expression "life-long learning" that is such a strong
and popular theme in contemporary education talk, and its connection
with this understanding of "life-long dying": life long learning, life long
dying? Is the learning in the dying, I wonder? I suspect so.) Life, as Karl
Rahner recognised, is, in a true sense, a process of dying[15]. We are dying
all our lives, and all those daily dyings, all the little deaths that we experience in the course of a lifetime, are really paschal moments, effecting
at least partial transfigurations. The moment of death is the definitive
completion, the consummation, of a process that unfolds through the
course of one's whole life, a process which expresses what Rahner
describes as our "fundamental option", one's choice or rejection of entry
into the divine communion[16]. At the core of life itself, then, we find the
Paschal Mystery – the mystery that it is in giving that we receive, that it
is in dying that we are born to new life.

This surrender of autonomy of existence, that is necessary if we are to
respond to the gift of God's self-communication and enter into the divine
communion, this fundamental option of assent to the offer of communion, finds singular opportunity for expression in our lives in the self
transcending dynamic of conversation. In conversation, we enter into a
dynamic event that is necessarily other-centred and self de-centred, which

---

15. See, for example, K. RAHNER, *On Christian Dying*, in *Theological Investigations*,
Vol. VII, London, 1971, pp. 287-291. See also *On the Theology of Death*, New York,
1961.

16. ID., *The Fundamental Option*, in *Theological Investigations*, Vol. VI, London,
1969; New York, 1974, pp. 181-188.

requires an unconditional acceptance and an essential orientation and openness toward the other, in a dynamic exchange of gift and thanksgiving, offer and response, a surrender of any sense of self-sufficiency and autonomy. Together in conversation – I and you – we enter a radical order of coexistence, a shared humanity, a unity-in-difference, a common hope, a com-passion. This is the conversational event. This is the moment of grace. And again the analogical imagination recognizes that, because it means love, and conscious mutual indwelling, it offers an analogy of the Trinitarian mystery.

There are undoubtedly real risks in conversation, all the risks of love. The outcome is uncertain; where the conversation will lead, no one knows (and that's an aspect of the paschal character of conversation); only the future will tell. Our human conversation is never really finished; there are at best provisional outcomes, closer approximations to the truth, along the way. But one thing is certain: the truth is discovered, life transforming truth, the truth that sets us free, the truth that does justice, only in this deep kind of genuine and grace-filled mutual engagement that is conversation, and that occurs when we, I and Thou, together yield to those transcendental precepts that are the hallmark of authentic selfhood and intersubjectivity: Be attentive, Be intelligent, Be reasonable, Be responsible[17].

The uncanny paradox so clearly identified by Lonergan is that truth is the fruit of genuine subjectivity, that "objectivity is simply the consequence of authentic subjectivity, of genuine attention, genuine intelligence, genuine reasonableness, genuine responsibility"[18]. Genuine attention involves attending, with openness and respect, to what the other has to say; it also acknowledges the blindspots, even biases and prejudices, in one's own understanding and one's own tradition: the logs in one's own eye! Genuine intelligence includes a readiness to grasp hitherto unnoticed or unrealized possibilities, along with a healthy suspicion of previous understandings in regard to unacknowledged biases. Genuine reasonableness demands the evaluation of the evidence, especially new evidence, however disturbing to past positions it might be. Genuine responsibility demands founding one's decisions and commitments on a discernment of what genuinely advances our understanding of the truth and the flourishing of authentic human well being and, indeed, the well being of all creation.

There is no need to fear pluralism in our conversation. The Christian tradition itself is a tradition of pluralism, from the very beginning in

17. B. LONERGAN, *Method in Theology*, New York, 1972, pp. 53, 55, 231.
18. *Ibid.*, p. 265.

the New Testament itself, and in the ongoing conversation through the centuries. Pluralism is, after all, to be expected, given that modern consciousness is differentiated in manifold diversity[19]. Pluralism is no more and no less than the fruit of variously differentiated converted consciousnesses, addressing and expressing the truth, meaning, and value we seek in their variously differentiated ways. Pluralism does not mean the end of communication and conversation. Rather, pluralism necessitates conversation. It demands an exploration of the diversity of understandings in the search for ever closer approximations to the truth. Pluralism itself demands the conversation that theology has come to be.

Neither does pluralism, nor the necessity of one's essential openness to conversion, to new understandings, and ever closer approximations to the truth in our conversation, entail a descent into relativism, for conversation demands a faithful holding to one's position and a commitment to the truth as one understands it, until one finds good reason to change it, should the evidence warrant it! There is no conversation if one has nothing to say, no position to hold, no conviction to defend, no understanding of truth to argue. Genuine conversation brooks no forsaking of one's particular vision and one's tradition for the sake of a cheap harmony or an indifferent tolerance. It countenances no kind of lazy pluralism, but demands real judgements of meaning and of value. But always "speaking the truth in love" (Eph 4,15); the love that bears all things, believes all things, hopes all things, endures all things; the love that never ends (1 Cor).

Conversation, like the analogical imagination, is itself a paschal reality. It demands a readiness to yield oneself to the dynamic of self-transcendence. There is indeed no other way to the truth we seek than the way of conversation. As David Tracy has noted, a community, a tradition, ultimately lives by the quality of its conversation, or it disintegrates and dies[20]. Our personal and communal well-being depends on it. The theological enterprise, the personal enterprise, the cultural enterprise, the peace enterprise are all inherently conversational enterprises; their success fundamentally depends on the quality of our conversation.

Again, the analogical imagination recognises our human conversations as a participation in the divine "conversation" that is trinitarian being, recognises them indeed in terms of the dance of the divine perichoresis, with its dynamic back-and-forth exchange of offer and response, gift and thanksgiving. It recognises that our conversations, even and indeed especially the most difficult ones, take place within that horizon of unbounded

19. *Ibid.*, pp. 85-99.
20. TRACY, *Plurality* (n. 1), p. IX.

self-yielding self-surrendering love that is the dance of the divine Three. Therein lies our hope. Yielding ourselves to the rhythm and movement of conversation, in an unceasing exploration of new possibilities in the search for truth, with the subject matter at hand imposing its own rhythm on us and with questioning constituting the movement, we enter the dance that is conversation, the conversation that is love, the love that is the divine communion.

X. SOME CONCLUSIONS – TRINITY AND CONVERSATION

We began our paper with a reflection on how rare and elusive a phenomenon conversation actually is, despite all the words and communications that abound in our world. The very notion of conversation is in fact a radical one, radical in terms of the respect for, openness to and welcome of the other it requires, radical in terms of the self-transcendence on which it relies, and in terms of the openness to conversion, an openness to the possibility of radical change in one's understanding of reality, and indeed of the reality that is oneself, which it requires. Yet how we long for conversation – long for this sense of shared humanity and radical coexistence, this unity in difference. And how we long for the meaning, truth, and value which emerges in conversation, long for that truth that sets us free.

I find it interesting to ponder this yearning for conversation that motivates our conference theme. It surely speaks of and from our longing for community, for communion, for genuine engagement with each other and with our God and for understanding, truth, meaning and love. It speaks just as potently of our disappointment that our day to day experience of the world is not thus, that too often our experience is one of a world of lack of genuine engagement with each other, lack of community, lack of meaning, and, in these recent weeks, of fear and dread of horrors yet to come. René Girard speaks of the human condition in terms of distorted desire, of rivalry, jealousy, and envy, that expresses itself in violence and victimization of the other[21]. Certainly, there is violence in our world, and seemingly intractable ethnic and inter-religious conflict. No wonder that such experience expresses itself in a longing for conversation, for community, for meaning, for peace and for love. It is perhaps not surprising

---

21. See, for example, R. GIRARD, *Job. The Victim of His People*, Stanford, CA, 1987; *A Theatre of Envy*, New York, 1991; G. BAILIE, *Violence Unveiled. Humanity at the Crossroads*, New York, 1997; J. ALISON, *Raising Abel. The Recovery of the Eschatological Imagination*, New York, 1996, and *The Joy of Being Wrong. Original Sin Through Easter Eyes*, New York, 1998.

then that the question of the Trinity-Conversation connection should emerge at this point on the theological landscape.

I shall draw to a close with three points in conclusion, and a question.

1. *Our Understanding of the Trinitarian Communion Illuminates the Meaning and Role of Human Conversation*

Our exploration of the interconnection of Trinity and Paschal Mystery leds us to an understanding of the mystery of the Trinity as a mystery of relatedness, of other-regarding other-centredness, for the Paschal Mystery reveals the mystery of trinitarian communion as a mystery of self-surrendering self-giving love, of the divine person as being-in-and-for-another, not in any autonomy or independence of existence but in a dynamic interpersonal and inherently relational exchange of life and love. Our exploration, and what it reveals of trinitarian relationality and personhood, surely hones our understanding of and respect for the nature and demands of authentic conversation. Moreover, the profoundly trinitarian character of our Christian faith, as revealed to us in the Paschal Mystery, clearly inspires a profound respect for diversity, motivates a quest for unity, and impels us as Christians to conversation. On the one hand, it inspires us to bring to our conversations a trinitarian imagination (for the Trinity inspires us to imagine the world otherwise and to work to make all things new), a trinitarian agenda (motivating us to bring about a better and more just world for everyone) and a trinitarian praxis (for the self-yielding, other-regarding relationality that characterizes trinitarian being serves as a model for the praxis of conversation). On the other hand, it alerts us to the dangers of any one-sidedness in our conversations, be they within the Church, with other faiths, in society or in politics generally. Indeed, it motivates us to a politics of conversation, as distinct from a politics of rhetoric, a politics of genuine engagement, active listening, empathic imagination, compassion, and humble recognition that the other's actions – all of them – are linked to ours.

2. *The Analogical Imagination Recognises Human Conversation as a Participation in the Divine Communion*

The analogical imagination and its inherent self-negating dynamic also impels us to conversation, for it is deeply conscious that I not only know the other through analogy with my own experience; I only know myself, I only know anything at all, in relation to the other, in community. The analogical imagination also recognises that human conversation, as human interpersonal event, is analogically related to and takes place within the divine communion, the divine interpersonal event. As Balthasar would express it, it is a case of our conversation within their "conversation"; our conversation takes place within the primordial inner-trinitarian "conversation" between God and God. Our human conversation, as the analogical imagination envisions it, is indeed a participation in the divine "conversation" that is trinitarian being, a participation in the divine communion that is perichoresis, with its dynamic back-and-forth exchange of offer and response, gift and thanksgiving. It takes place within that dynamic horizon of unbounded love that is the dance of the divine Three. As we yield ourselves to the rhythm and movement of conversation, in an unceasing exploration of new possibilities in the search for truth, we enter the *dance* that is conversation, the conversation that is love, the love that is a participation in the divine communion, the divine conversation.

3. *The Church's Conversations – A Trinitarian Imagination*

The events of September 11 surely motivate us to interfaith conversation; as Hans Küng once commented, there can be no peace between nations without peace among the religions. Our exploration of the Trinity-conversation connection alerts us to the dangers and limitations of any one-sidedness in our conversations and indeed in our ecclesiology, warning us in no uncertain terms, for example, of the dangers of an ecclesiology conceived, say, only in terms of Christ (Christomonism) or the Spirit (pneumatomonism) and inspiring us to cultivate a trinitarian imagination in our interfaith (and indeed in all our) encounters. Our struggle to cultivate a trinitarian imagination is further motivated by our understanding that the conversation that is the Church's life and vocation – conversation with each other, with our young people, with the alienated, with other faiths, with the world – is not just an image of, but a real participation in, the divine communion, the "conversation" of Father, Son and Holy Spirit. It speaks out of the abiding silence of the Father, in a Word of hope, and in a Spirit which keeps on inspiring us to the love that is conversation, engagement, and praxis. The scope of our conversation, the range of our concerns, is itself trinitarian-inspired and motivated; it includes God, human being, all creation, the whole cosmos, salvation, ultimate reality, human destiny, with no one, no place and no thing excluded from our concern. The aim of our conversation is an ever closer approximation to the truth. Our hope in the process is ever more authentic human existence, human flourishing and the enrichment of the cosmos – ultimately our entry into the divine trinitarian communion of life and love, that conversation which is the divine life. Throughout, indeed within this very process, motivating us to ever deeper conversation, to ever more grace-filled engagement with each other, inspiring us in the search for ever closer approximations to the truth, the formation of human community and ultimately our entry into the divine communion, is the Trinity itself.

4. A Concluding Suggestion

Taking the perspective of classical trinitarian theology, the psychological analogy can easily be transposed into the inter-subjective analogy of conversation, taking the phenomenon of human conversation as analogy for the inner-trinitarian communion. This kind of exploration of the analogy, while paying due considerations to the similarities and the ever greater dissimilarities, leads one to a range of implications for ecclesiology (the relationships in the Church as well as for the Church in the World) and for Christian life and spirituality. The results, I suggest, are neat and refined, perhaps all rather predictable, not particularly new or especially challenging, suggesting nothing much more perhaps than human civility might demand of us as social beings.

But, like Balthasar, it seems to me that the analogy of human conversation utterly pales as image of trinitarian life, in comparison with the revelation of the Trinity which is given to us, given indeed to excess, in the mystery of Jesus' Paschal Mystery. The sheer drama of the Paschal Mystery, I suggest, urges our exploration of the Trinity-Conversation connection to another dimension altogether, immeasurably beyond the play of word and meaning that we recognise as conversational, to an utterly life-transforming engagement, an engagement that involves a radical transfiguration, which presents itself to us in the form of death-like annihilation, and which leads to communion built on radically self-surrendering kenotic love. If nothing else, the Paschal Mystery reminds us that our conversation takes place around the crucified!

While conversation certainly illumines the trinitarian mystery that is revealed to us in the Paschal Mystery, the Paschal Mystery, it seems to me, explodes the very notion of conversation as we know it. At the very least, the Paschal Mystery demands not just a conversational ideal, but a genuinely conversational self; not just the occasional play of engagement in conversation in our lives but a truly conversational life, a life that is characterised by unconditional other-regarding, other-welcoming, other-centredness, that kind of being-for-one-another which is revealed for us in the Paschal Mystery as the essence of inner-trinitarian personhood and life, and that costs us not less than *everything*.

Like the footwashing, the sheer drama of the encounter and the utter radicality of the engagement that is so powerfully and startlingly revealed in the Paschal Mystery simply breaks out of and just cannot be confined within the notion of conversation. Though useful and, within its limits, a constructive theme, and indeed a metaphor that is amenable to the development of a research programme as has been proposed, conversation is, I suggest, rather too weak and too limited a notion to encapsulate the sheer drama and the mystery and the glory that has manifest itself to us. Recall the paschal character of conversation itself. Here, the Paschal Mystery also alerts us to the paschal character of Systematics itself – that no system, no notion, no metaphor is adequate to the magnificent task that is ours in Systematics. In proceeding then to develop a research programme with the notion of conversation as its foundation, let us not forget or overlook its limitations.

"The Word became flesh and dwelt among us, full of grace and truth" (John 1,14). Our redemption consists not in words spoken by the incarnate Word, but in the wordless acts of boundless all-embracing undying love. Love is *id quo maius cogitari nequit*, the Love that never ends, that knows no bounds, that refuses to be anything but love, the love that enters into conversation with us, the love that is so tangibly, so radically and so utterly unexpectedly disclosed to us in the Paschal Mystery – and in the footwashing.

Australian Catholic University   Anne HUNT
Aquinas Campus
1200 Mair Street
Ballarat Vic 3350
Australia

DYSFUNCTIONAL CONVERSATION IN ISAIAH 24

I. INTRODUCTION

There are many places in the collection of literary documents we refer to as the Hebrew Bible in which conversation, such as it is, between the deity and his worshippers is clearly dysfunctional. One characteristic (form-critical) feature of the so-called lament psalms, for example, is their initial expression of the experience of the absence and ultimate silence of God in dire circumstances, a situation in which the conversation between both parties becomes rather one-sided, often expressed in the form of a question: "How long, O Lord will you remain at a distance and refuse to answer?". The prophets as "speakers of the unspeakable" (see below) often immerse themselves in the dysfunctional relationship between YHWH and his people, giving voice to the other side of the conversation between them or the apparent lack thereof.

The present paper will endeavour to show that the prophet in Isaiah 24 intended to portray the relationship between his people and his/their God as a three-sided conversation, including the earth as representative of God's creation. Where the human relationship with God dysfunctioned and became infertile so the relationship with the earth dysfunctioned and became infertile. As is clearly the case elsewhere in the prophetic books and indeed throughout the Hebrew Bible, reference to the dysfunctional conversation between God and his people in Isaiah is a delicate matter, one which the author(s) often handled by resorting to the use of metaphorical language. The metaphorical language found in Isaiah 24 would tend to suggest that God metaphors are primarily relational metaphors and not exclusively intended to inform or educate their audience about the characteristics of the divinity alone.

Based on a literary examination of the text of Isaiah 24, the paper will thus conclude that the prophetic (metaphorical) portrayal of the divine-human relationship must include earth as an indispensable dialogue partner, that conversations within this three-sided relationship frequently dysfunctioned and that the prophetic participation in and portrayal of these dysfunctional conversations in the Hebrew Bible often resorts to metaphor.

II. PROPHETIC DISCOURSE AS CONVERSATION

Ferdinand Deist notes "... if one wants to understand prophetic speech as 'dialogue' one has to answer the question: who were the prophets, that is, what was their social location? Secondly, one would have to evaluate the effectiveness of their speech in their own societies: how successful was their "dialogue"? Thirdly, given the present view of "Israelite prophecy", in what manner can the prophetic books assist contemporary dialogue between Christianity and secular society?"[1]. While these are clearly important questions with respect to the assumptions made concerning the socio-cultural role of the so-called "writing prophets", the present contribution wishes to focus primarily on the prophets as "the receivers and public announcers of God's message", and on prophetic speech as "a religious discourse that responds to political and social situations as a proclamation of God's judgment or reward"[2]. To what extent can we consider *such* prophetic discourse a conversation or dialogue, and, if we can, what part does the prophet have to play in that conversation? While in the prophetic texts as a whole the prophet is alone in speaking, and we may be thus tempted to hear his words as a monologue – they are ultimately his or his followers' or a later redactor's words – he does place words in the mouth of two notable others: God and the people. The common and familiar expression designed to introduce divine elocution "Thus says the Lord" is frequently followed by or preceded by a statement of the Lord spoken in first person speech by the prophet. Isaiah 1,2 provides a good example of what I mean, although the designation of speaker is rarely left undisputed: "Hear, O heavens, and listen, O earth: *for the Lord has spoken*: I reared children and brought them up but they rebelled against me"[3]. If one can determine a conversation to be *at least* a dialogue between *at least two* parties, establishing a relationship between the two or more participants, then prophetic discourse is a conversation and one would be correct in determining the role of the prophet as one of a conversation partner representing, for the most part, the Lord and perhaps himself. The addressees of this word of the Lord, the other side of the conversation, are the actual

1. F. DEIST, *Prophetic Discourse: Dialogue, Disaster or Opportunity?*, in *Scriptura* 57 (1996) 179-192, p. 179.
2. Y. GITAY, *The Realm of Prophetic Rhetoric*, in S.E. PORTER – T.H. OLBRICHT (eds.), *Rhetoric, Scripture and Theology. Essays from the 1994 Pretoria Conference* (JSNT SS, 131), Sheffield, pp. 218-229, esp. 219, 227.
3. Heaven and earth here clearly represent a meristic form of address, intended to include the whole world in the prophet's range of addressees.

audience, the presumed audience, the historical audience, the actualised audience, the present day audience, most of whom, if not all, consider(ed) themselves part of the conversation with the Almighty (in the form of the prophet). Thus one can say that the conversation already has *at least* three actants: the prophet, the people (us) and God. The content of the conversation as such, however, makes it clear that other actants constituted genuine participants, one of which, namely earth, will be an additional focus of the remainder of our paper.

First of all, however, we need to take a look at some of the principles governing our understanding of metaphor and the prophet's use thereof.

Metaphor: The Prophet Places Words Where There Is No Mouth!

Any attempt to deal with the metaphorical content of a piece of biblical Hebrew poetry (henceforth BHP) such as Isa 24 requires that we try to determine what we mean by metaphorical speech in the first place, how we can distinguish it from other figurative manners of speech employed in poetry, how it functions and what the intention of the author(s/redactors) may have been in employing it[4]. At the same time, the fact that we are dealing with BHP within a larger prophetic context requires that we not only delimit our focus text and review our text-critical options as part of a more technical exegetical endeavour, but that we also endeavour to discern its primary structuring features as poetry (colometry, parallelism etc.) prior to any further engagement with its non-structuring features such as metaphor[5]. While it is apparent that both structuring and non-structuring aspects of BHP function together and are interrelated[6], the identification of non-structuring features such as metaphor is often not as simple as many a commentary would suggest[7]. In order to proceed, therefore, we need to establish some parameters: Which *definition* of metaphor should we maintain? What should we be looking for in *identifying* metaphor in BHP? How should we go about *categorising* the metaphors we find? How should we ultimately *interpret* an author's use of metaphors? The methodology we will follow in

---

4. For a more detailed examination of these important questions see B. DOYLE, *The Apocalypse of Isaiah Metaphorically Speaking. A Study of the Use, Function and Significance of Metaphors in Isaiah 24–27* (BETL, 151), Leuven, 2000, pp. 49-144.

5. W.G.E. WATSON, *Classical Hebrew Poetry: A Guide to Its Techniques* (JSOT SS, 26), Sheffield, ²1995, pp. 16-20.

6. Cf., in the case of metaphor and parallelism, A. BERLIN, *On Reading Biblical Poetry: The Role of Metaphor*, in J.A. EMERTON (ed.), *Congress Volume, Cambridge, 1995*, Leiden, 1997, pp. 25-36.

7. See the majority of commentaries which speak here of metaphor but with no further explanation.

the present contribution, therefore, is a simple one based on the four afore-mentioned questions. It will be an endeavour to confront the text of Isa 24,4 from a variety of different perspectives with a view to the iden-tification, categorisation and interpretation of its metaphorical language as a constitutive part of a dysfunctional conversation illustrating a dys-functional relationship between God, the earth and the people.

While there are many definitions of metaphor available[8], we opt for the following definition taken from Daniel Bourguet's *Des métaphores de Jérémie* for the simple reason that it was conceived in the specific con-text of the analysis of BHP:

> ...le fait de décrire intentionellement, de manière médiate ou immédiate, une métaphorisé dans les termes d'un métaphorisant qui lui ressemble et qui appartient à une autre isotopie[9].

Three terms in Bourguet's definition require further explanation: *métaphorisé*, *métaphorisant*[10], and *isotopie*. The term *métaphorisé* is roughly equivalent to the "tenor" or the "principle/primary subject" as Max Black would put it. The term *métaphorisant*, on the other hand, is akin to the "vehicle" or Black's "subsidiary/secondary subject"[11]. The term *isotopie* refers to a sector of vocabulary associated with a par-ticular subject and is roughly equivalent to Kittay and Lehrer's "seman-tic field"[12]. Biblical Hebrew particularly lends itself to the establishment of *isotopies* because of the polysemic character of many of its lexemes. Following Bourguet's definition, therefore, a biblical metaphor must employ two distinct isotopes, two distinct domains of knowledge, that of the *métaphorisé* and that of the *métaphorisant*. Distinction in isotope is thus an essential dimension of metaphor. Where there is no distinction in isotope one is probably dealing with simple comparison or indeed simile.

---

8. See P.W. MACKY, *The Centrality of Metaphors to Biblical Thought. A Method for Interpreting the Bible* (Studies in the Bible and Early Christianity, 19), Lewiston – Queen-ston – Lampeter, 1990.

9. D. BOURGUET, *Des métaphores de Jérémie* (Études Bibliques, 9), Paris, 1987, p. 10. Bourguet's definition is a refinement of that proposed by Paul Ricœur.

10. With the exception of *isotopie*, Bourguet's terminology is difficult to translate into English without resorting to the use of awkward neologisms.

11. M. BLACK, *Metaphor*, in ID. (ed.), *Models and Metaphors: Studies in Language and Philosophy*, Ithaca, NY, 1962, pp. 25-47; originally published in *Proceedings of the Aris-totelian Society* 55 (1954) 273-294. Cf. also ID., *More About Metaphor*, in A. ORTONY (ed.), *Metaphor and Thought*, Cambridge, ²1984, pp. 19-43.

12. E.F. KITTAY – A.A. LEHRER, *Semantic Fields and the Structure of Metaphor*, in *Studies in Language* 5 (1981) 31-63; cf. also E.F. KITTAY, *Metaphor. Its Cognitive Force and Linguistic Structure*, Oxford, 1987, pp. 214-257 ("Semantic Field Theory"). Kittay and Lehrer also speak of a "recipient field" and a "donor field" which once again are rough equivalents of Bourguet's *métaphorisé* and *métaphorisant*.

While Bourguet – and indeed many others if the commentaries are anything to go by – would maintain that Hebrew comparative particles (and other comparative terms and expressions – A is like/as B) are a significant formal indicator of the presence of metaphor in biblical poetry, bringing distinct isotopes together and allowing them to interact, we are inclined to lay greater emphasis on the various structuring devices of Hebrew poetry (especially parallelism in all its forms[13]) which tend to function in the same way. A. Berlin maintains that metaphor and parallelism are two sides of the same coin because both bring together terms/ideas/images (isotopes) which are distinct yet similar. We still have to account, however, for the aspect of similarity within Bourguet's theory. Bourguet insists that a level of resemblance is an essential element in the relationship between the distinct isotopes of the *métaphorisé* and the *métaphorisant*. He refers to this area of cross-reference as the *foyer*, the seat or heart of the metaphor. It consists, he maintains, of a certain level of repetition (akin thus to parallelism in BHP) which can be both literal or implied. For Bourguet, this aspect of metaphor serves to distinguish it from other figures of classical rhetoric such as metonymy or synecdoche[14].

The insights of P.W. Macky are also worthy of note in the process of analysing the metaphorical language in a biblical text. Macky insists that metaphors are not words but expressions or statements. The word "rock", for example, is not a metaphor but the expression "YHWH is a rock" clearly is (two distinct isotopes). In other words, our focus of attention in exploring a piece of BHP for metaphorical content should not be individual terms (a single *métaphorisé* and a single *métaphorisant*) but speech acts, broader metaphorical statements (an *énoncé métaphorisé* and an *énoncé métaphorisant* as Bourguet would put it) in which distinct isotopes are brought into interaction by the structuring poetic context.

Since Max Black's studies[15] were published in the sixties and seventies, commentators have tended to speak of metaphorical speech as "interaction" between distinct isotopes or knowledge domains whereby one isotope (in our case the *métaphorisé*) is understood/structured in terms of the other (the *métaphorisant*). Exploiting his/her poetic skills, the biblical author laid down structural foundations whereby isotopes that explicitly differ yet enjoy some degree of cross-reference are allowed to

13. In line with and beyond Berlin.
14. The former is based on attribution or relationship between the terms concerned, the latter on contiguity between them. Neither is based on resemblance and distinction combined.
15. See note 11.

encounter one another in an interaction that ultimately informs the reader/listener concerning, at least for the most part, the *métaphorisé*. In the text we will examine below, this interaction serves as an invitation to the reader/listener to explore relationship.

As a more or less fixed entity, the biblical text provides us with a source in which we can explore for intentional juxtaposition of distinct isotopes which have a point of resemblance, in other words for metaphorical speech. With this in mind we turn to the text of Isa 24,4-6 and its metaphorical language.

III. WORKING TRANSLATION *ISA 24,4-6*

4a She wails, she withers, the land.
  b She is weak, she withers, world.
  c They are weak, the high place[s], the people[16] of the land.
5a And the land is polluted under her inhabitants.
  b For, they have transgressed laws, by-passed precept[s],
  c [for] they have broken the covenant everlasting.
6a Therefore, a curse consumes land,
  b and they are held guilty, those who dwell in her.
  c Therefore, they diminish, those who dwell in land,
  d and what remains is a single man, a mere few.

1. *Delimitation of Metaphorical Statement*

The passage under consideration is to be found at the beginning of the so-called Apocalypse of Isaiah (chapters 24–27) in which the prophet

---

16. According to D. BARTHÉLEMY (*Critique Textuelle de l'Ancien Testament, 2. Isaïe, Jérémie, Lamentations* [OBO, 50/2], Göttingen, 1986, pp. 172-174), the variety of readings of this expression are based on the fact the MT has a plural verb followed by a singular subject which consists of two nouns in the construct state, the second of which has a collective significance. This, he maintains, constitutes a *lectio difficilior* which has led to harmonisations and contradictory interpretations on the part of the witnesses and later translations, and in some cases to the omission of the term עם (1QIsaᵃ, Pesh.). While following the MT, Barthélemy and his team ultimately opt for the association of the term עם with מרום, leaving the reference to "people" explicit and translating the expression as a reference to the élite of the land. Objections to this perspective maintain, however, that the whole population is affected by the calamity and not just the élite. The parallelism is inclusive of people/inhabitants and land. I interpret the term as "high place", which, according to NIDOTTE (8123 [SMITH/HAMILTON]) occurs with some frequency in BI (16x). The notion of "high place" might suggest that both Jerusalem and the surrounding land are included in this weakening and withering.

confronts his audience with an impending period of all-embracing devastation and ruin. Several commentators establish vv. 4-6 as the second sub-division of the first textual unit of chapter 24, namely vv. 1-13[17]. In vv. 1-3, the prophet initiates the conversation by announcing in 3rd person speech that the earth and its inhabitants are to be utterly destroyed by a hostile YHWH who is the functionally acting subject of the impending devastation. The prophet employs language from the isotope of an attacking army destroying everything in its path and deporting prisoners and allows it to interact with the isotope of the divine thus inviting the audience to view YHWH as a hostile invader. The subject changes in the present verses from YHWH to "wailing earth" / "inhabitants" who pick up the conversation. Thus the metaphorical statement in vv. 4-6 moves its focus from the isotope of the divine (hostile YHWH) to the isotope of "earth" / "world" (and its "inhabitants" / "dwellers" [always together with "earth"]). This isotope – "earth" / "world" – thus constitutes the *métaphorisé* while the isotope of "wailing" / "withering" / "being weak" / "polluted" / "consumed" / "held   guilty" / "diminished" / "a remainder" constitutes the *métaphorisant*. The entire image in these verses, while alternating between earth and inhabitants as in vv. 1-3, dwells more on the earth and what is happening to it as a result of human failure and transgression than on the inhabitants and what is happening to them as a result of earth's destruction (vv. 1-3)[18]. From a structural/colometric perspective, vv. 4-6 also constitute a concentric pattern of bicola ([abcb'a']) turning around v. 5bc which appears to be quite "literal" language and not intended to be part of the metaphorical statement ([a]: 4ab; [b]: 4c-5a; [c]: 5bc; [b']: 6ab; [a']: 6cd). The concentric shape of the metaphorical statement is based on the interplay between the *énoncé métaphorisé* and the *énoncé*

17. For example, E.J. KISSANE, *The Book of Isaiah*, Dublin, 1960, p. 273; P. REDDITT, *Isaiah 24–27: A Form Critical Analysis*, Diss., Vanderbilt University, 1972, pp. 73ff.; A. SCHOORS, *Jesaja* (BOT, IX), Roermond, 1972, p. 144 (sub-division of vv. 1-6); H. WILD-BERGER, *Jesaja 13–27* (BKAT, X-3), Neukirchen – Vluyn, 1982, p. 912; D.J. LEWIS, *A Rhetorical Critical Analysis of Isaiah 24–27*, Diss., The Southern Baptist Theological Seminary, 1985, pp. 49ff. (vv. 4-6 constitute the first of three strophes dividing up vv. 4-13; D.G. JOHNSON, *From Chaos to Restoration. An Integrative Reading of Is 24–27* (JSOT SS, 61), Sheffield, 1988; = revised version of *Devastation and Restoration, A Compositional Study of Isaiah 24–27*, Diss., Princeton Theological Seminary, 1985, p. 21 (vv. 4-6 are a distinct pericope but they share vocabulary and tone with vv. 7-12); P. HÖFFKEN, *Das Buch Jesaja Kapitel 1–39* (NSKAT, 18-1), Stuttgart, 1993, p. 177; P. MOTYER, *The Prophecy of Isaiah*, Leicester, 1993, p. 198 (a sub-division of vv. 1-20). Authors arrive at their divisions on a variety of different textual bases (genre, structure, syntax, semantics etc.).

18. Syntactically speaking the use of asyndetic *qatals* (cf. *Indicators* below) demarcates the unit from what precedes it (*w*[e]*qatals*) as does the change of actant in v. 7 ("earth" / "inhabitants" to "wine" / "joy" / "mirth").

métaphorisant. Thus the structural pattern leads us to view certain terms metaphorically because of their parallel relationship with other more clearly figurative language.

2. *Indicators*

It is clear that the metaphorical statement in vv. 4-6 has no formal indicators in the form of comparative particles (and their equivalents) and is thus, in Bourguet's terminology, a "short" metaphor presenting a "short shock". The *métaphorisé* is "earth" / "world" and its "inhabitants" which featured also in vv. 1-3. The alternation between earth and inhabitants continues here while the structure of the unit places the inhabitants of earth in a central position as was also the case in vv. 1-3. In both the first unit and the present unit these statements do not appear to constitute metaphorical language although they are "sandwiched" within an evidently metaphorical statement. The "dwellers of the earth" in the present metaphorical statement are only presented in relation to "earth" and not independently, they respond in the conversation in the same way as "earth" does. While "inhabitants" may be considered part of the *énoncé métaphorisé*, the primary focus thereof is clearly "earth". The *énoncé métaphorisant* is spread out over a number of verb forms in these verses and includes "wailing", "withering", "being weak", "polluted", "consumed by curse" [indirectly also "being held guilty", "diminishment", "remaining few"], all of which are part of the isotope of "mourning" / "sin" as well as that of "desolation"[19]. Evidently, therefore, the

---

19. √אבל is used for external acts of mourning or mourning customs (cf. Gen 37,34; 2 Sam 13,31-37) and not usually for the inner feelings associated therewith although this is not excluded. Elsewhere it refers to the devastation of nature and vegetation due to drought (cf. Isa 33,9; Jer 4,28; 12,4.11; 23,10; Hos 4,3) where it is often paralleled with √יבש "to dry up" (Jer 12,4; 23,10). It can also mean "to be desolate" when paralleled with √שמם (Jer 12,11) (cf. TDOT I 45-47 [BAUMANN]; DCH I 106-109; NIDOTTE 61 [OLIVER]); √אמל likewise can refer to both humans and natural phenomena and can imply both emotional feebleness (Ezek 16,30) as well as "being dried up" (parallel √יבש Joel 1,12; Isa 16,8; 33,9; cf. DCH I 314; HALOT 63; NIDOTTE 581 [HAYDEN/TOMASINO]). Like אבל, אמל also has a secondary connection to the notion of "shame" (respectively Isa 33,9; Jer 15,9) which surely has relevance in the present context. The notion of "diminishment", or "dwindling" is likewise part of the semantic field of this term (cf. 1 Sam 2,5; Isa 19,8; Jer 18,9; Hos 4,3); √נבל has the general meaning of "to sink" / "to drop down" and can apply, once again, to humans (from "exhaustion" Ex 18,18; from "discouragement" 2 Sam 22,46; figuratively: of "a good man" Ps 1,3; of "Israel" Jer 8,13; of "the wicked" Ps 37,2). The usual subjects are natural, such as trees (Isa 1,30; Ezek 47,12), leaves etc. (cf. NBDB 5034; NIDOTTE 5570 [HAYDEN]); √חנף means "to make godless" / "to profane" and can be applied to persons (Jer 23,11) and (passively) to earth (Jer 3,1; Ps 106,38; cf. NBDB 2610; HALOT 335; NIDOTTE 2866 [AVERBECK]); √אכל basically means "to eat" and

métaphorisé and *métaphorisant* are both present although this is not always the case[20].

The isotope of "earth" / "world" is clearly distinct from that of "sin" / "mourning", the former being solid, corporeal, inanimate reality (no matter how far it extends), the latter turning around negative concepts ("withering" / "languishing", "being weak", "polluted", "consumed", "guilty" [also "diminished", "remaining"]) and expressed negative emotion ("wailing") more usually associated with sentient, human reality. The lack of formal indicators is certainly made up for by the abundance of informal indicators of the presence of metaphor. Syntactic surcharge is evident via the simple (asyndetic) juxtaposition of terms from both isotopes ("earth wails") while consistent parallelism between the cola contributes to the confrontation of the terms in question with one another (both within the isotope and outside it) and heightens the metaphorical "tension".

Based on what we have noted so far, it is apparent that the metaphorical statement as such extends to v. 6. In vv. 7-13, a new *métaphorisé* is introduced ("wine" / "joyful noise" which itself constitutes an *énoncé métaphorisant* with YHWH as the "silent" *métaphorisé*) and the entire metaphorical statement takes a different turn. It is also evident that we are

---

frequently occurs together with שׁתה√ ("to drink") as a sign of human well-being and happiness (Isa 21,5; Jer 15,16). Its negative side suggests the notion of being "destroyed" or "devoured" and is frequently used with "locusts" as subject as they desolate and destroy the land (Ex 10,5.12.15; Joel 1,4; 2,5; Am 4,9; 7,2; Ps 105,35) and its natural produce (grass: Gen 3,18; Ex 10,12.15; Am 7,2; Ps 105,35) or with "fire" / "flame" which burns up and destroys the earth (Isa 1,7) or human persons in one form or another (Dt 7,16; Zech 12,6; Ps 14,4; Hab 3,14; Prov 30,14 etc.; cf. DCH I 240-248; TDOT I 236-241 [OTTOSSON]; NIDOTTE 430 [O'CONNELL]). אשׁם√ in its *qal* form basically means "to be guilty" and mostly refers to human persons (Ezek 6,6; Hos 10,2 etc.). It can also refer to a country (Judah Hos 4,15; Ephraim Hos 5,15; Samaria Hos 14,1 – signifying both territory and nation; cf. DCH I 414-415; NIDOTTE 870 [CARPENTER/GRISANTI]). In Ezek 6,6, אשׁם√ is parallel with חרב√, which usually suggests "to be dried up" (of "waters" / "rivers": Gen 8,13; Isa 19,5; Ps 106,9; Jer 51,36 etc.) or (חרב√ II) to be laid waste, depopulated ("sanctuaries" Am 7,9; "cities" Jer 26,9; Ezek 6,6; "nations" / "lands" Isa 37,18; 42,15; cf. NBDB 2717). Like אמל√ and אבל√ there is also a secondary association with sin (parallel חטא√ Lev. 4,22) and "being unclean" / "shame" (parallel טמא√, referring to Jerusalem); חרר√ (NDBD 2787 I; NIDOTTE 3081 [WAKELY]) basically means "to be scorched" / "to burn" which can apply to human beings ("burn with fever" Job 30,30) or to nature ("the vine" Ezek 15,4.5); nominal form signifies a "parched place" (Jer 17,6 where it is parallel to עבר√ and figurative for the life of the godless); שׁאר√ has developed theological connotations which tend to shroud its original, more neutral meaning, namely "to be left over/alive" from a larger group (of people) or natural condition (land) after famine, plague or other disaster (human bodies and lands Gen 47,18; the land Ex 10,15; Josh 13,1ff., cities Jer 34,7; people Gen 7,23; Ezek 9,8 etc.; cf. TWAT VII 935ff. [CLEMENTS]; NBDB 7604 I; NIDOTTE 8636 [PARK]).

20. They may indeed be simply implied by the context.

dealing here with dependant and therefore figurative speech. All of the verb forms of the *énoncé métaphorisant* can only apply to the *métaphorisé* (earth) because of their already established connection with human persons and their psychological/physical states. In light of the double meaning associated with the terms involved in the *énoncé métaphorisant* it is possible to envisage much of the present metaphorical statement in more literal terms, viewing it as a statement of the dry and empty earth in time of drought. Oddly enough, however, the two terms "earth" / "world", according to the scheme proposed by Watts[21], tend to refer more to the civilised world than to the cultivable soil (cf. אדמה) which one would associate with the effects of drought. In this light, therefore, it becomes more difficult to reduce to literal speech and we must regard the metaphor of languishing, wailing earth as "profound" rather than "superficial".

The analogical relationship between the *métaphorisé* and the *métaphorisant* appears to be "neutral" in that it has both "positive" and "negative" dimensions. Both similarity and difference between the *métaphorisé* and the *métaphorisant* are rooted in the possibility of interpreting the isotope of the *énoncé métaphorisant* in both physical (non-human) and psychological (and thus human) terms. As with the focal metaphor in vv. 1-3, the level of analogical resemblance/difference is what allows the *métaphorisant* to provide insight into the *métaphorisé*.

3. *Type*

The primary core of the metaphorical statement in these verses appears to be located in the isotopic cross-reference contained within the terms of the *métaphorisant* ("wailing", "withering", "being weak", "polluted", "consumed by curse": terms from the isotope of "mourning" / "sin" as well as that of "desolation"), in the ambiguity of the "lamenting" (psychological) and "parched" (physical) earth. K.M. Hayes[22] is correct (and not alone[23]) in pointing out that some of the verbal roots involved in our metaphorical statement have a double meaning (overlapping isotopes) which has found its way into the dictionaries (i.e. it has been lexicalised): the physical/earthly (e.g. "to dry up") and psychological/human "to mourn" (ritually as well as interiorly). It is within this ambiguity that we

21. J.D.W. WATTS, *Isaiah 1–33* (WBC, 24), Waco, TX, 1985, pp. 316-317.

22. K.M. HAYES, *"The Earth Mourns": Earth as Actor in a Prophetic Metaphor*, Diss., Catholic University of America, 1997, pp. 14-24, 187ff.

23. Cf. W. MARCH, *A Study of Two Prophetic Compositions in Isaiah 24:1–27:1*, Diss., Union Theological Seminary, 1966, p. 27.

must search for the primary isotopic cross-reference between the *métaphorisant* and the *métaphorisé*. The ambiguity as such, however, makes the metaphor quite complex and, I believe, "dual direction", the *métaphorisé* ("earth" / "world" and its "inhabitants") and the *métaphorisant* in part informing one another. The primary core or isotopic cross-reference is evidently "absent" in that it does not rest in the so-called "middle ground" of resemblance between the *métaphorisant* and the *métaphorisé* but is contained or "hidden" within the ambiguity of *métaphorisant* itself. It is thus the ambiguity established by the terms of the two overlapping isotopes (the *métaphorisant*: mourning/desolation) that makes it possible to view this as a metaphorical statement concerning earth and its inhabitants (the *métaphorisé*). While not specifically a "word-play" core as it is defined by Bourguet, the isotopic cross-reference hidden within the terms of the *métaphorisant* is clearly supported and underlined by their phonetic similarity (esp. אבל, אמל).

Hayes has also suggested that we are dealing here with a "dead" metaphor, originally derived from observations that ritual actions of a mourner mimic the state of the earth in periods of drought[24]. If one were to accept that the metaphor in question is "dead", however, then one would have to accept, along with Ricœur[25], that it no longer functions as a metaphor and this seems far from the case in the present text. According to Black[26], the reader/listener would not recognise the etymology of the term(s) employed in the *énoncé métaphorisé* where "dead" metaphors are concerned (he calls them "extinct"). The very fact that the ambiguity of the terms involved here has been lexicalised suggests that the listener reader would be well aware of their dual significance and quite aware that they were being employed metaphorically. In Black's terms this would make our metaphor "active" and both "emphatic" (a genuine interaction metaphor) and "resonant" (rich in interpretative implications).

It may be possible to discern a metaphor of the A is B type in the present text, namely "earth is mortal". It is also possible to turn the entire concept around and suggest that "mortals are earthly". The link between "earth" and "people" is established in the primary metaphorical core and in the structure of the text: what the people do has an effect on the earth (pollution) – the earth's condition has an effect on the people ("guilt", "burned up"). In this sense the metaphor works in two directions and thus serves to underline the intimacy of the relationship between people

24. HAYES, *"The Earth Mourns"* (n. 22), p. 20.
25. P. RICŒUR, *La métaphore vive*, Paris, 1975, p. 370.
26. BLACK, *More about Metaphor* (n. 11), p. 25.

and earth (or people and land). The fact that the *métaphorisé* is a well-known reality and the *métaphorisant* both physical and non-physical (emotional) at the same time allows for further possibilities in interpreting the metaphorical statement.

In terms of Lakoff and Johnson's categories of metaphorical concepts, the metaphorical statement in vv. 4-6 would appear to be "structural" in that it encourages us to structure our understanding of earth/world (and its population) in terms of mourning ritual/pollution/sin. The presence of ambiguity in the *métaphorisant* also allows for the possibility of the metaphor being "Twice True", i.e. both a literal statement about the earth (it is devastated, dried up) and a metaphorical one (it is in mourning). Nelly Stienstra's observation that certain metaphors are culture-dependant and others culture-exceeding also seems relevant here. Since the core of the metaphor is locked or hidden in the terms of the *énoncé métaphorisant* it is evident that modern readers, unfamiliar with mourning rituals of the Ancient Near East, would only partly understand the full extent of the metaphor (perhaps more as "humans are earthly" than as "earth is mortal"). To this extent the metaphor is predominantly culture-dependant.

We noted above that Hayes was of the opinion that the metaphor of the "mourning earth" has its roots in a "dead" metaphor. Macky's broader set of categories, which sets metaphorical usage on a continuum running from "novel" to "retired", obviates the need for a "dead" or "alive" debate. The analogy between mourning patterns/rituals and the parched earth may at one time have been more evident than it is today. In a certain sense, the modern reader would probably be inclined to see the metaphor as "novel" since it draws our attention to a similarity which we did not already know. At the same time, the fact that the ambiguity in the *métaphorisant* has, to a certain extent, been lexicalised, suggests that even the modern reader would ultimately be able to find his/her way into the metaphor without too much difficulty. The "dual direction" of the metaphor might even lead the modern reader into establishing analogies at a "novel" psychological level (e.g. parched/scorched earth as metaphor for traumatised human psyche). For the author and his first "audience", however, the content of the metaphorical statement in vv. 4-6 was probably quite evident, the metaphor thus being "familiar" according to Macky's categories. As he notes, however, the positive and negative analogy between the *métaphorisé* and the *métaphorisant* was still enough to invite the reader/listener to approach this speech act as metaphorical and thereby explore the image offered by the author. In this sense the metaphor in these verses is not "ornamental" but "comparative" in that it invites its audience to explore the analogy (+ and -) between *métapho-risé* and *métaphorisant*. Macky also points out that such "familiar" metaphors abound in the OT. We can certainly go along with Hayes in part in that the core of our metaphorical statement here seems to have been well on its way to "retirement", i.e. to independent, literal use.

4. Author's Purpose/Interpretation

For what type of speech has the author employed a metaphorical statement? Clearly the metaphor is evocative of human emotion associated with mourning and the speech act might thus be described as "expressive". As we have already noted, however, the emotional dimension of the metaphor seems to take a secondary position to expression of mourning in ritual form. It would also appear that the present metaphor is pedagogical in that it intends to illuminate the consequences of sin/transgressing with regard to ancient laws, precepts and covenant. At the same time the author may have employed this particular metaphor for the purpose of stimulating a sense of mourning in his audience related to a new awareness (transformation) of their misdeeds. In this way, one might categorise the speech act as "affective" as well as "pedagogical" and, thus, ultimately "transformative". In the last analysis, however, the primary aspect involved in the author's use of metaphor would appear to be "relational" in that the triangular relationship between earth/people/God is understood to be open to change (for good or bad) by the deeds of any one of the parties involved[27].

Given the concentric structure of the present unit it seems reasonable to assume that the author has employed a rather elaborate metaphorical statement to shed light on a "real" (if primarily theological) situation of transgression and its consequences. The metaphor ultimately continues on from the announcement of judgement begun in vv. 1-3 in which the metaphor of "YHWH as enemy" took centre stage and the foundations of the clearly dysfunctional conversation were laid. To a certain degree, therefore, vv. 4-6 (esp. 5bc and 6a) present the audience with a particular argument or communicate information (transgress and you will suffer the consequences) but this "presentative" (or "cognitive") dimension of the text remains secondary. The primary focus of the author is on the results of the judgement announced in vv. 1-3 which turn around the inharmonious triangular relationship between earth (including its "high places", which we take to mean "heavens"[28]), inhabitants and God who

27. MACKY, *Centrality* (n. 8), p. 17.
28. Cf. L.A. SNIJDERS, *Jesaja*. Deel I (POT), Nijkerk, 1969, pp. 235-236; SCHOORS, *Jesaja* (n. 17), p. 145.

ultimately brings about judgement. Although not directly mentioned in these verses, God is present in the conversation in the person of the prophet as well as in the various allusions to breaking covenant. The relationship between God and humans is disturbed, and this reveals itself in the relationship between humans and earth insinuated by the metaphor. Earth dries up (natural phenomenon) and mourns (human phenomenon). Humans pollute the earth instead of cultivating it and as a consequence they too are diminished, dried up, scorched; they too wail along with the earth[29]. While the author is clearly offering a judgement of the situation, evaluating what he sees, and inviting his audience to reflect on what he says and ultimately change their ways, his primary purpose here seems to be relational. He invites his audience to explore their relationship with earth and with God, cunningly establishing a triangular relationship between them: between humans and earth via the metaphorical statement and between God and humans/earth via the allusions to broken covenant.

As with vv. 1-3, the author has provided us with a sufficiency of signs, permitting us to gain access to what one might call the "speaker's meaning" in the context of a conversation. From the field of potential meanings surrounding the terms of the *énoncé métaphorisant*, the author has selected a double focus, encouraging his audience to view the earth/world in human terms and, by extension, to view humans in earthly terms. By employing these metaphorical terms in the context of a central statement about the transgression of laws and the breaking of covenants (5bc), the author sets up a two-way image of dysfunctional relationship: between God & his people (humanity?) and between the people and the earth (and vice versa). Since the significance of the terms involved is partly accessible to the modern reader, even beyond the cultural gap which separates us from these texts, it remains possible for audiences of any age to have what Macky calls participant knowledge of the author's/speaker's meaning and gain (limited) access thereto. In line with Macky's approach to the imaginative re-construction of the speaker's meaning, it is possible, to a degree, to stand in the author's place and understand his statement before evaluating it and interpreting it. The statement and its terminology is not obscure and, at the same time, the author employs his stylistic skills to call our attention to the essentials of his speech act. While acknowledging the mystery involved in the process of meaning, it seems possible and is perhaps

29. Note the inclusive effects of v. 4ab (withering earth) and v. 6cd (burned up, diminished humans).

even essential, at least in these verses, to restate the entire metaphorical statement in a way which explicitly unlocks the ambiguous content of the *énoncé métaphorisant*. Knowing that these terms have an earthly and a human referent has in fact led us to reduce the metaphorical statement to the A is B type (see above). Taking all the factors into consideration we can now nuance that statement: for God, earth is mortal – for God, humans are earthy, both earth and its inhabitants are mutually destructive when their relationship with God is severed.

IV. Conclusion

The metaphorical statement we have been examining has its context in a particular prophetic discourse (the so-called Apocalypse of Isaiah) in which three primary elements are invited by the prophet to respond to one another in a dysfunctional conversation reflecting a dysfunctional relationship. The conversation begins with YHWH who is presented in metaphorical terms as a hostile invader. The present passage is a first response in the conversation. The "earth mourns", "the world is weak". The prophet places words (of mourning) where there is no mouth and has humans behave as nature does when faced with devastation. Ultimately it is the inhabitants of the earth who serve in the prophetic discourse as the pollutant that brought about this devastation by their transgressions. In the remainder of chapter 24, the author employs further metaphors for the earth, serving to continue the dysfunctional conversation: "the vine languishes" (24,7); "the earth staggers like a drunkard" (24,20a); "the earth falls and will not rise again" (24,20cd); "the moon is abashed and the sun ashamed" (24,23ab). Later in the textual complex, however, the relationship and conversation between YHWH and his people becomes more functional and earth responds in a variety of metaphors for fertility: "the earth will give birth to those long dead" (26,19d); "the earth will disclose the blood shed on it". The final chapter of the textual complex known as the Apocalypse of Isaiah contains a more heartening metaphor in which the people are presented as a vine (the second Song of the Vineyard) that has a choice to respond to the caring attention of the vine-keeper in two ways: by producing "thorns and briar" or by "clinging" to the vine-keeper and "making peace" with him (27,2-6). It is evident, therefore, that the three-sided conversation between God, the people and the earth often expressed in metaphorical terms in prophetic discourse can be grounded in both dysfunctional and functional relationships. Where the relationship functions there is fertility (both earthly and human) and peace but where it does not, the conversation resorts to hostile metaphors and earth responds in terms of mourning and lament to its infertile condition.

Faculteit Godgeleerdheid   Brian DOYLE
K.U. Leuven
St.-Michielsstraat 6
B-3000 Leuven
Belgium

FROM CONVERSATION ABOUT GOD
TO CONVERSATION WITH GOD

THE CASE OF JOB

In his presidential address to the third LEST congress, Jacques Haers pointed to the importance of narrativity as one of the key methods to develop the new theological research programme or paradigm which was the topic of the aforementioned congress, viz., the paradigm based on the root metaphors of "connectedness" and "conversation"[1]. Theology in a contemporary context should engage in the confrontation with its own narratives, as validated by a religious community that is the keeper of these narratives but which, at the same time, is also constantly renewed by these narratives.

Among these narratives, those biblical occupy an important, if not the primary, position[2]. In his opening speech to the same congress, Mgr. Van den Berghe, bishop of Antwerp, mentioned some biblical narratives recounting conversations with God. Referring to Abraham's conversation with God about the fate of Sodom and Gomorra, and to Jesus' conversations with his Father, he stressed the importance of conversation in the founding biblical narratives of the Judaeo-Christian tradition.

One of the founding biblical narratives on theological conversation about God and on conversation with God is, without doubt, the book of Job. Indeed, in few biblical books, if any, does conversation occupy the same central position as in the book of Job. The book may be considered one extended conversation, albeit with shifting participants. Therefore, it stands to reason that a reflection on the conversations in the book of

---

1. Cf. J. HAERS, *Defensor vinculi et conversationis. Connectedness and Conversation as a Challenge to Theology*, in this volume, pp. 1-40.

2. In his presidential address to the 1990 SBL Annual Meeting in New Orleans, Walter Brueggemann made a strong plea not to limit the exegetical interpretation of texts to a purely descriptive activity. The metaphors and images of the biblical texts themselves urge readers and exegetes to allow for a spill-over of meaning into new contexts. Interestingly, Brueggemann does not view this opening of the text's meaning as an "application" of the text in contemporary contexts, but as the opening of a "rhetorical field" in which a dialogue with the text in a given context is made possible. W. BRUEGGEMANN, *At the Mercy of Babylon. A Subversive Rereading of the Empire*, in *JBL* 110 (1991) 3-22, pp. 20-21.

Job, as one of the biblical narratives about the conversation about God and with God, should be included in the articulation of the fresh, relational approach to theology for which Jacques Haers called in his presidential address. The present article attempts to be a modest contribution to this approach.

There is no need to deal with the narrative of the book of Job at great length; its basic outline is well-known[3]. The book opens with a conversation between God and one of his celestial courtiers, the satan, about the integrity of Job (1,6-12; 2,1-7). After all calamities have fallen on him, Job argues with his wife (2,9f.) and with his friends (4,1–26,14; 32,1–37,24), about his innocence and the correspondence between good behaviour and prosperity, or the lack thereof. Finally, God speaks, first to Job (38,1–40,2; 40,6–41,26), who replies twice very briefly (40,3ff.; 42,1-6), and then, finally, also to Job's friends (42,7f.).

In this article, I will focus on God's final words in the book, particularly on his evaluative statement concerning the friends in 42,7b, which is also repeated in the following verse. In these verses, God tells Job's friends that his anger is aroused against them, because they have not spoken as Job has. The complete text of the verse runs as follows in the New Revised Standard Version[4]:

> After the LORD had spoken these words to Job, the LORD said to Eliphaz the Temanite: "My wrath is kindled against you and against your two friends; for you have not spoken of me what is right, as my servant Job has."

As Stanley Porter has argued in his 1991 article on the verse, God's statement, and one's understanding of it, determines to a large extent how one interprets the book of Job as a whole[5]. The verse serves as a retrospective hermeneutic key for the whole book, as it clearly favours Job's words over that of the friends. It is the key to evaluating all the conversations that have taken place in the book, and even the role of conversation as such.

Grammatically speaking, the Hebrew causal clause in 42,7b is simple enough. Nonetheless, it confronts the interpreter with two major problems. The first is a problem of reference: which words of Job are being commended by God, and which words of the friends are being rebuked?

---

3. Cf. N. HABEL, *The Book of Job* (OTL), Philadelphia, PA, The Westminster Press, 1985, pp. 25-35; J. HARTLEY, *The Book of Job* (NICOT), Grand Rapids, MI, Eerdmans, 1988, pp. 35-50; D. CLINES, *Job 1–20* (WBC, 17), Dallas, TX, Word Books, 1989, pp. xxxiv-xlvii; E. VAN WOLDE, *Mr and Mrs Job*, London, SCM Press, 1997, pp. 1-5.

4. All biblical quotations are taken from NRSV unless stated differently.

5. S. PORTER, *The Message of the Book of Job. Job 42:7b as Key to Interpretation?*, in *EQ* 63 (1991) 291-304.

It seems out of the question that God's final speech would mean that every word the friends spoke was wrong and that every single one of Job's words was right. It should be noted in this regard that, in the preceding chapters, Job himself was called to order by God, while Job acknowledged having spoken בלי דעת "without knowledge" (42,3). It should come as no surprise, then, that the scholarly proposals on this matter of reference show large variety. The late David Wolfers even contended that "it is open to every interpreter to state his own opinion as to what it was that Job said which drew this remark from the Lord, and what the friends"[6]. I do not fully endorse this relativistic attitude, as I will show.

Without going into detail, the major scholarly proposals on this question of reference can be presented as follows[7]. For some, the words which God refers to are Job's words in the prologue in which he initially praises God, in spite of his suffering[8]. Others consider the reference to be to Job's speeches in the dialogue with his friends. God would, then, commend the fact that Job was an impatient protester, rather than a pious hypocrite, as Marvin Pope contends[9]. Many other authors follow a similar reasoning in asserting that God prefers Job's vigorous defence of his own integrity, to the friends' sterile dogmatic deductions[10]. To quote Norman Habel, "The blunt and forthright accusations of Job from the depths of his agony are closer to the truth than the conventional unquestioning pronouncements of the friends"[11]. Some, usually older, authors hold that only Job's responses to God at the end of the book (40,4f. and 42,2-6), in which Job retracts from what he said, contain Job's "truth" about God[12]. It is Job's

6. D. WOLFERS, *Deep Things out of Darkness: The Book of Job. Essays and a New English Translation*, Grand Rapids, MI, Eerdmans; Kampen, Kok – Pharos, 1995, p. 462.

7. For a recent, extensive discussion of the proposed solutions, see PORTER, *Message* (n. 5), pp. 294-300 and M. OEMING, "*Ihr habt nicht recht von mir geredet wie mein Knecht Hiob*". *Gottes Schlusswort als Schlüssel zur Interpretation des Hiobbuchs und als kritische Anfrage an die moderne Theologie*, in *Evangelische Theologie* 60 (2000) 103-116, pp. 104-112.

8. Reference is made, then, to the famous Joban dictums in 1,21 and 2,10, respectively: "Naked I came from my mother's womb, and naked shall I return there; the LORD gave, and the LORD has taken away; blessed be the name of the LORD" and "Shall we receive the good at the hand of God, and not receive the bad?".

9. M. POPE, *Job* (AB, 15), Garden City, NY, Doubleday, 1986, p. 350. See also VAN WOLDE, *Mr and Mrs Job* (n. 3), p. 144.

10. J. Moster adds to this that the friends are being punished by God because as "dogmatic fanatics" they were so intolerant of Job, rather than bringing "comfort and hope to sufferers". Cf. J. MOSTER, *The Punishment of Job's Friends*, in *JBQ* 25 (1997) 211-219, esp. 219.

11. HABEL, *Job* (n. 3), p. 583.

12. See, e.g., G. FOHRER, *Das Buch Hiob* (KAT, 16), Gütersloh, Gerd Mohn, [1963], ²1989, p. 539.

conversion, then, that is commended by God. In his article on the verse, which I mentioned earlier, Stanley Porter suggests that reference is made to both Job's words in the dialogues with the friends and his final answers to God. Porter contends that Job was right to protest against unjust suffering in the dialogues with the friends, but that he was also correct in recognising, at a later point, that he is only a human being and that the issues of justice and suffering are ultimately God's concern[13]. It is clear, then, that scholars are divided on the question of why exactly Job's words are commended and those of the friends not.

To my mind, the problem described above is closely related to a second problem with which the verse confronts us, i.e., the interpretation of the Hebrew preposition אל. In contemporary translations and commentaries, this preposition is invariably interpreted as "about" or "of". The clause as a whole is read as "you have not spoken *of me* what is right" (italics mine). The preposition אל usually means "towards", but, as some commentators have correctly remarked, it often takes the meaning of "about", especially in later biblical texts[14]. This latter interpretation of the preposition is usually preferred in this verse, often without further discussion, because the friends have not spoken to God at all, and, therefore, cannot be blamed for not having said the correct things to God.

I would, however, like to reconsider the issue, asking if it is not possible to read the preposition in its most obvious meaning, i.e., "towards", as Karl Budde did at the end of the nineteenth century[15], and as Manfred Oeming recently suggested[16].

---

13. PORTER, *Message* (n. 5), p. 303.

14. See, among others, P. DHORME, *Le livre de Job* (ÉB), Paris, Gabalda, 1926, p. 592; J. KROEZE, *Het boek Job* (Commentaar op het Oude Testament), Kampen, Kok, 1961, p. 470. For a grammatical treatment of the syntax and meaning of the preposition, see P. JOÜON – T. MURAOKA, *A Grammar of Biblical Hebrew* (Subsidia biblica, 14), Rome, Pontificio Istituto Biblico, 1996, pp. 485f.

15. K. BUDDE, *Das Buch Hiob, übersetzt und erklärt* (Göttinger Handkommentar zum Alten Testament), Göttingen, Vandenhoeck & Ruprecht, 1896. Budde somewhat artificially explained the use of the expression "speaking to God" in this verse with the observation that all speaking is ultimately heard by God and is, therefore, in some sense directed to God. Because of the artificiality of the argument, Duhm discarded this interpretation. Cf. B. DUHM, *Das Buch Hiob erklärt* (Kurzer Hand-commentar zum Alten Testament), Tübingen, Mohr, 1897, p. 204, which led Budde to completely strike out the prepositional clause in the second edition of his commentary (1913), albeit on a very narrow text-critical basis.

16. OEMING, *Gottes Schlusswort* (n. 7), pp. 112ff. Oeming's enthusiasm for having discovered something that others "immer und immer wieder übersehen haben" (112) should be somewhat dampened. A considerable number of scholars considered the possibility of reading the preposition as "towards" in this verse, but – with the exception of Budde – without ever adopting it. For example, P. SZCZYGIEL, *Das Buch Job* (Die Heilige Schrift des Alten Testamentes), Bonn, Hanstein, 1931, p. 242, reads the Masoretic text as "zu mir" but chooses to emend the text, while KROEZE, *Job* (n. 14), p. 470 discusses the

A first, oblique justification of this reconsideration is that none of the major old versions interpreted the preposition of the verse as "about". The Greek Septuagint (ἐνώπιον) and the Syriac Peshitta (ܡ݂ܰܕ) translated the preposition as "before" or "in the presence of", a translation also adopted by Jerome in his Vulgate, in which he renders it as *coram*. The standard (Rabbinic) Targum of Job[17], on the other hand, has the preposition לות, which can mean "before", but which should be interpreted as "towards" in the present verse, as the English edition of the Targum has correctly done: "for you have not spoken (with) understanding towards me as my servant Job"[18]. It is clear, then, that the interpretation usually offered in contemporary exegesis is not as self-evident as the unanimity among scholars might suggest.

My main argument for considering the possibility of reading the preposition as "towards" is found in the Hebrew text itself, however. First, in all the other cases within the book of Job where the preposition אל is used with the verb דבר "to speak", its meaning is indisputably "towards" (2,13; 13,3; 40,27; 42,7.9)[19]. As these instances show, this is even the case in the immediate context of the sentence under investigation in the present article (42,7.9). Furthermore, when the cognate verb אמר "to say" has the preposition אל in the book of Job, the latter always has the meaning of "towards" (1,7.8.12; 2,2.3.6.10; 9,12; 10,2; 34,31). Statistically speaking, not much weight can be attributed to the evidence adduced here, taking into account the small number of cases[20].

---

interpretation of the preposition – including the possibility of "to me" – at some length, only to choose for the traditional interpretation reading "about me". Nonetheless, Oeming was the first, to my knowledge, to interpret the verse as commending Job's conversation with God, while Budde thought reference was made to the dialogues of Job and his friends, which happened to take place before God and were, hence, indirectly also addressed to God.

17. Unfortunately, in the Targum of Job discovered in Cave 11 from Qumran (11QtgJob = 11Q10), the verses 42,7-8 are not preserved (end of column xxxvii is lacking), although the preceding and following verses are. See F. GARCÍA MARTÍNEZ – E. TIGCHELAAR, *The Dead Sea Scrolls. Study Edition. Volume 2*, Leiden, Brill; Grand Rapids, MI, Eerdmans, 1998, pp. 1200f.

18. C. MANGAN – J. HEALEY – P. KNOBEL, *The Targums of Job, Proverbs, Qohelet* (The Aramaic Bible, 15), Collegeville, MN, The Liturgical Press, 1991.

19. OEMING, *Gottes Schlusswort* (n. 7), p. 113 n. 43 also includes two instances of the noun דבר with the preposition אל in his list of cases (viz. 4,2.12). Even if these instances are not strictly speaking illustrations of the use of the preposition with the verb, they do strengthen the semantic argument made here.

20. For this reason, I consider Oeming's discussion of the verse insufficient. Even though I fully endorse his conclusions, his arguments, viz., the statistics of words for "speaking" with the preposition אל in the book of Job, and the (oblique) support of the Septuagint and the Vulgate, are not decisive for his case.

A much stronger argument, to my mind, is the occurrence of the same expression "to speak to" with the same addressee "God" in Job 13,3. In the opening verses of chapter 13, the immediate context of the verse in question, Job asserts that his friends do not have more experience or knowledge than he has, in other words, that they are equals as far as experience and wisdom is concerned. The great difference between them is – still according to Job himself – that he is willing to speak with God (13,3), while his friends fabricate lies in the name of God (13,4). Job blames his friends for taking God's part, for defending God's case, while he himself wants to talk to God. This desire is regularly repeated in the book of Job[21], but it is made most explicit in 13,3 which runs as follows:

But I would speak to the Almighty, and I desire to argue my case with God.

Thus, Job explicitly opens his conversation with God, who, after many chapters of silence, will eventually answer Job (38–41). Desiring to speak to God is not a minor thing, however; only very few people in the Hebrew Bible are said to have a conversation with God. If we take a look at the use of the expression at hand here, i.e., … דבר אל /ל "to speak to" with God as the addressee, we learn that only Abraham, Moses, Joshua and David are ever mentioned as the subject of such a phrase[22]. Many more people, of course, say things to God, but this is not the same thing as engaging in a conversation with him[23]. What Job asks for in 13,3, i.e., to speak to God, is a rather extraordinary thing to do, then. Since the expression "to speak to God" only occurs twice in the whole book of Job, in 13,3 and 42,7, I take the former verse to be of particular significance in trying to determine the meaning of the expression in 42,7, the verse under discussion in this paper. Could it not be that God commends Job's desire to speak to and with him, unlike the friends who only speak about him or for him, as is said in 13,4.7-10?

The semantic correspondence of a single expression across two verses alone cannot be conclusive in settling the question. The first interpretative question concerning verse 42,7, which I discussed before, should

21. Job 9,14-16; 13,3; 13,14-22; 23,3-7 *et passim*.

22. Gen 18,27.29.31 (Abraham); Num 27,15; Deut 3,26 (Moses); Josh 10,12 (Joshua); 2 Sam 7,20; 22,1 = Ps 18,1 (David).

23. In contrast to the verb אמר "to say", the verb דבר "to speak" designates the act of speaking, rather than the content of what is said. For that reason, the verb often has the meaning of "holding a conversation", "conversing with" (see TWAT II, cc. 105f.). Having a conversation with God could not be endured by people, except for a few exceptions, as Ex 20,19 makes clear: "[…] do not let God speak [דבר] to us, or we will die" (see TWAT II, cc. 110f.).

also be taken into consideration: can the difference between the way in which the friends speak and the way in which Job speaks, to which God refers in 42,7, be interpreted as the difference between speaking about God and speaking to or with God? To my mind, the text of the book provides enough evidence to answer this question affirmatively. The friends, to begin with, never address God in the whole book, although they speak about him and speak on his behalf. Job, on the other hand, does address God explicitly in the second person. Andrew Steinmann has recently demonstrated the structural importance of these addresses in the book of Job: in the first four replies of Job to the friends, Job turns from speaking about God to speaking to God (7,12-21; 10,1-19; 13,17–14,22; 17,1-5), whereas, in the second set of four replies, he does not address God explicitly any longer[24]. That Job, at a certain point, ceases to speak to God does not mean he has given up on his desire to converse with God. On the contrary, he waits for God to enter into the conversation, as I will show below. The four occasions on which Job speaks to God show a clear development. In these instances, Job desperately seeks to talk things out with God, he seeks to present his case to God himself, bombarding him with questions. This resolution to talk with God reaches its climax in chapters 13 and 14, the opening verses of which I discussed above. As Marvin Pope has shown in his commentary, Job even offers God the choice of roles in which they will be speaking: either Job will ask questions and God will answer, or vice versa: "God may choose to be either appellant or respondent [...] so long as he agrees to come into court"[25]. From this point on, Job only addresses God once more, very briefly (17,1-5), and waits for God to come into the conversation. But God remains silent for twenty-three more chapters.

During this divine silence, Job frequently repeats his desire to speak with God, e.g., in the desperate outcry in 23,3[26], but he does not address God again. He, instead, turns to oaths, as John Hartley has demonstrated, with which he puts his own existence at risk, and shows "that his deepest desire is to have a genuine relationship with God for its own sake"[27].

24. A. STEINMANN, *The Structure and Message of the Book of Job*, in *VT* 46 (1996) 85-100, pp. 94f.

25. POPE, *Job* (n. 9), p. 101.

26. The verse reads "Oh, that I knew where I might find him, that I might come even to his dwelling".

27. J. HARTLEY, *From Lament to Oath: A Study of Progression in the Speeches of Job*, in W. BEUKEN (ed.), *The Book of Job* (BETL, 114), Leuven, University Press – Peeters, 1994, pp. 79-100, here p. 88.

It is clear, then, that Job's speaking differs profoundly from that of his friends: not only is he the only one to address God[28], but he also makes the encounter and conversation with God his primary objective. The evolution of Job's own speeches, together with the semantic parallel between 42,7 and 13,3, strongly suggest that God commends not so much what Job said, but the fact that he spoke to God. Similarly, the friends are not blamed for not having said correct things about God, but for not having spoken to God at all, which would have been the appropriate thing to do.

This does not mean that God also agrees with the content of Job's words, as God's extended answer to Job shows. For Job and for us readers, the fact that God finally answers comes as a relief, after Job had asked so much for it. The way in which God's answer is introduced is remarkable when compared to the introduction of the argumentative turns in the dialogue between Job and his friends (4–37). In this dialogue, the interlocutors' turns are invariably and stereotypically introduced with the phrase ויען ... ויאמר "X answered and said"[29]. Only in the communication between God and Job[30] (as well as twice in the discussion between God and the satan[31]), is this phrase extended with a direct object: ויען ... את ... ויאמר "X answered Y and said". This remarkable change in the introductory formulae indicates that God is the first one to truly answer Job and to address him personally. God, thus, eventually engages in the communication, but does so on his own terms. He immediately turns around Job's relentless asking, by stating that he is the one that will ask the questions, and that Job must answer if he can[32]. God turns around the perspectives: reality will not be looked at from Job's point of view, but from God's, which immediately confronts Job with his own ignorance. And Job accepts this reversal of perspectives in his final reply to God (42,1-6), first by admitting his ignorance, and then, by explicitly, though very briefly, taking over God's perspective, as Ellen van Wolde has convincingly concluded on the basis of a comprehensive text-syntactical and semantical analysis of the pericope[33]. Since these verses

28. See also H. PREUSS, *Theologie des Alten Testaments II*, Stuttgart, Kohlhammer, 1992, p. 138, where the author remarks that God acknowledges Job as the one "der zu Gott hin, nicht nur über ihn gesprochen hat, was ihn zugleich von den Freunden und ihren Argumentation abhebt".

29. In Job 4,1; 6,1; 8,1; 9,1; 11,1; 12,1; 15,1; 16,1; 18,1; 19,1; 20,1; 21,1; 22,1; 23,1; 25,1; 26,1; 32,6; 34,1; 35,1.

30. Job 38,1; 40,1; and 40,6 (God answers Job); Job 40,3 and 42,1 (Job answers God).

31. Job 1,9; 2,4.

32. POPE, *Job* (n. 9), p. 291.

33. E. VAN WOLDE, *Job 42,1-6. The Reversal of Job*, in W. BEUKEN (ed.), *The Book of Job* (n. 28), pp. 223-250, here p. 250: "Through the speech of YHWH and the game of

directly precede the verse I have been discussing in this paper, I agree with many commentators that these last words are also referred to in God's appraisal of Job: as a result of Job's willingness to converse with God, he got to hear God. How God spoke to him was not at all as he had expected, but Job accepted this and followed God in this reversal of direction. Undoubtedly, then, Job's words to God in 42,1-6, which substantiate his reversal, are also commended by God in the next verse.

In this sense, Job not only differs from the friends in his way of speaking, but also in his vision of God. The friends only have a view on God, whereas Job has a vision of God and even briefly comes to see through the eyes of God. If I may borrow the words of the French philosopher Jean-Luc Marion, the friends have an idolatrous view of God, limiting God to their own concepts, and thus making God the mirror for their own social and religious outlook[34]. By doing so, they make the invisible God unreachable for Job, or, using Marion's wordplay, they make the *invisible invisable*[35]. Job, on the other hand, also has his idolatrous views on God[36], but challenges God to enter into an encounter, more specifically, into a case before court, convinced as he is of his own innocence. By this, he leaves the initiative with God. Unexpectedly, God takes the initiative and reveals himself from his own perspective, by pointing to creation

question and answer that is central to it, through the experience that in that one speech YHWH keeps reversing the roles between himself and Job, Job can detach himself from his own referential point of view and begin to look through different eyes".

34. In a number of publications, especially in the first two chapters of his *Dieu sans l'être* (Quadrige, 129), Paris, Presses Universitaires de France, 1991, Jean-Luc MARION proposes the distinction between idol and icon as two modes of being of (religious) concepts. Icons and idols do not differ in what they are, but in how they appear to those (conceptually) looking at them. The characteristics of the idol are that it offers a ground on which the human look may rest. In this way, it becomes a mirror, reflecting the look of the beholder, but, at the same time, blocking the ability of the person to look beyond it: "L'idole joue ainsi comme un miroir, non comme un portrait: miroir qui renvoie au regard [...] l'image de sa visée [...]" (*Dieu sans l'être*, p. 21).

35. See also the discussion of Marion's thought in S. VAN DEN BOSSCHE, *Presentie in differentie. Vier essays over de godsontmoeting in een postmoderne context*, Leuven, Dissertation, 2000, pp. 87f.

36. Job does not differ from his friends in this, as Jürgen van Oorschot has correctly observed. See J. VAN OORSCHOT, *Gott als Grenze. Eine literar- und redaktionsgeschichtliche Studie zu den Gottesreden des Hiobbuches* (BZAW, 170), Berlin – New York, de Gruyter, 1987, p. 197: "Mit diesen Fragen [in 38–41] prangert die Rede Gottes an, daß Hiob und die drei Freunde aus einem Wissen um Gott ein Wissen über Gott gemacht haben [...]." and pp. 202f.: "Ihre selbstgerechten Urteile verfehlen die Wirklichkeit genauso wie Gott, der hinter ihrem Gottesbild zu verschwinden droht. Indem Gott erscheint und Hiob zurechtweist und belehrt, entzieht er ihm und den Freunden ihr Bild von Gott. Erst dadurch wird Hiob befreit zur Begegnung mit Gott und zur Annahme seines Schicksals. Die Fragen nach dem 'Warum' und 'Wozu' des Leidens können offenbleiben, denn sie haben ihre verletzende Schärfe verloren".

from his point of view. This vision of nature becomes for Job the icon – continuing the use of Marion's vocabulary – through which he can suddenly suspect something of the way in which God looks at the world and at him, effecting a fundamental reversal in Job[37].

This reversal, although the direct result of God's initiative, was only possible because Job was willing to speak to God. And for this willingness, he is commended in 42,7, in contrast to his friends.

Theologische Faculteit Tilburg   Pierre VAN HECKE
Universiteit van Tilburg
Academielaan 9
NL-5037 ET Tilburg
The Netherlands

37. The reversal of viewing perspective, which according to van Wolde (*Reversal* [n. 33]) constitutes the major change which Job underwent in the book, is also the main phenomenological characteristic of an icon as Marion understands it. "L'icône ne résulte pas de la vision, mais la provoque", the author states in *Dieu sans l'être* (n. 34), p. 28. At the same time, the icon of creation does not make visible what was invisible and incomprehensible to Job. On the contrary, Job admits his own inability to understand, but, by adopting God's perspective, he is able to see things in their incomprehensibility, and to revoke his desire to have ultimate understanding. In his highly intricate language, Marion describes the functioning of the icon in precisely these terms: "L'invisible demeurt toujours invisible; non pas invisible parce qu'omis par la visée (invisable), mais parce qu'il s'agit de rendre visible cet invisible comme tel – l'inenvisageable". Job's final reversal may, therefore, be described as turning from the idolatrous to the iconic, as a result of God's engaging in conversation with Job.

CONVERSATIONS ABOUT POVERTY IN THE LUKAN COMMUNITY

I. INTRODUCTION

The question of poverty and wealth is an important aspect of Lukan theology and his community[1]. Next to James and John, the prophet and author of Revelation, Luke is the central author to deal with issues of poverty and wealth in the New Testament. He develops his viewpoint on a theology and spirituality of poverty as a precondition for Christian community in both of his writings, the Gospel and Acts.

In this paper, we will investigate the methods of communication Luke used to convince his community[2] to put a particular Christian lifestyle into practice. Although Luke did not choose the *genre* "letter", the most obvious form of correspondence, to formulate his message to his community, the *genre* "Gospel" keeps up a process of correspondence. Different levels of communication can generally be found in a narrative[3]. The first level is the intercommunication between the actors in the text. The way they speak, the quality and quantity of their speech, and their proposed actions can be analysed. The second level of communication is

---

1. H.-J. KLAUCK, *Die Armut der Jünger in der Sicht des Lukas*, in *Claretianum* 26 (1986) 5-48; = ID., *Gemeinde, Amt, Sakrament. Neutestamentliche Perspektiven*, Würzburg, Echter, 1989, pp. 160-194, p. 160, points out, that no other topic dominates the Gospel more than the question of what a Christian should do with his property.

2. Apart from the different levels of communication to be found in a text there is an initial process of communication between Luke and his social-historical and religious background. Before and whilst writing his Gospel, he is influenced by the Hellenistic and Jewish culture, literature and society, his own personal heredity, the questions of his community; and finally by the inspiration of the Holy Spirit. How far it is possible to trace these influences in Luke and Acts is a point of discussion in exegesis (*Traditionsgeschichte*). This specific topic cannot be treated in our paper.

3. Luke, as the greatest narrator of the NT, does not relate his theology to his addressees with doctrines, but with one of the most picturesque narratives of the NT. He provides with them his theology and ecclesiology. He is no naive narrator, indeed his narratives affirm theological reflections. Cf. J. ROLOFF, *Die Kirche im Neuen Testament* (GNT, 10), Göttingen, Vandenhoeck & Ruprecht, 1993, p. 191 (his main emphasis is not on social aspects of the Lukan community but on the concept of the history of salvation and the continuity between the OT and NT. Furthermore, he underlines guidance through the Spirit and the historical dimension of the Church and its structure, built on twelve apostles and the special offices within the community).

to be found in the correlation between different pericopes. It is the creative task of the (implied) reader to recognize the various connections between subjects, motives, and interactions in the text. This is where the third aspect of communication starts to develop: the dialogue between the text and the reader (pragmatic dimension).

These three levels of communication will be exemplified in this paper by consideration of the dialogue between three pericopes in Luke. First, we will analyse Jesus' encounter with the rich, nameless anonymous Jewish ruler (Luke 18,18-27) who asked him which commandments should be kept in order to inherit eternal life. He left with sadness[4] because the burden of selling all his material goods and giving the proceeds to the poor was too much for him. Who is taking the initiative in the dialogue? What are the motives of this person? How can the relation between the questions and the answers, the quality and quantity of direct speech best be described?

The second step will be to take a fresh look at the pericope of Zacchaeus, the rich tax collector, who tries to see Jesus (Luke 19,1-10). His delight at Jesus' visit to his home and the salvation received there enables him to give half of his possessions to the poor. How can the communication be described in this pericope? What is the relation between action and speech?

Third, we will bring both pericopes in connection with each other to see how they deal with the topic of poverty. We will argue the thesis that there is an implicit dialogue between the rich, anonymous Jewish ruler and the rich tax collector Zacchaeus. Both are anti-types: the first is not ready to give his possessions to the poor; he is only interested in an intellectual dialogue with Jesus about religion and its commandments, without being challenged personally. Zacchaeus, unlike the Jewish ruler, is seeking to see Jesus and longing for salvation in his life. He is open to an encounter and conversation that changes his life completely. Thus, conversation works on a basis of contrast between both pericopes.

Within the course of Luke's narrative composition, both pericopes are placed in close relation with each other. It is easy for the reader of the Gospel to link them with each other. The delighted Zacchaeus reminds him/her of the sad rich man a few verses earlier. The reader who has read the Gospel in its entirety will still have the inaugural preaching of Jesus

---

4. Another example of sadness is the wife of Lot (Luke 17,32 – Gen 19,26: καὶ ἐπέβλεψεν ἡ γυνὴ αὐτοῦ εἰς τὰ ὀπίσω καὶ ἐγένετο στήλη ἁλός) who lost all her possessions. Cf. L.T. JOHNSON, *The Literary Function of Possessions in Luke-Acts*, Diss. New Haven [Yale University], 1976, Missoula, MT, 1977, p. 62: "… she identified her being with her having".

in the synagogue of Nazareth in mind (Luke 4,16-21), where he proclaims good news to the poor. According to Luke, the social programme can be described as social compensation between the rich and poor members of his community, that can have the giving of half of one's material goods to the poor, as Zacchaeus did, as a consequence[5]. Christians who search for and follow Jesus, as the tax collector did, implement Luke's social programme for the poor in their community. Thus, they are able to share the joy of salvation with each other.

Communication takes place on three planes within the Gospel of Luke: first, between the actors (Jesus, Jewish ruler, Zacchaeus etc.) of the individual pericopes. Secondly, on the level of the narrative unity of the Gospel (and the Acts). And finally, between the reader and the text. Luke tries to persuade his addressees not by imposing ethical rules on them, but by telling stories with good and bad examples. The dialogue between the text and the reader never finishes. Bible texts always remain open to new situations and life-decisions.

II. METHODOLOGICAL CONSIDERATIONS

Luke has chosen the narrative *genre* to correspond with his community. It is based on different rules to the rhetoric of a letter. Since the request of this conference is the correlation between theology and conversation the approach of this paper is based on a theory of communication[6]. How does conversation come about in a narrative? What relevance does the biblical text have for theological discussions nowadays? Different theories of communication exist among New Testament scholars and it is not the right place to discuss them here. We shall limit ourselves to presenting a thorough outline of the main aspects.

The process of communication between Luke and his addressees is analysed in an article of F. Mussner who refers to the theory of P. Ricœur, one of the most important authors on this topic. He describes the language of Luke as a *"Zielsprache"* with the aim of challenging the readers.

---

5. This programme is already developed in the proclamation of John the Baptist Luke 3,11: "He who has two coats, let him share with him who has none; and he who has food, let him do likewise". Sharing the half of the clothes, food and money with needy people is one aspect of the Lukan concept against poverty. It is a kind of compensation between rich and poor people in the community.

6. Cf. F. MUSSNER, *Die Gemeinde des Lukasprologs*, in *SNTU/A* 6/7 (1981/82) 113-130, pp. 117-120, who refers to the theory of P. Ricœur.

Amongst the exegetical methods it is the pragmatic approach that deals with this aspect of exegesis.

Mussner describes the process of communication in Luke with regard to the situation of Luke's addressees, his intention and narrative. His arguments are based on the key verses of the prologue Luke 1,1-4 depicting the reader's situation[7]. Luke is writing his Gospel for *an implied reader*[8] called Theophilus. So we read in Luke 1,3: "I too decided, after investigating everything carefully from the very first, to write an orderly account for you, most excellent Theophilus"[9] (1,4). Theophilus is a personified representative of the Lukan community, one of the pious Gentiles who had already come into contact with the Jewish religion[10].

Luke's *motivation* for compiling a new Gospel is disclosed in 1,3: "it seemed good to me also, having followed all things closely for some time past, to write an orderly account ...". The study of the tradition and his addressee Theophilus motivated him to write an orderly account of what has been accomplished. Luke's *intention* "so that you may know the truth concerning the things about which you have been instructed" is closely connected with his motivation. The particular situation of the *addressees*, the Lukan community, is further elaborated from this remark and other information in the prologue. The community had already been instructed about the life of Jesus (1,4), but they had become unsure in their faith. Therefore, they needed to be strengthened (by a new Gospel) in their trust in Christ and their participation in an eschatological and ecclesiological "we"/community[11].

The issue of wealth and poverty in the Lukan community is specific to their own particular situation. It has religious and social aspects. Poverty is an expression of the addressees' piety, it is one way of following Jesus on his path through suffering to salvation. This piety of

7. Cf. R. DILLMANN, *Die lukanische Kindheitsgeschichte als Aktualisierung frühjüdischer Armenfrömmigkeit*, in *SNTU/A* 25 (2000) 76-97, pp. 86-93. Cf. also R. DILLMANN, *Das Lukasevangelium als Tendenzschrift. Leserlenkung und Leseintention in Luke 1,1-4*, in *BZ* 38 (1994) 86-93.

8. C. KAHRMANN – G. REISS – M. SCHLUCHTER, *Erzähltextanalyse. Eine Einführung in Grundlagen und Verfahren. Bd. 1-2* (Athenäum Taschenbücher, 2121/2132), Kronberg, 1977, distinguishes between "fictive narrator" and "address", "abstract author" and "abstract address", "real author" and "real reader", "historic author" and "historic reader".

9. Cf. also the reference to this verse in the prologue of Acts 1,1: "In the first book, o Theophilus, I have dealt with all that Jesus began to do and teach".

10. Cf. H.-J. KLAUCK, *Magic and Paganism in Early Christianity. The World of the Acts of the Apostles*. Translated by B. MCNEIL, Edinburgh, T & T Clark, 2000, p. 4.

11. Cf. MUSSNER, *Gemeinde* (n. 6), pp. 121-130.

poverty has social consequences for Christians living together in a society of rich and poor[12]. Both the social life of society and the Christian community are challenged. Thus, Luke's theology of poverty has an ethical and parenetical accent.

One can ask why Luke, the author, is so much interested in the topic[13]. Is it possible to read between the lines – with a sort of "mirror reading" – and deduce the situation of the Lukan community and their problems regarding poverty and wealth[14]?

Some methodological considerations are therefore crucial. We have to ask how communication happens in Luke's narrative. The first level of communication is to be found prior to the text: The narrator Luke is influenced by various oral and written sources. The Gospel of Mark[15], the Saying Source Q, his background, the issues of his community, the Hellenistic culture, literature and society[16], the OT writings (LXX)[17], and, last, but not

12. D.P. SECCOMBE, *Possessions and the Poor in Luke-Acts* (SNTU.B, 6), Linz, 1982, p. 23, proposes that "Luke uses 'the poor' as a characterization of Israel in her need of salvation". He discusses different attempts to identify the poor (as the pious, as a particular social group, as radical followers of Jesus, as heirs of salvation, and as Israel).

13. This question is asked by KLAUCK, *Armut* (n. 1) pp. 187-194. He solves this problem by combining the topics poverty and celibacy.

14. Concerning the theory of a mirror-reading in Luke cf. A. DENAUX – J. DELOBEL, *De oorspronkelijke bestemmeling van Lukas-Handelingen: De "gemeente van Lukas"?*, in J. DELOBEL – H.J. DE JONGE – M. MENKEN – H. VAN DE SANDT (eds.), *Vroegchristelijke gemeenten tussen werkelijkheid en ideaal*, Kampen, Kok, 2001, pp. 115-133, esp. 116-118.

15. The communication with the Gospel of Mark can be considered by a synoptic comparison. The redactional changes of Luke portray his technique of communication with Mark: He sharpens the preference in his sources and adds more material with regard to poverty and richness. Cf. P.F. ESLER, *Community and Gospel in Luke-Acts. The Social and Political Motivations of Lucan Theology* (SNTS MS, 57), Cambridge, Cambridge University Press, 1987, pp. 165-169, who discusses the redactional work of Luke on Mark and Q. Some pericopes reveal an intensification of the topics poverty and wealth. Different opinions exist among exegetes concerning Luke 4,16-30, a pericope with programmatic function in Luke. Some suggest that Luke relies on Mark, others argue that it is a free reworking of the Markan parallel (J. Fitzmyer), and those who prefer non-Marcan sources (H. Schürmann) try to demonstrate the existence of Aramaisms. Anyway, Luke presents a very radical pericope at the beginning of Jesus' public ministry. The poor have a special place in the scheme of salvation.

16. ESLER, *Community* (n. 15), pp. 169-171, discusses the social setting of Luke's theology of poverty. He criticizes the fact that very few Lukan commentators (J.J. Degenhardt, G.E.M. de Ste Croix, R.J. Karris) have attempted to relate Luke's theology with the realities of a Hellenistic city of the Roman East. The social background with which Luke is in touch is very important to understanding what poverty and wealth meant at this time. Furthermore he describes the social stratification of the Hellenistic cities with its experience of poverty (cf. 171-179). Especially his description of existence as a day-to-day struggle of those who were hired in a daily basis explains the parable of the labourers in the vineyard in Matt 20,1-16.

17. Cf. S.J. ROTH, *The Blind, the Lame, and the Poor. Character Types in Luke – Acts* (JSNT SS, 144), Sheffield, JSOT Press, 1997, p. 80, points out that the authorial audience

least, the inspiration of the Holy Spirit must all be taken into consideration. The effect of the written sources is certainly easier to construe.
To explore Luke's background, the issues generated by his community,
culture and society prove to be more problematic. Non-biblical writings
that have been handed down to us give an impression of Hellenistic society, but we have no further information about the personal background of
Luke and the questions of his community. All we can do is deduce possible questions from his narrative – which can be a vicious circle.

After investigating the different influences on Luke the next step is to
analyse his narrative(s). Verbal (direct and indirect speech) and non-
verbal communication (facial expression, gesture, movement, emotions,
expressions of time, place, characterization of persons[18]) are the two
major techniques of communication in a narrative. Closely connected
with them is the analysis of the correlation between different pericopes
and their position in the narrative. For our considerations all pericopes
touching the topics of "wealth" and "poverty" are relevant.

Finally, the last level of communication is between the text and the
reader. Every text is written by an author and focuses on a specific group
of recipients. This communication can be analysed by a "reader-response-
analysis", a "reader-response-criticism"[19] or "mirror-reading". This method
is "rooted in a philosophical approach to language that evaluates language
on the basis of its function in the speech act"[20]. Two main questions are connected with it: "What is the immediate effect on the reader during the reading process? and What is the rhetorical significance of the positioning of
the episodes and the sequence of events in the narrative?"[21]. The most
problematic and uncertain aspect of this approach is the fact that every
reader is different, each person understands the text from the background

should concretise special characters on the basis of the LXX. His viewpoint is not the conversation between the author and the LXX that is more based on facts.

18. ROTH, *Blind* (n. 17), p. 76: "It should be kept in mind that no actual human being
is ever so simple as the roundest of characters in a narrative. No narrative, not even modern narratives intended to be biography, can ever display the fullness of personality traits,
the interweaving of relationships, the points of view, the predictability and unpredictability of actions, all of the enormous complexities that make up a human being. Characterization, then, is always fictive (and rhetorical)". Furthermore Roth points out that there are
differences between ancient and modern characterization of characters. Ancient characters
are "flat", "static", and quite "opaque". "Modern characters, however, are products of
our cultural paradigm [...]" (*ibid.* p. 77). He distinguishes between illustrative and
representational characterizations (78).

19. Roth uses the expression "audience-oriented criticism" "because 'audience' better expresses the oral character of ancient reading". Cf. *ibid.*, p. 57.

20. *Ibid.*

21. *Ibid.*, p. 64. The linearity of the reading process is challenged by this question.

of his/her own experience and cultural background[22]. The image of a fictive or "mock reader" (Gibson) is also the "product of interpretation and not something independent of, or prior to, interpretation"[23].

Thus, the "mirror-reading" method harbours the risk of the reader filling the gaps of a text with his/her own ideas or even attempting to make the narrative coherent[24]. Projections of personal ideas and weaknesses into the text are latent dangers. It is the most problematical step in interpreting a text, especially if the reaction of its first recipients has not been passed on to us by textual witnesses, thus revealing something of its *"Wirkungsgeschichte"*. Methodologically that means that the addressees, their situation[25] and probable response are to be deduced from the primary texts, namely the Gospel of Luke and Acts. This raises many questions: Did Luke write his Gospel for the poor, the rich, or for both[26]? Does he speak to the leaders of his community or to "the people"[27]? Again, this methodological approach can cause us generate very subjective and prejudiced hypotheses, hence our consideration must be to analyse the texts accurately.

In subsequent parts the two chosen pericopes on "poverty" and "wealth" will be analysed before trying to make a summary regarding our two issues. We have to concentrate on the interpretation of the two aspects "conversation" and "theology of poverty" in the Lukan community. For that reason we will examine the different levels of correlation between the texts.

22. *Ibid.*: "... reading is a temporal experience of discovery". Memory (recollection of what has already transpired in the narrative – "intratextual allusion" – reader competences – "extra-textual repertoire") and expectation are the two main activities of reading. Anticipation and reverberations of the text correspond to this reader activity.

23. *Ibid.*, p. 61. The distinction between the real reader and a constructed implied reader is good.

24. In the pastoral framework it is an often used creative method.

25. Cf. the connection between poverty/wealth and persecution in the position of W. SCHMITHALS, *Das Evangelium nach Lukas* (ZBK.NT, 3,1), Zürich, Theologischer Verlag, 1980, pp. 12f, 80, 144, 159, 162, 171, 182, 213. G. THEISSEN, *Studien zur Soziologie des Urchristentums* (WUNT, 19), Tübingen, Mohr, ²1983, p. 104, supposes the situation of radical wanderings. One can also find the rejection of any historical question towards Luke: L.T. JOHNSON, *Function* (n. 4), interprets the Gospel merely as a "story", the poor are degraded to symbolic roles. Cf. the summary of SECCOMBE, *Possessions* (n. 12), pp. 16f. A general outline of the social world in Ancient Christianity gives ESLER, *The First Christians in their Social Worlds. Social-scientific Approaches to New Testament Interpretation*, London, Routledge, 1994.

26. Cf. SECCOMBE, *Possessions* (n. 12), p. 12f. Seccombe's thesis is that Luke uses the poor to characterize Israel in her need of salvation.

27. This is the thesis of J.J. DEGENHARDT, *Lukas – Evangelist der Armen. Besitz und Besitzverzicht in den lukanischen Schriften. Eine traditionsgeschichtliche Untersuchung*, Stuttgart, Verlag Katholisches Bibelwerk, 1965, p. 216 and passim. Cardinal Degenhardt identifies μαθηταί with church leaders and λαός with ordinary Christians.

III. THE CONVERSATION BETWEEN A CERTAIN JEWISH RULER
AND JESUS (LUKE 18,18-27)

First, we will analyse the pericope of a certain Jewish ruler and Jesus in Luke 18,18-27. As communication takes place on different planes, the dialogue between Luke and one of his sources, the Gospel of Mark, must be taken into consideration in our discussion. Another aspect will be the description of various techniques of communication in the pericope. And the final plane of communication is to be found in the correlation between this pericope and others in the Gospel of Luke. Of course, only a few significant points can be chosen for this presentation, others are mentioned in the footnotes.

The Synoptic comparison of the Lukan and Markan (Mark 10,17-22) versions highlight various differences. The rich man does not disappear after his conversation with Jesus (cf. Mark 10,22). The problem of the rich man remains present to the Lukan community for the time being[28]. Furthermore, Luke omits the reaction of Jesus' disciples (cf. Mark 10,23-27.28-31).

The pericope is ordered towards the pivotal verse 25: "For it is easier for a camel to go through the eye of a needle than for a rich man to enter the kingdom of God". Vv. 24.26f. embraces the topic of salvation: the rich have problems reaching it (v. 26), but salvation is possible with God. The command to possess nothing in v. 21-23 is linked to Peter's advice that the disciples avoid having any property. Rules for living together are to be found in v. 20.29. And the last correlation is between v. 18f. and 30, with the question of how to inherit eternal life and Jesus' answer that one has to leave everything to come to eternal life[29].

The initiator of the dialogue with Jesus is a person who is only characterised as a certain ruler (ἄρχων[30]) (v. 18), who was very rich (v. 23). He does not introduce himself by name nor does Jesus address him by name. He remains nameless throughout the narrative. His abode and profession are not mentioned, but it is apparent that he grew up and was educated within the Jewish tradition. He is mainly characterized by his existential question of how to reach eternal life[31]. In his eyes salvation is

---

28. Cf. ESLER, *Community* (n. 15), p. 185, who refers to an article of S. Legasse.

29. Cf. to this structure the scheme of H.-J. KLAUCK, *Armut* (n. 1), p. 178.

30. Cf. also Jaïrus who is called ἄρχων (Luke 8,41). The description of him is completely positive. SECCOMBE, *Possessions* (n. 12), p. 120, brings this argument into consideration. Furthermore he argues that Luke's description of pious characters (as Zechariah and Elizabeth) is compatible with the self-image of the certain Jewish ruler.

31. Another example for this questioning is the lawyer in Luke 10,25. He is given the same answer as the rich ruler in our pericope.

accessible by fulfilling the Jewish commandments. The connection between his fear and hope for salvation is obvious.

In this pericope conversation stays on the level of a spoken dialogue, there are no other interactions between the two persons engaged in the conversation. The first answer given by Jesus is a long quotation from the Old Testament commandments of Moses. This reply matches the impersonal character of the question. The second part of the conversation remains on the same level: the nameless ruler answers that he has fulfilled all the Jewish commandments. Hence Jesus gives him a new and radical commandment: to sell all his possessions to the poor and to follow Him. The ruler gives no reply to this request. It is Luke's commentary that explains his reaction of sadness because of his wealth. Meanwhile he does not disappear from the narrative as happens in the Synoptic parallels. He remains as a witness to the following dialogue about the conditions of salvation.

The first verse of the second part acts as a transition. It bridges between the witnesses' question about, the conditions for salvation and, at the same time it offers consolation to the rich man: what is impossible with men is possible with God. Jesus' reply is a repetition of what had already been said at the proclamation of his birth to Virgin Mary (1,37). The reader can link both pericopes to each other and realise that salvation comes in unexpected ways.

Jesus' call for the rich ruler to return home, sell his belongings and distribute the proceeds to the poor seems to be an essential precondition for discipleship. In Luke 9,57-62 two men encounter Jesus and are asked to follow him immediately. They are not permitted to set things in order at home. The first is not allowed to bury his father (v. 59), and the second cannot say farewell to his family and relations (v. 61). Jesus' negative response is conditioned by the importance of the kingdom of God. Everything else is secondary, subordinated to this primary goal.

The pericope of the rich ruler who is told to go home and sell his belongings seems, at first glance, to contradict this command. D.P. Seccombe tries to find an explanation: "It seems there is something about the ruler which makes his service unacceptable until he has disposed of everything he owns"[32]. But is this interpretation appropriate? Do both pericopes target the same point? Important differences are recognizable. Those who asked Jesus for permission to go home before following him wherever he goes (Luke 9,57ff.) were already accompanying him on his way.

---

32. SECCOMBE, *Possessions* (n. 12), p. 126.

They had already left their belongings and families behind them. Their question concerns the last radical step of following Jesus everywhere. The rich ruler, on the contrary, appears in the Gospel for the first time. He had not been following Jesus hitherto but was consulting him for the first time as a religious teacher. He is not yet a disciple and is not yet freed from personal relationships and belongings. For that reason he is instructed to sell everything in order to become free to follow in Jesus' footsteps. Poverty, in this context, means obeying God's commandments and following Jesus in freedom from worldly ties. Success, wealth, and belongings hinder the rich ruler from inheriting eternal life. His sadness (περίλυπος) is a sign of his fixation on his present life, whereas happiness, on the other hand, is a sign of being blessed (μακάριος)[33].

IV. THE CONVERSATION BETWEEN JESUS AND THE TAX COLLECTOR ZACCHAEUS (LUKE 19,1-10)

The pericope of the tax collector Zacchaeus is part of the Lukan *Sondergut* and reveals typical aspects of the Lukan theology. Communication takes place on several planes. Luke introduces him as a man called Zacchaeus, living in Jericho as the chief tax collector who had attained prosperity. He has a name and is a well-known man in Jericho. His name, his place of residence and his profession are mentioned. He has a complete identity as a well-known person. The starting point of communication here is an action of Zacchaeus. He was trying to see Jesus and climbed up a sycamore to get a better view. The process of communication is opened by a non-verbal action of Zacchaeus. His desire to seek and see Jesus is crucial for the following conversation. The further

33. According to Luke 6,20-22 those are blessed who are not on the bright sight of life: the poor, those who weep, who are hated. They can rejoice in heaven and leap for joy (χάρητε ἐν ἐκείνῃ τῇ ἡμέρᾳ καὶ σκιρτήσατε). A great reward in heaven is promised to them (v. 23). "This story, more than that of the ruler, provides some parallel to the early church where salvation was accompanied by spontaneous joy and generosity" (*ibid.*, p. 132). The saying "for out of the abundance of the heart his mouth speaks" (ἐκ γὰρ περισσεύματος καρδίας λαλεῖ τὸ στόμα αὐτοῦ. Luke 6,45) underlines this view: if someone's heart is fixed on his belongings, his mouth cannot proclaim the Kingdom of God – maybe it is possible to describe the Lukan point of view in this summary. "Jesus is unwilling to have a follower with divided loyalties and interests" (SECCOMBE, *Possessions* [n. 12], p. 127). Wealth, then, is a barrier to entry into the Kingdom.

Poverty has different aspects in Luke: it has a religious element as a prerequisite for following Jesus. Furthermore it has a social element as a consequence of the Christian faith: social compensation and sharing of private property in the community is a sign for authentic faith. Both aspects – the religious and the social – are thus connected with each other.

development of the narrative is in complete paradox to his expectations: instead of getting a view of Jesus on his own, Jesus looks up at him and asks him to come down. Zacchaeus has to accept his smallness and low-liness in order to encounter Jesus; climbing up is the wrong method. Then Jesus opens the dialogue while Zacchaeus keeps silent.

The end of the pericope includes a conflict between Jesus and the wit-nesses to his visit at Zacchaeus' house. They grumble against him for visiting a sinner (Luke 19,7). At this moment Zacchaeus speaks the only words of the whole pericope as he addresses Jesus saying: "Look, half of my possessions, Lord, I will give to the poor; and if I have defrauded anyone of anything, I will pay back four times as much" (Luke 19,8). Jesus responds to this expression of Zacchaeus' repentance with an inter-pretation of the inner process. He formulates this impersonally in the third person singular[34] without addressing either Zacchaeus or the observers directly. "Today salvation has come to this house, because he too is a son of Abraham" (Luke 19,9).

"Presumably Zacchaeus remains materially in a comparable situation to where he began, though he has expressed his love and joy in a con-crete manner"[35]. I cannot agree with this position completely. Zacchaeus' promise (19,8) is not just a spontaneous decision at the moment of Jesus' visit. Certainly the present tense of the two verbs δίδωμι and ἀποδίδωμι could evoke the impression of a single action. But the emphasis in the pericope relies on the "today" of salvation: σήμερον σωτηρία τῷ οἴκῳ τούτῳ ἐγένετο (19,9). As salvation is an ongoing process, this reaction to Jesus' hospitality will continue.

V. The Communication between the Two Pericopes
Luke 18,18-27 and Luke 19,1-10

Both pericopes are related to each other by their motives of wealth and poverty, and further by the issues of discipleship and gaining salvation. Furthermore they are connected with each other by the structural char-acterisation as antitypes.

---

34. Cf. J. Dupont, *Le riche publicain Zachée est aussi un fils d'Abraham (Luc 19,1 10)*, in C. Bussmann – W. Radl (eds.), *Der Treue Gottes trauen. Beiträge zum Werk des Lukas*. FS G. Schneider, Freiburg – Basel – Wien, Herder, 1991, pp. 265-276, p. 265.
35. Seccombe, *Possessions* (n. 12), p. 132.

Comparing both pericopes one has to take into consideration the different *genre* of both to uncover the main issue. The first pericope is comparable to a vocation narrative that has the intention of calling a person in a special way to follow Jesus. The second one is a typical example of hospitality in the Gospel of Luke. Jesus' visiting a home reveals the presence of God.

Communication between both pericopes works by the contrast between the different responses of the two men to Jesus[36]. The sadness of the rich man finds its expression in his silence, the joy of Zacchaeus opens his mouth for words of justice towards those whom he had defrauded. Sadness changes nothing, but joy changes the life of the tax collector and others. An intellectual search for salvation fails to achieve its aim, but the desire to encounter Jesus in the deepest corners of the heart changes a whole life.

Communication also works by cross inference: both pericopes touch the subject of poverty and riches (18,23: ἦν γὰρ πλούσιος σφόδρα and 19,2: καὶ αὐτὸς πλούσιος). Jesus' promise "What is impossible with men is possible with God" (18,27) is affirmed by the example of the rich tax collector. Salvation is possible for the rich – if they seek to see and receive Jesus into their life. Poverty as a condition of imitating Jesus in order to reach salvation has a personal dimension. The individual measure of poverty depends on the depth of the relationship with Jesus. Imitating Jesus and seeking salvation is not an intellectual but an existential persuit. These aspects of Luke's theology of poverty can be explored by comparing the planes of communication in both pericopes and the relation of both to each other.

VI. The Relation between the Two Pericopes and the Rejection of Jesus at Nazareth (Luke 4,16-30)

Luke 4,16-30 has a programmatic function in the Gospel as Jesus reveals mission there[37]. The interpretation of the Old Testament quotation

---

36. *Ibid.*: "The stories should, therefore, be treated as paradigms of response".

37. The text contains different exegetical problems: The quotation of Isa 61,1f. LXX is suddenly interrupted by an addition of Isa 58,6. The exact wording καλεῖν of the LXX is substituted by κηρύσσειν. (Cf. R. Albertz, *Die "Antrittspredigt" Jesu im Lukasevangelium auf ihrem alttestamentlichen Hintergrund*, in ZNW 74 [1983] 182-206, p. 182). Albertz decides that the variations are consciously done by Luke to liberate the OT promises from their original background and open them for the new situation (*ibid.*, p. 190).

within the inaugural speech is pertinent to our question: "The Spirit of the Lord is upon me, because he has anointed me to preach good news to the poor. He has sent me to proclaim release to the captives and recovering of sight to the blind, to set at liberty those who are oppressed to proclaim the acceptable year of the Lord". Who are the poor, the captives, the blind, and oppressed in the Lukan community? To get the point of Luke's social programme against poverty we have to analyse the members of this group first, whose identity has hardly been discussed among exegetes.

Exegetes are of differing opinions concerning the definition of these people: they are supposed to be the devout of the Old Testament, the godly poor, the social poor, the ill or maladjusted[38].

In the book of Isaiah the poor are no longer those who lament the destruction of Jerusalem. The cited text Isa 58,1-12 has a concrete social-ethical background. The τεθραυσμένοι are those who are financially ruined. Luke has chosen a quotation about poverty from Isaiah, which has the most numerous references to this topic of all the prophetic books[39]. It is *the* characteristic of Isaiah that he identifies the poor with the people of Israel[40]. The theology of the poor in Isaiah means that the abused/downtrodden are special friends of JHWH, they can expect the special mercy and help of God in their life and trust in his protection. Zion and the suffering servant are called the afflicted. The poor are recognized as those who completely trust in God's consolation and mercy[41]. One main aspect of Isa 61,1-3 is that the message of salvation and liberation is only told to the poor and not to the whole people of Israel after the exile. The poor in 61,1f. are not the humiliated but those who do not have the barest necessities to live.

Thus, the OT quotation in Jesus' inaugural speech intends to present the social aspect of his mission. The poor (πτωχός) in Luke are always the socially underprivileged/deprived (Luke 1,53; 6,20.24-26.34-38; 7,22; 16,9; 18,22) – on the other hand it means that the rich are those who are economically rich[42]. Therefore Jesus' proclamation of liberation and salvation has a social and religious aspect.

---

38. Cf. ALBERTZ, *Antrittspredigt* (n. 37), pp. 184f.

39. Cf. U. BERGES, *Die Armen im Buch Jesaja. Ein Beitrag zur Literaturgeschichte des AT*, in *Bib* 80 (1999) 153-177, p. 159.

40. *Ibid.*, p. 161.

41. *Ibid.*, p. 166-168.

42. Cf. ALBERTZ, *Antrittspredigt* (n. 37), pp. 191-206. Cf. KLAUCK, *Armut* (n. 1), pp. 173f., who deduces from the article of Albertz, that the social terms in Luke are to be taken literally.

VII. CONNECTION WITH OTHER PERICOPES IN LUKE AND ACTS[43]

Before coming to a conclusion our last step is to check if the Lukan social concept of poverty can also be found in other parts of the Gospel and in his second book, the Acts of the Apostles[44]. Certainly, this is not the main goal of this paper, but a short overview of the significant texts in Luke and Acts may confirm our thesis that Luke develops a concrete social programme against poverty through a narrative approach[45]. Our main question is whether Luke develops a social programme of selling all property and expects a life of poverty or if he demands the giving away of half of our property or any other individual measure? We find examples for both in the Lukan writings[46]. Can we get a clear answer from a narrative? A narrative is normally open to different interpretations; it does not comprise a doctrine.

Other rich people who provide for the Lukan community are mentioned in the book of Acts. Zacchaeus and the Ethiopian chamberlain (Acts 8,27-40) can be compared with each other. They support the community with their wealth and they do not live as poor people. Neither give up their professions and careers as tax collector or chamberlain. After encountering Jesus as their redeemer – whilst reading in the scripture or meeting him or one of his apostles personally – and having

43. Of course, the unity of Luke-Acts is not a consensus in the exegesis. Arguments pro unity can be found in J. VERHEYDEN (ed.), *The Unity of Luke-Acts* (BETL, 142), Leuven, Uitgeverij Peeters, 1999. Disagreement with this position J. Schröter presented in his actual paper during the CBL 2001. He reduces the unity of both writings on the level of content, the pragmatic aspect is excluded. He especially refers to R. TANNEHILL, *The Narrative Unity of Luke-Acts. A Literary Interpretation*, Philadelphia, PA, Fortress, [2]1990, and mentions the following characteristics of Acts that differ from those of the Gospel: redundancy, speeches of the actors, "we-passages". Furthermore Luke substitutes the baptism of John through the baptism of the Holy Spirit, the restitution of the βασιλεία τοῦ Ἰσραήλ through the commandment of witnessing (ἔσεσθέ μου μάρτυρες), and the performing Spirit instead of Jesus.

44. We will seek for aspects of continuity as we can find them within the topic of the history of salvation. KLAUCK, *Armut* (n. 1), pp. 165-169, first points out that the topic of poverty is not visible in Acts. But at the second view he reveals several pericopes about the danger of property: Judas, Hananias and Sapphira, Simon Magus are examples among the Christians. Moreover he analyses the special sensitivity of Luke for the social question: the distribution for the widows by the chosen Seven (Acts 6,1ff.) and Tabita (Acts 9,39), the centurion Cornelius, Maria – the mother of John Mark – (12,12) and last but not least the example of the apostles Peter, John and Paul.

45. The article of DILLMANN, *Kindheitsgeschichte* (n. 7), pp. 76-97, illustrates the theology of poverty in the Lukan childhood narrative.

46. Examples for those who give their whole property are: the poor widow, the disciples, Barnabas – examples for those who give a part are Zacchaeus, Hananias and Sapphira. Jesus asked people to sell everything – others give everything on their own. On the basis of these pericopes one cannot conclude that two different social models of following Jesus exist in the Church.

come to an understanding of the Good News they share their prosperity with the poor of the Christian community. Zacchaeus even practises justice towards those whom he had discriminated against previously. His change of lifestyle is a proof of this conversion from self-centredness to selflessness. His life became a vivid symbol of Jesus' commandment of love. Zacchaeus does not literally fulfil the Jewish law by giving one tenth (18,12) but by giving a quarter of the demanded taxes back to those whom he had defrauded, following the law of love.

There are only a few other examples of rich people in the Gospel; the reader encounters more often the poor people whom Jesus helped. We can regard the tax collector Levi as belonging to this group, who leaves everything behind in order to follow Jesus (5,27-32) – although there is no explicit mention of wealth in the text. Another such person is the centurion of Capernaum who built synagogues for the Jews because of his love for this people and who cared for his slave (7,2-10 – 7,2: δοῦλος κακῶς ἔχων ἤμελλεν τελευτᾶν)[47].

Among the group of rich people there are several women in the Lukan community who take care of Jesus[48]. The sinful woman who anoints Jesus with expensive oil (7,36-50) gives of her property to express her love for Jesus. Luke mentions other women who follow Jesus, serving him or/and the community with their property (Luke 8,1-3: provide for/διακονέω) – certainly Peter's mother in law, too (4,38-41: serve/διακονέω) and Martha who serves Jesus and his disciples (10,38-42: serve for/διακονέω). The Greek verb διακονέω includes personal services and financial support.

Other examples of people mentioned in the Gospel of Luke who helped with their financial resources are the merciful Samaritan helping the man who fell amongst robbers (10,25-37). He is fulfilling the commandment of 6,35: "to do good, and lend, expecting nothing in return"[49]. The opening dialogue to this parable is comparable with the conversation between the rich man and Jesus about the Jewish law. The prodigal son and his merciful father (15,11-32) and the parable of the rich man and the poor man Lazarus (16,19-31) are oppositional examples. The rich people and the poor widow giving money in the temple (21,1-4) are used by Luke to show the real meaning of almsgiving.

In the book of Acts Judas is an example of someone who made money by practising injustice (Acts 1,15-20), but this led to his perdition.

47. Cf. KLAUCK, *Armut* (n. 1), p. 162.
48. *Ibid.* The author underscores that Luke gives the impression of social high situated women.
49. *Ibid.*, p. 163. The same commandment of humility and hospitality is fulfilled in the parable of the great dinner (Luke 14,15-24).

His wealth did not make him happy. The ideal of the Lukan community sharing possessions among the members also provokes conflicts (Acts 2,45; 4,34[50].36-37). One example Luke tells his community is that of Hananias and Saphira (Acts 5,1-11) who keep part of the money they got after selling some of their possessions[51] – they are antitypes to Barnabas (Acts 4,36f), who sold his field, and brought the money to the apostles. Ananias and Sapphira (Acts 5) do not give an example of giving everything away. They are punished for their attempt to keep part of their income secret. This pericope does not intend to ask people to give the whole of their material goods away but warns Christians against being dishonest, not telling the truth and keeping secrets. The sin of Ananias and Sapphira is not their wealth but their antisocial behaviour towards the community. Other positive examples are Tabita, who gave money (Acts 9,36-43), and Cornelius, the centurion (Acts 10,1-48). Further rich women who provide for the community are mentioned in the Book of Acts (Acts 13,50). Among those mentioned explicitly are Lydia (16,14) and Priscilla (18,1-11).

Luke's ethical concept is based on the Hellenistic ethic of friendship. This can be seen in the context of Jesus' commandment to love one's enemy in Luke 6,27-38[52]. Luke asks to "give, and it will be given to you; good measure, pressed down, shaken together, running over, will be put into your lap. For the measure you give will be the measure you get back" (6,38).

VIII. Contributions to Poverty and Wealth in the Lukan Community

What is the Lukan concept of poverty and wealth? What is the social programme to be seen in the Lukan community? Is it his one hundred percent programme of 18,22 or the fifty percent programme of 19,8? Different answers concerning Luke's social programme are to be found in

50. Acts 4,34: "There was not a needy person among them" (οὐδὲ γὰρ ἐνδεής τις ἦν ἐν αὐτοῖς). KLAUCK, *Armut* (n. 1), p. 161, underlines that the Lukan concept is based on Dtn 15,4a: "But there will be no poor among you" (ὅτι οὐκ ἔσται ἐν σοὶ ἐνδεής).

51. P. DSCHULNIGG, *Die Erzählung über Hananias und Saphira (Apg 5,1-11) und die Ekklesiologie der Apostelgeschichte*, in H.J.F. REINHARDT (ed.), *Theologia et Jus Canonicum*, FS H. Heinemann, Essen 1995, pp. 59-71.

52. Cf. KLAUCK, *Armut* (n. 1) and M. EBNER, *Feindesliebe – ein Ratschlag zum Überleben? Sozial- und religionsgeschichtliche Überlegungen zu Matt 5,38-47/Luke 6,27-35*, in J.M. ASGEIRSSON – K. DE TROYER – M.W. MEYER (eds.), *From Quest to Q*. FS J.M. Robinson (BETL, 146), Leuven, Uitgeverij Peeters, 2000, pp. 119-142.

the various exegetical discussions. One position declares the topic to be a literary pattern. Thus poverty is no more than a symbol of acceptance or rejection of the authority of Jesus[53]. Another thesis defines the poor as the people of Israel, oppressed by its enemies[54]. W. Stegemann presented an interesting approach. He discussed the problem of poverty on the background of the Lukan community. His thesis was to present Luke as theologian of the rich rather than of the poor. His aim was to challenge the rich of his community, to make them realize that wealth was not a sign of God's special mercy and that (charitable) loving trust was a sign of true Christian faith. The Lukan theology of poverty can be described as social compensation between rich and poor. One positive example for this group of rich people is Zacchaeus[55].

At the beginning of our paper we underlined the fact that every reader understands writings according to his own background and experience. This is also observable among exegetes. Scholars of First World nations, in particular, minimize the Lukan theology of poverty and his criticism of wealth. Exegetes of South-America and other poor countries of the world, on the other hand (or: in sharp contrast to this), accentuate the Lukan approach as a social programme against poverty. A comparison of these two explanations and their relation to differing cultural backgrounds reveals how biblical texts lend themselves to varying interpretations. Interpretation is dialogue with a text and depends on the personal experience of the interpreter.

Let us sum up what we can say about poverty in the Lukan community:

– Those rich people who represent the bad paradigm of keeping their wealth for themselves remain nameless in the Gospel. Luke does not

53. L.T. JOHNSON, *Sharing Possessions. Mandate and Symbol of Faith* (Overtures to Biblical Theology, 9), Philadelphia, PA, 1981, pp. 11-29.

54. Cf. SECCOMBE, *Possessions* (n. 12), p. 95: "There is nothing socio-economic or socio religious about Luke's use of "poor" terminology in the passages we have considered. To seek to ground a liberation theology, or an ethic of poverty, upon these texts would be to misunderstand and misuse them". The thesis of DEGENHARDT, *Lukas* (n. 27) distinguishes between the disciples with a special vocation (the services in the [catholic] church) and the regular Christians. Radical poverty is only demanded from the services in the church. The normal Christians can follow Jesus without obeying to this commandment. By the way, Degenhardt does not analyse Luke 19,1-10 in his PhD. The position of SCHMITHALS, *Lukas* (n. 25), 12f.80.144.159.162.171.182.213, is stranger. He supposes a situation of persecution in which Christians lost their complete property. THEISSEN, *Studien* (n. 25), p. 104, supposes the situation of radical wanderings.

55. Cf. W. STEGEMANN, *Nachfolge Jesu als solidarische Gemeinschaft der reichen und angesehenen Christen mit den bedürftigen und verachteten Christen – Das Lukasevangelium*, in L. SCHOTTROFF – W. STEGEMANN, *Jesus von Nazareth – Hoffnung der Armen* (Urban TB, 639), Stuttgart, Kohlhammer, [2]1981, pp. 89-153.

confront the rich members of his community with explicit people in his Gospel – in Acts he merely mentions Judas as a person who received unjust wealth. On the contrary he does mention a few specific persons who gave an excellent example of Christian faith and lifestyle.

– The giving of possessions includes the giving of part of one's own life. The question of how to balance poverty and riches in life challenges a person's whole existence.

– Poverty has a personal dimension: Based on Jesus' words and deeds, Luke does not demand total poverty from the members of his community. Each of them has to decide his/her own measure of giving possessions to the poor. Their personal relationship with Jesus, the depth and power of their own faith serves as a yardstick for their decision.

– Poverty includes the aspect of justice: Any wealth that is founded on injustice is a sign of an imbalanced relationship towards one's neighbour. Luke does not condemn wealth in general, but he is extremely critical of any wealth amassed by injustice towards the suffering poor. The building up of career and property at the cost of the poor even if only by neglect is sin and excludes from life. This is visible in the subsequent three examples: the rich man who did not share his luxury with the poor Lazarus, the rich man who wanted to reach eternal life but left Jesus with sadness, and finally Judas who bought a field from the money gained by his betrayal and died – here the word injustice (ἀδικία) explicitly occurs (Acts 1,18).

– Richness constitutes a danger to faith[56].

– The Lukan concept against poverty is to give half of everything – clothes, food and money – to the poor. But this "half" is only an indication. It can be exceeded by giving everything, as the widow in the temple did (21,1-4) and as Luke asked Jewish ruler to do (18,18-30). With these rules Luke develops the ideal of social compensation in his community[57]. That means that the poor are no longer objects of charity and mercy, but the real subjects of salvation[58]. Imitating Jesus through radical poverty is not the prerogative of a specific group of people or office in the Lukan community.

56. I.H. MARSHALL, *The Gospel of Luke. A Commentary on the Greek Text* (NIGTC), Exeter, Paternoster Press, 1978, p. 326.
57. Cf. KLAUCK, *Armut* (n. 1), p. 171.
58. Cf. *ibid.*, p. 172. He emphasizes that the evolution of the poor to subjects of salvation encloses a christological dimension: Jesus Christ shared the life with the poor (*ibid.* 174). Following the poor man of Nazareth means to be poor, trustworthy and convincing witnesses of his message.

- According to Luke, Jesus is not against having possessions. His criticism has religious, social and ethical connotations.
- In the context of poverty and wealth almsgiving is important.
- The social concept of poverty in the Lukan community is realistic. Based on the good news of Jesus Christ who refers to Isaiah's social concept against poverty, Luke asks his community to practice fair commerce. He does not propose members of the community to give their whole wealth to the community but that they be honest towards each other. Truthfulness signals humanity and openness towards God and neighbour. It is a precondition for following Jesus Christ and being able to live in a Christian community.
- This objective is transmitted to the Lukan community by telling narratives of various people who tried to follow the example of Jesus' life and to fulfil his commandments:
- Conversation does not merely take place in direct speech but also in non-verbal forms of communication – as it is particularly perceptible in the encounter between Jesus and Zacchaeus.
- One characteristic of a narrative is its openness. Therefore, we have to ask the hermeneutical question: Can we develop a social theory/ doctrine or programme from a narrative?
- Luke addresses his theology of poverty to the rich and poor of his community. He encourages the poor and he criticizes the rich, he enlightens both about the necessity of repentance[59].

According to Luke, the call of the first disciples accentuates this social aspect of compensation: Simon is the owner of different boats (5,3.7 – one of the boats, the other boat). James and John, the sons of Zebedee, were his partners (5,10) – Luke already speaks of Simon's partners in 5,7 without mentioning their names. Anyway, his business is based on partnership, although he is the owner of the boats. They share in his prosperity. And it is obvious that Simon's decision to follow Jesus as his disciple is not made without considering his fellow workers. Together they leave their belongings. It is a common decision. Following their call,

---

59. In this context ESLER, *Community* (n. 15), p. 187, mentions the parable of the Lost Sheep (15,4-7) and the Lost Drachma. The first parable, which has a parallel in Matt, describes the situation of a well-situated man, an owner of hundred sheep. The second parable, Sondergut of Luke, portrays a woman who has only ten drachmas, the income for ten days' labour. Both pericopes show the joy in heaven at the repentence of one sinner. The first pericope exemplifies the topic for the rich, the second for the poor members of the Lukan community. It is hardly discussed among New Testament scholars to whom Luke destined his theology of poverty. Cf. SECCOMBE, *Possessions* (n. 12), pp. 12f: "For whom did Luke write? For rich, for poor, or for both?".

James and John remain Simon's partners as is observable in various pericopes in Luke. Simon, James and John are mentioned first in the list of
the twelve chosen apostles (6,14). They are the only companions to follow Jesus into the ruler's house to restore his daughter to life (8,51) and
they are witnesses to his transfiguration (9,28). In Luke 18,28 Simon
speaks for the whole group of Jesus'. Simon and John are sent by Jesus
to prepare the passover (22,8). Discipleship with the precondition of radical poverty is not a lonesome way, it is related to companions and a
community. Only together it is possible to radically follow Jesus.

Theologische Fakultät Paderborn   Beate KOWALSKI[60]
Kamp 6
D-33089 Paderborn
Germany

---

60. I cordially thank Helen Leith for refining my English for this article.

METAPHOR AS APT FOR CONVERSATION

The Inherently Conversational Character
of Theological Discourse

It has been suggested in a number of the papers at this conference that conversation, connectedness, encounter and relation are apt metaphors for the theological task in the twenty-first century – particularly apt for addressing pressing problems, which, if not unique to our day, at least have a new post-modern twist. Jacques Haers has proposed these as the root metaphors for a collaborative research program. Papers have investigated the aptness of the metaphors and made compelling cases for them as key paradigms for theological thinking. I suggest to the contrary that we reverse the formulation of the theme. Rather than focus attention on how conversation and encounter are apt metaphors for the theological project, we should consider how apt metaphor is for conversation. In fact, some conversations and related encounters, among which the religious and theological are included, could not take place without a metaphoric process. Properly speaking, talk of God is always rooted in and essentially related to a metaphoric process. That is my first claim.

My aim in this initial reversal, however, is not to undercut the conference theme. The metaphoric process reveals itself to be intrinsically conversational. The metaphoric act presupposes dynamic shifts in shared fields of meanings that can only be undertaken and grasped through ongoing interaction in language and in connectedness with others. Moreover encounter (in the most proper sense of the term) with God and with the neighbour is mediated by a metaphoric process. The research program envisioned in Professor Haers's paper and many of the others is more radical than the investigation of apt metaphors – even if we conceive them as root metaphors. To opt for such root metaphors is to call for *teshuva*[1]: a metaphoric turning or conversion in thinking and living. My second objective is to elaborate a bit on these contentions.

---

1. For a discussion of the Buber's use of the term and an argument that God-talk involves such a "turning" (although described as grammatical, not metaphorical) see N. Lash, *Easter in Ordinary: Reflections on Human Experience and the Knowledge of God*, Notre Dame, IN, University of Notre Dame Press, 1988, pp. 193 ff.

Inattention to this essentially conversational dynamic of our metaphoric discourse about God is at the root of significant confusions in religious and theological thinking. This occasion does not offer the opportunity to discuss specific cases at length, but I will cite instances, one of which I have analysed more fully in a recent issue of *Theological Studies*[2]. Developing these points, hopefully, will give some justification for concluding that conversation and encounter are not merely apt metaphors for theological thinking. Theological thinking as inherently metaphoric is, when successful, intrinsically conversational and fundamentally directed toward encounter with God and neighbour as other and mystery. Attention to the logic of this essentially conversational dynamic is crucial to understanding how we think and talk about God and how we relate to neighbour – especially in our pluralistic world with its many intersecting but also disparate conversations.

My remarks here are part of a larger project to analyse the metaphoric turn in God-talk as a way to rethink the doctrine of analogy. In light of that broader argument, I will take the liberty of making presuppositions that a fuller treatment of the issues would need to justify. A brief acknowledgment of these assumptions must suffice to situate the context and basis for the case I am making.

In Catholic theology, the appeal to analogy has played a pivotal role in explaining how understanding and language can meaningfully refer to God whose reality transcends human grasp. The "received" tradition traces the Catholic position to Thomas Aquinas's theory of analogy. However, convincing arguments have been made that Aquinas never proposed an explicit theory or even appealed to analogous uses of language in a consistent way over the course of his career[3]. Perhaps more importantly, the use and understanding of analogy in Catholic theology has gradually moved away from the scholastic conceptual framework of the received tradition. This shift in understanding, however, has not been adequately articulated or explained. Often it is not even acknowledged[4]. This became

---

2. R. MASSON, *Analogy and the Metaphoric Process*, in *TS* 62 (2001) 571-596.

3. For a treatment of this issue see D. BURRELL, *Aquinas: God and Action*, Notre Dame, IN, University of Notre Dame Press, 1979, p. 55.

4. For example, the *Oxford Dictionary of the Christian Church* (3rd ed., 1997) does not note this shift or its import. George Klubertanz's article in the *New Catholic Encyclopedia* (1981) details the historical development of the notion of analogy in Thomistic thought without acknowledging the difference between such accounts and the way appeals to analogy actually work in contemporary theological figures like Karl Rahner or the influential philosopher of the doctrine, Erich Przywara. Contemporary theologians, like Elizabeth Johnson, who self-consciously have appropriated this transition in understanding continue, nevertheless, to explain analogy in traditional conceptual language which conceals both the shift itself and its significance.

evident to me in my own investigations of Karl Rahner's theology. His use of analogous language is far more subtle, innovative and effective than his explanation of analogy. Inattention to such unarticulated but fundamental moves in his thought is the source of significant misunderstanding among some commentators and critics[5]. I believe that this is not a peculiarity of Rahner or others indebted to Thomistic tradition but is true in general of theological and philosophical reflection on analogy. By and large, explanation has not matched the exercise of the analogical imagination. Nor has the connection between the analogical imagination and metaphoric imagination, or their relationship with the dialectical imagination, been explained satisfactorily.

In this context, the theory of metaphoric process and understanding of analogy advanced in the interdisciplinary reflections of the theologian and literary theorist, Mary Gerhart, and the physicist, Allan Russell, stand out as a unique contribution[6]. Their conception offers an innovative, perspicuous, coherent and persuasive explanation of what happens when believers and theologians stretch language, and are stretched by language, to speak and think of God. Perhaps familiarity with their position cannot be taken for granted. It is not clear that their position is known widely outside American theological circles[7]. More significantly, it is not clear how many, even in American circles, appreciate the significant potential of Gerhart and Russell's contribution beyond its immediate pertinence to the dialogue between science and religion. Their publications have, for the most part focused on that issue and related methodological concerns[8]. The theological illustrations they offer, while suggestive, are limited to brief sketches. Their studies do not directly address the conceptual confusion surrounding theological appeals to analogy and do not test in any

5. The case for this claim will have to be made in other places but I believe an examinations of the writings of what might be called a "Yale school" interpretation of Rahner in the 1970's and 1980's, Thomas Sheehan's influential analysis of Rahner's philosophical roots, and Roger Haight's appropriation of Rahner's theology of symbol would show that all miss the metaphoric shift intrinsic to Rahner's argumentation.

6. See M. GERHART – A. RUSSELL, Metaphoric Process: The Creation of Scientific and Religious Understanding, Fort Worth, TX, Texas Christian University, 1984; and their further elaborations of the theory in The Cognitive Effect of Metaphor, in Listening 25 (1990) 114-126, and New Maps for Old: Explorations in Science and Religion, New York, Continuum, 2001.

7. For example, their work is not cited in any of the essays in recent collection edited by Leuven's professors, L. BOEVE – K. FEYAERTS (eds.), Metaphor and God-talk, New York, Peter Lang, 1999.

8. The one instance of extended analysis of which I am aware is the fourth chapter of New Maps for Old [originally published with Joseph P. Healey in Semina 61 (1993) 167-182] analysing the metaphoric process implicit in the Mosaic identification of Yahweh and El.

detail the theory's ability to explain the conceptual moves of specific theologians and do not explore the theory's potential to resolve particular theological controversies. So my larger project entails, in part, establishing how and why I think their theory can be helpful in addressing such issues. Moreover, although the case I will make here for the inherently metaphoric and conversational character of theological discourse presupposes their theory, it also seeks to illustrate its explanatory power and in that way to argue for it. Whether the specific details of their theory merit this close attention will hinge in the end on the theory's ability to clarify such issues. The *Theological Studies* article I mentioned was one foray in that direction. What follows is another limited engagement.

I. THE METAPHORIC PROCESS ACCORDING TO GERHART AND RUSSELL

Gerhart and Russell's proposal summarizes and builds on an extensive body of research in philosophy and literature on metaphor. The focus of concern, as they have been at pains to emphasize, however, is not on metaphor or analogy as such, but on the fundamental epistemological process underlying the creation of new understanding in science and in religion. Metaphors have a part in their understanding in so far as they are manifestations of that epistemic process. But the decisive step in their theory is the role which the underlying process plays in changing the fields of meanings in an inquiry. Rather than merely augmenting what is already known, the metaphoric process creates the possibility for new meanings and understanding. Paul Ricœur comments that this is the "most remarkable contribution" of their proposal[9].

Their argument presupposes that our inquiries about the world and ourselves take place in what can be imagined as cognitive spaces or worlds of meanings. These worlds of meanings are composed of networks of interrelated concepts. Physics, theology, a religion, or common sense, as defined by a particular time and culture, are examples of such fields of meanings. The concepts within these fields do not stand directly for things in themselves, but for our notions of these things. These notions are defined by their interrelation with other notions. For example, to get some conception of "house", one must have other notions available (lumber, bricks, wall, window, roof, and so forth). These other notions are variable, as well as the relations between them, so meaning "arises out of the interaction of concepts and relations, and is expressed in the topography

---

9. GERHART – RUSSELL, *Metaphoric Process* (n. 6), p. xii.

of the field. Necessary concept changes, such as those which might arise from a new experience, alter relations; and changes in relations, such as occur when one attempts to understand an experience in a new way, relocate old concepts"[10]. Consider the difference in the concept that "bungalow" would call to mind by the interaction of such notions: in India (a thatched or tiled one-story dwelling surrounded by a wide veranda), in Aberdeen, Scotland (a small granite cottage huddled between similar structures) or in New England (a single story wood framed home). Even among those who share a world of meanings, the understandings of such notions can vary somewhat from person to person, depending on factors such as background, education and linguistic sophistication. Moreover, meanings can change over time if new associations are made between existing notions, or if a new notion is added to a field of meanings. In the Gospels, when Jesus identifies the notion of Messiah with that of the Suffering Servant, the association significantly alters not only these notions but, as well, a host of other notions related to the idea of eschatological expectation (a field of meanings), if not the very fabric of Jewish faith (a still broader field of meanings)[11].

In the view of Gerhart and Russell, a world of meanings is made up of collections of such fields of meanings and it "comprises the basis for an individual's idea of the way things are"[12]. The theory regards the individual's or community's construal, when it is successful, as corresponding in a genuine but complex way to reality. On the other hand, the theory also holds that "worlds of meaning are culture-bound. Within a particular culture, persons have worlds of meanings that have the same general topography despite the fact that a particular field of meanings possessed by one person may be completely absent in another"[13]. These construals take place in conversation – in ongoing interaction in language and in community with others.

What interests Gerhart and Russell is how new understandings and meanings develop among people who share such a world of meanings. They distinguish the discovery of new meanings from the acquisition of new knowledge that involves merely an addition of data that does not

---

10. Id., *The Cognitive Effect of Metaphor* (n. 6), p. 119.

11. To what extent such alterations in meaning were effected, whether by Jesus or later interpreters, with what justification and with what success are of course the fault lines of disagreement from which Christianity developed as a new religion and that continue to divide traditions of beliefs and schools of scholarship. That different historical and theological answers to such questions are possible, does not alter the fact that a metaphoric identification underlies the possibility of such new meanings and understandings.

12. *Ibid.*, p. 120.

13. *Ibid.*

change the notions or fields of meanings themselves. For example, we can learn of new cities or new planets and so gain additional information for ourselves or the field of astronomy. In doing this, however, we usually do not change the notions of "city", "planet", or "solar system". In contrast, Copernicus's insistence that the sun is the centre of the universe or Newton's insistence that the mechanical laws of the heavens are identical with the mechanical laws of the earth, created new understandings that changed fundamental notions within physics and indeed changed how ordinary people understood things. Much of the routine work of scientists and theologians is devoted to the former sort of acquisition aimed at expanding the current knowledge base. Insights of the latter sort are occurrences of genius and discovery typically associated with more extraordinary and consequential developments in a discipline.

Analogy, broadly conceived, plays a key role in both processes. A crucial element of Gerhart and Russell's proposal is the suggestion that we distinguish between three different though related ways of making an "analogy" that we can designate as "analogy", "simile", and "metaphor".

In Gerhart and Russell's scheme "analogy" and "simile" are conceptual tools that often play a key role in the former task, the acquisition of additional information. Analogy in this definition involves the use of some feature common to two known realities to extend or expand our knowledge of either one of them, or, in some cases, both of them. Successful analogies between the operations of the human mind and computers, for example, could lead either to a better grasp of how the mind works, to the development of more sophisticated software, or to an enriched understanding of both minds and computers.

Sometimes, only one of the analogues in question will be known. In that case, a known feature of one reality tells us something about another reality that is unknown. This is what Gerhart and Russell understand to be the defining characteristic of simile. "So when Max Black wrote, 'The chairman plowed through the discussion', he created a text that instructs the reader who does not know how the discussion proceeded, and who now, on the comparative basis of the simile, does know"[14]. It is important for our exploration of the conversational character of such conceptual and linguistic moves to observe that whether Black's proposition functions as an analogy or simile depends on the state of knowledge of the persons involved. A person who was present at the chairman's discussion would be in a position to agree with Black's analogy or, as we say, to "get"

---

14. *Ibid.*, p. 116 quoting M. BLACK, *Models and Metaphors: Studies in Language and Philosophy*, Ithaca, NY, Cornell University Press, 1962, p. 13.

the analogy and acquire a deeper insight into the event. That person, however, would not be acquiring new information about something unknown. Therefore, in Gerhart and Russell's account, for that person the proposition would be an analogy, not a simile.

Gerhart and Russell note that with these definitions a great many of the comparisons we ordinarily think of as metaphors are, in their theory, either analogies or similes. As I mentioned previously, they are not proposing that literary concepts of metaphor need to be changed or abandoned. Their description of the "metaphoric process" is not intended as a comprehensive theory of metaphor or metaphorical usage. Rather, the goal is to direct our attention to an epistemological process that involves a third kind of analogy where, given the normal understanding of the notions within or between fields of meanings, there is no acknowledged similarity between a known "x" and "y". When such a situation obtains, saying that "x is y" forces an analogy between the two knowns that is uncalled for "thereby *creating* a similarity or analogy where none existed"[15]. The distinguishing character of what Gerhart and Russell label the metaphoric process is that it distorts the given world of meanings. Once one gets the point of the metaphor – gets the point of affirming that "x is y"then "x", "y", and the coordinates (or field of meanings) in terms of which we had formerly understood them, are comprehended in a new way which makes it possible to conceive notions, understand relations, and envision as logical what could not have been so grasped before the metaphoric act. Gerhart and Russell stress "it is of particular importance to see that it is the theoretical structure of the meanings involved in metaphor that makes new knowledge possible. The distortion of the fields of meanings by means of the metaphoric process is a structural change that demands that other meanings and understandings have to be changed in the wake of the metaphor"[16]. They contend, "This is what is so different about the metaphoric process. The analogical process, on the other hand, is an extension of meaning (as distinct from the creation of new meaning). The increased knowledge from analogy is primarily in terms of the original understandings"[17].

Take the example of the early Christians' affirmation that "Jesus is the Messiah". Given the images current in the eschatology of the day, affirming that God was victorious in the crucified son of a carpenter from Nazareth was uncalled for. In fact, most of the key eschatological images

15. *Ibid.*, p. 121.
16. ID., *Metaphoric Process* (n. 6), p. 119.
17. *Ibid.*

by which Jesus is identified in the Gospels have something of this metaphoric dimension. By ordinary logic he was not a victorious King of Israel; he was not a Son of Man who descended gloriously from the heavens; he was not acknowledged by his people nor did he vanquish their enemies. To affirm that Jesus is the Messiah is to force an analogy between him and Israel's expressions of hope and trust in God. Forcing the analogy requires us to understand differently both Jesus and that hope itself. Affirming that Jesus is the Messiah, if taken seriously, forces a thoroughgoing revision of the field of meanings operative in Palestinian Judaism, or at least those operative in the narrative worlds of the New Testament. Given that shift in meaning, it is appropriate to say that Jesus literally and properly is the Messiah.

According to Gerhart and Russell, Copernicus brought about a similar shift in scientific understanding.

> The sun (not the earth) is the center of the solar system." This is not a simile, nor is it an analogy. Furthermore, there is nothing unknown or ambiguous about "the sun", nor about "center of the solar system." To insist, on the basis of no observational evidence, that one of the concepts is the other, conforms to our description of the linguistic expression of a metaphoric act. The identity between two hitherto different but known concepts changed a host of relations in fields of meanings and reformed the topography of the world of meanings. Testimony to the outrageous act is amply given in history's descriptions of the reaction of religious authorities[18].

They argue that Newton's equation of the mechanical laws of the heavens with the mechanical laws of the earth "had perhaps an even more profound effect on our lives"[19] and that it was in similar ways metaphoric.

To summarize, in Gerhart and Russell's theory a distinction must be made between two different epistemological processes that use analogies. What they refer to as the "analogical act" involves recognition of similarities within or between given fields of meanings. These are what we ordinarily regard as analogies, similes and, in many instances, metaphors. When successful, the analogical act expands meanings within those fields without distorting the fields themselves. The "metaphoric act" also involves the recognition of similarities, but these similarities are the result of a "disruptive cognitive act" that forces an uncalled-for analogy within or between the fields of meanings – a distortion of one or both of these fields in order to achieve the required analogy. When this distortion is

---

18. ID., *The Cognitive Effect of Metaphor* (n. 6), p. 124.
19. *Ibid.*

productive it creates new understandings and meanings. For example, a new world of meanings, in fact a new religion, is created if one takes as true the affirmation that Jesus is the Messiah.

II. The Metaphoric and Analogical Acts as Inherently Conversational

These distinctions between the analogical act and the metaphoric act cannot be determined apart from the knowing processes of the persons entertaining them. Metaphoric and analogical construals take place in ongoing interaction in an already-given world of meanings and in community with others. These are inherently conversational processes. For example, as a successful metaphoric act gains acceptance and begins to effect permanent transformations in a field of meanings, the uncalled-for analogy becomes more and more obvious. After a while, it is taken for granted. It becomes a "given" in the new but now stabilized field of meanings. The metaphor dies or perhaps more accurately is transformed into an analogy, simile, or univocal concept. It was a metaphoric act for Copernicus, and those who accepted his affirmation, to insist the sun is the centre of the solar system, or for Newton, and Newtonians, to insist on the identity of heavenly and earthly mechanics. Such insistence would not constitute a metaphoric act today.

That the propositions could be metaphoric for Copernicus and Newton but univocal for us demonstrates that whether the act terminates in metaphor, analogy, simile, a univocal concept or an equivocation is determined in part by the knowledge state of the person entertaining it. As we saw with Black's example of the chairman ploughing through a discussion, an analogy becomes a simile if the people entertaining the proposition were not at the discussion. Likewise, the persons must know both sets of relations for a metaphoric proposition to create a distortion in their fields of meanings. If they know only one of the two metaphoric elements, the proposition "functions as an analogy, since the unknown element is free to move within the field. Such freedom removes the possibility of tension or distortion of the field of meanings"[20]. Alternately, if the persons involved have different linguistic sensitivities or only appear to share fields of meanings, and because of different backgrounds or presuppositions understand one or the other of the terms differently, then

20. *Ibid.*, p. 121.

what for one person is a metaphor, for a second could be merely an analogy, while a third might take the proposition as univocal.

Let me illustrate with the example I mentioned of the Christian's insistence that crucified Jesus is the Messiah. There are a number of ways of reading this affirmation. The reading I recommended above would construe the affirmation as metaphoric. The metaphoric reading challenges us to reconfigure fundamentally the fields of meanings involved in understanding Jesus, God's love, and humanity's relation to both. When Saint Paul, in the first letter to the Corinthians, acknowledged that this insistence is "illogical to those who are not on the way to salvation" (1 Cor 1,18)[21], he recognized the necessity for fundamental changes in the fields of meanings associated with these concepts – indeed, the rhetoric of his argument presupposes and plays on the this conceptual reconfiguration.

But, as Paul's admission allows, this is not the only logical reading possible. The proposition could also be conceived in Gerhart and Russell's terminology as analogical. On the analogical reading, there are some ways in which Jesus' activities and his impact were similar to the activities and impact associated with a New David, a Son of Man descending from the clouds of heaven, or the promised Messiah. But there are also obvious ways in which the analogy does not apply. So he is not literally the Messiah. Understood in this way, the analogy proposes to communicate a deeper insight into the events, similar to what we saw with Black's proposition about a chairman ploughing through a meeting. Read as an analogical metaphor, the insistence that the crucified Jesus is the Messiah, however, does not require any realignment of our fields of meanings. It may add to knowledge but it does not create new meanings. It is similar to information acquired from learning about the existence of new cities; it is different from the creation of new understanding in the Copernican assertion that the Sun *is* the centre of the universe.

It is possible to imagine several people disagreeing about whether and how such an analogical reading of Jesus as Messiah applies. The first might believe the analogy is warranted. Perhaps this person would be intent on showing how Jesus fulfilled what is essential about the scriptural prophecies, even if Jesus did not literally descend from the heavens. For such a person, the identification of Jesus and the Messianic expectations is not simply univocal, but it is not merely a metaphorical trope either. That person's problem is to explain how this middle point is not an equivocation. It is possible to imagine a second more liberal believer

21. The Jerusalem Bible.

who holds that Jesus is the Messiah but who sees this affirmation as more metaphorical and figurative. That person faces the charge of relativizing the Christian faith's claim. There is the third possibility of a secular historian who does not believe that Jesus is the Messiah but who judges that the affirmation is warranted, or at least makes sense, but only figuratively. A fourth possibility is a more sceptical counterpart who holds that the identification of Jesus with such Messianic concepts is historically implausible, and that using the term figuratively is thus misleading and unjustified. Finally, there is the possibility of non-believers (for example, Jews or Muslims) who regard the analogy as untrue, even though such persons might have great respect for Jesus as a person and religious figure. Despite the real differences between each of these positions, all understand the affirmation, Jesus is the Messiah, as analogical in Gerhart and Russell's sense. What is in dispute between them is quite different than what is at issue on the first reading as a metaphoric analogy. This is true even though the believers who read the affirmation as an analogical metaphor might also cite Paul's text from 1 Corinthians for support.

There are still other possibilities. We can envision a person whose understanding of Messianic hope and images is learned from a very limited reading of the New Testament. Or we can consider someone raised in the Jewish faith who learned about Jesus or the significance Christians attribute to Jesus by associating the concepts of Davidic promise and Messianic expectation with him. In these cases, we would have instances of what Gerhart and Russell call similes. The one analogue provides information about the other. There is an expansion of information but not a creation of new understanding or fields of meanings.

Finally, there is the possibility of persons who interpret confession of Jesus' lordship as asserting a univocal identification of Jesus and the concept of Messiah without a sense of the complexity involved in the affirmation. There are both believers and sceptics who assume that this sort of univocal identification is the decisive question. And what is at issue for them is distinct from what is at issue in either an analogical reading or a metaphoric reading.

The point of laying out all these possibilities is to illustrate that the same affirmation can be understood as an instance of metaphoric understanding for one person, analogical understanding for a second, and univocal understanding for third. On each of these readings what counts for the truth of the affirmation and what constitutes equivocation varies significantly. Hence "reception" has to be taken into account to understand what is being signified. Reception is but one side of the give and take of conversation. Getting the meaning of a metaphoric act, or generating it in the first place, presupposes dynamic and fundamental shifts in shared fields of meanings that are grasped in ongoing dialogue. So the generation and sustaining of metaphoric meaning requires a give and take between conversation partners, between their fields of meanings, and between their worlds and those networks of meanings. Moreover, where there is conversation, shared fields of meanings, and ongoing fundamental shifts in some of these meanings, there is also the possibility that one party might get the other's analogy differently, get it wrongly or might not get it at all because a metaphoric shift is not recognized, not accepted or confused with an analogical shift. The point at issue between these positions has as much to do with how something is said – and heard – (as metaphoric, analogical or univocal) as it does with what is said. Fundamental disagreement about the former is likely to preclude or at least confuse meaningful resolution of the latter.

The research program Haers proposes requires attention to this connection between the metaphoric process and conversation. This connection has positive and negative aspects. Both underline the intrinsic and mutual connection between metaphoric process and conversation. Positively, the metaphoric invitation to force an uncalled for analogy and the consequent shifts in shared fields of meanings is key to the generation of new knowledge among conversation partners. It enables conversation partners to recognize, say, and explain something new which they could not have understood or said before. The conversation could not advance in this new direction without the metaphoric act. For example, the generation of Christian faith and community presupposes and is effected in the metaphoric proclamation of Jesus as Lord. And likewise, the metaphoric act could not take place without a community in conversation, just as the proclamation of Jesus as Lord, presupposes a community whose field of meanings and whose experience of Jesus allow for the possibility of recognizing the affirmation's force. Moreover, if the metaphoric act is to continue to carry its force, and so its meaning, the community's conversation must have resources to sustain the new meaning and communicate it. The liturgical retelling of the Gospels and development of doctrine thus work to revivify the revelatory and extraordinary character of the Christian community's confession.

Negatively, the possibility for missing or mistaking metaphoric shifts in fields of meanings provides the potential for misunderstandings that can confuse or preclude genuine conversation. The force of a metaphoric shift in meanings is an invitation and conceptual move that can be missed, refused or confused (taken as mere analogy or simile). The point, here, would be missed if we simply thought it a matter of misunderstanding caused by people having different presuppositions. Difference in presuppositions could be taken merely to mean either knowing different things within a shared field of meanings or having different fields of meanings. The creation of new knowledge in the metaphoric act is different than what is at issue in those two instances. In the first, the matter has to do with expanding knowledge within a given field of meanings. (Learning more facts about Jesus.) In the second, the matter could concern simply a expansion of one's fields of meanings. (A Christian learns how Jews and Muslims understand holiness.) Although there is an expansion of meaning in both cases, neither requires a reformulation or shifts in fields of meanings, and so neither would be metaphoric. (One can learn what it means, at one level at least, for Christians to say "I believe Jesus is Lord", without getting the metaphoric force of the affirmation.)

III. THE METAPHORIC AND CONVERSATIONAL DIMENSIONS OF GOD TALK

Had we the time, I would want at this point to demonstrate how theological discussion gets into trouble when we are inattentive to the metaphoric character of God-talk and its intrinsically conversational dimensions. The article in *Theological Studies*, to which I referred previously, examines one illustration: Joseph Bracken's "Process" response to Elizabeth Johnson's revised "Thomist" account of divine providence. Bracken's critique misses altogether her argument's metaphoric thrust. The issue for him is whether "process" or "substance" provides the more apt metaphor for God. Johnson's position presupposes a more fundamental shift in understanding how we talk about God in the first place. Her revision of Thomism presupposes that Aquinas himself stretched language, and that we must stretch language today, not to identify *esse* or substance as the best analogy for God, or to identify any analogy for God as best, but to identify God as unlike any other being or substance. On this point, at least, my interpretation of her argument is in agreement with Denys Turner's interpretation in this volume of classical, late antique and medieval apophaticism. I think I could also enlist support from Turner's paper for emphasizing, in response to Bracken, that stretching language this way, though a rejection of the kind of ontotheology advance in Process Theology, is not an abandonment of rigorous philosophical argumentation about God's existence and identity. Turner's argument supports, further, my contention that we speak properly of God only when we are brought by such argumentation to the recognition, that God is beyond the grasp of our conceptions.

Turner shows that the point of Pseudo-Denys "is to demonstrate that our language leads us to the reality of God when, by a process simultaneously of affirming and denying all things of God, by, as it were in one breath, both affirming what God is and denying, as he puts it, "that there is any kind of thing that God is"[22], we step off the very boundary of language itself, beyond every assertion and every denial, into the "negation of the negation" and the "brilliant darkness"[23] of God"[24]. Turner offers a similar reading of Aquinas: "So what the five ways prove is *simultaneously* the existence of, and the unknowability of, God: God is shown to exist, but what is also shown is that, in *that* case, we have almost lost our grip on the meaning of "...exists" as predicated of God"[25].

I do not know whether Professor Turner would find helpful my further description of such language as metaphoric, but the case he makes certainly fits the paradigm. He does not hesitate to affirm that for Pseudo-Denys and Aquinas the principle of apophaticism is necessarily at the same time the general principle of cataphaticism. He shows how the logic of this argumentation entails a "paradoxical conjunction of opposites". He insists that for Aquinas "God must be thought of as off *every* scale of sameness and difference and thus beyond 'every assertion ... beyond every denial'"[26]. Turner insists (and I would concur) that such claims are neither leaps of "atheistical deconstruction" nor exercises in a "foundationless, anti-metaphysical" apophaticism. Nevertheless, in the end, the conceptual moves are intended to get us to the realization that when we speak of God, we are talking about one who is not like any other and we are using our ordinary language in a way that is significantly different from other ways of signifying. The force of this argument requires that the logic of description in God's case is not what it is in every other case. Inattentiveness to this metaphoric move and its necessary relation to its roots in the soil of medieval metaphysics and vocabulary (fields of meanings) is precisely what Turner faults in both the apophaticism of Derrida and some contemporary spiritualities. The issue here, as in the Bracken-Johnson discussion, is not just that parties in dispute apparently have different concepts of being or of apophaticism. One discussion partner does

---

22. DIONYSIUS AREOPAGITA, *The Complete Works*, trans. C. LUIBHEID, New York, Paulist, 1987, p. 98.
23. *Ibid.*
24. Compare the contribution by Denys Turner on *Atheism, Apophaticism and "Différance"* in this volume pp. 689-708, esp. 691.
25. *Ibid.*, p. 701.
26. *Ibid.*, p. 702.

not recognize the metaphoric moves operative in the other's fields of meanings and so misses the force and logic of the other's arguments.

In the article mentioned earlier, I show how David Burrell and Karl Rahner's readings of Aquinas led them to conclude as well that, properly speaking, talk of God always entails this logical difference from talk about every other reality. That is what Rahner meant when he insisted that affirmations properly apply to God only as mystery. I take this to be the ultimate meaning of his claim, shared by many other Catholic theologians, that talk of God is necessarily analogical. The reason for describing this talk further as metaphoric, besides distinguishing it from misguided attempts to find a "most apt analogy", is to indicate that the positive insight and knowledge is achieved through the distortion in accustomed fields of meanings. The new understanding is brought about by the stretching of language itself and not with some new concept or analogy for grasping God[27]. It is the forcing of the analogies that open up the possibility for new meaning – for using everyday language to speak towards what is beyond its ken. This is why properly speaking, at least in the Christian conception, talk about God is inherently rooted in and essentially related to a metaphoric process and why I suggest that inattentiveness to this process and its essential conversational character is a source of theological confusion.

I do not suppose for a moment that recognition of this metaphoric dimension in itself is all that we need to clarify our theological muddles. Turner wondered at the conclusion of his paper what Christoff Schwoebel could possibly mean when he said "that it was a mark of our philosophical sinfulness that we make the pattern of our existence to be the pattern of the divine – as if there were some, even notional, alternative state of affairs, some other, *pre*-lapsarian possibilities of language about God from which we have fallen away"[28]. One might address a similar question to Anne Hunt who concluded that the Paschal Mystery "explodes the very notion of conversation as we know it"[29]. Schwoebel's recommendation

---

27. The limitation of Wim A. de Pater's analysis of the analogy of attribution, from this perspective, is that it does not draw attention to this shift in fields of meanings although I believe it, like Burrell's position, presupposes such a shift. My aim is not to take exception to such interpretations but rather to point to this further aspect and its importance for clarifying what is going on in God-talk. See W. DE PATER, *Analogy and Disclosures: On Religious Language*, in *Metaphor and God-talk* (n. 7), pp. 33-44.

28. Compare the question by D. Turner on p. 706 of this volume, referring to C. SCHWÖBEL, *God as Conversation. Reflections on a Theological Ontology of Communicative Relations*, pp. 53-55 (IV. *Disrupting the Conversation: Sin*).

29. Compare the article by Anne Hunt on *Trinity and Paschal Mystery: Divine Communion and Human Conversation*, in this volume, p. 96.

looks to me a classic Lutheran metaphoric turn and Professor Hunt proposes a variation on a turn of thought recommended by von Balthasar. Whether and how others of us might accept such recommendations will not be resolved simply by noting their metaphoric character. To show that their affirmations are metaphoric does not prove them true. On the other hand, if I am correct about the metaphoric character of their positions, genuine engagement with their claims presupposes recognition of this metaphoric thrust.

IV. CONCLUSION

If talk of God is intrinsically metaphoric in this way and, as Karl Rahner persuasively argued, the human person is defined intrinsically by openness to God, there is a sense too in which the identity of the other, our neighbour, is also beyond any adequate grasp of our conceptualizations. But as Professor Haers indicated so clearly in his paper, for me even to state the issue this way suggests that encounter with neighbour begins with myself and entails merely my finding things in common with the other. This makes it sound as if I am in a position to get an adequate grasp of my connectedness to God and neighbour; the task is merely to find the right analogies for comprehending them. But as long a I begin with myself as privileged centre for encounter and presume that the God or neighbour can come within my grip, there is no space for the claim of our prior connectedness and for genuine encounter with them as irreducible other to emerge. There is a metaphoric thrust to the Christian claim that in Christ we are all sisters and brothers, or to the confession (shared with Jews and Muslims) that we are all children of God. To get the point entailed in these affirmations requires a fundamental shift in our field of meanings. For the point is not that we are "like" sisters and brothers, but that we "are". Although I agree with Professor Haers that it would be misleading to describe this fundamental conviction as a paradigm change, since it is central to the core of Christian faith and not something new, the notion is also more than a mere metaphor, albeit a root one. Hence I think it important to add, what I hope is not an imposition on Professor Haers's argument but a kind of "midrash", that to opt for such an affirmation as a root metaphor is to call with the prophets for *teshuva*: a turn or conversion in thinking and living. It requires such a turn because a thinking and living which seeks to centre itself in the "other", rather than the in the "I", requires an openness to the gift of the other and the givenness of our prior connectedness. It is not something that the "I" can establish for itself. The "turning" is never complete because no conversion can ever capture the neighbour or God. The turning is metaphoric because it requires a radical shift in our fields of meanings about self, God and neighbour.

This then is the brief for my suggestions at the beginning of the talk. Properly speaking, talk of God is always rooted in and essentially related to a metaphoric process. Conversation and encounter, consequently, are not merely apt metaphors for theological thinking. Theological thinking as inherently metaphoric, when successful, is intrinsically conversational and fundamentally directed toward encounter with God and neighbour, as other and mystery. Attention to the logic of this essentially conversational dynamic is crucial to understanding our thinking and talk about our encounter with God and neighbour – especially in our pluralistic world with its many intersecting but also disparate conversations.

Department of Theology   Robert MASSON
Marquette University
100 Coughlin Hall
P.O. Box 1881
Milwaukee, WI 53201-1881
U.S.A.

APOPHATIC ASPECTS OF THEOLOGICAL
CONVERSATION

I. INTRODUCTION

In this paper I am going to explore the contribution of the apophatic tradition to contemporary theological conversation. I employ a method called the *apophatic* way, which is to a degree a Greek alternative of the Latin *via negativa*. I say "to a degree", because there are also striking differences between these two methods, which are significant for my exploration. While the *via negativa* is rooted more in speculative thinking and is concerned with what cannot be said, mainly in the area of what cannot be said about God[1], the *apophatic* way comes from a tradition of contemplative thinking, and emphasizes not only what cannot be said, but also what kind of conversion is needed so that we will move from living in a lie to living in truth, from forgetting our roots to rediscovering them in our memory, from being separated from communion with God and with other people to being included[2]. Contemporary interest in negative theology often does not appreciate the differences between the Western and the Eastern approaches[3]. It is predominantly concerned with what cannot be said about God, or in other words, where our speech about God ceases to be helpful. Yet, the negative has also liberating aspects, and this is where my interest lies – in the ability to subvert the definitive descriptions, the clearly divided relations of power,

---

1. In AQUINAS the negativity is related to the deceptions that human knowledge as such is liable to (see *Summa Theologiae* I-II, q.q, a.8) and to the disjunction between knowing corporeal matters and spiritual matters (see *Summa* I, q. 84, a. 6).

2. Here we find the three Platonic principles, katharsis, anamnesis, and methexis implicitly present. For *anamnesis* see PLATO, *Meno* 81; *Phaedrus* 92.A; for *katharsis* see *Sophist* 229.d; 231.e; for *methexis* see *Parmenides* 229.d. References are taken from E. HAMILTON – H. CAIRNS (eds.), *Plato: Collected Dialogues including Letters*, Princeton, NJ, Princeton UP, 1996.

3. To a degree we can say that the Eastern approach is inspired by the Platonic philosophy of essence and its emphasis on the participation in the divine essence, while the Western is inspired by the Aristotelian philosophy of categories with the emphasis on the relationships of causality in our existence. Yet this distinction is inadequate when it comes to Augustine and thinkers inspired by him, such as Bonaventure. There we have a Western version of Platonism. Also Western mystics, such as Ignatius of Loyola, John of the Cross, Theresa of Avila or Meister Eckhart, subvert the simple distinction.

the captured and controlled presence or absence of God. The liberating negative, as will be shown, opens and guards spaces for conversation, for communication.

My paper starts with patristic theology, in order to emphasize the long roots of the subject. The first part examines the apophatic method which we find in Gregory of Nyssa, and elaborates on the aspects which can provide a contemporary theological conversation with the liberating negative. In the second part, I look at the appropriations of the liberating negative among contemporary western theologians, Jean-Pierre Jossua, Jean-Luc Marion and Louis-Marie Chauvet in particular.

II. The Apophatic Way in Gregory of Nyssa

Gregory of Nyssa (c.330–c.395) is best known for his contributions, along with his brother, Basil, and their friend, Gregory Nazianzen, to the Trinitarian formulations of the Council of Constantinople. However, my main concern in what follows is another aspect of Gregory's theology. I wish to consider Gregory's understanding of apophaticism, which developed as a response to two key controversies of his time, one with Eunomius (d.394/5), a representative of radical neo-Arianism[4], the other with the late teaching of Origen (c.185–c.254), who was previously a source of great inspiration for Gregory. Here, Gregory formulated his teaching on God's infinity, on the one hand, and the infinite progress of humanity on the way to God, on the other. Before examining these areas, let me first offer a definition of the apophatic way which I associate with Gregory[5].

The word apophatic, in Greek *apophatikè*, comes from *apophasis*, which has two basic meanings, namely revelation and negation[6]. The apophatic way, then, includes both of these meanings. It is a complement

---

4. Gregory opposed the heresies of both Arius and Eunomius. Arius's claim that there is an essential difference between the ungenerate nature of the Father and generate nature of the Son (refused in 321 – and opposed by the Council of Nicea in 325) is radicalised by Eunomius's assertion that the "ungenerate" is not only the fundamental characteristic of God but also God's essence (*ousia*). Eunomius brought a form of negative theology, which claimed superiority to the affirmative theology, because of its privileged knowledge of the negative name of God.

5. For a more detailed argument for placing Gregory within the apophatic tradition, see my paper *The Apophatic Way in Gregory of Nyssa*, in P. Pokorný – J. Roskovec (eds.), *Philosophical Hermeneutics and Biblical Exegesis*, Tübingen, Mohr Siebeck, 2000, pp. 323-339. The analysis of Gregory's position in this article is partly taken from there.

6. The word revelation comes from *apophainomai*, while the word negation from *apophèmi*.

and a critique of the kataphatic way, the "positive" symbolic content of theology, and as such the apophatic way questions all our concepts of God, ourselves and the world. It negates definitive descriptions in order to open windows for transcendent revelation and for immanent conversion, both of which are necessary for the human journey towards God and for communion with God[7]. Such an understanding of apophaticism, of which Gregory is a significant proponent, stems from the Greek Fathers, from the tradition of the Alexandrian school, in particular Origen and Clement, and emphasises the infinity and incomprehensibility of God. As such it is firmly rooted in biblical exegesis and careful not to claim any sort of higher knowledge but rather is seen as a complementary discourse[8].

Gregory's notion of God's infinity developed in opposition to Eunomius's argument that God could be perfectly known by human reason, provided it knew the definitive name of God and held a correct doctrine. This, according to Eunomius, meant naming God the Ungenerated and recognising, thus, his one single supreme essence. The Son of God, then, was created by the Father and not of his essence, and neither was the Spirit, who was created in turn by the Son. Gregory's reply, *Contra Eunomium* (c.382), is heavily tied up with his defence of the Constantinopolitan position on the divinity of the Son and the Spirit. But in it, Gregory also argues strongly that to call God unbegotten, or ungenerated Being, is not the definitive way of naming God and does not give us access to God's essence, as this is, indeed, something beyond our reach[9]. Over against this designation, he says that the most important attribute of God is his infinity[10], as it does not betray the fact that our knowing God always includes leaving behind what we think we have grasped and moving beyond that.

When we come to the second polemics, which gave rise to Gregory's understanding of the infinite progress of the human soul on the journey towards God, we have to be aware that there are different starting points.

---

7. See V. Lossky, *Orthodox Theology: An Introduction*, Crestwood, NY, St. Vladimir's Seminary Press, 1978, pp. 32-33.

8. As Lenka Karfíková argues, "Gregory does not wish to develop a system of apophatic theology only in the sense of private or negative statements, as we can find with the Arians. Gregory explicitly rejects Eunomius's "technology" of negative statements as meaningless and says that positive statements have generally a priority over the negative ones", L. Karfíková, *Řehoř z Nyssy* [Gregory of Nyssa], Praha, Oikúmené, 1999, p. 186.

9. See Gregory of Nyssa, *Contra Eunomium libri I et II*, ed. W. Jager, Leiden, GNO II, 1960, pp. 3-311: II.3.

10. *Ibid.*, I. 673.

Gregory's relationship to the tradition of the Alexandrian school, and, in particular, to Origen is a great deal more complex. Much of Gregory's theology was influenced by these sources. He took from them the allegorical interpretation of scripture, their teaching on human freedom (with its denial of any form of determinism), and the concept of eschatological hope when all will be well in God[11]. However, in one area, Gregory found himself in disagreement with Origen. This was over Origen's idea of a cyclical cosmos, where the soul becomes sated with contemplation of God and falls back into created matter once again, to begin the process of returning to God. It is effectively a version of reincarnation, and Gregory rejects it[12]. This doctrine of Origen led Gregory to develop his own response which was based on the concept of epektasis[13]. With this, Gregory refers to the constant striving and straining of humankind on the never-ending journey towards God, which does not end even after resurrection, but, rather, enters into a new phase.

For Gregory God cannot be understood as a composition in human terms. Rather, God must be understood precisely in terms of an infinity (the immediacy, that is, the unmediatedness of God), within whom are inner relationships and inner communication. Furthermore, this inner life of God, although it remains unbounded by time and space, is not something which is therefore totally alien to creation. For we can experience its effects on us, such as mercy, goodness, love. This ability to experience the effects of God's infinity leads Gregory to posit that we are enabled to participate infinitely in God's infinity[14]. To this participation in God's infinity, though, we must necessarily bring our createdness, with all its implications of bodily existence rooted in particular times and spaces. Thus, the infinite human journey is one which involves both this mediatedness and the challenge posed to it by the participation in the infinity of God. It is through this encounter between the mediated and the unmediated that spiritual progress is made.

In this context Gregory also considers the nature of human and divine communication. He sees communication as related to the inner life of

---

11. We find in Gregory a similar position to Origen's teaching on apokatastasis, namely, that all will be well in God in the end, which included the conversion and inclusion of everything and everyone, including all people, but also all the dark forces, even Satan. Gregory's position runs on similar lines, but, perhaps, as it remained less explicit, it avoided condemnation, which Origen's teaching on apokatastasis did not.

12. In this, Gregory keeps with the anathema of Constantinople, which we know from the Edict of Justinian in 542. See KARFÍKOVÁ, Řehoř z Nyssy (n. 8), p. 25.

13. This concept Gregory takes from Phil 3,13: "epekteinomenos" – striving toward that which is coming to it.

14. See KARFÍKOVÁ, Řehoř z Nyssy (n. 8), p. 195.

God. Even if, in principle, knowledge of that inner life is beyond us, we are included in it. Gregory wants to maintain the fundamental difference between human and divine communication, but he differs here from later Western thinkers like Aquinas. Gregory does not explain the difference by means of analogy[15]; he simply states the incompatibility, which can be bridged from God's side, as God enters into relationship with us, as God reveals his plans, his actions and himself to us. It is the gift, which does not remove the paradox, a knowledge of the unknowability, a seeing of the unseeable, a grasping of the still ungraspable.

III. Appropriation of the Apophatic Elements in Contemporary Theology

In this part, I intend to look at three French thinkers: Jean-Pierre Jossua, Jean-Luc Marion, Louis-Marie Chauvet. All three are involved in a critique of traditional metaphysics, or onto-theology[16]. With Jossua, I will look at how the theme of apophaticism is present in the main features he identifies as necessary for living the life of a witness to the good news of the Gospel. From Marion, I will take the critique of conceptual idolatry and the notion of theology as a discourse grounded in a gift. Finally, Chauvet will provide an analysis of the symbolic order within which he situates the possibility of human conversion.

1. Jean-Pierre Jossua, The Condition of the Witness

The first negative moment we find in Jossua's book, *The Condition of the Witness,* is rejecting the notion of a Christian faith as a flight from the world. To do this is to ignore, if not reject, the Biblical tradition, which sees salvation as rooted firmly in actual human existence. It is real people, who encounter Jesus as he moves around Galilee, who experience his healing acceptance, and who come to follow him. Thus, to be Christian is to be human:

> Ultimately, "Christian" is never more than an adjective: it is applied to one and the same integral human subject who, on becoming a believer, can be considered and named from the perspective of faith. It is not that being human and being a Christian are purely and simply identical: there are

15. See G.J. HUGHES's analysis of Aquinas's analogical language in *Aquinas and the Limits of Agnosticism*, in G.J. HUGHES (ed.), *The Philosophical Assessments of Theology*, Washington, Kent & Georgetown University Press/Search Press, 1987, pp. 37-63.

16. By onto-theology are meant the approaches which aim at explaining the totality of being.

aspects of Christian experience which at particular moments go beyond what humanity understands by living, which is historical and even go beyond every intrinsic possibility of our species. However, these aspects are realised in human beings, so human beings must be capable of them, and that includes the unique achievement, unprecedented for a man, of being Son of God![17]

There are two ways of interpreting Jossua. Superficially it would be possible to detect in him a return to the Protestant liberalism of Harnack, the brotherhood of Jesus and the fatherhood of God[18]. So, when he writes, for example, "Brotherhood, gentleness, service, forgiveness, contagious peace, the purity of a tranquil heart, a concern for human dignity and justice, seem to me to represent the better things of this earth – provided that they are not based on the fear of pleasure and the rechanneling of aggression"[19], we might, with the possible exception of the exceptive clause at the end, be reading any exponent of *fin-de-siècle* liberal Protestantism.

Yet this would remain a superficial reading of Jossua. His book is not just about the nice side of Christianity, for to be a witness (*martyros*) is not simply about what is nice, but about the possibility of rejection, of suffering, of failure. Rather, we can see Jossua as being much more closely related to the apophatic tradition of Gregory. The quotation above shows how important it is for Jossua that we are human beings – we do not come to(wards) God despite our humanity but because of it, through it. This journey is one in which we travel as mediated and limited yet as infinitely blessed, bringing our humanity into God (and Jossua quotes the old Patristic dictum "That which is not assumed is not saved"). Jossua in his language echoes themes which were considered in Gregory's accounts of our journey towards God, which does not remove the difference between the *adiasthematicity* of God and *diasthematicity* of us creatures[20], but precisely allows us to bring all our createdness into God. Jossua emphasizes that this full embracing of humanity, in all its variety and with all its challenges, is something which we see in Jesus of Nazareth, and from this angle, he reads the story of God becoming a man. He says that among the things which make Jesus of Nazareth an unforgettable

17. J.P. JOSSUA, *The Condition of the Witness*, London, SCM, 1985, p. 36.
18. See, A. VON HARNACK, *What is Christianity?*, London, Williams & Norgate, 1904, p. 305. A. Loisy critisized this position as a "sentimental-filial confidence in God, the merciful Father" (A. LOISY, *The Gospel and the Church*, Philadelphia, PA, Fortress Press, 1976, pp. 14-15).
19. JOSSUA, *Witness* (n. 17), p. 33.
20. *Diasthematicity* is the term used by Gregory with reference to creation. By it he means spreading through time, moving from the past to the future. God is for Gregory *adiasthematic*; uncircumscribed by time.

figure is his "acceptance of the other as he or she is, no matter what. Here we find pity – an admirable word, degraded by condescension, rejected by wounded pride; but it is the word which expresses total understanding, total solidarity with the suffering of our kin"[21].

In Jossua, then, the apophatic element resides in his rejection of conceptual schemes of reality as the first referent to discuss the relationship between God and humanity. It is all too easy to become tied to the scheme and lose sight of the real person and indeed the real God who are in fact the bedrock of our reality. If we want to take incarnation seriously, and be witnesses to the incarnated God, we also have to take on ourselves the risk of history and humanity, the risk of the real relationships and situations we encounter, and thus allow a conversion to reality to happen, which ultimately is a conversion to God.

2. Jean-Luc Marion and the Critique of Conceptual Idolatry

We can start our investigation of Jean-Luc Marion by drawing attention to his use of the concept of *epektasis* which we saw previously in Gregory, who himself took it from Phil 3,13. This striving towards God plays an important role also for Marion, even if he emphasizes more its eschatological dimension – an anticipation of the future, which is concretely lived[22]. Marion employs the concept of *epektasis* when he speaks about the eucharist, which, according to him, "constitutes the first fragment of the new creation", and which "anticipates what we will be, will see, will love... facing the gift that we cannot yet welcome, so, in strict sense, that we cannot yet figure", and he concludes with a quotation from Proust: "In this way, 'sometimes the future lives in us without our knowledge of it'"[23].

The reason for this in Marion is also closely linked to one of Gregory's themes, especially in his anti-Eunomian works, namely the critique of absolute concepts. Gregory rejected Eunomius' fixing on unbegottenness or uncreatedness as the absolute names for God, as if in calling God unbegotten all that could be said about God had been said. Marion does not fix on this concept but his critique is perhaps even more radical. For he criticises the very concept of Being. This echoes Lossky's definition of apophaticism, where he emphasizes that in following this way, "One finally excludes being itself. God is none of all this"[24]. Marion argues that

21. JOSSUA, *Witness* (n. 17), p 34.
22. See J.-L. MARION, *God Without Being*, Chicago, IL – London, University of Chicago Press, 1991, p. 174.
23. MARION, *God Without Being* (n. 22), p. 174; he quotes M. PROUST, *À la recherche du temps perdu*, Paris, Pléiade, 2, 1954, p. 639.
24. LOSSKY, *Orthodox Theology* (n. 7), p. 32.

being runs the risk of becoming an idol for us. It is possible to forget the infinite depths of God and ignore it or seek to reduce it to something manageable by applying the concept of being. With that, we hope to define or measure the dimensions of God – God is like other being, only infinitely so. However, that Marion is, perhaps unwittingly, operating in the same apophatic tradition as Gregory is clear from the way in which he distinguishes the idol from the icon:

> in the idol, the reflex of the mirror distinguishes the visible from that which exceeds the aim…; in the icon, the visible is deepened infinitely in order to accompany, as one may say, each point of the invisible by a point of light. But visible and invisible thus coexist to infinity… The invisible of the icon consists of the intention of the face. The more the face becomes visible, the more the invisible intention whose gaze envisages us becomes visible. Better: the visibility of the face allows the invisibility that envisages to grow[25].

And the problem with the idol is this: "[it] places its centre of gravity in a human gaze; thus, dazzled as it may be by the brilliance of the divine, the gaze still remains in possession of the idol, its solitary master"[26]. In other words, the infinite transcendence and otherness and incomprehensibility of God is reduced to the finite and ultimately false security of the known.

It is not just sight that enables us to (not) know God, but also language. One of Marion's key arguments is that, paradoxically, any attempt to speak about God in definitively constructed propositions will always end up in the disappearance from our conversation of silence: "[t]he surprising thing, therefore, is not our difficulty in speaking of God but indeed our difficulty in keeping silent"[27].

So, if the human condition is one which is prone to idolatry, how are we to set about freeing ourselves from this temptation? What is necessary, for Marion, is ultimately a conversion, a line, which was present in Gregory and which Lossky summarizes as follows: "in His own nature He is the unknowable. He 'is not'. But here is the Christian paradox; He is the God to whom I say 'Thou', Who calls me, Who reveals Himself as personal, as living"[28]. For Marion this conversion is from one of seeking to talk about God to one where, in silence, God is allowed to speak, to reveal himself. And when God is allowed to do this, then the human being is allowed to accept this revelation as gift and respond

25. MARION, *God Without Being* (n. 22), p. 20.
26. *Ibid.*, p. 24.
27. *Ibid.*, p. 55.
28. LOSSKY, *Orthodox Theology* (n. 7), p. 32.

adequately to the giver, in charity and in holiness. "In short, *theology cannot aim at any other progress than its own conversion to the Word*"[29].

Acceptance of this Word, of its revelation, according to Marion, is possible only when we acknowledge it as a gift and respond in thanks to the giver. So it is not surprising that at the heart of Marion's work is a reflection on the eucharistic role of theology[30]. Compared to Gregory, Marion is more concerned with the community than with the individual. For him the community is always engaged in a journey (always and necessarily in some sense unsuccessful or at least incomplete) towards an encounter with the face of the Lord[31]. And here the notion of *epektasis* returns. For this journey is indeed always incomplete, the receiving community does not have (never will have) the final full presence of God under its control. To do this would be to reduce God again to an idol[32]. To accept God in his fullness is to relinquish all hope of ever encountering God in his fullness. Receiving of the gift transforms us, but it does not destroy either the otherness of the giver or the reality of human spatio-temporal existence. It is not that in the moment of receiving the gift we are temporarily removed from the limits of human existence, but rather that we bring our createdness to God and it is that createdness which receives the gift. Here again Marion and Gregory are in close agreement.

The danger always remains that in attempting to name God or to conceptualise God, God is somehow made smaller, reduced to a more manageable reality, which will serve as an excuse to escape from our actual day-to-day reality. However, the gift is not about escape, but about entering into the holiness and charity of the given moment:

> The eucharistic presence comes to us, at each instant, as the gift of that very instant, and, in it, of the body of the Christ in whom one must be incorporated. The temporal present during which the eucharistic present endures resembles it: as a glory haloes an iconic apparition, time is made a present gift to let us receive it in the eucharistically given present"[33].

So, the journey of conversion (what Gregory calls "spiritual progress") is stressed, the impermanency of the traveller in place of the permanency

---

29. MARION, *God Without Being* (n. 22), p. 158.
30. *Ibid.*, p. 163.
31. *Ibid.*, p. 165.
32. Within this discussion Marion situates his critique of the theory of transubstantiation, see *ibid.*, p. 168.
33. *Ibid.*, p. 175.

which no longer perceives any need for conversion. We have received the first gift, of sustenance on the journey, but not the second, if gift it is, of a final and permanent resting place where all striving is over.

3. *Louis-Marie Chauvet and Human Conversion within a Symbolic Order*[34]

As with Marion, Chauvet is concerned with a critique of any attempt to imprison reality within conceptual schemes[35]. He argues that there is a tendency on the part of metaphysicians to understand being as their stock-in-trade. But in doing that they are prone to forget that being is also an event in which something is revealed to us and that therefore the event is one which remains dynamic. The underlying reason for this dynamic is, according to Chauvet, grace, which he sees as irreducible, "always preceding and necessitated by nothing"[36]. Heavily influenced by Heidegger, he speaks of being as a fundamental openness, "an attitude of listening and welcome towards something ungraspable by which we are already grasped; ... a gracious attitude of "letting be" and "allowing oneself to be spoken" which requires renouncing all ambition for mastery"[37]. The symbolic language which we need to talk about being will have to include the features of being mentioned above.

Thus it is that Chauvet gets to his symbolic order, one based on grace, and within which our existence is situated. Lossky, from an Orthodox perspective, speaks of the dialectics between the apophatic and kataphatic traditions. Chauvet, from a Western perspective, says much the same thing using, however, the language of the presence and absence of God. For him, this dialectic plays a crucial role in our conversion on the journey towards God, as it does for Gregory.

In order to illustrate this point, Chauvet has recourse to the story of the disciples on the road to Emmaus. In his interpretation the key question is

---

34. For a more detailed analysis of Chauvet's position, see my article *The Symbolic Nature of Existence according to Ricœur and Chauvet*, in *Communio Viatorum* 43 (2001/1) 39-59.

35. Yet, in contrast to Marion, Chauvet does not hold a strong category of presence, but rather a dialectics presence-absence, see S. VAN DEN BOSSCHE, *God Does Appear In Immanence After All: Jean-Luc Marion's Phenomenology as a New First Philosophy for Theology*, in L. BOEVE – L. LEIJSSEN (eds.), *Sacramental Presence in a Postmodern Context* (BETL, 160), Leuven, Leuven University Press – Peeters, 2001, pp. 325-346.

36. L.-M. CHAUVET, *Symbol and Sacrament: A Sacramental Reinterpretation of Christian Existence*, Collegeville, MN, The Liturgical Press, 1995, p. 446.

37. *Ibid.*, p. 446.

"How does one pass from non-faith to faith?"[38]. As Gregory did with Moses[39], Chauvet here uses a narrative theology, or at least a theology based on a concrete story. Thus, his speculation can be rooted in a particular experience. He is especially interested in how this conversion happens. The disciples on the road are in the sealed tomb where they think Jesus's dead body lies. They have abandoned hope, abandoned all they had experienced previously. They are people without a future[40].

The first feature of conversion is the transition from a closed relationship between two people to an open one involving three. The two open themselves up to a stranger. He enters into conversation with them, and lets them name their situation, lets them tell their story. He first appeals to their memory, then makes a link with the Scriptures: "remember ... slow of heart, all that the prophets have declared, everything must be fulfilled"[41] and offers a rereading of all the Scriptures[42]. Chauvet says, "Instead of holding forth with self-assured pronouncements on God, one must begin by listening to a word as the word of God. The reference to the Scriptures as a third agency plays a role that is of capital importance here. In allowing Jesus to open the Scriptures for them, the two disciples begin to enter into an understanding of the real, different from that which they had previously thought evident"[43]. They urge the stranger to stay, and in his breaking of the bread, when his word becomes flesh, their eyes begin to open; they recognize the stranger in his radical strangeness. But their eyes open to an emptiness: he has vanished from their sight. It is, however, an emptiness full of presence. The disciples recognise the Risen Lord, they receive it as a gift of the good news and return it as a gift in terms of Christian witness. Chauvet emphasises that one is not possible without the other. Here he is in close agreement with Jossua: "In the last analysis, faith can only exist if it expresses itself in a life of witness"[44].

This conversion does not aim at removing the experience of absence or emptiness or of not being able to grasp, but neither does it make that its highest point. As with Gregory's critique of Eunomius, it is not a question of the negative being better than the positive, replacing one hegemony

---

38. *Ibid.*, p. 161.
39. See GREGORY OF NYSSA, *The Life of Moses*, New York – Ramsey – Toronto, Paulist Press, 1978.
40. CHAUVET, *Symbol and Sacrament* (n. 36), p. 168.
41. Luke 24,6.25-27.
42. See Luke 24,44-45.
43. CHAUVET, *Symbol and Sacrament* (n. 36), p. 168.
44. *Ibid.*, p. 169.

with another. Rather it is the recognition that the privileged place of his presence is at the same time the most radical mediation of his absence[45].

This fact Chauvet applies to the Church as the corporal expression of Christianity. Too often the Church or Christians have sought to witness to the gospel, to the truth of salvation, to the gift of faith, as something which they have and which others do not have. Thus, we become the masters, the possessors of the answer to those who may or may not realize that they have a question. But at the heart of what Chauvet is arguing is that we remain always witnesses of some(thing) which we cannot have. And this is precisely what is constitutive of grace. We are enabled to belong by grace, but grace also means that the dynamics of belonging are such that we do not have (and radically, that is to say, definitively do not have) that to which we belong. We witness to it, and our witness is to that towards which we move, not that within which we already are.

IV. CONCLUSION

In conclusion, then, I wish to draw together some of the apophatic aspects of theological conversation. The basic need which has been clear in different ways in Gregory, Jossua, Marion and Chauvet is for permanent conversion. As in the New Testament[46], also here the conversion – *metanoia* – is more than a single movement, single action. It is a part of the whole of our communication with God as well as with people and with the whole of creation. Such communication includes all human activities, their glory, as well as their subjection to a falling away from what they could be, subject to *hamartia*, sin, a failure to hit their target, to achieve their objectives.

This conversion of communication is needed in several areas. First, as we have seen, there is a fundamental need to recognize that none of us is the owner of the mystery we talk about. There is no them and us in this sense. Neither theologians nor Christians in general are the controllers and owners of the Christian message, and even less of the mystery of God become human in Jesus Christ. We all participate in the mystery, but we cannot hope to give a definitive account of it. All we can (but also therefore what we must) do is witness to it.

Secondly, there is the need to remember that we are on this journey towards God, experiencing this *epektasis*, this striving and straining for

45. *Ibid.*, p. 509.
46. See Matt 4,17; Mark 1,15; Luke 13,3; 15,7; Acts 2,38; 3,19; 17,30 etc.

God. But this straining and striving is not some temporary state, which would be overcome when we get better. It is at the heart of what it is to be human, and what it is to be human does not end with death. Our journey towards the infinite otherness and transcendence of God is itself a never-ending one, one of progress with others on the way, but never arriving, as the disciples on the road to Emmaus never really get home. Every moment of recognition, of seeing, is a moment of non-recognition, of not-seeing. The journey continues without end.

Finally, there is a time for speaking and a time for being silent. Of the first we are perhaps already sufficiently aware. But, of course, communication, if it is to be communication and not simply one way information transfer, must involve dialogue. And dialogue means silence on one side while there is talking on the other. So, if we are not to silence others and not to silence God, we must learn ourselves to keep silence, and in so doing, we may also learn to talk[47].

Protestant Theological Faculty   Ivana NOBLE (DOLEJSOVA)
Charles University
P.O. Box 529, Černá 9
115 55 Prague 1
Czech Republic

---

47. This point is elaborated in my book *Accounts of Hope: A Problem of Method in Postmodern Apologia*, Bern – Berlin – Bruxelles, Peter Lang, 2001.

IN CONVERSATION WITH THE PAST?

RICŒUR, THEOLOGY, AND THE DYNAMICS OF HISTORY

I. INTRODUCTION

One of the tasks of philosophy of religion is the critical examination of current religious concepts. As part of this task, I will examine the concept of conversation in theology, focusing on the idea of a conversation with the past.

As a starting point for this examination, we need a definition of the notion of conversation. For the moment, I leave the field of theology aside and turn to a recent encyclopaedia of rhetoric. According to the lemma concerned, conversation may be defined as "the art of keeping company, which is devoted to the physical and mental representation of oneself, in contact with others"[1]. I use this definition as a starting point for our examination, because it summarizes in a few words some notions that we, intuitively, associate with conversation. Of course, conversation has to do with talking, with dialogical interaction. However, a conversation is open to more than two participants, and hence we should not limit conversation to the pattern of dialogue. Furthermore, a conversation has a distinctively temporal structure. A conversation may be deepened; it may lose momentum, or become stronger. A conversation is a linguistic relation, developed in time. Conversation is also more than the exchange of linguistic messages; it is an art, it is a praxis that can be developed. Moreover, conversation is more than an exchange of words. It is just as much a matter of body language. Even more fundamentally: conversation has to do with the representation of ourselves to others, and the representation of others in our world of living. All these facets are summarized in the above definition.

The question for systematic theology is whether this notion of conversation occupies a place in theology. By examining the idea of a conversation with the past, I intend to make a contribution to this question.

---

1. "...die Kunst des Umgangs, die sich der körperlich-geistigen Repräsentation des Selbst im Kontakt mit dem bzw. den anderen widmet", K.-H. GÖTTERT, *Konversation*, in G. UEDING (ed.), *Historisches Wörterbuch der Rhetorik, Bd. 4*, Tübingen, Max Niemeyer, 1998, pp. 1322-1333, esp. 1322.

This goal may raise some questions, for it seems obvious that there is a place for conversation in theology. There is, at least, a pressing need for dialogue and conversation, as opposed to violence. As the many religious conflicts today demonstrate, conversation is highly desirable. It is not only desirable; there are even good reasons to assume that conversation is a necessary notion for theology, as the many case-studies of this conference attempt to show.

Still, there is a need for critical examination of this issue. I consider the widespread use of the notion of conversation as an argument for consideration. Every accepted notion is open to critical and systematic examination. My contribution to such an examination does not consist merely of a conceptual analysis. I will rather proceed by focusing upon the aspect of representation. Our definition uses representation as a main characteristic of conversation. Conversation is representation in relationships; it has to do with the art of keeping company. Consequently, our examination should focus on the possibility of keeping company and establishing a relation of representation. To this end, I propose the field of history as an area of thought in which the possibility of representation and company is put to the test. History is pertinent to our question, because it does not exclude the possibility of conversation *a priori*, but also shapes our awareness of the difficulties of keeping company. Though a conversation does not need complete understanding, there must be a certain common ground, to which the conversation partners can refer. On the one hand, such a familiarity may be supposed to exist in one's past, the tradition to which someone belongs. On the other hand, one may doubt whether any familiarity exists in a conversation with the past. For how can one be in touch with something that is, by definition, not present?

This dilemma forms the subject matter of this paper. We will first consider some arguments for and against the possibility of a conversation with the past (§2). Once these arguments are presented, we turn to the field of philosophy of history, as treated in a recent book by Paul Ricœur (§3). The materials of this book will lead us to a final section on conversation and theology (§4).

II. IN CONVERSATION WITH THE PAST: ARGUMENTS PRO AND CON

In favour of the notion of a conversation with the past, one could argue that such a conversation is both desirable and necessary. Conversation with the past is highly desirable, especially after events of war and terror, when the question arises as to what we can learn from the past.

Every commemoration of war expresses: never again. Such use of history is a matter of formative education[2]. We may learn from the faults and errors of the past for our present and future political decisions. One may demand from political leaders a certain predilection for the past. If one should learn from the past, there must be an intense exchange. Conversation with the past is, for a large part, an instructive discourse. Reading historical sources and talking with witnesses broaden the individual memory into a collective memory[3]. The contribution of such witnesses is an edifying experience, highly needed, especially in the formation of youth.

We can go even one step further by stating that conversation with the past is not only desirable, but also necessary; one cannot escape communication with history. An entire current of historicism has given us at the very least the conviction that history is more than an illustration of general insights. History does matter. We are, as Wilhelm Schapp put it, "entangled in histories"[4]. Schapp comes to this insight from a Heideggerian approach. When being has a history, the human being reflects this character and is full of stories and history. This perspective replaces the traditional, metaphysical perception of being and nature. Thus, it becomes essential for recent postmodernism that there is "nothing but history", as the title of a book by David Roberts puts it[5]. We cannot surpass the bonds and dynamics of history in any supra-historical structure or conception. In other words, history determines our nature and identity[6]. To a large extent we are formed by what the past has brought to us. History also provides a wide spectrum of role models, alternative forms of behaviour and patterns of experience. Paul Ricœur once spoke of narrative as a "laboratory of forms"[7]. A narrative provides us with possible forms of behaviour that we can explore by reading, more than we could do by our own living. History is part of narrative, in this respect. It offers patterns of action by which we can be shaped and transformed.

Despite this intertwining of history and human existence, we can raise many arguments against the notion of a conversation with the past, as

2. Cf. K. REPGEN, Vom Nutzen der Historie, in A. FÖSSEL – C. KAMPMANN (eds.), Wozu Historie heute? Beiträge zu einer Standortbestimmung im fachübergreifenden Gespräch (Bayreuther historische Kolloquien, 10), Köln, Böhlau, 1996, pp. 167-183.
3. Cf. M. HALBWACHS, La mémoire collective, Paris, PUF, 1968, pp. 36-37.
4. W. SCHAPP, In Geschichten verstrickt, Wiesbaden, Heymann, 1976.
5. D.D. ROBERTS, Nothing But History. Reconstruction and Extremity after Metaphysics, Berkeley, CA, University of California Press, 1995.
6. Cf. H. LÜBBE, Identität durch Geschichte, in ID., Geschichtsbegriff und Geschichtsinteresse. Analytik und Pragmatik der Historie, Basel – Stuttgart, Schwalbe, 1977, pp. 145-154.
7. P. RICŒUR, Soi-même comme un autre, Paris, Seuil, 1990, p. 139.

well. I note three problematic areas. The first has to do with a general crisis in philosophy concerning the possibilities of representation. How can we conceive "real presences" in our culture, which has become weary with over-extensive metacriticism? It is clear that new ways should be sought to overcome these problems of metacriticism[8]. This problem is a critical one, especially in theology[9].

A second field of problems relates to the idea of history. In 1992, for example, Francis Fukuyama formulated his insight in "the end of history"[10]. His argument leant heavily on the insights of earlier philosophers like Derrida, Foucault, and Baudrillard. With their sharp deconstructions, they have exposed the impossibility of any ideology-free view of history. What the postmodernists have revealed is the impossibility of establishing ends in history. History has no end. At most it has ends. Or perhaps the singular "history" is wrong itself. There are only many histories with many ends. If we may question the possibility of representation in our first area of problems, we are now confronted with the question whether there *is* something to be represented. Do we have the possibility of conceiving history as our partner in conversation, when there is no singular concept of history with a clear goal?

A third problem relates to the notion of conversation. This notion meets the same critical approach of postmodernists as the notion of history[11]. The notion of conversation rests upon at least three assumptions. First, conversation or dialogue has to do with intentional speech; but it is precisely the use of intentional meaning in speech that may be fundamentally deconstructed as an arbitrary act. Second, conversation is a form of oral discourse. Hermeneutics and deconstruction have taught us to be suspicious of the supposed directness of oral communication. At least there are good reasons to separate oral and written discourse. One can even posit the primacy of written discourse in regard to oral discourse. However, the living presence of a speaker in words and in body disappears in written discourse. Third, conversation depends upon an idea of mutuality. Again, it is deconstruction that has brought into hermeneutics the creative function of ruptures and the far more intricate kinds of relation that govern meaning. Dialogical philosophy has appeared to be a naïve notion that cannot stand the test of critical analysis. Conversation is not so immediate and

8. Cf. G. STEINER, *Real Presences. Is There Anything In What We Say?*, London – Boston, Faber & Faber, 1989.

9. Cf. L. BOEVE – L. LEIJSSEN (eds.), *Sacramental Presence in a Postmodern Context* (BETL, 160), Leuven, Leuven University Press – Peeters, 2001.

10. F. FUKUYAMA, *The End of History and the Last Man,* London, Hamilton, 1992.

11. Cf. the article of Lieven Boeve in this volume, pp. 189-209.

innocent as it might seem at first sight. How can we then conceive of any "keeping company", except in a derived sense? If the notion of conversation can be maintained only with the help of analogies and derivations, we should at least look for other notions that are more suitable, and perhaps even drop the possibility of direct company altogether[12].

Even if one does not accept post-modern criticism, there are good reasons to maintain that conversation is at least an unworkable notion for philosophical analysis. This is John Searle's contribution to the subject matter as a philosopher of language. Regarding speech act analysis, the notion of conversation cannot be approached in a satisfactory manner[13]. The main problem for any speech act analysis is, that the response to a speech act within a conversation cannot be explained from the intention of the initial speech act alone. We need to refer to the conversational context. However, this leads to an infinite order of regression. This regression can only be stopped by assuming an unintentional background, which lies outside the capacity of speech act analysis. I note that speech act analysis already falters at the regressive movement of conversation. This is to say nothing of the progressive movement of conversation, which seems to lie completely outside the realm of speech act analysis, but is such an essential component of conversation. If conversation is a philosophical reality, then we may conclude that it is rather a phenomenon beyond analysis than a notion to be used as a conceptual model.

Our hesitation concerning the notions of history and conversation makes us reluctant to posit the idea of a conversation with the past. So many questions arise in connection with the two words, all centred on the idea of representation. For how can the past be represented? One can speak with older people as witnesses of times past. However, one speaks to persons in the present. At most, these persons symbolise the past. They make present a former reality. Strictly speaking, this is not a conversation with the past; it is a conversation with present persons, who manifest traces from the past. Only the traces are present, not the acts of speakers from the past. How can we have a mutual relation to someone or something (a text, an archaeological source) that is not present itself? We can develop some mutual relation to a text. Gadamer's idea of a fusion of horizons between text and reader is based upon such a relation.

---

12. Against the basic idea of, e.g., H.-G. GADAMER, *Wahrheit und Methode. Grundzüge einer philosophischen Hermeneutik*, Tübingen, Mohr, ⁶1990; W.C. BOOTH, *The Company We Keep. An Ethics of Fiction*, Berkeley, CA, University of California Press, 1988.

13. J. SEARLE, *Conversation*, in ID., *et al.* (eds.), *(On) Searle on Conversation*, Amsterdam, John Benjamins, 1992, 7-29.

However, as readers, we only approach a present text, or a present archaeological finding. The past only achieves a sense of presence through interpretive acts. These acts establish a presence in the present, with which we can keep company; but we can only imagine that we reach the past through this company. The original speakers or agents have disappeared from our imaginative company and we miss the mutuality to them that is essential for a real conversation.

I can only imagine the idea of conversation as an analogical notion. However, the question arises then whether there are other notions to be put forward that better conceptualise the intention of relating human beings in the present to the meaning of the past. There are many such notions. My relation to the past can be viewed as looking in a mirror. The mirror of the past is a common metaphor, which does not possess the connotations of mutuality and presence implied by the notion of conversation, while it does express the close-knit connections of past and observer[14]. Another possibility is the idea of remembrance[15]. The past can be remembered in the present. Related to this notion is the metaphor of traces of the past that must be found and valuated by remembrance in the present. A fundamentally ethical aspect is attached to the idea of remembrance. Remembrance becomes a task, a duty of reordering, re-membering the traces that have been dispersed[16]. One could also present the notion of an inheritance that comes from the past to present heirs[17]. Such models displace a clear awareness of a relation to the past, without the problems of the idea of keeping company. We commemorate, because the persons to be remembered do not live anymore. We receive an inheritance, only because the testator has passed away and is not present anymore.

14. Cf. F.R. ANKERSMIT, *De spiegel van het verleden. Exploraties I: Geschiedtheorie*, Kampen, Kok Agora; Kapellen, Pelckmans, 1996.
15. Cf. the position of remembrance in culture in O.G. OEXLE (ed.), *Memoria als Kultur* (Veröffentlichungen des Max Planck-Instituts für Geschichte, 121), Göttingen, Vandenhoeck & Ruprecht, 1995; J. ASSMANN, *Das kulturelle Gedächtnis. Schrift, Erinnerung und politische Identität in frühern Hochkulturen*, München, Beck, 1992. For remembrance as a subversive notion: W. BENJAMIN, *Geschichtsphilosophische Thesen*, in his *Zur Kritik der Gewalt und andere Aufsätze*, Frankfurt a. M., Suhrkamp, 1965, pp. 78-94; for theology J.B. METZ, *Glaube in Geschichte und Gesellschaft. Studien zu einer praktischen Fundamentaltheologie*, Mainz, Matthias-Grünewald Verlag, 1977.
16. E. WYSCHOGROD, *An Ethics of Remembering. History, Heterology, and the Nameless Others* (Religion and Postmodernism), Chicago, IL, University of Chicago Press, 1998.
17. E.g., in the philosophy of E. BLOCH. Cf. the collection of his *Religion im Erbe. Eine Auswahl aus seinen religionsphilosophischen Schriften*, München – Hamburg, Siebenstern, 1959, and esp. the preface of J. MOLTMANN, pp. 7-14. Recently, H.J. ADRIAANSE, *After Theism*, in H. KROP et al. (eds.), *Post-theism. Reframing the Judeao-Christian Tradition*, Leuven, Peeters, 2000, pp. 33-61, esp. 44-59.

Now, when such excellent alternative notions and metaphors are available, the idea of a conversation with the past might fade into the background of philosophical and theological interest. Nevertheless, something may be said in favour of the idea of a conversation with the past. However, we should not look for a clear model of interaction to be applied, but rather for some inherent traits in history. At this point, philosophical analysis receives a new function, in describing a dynamic that otherwise remains hidden from view.

III. Ricœur: Memory, History, Oblivion

I commence a philosophical search for the dynamic of conversation with history by turning to a recent book of Ricœur: *La mémoire, l'histoire, l'oubli*[18]. This book is suitable for our search because Ricœur shows a refined sensitivity into the many layers of philosophical interest into history. There are at least three levels of thinking in the philosophy of history. I will go through these levels and mention the possibilities of conversation in them.

Ricœur starts his treatment of a philosophy of history with a phenomenology of remembrance. It seems to be a general feature of human existence to grasp the past by remembering. The phenomenological questions that Ricœur raises concern the "what?", "how?", and "who?" of remembering. In examining the "what?" of remembering Ricœur comes upon the large gap between past and present. The idea of representation is a fundamental problem. The past cannot be made present sufficiently. Concerning the "how?" of remembering, Ricœur discusses a wide repertory of mnemonic devices developed in human culture. These devices, however, also show the danger of remembering. Memory is abused for all kinds of political aims[19]. There is a large distance between present and past, and any forced use of mnemonics increases that distance rather than establishes a firm connection between the two. This conclusion leads Ricœur once more to the importance of inquiring into the "who?" of remembering. At this point, Ricœur is faced with the dilemma of individual and collective memory. What has the primacy in remembering:

---

18. P. Ricœur, *La mémoire, l'histoire, l'oubli* (L'ordre philosophique), Paris, Seuil, 2000.

19. There are many places in the book where Ricœur shows his aversion to public commemorations with a political view, e.g., *La mémoire*, pp. 110-111 and pp. 532-535 (following Pierre Nora).

the individual or the collective? Ricœur introduces a third notion: the neighbour. The category of the neighbour forms an intermediate level between individual and collective. It is on this level that a human being is confirmed in his or her existence[20].

This is also the point where our interest into a conversation with history takes hold. The questions as to "what" and "how" only stress the distance from the past and the abusive attempts of surpassing that distance. The question as to the "who" of remembering leads us to a certain reciprocity. The remembering subject must be confirmed in his or her identity as remembering agent. This is fulfilled in contacts with neighbours, who have the ability to address the remembering subject in his or her essence. This reciprocity comes close to our notion of conversation.

There is however, another level in the philosophy of history, in which the pendulum switches to the side of distanciation. This is the level of historiographic epistemology. From the field of testimony we turn to a field of notions like representation and truth. The "historical operation", the act of the historiographer, is, as these word-fields show, very different from the act of remembering. It is an operation with different aims, namely the aim of documentation, explication, and, finally, representation[21]. While the first two steps receive most of the historians' interest, the methodological *pièce de resistance* is given in the notion of representation. Here lies the frequently hidden claim of a historian that his methods allow him to deal with hard facts. When Ricœur places representation as a third step, after the operations of documentation and explication, it may be clear that the idea of representation has lost any connotation of primary, directly accessible facts. Rather than using the term representation, Ricœur turns, consequently, to the word *représentance*, "representation by replacement"[22]. Representation is an act of replacement, *lieutenance*. As such, it does not deal with bare facts, but rather with a narrative framework. The historian displays a certain representative tendency, which marks his or her work.

I must admit that I see few possibilities for conversation in this representative tendency. Clearly, history cannot deal with bare facts; it is a triple act, unfolded in a horizon of representative tendency. This situation asks for an explicative model like conversation. For conversation has to do with an intention, a tendency of representation over against others, as our initial definition put it. However, as regards the level of epistemology,

---

20. RICŒUR, *La mémoire* (n. 18), p. 161.
21. A tripartition of history by Michel de Certeau.
22. RICŒUR, *La mémoire* (n. 18), pp. 359-369.

I see rather the wish for a conversation-like model than the possibility of grounding the notion of conversation.

Ricœur turns to a third level, the hermeneutical level that considers the possibilities of understanding behind the historiographic act. Here we enter the realm of the historical condition of human existence. Ricœur uses elements of Heidegger's *Sein und Zeit* in order to describe the existentials of this historical existence. He brings in an emphasis of his own by contradicting any tendency to totalization on this level. The fundamental term of this part is oblivion. Oblivion is a regretful circumstance; sometimes it has the form of enforced amnesia, but there is also a form of happy forgetfulness, which forms a counterpart to the claims of memory. Thus, the historical act is placed between the poles of memory and oblivion. Their interaction constantly determines the possibilities and limits of history. The notion of oblivion undermines the ideal of communication. The historian constantly encounters the fact that he or she must communicate extremes from history that simply are too harsh for words. Dark events like "Auschwitz" cannot be put to words, yet they still need to be told. They are, as Ricœur puts it, not transmittable, but that does not imply that they should be not speakable[23]. However, other modes of speaking must be sought. Ricœur calls them the optative mode, or the eschatological mode. Between the poles of remembrance and forgetfulness, the historical speaking is bereaved of its naiveté, and is forced to search other languages, in a tempered mode of speaking, *sotto voce*.

This tempered mode of appeasement finally leads Ricœur to the subject of forgiving. Forgiveness as such is not the object of the historian's interest. Ricœur is, using an analysis of Derrida, very sceptical about the possibility of forgiveness. One cannot shape a "politics of forgiveness". Still, an agent can be called to account for his deeds. Moreover, he or she may be addressed on account of his or her identity behind the acts committed. As for Ricœur, that final address is the only way to forgiving. Speaking about agency must be left aside in order to address the issue of regeneration. An agent of evil deeds must be disassociated from his or her deeds to become another person. A voice from the past must address the agent on a basic potentiality: "tu vaux mieux que tes actes", you are worth better than your deeds[24]. Certainly, this is not a simple manner of forgiving. But, given the impossibility of forgiveness as an act that restores former deeds, it is the only way out of revenge and exasperation.

23. *Ibid.*, p. 584.
24. *Ibid.*, p. 642.

I refer to the communicative aspect of forgiving here. Ricœur presents forgiveness as a matter of an address to an agent. There is no simple dialogue with the past, but there comes a voice from history that addresses a human being concerning capacities that go deeper than his or her deeds. That comes close to an idea of conversation. However, it is a conversation without an imperative mode. It is a deep voice, behind the horrible acts of the past. It is a voice that only sounds in an optative mode. It is, in other words, a horizon to which our speech orients itself, without actual fulfilment. It should not even be realised as a normal speech act. If history speaks to the heart, it cannot be ordered, manipulated into a politics of forgiveness. It necessarily has to remain a communicative address at a distance. However, it is an address that so strongly asks for a response, that I cannot do other than relate the word conversation to it. We can view it, in other words, as a "conversational move", a communicative address that asks for response.

If we should envisage a conversation with the past, it is on this fundamental level of addressing an identity beyond common agency, only. This is, to paraphrase Ricœur, a non-transmittable range, but not a range without speaking – and not without a move towards conversation, either, we add. What is more, we have now reached a conversational move that is necessarily without present aspects. Only this form of conversation, as a voice from the dark, not to be reached, can offer a real contact with the past as past, without presence in the present.

IV. CONCLUSION: THEOLOGY AND THE CONVERSATION WITH THE PAST

It is interesting to note that, once Ricœur treats the possibilities of a speech of forgetfulness and of forgiving, all kinds of biblical allusions emerge. Throughout the book, we read of Ecclesiastes, the Song of Songs, 1 Corinthians 13, or of remembrance and of forgiveness and repentance in the Abrahamitic religions. The mode of historical speaking, once history is brought under the pole of forgetfulness, is alluded to as an eschatological mode. This brings us to the question of how theology relates to the problem of conversation and history.

I know of one major theological proposal that accounts for both the possibilities and the limits of the notion of conversation in theology[25].

---

25. In this section, I pass over the proposal of W. PANNENBERG, Sprechakt und Gespräch, in his Anthropologie in theologischer Perspektive, Göttingen, Vandenhoeck, 1983, pp. 351-365. Cf. the volume of K. STIERLE – R. WARNING (eds.), Das Gespräch (Poetik und Hermeneutik), München, Wilhelm Fink, 1984, pp. 65-76. Pannenberg translates

I mean David Tracy's presentation of conversation as a model for theology in *Plurality and Ambiguity*[26]. For Tracy the model of conversation expresses the conviction that the essence of a human being as an interpreting being, emerges in questioning. "We learn to play the game of conversation when we allow questioning to take over. We learn when we allow the question to impose its logic, its demands, and ultimately its own rhythm upon us"[27]. We can converse with other people, but also, and this is the kernel of Tracy's hermeneutic, we can converse with texts. "In conversation we find ourselves by losing ourselves in the questioning provoked by the text"[28]. The most challenging conversation is given in interaction with the classical texts. Religion, as living with the classics, is, for that reason, the ultimate test of any hermeneutic. Thus, for Tracy, conversation is not a by-product of another interpretive move, but is essential for hermeneutics, both philosophical and theological. Tracy confronts this idea of conversation with the situation in culture as it is sketched by the postmodernists in words like plurality and ambiguity.

In his confrontation of conversation with these notions, the subject of history also comes up. For Tracy, the question of history is a form of most radical ambiguity[29]. He believes that the model of conversation can stand up to the test of history, even with all the forms of ideology-criticism that he is aware of. Nevertheless, it is remarkable that the word conversation itself hardly occurs in the chapter on history. When it occurs, it is in connection with the topic of interaction with the classics of a tradition. However, there is more to history than dealing with classical texts. Tracy does not provide us with insights into how to interact with past events and experiences. The past and history remain a form of otherness with which Tracy cannot adequately deal. For Tracy the consequences for interpretation of this otherness are put totally at the side of the interpreter. It is his or her identity that has to be transformed in order to understand the past. Ricœur's model of thinking history is more radical, in this sense that it also turns to history itself. Another voice in history has to be sought, another mode of speaking that comes history itself.

Gadamer's idea of successful conversation in interpretation to the act of conversation itself. A successful conversation gives way to a sense of wholeness, which transcends the intentions of the speakers. For Pannenberg, this transcendent move is a religious dimension of speech, an idea for which he is dependent upon Schleiermacher.

26. D. TRACY, *Plurality and Ambiguity. Hermeneutics, Religion, Hope*, San Francisco, CA, Harper & Row, 1987.

27. *Ibid.*, p. 18.

28. *Ibid.*, p. 19.

29. *Ibid.*, p. 66.

It is remarkable to notice that Tracy's book ends with a chapter on religion and hope. Ultimately, it is in the horizon of religious hope that fundamental meaning is created. This comes close to what Ricœur writes on the eschatological mode. In my opinion, however, Ricœur is more aware of the consequences of speaking from this mode on the possibilities of a conversation with the past. History is not a radical example of a cultural situation that can also be met in other forms of plurality and ambiguity. History is the phenomenon of ultimate otherness, which continuously puts traces of representation into human existence.

The dynamics of remembrance and forgetfulness that follow from the representative urge in history determine the possibilities and limits of the notion of conversation. Especially in theology, we should take these possibilities and limits seriously. The ultimate goal of theological thinking, as appears on account of the subject of history, is not a matter of enlightenment and emancipation, as Tracy likes to have it[30]. The task of theology is to search for a language of otherness in the phenomena of human existence and culture, using the symbols and experiences of the field of religion. The subject matter of a conversation with the past makes up the field *par excellence* to fulfil this task.

Faculteit der Godgeleerdheid   Theo L. HETTEMA
Universiteit Leiden
Postbus 9515
2300 RA Leiden
The Netherlands

30. *Ibid.*, p. 80.

THE END OF CONVERSATION IN THEOLOGY

CONSIDERATIONS FROM A POSTMODERN DISCUSSION

In this paper I will compare the concepts of conversation used by Jürgen Habermas, Jean François Lyotard and Richard Rorty. I will highlight in a particular way the discussions in which they have engaged one another. At the same time, I will attempt to evaluate the relevance and challenge of these concepts for contemporary fundamental theology. I will try to show that these concepts of conversation first of all teach us something about the present context and its critical consciousness, and also, more specifically, shed light on the use of concepts of "conversation" in Christian theology – the theme of this conference. My thesis runs as follows: the end of conversation in theology is that, at least at a certain stage, it should end.

For these three authors it is fair to say that their concept of conversation is crucial in their philosophical positions. First, it serves them as a reading key to evaluate the history of philosophy and the panorama of current philosophical thinking. Second, it helps them to develop their own thinking patterns, and to sustain their post-metaphysical claims, in positioning their thinking after the "linguistic turn" and in changing from a subjectocentric to an intersubjective focus. Rationality for them is grasped in language games and interactions between the participants in the conversation. These striking similarities, however, should not serve to disguise the deep differences between the three philosophers. Conversation is not only what unites them, but also what divides them. Moreover, it would seem that precisely the discussions they have had with one another, are most enlightening in our efforts to grasp what is at stake in our postmodern condition.

For theologians, there are at least two good reasons to delve into these discussions between Habermas, Lyotard and Rorty. *First of all*, in developing their diverse concepts of conversation all three – without exception – apply it to evaluate the state and future of Christianity in a negative way, each in this regard being more outspoken than the other. For theology it is important to have a clear perspective on the nature and background of these criticisms and to evaluate the way in which they affect Christianity. *Secondly*, according to its nature, fundamental theology is "fides quaerens intellectum" – faith in search of understanding – and it proceeds by relating to the prevailing critical consciousness, i.e. the contextual philosophical thinking patterns, to constitute this "intellectum". Changes in this contextual critical consciousness have urged theology time and again to "recontextualise": in order to be able to demonstrate its own plausibility and rationality theology needed to seek a new relation to the changed context and the rationality operating therein[1]. As all three of the philosophers under consideration claim that with their thinking a contextual change is occurring, an investigation into the possibilities they offer for a contemporary recontextualisation could offer new perspectives for a so-called "postmodern" theology, that is, a theology which relates to the postmodern context.

I. Conversation as Communication: Habermas' Attempt to Save the Modern Emancipatory Project

The point of departure of Jürgen Habermas' philosophical position is not the subject (as in modern philosophy), but intersubjective interaction. In this interaction, speakers seek mutual understanding and pronounce statements that make claims to validity. A consensus is reached if statements that are in principle amenable to critique are recognised intersubjectively as valid; this means that they are commonly received as either propositionally true (facts), normatively correct (ethical judgements), or subjectively authentic (self-expression). Because of the necessity of general consent, there is always the risk of dissent in communicative action. This risk, however, is considerably restricted in everyday language use by a massive background consensus, consisting of commonly shared, unproblematic convictions.

Habermas' appeal to communicative interaction stems from his programme to safeguard the inner bond between modernity and rationality and to defend the modern project against all critics who reject modernity-in-itself[2]. He therefore proposes an encompassing paradigm change[3].

1. For the concept of "recontextualisation", see L. BOEVE, *Interrupting Tradition: An Essay on Christian Faith in a Postmodern Context* (Louvain Theological and Pastoral Monographs, 30), Leuven, Peeters; Grand Rapids, MI, Eerdmans, 2002, chapter 1.
2. And this against those who plead for "das Andere der Vernunft", instead of a terroristic and violent (because logocentric and subject-centred) reason which is done away with; cf. J. HABERMAS, *Der philosophische Diskurs der Moderne*, Frankfurt am Main, Suhrkamp, 1985, p. 352 ff., with reference to H. BÖHME – G. BÖHME, *Das Andere der Vernunft: Zur Entwicklung von Rationalitätsstrukturen am Beispiel Kants*, Frankfurt am Main, Suhrkamp, 1983.
3. Habermas already treated this paradigm change in his reworking of Mead in his *Theorie des kommunikativen Handelns*, II, Frankfurt am Main, Suhrkamp, 1981, ³1985

He replaces the modern epistemological privilege of the subject and its knowledge of the object with a paradigm in which interpersonal relationship (communication) and consensus-formation are fundamental in the process of discerning cognitive, ethical and aesthetic truth claims. Thus, rationality no longer originates from subjectivity, but from intersubjectivity. He couples this transition with another, namely the move from a philosophy of consciousness to a philosophy of language, in which subject-object relationships are replaced by linguistic relationships. In this perspective, Habermas opts for a procedural rather than a material concept of rationality: post-metaphysical thought does not have any privileged access to the truth, but considers the conditions within which it can be validly discussed. With this, the primacy of theory over praxis is rejected and the pre-reflexive, everyday linguistic relationship is re-valued as the starting point of sound philosophical reflection. This also implies that reason is not acquired by abstraction from its historical, concrete embeddedness: in place of classical attributes, finitude and historicity function as its characteristics.

In daily communication, which is concentrated on consensus-formation, rationality can be discovered in the universal validity claims linguistically articulated in concrete dialogue (claims to propositional truth, normative correctness, and subjective authenticity, respectively) that aim at intersubjective recognition. This is no "reine Vernunft", but a rationality always incarnated in communication and in the structures of the lifeworld. Hence, this rationality never appears optimally but is always contaminated and infected, because it always stems from particularised conditions. Its validity claims appeal to a certain generality that is always contained in local contexts. However, it is not a transcendental consciousness leading to uniformity. It is rather the ever particularised prereflexive totality of traditions, solidarities and experiences of the "lifeworld" which functions as the source for the validity claims. To this extent, the "lifeworld" is not arbitrarily at the disposal of the subject, but is the pre-given background in which communication happens.

(chapter 5). He elaborates on the philosophical clarification of the paradigm change, not only in *Der philosophische Diskurs der Moderne* (n. 2), but likewise in *Nachmetaphysisches Denken. Philosophische Aufsätze* (Frankfurt am Main, Suhrkamp, 1988), especially in the articles: *Der Horizont der Moderne, verschiebt sich* (11-17), *Motive nachmetaphysischen Denkens* (35-60), the often cited *Handlungen, Sprechakte, sprachlich vermittelte Interaktionen und Lebenswelt* (63-104) and *Die Einheit der Vernunft in der Vielfalt ihrer Stimmen* (153-186), among others. What he demonstrates in the first two mentioned articles, he draws out in the philosophical development of his theory of communicative action: the lessons of the twentieth century rejection of metaphysics as identity-logical, totalising, subject-centred, logocentric theoretical thought.

Habermas considers this procedural communicative concept of rationality to be capable of defending the unity of reason in the multiplicity of its voices. He profiles it first against those who plead for recovering a pre-Kantian and/or metaphysical unitary thought. It is also contrasted against those who maintain irreducible multiplicity and radical contextualism, whereby claims do not transcend the local level. In this regard Habermas judges the postmodern attempts to save "difference" as structurally analogous to neo-conservative positions. In the end, postmodern philosophers of difference cannot hold on to the critical power that such thinking claims; irreducible multiplicity and radical contextualism then become functionalised as support for a neo-conservative ideology. For Habermas, the many voices can make claims to validity only within the irreducible framework of communicative (inter)action. The unity of reason is not the destruction but the source of its many voices. Normative universalism is not the deathblow but the guarantee of an advanced individualisation. Unity and multiplicity can only be held together dialectically. "For the transitory unity that is generated in the porous and refracted intersubjectivity of a linguistically mediated consensus not only supports but furthers and accelerates the pluralisation of forms of life and the individualization of lifestyles. More discourse means more contradiction and difference. The more abstract the agreements become, the more diverse the disagreements with which we can *nonviolently* live"[4].

What Habermas defends, therefore, is a "weak, but not defeatist" concept of reason incarnated in the linguistic praxis of communication. Such a concept prevents both from sinking away in the complete contingency of the diverse particularistic contexts, and from holding on to the claim of metaphysics to materially encompass the whole of truth. In this regard Habermas points to the idea of "intact inter-subjectivity" that appears in the investigation into the conditions of a dialogue oriented towards consensus-formation. This idea does justice to both the interaction itself and the identity of the participants in the interaction. However, this idea should not be projected as the utopian vision of a promising future: "it contains no more, but also no less, than the formal characterization of the necessary conditions for the unforeseeable forms adopted by a life that is not misspent"[5]. These conditions can be realised only when

---

4. HABERMAS, *Die Einheit der Vernunft* (n. 3), p. 180. E.T. from *Postmetaphysical Thinking: Philosophical Essays*, transl. W.-M. HOGENGARTEN, Cambridge, MA, MIT, 1992, pp. 115-148, esp. 140.

5. "... die formale Charakterisierung notwendiger Bedingungen für nicht antizipierbare Formen eines nicht-verfehlten Lebens", from HABERMAS, *Die Einheit der Vernunft* (n. 3), p. 186. E.T.: *Postmetaphysical Thinking* (n. 4), p. 145.

partners in communication take up their responsibility in solidarity. It is this project of modern humanism, which Habermas refuses to give up: the striving for human autonomy and self-realisation anchored in communicative rationality. This modern project is not yet complete[6].

No Theology with Habermas?

Contrary to the opinion of many theologians, conversation as communication does not really have anything to offer Christian faith and theology – at least not according to Habermas[7]. Precisely by engaging communication, the "truth" of Christian tradition and theology becomes generalised. Christian narrativity is then stripped of its particularity and transformed into a universally communicable kernel of valid cognitive, normative and authentic statements. Theological truth claims cannot survive outside the particularity of the Christian discourse. If there is a role left for Christianity, then it is a provisional one. As far as Habermas is concerned, as long as traditions have not been transformed by communicative interaction into sets of valid statements, traditions can keep on transmitting their contents and attitudes. "The process of a critical appropriation of the essential contents of religious tradition is still underway and the outcome is difficult to predict. […] As long as religious language bears within itself inspiring, indeed, unrelinquishable semantic contents which elude (for the moment?) the expressive power of a philosophical language and still await translation into a discourse that gives

---

6. Compare ID., *Die neue Unübersichtlichkeit: Die Krise des Wohlfahrtsstaates und die Erschöpfung utopischer Energien*, Frankfurt am Main, Suhrkamp, 1985. Habermas describes what remains of utopian consciousness: no longer the unfolded utopia of the labourers' society projected onto the future and concretely designed that would expand via functionalistic rationality a humane society of equality and freedom. What remains is a sort of formal utopia of the communication-society, something that submits to general description and thus is not to be obtained as such, an "ideal conversation situation". "[W]as sich normativ auszeichnen läßt, sind notwendige, aber allgemeine Bedingungen für eine kommunikative Alltagspraxis und für ein Verfahren der diskursiven Willensbildung, welche die Beteiligten *selbst* in die Lage versetzen könnten, konkrete Möglichkeiten eines besseren und weniger gefährdeten Lebens nach *eigenen* Bedürfnissen und Einsichten aus *eigener* Initiative zu verwirklichen" (pp. 161-162).

7. Cf. HABERMAS, *Transcendence from Within, Transcendence in this World*, in D.S. BROWNING – F. SCHÜSSLER FIORENZA (eds.), *Habermas, Modernity, and Public Theology*, New York, Crossroad, 1992, pp. 226-250. For more information about the usage of Habermas' thinking in theology, see further to the collection we quoted also: E. ARENS (ed.), *Habermas und die Theologie: Beiträge zur theologischen Rezeption, Diskussion und Kritik der Theorie kommunikativen Handelns*, Düsseldorf, Patmos, 1989 (with bibliography) and H. DÜRINGER, *Universale Vernunft und partikulare Glaube. Eine theologische Auswertung des Werkes von Jürgen Habermas* (Studies in Philosophical Theology), Leuven, Peeters, 1999.

reasons for its positions, philosophy, even in its postmetaphysical form, will neither be able to replace nor to repress religion"[8]. But it seems only to be a question of time before such a functionalised religion will disappear.

II. Communication as Conversation: Rorty's Anti-Foundationalist Plea for Contingency, Irony and Solidarity

Richard Rorty's philosophical theory rests essentially on an anti-foundational claim: there is no foundation in reality or in the subject that forces us to choose one description of reality over another. Descriptions are not "mirroring nature"[9]. They refer more to the community in which they function than to "reality" – rather to solidarity among the community members than to objectivity. Descriptions are both the result of communal conversation and sustain this conversation. Evolution in descriptions is a process of the emergence of new metaphors that generate new possibilities for description and bring about a situation in which the old ones stop describing in a correct way – and this according to the standards valid in the community (or for the individual). Language, the self and the community are contingent, and dependent, upon a commonly accepted background, even if one is distancing oneself from it.

Descriptions stem from the basic or final vocabularies by which individuals and communities live. In this regard Rorty distinguishes between vocabularies that serve private goals and those serving public goals. Both goals should not be confused. This enables him also to make a distinction between two kinds of philosophers and authors, each of them serving a different kind of goal. (1) Kierkegaard, Nietzsche, Baudelaire, Foucault but also Lyotard are protagonists of individual autonomy. According to Rorty, they plead for creative self-description, for new metaphors to affirm one's own identity, unbound and not controlled by the community. The individual's quest for identity then results in attempts at self-description in which individuals constitute their being different from one another. For Rorty such a self-description has no ground, it is merely profiled

8. Cf. HABERMAS, *Transcendence from Within, Transcendence in this World* (n. 7), p. 237. See also F.P.M. JESPERS, *De theologische receptie van de latere Habermas*, in *Tijdschrift voor theologie* 35 (1995) 176-185, esp. p. 184-185.

9. Cf. Rorty's first main work R. RORTY, *Philosophy and the Mirror of Nature*, Princeton, NJ, Princeton University Press, 1979.

within language and thus is contingent – Rorty labels the one who is conscious of the contingency of his auto-constitutive description an *ironist*. (2) Authors such as Marx, Rawls and Habermas, on the other hand are *liberals*. They serve public goals, as the fruit of the social conversation that results from the liberal revolution of the polity in modernity; that which stems from this conversation as consensus is taken by the participants as true, good and right. The only legitimation of this consensus is that it functions, and that it prevents cruelty as much as possible. The liberal democratic society is merely the outcome of a long process of trial and error and does not in any way reflect a presupposed nature or essence of what a society ought to be. As a result, the postmodern person *par excellence* is the *liberal ironist*: the one who succeeds both in shaping him/herself creatively in an original final vocabulary and in making space in this final vocabulary with regard to the public objectives of the liberal utopia[10].

In short, for Rorty communication is conversation between those who belong to a community. Its result is what the community holds as true, good and authentic – without that, there would be a necessity for this consensus to be founded on anything more than such mere intersubjective consent. This, for example, is what the liberal democratic political system is about: the conversation between different individual and social final vocabularies trying to constitute a common discourse in convincing one another of the suitability of one's position.

No more Christianity with Rorty

In reference to Hans Blumenberg[11], Rorty argues that the insight into the contingency of language, and thus of the results of conversation, is

10. In *Contingency, Irony, and Solidarity* (Cambridge, Cambridge University Press, 1989) Rorty qualifies his own thinking as *ironic theory*, a tradition that he traces back to authors like Hegel, Heidegger, and Derrida. This tradition has as its object the deconstruction of metaphysics – i.e. of the canon from Plato to Kant – and has as its goal an understanding of the metaphysical impulse such that people are freed from it. This is what all ironists do: creatively redescribe themselves and the history from which they arise, so that their own autonomy is re-established. So doing, philosophy no longer has any political vocation: it becomes a form of literary criticism. On the political level Rorty sees a role for literature, and especially for the novel – besides television, film, docudrama, etc. – to help us to be less cruel. The novel plays this political role, for instance, when it describes to us the (pernicious) effects of our institutions and practices on other people, or indicts the inherent cruelty of certain private ironic redescriptions; or narratively renders from the perspective of the victim the cruelty that it overcomes.

11. Rorty refers to H. BLUMENBERG, *The Legitimacy of the Modern Age*, Cambridge, MA, MIT, 1982.

the outcome of the secularisation of the pre-modern world. In modernity, the love for God is replaced, first, by the love for the truth about the world (science) and, later, by the love for our own inner wealth, our Self (romanticism). However, in our postmodern era the "World" and the "Self" have lost their quasi-divine status as unassailable criteria. A new "de-divinisation" tackles the "need" to worship something outside or inside us, and urges the complete contingency of the universe. Language, consciousness, truth, community and culture are "a product of time and chance", the result of a coincidental convergence of circumstances[12].

The consequences for Christianity are devastating. (1) For Rorty, the era of religion is behind us. Like August Comte, Rorty situates religion before the modern metaphysical era, which is presently coming to an end. Both are outdated ways of thinking reality as a whole[13]. (2) Christianity tries to unite private and public goals in one vocabulary and to do away with the insurmountable distinction between the two: the Christian is called to individual perfection by means of love of neighbour[14]. In Rorty's opinion such unified vocabulary is not possible because one of the two categories of objectives is always undervalued. (3) If one considers Christianity as a mode of private self-description, then one must concede that it shares in the evils of correspondence-thinking. It gives a feeling of power over oneself, the world, reality. Christianity (like Marxism) then is a way of describing oneself, a redescription whereby the dramatic force is expressed by the word "conversion": one turns away from a false description (inspired by evil, the devil, etc.) towards a (real!) description of the true self. Such insight proffers power: the believer begins to believe "that his [or her] acceptance of that redescription seals an alliance with a power mightier than any of those which have oppressed him [her] in the past"[15]. For Rorty, Christianity has no real chance of survival – insofar as it still is alive – considering the widespread factual secularisation of Western populations. Should an ironic mentality permeate these populations, Christianity will be definitively finished. It will be exposed and put aside as an essentialistic correspondence theory uniting the redescription of the

12. RORTY, *Contingency, Irony, and Solidarity* (n. 10), p. 22.
13. Cf. *ibid.*, p. 68.
14. Cf. *ibid.*, p. xiii, p. 187: in Christianity the questions: "who am I?" and "how do I live with others in community?" are answered together. This altruistic directedness ensures that a postmodern liberal redescription of Christianity can indeed, along the lines presented above, describe Christianity as an articulation and a practical filling-out of a longing for as little cruelty as possible. However, Christianity itself did not know that this was the goal (p. 90).
15. *Ibid.*, p. 90.

private with the public. But we have to admit that the reaction of theologians concerning the relevance of Rorty for theology is analogous. The theologians who take Rorty as their favourite "ancilla" are few indeed[16].

III. COMMUNICATION VERSUS CONVERSATION: HABERMAS VERSUS RORTY

Habermas' attempt to defend justice, via philosophy, as the goal of the public forum, is resolutely denounced by Rorty[17]. After all, in order to realise this objective, Habermas needs to take refuge in an essentialist approach to language, communication and the consensus resulting therefrom. Rorty indeed also subscribes to dialogue as a political model and considers the consensus that results from it as true, normative and authentic. He rejects, however, the founding of this model in the ultimate convergence to which non-hegemonical communication leads and which presupposes a kind of general background layer of knowledge, normativity, and authenticity which then would be set free by communal communicative action. Moreover, from Rorty's perspective, such a philosophical project leaves no space open for the individual's radical creative self-description. The public goals then ultimately outflank the private ones.

Habermas, for his part, does not so much criticise Rorty for distinguishing between public and private goals, but for his stringent rejection of every legitimation strategy except for the pragmatic. For Habermas, legitimation strategies cannot be reduced to mere social practices. People are reflexive participants in the dialogue. They make a distinction, even in their daily communication, between what they consider as "valid" and what they consider "socially accepted". At the same time, the distinction between what is an opinion and what is a conviction rests on this. "From the perspective of the first person, the question of which beliefs are justified is a question of which beliefs are based on good reasons; it is not a function of life-habits that enjoy social currency in some

---

16. See e.g. the presentation and evaluation of applying Rorty's thinking in theology by F.P.M. JESPERS, *Contingentie, contextualiteit en godsdienst bij Rorty*, in *Bijdragen* 54 (1993) 234-253.

17. Habermas and Rorty met in May 8-9, 1995, in Warsaw; their discussions are published in J. NIZNIK – J.T. SANDERS (eds.), *Debating the State of Philosophy: Habermas, Rorty, and Kolakowski*, Westport, Praeger, 1996. See also R. RORTY, *Habermas, Derrida and the Functions of Philosophy*, in ID., *Truth and Progress* (Philosophical Papers, 3), Cambridge, Cambridge University Press,1998, pp. 305-326.

places and not in others"[18]. As for Habermas, whoever maintains that philosophy has no longer a role to play in the public sphere (as Rorty does), sings in the choir of the neo-conservatives who try to make such politically translated irrationalism acceptable on a grand scale.

IV. A PLURALITY OF DISCOURSES AND THE *DIFFÉREND*: JEAN-FRANÇOIS LYOTARD RESISTING MASTER NARRATIVES

For Jean-François Lyotard[19] an expectation is opened with every phrase, which can never be fulfilled by the next phrase. When a phrase has happened, the nature of the following phrase is *in se* completely arbitrary. *That a phrase* has to follow is necessary, *which phrase* should follow, is contingent, and depends on the discourse which succeeds in establishing the chain. Each phrase once it is uttered, therefore, opens up an expectation – a *différend* – that can be closed by a multitude of new phrases, all belonging to different discourse genres. However, in an all too-determining fashion phrases and discourses transform this *différend* into a litigation, thereby doing injustice to the unpresentable openness of the expectation by fixing it in words and phrases. Phrases determine what is at stake; discourses link phrases to each other in order to reach the discourse's goal.

It is the task of contemporary philosophy to bear witness to the *différend*, i.e. this untimeable and ungraspable moment that separates two phrases, which is forgotten with each new phrase. Philosophy attempts to remind us that while concatenating phrases in discourses we tend to forget, and that often even this forgetting is forgotten. The latter is definitely the case with grand or master narratives. These are hegemonic discourses which immediately transform *différends* into litigations by regulating every concatenation of phrases on the basis of its own logic. Philosophy is therefore first of all the critique of master narratives.

1. *Christianity is a Master Narrative*

From the perspective of this thinker of difference, i.e. of the *différend*, Christianity offers the master narrative par excellence. In *"Le différend"*,

---

18. HABERMAS, *Questions and Counterquestions*, in R.J. BERNSTEIN (ed.), *Habermas and Modernity*, Cambridge, Polity Press, 1985, pp. 192-216, esp. 195. Cf. HABERMAS, *Debating the State of Philosophy*, pp. 18-24.

19. Cf. J.-F. LYOTARD, *Le différend*, Paris, Éditions de Minuit, 1983.

Lyotard writes about Christianity[20]: "Le récit chrétien à Rome a vaincu les autres récits parce qu'en introduisant l'amour de l'occurrence dans les récits et les narrations de récits il désignait l'enjeu du genre [du récit] lui-même. Aimer ce qui arrive comme un don, aimer même le Arrive-t-il? comme la promesse d'une bonne nouvelle, cela permet d'enchaîner sur tout ce qui arrive, y compris les autres récits (et ultérieurement les autres genres même)"[21]. So doing, Christianity recuperates from the very beginning the event of the *différend*. Lyotard thus estimates the Christian narrative as a closed, hegemonic, narratively structured discourse of the Idea of love. Stemming from a particular narrative tradition, in a plurality of small narratives, Christianity developed the "virtue of love" into a universal *regulativum*. This love, understood as a general principle, transcends the particularity of the traditional instances (addressors, addressees, etc.). The ground of the commandment of love is the revealed primordial narrative of the God who is love but who does not receive love from his children in return. The commandment, revealed by God to all creatures in the revelatory narrative, is formulated in a circular way: "if you are loved, you must love; and you will be loved, only if you love." Small narratives concerning sin and conversion function as examples of this love. The instances of a particular narrative tradition are thus universalised.

2. Habermas still Tells an Emancipatory Master Narrative

The same holds true for the modern master narratives constitutive of what Habermas coins "the modern project". First, Lyotard is convinced that this project is not unfinished and abandoned, as Habermas opines, but destroyed[22]. This project can no longer be started again, but has entered

---

20. Cf. *ibid.*, pp. 229 ff, nr. 232-235. Other short notes on this matter, amongst others, in *Missive sur l'histoire universelle*, in *Le postmoderne expliqué aux enfants. Correspondance 1982-1985*, Paris, Galilée, 1986, pp. 43-64, esp. 47; and in *Moralités postmodernes*, Paris, Galilée, 1993, particularly in *Mur, golfe, système* (65-77), p. 74; *Une fable postmoderne* (79-94), p. 90, and *Intime est la terreur* (171-184), p. 182. With regard to the relation between Judaism and Christianity (and the dialectical sublation of Judaism in the latter), see J.-F. LYOTARD – E. GRÜBER, *Un trait d'union*, Sainte-Foy, Le Griffon d'argile, 1994.

21. LYOTARD, *Le différend* (n. 19), p. 229, nr. 232. E.T.: "The Christian narrative vanquished the other narratives in Rome because by introducing the love of occurrence into narratives and narrations of narratives, it designated what is at stake in the genre itself. To love what happens as if it were a gift, to love even the *Is it happening?* as the promise of good news, allows for linking onto whatever happens, including other narratives (and, subsequently, even other genres)" (*The Differend. Phrases in Dispute*, transl. G. VAN DEN ABBEELE, Manchester, Manchester University Press, 1988, p. 159).

22. Cf., among others, LYOTARD, *Apostille aux récits*, in ID., *Le postmoderne expliqué aux enfants* (n. 20), pp. 38-39.

a process of self-destruction. Moreover, due to numerous counter-examples the modern master narratives have lost their plausibility[23]. And secondly, the discourse of communicative action should be analysed as a master narrative. Herein a diversity of language games is profiled, so to speak, meta-prescriptively in one grand encompassing narrative. For Lyotard, Habermas' *Diskurs*-model, taking the very possibility of a universal consensus as its starting point, is bankrupt from the very start. For this purpose, everyone would first have to reach an agreement concerning the meta-linguistic rules for all discourses, and secondly, it must be assumed beforehand that dialogue leads to consensus. The heterogeneity of the discourses and the search for dissent (as in *La condition postmoderne* where Lyotard describes "paralogy" as the motor for scientific development), however, make the striving for consensus extremely dubious. Habermas' solution still resembles an emancipation-narrative, in which a universal subject moves to freedom via a universally shared consensual knowledge. Because such a consensus model does not suffice for Lyotard, a reflection on justice has to start from *dissensus*[24].

V. Conversation Is but One Discourse Strategy: Lyotard Versus Rorty on the "Other"

1. *Rorty versus Lyotard*

Rorty considers Jean-François Lyotard an ironic philosopher, an aesthetical thinker: by attempting to bear witness to the *différend*, the non-presentable, one creates one's own vocabulary. However, Lyotard falsely assumes that his philosophy of the private would also apply for public goals. Lyotard's plea for *dissensus* is perhaps interesting, Rorty concedes, but as concerns the political, the establishment of consensus is of capital importance. Rendered in terms of the aesthetic categories of the "beautiful" and the "sublime" (which Lyotard favours as well[25]): "Social purposes are served, just as Habermas says, by finding beautiful ways of harmonising interests, rather than sublime ways of detaching oneself from

---

23. See Lyotard, *Le différend* (n. 19), p. 229, nr. 232.
24. Lyotard's criticism of Habermas in *La condition postmoderne* was accompanied by the promise to conduct a more thoroughgoing reflection on justice – a promise which a few years later resulted in *Le différend*.
25. See, e.g. Lyotard, *Le sublime et l'avant-garde* and *Représentation, présentation, imprésentable*, in *L'inhumain. Causeries sur le temps*, Paris, Galilée, 1988, resp. pp. 101-117 and 131-139; *Leçons sur l'Analytique du sublime*, Paris, Galilée, 1991.

others' interests. The attempt of leftist intellectuals [like Lyotard] to pretend that the avant-garde is serving the wretched of the earth by fighting free of the merely beautiful is a hopeless attempt to make the special needs of the intellectual and the social needs of [his/]her community coincide"[26]. In other words: the thinking of Habermas and Lyotard illustrate for Rorty the radical and irreconcilable distinction between private and public objectives.

Rorty thus critiques the political pretension of Lyotard's ideas[27]; especially since Lyotard, out of fear of lapsing into a meta-narrative, treats all political narratives in one and the same way. But politics cannot do without narratives; more so, all politics is woven into a narrative. These narratives, however, do not necessarily have to be meta-narratives. The fall of metaphysics does not drag the western political project down along with it. The narrative we tell in order to recommend western parliamentary democracy as the best model till now does not have to proceed from any correspondence between that political model and the essence of all social life. The narratives of other peoples and other models can also inspire us to enrich our model, even if we necessarily approach these other narratives ethnocentrically. Moreover, our western political narrative should not be identified as a narrative of emancipation, as Lyotard opines, but rather as a narrative of cosmopolitanism. The liberal utopia pictures a society wherein everyone can say what he or she wants to say about society in an open, free conversation. That we are able to understand each other in such a dialogue goes hand in hand with Rorty's assumption that we have more words in common in our different vocabularies than not in common. And this is likewise valid for the dialogue with other cultures, the Cashinahua-Indians[28], for instance. Because Lyotard proceeds from incommensurability between the different genres, he assumes that these Indians can be converted to cosmopolitanism only by violence, not by persuasion-in-dialogue. Rorty, on the contrary, states that even language

---

26. RORTY, *Habermas and Lyotard on Postmodernism*, in ID., *Essays on Heidegger and Others* (Philosophical Papers, 2), Cambridge, Cambridge University Press, pp. 164-176, esp. 176. The text goes further: "Such an attempt goes back to the Romantic period, when the urge to think the unthinkable, to grasp the unconditioned, to sail strange seas of thought alone, was mingled with enthusiasm for the French Revolution. These two, equally laudable, motives should be distinguished."

27. For the following paragraph see RORTY, *Cosmopolitanism without Emancipation: A Response to Jean-François Lyotard*, in *Objectivity, Relativism, and Truth* (Philosophical Papers, 1), Cambridge, Cambridge University Press, pp. 211-222. Here, Rorty critically discusses (alongside *Le différend*) Lyotard's *Missive sur l'histoire universelle* (in *Le postmoderne expliqué aux enfants*, pp. 43-64). These articles of Lyotard and Rorty, and a discussion between the two, originally appeared in *Critique* 28 (1985) nr. 456.

28. Example by Lyotard in *Le différend* (n. 19), pp. 224-225, nrs. 222-225.

games that are responsible for cultural difference are not totally incommensurable; they might well be untranslatable, but surely learnable, as well – they can be explained to us. Rorty thus refuses to consider the phrase "there is no pre-given language to which every differentiation can be translated" as equal to "there are languages that cannot be learned". The difference between languages is consequently best compared to the distinction between an old vocabulary and one that is metaphorically renewed. Incommensurability is, therefore, a temporary problem. Does Rorty then address every *différend* with litigation? Not automatically, in his opinion; rather it is his conviction "that political liberalism amounts to the suggestion that we try to substitute litigation for *différends* as far as we can, and that there is no *a priori* philosophical reason why this attempt must fail, just as (*pace* Christianity, Kant, and Marx) there is no *a priori* reason why it must succeed"[29]. If a universal history is written, then this will only be possible when a generalised cosmopolitanism is established in the encounter between people and cultures, whereby this establishment takes place more through persuasion than through violence. May 1968 is in that regard not a counter-example for the utopia of liberalism; only a better, more convincing utopia can take its place.

More generally, Rorty reproaches the French philosophers for fostering difference too much[30] and being insufficiently concerned with laying down connections in order to bring about agreement and convergence. The image of the archipelago depicts, for Lyotard, the insurmountable diversity of discourses. Rorty likewise acknowledges the archipelago as an image for diversity but nonetheless will propose that we build bridges and viaducts across the waters that divide the diverse islands, however difficult this may sometimes seem. For the French, according to Rorty, postmodernity is in the first place a decisive change in our culture, whereas, for him, it is rather about "the gradual encapsulation and forgetting of a certain philosophical tradition"[31].

2. *Lyotard versus Rorty*

Lyotard does not agree with Rorty's critique[32]. What strikes him especially is the "*différend*" separating him from Rorty. Rorty speaks of

---

29. RORTY, *Cosmopolitanism without Emancipation* (n. 27), p. 217.

30. In this regard, see also the introduction of RORTY, *Essays on Heidegger and Others* (n. 26), p. 4.

31. RORTY, *Cosmopolitanism without Emancipation* (n. 27), p. 222.

32. Cf. *Discussion entre Jean-François Lyotard et Richard Rorty*, in *Critique* 38 (1985) nr. 456, 581-584; Lyotard's interview with Willem VAN REIJEN and Dick VEERMAN:

languages, Lyotard of genres of discourse or discourse strategies (within language): the latter distinguish themselves from each other by their objectives, while Rorty's languages each have their different history. With a change of discourse genre, one does not translate, but one transcribes, whereby one wins (another objective is served by the other discourse into which one has changed the original one) and loses (the objective of the original genre). One can make translations between different languages (natural languages, "language" in the literal sense of the word), however not between different genres of discourse. An aesthetic question is not solved in a cognitive discourse. "Entre les Cashinahua et nous, il existe une différence de genres de discours, et elle est fondamentale"[33]. Here, Rorty's plea for convergence and consensus betrays a "soft imperialism": "l'impérialisme conversationnel de Rorty", even when (physical) violence is avoided and only persuasion is applied; after all, persuasion implies "mental violence", because it presupposes a privileged role for conversation (persuasion-in-dialogue)[34]. In what follows, we will first review two analytical reflections of Lyotard concerning "conversation" and "translation" and then a few critical notes regarding the privileging of conversation.

Conversation ("interlocution", argumentation, dialogue, or discussion) is, as far as Lyotard is concerned, only a genre among other genres, namely the genre that provides the procedural rules that condition the consent of the addressee with regard to what is said by the addressor. Conversation as genre includes "la procédure de levée du dissentiment qui caractérise le rapport des interlocuteurs en début de discussion"[35]. For Rorty, Lyotard comments, the goal of conversation, as privileged genre of the public domain, is to persuade the other of the truth of what

---

De Verlichting, het verhevene, filosofie, esthetica. Interview en uitwisseling van gedachten met Jean-François Lyotard, in W. VAN REIJEN, *De onvoltooide rede. Modern en Postmodern*, Kampen, Kok, 1987, pp. 63-117, esp. 108-115; and LYOTARD, *Un partenaire bizarre*, in *Moralités postmodernes*, pp. 111-130. On Lyotard's doubt regarding consensus and communication as conditions for actual establishment of communities, cf. his *Postscriptum* in *Pérégrinations. Loi, forme, événement*, Paris, Galilée, 1990, pp. 85-87.

33. *Discussion* (n. 32), pp. 581-582. ET: "Between the Cashinahua and us, there is a fundamental difference between the discourse genres".

34. *Ibid.*, p. 582.

35. LYOTARD, *Un partenaire bizarre* (n. 32), pp. 114-115. Formulated still more sharply: seeing that the sublation of a dissensus differs in strategy if it is about the solving of a sum, the viewing of a sculpture, the explanation of a physical phenomenon, or deciding whom to vote for at an election, it is even commended to speak of diverse conversation-genres: in view of their diverse objectives, they also differ in strategy as to the realisation of the objective and are not to be reduced as such to one genre.

the "I" says. Reducing all communication to this genre implies, however, that all genres are forcedly integrated and thus that all other goals of the other genres are subordinated. "Dans tous les cas de discussion, chacun vise à persuader l'autre que ce qu'il dit est vrai. [...] C'est n'admettre qu'une seule procédure, la persuasion, et qu'un seul enjeu, la véridicité"[36].

The problem of such a reductive homogenisation is expressed in the meaning of *translation*. As already mentioned, Lyotard disputes the idea that phrases from one genre of discourse can be translated integrally and without damage into another. How, for instance, can an experience of beauty be cast in concepts and argumentations so much so that someone can be convinced of the beauty of a painting?[37] A transfer (of phrases) from one genre to another (in this case, to conversation) is indeed possible, but such transferences can hardly be called a faithful translation, considering that the objectives of the genres of discourse differ. Rather, a phrase that is taken up from one discourse and applied in another is placed there, in a manner of speaking, between quotation marks[38]. If a transfer to the genre of conversation is indeed equated with translation – whereby one mistakenly proceeds from the assumption that everything that is translated can be preserved – then the conversation indeed functions as a meta-discourse, as a discourse that is capable of removing the incommensurability between the genres of discourse[39].

But is this possible? Lyotard offers a fourfold negative response. (1) As far as Lyotard is concerned, Rorty is right when he considers conversation as the only alternative to violence at this moment; liberal democracy offers the best opportunities in order to avoid violence. But politics does not live by conversation alone. The search for consensus is surely one of the most important political tasks, but politics is not to be reduced to this genre. Other genres likewise come into the picture; such as, for instance, that of obligation (the formulation of the ideal of justice

36. *Ibid.*, p. 117. ET: "In discussions one always strives at convincing the other that what one says is true. [...] It is permitting only one single procedure, persuasion, and only one objective, veridicality".
37. Cf. *ibid.*, pp. 117-118.
38. Comparing, for example, the way in which phrases and narratives function in the (oral) narrativity of the tribe and the way in which the very same phrases and narratives are written into a book by the cultural anthropologist, in the framework of an investigation, for instance, into the way in which cultural knowledge is transmitted; or how the phrase "smoking is bad for your health" functions differently in a scientific discourse than in a discourse of the father who catches his precocious son of thirteen smoking a cigarette.
39. As Lyotard states in *Un partenaire bizarre* (n. 32), p. 117: "La procédure de la persuasion, selon Rorty, [...] [s'autorise] [...] d'une sorte d'évidence universelle".

to which the community aspires): its normative value – also in conversation – is valid only when its content is not open for discussion time and again. And in the end this is likewise so with Rorty. Even with him, the discourse of obligation emerges in the discourse of conversation, thus showing the limit of the discourse of conversation: "Ici la discussion rationnelle ou l'interlocution argumentative est constituée elle-même en idéal de justice. La façon de procéder vient occuper la place de ce qu'il s'agit d'atteindre par la procédure"[40]. (2) Lyotard's second argument against a presupposed priority of conversation is situated on the level of the relationship of addressor and addressee in phrases (and genres of discourse). In conversation, the "other" as "you", who is in conversation with the "I", is immediately taken up as (an equal) conversation partner in the "we". This "we" is "une sorte de préconsensus interlocutaire"[41]. If, however, one goes so far as to promote conversation as the privileged genre, then this "we" becomes a "pré-consensus" that precedes all speaking. For Lyotard, this is manifestly disputable. Certain genres do not start with a "we", surely not with a "we" whereby the "I" and the "you" are able (and need) to shift positions unlimitedly and simultaneously, from addressor to addressee and vice versa, as in conversation. Such a "we" is not present in the genres of discourse of, for instance, "faire croire", "faire trembler ou pleurer" (through poetry), or "faire faire". Moreover, there are genres where the "you" is barely present: reflection, writing, and so forth[42]. Furthermore, if persuasion is really the objective of conversation, the "we" – which is of exceptional importance for the "liberal" Rorty – is constituted in an unbalanced way: the "I" weighs more than the "you"; a counter movement from the "you" is actually not presupposed. (3) Thirdly, it is far from clear for Lyotard that all consensus is necessarily a consequence of dialogue. With regard to aesthetic judgement, for instance, he argues that conversation about it is possible, but that it is not constitutive of the aesthetic judgement itself. (4) Finally, the attempt in conversation to transpose différends into litigations as much as possible proceeds from the presupposition that convergence and communicability are of high priority[43]. But why, asks Lyotard, is convergence to be preferred? Even within one single individual, several addressors have the floor and, even there, convergence per se is not a must. Perhaps

40. Ibid., p. 121.
41. Ibid., p. 122.
42. Lyotard adds that Rorty's writings are likewise not a discussion, but rather a taking hostage of the reader who is not his conversation partner (ibid., p. 125).
43. See also LYOTARD, Intime est la terreur, in Moralités postmodernes (n. 20), pp. 171-184, esp. 178.

the other can simply not enter into conversation with us. This does not mean that we must exclude the other's language game or that we need to characterise his game as a non-game and then just look for someone else who indeed wants to play the game with us. To do so is to violate the other, and destroy the event. We do better learn the game of the other, as something new, something unknown, as an occurrence, an event. This is really what writing and thinking is about: "[faire] à [n]ous-même violence pour essayer d'apprendre les mouvements que [n]otre partenaire silencieux impose ... aux mots et aux phrases, et que [nous ignorons]"[44]. This is an encounter with the unnameable partner, who cannot be locked up in an interlocutory "we", one with whom one cannot play, who is not or cannot be a conversation partner. "Augmenter la capacité de discuter est bien; augmenter la passibilité à l'événement n'est pas moins bien"[45].

In short, what actually disturbs Lyotard is the dominating "I"-involvement in Rorty's thought, where he preaches an enforced "conversational" cosmopolitanism. This "I"-involvement expresses itself in the persuasive character of the conversation – the "you" must be convinced of the right of the "I"; but also in translating to oneself what the "you" says, without taking the heterogeneity of its discourse into account. By locking up the "you" in the "we", every appeal from the "you" as other is eliminated – every event, where the "you" is the unnameable partner, is already enfeebled in advance.

VI. Some Theological Considerations

We first summarise the findings stemming from the conversation of, and with, Habermas, Rorty, and Lyotard.

– Conversation as communication (Habermas) strives at the construction of intersubjectively acknowledged true, normative and authentic statements. The logic of communicative action de-particularises the layers of truth, normativity and authenticity embedded in the traditions of our lifeworlds and transforms them in argumentatively legitimate claims to universal validity. Conversation here, according to Habermas, is the end of theology.
– This is also the case for Rorty. Conversation is what keeps the community going, the constitution of a common "we". Striving for universalisation is only striving to enlarge this "we" to a "cosmopolitan

44. Lyotard, *Un partenaire bizarre* (n. 32), p. 129.
45. *Ibid.*, p. 130.

we". The claims stemming from conversation are only legitimated because they are the result of intersubjective consent, no matter how this consent is realised, and nothing more; there is no objective ground to sustain our truths, our norms, our authentic expressions. Also, here conversation is the end of theology. It is not its particularity which is questioned here, but its claims to speak about something which or someone who, transcends language. Rorty rejects its metaphysical orientation as something outdated. The secularisation of Western societies will progressively extinguish Christianity.

- Lyotard's criticism of Christianity and theology also focuses on this metaphysical orientation, which he labels as characteristic for grand narratives. But the source of his criticism is different. It does not stem from "conversation", but from the consciousness of that which is also too easily forgotten in conversation, certainly in the persuasion-in-conversation as profiled by Rorty. Theology serves the Christian master narrative by too quickly identifying the *différend* as a gift, to be situated within the dynamic of divine love. Lyotard thus criticises the fact that Christianity as a particular narrative does not sufficiently bear witness to the *différend*.

From a theologian's perspective, some lessons can be learned from these three philosophers.

- Habermas once again warns theologians that engaging modern thinking is not without any risks for the particularity of the Christian tradition. Through communicative action, the wisdom of narrative religious traditions is transformed into statements to be tested as regards their validity. By retrieving these statements from their original – premodern – origins, such operations do away with the particularity of the traditions (and thus with the traditions themselves). It would seem, therefore, that theologians should be aware that they cannot go all the way with Habermas. No matter how interesting and useful his thinking patterns may be, e.g. in the domain of pastoral ecclesiology, Habermas' proposals result in the phasing out of Christianity as a particular and recognisable narrative. Unless, of course, the theologians' appreciation of Christianity's particularity is equally minimal.
- Rorty's critique of Christianity can be linked to the ontotheological criticism of Christian theology that a lot of continental philosophers venture. Christianity too rapidly tends to diffuse universal truth claims without taking into account the irreducibly particular history and context they come from. The radical historical and contingent, contextual and communitarian dimension of the Christian narrative may no longer

be overlooked. The question with which theologians are left when they intend to go beyond Rorty's particularism, is then: how to safeguard at all the Christian truth claim without relativising or forgetting its radical particularity and contextuality?

– Lyotard's lesson for theology is at first sight similar. Theology has to fight the ontotheological impetus by which it seems to be possessed. Theology too easily falls prey to the trap of structuring its discourse as a closed narrative, identifying and encapsulating the *différend* from the very beginning as something known, which functions in the narrative. But the *différend*, for Lyotard, is not to be functionalised. Even if one, when using language and linking phrases, cannot but forget the *différend* (by transforming it in litigation), we should learn to do this in a way which does not forget this forgetting. At least this is the task for philosophy: bearing witness to the *différend*, by trying to evoke in its discourse that which both enables and escapes this discourse. That is why, when looked at more closely, the philosophy of Lyotard not only teaches theology that as a particular narrative it risks encapsulating the *différend*. It also presents a way of thinking which enables the conceptualisation of particularity and truth in a new way, which prevents an immediate falling back into ontotheology.

Conversation is the end of theology. That is what Habermas and Rorty teach us. And perhaps they are right. There is of course conversation in theology, between theologians, of theology with the magisterium, with the church communities – and we can apply more or less the criteria for good conversation elaborated by both thinkers. But do their concepts of conversation also apply to conceive of the first theo-logy: God addressing Godself to his people? Perceived from a dialogical relationship of (equal) partners the relation between God and human beings is probably misconceived. God then is too easily treated as an "other for us", enclosed in the discourse strategy into which we force God. It is here that Lyotard's criticism of Habermas and Rorty becomes relevant for theology, and that his thinking may serve us as a strategy to reconceive our theological conversation to and on God.

Of course God has revealed Godself as an "other for us" but could only do so because God is other than us. At the same time, God enables and escapes all God-language. Here a linguistic structure becomes apparent, similar to that underlying Lyotard's paradigm of philosophy[46].

---

46. For a more concise discussion of the way in which theology and philosophy relate here to each other, see my *Method in Postmodern Theology: a Case Study*, in

Homologous to the "philosophical" way in which he tries to bear witness to that which "happens" in the linking of phrases, the *différend* – an exercise in, as Derrida attempted, "comment ne pas parler" – theologians link phrases to each other to confess the God who reveals Godself in history, but can never be grasped or encapsulated in it. However, Lyotard also needs phrases to bear witness and his narrative is no less particular than any other. This linguistic structure could be framed an "open narrative": particularity opening itself towards that which accompanies the narrative without ever being grasped by it. As an open narrative, Christian theology no longer offers a description of God's engagement in history, but is a bearing witness to it, being conscious that each phrase, each discourse, already determines too much that which finally escapes all determination. Christian truth claims, then, do not function in their own right, as statements "containing" the truth they express. Their truth is related to the way in which they succeed in referring to that which is already forgotten when the first word is uttered. Indeed, in all too contingent, contextual and particular narratives (lesson from Rorty) Christians bear witness (lesson from Lyotard) to that which they have come to know through their narratives as the God of Jesus Christ.

What is the end of conversation in theology? Probably that, at a certain stage, it should end and leave room for the God who cannot be grasped by our words, phrases, and narratives – although this God can only be referred to by these same particular words, phrases, and narratives.

Faculteit Godgeleerdheid   Lieven BOEVE
K.U. Leuven
St.-Michielsstraat 6
B-3000 Leuven
Belgium

L. BOEVE – J.C. RIES (eds.), *The Presence of Transcendence: Thinking "Sacrament" in a Postmodern Age* (Annua Nuntia Lovaniensia, 42), Leuven, Peeters Press, 2001, pp. 19-39.

BODIES AND PERSONS, RESURRECTED AND POSTMODERN

TOWARDS A RELATIONAL ESCHATOLOGY

I. INTRODUCTION

A major problem for contemporary Roman Catholic theology is the development of a plausible understanding of the reality of life after death. Can it speak meaningfully about the eternal life in God which is promised for believers and do so within a postmodern culture which is critical of both transcendence and of unified notions of the self?

On this issue, current Roman Catholic eschatology is in disarray. The problems are rooted not only in the fact that the *eschata* are fundamentally mysteries that lay beyond any humanly-achieved certainty. There are also major questions concerning the relative appropriateness of the images, language, and categories to be used for liturgical and personal prayer, for preaching, and for theological reflection upon eternal life. Crafting a contemporary eschatology has been made more difficult due to the demise of theology's traditional dualistic anthropology and by the fact that the theological discussion of "personal identity" has lagged behind the contemporary philosophical discussions of subjectivity and alterity.

This disarray is most evident in the Church's "eschatology in practice", the current funeral liturgy celebrated according to the revisions laid out in the *Order of Christian Funerals* (1970)[1]. These were carried out in the light of the ambivalent approach to the Catholic tradition which has continued to characterize the reception of Vatican II over the past three decades. On the one hand, there has been the welcome return to biblical roots and to the Christological focus of the early Christian tradition, with a special emphasis on the centrality of the paschal mystery. On the other hand, there has been the rejection of what one commentator has called the "distorted and dualistic anthropologies of body and soul," that is, older

---

1. The text can be found in *The Rites of the Catholic Church, Volume I*, Study Edition, Collegeville, MN, Pueblo – Liturgical Press, 1990, pp. 909-1118.

eschatological perspectives which over-emphasized the spiritual dimension of human life and focused on the spiritual survival of the individual,
to the detriment of human embodiment and historical experience[2].

The rejection of dualism is evident especially in the liturgy, where the
word "soul" hardly appears (it is confined to certain biblical texts in the
lectionary and to the "song of farewell" sung at the final commendation).
The result is a liturgy which is obviously catechetical, emphasizing the
credendum that the reality of the resurrection of Christ is the condition
for the possibility of our own resurrection. But it is also unusually exhor-
tatory, urging that the predominant affective stance of the believer in the
face of death and loss be one of peace and quiet confidence in the power
of God to overcome the finality of death and grant eternal life. The consolation which the mourners desire is understood to be assured by the
already-accomplished salvific effects of Christ's resurrection[3]. While not
completely ignoring grief, the liturgy downplays any recognition of the
emptiness, heavy sadness, or desperate lamentation that also may characterize the affective state of the mourners. Despite the care taken in
underlining the community's hope, the liturgy's consistent emphasis on
the resurrection becomes, in its cumulative effect, an *overemphasis* which
skirts quite close to proclaiming a realized eschatology.

This is problematic at least on two counts. First, it creates a great dis-
sonance between the liturgy and the most recent statements on eschatology by the Congregation for the Doctrine of the Faith (1979) and the
International Theological Commission (1992), both of which affirm
eschatological doctrines in their traditional expressions (including the use
of "soul" and the existence of the "interim state") and which take issue
(in the case of the ITC, strong issue) with the theory of "resurrection in
death"[4]. Secondly, it directly contradicts the empirical evidence which is

2. D.A. LANE, *Keeping Hope Alive: Stirrings in Christian Theology*, New York –
Mahwah, NJ, Paulist Press, 1996, p. 40.

3. Clearly those responsible for the revisions have taken seriously the mandate of
Vatican II's *Constitution on the Sacred Liturgy* that "the funeral rites should express more
clearly the paschal character of Christian death" (*Constitution on the Sacred Liturgy
"Sacrosanctum Concilium"*, §81, in N.P. TANNER (ed.), *Decrees of the Ecumenical Councils*, 2 vols., London, Sheed and Ward; Washington, DC, Georgetown University Press,
1990, vol. 2, p. 835 [Latin orig. and Eng. trans. on facing pages]).

4. SACRED CONGREGATION FOR THE DOCTRINE OF THE FAITH, *Recentiores episcoporum
synodi* (11 May 1979), in *Acta Apostolicae Sedis* 71 (1979) 939-943; English translation,
The Reality of Life after Death, in A. FLANNERY (ed.), *Vatican Council II: More Post-
conciliar Documents*, Grand Rapids, MI, Eerdmans, 1982, pp. 500-504; INTERNATIONAL
THEOLOGICAL COMMISSION, *De quibusdam quaestionibus actualibus circa eschatologiam*,
in *Gregorianum* 73 (1992) 395-435; English translation, *Some Current Questions in Eschatology*, in *The Irish Theological Quarterly* 58 (1992) 209-243. The case for "resurrection

there before the mourners, namely, the corpse in a casket in the center aisle of the church. The presence of the literal "remains" of this particular historically-performed individual life is proof that the cosmos is *not yet* fully redeemed. The grief of the mourners is a response to this brute fact as well as to the fact that death has ruptured the loving relationship that they have had with the one who has died.

If anecdotal evidence about the "eschatology" of popular piety is any clue, it is a good bet that the mourners understand this situation in terms of a traditional and persistent body-soul dualism which remains unaffected by theological trends. A phenomenology of the liturgical situation, then, would show that there are at least *three* different eschatologies in play at every Catholic funeral. In the background there is the "official" eschatology of the Vatican statements which asserts the continuing validity of the traditional interpretations of the interim state and of the creedal profession of the resurrection of the body as "referring to *the whole person*", and maintains the necessity of using "soul" to refer to the "spiritual element [which] survives and subsists after death"[5]. Next there is the spirit-matter dualism of popular piety. Finally there is the quasi-realized eschatology of the liturgical texts with their virtual abandonment of "soul" language.

By abandoning "soul" language out of fear of lapsing into dualism, the Church in its liturgy loses its ability to address what "soul" symbolized in an older theological anthropology and continues to symbolize within popular culture and piety, namely the mysterious depth of individual identity which has come to be valued and beloved within a particular family and a particular community, as well as the unique cluster of relationships and bodily performances which have served to constitute and expand that identity. In turn the Church loses its capacity to respond to the mourners' shock that this unique and beloved "I" has been torn out from its embeddedness within a particular community of love and care. When death comes, the network of relationships which help to

in death" has been argued most notably by Gisbert Greshake; cf. G. GRESHAKE – G. LOHFINK, *Naherwartung–Auferstehung–Unsterblichkeit: Untersuchungen zur christlichen Eschatologie* (Quaestiones Disputatae, 71), Freiburg/Br., Herder, ⁴1982 (orig. 1974); G. GRESHAKE – J. KREMER, *Resurrectio mortuorum: Zum theologischen Verständnis der leiblichen Auferstehung,* Darmstadt, Wissenschaftliche Buchgesellschaft, 1986; reprint 1992.

5. *The Reality of Life after Death* (n. 4), pp. 501-502, nos. 2, 3, and 7. See especially the conclusion of no. 3: "Although not unaware that this term [soul] has various meanings in the Bible, the Church thinks that there is no valid reason for rejecting it; moreover, she considers that the use of some word as a vehicle is absolutely indispensable in order to support the faith of Christians" (p. 502).

constitute not only the identity of the deceased but also the identities of the mourners appears to be ruptured with tragic finality. It is ironic that body-soul dualism, rightly criticized for being un-biblical, extrinsicist, ahistorical, and dis-incarnational to the point of gnosticism, was actually better able to explain the empirical evidence of death and the shattering loss of personal contact with the deceased's uniquely constituted self. It provided, in other words, a *metaphysical* as well as an *aesthetic* framework within which the experience of the mourners "made sense"– not by explaining fully the mystery of the afterlife but by providing a conceptual and compositional framework wherein the deceased, the grieving survivors, and the ecclesial community at large related to each other in a position of exquisite equipoise over against the horizon of the terrible ("Dies irae") and merciful ("Requiem aeternam dona eis, Domine") judgment of God.

The purpose of this paper is to address these problems in eschatology. I wish to sketch out a constructive position which attempts to do justice to the church's creedal affirmation of "the life of the world to come", to contemporary philosophical and aesthetic discussions of "self", "other", and embodiment, and to the affective needs of believers. The paper has two parts. In the first part, I will argue for a four-fold sense of the body (analogous to the senses of scripture) which articulates the performative, ecstatic, and pluriform nature of embodiment. In the second part I will investigate the affective function which "soul" played in older Catholic eschatology and then will attempt to retrieve this function (and perhaps "soul" itself) in a more contemporary way.

It is not my wish to bring back an outmoded body-soul dualism, the dis-embodied soul, or the "ghost in the machine" imagery that we have inherited from Descartes. These anthropologies are all inadequate and betray our historically-situated lived experience. Rather, I want to win back for eschatology an acknowledgment of the *duality* of embodied human experience and retrieve the functions which "body" and "soul" played previously in helping us imaginatively articulate that duality.

II. Performed Embodiment

One way of understanding the issues surrounding embodiment is to interpret the body along the lines of the medieval method for interpreting Scripture. Just as the medievals asserted the four-fold sense of Scripture, one can assert a *four-fold sense of the body*. Remember the little verse which summed up the principle:

Littera gesta docet, quid credas allegoria,
moralis quid agas, quo tendas anagogia[6].

The literal teaches events, the allegorical what you should believe,
the moral what you should do, the anagogical that toward which you
    should strive.

Accordingly, the real truth of a Scriptural text turns out to be a *multi-valent* truth. Such a schema can be applied analogously to the body and in order to help disclose the body's non-negotiable multivalent character. The *literal* meaning of the body is its biological or material-empirical substratum. The *allegorical* meaning can be seen as the meaningfulness of bodily gestures and embodied actions. The *moral* meaning would be the humanizing or dehumanizing character of those actions. Finally, the *anagogical* meaning would refer to the ultimate intentional goal of all of the body's possibilities of transformation, namely *theōsis,* the union with God promised to us by our baptism into the dying and rising of Christ. However, just as the hegemony of the modern historical-critical method has reduced the four senses of Scripture down to one, namely the *literal* (which is then further identified with the *historical*[7]), so too a similar fate has prevailed for the contemporary body: its "true meaning" for most people has been reduced to its *literal* meaning, and the literal has been made equivalent to the "fact" of its biology. How do we open up our understanding of the body beyond the literal sense?

First, our eschatology must be anchored in a strong theory of the resurrection of Jesus. By "strong" I do not mean a literalist or physicalist reading of the resurrection narratives. Rather, I mean a theory which does three things: (1) it affirms the resurrection as an event which happens both to Jesus himself and to his disciples; (2) it sees the empty-tomb narratives and the appearance narratives as interlocking evidence not to be separated, and (3) it affirms the true bodily resurrection of Jesus, the eschatological transformation of his corporeal identity. Without such an understanding of the resurrection of Jesus, it would not even occur to us to raise questions about embodiment, its permutations, and its transformational possibilities.

I find a strong theory of resurrection in a place where many might least expect it: in the Christology of Edward Schillebeeckx. One can prescind

---

6. See H. DE LUBAC, *On an Old Distich: The Doctrine of the "Fourfold Sense" in Scripture,* in ID., *Theological Fragments,* trans. R. HOWELL BALINSKI, San Francisco, CA, Ignatius Press, 1989 (orig. 1948), pp. 109-127.
7. See F. SCHÜSSLER FIORENZA, *The Crisis of Scriptural Authority: Interpretation and Reception,* in *Interpretation* 44 (1990) 353-368.

from his specific and controversial starting point (the conversion of Peter and the other disciples occasioned by their experience of forgiveness) and retrieve from his argument the more central affirmation of the fundamental structure of the resurrection experience. These two passages indicate what I have in mind.

> It is evident from that analysis of the Easter experience that the objective cannot be separated from the subjective aspect of the apostolic belief in the resurrection. Apart from the faith-motivated experience it is not possible to speak meaningfully about Jesus' resurrection. ... Without being identical with it, the resurrection of Jesus – that is, what happened to him, personally, after his death – is inseparable from the Easter experience, or faith-motivated experience, of the disciples. ... Besides this subjective aspect it is equally apparent that ... no Easter experience of renewed life was possible without the personal resurrection of Jesus – in the sense that Jesus' personal-cum-bodily resurrection ... "precedes" any faith-motivated experience[8].

> I am concerned ... with a theological clarification for modern men [and women] which will make it understandable why the first Christians seized on the model of the appearances of God and angels in the Old Testament in order to express their Easter experience. Here I will concede that this need not be a pure model; it can also imply a historical event[9].

By relying upon a phenomenological theory of constituted knowledge and a hermeneutical theory of experience, Schillebeeckx clarifies the structure of the experience. It includes what he calls (for lack of a better term) the "subjective element"; one would include here the disciples' experiences within Second Temple Judaism and its prevailing eschatological mind-set[10], their fundamentally holistic understanding of person, and their memories of Jesus, including his Kingdom proclamations, his lifestyle, and his horrific death. The disciples thus have a set of culturally-situated and articulated religious expectations over against which they understand any act of God which touches their experience. There is a non-negotiable "objective" element as well, what I would term the "non-I catalyst". This serves to shatter their expectations and take their understanding of Jewish eschatology, of personhood, and of Jesus himself in an unexpected direction.

---

8. E. SCHILLEBEECKX, *Jesus: An Experiment in Christology*, trans. H. HOSKINS, New York, Seabury – Crossroad, 1979, p. 645.

9. E. SCHILLEBEECKX, *Interim Report on the Books "Jesus" and "Christ"*, trans. J. BOWDEN, New York, Crossroad, 1981, p. 147 n. 43.

10. Cf. E.P. SANDERS, *Judaism: Practice and Belief, 63 BCE – 66 CE*, London, SCM Press; Philadelphia, PA, Trinity Press International, 1992, pp. 279-303; J.P. MEIER, *A Marginal Jew: Rethinking the Historical Jesus. Volume 2: Mentor, Message, and Miracles* (The Anchor Bible Reference Library), New York, Doubleday, 1994, pp. 237-270.

This objective, non-I element forces the disciples in their constitution of this experience to stretch all these traditional categories to fit something new, unprecedented. The fact that the gospel narratives (and Paul) purposely employ the language of vision and body for their testimony and that they "misuse" apocalyptic language, (e.g., alongside the belief that *all* will rise at the end of time, they make the claim that *one* has risen before all) are factors which force one to ask what kind of an experience would act as a catalyst for *this particular form* of consistent testimony, rather than the language of the martyred prophet or the continuation of the "cause" or "memory" of Jesus[11]. It must be an experience that can be constituted only in this fashion – that is, one for which the language of person, vision, body, unfamiliarity, familiarity, and "Jesus" is relatively appropriate. It is the experience of the "body as a symbol" of Jesus' self[12], the self which is consistent throughout the transformation and whose corporeal symbol, which bore the developed constitution of Jesus' self-identity through his human actions, still communicates his unified individuality and provokes continued relationships with his disciples. But the texts also articulate a crucial experienced difference. This is not simply the familiar Jesus but an identity which has been transformed: he frightens some, goes unrecognized by others, walks through closed doors. The narratives want to have it both ways, unfamiliar presence *and* good old Jesus, in order to communicate that this is indeed Jesus, but somehow different from the pre-Easter Jesus. The narratives, across the various gospel traditions, assume that only the use and the conscious misuse of the language of corporeality can get a handle on this experience.

This must make us pause and ask: what kind of bodiliness is this? How can corporeality support such a transformation which has been

---

11. Fundamental theological examinations of the resurrection of Jesus as the ground of Christian faith which go back no further than the New Testament narratives themselves, due to the difficulties involved in interpreting the narratives and the evident diversity of historical reconstructions of the events behind the narratives (most notably the analysis offered by F. SCHÜSSLER FIORENZA, *The Resurrection of Jesus and Roman Catholic Fundamental Theology*, in S.T. DAVIS – D. KENDALL – G. O'COLLINS (eds.), *The Resurrection: An Interdisciplinary Symposium on the Resurrection of Jesus*, Oxford – New York, Oxford University Press, 1997, pp. 213-248), offer valuable insights into the relationship between early Christian testimonies and Christian faith. But they fail to take the next logical phenomenological step and ask about the *quality of the experience* which was the catalyst for the text – that is, they fail to determine, as far as the evidence permits, what kind of experience(s) would give rise to these *specific* testimonies and to the *specific* choices of language and literary genre that appear in the New Testament.

12. S. SCHNEIDERS, *The Resurrection of Jesus and Christian Spirituality*, in M. JUNKER-KENNY (ed.), *Christian Resources of Hope*, Collegeville, MN, Liturgical Press, 1995, pp. 81-114, at 97.

promised to those who commit themselves to the values of the Kingdom of God? Do we have any hints from our own experience that corporeality has other modes beyond the literal-biological? If we do, then we will be able to confirm at the very least the open, multivalent *possibilities* which the resurrection narratives sketch out, even if the New Testament's further claim that they are realizable only by the gracious love of God must be left to faith and to the future.

Here is where we need to turn to postmodern theory for some hint as to how to articulate a dynamic and intentional way of considering bodies which gets a handle on our problem in a way that the New Testament cannot. Judith Butler has argued that gender is bodily performance, an inscription upon the body of social roles which are internalized but always infinitely revisable. What heretofore has been considered part of the inherent substantial identity of a person mirrored outwards is for Butler a collection of bodily gestures and social practices really mirrored inwards, an internalized identity giving the appearance of some inward organizing principle, but really being nothing but a performative fiction sustained through corporeal signs[13], Butler treats the body as other than an established material-empirical meaning. "The body is not a 'being', but a variable boundary, a surface whose permeability is politically regulated, a signifying practice", and thus gender is "*a corporeal style,* an 'act', as it were, which is both intentional and performative, where *'performative'* suggests a dramatic and contingent construction of meaning"[14]. Gender, in this analysis, is a set of stylized acts repeated over time, "a constituted *social temporality*"[15].

Many such understandings of "body" as essentially incarnate intentional performance have their ultimate source in the phenomenology of Maurice Merleau-Ponty. He not only saw the body as a series of intentional actions sedimented in time and united by a consciousness which itself was temporal in structure, but realized that the body was conscious of the world in a way different from and prior to logical consciousness[16]. Whether or not one agrees with Butler on the point that there is no internal organizing principle (I disagree with her, as the following section will show), she makes it clear, as does Merleau-Ponty, that bodies are more than their biological substratum. In fact, our bodies are performances of

13. J. BUTLER, *Gender Trouble: Feminism and the Subversion of Identity,* New York, Routledge, 1990, p. 136.

14. *Ibid.,* p. 139.

15. *Ibid.,* p. 141.

16. M. MERLEAU-PONTY, *Phenomenology of Perception,* trans. C. SMITH, London, Routledge and Kegan Paul, 1962, especially part one, chapter one and part two, chapter three.

our intentional relationships with the world which both reveal the world to us and reveal our intentional desires to the world. Our bodies bear the traces of previous performances and open us up to new configurations. Such a view goes a long way in restoring one of the four senses of the body we mentioned earlier, the allegorical, where bodily actions have meanings and effects directed not just outwards towards others and the world, but back toward ourselves as well.

But this is not the whole story. The body does not simply dissolve into infinitely malleable discourse. In a survey of contemporary theories of the body, Caroline Bynum has pointed out how many ancient and medieval discussions, from Origen to Thomas Aquinas, had concerns that are surprisingly similar to Butler's, though for vastly different reasons: they were trying to pack as many personal bodily characteristics as possible into the soul in order to explain how the self persists after death[17]. But they encountered the same problem that afflicts Butler's theory as well, the material resistance and limits of the lived body-experiences such as death, pleasure, weight, the fact that bodies are not simply infinitely revisable rhetorical projects. "Both Butler and Origen speak of a labile, active, unfolding body that somehow becomes more what it is by behaving as it does; both have trouble explaining how what we think of as 'physical stuff' fits in"[18].

My suggestion, that we understand the body as intentionality-in-time, supports such intuitions of corporeal openness and of resistance. It also accounts for the fact that the body at times outruns our intentions and, to some degree, has a life of its own. I am my body, and yet I am also not my body. Think about the sinus headache you wake up with and the recalcitrant body which you have to drag out of bed by sheer force of will. Think of skin: the same skin which touches fabric to feel texture is used to hold a child in order to give comfort; in the midst of an intimate encounter with another it can go electric, driving us with passion that is difficult to control. The body can reveal meanings and configurations that are even surprising to us and provides a depth of connection to the world and to others which outstrips any merely material-empirical attempt at description.

Let me summarize this section on bodiliness. We intended to find out whether the body has more than simply a literal, biological, material-empirical sense, and to some extent we have succeeded. Contemporary

17. C. BYNUM, *Why All the Fuss about the Body? A Medievalist's Perspective*, in *Critical Inquiry* 22 (1995) 1-32, at p. 21.
18. *Ibid.*, p. 30.

theory about the body, emphasizing the performative nature of embodiment and the residual bodily effects of these performances, discloses the allegorical sense of the body, the extended depth of bodiliness as experienced through its meaningful practices. The body is not closed in upon its apparently stable materiality and is more than a commodified object. Rather, the body is open beyond itself by its pluriform possibilities and intentional desires and even defined to some degree by those desires and their fulfillment. A strong theory of the resurrection brings us even further, and allows us to grasp in faith that this symbolic depth of the body with its pluriform possibilities was once confirmed by God and fulfilled by the power of God in the risen Jesus. This is the anagogical sense of the body, God's promise for our embodied selves made manifest in the glorified body of the Lord. We are promised, then, that our constituted embodied selves, with all of their history, will be redeemed and transformed.

III. THE RETRIEVAL OF THE FUNCTION OF "SOUL"

As "the story of divine love calling creation back from death", eschatology has always drawn upon "a repertoire of images that is endlessly varied and at times seemingly at variance with itself"[19]. Part of this repertoire is the language of "soul" properly understood as an imaginative metaphorical construct which refers "to my whole self, gathered together"[20]. Thus, despite the world-denying ways in which it has been used, "soul" language has played a crucial aesthetic role by offering religious experience a way to imagine everyday life "otherwise".

This *aesthetic* function gets to the heart of eschatological hope. Eschatology is an argument against closure, against understandings of the self which identify "person" with finitude, with closed-in self-sufficiency, and with "bodiliness" in the literal, biological sense. It is also a strategy of critique and resistence to the over-arching consumer logic, the loss of historical consciousness, and the relentlessly immanentist and claustrophobic view of the self which characterizes much contemporary culture and contemporary theory.

One of Catholic eschatology's concerns, then, is to defend the *duality* of the self – view of self-identity which is not reducible to finite material-empirical constraints – while respecting Catholicism's commitments

---

19. C. ZALESKI, *The Life of the World to Come. Near-Death Experience and Christian Hope*, New York – Oxford, Oxford University Press, 1996, p. 81.
    20. *Ibid.*, p. 60.

to incarnation and sacramentality. Theology's task is to assess the experience of embodied self-identity and discern the ground of unified and unique individual freedom within the historically- and socially-situated embodied self. Eschatology thus shares some of the concerns of contemporary philosophy to defend individuality and human freedom over against characteristically post-structuralist attempts to subvert subjectivity and make it merely an effect of discourse or social construction. Manfred Frank, for example, has posed this dilemma which faces all those who seek to describe the self as both situated and free:

> How can one, on the one hand, do justice to the fundamental fact that meaning, significance, and intention – the semantic foundations of every consciousness – can form themselves only in a language, in a social, cultural, and economic order (in a structure)? How can one, on the other hand, redeem the fundamental idea of modern humanism that links the dignity of human beings with their use of freedom, and which cannot tolerate that one morally applaud the factual threatening of human subjectivity by the totalitarianism of systems of rules and social codes[21]?

A hermeneutical approach which views "I" as a constituted self is particularly valuable here. Hans-Georg Gadamer's dialectical understanding of experience provides a way to uncover the constitution of historically-conscious self-identity over time and the non-negotiable role played by in that constitution by our relations with others[22]. Experience is primarily structured by means of an "outward" motion away from the self which relies on a field or "screen" of expectations based on one's previously-acquired fund of experience. These act as a horizon over against which one discovers what is other than the self. The "otherwise" or new element is then brought back to the self to be integrated with the previously-acquired fund of experience. Whatever is "new" can only be recognized as such if it is *other than* or *shatters* one's expectations. Without the shattering effect, one would not be able to recognize the "new" or the "different"; one would not have an "experience" at all, but simply repetition. The "otherwise" of experience is the crucial event and discloses two further aspects of experience. First, every experience is both positive and negative; we *know* more and *are* more than we were before, but we also realize that we do not know and are not everything – there is always something new to encounter and limits that need to be shattered if one's

21. M. FRANK, *What is Neostructuralism?*, trans. S. WILKE – R. GRAY (Theory and History of Literature, vol. 45), Minneapolis, MN, University of Minnesota Press, 1989, p. 6.

22. For Gadamer's theory of experience, see H.-G. GADAMER, *Truth and Method*, 2nd rev. ed., trans. rev. J. WEINSHEIMER – D.G. MARSHALL, New York, Crossroad, 1989, pp. 346-362.

identity is to develop. Next, what provokes the shattering cannot be ourselves (since it must be other than our hitherto-constituted identity) but must have its source in what is other than the self, the "non-I". Thus others (as well as the world) are implicated in my very self-identity – I cannot be "I" without a relation to an "other/Other". The truth of the self, then, is a reality constituted over time in a relational setting. This mirrors Gadamer's primary model of conversational play in the constitution of the truth of a work of art. In the same way as tradition is seen by Gadamer as a "history of effects" *(Wirkungsgeschichte)* construed as meaning projected beyond texts, so too the self, with all its relationships, can be viewed as an ensemble of effects projected beyond the material-empirical substratum of the body and unified by self-consciousness.

But this is not an immediately transparent self. It is, rather, a self characterized by a lack, a non-presence, a self whose final significance is never settled because it is constituted over time. The truth of the self always remains relative to the interpretation of its partial significations, which are the only ones in our grasp[23]. It is an embodied self which is visible in its incarnate actions, yet also ineffable. In attempting to defend the self against "the postmodern declaration of its death"[24], Manfred Frank has pointed to the importance of the individual's freedom, rooted in self-consciousness, which can never be grasped as a perceived object in reflection and which exists prior to any structured systems of signs[25]. "Every human practice," he argues, "participates in two orders", structuring and application[26]. Structure is the sphere of universal certainty and the homogeneous, the formation of general concepts and conventions which attempt to order experience by emphasizing what is "the same". Application, on the other hand, is the realm of individual experience which can never be predicted, never reduced to a rule. While structure may be conveyed by a tradition, application by an individual within the

23. M. FRANK, *What is Neostructuralism?* (n. 21), pp. 363-364.
24. See ID., *Die Unhintergehbarkeit von Individualität: Reflexionen über Subjekt, Person und Individuum aus Anlaß ihrer "postmodernen" Toterklärung,* Frankfurt am Main, Suhrkamp, 1986.
25. ID., *Stil in der Philosophie,* Stuttgart, Reclam, 1992, pp. 49-52; English translation of the complete work: *Style in Philosophy,* trans. J. JANSEN – M.K. SHIN, in *Metaphilosophy* 30 (1999) 145-167 and 264-310, at pp. 264-266; English translation of Part II: *Toward a Philosophy of Style,* trans. R.E. PALMER, in *Common Knowledge* 1 (1992/1) 54-77, at pp. 54-56 (hereafter I will cite only the Palmer translation, which is more accurate). See also M. FRANK, *What is Neostructuralism?* (n. 21), pp. 362-366, as well as A. Bowie's summary of Frank's position in the introduction to M. FRANK, *The Subject and the Text: Essays on Literary Theory and Philosophy,* trans. H. ATKINS, ed. A. BOWIE, Cambridge, Cambridge University Press, 1997, pp. xx-xxvi, xxxi-xxxvi.
26. FRANK, *Toward a Philosophy of Style* (n. 25), p. 54.

individual's specific situation ensures "the irreducibility of the individual to the universal"[27]. The combination of structure and application Frank calls "style". It is the task of "style" to highlight the irreducibly individual aspects of human activity.

The individual's critically discerning application is a manifestation of individual freedom and a basic human right which cannot be obliterated by arguments which attempt to render the self totally determined by its social setting (e.g., structuralist and poststructuralist arguments for the linguisticality of experience)[28]. Against these, Frank argues for a postmodern subjectivity invested with freedom:

> What comes forward here on a very basic level is the freedom possessed by human beings, a freedom made manifest in the *unforseeability of interpretation*. Interpretation is neither determined solely by the object nor is it simply derived from the concept through which a "community of investigators" or of "speakers/interlocutors" has somehow "codified" it into something "intersubjectively sharable"[29].

He makes a strong case for what he calls the "nondeducible process of individuation, a process that relates and connects a canonical structure to a lived experience, an experience never to be identically repeated", that is, the individual subject's existence already before all signs and structures, since signs and structures are artificial and are empowered by meaning-giving subjects whose self-consciousness is recognized prior to all differential representations and significations[30].

Here, then, are two contemporary ways of unblinkingly acknowledging the *duality* of human experience without falling into dualism. The desire of both these theories to describe the self as constituted by non-closure or transcending intentionality parallels the desire of eschatology to speak of the individual self whose identity persists beyond the closure of death. But it is only a parallel, not an equivalence; to demonstrate non-closure does not prove the persistence of the self after death. The character of life after death remains a mystery beyond any extrapolation from finite

---

27. *Ibid.*
28. Frank has labeled such determinist arguments "linguistic idealism": "For the old idealists, everything of which we are conscious was supposed to exist immanently in consciousness itself; for the new linguistic idealists, everything that becomes intelligible by means of language is itself something linguistic" (*The Subject v. Language: Mental Familiarity and Epistemic Self-Ascription*, trans. L.K. SCHMIDT – B. ALLEN, in *Common Knowledge* 4 (1995/2) 30-50, at p. 33.
29. M. FRANK, *Toward a Philosophy of Style* (n. 25), p. 54 (my emphasis).
30. *Ibid.*, pp. 55-56; see also A. Bowie's introduction to *The Subject and the Text* (n. 25), pp. xxv-xxxvi.

experience. Only the revelation of human destiny through the resurrection of Christ gives us the freedom to imagine eternal life with God as a real human possibility.

But we can use a philosophical anthropology as one aspect of a theological anthropology and eschatology which attempt to make the mystery intelligible insofar as this is possible. Both Gadamer and Frank suggest a model of the self as an ensemble of events, effects, and relationships constituted and played out over time, whose identity, while incomplete, is nonetheless composed of both exteriority (structure) and interiority (intentional self-consciousness). Both qualities are temporal, each quality is the condition for the other, and neither is reducible to the other. Frank's use of the term "style" – the intersection of socially-constructed code and unique application resulting in the "unforseeability of interpretation", an irreducibly individualized constitution of real meaning which nonetheless is intersubjectively sharable – comes close in tone to the religiously imaginative use of "soul" to stand for the uniquely constituted and deeply unified "I" which is nonetheless recognizable as a human among humans. "Style" and "soul" symbolize the intersubjectively sharable incarnated depth of the self. They are ways of aesthetically representing the unique-yet-relational "I" which is a real projection beyond the immediately perceptible.

And it is the anticipated or experienced loss in death of this unique ensemble of embodied experiences (both our own style/soul as well as that of those we love) which fills us with dread. We feel tragically lost when we face the dissolution of our own proper self or the dissolution of the beloved other's self who is part of me and whose effects are part of my own proper "style". And this is why "soul" with its connotations of depth, of hard-won personal integration, of irreplaceable uniqueness remains a valuable aesthetic and affective symbol which can express both our limitless love and our devastating loss. To lament along with Job that "my soul is weary of life" (Job 10,1) or to pray along with Mary "my soul magnifies the Lord, my spirit rejoices in God my savior" (Luke 1,46) is to symbolize more than to say "I loathe my life" or "I acclaim the greatness of the Lord, I delight in God my savior"[31]. We have experienced too many commodified or self-centered "I"s to hear in the latter phrases anything more than the flat indication of personal space. What we mourn in the death of a loved one is the dreaded loss of an irrepeatable

---

31. "I loathe my life" is the New American Bible's translation of Job 10,1; "I acclaim..." is the translation of Luke 1,46 from *Psalms for Morning and Evening Prayer,* Chicago, IL, Liturgy Training Publications, 1995, p. 267.

incarnate configuration of personal experiences, of an "incarnate personal style" – the loss of an embodied spirit in the world who loved us and strained toward God. In the presence of death, why should we not be sad, or in torment, or wailing in lamentation? And why cannot the Church, secure in its belief in the resurrection, still meet us through the liturgy where we are in the "not yet", acknowledging our pain in the midst of an extravagant richness of liturgical symbolism which does justice to the mystery of life and death?

Eschatology is an argument against closure. The bodily resurrection of Jesus is a sign of the duality of self-identity and is a witness against the collapse of "self" into the literal, biological sense of bodiliness. Thus, if these anthropological arguments are to have the desired effects of supporting a contemporary Catholic eschatology and providing a meaningful elucidation of the character of life after death, then they must reflect the Catholic commitment to incarnation and to sacramentality and contribute to a deepening of theological anthropology. They must grapple with both the message of revelation and the presuppositions (even the ideologies) of contemporary culture. If our best eschatological assertions can only be the result of the extrapolation of our embodied temporal experience seen in the radiance of revelation, then we owe ourselves an understanding of embodied, relational personhood which not only supports a liberating praxis in this life, but a liberating redemptive performance by God in union with our truly lived selves in the life of the world to come[32].

Department of Theology and   Anthony J. GODZIEBA
Religious Studies
Villanova University
800 Lancaster Avenue
Villanova, PA 19085-1699
U.S.A.

32. My thanks to Francis Schüssler Fiorenza, Anne Clifford, and Kevin Hughes for their comments on earlier versions of this paper.

RELATIONSHIP IN GOD AND THE SALVATION OF HUMANKIND

THE THOUGHT OF WALTER KASPER

Inspired by the theology of Walter Kasper, this article focuses on the relation between the inner conversation in God and the history of salvation. Modern philosophy – modern personalism – takes its starting point in the human *subject* and more especially in the idea of *freedom* and tries then to think of *being (God)* in the horizon of freedom[1]. The study and treatment of the modern complex of problems is for Kasper one of the most important tasks of contemporary theology. Kasper wants to define God's essence against the background of the modern philosophy of personal freedom[2].

Modern personalism has made clear that a human person cannot exist but in relation: personality cannot exist but as inter-personality, subjectivity as inter-subjectivity[3]. Every human person is a *vis-à-vis* of another one and vice versa.

I. RELATIONSHIP *WITHIN* GOD AS A CONDITION OF POSSIBILITY FOR THE TRANSCENDENCE OF GOD

It is the indisputable conviction of the Old Testament that Yahweh is one and unique (Deut 6,4). However, within the framework of modern

---

1. W. KASPER, *Der Gott Jesu Christi*, Mainz, 1982, pp. 193 ff.
2. Cf. *ibid.*, pp. 192 ff.: When Kasper makes an attempt at placing the definition of God's essence in the horizon of the modern philosophy of freedom, he also wants to do justice to the claims of the traditional definition of God's essence in the horizon of metaphysics; at the same time, he wants to do more justice to the biblical foundations. At the start Kasper stays in line with J.E. Kuhn of the Catholic Tübingen School of the nineteenth century. Ultimately, he will opt, under the influence of the later philosophy of F.W.J. Schelling (1775-1854) and in critical distinction from Kuhn, whose thoughts at the end for Kasper are too idealistically linked, for a post-idealistic start that is more aware of the facticity of reality as both incapable of being derived from spirit and as nonetheless a given that cannot be ignored. Cf. *ibid.*, p. 140. Cf. ID., *Vorwort. Zur gegenwärtigen Situation und zu den gegenwärtigen Aufgaben der Systematischen Theologie*, in ID., *Theologie und Kirche I*, Mainz, 1987, p. 17. Cf. ID., *Das Wahrheitsverständnis der Theologie*, in ID., *Theologie und Kirche II*, Mainz, 1999, p. 43.
3. ID., *Der Gott Jesu Christi* (n. 1), p. 353.

personalism an isolated (unipersonal) God is inconceivable[4]. Once God
is considered initially as personal, the oneness and unicity of God can
impossibly be thought of as the designation of a solitary God. God must
be thought of as a relational entity, as a person.

The understanding of God as free person inevitably must lead to
the question: who is God's appropriate *vis-à-vis* (in German his
"entsprechende Gegenüber")? There cannot be an I without a thou.
Given that a human person, the people, or the human race are God's only
vis-à-vis, then man would be an imperative partner of God. Man could
then not longer be seen as the one who is loved with a boundless free and
gracious act but rather as a need of God and a supplement of God. If the
only counterpart for God is the human race, then the relation becomes an
imperative one and God loses his absolute freedom, in other words his
transcendence[5].

In a certain sense this is the problem shown by Fichte: because of the
fact that "persons" only exist in relation to other persons of our world,
Fichte concluded that personality means at the same time that God would
be limited and conditioned and that therefore it cannot be applied to God[6].
Here we have the deepest reason why the theistic view with its unipersonal God is untenable[7]. A unipersonal view will be intrinsically forced
to search for God's partner; such a unipersonal view will necessarily
accept the world or man as God's appropriate partners, but, at the same
time, by setting up that imperative relationship, God's freedom in love,
i.e. his transcendence, will no longer be preserved[8]. If God's essence is
only overflowing love upon the world, then He can only exist on the condition that world and man exist. Consequently God's existence depends
on man's existence and in fact God is no longer God. If God is to keep
his Godness and not become dependent on the world or man, then he
must be co-existent (in German "Mitsein") within himself[9]. God must be
thought of as relational within Himself, as an intra-relational person.
In other words: God must be love (cf. *infra*).

So we can ask: who is the adequate recipient of the love which is
God himself? If God's inner nature is nothing but a pure loving outpouring of himself upon the world and man, then God can impossibly

4. *Ibid.*, p. 353.
5. *Ibid.*, p. 297.
6. *Ibid.*, p. 194.
7. *Ibid.*, pp. 294-295.
8. *Ibid.*, p. 364.
9. *Ibid.*, p. 373.

exist without the world. But is a God who cannot live without the world still God [10]? Is God still God if he needs the human race and the world to be himself? So, God must be love within himself: he must be communication and self-emptying within himself. We have to presuppose an intra-relational, inner-divine love within God himself as an imperative condition for the possibility of preserving his absolute transcendence. In *Der Gott Jesu Christi* Kasper concludes: "Will man die biblische Botschaft von Gott als absoluter Person und volkommener Freiheit in der Liebe auch im Denken konsequent durchhalten, dann wird das trinitarische Bekenntnis der Bibel für das gläubige Denken plausibel"[11].

God's oneness must be thought of as love that exists only in the giving of itself. Kasper here speaks of God as "communion-unity" ("Communio-Einheit")[12]. In God the communion of love is not one of separate beings, as it is among men, but a communion within a single nature. This is why in his farewell prayer Jesus says "All I have is yours and all you have is mine" (John 17,10). In his *De Trinitate* Saint Augustine has formulated this view: "The Trinity is the one and only God, and the one and only God is the Trinity"[13]. For Kasper concrete monotheism cannot be thought of as in the way of the doctrine of the Trinity and vice versa: "Die Kirche will nicht trotz der Trinitätslehre auch noch an der Einheit Gottes festhalten. Sie will vielmehr gerade in der Trinitätslehre am christlichen Monotheismus festhalten. Ja, sie hält die Trinitätslehre für die einzig mögliche und konsequente Form des Monotheismus"[14].

II. TRINITARIAN RELATIONSHIP WITHIN GOD AS A CONDITION OF POSSIBILITY FOR THE SALVATION OF HUMANKIND

Only because God is God – the transcendent one, the absolute person – and not in an imperative dependent relation with man and world, (only then) can He be the Saviour of man and world. Only because God is love within himself, can He be conceived as not being imperative but free and gratuitous. Only because God is love within himself, (only then)

10. *Ibid.*, p. 198.
11. *Ibid.*, p. 364.
12. *Ibid.*, p. 373.
13. AUGUSTIN, *De Trinitate*, I, 4.
14. KASPER, *Der Gott Jesu Christi* (n. 1), p. 360.

can the outpouring of his love upon the world be saving love for us[15]. He can be this when his relational life *ad intra* is similar to his relational life *ad extra*. God's self-communication in the history of salvation through the Son in the Spirit would not really be God's own self-revelation unless it also belongs to God's internal life, in other words, unless the economic Trinity *is* also the immanent Trinity[16].

Moreover, only the true God, God as God, the transcendent God – not the solitary one, not the one who is dependent on the world or man – can save the world. The only way to think of man's salvation is as salvation comprehended as God himself; salvation, understood as a created gift ("gratia creata") distinct from God's nature, can impossibly be certified as man's true salvation. "Das Handeln Gottes durch Jesus Christus im Heiligen Geist ist deshalb nur dann Gottes Heilshandeln, wenn wir es dabei mit Gott selbst zu tun bekommen, wenn dort Gott selbst als der, der er an sich ist, für uns da ist. Die ökonomische Trinität würde also jeden Sinn verlieren, wenn sie nicht zugleich die immanente Trinität wäre"[17].

Since in Jesus Christ God has revealed himself definitively and eschatologically, consequently this theo-logical characteristic of the person of Jesus Christ implies that in Jesus Christ God must have communicated himself unreservedly. In the Christ-event there cannot be some unilluminated and hidden part (*Deus absconditus*) "behind" the illuminated and visible reality (*Deus revelatus*). Rather, the *Deus absconditus* is the *Deus revelatus*. The mystery of God is the mystery of our salvation. In the words of Kasper: "Die Wesensaussage ohne die Heilsaussage wäre eine abstrakte Spekulation; die Heilsaussage ohne die Wesensaussage kraftlos und unbegründet"[18]. It was the purpose of K. Rahner (1904-1984) to link again the doctrine of the Trinity with the history of salvation.

1. *The Economic Trinity Is the Immanent Trinity: Need for Differentiation*

But the identification of the immanent and the economic Trinities is of course open to various misinterpretations[19].

---

15. *Ibid.*, pp. 360-361.
16. Cf. *ibid.*, pp. 365 ff.
17. Cf. *ibid.*, pp. 333 ff., esp. p. 334.
18. ID., *Jesus der Christus*, Mainz, 1992[11], p. 201. On the level of Christology Kasper stresses that a functional Christology may never be played off against an ontological Christology. Jesus' pro-existence presupposes his pre-existence. Cf. ID., *Christologie und Anthropologie*, in *Theologie und Kirche I* (n. 2), pp. 194-216, esp. 215-216.
19. ID., *Der Gott Jesu Christi* (n. 1), pp. 335 ff.

(i) If people – on the score of the presumed identity – consider the economic Trinity only as a temporal manifestation of the eternal immanent Trinity, they deprive the economic Trinity of its proper historical reality.

(ii) Today, of course, the opposite misinterpretation is more frequent: the dissolution of the immanent Trinity in the economic Trinity. In eternity the "personal" distinctions would then at best be modal, and would be constituted truly personal only in history. This is the case in the theology of Piet Schoonenberg (1911-1999). For Schoonenberg there is no other way to know God in his own immanent – and for us transcendent – Trinity than on the basis of his economic Trinity in the Christ-event[20]. All that can be said about the immanent Trinity, has been said about the economic Trinity and can never injure the latter[21]. The question whether God is triune from the beginning – i.e. independent of the Christ-event in the history of salvation – is for Schoonenberg a question which has nothing to do with our salvation[22]. Only on the basis of the certain premise of the history of salvation, could one justify either an affirmation or a denial concerning the possibility of the immanent Trinity. Schoonenberg accepts only one such premise: the impossibility of the Son as a person with a complete self-awareness and a complete freedom. Otherwise the primary certainty that Jesus is one human person[23] (with freedom and self-awareness) would be deprived and the risk of a three-theism would not be imaginary.

Here we recognize Schoonenberg's preference for a christology "from below" (here, of course, in the case of the doctrine of the Trinity). The (for Schoonenberg) meaningless question whether God is triune, independent of his self-revelation in the history of salvation can according to Schoonenberg only get an adequate answer if man could enter into the mysterious relation between God's immutability on the one side and his free self-revelation on the other side. Since this relation can never be

---

20. Cf. P. SCHOONENBERG, *De Geest het Woord en de Zoon. Theologische overdenkingen over Geest-christologie, Logos-christologie en drieëenheidsleer*, Averbode – Kampen, 1991, pp. 153-154.

21. Those are the two – what Alfred Kaiser calls – "hermeneutische Grundregeln" of Schoonenberg, in this context applied to the Trinity. Cf. SCHOONENBERG, *Hij is een God van mensen. Twee theologische studies*, 's-Hertogenbosch, L.C.G. Malmberg, 1969, pp. 79 ff. Cf. A. KAISER, *Möglichkeiten und Grenzen einer Christologie "von unten". Der christologische Neuansatz "von unten" bei Piet Schoonenberg und dessen Weiterführung mit Blick auf Nikolaus von Kues*, Münster, 1992, p. 153.

22. Cf. P. SCHOONENBERG, *Jezus, de mens die Gods Zoon is*, in *De Heraut* 99 (1968) 37-39.

23. ID., *Hij is een God van mensen* (n. 21), pp. 66-74.

accessible for any human person, the initial question always stays "unbeantwortet und unbeantwortbar"[24].

At this point Kasper's criticism enters into the discussion. When Schoonenberg says that the distinction between Father, Son and Holy Spirit is *personal* on the level of the history of salvation, but at best *modal* on the level of the immanent Trinity[25], this statement contradicts his former conviction of the inaccessibility of the immanent intra-divine mystery (cf. *supra*)[26]. If it is true that God has revealed himself in an eschatological-definitive way as outpouring of love in Jesus Christ, then this self-communication of God between the Father and the Son must be the eternal nature of God himself[27]. Schoonenberg's statements – (a) that the immanent Trinity as such has never existed; and (b) that the economic Trinity and the immanent Trinity are "equally-eternal"; and (c) (in line with Karl Rahner) that the economic Trinity is the immanent Trinity[28] with the implication that the eternal *(modal)* Trinity constitute themselves as truly *personal* just in and through history (cf. *infra*) – ultimately lead to an absorption of the immanent Trinity into the economic Trinity.

(iii) Finally, Rahner's theological axiom is totally misused when someone, so to speak, only wants to be occupied with the salvation of humankind and consequently considers exclusively the Trinity in the economy of salvation. By eliminating the considerations of the Trinity in God's immanent nature, he simultaneously deprives the economic Trinity of all meaning and significance. For the latter, Kasper says, only has meaning and significance if God has communicated himself in the history of salvation as the one who he is from eternity. The identification

24. Cf. SCHOONENBERG, *Trinität – der vollendete Bund. Thesen zur Lehre vom dreipersönlichen Gott*, in *Orientierung* 37 (1973) 115-117.

25. Cf. *ibid.*, p. 116.

26. Cf. KASPER, *Jesus der Christus* (n. 18), p. 215: Kasper means that the inherent contradiction in Schoonenberg's theology has been rooted in his philosophical a priori that looks for the relation between God's immutability on the one side and his free self-determination on the other side. According to Kasper, it is not the task of theology to take an abstract philosophical a priori as its starting point, but rather the conviction of the New Testament that God has revealed his deepest nature – God is Love (1 John 4,8.16) – in Jesus Christ in an eschatological-definitive way.

27. Cf. *ibid.*, p. 207 and p. 215: Precisely from the eschatological and definitive character of the person of Jesus Christ ("Jesus ist der Christus" is for Kasper the "Kurzformel" of theology). Kasper also will interpret the idea of Christ's pre-existence. If God has communicated himself in an unsurpassable and definitive way in Jesus Christ, then Jesus himself must belong to the definition of God's inner nature. The concept of the pre-existence expresses in a deeper way the eschatological aspect of the person and the work of Jesus Christ and is consequently always soteriologically determined.

28. Cf. SCHOONENBERG, *De Geest het Woord* (n. 20), pp. 202 ff.: in Dutch Schoonenberg uses the word "gelijkeeuwig".

only has significance if God does not simply *show* himself historically to us as Father, Son and Spirit, but *is* really and eternally the triune God[29].

2. *The Economic Trinity Is the Immanent Trinity: History as Differentiation and Determination*

According to Kasper, theology can escape such misinterpretations – which lead to the dissolution or absorption of the immanent Trinity – when the "is" of the axiom (the immanent Trinity "is" the economic Trinity) is not comprehended in the sense of the mathematical law A=A. The "is" in the axiom must be understood not as an essential and solid identification but rather as a "non-deducible, free, gracious, historical presence of the immanent Trinity in the economic Trinity". Kasper will reformulate Rahner's basic axiom in line with his "historical"[30] interest: "In der heilsgeschichtlichen Selbstmitteilung ist die innertrinitarischen Selbstmitteilung in einer neuen Weise in der Welt present: unter geschichtlichen Worten, Zeichen und Taten, letztlich in der Gestalt des Menschen Jesus von Nazaret"[31].

The immanent Trinity – the inner life of the triune God – is the transcendental condition of the possibility of God's self-revelation in salvation history in Jesus Christ through the Holy Spirit[32]. The non-deducible and new aspect of this Christ-event is the ultimate hope for mankind and the world. Only a new and non-deducible event can assure a hopeful future for humankind.

As a result of his study of the late philosophy of F.W.J. Schelling (1775-1854)[33] Kasper recognizes the awakening of the unfathomable and underivable facticity of reality: "Es wurde die Einsicht bestimmend, daß die menschliche Vernunft radikal über sich selbst hinaus verweist. Sie kann sich weder selbst begründen noch sich selbst erfüllen. In ihrer unableitbarer Faktizität ist sie ganz auf die Geschichte und die ihr in und aus der Geschichte begegnenden Sinnantworten verwiesen. Sie kann nicht

29. KASPER, *Der Gott Jesu Christi* (n. 1), p. 336.

30. Cf. T. PRÖPPER, *Freiheit als philosophisches Prinzip der Dogmatik. Systematische Reflexionen im Anschluß an Walter Kaspers Konzeption der Dogmatik*, in E. SCHOCKENHOFF – P. WALTER (eds.), *Dogma und Glaube. Bausteine für eine theologische Erkenntnislehre. Festschrift für Bischof Walter Kasper*, Mainz, 1993, pp. 165-192, esp. 165: one of the characteristics of the Catholic *Tübingen Schule* was the unity of historical and speculative thinking.

31. KASPER, *Der Gott Jesu Christi* (n. 1), p. 336.

32. ID., *Jesus der Christus* (n. 18), p. 218.

33. Cf. ID., *Das Absolute in der Geschichte. Philosophie und Theologie der Geschichte in der Spätphilosophie Schellings*, Mainz, 1965.

mehr deduktiv von einer selbst sicheren Subjektivität bzw. Rationalität ausgehen"[34].

In the philosophy of all the post-idealistic thinkers Kasper finds "das Unvordenkliche, die Unableitbarkeit und geschichtliche Faktizität der Wirklichkeit"[35]. Finally this insight among other things will bring Kasper to a more differentiated position concerning the relation between the immanent and the economic Trinities or even between anthropology and Christology[36]. According to Kasper, the young Rahner in his thinking about the relationship between history and transcendentality paid too little attention to the fact that the content of history implies a determination ("Determination") of the transcendental conditions of possibility of understanding and that the content of history is not derivable from those conditions[37]. Kasper writes in his article *Das Wahrheitsverständnis der Theologie:* "Es gelingt Rahner nicht immer, die geschichtliche Unableitbarkeit und Einmaligkeit der Offenbarungswahrheit zu wahren, sosehr er dies prinzipiell selbstverständlich will"[38].

At this point Kasper asks the question "Doch wäre hier nicht zu differenzieren". Kasper remarks that Rahner's Christology is still too closely linked to an idealistic philosophy of identity and identification of being and consciousness; not only with regard to the relation between the immanent and economic Trinities (cf. supra), but also with regard to the relation between anthropology and Christology. Where Rahner defines Christology as "the unique highest instance of the essential realization of human reality" or in other words as "a self-transcendent anthropology" and the latter as "a deficient Christology", Kasper defines (in line with his emphasis on differentiation and determination) Christology as "a substantial determination of anthropology which as such must remain open" and anthropology as "the grammar which God uses to express himself"[39].

34. ID., *Zustimmung zum Denken. Von der Unerläßlichkeit der Metaphysik für die Sache der Theologie.* Abschiedsvorlesung an der Katholisch-Theologischen Fakultät der Eberhard-Karls-Universität Tübingen am 6. Juni 1989, in ID., *Theologie und Kirche II* (n. 2), pp. 11-27, esp. p. 23.

35. ID., *Das Wahrheitsverständnis der Theologie*, in ID., *Theologie und Kirche II* (n. 2), pp. 28-50, esp. p. 43.

36. In the context of this article, the development of the implications and consequences of this insight would lead us too far. Cf. on this subject ID., *Freiheit als philosophisches und theologisches Problem in der Philosophie Schellings*, in ID., *Glaube und Geschichte*, Mainz, 1970, pp. 33-47. Cf. ID., *Jesus der Christus* (n. 18), pp. 62 ff; *Der Gott Jesu Christi* (n. 1), pp. 140 ff.

37. Cf. ID., *Jesus der Christus* (n. 18), pp. 59-61.

38. ID., *Das Wahrheitsverständnis der Theologie* (n. 35), p. 44.

39. Cf. ID., *Jesus der Christus* (n. 18), pp. 59-61.

More than Rahner, Kasper focuses on the relation between God and man inside a historical horizon: he understands history as a process of reciprocity between subject and object. In this process man determines the world and the world determines man[40].

3. *History as a Process of Reciprocal Determination in Freedom*

Inspired by the Catholic Tübingen School of the nineteenth century Kasper views the human person in the horizon of the concept of "historicity" ("Geschichtlichkeit"). Where there is history, there is freedom, and vice versa. In line with the *Tübinger Schule* and with the late Schelling, Kasper takes the idea of freedom as his starting point and he develops his theology in a historical horizon. Being fundamentally conditioned on the one side and absolutely unconditioned on the other side, human freedom always exists in a dialectic of historically existing freedom. That is the paradoxical situation of every human being[41].

On the one hand, by reason of his freedom, man overreaches all that exists, the whole of reality. He lives by wishful thoughts and images of a successful existence. He overreaches all facts and asks about the meaning of existence, about the significance of the entire reality. We can say: on the one hand, that man is greater than reality. He always experiences a greater possibility than reality, and that possibility is the stage of his freedom of action.

On the other hand reality is greater than man. Man is always pre-given to himself in his freedom. He cannot yet deduce the pure fact of his existence. Here reality precedes man: in the end, ultimately in the phenomenon of death, reality surrounds man and is greater than man.

How is human existence possible in this aporetic historical situation? How can human freedom reach its fulfilment and how can human hope get its answer? To avoid that the paradoxical human situation would end in absurdity and to assure that the definitive goal of human freedom would be accessible, there must be an absolute self-communicating freedom which is not only intentionally unconditioned and absolute (as the freedom of every human being), but also in reality actually is unconditioned and absolute[42]. According to Kasper, human freedom is possible only if – ultimately – absolute freedom rules in reality as a whole. The entire reality is defined by freedom and relation; and this relation is the guarantee of man's hope, the guarantee also of a happy ending for

---

40. Cf. *ibid.*, p. 63: here again we find the "Determinationsdialektik" of J.E. Kuhn.
41. PRÖPPER, *Freiheit* (n. 30), pp. 169-170.
42. Cf. ID., *Jesus der Christus* (n. 18), pp. 65-66.

man's freedom and relationship. The absolute relation is the condition
for the relations between human persons. Kasper will say that, in the core,
reality is defined by relation, i.e. a triune relation: "Die Ausbildung der
Trinitätslehre bedeutet nämlich den Durchbruch (...) zu einem Wirk-
lichkeitsverständnis unter dem Primat der Person und der Relation"[43].
Only if the triune God exists as absolute creative freedom in love in history can the world be a possible realm of man's freedom. But this freedom is underivable ("unableitbar") for man: It is the substantial under-
ivability of the Christ-event. This non-deducibility of the Christ-event
– understood as the incarnation of the absolute freedom – is for Kasper
the last hope for mankind and the world. "Die Freiheit Gottes erweist
sich also – anders als der atheïstische Humanismus meint – nicht als
Grenze der menschlichen Freitheit, sondern als deren letzter Grund. Nicht
daß Gott tot ist, sondern daß er ein lebendiger Gott der Geschichte ist,
ist deshalb die Hoffnung des Menschen"[44].

4. A Trinitarian Ontology of Love

In short we could say that Kasper, preferring a post-idealistic personal
connection[45], starts with the idea of freedom; no longer the abstract
freedom of idealistic thought, but the concrete historically existing human
freedom. Such a freedom is both contingent and (intentionally) unconditioned: it cannot reach its own fulfilment. This freedom can only get the
adequate answer in relation to a freedom that is not only absolute with
regard to the intention but also with regard to reality. Hence human freedom refers to an absolute freedom in love as the last condition and ground
of its fulfilment.

Kasper also defines anthropology as the "grammar" used by God for
his self-communication as freedom in love. Each "grammar" as such is
still open to and available for many pronouncements. In the end
the human freedom cannot reach its own fulfilment (cf. supra). With
J.E. Kuhn Kasper confirms in that sense: "Nach ihm (Kuhn) erfährt das
unbestimmt allgemeine, leztlich offenbleibende Geheimnis, in welches
das Denken am Ende hineinverweist, durch die Offenbarung seine letzte
konkrete Bestimmtheit (Determination). 'Der concrete Gedanke' in dem
sich das Denken vollendet wiederfindet, "ist der in Christus, als seinem
ewigen Sohne, sich zeitlich offenbarende Gott""[46]. The revelation of the

43. ID., *Der Gott Jesu Christi* (n. 1), p. 377.
44. ID., *Jesus der Christus* (n. 18), p. 66.
45. ID., *Der Gott Jesu Christi* (n. 1), p. 364, n. 199.
46. ID., *Zustimmung zum Denken* (n. 34), p. 25.

triune God is the ultimate answer to the question that every human being not only asks himself, but actually is – "Die unbegrenzte, aber unbestimmte Offenheit der Vernunft wird so durch die Offenbarungswahrheit konkret bestimmt. Theologische Wahrheit ist also, so könnte man Kuhn zusammenfassend interpretieren, die gnadenhafte Bestimmung der unbestimmten Offenheit menschlicher Vernunft und menschlicher Wahrheitssuche"[47]. In a paraphrase Kasper rightly states that God's free self-communication in love (i.e. "gratia") presupposes human freedom and fulfils human freedom (i.e. "natura")[48].

The self-revealing God is freedom in love and freedom can only be answered and fulfilled by freedom. True freedom is not the modern emancipated freedom, but liberated freedom, a freedom set free and given by another (absolute) freedom[49]. True freedom presupposes a radical new beginning, a "Neuanfang" as Kasper says. True freedom presupposes an absolute freedom that is co-existent within itself, a trinitarian freedom in love.

The question of the ontological implications of this affirmation brings him to a relational ontology or metaphysics of love in which the human person is the core of thinking, and love is the deepest sense of all reality[50]. Love is capable of combining unity and diversity in the relation between the divine persons, in the relation between God and humanity, between people, between the different religions. "Die tiefste Begründung dafür, dass das Bekenntnis zu dem einen Gott Vielfalt nicht aufhebt, sondern gewissermaßen einschließt, liegt im trinitarischen Bekenntnis zu dem einen Gott in drei Personen. Es ist die Auslegung der biblischen Aussage: "Gott ist Liebe" (...). Denn es besagt, dass der eine und einzige Gott kein einsamer Gott ist, sondern von Ewigkeit her sich verschenkende Liebe, in der sich der Vater dem Sohn und Vater und Sohn im Heiligen Geist mitteilen. Jede der drei Personen ist ganz Gott, ganz unendlich, und doch gibt jede der anderen Raum, indem sie sich mitteilt und dadurch entäußert. In dieser kenotischen Weise ist Gott Einheit in der

---

47. ID., *Wahrheitsverständnis der Theologie* (n. 35), p. 46.
48. ID., *Theologische Bestimmung der Menschenrechte im neuzeitlichen Bewußtsein von Freiheit und Geschichte*, in ID., *Theologie und Kirche I* (n. 2), pp. 184-185.
49. ID., *Jesus der Christus* (n. 18), pp. 185, 229.
50. ID., *Christologie und Anthropologie* (n. 18), pp. 194-216, esp. p. 216. Such a trinitarian relational ontology cannot be reached by deducing ("deductio") universal claims of truth from an a priori transcendental experience, but by reducing ("reductio") the historically given claims of revelation to the conditions which must be there in order for that, what is to be what it is. Kasper speaks here of the "transcendental method" in theology. For additional explanation Cf. ID., *Postmoderne Dogmatik. Zu einer neueren nordamerikanischen Grundlagendiskussion*, in *Internationale Katholische Zeitschrift Communio* 19 (1990) 298-306, esp. p. 304. Cf. ID., *Wahrheitsverständnis der Theologie* (n. 35), p. 44.

Vielheit. (...) Die Almacht der Liebe (...) kann sich hingeben und weggeben und ist eben in dieser Hingabe sie selber. Solche Entäußerung ist nur dann wahr und echt, wenn die Gottheit des ewigen Logos die Menschheit nicht aufsaugt (...), sondern in ihrer Eigenheit annimmt und sie in ihr Eigensein freigibt"[51].

Trinitarian theology, as well as Christology, presents a model of unity which is not totalitarian; a unity which fulfils the other and sets the other free not by losing its own identity, but by finding its own and deepest nature[52]. As the unity and diversity in Christ has its transcendental-theological condition of possibility in the unity and diversity in the trinitarian God himself, so the historical reality ("Geschichte") of human beings (as the "grammar of Christology") has its fulfilment in the revelation of the triune God in Jesus Christ through the holy Spirit.

III. CONCLUSION: THE TRANSCENDENCE OF GOD AS THE SAFEGUARDING OF THE TRANSCENDENCE OF MAN

The Old Testament states that God is one and unique. If God is not to be understood as a solitary narcissistic being, then God can only be conceived as co-existent (relational). And if God is not to be understood as a dependent being, then God can only be conceived as co-existent within himself (intra-relational). That co-existence within God's essence is the necessary condition for the realisation of the salvation of humankind, i.e. the freedom and transcendence of humankind. Only when God can be absolutely God, can man be totally man. With Kasper we can conclude: the transcendence of God — his inner-divine trinitarian relationship – is the condition of possibility for the safeguarding of man's transcendence. "Gerade die Anerkennung des Gottseins Gottes führt zur Vermenschlichung des Menschen"[53].

Faculteit Godgeleerdheid   Kristof Struys
K.U. Leuven
St.-Michielsstraat 6
B-3000 Leuven
Belgium

51. ID., Jesus Christus. Gottes endgültiges Wort, in Internationale Katholische Zeitschrift Communio 30 (2001) 18-26, esp. pp. 24 ff.
52. Cf. ID., Wahrheitsverständnis der Theologie (n. 35), p. 49: Hans Urs von Balthasar was the one who pointed out that the christological structure of theological truth is grounded in the trinitarian structure.
53. ID., Der Gott Jesu Christi (n. 1), p. 383.

CATHERINE MOWRY LACUGNA'S CONTRIBUTION TO A RELATIONAL THEOLOGY

Catherine Mowry LaCugna would surely have been delighted that relational theology is the theme of this conference, and had her life not been tragically interrupted by cancer she would undoubtedly have come here this week to listen, to learn, and to share with you her own reflections on the topic at hand[1]. LaCugna's work in trinitarian theology, indeed, makes an important contribution to our conversation. The contemporary movement towards relational theology rides in part on the wake of the renaissance of the doctrine of the Trinity which has been rescued from the appendix of Schleiermacher's *Christian Faith* and from the confines of the neo-Scholastic treatise *De Deo Trino* and restored to its rightful place as the cornerstone of Christian systematic theology. LaCugna's *God for Us: The Trinity and Christian Life* has proven to be a landmark work in this revitalization[2]. This book, according to Michael Downey, "did more, perhaps, to stimulate thinking and discussion about the doctrine of the Trinity in Roman Catholic circles in the United States than any theological work since Karl Rahner's *The Trinity*"[3]. LaCugna wrote from the conviction that the paradigm of the economic and immanent Trinity that Rahner himself had used needed reconceptualization, and she proposed the patristic distinction of *oikonomia* (the mystery of salvation) and *theologia* (the mystery of God) as an alternative framework for contemporary trinitarian theology. This framework, she believed, can simultaneously revitalize the doctrine of the Trinity and support the development of a relational theological ontology.

1. Catherine Mowry LaCugna died in 1997. Memorials include N. DALLAVALLE, *In Memory of Catherine Mowry LaCugna (1952-1997)*, in *Horizons* 24 (1997) 256-257; L. CUNNINGHAM, *God Is For Us*, in *America* 176 (1997) 6-7; R. MCBRIEN, *Catherine Found Words to Explicate the Trinity*, in *National Catholic Reporter* (July 4, 1997) 18.

2. C.M. LACUGNA, *God for Us: The Trinity and Christian Life*, San Francisco, CA, HarperCollins, 1991.

3. M. DOWNEY, *Altogether Gift: A Trinitarian Spirituality*, Maryknoll, NY, Orbis Books, 2000, p. 12.

I. THE LIMITATIONS OF THE PARADIGM OF THE ECONOMIC
AND IMMANENT TRINITY

LaCugna advocated a new approach to trinitarian theology that would avoid some of the aporia of the discourse of the immanent and economic Trinity which structures much contemporary trinitarian thought. According to Pannenberg, a distinction of the essential and economic Trinity is traceable to the eighteenth-century theologian J. Urlsperger[4]. Within Roman Catholic theology, it has been in widespread use since the publication of Rahner's influential 1967 essay *The Trinity*[5]. LaCugna acknowledged that the paradigm of the economic and immanent Trinity has enabled important contributions to contemporary theology, particularly through Rahner's own work and the ensuing discussion of his seminal *Grundaxiom* – "The 'economic' Trinity is the 'immanent' Trinity and the 'immanent' Trinity is the 'economic' Trinity"[6]. Rahner reaffirmed that soteriology is decisive for theology and fostered a renewed appreciation of the mystery that God is by nature self-communicating and self-expressive. In so doing, he revitalized Catholicism's theology of God[7]. At the same time, LaCugna was convinced that Rahner's clarion call for a renewal of trinitarian theology required the construction of a trinitarian paradigm that prescinded from the very language of the "economic Trinity" and the "immanent Trinity" that Rahner himself had used. "I was more and more convinced," she stated in a reflection on the genesis and development of her own theology, "that the crucial aporia of the modern doctrine of the Trinity lay in or around the terms immanent and economic"[8].

For reasons that I have explicated in detail elsewhere[9], LaCugna found the terminology of the "immanent Trinity" and the "economic Trinity"

---

4. W. PANNENBERG, *Systematic Theology I*, trans. Geoffrey Bromiley, Grand Rapids, MI, Eerdmans, 1991, p. 291 n. 111. Reference is to J. URLSPERGER, *Vier Versuche einer genaueren Bestimmung des Geheimnisses Gottes des Vaters und Christi* (1769-1774); ID., *Kurzgefasstes System meines Vortrages von Gottes Dreieinigkeit* (1777). It is anachronistic to interpret patristic or medieval theology using the terminology of the immanent and economic Trinity, although this is now standard practice.

5. K. RAHNER, *Der dreifaltige Gott als transzendenter Urgrund der Heilsgeschichte*, in H.U. VON BALTHASAR – J. DAVID – A. DEISSLER, *Die Heilsgeschichte vor Christus* (Mysterium Salutis: Grundriss heilsgeschichtlicher Dogmatik, 2), Einsiedeln, 1967, pp. 317-401, translated by J. Donceel as *The Trinity*, New York, Crossroad Herder, 1970 and 1997.

6. *Ibid.*, p. 22.

7. LACUGNA, *God for Us* (n. 2), pp. 210-211 and pp. 230-231.

8. LACUGNA, *Discussion of God for Us*, text of lecture at Duke University, November 11, 1993, p. 2.

9. E. GROPPE, *Catherine Mowry LaCugna's Contribution to Trinitarian Theology*, in *TS* 63 (2002) 730-763.

imprecise and misleading. This discourse can create the false impression that there are two Trinities that somehow must be related to one another[10]. In so doing, this discourse impedes the doxological character of theology, which can become an intellectual exercise in thinking about two reified Trinities rather than an act oriented to the worship of the unobjectifiable and incomprehensible God. The paradigm of the economic and immanent Trinity also perpetuates the use of a theological ontology of substance insofar as the immanent Trinity is typically designated the ontological, substantial Trinity (God *in se*) in contrast to the revelatory or economic Trinity[11]. The limits of substance ontology have been noted by a variety of contemporary theologians[12]; LaCugna's own search for an alternative to an ontology of substance was rooted, as we shall see, in her conviction that this ontology is insufficiently informed by soteriology. In similar vein, LaCugna believed that the paradigm of the economic and immanent Trinity problematized the theology of God's freedom[13]. Many theologians qualify Rahner's *Grundaxiom* with an emphasis on the nonidentity of the economic and immanent Trinity in order to preserve the freedom of God's acts of creation and redemption[14]. This safeguard, however, establishes an opposition between God's being and God's free actions, whereas LaCugna believed that the God revealed in the incarnation and paschal mystery of Jesus Christ is a God who acts in the freedom of love and that this love is indistinguishable from the divine being[15]. In addition, LaCugna was convinced that the paradigm of the economic

---

10. LaCugna, *God for Us Review Symposium*, in *Horizons* 20 (1993) 135-142, p. 139; EAD., *Discussion of God for Us* (n. 8), p. 5.

11. *Ibid.*

12. See, for example, J.A. BRACKEN, S.J., *The Triune Symbol: Persons, Process and Community* (CTS Studies in Religion, 1), Lanham, MD, University Press of America, 1985, pp. 5, 20-21, 51; J. MACQUARRIE, *Principles of Christian Theology*, New York, Charles Scribner's Sons, ²1977, p. 109; J. MOLTMANN, *The Trinity and the Kingdom*, San Francisco, CA, Harper and Row, 1981, p. 19; T. PETERS, *God as Trinity: Relationality and Temporality in Divine Life*, Louisville, KY, Westminster/John Knox Press, 1993, pp. 30-34; M.H. SUCHOCKI, *Introduction*, in J.A. BRACKEN, S.J. – M.H. SUCHOCKI (eds.), *Trinity in Process: A Relational Theology of God*, New York, Continuum, 1997, pp. vii-xiii. For a critique of some of these criticisms of the metaphysics of substance, see W. ALSTON, *Substance and the Trinity*, in S.T. DAVIS – D. KENDALL – G. O'COLLINS (eds.), *The Trinity: An Interdisciplinary Symposium*, Oxford, University Press, 1999, pp. 179-201, esp. 193-201.

13. LaCugna, *Horizons Review Symposium* (n. 10), p. 139. See also *Discussion of God for Us* (n. 8), p. 5.

14. Y. CONGAR, *I Believe in the Holy Spirit III*, New York, Seabury, 1983, p. 13; J. THOMPSON, *Modern Trinitarian Perspectives*, New York, Oxford University Press, 1994, p. 27.

15. LaCugna was not alone in her concern to express theologically the indivisibility of God's being, God's freedom, and God's love. Jüngel and Moltmann have voiced similar concerns. See E. JÜNGEL, *God as the Mystery of the World*, Grand Rapids, MI,

242   E.T. GROPPE

and immanent Trinity inhibits the realization of the practical and soteriological implications of the doctrine of the Trinity[16]. Rahner himself used
the axiomatic identity of the immanent and economic Trinity to stress the
indelibly soteriological (hence, practical) character of trinitarian theology. As noted above, however, many of the theologians who draw on
Rahner's work question his formulation of axiomatic identity in order to
express more clearly the freedom of God. Once this distinction of the
economic and immanent Trinities is emphasized, soteriology (in the form
of reflection on the economic Trinity) is structurally disjoined from theology proper (reflection on the immanent Trinity) and this can hinder the
expression of trinitarian theology's fundamentally practical character.

II. OIKONOMIA AND THEOLOGIA AS ALTERNATIVE PARADIGM

All theological frameworks and all theological terms have their shortcomings and must be used with nuance, contextualization, and caveat[17].
Careful use of the paradigm of the economic and immanent Trinity can
alleviate some of the difficulties discussed above. Indeed, this paradigm
is commonly used as a structural scheme in contemporary trinitarian theology and it has not prevented substantive contributions to this field by
numerous theologians. LaCugna believed, nonetheless, that the liabilities
of the paradigm of the economic and immanent Trinity were weighty
enough to warrant explorations of other frameworks. "... I have suggested," she wrote, "a moratorium on the terms 'economic and immanent
Trinity', as one step to greater precision", and she invited theologians to
develop alternative approaches[18].

This point bears reiteration, for LaCugna has sometimes been interpreted using the very terminology of the economic Trinity and immanent
Trinity that she herself sought to transcend. Colin Gunton, Joseph

Eerdmans, 1983, p. 371; MOLTMANN, The Trinity and the Kingdom (n. 12), pp. 52-56, 151,
153.
    16. LACUGNA, Horizons Review Symposium (n. 10), p. 139. See also Discussion of
God for Us (n. 8), p. 5.
    17. On the difficulties and inevitable distortion occasioned by all theological models,
see C.M. LACUGNA – K. MCDONNELL, Returning from "The Far Country" : Theses for a
Contemporary Trinitarian Theology, in SJT 41 (1988) 191-215, pp. 204-205.
    18. "This is not," she continued, "because, as Finan fears, I do not believe in the
immanent Trinity; as Haight acknowledges, 'The inner nature of God is of course revealed
in this interaction with us on the supposition that it is no other God that so acts'".
LACUGNA, Horizons Review Symposium (n. 10), p. 139. Reference is to essays by Barbara
Finan and Roger Haight in the same symposium. On this point see also LACUGNA, God
for Us (n. 2), p. 223, p. 234 n. 7 and n. 227.

Bracken, Paul Molnar and Thomas Weinandy are among those who express concern about what appears to be LaCugna's reduction of trinitarian theology to a merely economic plane[19]. It is not the case, however, as Gunton and others fear, that LaCugna limits her theology to the economic Trinity and casts doubt on the necessity of a doctrine of an immanent or ontological Trinity[20]. Nor is it the case that she establishes a disjunctive opposition between the immanent and economic Trinity[21]. Rather, LaCugna prescinded from the very discourse of both the economic and immanent Trinity and proposed the following alternative structuring paradigm for contemporary trinitarian theology: the inseparability of *theologia* (i.e. the mystery of God) and *oikonomia* (i.e. the mystery of salvation)[22]. The term *"theologia"* is not simply a substitute for the term "immanent Trinity" nor is *"oikonomia"* identical in meaning or function to the term "economic Trinity"[23]. Rather, in LaCugna's work, *theologia* refers to the mystery and being of God[24]. *Oikonomia*, in turn, is the "comprehensive plan of God reaching from creation to consummation, in which God and all creatures are destined to exist together in the mystery of love and communion"[25]. *Theologia* and *oikonomia* are distinct but inseparable dimensions of trinitarian theology that cannot be divorced from one another[26]. *Oikonomia* is the plan of God (Eph 1:3-14) and as such participates in *theologia*, for the plan of God is one dimension of the mystery of God, an expression of God's being. Insofar, however, as the divine plan includes what is other than God – creation, time, space, history, personality – *theologia* is distinct from *oikonomia*. *Theologia* is

19. These critiques are found in varied forms in J. BRACKEN, *Trinity: Economic and Immanent*, in *Horizons* 25 (1998) 7-22; C. GUNTON, *The Promise of Trinitarian Theology*, Edinburgh, T &T Clark, ²1997, pp. xv-xxxi; P. MOLNAR, *Toward a Contemporary Doctrine of the Immanent Trinity: Karl Barth and the Present Discussion*, in *SJT* 49 (1996) 311-357; T. WEINANDY, *The Father's Spirit of Sonship*, Edinburgh, T & T Clark, 1995, pp. 123-136.

20. GUNTON, *Promise of Trinitarian Theology* (n. 19), p. xvii.

21. D. CUNNINGHAM, *These Three Are One: The Practice of Trinitarian Theology*, Malden, MA, Blackwell Publishers, 1998, p. 37.

22. This is not to say that she completely avoided using the terminology of economic and immanent Trinity, which she continued to employ even in *God for Us* in order to engage in conversation with theologies structured in these terms. When she was stating her own positions, however, she did so using an alternative framework.

23. The terminology of economic and immanent Trinity, LaCugna wrote, "is imprecise and misleading, and not equivalent to the distinction between *oikonomia* and *theologia*". LACUGNA, *Horizons Review Symposium* (n. 10), p. 139.

24. LACUGNA, *God for Us* (n. 2), p. 223. Elsewhere she described *theologia* as a reference to God's eternal being. *Ibid.*, p. 23.

25. *Ibid.*, p. 223.

26. LaCugna wrote of the "inseparability" and "essential unity" of *oikonomia* and *theologia*. *Ibid.*, pp. 4, 211, and 229.

irreducible to *oikonomia* and yet remains inseparable from it, for it is God who has desired to extend God's life to the creature. "*Theologia* is fully revealed and bestowed in *oikonomia*, and *oikonomia* truly expresses the ineffable mystery of *theologia*"[27].

What does this mean concretely? It means, for example, that in response to the question "What is the doctrine of the Trinity?" the standard short formulaic responses "God is one being in three persons" or "God is Father, Son and Spirit" are incomplete and should be expanded to include more explicit reference to the divine economy. The doctrine of the Trinity, one might say, is the doctrine that God creates and redeems the cosmos in the power of the Holy Spirit through the eternal Word incarnate in Jesus Christ. Or, as LaCugna herself wrote, "the doctrine of the Trinity, which is the specifically Christian way of speaking about God, summarizes what it means to participate in the life of God through Jesus Christ in the Spirit. The mystery of God is revealed in Christ and the Spirit as the mystery of love, the mystery of persons in communion who embrace death, sin, and all forms of alienation for the sake of life"[28]. This short statement, while not a comprehensive trinitarian theology, is suggestive of what it means to maintain the inseparability of *theologia* and *oikonomia*.

The difference between the paradigm of the economic and immanent Trinity and LaCugna's own approach may be graphically portrayed as follows[29]:

The Immanent and Economic Trinity

immanent Trinity = Father, Son, and Spirit *in se*
economic Trinity = Father, Son, and Spirit *ad extra*

Oikonomia and *Theologia*

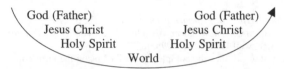

These graphic depictions are coarse representations that cannot do justice to the complexity and nuance of a developed theological system, but they may at least help us to visualize in a rudimentary way the difference between the paradigm of the economic and immanent Trinity and

27. *Ibid.*, p. 221.
28. *Ibid.*, p. 1.
29. *Ibid.*, pp. 222-223.

LaCugna's proposed alternative. In the former, we may be led to conceptualize the Trinity in a reified way as a discrete entity – or even two discrete entities. In the latter, in contrast, we see not an objectified Trinity but the dynamic trinitarian movement of God who acts through Jesus Christ in the Holy Spirit. In the first schema, it is possible to focus our attention either on the immanent (ontological) Trinity or the economic (biblical or revelatory or soteriological) Trinity, and there is nothing to prohibit us from thinking about one Trinity apart from the other. If, in contrast, one were to articulate the theology implicit in the latter diagram, one must somehow express the inseparability of the ontological and the soteriological dimensions of trinitarian theology. The God whose very *esse* is to be (Ex 3,16) *is* the God who creates and redeems the world through Jesus Christ and the Holy Spirit in an ecstatic movement *a Patre ad Patrem*.

LaCugna identified several merits of the paradigm of *oikonomia* and *theologia* that contribute to its serviceability as a framework for contemporary trinitarian theology. First, it is consistent with biblical, creedal, liturgical, and ante-Nicene theological formulations in a way that Urlsperger's 18th century language of the essential Trinity and the economic Trinity is not[30]. Second, the axiomatic affirmation that *theologia* is given in *oikonomia* and *oikonomia* expresses *theologia* maintains the fundamental insight that classical trinitarian theologies have sought to express: the economy of salvation is grounded in the eternal being of God, and God is not other than God has revealed God's mystery to be in the incarnation of the Word and the gift of the Holy Spirit[31]. Finally, the principle of the unity of *theologia* and *oikonomia* ensures that soteriology will not be divorced from theology proper. Indeed, LaCugna noted that her principle could be restated as follows: "Theology is inseparable from soteriology, and *vice versa*"[32].

LaCugna's emphasis on the inseparability of *theologia* and *oikonomia* has precedent in the tradition. Some of the earliest patristic trinitarian reflections that use the terminology of *theologia* and *oikonomia* do so in a manner that implies the inseparability of these two dimensions of the Christian mystery[33]. LaCugna's principle also has basis in the repeated affirmation of many layers of the Christian tradition that the trinitarian

---

30. LaCugna, *Horizons Review Symposium* (n. 10), p. 137.
31. Ead., *God for Us* (n. 2), p. 224.
32. *Ibid.*, p. 211.
33. See for example R.J. Kees, *Die Lehre von der* Oikonomia Gottes in der Oratio catechetica *Gregors von Nyssa* (Supplements to Vigiliae Christianae, 30), Leiden, E.J. Brill, 1995.

missions cannot be separated from the processions even as they are distinguished from them[34]. Her principle is also grounded in developments in contemporary Christology which stress the indispensability of soteriology to Christological method. Walter Kasper emphasizes contra the neo-Scholastic division of the doctrines of Christ's person and work that the ontological question of who Jesus Christ is cannot be addressed apart from consideration of Christ's salvific life, death, and resurrection. "Christology," he writes, "and soteriology (that is, the doctrine of the redemptive meaning of Jesus Christ) form a whole"[35]. If this principle holds true in Christology, LaCugna determined, it must also hold true in trinitarian theology. "There can be no sure basis for the truth claims of any contemporary christology unless it can be *theologically* substantiated that the distinction between being and function no longer holds. That is, if it is true for Christ, it must also be true for God. Or, better, it can be true for Christ only because it is already true of God"[36]. LaCugna did not argue for the reduction of theology to a merely functional (rather than ontological) plane, an approach she explicitly warns against[37]. She did emphasize that ontology and soteriology cannot be separated. Theology must be ontological in character, and theological ontology must be is forged in a soteriological key.

Indeed, as LaCugna observed, *oikonomia* and *theologia* have always been united in the church's liturgical worship and the domestic prayer of the Christian home. In the act of doxology, the inseparability of *oikonomia* and *theologia* is not simply a theological principle but a lived reality. The praise of God is rooted in *oikonomia* and reaches to *theologia*:

> Praise is always rendered in response to God's goodness to Israel, or God's majesty in creation, or God's faithfulness to the covenant, or God's peacemaking in the heart of the sinner, or God's face seen in Christ. Praise is offered because in the concrete aspects of God's life with us we experience God's steadfast love, God's gracious and everlasting presence. (...) The

34. This is evident both in biblical passages such as Eph 1,3-4 and in systematic theological reflections such as those of Thomas Aquinas, who surmised that God wills Himself and all things by one act of will. AQUINAS, *Summa Contra Gentiles*, 75 and 76. In our own era, Yves Congar insisted, "Let us remember that the Logos is, in the eternal present of God, conceived *incarnandus ... crucifigendus, primogenitus omnis creaturae, glorificandus ...*". Y. CONGAR, *The Word and Spirit*, San Francisco, CA, Harper and Row, 1984, p. 11. Von Balthasar writes of the identity of the mission (*missio*) of the Son "with the person *in* God and *as* God (*processio*)". H.U. VON BALTHASAR, *Theo-Drama III*, trans. G. HARRISON, San Francisco, CA, Ignatius Press, 1992, p. 533.
35. W. KASPER, *Jesus the Christ*, trans. V. GREEN, Mahwah, NJ, Paulist Press, 1976, p. 22.
36. LACUGNA, *God for Us* (n. 2), p. 7.
37. *Ibid.*, p. 4 and p. 227.

praise of God is possible *only if* there is a real correspondence between "God" and "God for us" (...). The God of saving history is the same God from all eternity, and the God of our future. There is no reason to think that by recounting God's deeds, anyone other than God *as God* is intended as the object of praise (...). The close relationship between soteriology and doxology, between salvation and praise, confirms the proper connection between *oikonomia* and *theologia*, essence and energies, which are inseparable in theology[38].

Theology is ultimately not speech about God nor even speech about the God-creature relation but an expression *of* the God-creature relation which reaches its climax in the creature's praise and glorification of God. Theology culminates in the *actuation* of creation's being-towards God in the act of praise and thanksgiving. "[T]he giving of praise to God", LaCugna wrote, "has the power to bring about our union with God, to put us back in right relationship with God (...). By naming God as recipient of our praise, we are redirected away from ourselves towards God"[39].

III. A RELATIONAL ONTOLOGY

It is the axiomatic inseparability of theology and soteriology – of *theologia* and *oikonomia* – that leads LaCugna to a critique of a metaphysics of substance and the development of a relational ontology[40]. Soteriological affirmations, LaCugna maintained, must have an ontological basis, and there is widespread agreement on this point amongst the theological community. Yet LaCugna took this principle one step further: if it is indeed true that the economy reveals God as God truly (ontologically) *is*, than ontology itself must have an intrinsically soteriological dimension. This principle lies at the heart and core of LaCugna's relational ontology. Not only does soteriology require an ontological foundation, but *soteriology itself must be decisive in our formulation of ontological statements about the being of God:*

---

38. *Ibid.*, p. 337, pp. 348-349.
39. *Ibid.*, pp. 338-339.
40. Some commentators critique *God for Us* for what appears to them to be a lack of adequate ontological foundation. It is my hope that the above exposition will help clarify the ontological basis of LaCugna's theology. For critiques, see MOLNAR, *Towards a Contemporary Doctrine* (n. 19), p. 323; GUNTON, *Promise of Trinitarian Theology* (n. 19), p. xvii; B. LESLIE, *Does God Have a Life? Barth and LaCugna on the Immanent Trinity*, in *Perspectives in Religious Studies* 24 (1997) 377-398, pp. 388-398; WEINANDY, *Father's Spirit of Sonship* (n. 19), p. 131.

> ... the doctrine of the Trinity is meant to express that who and what God is *with us* (as redemptive love) is exactly who God is *as God*. God can draw completely near to us, share history with us, and never be diminished either as mystery or as God. Indeed, one might add that God is Absolute Mystery not because God remains locked in other-worldly transcendence, but because the transcendent God becomes also absolutely immanent[41].

The economy of creation and redemption reveals that "God is not self-contained, egoistical and self-absorbed but overflowing love, outreaching desire for union with all that God has made"[42]. God's love for us is by no means exhaustive of the divine being but it is nonetheless inseparable from it, and a theological ontology must express this:

> It would be improper theologically to assume that the One who (supposedly) could be known in abstraction from his/her relationship with creation would be *God*! For if the very nature of God is to be related as love – and this, after all, *is* the fundamental claim of a trinitarian theology – then one cannot prescind from this relatedness and still hope to be making statements about the relational God. Far from devolving into a theological agnosticism, a trinitarian theology of God can affirm with confidence that God *is* who God reveals Godself to be[43].

A metaphysics of substance which presumes that a being is constituted as a particular kind of being by virtue of that which it is *in se* – in distinction from all its relations to other beings which are accidental to its nature – is a metaphysics that is limited by its very structure from articulating a thoroughly soteriological ontology. God as revealed in the Covenant with Israel, in the incarnation of the Word and in the gift of the Holy Spirit *is* God as God eternally *is* and hence the ultimate ground and foundation of reality is not an "in itself" or a "by itself" or a "for itself" but rather a person (God) turned towards another in ecstatic love. "Person, not substance," LaCugna concludes, "is the ultimate ontological category" and God's To-Be is To-Be-in-Relation and To-Be-in-Communion[44].

---

41. LaCugna, *Problems with a Trinitarian Reformulation*, in *Louvain Studies* 10 (1985) 324-340, p. 330. On this point see also *God for Us* (n. 2), p. 322.

42. Ead., *God for Us* (n. 2), p. 15.

43. Ead., *Problems with a Trinitarian Reformulation* (n. 41), p. 340.

44. Ead., *God for Us* (n. 2), p. 14 and p. 250. It is notable here that LaCugna replaces substance with person – not relation – as the ultimate ontological category. In response to Clarke who argues that "relation" cannot stand alone but needs something to ground it, LaCugna would surely agree. In contrast to Clarke, she finds this ultimate ontological ground not in the category of substance but in the category or person – or more precisely, in the very person of God – rather than in the category of relation. For Clarke's position, see W.N. Clarke, *Person and Being* (The Aquinas Lecture, 1993), Milwaukee, WI, Marquette University Press, 1993.

If God's To-Be is To-Be-in-Communion, what then of the ontological distinction of God and creation that is so foundational to Christian theology? What of the freedom and gratuity of God's creative act, and the temporality of creation? LaCugna's relational ontology maintains these fundamental dimensions of Christian theology, even as it transposes them into a new key. Within the metaphysics of substance that has been prevalent in Catholic theology, God *in se* is distinguished from the creature *in se*. Within LaCugna's ontology of person and relation, in contrast, God and creature are distinguished not as two qualitatively different kinds of being-in-itself but as two qualitatively different persons-in-relation[45]. The very category of relation that is so central to LaCugna's theology is, notably, a term of both communion and distinction. God and creature are not identical but rather related. This relation between God and creature, furthermore, is not strictly reciprocal, for God's relation to us is of a qualitatively different character than our relation to God. God, LaCugna explained, "belongs to the sphere of infinite relatedness, infinite capacity for relationship, infinite actuality of relationship, both to past, present, and future reality"[46]. Human persons, in contrast, relate to others in a manner limited by our embodiment and our historical, cultural, and linguistic conditions[47]. "In God alone," LaCugna continued, "is there full correspondence between personhood and being, between *hypostasis* and *ousia*"[48]. In human persons, in contrast, personhood and relationality are imperfectly realized. God alone is the Unoriginate Origin, the source (*archè*) of the begetting of the Son, the breathing forth of the Holy Spirit, and the gracious acts of creation and redemption. "God does not have to be loved in order to love. This is not the situation of the creature who learns to love in response to being loved. God *is* Love itself and the origin of Love, that is to say, God is the origin of existence"[49]. We, in turn, are the awed recipients of the love of God, "destined and appointed to live for the praise of God's glory"[50].

---

45. It is my hope that this will clarify LaCugna's position on an issue that has fostered some concern among her commentators. Barbara Finan cautions that LaCugna "may be too close to abandoning the radical distinction between God and us in her efforts to affirm that God is for us". B. FINAN, *Horizons Review Symposium* (n. 10), p. 134. Bracken believes LaCugna's approach runs the danger of monism, and Molnar and Gunton describe LaCugna's theology as pantheistic (Molnar) or at least as potentially so (Gunton). BRACKEN, *Trinity: Economic and Immanent* (n. 19), p. 21 n. 30; MOLNAR, *Toward a Contemporary Doctrine* (n. 19), pp. 313 and 319; GUNTON, *The Promise of Trinitarian Theology* (n. 19), p. xviii.
46. LACUGNA, *God for Us* (n. 2), p. 292.
47. *Ibid.*, p. 292.
48. *Ibid.*, p. 305.
49. *Ibid.*, p. 303.
50. Eph 1,12. Cited in LACUGNA, *God for Us* (n. 2), p. 342.

LaCugna's relational ontology maintains not only this axiomatic ontological distinction between God and creation but also Christianity's long-
standing affirmation of the freedom and gratuity of God's act of creation,
an affirmation forged by patristic theologians in counter-distinction to
Neo-Platonic philosophies of emanation. If *theologia* is truly inseparable
from *oikonomia*, one might inquire, is God compelled to create and
redeem the world? Does creation become a demiurgic emanation of
God's being removed from the domain of God's will? For LaCugna, the
answer is clearly "no". God is not compelled to create the world and creation is not removed from the domain of God's will. Creation is a freely
willed act of God. Indeed, it is precisely because God *has* freely created
and redeemed the world that LaCugna believed that this reality – this
mystery – must shape trinitarian theology in a formative way if indeed
our theology is to speak as truthfully as possible of the God who has been
revealed to us. According to Robert Sokolowski, the ontological distinction of God and creation is a "distinction between the world understood
as possibly not having existed and God understood as possibly being all
that there is, with no diminution of goodness or greatness"[51]. LaCugna's
approach allows for contemplation of this possibility but – unlike
Sokolowski – she does not establish the possible non-existence of creation
or the self-sufficiency of God as the ultimate meaning of the God/crea-
ture distinction. We can certainly contemplate the possibility that the cosmos might never have been, that God might have been all that there is –
an odd form of "thought" that requires negating ourselves and our very
thoughts of possible non-existence even as we "think" them. Yet this
self-negating intellectual exercise ends not in negation but rather culminates in awe and wonder with the affirmation that the cosmos in all its
multitude of creatures *does* exist and *was* created by God. This affirmation tells us something about the character of our own existence – specifically, that it is rooted in grace – and also tells us something about the
character of God. God is not a deity of self-enclosure nor self-satisfac-
tion but the God of ecstatic love – Bonaventure's *fontalis plenitudo*. For
LaCugna, God's creative ecstasy in no way jeopardizes the freely willed
character of creation, but it does require a refinement of some ideas about
the meaning of freedom that have become commonplace in western culture in which we have become accustomed to think of freedom as autonomy and self-sufficiency. In the acts of creation and redemption, God's

---

51. R. SOKOLOWSKI, *The God of Faith and Reason: Foundations of Christian Theology*, Notre Dame, IN, University of Notre Dame Press, 1982, p. 23.

freedom is revealed to us as the freedom of love. "Love", LaCugna stated quoting John Zizioulas, "is identified with ontological freedom"[52].

If God's freedom is the freedom of love, and God's To-Be is To-Be-in-Communion, is creation then eternal? The question of the eternity of creation has been a perennial topic of discussion amongst both theologians and philosophers and there are a wide variety of perspectives on this matter[53]. Today, these inquiries proceed in conversation with contemporary physics and cosmology which teach us that time itself cannot be abstracted from space but is part of a space-time continuum[54]. LaCugna herself did not explicitly address the issue of the eternity or temporality of creation within her published writings, so one can only speculate as to what her position might have been given the basic principles and framework of her theology. From this perspective, the space-time continuum is not a random phenomenon of cosmic auto-genesis but the creation of God. God's eternity is not unending space-time, nor infinite space-time, but something qualitatively different, an attribute of the God who is the Unoriginate Origin of all creation[55]. The being of God is eternal, whereas the being of creation is delimited by the space-time continuum. At the same time, LaCugna's framework allows for the affirmation that God is eternally creating space-time through the Word and the Spirit. God is eternally in relation to the space-time that God has created, and creation exists (temporally and spatially) only in relation to the eternity of God. This particular interpretation of LaCugna's theology provides a way to account for the testimony of both Scripture and tradition that creatures – although not themselves eternal – have an inclination to eternity and ultimately can share in the eternal life of God. If there is an absolute ontological divide between God and creature this would be hard to conceive. From the perspective of LaCugna's approach, however, creatures can be understood to

52. LaCugna, God for Us (n. 2), p. 261. She cites J. Zizioulas, Being as Communion, Crestwood, NY, St. Vladimir's Seminary Press, 1985, p. 46.

53. For an overview of wide-ranging views on this matter in both theology and philosophy see the "Classification of Cosmogonic Views" in F. Kovach, The Question of the Eternity of the World in St. Bonaventure and St. Thomas – A Critical Analysis, in R.W. Shahan – F.J. Kovach (eds.), Bonaventure and Aquinas: Enduring Philosophers, Norman, OK, University of Oklahoma Press, 1976, pp. 155-186, esp. 155-162.

54. P. Davies, God and the New Physics, New York, Simon and Schuster, 1983, p. 18.

55. Notably, LaCugna avoided spatial metaphors in her discussion of the mystery of God. She was particularly averse to the expression the "inner life of God". "...[T]here is nothing 'in' God", she wrote, "as if God were something into which something else could be placed, whether it be attributes or relations or a trinity of persons. The world is neither inside God, nor is the world outside God, as if there were a horizon separating God and the world. The nonmateriality and simplicity of God rule out any such crude interpretations". LaCugna, God for Us (n. 2), p. 225.

have an ontological relation to eternity. As Gregory of Nyssa writes: "Since, then, one of the excellences connected with the Divine nature is also eternal existence, it was altogether needful that the equipment of our nature should not be without the further gift of this attribute, but should have in itself the immortal, that by its inherent faculty it might both recognize what is above it, and be possessed with a desire for the divine and eternal life"[56]. LaCugna's ontology allows us to understand the "equipment" for eternity of which Gregory spoke in relational terms.

IV. AN ILLUSTRATION OF THE CONTRIBUTION OF LACUGNA'S APPROACH

LaCugna's work is a rich resource that can contribute constructively to challenges currently facing systematic theology in such areas as Christology, pneumatology, ecclesiology, and theological anthropology. Here I will highlight only very briefly one of the many ways in which LaCugna's work can be of service. One of the recurring themes of this conference has been the need for a reunification of theology and spirituality. The lamentable separation of theology and spirituality has a long history, and a variety of factors contributed to this rent in the fabric of Christianity. As Paul Verdeyen explains, a major factor was the rise of scholasticism in the thirteenth century. Scholasticism's dialectic method nurtured a finely honed reason but neglected the affective and relational dimensions of theology. Reason was then susceptible to truncation from wisdom and love – thereby divorcing spirituality and theology[57]. Overcoming this divorce will require a reintegration of the rational, affective and relational dimensions of the Christian life and a reintegration of reason, wisdom and love. LaCugna's trinitarian theology and relational ontology are eminently suited to this task[58]. The ontological categories of her theology

---

56. GREGORY OF NYSSA, *The Great Catechism*, in *Select Writings and Letters of Gregory, Bishop of Nyssa*, trans. WILLIAM MOORE (NPNF Vol. V), Grand Rapids, MI, Eerdmans, 1988, p. 404.

57. See P. VERDEYEN, *La séparation entre théologie et spiritualité: Origine, conséquences et dépassement de ce divorce*, in this volume, pp. 675-688.

58. For some of LaCugna's explicit reflections on spirituality, see LACUGNA, *God for Us*, pp. 319-417; C.M. LACUGNA – M. DOWNEY, *Trinity and Spirituality*, in M. DOWNEY (ed.), *The New Dictionary of Catholic Spirituality*, Collegeville, MN, Liturgical Press, 1993, pp. 968-982. LaCugna delivered an address on "Spirituality for the Twenty-First Century" to the Northwest Conference on Women in Seattle, Washington, April 18-19, 1997. She also gave workshops on spirituality for the Carmelites in Indianapolis, IN and the monastic community of New Melleray, IA.

– person, relation, communion – are not only capable of supporting reflection on wisdom and love but by their very character *require* inclusion of these dimensions of the Christian life in their explication. If to-be is to-be-in-communion, then reason's pursuit of the true and the real is inseparable from love's pursuit of the beloved.

From this perspective, the writings of the great spiritual masters cannot be dismissed as mere spirituality but are crucial resources for the development of a systematic theological ontology. Consider, for example, the following passage from John Ruusbroec's *Spiritual Espousals*:

> In this storm of love two spirits struggle – the Spirit of God and our spirit. God, by means of the Holy Spirit, inclines himself toward us, and we are thereby touched in love; our spirit, by means of God's activity and the amorous power, impels and inclines itself toward God, and thereby God is touched. From these two movements there arises the struggle of love, for in this most profound meeting, in this most intimate and ardent encounter, each spirit is wounded by love. These two spirits, that is, our spirit and God's Spirit, cast a radiant light upon one another and each reveals to the other its countenance. This makes the two spirits incessantly strive after one another in love. Each demands of the other what it is, and each offers to the other and invites it to accept what it is. This makes these loving spirits lose themselves in one another. God's touch and his giving of himself, together with our striving in love and our giving of ourselves in return – this is what sets love on a firm foundation. This flux and reflux make the spring of love overflow, so that God's touch and our striving in love become a single love. Here a person becomes so possessed by love that he must forget both himself and God and know nothing but love. In this way the spirit is consumed in the fire of love and enters so deeply into God's touch that it is overcome in all its striving and comes to nought in all its works. It transcends its activity and itself becomes love above and beyond all exercises of devotion. It possesses the inmost part of its creatureliness above all virtue, there where all creaturely activity begins and ends. This is love in itself, the foundation and ground of all the virtues[59].

This passage from the 14th century Flemish mystic employs the language of encounter – striving, storming, demanding, touching, giving, flux and reflux. Ruusbroec's language is also the language of communion, indeed a communion so profound that "God's touch and our striving in love become a single love". From the perspective of LaCugna's relational ontology, this mystical spirituality is a wellspring of theological wisdom, for Ruusbroec's relational language tells us not only about his own spiritual experience but also something ontologically true about who

59. J. RUUSBROEC, *The Spiritual Espousals and Other Works*, trans. JAMES WISEMAN, New York, Paulist, 1985, p. 115.

God really is and who we are in relation to God. Given the inseparability of *theologia* and *oikonomia*, there is not some other, truer God beyond
the God in whose love Ruusbroec is consumed – a God whom we might
access by some form of theological abstraction – but rather the God
whose spring of love overflows is God as God really is.

LaCugna's theology, in sum, calls us to contemplate the mysteries of
Christianity with new eyes, to see them not through the lens of the language of the immanent and economic Trinity nor the categories of a substance metaphysics. Instead, she invites us to see reality through the
ancient paradigm of *oikonomia* and *theologia* and through the categories
of a relational ontology. She is recommending what Thomas Kuhn calls
a paradigm shift[60], a shift that requires relinquishment of categories and
manners of thought to which we have become accustomed, but a shift that
can lead us to a renewed encounter with God's inscrutable and unfathomable love, a love that calls a world fractured by injustice and violence
to live in right-relationship and communion.

Department of Theology   Elizabeth T. GROPPE
Xavier University
3800 Victory Parkway
Cincinnati, OH 45207-4442
U.S.A.

    60. T. KUHN, *The Structure of Scientific Revolutions*, Chicago, IL, University of
Chicago Press, 1996.

THEOLOGY CONSTITUTED BY COMMUNICATION IN MULTIPLE CAUSALITY

KLAUS HEMMERLE'S TRINITARIAN ONTOLOGY AND RELATIONAL THEOLOGY

If we want to discuss relational theology in the German-speaking world, we should not forget the theologian and bishop Klaus Hemmerle (1929-1994). He was a theologian who tried to think about faith in the field between academic theology, philosophy, ecclesiastical practice and spirituality in a highly original manner. A summary of his thinking just at the end of his academic career is contained in a little book published in 1976 and dedicated to Hans Urs von Balthasar who celebrated his 70th birthday: *Theses for a Trinitarian Ontology*[1]. This essay makes "relation" a central term and a fundamental category of ontology and therefore of theology too.

The following contribution consists of five steps: 1) general considerations about the relationship between theology and ontology; 2) an examination of the approach of Klaus Hemmerle and his trinitarian ontology; 3) a presentation of the most fundamental categories and terms of this ontology, utilizing, as one example, the spoken word; 4) a consideration of the consequences of these categories for theology; and finally, 5) an examination of the efficiency of these categories with reference to a topic of great importance for the church and theology today – the question of authority.

---

1. The *Thesen zu einer trinitarischen Ontologie (Theses for a Trinitarian Ontology)* was first published in Einsiedeln, Johannes-Verlag, 1976; it was reprinted in K. HEMMERLE, *Ausgewählte Schriften* (hg. R. FEITER), vol. 2, Freiburg, 1996, pp. 124-161 – This is the edition I will quote. Concerning the intellectual and spiritual biography of Klaus Hemmerle and the central importance of the Fokolare-Movement cf. A.P. FRICK, *Der dreieine Gott und das Handeln in der Welt. Christlicher Glaube und ethische Öffentlichkeit im Denken Klaus Hemmerles,* Würzburg, 1998, pp. 13-115, esp. 60-76; cf. also the biography by W. BADER – W. HAGEMANN, *Klaus Hemmerle. Grundlinien eines Lebens,* München, 2000. For the interpretation of the *Theses,* cf. FRICK, *Der dreieine Gott,* pp. 92-106; and M. BÖHNKE, *Einheit in Mehrursprünglichkeit. Eine kritische Analyse des trinitarischen Ansatzes im Werk von Klaus Hemmerle,* Würzburg, 2000. H.U. v. BALTHASAR answered Hemmerle in his *Theodramatik.* Vol. 4, Einsiedeln, 1983, pp. 64-65 and developed his own version of a trinitarian ontology – cf. *ibid.,* pp. 53-95.

I. Why must Theology Care about Ontology?

What is theology useful for? What is it able to accomplish? During the last fifty years these questions have been answered in different ways. Some theologians say that theology has to be liberation theology – it is useful, if it helps to establish social structures which enable people to live in a really human way. Others consider theology useful if it sets free the therapeutic effects of religion. Whatever the truth of such conceptions, if theology wants to be Christian theology, it must prove useful in an even more basic manner. It must be able to communicate the Word of God in human language.

Whenever we communicate something in human language, the language used is always a particular and distinct human language, bringing with it a specific history and cultural heritage. It will also bring along ontological implications, i.e. convictions about reality and its basic structure, convictions about the essential structure of what there is. Whoever uses a certain language moves within the framework of a certain kind of ontology, whether one wants to do so or not. Normally one does not choose one's ontology just as one does not choose one's language. Theology cannot escape this basic fact either. There is no theology, there is not speaking about God, without ontological implications.

This fundamental connection between statements of faith and ontology is fairly well proven by the history of Christian theology. The decisions of the councils during the first five centuries offer a good example of the ways theology made use of the ontologies it found within the Hellenistic culture. In this process a twofold motion can be recognised: on the one hand, theology took over the terms and categories of a mainly Platonic ontology; on the other hand, these categories and terms were changed and interpreted in a new manner. In order to express the meaning and the dignity of Christ within the context of Hellenistic culture, it was necessary to use Hellenistic terms, but if the contents of faith required modifications, the contents and the usage of the terms were changed. Klaus Hemmerle, certainly not the first to observe these facts, characterises the whole process as the "strenuous elaboration of the basic terms for trinitarian theology and Christology, which the philosophy of those days could not offer"[2].

If it is right that there is no theology without ontology, then it will prove useful for theology to care about ontology, and there are at least three reasons for doing so. In the first place, by reflecting on ontology, the unavoidable ontological dimension of every theological discourse can

2. K. Hemmerle, *Thesen* (n. 1), p. 131.

be disclosed. Secondly, in doing so, one can find the range of possibilities for making theological assertions. It is the consciously chosen or the
unconsciously adopted ontology which determines what can be said
within a certain language. Finally, a reflection on ontology helps to take
into account the fundamental changes in the understanding of ontological categories and their effects on theological language. In a brilliant essay
about the history of ancient Christology and the possibilities of translating their assertions into the context of modern philosophy, the philosopher
and theologian Bernhard Welte, one of the teachers of Klaus Hemmerle,
has shown the necessity for doing so[3].

II. TRINITARIAN ONTOLOGY, ITS ORIGIN AND ITS JUSTIFICATION

Klaus Hemmerle's *Theses for a Trinitarian Ontology* begins with a
clear-cut conviction: "We need ontology. This is a theological and a philosophical postulation as well"[4]. But even more: "The kind of ontology
which is necessary today, is a radical one, it is a fundamental ontology"[5].
Such is the kind of ontology that Hemmerle wants to offer in his *Theses*.
He is quite conscious of the fact that a trinitarian ontology is not something
completely new. He explicitly refers to Augustine of Hippo, Bonaventure,
Thomas Aquinas and Nicholas of Cusa. But Hemmerle considers these
drafts to be attempts which "still did not reach the end they aimed at"[6].
    Hemmerle's trinitarian ontology begins with the distinguishing Chris-
tian[7]. For Hemmerle this is found in the "middle of the Christian"[8], in
the revelation of God in Jesus Christ. At this point of history God reveals
himself as God who gives himself and his life for us. In order to describe
this event in a phenomenological manner Hemmerle uses the term of
"giving-oneself". Trinitarian ontology has its "starting point in love, in
giving-oneself"[9]. This is the central key for understanding this kind of

---

3. Cf. B. WELTE, *Homoousios hemin. Gedanken zum Verständnis der theologischen
Problematik der Kategorien von Chalkedon*, in A. GRILLMEIER – H. BACHT (Hg.), *Das
Konzil von Chalkedon*, vol. 3, Würzburg, 1954, pp. 51-80. Concerning the influence of
Welte on the thinking of Hemmerle cf. BADER – HAGEMANN, *Klaus Hemmerle* (n. 1),
pp. 43-49; and FRICK, *Der dreieine Gott* (n. 1), pp. 15-33.
    4. *Thesen* (n. 1), p. 125. Hemmerle defines the term ontology in a classical manner:
"Lehre vom Seienden und vom Sein" (124) cf. also *ibid.*, p. 126.
    5. *Ibid.*, p. 126.
    6. *Ibid.*, p. 140.
    7. Cf. *ibid.*, p. 133: "Der Einsatz beim unterscheidend Christlichen"; and: "Eine neue
Ontologie ist gesucht, eine Ontologie, die beim Proprium des Christlichen ansetzt".
    8. *Ibid.*, p. 138.
    9. *Ibid.*, p. 140: "Ansatz bei der Liebe, beim Sich-Geben".

ontology. In the light of the divine giving-oneself, "being, thinking and occurring discloses itself in its structure"[10]. Trinitarian ontology is the attempt, "to understand anew and without shortcomings in a phenomenological manner all that is in the light of love and giving-oneself"[11]. Trinitarian ontology is seeing reality as something which is because it is giving-itself.

Such a kind of ontology sees each kind of being not as a thing, but as an "occurrence", as an "event"[12]. For Hemmerle, trinitarian ontology is an "ontology of occurrence, of relation"[13]. In this kind of ontology "occurrence, but not understood in the Aristotelian way" and "relation, but also not understood as a category or even the most weakest accidental characteristic any longer, are given a central place"[14].

At first sight it might be irritating that a philosopher begins with theological premises. But such a beginning is quite legitimate. As the most basic and foundational discipline, ontology cannot be founded on principles laid somewhere else and before. The legitimation of ontology does not lie in its principles, but in its ability to make reality understandable. As in the case of scientific theories, one has to make a clear distinction between the "context of invention" and the "context of justification". Concerning the invention of the basic categories of trinitarian ontology, there is no doubt that they are founded in the Christian faith in the triune God. Concerning the systematic justification of trinitarian ontology, Hemmerle emphasises the fact that the plausibility of this kind of ontology is only perceived by someone "who gives himself to this divine giving-oneself and who enters not only with his thinking but with his whole existence in all its dimensions into this movement of giving-oneself"[15].

---

10. *Ibid.*, p. 150.

11. *Ibid.*, p. 141: "Es geht indessen nicht darum, das Phänomen Liebe, Sich-Geben einzubringen in eine umgreifende Phänomenalität dessen, was ist, sondern umgekehrt die Phänomenalität all dessen, was ist, aus der Liebe, aus dem Sich-Geben neu und unverkürzt zu lesen".

12. *Ibid.*, p. 142: "Die 'Sache', die das Hauptwort Leben meint, ist der Vorgang, das Geschehen, verbal verstandenes Leben".

13. *Ibid.*, p. 147: "Ontologie des Vorgangs, der Beziehung".

14. *Ibid.*, pp. 140-141: "Denn wenn das Bleibende die Liebe ist, dann ist die Verlagerung des Schwerpunktes aus dem Selbst ins Andere, dann ist die (nicht mehr aristotelisch verstandene) Bewegung, dann ist die (ebenfalls nicht mehr als Kategorie, gar als seinsschwächstes Akzidens verstandene) relatio in die Mitte gerückt". With this accent on relation Hemmerle positions himself within a broad tendency in theology. As an example one can quote Walter Kasper: "Weder antike Substanz noch neuzeitliches Subjekt sind das Letzte, sondern die Relation als Urkategorie des Wirklichen", in W. KASPER, *Der Gott Jesu Christi*, Mainz, 1982, p. 354; Kasper himself refers to Joseph Ratzinger.

15. *Thesen* (n. 1), p. 151: "Sie erschließt sich nur dem, der diesem göttlichen Sich-Geben sich selber gibt, der in die antwortende Bewegung des Sich-Gebens nicht nur sein

Trinitarian ontology (as every kind of ontology) is based on an option, and one must share this option in order to participate in its disclosing capability[16].

With regard to this capability of trinitarian ontology to disclose reality, Hemmerle is very confident. He is quite sure that it can meet the challenge which is given with "the weakness of thinking and being, the questionable character of subject and substance, the fading away of God, of the world, of man, all that threatens freedom and meaning"[17]. The ultimate reason for this capability is the cross of Jesus and his kenosis – this is the "deepest point of trinitarian ontology", and therefore "all limitations and all contradictions are included in the event of divine giving-oneself"[18].

III. THE SPOKEN WORD: AN EXAMPLE FOR TRINITARIAN ONTOLOGY

As it is not possible to present the dense *Theses for a Trinitarian Ontology* of Klaus Hemmerle in an adequate way, I will illustrate the basic categories of this ontology by means of an example given by Hemmerle himself – the spoken word. Hemmerle declares: "I speak the word, it begins its existence in me, I disclose myself in the word"[19]. Therefore I am the origin of my word – but I am not alone the origin of it. Besides me there is something else – "language is the origin of my word"[20]. Without the language I have learned I could not say my word. But this is not the final explanation either: "You to whom I am speaking, you the one I address, you are the origin of my word"[21]. What I say and the way I say it all depends on the person I address with my word.

With the help of this example Hemmerle illustrates his thesis: "A thing, a subject, a being can only understand itself and can only

Denken, sondern seine Existenz, und sie nicht nur privat, sondern in allen ihren Bezügen einbringt".
16. Cf. *ibid.*: "Wer aber aus der unableitbaren und unabnehmbaren Entscheidung des Glaubens an die Liebe die Konsequenz der liebenden Selbstaufgabe zieht, der entdeckt in den Dingen, in den Verhältnissen, in den Bereichen und Vollzügen dieser Welt, was sie zutiefst *von sich her* sagen und zeigen".
17. *Ibid.*, p. 152.
18. *Ibid.*, p. 153: "Es ist indessen, theologisch gesehen, der tiefste Punkt einer trinitarischen Ontologie, daß in der Kenosis des Sohnes alle Endlichkeiten und Widersprüchlichkeiten aufgenommen sind ins Ereignis des göttlichen Sich-Gebens".
19. *Ibid.*, p. 143.
20. *Ibid.*
21. *Ibid.*, p. 144.

perform itself in an act. This act is the constitution, the communication, the marking off and the insertion into a comprehensive context. Outside this act there 'is' nothing. But this act is not a degradation of standing in itself, but its constitution"[22]. We could simplify this rather dense formulation in the following way:

a) Reality which is recognised and named as a distinct kind of reality must be understood as an *event* (Ereignis). It is not simply something, but it is something in the act of occurring.
b) In this event, being presents itself as a *relational event* (Beziehungsgeschehen) which has different origins. This relational event occurs in a threefold movement "leading to each other, into each other and from each other"[23]; it is "unity in multiple causality"[24].
c) Reality seen and named as reality is reality in relation to a subject. But this subject only recognises reality if it engages in reality. Trinitarian ontology characterised by Hemmerle as "an act and in act"[25] therefore needs a specific mode of thinking: one must "enter into its rhythm with one's thinking, talking, and with the whole being"[26]. Only in this way can I recognise reality and its specific constitution. Therefore trinitarian ontology is not only characterised by specific "contents of thought" but also by a specific "mode of thought"[27].

Summing up one can say that reality as a whole "finds its fulfilment and realises its essence by realising its relationality and its transcendence, its having itself by giving-oneself, its moving to each other and its being for each other"[28].

This special way of thinking based on the fundamental categories of event and relation provokes the question of whether this is not fatal to all that is consistent and continuous. For Hemmerle this would only be the

22. *Ibid.*, p. 142: "Ein Ding, ein Subjekt, ein Seiendes läßt sich nur verstehen und kann sich nur vollbringen in einem Akt. Und dieser Akt ist Konstitution, Mitteilung, Abgrenzung und Einfügung in einen umgreifenden Zusammenhang. Außerhalb seines Aktes 'ist' nichts – wobei Akt nicht die Nivellierung des Standes in sich selber bedeutet, sondern gerade seine Konstitution".

23. *Ibid.*, p. 142.

24. *Ibid.*: "Einheit in Mehrursprünglichkeit".

25. *Ibid.*, p. 159: "Trinitarische Ontologie als Vollzug und im Vollzug ...".

26. *Ibid.*, p. 157: "Trinitarische Ontologie ist nicht nur Denkinhalt, sondern auch Denkvollzug. Sie denken heißt: mit dem Denken, mit dem Sprechen, somit aber mit dem Dasein selbst einsteigen in ihren Rhythmus".

27. *Ibid.*

28. *Ibid.*, p. 151: "Alles erfüllt sich und vollbringt sein Eigenstes, indem es in seine Beziehentlichkeit, in sein Über-sich-hinaus, in sein Sich-Haben im Sich-Geben, in sein Zu- und Füreinander tritt".

case, if event and multiple causality were made "principles of deduction, elements of a system"[29]. But, according to Hemmerle, such a move would not be right. Instead, this model of multiple causality is an invitation to enter the game of mutual relationality in the specific mode of thought appropriate to trinitarian ontology. If one does, then one can say: "Giving does not hold onto what it has, but it contains what it gives"[30]. As Hemmerle puts it: There is "no standing outside going, no finding hold but in transcendence, no finding position but in relation to something beyond it. But it is exactly in this way that consistency, being itself and being different is established"[31]. This is illustrated by the spoken word: The word is completely event and relation, but exactly in this event and in this relationality the word has its being. Therefore relation and movement "are not established as a new principle, by which one can deduce everything in a lonely manner. There is only one thing one can do: entering into the movement, which agape, love, itself is. This movement is the rhythm of being, it is the rhythm of giving which gives itself"[32]. What being is can be seen in its act; entering this act is the genuine possibility to understand being. Every assertion based on this act of understanding, but separated from it, must be seen as a secondary abstraction.

IV. RELATIONAL THEOLOGY: THEOLOGY BASED ON THE GIVING-HIMSELF OF GOD

As it should have become clear by now, trinitarian ontology owes its existence to an insight of Christian faith and theology: God is triune, the mystery of the triune God "is love, is giving-himself"[33]. This is the starting point for the "new of this new ontology"[34]. And starting from this point of departure "being, thinking and happening disclose themselves in their structure"[35]. But if this is true for reality as a whole, it is also true for theology.

---

29. *Ibid.*, p. 145.
30. *Ibid.*, p. 146.
31. *Ibid.*
32. *Ibid.*, p. 141: "Aber Beziehung, Bewegung werden nicht als ein neues Prinzip statuiert, aus dem sich alles doch wiederum in einsamer Deduktion ableiten ließe. Nur eines bleibt: Das Mittun jener Bewegung, welche die agape selbst ist. Diese Bewegung ist der Rhythmus des Seins; es ist der Rhythmus des Gebens, das sich selber gibt".
33. *Ibid.*, p. 150: "Das Neue der neuen Ontologie ist ihr Ansatz in einer Tiefe, die sich von unten nicht aufschließen läßt: beim dreifaltigen Geheimnis Gottes, das uns im Glauben offenbar ist. Das Geheimnis dieses Geheimnisses heißt Liebe, Sich-Geben".
34. *Ibid.*
35. *Ibid.*: "Von hier aus aber schließt sich alles Sein, alles Denken, alles Geschehen in seiner Struktur auf".

This is the reason why Hemmerle in his *Theses* sketches theology as an event in relationality right from the beginning. If Christian theology is the result of reflecting about the Word of God, it is characterised – according to Hemmerle – by a "twofold apriori": the "apriori of the divine with respect to the human and the apriori of the human with respect to the divine"[36]. Or the other way round: "Every word of revelation and each kind of theology is moving in two opposite directions: The word of God enters the context of human possibilities of understanding"[37]; and the human way of understanding and thinking takes its measure from the word of God, "which enters the possibilities of this way of understanding and transcends them at the same time"[38]. Characterised in this way, speaking about God on the basis of revelation presents itself primarily not as an ensemble of sentences combined in an understandable structure of argumentation, but as an event and as a unity in multiple causality.

In the final section of his *Theses* Hemmerle explicitly talks about the consequences of trinitarian ontology for theology. One of these consequences is the "unity of theory, spirituality and community"[39]. At first glance this combination of realities seems to be incidental. But it is a precise characterisation of theology seen in the light of trinitarian ontology. Why?

In order to answer this question one has to remember that Christian theology does not only have the task to *talk about* the Word of God, but also to pronounce the Word of God in human language. But this cannot be performed by an autonomous subject; it is only possible in the field opened by the community of faith, by the church. It is the church which is testifying the Word of God through the centuries by means of a multitude of witnesses and testimonies. Using the words of Hemmerle: If we are talking about the revelation of God, if we are talking about the giving-himself of God, theology must not "lose anything of the tradition of this giving-himself. Theology must receive the one, God's giving-himself, and it must open it to understanding"[40]. And at the same time theology has to "look with God into the direction where his love looks, where he is giving himself and where he wants to give himself: to the human beings, to the

---

36. *Ibid.*, p. 130: "In Offenbarung und Theologie waltet so ein doppeltes Apriori: das Apriori des Göttlichen fürs Menschliche und das Apriori des Menschlichen fürs Göttliche".
37. *Ibid.*, pp. 129-130.
38. *Ibid.*, p. 130.
39. *Ibid.*, p. 159.
40. *Ibid.*, p. 160: "Denn wenn Gott sich gegeben hat, dann kann sie nichts von der traditio dieses Sich-Gebens zu Boden fallen lassen. In allem muß sie das Eine, Gottes Sich-Geben, verdanken und aufschließen".

world"[41]. There is no doubt that this complex operation presupposes a multiple co-operation. Theology is unity in multiple causality *par excellence*. And this is, according to Hemmerle, the basis for a new definition of an ecclesiastical habit or attitude: Theology "is not only ecclesiastical in its careful attempt not to contradict the doctrine of the church; it is actively ecclesiastical as the expression of living unity and as the opening of living unity"[42].

But as the history of the church tells us, being a community is not self-evident. Very often life in the church is characterised by indifference or even confrontation. In order to become a living unity the church needs a spirituality of community. For Hemmerle such a kind of spirituality is defined by "service"[43]: "The highest dignity, the highest right, the highest initiative of everybody, where one cannot be substituted, is to love first, is to serve first"[44].

V. A RE-EXAMINATION: IDENTITY AND AUTHORITY IN THE CHURCH

In judging the *Theses* of Hemmerle, philosophers and theologians are ambiguous in their statements. On the one hand, they have to esteem the ingenious character of these thoughts – a "fascinating model of thought"[45]. On the other hand Hemmerle does not make it easy for his readers by using a language quite of his own. The "brilliance of language" is combined with a "very individual style of language"[46], which must be seen even as hermetic[47]. Sooner or later, then, one might wonder if it is worthwhile to engage with the thoughts of Hemmerle. Certainly this will be necessary if one wants to demonstrate that his kind of ontology has helpful consequences for the idea and practice of theology. Such an assertion must be proved.

In the last section of this paper we will attempt such a proof. We will do so by applying Hemmerle's trinitarian ontology to the question of authority. We want to find out, how ecclesiastical authority can safeguard identity in faith. Many things in present theory and practice of the church

---

41. *Ibid.*
42. *Ibid.*: "Solche Theologie ... ist nicht nur kirchlich in der Vorsicht, doch ja nicht der Lehre der Kirche zu widersprechen; sie ist aktiv kirchlich als Ausdruck gelebter Einheit und als Eröffnung gelebter Einheit".
43. *Ibid.*, p. 161.
44. *Ibid.*
45. BÖHNKE, *Einheit in Mehrursprünglichkeit* (n. 1), p. 274.
46. *Ibid.*, p. 23.
47. Cf. *ibid.*

can be understood as an attempt to safeguard Christian identity in the context of a great number of competing religious and other ideas. The terms "progressive" and "conservative" are labels for different strategies in order to reach this aim – either by preserving what has developed through the centuries or by adaptation to the present time and to the future.

At the same time this problem affects theology and its constitution. The question of identity is not only a question *for* theology, but a question *of* theology as well. It is the question of how theology can remain a special way of communicating the Word of God.

1. *Identity Safeguarded by Authority*

Theologically and practically it is quite clear that it is not enough to quote texts in order to safeguard identity. Texts always need interpretation. And in order to keep interpretation within a certain framework, and in order to keep texts from losing their meaning, it seems quite reasonable to have an authority responsible for ultimate and definite decisions. On the bases of scripture and tradition, authority is a means for safeguarding identity in doctrine. This at least is the proposal made by the Second Vatican Council[48].

The significance of authority for faith and theology was established in a specifically pointed way in Catholic theology during the last centuries. According to this theological doctrine we do not believe what God has revealed because of our insight into the truth of God's revelation but because of the authority of the revealing God[49]. Faith, and, therefore, the basis of theology, too, are legitimated and safeguarded in their identity by the authority of those instances which warrant faith and its contents. And the sum of those instances and their authority is the authority of the church. This understanding of external legitimation of faith as independent from its contents has been proven dysfunctional[50]. Therefore it became necessary to find an alternative method and to legitimate assertions of faith and theology by referring to the plausibility of their contents. But this also proves problematic[51]. Plausibility is not a guarantee for truth – neither within faith nor without. For example: I do not believe that Jesus has risen from the dead because this sounds plausible but because

48. Cf. SECOND VATICAN COUNCIL, *Dei Verbum*, 10.
49. Cf. FIRST VATICAN COUNCIL, *Dei Filius*, Chapter 3 (DS 3008).
50. For this kind of legitimation one has coined the term "Extrinsezismus" – cf. M. SECKLER, *Fundamentaltheologie: Aufgaben und Aufbau, Begriff und Namen*, in W. KERN – H.-J. POTTMEYER – M. SECKLER (Hg.), *Handbuch der Fundamentaltheologie*, vol. 4, Freiburg, 1988, pp. 451-514; esp. pp. 511-513.
51. Cf. H.U. v. BALTHASAR, *Glaubhaft ist nur Liebe*, Einsiedeln, 1975, pp. 8-32.

it is testified to me as part of the revelation of God. This is the reason for taking into account what seems to be the result of the history of theology, namely, that with respect to faith and theology, one cannot renounce authority. One cannot safeguard the identity of faith and theology without the authority of instances which testify faith[52]. The question only is, how authority functions or should function.

2. The Risk of Klaus Hemmerle – Not without Precaution

As far as the question of identity is concerned, trinitarian ontology is a risky enterprise. It is Klaus Hemmerle himself who formulates the objection that in his kind of ontology the consistency of reality and the question of identity are not taken seriously enough and dissolved completely[53]. If everything is an event, what remains in order to found identity? Does not trinitarian ontology bring theology to a kind of actualism, which leaves faith without any security?

As far as this question is concerned, Hemmerle hints at the fact that within the framework of trinitarian ontology identity is defined in a new manner[54]. Identity is no longer a matter of conformity, but it reveals itself in the act of occurring. Identity is "experienced as increase, as dramatic change. Life is identical with itself in its development and in its growth, life remains life by becoming more life"[55]. Two other examples: "Language remains language by being spoken again and again, by saying more and more, by addressing the other more and more. Time remains time by pushing ahead for future and even more future"[56]. Hemmerle, himself a musician, reminds us of a last example which makes his thesis plausible: "I only play Mozart well, if Mozart remains Mozart. But if I play Mozart very well, then Mozart becomes even more Mozart and I become more myself"[57].

But what is the importance of these examples? Are they more than an invitation to a kind of confidence that identity can be preserved, even if I do not repeat the same all the time? Questions remain. What does the comparison with music mean for theology? Is it not necessary to have a score and to be faithful to it in order to be sure that you really play Mozart?

---

52. One has only to remember the doctrine of the loci theologici as it was introduced by Melchior Cano: He does not simply speak about Scripture, tradition, the pope, the councils, but of the *authority* of Scripture, the *authority* of traditions and so on – cf. B. KÖRNER, *Melchior Cano, De locis theologicis. Ein Beitrag zur theologischen Erkenntnislehre*, Graz, 1994.
53. Cf. HEMMERLE, *Thesen* (n. 1), p. 145.
54. Cf. *ibid.*, p. 144.
55. *Ibid.*
56. *Ibid.*
57. *Ibid.*, p. 145.

If we examine the *Theses for a Trinitarian Ontology* thoroughly, we find that the ideas of Hemmerle are risky, but – at least with respect to theology and its centre and framework – not without precaution. God has given himself in Jesus and has revealed himself as the triune God and eternal love – this is the decisive insight and the foundation of trinitarian ontology. This insight is not only the background of his kind of ontology, but the hermeneutical key which determines the contents of it. And it is the key which determines everything which is reconstructed in the light of trinitarian ontology. This key is taken from the centre of Christian faith. Interpretation, at the same time necessary and dangerous for theology, therefore has a framework and a centre right from the beginning, which prevents it from becoming a game without limitation.

But the christologically founded giving-oneself does not only determine the contents but also the spirituality of those instances which testify faith and make theology an event caused by the interplay and unity of these instances. Therefore, according to Hemmerle, it is possible to understand theology as being "ecclesiastical as expression of living unity and of the opening of living unity"[58]. It is decisive that the interplay within the church is stamped by a spirituality of unity. And this is also true for those instances which have the authority of final decisions.

3. *Authority in the Light of Trinitarian Ontology*

For Hemmerle it is self-evident that a community "cannot exist without authority and something obligatory"[59]. Furthermore, the Christian "knows and makes the experience that the measure of community is the love of him who has given himself away without restriction and whose love is the outmost claim"[60]. In other words, living and exercising authority in the church must be stamped by the spirituality of giving-oneself. It must be stamped by God, "who has given himself away without restriction, whose love is the outmost claim"[61]. Such an authority proves true by opening possibilities of faith. Even authority becomes what it is by the interplay: love as giving-oneself is not only a requirement for those who have authority, but also for those who are determined by authority.

---

58. *Ibid.*, p. 160.
59. *Ibid.*, pp. 160-161: "Gemeinschaft selbst – in der Kirche, aber auch in der Gesellschaft – tritt unter dasselbe Gesetz. Ihr Leben ist nicht ins Belieben und Verfügen ihrer Mitglieder gestellt. Sie kennt Maßstäbe, sie kennt Autorität, sie kennt Verbindlichkeit. Der Christ weiß und erfährt, daß das Maß aller Gemeinschaft die Liebe dessen ist, der sich bis zum äußersten gegeben hat und dessen Liebe äußerster Anspruch ist".
60. *Ibid.*
61. *Ibid.*, p. 161.

With this concept of authority, two problematic extremes can be avoided: on the one hand, an authoritarian attitude emphasising formal authority, on the other hand, an attitude which allows everything with the confidence that truth will prevail. But such confidence has no foundation in history. There will always be voices which know how to use a vacuum of authority. But an authoritarian attitude and loveless conflicts do not prove apt for finding out what is true either. Anger always prevents people from having a clear view of the traces of truth "on the other side"; often it introduces alien interests into the discussion, and in most cases, it does not lead to common insight, but to a contradiction of positions.

The only solution seems to be that, in the light of trinitarian ontology, the transmission of faith and theology correspond to the nature of the church and that they become "the expression of living unity" and "the opening of living unity"[62] too. The necessary effort to live unity becomes concrete in the attempt to understand the other in spite of all differences and contradictions, in the attempt to recognise what is true and must be accepted, and, last but not least, in the attempt to respect and accept the other and his role. A spirituality of unity as conceived by Hemmerle does not make instances superfluous which have the task to make definite decisions. Such a spirituality cannot and should not avoid disputes, but it will help to carry them on in a manner which makes clear that the principles of Christian doctrine are observed even in discussion and conflict.

Seeing the transmission of faith and theology in this way, we have found what the German theologian, Hermann-Josef Pottmeyer, postulated on the basis of hermeneutical reflections in his essay on "Norms, criteria and structures of tradition". In order to safeguard an effective transmission of revelation there is, according to Pottmeyer, the need of authentic witnesses of faith, who do not only speak about something, but who also testify to this by their lives. As Pottmeyer puts it: An authentic testimony of faith becomes reality "in the personal co-act of the self-delivery of Jesus Christ"[63]. And as the transmission of revelation and faith occurs in the interplay of many, authentic transmission happens at last "as the unity of testimony and witnesses in the community of witnesses" and in this way it then becomes "the epiphany of the Kingdom of God in the midst of history"[64]. In this case the Kingdom of God is not only something the witnesses are talking about, but also something which becomes

---

62. *Ibid.*, p. 160.

63. H.-J. POTTMEYER, *Normen, Kriterien und Strukturen der Überlieferung*, in KERN – POTTMEYER – SECKLER (Hg.), *Handbuch der Fundamentaltheologie*, vol. 4 (n. 50), pp. 124-151, esp. p. 151.

64. *Ibid.*

visible in their common life and testimony. In Hemmerle's terms, the Kingdom of God becomes visible because the common life of the witnesses is stamped by a spirituality of unity.

VI. THE RESULT: POSSIBILITIES, DANGERS AND SAFEGUARDS OF A RELATIONAL THEOLOGY

Reviewing the way we have followed, we can sum up the major insights which seem to be important for the idea and practice of a relational theology:

a. Reconstructing theology in the light of trinitarian ontology means understanding theology primarily as an *event* (Geschehen) conditioned by historicity, i.e. by the circumstances which characterise its origin and have to determine its interpretation.
b. The central model of understanding offered by trinitarian ontology – unity in multiple causality (Einheit in Mehrursprünglichkeit) – helps to reconstruct theology as an *event in relation,* i.e. as an event which is the result of the interplay of several origins.
c. Understanding theology as an event in relation discloses the *inherent weakness* of theology: if it depends on a number of origins, it is exposed to the danger of losing its identity in the hermeneutical game of interpretation.
d. Hemmerle's draft also makes clear, what can give *coherence, stability and identity* to theology. There are three necessary presuppositions: 1) Formally speaking, the identity of faith and theology depends on the recognition of *authority* and *obligation* by all who are involved in the process of formulating assertions of faith and theology; 2) This obligation comprises a *spirituality of community* which stamps the different instances responsible for the transmission of faith and for theology; 3) Finally, theology under the presupposition of historicity depends more than ever on a commonly accepted *hermeneutical key*; it depends more than in pre-modern times on a clear definition of the presuppositions of faith.

Institut für Moraltheologie und Dogmatik   Bernhard KÖRNER
Karl-Franzens-Universität Graz
Universitätsplatz 3
A-8010 Graz
Austria

CONVERSATIO CORDIUM

CONVERSATION AS BASIC PRINCIPLE
OF NEWMAN'S TRINITOLOGY

Cor ad cor loquitur

I. PRELIMINARY REMARKS

In 2001, the Church celebrated the bicentenary of the birth of John Henry Newman. He may rightly be called one of the forerunners of the Vatican Council II and the theology of our time. His age, the Nineteenth Century was very different from ours yet his lifelong, earnest search for truth made him a contemporary thinker with our age who may help us in our own study of theology. Let me compare the *intellectual context* of his age and ours.

1. In the past decades we have been experiencing the *discovery of the Holy Trinity* in theology. Today's reflection on God is no longer simply based on the one divine substance, not even simply on the distinction of the persons, but on their mutual intercourse, relationship. A great number of monographs have recently been written about the Trinity, the division between the chapters *De Deo Uno* and *De Deo Trino* seems to be more and more obsolete. "Suddenly we are all trinitarians", partly because of the growing influence of Eastern Orthodox theology, partly because of the growing awareness of the Holy Spirit's presence and role[1].

There is a new "social image of the Trinity" emerging in today's theological thinking, a type of "communion trinitology", based also on the new approaches of the notion "person". Joseph Bracken already in the 1970s pursued a communitarian model of the Trinity: "The nature or essence of God is to be an interpersonal process, i.e. a community of three divine persons who are constantly growing in knowledge and love

---

1. E.C. GUNTON, *The Promise of Trinitarian Theology*, Edinburgh, Clark, 1997, p. xv.

of one another and who are thus themselves in process even as they constitute the divine community as a specifically social process"[2].

Newman lived and worked in a dry and dark period of theology, where
monotheism overshadowed the mystery of the Holy Trinity, its doctrine
was taken as abstract ideology and empty formula. Karl Rahner rightly
speaks about "the forgotten Trinity", claiming that hardly any believers
would notice the disappearance of the three Divine Persons in religious
literature[3]. Newman studied the Eastern Fathers, first of all in the ante-
Nicene period, and though he did not develop their notions and statements summed up in the Nicene Creed, his whole theology is centred on
the salvific economy of the Triune God.

2. In the field of philosophy and anthropology the human person has
recently been discovered in his/her social and communal relations: *person as being-in-communion*[4]. This new approach of the person is enriched
by recent Trinitarian theology and vice versa: trinitology has given new
insights to the analysis of the "person". As Nicolas Lossky writes: "God,
in His Trinitarian life, thus becomes the perfect prototype of unity in diversity, of personhood. In this perspective, a "person" is by definition a
being-in-communion, a relational being who cannot be saved by himself
alone"[5]. The principle of dialogue, of communication, of conversation
provides a new approach both for philosophy and theology and gives a
new impetus to Trinitarian theology as well. New ways of finding truth
have been discovered in the recent past: knowledge is no longer viewed
simply as a collection of objective and unquestionable statements, it always
has a subjective element: the person who is searching, who is making

2. J. BRACKEN, *The Triune Symbol: Persons, Process and Community*, Lanham, MD,
University of America Press, 1985, p. 7. Cf. J. O'DONNELL, *The Mystery of the Triune God*,
London, Sheed and Ward, 1988, p. 106.

3. K. RAHNER, *Der Dreifaltige Gott als transzendenter Urgrund der Heilsgeschichte*,
in J. FEINER – M. LÖHRER (eds.), *Mysterium salutis: Grundriss heilsgeschichtlicher Dogmatik*, II, Einsiedeln – Zürich – Köln, Benziger Verlag, pp. 317-347, esp. 319. It is impossible to enumerate even the most important monographies about the Holy Trinity published in the recent past. For my purposes the most useful books were: G. GRESHAKE, *Der
Dreieine Gott*, Freiburg, Herder, 1997; J. MOLTMANN, *Trinität und Reich Gottes*, München,
Kaiser, 1980; *In Comunione con la Trinita*, Roma, Editrice Vaticana, 2000; V. LOSSKY,
The Vision of God, New York, SVS Press, 1983; O'DONNELL, *Mystery* (n. 2); GUNTON,
Promise (n. 1); T.W. WEINANDY, *The Father's Spirit of Sonship*, Edinburgh, Clark, 1995.

4. See among others: J.D. ZIZIOULAS, *Being as Communion*, London, Darton, Longman and Todd, 1985.

5. N. LOSSKY, *The Oxford Movement and the Revival of Patristic Theology*, in P. VAISS
(ed.), *From Oxford to the People*, Leominster, Gracewing Fowler Wright Books, 1996, pp.
76-82, esp. 77.

statements, who strives to depict multidimensional reality as a symphony of one-dimensional approaches in continuous conversation with others.

Newman lived in a rationalistic and individualistic age when autonomy and independence seemed to be the basic characteristics of personhood, when natural sciences seemed to determine exclusively the methods of searching for reality. Yet for him truth was not an abstract notion but a living reality, in the end, the Living Personal God himself, whom he tried to find in the growing light of faith and imagination: *"ex umbris et imaginibus in veritatem"*.

His Trinitarian horizon of Christian faith and his extremely personal and conversational approach to revelation encouraged me to study his insights and experiences from the point of view of theology and conversation.

II. NEWMAN'S TEACHING ON THE IMMANENT TRINITY

Newman's greatest theological adventure was the study of the Alexandrian Fathers. Instead of elaborating a theology of his own, he summed up their teaching in a clear system and proved that they were in complete conformity with their forerunners in the Second and Third Centuries as well as in conformity with Scripture. His Trinitology sums up that of the Church Fathers: God is One in three persons. Newman does not examine in detail their eternal immanent relationships, the life of the Trinity *ad intra*. His teaching about the immanent Trinity is rather rudimental and simple, concentrating on the fundamental dogmas and reverting to the mystery of the Triune God that he can celebrate and glorify[6]. Still it has some *characteristics* worth noticing.

1. Newman is inclined to take the line of *apophatic theology*[7]. No human word can express the Divine Mystery. "The word "Trinity" belongs to those notions of God which are forced on us by the *necessity of our finite conceptions*"[8]. Not even dogmas or the words of the Scripture can adequately convey God's reality. "Let the Catholic dogmas as such, be freely admitted to convey no true idea of Almighty God, but only an earthly one, gained from earthly figures"[9]. "The Catholic dogmas are, after all, but

---

6. PS VVI, p. 327. For these abbreviations, see the appendix.
7. I. KER, *Newman on Being a Christian*, London, Harper-Collins, 1990, pp. 22-23.
8. GA, p. 50.
9. US, p. 340.

symbols of a Divine fact [...]"[10]. He further on claims that "we may, without irreverence, speak even of the words of inspired Scripture as imperfect and defective"[11]. All this does not mean that we know nothing about God. Yet Newman prefers images to notions and insists on going beyond ideas to reality, and of connecting theology to religion. The Nicene Creed is for him not an abstract formula of dogmatic statements, or a conceptual synthesis but a "hymn of praise", a "song of love". Rahner would speak about "kneeling theology".

2. Consequently, Newman is not concerned so much about different and sometimes erroneous definitions and ideas used even by Ignatius or Origen or Athanasius or any other of the orthodox Church Fathers. What is important for him is the *continuous and stable tradition* based on the Scriptures and developed by the ecumenical councils. "It may be asked, whether the mistake of words and names for things is not incurred by orthodox as well as heretics, in dogmatizing at all about the secret things which belong unto the Lord our God". "Our anathemas, our controversies, our struggles, our sufferings, are merely about the poor ideas conveyed to us in certain figures of speech"[12]. Writing about the Alexandrians he dedicates a whole chapter to the "Unadvisable terms and phrases in early writers"[13].

3. Newman sees the main proof for Catholicism in its very *tradition* so solid and stable throughout the centuries: in that continuous exchange of ideas, that never-ceasing *theological and spiritual conversation* and worshipping within the church, based on revelation. In that conversation even "the greatest Fathers and Saints had sometimes been in error, i.e., "they did not in their expressions do justice to their own real meaning". Yet the church as such is growing in faith: "as time goes on, revelation, what was given once for all is understood more and more clearly". In this huge conversational learning process heresy will clearly be separated from orthodoxy, even if the orthodox Fathers "spoke inconsistently, because they were opposing other errors, and did not observe what they said. When the heretic Arius arose, and they saw the use which was made of

10. US, 331. Ker quotes the *Grammar of Assent*: "the dogma is 'addressed' to the 'imagination', not the pure intellect, and is intended to 'excite our devotion', not to 'interest our logical faculty'". Cf. I. KER, *The Fullness of Christianity*, Edinburgh, Clark, 1993, p. 87.
11. US, p. 266.
12. US, pp. 338-339.
13. TT, pp. 162f.

their admissions, the Fathers retracted them"[14]. Analysing the crystalli-
sation process of orthodoxy in the course of doctrinal development he
remembers also the victims of this intellectual struggle for truth: "It is a
solemn and pregnant fact, that two of the most zealous and forward of
Athanasius' companions in the good fight against Arianism, Marcellus
and Apollinaris, fell away into heresies of their own; nor did the Church
spare them, for all their past services"[15].

4. Living tradition in the faith and teaching of the Church is not only syn-
chronic, but also diachronic, connecting different ages and schools of
theology in different cultural and intellectual settings. Newman employs
a historical approach and connects it with his theological method, comparing different views and finding out their common and orthodox meaning[16]. In his famous book about the *Arians of the Fourth Century* and in
his treatise about *Primitive Christianity* he describes the development of
Catholic faith, "the public tradition" throughout the centuries. He quotes
Vincent of Lérins: "thou must not be an author, but a keeper, not a
beginner, but a follower, not a leader, but an observer. Keep the
deposit"[17].

5. Newman's teaching about the immanent Trinity does not bring us much
novelty in its content. However, in dealing with the development of teaching in the Third and Fourth centuries he provides us an excellent example of *conversational theology*. He recollects the teachings of the Alexandrian school from Origen to St. Dionysius, St. Gregory Thaumaturgus,
etc. up to Athanasius and that of the Asian Fathers. Christ is "the Only-
begotten as ever co-existing with God", Origen said. Newman quotes
Dionysius: "Whereas the Father is eternal, the Son is eternal [...] Since
there is a parent, there is also a child". And Gregory: "One God, Father
of a Living Word, of an Only-begotten Son"[18]. This is how he summarizes
the fundamental faith of the Church, accepted and preached always and
everywhere: Christ is "God from God". The doctrine of the Lord's divinity "led to the summoning of the first Ecumenical Council in A.D. 325".
The council "pronounced that that doctrine concerning our Lord, such as
we hold it now was a doctrine taught by the Apostles in the beginning.

14. MD, p. 119.
15. HS, Vol. I, p. 400.
16. Cf. his marvellous essay on *Our Lord's Incarnation and the Dignity of His Blessed
Mother and of All Saints*: Dev., p. 135.
17. HS, Vol. I, p. 388.
18. TT, pp. 194f.

This was their concurrent and energetic testimony, as history records it"[19]. The Nicene Creed is *a relevant model of sound conversational theology* and – what is more – of the conversational-communicational faith of the church as communion. So "we are introduced to the ineffable, the adorable, the most gracious dogma of a Trinity in Unity [...]"[20].

6. In his ideas about the *life of the immanent Trinity in eternity*, before the creation mirrors the "intellectual mysticism"[21] in the Alexandrian fathers, Newman claims that the Divine Persons were "alone but not solitary", in eternal joy of their "ineffable intimacy of union", "the ineffable mutual love", in complete freedom and perfection[22]. "The Son was from eternity in the bosom of the Father, as His dearly-beloved and Only-begotten. He loved Him before the foundation of the world. He was in the Father and the Father in Him. [...] And in this unspeakable Unity of Father and Son, was the Spirit also, as being the Spirit of the Father, and the Spirit of the Son; the Spirit of Both at once, not separate from them, yet distinct, so that they were Three Persons, One God, from everlasting"[23]. He stresses that the Triune God did not need anything or anybody else. "Why should He seek external objects to know, to love, and to commune with, who was all-sufficient in Himself. [...] He was not solitary, but had ever with him His Only-begotten Word in whom he delighted, whom he loved ineffably, and the Eternal Spirit, the very bond of love and peace"[24].

Most of Newman's commentators claim that his Trinitology was based on the Eastern tradition, primarily the teachings of the Cappadocians[25]. He does not go further in guessing what this everlasting life before creation was like, he does not use any metaphors like Augustine or many others. He insists that this was the most perfect and joyful life of Infinite Love, in a certain state of rest, of repose. We may add: in a silent communication of love, in loving silence that is the strongest communion of the persons loving each other. Newman expresses it thus: "He His own Temple, His own infinite rest, His own supreme bliss, from eternity". This rest was finished by the work of creation and redemption, by the

19. Ess., Vol. I, p. 130.
20. OS, p. 185.
21. Lossky, *Vision* (n. 3), p. 103.
22. OS, p. 79.
23. PS VI, p. 364.
24. PS VI, p. 365.
25. E.g. J. Honoré, *La pensée Christologique de Newman*, Paris, Desclée, 1996, p. 46. Cf. also C.S. Dessain, *Cardinal Newman and the Eastern Tradition*, in *Downside Review* 94 (1976) 83-98.

divine drama, freely determined by God. "The whole economy of redemption is a series of great and continued works. [...] They began out of rest, and they end in rest"[26].

III. The Economy of Salvation by Christ and the Holy Spirit

Pierre Masson in analysing Newman's pneumatology claims that his point of departure is that of the doctrine of Justification[27]. Yet the economy of salvation, the "theodrama" began already with the creation of the world. "After an eternity in which God was the sole Being in existence, God wanted to surround Himself with creatures destined to live for ever. [...] Then he passed from a state of repose to an age of unintermitted, everlasting action"[28]. The three "divine agents" – a favourite expression of Newman – acted and have been acting in complete harmony. Using the metaphor of St. Ireneus, God Father acts with his two hands: the Son and the Spirit.

The acting God is an agent, a person, not a principle, claims Newman. In his controversies with the philosophers and liberal theologians of his time he forges a new term, indicating his method: *"personation"*[29]. Based on revelation Newman expounds the economy of salvation in its historical development. "Christ's original descent to the creature is the channel of our knowledge"[30]. Thus we have the opportunity to meet the self-revealing, self-giving God, the economic Trinity and life in communion with Christ by the Spirit. Most of Newman's work is centred on this mystery. God's aim is to extend his loving communion outside the Trinity. That is why he creates the world and human beings in it. Divine communion and communication is extended to the created world from the beginning. The aim of this communication is nothing less than the final perfection of the world: elevating all humans into that divine communion[31]. In the words of St. Athanasius: our deification[32].

This divine drama of economy unfolds in four acts: 1. Creation/condescension. – 2. Incarnation: full humanity, full divinity, yet in one

---

26. PS VI, p. 354.
27. P. MASSON, *Newman and the Holy Spirit*, Taipei, Yeh Yeh Book, 1982, p. 47.
28. Ari., p. 9. *The Doctrine of the Primogenitus.*
29. Thomas Weinandy in his book about the Holy Spirit used the same term, without referring to Newman: "While the Spirit 'persons' the Father as Father and the Son as Son, he does so only he is equally and simultaneously substantiated or 'personed' by the Father and the Son". WEINANDY, *The Father's Spirit of Sonship* (n. 3), p. 74.
30. *Ibid.*
31. MASSON, *Newman and the Holy Spirit* (n. 27).
32. LOSSKY, *Vision* (n. 3), p. 69.

divine person. – 3. Christ's atoning sacrifice. – 4. Justification: the
indwelling of the Spirit in the faithful. Let us follow Newman's ideas in
his economical – and conversational – trinitology.

1. *Condescension*

Newman thoroughly analyses the ideas of the Alexandrian Fathers
about the only-begotten and the first-born Christ. He quotes the expression of Athanasius about creation: "By the condescendence *synkataba-*
sis of the Word the creation also is made a son through Him". He adds:
God elevated the universe in the Divine Son, impressing His own likeness upon it. "Thus the Only-begotten of the Father imputes his Divine
Sonship to the universe, or rather makes the universe partaker of His
Divine Fulness, by entering or being born into it". So Christ became the
First-born of the creation and afterwards the First-born of the predestinate.

Newman admits that this doctrine expounded by Athanasius, confirmed
by Augustine and Thomas is very unlike Arianism, but had a direct
resemblance to the Semi-Arianism. He claims it to be "true doctrine, but
incautiously worded and imperfectly explained"[33].

The condescension of the Son in creation was but the prelude of his
incarnation in the fullness of time. "While the creation was exalted into
sonship, the Son, in exalting it, was lowered". The real condescension of
the Son was his incarnation.

2. *Incarnation*

Newman writes extensively about the earthly life of the incarnate Son.
He meditates frequently about Christ's voluntary self-abasement, his
deliberate choosing a low estate, poverty[34]. Christ "left his heavenly glory
and came down on earth"[35], "humbled himself unto his own sinful creation, refused the world's welcome, lived as a pilgrim"[36]. Newman gives
a moving description about Christ's humility[37], he confesses undoubtedly
the *full human nature of Christ*, yet there are some phrases where a slight
reminiscence of monophysitism is to be detected[38]. We must not forget

---

33. *Ibid.*, p. 69
34. PS IV, p. 240.
35. PS VI, pp. 41ff.
36. PS V, pp. 94ff.
37. HONORÉ, *La pensée christologique de Newman* (n. 25), pp. 82-84.
38. "In his Christology Newman so emphasized the divinity of Christ as to risk down-
grading his humanity, partly because of the influence of the Alexandrian Fathers, especially
St. Athanasius, and partly because he was extremely anxious to rebut any diminution of

that he followed the heritage of the Alexandrian school! "He was so separate from the world, so present with the Father even in the days of his
flesh [...] He lived out of the body while He was in it [...] He took human
nature like a garment"[39].

Newman would not explore the term *unio hypostatica*, yet he sticks
to the "essential doctrine that the Person of Christ is divine, and that into
His Divine personality he has taken human nature. In other words, the
Agent [...] is God, though God in our flesh, not man with a presence
of divinity"[40]. He stresses that it was "the Eternal Word of God who
acted through the manhood which He had taken [...] when He suffered,
it was God suffering"[41]. Newman uses vivid expressions imagining how
God could be refused and tortured in Christ. "God the Son suffered in
that human nature which He had taken. The officer lifted up his hand
against God the Son [...] That Face, so ruthlessly smitten, was the Face
of God Himself [...] It was the Blood, the sacred Flesh, and the Hands
and the Temples, and the Side, and the Feet of God Himself [...]
Almighty God Himself, God the Son, was the Sufferer"[42]. In that respect
the famous Newman scholar, Ian Ker, may be wrong claiming that
incarnation itself was more important for Christ than crucifixion: "Newman disliked too much explicit attention to be paid to the cross of
Christ"[43].

It can hardly be imagined what it meant for Christ to *go through human
sufferings with his divine personality*. "Christ's soul felt more than that of
any other man, because His soul was exalted by personal union with the
Word of God. Christ felt bodily pain more keenly than any other man [...]
He looked pain in the face. He offered His whole mind to it, and received
it, as it were, directly into His bosom, and suffered all He suffered with a
full consciousness of suffering. [...] He willed to the full sense of pain"[44].

Newman believed in the full humanity of Jesus, and he meditates a
great deal Christ's tremendous suffering at the end of his life, *viz.* his
being *deprived of the light of the presence of God*. "He had in the course
of his ministry fled from men to God. He had taken refuge [...] in Divine
Communion". Yet "when it pleased Him, He could, and did, deprive it

Christ's divinity by the liberal theologians of the day". KER, *Newman on Being a Christian* (n. 7), p. 40.

   39. PS VI, pp. 73ff.

   40. Ess. II, p. 203.

   41. PS VI, pp. 73ff.

   42. *Ibid.*

   43. KER, *Newman on Being a Christian* (n. 7), p. 43.

   44. MD, pp. 433ff. Cf. R. STRANGE, *Newman and the Gospel of Christ*, Oxford, 1981,
p. 89.

of the light of the presence of God. This was the last and crowning misery that He put upon it [...] He deprived Himself of this elementary consolation, by which he lived"[45].

3. *Atonement*

Newman meditates on the threefold office of Christ, as priest, prophet and king. He adds: in these he represents the Trinity: the Father is the king, the Son the priest, the Holy Ghost the prophet[46]. His active life was crowned by his sufferings, ending on the cross. Yet Newman sees the unique importance of this: "Christ was not only a martyr, He was an Atoning Sacrifice"[47]. "Christ's death was not a mere martyrdom [...] As He was not a mere man, so he was not a mere Martyr. Man dies as a Martyr, but the Son of God dies as an Atoning Sacrifice"[48]. Atonement was the common act of the three Divine Persons: Christ's death was not the tragic though heroic end of an exceptional life, but the greatest act in the economy of salvation, continued in his resurrection, ascension into heaven and the outpouring of the Holy Spirit.

Newman meditated upon Christ's life and suffering of deep sympathy and compassion. In addition to the sermons his prayers give insight into his heart. This is how he prayed on the feast of Ascension. "O God in our flesh, we will cling into the skirt of Thy garments, [...] for without Thee we cannot ascend. Oh inexpressible ecstasy, after all trouble. [...] Deus cordis mei. [...] Thou art the God of my heart"[49]. In other places he meditates upon God's sympathy, hidden from us. "It is the love of God, the bowels of compassion of the Almighty and Eternal, condescending to show it as we are capable of receiving it, in the form of human nature"[50]. What else can this mutual sympathy of God and the human soul be than the deepest communication possible?

4. *The Holy Spirit Justifying*

Newman is clear about the drama of salvation. Christ led a hidden life on earth; the Holy Spirit continued his mission after his resurrection and ascension. They acted as different actors in the same drama, taking over each other's ministries or offices. Atonement was followed

---

45. MD, pp. 413-431.
46. SD, pp. 52-63.
47. PS II, p. 42.
48. PS VI, p. 70.
49. MD, p. 534.
50. PS III, p. 133.

by justification, where the main agent is the Spirit of Christ. "Christ's mission ended when He left the world; He was to come again, but by his Spirit. [...] There was but One Atonement, there are ten thousand justifications". Our individual justification, continues Newman, "must be a spiritual, ubiquitous communication of that Sacrifice continually"[51]. Masson suggests that Newman's doctrine on justification, even the term "justification" may seem unattractive to our ears. "The word is less used in Catholic teaching, but has become current in Protestant circles"[52].

Newman did not hesitate to use that term. "Christ atoned in His own Person, He justifies through his Spirit", so that his grace should be "diffused, communicated, shared in, enjoyed"[53]. Newman presents us a complete, up-to-date doctrine on justification acceptable for Catholics and Lutherans: he may be called the forerunner of the joint agreement on Justification in Augsburg, 1999. A few quotations can show what justification means to him concretely: the indwelling of the Holy Spirit in each baptised individual person, that is, the continuous and most intimate communication of Christ's Spirit with each member of the faithful[54]. "The presence of the Holy Ghost shed abroad in our hearts [...] makes us righteous, and our righteousness is the possession of that presence"[55].

The communication of the risen Christ is no mere pious fancy or mystical experience; it is achieved by the *sacraments*, first of all by baptism and Eucharist. Newman had already discovered the "mystical or sacramental principle" in the Alexandrian fathers[56]. "His atonement is applied [...] in the flesh and blood of the risen Lord, first sacrificed for us, then communicated to us. [...] The body and blood of the Word incarnate is in some real, though unknown way, communicated to our souls and bodies". Newman adds: this is a mysterious communication: "no words can reach what is intended", still "there is a real gift of communication"[57]. The Spirit is the only One, who can "bring our souls into God's presence, while our bodies are on earth", by "divinely made impressions". "He makes Christ present with us, by making us present in Christ"[58]. In the economy of salvation the first communicator was Christ,

---

51. Jfc., p. 205.
52. MASSON, *Newman and the Holy Spirit* (n. 27), p. 141.
53. Jfc., p. 207.
54. For a more detailed explanation see MASSON, *Newman and the Holy Spirit* (n. 27), p. 145.
55. *Ibid.*, p. 137.
56. KER, *Newman on Being a Christian* (n. 7), p. 107.
57. Ess. I, vol. I, p. 248.
58. PS VI, pp. 127ff.

who began conversation with us, his work is followed and completed by the Holy Spirit, the everlasting communicator, who continuously converses with us.

IV. LIFE IN CHRIST, LIFE IN THE SPIRIT

The economy of salvation is not a drama performed for us as audience, but a drama in which we are all invited to take part. It is not a memory of past events, but an everlasting presence. The immense universal theodrama is continued in each individual soul. This is the actual place for Newman's most personal reflections.

1. *Divine Calls and the Human Response of Faith.* One of the recurring expressions of Newman is "call". There are Divine calls in Scripture. "All through our life Christ is calling us. [...] We are all in course of calling, on and on, from one thing to another, having no resting place, but mounting towards our eternal rest. [...] The accidents and events of life are one special way in which the calls I speak of come to us"[59].

The calls of Christ should be listened to and answered positively, in faith and obedience. However, he may be refused and conscience thereby silenced. "If the Gift be resisted, it gradually withdraws its presence"[60]. Newman speaks extensively about faith and obedience, as the right response to Christ's calls, and as the *conditio sine qua non* of Christian life. "Faith consists in venturing on Christ's words without seeing"[61]. Newman gives also the basic requirements of faith: We need "some little sympathy, some little love, some little awe, some little repentance, some little desire of amendment, in consequence of what He has done and suffered for us"[62]. The difficulty is, that "we have stony hearts, hearts as hard as the highways. [...] Yet we must have tender, sensitive, living hearts [...]"[63].

The surest remedy for disobedience is contemplation. We have to make "continual efforts all through the day to think of Him, His love, his precepts, his gifts, His premises". Meditation is "able to soften our hard hearts", so "little by little we shall gain something of warmth, light, life and love"[64].

---

59. PS VIII, p. 24.
60. PS III, p. 267.
61. PS IV, p. 300.
62. PS VI, p. 40.
63. PS VI, p. 41.
64. *Ibid.*, p. 43.

2. *Conscience* is the innate sensor of divine calls in us. Newman is perhaps best known for his idea of conscience. "Conscience is the connecting principle between the creature and his Creator"[65]. "Our great internal teacher of religion is [...] our conscience. Conscience is a personal guide"[66]. It is the human organ listening to the call of God and responding to it, the organ for our conversation/communication with God, the organ which helps us to be in communion with God, enjoy his indwelling, his presence in us. "Thus a man is at once thrown out of himself, by the very Voice which speaks within him". The "inward voice of conscience", "the light of conscience" is the true Light, which "enlighteneth every man that cometh into this world". "It is more than a man's own self. He may silence it in particular cases or directions, he may distort its enunciations, but he cannot emancipate himself from it. He can disobey it, he may refuse to use it, but it remains"[67].

3. *Holiness* is the most personal aim of Newman and it should be the aim of all believers. "Faith is to love as religion to holiness"[68]. This is the result of justification: a new creation is born in unity with the indwelling and glorified Christ. Christians are "taken into Christ, existing in Christ, as already in their mortal life they "have their being" in God"[69]. Christians are called to holiness, i.e., to grow in faith, love and obedience. "We pass from one state of knowledge to another. We are introduced into a higher region from a lower, by listening to Christ's call and obeying it"[70]. God makes us acquainted with more and more truths. "God seems to speak in them". "God may be bringing us into a higher world of religious truth. Let us work with him"[71]. This is the continuous existential communication between the self-giving God of revelation and the human heart opened by faith, the *ontological conversation* between God and his human partner called to communion.

4. *The words of prayer* are the most adequate answers to God's call. Newman is at his best in his prayers: his inner life, his intimate connection to God is mirrored in these texts. This is a real conversation of love, an intense and never ceasing contact between two persons in the

---

65. GA, p. 117.
66. GA, p. 389.
67. PS II, pp. 18, 64.
68. PS IV, p. 313.
69. Jfc., p. 201.
70. PS VIII, pp. 23-32.
71. *Ibid.*, p. 30.

communion of love. In most cases Newman is asking something, but what he is begging for is nothing other than God himself, his presence. His greatest and only desire is to see "the King in His beauty"[72]. "May I fix my heart on my true love?"[73]. "His eyes rivet me and move my heart. His breath is all fragrant, and transports me out of myself. Oh, I will look upon that face for ever, and will not cease"[74]. "I worship Thee with all my best love and awe, with my fervent affection, with my most subdued, most resolved will. [...] Make my heart beat with Thy Heart"[75]. "Give me that open-hearted sincerity which I have desired. Teach me to love Thee more"[76]. The final aim of Newman is complete unity with God, though he is well aware of the infinite difference between a creature and his Creator. "Thou shouldst grant me to have not only the sight of Thee, but to share in Thy very own joy!"[77]. "Let me be partaker of that Divine Nature in all the riches of Its attributes. [...] Teach me and enable me to live the life of Saints and Angels"[78].

5. *Communication*, however, creates both a vertical and horizontal line of communion. A Christian must not remain an isolated individual; he or she is member of a great communion, of the *Body of Christ*. Divine communication is continued on earth in the historical and human, sacramental communication of the *church*. Christ "does not look at us as mere individuals, but as a body, as a certain definite whole"[79]. "His gracious purpose was to make them one, and that by making earth like heaven. [...] All of us, and every one, and every part of every one, must go to make up His mystical body, [...] thus setting up a new creation in unity"[80].

"Christ came, but not to make us one, but to die for us: the Spirit came to make us one in Him who had died and was alive, that is, to form the Church. [...] We are living stones. [...] The communion of Saints with each other, and in the Holy Trinity, in whom their communion with each other consists"[81].

72. J.F. CROSBY, *God as Mysterium Tremendum in Newman*, in *Newman-studien* 10 (1978) 105-119, p. 110.
73. MD, p. 312.
74. MD, p. 409.
75. MD, p. 573.
76. MD, p. 582.
77. *Ibid.*, p. 590.
78. *Ibid.*, p. 596.
79. PS II, p. 120.
80. Jfc., p. 200.
81. PS IV, p. 171.

V. CONCLUSION

We have tried to follow the footsteps of Newman in his interpretation of the interaction between the self-giving, revealing God and human persons in the economy of salvation. One may object that our understanding is forced and misinterprets his theology and his personal and intimate approach to God. Nevertheless, Newman himself made a distinction between true and false communication, between empty notional theology and religious faith. Theological conversation must not remain a mere chatting or idle discussion, it must have its source and origin in the triune conversation of God. It must tend towards its ultimate goal, the participation in divine communication, in the triune God. It must end in praise, hymn of love. We have to give our assent not to notions, but to the mystery of God. "Not only do we see Him at best only in shadows, but we cannot bring even those shadows together, for they flit to and fro, and are never present to us at once. [...] Our image of Him never is one, but broken into numberless partial aspects, independent of each"[82]. That is why different views have to be put together in a joint effort of believers and theologians. Newman concludes: our efforts are but faint reflections of the Mystery, but they are "sufficient for faith and devotion". The Athanasian Creed "is a psalm or hymn of praise, of confession, and of profound, self-prostrating homage, parallel to the canticles of the elect in the Apocalypse"[83]. Newman used a lot of different names to express "the original revelation as it took form quietly and mysteriously in human minds: [...] Christ dwelling in us by faith, an Impression caused on our minds and hearts by God's word, inward knowledge, the Master of the Gospel, the echo in our hearts of the living Word"[84].

Newman's continuous and committed search for truth opened new ways towards a *communicative theology* and through communication to a *personal ontology*. Both concepts challenge theologians of our time to elaborate a more appropriate approach to a fuller understanding of God's loving communication in the Trinity and towards his creatures[85].

82. GA, p. 131.
83. GA, p. 133.
84. H.F. DAVIS, *Newman and the Theology of the Living Word*, in *Newman-studien* 6 (1964) 167-178, p. 167.
85. Among several sketches and attempts see e.g. J.D. ZIZIOULAS, *On Being a Person. Towards an Ontology of Personhood*, in *Persons, Divine and Human. King's College Essays in Theological Anthropology*, Edinburgh, 1991, p. 33.

Newman "disliked too much speculation in theology"[86] and sharply criticised shallow philosophers and liberal theologians who disobey their conscience. "A liberal theologian is a critic and a judge, not an inquirer, and he negotiates and bargains, when he ought to be praying for light. And thus he learns nothing rightly, and goes the way to reject a divine message". His manifesto was: "I wish to deal, not with controversialists, but with inquirers"[87]. In his long life full of controversies Newman proved to be a steadfast inquirer of the Truth in continuous conversation with God and his fellow-inquirers.

APPENDIX: ABBREVIATIONS OF NEWMAN'S WORKS

References to works published during Newman's lifetime are to the uniform edition, which was published by Longmans, Green & Co. of London between 1868-1881, otherwise the complete reference is mentioned in the list below

PS   *Parochial and Plain Sermons*
GA   *Grammar of Assent*
US   *Fifteen Sermons Preached Before the Universoty of Oxford*
TT   *Tracts Theological and Ecclesiastical*
MD   *Meditations and Devotions* (London, Burns and Oates, 1964)
HS   *Historical Sketches*
Dev. *An Essay on the Development of Christian Doctrine*
Ess. *Essays Critical and Historical*
OS   *Sermons Preached on Various Occasions*
Ari. *The Arians of the Fourth Century*
SD   *Sermons Bearing on the Subject of the Day*
Jfc. *Lectures on the Doctrine of Justification*

Sapientia School of Theology	László LUKÁCS
Ferenciek tere 7-8
H-1053 Budapest
Hungary

86. DESSAIN, *Cardinal Newman and the Eastern Tradition* (n. 25), p. 88.
87. *Ibid.*

TRINITARISIERUNG DER KOMMUNIKATION
IN DER POSTMODERNE

I. GRUNDMERKMALE DER POSTMODERNE

Der Mensch des dritten Jahrtausends wird ein religiöser Mensch und, wie schon Karl Rahner vorausgesehen hat, ein Mystiker sein. Aber wo dieser Mensch die Materie um seine Bedürfnisse zu stillen schöpfen wird, das darf uns nicht gleichgültig sein. So stellt jede Zeit das Christentum und seine Theologie vor neue Herausforderungen. Und eine solche Herausforderung in unserer Zeit ist auch die Postmoderne. Johann Baptist Metz sagt: »Tödlicher als der Verdacht, ungleichzeitig zu sein, wäre für das Christentum der Verdacht, überflüssig geworden zu sein«[1]. Ohne hier in die Details der Postmodernitätsdebatte einsteigen zu können, ist es doch wichtig, einige wenige Grundmerkmale der Postmoderne zu erwähnen, um dann (als geeignetste und fruchtbarste) die trinitarisch geprägte Kommunikation mit ihr vorzuschlagen[2]. Hier möchte ich darauf aufmerksam machen, dass die Postmoderne in den post-kommunistischen Ländern eine besondere Prägung hat!

1. Individualisierung

Das Subjekt, das seit der Aufklärung Träger der intellektuellen und politischen Emanzipation war, ist sich selbst fraglich geworden[3]. So hören wir von einer »Desidentifizierung«, von einer »pluralen Identität« des Menschen, von einem in sich selbst »gespaltenen« Menschen, ja von einem »radikalen« Menschen, der ein Individuum, ein »depersonalisierter« Mensch ist[4].

---

1. J.B. METZ, *Gotteskrise. Versuch zur »geistigen Situation der Zeit«*, in ID. et al., *Diagnosen zur Zeit*, Düsseldorf, Patmos, 1994, pp. 76-92, esp. 92.
2. Vgl. I. SANNA, *L'antropologia cristiana tra modernità e postmodernità*, Brescia, Queriniana, 2001, pp. 146-250 und dort angegebene Literatur.
3. Vgl. A.W. MUSSCHENGA, *Persönliche Identität in einer individualisierten Gesellschaft*, in *Concilium* 36 (2000) 144-151; J.C. NYÍRI, *Religiöser Individualismus in einer Welt ohne Zentrum. Globale und lokale Gemeinschaften im Zeitalter der Vernetzung*, in T. FAULHABER – B. STILLFRIED (eds.), *Wenn Gott verloren geht. Die Zukunft des Glaubens in der säkularisierten Gesellschaft*, Freiburg–Basel–Wien, Herder, 1998, pp. 86-96.
4. Vgl. SANNA, *L'antropologia* (n. 2), pp. 337-383; O. MEUFFELS, *Theologie der Liebe in postmoderner Zeit*, Würzburg, Echter Verlag, 2001, pp. 13-41. Der Autor entwickelt in

2. Sprache als Grund der Missverständnisse

In der Postmoderne entsteht die Frage, ob wir eigentlich von Gott reden können, weil die Sprache der Grund aller Missverständnisse ist, besonders wenn es um ein so großes Geheimnis (Wirklichkeit) geht. »Gott soll jetzt nicht bloß vor allen menschlichen Funktionalisierungen, sondern auch vor allen sprachlichen Begriffen bewahrt werden«[5]. Gott ist »der Unbegreifliche«! Die Sprache selbst bietet kein verläßliches Bezugssystem zur Wirklichkeit mehr.

3. Pluralität

Walter Kasper stellt fest, dass Postmodernismus nicht nur Akzeptanz und Toleranz von Pluralität, sondern eine grundlegende Option für den Pluralismus ist. Wahrheit, Menschlichkeit, Gerechtigkeit gibt es nur im Plural. »Ganzheit ist nur via Differenz einzulösen«[6]. Das Schwergewicht postmodernen Denkens liegt zunächst nicht auf dem Ganzen, sondern auf der Pluralität. »Die Postmoderne beginnt dort, wo das Ganze aufhört«, sagt Welsch[7].

4. Mythische Wahrheit

In der Postmoderne gilt es, dass die mythologische Wahrheit letztlich nicht in die logische Wahrheit »übersetzbar« ist. »Die Postmoderne ist auch als ein Aufbegehren gegen den Totalitätsanspruch der Vernunft zu verstehen. Sie will das wirkliche oder vermeintliche Monopol des Logos durchbrechen. Hicks Begriff der »mythologischen Wahrheit« kann als ein solcher Versuch interpretiert werden. Es gibt nicht nur die Wahrheit des Logos, es gibt auch eine Wahrheit des Mythos«[8].

5. Verabschiedung von Meta-Erzählungen

Was für die Postmoderne das unterscheidende Charakteristikum ist, ist *der Zweifel an allen großen Erzählungen*: des Christentums über die

---

seinem Buch die These, dass nur die Liebe die richtige Antwort auf die Fragen der Postmoderne ist.

5. W.G. JEANROND, *Zur Hermeneutik postmoderner Öffentlichkeit: Gottesbegriff und Alterität*, in E. ARENS – H. HOPING (eds.), *Wieviel Theologie verträgt die Öffentlichkeit?*, Freiburg – Basel – Wien, Herder, 2000, pp. 82-100, esp. 96.

6. W. KASPER, *Die Kirche angesichts der Herausforderungen der Postmoderne*, in ID., *Theologie und Kirche*, Bd. 2, Mainz, Matthias-Grünewald, 1999, pp. 249-264, esp. 253; vgl. H. BÜRKLE, *Das Absolute im Abseits*, in *IKZ* 25 (1996) 310-321.

7. W. WELSCH, *Unsere postmoderne Moderne*, Weinheim, VCE, 1987, p. 39.

8. KASPER, *Die Kirche angesichts der Herausforderungen der Postmoderne* (n. 6), p. 256.

Erlösung, der Aufklärung über die Emanzipation des Menschen, der Idealismus über den Geist (Hegel) und der Materialismus über die Praxis (Marxismus). Alle diese Meta-Erzählungen haben nach Lyotard in der Postmoderne ihre Glaubwürdigkeit verloren[9]. »Lasst mich mit den großen Erzählungen in Ruhe« – dies ist das Credo vieler Menschen in der Postmoderne.

6. Eklektizismus und Synkretismus

Ästhetisches Weltverhältnis nimmt Dinge in ihrer Vielfalt wahr, läßt sie auf sich wirken, bewertet sie nach ihrem subjektiven Erlebnisgehalt, entscheidet sich mehr oder weniger eklektisch für das, was einem selbst am ehesten zu entsprechen scheint, lässt die Widersprüche zwischen dem vielen stehen. Wo die Dinge derart gleichgültig nebeneinander stehenbleiben, ist die Gefahr groß, dass das Bekenntnis zur Pluralität und Toleranz zu Gleichgültigkeit, Desinteresse und Relativismus verkommt[10].

7. Religion ohne (persönlichen) Gott

Joseph Ratzinger hat auf den engen Zusammenhang neuer Religiosität mit der New-Age-Bewegung hingewiesen. Er versteht sie als eine »bewusst anti-rationalistische Antwort auf die Erfahrung des 'Alles ist relativ'[11]. Es ist eine Religiosität, die sich kaum in satzhaften Bekenntnissen äußert, vielfach im vagen, diffusen Glauben an eine »höhere Macht« befangen bleibt, ja, es ist weitgehend eine Religion ohne Gott. Johann Baptist Metz spricht daher von »einer Art religionsförmiger Gotteskrise«[12].

Es geht um das Glaubensgefühl, um den Glauben, der einerseits gefühlsvoll, stark emotional gefärbt ist, andererseits ist es aber eine richtige kollektive »Mystik«. Es ist nicht einfach, eine allgemeingültige Note dieser neuen Religion, zu geben. Diese Religion entwickelt sich noch weiter und nimmt immer neue Formen an. Mit ihrer Hilfe können wir ein neues Bild vom Menschen entdecken, und ein neues Bild von Gott. Dieser Gott wird anziehend wirken. In diesem Rahmen gibt es keinen Raum für die Institution.

---

9. Vgl. J.-F. LYOTARD, *Das postmoderne Wissen. Ein Bericht*, Graz-Wien, 1986, p. 14.

10. Vgl. J. RATZINGER, *Zur Lage von Glaube und Theologie heute*, in *IKZ* 25 (1996) 359-372, esp. pp. 360-362.

11. *Ibid.*, p. 365; vgl. SANNA, *L'antropologia* (n. 2), pp. 280-335.

12. METZ, *Gotteskrise* (n. 1), p. 77; RATZINGER, *Einführung in das Christentum. Mit einem neuen einleitenden Essay*, München, Kösel Verlag, 2000, pp. 19-26; E. SCOGNAMIGLIO, *La Trinità nella passione del mondo*, Milano, Edizioni Paoline, 2000, pp. 19-106.

8. *Die nachgeschichtliche Zeit*

Das Ende der Ideologien, der utopischen Leitbilder wirft den Menschen nun zurück in den Mythos, in die auserlesene Erfahrung des gegenwärtigen Augenblicks des Lebens. Mit der Wiederkunft des Mythos und des zyklischen Weltbilds ist auch das Ende des linearen, auf Fortschritt ausgerichteten Geschichtsbildes verbunden. Denn dort, wo alles immer gleich ist, wo sich alles in ewiger Wiederkehr zu replizieren beginnt, erübrigt sich auch die Geschichtsschreibung. »Posthistorie« ist aus dieser Perspektive gleichbedeutend mit der Postmoderne. Die Geschichte, die erst im 20-sten Jahrhundert ihren entscheidenden Platz gefunden hat, ist jetzt mit der Postmoderne als ein nicht nutzbares Mittel in die Ecke gestellt. Jetzt ist die Zeit des unbegrenzten Experimentierens, eine mythisch-dionysische Zeit ohne Finale, »the future is now«[13]. So wird die Postmoderne als das Ende der Vorstellung von geschichtlicher Finalität begriffen.

Unsere Zeit ist gekennzeichnet durch einen Ausfall der Eschatologie. Der Mensch der Postmoderne oder der Posthistorie hat sich auf der Zeit, derer Charakteristikum Exodus und Adventus ist, verzichtet und den gegenwärtigen Zustand für Ziel erklärt. Der Verlust der eschatologischen Hoffnung hat so in unseren westlichen Gesellschaften (im Gegensatz zu einer angeblichen Jenseitsvertröstung in vergangenen Jahrhunderten) eine starke Diesseitsvertröstung zur Folge.

9. *Der nihilistische Grundzug der Postmoderne*

Nicht das Neue ist so ein Kennzeichen der Postmoderne, sondern – im Anschluß an Nietzsche – die Einsicht in die ewige Wiederkehr des Gleichen. Das ist die Vollendung des Nihilismus: »Der vollkommene Nihilist ist derjenige, der begriffen hat, dass der Nihilismus seine (einzige) Chance ist«[14]. Für Vattimo ist der Tod Gottes, den Nietzsche verkündete, identisch mit der Überflüssigkeit letzter Werte und Ursachen. Das postmoderne Denken hat (aufs Ganze gesehen) eine innere Affinität zum Nihilismus. Diese Affinität hat neben der Verabschiedung des Glaubens an letzte Ursachen und letzte Werte insbesondere mit dem Aufgeben der Hoffnung auf ein Finale der Geschichte und damit auf einen letztgültigen Sinn der Geschichte zu tun (vgl. *Fides et Ratio*, 91).

---

13. Vgl. METZ, *Gott. Wider den Mythos von der Ewigkeit der Zeit*, in T.R. PETERS – C. URBAN (eds.), *Ende der Zeit? Die Provokation der Rede von Gott*, Mainz, Grünewald, 1999, pp. 32-49, esp. 48-49.

14. G. VATTIMO, *Das Ende der Moderne*, Stuttgart, 1990, p. 23.

II. DER DREIEINIGE GOTT ALS GRUND DER KOMMUNIKATION

In dieser paradoxen Zeit der wirtschaftlichen und politischen Globalisierung[15] einerseits und der kulturellen und religiösen Privatisierung andererseits, hat es die christliche Theologie nicht leicht, sich sowohl den akuten Bedürfnissen unserer Zeit zu stellen als auch den Fragehorizont unserer Zeitgenossen herausfordern und erweitern zu helfen und mit ihnen in eine fruchtbare Kommunikation zu treten. Als Ausgangspunkt nehmen wir den trinitarischen Glauben und als Vermittlung die trinitarische Sprache.

Jürgen Moltmann betont, dass wir die Wiederentdeckung des dreieinigen Gottes brauchen, des Gottes, der kein einsamer, nichtgeliebter Herrscher im Himmel ist, der sich alles wie irdische Despoten unterwirft, sondern ein Gott der Gemeinschaft, reich an Beziehungen, ein Gott der Liebe ist[16]. So erweist sich die Trinität auch als hilfsreichstes Modell, um Einheit und Verschiedenheit in allen Lebensbereichen besser begreifen zu können. Dieses trinitarische Modell »bedeutet den Abschied von jeglichem totalitären Unitarismus und Fundamentalismus, der die Verschiedenheit zugunsten einer gewalttätigen Einheit unterdrückt, wie die Therapie gegenüber einem Pluralismus, welcher sich zur Beliebigkeit verflüchtigt und am Ende in Nihilismus auflöst. Dies gilt für das Denken ebenso wie für den Bereich der Politik und nicht zuletzt für ein angemessenes Verständnis der Einheit der Kirche in der Vielfalt der Ortskirchen. Nicht der abstrakte Monotheismus, sondern der konkrete trinitarische Gottesglaube ist demnach die Antwort auf die geistige Not unserer Zeit«[17]. Darum möchte ich hier nur flüchtig von diesem trinitarischen Gott reden. Mich interessiert, was diese Trinitarität für ihn und was für uns Menschen bedeutet[18]. Ich bin nämlich überzeugt, dass die Trinität die Antwort auf die Herausforderung durch die Postmoderne und die trinitarische Sprache die geeignetste für die Kommunikation mit ihr ist.

---

15. Moltmann spricht von »globaler Vermarktung aller Dinge«. Vgl. J. MOLTMANN, *Gott im Projekt der modernen Welt*, Gütersloh, Chr. Kaiser, 1997, pp. 141-142.

16. *Ibid.*, p. 97; vgl. G. GRESHAKE, *Der dreieine Gott. Eine trinitarische Theologie*, Freiburg – Basel – Wien, Herder, 1997, pp. 197f; M.G. MASCIARELLI, *»Trinità in contesto«. La sfida dell'inculturazione al riannuncio del Dio cristiano*, in A. AMATO (ed.), *Trinità in contesto*, Roma, LAS, 1993, pp. 71-125.

17. W. KASPER, *Theologie und Kirche* (n. 6), p. 263; vgl. B. KOERNER, *Die Suche nach dem, was gilt und trägt. Christen zwischen postmoderner Beliebigkeit und Fundamentalismus*, in *Ökumenisches Forum* 19 (1996) 87-101.

18. Mit David S. Cunningham möchte auch ich behaupten: »The doctrine of the Trinity – despite the abstract language which it often must employ – is not just something that Christians *think*; it is also something that they *do*«: D.S. CUNNINGHAM, *These Three are One. The Practice of Trinitarian Theology*, Malden, MA, Blackwell Publishers, 1998, p. ix; vgl. den dritten Teil: *Living Water: Trinitarian Practices*, pp. 233-335.

1. Liebe als grundlegende Kommunikation in Gott

In der Behauptung: »Gott ist Liebe« (1 Joh 4,8.16), erkennt man einen trinitarischen Satz, der einer trinitarischen Auslegung bedarf[19]. Liebe ist nie unpersönlich, deshalb setzt sie die Personen, die diese Liebe in gegenseitiger Schenkung und Dialog leben, voraus. Die Erfahrung des sich schenkenden und des dialogisierenden Gottes, der nicht nur Logos, sondern Dia-logos, sogar Tria-logos ist, macht klar, dass es »in dem einen und unteilbaren Gott das Phänomen des Dialogs, des Zueinander von Wort und Liebe gibt«[20]. Liebe ist höchst persönlich und personifizierend. Moltmann macht uns aufmerksam auf die der Schöpfung zugewandte Seite des perichoretischen Gotteslebens und der Gottesliebe, wenn er sagt: »Die perichoretische Einheit des drei-einigen Gottes ist in dieser Hinsicht eine *einladende und ver-einigende Einheit* und als solche eine *menschen- und weltoffene Einheit*«[21]. Deshalb dürfen wir den trinitarischen Begriff der Einheit des drei-einigen Gottes nicht ausschließend, sondern wir müssen ihn einschließend, einladend und befreiend verstehen. Das meint Moltmann mit dem Ausdruck »offene Trinität«. »Die Trinität ist »offen« nicht aus Mangel und Unvollkommenheit, sondern im Überfluß der Liebe, die den Geschöpfen Lebensraum für ihre Lebendigkeit und Freiraum für ihre Entfaltung gibt«[22].

2. Trinitarische Kommunikation zwischen den Menschen und Gott

Gottes trinitarische Liebe ist die tiefste Grundlage (Matrix[23]) und der Ausgangspunkt der agapischen Anthropologie und der aus dieser abstammenden agapischen Ethik und Moral. Klaus Hemmerle betont, daß wir nicht nur Gott, sondern auch den Menschen in seiner Beziehung zu Gott und zum Menschen »sub specie Trinitatis« behandeln müssen, was auch »proprium« des katholischen Glaubens ist, der von der »trinitarisch-ontologischen Liebe« ausgeht[24].

---

19. Vgl. C. SORČ, *Die Liebe als Prinzip christlicher Theologie und Praxis*, in ThQ 181 (2001) 33-49.
20. RATZINGER, *Einführung* (n. 12), p. 170.
21. MOLTMANN, *Gott* (n. 15), p. 110.
22. ID., *Erfahrungen theologischen Denkens*, Gütersloh, Chr. Kaiser, 1999, pp. 282f.
23. Vgl. MEUFFELS, *Theologie der Liebe* (n. 4), pp. 35-36.
24. Vgl. K. HEMMERLE, *Dreifaltigkeit: Lebensentwurf für die Menschen aus dem Leben Gottes*, in ID. (ed.), *Dreifaltigkeit – Schlüssel zum Menschen, Schlüssel zur Zeit*, München – Zürich – Wien, Neue Stadt, 1989, pp. 72-73; vgl. auch M. BÖHNKE, *Einheit in Mehrursprünglichkeit. Eine kritische Analyse des trinitarischen Ansatzes im Werk von Klaus Hemmerle*, Würzburg, Echter Verlag, 2000, pp. 64-136.

Der Mensch ist eine Person soweit, wie er, durch den persönlichen Ruf Gottes des Schöpfers, ins Leben gerufen wird. So war die Schöpfung die erste Liebesansprache, mit der sich Gott zum Menschen zugewandt hat. Durch diesen Ruf ist der Mensch eine Person geworden. Eine Person, die Gott fähig ist! Der Mensch wurde in eine dialogische Beziehung mit Gott gestellt, und die ganze Erlösungsgeschichte ist eine Rettung der Persönlichkeit des Menschen, eine Wiederherstellung jenes Liebesdialoges, ohne dessen der Mensch als Person verstümmelt wäre. Von dieser liebevollen Beziehung des Menschen zu Gott hängt seine Fähigkeit des Dialoges mit den Mitmenschen und der Schöpfung ab.

In der Vereinigung mit Gott verwirklicht sich der Mensch, in Gott findet er sich selbst, denn, wenn er zu Gott kommt, kommt er zu sich: er ist ja aus der Liebe und für die Liebe geschaffen. Hier geht es nicht um »einen Menschen ohne Eigenschaften« (Robert Musil), sondern um einen »einmaligen Menschen«, der hoch geschätzt ist. Christen leben ihre Beziehung zu Gott in Gemeinschaft mit den anderen, oder sind sie keine Christen. Wir sollen nicht vergessen: »Gott, der Ganz-Andere als wir, erscheint am Ort des Andern, im 'Sakrament des Bruders'«[25].

3. *Die trinitarische Kommunikation in Gemeinschaft der Menschen*

Die liebevolle Einheit der Heiligen Dreifaltigkeit ist so auch ein Modell für jedes Mit-Sein und »Für-andere-da-Sein«. Auf den Menschen und auf die Gesellschaft wirkt sie kritisch und anregend. Dietrich Bonhoeffer hat das treffend ausgedrückt: »Unser Verhältnis zu Gott ist kein »religiöses« zu einem denkbar höchsten, mächtigsten, besten Wesen ... sondern unser Verhältnis zu Gott ist ein neues Leben im 'Dasein-für-andere'«[26]. Die Gemeinschaft der Menschen, die eine trinitarische Kommunikation entwickeln und leben, ist so: eine Gemeinschaft in der Verschiedenheit und eine Verschiedenheit in der Einheit; eine offene und einschließende Gemeinschaft; eine personifizierende Gemeinschaft; eine kommuniale Gemeinschaft, eine befreiende Gemeinschaft und eine lebens- und zukunftoffene Gemeinschaft.

Hier spielt die dialogische Dimension des menschlichen Lebens; das dialogische Verhältnis zwischen Generationen, zwischen Ständen, Kulturen, Nationen, Religionen und Weltanschauungen eine sehr wichtige Rolle. Das zweite Vatikanische Konzil behauptet nicht umsonst, dass »der Mensch in den Tiefen seiner Natur ein Gemeinschaftswesen ist,

---

25. H.U. VON BALTHASAR, *Glaubhaft ist nur Liebe*, Einsiedeln, Johannes, 1963, p. 100.
26. Zitiert nach G.L. MÜLLER, *Der Anonyme Gott*, in S. PAULY (ed.), *Der ferne Gott in unserer Zeit*, Stuttgart – Berlin – Köln, Kohlhammer, 1998, p. 49.

und dass er ohne mitmenschlichen Beziehungen weder leben noch seine Gaben entwickeln kann« (GS 12; vgl. GS 24). Es gibt keinen, der in der agapischen Gemeinschaft ohne Bedeutung wäre. In ihr werden alle Wertmodelle der sogenannten bedeutsamen, elitären, erfolgreichen Gesellschaft auf den Kopf gestellt[27]. Hier hat der Mensch seinen Wert in sich selbst, in seinem ontologischen Sein.

Die Zukunft der Menschheit liegt im Freiheit stiftendem Zusammenleben der Kulturen, Nationen (Respektierung der Minderheiten) und Völkern. Diese Lebenskommunikation kommt nur im Pfingstmodell und nicht im Modell des Turms von Babylon zur Geltung. Moltmann hat recht, wenn er eine personale Gemeinschaft einer Gemeinschaft der Individuen entgegenstellt: Eine Person ist im Gegensatz zu einem Individuum ein menschliches Dasein im Resonanzfeld seiner Sozialbeziehungen und seiner Geschichte. Sie hat einen Namen, mit dem sie sich identifizieren kann. Eine Person ist ein Gemeinschaftswesen«[28]. Also nur eine Globalisierung, die alle diese Komponenten enthält, ist eine christliche, evangeliumgemäße Globalisierung. So können wir von einem christlichen Programm der Einheit in Verschiedenheit, von einer pluralen Einheit sprechen; von eine Pluralität, die weder in die Atomisierung führt, noch den Moloch einer künstlichen Vereinheitlichungstendenz zur Folge hat. Mehr als um Globalisierung und Pluralisierung, bemüht sich der Christ um die Trinitarisierung der Kommunikation in der Gesellschaft und besonders in der Kirche.

4. Die trinitarische Kommunikation in der Kirche

Die trinitarische Struktur der Kirche gründet in der Tatsache, daß die Kirche eine Schöpfung der Heiligen Dreifaltigkeit ist: »Ecclesia de Trinitate«. Die Struktur und die Sendung der Kirche sind in ihrem Ausgangspunkt eingegeben: Die Kirche ist also die kommunikale Gemeinschaft, die die Unterschiede nicht abschafft, sondern sie annimmt, sie anregt[29]. Der Grund der Kircheneinheit und Kircheneinmaligkeit ist in

---

27. Vgl. J. MOLTMANN, *Der Geist des Lebens*, München, Chr. Kaiser, 1991, pp. 205-207.

28. ID., *Erfahrungen* (n. 22), p. 290.

29. Vgl. B. NITSCHE, *Die Analogie zwischen den trinitarischen Gottesbild und der communalen Struktur von Kirche*, in B.J. HILBERATH (ed.), *Communio – Ideal oder Zerrbild von Kommunikation?* (QD, 176), Freiburg – Basel – Wien, Herder, 1999, pp. 81-114; R.J. SCHREITER, *Globale Kommunikation und neue Katholizität*, in ARENS – HOPING, *Wieviel Theologie verträgt die Öffentlichkeit?* (n. 5), pp. 101-112; A. ECKERSTORFER, *Kirche in der postmodernen Welt. Der Beitrag George Lindbecks zu einer neuen Verhältnisbestimmung der Kirche zur Welt* (Salzburger theologische Studien, 16), Innsbruck – Wien, Tyrolia Verlag, 2001, pp. 114-163. Eine gute, ökumenisch geprägte Studie über communitarische

der Einheit und Einmaligkeit der Heiligen Dreifaltigkeit verankert. »Ecclesia de Trinitate« ist Kirche als communio, koinonia, die eine perichoretische Einheit und Vielfalt enthält und herstellt[30]. Die Kirche wird vom Heiligen Geist »vereinigt« und »versammelt« (vgl. LG 4). Sie aber versammelt nach diesem Vorbild und mit der Hilfe des Heiligen Geistes alle Nationen um ihren Gründer Jesus Christus, der gekommen ist, um die verlorenen Schafe zu sammeln und sie zum Vater zu führen. Die Kirche ist also eine Erlösungswirklichkeit, durch die Gott auf verschiedene Weise die Menschen einlädt und in sein Reich führt. Ihre communio Struktur wiederherstellt und verlangt von ihr die kommunikale Beziehungen, welche die Beziehungen der Liebe sind.

III. DIE AUSSICHTEN DER TRINITARISCHEN KOMMUNIKATION

Den wichtigen Beitrag des Christentums zur Postmoderne können wir in drei Worten ausdrücken: *Einmaligkeit, Kommunio* und *Zukunftsoffenheit.* Und alle diese Wirklichkeiten sind realisierbar nur in den Koordinaten der Trinitarisierung der Kommunikation.

1. *Einmaligkeit*

Die Trinität ist nicht nur »Vorbild« der Gemeinschaft, sonder auch des existentiellen Daseins! Gisbert Greshake betont mit recht: »In der Offenbarungsgeschichte zeigt sich eine 'Pluralität' in Gott, vor allem in der *dialogischen* Beziehung zwischen Jesus und seinem Vater sowie im interpersonalen Wir von Vater und Sohn, das sich den Jüngern eröffnet (Joh 17). Geschieht also das Offenbarwerden Gottes in 'interpersonaler' Pluralität, so zeigt sich eben darin, dass Gott auch in seinem inneren göttlichen Leben als interpersonale Einheit zu verstehen ist«[31]. Schon ein flüchtiger Blick in das »trinitarische« Leben des menschgewordenen Sohnes Gottes zeigt uns, dass die Einheit Gottes nicht nur eine nummerische, sondern eine ontologische und agapische Einheit ist (der Vater, der Sohn und der Heilige Geist *sind* ein Gott!). Wir haben eine solche

---

Ekklesiologie bei Ratzinger und Zizioulas hat geschrieben: M. VOLF, *Trinität und Gemeinschaft*, Mainz, Grünewald; Neukirchen-Vluyn, Neukirchener Verlag, 1996.
    30. Vgl. KONGREGATION FÜR DIE GLAUBENSLEHRE, *Schreiben an die Bischöfe der katholischen Kirche über einige Aspekte der Kirche als Communio*, p. 3; L. LIES, *Koinonia und Perichorese*, in J. SCHREINER – K. WITTSTADT (eds.), *Communio sanctorum. Einheit der Christen – Einheit der Kirche* (FS für Bischof Paul-Werner Scheele), Würzburg, Echter Verlag, 1988, pp. 338-354.
    31. GRESHAKE, *Der dreieine Gott* (n. 16), p. 172.

Einmaligkeit der Person erfahren, welche die Liebe, die Offenheit, den Dialog, die Kommunikation und die Verantwortung kennzeichnen. Nur in diesen Kategorien können wir vom Gott der Offenbarung und Selbstmitteilung[32], von Christi Einmaligkeit und von seinem Universalcharakter sprechen. Die Person setzt ihre Unersetzbarkeit in ihrem extatischen Leben durch, ohne ihre eigene Identität zu verlieren. Hier geht es nicht um eine Isolierung und Selbstzufriedenheit, aber auch nicht um eine Entpersonalisierung bis zur Unterordnung, Verschwinden oder Auflösung in einer alles aufzehrenden Wirklichkeit[33].

Diese trinitarischen »Grundsätze« gelten per analogiam auch für den Menschen, der nach Gottes trinitarischem Bild geschaffen ist (wir sprechen von einem »trinitarischen Mensch«), und endlich für die ganze Schöpfung, die aus den Händen eines solchen Gottes kommt und »vestigia Trinitatis« trägt[34]. Trinitarisch-kommuniale Wirklichkeit nimmt der personal-existentiellen Dimension des Lebens gar nichts ab. Im Gegenteil: nur als einmaliges Wesen kann sich der Mensch ganz in die Gemeinschaft einfinden. Noch mehr: Die Gemeinsame und die existentielle Dimension des Lebens sind aufeinander hin ausgerichtet und setzen einander voraus[35].

So kommt trinitarische Theologie dem Menschen der Postmoderne entgegen im Suchen Gottes, der selber Person ist und der personifiziert, aber auch im Suchen seines eigenen Bildes, in welchem er sich nicht als ein »Spielzeug der Götter oder der Gefühle«, auch nicht als in sich selbst »zerspaltenes« Wesen erkennt, das angesichts einer Ausweglosigkeit lebt, sondern als Wesen, das aus der Liebe und für die Liebe ins Leben gerufen ist, als ein sinnvolles Wesen mit einer unbegrenzten Zukunft vor sich. Die Liebe ist auch die, die »den anderen als den Anderen zulässt und gerade in der bleibenden Differenz die Möglichkeit zur einheitlichen Gemeinschaft sucht, in der das Einzelsubjekt seine Identität findet«[36]. Bleibt also festzuhalten, dass in der Liebe »der sinngebende Grund, die

32. Vgl. K. RAHNER, The Trinity, New York, Crossroad Herder, 1997, pp. 82-99; K. BARTH, Die Kirchliche Dogmatik. Die Offenbarung Gottes, I,1 (Studienausgabe), Zürich, Theologischer Verlag, 1987, pp. 311-367; C.M. LACUGNA, Dio per noi. La Trinità e la vita cristiana, Brescia, Queriniana, 1997, pp. 211-241.

33. Gründlicher beschäftige ich mich mit diesem Thema in meinem Aufsatz Die Perichoretischen Beziehungen im Leben der Trinität und in der Gemeinschaft der Menschen, in EvTh 58 (1998) 100-119.

34. Wir können von einem »trinitarischen Menschen« sprechen. Vgl. SANNA, L'antropologia (n. 2), pp. 435-469; vgl. auch meinen Aufsatz Die trinitarische Dimension des menschlichen Lebens, in Folia theologica 10 (1999) 37-54.

35. Vgl. H. SCHMIDINGER, Der Mensch ist Person. Ein christliches Prinzip in theologischer und philosophischer Sicht, Innsbruck – Wien, Tyrolia Verlag, 1994, pp. 125-150.

36. MEUFFELS, Theologie der Liebe (n. 4), p. 36; vgl. pp. 136-165.

kraftspendende Quelle und die Erfüllung verheißende Hoffnung aller menschlichen Kommunikation liegt, die diesen Namen verdient«[37]. Weil der Mensch ein dialogisches Wesen ist, kann er in Kontakt mit Gott und mit anderen Menschen treten und das Wort (das aber nicht die einzige Möglichkeit des Kommunizierens ist) als Träger einer inhaltsreichen Botschaft und nicht als Grund immer neuer Mißverständnisse entdecken. Der Andere (Mensch oder Gott) ist nämlich kein Umweg, sondern ein »Abkürzungsweg« zu mir selbst! So soll das Christentum in unserer Zeit *die ganze Wahrheit* vom Menschen, von seinen trinitarischen Koordinaten verkündigen.

2. *Kommunikation*

Die Person kommt zu ihrer vollen Verwirklichung in der Treue zu ihr selbst, was aber auch ein Sich-einstellen auf einen Anderen und ein Eintreten für die Gemeinschaft der Personen einschließt (agape). »Indem sich also der Mensch in unverwechselbarer Individualität selbst bestimmt, tut er dies bereits unter der Voraussetzung, dass er in wechselseitiger Beziehung zu anderen Menschen steht. In der Kommunikation liegt nicht allein ein Ermöglichungsgrund seiner Freiheit, sondern zugleich auch der Bereich der Erfüllung von Freiheit«[38].

Unser Ausgangspunkt ist wieder die dreieinige Personalität Gottes[39]. In Gott (wir können auch sagen: in Gottes communio, koinonia) bewahrheiten sich alle drei Personen auf höchste Weise (nämlich göttliche!). Wir haben auch gesehen, dass die heilige Trinität nicht eine in sich selbst geschlossene Wirklichkeit der selbstgenügsamen göttlichen Personen ist, sondern eine aus ihrem Wesen her nach außen offene Einheit der drei Personen. Die Trinität ist so keine exklusive und monologische, sondern inklusive, einschließende, einladende, dialogische Einheit, was wir mit dem Begriff »communio« (auch »communicatio«, koinonia; vgl. 2 Kor 13,13) aussagen möchten. In der trinitarischen Gemeinschaft verwirklicht sich die Einheit in Verschiedenheit und Anderssein und Verschiedenheit in Einheit. »Die Idee der Gemeinsamkeit, die ihre Quelle in der christlichen Offenbarung und das höchste Vorbild im dreieinigen Gott hat (vgl. Joh 17,11.21), ist niemals Einebnung in der Uniformität oder erzwungene Angleichung oder Vereinheitlichung; sie ist vielmehr Ausdruck des Aufeinander-Zustrebens einer vielgestaltigen

---

37. SCHMIDINGER, *Mensch* (n. 35), p. 146.
38. *Ibid.*, p. 143.
39. Vgl. GRESHAKE, *Der dreieine Gott* (n. 16), pp. 90-94.

Vielfalt und wird daher Zeichen des Reichtums und Verheißung der Entfaltung«[40]. So können wir von einem »trinitarischen Model« sprechen,
das allein es ermöglicht, dass »jeder einzelne auf seine Weise Ursprung
der Gesellschaft ist und die Gesellschaft doch mehr ist als die Summe
der einzelnen, dass die Gesellschaft ein eigenes, gemeinsames Leben hat
und dieses doch das Leben eines jeden einzelnen ist. Ich, der Andere und
das Ganze werden je zum Ausgang, zum Ziel und zur Mitte der Bewegung«[41]. In diesem Sinn verstehen die Christen die Pluralität, lehnen
aber die Pluralität als Ausrede für allerlei Entfernung und Entfremdung
ab. Die trinitarische Kommunikation stellt die Versöhnung von individu-
eller Freiheit und sozialer Gemeinschaftlichkeit und so ein echtes und
ursprüngliches Menschensein wieder her, das sich nur in Gemeinschaft
mit anderen verwirklichen kann. Darum ist es die Aufgabe der Kirche –
ekklesia, die individuelle Freiheit des Menschen ernst zu nehmen und sie
zu einer kommunikativen und solidarisch gelebten Freiheit umzuwan-
deln.

Als wir die Globalisation als jene Art des Zusammenseins, das immer
mehr in unserer Gesellschaft zur Geltung kommt, erwähnt haben, haben
wir auch auf ihre Entwertung des Einzelnen (des Menschen, des Volkes
u.a.), des Andersseins, besonders aber jedes Andersseins, das nicht in
schon vorgefertigte Schablonen paßt, aufmerksam gemacht. Die trinitarische Gemeinschaft ist auf einem anderen Fundament begründet, darum ist
sie eine unentbehrliche Alternative für Globalisation sowohl im Bereich
des Glaubens, wie auch im Bereich der Kultur, der Politik und der Wirt-
schaft. Trinitarische Gemeinschaft ist solidarisch, weil in ihr die Anderen
und die Gesellschaft nicht nur ein Mittel für meine eigene Fortentwick-
lung, meinen eigenen Interessen unterworfen, sondern auch »ein Raum«
der Verwirklichung menschlichen Dienens und der Proexistenz sind[42].

3. Zukunftsoffenheit

Die Trinität ist der Anfang, der Wirkungskreis und das Ziel der ganzen
Geschichte. Im Licht dieser Realität findet die Geschichte ihre echten,
ewigen Perspektiven. Das bezeugt uns die Erlösung, dessen Ziel die
Seligkeit ist. Christliche Verkündigung ist nämlich die Verkündigung

---

40. JOHANNES PAULUS II, *Der Dialog zwischen die Kulturen. Für eine Zivilisation der
Liebe und des Friedens*, p. 10.
41. K. HEMMERLE, *Thesen zu einer trinitarischen Ontologie*, Einsiedeln, Johannes,
1976, p. 68.
42. Vgl. J. SPLETT, *Leben als Mit-sein. Vom trinitarisch Menschlichen*, Frankfurt am
Main, Verlag Josef Knecht, 1990, pp. 73-89.

von »der Zeit, die auf eine Vollendung ausgerichtet ist«[43]. Denn die christliche Botschaft ist eine Botschaft von der »Zeit mit Finale«. Sie ist eine Botschaft von der befristeten Zeit und äußert sich in einer primär gedächtnisorientierten Kultur. Im Gegensatz dazu ist die Botschaft vom Tod Gottes eine Botschaft von der Zeit ohne Finale und drückt sich in einer Kultur des Vergessens (»selig die Vergesslichen«, sagt Nietzsche), in Formen »kultureller Amnesie« aus[44]. So stehen heute die Kirche und die Theologie vor der Herausforderung, im postmodernen Disput das christliche Geschichs- und Zeitverständnis neu zur Geltung zu bringen, das heißt, Geschichte neu als Ort der Heilsgeschichte verständlich zu machen. Die Theologie muss angesichts der nihilistischen Sinnentleerung der Geschichte die christologische und eschatologische Hoffnungsperspektive des Evangeliums neu in das Gespräch unserer Zeit einbringen[45]; die Perspektive, die eine fruchtbare und sinnvolle Kommunikation eröffnet. Diese Kommunikation ist so in der Geschichte begründete, in der Geschichte verbreitete und für die Zukunft geöffnete Wirklichkeit.

Hier steht im Mittelpunkt Jesus Christus als »Fülle der Zeit«, als »eschatos«, als »ultimum novum« in seiner geschichtlichen Einmaligkeit, wie auch in seiner universalen Bedeutung – also »concretum universale«[46]. Mehr biblisch ausgedrückt: man muss vom »Ein-für-allemal« und von der eschatologischen Dimension des Christusgeschehens sprechen. Wir müssen sagen, dass nach Gottes Menschwerdung nicht mehr die Heimatlosigkeit, Seelenlosigkeit, Beziehungslosigkeit, Ziellosigkeit und Sinnlosigkeit in der Welt herrschen, gegen welche die Postmoderne kämpft, sich ihnen aber oft unterwirft.

Im Anschluss an das Zeugnis der Heiligen Schrift haben die Kirchenväter herausgestellt, dass mit der Menschwerdung des ewigen Sohnes Gottes die Weisheit Gottes, in der alles geschaffen ist, in ihrer Fülle in die Geschichte eingetreten ist, so dass sich Gott in Jesus Christus nicht nur endgültig und unüberbietbar selbst veroffenbart hat, sondern dem Menschen und der Welt auch letztgültig gezeigt hat, wer sie selbst sind und wozu sie berufen sind. So ist Jesus Christus Anfang, Mitte und Ziel

---

43. Vgl. C. SORČ, *La historia en su dimensión pericorética*, in *Estudios trinitarios* 33 (1999) 133-146.

44. Vgl. METZ, *Gott* (n. 13), pp. 41-65; ID., *Zum Begriff der neuen Politischen Theologie*, Mainz, Grünewald Verlag, 1997, pp. 149-155, pp. 184-192.

45. Vgl. C.M. MARTINI, *Quale belezza salverà il mondo*, Milano, Centro Ambrosiano, 1999.

46. Vgl. H.U. VON BALTHASAR, *Christus Alpha und Omega*, in *IKZ* 25 (1996) 322-328; G. RUGGIERI, *Pour une logique de la particularité chrétienne*, in ASSOCIATION EUROPÉENNE DE THÉOLOGIE CATHOLIQUE, *Cultures et théologiques en Europa*, Paris, Cerf, 1995, pp. 77-108.

aller Wirklichkeit, die Achse und der Konvergenzpunkt der gesamten Menschheitsgeschichte. Dieses christliche Geschichtsverständnis ist kein Mythos, aber auch keine »Meta-Erzählung«, sondern Memoria passionis, Überlieferung (paradosis), Erzählung (narratio) von Tod und Auferstehung Jesu Christi[47]. Die gesamte Geschichte ist im Lichte Jesu Christi nicht nur als Siegergeschichte, sondern auch und vor allem als Leidensgeschichte zu verstehen. »Die Kirche steht ja nicht über, sondern unter jener Autorität der Leidenden, die Jesus in der Gerichtsparabel der sogenannten »kleinen Apokalypse« von Mt 25 zum Kriterium des Weltgerichts gemacht hat: »Was immer ihr dem Geringsten getan oder nicht getan habt ...« Der Gehorsam dieser Autorität der Leidenden gegenüber kann von keinem Diskurs und keiner Hermeneutik hintergangen werden«[48]. So ist die Kirche »Tradentin einer gefährlichen Erinnerung in den Prozessen der Modernisierung«, zugleich aber ist sie in der Kraft »memoriae resurrectionis«, Tradentin einer unerschütterlichen Hoffnung für alle Menschen. Der Ort der Kirche ist also unter dem Kreuz ihres Herrn und Hauptes, aber auch unter den Kreuzen aller ihrer Glieder. Gottes »Praxis« ist die höchste Autorität für kirchliche und menschliche Praxis!

Christliches Geschichtsverständnis steht also jenseits des Dilemmas von säkularisierten innergeschichtlichen Utopien einerseits und nihilistischer Sinnentleerung der Geschichte andererseits. Es hält fest am je einmaligen Wert und an der je einmaligen Würde jedes einzelnen Menschenlebens. Die Nachfolge Jesu und das Streben nach einem Leben aus seinem Geist der Liebe ist darum die wahre Erfüllung des Menschenlebens. Hierfür glaubwürdig Zeugnis abzulegen ist die entscheidende Antwort der Theologie und der Kirche auf die Herausforderung der Postmoderne, die Antwort, die nur in einer trinitarischen Kommunikation mit ihr realisierbar ist.

Theological Faculty   Ciril SORČ
University of Ljubljana
Poljanska 4
1000 Ljubljana
Slovenia

47. In der Enzyklika *Fides et ratio* lesen wir: »Der gekreuzigte Sohn Gottes ist das geschichtliche Ereignis, an dem jeder Versuch des Verstandes scheitert, auf rein menschlichen Argumenten einen ausreichenden Beleg für den Sinn des Daseins aufzubauen. Der wahre Knotenpunkt, der die Philosophie herausfordert, ist der Tod Jesu Christi am Kreuz. Denn hier ist jeder Versuch, den Heilsplan des Vaters auf reine menschliche Logik zurückzuführen, zum Scheitern verurteilt« (*Fides et ratio*, 23); vgl. SCOGNAMIGLIO, *Trinità* (n. 12), pp. 47-54.

48. METZ, *Gott* (n. 13), p. 41.

KENOSIS: METAPHOR OF RELATIONSHIP

This paper will argue that kenosis, as a metaphor of the divine mode of relating, is a model for human ways of relating that are inclusive and reverent.

As the theme of this conference recognizes, conversation is being increasingly acknowledged as of vital importance, both for theology and for all forms of human relating and endeavor. At this crossroads in human history, we are finally, belatedly realizing the urgency of fostering understanding through communication, for the sake of justice and peace. When we engage in dialogue with one another new vistas of understanding, new possibilities for enriching our human community can be opened up; but if dialogue breaks down our best hope for reaching and touching each other is subverted, and we all die a little as a result. *Conversation* is an indispensable paradigm of the kind of exchange in which we need to engage if we are to survive at all, let alone in a way that ensures the dignity and rights of all creatures.

This section of our conference program – "Conversation and Trinity" – points out that recent theology has emphasized the significance of trinitarian relations for our envisioning of creaturely relations; it notes that the "idea of conversation provides opportunities to elaborate on the immanent and economic love relationships in the Trinity". This paper is one effort at such an elaboration. To engage in such an attempt is not an idle exercise. Jürgen Moltmann has argued that there is a "reciprocal relationship" between our theology and our anthropology[1]. Elizabeth Johnson maintains that the "symbol of God ... functions in social and personal life to sustain or critique certain structures, values, and ways of acting ... Specific ideas of God support certain kinds of relationship and not others"[2]. Our understanding of the trinitarian relationships, therefore, can have significant implications for our understanding of human relationships.

---

1. J. MOLTMANN, *The Crucified God. The Cross of Christ as the Foundation and Criticism of Christian Theology*, trans. R.A. WILSON – J. BOWDEN, New York, 1974, p. 267.
2. E.A. JOHNSON, *She Who Is. The Mystery of God in Feminist Theological Discourse*, New York, 1992, p. 36.

My question in this paper, then, is this: What is it that we not only *can*, but *need* to learn from our trinitarian God about the art of conversation? I suggest that conversation is indeed an art and that we, as individuals, as societies, and as church, do have a lot to *learn* here. Many of us seem to have little trouble *talking*; this is the age of self-expression and freedom of speech, the right to which is held sacred in our culture of individualism. But *talking* and *expressing ourselves* are not the same as *conversing*. Furthermore, what *we* take for granted as a right is systematically denied by many others. Acknowledging the vital urgency of conversation unleashes a serious challenge: What about those who are excluded from the conversation, those who are not heard, who are denied a voice, whose voices are drowned out? What of those who are overlooked as insignificant, all the "invisible" people? What of the voiceless creation itself, the creatures who have no power to protest our devastating assaults on them and on the life systems that sustain us all. Almost daily we hear accounts of those who are marginalized and denied a voice because of race, gender, age, ethnicity, class, heritage or biological status; and experience has taught us that there are countless more, of whose existence we may never even become aware. What is the theological challenge posed by this exclusion of so many from the table of conversation, which in very concrete terms translates into exclusion from the table of life?

The search for an answer begins with reflecting upon the patterns of relationship modeled by God. Careful attention to God's ways with the world reveals an astounding inclusiveness. One could say that creation itself is the originating act of inclusiveness, the primal call to relationship, God's very desire for the radically Other bringing into being the things that did not exist (Romans 4,17). Almost every page of the Bible expresses a lively conviction of God's intimate involvement in creaturely life.

It is significant that this involvement is not simply unilateral. In the Hebrew Bible, many of the narratives, the metaphors, the words of the prophets convey a profound sense of God's *being affected* by human actions. One author argues that this reflects a crucial experience and conviction about how God chooses to relate to human beings: by the act of entering into relationship, God determines to take human beings seriously and allow them to make a real difference to the shape of the relationship; if such is not the case, then all the ways that God invites human participation and response are misleading and dishonest – they lack integrity[3]. The primary symbol of Israel's life before God is one of

3. T.E. FRETHEIM, *The Suffering of God. An Old Testament Perspective* (Overtures to Biblical Theology, 14), Philadelphia, PA, 1984, pp. 36-37; 46-48.

inclusive relationship, and throughout their history the people's role in the Covenant – keeping the Torah – is taken very seriously: God insists on a fidelity from them that corresponds to God's own.

Another important biblical symbol is the *word of God*. God speaks and calls to creatures, in often passionate language, and yearns for their response. God *addresses* creation, in command, in creativity, in entreaty, in love, in warning, and in power; God's word brings all things out of nothing and accomplishes everything which it is sent out to do (Isaiah 55,11). This makes all the more significant the pervasiveness of the conviction that God also *listens* and *hears*. God *hears* the cry of the afflicted Israelites in Egypt (Exodus 3,7). God is affected by the voice of the slain brother's blood crying from the earth (Genesis 4,10). God hears the crying of the thirsty child Ishmael in the wilderness (Genesis 21,17). The examples are too numerous to cite exhaustively, because this is such a fundamental feature of biblical religion. The psalms, the most powerful prayers in our tradition, are saturated with the confidence that God is listening (or is *supposed* to be listening!). Psalm 34, for example, insists repeatedly that God *hears* the one who is suffering poverty and misfortune, a conviction echoed elsewhere, as well (e.g., Sirach 35,13-18). Moving into the New Testament, we find Jesus urging his followers to "pray always", telling them, "Ask and you will receive" (Luke 11,9), and presenting the story of the persistent widow to drive home the point that God does listen and respond (Luke 18,1-8).

This biblical insistence that God listens and hears might seem problematic in light of the manifest exclusion of so many from the fullness of life, but it reflects what seems to be a very deep-seated religious experience: that God is touched by and responsive to the human word. Nevertheless, our actual knowledge of the injustice that pervades the world tempts us to wonder whether God hears even those who are voiceless, and sees those whom no one else sees. What are we to make of the scriptural assurance in the face of so much evidence to the contrary, evidence that seems to indicate that so many are not heard? Perhaps it challenges us to a deepening of the question: not *whether* God hears, but – returning to the fundamental question of this discussion – *how* God hears.

In order to reflect on this, I will focus my discussion of the divine inclusiveness on another scriptural metaphor, that of the *kenosis* or *self-emptying* of Christ. I make the disclaimer that my approach to this image is not that of the exegete, but that of the systematic theologian looking for deeper theological connections and implications. The metaphor of kenosis is found in the christological hymn in Philippians 2,6-11, which recounts that Christ, though he was in the form of God, did not grasp equality with God, but emptied himself, took the form of a slave, humbled himself, and became obedient unto death (even on a cross); and that therefore God highly exalted him and gave him the name above every name, so that at his name every knee should bend and every tongue confess his lordship to the glory of God the Father.

If the phrase, "he emptied himself", is interpreted as referring to the incarnation, as has traditionally been the case, it suggests something significant about God's manner of relating. Christians believe in the incarnation as the unsurpassable event of God's self-communication. John's Gospel depicts it as God's *Word* becoming flesh. Yet, if one may be forgiven for mixing metaphors and scriptural texts, the Philippians passage qualifies this by suggesting that God's self-utterance, taking the form of self-emptying, is anything but an act of naked self-*assertion*. Even Saint Augustine – who, in adhering to the traditional position that there was no true *emptying* of Christ's divinity[4], inverted the meaning of kenosis to signify that Christ *added* a human nature to his divine one[5] – understood the incarnation to entail an act of divine *humility*[6]. The passage suggests that God's coming among human beings is humble, even hidden, not taking the form of dominating power, but of humility, weakness, and obedience – the form of a slave.

This is a significant critique of an all-too-human tendency to valorize power, self-assertion, success and self-aggrandizement, a tendency which would find its religious legitimation in the "theology of glory". In our theological history, this critique is taken up by Martin Luther[7], as is well known, and by Jürgen Moltmann[8], among others (not to mention the Apostle Paul). The kenotic God manifests a way of relating to humans and their history which is quite different from our customary patterns of egocentric self-assertion. Insofar as this is the case, this metaphor provides a valuable and necessary critique of human relationships.

But it is unsatisfactory and even dangerous to stop here. Particularly in light of the concerns of this paper, it is imperative that we examine the

---

4. See, e.g., CHRYSOSTOM, *Homily 7 on Philippians*, in P. SCHAFF (ed.) *Homilies on the Epistle of St. Paul the Apostle to the Philippians*, trans. W.C. COTTON, with additional notes by J. BROADUS (A Select Library of the Nicene and Post-Nicene Fathers of the Christian Church, 13), Grand Rapids, MI, 1956, p. 215.

5. AUGUSTINE, *Sermon 183* (on 1 John 4,2), in *Selected Sermons of St. Augustine*, trans. and ed. Q. HOWE, Jr., New York, 1966, p. 77.

6. G. BONNER, *Christ, God, and Man in the Thought of St. Augustine*, in *Angelicum* 61 (1984) 268-294, p. 275.

7. M. LUTHER, *The Heidelberg Disputation,* in *Early Theological Works*, ed. and trans. J. ATKINSON (Library of Christian Classics, 16), Philadelphia, PA, 1962, theses 19-21.

8. MOLTMANN, *The Crucified God* (n. 1), pp. 207-214.

implications of the divine self-emptying more carefully, lest this metaphor unwittingly encourage precisely the distorted forms of relationship we must call into question. In the Christian tradition kenosis is a key symbol of the self-sacrifice, humility, obedience, and submissiveness which characterize Christ and are urged upon his followers. Indeed, its context in the Letter to the Philippians makes it clear that Paul's intention in quoting the hymn is to urge his readers to Christ-like humility, service (vv. 3-5) and obedience (v. 12)[9]. One commentator believes that the "language used to describe Jesus' actions qualitatively in 2,6-8 is drawn from the language of early Christian paraenesis"[10]. Jesus' example not only models but also reinforces what Christians are taught concerning the Christian way of life. In this regard it is also worth paying special attention to the language which qualifies the meaning of his self-emptying by stating that Jesus took the form of a *slave*. Whether *slave* is intended here to describe the human condition, especially as disobedient and sinful, or whether it is a reference to Christ's ministry of service[11], this terminology – particularly when used to name the state he voluntarily assumed – surely cannot have failed to make a profound impression in a society where slavery was an all too real fact of life for thousands of people. The impact of this word is heightened in recalling the conditions of slavery: the slaves' powerlessness and total lack of rights; their entrapment in a social structure of exploitation and violation[12]; their vulnerability to sometimes inhuman cruelty and even execution – on suspicion of rebelling against their fate or even merely on the whim of their masters[13].

It is this model of Christ's submissiveness, with all these implications, which is raised up, and has continued to function, as a fundamental paradigm for Christian faith and life. Down through the ages, the conviction

9. Although there are a variety of interpretations regarding Paul's intentions in setting Christ's kenotic history before his readers, they all converge on the notion that the Philippians passage appeals to Christians to imitate or conform themselves to Christ in his self-effacing, obedient submission. Bloomquist surveys the various approaches in G. BLOOMQUIST, *The Function of Suffering in Philippians* (JSNT SS, 78), Sheffield, 1993.

10. L.W. HURTADO, *Jesus as Lordly Example in Philippians 2:5-11*, in P. RICHARDSON – J.C. HURD (eds.), *From Jesus to Paul. Studies in Honour of Francis Wright Beare*, Waterloo, 1984, p. 126.

11. G.F. HAWTHORNE, *Philippians*, in D.A. HUBBARD – G.W. BARKER – R.P. MARTIN (eds.), *Word Biblical Commentary*, Waco, TX, 1983, pp. 78, 87.

12. C.F.D. MOULE, *Further Reflections on Philippians 2:5-11*, in W.W. GASQUE – R.P. MARTIN (eds.), *Apostolic History and the Gospel. Biblical and Historical Essays Presented to F.F. Bruce on His 60th Birthday*, Grand Rapids, MI, 1970, p. 268.

13. See the Chapter, *The "Slaves' Punishment"*, in M. HENGEL, *The Cross of the Son of God* (Containing *The Son of God, Crucifixion, The Atonement*), trans. J. BOWDEN, London, 1986, pp. 143-155.

that following Christ means conforming to the Christlike virtues of humility, obedience and self-sacrifice has been deeply impressed upon the Christian psyche[14]. It has fostered the notion that to be a good Christian, to be a good *person*, one must deny and efface the self. According to Joanne Carlson Brown and Rebecca Parker, "Those whose lives have been deeply shaped by the Christian tradition feel that self-sacrifice and obedience are not only virtues but the definition of a faithful identity"[15]. There is thus an almost overpowering moral pressure, which can operate on the psychic level even when one "knows better", to regard any form of self-concern or refusal to be submissive as unworthy and selfish.

This means that care must be taken to avoid turning the metaphor of kenosis into indoctrination toward destructive forms of relationship. The Christian emphasis on self-sacrifice and obedience can all too easily be subverted to legitimate the sufferings of the oppressed and condition them to accept their lot patiently as God's will. One could mention in this connection reports by counselors concerning abuse victims who see their suffering as deserved, as salvific, or otherwise justifiable[16]; or the ways that texts such as Romans 13,1-7, urging subjection "to the governing authorities", have been used to validate oppressive political regimes[17]; or the use of the Suffering Servant text of Isaiah 53 to justify the suffering of black people as divinely-willed vicarious suffering for the salvation of their white oppressors[18] – to specify just a few instances of the dangerous misuse of these Christian values.

Furthermore, self-sacrifice, in and of itself, is not necessarily unmixed benevolence. For it can mask attitudes that are in fact unloving and reinforce relational structures that undercut the dignity and well-being of all involved. As Christine Gudorf puts it, "When we assume that to do the hard, self-sacrificing thing is to do the loving thing, we have, in fact, defined the interest of the other in terms of

14. It should be noted that the Philippians passage is only one of several which define followers of Christ in terms of these qualities.

15. J.C. BROWN – R. PARKER, *For God So Loved the World?*, in J.C. BROWN – C.R. BOHN (eds.), *Christianity, Patriarchy, and Abuse. A Feminist Critique*, New York, 1989, 1-30, p. 2.

16. See J.N. POLING, *The Abuse of Power. A Theological Problem*, Nashville, TN, 1991, p. 40.

17. See J. BOTHA, *Subject to Whose Authority? Multiple Readings of Romans 13* (Emory Studies in Early Christianity, 4), Atlanta, GA, 1994. For a history of how this text has been used in relation to specific political situations, see also U. WILKENS, *Der Brief an die Römer (Röm 12–16)* (Evangelisch-Katholischer Kommentar zum Neuen Testament 4/3), Zürich – Einsiedeln – Köln, 1982.

18. This is Washington's position in J. WASHINGTON, *The Politics of God*, Boston, 1969. Washington is himself a black theologian.

ourselves, and not in terms of the person and conditions of the other"[19]. Or as Gene Outka says, "Self-sacrifice must always be purposive in promoting the welfare of others and never simply expressive of something resident in the agent"[20]. We can be tempted to think we are doing good when in actuality we are imposing our own perceptions and agenda on others, rather than respecting their radical otherness and particularity; or we may be undercutting, rather than supporting, their autonomy. If this is not taken into consideration, we run the risk of turning kenosis into an image of a self-indulgent projection of the Self upon the Other, what Catherine Keller describes as a "narcissistic merger"[21].

The preceding remarks are meant to underscore the need for caution in light of the ways the image of Christ's self-emptying can function as a model of distorted relationship patterns: either passive submissiveness to oppression or misguided self-sacrifice and "charity". With regard to the present topic of discussion, we must take care that a *self-effacing* Christ does not encourage the voiceless to remain silent or justify a refusal to listen by the powerful. Alternatively, we must take care that a heroically *self-sacrificing* Christ does not promote attitudes and patterns of acting which fail to be open to the particular truth of the voiceless. Since the image of kenosis and its related ideals are so central and loom so large in the Christian ethos and imagination, it is absolutely essential to engage in a critical re-appropriation of them which can, if possible, transcend their potential for harm and mine their even deeper potential for good. In fact, as I hope to show, it is only by doing so that we can enter into a deeper appreciation of the true significance of Christ's self-emptying.

One step toward this critical reappropriation involves seeing the metaphor of kenosis as a pointer to the divine way of relating. First of all, if we interpret kenosis in the traditional sense of incarnation, it entails that God is not distant and disengaged from the world, but has become profoundly, personally, immediately involved in its history and destiny.

19. C. GUDORF, *Parenting, Mutual Love, and Sacrifice*, in B.H. ANDOLSEN – C.E. GUDORF – M.D. PELLAUER (eds.), *Women's Consciousness, Women's Conscience. A Reader in Feminist Ethics*, Minneapolis, MN, 1985; reprint, San Francisco, CA, 1987, 175-191, p. 184.

20. G. OUTKA, *Agape. An Ethical Social Analysis*, New Haven, CT, 1972, p. 278, quoted in GUDORF, *Parenting, Mutual Love, and Sacrifice* (n. 19), p. 183.

21. C. KELLER, *Scoop up the Water and the Moon Is in Your Hands. On Feminist Theology and Dynamic Self-Emptying*, in J.B. COBB, Jr. – C. IVES (eds.), *The Emptying God. A Buddhist-Jewish-Christian Conversation* (Faith Meets Faith Series), Maryknoll, NY, 1990, 102-115, p. 108.

The Philippians passage portrays this in the symbolic terms of Christ emptying himself, leaving the divine sphere and becoming part of ours, followed by his exaltation in which all of creation is caught up in the culmination of his lordship.

But the divine relational inclusiveness can also be elaborated in another way. What is sometimes overlooked about the Christ hymn in Philippians is that it is not just about what *Christ does*. It is not a narrative of a chain of events involving only a single subject, or a drama internal to Christ's person entailing some sort of "transaction" between his human and divine natures. Rather, it is a depiction of a *dialogue*, a *reciprocal interaction*, a "trinitarian drama", as Moltmann has put it. In the first part of the narrative, Christ is the active one, emptying himself, humbling himself, becoming obedient; in the second part, God is the active one, responding to what Christ has done by exalting him and giving him the name above every name. Moltmann therefore notes that "kenosis is only ... one side of the story", a side related in light of the other side, "in the light of the exaltation of Christ"[22]. What this means, among other things, is that Christ's self-emptying is a constitutive moment of a more comprehensive event of mutual exchange and reciprocal relating. Christ empties himself of everything (for God) and God in turn gives "everything" (i.e., universal lordship) to Christ. Through their interaction, something new takes place: God's incarnate entry into creation and the gathering of all creation into the purview of Christ's lordship. And the scope of the interaction extends even further backward and forward in time if we heed the emphasis both on Christ's obedience and on a future fulfillment of his lordship. Obedience is a form of *response*; the Latin root of "obey" (*oboedire*) means "to listen to", implying that there is *someone* who is listened to and an "event" (a command, request or word of love) to which the obedience is a response[23]. At the end of the passage is the implication that even the acknowledgment of Christ's lordship by the entire cosmos (which is yet to come?) is not an end in itself, but serves the ultimate purpose of glorifying the Father. (This is similar to the pattern in 1 Corinthians 15,24-28 where God puts "all things in subjection"

---

22. I am directly indebted to Moltmann for the basic insight which led to this "dialogical" interpretation of Philippians 2,6-11, and which I discussed with him in several conversations in Tübingen during the Fall of 1991 and the Spring of 1993; the passages in quotations are from conversations on 15 November 1991 and 18 June 1993 respectively.

23. Although the Philippians passage is not concerned with specifying the recipient of Christ's obedience, I would argue that it is rendered to God, especially since God is the one who responds, in the second part of the hymn, to all that Christ has done in the first part.

to Christ so that, after all enemies have been destroyed, Christ may deliver the kingdom over to the Father and "God may be all in all"). A pattern thus becomes evident, according to which, in his self-emptying, Christ *listens* and responds to the Father, and the Father then responds to Christ, in an ongoing interaction oriented toward future culmination.

Interpreted along these lines, kenosis is a key to the form of the dialogue between Jesus and the Father, helping to underscore the mutuality and reciprocity of their relationship as enacted in this passage. Both engage in a pattern wherein each in turn is active and passive, each gives and then receives, and then gives again. Gift follows upon gift, each time graciously accepted. Their "posture" toward each other is one of openness and mutuality, of total outpouring of self and total welcoming of the other. The metaphor of kenosis points to the radically generous and unreserved character of this openness: in emptying himself, Christ truly turns away from himself, in both his giving and receiving, to focus on his Other, the Father. The kenotic imagery even suggests that his emptying of self creates the room, the empty space that can then be filled with what the Father would give.

In every act of giving, the acceptance of the gift is crucial, for only in this is the giving completed. Only in the acceptance is the value of both giver and gift affirmed; for the way the gift is received reflects the recipient's attitude toward the giver. In other words, *the readiness to receive, the making of that empty space, is just as crucial, just as much an act of love, as the act of giving itself. Openness to and reverence for the Other may be the most profound form of love,* for without these we risk denying the unique truth and worth of the Other precisely as one who is other and different than ourselves. I would argue, then, that Christ's openness to the Father, and the Father's openness to Christ, may be one of the most profound points of significance in understanding the meaning of kenosis.

Where the kenosis of Christ entails his entry into human history we find further evidence of his self-emptying openness. Though circumstances do not permit elaborating this in great detail, everything in Jesus' ministry – his teaching, healings and exorcisms, his table fellowship, his reaching out to people and breaking down barriers between them – points toward the fostering of relationship, relationship among human persons, and, in this, relationship with the Father through Jesus himself. In light of this communion-building intentionality of his ministry, it is interesting that one recent interpretation of kenosis stresses Christ's generosity: his emptying himself is to be understood by way of contrast to a possibility presented in the previous verse, the possibility of counting his "equality with God" as "something to be grasped", that is, as something to be regarded possessively, for selfish exploitation[24]. His self-emptying thus entails the *opposite* of grasping possessiveness, namely open-handed generosity. As C.F.D. Moule puts it, Christ "recognized equality with God as a matter not of getting but of giving"[25]. What the kenosis hymn thus hints at is concretely embodied in Christ's ministry: his generosity with what is most deeply his, his inclusive openness in inviting others to share his relationship with the Father.

With these reflections I have only begun to explore the possibilities for finding meaning in kenosis as a metaphor of relationship, and I have not yet said anything about the role of the Holy Spirit. To do justice to the latter would require much fuller treatment than I can give it here, but I will indicate at least the direction such reflection might take. The Spirit is the Giver of Life, the one who empowers all things to be and to live and to thrive. The Gospels portray the Spirit as the one in whose presence and power Jesus' relation to his Father and his ministry of inclusiveness unfold. And in the Letter to the Romans, it is the Spirit who is poured out and given (5,5), who gives life, dwells in us, makes us children of God, and enables us to cry, "Abba! Father!" (see 8,11-17) – all the gifts that actualize our sharing in the Son's relationship with the Father. It is legitimate to say, then, that it is the Spirit who empowers the voiceless to speak and their hearers to listen, who empowers every act of participation and inclusiveness. It is the Spirit who prays deep within us when we do not even know how (Romans 8,26), and who thus leads the marginalized to the words they must speak and that must be heard. In all this, I believe we may imagine a self-emptying of the Spirit, pouring itself out so that others may thrive and their communion be accomplished.

The self-emptying of Christ opens our eyes to a vision of a God who is open and inclusive. In the incarnate one, God empties self into the world and the world in turn is drawn into the embrace of Father, Son and Spirit. The metaphor of kenosis shows in vivid terms that God is supremely relational, and that the form of God's relation to the world is self-emptying, a profound self-giving openness. God is open enough to the world in its otherness to invite it into God's own "space", into the dynamic life of the trinitarian relationships. God is creative and daring

---

24. P.T. O'BRIEN, *The Epistle to the Philippians. A Commentary on the Greek Text* (The New International Greek Testament Commentary), Grand Rapids, MI, 1991, pp. 212-216; R.W. HOOVER, *The HARPAGMOS Enigma. A Philological Solution*, in *Harvard Theological Review* 64 (1971), p. 118.

25. C.F.D. MOULE, *The Manhood of Jesus in the New Testament*, in S.W. SYKES – J.P. CLAYTON (eds.), *Christ, Faith, and History* (Cambridge Studies in Christology), Cambridge, 1972, 95-110, p. 97.

enough to utter God's word and then to listen attentively to the world's response.

Conversation, according to the *Oxford English Dictionary*, is the *reciprocal interchange* of ideas, which implies that everyone is given the chance to speak and to be heard, that no one is excluded or brushed aside. "Reciprocal interchange" entails a true giving and receiving, authentic speaking by and listening to, diverse voices. True and worthwhile conversation means speaking humbly and honestly, and listening with greatest care to those least likely to be heard – a listening inspired and empowered by the self-emptying of God.

Saint Francis Seminary   Jane E. LINAHAN
3257 South Lake Drive
St. Francis, WI 53235
U.S.A.

DIALOGICAL TRADITIONS
AND A TRINITARIAN HERMENEUTIC

During the second half of the twentieth century dialogue and communication became central categories for understanding the nature of revelation and the church among a growing number of Catholic theologians, as well as in ecumenical circles and in contexts where exchanges between members of diverse religious and cultural traditions took place. Vatican II marked a turning point for Catholics in this regard: a dialogical approach to tradition emerged as the point where God's revelation and the church's identity and mission intersect; simultaneously a new appreciation of the diversity of traditions within the Christian tradition, and the relationship between Christian traditions and other religious and cultural traditions was achieved, thanks to the work of countless scholars and church leaders. At the council, bishops and theologians committed to church renewal through retrieving forgotten traditional voices, and those seeking renewal by expanding the contemporary conversation, joined together to offer an alternative to the regnant neo-scholastic theology, which had neither promoted dialogue, nor achieved effective communication.

Vatican II represents an emerging consensus surrounding the realized assets and the unfolding promise of a dialogical and communicative approach to revelation and the church, to traditions, Catholic, Christian, religious, and cultural, that remains singularly important. But no less important are the ways that the confidence and hope in dialogue and communication have been called into question over the last thirty years. On one level, the newly found trust in the power of dialogue and communication to advance consensus in beliefs, mystical and interpersonal bonds of communion, and social action has been shaken by a contentious diversity of approaches to dialogue and communication and by contrasting hermeneutical strategies. Certain voices, partial truths, selective methods dominate in various ecclesial and social circles. On a far deeper level, however, proponents of dialogue are forced to confront deceptions and distortions at work in personal and communal relations. These corruptions of dialogue are the result of pernicious psychological and ideological dynamics, which can damage, scar, and sometimes destroy people, relations of intimacy, and communities. The assault on dialogue takes many forms. Truths spoken may be infected by lies that repress; disclosures that are partial and self-serving can amount to false witness. The very preconditions of genuine dialogue – honesty, integrity, justice – can be sacrificed in order to uphold the lie, deny the repressed, and defend one's personal or institutional image as pure and undefiled – and thus exempt from responsibility. Whether in interpersonal or institutional relations, desecrations of dialogue yield a bitter harvest: anger and hostility, disillusionment and cynicism. But the harder choice, possible only by grace, is to cultivate a realism about the travails of dialogue, a realism that demands honesty and mediates compassion in the midst of tragedy and brokenness, finitude and sin.

The challenge, then, is to construct a comprehensive and judicious theological hermeneutics that takes account of the *promise* of the dialogical and communicative approach to traditions and the *perils* that have always, and will in every age, threaten dialogue within Christian traditions and between religious and cultural traditions. One must savour the redemptive and sanctifying graces that are available through dialogue and communication, while confessing the brutal facts about distortion in the depths of the human psyche and in social relations. This essay will argue that ultimately nothing less than a Trinitarian hermeneutic that honours the work of the Trinitarian pleroma can fulfil the promise of a dialogical and communicative understanding of traditions. In order to confront the risks to that promise posed by distortions and betrayals of dialogue, isolated approaches to conversation, and restrictive hermeneutical strategies, there is need for a hermeneutic theory receptive and responsive to the Trinitarian self-communication of God in the church and the world. Such a theory should be judged by its ability to clarify and foster ongoing conversion to a catholicity in outlook that reveres the individuation of the other, and to a deepening communion with God and others that is the condition and culmination of genuine individuation. Such a theory must consequently be able to account for lifelong spiritual processes of purification that invariably include repentance, forgiveness, and reconciliation of individuals and communities. Such a hermeneutical theory ought to reflect the identity and economy of the triune God as a communion of persons. The personal and collective journey into the most profound mysteries of God, where the *apophatic*, the hidden, and the pernicious challenge every *cataphatic*, revealed, and graced word spoken and received, demands a Trinitarian hermeneutic, ecclesiology, and spirituality working in concert.

I. Toward a Dialogical Approach to Traditions:
The Argument Outlined

The overarching argument is advanced in four steps. The first three will simply be posited here, while the paper will be devoted to the last one.

First thesis: In order to realize the promise of a dialogical and communicative approach to Christian, religious, and cultural traditions, it is necessary at one level that we consolidate selected insights from a variety of theoretical approaches and models: interpersonal, social and institutional, and multi-cultural. Far too often people work out of one or two models and fail to account for important contrasting approaches to the phenomena of dialogical and communicative relationships. Hence one must search for connections between, and hybrid combinations of, various research projects into interpersonal and social dialogue and communication. I provisionally delineate these in terms of three trajectories of inquiry, informed by the work of three sets of social theorists: (1) personalists and their critics, who examine dialogue with the other as a necessary yet treacherous pathway to self-discovery, community building, and relationship with God (M. Buber and E. Levinas); (2) hermeneutical theorists, who debate about how dialogue takes place both between and among readers, texts, and traditions (H.G. Gadamer, H.R. Jauss, and M. Bakhtin); and (3) social communication theorists and their critics, who consider the requirements, risks, and illusions of reaching communal judgments and decisions through dialogue, as well as the possibility of cross-cultural exchange and conflict resolution (J. Habermas, F. Lyotard, and J. Dean).

Second thesis: The promise of dialogue and communication within Christian traditions and between religious and cultural traditions can be more fully actualised only by taking into account deeper, more obscure, and ominous insights into the deceptions and distortions that occur in interpersonal and social relationships. This requires exploring the depths and dark side of the human psyche and ideological power dynamics. Destructive powers and sinful patterns are at work both in interpersonal relationships, beginning with the family, and in larger social patterns of discourse. Religious traditions at times seem powerless to effect genuine change and may in fact contribute to the problem. It is in the face of these negative realities that one must explore to what extent dialogue and communication with family, friends, and religious communities, can penetrate into the opaque corners of personal and collective life, and foster healing, conversion, transformation, and growth.

Third thesis: The dialogical and communicative character of traditions calls for a hermeneutical approach that is comprehensive in scope, one that provides a framework that accounts for four sets of triadic relationships. First, the triadic relationship between authors (speakers), texts (messages), and readers (hearers), are the constitutive ingredients in meaning production and communicative action which resulting in judgments, decisions, and committed practices.

The second set of triadic relations conveys the inherent plurivocity or polyphony operative at each of the three levels of authors, texts, and readers. Comprehending the contributions of *authors* requires situating authors in communities and attending to the importance of the communal processes in the genesis (and transmutations) of texts and traditions. *Texts and traditions* are embedded in the social world of narratives and arguments, where one always encounters conflicting ideologies, negotiated settlements, and the alliances of characters and world views, where truth and righteousness can be victor, but where, just as likely, alien voices are muffled, sometimes to be forgotten. Texts and traditions are nothing, dead letters, mute, without the reception of these texts and traditions by *readers and hearers* who are thinkers and actors in various social and historical locations; their roles in the constitution of meaning must be acknowledged and clarified.

The third set of triadic relationships pertains to trialogue within the ecclesial community of interpreters, between the entire people of God, theologians, and bishops. Specifically, in the Catholic tradition, with analogues in other Christian communities, there is the teaching office of bishops acting collegially (with the bishop of Rome), the collaborative contributions of theologians, and the role of the entire people of God in the process of consultation with bishops and theologians, and the reception of teachings. The fourth, and final, set of triadic relations, and most important for this paper, concerns the trialogue of Christian traditions: the dialogue of Christian traditions (ecumenism); the dialogue of Christian traditions with other religious traditions (interreligious dialogue); the dialogue of Christian traditions with other cultural traditions (constitutive of the church-world relationship).

This kind of multi-leveled approach stands in contradistinction to author-centred (e.g., E.D. Hirsch), text-centred (e.g., H.G. Gadamer and P. Ricœur), or reader-centred (W. Iser and H.R. Jauss) approaches to hermeneutics that extol one approach and one ideal or pragmatic centre point as the privileged way to arbitrate between positions, or that judges the meaning of the texts based on the authority or claim of any one of the voices or groups posited in each triadic set. Instead, we need to posit and cultivate a genuinely dialogical approach that can field the insights and judgements of not only a variety of hermeneutical strategies, but of a diversity of voices behind and within texts and traditions, and the communities of interpretation which pass these texts and traditions on. Identifying these four triadic sets goes far to explain why the efforts and aims of hermeneutics can be so complex and maddening. But it also explains why and how there can be changes in understandings and applications, where those that are richer, fuller, and more demanding struggle against those that are poorer, leaner, and indulgent.

Fourth thesis: Nothing less than a Trinitarian approach to hermeneutics, one committed to exploring the dialogical and communicative implications of the works of the Creator, the Word/Wisdom made flesh, and the Spirit of life and holiness as a communion of persons, offers a rationale rooted in the most fundamental and most comprehensive Christian convictions for theses one, two, and three.

II. A TRINITARIAN HERMENEUTIC OF TRADITIONS IN DIALOGUE
A PRELIMINARY SKETCH

The task before us is to transpose Bonaventure's *Itinerarium mentis in Deum*, in terms of the human person's journey into the Triune God which takes place through dialogue with other individuals, family, friends, but also in significant ways through the dialogue of diverse traditions[1]. This dialogical process draws individuals and communities into the mystery of God. This is a mysterious and never ending journey beyond idolatry and projection into the truth of God. One lives into the truth of God through the light and consolation received through the many circles of dialogue that constitute a human life.

However, the journey into God's truth will inevitably lead through the dark nights and desolation associated with the suffering of dialogue thwarted. Here one encounters the way of Jesus: in the betrayal of dialogue, the agonic dialogue in the garden, the bankruptcy of dialogue in

---

1. Had space permitted, the distinctiveness of my approach could be clarified by comparatively scrutinizing the contributions of Friedrich Schleiermacher, H.R. Niebuhr, Hans Urs von Balthasar and Kevin Vanhoozer. My contention is, in brief, that each figure has made valuable contributions to this topic, but has fallen short of developing a fully dialogical approach to traditions and a Trinitarian approach to hermeneutics that can advance this agenda. Troubles sometimes lurk in their Trinitarian theologies, their theological hermeneutics, or their understandings of the dialogue of traditions. This limits these authors' ability to give due respect to the importance of distinctiveness (individuation) as well as dynamic relations (communion) at the same time in the divine reality and in the dialogue of traditions as these make possible the realization of divine and ecclesial identity and mission.

political and religious institutions bent on self-preservation, all of which culminate in the wretched silent dialogue of the cross. This way of the cross is the painful path on which dialogue with the other is desecrated and denied. God's most powerful word of dialogical communion restored, is, in a certain eschatological, proleptic sense, God's last word, which comes out of this void in dialogue defeated. The resurrection offer of restored and healed relations is constant, but one is frequently left with only fragments of dialogue regained, and at other times the reality of dialogue transfigured is known only by its absence.

This journey into the truth of God through the dialogue of traditions is also a journey into the truth of the human person and of human communities. One must find the words to speak of the self-referential and community-referential analogues to idolatry and projection, be it Thomas Merton's "false self" or talk of "false consciousness" of the conscience collective offered by various masters of suspicion. Here one must draw on the many ways of naming the pathologies, ideologies, and distortions that foil dialogue. Ultimately, there is no other pathway into genuine self and communal identity and mission than through the process of differentiation (individuation) that takes place through dialogue, and particularly through the suffering of dialogue, where negative contrast experiences reveal the *humanum* through the repressed and the excluded. The goal is the true self and the true community. Only by facing and working through the brokenness and distortion of dialogue, when that which has been denied or repressed, totalised or dismissed has been brought to light, can personal and collective differentiation occur. This way of the cross that dialogue will inevitably entail is the pathway toward mutual understanding and recognition, and inevitably includes ongoing repentance, forgiveness, and reconciliation.

A Trinitarian approach to interpretation honours the ways the triune God works in the world, in human communities, and in human persons. This requires, first, that attention be given in the process of interpretation to the ways the work of each person in the Trinity in the one economy of salvation is revealed in many economies. Second, there is a need to heed in interpretation distinctively Trinitarian truths about the importance of communion or unity between authors, texts, and readers, between authorized interpreters and audiences, which is often noted. The third and more recent realization is that a Trinitarian hermeneutics requires attending to differentiation that takes place in and through a dialogical communion of persons in the Triune God, the Trinitarian exchange (in the traditional language, perichoresis or circumincession, i.e., mutual interdependence of persons), one might say trialogue, which funds the dynamic of ever greater inclusivity (Catholicity) and ever greater communion that marks the divine identity and mission. This all needs further development.

First, honouring God as personal source of all that is, the one identified as Creator, usually Father, and more frequently Mother, the one who not only creates, but preserves, responds to creation, and calls into covenant, establishes certain hermeneutical requirements. This is often overlooked because the focus is usually on the hermeneutical implications of belief in Jesus Christ and the Holy Spirit. What does it mean to be mindful of God's identity as personal source of all that is in theological hermeneutics? It entails respecting and attending to the particularities of continents and geographical regions, of natural environments, climates, and seasonal patterns, of races, ethnic groups, and cultures, and all of the particularities of bodies and psyches, minds and freedom that contribute to the dignity and identity of individuals and families. To reverence the work of the Creator requires that interpreters "reverence the particulars" as these affect and leave their mark on texts and traditions. To affirm the significance of the Creator in hermeneutics neither relinquishes nor diminishes the importance of the Triune God as Creator, preexistent Wisdom and Word, creator Spirit. Indeed, it is always and finally through the economy of the Trinitarian mystery in history that the givenness of creation is redeemed, purified, and sanctified through a process of differentiation and reintegration. But this larger Trinitarian vision can only take place as the completion of the work of the Source of all that is.

Honouring the Word and Wisdom made flesh in Jesus Christ entails keeping alive the dangerous and consoling memory of the teachings, actions, death, and resurrection of Jesus as redemptive, healing, empowering. Affirming the christological principle requires accepting that the dialogical encounter of individuals and communities with the life-giving Word and Wisdom of God in Jesus is witnessed to in the scriptures as the living word of God, and passed on in and through the church as the living body of Christ. Consequently, the christological principle in hermeneutics issues forth in a comprehensive view of the generation, codification, transmission, and reception of biblical traditions, from the communal, authorial, and editorial passing on of oral traditions to written traditions and edited traditions that were eventually recognized as canonical traditions through ongoing reception of the entire people of God. This in turn requires adhering to the collective continuation and apostolic memory of the presence and agency of the risen Lord in the body of Christ in various communities around the world, and the saving power of this same risen Lord throughout the world even where Christ is not yet known or not acknowledged as Lord. The christological principle in hermeneutics includes a respect for both the exercise of the pastoral, prophetic, and priestly ministries shared by all the members of the church by baptism and for the important role of those who are office holders, specifically bishops, who represent Christ and the community in a special way and with special responsibilities amidst the communities of interpretation that constitute the church. The christological principle has proven to be as much a hurdle as a help in ecumenical dialogues. Protestants have used this principle, the *sola Christus,* to warrant their *sola scriptura* principle, while Roman Catholics have used belief in Christ, the head of the body, to warrant their emphasis on tradition, at times meaning by this the official interpretation of scriptures by the teaching office of the church made possible by the grace of office. But it is the doctrine of the totus Christus that must bind both scripture and communal interpretation together and offer the possibility of healing the breach between communities who have torn Christ apart.

Honouring the Spirit requires attentiveness to the presence and agency of God speaking in the new and in the future, where the wind of the Spirit blows in unexpected ways, just as the Spirit calls to mind forgotten truths, the memory of Jesus and his followers long lost; this recollection takes place when the ancient becomes new again and even a disturbing truth. Talk of the Spirit most often expresses the inspiration of the prophets, their words and their symbolic actions; yet just as important is the role of the Spirit in the reception of these words and actions. The Spirit is the guardian of the truth of faith in episcopal teachers when they speak in communion, but just as important the Spirit is the guardian of the truth of faith in the disciples when they listen and receive in communion. The Spirit gives power to the speaker and life-giving fruit to those who hear. The various charisms of the Spirit are evident in the prophetic and mystical voices in the midst of community as well as in the gift of ecclesial offices, and in every reception of these gifts. However, the presence and agency of the Spirit is not only present in church leaders and believers, but also throughout the world in social movements and world historical events. To honour the Spirit means to be receptive to voices speaking in unusual places and events beyond the borders of our communities.

A Trinitarian hermeneutic requires this kind of reflection on the hermeneutical repercussions of each of the persons of the Trinity. However, it is at least as important to consider the hermeneutical implications of the dynamic communicative relations that constitute the differentiation of identity and mission of the triune persons in communion. Here there is a need to identify the limitations of a venerable approach to the communicative character of God and suggest a more comprehensive alternative. Walter Kasper, Hans Urs von Balthasar, and Kevin Vanhoozer are recent spokespersons for an old tradition that speaks of the Father as the speaker, the Son as the message, and the Spirit as the reception of the message. This customarily provides the basis for claiming that the Son is obedient to the Father and the disciples are obedient to the Son and the representatives of the Son, scriptural representatives and institutional ones. While there is a profound truth in this formulation, it is not the full truth, and a partial truth can bring about a great deal of harm in matters hermeneutical and in matters ecclesiological. The simple truth of the matter, abundantly testified to in the scriptures, is that it is not only the Son who is obedient to the Father, but that the Father and the Son are both obedient to the Spirit who gives utterance to suffering and aspiring humanity and indeed to the incompleteness in the entire cosmos. The Father and the Son hear the cries of the poor and aspiring, they listen, receive, and respond; in short, they obey the voice of the Spirit. So too the Father hears and heeds the cry of Jesus, uttered in the Spirit, to the very end on the cross. The Spirit too hears and heeds, dutifully conveys and authenticates, the voices of the Father and the Son in their mutual dialogue. The Trinitarian mystery is one of mutual obedience. Differentiation and communion occur in the divine reality and in the church and the world through mutual obedience, understood as attentiveness, reception, and response. This provides a central principle in a Trinitarian ecclesiology and hermeneutics.

Hermeneutical theories, just like Trinitarian theologies, can suffer from abstraction. Ultimately, a Trinitarian approach to hermeneutics must be validated through the processes of interpretation in the dialogue of traditions between contrasting schools within individual faith communities, in ecumenical dialogues, and in interreligious dialogues. This means a Trinitarian hermeneutic must be validated in concrete practices of dialogue in traditions and between them. Moreover, it should be judged by how it addresses the most contested issues where the dialogue or traditions faces its most difficult obstacles; one thinks, for example, of the exercise of authority in ecumenical dialogues, addressing past offences among representatives of the Abrahamic traditions, Christianity, Judaism, and Islam, married and women clergy, and homosexuality. Any hermeneutic theory must ultimately be judged by whether it can advance the dialogue of traditions in the every day concrete lives of individuals and communities and in their most difficult interpretive conflicts.

In conclusion, consider ecumenical hermeneutics as one such valuable test case for some of the issues we have explored. Scholars engaged in ecumenical dialogues have for more than a decade been discussing their hermeneutical principles and practices. At the conference of Faith and Order in Santiago de Compostella in 1993 three different tasks were identified.

> (1) to overcome and to reconcile the criteriological differences with regard to a faithful interpretation of the one gospel, recognizing the multiform richness and diversity of the canon of the scriptures, as it is read, explicated and applied in the life of the churches, but at the same time strengthening the awareness of the one Tradition within the many traditions; (2) to express and communicate the one gospel in and across various, sometimes even conflicting contexts, cultures and locations; (3) to work toward mutual accountability, discernment and authoritative teaching and toward credibility in common witness before the world, and finally toward the eschatological fullness of the truth in the power of the Spirit[2].

Five years later Faith and Order Commission published *A Treasure in Earthen Vessels: An Instrument for an Ecumenical Reflection on Hermeneutics* (1998) which addressed the above three tasks. Accordingly, this text

> (1) examines the interpretation of scripture and Tradition in a more hermeneutically conscious way, especially with greater sensitivity to the conditions involved in interpretation; (2) explores the hermeneutical and theological significance of the fact that the ecumenical movement includes the participation of communities from many different cultures and contexts, and offers reflections which can lead to a more successful intercontextual dialogue; (3) explores three dimensions in the process of interpretation: the activity of discernment, the exercise of authority, and the task of reception (p. 138).

These statements by the Faith and Order Commission in large part are consistent with the Trinitarian hermeneutic introduced here. Moreover, it is particularly attuned to the concerns for diversification and unity, catholicity and communion (esp. §48, p. 152). However, this recent document rarely speaks in Trinitarian terms. Rather it speaks in each of the three sections of the document, back and forth, of the Son and the Spirit, not with perfect symmetry, but with a dynamic synergism in terms of texts and traditions, authors and audiences, contexts around the world that profess the one Gospel, the living Tradition of Christian faith.

There are a few noteworthy statements about the Trinity. We read: "The ecumenical recognition that those who have been baptized in the

---

2. Texts from the Fifth World Conference on Faith and Order are cited in *A Treasure in Earthen Vessels: An Instrument for an Ecumenical Reflection on Hermeneutics*, in P. BOUTENEFF – D. HELLER (eds.), *Interpreting Together: Essays in Hermeneutics*, Geneva, WCC, 2001, p. 138.

name of the triune God are brought into unity with Christ, with each other and with the church of every time and place challenges the churches to overcome their divisions and visibly manifest their communion in faith and in all aspects of Christian life and witness" (§58, p. 155). In addition, "the church is a communion of persons in relation; thus active participation and dialogue between communities, and within each community at all levels, is one expression of the church's nature. The divine being of the triune God is the source and the exemplar of communion" (§64, p. 157). There are paragraphs about ministry (§54-58, pp. 154-155), contextuality, and catholicity (§43, 45), that build on Trinitarian convictions. The conclusion to be drawn is that this document implicitly lends credibility to, if not confirms, the argument advanced above, that catholicity, communion and differentiation of persons in identity and mission are central hermeneutical consequences that follow from the doctrine of the triune God. However, I would also contend that a more explicit Trinitarian hermeneutic would enhance and strengthen the claims being made in this document.

In the end, the personal and collective participation in the divine identity and mission of the Triune God provides not only a depth grammar and rhetoric, but in fact a Trinitarian ontology for understanding the dialogical and communicative character of tradition, that is, of revelation and the church. Such a Trinitarian hermeneutic creates the conditions for realizing a generous catholicity in the dialogical and communicative life of the church through the ongoing process of conversion, repentance, and reconciliation among individuals and communities, and the conditions needed to advance communion by forming and deepening mystical, interpersonal, and social bonds, widening consensus in beliefs, and bringing about ever more effective social action.

Department of Theology   Bradford E. HINZE
Marquette University
100 Coughlin Hall
P.O. Box 1881
Milwaukee, WI 53201-1881
U.S.A.

SOME RECENT TRENDS
ON THE SACRAMENTALITY OF CREATION
IN EASTERN-ORIENTAL CHRISTIAN TRADITIONS

The world as sacrament is a rediscovered paradigm in contemporary discussions on sacramentology[1]. Although these studies unanimously recognize God's sacramental presence in the world, they differ in their response to this divine presence in the ethical, liturgical, and mystical domains[2]. This paper aims to discuss some recent studies on the sacramentality of Creation from the perspective of the Greek and Syrian Christian traditions. We shall first look at the works of Sophiologists and Neo-Patristic theologians of the Russian Orthodox tradition. Then we shall present a synthesis of their views based on the Syrian tradition of Saint Ephrem.

I. RUSSIAN SOPHIOLOGY

Russian "Sophiology", an offshoot of the Russian religious renaissance in the 19th century, is perhaps the first theological attempt, in the modern history of eastern theology, to bridge the gap between Creator and

1. See, for example, the following articles of K. IRWIN: *Sacramentality and the Theology of Creation: A Recovered Paradigm for Sacramental Theology*, in LS 23 (1998) 159-179; *The Sacramentality of Creation and the Role of Creation in Liturgy and Sacraments*, in K. IRWIN – E. PELLEGRINO (eds.), *Preserving the Creation: Environmental Theology and Ethics*, Washington, DC, Georgetown University Press, 1994, 67-111; *Liturgical Action: Sacramentality, Eschatology and Ecology*, in L. BOEVE – L. LEIJSSEN (eds.), *Contemporary Sacramental Contours of a God Incarnate*, Leuven, Peeters, 2001, 111-123. See also A. SCHMEMANN, *The World as Sacrament*, London, Darton, Longman & Todd, 1966; F.X. D'SA – I. PADINJAREKUTTU – J. PARAPPALLY (eds.), *The World as Sacrament: Interdisciplinary Bridge-building of the Sacred and the Secular*, Pune, Jnana-Deepa Vidyapeeth, 1998; J. CHRYSSAVGIS, *The World as Sacrament: Insights into an Orthodox Worldview*, in *Pacifica* 10 (1997) 1-24. The following articles of S. BROCK are also interesting: *World and Sacrament in the Writings of the Syrian Fathers*, in *Sobornost* 6 (1974) 685-696; *Humanity and the Natural World in the Syriac Tradition*, in *Sobornost* 12 (1990) 131-142.
2. While liberation theologians generally emphasize the ethical response to God's sacramental presence in the world, the liturgical theologians emphasize a liturgical response. The philosophical theologians in general accentuate the "mystery" dimension. Although attributed to different schools, the different responses are overlapping.

creation. The "sophiological" theory is based on an indigenous philosophy rooted in the religious experience of the Russian culture. Although
greatly influenced by the German idealism of Schelling and Hegel, and
by Rhineland and Protestant mysticism[3], Sophiologists criticized west-
ernizing tendencies in Russian society and explained the relation between
Creator and creation in terms of *Sophia*[4]. In this section, we shall briefly
discuss the works of Russian Sophiologists of the 19th century.

Vladimir Soloviev (1853-1900)[5], the father of Russian Sophiology,
used the metaphysics of "All-Unity" (God-manhood)[6] to relate *Sophia*
and *Logos*, and to explain the unity of Wisdom and the created world[7].
Soloviev presents *Sophia* as the universal substance that unites Father,
Son, and the Holy Spirit in the Trinity[8]. This divine *Sophia*, however, is
not only the unifying element of the Trinity. It is likewise operative in
God's ongoing act of creation, and in the Church, which particularly
shares the same spirit of wisdom as the Incarnate Son of God:

3. Among the German idealists, Schelling and Hegel had a great influence on Russian
thinkers. The early philosophy of art of Schelling, in particular, helped them to perceive
"absolute reality" vis-à-vis traditional Orthodox piety. But the influence of Schelling
started dwindling with the advent of Hegelianism in the 1840's. Cf. J. MEYENDORFF,
Visions of the Church: Russian Theological Thought in Modern Times, in *SVTQ* 34 (1990)
5-14, pp. 7-8. Their interest in Hegelianism was due to his adoption of the neo-Platonism
of Proclus and Pseudo-Dionysius.

Among the German mystics, the Catholic Rhineland mystics and the quasi-hermetic
Protestant mysticism of Jakob Böhme played an important role. Cf. R. WILLIAMS, *Eastern
Orthodox Theology*, in D. FORD (ed.), *The Modern Theologians: An Introduction to Chris-
tian Theology in the Twentieth Century*, Oxford, Blackwell Publishers, 1997, 499-512.

4. While the Byzantine tradition identifies *Sophia* with Christ, Russian Orthodoxy identifies it with Mary. For a detailed study of *Sophia* as applied in different theological traditions, see J. MEYENDORFF, *Wisdom-Sophia: Contrasting Approaches to a Complex
Theme*, in *Dumbarton Oaks Papers* 41 (1987) 391-401.

5. Soloviev tried to reconcile philosophy, theology and science in a great synthesis.
Influenced by the Slavophilists Aleksei Khomiakov (1804-1860) and Ivan Kireevskii
(1806-1856), he proposed mystical philosophy to overcome the impasse of modern thought
between empiricism and rationalism. The writings of Schelling and Jakob Böhme made a
strong impact on him.

6. Cf. S. HORUZHY, *Neo-Patristic Synthesis and Russian Philosophy*, in *SVTQ* 44 (2000)
309-328, pp. 314-315. According to Horuzhy, Plotinus introduced the metaphysics of "All-
Unity" as a philosophical category and Neo-Platonism elaborated it. Pseudo-Dionysius
appropriated it for Christian theology, though its elements were already present in St Paul.
This "All-Unity" metaphysics was taken up by Western authors, especially Eriugena,
Nicholas of Cusa, and Leibniz. Schelling and Hegel completed its elaboration. Horuzhy
also notes a similar Christian Platonism in Russian culture and Russian Orthodox spirituality, in its so-called "panentheist" ontology. Soloviev's metaphysics of "All-Unity" basically belongs to the German idealist school of Christian Platonism.

7. Although his teaching on Sophiology is found in many of his writings, a systematic
presentation could be seen in V. SOLOVIEV, *Russia and the Universal Church*, trans.
H. REES, London, Geoffrey Bles, 1948.

8. SOLOVIEV, *Russia and the Universal Church* (n. 7), pp. 156-157.

The Church, human society made divine, possesses fundamentally the same substance as the incarnate person of Christ or His individual Humanity[9].

Sophia is the ultimate source of all things. Moreover, the notion of *Sophia* gives a metaphysical justification to Goodness, and grounds Soloviev's social and personal ethics[10]. In spite of the criticism of his alleged Gnosticism, there has been a reappraisal of Soloviev's thinking in recent years[11].

Paul Florensky (1882-1943)[12] continued Soloviev's metaphysics of unitotality and tried to place the doctrine of *Sophia* in Orthodox liturgical tradition and patristic theology[13]. For him *Sophia* is a "fourth person". Although not consubstantial to the Divine Persons, *Sophia* is admitted to the Trinity by divine condescension. It is also part of the original nature of Creation. Richard Gustafson, in his introduction to the translation of Florensky's *The Pillar and Ground of Truth*, notes:

> From the view point of the theological Trinity *ad intra*, Sophia is the substance and power of being ... From the point of view of the economical Trinity *ad extra*, Sophia is the Body of Christ, The Church, the Virgin Mary[14].

Sergius Bulgakov (1871-1944)[15] used the doctrine of *Sophia* to present an explanation of the relationship between God, the world, and the human

9. *Ibid.*, p. 177.

10. MEYENDORFF, *Russian Theological Thought* (n. 3), p. 11.

11. Paulos Mar Gregorios includes Soloviev in the tradition of Gregory of Nyssa, Dionysius and Maximus. Cf. P.M. GREGORIOS, *The Human Presence: An Orthodox View of Nature*, Geneva, WCC, 1978, p. 80: "Especially in his insistence on man as mediator between God and creation, and on the redemption of creation being bound up with the redemption of man, Soloviev remains faithful to the authentic tradition which begins in this regard with the Apostle Paul in Romans and Colossians".

12. Florensky is well known as a mathematician, scientist, philosopher, and theologian. He also showed great interest in art and culture, working in all these fields until his execution by the communists in 1937. He tried to reconcile science and religion in his works. Inspired by the mystical monastic movement *Onomatodoxy* initiated by the Russian monks of Mount Athos and Caucasus which criticized Soloviev's dependence on Western philosophy, Florensky tried to explore the Sophiology of the Russian tradition. Like other Muscovite philosophers like Bulgakov, Ern and Losev, Florensky believes that the metaphysics of "All-Unity" should be complemented by the Palamitic concept of divine energy.

13. Florensky notes how *Sophia* became an object of contemplation in Greek Patristic Theology, an emblem of chastity and spiritual perfection in Slavic tradition, and the symbol of the unity of all creation in modern Russia. See P. FLORENSKY, *The Pillar and Ground of the Truth: An Essay in Orthodox Theodicy in Twelve Letters*, trans. B JAKIM, Princeton, NJ Princeton University Press, 1997, p. 282.

14. R. GUSTAFSON, *Introduction to the Translation*, in FLORENSKY, *Pillar and Ground* (n. 13), p. xxi.

15. Sergius Bulgakov began his career as a Marxist economist. Although he continued to cherish Marx's socialist ideal, he gave up Marxist ideology in 1903 because he found it difficult to combine Marxism with idealism. He later adopted the rational ethics of the Neo-Kantian philosophy. Soloviev and Florensky played a significant role in influencing

person that is consistent with Orthodox tradition and the challenges of contemporary technology[16]. For him, *Sophia* is the loving substance of the Trinity. The Holy Trinity is founded

> ... on the one life and one substance of the Divine Tri-unity, as well as on their mutual identity: God possess the Godhead, or he is the Godhead, is *Ousia*, is *Sophia*[17].

This does not mean a separate entity, a fourth hypostasis like in Florensky. Bulgakov thus explains the presence of *Sophia* in the Godhead:

> The living tri-unity of the Holy Trinity is founded on a single principle of self-revelation with one life in common, though in three distinct persons. The Holy Trinity has one *ousia*, not three, or three thirds of an *ousia* divided between three persons. It likewise possesses one Wisdom, not three, one glory[18].

But Bulgakov also sees *Sophia* present in creation. There is a difference, however, between heavenly *Sophia* and creaturely *sophia*. God's voluntary *kenosis* through creation made the created world the creaturely *sophia*. Bulgakov spoke of the presence of the heavenly *Sophia* in creaturely *Sophia*, in an effort to elaborate a theology consistent with Chalcedonian Christology, thus avoiding the errors of pantheism and

Bulgakov's thought. Although his works were condemned as heretical by both the Patriarch of Moscow and the émigré Bishops in 1935, he was later acquitted by Metropolitan Evlogy with whom he had worked in the Russian diaspora in Paris.

16. Bulgakov already provided in 1917 a biblical discussion of *Sophia* in *The Unfading Light: Contemplations and Speculations*, Moscow, Put, 1917. He developed this *Sophia* theme in a more systematic way in his trilogy: *The Lamb of God* (1933), *The Comforter* (1936), and *The Bride of the Lamb* (1945), dealing with the themes of Christ, the Holy Spirit, and the Church, respectively. These three works were later summarized in a single-volume work, *The Wisdom of God: A Brief Summary of Sophiology*, London, William and Norgate, 1937. A revised edition of this work is presently available under the title *Sophia, the Wisdom of God: An Outline of Sophiology*, Hudson, NY, Lindisfarne Press, 1993.

17. BULGAKOV, *Wisdom of God: Brief Summary of Sophiology* (n. 16), p. 59.

18. *Ibid.*, pp. 59-60. It seems that Bulgakov tried to replace the abstract notion of *Ousia* with the relatively concrete notion of *Sophia*. This was the reason for which he was accused of heresy. Apparently, Bulgakov was still struggling with the notion of *Sophia* in his earlier writings. Aidan Nichols notes a certain shift in Bulgakov's thinking. Bulgakov's early works present a "monistic sophiology" with only one *Sophia* presented as a *hypostasis* with two faces, created and Uncreated, while his later works "introduces a 'dualist' sophiology, in which the divine *ousia* and the being of creatures are clearly differentiated, and the wisdom theme is integrated with the doctrine of the Holy Trinity". Cf. A. NICHOLS, *Bulgakov and Sophiology*, in *Sobornost* 13 (1992/2) 17-31, p. 29.

According to Rowan Williams, as early as 1917 Bulgakov presented *Sophia* not as a *hypostasis*, to avoid tendencies to pantheism: "Sophia is not an objectified World-Soul, but the impulse in things toward harmony and order". From his 1925 essay on hypostasis and hypostaseity, Bulgakov insists that *Sophia* is not a person but an "ontological principle of life". Cf. R. WILLIAMS, *Eastern Orthodox Theology* (n. 3), p. 503.

Manichean dualism. The Incarnation is not the result of the Fall, but of God's "affirmation of the integral ability of divinity and humanity to co-operate, as represented in *Sophia*"[19]. Christ then is presented, not only as a model to be followed, but as the "one hypostasis who re-united within himself all persons, not as they were in sin, but as they were created to be"[20]. This view re-establishes synergy as the true road for humanization[21]. Deification, moreover, is not limited to humanity; it is extended to all of creation.

> The Church in the world is *Sophia* in process of becoming, according to the double impulse of creation and deification; the former imposes the conditions of the latter, the latter constitutes the fulfillment of the former. God created the world only that He might deify it and Himself become all in all to it[22].

The above survey shows how Sophiological theology endeavoured to find a rational account of the God-world-human relationship. The 19th century Russian Sophiologists, for their part, have presented *Sophia* as the principle grounding their cosmotheandric worldview[23]. This *Sophia*-based theology of creation, however, was criticized by the Neo-Patristic school that preferred to discuss the God-world-human relations in the terms of patristic theology and of the liturgical traditions of the Church. While the sophiological theology of creation is compared to Origenism, the Neo-Patristic synthesis is likened to Athanasian theology[24].

II. NEO-PATRISTIC SYNTHESIS

Among the Neo-Patristic theologians, Vladimir Lossky (1904-1958) proposed an anthropology based on the mystical and ascetic Orthodox traditions of Hesychasm and Palamism in particular[25]. Following the

---

19. BULGAKOV, *Social Teaching in Modern Russian Orthodox Theology*, in *Diakonia* 20 (1986), p. 122.

20. *Ibid.*

21. *Ibid.* Rowan Williams notes that Bulgakov's notion of "humanizing the world" distinguishes him from Soloviev and the Hegelian philosophers. Cf. WILLIAMS, *Eastern Orthodox Theology* (n. 3), p. 503.

22. BULGAKOV, *Wisdom of God: Brief Summary of Sophiology* (n. 16), pp. 202-203.

23. "Cosmotheandric worldview" is a term often found in the writings of Raimundo Panikkar. Cf. R. PANIKKAR, *Cosmotheandric Experience*, Maryknoll, NY, Orbis, 1993.

24. Cf. V. LOSSKY, *The Mystical Theology of Eastern Church*, Crestwood, NY, SVS Press, 1976, p. 62; J. MEYENDORFF, *Creation in the History of Orthodox Theology*, in *SVTQ* 27 (1983) 27-37, p. 32. This distinction is proffered by the critics of sophiology.

25. Although Lossky is greatly indebted to Dionysius the Areopagite for developing his mystical theology, his mystical-ascetic anthropology is based mainly on the Palamite distinction between God's nature and his energies. Hesychasm and Palamism are two

apophatic theology of Saint Dionysius the Areopagite, Lossky speaks of the incomprehensibility of the Trinity: "God is neither one nor many but that He transcends this antinomy, being unknowable in what He is"[26]. This divine incomprehensibility entails neither agnosticism nor refusal to know God. What Lossky proposes is knowledge (*gnosis*) by participation (*theosis*). He bases his explanation on the Palamite distinction between nature and energy, arguing that, while the divine nature remains inaccessible to human beings, God is accessible to human beings through his energies (divine operations) which are inseparable from his essence[27]. It is the responsibility of human beings then to participate in God (deification) through the divine energies.

Georges Florovsky (1893-1979) elaborated Lossky's doctrine and proposed an "energeistic ontology" to bridge the gap between the Creator and the creature. He notes a difference in nature between Creator and creation, arguing that these natures remain unchanged even in the deification: "Any transubstantiation of creaturely nature into the Divine is as impossible as the changing of God into creation"[28]. Adopting the Athanasian distinction between creation and generation, Florovsky explains that, while divine generation is an act of the divine nature, creation is an act of the divine will. For him, the act of creation is not done out of Creator's own substance, but is "heterogeneous to its Creator"[29]. The "creaturehood" of the creature is its own substance, giving it *creaturely freedom*. Thus, to be with God or not to be with God is not only one choice among many, but a necessary choice. Not to strive for deification would mean "death" for the human creature[30]. Death here does not mean the end of existence, but a separation of the creature from God[31]. God created human beings in freedom[32], so that human beings may ascend to God (*deification*) by their own efforts. Deification is the union of created energies with the divine energy.

movements started in the 14th century in Mt Athos. The distant origin of Hesychasm is traced back to the teachings of the Church Fathers like Gregory of Nyssa in the 4th century. Palamism is associated with Gregory Palamas (1296-1359) who was also one of the main proponents of Hesychasm. Both stressed the incomprehensibility of God's essence and of God's energy.

26. LOSSKY, *The Mystical Theology of Eastern Church* (n. 24), p. 31.

27. *Ibid.*, p. 70.

28. G. FLOROVSKY, *Collected Works of Georges Florovsky*. Vol. III: *Creation and Redemption*, Belmont, MA, Nordland Publishing Company, 1976, p. 47.

29. *Ibid.*, p. 48.

30. *Ibid.*, p. 49.

31. *Ibid.*, pp. 50-51.

32. *Ibid.*, p. 52. As Florovsky stresses the freedom of the creature, he also stresses the perfect freedom of God in His act of creation.

Alexander Schmemann (1921-1983), a leading exponent of contemporary Orthodox liturgical theology, places the God-world-human relationship in the liturgical and sacramental context. Schmemann looks at theology from a liturgical perspective and considered the eschatological belief of early Christianity as the principle that explains both the sacramental symbolism and the Christian worldview[33]. The eschatological sacramental symbolism and the eschatological worldview are instrumental to Schmemann in explaining the role of human beings in Creation. He emphasizes the centrality of human beings in Creation and their role as priests. Schmemann's anthropology does not follow the classic definitions of human being as *homo sapiens* and *homo faber*. He sees the human being primarily as *homo adorans*[34], underlining the human being's responsibility to thank God for his goodness manifested in creation. Schmemann makes it clear, though, that this priestly role is not primarily exercised in a cultic sense. He sees the priestly life as fundamentally a life in communion with God (*deification, divinization, theosis*). Thus, life in communion with Jesus or "sacramental living" is the main characteristic of the human being's priestly function. He also explains the priestly character of *leitourgia* in the Church, with its cosmic and eschatological dimensions, in terms of holding together the tension between elevating this world to the sphere of the divine, and of the divine descending into this world.

John Meyendorff (1926-1992) proposes both a "theocentric" anthropology and an "anthropocentric" cosmology based on the Incarnation to explain God-world-human relations[35]. He bases his theocentric anthropology on Irenaeus and Gregory of Nyssa. Irenaeus defined the human being in terms of communion with God. In this sense, the human being has not an autonomous and self-sufficient nature, but is to be understood in terms of his "internal relationship with God"[36]. For Gregory of Nyssa, the human being was created to enjoy the goodness of creation. Moreover,

---

33. Interestingly, Schmemann keeps a critical distance with regards to the "mysterio-logical" and "illustrative" sacramental symbolism of the patristic period. He prefers to go back to the "eschatological symbolism" of the earlier period. For a detailed study of these three types of sacramental symbolism in Schmemann, see my article *Sacramental-Liturgical Theology: A Critical Appraisal of Alexander Schmemann's Sacramentology of "Eschatological Symbolism"*, in *Questions Liturgiques/Studies in Liturgy* 82 (2001) 112-127.

34. A. SCHMEMANN, *Worship in a Secular Age*, in *SVTQ* 16 (1972) 3-16, p. 4; *Sacraments and Orthodoxy*, New York, Herder and Herder, 1965, p. 16.

35. MEYENDORFF, *Creation in Orthodox Theology* (n. 24), p. 34. For the patristic notion of "theocentric" anthropology see J. MEYENDORFF, *Byzantine Theology: Historical Trends and Doctrinal Themes*, New York, Fordham University Press, 1983, pp. 138-143.

36. *Ibid.*

it is the *imago Dei* in the human being that enables him to share in the Creator's freedom and self-determination. Likewise for Meyendorff, the image of God in the human being is not static givenness, but potentiality for growth towards God (*theosis*). This participation in God, moreover, is extended to the whole of creation.

Meyendorff's "theocentric" anthropology is based on the Chalcedonian Christology of the hypostatic union. The human and the divine natures in Jesus are not opposed to each other, as created nature is opposed to uncreated nature. Rather they form a dynamic union. On one hand, human characteristics are assumed by the *Logos*; on the other hand, man is deified. This deification does not mean the human being's absorption into God, but his true fulfillment[37].

Meyendorff's anthropocentric cosmology presents the centrality of human being in creation. It is the "theocentricity" of the human being that makes creation anthropocentric. Meyendorff bases the anthropocentrism of his cosmology both on the Genesis story of creation, where man is the ruler of creation, and on the Pauline doctrine of the "new creation" in Christ as it is expressed in Orthodox sacramental and liturgical traditions[38].

Thus the Neo-Patristic school, represented by Lossky, Florovsky, Schmemann, and Meyendorff, avoid speculative terms like *Sophia* to explain the presence of the divine in creation. Moreover, they stress the *creaturely freedom* that makes human beings responsible for working at their *deification*. These Neo-Patristic Orthodox theologians also stress the role of liturgical and sacramental traditions to keep human beings in communion with God. Although Meyendorff claims the predominance of the Neo-Patristic over the Sophiological School[39], one must appreciate the contributions of both schools to the theology of creation[40].

III. SYRIAN TRADITION

The sacramental worldview of the Syrian Fathers is based on Saint Ephrem's distinction between Creator and creation. Ephrem speaks of the ontological chasm between Creator and creation. He also insists on

---

37. *Ibid.*, p. 35.
38. *Ibid.*, pp. 35-36.
39. *Ibid.*, p. 33.
40. Paulos Mar Gregorios (1922-1996) notes this common view among different theologians: "human redemption is inseparable from the redemption of time and space as well as of 'things'". See GREGORIOS, *Human Presence* (n. 11), pp. 80-88.

the human being's incapacity to know God and to cross this ontological chasm. At the same time, he asserts that, while the transcendent Creator is hidden and unknowable to his creation, He is immanent in the world. Ephrem presents this "hidden" (*kasyuta*) but "revealed" (*galyata*) experience of God from two different perspectives: God's self-revelation from the human perspective, and God's actual being (*ituta*) from the divine perspective. On the one hand, the human experience of God depends on His self-revelation. In Saint Ephrem's view, there are the three ways in which God reveals Himself in Scriptures and in Nature: (i) through types and symbols, (ii) through the divine "names" or metaphors, and (iii) through the Incarnation. God's actual being, on the other hand, can only be experienced in a hidden and subjective manner[41]. The theological anthropology of the Syrian tradition is important in this context.

In order to understand the role in creation of the human being, it is important to know the significance of the human being's creation "in God's image" (Gn 1,26-28). In the Syriac Bible, the *Peshitta*, the verses alluding to man's dominion over the animal world immediately come after the verses describing the creation of man in the image of God. In Gn 1,26 "dominion" is expressed as "a consequence of humanity's being created in God's image"[42]. While the Alexandrians explain the creation of humankind "in the image of God" as an analogical "likeness" to God, the Syrians interpret it differently[43]. For the latter, the term "image of God" in Gn 1,26 is a metaphor for kingship and gives human beings the authority to rule over all of creation[44]. The Syrian Fathers sees God's creation of human beings "in his image" as the creation of "a

41. S. BROCK, *The Luminous Eye: The Spiritual World Vision of Saint Ephrem the Syrien*, Kalamazoo, Cistercian Publications, 1992, pp. 27-29. It is important to note that in the Syrian tradition – in Saint Ephrem in particular – Scripture and Nature are considered to be two sources of revelation. See, for example, EPHREM, *Hymns on Earth* 35.1; *Hymns against Heresies* 28.11-12.

42. BROCK, *Humanity and Natural World in Syriac Tradition* (n. 1), p. 132.

43. R. MURRAY, *The Image of God: Delegated and Responsible Authority*, in *Priests & People* 14 (2000) 49-54, pp. 50-51. According to Murray, this Alexandrian interpretation was continued in Western theology which generally interpreted "image" (*tselem* in Hebrew) in terms of the analogical "likeness" (*demuth*) of our spiritual and intellectual qualities to the divine operations. In the Augustinian tradition in particular, "image" defines human nature by spirituality and intellect, and views the rest of creation as mere resources for human use by virtue of man's spiritual superiority.

44. God's act of creation has conferred on the human being the qualities of wisdom, power and righteousness, which are attributes of "kingship". Thus, in the Near Eastern tradition, which associates God with the ancient concept of "kingship", the Old Testament ascribes royal images to God. In the Near Eastern tradition, kings were attributed a quasi-divine status. In places like Sumer and Babylon, kings were regarded as "living images" of the patron gods of their cities. For example, in Babylon the king was regarded as the

living image of himself on earth". This image has "a *viceregal* role, to govern all other creatures with responsibility to God"[45]. Therefore, human beings created in the image of God represent God in creation. In order to exercise this *viceregal* role, God gave them authority and free will. This understanding of delegated authority with free will has become the basis of the Syrian tradition, particularly in the writings of St. Ephrem[46]. Ephrem thus recognizes the royal authority implicit in Gn 1,26-28:

> *And God said, "Let us make man in our image".* According to what has been the rule until now, namely if it pleases God He will make it known to us, Moses explains in what way we are the image of God, when he said *"Let them have dominion over the fish of the sea, and over the birds, and over the cattle, and over the all earth".* It is the dominion that Adam received over the earth and over all that is in it that constitutes the likeness of God who has dominion over the heavenly things and the earthly things[47].

The authority and free will given to humanity entail responsibility to the divine source of this authority. Free will is the condition of our love for God and of our responsibility for creation[48]. Free will makes human beings different from other creatures:

> Man, owing to his Free will, can be like [other creatures], while they cannot become like him. On this account they have a (fixed) Nature, while we have Free will[49].

living image (the Babylonian word *salmu* is equivalent to the Hebrew *tselem* of Gn 1,26) of the city god Marduk. Murray notes that, in the Old Testament, "YHWH was celebrated with royal acclamations and all the symbolism of kingship". This is more clearly expressed in Psalms: "The Davidic kings claimed to be adopted sons of YHWH (Pss 2 and 110), while Psalm 89 celebrates, with close parallelism, first God in his supreme power and then the Davidic house to which YHWH promised eternal rule". MURRAY, *Image of God* (n. 43), p. 52.

45. *Ibid.* Murray criticizes some recent efforts to attribute the metaphor of "stewardship" to the human being, opting instead for the biblical metaphor of "kingship".

46. The Antiochene and Syrian notion of delegated authority with free will is seen in the writings of some Syrian authors who "compared humanity as God's image in creation to the statue of a king". See BROCK, *Humanity and Natural World* (n. 1), p. 132.

47. EPHREM, *Commentary on Genesis* I:1,29. Murray, in his translation of Gn 1,26 – see passages in italics – avoids the term "dominion"' and uses "authority" instead. In his opinion, the word "dominion" connotes ownership, while the Syriac *shultana* implies the "authority" that is delegated to human beings. The Syriac *shultana* (authority) corresponds to the Greek *exousia*, used in the New Testament. (Cf. "Authority" in Mk 1,22.27; 11,28; etc.). This "authority" is the source of one's personal freedom to act (1 Cor 8-9). Cf. MURRAY, *Image of God* (n. 43), p. 51.

48. Murray thinks that, among the Syrian Fathers, Saint Ephrem puts the greatest emphasis on free will. Cf. R. MURRAY, *Saint Ephraim's Dialogue of Reason and Love*, in *Sobornost* 2 (1980) 26-40, p. 29.

49. T. JANSMA, *Ephraem on Exodus II, 5: Reflections on the Interplay of Human Free will and Divine Providence*, in *OCP* 34 (1973) 5-28, p. 19.

Free will is given to all human beings in the same measure, although it can be obscured in people who are enslaved to sin[50]. Free will depends also on man's ability to contemplate the divine mysteries. It makes them different from other creatures and, thus, the image of God is actualized in creation[51]. The use and misuse of free will determines the human attitude towards the natural world. The individual is responsible for his response. The right response is essentially one of wonder (tehra)[52] and gratitude. The wrong response is the result of greed and arrogance. The right response is coupled with an awareness of a "hidden power" present in the natural world and in Scripture.

> The presence of this "hidden power" in the natural world lends to the natural world itself a sacramental character, which in turn requires that the natural world be used with reverence[53].

The use and misuse of free will also affects harmony in society and in creation. The harmony that is lost by the misuse of free will, however, can be recovered "through right choices and through the right use of creation"[54]. Brock notes a conditional and a reciprocal element in St. Ephrem's idea of authority:

> Rightly exercised, it will instil a love which results in harmony between ruler and ruled; wrongly exercised it instils hatred and sows disharmony[55].

In order to understand ethical responsibility for creation, it is also important to emphasize the interconnectedness of all beings in creation. Brock cites Ephrem's use of the image of human society as a body[56]. Ephrem extends Paul's allegory of the body in 1 Cor 12 and Rom 12 to the whole human race and even to animals[57]. The relationship of humanity to the animal world and to the whole of creation is also shown in Ephrem's commentary on Gn 1,26[58]. This interconnectedness of all beings

---

50. BROCK, *The Luminous Eye* (n. 41), pp. 35-36.
51. D. BUNDY, *Language and Knowledge of God in Ephrem Syrus*, in *PBR* 5 (1986) 91-103, p. 103.
52. BROCK, *The Luminous Eye* (n. 41), p. 68. The attitude of wonder is a key element in Ephrem's notion of the sacramentality of the world. This wonder is evoked not only by the Incarnation and the Eucharist, but also by the created world. Cf. BROCK, *World and Sacrament* (n. 1), pp. 694-695.
53. *Ibid.*, pp. 164-165. See also BROCK, *Humanity and the Natural World* (n. 1), pp. 138-139.
54. *Ibid.*, pp. 166-167. Ephrem presents Noah's generation as the best example of the use and abuse of free will. EPHREM, *Hymnen de Fide* 3.9.
55. ID., *Humanity and the Natural World* (n. 1), p. 135.
56. ID., *The Luminous Eye* (n. 41), p. 167.
57. MURRAY, *Image of God* (n. 43), p. 52.
58. BROCK, *Humanity and the Natural World* (n. 1), p. 135.

in creation makes solidarity with all creatures important. It is for this reason that interdependence binds us with love for everything[59]. For Brock, St. Ephrem sees interconnectedness on three levels: (i) within humanity as a whole; (ii) within creation as a whole (thus including between humanity and the environment); and (iii) between the material world and the spiritual world. This interconnectedness of everything in creation gives the human being an important role in recovering creation from the disharmony caused by human misuse of free will[60].

Before the Fall, all creatures and all the elements existed together in harmony in the cosmic and social realms. The misuse of free will led to cosmic disorder[61]. We also see efforts to restore this lost harmony, the potential for recovery being always present since the Fall[62]. Ephrem, in his *Commentary on Genesis*, sees a temporary restoration of harmony granted by God to Noah[63]. Restoration is also presented in the entry of the Hebrews into the Promised Land[64]. This Restoration is achieved in the salvific mission and death of Jesus. "The voice of creation cried to proclaim Him innocent", St. Ephrem says[65].

Jesus' restoration of creation is an important theme in the works of the Syrian Fathers. This restoration reinstated human beings in the paradise originally given to Adam. This redemptive experience is at the core of Syrian liturgical and sacramental celebrations, anticipating the Christian's participation in the *eschaton*. This is seen primarily in the sacraments of Baptism and the Eucharist. For the Syrian Fathers, the ultimate recovery of the lost harmony will take place only in the eschatological paradise[66]. By emphasizing the harmony that will take place in the eschatological paradise and its anticipation in the liturgical and sacramental celebrations, the Syrian tradition tries to find a balance between the ethical and liturgical responses to the sacramentality of creation.

---

59. ID., *The Luminous Eye* (n. 41), p. 167.

60. ID., *Humanity and the Natural World* (n. 1), p. 140.

61. EPHREM, *Hymnen contra Haereses* 28.9. The same theme is seen in his *Commentary on Genesis* II:31. See also his biblical narrative of *Commentary on Genesis* III:18. Cf. BROCK, *Humanity and the Natural World* (n. 1), p. 139; *The Luminous Eye* (n. 41), p. 165.

62. BROCK, *Humanity and the Natural World* (n. 1), p. 139.

63. EPHREM, *Commentary on Genesis* II:59-60.

64. BROCK, *World and Sacrament* (n. 1), p. 688. Saint Ephrem sees the escape from bondage in Egypt as representing the Christian's escape in Baptism from the clutches of both Satan and Death. EPHREM, *De Azymis*, III.

65. EPHREM, *Commentary on the Diatessaron* 21.5.

66. At the same time, he acknowledges its occasional anticipation on earth by the saints. BROCK, *The Luminous Eye* (n. 41), p. 165. Compare Ephrem's *Hymnen contra Haereses* 21.6, *Commentary on Genesis* II.9, and *Prose Refutations* 1, lxxxv-lxxxvi.

IV. CONCLUSION

The different theologies of creation we have reviewed attempted to explain the relation between God, the world, and human beings. In these different theological traditions, one sees a recognition of the sacred character given to creation and the unique position of human beings as God's representative. Although the eastern and oriental Christian traditions are often seen as overtly mystical and apparently unconcerned with the realities of the world, this study shows how these traditions show their concern for the world in their peculiar manner. While contemporary Western Christian theologians emphasize social concerns, Orthodox theologians generally emphasize the Christian faith as primarily a direct experience of the Kingdom of God, as it is sacramentally present in the Church. Without denying the Christian's responsibility for the world, they consider this responsibility as a demand that springs from life in Christ. It is not a flight from the realities of the world, but a deep commitment to it.

Desom P.O.   Mathai KADAVIL, OIC
Aluva 683 103
India

A CONVERSATIONAL GOD
AS THE SOURCE OF A RESPONSE ETHICS

In this paper, we intend to lay open the meaning of and implications for an ethics of biblical thought about God. As our starting point, we will sketch the three great paradigms or models that have determined ethical thinking in the West until the present. Arriving at the model of relational responsibility, we shall demonstrate how this relatively recent model of thought displays strong affinities with the manner in which the biblical tradition professes ever more clearly an interpersonal and dialogical God. We will pay special attention to the question as to what impact the relational, biblical approach to God has on ethics, out of which the response structure of biblical ethics is unequivocally made evident.

I. Self-Realisation, Law and Responsibility

According to H. Richard Niebuhr[1] we can distinguish three paradigms or models in Western history that develop in their own way a concept about ethics and the human person as an ethical subject.

1. *Self-unfolding*

First of all, we find in Greek thought "the image of man-the-maker", meaning to say the paradigm whereby the human person who designs and creates oneself is of central importance. "Know thyself" (*"gnothi seauton"*) counted as the essential condition in creating and designing oneself. This self-knowledge, according to Aristotle, must lead to an insight into the internal finality of human dynamism, which ends up in a teleological conception of the ethical task of the human person. A number of potentialities lie dormant in the person, which thus "ask" to be realised, and this according to a certain *"telos"* or "end-goal". Concretely speaking, this goal consists of the self-realisation of the subject. As a human person, one is faced

---

1. H.R. Niebuhr, *The Responsible Self: An Essay in Christian Moral Philosophy*, New York – Evanston, IL – London, Harper and Row, 1963, pp. 47-68.

with the task of working on oneself in such a manner, or rather to work making use of one's own capacities, so that one gives form and shape to oneself according to one's own human finality, and thus become fully or "truly" human. Thomas Aquinas, clearly influenced by Aristotle, maintains this finalistic, future-oriented conception of ethics. However, he no longer situates the "ultimate goal" of human becoming in the human person himself, but in the *"unio beatifica"* or the "beatific vision of the divine". Or rather, the perfection of the human person according to one's own inner finality lies precisely in the union with God, which can then be realised in a full way only after death – in the afterlife – and can only be anticipated in a partial way here below (it is likewise made possible by a sacramental life and a life "in union with God").

In the same line with Aristotelian thought lies the self-actualisation psychology of Abraham Maslow, Carl Rogers, Erich Fromm, Gordon Allport and others[2] who promote the unfolding of the inner, "true" self as the goal of human existence. The human person must be faithful to his or her inner essence or "nature". One discovers in the human person a longing for self-fulfilment, the inclination to actualise what one potentially is. This thought on self-unfolding formulates this inclination as the longing to become more and more that which one "idiosyncratically" is, that is to become according to one's utter and irreducible uniqueness that which one is capable of becoming. It is thus not surprising that "ideal" and "ideals" and personal responsibility for this "ideal" self or one's own qualitative human-becoming strongly come into the fore (cf. infra). Today, this thought related to self-unfolding is translated into the subjective terms of "happiness" and "becoming happy".

2. *External Law*

The second paradigm of the human person as an ethically acting subject, according to Niebuhr is "the image of man-the-citizen", i.e., the human who lives under the law and obeys laws, as these are promulgated especially in society but also in religion by a "legal" authority or "divine" will. In the "polis", all sorts of "Thou shalt …"-laws, but especially "Thou shalt not …"-prohibitions, are promulgated. We frequently find these rules, demands, permissions and obligations in the "mores" or the customary laws, and in all sorts of rules that are valid within the family, the neighbourhood or the small community, as well as in the broader social, economic and political community of the state, on the national, international

2. S.R. MADDI, *Personality Theories: A Comparative Analysis*, Dorsey Homewood, IL, 1980, pp. 80-155, 341-385.

and global levels. What is specific to this "legal" model is that our behaviour is governed by the rules and prescriptions that are promulgated by others. We can indeed rebel against them or subject ourselves to them, because they are reasonable and wise, that is, they both regulate society as well as create the space and the conditions for our own self-realisation (the latter implies that the first and second paradigms need to be combined). In contrast to the teleological-finalistic character of the first paradigm, we can call this second paradigm "deontological", precisely insofar as it is based on obligations and rules that must be executed. The question is not: "What should I do? What should I do at best? What is my goal, my ideal or telos?" (1st model), but rather: "What is the law that I must fulfil? What is the first and foremost law of my life?" In this model, responsibility consists in giving an account to the "lawgiver" for the good or bad accomplishment of the prescriptions and obligations.

3. *Interaction*

The third paradigm (one that is becoming increasingly prevalent today) is the paradigm of responsibility in the strict sense of the term. In the first paradigm, responsibility is experienced as a form of self-knowledge and self-growth, for which I myself have to guarantee: I am not only the starting point but also the goal of responsibility. According to the second paradigm, responsibility means that I must give an account to the "lawgiver" for executing or not executing the law[3]. In the third paradigm, responsibility is conceived of relationally, i.e., literally as giving an answer to a question that is posed, or as creatively responding to a summons that is directed towards us. We can likewise call it an interaction model. Life consists in giving answers to questions or problems that come to us, from reality, circumstances, nature, our life surroundings, or the people with whom we live. Human existence is no longer seen as the modeling of the self as "material" for a self-design, nor as obedience to the law, but as reacting to stimuli, challenges and claims that come to us and appeal to us "from elsewhere", especially from others – and for the religious person, from God as well. The image of the human person that is contained in this paradigm is "the human person as the giver of answers". We understand ourselves as responsive or responsorial beings, who, by means of our feelings, thoughts and actions do not so much work on ourselves or obey a certain law, as attempt to give an answer to that which befalls us or meets us as stimulus. The starting question for responsorial action is then

---

3. P. Ricœur, *The Just*, Chicago, IL – London, University of Chicago Press, 2000, pp. 13-19.

not so much "What is my goal?" or "What must I do?" in order to succeed in life, or "What are my duties?" to which I must comply in order
to be a good citizen or fellow human being, but rather: "What is happening? What comes to me from the situation, or literally from the "cir-
cum-stances"?" and: "What is expected of me here and how can I take
this up to the best of my abilities?" In the first model the concept of the
good as the "perfect" stands central; in the second model what is "correct" or "right" or that which "must" be according to the law; in the
third model what "responds" or "corresponds" to what is asked of me and
for which I must also give an account.

II. Covenant and Ethics as Interpersonal Relationship

This interactional and relational concept of ethics was introduced by
the so-called dialogical thinkers like Franz Rosenzweig, Martin Buber,
Gabriel Marcel, Maurice Nédoncelle, Emmanuel Levinas – to give but the
foremost names. It is not coincidental that these authors have their pre-
philosophical roots in biblical, Jewish or Christian thought. In the meantime, it has become clear that in biblical thought a relational image of God
and the human person occupies a central position, out of which a relational ethics of responsibility ensues. Or to put it differently: from the Old
Testament, a personal, or even more strongly, an "inter-personal" God,
ever more clearly comes to the fore, which has direct consequences for
the image of the human person and the ethics that is involved therewith.
To profess faith in a personal and "inter-subjective" God means, at the
same time, to conceive and live out of an ethics as an "inter-subjective"
and dialogical event. We would like to illustrate this fundamental idea,
first on the basis of the idea of the covenant and, subsequently, on the
basis of the prophetic calling wherein ethics, in an unusually acute way,
is couched as a personal and inter-personal event of responsibility.

1. At God's Initiative

The core idea of the concept of God in the Old Testament in general
and the Mosaic tradition in particular is the idea of a covenantal God[4].
God is not a highest principle of explanation, that on the basis of reason

4. H. Wattiaux, *Engagement de Dieu et fidélité du chrétien. Perspectives pour
une théologie morale fondamentale*, Louvain-la-Neuve, Centre Cerfaux-Lefort, 1979,
pp. 29-117.

is posed or derived as a conceptual tailpiece regarding our inner-worldly experiences. On the contrary, He directs himself to the people of Israel as a speaking Someone, with the explicit intention and question on establishing a covenant. God is not a solipsistic God, who in his transcendence would be unapproachably "solitary", and thus would have nothing to do with the world and especially with human beings, who stand for Israel. As a person – as Someone – He is inter-personal and at the same time conversational. He turns towards Israel and addresses them, whereby Israel itself becomes "someone": "I will be your God, and you will be my people". The human person is appealed to and invited to enter into a relationship. The word that God speaks expects an answer, literally a counter-word, whereby a covenant comes to be.

In this regard, the covenant begins with a heteronymous asymmetry: the origin of the covenant is not Israel, or the human person, or I-myself, but the "Other", Yahweh, who comes towards humans. In other words, the covenant rests on the *election* by Yahweh. Israel is "separated" from the peoples and "set apart" by Yahweh not simply in order to be a people, but God's chosen people. The covenant is not an agreement between equals. It is Yahweh who decides for the covenant, He is the One who *takes the initiative*. And so it was in the covenant with Noah (Gen 9,8vv) with Abraham (Gen 15,15 and 17), with Moses (Exod 24). In other words, the covenant is in the literal sense of the word "founded" – and this without any merit from Israel's side.

2. *Ethics as Response*

This, however, does not preclude a reciprocity between Yahweh and Israel, that is, between God and humans. Yahweh directs Himself to the people and addresses them, with the appeal to say "yes" to the covenant. Only when humans give their response can one effectively speak of a covenant. Moreover, this positive response to God's offer not only implies an "act of faith", namely an act of entrusting oneself to God as the One and Only, but also the realisation of certain earthly, inner-worldly affairs that have everything to do with the quality – the ethics – of human relationships, both among themselves as well as towards nature. In this regard, the covenant is anything but non-committal: it is not only God who engages Himself with the people, it is also Israel that must engage itself with God. Only by means of doing something, quite concretely by the doing of the Torah, does the covenant become real and also have a future. This fulfilment of the Law, of which the "Ten Commandments" or the Decalogue is an eminently concentrated form, thus "founds" and realises the covenant as much as God's initiative towards the covenant. Here, the obedience to the commandments in general, and especially to the commandments from the second tablet, is no longer an isolated affair (cf. the second paradigm), but is integrated into the relational and respon- sorial event of the covenant. From the side of God, there is the promise of love and faithfulness (*"chesed"*); from the side of humans, this implies the task of living lives of love and faithfulness. Sin, therefore, is not only a form of disobedience to the Law, but also and especially a form of unfaithfulness towards God. Moral evil doing is not simply an objective violation of an external prescription, but an affective and relational event whereby the violation hurts the partner and harms the trust given. It is therefore no coincidence that the covenant is expressed in marital terms whereby the fulfilment of the law and ethical action, are understood as a form of faithfulness towards God, and disobedience to the law is repeat- edly branded by the prophets as "adultery". By fulfilling the command- ments one not only acts ethically, but one also demonstrates one's soli- darity with and one's "heart" for God.

3. *Ethics as Intimacy with God*

In this manner, ethics acquires a religious and relational meaning. We can likewise call this the response structure of actions, just as religious belief itself has a responsorial structure. Fidelity to the Law is not sim- ply an ethical or social praxis, but a religious act, namely an act whereby Israel enters into relationship with God. Here, ethics is not in the first place directed towards self-fulfilment (although it is indeed its inadver- tent "outcome"), or towards the fulfilment of social obligations amongst the people. It is especially a specific and essential manner of relating one- self to God and thus being near God. On the basis of the personal and inter-personal concept of God, which essentially lies in the category of the covenant, ethics itself – as the doing of the Law – becomes an inter- personal event. By doing certain things, one gives a response to God whereby ethics acquires a religious meaning and bears witness to God who binds Himself with Israel, that is, with human beings. Throughout a history of falls and rises, infidelity and fidelity, ethics contributes to a solidarity between free partners who repeatedly choose for each other, and confess this choice before each other and – by means of all sorts of rituals – confirm and deepen it. The religious, mystical experience of God as Someone who addresses and calls human beings affords a very differ- ent meaning to ethics, a personalist and inter-personal tint and dynamism. The Law is no external, objective event any longer, but something that takes part in the life of faith as an inter-personal intimacy with God. In this regard, prayer, meditation and celebration are not the only ways of entering into intimacy with God. An ethics of love, of which the commandments in the Decalogue only indicate the minimal conditions, brings me just as well close to God, albeit in its very own way: "Whoever loves is a child of God, and knows God", says John after all (1 John 4,7).

4. *Personalising Dynamism*

This in its turn is connected to the ethical struggle against all depersonalisation of the human person, likewise or even especially if these depersonalisations ensue from one or the other religious experience. At the same time, this interpersonal concept of God implies, with its interpersonally interpreted and experienced ethics, a critique on all concepts of God that depersonalise and reduce God to an anonymous force of nature or cosmic energy. Naturally, we know both from philosophy and from the existential "wisdom" of the life of faith itself that the concept of person is a risky concept. "Negative theology" is thus a mainstay with regard to the personalist concepts of God. Iconoclasm or the destruction of "images of God" necessarily places that God as the first and final Being too much beyond and above the human person and the world, at the cost of his "immanence" or "essential-presence".

This critique should never lead to the concept of God as "infra-" or "sub-personal" or, still less, as an "un-personal" dynamism. These conceptions lead not only to a reduction of *"The"* (personal) Holy One of the Bible to *"the"* Sacred, but also to a depersonalisation of the human person. An un-personal concept of God reduces the human person to an element in an anonymous and "submerged" process of participation, albeit one that is awe-inspiring and fascinating. There is no recourse to or resistance against such "faceless deities".

This stands in sharp contrast to Jacob who did struggle with God, a story which not only presupposes a personal God but also personalises the human person, and moreover strengthens this personalisation. In this wrestling, a strong bond of intimacy grows between the struggling parties, without, however, an all-absorbing confusion or mix-up of one of the two. In the struggle, they remain radically distinct and yet thanks to this struggle, a strong bond deepens between them.

According to the biblical tradition, an un-personal God leads back to chaos, both on the religious and the personal levels, wherein all creatures disappear into "nothing", in the sense that they are "no-thing" (not-a-thing) and "no-one" (not-someone) any longer. Thanks precisely to the divine act of creation, they have received their separateness and uniqueness, and thereby are irreducible to each other and to God. This is the fundamental meaning of revelation. This presupposes the conquering of chaos and of the un-personal divine powers, wherein the human person is not only submerged but also made the victim "in fear and trembling".

Only when God reveals Himself by means of speaking, and thereby manifests Himself as Someone who directs Oneself to someone else, Israel, the human person, the transcendence of God and, equally, the personal fundamental structure of the human person as an independent and free being are respected. For it is precisely out of the person's irreducible being-person that one is able to give an answer, and thus accord the covenant with God its historical reality and reciprocity.

Moreover, thanks to this personal response, which also includes the tangible and visible fulfilment of the Torah, one bears witness to God's personal, or rather interpersonal being, which in its turn confirms and concretises the personal and conversational being of the human person, one's religiosity and one's ethics. In this sense not only is the covenant faith important for faith itself, but it implies at the same time an emancipatory meaning for the human person. The human person is not an unimportant element in a cosmic game, a number out of a series, but a special someone who, thanks to God's election, also acquires a unique meaning.

III. ETHICS AS VOCATION

This personalising and "inter-subjectivising" of human persons and their ethics in the idea of the covenant find an eminent deepening in the way in which the bible depicts the calling of the prophets[5]. The parallels between the covenant and prophetic calling are so manifold and striking that they are quite self-explanatory. It is important to keep in mind that the idea of the calling not only refers to the special manner of existence of a few "exceptional" people but, on the contrary, of human existence and ethics itself.

---

5. E. LEVINAS, *Otherwise than Being or Beyond Essence*, The Hague – Boston – London, Nijhoff, 1981, pp. 81-97, 140-152; ID., *Difficult Freedom: Essays on Judaism*, Baltimore, MD, Johns Hopkins University Press, 1990, pp. 85-96; ID., *Nine Talmudic Readings*, Bloomington, IN, Indiana University Press, 1990, pp. 120-135, 134-135; P. RICŒUR, *Le sujet convoqué. À l'école des récits de vocation prophétique*, in *Revue de l'Institut catholique de Paris* 28 (1988) 84-89.

1. *Heteronomous Vocation*

The first thing that strikes us is that the prophet is one "called" in the literal sense of the word. His calling begins not with himself, but with a radical Other, God, who calls him *"ex abrupto"* – "from elsewhere" – to something that does not correspond with his life's design and his plans. In the narratives of prophetic calling, we read each time: "The Word of Yahweh came to ..." or "The Word of Yahweh was directed to ...". In this regard, the prophet was not a prophet beforehand, but he only becomes a prophet in and through being called by someone else, namely the wholly Other. The origin of the prophetic calling is not in the king or in the established political order, as was the case among the so-called "court prophets"; much less does it arise from the innermost self of the one called. The calling begins in heteronomy and not in our human autonomy. The spoken Word of God comes first; it precedes all planning, all possible projects or dreams of the prophet.

In the New Testament as well, we find this radically heteronomous vocation experience, among others in the evangelical narrative of the annunciation of the angel to Mary (Luke 1,26-38). Here, the presupposed starting point is the life of Mary herself, who cherishes her plans and dreams, her personal life project. As a young woman – and in this she is the image of every human person – she has built up her options and her perspectives on life, and she wants to realise them. Among others, she was engaged to Joseph (Luke 1,27) and therefore had plans for marriage, with the accompanying dream for her own house and children. This is her, inalienable life, borne by a most personal commitment. But without taking account of this, the angel Gabriel breaks unannounced and unexpected into her life. In line with the Old Testament tradition, the angel is the one who acts in the name of God "towards human beings". The angel is the appearance, the turning of the face of the invisible and wholly transcendent God "towards human beings". In such manner God becomes present among people, without needlessly exposing His transcendence and surrendering His holiness. Moreover, the angel is also a messenger; in Greek and Latin the word "angel" means "bearer of news" (*"aggelos"*, *"angelus"*). This means that the angel is defined by words, or rather the word spoken not in its own name but in the name of the one who sends it. The angel is but a messenger because it has something to say "from God" to humans, just as happens in the story of Mary: the angel Gabriel went in and came to her and addressed the Word to her (Luke 1,28). This Word, as in the case of the prophets of the Old Testament, alludes to the heteronomous passivity of the fact of being called despite oneself. The Word of the angel, namely the Word of God to Mary, precedes the personal life project of Mary.

In this regard, the biblical idea of vocation is fundamentally distinguished from what we usually call ideal. In our Western culture, at least as this has been modelled since the Enlightenment and has grown to become our second nature – our cultural body – the term "ideal" is understood as a lofty expression and eminent realisation of the "self". As a conscious and free being, I design myself on the basis of my dreams and longings, my abilities and inabilities, that is, on the basis of my possibilities and limits, a specific task or life choice that only has meaning when it substantiates the best of myself (cf. the first paradigm). In this context, the Greek philosopher, Pindarus, is often cited: "What one *can* be, one *must* be"; Nietzsche is quoted as well: "Become what you are". The human person is called to be faithful to one's own "self", not so much one's superficial or fractured self but one's deeper, true self. And one can do so only by means of unfolding one's most individual of possibilities and gifts, and thus become that to which one is capable of becoming on the basis of one's own inner powers of growth.

The biblical idea of calling goes directly against this idea of autonomy and auto-realisation, whereby the word "*autos*" is centrally important, in the sense that the subject poses its own "self" ("*autos*") as the law ("*nomos*"), albeit that this auto-realisation is substantiated by means of the relationship with the world, others, the community and even with that which transcends us, and with God. It should be made clear – and this is certainly no comforting thought that would sound pleasant to our "(late-)modern" ears – that the idea of intentional and endeavoured self-fulfilment, subjective happiness, the unfolding of the personal "purpose" and "actualisation" actually falls outside of the biblical perspective. Put more strongly, from its particular perspective the bible uninhibitedly puts emphasis on the heteronomous character of the calling, in terms of both its origin as well as its goal. Calling – and therefore the meaning of my existence – does not arise out of myself, nor out of one or the other predilection or predisposition out of my own being, but out of the "other" than myself that makes a claim on me "despite of myself", concretely out of the totally Other who appeals to me with its Word.

2. *Called by a Sensitive God*

This heteronomy of being called despite oneself, however, is not blind fate, but refers to the address by Someone, a divine Thou, or rather a divine Third Party – a He/She, or rather a "One Over There" – who has spoken[6]. In any case, God is no anonymous principle but a person who addresses the word to a human being, who precisely through this word becomes a "prophet", literally one addressed by God and thus one who speaks for God to the world. It is literally about a calling, with the emphasis on the passivity of the "being called" – a passivity that precedes all activity. That is why the assent to the actively experienced calling is always "secondary" with regard to the One Who Calls. This implies that human existence as calling essentially has a response structure, meaning it can only concretise itself as a response (which is also a word) to some word that is spoken beforehand, that comes from someone else. The calling – and thus human existence itself – is a linguistic event whereby the spoken word takes central importance, and further whereby the passivity of being addressed by the other forms the basis of all that follows thereafter as an active response. What is unique to the spoken word – in Hebrew "*dabar*" – is that it does not arise from the innermost self of the one spoken to, as if it would have already been dormant in there before as a pre-given "idea" that only needed to be aroused. The word of the calling is utterly "external"; it comes "from outside", namely from the "spokesperson" who is radically separate from the one spoken to and maintains and strengthens its irreducibility precisely in the speaking, without excluding the possibility of a deep and even intimate relationship. The word of the calling occurs as that which is "objective" *par excellence*, and which comes to me from elsewhere and addresses me out of its separateness. As the most "foreign", it nestles itself at the same time in myself, whereby it shares in my intimacy. We can also label this as the paradox of a "foreign intimacy", which never loses its foreignness and thereby does not annul its intimacy or "inner depth".

6. Even when God is in the "third person", in the sense that He is not directly present but always withdraws Himself or, in other words, remains transcendent, this does not take away His "being-person". By means of His retreat in the past He does not become something or an impersonal event, but is and remains indeed a Someone who has directed His Word to humans. By means of the divine address, humans not only become someone, thus even persons as well, but they are likewise neither seized nor crushed by the word addressed to them, so much so that they acquire the necessary space and freedom for their personal and free response. The one who has spoken has already "passed by" and has withdrawn into the past, or as Levinas would say "in a past immemorial", in a past that is never past enough. And it is precisely in this transcendence, which displays a truly divine character, that the one called receives the freedom of the response. Cf. LEVINAS, *Of God Who Comes to Mind*, Stanford, CA, University Press, 1998, pp. 62-65.

3. *Mission Impossible*

The "intrinsically unique character" of the divine Word that makes the prophet a prophet reaches still farther. It enters into the existence of the one called as an unconditional word that summons and makes a claim, giving the person something to do, namely to speak out of and for God. This prophetic speaking is an action in the full sense of the word, since it is not simply about an informative or descriptive word, but about a performative or "transforming" word that incises into a situation and always brings with something, usually a crisis. In this regard, calling is mission. This task, however, is in the literal sense of the word a "mission impossible", a "non-possible" task since it does not ensue from the capability and the autonomy of the one called. The mission happens to the person as a *"Fremdkörper"* or as "chaos" in the literal sense of the word, i.e., a "disruption of order" which is not concerned with whether all this is possible, whether the one called is in the proper state or mood, and possesses the necessary capacities and talents, or whether the one called will be happy with it or will successfully accomplish one's life-project, and so on.

That calling, which immediately and essentially means mission, is likewise apparent in the call narrative of Mary. The mission that is entrusted to Mary consists in becoming the mother of Jesus. The "foreign" Word, that comes to her from God through the angel Gabriel, says: "And now, you will conceive in your womb and you will bear a son, and you will name him Jesus" (Luke 1,31). In this regard, Jesus is not the result of a conscious or "responsible parenthood", that in a "foreseen" manner, based on all sorts of motives and taking into account of all kinds of factors (such as medical, eugenetic, psychological, social, economic or demographic indications), plans and controls a pregnancy (think of the term "birth control"). On the contrary, Mary acquires a pregnancy that is entrusted to her, without her having foreseen, planned and pondered on this. Motherhood is literally "brought about" in her; she is appealed thereto "in spite of herself". And since Mary, just like all prophets, stands for every human being, this means that every person is called and sent in order to bear the "son of man", the other person, and bring him forth into the world. We can likewise call this the concept of "ethical motherhood": to bear the other in oneself until the other is born. And in connection with Mary, this ethical motherhood acquires a still stronger significance. The son whom she must bring forth into the world is indeed the Son, the Anointed One (Christ) of the Most High.

4. Election as Mission

Even so, heteronomy thus understood does not mean the alienation or the destruction of the prophet, and of the human subject in general. Throughout the calling, on the contrary, the one called receives his or her uniqueness. God does not address his Word to humans as such, but quite singularly to a concrete someone. The calling is an election, which quite concretely designates and makes a claim on someone. The word of God comes to someone, who is addressed by name, and who therefore cannot be mistaken for anyone else. In every call narrative, the prophet is addressed by his unique name. For instance: "Hosea" (Hos 1,1), "Joel" (Joel 1,1), Micah (Micah 1,1), Zephaniah (Zeph 1,1). Likewise, along with the name, the prophet is situated in time and space. Concretely, someone is particularly called in a well-defined moment and in well-defined historical circumstances in order to take up a very singular mission from God: "Now the word of the Lord came to Jonah son of Amittai" (Jonah 1,1); "The word of the Lord that came to Hosea son of Beeri, in the days of King Uzziah, Jotham, Ahaz, and Hezekiah of Judah, and in the days of King Jeroboam son of Joash of Israel" (Hos 1,1); "The word of the Lord that came to Joel son of Pethuel" (Joel 1,1); "The word of the Lord that came to Micah of Moresheth in the days of Kings Jotham, Ahaz, and Hezekiah of Judah" (Micah 1,1); "The word of the Lord that came to Zephaniah son of Cushi son of Gedaliah son of Amariah son of Hezekiah, in the days of King Josiah son of Amon of Judah" (Zeph 1,1); "In the eighth month, in the second year of Darius, the word of the Lord came to the prophet Zechariah son of Berechiah son of Iddo" (Zech 1,1). The vocation visions of Isaiah and Ezekiel as well are personally and historically dated. Isaiah receives his vocation vision "in the year that King Uzziah died" (Isa 6,1). And the priest Ezekiel, who is identified as the son of Buzi, receives his vision during his stay amongst the exiles by the river Chebar in the land of the Chaldeans, namely on the fifth day of the fourth month of the thirtieth year, that was at the same time the fifth year of the exile of Israel's king Jehoiachin (Ezek 1,1).

Indeed, we find a similar individualisation among all the prophets. In this manner, the prophet is accorded his uniqueness. It is not a uniqueness that is determined by a number of objective coordinates, qualities and characteristics, social situation and status, or by proficiency or realisations, but a uniqueness that is constituted by the calling itself – the fact of having been called. Since the prophet is called personally, he must also respond personally. He cannot be replaced by anyone at all; he cannot shift the claim to anyone else. He must act as the one and only

– the unique one – who must respond. Notwithstanding the heteronomy of the vocation, he is indeed "set apart" or "set aside": the only one in the world to reply. Thereby he acquires a "singular" uniqueness and dignity. His is an irreplaceable task: not as self-determination and mastery but as a designation "despite oneself". He is not at the origin of his election; he is set apart *by someone else*. And thereby as a human being, he becomes "unique", separated from the grey egalitarian masses, or "made singularly unique" as Kierkegaard would put it, without this uniqueness referring back to his knowledge or capabilities.

This is likewise the case with the calling of Mary, as discussed above. The Word of the Lord is not simply an empty Word, meant for humans in general, but it is a Word directed and intended for someone in particular, in this case Mary. Her personal and historical designation does not simply happen casually or carelessly, but thoroughly and with a great deal of ascertainable data. There is no mistake possible; we know clearly who this Mary is: "In the sixth month the angel Gabriel was sent by God to a town in Galilee called Nazareth, to a virgin engaged to a man whose name was Joseph, of the house of David. The virgin's name was Mary" (Luke 1,26-27). Likewise, she is addressed personally, and this happens twice: "Greetings, favored one! The Lord is with you" (Luke 1,28); "Do not be afraid, Mary, for you have found favor with God" (Luke 1,30). And the mission, the exceptional pregnancy, which is accomplished in and entrusted to her, is indeed *her* pregnancy, to which she is personally called and chosen. Precisely out of this election for a heteronomous mission does her dignity flow forth!

Nonetheless, this election should not be understood as a privilege in which the one called can take pride and to which one can refer in order to be "secure" or ensure oneself of a future reward or redemption. The one called has been called only because she has been claimed despite herself, and in this claim she is sent not to be concerned about personal matters, but to involve herself in the fate of others. The uniqueness of the one chosen, which only comes to be in the election by a radically "other", can never be described in terms of privileges, but only in terms of a personal responsibility for others than oneself. The election does not so much express the pride of one chosen, but the humility of a servant. It is no pretentious awareness of exceptional "rights" but of exceptional – literally "out-of-the-ordinary" – and thus unheard of, even "impossible" duties. The mission and its specific, altro-centric content is, in other words, an essential dimension of the prophetic calling, just as the election. No election without mission, whereby the one called is not directed to oneself but is de-centred, directed away from oneself towards the others. As one called, the human person is "inspired", literally moved and "aroused". He or she is always chosen in order to be sent to others. Moreover, the prophetic mission always involves the wholeness and salvation or healing of others. Even if it consists in articulating a fulminating judgment and calling forth even calamity onto a certain people or even Israel, it is always about a judgment and a "punishment" that concerns evil and crime which is counter to the deepest being of God. Furthermore, the judgment is always articulated with the intention that the "wrongdoer" is converted so that he would be able to receive the mercy and salvation of God.

5. *An Ethically Qualified Heteronomy*

This implies that the heteronomy of God's calling Word is a qualified heteronomy. God is not a highest principle of being that only has a formal or intellectual significance in explanation of what we do not understand in this world. He is no "unmoved Mover", but on the contrary the "Moved One", the Non-Indifferent One *par excellence*, who binds Himself with humans and with the world, and who is affected by what takes place in this world. God is not merely this or that; He is the Good *par excellence*. That is why in the biblical tradition, He is each time characterised in ethical terms. First of all, with positive ethical terms: the Just One, the Faithful One, the Merciful One, the Patient One, the Loving One, and so forth. This applies not only for the Old but likewise for the New Testament. When Jesus talks about the Kingdom of God, or rather about God's reign, he turns this category inside-out, as it were, by connecting "lordship" to a serving and liberating relationship with people, in particular with the poor, the weeping, the hungry, the oppressed (cf. the Beatitudes). God is not a far and inaccessible being, but a "touchable" and "touched" God, in short, an associated God, or rather a God who associates Himself time and again, a God who enters into and binds Himself with the small and the vulnerable in their history. This does not deny that the Bible, especially the Old Testament, also speaks of God in negative ethical terms, insofar as God not only bends mercifully towards the victim of repudiation and abuse, but at the same time gets angry about the violation of trust, of justice and of love. Upon closer inspection, the expressions of God's indignation and judgment, which are often strongly laden with verbal violence, likewise convey God's utterly ethical positivity. With this, the paradox comes to the fore that the ethically laden positivity of God is precisely grace for human beings. As a human being, what I experience as grace from an "other" is the ethical task and commitment of that other. When the other – God, but also my fellow humans – comes towards me out of his or her ethical movedness and solidarity, I may experience this as a great grace and blessing, whereby I – despite myself – find love and through this love I receive my self-esteem and self-worth, or stronger still my utterly positive uniqueness.

Out of this inextricable interwovenness of election and mission, bearing the stamp of the ethically qualified and thus gracious God, it would seem that the prophet – and in him, each one who is called, each person – is, despite himself, dedicated towards "the good". This "devotion" to the Good precedes free choice. The one called "finds" oneself in an alliance with the Good, even before one has any awareness of it. In the prophetic narratives, the prophet is made to be involved with the other than oneself by the radically Other, God. It is precisely this heteronomous dedication to the good for others – not for oneself – that lies at the foundation of this "foreign" fundamental structure of the mission, and of human existence itself. The one called is put on the track towards others, and that is precisely his or her election in which a "covenant" takes place, which in no way can be traced back to his or her free choice. As one called, the human person stands in a "covenant-bond" with the other than oneself, even before he or she can enter into an "obligation" with others.

This heteronomous dedication to the other than oneself – to the Good – is likewise apparent in the first calling of Jesus himself, just as this comes to the fore in the already mentioned narrative of the annunciation to Mary. The starting point of Jesus' calling does not lie in the desire or a future dream of Mary regarding her child, but in the action of an angel who pronounces God's destination for one who has not yet even been conceived. After the annunciation of the angel Gabriel, Mary is "promised" by God that she will become pregnant and shall bring forth a son to the world, to whom she must give the name Jesus (Luke 1,31). It does not end there, however, for about Jesus a destination, that is, a calling, is also pronounced. Not only before he was born, but also before he was "conceived", has his deepest being and meaning already been indicated: "He will be great and will be called the Son of the Most High (Luke 1,32a). Moreover, his mission is already assigned to him: "... and the Lord God will give to him the throne of his ancestor David. He will reign over the house of Jacob forever, and of his kingdom there will be no end" (Luke 1,32b-33). Above, we have already mentioned what this kingship will consist of, namely how it involves a very particular and paradoxical kingship, that is closely connected to the message he brings about God's liberating and serving reign that is near to people. In other words, Jesus is called and sent to embody and to proclaim God's radical *kenosis* or self-emptying. To put it differently, Jesus is the Anointed One, the Christ, who is moved and inspired by God Himself in order to show in deeds and words – where the deeds are indeed suited to the words – how God's royal majesty consists precisely in sloughing this majesty and in all humility identifying with the humiliated, the excluded, the injured, the imprisoned and all those delivered unto suffering and death.

6. *No Alienation*

Does not this heteronomous dedication, however, mean a negation or, stronger still, a destruction of the freedom of the one called, and thus of human dignity? It is not because calling, election and mission do not find their origin and meaning in free choice that the one called no longer possesses freedom in order to respond and in order to take up his calling as mission. Freedom is no longer first, but it is precisely evoked as the possibility "to respond" and via this response concretely authenticate the mission. The one called is no "slave" of the good. The attachment to the Good, not to be understood in the active sense ("I attach myself to ...") but in the passive sense as being attached to the Good ("I am being, or better still, I have been attached to ..."), is not coercion that negates freedom but a "being applied to the Good" that precisely evokes and invites freedom in order to take upon oneself and embody this movedness. The dedication to the Good "despite myself" never becomes real "without myself". Becoming heteronomously involved in an "impossible" mission precisely requires a response in order to become effective. Freedom no longer takes first place; it is no longer the principle and alpha of all, but yet it is not eliminated. On the contrary, it is wholly incorporated. In other words, the heteronomous movedness by the good, out of which ensues the "must" in doing the good, should not be understood as a naturally necessary must. If you hold a stone on high and you let go of it, then it must fall. This is an unavoidable, natural must, which is precisely the opposite of an ethical must. The "must" in responding to the call, the must in fulfilling the mission as the salvific concern for others, is an ethical must, out of which all necessity – in the sense of not being able to do otherwise – is absent. The one called must say yes to the mission entrusted to him or her, but he or she can say no. That is one's fundamental freedom, which in no way destroys the preceding bondedness to the Good but, on the contrary, endorses it.

This freedom, however, is also essentially the possibility of not fulfilling the mission as dedication to the Good, that is, to flee from it, or to do as if one has not heard or seen it, to withdraw in sleep, to relegate everything to someone else, to trivialise the mission, and so on.

This "withdrawing" hesitation and even attempts at escape can also be found in a number of prophetic narratives, which in their turn depict in an exemplary way the resistance of every human being to experiencing one's existence as an "impossible mission" towards the other than one-self. A number of prophets have resisted, just as we all do, the imposed mission and thus formulate all sorts of objections and diversions. As an illustration, we refer to Moses, the first and greatest prophet, who says: "Who am I that I should go to Pharaoh, and bring the Israelites out of Egypt ... But suppose they do not believe me or listen to me ... I have never been eloquent ... Please send someone else" (Exod 3,11; 4,1,10,13). Or Jeremiah: "... I am only a boy" (Jer 1,6). And Ezekiel: "I went in bitterness in the heat of my spirit, the hand of the Lord being strong upon me" (Ezek 3,14). The direct or indirect and veiled forms of refusal, hesitation or questioning essentially belong to the freedom of the one called. His or her freedom is a radically demanded, and yet not imposed freedom in order to take upon oneself the mission. And since the mission is essentially "impossible", i.e., it does not flow forth from the wishes and capacities of the one called, and thus does not take them into account, it is understandable that freedom feels attracted or "tempted" to push away the mission or "to make a wide detour around the mission", just as the priest and the Levite both did in the narrative of the Good Samaritan when confronted with the wounded person lying on the road, which breaks into their existence as an unforeseen calling and makes them responsible despite themselves for the suffering other (Luke 10)[7]. Naturally, this temptation should not be understood as a "natural cause" that destroys freedom; it is only a "circumstance" that does not make the free choice for the Good more self-evident and easy.

7. *Establishment of Creative Freedom*

Both the elements of doubt and critical questioning, as well as those of free endorsement and concrete fulfilment, can be found in the call narra-tive of Mary, although we can easily overlook them in our reading. To the announcement of her future motherhood, she does not simply answer in

7. Indeed, the narrative of the Good Samaritan can also be read as a call narrative in line with the prophetic idea of calling. The three travelers, the priest, the Levite and the Samaritan are, despite themselves – in spite of their personal life projects – called by the appearance of the other in need in order not to leave the other to his fate, meaning to say to be delivered unto suffering and death, but to take up responsibility for the other and per-form concrete care. The other appears here simply as an appeal or a calling, whereby inter-personal ethics appears to have a response structure as well. For lack of space in this paper, we cannot further develop these ideas here.

blind obedience with an unreflective or slavish yes, but she explicitly poses a critical question. She says to the angel: "How shall this be since I have no husband?" (Luke 1,34). She means that God asks of her something "impossible", God assigns her something that is not in line with her possibilities at present: "how can I become pregnant since I have had no relations with a man?". It is apparent from this how Mary is not a submissive "yes-person", who always acquiesces with what is asked of her with eyes shut and bowed back. She is an adult young woman who is aware of what "happens to her" and hence with wide-open eyes and her irreducible independence dares to ask for some clarification. The angel burdens her with a task that is, quite simply, not possible due to her "natural" or current possibilities. In this way, her critical question brings into focus again the heteronomous character of the call entrusted to her. Her mission does not arise from what Mary is or what is possible in her situation, but radically enters into her existence "from elsewhere" without making the call dependent on certain conditions that should have been fulfilled first. No pre-investigation or pre-selection has previously taken place for the most suitable candidate. On the contrary, we regularly note in the Bible that it is precisely the less capable and the least prepared who are chosen – against all logic – in order to fulfil an impossible, divine mission. For instance, Moses noted of himself, as we saw above, that he was unsuitable to argue for setting his people free from Egypt since he was a stammerer.

This "questioning" likewise means that her freedom is not eliminated. Mary's request for clarification means that she is not coerced, but that she can respond to the calling out of "herself". In that sense, her mission is not a coercion that negates or destroys her freedom. On the contrary, it is an appeal that addresses her freedom by means of a claim and at the same time leaves it be, not so much to be free to do whatsoever, but to be free in order to acquiesce to her calling. In this sense we can say that the call is a powerful performative word that transforms her into "another being", that she herself then, in full freedom, can appropriate and, in free surrender, can substantiate.

After her critical question, Mary says yes in full freedom to the mission that is entrusted to her "from elsewhere" – from God. Moreover, she does not simply say "yes": her yes is not a formal or merely verbal yes, but an incarnated obedience. That is why she says yes to the divine calling with her whole being, with her whole body. Only by making herself available in a full sense, including her body, can Mary really substantiate her mission to be the mother of Jesus. This, likewise, applies to every call: a mission that is accepted can only be realised when it is accomplished in a concrete, incarnated and earthly manner.

From this it is apparent how the "obligated" but "non-enforced" choice for the Good does involve freedom as a response in yet a different way, namely as the creative realisation of the mission, to which despite oneself one is dedicated "from elsewhere" – by the wholly Other and at the same time intimately Near One. The accomplishment of the impossible task requires the effort of all strengths, possibilities and capabilities which one has at one's disposal, and which one has acquired and developed in the "natural" care for oneself. Once again, freedom comes in second place, but this does not mean that it is unimportant. On the contrary, it is an utterly indispensable condition in order to give concrete form and shape to the entrusted mission, attuned to the circumstances of time and space. In the context of call and mission, autonomy has indeed become an "inspired" autonomy, and it can no longer proclaim itself as the *"Ein und Alles"* of meaning and action. However, autonomy is anything but trivialised or minimised. It is a called freedom, which belongs essentially to the mission just as the heteronomous origin and finality of the calling. Dedicated despite oneself to the other than oneself, but therein promoted to the unique possibility of making visible and tangible the heteronomous attachment to the Good in a unique, "brilliant" way. Thus inspired freedom should and can bear witness to the Good, to God Himself in this world.

IV. CONCLUSION: THE RESPONSIVE DYNAMISM OF ETHICS

From a reflexive, philosophical deepening of the fundamental biblical categories of covenant and prophetic calling, it has become clear how the relational understanding and experience of God has far-reaching consequences for the view of the human person and ethics. If God is thought of and experienced as both the personal and interpersonal Word, then human existence appears as a call, and ethics as a mission that not only belongs integrally to that call, but itself also acquires a relational meaning, both human as well as religious. By keeping the commandments (Torah) and taking up with full dedication the entrusted mission (for one's fellow humans and the world), the person not only establishes a covenant with God, but his or her existence and actions likewise acquire a "covenantal" significance. In themselves they become a relational event, in the sense that they are a way of entering into relationship with God and of unfolding this relationship as well. This implies at the same time that by means of this religious covenant relationship, human life and action also acquire an interpersonal character. Thanks to the calling by someone else, the person becomes a unique being that is at the same time made exceptional in this uniqueness without being locked up in oneself. By means of the heteronomous election, I become involved in the other than myself, and that gives to my uniqueness its responsorial and dialogical structure. By fulfilling the Law and by letting myself as the one called enter into the life of the other than myself, I do not only enter into a relationship with the others, but my being and actions likewise become a way of becoming "intimate" with God, the most Foreign of all and yet the most Near One. From the world, its circumstances and especially from the wounded and suffering other, His Word touches me whereby I am moved and sent, away from myself, in order to be His healing and salvation for every one who lies across my path and thus becomes my divine calling.

Faculteit Godgeleerdheid   Roger BURGGRAEVE, S.D.B.
K.U.Leuven
St.-Michielsstraat 6
B-3000 Leuven
Belgium

LA MÉTHODE SCIENTIFIQUE ET LA STRUCTURE
DE L'ACTE DE FOI

Le succès actuel des sciences masque une crise de la méthode scientifique qui n'est pas sans rapport avec la crise de la foi. En effet, historiquement, l'apparition de la méthode scientifique est, pour une part, redevable au travail de l'acte de foi chrétien au sein de la culture. En retour, ce dernier s'est développé comme une dynamique de vie marquée par la démarche critique de la raison. La crise des sciences tient au déplacement du sacré en relation avec la perte de vue du caractère révolutionnaire de l'acte de foi. En ce sens, la méthode scientifique et l'acte de foi constituent deux pôles anthropologiques en tension dialectique au service de l'homme.

I. L'EXPLOSION DU DÉVELOPPEMENT SCIENTIFIQUE AU XXE SIÈCLE

Le XIXe siècle fut le siècle de la montée en puissance des sciences associées à l'industrialisation des sociétés occidentales. Cette évolution fut telle que quelques-uns parmi les plus grands chercheurs de la fin de cet âge d'or de la foi en la science affirmaient qu'il ne restait presque rien à découvrir. Et pourtant, rétrospectivement, c'est le XXe siècle qui apparaît comme le siècle de l'explosion des découvertes scientifiques, découvertes aussi bien théoriques que pratiques.

Dans le monde de la physique, la relativité restreinte puis la relativité générale ont constitué la première grande révolution conceptuelle du siècle écoulé[1]. Elles ont mis en relation étroite les concepts newtoniens d'espace, de matière et de temps. Ce faisant, elles les ont transformés radicalement. Espace, matière et temps sont pensés désormais comme les paramètres d'une structure de l'univers obéissant à des lois particulières. Mais la surprise fut bien plus grande encore lorsqu'apparut la mécanique quantique[2]. Les concepts d'espace, de matière et de temps, même travaillés par la mécanique relativiste, ont volé en éclats. Dans ce

---

1. Leur découverte par Albert Einstein remonte respectivement à 1905 et 1915.
2. L'apparition de la mécanique quantique remonte à 1924.

nouveau cadre, la localisation n'est plus pensable qu'en terme de densité de présence. Un siècle plus tard, les conséquences philosophiques de tous ces bouleversements ne sont pas encore réellement prises en compte.

À ces découvertes en physique, il faut ajouter la révolution dans le champ des mathématiques et de la logique opérée par le théorème de Gödel. Au tournant du siècle, le problème des fondements des mathématiques fut posé par Hilbert sans qu'aucune solution ne lui fût apportée. C'est finalement le logicien Kurt Gödel qui mit un terme à la question en démontrant que «toutes les formulations axiomatiques consistantes de la théorie des nombres incluent des propositions indécidables»[3]. En d'autres termes, on ne peut pas déterminer tous les axiomes nécessaires pour fonder la théorie des nombres entiers. Ou encore, il existe, dans tout système se rapportant à la théorie des nombres entiers, des propositions dont on ne peut savoir si elles sont vraies ou fausses. La logique et les mathématiques ont ainsi assumé de l'intérieur des limites formelles.

Il n'est pas possible de parcourir le siècle sans mentionner les découvertes de la biologie. Celle-ci héritait de la théorie transformiste de Lamarck et de la théorie de la sélection naturelle de Darwin. Mais le tournant de la biologie s'est opéré grâce à la découverte de l'ADN qui en a modifié à jamais les perspectives[4]. L'étude des espèces vivantes comme celle de leur évolution n'a pas fini d'en porter les conséquences. Le séquençage du génome humain s'inscrit dans la logique de cette révolution. Les perspectives ouvertes par ce travail ne sont pas encore toutes soupçonnées[5]. À cela, il faut ajouter l'ouverture de l'immense chantier de l'étude du système cérébral.

Enfin, sans rechercher une quelconque exhaustivité, il n'est pas possible d'oublier l'ordinateur. Il apparaît au commun des mortels comme une prouesse technique. Mais il n'est pas que le produit des avancées technologiques, il est surtout le résultat des découvertes de la logique[6]. La révolution en cours est celle de la numérisation croissante de modèles

---

3. D. HOFSTADTER, *Gödel, Escher, Bach – Les brins d'une guirlande éternelle*, trad. J. HENRY et R. FRENCH, Paris, InterÉditions, 1986 [*Gödel, Escher, Bach: an Eternal Golden Braid*, New York, Basic Books, 1979], p. 19. La démonstration du théorème remonte à 1931.

4. La découverte de l'ADN par Grick et Watson remonte à 1953.

5. Le débat sur la grammaire universelle innée de Noam Chomsky vient d'être relancé par la découverte de gènes qui joueraient un rôle précis dans la structuration de la zone langagière du cerveau par Anthony Monaco (Oxford, 2001).

6. Alan Turing et John von Neumann ont bouleversé la notion d'intelligence en proposant la numérisation de fonctions intellectuelles et leur implémentation sur un support quelconque.

sensés reproduire des actes humains. Sans ces capacités nouvelles qui se présentent comme des prothèses de l'intelligence humaine, la recherche scientifique ne pourrait développer les programmes qui font les sciences d'aujourd'hui.

Ces succès sont devenus une réalité palpable pour tous les habitants du monde. Il n'est bientôt plus une zone de la planète qui ne connaisse l'électricité ou la mise en relation de ses habitants grâce aux ondes électromagnétiques. C'est la nouveauté du XXᵉ siècle. La science est sortie définitivement de ses laboratoires pour entrer dans la vie quotidienne. Le succès de la science est manifeste à travers sa performativité technique.

Appelée technoscience, cette association de la recherche scientifique et des réalisations technologiques est une approche nouvelle de la réalité scientifique elle-même. Jusqu'alors, XIXᵉ siècle y compris, une science pure pouvait s'élaborer en laboratoire. Dans un second temps, apparaissait la question de ses applications technologiques. La science se distinguait de ce qu'elle permettait. Et réciproquement, on pouvait réfléchir aux applications techniques sans que la recherche s'en trouve affectée. Or la situation actuelle a provoqué un bouleversement de cette vision. La recherche reste pour une part à l'origine des applications technologiques. Mais pour une autre part, elle en dépend. Les recherches contemporaines en physique comme en biologie n'ont fait des bonds en avant extraordinaires durant les deux dernières décennies que grâce aux capacités techniques des machines qu'elles utilisent. Une véritable imbrication des développements de la recherche et des évolutions technologiques est la nouvelle donne de la recherche scientifique.

En cela, la technoscience manifeste le succès des sciences comme jamais jusqu'à maintenant. Ce qui pourrait apparaître comme un cri de victoire positiviste et scientiste est largement atténué par un nombre importants d'effets pervers de cette même technoscience. Le premier ébranlement spectaculaire s'est produit avec l'utilisation de l'armement atomique. Son effet fut de pointer que l'utilisation des technologies et l'orientation des crédits de la recherche pouvaient servir des intérêts politiques. Ce fut alors avec terreur qu'on découvrit comment le régime nazie s'était asservi la recherche scientifique et l'avait pervertie. Dès lors, la science avait perdu son *aura* scientiste de pure servante du progrès de l'humanité en marche vers le bonheur. À cela, s'est ajoutée la prise de conscience de la crise écologique provoquée, pour une part, par les technologies destinées au service du monde économique. Et depuis deux décennies, les découvertes dans le domaine du génie génétique ne laissent pas d'inquiéter compte tenu des dérives dont elles peuvent faire l'objet.

Un autre effet important de cette évolution touche la méthode scientifique elle-même. En effet, la conjugaison du développement de la technoscience et de ses effets pervers a occulté le fondement des sciences modernes. Le succès actuel des sciences n'est plus lisible pour le grand public en tant que fruit d'une méthode. Il apparaît souvent comme le produit d'une puissance technologique et économique, la preuve en étant apparemment fournie par les effets pervers. Or cette occultation de la méthode a des effets extrêmement importants en termes d'épistémologie et d'anthropologie.

II. L'AVENIR DE LA MÉTHODE SCIENTIFIQUE

Cette occultation de la méthode scientifique possède trois origines: la puissance des technosciences, les effets pervers du développement scientifique et la recherche épistémologique. Les deux premières, pour importantes qu'elles soient, ne sont qu'une des facettes de la critique de la rationalité moderne. La puissance des technosciences est l'effet combiné de la recherche, des choix politiques et du lien que la science entretient avec les puissances économiques[7]. La force de la critique venant des épistémologues eux-mêmes est bien plus radicale. Elle pose la question fondamentale de la valeur de la méthode.

Dans le contexte contemporain, certains épistémologues se sont penchés sur l'histoire des sciences et sur la sociologie du milieu des chercheurs[8]. Ils en viennent à nier qu'existe une méthode scientifique. Paul Feyerabend n'hésite pas à affirmer que «la science est une entreprise essentiellement anarchiste»[9]. Pour étayer cette assertion, il s'appuie sur une histoire des sciences, créatrice, indépendamment de l'application d'une quelconque méthode. Il suggère même que toute idée de méthode ne peut qu'être un frein à la découverte scientifique. L'intérêt de sa position est de finir de dégager la science d'une conception dirigiste qui s'était

---

7. L'orientation des crédits de recherche et le poids des sociétés multinationales constituent un facteur majeur de la constitution de la figure actuelle des technosciences. L'idéologie de cette évolution avait déjà été analysée par l'école de Francfort.

8. Deux figures de cette recherche sont intéressantes: Paul Feyerabend qui propose une critique radicale de la notion même de méthode (cf. P. FEYERABEND, *Contre la méthode. Esquisse d'une théorie anarchiste de la connaissance* [«Science ouverte»], Paris, Éd. du Seuil, 1979 [*Against Method*, London, New Left Books, 1975]) et Bruno Latour qui fonde son épistémologie sur la sociologie (cf. B. LATOUR – S. WOOLGAR, *Laboratory Life. The Construction of Scientific Facts*, Princeton, NJ, Princeton University Press, 1986 [*La vie de laboratoire*, Paris, Éd. de La Découverte, 1988]).

9. FEYERABEND, *Contre la méthode* (n. 8), p. 13.

imposée avec les notions de plans de recherche et avec les cadres institutionnels de la recherche. Néanmoins, plus qu'un apport sur la question de la méthode, il s'agit plutôt d'un constat d'ensemble qui ne remet pas en cause les éléments nécessaires au développement scientifique. Paul Feyerabend entre en débat avec d'autres épistémologues qui avaient dégagé la structure de la méthode mise en œuvre. Leur figure de proue est Karl Popper qui a dégagé une histoire formelle des théories[10]. Loin d'être une négation de l'histoire réelle, l'histoire formelle sert la recherche qui doit se donner un protocole rigoureux sans lequel la notion même de science moderne s'écroule.

Analysant le concept de théorie, Karl Popper désigne celle-ci métaphoriquement comme «un filet destiné à capturer «le monde»; à le rendre plus rationnel, l'expliquer et le maîtriser [filet dont] nous nous efforçons de resserrer de plus en plus les mailles»[11]. La théorie est un système symbolique, au sens logico-mathématique en rapport d'homologie avec une réalité découpée. Elle permet de construire des expériences reproductibles par quiconque et de recueillir les donnés fournies par les instruments de mesure. Deux hypothèses se présentent: soit les résultats s'inscrivent sans difficulté dans la théorie (ils n'apportent pas d'informations substantiellement nouvelles pour la théorie), soit ils ne s'inscrivent pas dans la théorie. Dans ce dernier cas, soit la théorie est amendée pour intégrer les résultats, soit elle ne peut pas les intégrer. Il s'agit alors d'une véritable information concernant la théorie. Celle-ci est falsifiée. Elle doit être remise en cause. Mais dans l'attente d'une théorie meilleure pouvant intégrer la précédente ainsi que les nouveaux résultats, elle sera conservée. Parallèlement, la recherche d'une théorie nouvelle va se développer.

Ainsi, la méthode scientifique est fondée sur une approche de la réalité extrêmement modeste. La réalité est découpée selon le décryptage que peut en fournir une théorie[12]. Une théorie est un outil heuristique qui permet de monter des expériences, c'est-à-dire de confronter des hypothèses avec la réalité analysée. Lorsque l'expérience réussit, l'information sur l'hypothèse est nulle: celle-ci n'est pas remise en cause. Le progrès a lieu lorsqu'une hypothèse est rejetée au vu des résultats de l'expérience.

10. K.R. POPPER, La logique de la découverte scientifique, trad. N. THYSSEN-RUTTEN – P. DEVAUX («Bibliothèque scientifique»), Paris, Éd. Payot, 1984 (1973) [Logik der Forschung, Vienne, 1935; The Logic of Scientific Discovery, London, 1959, 1968]. Karl Popper doit beaucoup au scientifique, épistémologue et historien des sciences français, Pierre Duhem (1861-1916).
11. POPPER, La logique (n. 10), p. 57.
12. Ce découpage est à penser selon des dimensions du réel qui puissent satisfaire à des critères d'universalité. Il ne s'agit pas du simple découpage d'un secteur arbitraire de la réalité.

Cette possibilité de falsifier l'hypothèse est le cœur de la démarche scientifique. En ce sens, les hypothèses restent du côté de l'heuristique. Considérées comme hypothèses herméneutiques, elles doivent être indexées par un coefficient de caducité dont l'importance dépend du degré de résistance de la théorie dans sa confrontation avec le réel[13]. Le progrès de la connaissance scientifique procède négativement. La science sait ce qu'elle ignore, elle pose des hypothèses d'interprétation des phénomènes et reste en deçà d'une éventuelle connaissance métaphysique du monde.

Dès lors, les critiques visant la méthode scientifique ne peuvent satisfaire le chercheur qui connaît les limites de son savoir. Elles touchent davantage la version positiviste du développement scientifique que son fonctionnement théorique réel. D'ailleurs, la critique de la science triomphante possède la structure de la méthode scientifique elle-même. Ce qui est visé est donc bien une philosophie qui déborde largement le champ des sciences. Cette philosophie de facture scientiste est l'instrument idéologique des puissances financières dont l'intérêt n'est pas la recherche fondamentale[14]. Lorsque cette critique s'étend à la méthode elle-même, l'enjeu est bien plus grave. Il faudrait rechercher qui a intérêt à cette remise en cause de la méthode. Qui, sous couvert de recherche d'une nouvelle sagesse pour le monde, ou de mise en lumière de la valeur des sagesses traditionnelles[15], a intérêt à nier la valeur de la démarche critique de la raison? En aucune manière, il ne s'agit de dénier aux sagesses traditionnelles leur valeur éthique et spirituelle. Mais il est nécessaire de critiquer une acceptation naïve de ces sagesses pour le seul motif qu'elles seraient traditionnelles[16]. L'un des acquis de la modernité est le recueillement critique de la tradition. Plutôt que d'un retour à un supposé âge d'or disparu, ne vaudrait-il pas mieux en extraire les valeurs dans une acceptation critique fondée sur une démarche rationnelle? Jusqu'alors, seule la méthode scientifique a permis de tracer des frontières plus claires entre une connaissance éprouvée et un pseudo-savoir dont la seule garantie de véracité était l'ancienneté.

---

13. Le caractère falsifiable d'une théorie en exprime la scientificité. Parce que le marxisme comme la psychanalyse sont des théories holistiques dépourvues de ce caractère, K. Popper leur dénie toute qualification scientifique.

14. Il suffit de connaître les difficultés financières de la recherche en mathématique pure pour s'en convaincre.

15. Ces sagesses peuvent être extraites du patrimoine littéraire de l'humanité. Mais ce sont aussi des sagesses reconstruites qui sont convoquées (cf. les cultures africaines ou amérindiennes).

16. Ce phénomène peut s'expliquer comme une manifestation du complexe culturel engendré par la négation de la valeur cognitive des autres cultures à l'époque du positivisme triomphant.

Touchant ainsi au problème de la connaissance du monde par l'homme, cette question épistémologique est en réalité une question anthropologique. Le premier point soulevé est celui de la place allouée aux connaissances scientifiques dans la démarche de connaissance de l'homme. Le second point qu'il faut mettre en exergue est celui de la vérité. Une affirmation, un système d'interprétation sont des prises de paroles provisoires au service d'une dynamique de recherche de la vérité, ceci en confrontation avec le réel[17]. Le monde humain est autant un monde construit qu'un monde reçu. Le degré d'opérativité de l'homme en situation dépend directement du degré d'homologie de sa théorie du monde avec la réalité qu'il rencontre.

III. L'ÉMERGENCE DE LA RATIONALITÉ SCIENTIFIQUE

Sans vouloir reprendre toute l'histoire de la raison occidentale au cours de laquelle est apparue la rationalité scientifique, il est important d'en relever deux moments fondateurs. Le premier moment est celui de la raison grecque. L'apparition de la philosophie et le développement de la science grecque fondent l'histoire de la pensée occidentale. Cette pensée se présente selon deux modalités qui se sont nourries l'une l'autre: le désir de connaissance de la nature et la recherche des principes au-delà de l'étude de la nature. Ce schéma hérité d'Aristote[18] a structuré toute la pensée occidentale. Cet héritage fut pour la Renaissance le point d'appui pour un bond en avant de la pensée. Cet héritage digéré par le christianisme a été la source d'un nouveau développement que celui-ci a permis.

En effet, les concepts centraux de la foi chrétienne sont entrés en rapport dialectique avec la raison venant de l'Antiquité. Deux d'entre eux ont joué un rôle déterminant dans l'évolution de la raison: celui de Dieu créateur et celui d'Incarnation. Le concept de Dieu créateur fut de toute première importance pour mettre un terme à la sacralisation du monde, à l'indistinction entre le monde des humains et le monde des dieux. Ainsi, selon l'interprétation classique de Gen 1, le principe du monde n'est pas en lui. Ce principe existe et est totalement distinct du monde. De plus, l'homme de Gen 1 est pensé comme le maître et le responsable de la nature dans laquelle il évolue. Cette transcendance de l'homme dans son univers matériel est fondée sur la transcendance divine de laquelle il tire

---

17. Cette approche traditionnelle de la vérité comme adéquation de la parole avec la chose reste pertinente pour embrayer la réflexion.
18. La structure de l'œuvre d'Aristote en *Physique* et en *Métaphysique* est celle qui, encore aujourd'hui, permet de comprendre les débats épistémologiques contemporains.

toute légitimité pour agir comme il l'entend dans le monde: il en est l'image. Il peut donc aussi étudier cet univers duquel tout sacré a été extirpé.

Le concept d'Incarnation a joué un rôle plus subtil. Il est venu appuyer la positivité du monde créé. Dieu qui a voulu le monde, le juge bon. Il lui donne ainsi une consistance et en fait une source d'intérêt pour l'homme. L'Incarnation amplifie cette attitude de Dieu par rapport au monde créé. Si le monde a eu le privilège d'accueillir son créateur, c'est qu'il mérite d'être pris en compte pour lui-même. Comment alors ne pas porter intérêt à ce qui intéresse au plus haut point le créateur lui-même? La grande différence est ainsi établie entre cette position et la position gnostique. Dans ce dernier cas, l'intérêt porté au monde ne peut qu'être un frein sur la route qui conduit à Dieu puisque le monde est lesté de négativité. Ainsi, avec l'affirmation chrétienne tenant ensemble la désacralisation du monde et sa positivité, la voie était ouverte pour le développement de la recherche scientifique.

Associée au travail de ces concepts sur la vision du monde, la foi confessée par le chrétien a joué un rôle essentiel dans le façonnement de la raison. La foi a rencontré l'avènement d'une rationalité qui s'affrontait à la connaissance de l'univers avec ses instruments propres. Quelques siècles plus tôt, Thomas d'Aquin avait posé les bases d'une articulation de la foi et de la raison. Il avait montré que cette dernière était apte à déployer toutes ses virtualités dans son champ propre. Dès lors, la foi et la raison fonctionnaient comme deux principes de connaissance. La première est la seule à permettre l'accès à une connaissance appartenant à l'ordre de la révélation. La seconde a toute légitimité pour explorer ce qui relève de l'ordre de la création. Elle peut même aller à la limite que constitue l'affirmation de l'existence de Dieu[19]. Il ne faut pas sous-estimer cette préparation intellectuelle lorsqu'apparaît le conflit autour de Galilée. Le conflit relève de l'absence de cohérence entre la logique institutionnelle et la logique intellectuelle qui travaillait les esprits en profondeur.

Cette logique intellectuelle était le fruit de la rencontre entre l'esprit grec et la dynamique existentielle instaurée par la foi chrétienne. La foi est l'acte de confiance radicale en Dieu manifesté efficacement comme sauveur en Jésus-Christ. Elle constitue le fondement de la vie humaine parce qu'elle s'enracine dans l'expérience pascale. Elle est l'entrée dans la Pâque même de Jésus. Celle-ci fournit la structure de cet acte de foi. Les commentaires de Paul sur l'indissociabilité de l'expérience du croyant et de celle de Jésus montrent comment le passage de la mort à la vie

---

19. Cette position sera celle de Vatican I dans *Dei Filius*.

(*Rm* 6), l'abandon du vieil homme au profit de l'homme nouveau (*Rm* 8) manifestent l'œuvre de l'Esprit au cœur du croyant. Cette œuvre de l'Esprit concerne la raison, caractéristique de l'homme. Elle installe au cœur du fonctionnement de la raison une dynamique qui ne s'y trouvait pas forcément. Elle offre même à la raison une autorité qu'elle n'a plus besoin d'aller chercher dans la tradition[20].

Finalement, c'est dans l'acte de foi que s'enracine la possibilité d'une rationalité critique forte. L'acte de foi suppose l'écart entre Dieu et l'homme pour une relation d'alliance. Cet écart permet la relation entre les deux partenaires et fonde l'autonomie de l'homme. La foi, comme confiance radicale en Dieu qui sauve, libère l'homme de tout envahissement de sa vie par l'angoisse du salut et de sa quête[21]. La foi, comme acte de confiance, redonne consistance à la raison en la libérant d'une quête de salut de type gnostique et en installant en son cœur l'autorité qu'elle tire de la dynamique de la résurrection. Par le fait même, elle lui permet de se déployer pour une quête plus gratuite. La foi, comme acte de confiance, permet d'approcher le monde sans crainte. Le fondement de la positivité du monde réside dans l'assurance que Dieu en se donnant à lui le valorise d'une manière maximale.

Ainsi la foi a permis à la raison d'assumer l'héritage grec pour ouvrir un nouveau chemin de connaissance. Dès lors, elle est entrée de plus en plus fortement en relation dialectique avec la raison. Elle a nourri cette dernière en l'ouvrant au monde, en la libérant de la question de ses fondements. En fécondant la raison, la foi a aussi bénéficié de la transformation de la rationalité.

IV. La foi comme dynamique existentielle

Le heurt frontal des sciences avec l'Église ne met pas en cause l'articulation fondamentale entre la foi et la raison. Le cas Galilée est avant tout le choc entre une première mise en forme des sciences de la nature trouvant son autorité dans la raison mettant à l'épreuve un réel qui résiste, et une conception totalisante du monde. Le nouveau rapport à la réalité, défendu par Galilée, mettait en cause l'autorité de l'Église arc-boutée sur la vision du monde et la métaphysique d'Aristote et une lecture non critiquée des Écritures. Il n'était donc pas question de la foi en tant que telle

20. La modernité est caractérisée par le déplacement de l'autorité de la tradition et des puissances établies en direction de la raison individuelle et collective.
21. Cette problématique que Luther a fait éclater au grand jour est bien présente dans les Écritures.

mais bien plutôt de l'autorité. Le conflit a porté sur l'instance qui a autorité: la raison ou l'Église comme institution. Fondamentalement, la question avait été résolue par Thomas d'Aquin, mais les résistances institu-
tionnelles prévalaient encore[22]. Le problème était plus politique que
doctrinal. Le même type de fonctionnement a dominé la querelle virulente
autour de l'évolution. En l'occurrence, le statut des différents types de
récits bibliques et le rôle des représentations théologiques étaient en cause.

Dans cette controverse difficile, l'acte de foi s'est trouvé en première
ligne. Deux grands types d'attitudes sont apparus. Le premier rassemble
toutes les tentations fidéistes. Ces attitudes ont touché un certain nombre
de croyants. Pour ceux-ci, compte tenu de la difficulté de l'articulation
de la foi et de la raison, un fonctionnement rationnel spécifique a été
promu pour penser la foi. Il était fait d'une autorité incontestée, recon-
nue soit à l'institution (pour la version catholique), soit aux Écritures
(pour la version protestante), parce qu'elle exprimait parfaitement la
volonté de Dieu[23]. Ils se fondaient sur le fait que ces autorités relevaient
d'une approche rationnelle spécifique légitime, car Dieu est de l'ordre du
mystère. Cette approche schizophrénique n'a pas renforcé l'acte de foi sur
le long terme. Elle l'a plutôt fragilisé en le cantonnant dans un registre
non rationnel.

L'autre type d'attitudes rassemble tous ceux qui refusent de s'en tenir
à la surface de la confrontation. S'inscrivant dans la longue tradition
représentée en particulier par les pères orientaux, des croyants ont fait le
pari qu'une structure anthropologique unique doit prévaloir lorsqu'il s'agit
d'aborder une réalité quelle qu'elle soit. La raison humaine est une parce
que c'est le même homme qui est créature de Dieu et qui est appelé à la
vie éternelle. Il y va du respect de l'homme comme unité rationnelle[24].
Dès lors, la démarche critique fondée sur le rapport au réel retrouvait sa
place dans l'acte de foi. La confiance radicale de l'homme en Dieu est
apte à porter la démarche rationnelle la plus exigeante, telle qu'elle
s'exprime dans le protocole de l'expérimentation scientifique.

La théorie scientifique trouve son homologue chez le croyant dans
l'articulation rationnelle du récit de sa vie comme cadre d'interprétation.

---

22. La controverse pouvait s'installer dès lors que deux lectures de Thomas d'Aquin
sont possibles: l'une porteuse d'avenir, qui concerne l'articulation de la foi et de la raison
à reprendre selon les contextes; l'autre qui était sa mise en application avec les matériaux
de l'époque et une vision du monde figée.

23. Il faudrait croiser ces sources d'autorité avec une autre: l'émotion. Elle a joué un
rôle important dans l'apparition des courants piétistes coulés dans les réactions de la société
face à la rationalité moderne.

24. La solution thomiste de l'âme spirituelle pour désigner cette unité avait été mise à
mal par le dualisme cartésien.

L'objectivité de la relation du croyant avec Dieu n'est pas du même type que celle qui régit les phénomènes. Elle n'est pas non plus de l'ordre d'une subjectivité enfermée sur elle-même, d'une subjectivité réduite à l'imaginaire. Pour comprendre sa propre vie sous le regard salvifique de Dieu, le croyant est conduit à élaborer un cadre d'interprétation qui lui permette d'agir en ce monde. Ce cadre est construit au carrefour de son propre itinéraire, de l'écoute de la Parole faite chair, grâce aux Écritures et de sa relation avec la communauté de ceux qui, comme lui, sont à l'écoute de la Parole. Ainsi, le croyant élabore pour lui-même un système de représentations et de valeurs qui lui permet de trouver une position d'équilibre et une posture opératoire dans le monde.

Si ce système est pour le croyant un enfermement dans une conception du monde intangible, il se sclérose. Mais si cette vision du monde qu'il se donne est sans cesse remise en question par la confrontation avec la Parole et la réalité de la rencontre de l'autre, figure du Christ qui vient, elle joue un rôle essentiel d'équilibre pour la conduite de la vie. Elle est alors au service de la dynamique pascale de l'existence chrétienne. La vision du monde que le croyant s'est donnée peut être remise en chantier sans qu'il soit déstabilisé si la distinction entre la confiance radicale en Dieu et l'expression qu'elle prend est bien faite. La représentation doit sans cesse être critiquée pour que la dynamique de vie qu'inaugure l'acte de foi puisse se déployer. Le réel auquel se confronte le croyant est celui de sa vie concrète et de la Parole. Ce réel qui sans cesse résiste le provoque à mettre sur pied de nouvelles hypothèses interprétatives. En tant qu'hypothèses, ces interprétations permettent au croyant d'une part de se positionner dans le monde et d'autre part d'explorer le mystère de Dieu.

En transposant le caractère négatif des connaissances scientifiques à la recherche spirituelle, se trouve clairement maintenue la distinction entre le champ des représentations religieuses et la réalité de Dieu. Cet écart est structurellement le même que celui qui sépare le phénomène de la réalité dont il est le phénomène[25]. Le croyant s'inscrit ainsi dans la grande tradition apophatique qui, tout en s'appuyant sur la Parole faite chair, a toujours dénié au discours la capacité de définir Dieu lui-même. Cette attitude n'est pas purement une prise de position épistémologique. Elle constitue aussi la structure anthropologique nécessaire à une conception de l'acte de foi comme dynamique de vie. Elle est à la base de la structure rationnelle du croyant, configuré au Christ en son existence pascale.

---

25. La question du rapport du phénomène avec le noumène dans la perspective kantienne est laissée de côté ici. Du point théologique, il faut veiller à une articulation sans laquelle la notion d'Incarnation serait tirée du côté du docétisme.

Du côté de l'homme, c'est la seule issue qui lui soit offerte. Elle lui permet de se tenir en éveil et fait de lui un être vivant. L'éveil est stimulé par le fait qu'aucune hypothèse interprétative ne constitue la vérité. Elle constitue seulement la meilleure mise en forme rationnelle du récit de sa propre vie. Cette solution fait aussi de l'homme un être de questionnement qui, sans cesse, invente des solutions aux problèmes qu'il rencontre et dépasse les questions qu'il se pose par de nouvelles questions[26]. Le fondement dans l'acte de foi de la possibilité d'entrer sans cesse dans un nouveau questionnement offre un statut nouveau d'être vivant à l'homme. La foi retrouve son caractère de source de vie chez celui qui domine les interprétations successives qu'il fait de sa propre vie en référence au Christ par des dépassements sans cesse renouvelés.

V. LA CRISE DES SCIENCES ET LA CRISE DE LA FOI

Il peut paraître étonnant de mettre en relation la crise que traversent les sciences contemporaines et la crise de la foi dans le monde moderne. Or l'anthropologie sous-jacente à l'épistémologie des sciences en relation étroite avec l'anthropologie nécessaire pour penser l'acte de foi justifie ce rapprochement.

La crise des sciences trouve son caractère le plus radical dans la remise en cause de la méthode scientifique elle-même. Elle constitue un problème philosophique de premier ordre relevé par Husserl: «Cette expression, qu'on entend aujourd'hui partout, n'est-elle pas outrancière? Car la crise d'une science, cela signifie rien de moins que le fait que sa scientificité authentique – ou encore la façon même dont elle a défini ses tâches et élaboré en conséquence sa méthodologie – est devenue douteuse»[27]. Husserl fait porter la question sur des points importants de méthode: la place des mathématiques, le dualisme cartésien (l'esprit, sujet de la connaissance, et l'étendue soumise à la description mathématique), la négation de la vie nécessaire pour faire de la science[28], le sujet de la connaissance. Il n'est pas sûr que l'ouverture philosophique que

---

26. Cette démarche typiquement philosophique, caractéristique de l'homme, est ainsi pleinement assumée par le croyant.

27. E. HUSSERL, *La crise des sciences européennes et la phénoménologie transcendantale*, trad. G. GRANEL («Tel», 151), Paris, Gallimard, 1993 (1976) [*Die Krisis der europäischen Wissenschaften und die transzendentale Phaenomenologie*, Husserl-Archief te Leuven and La Haye, Martinus Nijhoff, 1954], p. 7 (texte publié pour la première fois à Belgrade en 1936).

28. Cette question apparaît au cœur de l'épistémologie de la biologie.

propose Husserl pour résoudre cette difficulté épistémologique réponde à la question. Elle a le mérite de situer les sciences dans une conception beaucoup plus vaste de la connaissance. Elle permet, en particulier, de sortir du scientisme. Mais il n'est pas sûr qu'elle apporte des éléments nouveaux quant à l'épistémologie propre aux sciences.

Ce courant philosophique contribuant à lutter contre le scientisme a été exploité, malgré lui, par les défenseurs de pseudo-savoirs rejetant toute analyse rationnelle de la réalité. On trouve même un certain retour à une conception magique du rapport de l'homme au monde. L'existence des croyances, mise en relief par l'anthropologie, encourage certains à vanter le retour à l'asservissement de la raison à la nature re-sacralisée. Les plus radicaux remettent en cause toute possibilité de la modernité de résoudre ses propres difficultés. Ils en appellent à un retour à une situation typiquement pré-moderne de la raison. Ils prennent bien soin également de ne pas en analyser toutes les conséquences. Cette question est bien anthropologique. Mais elle est également théologique.

Le passage d'une raison fonctionnant uniquement sur la base d'une confiance en une autorité extérieure à elle-même à une raison s'affrontant au réel s'est opéré grâce à la libération de la raison de toute autorité autre que celle du Christ donnée dans l'acte de foi. Le retour à une raison qui sacraliserait le monde et nierait sa propre capacité à la rigueur de l'affrontement avec la réalité serait le signe d'un déni de libération de la raison. La libération s'était opérée par la séparation entre Dieu et sa créature et par l'assurance que la raison trouvait son fondement dans une confiance radicale en son salut, la libérant par le fait même de l'épreuve épuisante de se sauver par elle-même. La crise est théologique dans la mesure où l'on change de paradigme religieux en re-sacralisant le monde et en affaiblissant la foi dans le salut déjà acquis en Jésus-Christ.

La crise de la foi sous-jacente à la crise de la rationalité scientifique ne se manifeste pas tant par la sécularisation que par le «retour du religieux» souvent repéré dans les sociétés occidentales. En effet, la sécularisation entretient un rapport étroit avec la désacralisation du monde opérée par l'acte de foi. En ce sens, elle possède une positivité qu'aucune autre société humaine n'a autant développée que les sociétés marquées par le christianisme. Dans ce monde sécularisé, les Églises n'ont pas encore terminé de rebâtir leur structure symbolique. Elles sont restées à mi-chemin entre une conception qui en fait des religions, re-sacralisant du même coup le monde. Dans ce contexte, le retour du religieux est bien plus le symptôme d'un besoin de sacré destiné à compenser l'ébranlement qu'a subi l'acte de foi. Il risque souvent de fermer le chemin de la foi plus que de l'ouvrir. En particulier, en liant l'individu, il ne le libère pas; en mêlant Dieu au monde, il ne libère pas l'homme du monde; en figeant la recherche sur un moment, il n'ouvre pas à la transcendance radicale caractéristique du christianisme.

La crise de la foi se manifeste donc par ces difficultés de l'homme à se situer dans le monde. Elle apparaît dans la faiblesse de la confiance que l'homme accorde à la raison. Aussi étrange que cela puisse paraître, l'affaiblissement de la vigueur rationnelle n'est plus le signe de la force de la foi qu'a voulu y voir trop souvent le christianisme. Au contraire, il est le symptôme d'une raison qui n'est plus travaillée par la dynamique pascale.

VI. LE DESTIN COMMUN DE LA RATIONALITÉ SCIENTIFIQUE ET DE L'ACTE DE FOI

Rien n'autorise à ramener la rationalité scientifique à l'acte de foi et réciproquement. Mais tout permet de soutenir qu'une dialectique féconde les lie. L'acte de foi a joué un rôle dans l'avènement de la rationalité scientifique. Et en retour il a été fortifié comme dynamique de vie par la rigueur de la rationalité scientifique. La situation contemporaine de crise de ces deux réalités a des racines anthropologiques communes. Le service que le christianisme peut rendre à la raison humaine est de l'alerter sur les principes théologiques en cause dans cette crise.

Poser ainsi la question, c'est la poser d'abord dans un cadre philosophique. En première approximation, le théologique désignera le discours sur le divin et le sacré. Et la question philosophique qui se pose peut s'énoncer ainsi: Y a-t-il divers types de sacré dans le monde et où sont-ils situés? Dans la mesure où le sacré envahit complètement le monde, la liberté de l'homme en quête de connaissance se trouve mise à mal. L'homme retrouve la situation de ses ancêtres en perpétuelle lutte contre des forces qu'il ne domine pas, sans certitude de remporter la victoire. C'est aussi la porte ouverte à diverses attitudes révérencieuses vis-à-vis du monde qui peuvent conduire à ce que la tradition chrétienne a désigné comme idolâtries. Et d'autre part, la distinction épistémologique entre réalité et imaginaire perd de sa pertinence. Dans ces conditions, la méthode scientifique reposant sur la confrontation d'un langage avec le réel perd également de sa pertinence. Si le sacré s'écarte de ce monde, en dehors du champ de la foi chrétienne, il n'a pas de lieu d'assignation précis. Il peut être radicalement évacué comme il peut être attaché à une réalité quelconque. Ainsi, par exemple, les partisans de l'égalité radicale entre l'homme et les animaux ont attaché le sacré à l'ensemble du monde vivant.

Poser la question dans le champ de la théologie chrétienne, c'est s'interroger sur le rôle de l'acte de foi dans la structuration de la raison humaine en quête de connaissance. Or l'acte de foi permettant une assignation du sacré hors du monde et reconnaissant comme sa seule figure, l'homme dans sa concrétude libère la raison pour son exploration du monde. Dénier tout sacré au monde et en reconnaître une figure dans l'homme ne conduit pas nécessairement à l'exploitation de la nature dénoncée par certains comme étant spécifiquement chrétienne. En effet, la désacralisation s'accompagne d'une anthropologie caractérisée par la responsabilité.

Réciproquement, le salut de la méthode scientifique pèse de tout son poids dans la structuration de l'acte de foi. La fascination pour le sacré n'est pas un chemin de foi puisqu'elle enclôt la raison dans un système symbolique ne permettant pas l'apparition d'une dynamique de vie. La méthode scientifique par son appel à la rigueur de la démarche et sa confrontation au réel est une école de la raison dans sa quête d'identité. La recherche même de Dieu ne craint ni la rigueur, ni l'affrontement au réel.

Dans une dialectique forte, la méthode scientifique comme école de la raison et l'acte de foi comme dynamique de vie ont un destin commun. Rien n'autorise à les opposer. Tout conduit à les garder en tension dialectique afin de féconder la recherche humaine contemporaine.

7, place Saint Irenee   Bernard MICHOLLET
F – 69005 Lyon
France

FUNDAMENTAL THEOLOGY
AND CLINICAL GENETICS IN CONVERSATION

I. INTRODUCTION

A recent study from the United States shows that people who go to church regularly live longer than those who do not[1]. In 2001 the results of a masked random sample showed the positive influence of prayer on the success of *in vitro* fertilisation and embryo transfer[2]. Faith seems to be a key to good (reproductive) health. At first glance, the relationship between health and genetic health on the one hand, and religion, faith, theology on the other hand seems to be clear. A closer look however demonstrates that conversation between fundamental theology and genetic research is not very well developed. In this chapter we want to explore this relationship, after having presented briefly the worldwide human genome enterprise. In a last section we will elaborate new ways to enhance the mutual exchange between theology and genetics.

II. THE HUMAN GENOME PROJECTS

The concerted effort in the biological and political communities to map and sequence all the DNA that comprises the human genome has come to be known popularly as the Human Genome Project. As the Human Genome Project continues to progress, the complex issue of how the knowledge derived from this research should be used becomes increasingly pertinent. In fact, one cannot speak about *the* Human Genome Project[3]. The Human Genome Project is in reality a two-tiered entity comprised of scientific and political levels and made up of at least three

---

1. *The NHS as a Theological Institution. The Ideal Remains Strong, but the Practice too has to Measure up*, in *British Medical Journal* 319 (1999) 1588-1589.

2. K.Y. CHA – D.P. WIRTH – R.A. LOBO, *Does Prayer Influence the Success of in Vitro Fertilization Embryo Transfer? Report of a Masked, Randomized Trial*, in *Reproductive Medicine* 46 (2001) 781-787.

3. R. BENSON, *Unwinding the Double Helix. The Ethical and Theological Implications of the Human Genome Projects: A Moral Analysis for a Personalist and Interdisciplinary Perspective*, Ph.D. Thesis, Leuven, 1993, p. 112.

distinct enterprises. First, there are the human genome *initiatives*. Under this umbrella are all those scientific endeavours that were previous to and contemporaneous with human genome projects and include studies that are of or can be related to human genome analysis. Second, there are a number of autonomous national or regional human genome *projects*. This term describes a chimera of scientific and political projects at different levels. They are an attempt to co-ordinate, with government funds, a concerted effort to map and sequence all or part of the human genome and engage in necessary related research. It is more technology than pure research. Overall its goal is to produce a resource that will serve future biological and biomedical research. The third level concerns a loose international confederation of scientists and governments joined in an unofficial co-operation in what could be termed the human genome *programme*. Perhaps the most obvious example at this level and its most active proponent is the Human Genome Organisation[4]. HUGO (its acronym) is ostensibly an absolutely apolitical and purely scientific organisation devoted to facilitating international scientific co-operation among individuals and countries engaged in human genome research. International co-ordination and the setting of guidelines for sharing of materials and information are some of the areas of particular concern to HUGO. The founding president of HUGO, Victor McKusick, considered it the "United Nations of the human genome". In reality it sometimes resembled more the League of Nations, a congress of independently planned national efforts, than the hoped-for coherent plan[5].

When people think of the Human Genome Project, most think of the U.S. Human Genome Project. Begun in 1990, the U.S. Human Genome Project is a thirteen-year effort co-ordinated by the Department of Energy and the National Institutes of Health[6]. The project was originally planned to last fifteen years, but effective resource and technological advances have accelerated the expected completion date to 2003. The project goals are to:

– *identify* all the approximate 30,000 genes in human DNA,
– *determine* the sequences of the 3 billion chemical base pairs that make up human DNA,
– *store* this information in databases,

    4. V. McKusick, *The Human Genome Organisation: History, Purposes and Membership*, in *Genomics* 5 (1989) 385-387; see also http://www.gene.ucl.ac.uk/hugo/.
    5. R. M. Cook-Deegan, *Genome Mapping and Sequencing*, in W.T. Reich (ed.), *Encyclopedia of Bioethics*, New York, Simon & Schuster Macmillan, ²1995, pp. 1011-1020, p. 1015.
    6. Cf. http://www.ornl.gov/TechResources/Human_Genome/project/about.html.

- *improve* tools for data analysis,
- *transfer* related technologies to the private sector, and
- *address* the ethical, legal, and social issues (ELSI) that may arise from the project.

To achieve these goals, researchers are also studying the genetic makeup of several non-human organisms. These include the common human intestinal bacterium *Escherichia coli*, the fruit fly, and the laboratory mouse.

The Feb. 16, 2001, issue of *Science* and Feb. 15, 2001, issue of *Nature* contain the first analyses of the working draft human genome sequence. The *Nature* papers include initial sequence analyses generated by the publicly sponsored Human Genome Project, while the *Science* publications focus on the draft sequence reported by the private company, Celera Genomics. Because of the importance of these landmark papers, both *Science* and *Nature* have provided free and unrestricted access to all articles[7].

III. GENETICS AND THEOLOGY

A unique aspect of the U.S. Human Genome Project is that it is the first large scientific undertaking to address the ethical, legal and social implications (ELSI) that may arise from the project. The ELSI program was an unprecedented effort by a scientific research initiative to analyse the impact of its work on social issues. 3% to 5% of the annual Human Genome Project budgets are devoted to studying the ethical, legal, and social issues surrounding the availability of genetic information. One million dollars (US) has been spent on ELSI research to date. This represents the world's largest bioethics program, which has become a model for ELSI programs around the world.

An interesting question regarding this research is how societal decisions regarding genetics are influenced by religious beliefs. Religious perspectives could offer a unique contribution to discussing the ethical, legal and social implications of the Human Genome Projects. However, the literature that examines religious values and opinions formed about the Human Genome Project has been scant. Some of the existing literature presents ethical and religious reflections on gene therapy and examines the role of religion in analysing ethical issues in human gene therapy[8].

---

7. http://www.nature.com/genomics/human and http://www.sciencemag.org/content/vol291/issue5507/.
8. J. NELSON – J. ROBERT, *The Role of Religions in the Analysis of the Ethical Issues of Human Gene Therapy*, in *Human Gene Therapy* 1 (1990) 438; J.M. GUSTAFSON, *Genetic*

Other publications are religiously based commentaries on genetic technology and policy or are discussion papers from religious conferences or
official policy statements of various religious denominations. One interesting American study attempted to map attitudes and beliefs of religious
leaders about the Human Genome Project[9]. In this study it is significant
that only a minority of the respondents were familiar with genetics
research and the Human Genome Projects. Nevertheless they had strong
opinions about the topic. The overwhelming majority wanted more dialogue and information about this research and realised that future ethical
dilemmas should be addressed now. Salient topics of consideration to
frame future discussions on policy regarding genetic technology were
identified.

Beyond these writings we can state without exaggeration that theology
is not a major player in a much-debated area such as genetics. An Internet search with the keywords theology and genetics yields a very small
field of results. Not much is being published on the relationship between
genetics and theology. On the other hand, in the contemporary ethical
debate on gene technology there are contributions by theologians. However, these entail at least two restrictions:

First, when theologians write on this topic, they are not usually identifying themselves *as theologians*, but as ethicists, employing the methodology of philosophy. This means that their object (explanation of the
moral experience), their aim (sensitisation of the moral experience), and
their instruments are the same as those of moral philosophers[10]. What is
striking in their arguments on the ethics of genetics is that even though
they have been trained as theologians, virtually all of their analysis is carried out employing secular philosophical arguments. Many theologically
trained ethicists – among them Albert Jonsen, James Childress, Robert
Veatch, Thomas Shannon, John Flectcher – are making use of philosophical categories in most of their work. Walters explains that the reason for this trend toward non-theological casuistry is undoubtedly complex. "All of the theologians mentioned are deeply involved in the
public-policy debates. Further some forms of genetic intervention begin
to look more and more like a simple extension of traditional medical

Therapy: Ethical and Religious Reflections, in *Journal of Contemporary Health Law and
Policy* 8 (1992) 183-200.

    9. K.L.D. PHAN – D.J. DOUKAS – M.D. FETTERS, *Religious Leaders' Attitudes and
Beliefs about Genetics Research and the Human Genome Project*, in *Journal of Clinical
Ethics* 6 (1995) 237-246.

    10. R. JANSSENS – H. TEN HAVE, *Medische ethiek en zorgpraktijk. Een diagnose vanuit
moraaltheologisch perspectief*, in *Tijdschrift voor Theologie* 39 (1999) 162-177.

practice"[11]. Other forms or possible uses of genetic means to enhance human capabilities are usually labelled eugenics and rejected as ethically unacceptable, without sustained theological discussion.

Our second restriction concerns the field of application. For some specific genetic topics such as germ-line gene therapy and cloning one can find more theological arguments[12]. Theologians see the question of genetic interventions in the context of evolution, the divine role in creating and sustaining the world, and human responsibility *vis-à-vis* the entire creation. Thus, this mode takes the long view in examining the question of genetic intervention. In the 1960s this so-called cosmic theology was represented by thinkers like Paul Ramsey, Karl Rahner, and James Gustafson. An essay presented by James Gustafson[13], a 1993 book by Ronald Cole-Turner[14] and J. Robert Nelson's 1994 book[15] helpfully remind us that cosmic theology did not end with the writings of the late 1960s. It is in this context that the famous aphorism of the late Paul Ramsey can be situated: "Human beings ought not to play god before they learn to be human beings, and after they have learned to be human being, they will not play God"[16]. For Ramsey "to play God" certainly meant to convey a negative moral connotation and his theological statement was aimed at limiting human efforts in the entire arena of genetic manipulation. Of course, where one stands on this question is partially determined by which model of the *imago Dei* one adopts. Because the stewardship model tends to limit human activity through its emphases on conserving and preserving creation, the charge of improperly playing God will frequently be raised by those who argue for a created co-creator model. It is clear that there is no common understanding of what "playing God" means[17]. Some find the phrase not very helpful and believe that bioethical discussions could be enhanced without its use, while others

11. L. WALTERS, *Human Genetic Interventions and the Theologians*, in L.S. CAHILL – J.F. CHILDRESS (eds.), *Christian Ethics: Problems and Prospects*, Cleveland, OH, Pilgrim Press, 1996, pp. 235-249.

12. J.J. WALTER, *Theological Issues in Genetics*, in *Theological Studies* 60 (1999) 124-134.

13. J.M. GUSTAFSON, *Where Theologians and Geneticists Meet*, in *Dialog* 33 (1994) 1, 7-16.

14. R. COLE-TURNER, *The New Genesis: Theology and the Genetic Revolution*, Louisville, KY, Westminster John Knox, 1993.

15. J.R. NELSON, *On the New Frontiers of Genetics and Religion*, Grand Rapids, MI, Eerdmans, 1994.

16. P. RAMSEY, *Fabricated Man: The Ethics of Genetic Control*, New Haven, CT, Yale University, 1970, p. 138.

17. L.S. CAHILL, *Playing God: Religious Symbols in Public Places*, in *Journal of Medicine and Philosophy* 20 (1995) 341-346.

argue it can serve as an important and distinctively theological perspective from which to assess scientific and technological innovations.

Aside from the "playing God" metaphor, other theological categories are discussed by theologians in the context of genetic interventions. These include creation, fall, incarnation, redemption and eschatology. These doctrinal expressions themselves have been based on certain models of God and of how the divine relates to and acts in nature and history. It could be interesting to see how the use of the framework of these five-fold Christian mysteries shows how moral judgements on, for instance, germ-line therapy rely upon and are authorised by certain theological beliefs and interpretations, for example, the issue of creation[18].

This doctrine of creation is actually a complex set of interpretations of who God is and how the divine directs human history and acts within it (divine providence). These theological interpretations have anthropological counterparts that attempt to understand both how we as created beings stand in the image of God (*imago Dei*) and how we are to evaluate the significance of physical nature and our bodily existence. In the great Christian tradition we can distinguish two main theological models of God, creation and divine providence. We will briefly indicate the meaning of these models and what the different implications are in the discussion on germ-line gene therapy. In one model, God is considered as the creator of both the material universe and humanity and the one who has placed universal, fixed laws into the very fabric of creation. As Lord of life and death, God possesses certain rights over creation, which in some cases has not been delegated to humans for their exercise[19]. Both physical nature and humanity are created in their complete and final forms. In the other theological model the divine continues to create in history (*creatio continua*) and God's actions, both in creation and in history, continue to influence the world process, which is open to new possibilities and even spontaneity. Thus God is not understood as having placed fixed laws into the fabric of creation. This implies that his purposes are not as clearly discernible as in the first view. As an anthropological counterpart to their interpretations of the divine, Christians have consistently understood all humanity to be created in the image and likeness of God (Gen 1,26-27). Related to the two former views on God, at least two different interpretations of how humans stand in that image can be

---

18. J.J. WALTER, *"Playing God" or Properly Exercising Human Responsibility*, in *New Theological Review* 10 (1997) 39-59.

19. J. JANS, *God or Man? Normative Theology in the Instruction* Donum Vitae, in *Louvain Studies* 17 (1992) 48-64.

distinguished. In the first view humanity is defined as a steward over creation. The ethical responsibility of humans, then, is primarily to protect and to conserve what the divine has created and ordered. Stewardship is exercised by respecting the limits placed by God in the orders of biological nature and society[20]. In the second interpretation of *imago Dei* humans are defined as co-creators or participants with God in the continual unfolding of the processes and patterns of creation. Though humans are not God's equals in the act of creating, they do play a significant role in bringing creation and history to their completion; they are created co-creators[21].

These diverse models of God and humans almost inevitably lead to different moral evaluations about therapeutic interventions into the human genome. If, as in the first perspective on God and humans, we are only stewards over both creation and, by extension, our own genetic heritage, then our moral responsibilities do not include the alteration of what the divine has created and ordered. Our principal moral duties are to remain faithful to God's original creative will and to respect the laws that are both inherent in creation and function as limits to human intervention. One would likely judge as human arrogance the attempt to alter permanently the genetic structure of the human genome even to cure a serious disease[22]. As a consequence of the second view on the Creator and *Imago Dei*, part of the human responsibility in bringing creation to its completion might even include permanently overcoming the defects in biological nature that remain contrary to God's purposes. Because creation was not made perfect from the beginning, one can discern certain elements in the created order, like genetic diseases, that are disordered. Because disordered aspects of creation cause great human suffering, they are judged to be contrary to God's final purposes and so can be corrected by human intervention[23].

So, a Christian interpretation of the significance and value of both Creation and Image of God plays an important role in arriving at moral judgements on gene therapy and human cloning.

The same could be said of the other concepts: fall, redemption, incarnation and eschatology. It is important to clarify how theology might play

20. T.A. SHANNON, *What Are They Saying About Genetic Engineering?*, New York, Paulist, 1985, p. 21.
21. P. HEFNER, *The Evolution of the Created Co-Creator*, in T. PETERS (ed.), *Cosmos as Creation: Theology and Science in Consonance*, Nashville, TN, Abingdon, 1989, pp. 211-233.
22. WALTER, *"Playing God" or Properly Exercising Human Responsibility* (n. 18), p. 45.
23. T. PETERS, *"Playing God" and Germ-line Intervention*, in *The Journal of Medicine and Philosophy* 20 (1995) 365-386, p. 302.

a role in these discussions. However, this is only one part of the meeting point between theologians and geneticists. In the eyes of most geneticists this is not always the part that is of most interest for their activities. Rather, this approach shows the openness of theologians for the domain of genetics but contributes more perhaps to theology than to genetics. The contribution of this input of theology is not always very clear for clinical geneticists. This does not mean it is not important, but in a conversation it is also important to see what the contribution of the other party might be. So we try as theologians to develop another kind of contribution: a conversation that is not only clarifying for theological categories and debates, but that also tries to form a contribution at the level of clinical genetics.

The question before us is; is there a role or place for theology in the domain of clinical genetics and genetic counselling and in what may this contribution consist? The answer is far less evident than in the case of gene therapy and cloning. How could theology as a specific discipline, for instance, fit in the practice of genetic counselling, in the ethical questions of non-directivity, informed consent, privacy, etc? As stated before, in bio-ethical or clinical genetics journals you will hardly find an article or contribution that covers the possible role of theology in clinical genetics. This indicates for theologians the challenge to make this influence explicit.

Our presupposition is that if we are thinking theologically about the ethical problems of genetics, it is out of a framework, context, or story that we will think; as Christians it is the Christian story[24]. The Christian story tells us the ultimate meaning of the world and ourselves. In doing so it tells us the kind of people we ought to be, the goods we ought to pursue, the dangers we ought to avoid, and the kind of world we ought to seek. It provides the backdrop or framework that ought to shape our individual decisions. When decision-making is separated from this framework, this narrative tradition, it loses its perspective. It becomes a kind of contracted etiquette with no relation to the ultimate meaning of persons.

This position leads to the assertion that stories and theology are utterly essential to bioethical discussions. It does not give us concrete answers or ready-made rules. Rather, it tells us who we are, where we come from, and where we are going. It is due to such understandings that our concrete ethical deliberations can remain truly humane and promote our best interests.

---

24. R.A. MCCORMICK, *Theology and Biomedical Ethics*, in *Église et Théologie* 13 (1982) 311-331.

One could understand this also as a plea for a broad bioethics, in contrast with a narrow one. The former could be described as a kind of procedural ethics that is based on the presupposition that ethics has to function independent of a vision of the person and that it has to limit itself to a *lingua franca* of some minimal principles that make a kind of thinking economy possible; some call this "moral engineering"[25]. We are in favour of the idea that Christian inspiration may play a role in the context of clinical genetics because the Christian tradition offers a context, a story, a broader framework that consists, among others, of the following factors: all humans have the same inherent value, the task of responsibility, the ideal of universal *caritas*, the respect for human dignity, the preferential option for the poor, the fundamental value of health, etc. It is, however, important that these values are developed in critical dialogue with other stories and frameworks. It is important that medical ethics always brings up the "most human desirable", but from a realistic perspective, wherein the "most human feasible" comes as close as possible to the "human desirable". This approach implicates an integration of broad and narrow orientations in bioethics: an integral approach to moral reality.

We would like to illustrate this approach with a specific issue within clinical genetics that becomes very important and questioned: the preference not to know.

IV. THE PREFERENCE NOT TO KNOW

In this section we want to develop the idea that there are, in our opinion, possible contributions of theology for clinical genetics. This position can be distinguished from theologians that think and write *de facto* as philosophers and from a theological reflection due to new genetic technologies that mainly contributes to theology itself and not to clinical genetics. In order to illustrate this conversation between theology and genetics, we – rather paradoxically – focus on an ethical principle that has become very important within clinical genetics: the right or preference not to know.

Aristotle begins his work on metaphysics with the statement that all human beings by nature desire to know[26]. It seems that every form of

25. A. CAPLAN, *Applying Morality to Advances in Biomedicine: Can and Should This be Done?*, in W.B. BONDESON, *Knowledge in the Biomedical Sciences*, Dordrecht, Kluwer, 1982, pp. 155-168.

26. ARISTOTLE, *The Metaphysics*, trans. J.H. MCMAHON, Buffalo, Prometheus Books, 1991.

knowledge is considered a good. The question is whether all people really desire to know, and, more specifically, if there is a desire to know about the genetic status of ourselves or of someone else. Is it better as a parent to know that your child will have an increased risk of a genetic disorder, or is it better not to know? Does knowledge bring happiness? The answer is not certain, and certainly not when it is a matter of disorders afflicting a future son or daughter. This is what clinical practice has shown. An international study among geneticists also showed that two-thirds of them are of the opinion that persons at risk should only be informed of their test result if they explicitly stated that they wanted to know it and that they should not be informed if the patient does not want to be, because of the patient's right not to know[27].

Based on the ethos of patients and clinical geneticists, there seems to be a great deal of receptiveness to a person's choice not to know. For children of the Enlightenment, this might seem strange upon first examination. Modern thinkers tend to argue that, for ethical reasons, a person should give up the right not to know, since they believe this right legitimates obscurantism and irresponsibility. They argue for the right *and* the duty to know[28]. As a result, they characterize the right not to know as a "naïve claim". A further argument against the right not to know is based on public health: the importance of health at the community level has greater weight in this view than any individual objections. Must we conclude from this that the wish or the right not to know is morally unwarranted? We do not think so. In our opinion, fundamental theology can contribute to this topic something that is of the utmost importance to the clinical geneticist. We will indicate moral theological grounds for the wish or the right not to know. We shall focus attention primarily on the development of a position based on a Christian view of humanity and health. In doing so, we will use the expression "the *right* not to know", which is current in the literature, rather than constantly adding "the *wish* not to know", without pretending to make any claims about the legal status of this "right" or the degree of its enforceability.

The concrete domain of application of the right not to know is quite heterogeneous. This means a conflict can arise, for instance, between the parents' right not to know, on the one hand, and the rights of their children — grown children, young children or unborn children — on the other

27. D.C. WERTZ – J.C. FLETCHER, *Ethics and Human Genetics. A Cross-cultural Perspective*, Berlin, Springer Berlin, 1989.

28. G. HOTTOIS, *Essais de philosophie bioéthique et biopolitique*, Paris, Vrin, 1999; R. RHODES, *Genetic Links, Family Ties, and Social Bonds: Rights and Responsibilities in the Face of Genetic Knowledge*, in *Journal of Medicine and Philosophy* 23 (1998) 10-30.

hand. Take as an example the situation of the grandson of a patient (grandfather) with an autosomal dominant condition, Huntington's chorea. The grandson wants to know whether he carries the gene because he has a 25% risk of being a pre-symptomatic carrier of the disease. However, his father (50% risk) does not want to know if he carries the gene. The father is worried about having a mental breakdown if it were to turn out that he does carry the gene, so he does not want to cooperate in the test for the benefit of his son. How should this situation be resolved? If the grandson is tested and is positive as a carrier, then it is immediately clear that the father is also a carrier. In practice, it seems that it is difficult to keep this information hidden from the father. Can the father appeal to the right not to know and on these grounds refuse to cooperate in generating precise information for his son? A conflict can also arise between the patient's right not to know and the interests of unrelated third parties. The debate about the right not to know can also be relevant in connection with future parents, unborn children, family members and participants in genetic screening programs. For instance, do parents have the right not to know whether a fetus in the uterus has Down's syndrome if a pre-natal test that can provide this information is available?

In general one can say that, in the case of the right not to know about genetic information, a distinction can be drawn between the possibility of being spared knowledge of available information and the right to determine oneself whether certain information is produced in the first place. For instance, consider people who have taken part in a genetic test. During the period before the test results are known, they are overcome by feelings of anxiety about the risk of being confronted with the possibility of positive test results. In such a case, they could choose not to be informed of the available results. This could also be the case for a couple where one of them has undergone a genetic test and the other one has not. The one not tested can request not to be informed of the result of the other one's test.

In addition to refusing available information, there is also the possibility that unexpected or indirect information comes to light by accident. It can happen, for example, that in testing for a specific congenital illness, it turns out that the legal father is not the biological father. Both of these cases show that it is not always advantageous for people to be informed about the risk they are subject to and the associated decision scenarios.

The following reflections are guided by a personalist approach to human beings and medical practice. In other words, an action is morally legitimate if it promotes human dignity, which means it is beneficial for the person as a bodily subject and for the person's relations with the world as God's creation, with other people, and with the community to which the person belongs[29]. This integral view of the person rejects a purely biological and vitalist conception of health and disease. Health is not only a matter of the prevention and cure of illness, but also a matter of care and of the fact that health has to do with good relations between the whole person and the context of the community. From a Christian perspective, health aims at an optimal functioning of the human person with a view to meeting social, spiritual, physiological and psychological needs in an integrated manner. A personalist view, therefore, implies a certain idea of disease and health. It is a comprehensive idea of health that is oriented not only towards bodily functioning but also includes moral integrity and responsibility for one's own behavior in its conception of a healthy life.

In the Christian narrative tradition a person can only be understood in terms of his or her final destiny[30]. This means that, in a biblical-religious context, disease and health are considered from the point of view of aims; they are part of a teleological structure. This means that disease and health only receive their proper meaning in the perspective of the final destiny of human life. The teleological structure of human life shows that a healthy life is not to be equated with a good life. This implies that the "sanctification" of a person does not coincide with his or her healthy constitution. Health is not a sign of individual perfection. It is an empty possibility, a potential that can be fulfilled either for good or for evil. It is only in striving for perfection that health acquires its meaning.

In line with the Christian notions of disease and health, one could say that health is a fundamental good for which a person should provide the necessary care. It is a capital that God has entrusted to human responsibility. Health acquires significance in light of what human beings should pursue. However, this care should not lead to the cultivation of health as an absolute or supreme value. Health is a penultimate value, more like grace than virtue, and something given to us as a sign that we must make more of our lives[31]. This implies that the health goals one aims at must be realistic. One of the conditions of human health is that people learn how to live with disease and imperfection. Health also involves the ability to live with a certain degree of renunciation, sympathy and suffering and to integrate this into one's life project. These qualifications applied

29. F. BÖCKLE et al., Personalist Morals: Essays in Honor of Professor Louis Janssens, Leuven, University Press, 1988.
30. M.A.M. PIJNENBURG, Verdelen van de gezondheidszorg. Een bezinning vanuit christelijk perspectief, Zeist, Kerckebosch, 1991.
31. U. EIBACH, Gentechnik: der Griff nach dem Leben. Eine ethische und theologische Beurteilung, Wuppertal, Brockhaus, 1986.

to health in the Christian tradition do not amount to a neglect of health but are attempts to prevent health and healthcare from becoming so predominant that they lose their status as instrumental values. One could say that, in doing this, the Christian view of disease and health makes visible a hidden value of sickness. Sick people show the healthy that ability and accomplishment are not everything in life. They remind healthy persons of the finitude and thus the true value of human existence; the sick are like a *memento mori*. True humanity begins with the acceptance of one's own dependence. It is clear that this personalistic view of humanity and health provides room for not knowing about certain genetic information. If health is more than merely the lack of bodily disease, if it is placed within a teleological context, then people may choose not to know. In this way, for example, a couple might choose not to take part in a prenatal test for Down's syndrome or they might choose not to know the results of such a test.

This choice not to know, however, must not be interpreted as a choice of obscurantism or ignorance. Rather, it is based on the belief that people are not completely responsible for everything that exists. If there were no room for the choice not to know, we would not be able to understand suffering that simply overcomes someone, since all suffering would be willfully committed. In fact, in this sort of reasoning one's own responsibility is moralized. People can be held morally responsible when they alleviate or fail to alleviate suffering using knowledge that it is possible to generate. Here, responsibility is infinitely extended. Nothing any longer simply overcomes us. One could speak of a moral hypertrophy of responsibility[32]. Accepting this is a significant cause of the pressure to seek out ever more potentially available genetic information. If we assume that every disease or behavior can be predicted using genetic tests, then people who do not take advantage of the information that such tests can provide cannot claim that they passively undergo the disease.

V. CONCLUSION

Since the official start of the combined Human Genome Project in 1990, it has been recognized that there are many issues of non-scientific

---

32. H. TEN HAVE, *Living with the Future: Genetic Information and Human Existence*, in R. CHADWICK – M. LEVITT – D. SHICKLE, *The Right to Know and the Right Not to Know*, Aldershot, Aveburry, 1997, pp. 119-127.

nature connected with this project. A significant part of the genome funds has been and should be spent to these important issues. The scientific breakthroughs that are being made today because of this research present us with extraordinarily important and far-reaching moral questions. Ethicists have for instance argued morally in favor or against the implementation of somatic cell therapy, forms of enhancement genetic engineering, germ-line gene therapy, etc. It also involves a theological problem of whether or not we have now entered the realm of "playing God" by using this technology. Is performing gene therapy on humans contrary to God's intentions and purposes, and therefore an act of usurping God's rights over creation? Moral theologians, reflecting on this topic, have sought to show how Christian moral decision-making on the new genetics is contextualized by specifically theological beliefs. Answers to the above questions are primarily being decided within the broader context of several theological affirmations of doctrinal themes that are interpretations of religious experience. In a certain way, questions in the genetic domain are the start of a theological reflection and explanation focused on theologians.

In the second part of this article we have tried to develop a different approach, whereby theology aims to come to a truly interdisciplinary conversation with clinical genetics that also has consequences and practical implications for clinical practice. We have elaborated this approach in one example, the right not to know. Increasingly, authoritative international documents and clinical practice both recognize the right not to know. However, theoretical considerations related to the right not to know are still at an early stage of development. Opponents stress the duty to know and the importance of public health. Drawing inspiration from Christian anthropology, we believe that people can choose to consider health – certainly in the purely biological, physical or genetic sense – not as life's ultimate goal, and thus to refuse certain medical and/or genetic information that may be generated or made public. This does not mean, however, that we consider this wish to be an absolute right. In certain cases, the damage a person might do to himself or others can function as a limitation on the right not to know. In the case mentioned above of the father who does not want to cooperate in obtaining accurate test results for his son, the father's right not to know comes into conflict with the son's desire to know. This conflict situation cannot simply be resolved by invoking the right not to know. Here a proportional weighing up of values has to be considered. The right not to know can also come into conflict with the responsibility of the physician who must ensure that the patient is properly informed and who may consider certain information to be so important that he or she feels obligated to communicate it. Nevertheless, we have established that, from a Christian theological point of view, it can be ethically legitimate to refuse certain medical or genetic information.

Centrum voor Biomedische Ethiek en Recht   Kris DIERICKX
K.U. Leuven
Kapucijnenvoer 35
B-3000 Leuven
Belgium

II

REFLECTING ON THE CHURCH AND THE WORLD

CONVERSATION AND ECCLESIOLOGY

THE CHURCH IN THE WORLD

A DIALOGUE ON ECCLESIOLOGY

This session invites us to a conversation on "The Church in the World: A Dialogue in Ecclesiology". When I first received the invitation from the organisers of LEST III to make this presentation, the topic proposed was: "The Church and the World: A Dialogue on Ecclesiology". Something inside me registered unease about this formulation. I paid attention to it, and, in accepting the invitation, I rephrased the topic thus: "The Church in the World: A Dialogue on Ecclesiology". But after I had done that and sent it back as my accepted topic, I was left with a problem. In this reformulation, I had eliminated what were apparently the dialogue partners, the church and the world. Who now was to dialogue with whom on ecclesiology, on whose behalf, from whose perspective and for what purpose? These questions are relevant since neither the church nor the world is a vocal person. I do not have the answers, but I leave you with the questions. Maybe together we will discover some answers in the course of the conversation.

My second observation is that this seminar is an "Encounter in Systematic Theology" on a subject that clearly has a systematic thrust. Ecclesiology is a dimension of fundamental theology. It belongs to the foundations of our Christian belief. While I accepted the invitation to participate, I could not help wondering all along what I was coming to do here as a biblical scholar. Since the conference began, and I have listened to the terminologies and frames of reference of the various discourses, my doubts have been confirmed more than ever. I share this in order to invite you to enter consciously into my own frame of reference as part of the dialogue. The Bible is not a systematised book (however much we biblical scholars may want to consider its study a science). Rather, it deals with stories, images, allusions, parables, prayers, and so forth, and (note this), it is often repetitive, for memory and emphasis. The entire Bible itself is essentially a powerful story of God's incredible love for humanity shown through creation, redemption and sanctification.

In keeping with this biblical character and the conversational thrust of LEST III, we adopt the narrative as our basic methodology. We conduct our dialogue in the form of stories and images that each of us may relate to in a parabolic way, that is, place alongside his/her personal experiences of the church in the world, in our diverse geopolitical, socio-cultural and ecclesio-theological contexts. We may recall that as disciples of Jesus, we are essentially and by nature part (not the sum total) of God's own gathering (*ekklesia*). With the rest of humanity, we are God's tilling, planting, building (1 Cor 3,9) and work of art (Eph 2,10). As believers we have the additional privilege of being a city set on a hilltop to be seen clearly by the world, provided we understand what a responsibility that places on us. In this biblical narrative approach, we do not systematise the discourse or ask how one image follows from or leads to another. Rather we stay open and tuned to the Holy Spirit whom we have invited to lead us in this session[1]. We pay keen attention to how and where She may choose to lead us as She blows freely where She wills (John 3,8), in the great act of bringing to birth a new church in the world.

We are talking about "the world". The world in this dialogue is the real world, the physical, geopolitical, social and cultural world. We are concerned with the world's value systems, its ideologies, symbols, language and diverse ways of organising life. Most importantly, we appreciate the world's struggle to respond to God's Spirit ever present and at work in it, enabling it to make its contribution, as, with the entire creation, it continues to groan in one great act of giving birth to a new self (Rom 8,21-22). It is a world whose rich multiple cultures, religions, ethnic and racial groups are increasingly being recognised and accepted. The citizens of this world today call themselves "the human family" and "global village" (and we are part of that family and village, for better or for worse). They have even drafted a Charter (Universal Declaration of Human Rights) to ensure that none of their citizens is discriminated against on the basis of race, sex, religion, colour, and so forth. Historically, this world is older than the church. The world existed before the church; the church came to birth and exists in the world. This relationship of "seniority" of the world to the church, as we would say in Nigeria, is an important aspect of dialogue.

We are talking about "the church". In his recent discourses on ecumenical and interfaith dialogue, John Paul II seems to accept the church

---

1. The presentation began with a triple invocation of the Holy Spirit, in line with the spirit of the conference, which sought to combine theology and spirituality. The invocation was made in the presenter's language, Ibibio, and the audience was invited to take part in singing in their own native languages or humming along with the presenter as the Spirit moved them. The invocation was "Di, O di. (twice). Di, Edisana Spirit. (Come, O come [twice]. Come, Holy Spirit). Since the conference was advertised as a conversation, the presentation maintains the conversational tone throughout. A marked feature of this conversational tone is the use of "we" throughout (inviting us to a common search) and other personal pronouns where necessary.

at three levels: "the Church of God" (embracing all humanity), "the one Church of Christ" (made up of all the Christian churches) and "the Roman Catholic Church" of which he is directly the head[2]. The order in which these three are listed here reflects a primacy of hierarchy and a primacy of service. The Roman Catholic Church (being the greatest among them, the one that can trace its line of succession directly to Peter), has the primacy of service, according to Jesus' criterion of greatness: "The greatest among you shall be your servant/slave" (Matt 23,10 par.; Cf. John 13,12-18). In our dialogue we will visit the church at all three levels, but our primary focus will be the Roman Catholic Church. The word "Roman" in the designation is important. We will pray to be delivered from the temptation of restricting the church to just ourselves (Roman Catholics). For, if the church is the *ekklesia tou theou*, God's gathering and reconciling of humanity to the divine self in Christ (2 Cor 5,19), born of a woman (Gal 4,4) the fulfilment of God's first act of grace to redeem fallen humanity (Gen 3,15), then we cannot restrict this church to the Roman Catholic Church or even to the one Church of Christ[3]. We pray for the grace to embrace this world, all its peoples and our disputed "sister churches" in God and Christ as we meet the challenge of being church in today's multifaceted world.

We are interested in "dialogue", the genuine effort to engage one another "through the word" (*dia logos*) on what it means to be church in today's world. "Word" here is taken with a capital and small letter. We have recourse to the Word who is life, the God-Word who pitched his tent among us and alone uniquely and unequivocally reveals God and God's purposes for humanity (John 1,1-5.14.18). We will pay attention to this Word in his actions and teaching. We will reflect on some of the images he gives to help us understand better how to be church in the world. Such images – light of the world, salt of the earth, leaven buried in a measure of flour, the mustard seed that provides a home for all the birds of the air – point our dialogue towards an ecclesiology that empowers and fosters growth in persons, all persons, including those within our church, as essential to our participation in God's loving activity of gathering together all God's scattered children (John 11,52).

---

2. JOHN PAUL II, *To the Bishop Friends of the Focolare Movement, "The Ecumenical way is the Church's way"*, in *L'Osservatore Romano*, No 3 (1674), 17 January 2001, p. 6.

3. On this divine work of reconciliation, see further John 11,52; 12,32; 21,21; and the commentary on the issue in T. OKURE, *John*, in W.R. FARMER et al. (eds.), *The International Bible Commentary: A Catholic and Ecumenical Commentary for the Twenty-First Century*, Collegeville, MN, The Liturgical Press, 1998, 1438-1502, esp. pp. 1483-1484.

We also pay attention to our human word, how our language of discourse about ourselves as church and about the world, with its underlying philosophies and ideologies, can promote or hinder our growth as church. In a genuine dialogue, the partners do not know from the start what issues will arise as they engage one another, nor do they pre-empt the outcome of the dialogue before it begins. Rather, they commit themselves to stay open and listen to one another in freedom. As they listen, they are led to re-evaluate their current positions, to consider other possibilities and perspectives on the same, and to gain new insights about one another's position. Such mutual listening attracts the possibility of the dialogue partners changing their own personal and communal views as a consequence. In other words, by "agreeing to engage in dialogue, one is agreeing to the possibility [at least] that one's views and positions will be modified", even if not radically changed[4]. This comment on interreligious dialogue applies equally to the dialogue on ecclesiology. Openness is an essential prerequisite and a lasting condition for any meaningful dialogue[5]. In our conversation we need to ask: "Who dialogues with whom on ecclesiology within the church? Through whose word is the dialogue conducted, for what purpose and for whose benefit? How does our perception of church (made up of clergy and laity) affect our internal relationships and consequently our dialogue with the world"?

Lastly, we are concerned with ecclesiology, the prayerful study of what it means to be church. John Paul II sees *missiology* as having been inserted into that of *ecclesiology* (*RM*, 32.3). By this we understand that the study of mission *ad gentes* is an important means by which the church can renew itself and the faith of believers and increase in membership. The reverse is also true, that by making a serious effort to understand and be the kind of church which God and Christ want, the church can increase in membership. So ecclesiology invites us to give all that it takes to understand ourselves as church in the twenty-first century in the light of the gospel. Such understanding will require, even impel us to redress the cumulative "deviations from the gospel" that we entertained over the centuries so as to rediscover our authentic self as God's church.

The ecclesiology that inspires our conversation draws inspiration from the New Testament images of the church already mentioned and such others as the body of Christ (Cor 1,12; Col 1,15-20), the branches of his

4. C. GILLES, *Pluralism: A New Paradigm for Theology* (Louvain Theological and Pastoral Monographs, 12), Louvain, Peeters Press; Grand Rapids, MI, Eerdmans, 1993, esp. Chapter 2, "Nature and Direction of Dialogue", p. 43.

5. Cf. JOHN PAUL II, *Novo Millennio Ineunte* (*NMI*), Vatican City, Libreria Editrice Vaticana, 2001, no. 56.

vine (John 15,1-8), the net which catches all kinds of fish but where the fishers do not sort out the good ones and reject the bad (John 21,6.8.11), contrary to what obtains in the parable (Matt 13,47-50). This Johannine post-Easter account (whether it is his version of the pre-Easter one narrated in the Synoptic Gospels or a totally different one), mentions no sorting out of the fish. Instead the account emphasises the abundance of the catch despite its being daytime, and marvels that despite the abundance, the net did not break. This inclusion of all the fish caught may likely reflect a new, post-resurrection understanding within the church that Jesus' mission (which embraces that of the disciples, the institutional church), is essentially a gathering into one of all God's scattered children and drawing them in him to the divine self (John 11,52; 12,32) and to one another[6]. If so, the account sheds significant light on how we understand Jesus' *ekklesia* and develop an ecclesiology, which fosters this *ekklesia* in today's world.

As we converse on the problematic of the church in the world, and the world in the church, it is important that we see ourselves individually and collectively as this church, in this world, within our individual and collective concrete life situations. Both aspects (individual and communal) are important. For as *Redemptor Hominis* (*RH*, 13), following *Gaudium et spes* (*GS*, 22) observes, "by his Incarnation, the Son of God, in a certain way united himself with each person". Consequently, the individual is the route, which the church needs to travel in the work of evangelisation. The individual is not only the route to travel, but also the goal of the church's missionary activity in the world. The church, the community itself is made up of individuals who follow the Way, Christ. This awareness calls us to reckon with the diverse socio-cultural settings of the church as an important aspect of our conversation on ecclesiology[7].

Our leading thought in this dialogue is that whatever its form, a dialogue on ecclesiology urgently needs to happen within the church itself. Our church, like today's world, takes dialogue seriously. But the focus of such dialogue is often, if not always, *ad extra*, engaging a wide range of peoples, issues and structures outside the church. To implement the

---

6. See further OKURE, *John* (n. 3), p. 1501; A. KÖSTENBERGER, *The Missions of Jesus and the Disciples according to the Fourth Gospel. With Implications for the Fourth Gospel's Purpose and the Mission of the Contemporary Church*, Grand Rapids, MI – Cambridge, U.K., William B. Eerdmans Publishing Company, 1998.

7. We use dialogue and conversation interchangeably in the presentation, as does the seminar itself, though some may disagree that the two are synonymous. Perhaps failure to see dialogue as conversation – free and unprejudiced – has been largely responsible for the fruitlessness of most of our dialogues.

directives of the Second Vatican Council, the church has set up pontifical Councils for promoting ecumenical dialogue (with older Christian
churches), dialogue with Pentecostal/Charismatic Churches, interfaith dialogue (with the world's religions), and dialogue with the world[8]. There
appears, however, to be no noticeable body established to promote dialogue *within the church itself*. Yet this dialogue *ad intra* is very much and
urgently needed on the same universal, catholic scale as these other dialogues. Current questions about the nature of the church, the place of
women in the church, the priest-laity divide, and the laws and structures
by which we govern ourselves as church call for serious and systematic
dialogue *ad intra*.

We posit that the dialogue *ad intra* is indispensable and perhaps even
long overdue. Such a dialogue should even enhance our understanding
and commitment to those other dialogues. Here, as in evangelisation,
"People today put more trust in witnesses than in teachers" (*RM*, 42.1-2)[9].
Some African theologians and ecclesiologists call for this type of dialogue when they speak of the church's need to listen to the grassroots people and their needs, respond concretely to alleviate their sufferings and
offer the opportunity for participatory leadership[10]. Readiness to identify
and effect the necessary corrections in the church's own self-
understanding and its mission vis-a-vis the world will be a welcome result
of this dialogue. The *Mea Culpa's* of John Paul II have already boldly and
courageously spearheaded us in this direction[11]. The need for the church
to assume the responsibility to apply internally (to itself) all its rich teachings and advice to the secular world (e.g., its teachings on human rights,

---

8. On these various dialogues see *Gaudium et spes*, 92; JOHN PAUL II, *RM*, 55-57;
NMI, 54-56; *Ut unum sint*, Part II; ID., *Dialogue between Cultures for a Civilization of
Love and Peace*, Vatican City, Libreria Editrice Vaticana, 8 December 2000, with reference to the UN declaration of 2001 as the "International Year of Dialogue among Civilizations"; F. GIOIA (ed.), *Interreligious Dialogue: The Official Teaching of the Catholic
Church (1963-1995)*, Boston, Pauline Book & Media, 1995; incredibly, the volume has
xxxiii, 694 p.; the Pontifical Council for Interreligious Dialogue [PCID] devotes its regular journal *Pro Dialogo* to the activities of the Council worldwide.

9. See further, *EN*, 41, 1-2; *LG*, 28, 35, 38; and *Populorum progressio*, 21, 42.

10. Cf. E.E. UZUKWU, *A Listening Church: Autonomy and Communion in African
Churches*, Maryknoll, NY, 1996, esp. chs. 5 and 6; G. EHUSANI, *A Prophetic Church*, Ede,
Osun State, Nigeria, Provincial Pastoral Institute Publications, 1996; J. HEALEY, *Today's
New Way of Being Church: Pastoral Implications of the Small Christian Community Model
of Church in the World Church Towards the 21st Century*, in C.H.I.E.A. *African Christ-
ian Studies* 7 (1991) 63-77.

11. See L. ACCATTOLI, *When a Pope Asks Forgiveness: The Mea Culpa's of John
Paul II*, trans. J. AUMANN, OP, Boston, MA, Book & Media Center, 1998, esp. pp. 67-79,
where the author underscores how the Pope had to go it alone in asking for pardon against
the fears and even the opposition of some in the Roman Curia.

social and theological justice, freedom of speech and conscience and its encouragement of women to resist all forms of oppression) cannot be overemphasised. Here too the adage holds good, that example speaks louder and works more effectively than the precept.

The NT church offers a foundational model for the desired dialogue on ecclesiology. In this NT model (e.g., of the vine and branches, the body and its members), the various organs, joints and structures live in constant dialogue with one another and with their head or source, Christ. He supplies them with energy, assigns each its function and keeps the entire body together so that it grows internally even as it participates in God's mission in the world. The Eucharist, source and summit of Christian worship (*SC*, 10), enacts this life-giving unity on a daily basis and most solemnly weekly as it commemorates the Lord's Supper and Day (cf. *NMI*, 35-36). The liturgical dimension is an essential aspect of the dialogue on ecclesiology. Instead of defining God and one another, often with an air of superiority, we are invited by the liturgy to "discern [and respect] the body", to know that this body belongs to Christ, be it his body the church (1 Cor 11,29) or his cosmic body (Col 1,15-20). The latter, of necessity, embraces the church itself, since Christ cannot be divided (1 Cor 1,13). LEST III is conscious of this liturgical dimension by its concern to marry theology with spirituality. Worship draws the attention of all away from the self, from others and from futile attempts to define God, with their attendant quarrels, and refocuses it on Christ and on God where the action lies. They alone build the church and the world. Jacob typifies this. He spent the entire night struggling with God, only to have his hip dislocated for his pains. He then converted his energy into worship and named the place for God, after God had first given him a new name and a new self. From then on he was longer the supplanter, expert in dealing craftily with his father, brother and in-laws, but became a new person, Israel, one in whose life God prevails, by God's pure act of grace (Gen 33,24-30).

The rationale for our dialogical thrust here proposed is that both the church and the world have a common, divine origin, God. God, not human beings, created the world (Gen 1,1–2,4a), and builds the church. God's ultimate plan is the salvation and restoration of the world, which includes the church. The church exists in function of this plan, and as part of it. Therefore it is unrealistic to view the church and the world *a priori* as existing in opposition to each other. The church is very much in the world and part of the world, its unique mission to the world notwithstanding. The world is equally very much in the church and part of the church, its sinfulness notwithstanding. Awareness of this truth calls us to radically review our perception of the church-world relationship as a sound basis on which we build or structure a dialogue that is fair to and liberating for both the church and the world, for the better integration of the church in the world, like the leaven in the dough, or the salt in the food. A dialogue on ecclesiology needs to highlight the mutuality of presence and influence between the church and the world. However, since the presence and influence of *the world in the church* has to date received little or no attention, our conversation will focus on this aspect to underscore the consequential urgency for internal dialogue in the church.

With these introductory observations, we may now give flesh to some of the issues here raised, as the circumstances will permit. Conversations are open-ended, not only in terms of content, but also because the issues they raise often call for other, at times equally open-ended sessions. So we do not expect that we will address all the issues raised. These issues themselves do not exhaust the possibilities of what could be considered in a dialogue on ecclesiology. Our selected areas of focus will include a closer look at the traditional approaches to the church-world relationship, salient issues for the dialogue *ad intra*, obstacles to such a dialogue and resources for addressing them, and finally, some signs of hope that the proposed dialogue is possible, even in progress, the age-old obstacles notwithstanding.

I. TRADITIONAL APPROACHES: THE CHURCH AND THE WORLD

The discourse on the church-world relationship is as old as the church itself. In our era, the Second Vatican Council, successive popes and theologians have devoted sustained effort to articulating the problem. Among the major works are *Lumen gentium (LG)*, *Gaudium et spes*, *Ad gentes (AG)*, *Apostolicam actuositatem (AA)*, of Vatican Council II; *Evangelii nuntiandi (EN)* of Paul VI; and, for our prolific writer and energetic Pope John Paul II, *Redemptor Hominis (RH)*, *Redemptoris missio (RM)*, *Christifideles laici (CL)*, *Tertio millennio adveniente (TMA) and Novo millennio ineunte (NMI)*. These conciliar and postconciliar documents themselves drew inspiration from such earlier papal works as *Evangelii praecones* of Pius XII, *Rerum Ecclesiae* of Pius XI and *Mystici Corporis* of Pius X[12]. Long before, Augustine of Hippo had elaborately treated this

---

12. SECOND VATICAN COUNCIL, *Lumen gentium, Gaudium et spes*, and *Ad gentes*, in A. FLANNERY (ed.), *Vatican Council II*. Two Volumes. I: *Conciliar and Post-Conciliar Documents*, Dublin, Dominican Publications, E.J. Dwyer Pty. Ltd., Fowler Wright Books Ltd, 1988, pp. 350-426, 903-1014, 813-856, respectively; on norms of implementation of Paul VI, *Ecclesiae Sanctae III* (6 August 1966) 857-862; for the works of John Paul II,

issue in his *City of God*. The dominant impression conveyed by this literature on the church-world relationship is one of dualism or polarity. On one side is the church: holy (divine), apostolic, catholic (universal), built on Peter the rock, filled with good things for the world and commissioned and sent by Christ to enlighten and redeem this world. On the other is the world: sinful, godless, earthly, standing very much in need of salvation of which the church is the ordinary or principal means.

This view equally gives the impression that the church itself does not need redemption. She is the spotless Bride of Christ who gave his life to make her perfect (Eph 5,25-27). The controversial Declaration *Dominus Iesus* of the Congregation for the Doctrine of the Faith, has recently added its own "unique" coloring to this view, by re-emphasising the Church's unicity and salvific universality for human (or the world's) salvation alongside that of Christ[13]. This emphasis is not a construct of the Congregation. The teaching Magisterium sees the world's need of God's salvation (offered in and through Christ and uniquely mediated by the church under the guidance of the Holy Spirit), as the driving force of missionary undertaking, one which makes the church's mission imperative even in this age of religious pluralism and freedom of worship. *RM*, for instance, "has as its goal an interior renewal of faith and Christian life", through missionary activity. This *"Faith is strengthened when it is given to others!"* (2.3). The Church's primary mission is "to point the awareness of every human being and of the whole humanity towards the mystery of Christ" (4.1). But *"the church is also a sign and instrument of salvation"* (9.1)[14].

The church, however, does not have a monolithic view of the world-church relationship. The same documents also embody a positive view of this relationship. *Gaudium et spes* clearly proclaims that the church and the world have mutually benefited from each other. This conciliar document easily qualifies as the key text of the church's celebration of the world, with particular reference to its cultures. It is unsurpassed by previous documents for its positive and joyful recognition of the world's goodness and its influence on the church through its diverse cultures (*GS* 92). In the same spirit, *RM* speaks of the "marvellous achievements" of the world. Following its predecessors (*GS* 22, and *Mystici corporis* before it), John Paul II's first encyclical *Redemptor Hominis* (March 4,

see J.M. MILLER (ed.), *The Encyclicals of John Paul II*, Huntingdon, IN, Our Sunday Visitor Publishing Division, 1996; for a fuller list of these papal works, see *RM*, 2.2, no. 1.

13. The sub-title of the document is "On the Unicity and Salvific Universality of Jesus and the Church", Vatican City, Libreria Editrice Vaticana, 2000.

14. A fuller list of other, specifically "missionary" goals of the encyclical is given in no. 2.5.

1979), which contains the agenda for his Pontificate, sees the human being as "the route" which the church needs to travel in mission. It proclaims that by his incarnation and redemption, Christ, the Son of God, has united himself in some sense with every human being (both the believer and unbeliever), irrespective of sex, race, class, religion, and so forth[15]. *Mystici Corporis* saw every human being as "Christ's brother [and sister] according to the flesh".

These breakthroughs notwithstanding, the dualistic picture dominates the documents and our thinking about the church-world relationship. This thinking assumes that the church exists apart from the world, and the world apart from the church. On the basis of this ontological difference one can then judge other differences between the two, the influence of one on the other, and the caring role, which the church needs to exercise towards the world. Many of us would agree with *RM*, that this world "seems to have lost its sense of ultimate realities and of itself". It has deviated from the moral order, from the demands of justice and from social love. To get back on track, the world needs "Christ the Redeemer" proclaimed to it by the church. Thus while the church recognises the goodness in the world's cultures, it cannot lose sight of its essentially sinful nature and need of salvation. This conviction inspires undaunted commitment of John Paul II to dialogue with other faiths and the world's evangelists and its cultures, and his indefatigable missionary journeys to conduct this dialogue[16].

The church did not invent this dichotomy between itself and the world. Arguably it goes back to Jesus himself, and so commands serious attention. John's Gospel in particular proclaims this in the farewell discourses. Jesus' public accountability to God for his completed mission, his last will for his disciples (traditionally called his priestly prayer; John 17), seems to make this church-world divide its basic inspiration or *leitmotif*[17]. The world has not known God, but Jesus does, and so, understandably, do his followers. The world has nothing but hatred for his disciples to whom Jesus has revealed God's name and given God's word, even as it had nothing but hatred for Jesus himself. The disciples inevitably remain in the world, but they are not of the world. To be kept safe from the world seems to mean the same as being kept from the evil one, the prince of this world. The Holy Spirit will convict the world of sin because of its refusal to believe in Jesus, while the disciples who believe in him will

15. *RH*, 13-14; *RM*, 10.2; *NMI*, 49.
16. For a list of these journeys, see *TMA*, 24; *NMI*, 13.
17. On the import of this prayer in Jesus' mission, see OKURE, *The Johannine Approach to Mission: A Contextual Study of John 4:1-42* (WUNT, II/31), Tübingen, Mohr Siebeck, 1988, pp. 191-226. ID., *John* (n. 3), pp. 213-219 and pp. 1492-1494.

be co-witnesses with the Holy Spirit against the world (15,26; 16,7-11), and so forth. This motif appears in diverse ways in rest of the New Testament. 1 Peter urges believers to steer clear of the world and its ways, since they are already separated by virtue of their call and consecration as God's holy and "priestly people" (1 Pet 2,9-12). Paul, too, urges the Philippians not to imitate the world, but rather to redeem it by their exemplary conduct (Phil 2,15)[18]. Revelation sums up this dualism in its own inimitable way, by making the church-world divide its leitmotif (Rev 14,14-20).

Yet, as in the church's teachings aforementioned, the picture in these NT works is not one-sided. John's Gospel also gives the greatest affirmation of the world unsurpassed even by the constant refrain in Genesis 1 ("And God saw that it was good"). It declares that God loved the world to such an extreme that he gave his *monogenès* (a word impossible to translate in English). The idea is that God poured out the divine self, the replica and perfect representation of himself, his uniquely beloved Son, loved as no one else is loved (John 1,14.18). God did this, not to judge and condemn the world, but so that this world might be saved through him (3,16). The very presence of Jesus' disciples in the world after his departure is so that through them the world might believe that God did indeed send him (17,21c). Belief here, as in the ancient world, was not merely an intellectual assent to a creedal formula; it was the commitment and orientation of the self to a way of life, here the life of Jesus who is himself the Way and the Life (14,6). Upon the completion of his mission, Jesus sends his disciples as God had sent him (20,21-23) and commissions them to go out to the whole world and proclaim to it the good news of its liberation from sin, from all death-dealing or anti-life forces. They were to initiate and welcome all the nations into Trinitarian communion (for all were initially created in God's image and likeness) (Gen 1,26-27) and promote among them a life of ongoing discipleship (Matt 28,20).

Paul equally proclaims that the entire creation was subjected to decay, not of its own will (implying that the world is not guilty before God), but by the will of the one who thus subjected it in hope of giving it a new birth. This is the very letter in which Paul deplores the human depravity that occasioned God's anger but later gave place to God's righteousness because of his love for humanity. As believers, recipients of the first fruits of the Spirit, long for their full redemption in Christ, and wait in patient hope for it, so does the creation itself (Rom 8,21-22). The author of Revelation ends his vision by celebrating the birth of a new world, a new

---

18. See further Col 1,21-22; 2,13; Eph 2,1-10.

heaven and a new earth alongside that of the new Jerusalem/Church, the Bride of the Lamb (Rev 21–22). It ends with a curse on anyone who would dare to change anything in his work (22,18-19). This new/renewed heaven and earth are the permanent home and habitat of the new/renewed New Jerusalem, the Church, the Bride of the Lamb. In NT vision, therefore, it is actually impossible to separate the world from the church, no matter how much they may appear to exist in opposition. God's will for both appears to be that they should coexist as siblings, interweaving, not as ineluctable enemies (as in the relationship between the Israelis and the Palestinians).

Some scholars have noted that the sectarian spirit and dualism in the Johannine account of the farewell discourses belong to a later stage in the life of the church and were inspired by the persecution experienced by the church in the Johannine community. The value of this theory is that the apparent rejection of the world registered in the farewell discourses need not be interpreted as the heartbeat of Jesus' gospel. Rather, it draws attention to how the church's experiences in the world inevitably affects its own self-understanding *vis-à-vis* the world, either positively or negatively. The same applies to the other NT passages. The lesson here is that our dialogue on ecclesiology does not happen abstractly, but emerges concretely in the dynamics of actual world-church relationship. This awareness invites us to constantly review what motivates our perceptions of this relationship and assess whether or not they are inspired by or in keeping with the spirit of Jesus' gospel. In their symbiotic relationship, the church and the world emerge always as mutually dependent, nurturing and impacting, interpenetrating and interweaving one another, both positively and negatively. Neither in the teaching of the church nor in the NT then, do we get a monolithic view of the church and the world. The problem is that in addressing the issue we have tended to focus on the negative aspect. Time has perhaps come to radically review this.

We may press home this issue by emphasising that *first was the world, not the church*. The church came to birth after creation, so too the call of Abraham, proto-ancestor of Israel which is said to pre-figure the church, the new Israel. The church itself is located in the physical geopolitical world. When a diocese or parish is set up, it does not exist in a vacuum but is given clearly defined geographical boundaries. The people who make up the church are themselves already socialised into their different cultures, each with its value systems, language and frames of reference. Except in the area of jurisdiction, the boundaries between the secular and the spiritual, the church and the state, are often more ideological than real. The sustained struggle between the papacy and the medieval kings vividly reminds us of this truth, a struggle which eventually resulted in the creation of the Papal State, the Vatican City, the Seat (headquarters) of our Roman Catholic Church. As human beings, all members of the church exist in the real world. We are first socialised into our culture and its worldview before we are socialised into the church. How else do we understand life, our environment and the world, except through our cultural language, mindset and worldview? We are the church and we are the world.

II. The World in the Church: Influence of the Empire

We have said that *first was the world, not the church*. This can be concretely illustrated in the organisational structure of our church. In many respects, our Roman Catholic Church owes much of its organisational structure today to the "Donation of Constantine" and the legacy of the Roman Empire, what I may call the "illegal marriage" with the Empire. This influence applies in the liturgy with its Roman rite, and juridically in its canon law. The Lateran Palace seems to have been the dowry for this marriage. Today the Lateran Basilica has become the "mother church" of our Roman Catholic Church (because it is the Pope's own church and seat, *cathedra*). This designation sidetracks the Upper Room where Jesus had consecrated himself as bread and wine for the life of the world, and where the Holy Spirit gave birth to the church on mission. A "purification of memory" and an "examination of conscience" (*TMA*, 34) is needed here, not in order to cast stones at the past, but so as to respond like the prodigal son who, once he realised the height from which he had fallen said, "I will arise [leave this place] and return to my Father" (Luke 15,18). The church today badly needs this return to the spirit of the gospel in all humility and joy.

John of Paris (ca. 1250-1306) commenting on the "Donation of Constantine" observes that because He [Constantine] gave the western Empire to Sylvester and his successors and the imperial emblems such as his palace, crown and the like. Some people propose therefore that by reason of this gift, the pope is emperor and lord of the world and that he can appoint kings and get rid of them like an emperor, especially during a vacancy of Empire, and that he can be appealed to, just like the emperor[19]. John of Paris does not think it necessarily follows!

---

19. O. O'DONOVAN – J.L. O'DONOVAN (eds.), *From Irenaeus to Grotius: A Sourcebook in Christian Political Thought 100-1625*, Grand Rapids, MI – Cambridge, UK, William B. Eerdmans Publishing Company, 1999, p. 409.

This assimilation of the church and its leadership style to the ways of the Empire gave rise to a free and unchecked entry of the world into the church, as a modern author rightly observes. Constantine converted to Christianity and gave this religion privileged social status in his Empire. The church made *full use* of this privilege and much emphasis was laid on the organisational structure of the church, *following the example of the administrative structure of the Roman Empire*. Unity in organisation and structure was regarded as the embodiment of the inner unity of the Church. Constantine's victory had great significance because in its wake the face of the unity of the church changed structurally[20].

The author further notes that before Constantine, "the unity of the church was a unity of church and worship" (as opposed to unity of "organisational structure"). It would not be far wrong to note that this assimilation of the ways of the Empire deviated the church itself from being God's instrument of proclaiming the good news to all the nations, into becoming itself a kind of worldly Empire. We are yet to recover from the effects of this deviation.

The influence of the Empire is still at work, for instance, in the system of appointing Nuncios and Bishops (Local Ordinaries)[21]. As the emperor appointed governors and sent supervisors to the provinces, regions and tetrarchates (e.g., Pontius Pilate as governor of Judea, Herod as tetrarch of Galilee), so did Rome appoint and send Apostolic Nuncios/Papal Delegates to the different countries, as its representatives *in situ*. The same applied in the overall organisation of the local church into dioceses and parishes, governed by bishops appointed by Rome and assisted by priests. The practice is still with us today. It serves as a clear example of the interpenetration of the world in the church and the church in the world, the church taking from the cultural and political practices of the world the principles of its structural and organisational self-understanding. Much of the hierarchical structure of the church still in force today derives from this legacy of the Empire.

Not only did we borrow the current hierarchical structures of the church from that of the Roman Empire. The Empire also left the church with a

---

20. G. Gous, *Ten Memory Marks in Ecumenical History*, in C. Lombaard (ed.), *Essays and Exercises in Ecumenism*, Pietermaritzburg, Cluster Publications, 1999, 42-54, esp. p. 47; emphases mine.

21. *The Local Church and Catholicity: Acts of the International Colloquium, Salamanca, Spain April 2-7, 1991* (Reprints from *The Jurist* 52 [1992]), Washington, Catholic University of America, 1992; the work contains a wide range of essays on the appointment of bishops, papal legates and local bishops, the relation of the local church to and within the universal church (catholicity) and useful papal documents on these issues.

linguistic heritage and culture that lasted until Vatican Council II and its call for all round renewal, though the legacy is still very much alive. Latin became and remained until the *aggiornamento* of Vatican Council II the official language of the church for the Catholic Bible (the Vulgate of Jerome), for liturgical celebrations, the church's official documents (the *Acta Leonis* became the *Apostolicae Sedis* in 1909), for canon law and for theological discourse. The liturgical symbols, rites, rituals, garb (e.g., stole and chasuble) still dominantly in use today, reflect those used in the Roman "pagan" cults. The cult around the Emperor was in many respects transferred to the Pope, the highest authority in the Church, even God's representative. Roman jurisprudence gave birth to and informed much of Canon law in the 1917 and revised 1983 Codes. The word "Roman" in the Roman Catholic Church is not entirely fortuitous. It registers a reality of its historical development in many of its aspects that have lasted to this day. The church today, some thirty-five years after Vatican Council II is still struggling to become a truly universal Church, not just the Roman Church spread throughout the world[22]. The church encourages inculturation theologically and in principle but often discourages it when it comes to practice. Yet the Roman Catholic Church itself was, and in many ways still is, a church that fully inculturated in the culture of the Roman Empire without much hindrance.

This evidence, which is hardly exhausted, makes our church-world dichotomy highly questionable. This "perceived" dichotomy hides the crucial point that the world is very much in the church, in our self-organisation and in each member and community of the church, in much the same way as, and in some respects even more so than, the church is in the world. It was said of Rome that it had never been defeated by a foreign army, till it became Christian under Constantine. The effects of the marriage thus appear to have been mutually debilitating. We are not here offering a critique of these practices, but simply asking that we become aware of their active presence in the church. The focus on organisational structure (instead of "unity of worship") as the embodiment of unity was an unfortunate shift from the gospel. This issue figures among those things that John Paul II repeatedly describes as "deviations from the Gospel". The early church (Paul, for instance) spoke of the "unity of the Spirit in a bond of peace". Because there is "one body and one Spirit",

---

22. K. RAHNER, *Towards a Fundamental Theological Interpretation of Vatican II*, trans. L.J. O'DONOVAN, in *Theological Studies* 40 (1979) 715-727; Rahner notes that it is only since the Vatican Council that the Church which moved from the Jewish to the Hellenistic world in the first century is for the first time on the way to becoming a truly universal church.

all members of the "one body" are called to the "one hope" through the
same "one Lord, one faith, one baptism" (Eph 4,3-5). We need to dialogue on the diverse consequences of the entry of the Empire into the
church in order to discern better how its enduring dynamics have hin-
dered or can help us to become church in the twenty-first century, in our
essentially multi-cultural and multi-ethnic world.

III. ECCLESIOLOGICAL FRUIT OF THE LEGACY FROM THE EMPIRE

The division between priests and laity emerges as and seems to incarnate the worst fruit of this legacy of the Empire because of the hierarchical nature of our church, where the church seems to be coterminous
with the hierarchy. We look at some images that convey the unfortunate
fruit of this illegal marriage with the Empire. The first is the portrait of
the priest as painted by Archbishop Anthony D'Sousa of India. He rightly
observes, "The ecclesiology which governs our thinking is that the
Church is a hierarchy and the clergy, to whom the laity are clients". Consequently, the first concern of the priest is not building communities of
mature and responsible Christians, specifically Catholics, but "saving
individuals" alias "souls". The Archbishop gives a vivid picture of the
priest in his Indian context, which probably applies to priests worldwide,
except perhaps in the First World countries where the shortage of priests
has resulted in a better collaboration between priests and laity. The portrait is this:

> The priest ... today is expected to be a genius: a philosopher, a theologian,
> a man of God, a linguist, a musician, an anthropologist, an engineer, a doc-
> tor, a banker and what have you. Name a secular profession and in some way
> the priest is called upon to dabble in it in the line of his duty. Any wonder
> the priest is suffering from a massive guilt complex? He is made to feel:
> "without me you can do nothing". On him rest the church, the sacraments,
> the totality of relationship of man to God and God to man. And without
> him there would be no Church, no sacraments and, strangely, no religion[23].

The hierarchical structure of the church described in *LG* chapter three
and reinforced by *Christus Dominus* justifies this picture. The pyramidal
structure places the clergy at the apex as the "superior" and the laity, by
far the silent majority, at the base as "inferiors". The document designates
them as "subjects", not "inferiors", but the meaning is the same.

---

23. A. D'SOUSA, *Wanted: A Seminary for a New Way of Being Church*, in *Vidyajoti*
65 (2001) 60-65, p. 61.

This image contrasts sharply with that of the NT with its diversity of gifts among the members of the church as we find in Paul's letters. Here some are "apostles, some prophets, some evangelists, some pastors, some teachers". All these functions are given to different members in the community "to equip the saints for the work of ministry, for building up the body of Christ till we all attain to the unity of faith and of knowledge of the Son of God, to mature humanity, to the measure of the status of the fullness of Christ" (Eph 4,11-13). To this list 1 Corinthians adds "workers of miracles, healers, helpers, administrators, speakers in various kinds of tongues" (12,28), in the order of importance of the ministry (not of persons). It also adds a list of charismatic gifts given to different members of the community for "the common good", that of building up persons, not structures, in the community (1 Cor 12,4-11). We need all these ministries and gifts to grow into a mature church. In our current system all these and more secular ones are placed on the head of the poor priest. No wonder he can say without me you can do nothing, because without these gifts the body cannot grow. In the long run both the clergy/superior and the laity/subject suffer. So does the entire body (1 Cor 12,26).

The other image is from a conversation with a layman (male) in a parish that is run by a group of religious priests. It struck me that the issue arose in a parish run by a religious order since the religious are supposed to be less conscious of striving for the power and authority of the Empire model. The layman shared that in one of their many societies and lay associations in the parish, the members had a good idea of how to organise themselves more effectively for the growth of their members and the good of the parish. They worked this out in its details, then went to consult the parish priest for his approval before implementing it. The parish priest in question was mad that they had dared to develop their ideas before ever consulting him. So he scraped the entire project. In explanation of his action he told the people that the church was "autocratic". I said, "He meant hierarchical" because our church is not autocratic; but the layman insisted that he meant "autocratic". So I asked, "What did he mean by that?". He replied, "He meant that when the Pope speaks the bishops jump. When the bishop speaks the priests jump. When the priest speaks the people jump". So I asked "And who jumps when the people speak?". Perhaps God (who hears the cry of the poor) or Jesus (who stood up when Stephen was being stoned to death) jumps. The laypersons in question were highly placed professionals and executive directors in their secular professions. But they could not think within the church without the permission or approval of their parish priest.

We know of course that the church is not autocratic, nor does it approve this type of hierarchical frog jumping, where those at the base of the pyramid get the brunt of it all, especially if they are women. The problem is that if those who operate the system perceive their authority in this way, they will act accordingly. Nevertheless, the system itself is partly, if not largely, responsible for this. It gives the local ordinary absolute executive, administrative and legislative powers, which they exercise freely, and the priest models this at his own parish level. We no longer speak of the pope's fullness of powers, and have, since the pontificate of Paul VI, dropped the tiara, symbol of the Pope's triple powers. But the philosophy that inspired its usage is still very much operative, the documents that say the contrary notwithstanding. *Lumen gentium* still recognised that the Pope has "full, supreme and universal power over the church which he can always exercise unhindered" (*LG, 22*). Peter in the NT did not have or exercise any such powers, as we see for instance in the Council of Jerusalem (Acts 15,6-11) and similar instances. Those who operate the current system are socialised into this frame of mind right from the minor seminary. We need to humbly recognise and address this lasting fruit of the Empire's legacy with the freedom which Christ and the Spirit give, for the slave cannot remain forever in the house (John 8,34-36).

This priest-laity divide encapsulates the opposition that Vatican Council II sets between the church and the world in *Lumen gentium*. The Council views the world as the proper sphere of the activity of the laity. Their mission is to make Christ present there and penetrate the world's activities with gospel values (*LG*, ch. 4). The essence of their ministry is to sanctify the world. They do this not through the ministerial priesthood ("ministerial" being originally understood as servant or serving), but through their share in "the ordinary priesthood of Christ". This priest-clergy divide promotes a poor self-identity in the laity, as those who form a bridge between the church (the ministerial priests or clergy) and the world. The conception leaves them hanging in the air, belonging neither fully to the church nor fully to the world[24].

The overall impression is that the real church (understood in people's minds as the hierarchy and the clergy) is beyond the reach of the world and vice versa. This equation of laity-world, priest-church, raises the questions: Are the laity integral members of both the church and the world or merely a bridge between the two? Are the clergy themselves not

---

24. See further, K. KUNNUMPURAM, S.J., *Beyond the Clergy-Laity Divide*, in *SEDOS Bulletin* 32 (2000) 151-159; OKURE, *The Laity: People of God in the African Church*, in *SEDOS* 25 (1993) 161-166; ID., *The Priest in Nigeria Today: A Layman's Perspective, A Response*, in L.N. MBEFO – E.M. EZEOGU (eds.), *The Clergy in Nigeria Today* (SIST Symposium Series, 3), Enugu, Nigeria, Attakwu, 1994, 49-58.

in the world? The church here is not an ideological concept but a body made up of flesh and blood human beings (be it the church triumphant, suffering or militant). All its members are real people formed and conditioned by and in the world. The church itself cannot exist and function outside the reality called world from which it takes its diverse forms and models[25].

How do we conduct a dialogue in an essentially pyramidal system? It is very easy to roll down instructions from the apex to the base in such a system, but it is virtually impossible for the base to make its voice heard at the apex. The pyramidal structure essentially impedes dialogue. We need to emphasise that leadership is absolutely essential and indispensable for any group of persons. If a group does not select a leader, one will surely emerge, and it may not be to its liking. Jesus made clear and unmistakable provision for leadership in his *ekklesia*. The issue is the type of leadership that enables and empowers this *ekklesia* to truly become God's church, according to the mind of Christ.

The church of the Upper Room was a truly dialogical church (if we reject the word "democratic"). There, Jesus dialogued with his disciples when he constituted them as church by the Eucharist and by purifying them by means of "the word" (John 15,3). There, Peter and the 120 disciples dialogued and acted together under God's guidance in their selection of Matthias to replace Judas (Acts 1,15-26) and in the settlement of the first ethnic/racial dispute within the community that led to the election of the deacons (Acts 6,1-6). Pentecost, that gave divine tongue and voice to all present, happened in the Upper Room. Outside that room they all dialogued with their audience, from every nation under heaven to gather a rich harvest for God, under the leadership of Peter. That is how the church on mission came to birth (Acts 2). There, too, most likely, Peter defended himself before the brethren for having visited and eaten with Cornelius (Acts 11,1-17). There, the church held dialogically its first Council to resolve the question of their identity as Christians, distinct from followers of Judaism (Acts 15). Paul adopted the same dialogical and persuasive approach in dealing with the young churches that he founded. A church on mission, that today continues the mission of Jesus as exemplified by the first disciples, needs to return to its origins as a church in dialogue *ad intra*, if it is to be more truly itself

---

25. On these models, see A. DULLES, *Models of Church*, Garden City, NY, Image Books, 1974, expanded 1987; J.M. GUSTAFSON, *Treasure in Earthen Vessels: The Church as a Human Community*, New York, Harper, 1961, esp. pp. 105-107 where the author cautions against reductionism or seeing the church as merely a human community or as a doctrinal reductionism that ignores the human elements in it.

and of better service to its members and humanity. So we need to move beyond the Empire model and look for other models and ways of being church.

IV. BEYOND THE EMPIRE MODEL

The Empire hierarchical model of the past believed in the divine right of kings, the democratic model of today believes in the divinely human rights of every person (i.e., as made in God's image and likeness). The church has tended to monopolise this divine right for the hierarchy and clergy, who alone are held to be "configured to Christ". Commonly accepted in the past by the secular world, the hierarchical model of the Empire type has long given place in secular society to the democratic one. This new model rests on society's awareness of the fundamental human rights of every person. Society not only holds this belief. It has also legislated for its implementation through the UN Universal Declaration of Human Rights: Arts. 1 and 2: "All human beings are born free and equal in dignity and rights" and none shall be discriminated against on the basis of "race, colour, sex, language, religion, political opinion, national or social origin, property, birth or other status ...". In particular, the UN has taken a series of affirmative actions to implement this charter for the empowerment of women: the decade in solidarity with women, the convention for the elimination of all forms of discrimination against women, the Beijing conference, the appointment of Mary Robinson as the UN personnel for the promotion of human rights, and so forth. Other nations have followed suit. Some nation states have legislated for the inclusion of a minimum quota of women in politics especially in the diverse ministries of their government (in Malawi, for instance, at least a third of all public functionaries and ministers must be women by law). In the wake of the abolition of slavery, the US introduced the system of "busing" to eliminate the discrimination against Blacks. South Africa has legislated for the overthrow of apartheid by abrogating the laws and practices that enforced the evil system. Even if the success of this moves are questionable, the fact is that they have taken place, legally.

On the theological level, EATWOT (Ecumenical Association of Third World Theologians), for instance, ruled that at least a third of the membership from each region must be women. If that quota was not met, the region (Africa, Asia Latin America and the Minorities in the First World) was prevented from presenting new members for admission in the Association. As a result, the membership of the Association is now almost fifty-fifty, and the stipulation no longer holds since it has been overtaken. An effective dialogue on ecclesiology will require similar legislation if the new way of being church advocated by Vatican Council II (especially that the laity do not exist in function of the priest but derive their ministry from their baptism in Christ) is to take effect. This applies not only in the clergy-laity relationship, but also and most especially in relation to the status of women in the church. The issue of women in the church, who is woman, mother and teacher, requires a treatment all its own. If the church (made up of all of us) is woman and we are children of the church, then we are all women (at least our souls are brides of Christ). In the end we will all become woman, since the church, the heavenly Jerusalem, the Bride of the Lamb, is woman. This faith in the church as woman calls for a new type of dialogue on ecclesiology that addresses flesh and blood women's place in the church seen as the primary sacrament of Christ.

The unfortunate belief that the current hierarchical model is divinely willed and installed for all eternity has trapped and handicapped the church in many respects. One frequently hears the argument that "ordination is not a human right, but a vocation". Yet one has to be biologically a human male even to be eligible to be considered for this divinely willed and freely given vocation. If one is biologically a woman, one is automatically excluded by virtue of one's sex. A little girl in the confirmation class put it well. In answer to a visiting bishop's question, "How many sacraments are there?". She answered enthusiastically in all her innocence: "Seven for boys and six for girls". The Sacrament of Holy Orders is the only sacrament reserved solely for men, on the basis of sex. Is Christ then not present in the other sacraments (including the Eucharist) and in the church, woman, "mother"? Is it not this church, woman, mother who ordains all "her" ministers including the Pope? There is much confusion in these arguments *ad hominem* that needs to be sorted out in the light of Christ and the gospel. As in the past the church used the argument of the divine right of kings from secular society to buttress its claims and practices in the hierarchical system modelled after the Empire, it also needs to use or allow current democratic developments in secular society to influence its understanding and practice of this same system and so effect a renewal or bring about changes that are based on the gospel of Jesus.

A latecomer in accepting the UN Declaration of Human Rights (the church initially resisted it because of its secular origins), the church has now not only fully endorsed this Declaration. It has even emerged as its ardent champion, encouraging its observance by secular society. It has equally emerged as the champion of women's rights, especially in the pontificate of John Paul II who even sees himself as *"papa femi-nista"*. John XXIII spearheaded this change of papal attitude in *Pacem in terris* (1,39-42) where he saw the women's issue as one of the greatest signs of the times, and prophesied that now that women were aware of their dignity, they would no longer accept to be exploited and marginalized. Despite the laudable efforts of John Paul II on behalf of women, including his "apology" to women[26], these efforts are weakened by the sustained belief in the basic inequality of women to men in the church concretised in the ordination question. Since ordination includes all leadership roles as highlighted by Archbishop D'Sousa, it means in effect that women as a sex are by nature perpetual "subjects" to men in God's church, and God is supposed to be the author of this.

However ingenious the arguments advanced to get around the question, the basic question of women in the church is their "perceived" inequality with men as human beings, and *in Christ* (the praises of women in *Mulieris dignitatem* and other letters of John Paul II to women notwithstanding). We may ask this key question differently thus: Is Christ in women and are women in Christ? Is it really true of women that they are as equally configured to Christ at baptism (*Christianos alter Christos,* according to Augustine) as are men, as the church teaches and believes? If they are, what impedes Christ from operating through them in his own person as he operates through men? The consistent teaching of the church from the NT times and throughout history till today on the import of baptism needs to be revisited christologically with respect to women in the church. The church tends to have a selective memory when it comes to the place and role of women in the early church. A "purification of memory" urged by John Paul II (*NMI*, 6) is very much needed here; so too a sound theological understanding of what Jesus really intended for his brothers and sisters born of him (in his blood), made one with him and endowed with the gift of one and the same Holy Spirit without discrimination based on sex (Gal 3,25-29). We may need a Universal Declaration of the Divine Rights of Women in the Catholic Church ("divine" as persons created in God's image and likeness, and as persons incorporated into Christ and the Trinity at Baptism). Equally necessary is a radical review of our understanding of Christ's priesthood in the light of his person. He is God's gospel, the quintessence of God's definitive plan of salvation for humanity, by God's deliberate and predetermined will and

---

26. See ACCATTOLI, *When a Pope Asks Forgiveness* (n. 11), ch. 4.

intent born of woman (Gal 4,4). Ultimately, the priesthood is his, not that of human beings, male or female.

V. THE CHURCH AS SERVANT OF THE WORLD

Along with this, the church needs to be and be seen as the servant of the world helping it to attain to the perfection intended for it by God, Creator, Redeemer and Sanctifier. Perhaps this relationship of service best helps us to understand Jesus' description of his church as a city set on a mountain top (to give hope and sustain aspiration for a higher way of life), a lamp put on a lamp stand to give light to all in the house, and the salt of the earth, necessary for seasoning, sweetening, preserving the earth against actual and potential corruption. Our being light of the world and salt of the earth should help to liberate the world, to which we belong, from the darkness of sin, selfishness, terrorism and war and preserve it from actual and potential corruption (the worship of money), as it grows in sweetness. Salt sweetens and preserves food, but too much salt makes the food unpalatable, even injurious to health. Some scholars recall that salt was rare and very precious when Jesus first told the parable. So too was light. Light is a good thing in darkness, but light where there is no darkness is energy wasted, conversely too much light in a room at night can actually become a nuisance. Neither salt nor light is self-centered or self-serving. They exist for the benefit of those who use them.

This designation of the church as servant in a multifaceted manner is not independent of Jesus' own self perception in relation to the church and the world, as testified by his own disciples. Jesus is God's servant *par excellence* and the Saviour of the World (John 4,42; Acts 4,12). The church, his body is called to exercise Jesus' priestly, liturgical, prophetic and socio-political functions for the benefit of the world. Simeon described him as the glory of God's people, Israel, and the eye-opener of God's people (the Gentiles) worldwide. He opens their eyes to see their own innate God-given goodness, glory and destiny and so strive to reclaim them or attain them ever more fully. He also opens their eyes to see the dark side of their customs, norms, practices which are in opposition to God's gospel or good news for them. The church, Christ's body, should do likewise.

In the past we (the church) had fostered a type of self-definition or knowledge that prevented us from becoming aware of the full impact and scope of our calling to be servant to the world by the gospel message and the mission that Jesus commissioned his followers to undertake for the world: "Go out to the whole world" and proclaim the good news that now all were to become members of God's own household thanks to Jesus' accomplished mission as "Saviour of the world" (Matt 28,18-20; John 4,42). Salient features for this mission are worth recalling. Jesus asked the disciples not only to "go out" to the whole world and proclaim the good news, but also to "make disciples of all nations". Making disciples invites to communion among those who consider themselves as disciples of a given master. We had understood making disciples of all nations as bringing all the lost (the pagans) into the barque of Peter where they were sure to find salvation, since outside of that barque they were sure to drown or be condemned to eternal death (*extra ecclesiam nulla salus*). The understanding of the church as Peter's barque gave rise to going out to convert people by "making" them confess (as an article of faith), their discipleship of Christ. That approach was perhaps for its own time only[27]. Now is the time for noticing the other images, given us by Jesus, which call us to a different way of being church in and for today's world, and for understanding and regulating our mutual relationship as his disciples.

To make disciples of all nations implies that the church itself is a disciple, one who follows, learns step-by-step, to serve as Jesus did and thus enjoy Trinitarian communion (cf. 1 John 4,1-4). Jesus has programmatically drawn all things to himself, but only so that he might restore them to God who then becomes "all things in all persons" (1 Cor 15,28). The church, seen as God's gathering of humanity to the divine self (not to the Catholic or Christian Church) in and through Christ, is essentially called to enter into communion with the entire creation in a process of incarnation (self-emptying and selective assumption; Phil 2,5-11) so that the world may be saved "through us" who are branches of his vine and are enabled by God to bear lasting fruit. Emerging from the Jewish matrix stamped with its election theology, the church has clothed itself with the garb of election-ism and has worn that garb for almost 2000 years. Wearing that garb for so long, we became comfortable in it and failed to ask whether it enabled us to be identified as church, "God's gathering" of humanity into Trinitarian communion and wholeness. The garb of election (as "the new Israel of God") is fast wearing out, to be replaced by that of inclusiveness. Vatican Council II initiated the process by abolishing the former

---

27. S. BATE, *Matthew 10: A Mission Mandate for the Global Context*, in T. OKURE (ed.), *To Cast Fire Upon the Earth: Bible and Mission Collaborating in Today's Multicultural Global Context*, Pietermaritzburg, Cluster Publications, 2000, 42-56.

conception of the church as Peter's barque. The church now needs to commit itself to this new task of working for inclusiveness so that it may be able to conduct a fruitful dialogue with the world in the diverse contexts where it is located and nourished by the Spirit-filled resources of the world.

VI. Resources for a New Way of Being Church: Examples of Jesus and the Early Church

The church exists in the physical, geopolitical world; but it is not intended to be of the world. The world here is understood as those value systems that are hostile to Christ, God's gospel (Rom 1,1), and that may be present in the hearts its own members as in those of unbelievers. This gospel is the good news of God's liberation of humanity from bondage to racism, sexism, classism, isolationism, individualism, consumerism, and all the other "isms" that are the by-product of the anthropological sins of racism, sexism and classism (Gal 3,28). If the church, the body of Christ, is the visible presence in the world of Christ who is drawing all human beings and the entire creation to divine self, then that church has a duty to be in the world in much the same way as Jesus himself was and still is in the world, as word become flesh (incarnation/inculturation), as the light of the world and as God's agent of reconciling the world to the divine self (2 Cor 5,18-19). Jesus cited his own life as eloquent and irrefutable witness that he came from God and revealed God. John's Gospel traditionally viewed as the gospel on which the church roots its theological self-understanding, articulates this in many ways[28]. His claim to authenticity and the power of his authority rested on this irrefutable witness of his life, especially in his teaching and manner of relating to all classes of people in need. Even his opponents recognised this while rejecting his claim to divinity (John 10,33). Similarly, the life of the members of his body and their interpersonal relationship should become the primary means by which they convince the world of their authenticity and mission (John 17,21). Jesus designated his followers, the church, as the salt of the earth, the leaven of the dough and the city on a hilltop. As mustard seed this church participates in God's reign that grows (feeding on the God-given resources provided by the earth) until it becomes a home for all the birds of heaven to come and rest (Ps 103,12).

---

28. See in particular, John 10,37-38; 14,10-11.

It was not only the contemporaries of Jesus, even his opponents, who found his life faultless. In our days unbelievers have done the same. We recall Mahatma Gandhi, for instance, who loved the peace-loving Christ but had a question about Christians. Aloysius Pieris, a Sri Lankan Jesuit reported at a consultation on Inculturation organised by The Institute of Missiology, MISSIO Aachen in 1994, that he once sought to find out from a group of Buddhist monks whether they found anything unique about Jesus which they did not find in their own or other world religions (this was long before the days of *Dominus Iesus*). To this effect he gave them a copy of just the four Gospels, not the Bible or even the entire New Testament. The monks took a long time before they gave their answer. When they did, they gave it in the form of a huge tableau (a slide of which Pieris brought to the consultation). In the huge tableau the monks had all classes of people, men and women, all casts, high and low, standing beautifully dressed, looking hale and hearty. In the foreground was Jesus, dressed like a Sri Lankan servant, kneeling down washing their feet. When Pieris asked them to explain, they said what struck them was that all classes of people and castes were welcome by him, with equal respect. They found it particularly unique that women were at home in his company and played key roles in his life and ministry. The second thing that struck them was that Jesus, the master founder and guru should literally be the servant of his disciples (they understood servant here literally, not ideologically, or as a *theologoumenon*). This they also found to be very unique. Pieris commented that it was unique that the two things for which our church is not known, service and the substantial inclusion of women, should emerge as the two most striking, even unique aspects of Jesus and his mission that even unbelievers can recognise. There is a rich, objective resource here for our fruitful dialogue on ecclesiology.

Jesus' inclusion of women started at the incarnation since he chose to assume one hundred percent of his humanity, including his maleness, from a woman (Luke 1,26-38; Gal 4,4). He had women disciples who stood by him from the crib to the cross (the first real altar of sacrifice), whom he made the first witnesses of his resurrection (though characteristically, the church ingeniously left them out in the early Christian creed on the resurrection, held as of foundational importance for the Christian faith (1 Cor 15,3-8) and commissioned to announce that now he and all his followers were brothers and sisters (no longer just slaves or friends). These women, more than the men disciples, seemed to have understood what his mission was all about, service and ministering to others out of his own substance (Luke 8,1-3). Jesus loved them to the core and appreciated their love, and told them so by his actions, weeping when they wept (John 11,35), and interrupting his ascension to the Father to console them (John 20,17)[29].

We are speaking of leadership and strategies of empowerment for a new way of being church. Jesus had a very clearly defined hierarchical (if we must use that term) model of leadership, which, as we have seen, he personally, visibly practised and enjoined upon his church leaders (John 13, 20; Luke 22,24-27 par.). His early disciples picked up his leadership and hierarchical model. Paul articulates this well in his letter to the Corinthians: "What then is Apollos? What is Paul? Servants through whom you believed as the Lord assigned each. I planted, Apollos watered, but God gives the growth and increase" (1 Cor 3,5-6). There is no question here of their being everything without whom the Corinthians could do nothing. Rather, that role belongs to God who assigns each worker his/her respective roles and remains all in all. These church leaders are only God's fellow workers, servants. The Corinthian Christians are "God's field, God's building" (vv 7-9). The hierarchy that emerges from this servant model is the reversed pyramid with the apostles and leaders at the base: "Paul or Apollos or Cephas, ... all are yours; and you are Christ's; and Christ is God's" (reversed in the sense that the leaders have to decrease like the apex, so that the Corinthians may grow and expand into Christ, for God's glory). All this is from God. God calls, is ever faithful and will do it (1 Cor 1,9). So the service leadership role is crucial and indispensable for effective growth of the church. This leadership is not weak, passive or oppressive. On the contrary, because it is truly an empowering service, it can be very challenging and demanding of those led (2 Cor 10,1-12), since it is acting on trust from God, a trust that cannot be compromised (cf. 2 Cor 4,1-2).

Jesus did not simply prescribe this enabling or service type of leadership. He performed it himself for Peter. We recall the fishing episode in John 21. Peter and the other disciples had spent all night fishing, but caught nothing. Jesus, the light of the world comes to their aid at dawn and directs them to fish in the right way, that is with is enabling presence since without him they can do nothing (John 15,5). He is the irreplaceable source of their life and ministry, who supplies all their needs; if, as head he is ever replaced in his body, the church, the body will surely die. No matter how badly the leadership may have been exercised in the past,

---

29. For further on these issues see OKURE, *The Significance Today of Jesus' Commission to Mary Magdalene*, in *International Review of Mission* 81 (1992) 177-188; esp. p. 181; ID., *Contemporary Perspectives on Women in the Bible*, in *Bulletin Dei Verbum* 53 (1999) 4-11.

Jesus who builds his church was always irreplaceably present ("I am with you always until the end of time"; Matt 28,20). So after Jesus has enabled Peter to personally catch the fish and sustain his failed boast made before the Passion that he loved him more than all the others, after Jesus had then physically fed Peter and the other disciples, he gives him a triple charge (not to wear the crown or wield absolute powers), but to feed, tend and look after his little sheep and lambs. In the end he himself would follow the master to the point of death and resurrection. In short, Peter was to learn from his own experience of weakness and powerlessness and Jesus' enabling presence in his life to perform the same service to Jesus' sheep, his brothers and sisters, i.e., "strengthen his brethren" (Luke 22,32). He does not intimidate, silence, or beat them as the chief servant does to his fellow servants because the master is supposedly away (Matt 24,48-51). He is to feed and empower the brethren so they too become physically, psychologically, morally and spiritually mature (by finding non-threatening strategies for affirming them, liberating them from frustration, futility and any haunting sense of guilt for past deeds as Peter must have had because of his denial of Jesus).

The same applies in the dialogue with the Samaritan woman. Jesus invited the woman to consider other possibilities than the usual Jewish Samaritan quarrel over the question not of how to worship, but of the right place to worship. Jesus redirects her attention to the real issue, what it means to worship God. In this issue one pays attention, not to what the fathers of the race or the fathers of the church did, but to what God, the Father/Mother of everybody is doing; not on the worth of the ancestral or church traditions, but on the Spirit that God gives freely to all to enable them worship God in spirit and in truth (John 4,23-24). True worshipers transcend all quarrels about correct rituals of worship, which can get in the way and obscure the true nature of worship: redirecting one's entire life to God and embracing the other. When all are engrossed in God, they have little or no time to pick holes in each other's ways of worshiping. This does not mean anarchy in worship. True worship will generate that love which expresses itself in live-giving order and decorum in the worshiping community. The woman listened, accepted Jesus' invitation to take a new look at the situation and consider other possibilities of dealing with the age-old situation. Personally convinced, she ran to spread the good news to others and led them to Jesus. The dialogue resulted in the breakdown of centuries of old barriers. The woman dropped her water pot (symbol of the past and of her social enslavement), moved forward with joy to appropriate her new status as an apostle of her people. A new relationship ensued between her and her people and between her, her people and Jesus and his disciples. Jesus and the disciples stayed and dined, socialised with them for two days, the maximum allowed in the *Didache* for a genuine missionary to stay in anyone place without becoming suspect as an impostor.

Strategies of empowerment! How do we work them out today? How do we empower lay people to exercise their role and ministry as evangelisers of the world, if they are never given the opportunity to learn to speak and hear their voice, views, evangelising gifts affirmed and challenged where necessary by their leaders? Where will they acquire the confidence to enable them minister effectively or evangelise the world if they never have an opportunity to do so within the church (we are not just thinking of catechists who may function in places where the priest is not available)? How will they "sanctify the world", when they themselves are made to feel they need to be permanently sanctified as lay persons (non-experts) by the clergy? The Samaritan woman like the disciples on the ways to Emmaus felt within them that something new had happened to them. Their encounter with Jesus was transformative for themselves and their communities. The Samaritan woman and her people were outsiders. The Emmaus disciples were insiders, but the method and the strategies and result were the same. The dialogue freed them from isolationism and led them into communion.

We need Jesus' strategy if our dialogue is to promote this kind of way of being church. World statistics show that most of the founders and members of the Pentecostal and charismatic churches are former members of the Catholic Church. When they were members of the church, we hardly gave them a voice; now that they have left, we have established Councils to dialogue with them. In some contexts, ecumenical and interfaith encounters, they rank equal with our bishops, archbishops and cardinals (we may leave out the Pope here) as leaders of their churches. Let us dialogue with them within the church, so that our failure to do so may not continue to split up Christ's body. Interestingly, a number of the leaders of these new, breakaway churches are women whom we now recognize as persons and engage in dialogue.

VII. THE NEGLECTED IMAGES OF BEING CHURCH

We have mentioned these images all along, namely, light, salt, leaven, a city on a hilltop and mustard seed. Common to all of them is their usefulness to the people in whose function they exist, their unobtrusive method of operating, and their essentiality for those who use them.

The Dogmatic Constitution on the Church of Vatican Council II, sees the church primarily as the "light of the nations" (*lumen gentium*, inspired perhaps by the prophecy of Simeon; Luke 2,32). Simeon saw Jesus as the light to enlighten the Gentiles, not set in opposition to them. To be light is to establish a relationship that changes people's lives, especially, but not exclusively, the poor of God. As light of the world, Jesus is not in opposition to the world's peoples or nations, but to darkness, the opposite of light (John 1,5). His mission is to enlighten the nations, not to blame them for the darkness. Light and darkness are modes by which human beings live and operate in the world and in the church, and which both affect and reflect their actions, choices and value systems. This is the gist of Jesus' dialogue with Nicodemus (John 3,19-21). Light and darkness here get their meaning, identity and function in relation to the ethical, moral, human and religious values of persons, individually and collectively. So the tension between the spheres and the reality of light and darkness is one of relationship and influence. Christ, the light, "shines in darkness and the darkness could not overcome it" (John 1,5). This light enlightens every person who comes into and lives in the world, and this includes every person who makes up the institutional church. But to be useful, light must truly be itself, light, not darkness; otherwise it will be useless against or indistinguishable from the darkness. "If the light in you is darkness, what of your own darkness, how deep will that be?" (Matt 6,23 par.). "If the salt loses its flavour, what is there to season it or to make it salt again?" (Matt 5,13 par.).

Salt seasons the food; the leaven works within the measure of flour to make it rise and become the bread it is intended to be. The birds of the air that make their nests in the mustard seed, which becomes a big tree, do not thank it for the service, they take it for granted. If this is what Jesus calls us as church to be in terms of the world, then we need to review the endemic polarity we have set between the church and the world, and our general attitude towards the world. The images imply that, unique and distinct as we are, we find our meaning in terms of the world, not by being assimilated, but by interpenetrating and making a difference to it. What if, like Paul, we were to believe that we are for the world, the world is for Christ and Christ is for God? When all Christ's enemies have been subdued through the victory of his resurrection, he will restore all things to God who will then become all in all (1 Cor 15,28). This restoration is that church or kingdom that will embrace all the other human kingdoms or Empires and will itself stand forever.

This type of perception of the church-world relationship differs from the dominant one whereby we believe our mission is to teach, instruct, guide, correct and lead the world from sin to holiness or whereby we project the feeling that we, not Jesus, are the Saviour of the world. The church's belief that Jesus is the sole Saviour of humanity and the world is impeccably consistent and faultless. The problem is to match our belief with our actions. If Jesus is the Christ, then we are not the Christ. No Christian can debate the necessity of the church as God's instrument for salvation. But Jesus tells us that as servants, when we have done all that we are expected to do, we are to recognise that we were merely and essentially servants, servants of the world, of one another and of Christ. As church we have a vital role to play in the world, provided we are authentically light, salt and leaven in ourselves. These images invite us to reach out to enable people to see better who they are before God (people uniquely loved and endowed), and to assess and order aright their lives, relationships and undertakings in the light of Christ. As salt we are to enable them develop the seasoning in their lives, so that they may experience Christ, God's gospel. Equally, they need us as yeast to enable them grow, expand and open up and blossom before God. As we do all this and more by our manner of presence to the world, we do not lose sight that the world is also present to and ministering to us as church.

The basic question is whether the church can indeed be this kind of light in the world, whether it can play this function of helping the world to see aright what it is and what it should be. As salt can it serve to season the world and preserve its genuine goodness? As mustard seed (the church is minute in relation to the rest of the (non-Christian) world), can it open its heart to embrace equally all peoples of the earth so that the church itself might grow in stature, character and grace before God and human beings? As yeast can it be so mixed in the large measure of the vast "unbelieving world" till this world becomes leavened with God's and Christ's own goodness and so rises as leavened dough rises to become delicious bread for its citizens and really beautiful for God?

VIII. DIALOGUE AND INCULTURATION

Inculturation is a key dimension of a dialogue on ecclesiology. How can the church carry out its multi-faceted ministry to or in the world through (or by means of) the word? Word is a basic component of language. Throughout the world, the church, made up of individuals and communities in their concrete socio-cultural settings, operates through the language and cultures of its members in that particular place. Its primary task would be to listen to the aspirations of the peoples in the given culture and study how through it, through discoursing with them as Jesus did with his audience in his own time and country, it can enable and where necessary challenge them to respond to these aspirations in keeping with God's revealed plans and purposes for them. This would be a solid way of proclaiming the good news that "God has reconciled them to the divine self (not to the church) in and through Christ", and that the church itself shares in this reconciliation as a body that has openly accepted God's reconciliation in all the locations where believers exist. For we, though many, form one body, and like grains gathered from, yet located in, different parts of the world, we intensify and increase our effectiveness in being salt to the earth and light to the world until the whole batch of the world is seasoned and becomes bright with God's light and God's love.

More important, then perhaps, than a dialogue on ecclesiology directed towards the relation of the church to the world, what it means to be church in the world, is the need for those who belong to the church to devote substantial time and space to dialogue among ourselves on what it means to be church in the twenty-first century and how to be present to the world in a way that will show that the mission is that of Jesus and we are only a part of that mission and partners with him. The dialogue needs to be conducted on equal footing by all sectors of the church across barriers of race, sex, class, age, state in life, culture and nationality. This dialogue will substantially affect the current church structures, understanding of sacraments, canon law and all the other ways of being church inherited or originating from the negative influences of the Empire. In this dialogue, we will need to reckon with the innate power of structures to resist change, because change means the death of a given structure. Structure here is not only governmental, but attitudinal and architectural. The very way in which our churches and sacred places are structured exercise a powerful influence on the way we think, act and relate to one another when we assemble as church. The structure of the African concept of church as family is not pyramidal, but circular. Traditionally, African houses were built as compounds of round houses, which the expatriates liked to call "huts". Not only were individual houses round, the entire compound was built in a configuration of round houses forming a square. The main house was there but not to the detriment of other houses. The Trinitarian model of communion requires this form. Jesus tells us that he and the Father "are one" and that whatever belongs to the Father belongs to him and is taken at will by the Holy Spirit for the service of humanity.

Inculturation is the heartbeat of mission theology and methodology. It has been operative from time immemorial, even if it is only recently being recognised[30]. The churches in Africa and Asia, in particular, are asking that the traditional western church remember that what has come to be defined as church in terms raised here (structures, symbols, ritual, law of governance), were taken from the pagan Greco-Roman cultures, the matrix from which the western European culture emerged, not primarily from the Gospel of Jesus Christ. Consequently it is a cultural imposition on peoples of other cultural matrix to have to embrace these Eurocentric modes of being church to the detriment of their own cultural heritage. In key instances these later cultural referents may offer better or more gospel-based forms of being church and living the gospel than the inherited western referents. A key example is the essentially communitarian culture of Africa, with its high premium on hospitality, its strong sense of community that embraces the living, the dead (who are never really dead) and those yet to be born. It promotes a sense of corporate responsibility for the growth and survival of the "clan" and respect for nature[31].

IX. CHURCH AS FAMILY OF GOD

It would be inappropriate to conclude this conversation without taking a special look, however briefly, at the African situation. The African Synod held in Rome in 1994 on "The Church in Africa and Her Evangelising Mission: "You shall be my witnesses", Acts 1,8"), gave birth to *Ecclesia in Africa (EIA)*. Since then there has been "Ecclesia" in Europe, in Latin America and in Asia. The African bishops who assembled in Rome with other Bishops of the church adopted the model of "Church as Family of God" as the model that best fitted the African concept of being church (*EIA*, 63). The Synod further asked African and other theologians to assiduously and critically study this model so as to bring out its full implications for our being church in today's world. This is not the place to elaborate on the dimensions of this model. However, I simply note that the African family set up can and does offer a good model for the kind of dialogue *ad intra* and *ad extra* proposed in this conversation. This holds, though, like all other human concepts used to express the mysteries of the kingdom, this model needs to be purified, and

30. Cf. OKURE, *Inculturation: Biblical/Theological Bases*, in T. OKURE – P. VAN THIEL, et al., *32 Articles Evaluating the Inculturation of Christianity in Africa* (Spearhead, 112-114), Eldoret, AMECEA Gaba Publications, 1990, 55-88.
31. Cf. B. BUJO, *African Theology in Its Social Context*, Nairobi, Paulines Publications Africa, 1999, esp. Part II, Ch. II, "The Theology of Ancestors as the Starting Point for an African Ecclesiology", pp. 85-106.

the positive accentuated as the Synod also noted. "For this image emphasizes care for others, solidarity, warmth in human relationships, acceptance, dialogue and trust". The negative aspects to avoid include "ethnocentrism and particularism" to which we must add patriarchy and all it implies in the traditional African family[32].

Blood remains the basic and unbreakable bond between members of the African family, as perhaps of families in other parts of the world, especially the Third World. Because of this blood bond which unites the living, the living dead and those yet to be born, family members have a special concern for one another (even at the extended family level and clan) and owe it to themselves to keep alive the sound moral traditions of the family and transmit it in tact (i.e., with its own integrity) to future generations. Yet while blood unites, one can find within an African family adherents of different religions: Christians (Catholics, Protestants and Pentecostals), Muslims and followers of African Traditional Religions (ATR). Dialogue is a key tool that serves to remind members of the importance of this relationship. Family meetings and discussions are regular features of family life. Here every family problem is thrashed out in view of workable solutions. We cannot expect the model of the church as family to work or achieve its goals without building dialogue into it as its substantial fabric. The African Synod recognized this and so underscored the necessity for dialogue (*EIA*, 65). All categories of people are included, in a kind of reversed hierarchy, which starts with the vital ecclesial communities and the laity and ends with the clergy, with the bishops, the greatest, mentioned last (*EIA*, 88-98).

This diversity in the religious affiliation of the members does not militate against the unity, which the blood bond gives. The members do not see themselves at loggerheads with or as enemies of one another. The natural blood bond enables them to respect one another's religious orientation and yet to coexist harmoniously as members of the one family, one seeking the good of the other in the typical African anthropology: "I am because we are, and because we are I am". This does not mean that there are no tensions among the members or even modern exceptions, as we find among the fundamentalist groups both Christians and Muslims. Often this conflict comes from outside influence, rather than from the "native" African instinct. Religious affiliation apart, their common concern for one another's well being and the survival of the family binds them together and gives them the sustained energy to resolve conflicts and work for one another's good. It may happen that in the course of their

32. *EIA*, 63; Propositio 8.

mutual coexistence and influence, or in the course of sharing their faith with one another, conversions occur. But with and without conversions, these members do not condemn one another, or dismiss others as useless because they do not follow their own particular religion.

This model can be of immense value as we consider the church's presence and dialogue with and in the world. Is it not possible to focus, for a start, on basic human needs that bring people together and that are rooted on what the 1971 Synod considered a constitutive aspect of preaching the gospel? To be church is to be the good news to the world. The Synod declared concern with social justice [and we would add, the promotion of human rights of every individual], as being a constitutive aspect of proclaiming the gospel. The people at the grassroots are already doing this with great success[33]. In the peak of the Muslim fanaticism of the Maitasane type in Nigeria in 1986, an Egyptian Muslim told me in the flight from Cairo to Lagos: "The earth is for you and I to till, religion is for God". When asked to elucidate what he meant by this, he replied that what I or he believed was between each of us and God, but that we had a common mission from God to make the earth habitable and fruitful for both of us, regardless of our religious affiliations. "Tilling the earth" in this way will include looking after the earth itself and enabling it, as well, to take part in God's project of renewal.

The model of the church-as-God's family invites a broader conception of church beyond the Roman Catholic Church and the particular churches. The church in this model becomes all God's children scattered all over the world, living in the world, formed by and forming the world. Some scholars equate it with God's kingdom, God's reign on this earth as in heaven. When Jesus said, "The time is fulfilled and the kingdom of God is at hand, repent, believe the gospel" (Mark 1,15), he was not addressing the disciples/the church, but anyone who cared to listen and accept the call to return to their authentic self as God had destined for each individual and the human community at creation. The role of the church is to proclaim to all that they have indeed been reconciled to God and should live accordingly (2 Cor 5,18-19), as people reconciled to God and to one another. The polarity set between the church and the world and between the clergy and laity disappears in this model. The model holds great assets for developing a dialogical ecclesiology in the context of today's world

---

33. Examples include Development Education and Leadership Services (DELES), and other work with grassroots women; Cf. Ecumenical Association of Nigerian Theologians, *Grassroots Women Arise: Bulletin of Ecumenical Theology* 8 (1996); the entire issue is on this subject.

of religious pluralism. The ecclesiology built on church as God's family would extend beyond the Christian, ecumenical world to embrace all the inhabitants of God's *oikumene*[34]. Viewing the church as God's family is relevant not only for Africa but for the universal church (since the church is the body of Christ, the second person in God's Trinitarian family). This model should help us to commit ourselves wholeheartedly to promoting one another's maturity in Christ (as Catholics, Protestants, Pentecostals), and reach out in love (Christ's love) to peoples of other faith.

X. A NEW PARADIGM: THE WORLD'S PROPHETIC ROLE FOR THE CHURCH

In the past we erroneously believed that the church always gives the lead to the world in all things. But a careful and objective attention to the reality proves the contrary and calls us to be humble. In a number of respects the world has given the lead to the church, especially in matters pertaining to human dignity, rights and freedom of speech and of research. This is particularly true with respect to the world's attitude towards women. The secular world spearheaded this as we saw earlier. Our church has yet to come to grips with the irreversible progress, which the world has made in these matters, through the guidance of the Holy Spirit who anointed Jesus to set free the oppressed (Luke 4,18-19). All this is from God who works in both the church and the world to restore his entire creation. Put differently, both the church and the world are God's work and building; both tend towards God who concurrently sustains each in being according to the divine plan (cf. Rom 11,33-36). Both originated in God's love and are sustained or kept in being by that love. God seeks both the happiness of human beings and the beauty of the creation (Wis 11,24–12,1). The salvation of creation is part and parcel of human salvation. The full revelation of God's children means the setting free of creation from its bondage to decay (Rom 8,18-23). Revelation calls it the new heaven and the new earth, which appear concurrently with the Bride, the heavenly Jerusalem or church made perfect in love (Rev 21–22). God continuously acts in the world as in the church to bring it to perfection. In view of this, we need to humbly admit that the church has played and continues to play a prophetic role towards the church, beyond the cultural influence mentioned in *GS*. Prophetic here is understood in the scriptural way of speaking for (*pro-phinai*) God. We stand to gain by

---

34. Cf. K. RAISER, *To Be the Church: Challenges and Hopes for a New Millennium* (Risk Book Series), Geneva, WCC Publications, 1997.

our readiness to observe how God works in the world and to respond to God's working, his life giving and liberating activity as Jesus did (cf. John 5,19).

XI. Obstacles to Overcome in the Dialogue *ad intra*

In undertaking this dialogue *ad intra*, we will need to reckon with the power of structure and ritual to resist change and to inculcate and reinforce received theologies and ideologies. As contexts where we celebrate the sacred, rituals reinforce in a gentle, but powerful and living manner the theologies and ideologies they embody. Perhaps we need to recall how these two institutions (for want of a better word), structures and rituals played a major role in the condemnation and crucifixion of Jesus by the Jewish leaders, specifically in John's Gospel. John's Gospel attributes the condemnation of Jesus to the Scribes (the lawyers whose duty it was to maintain the tradition and its legal structures) and the Sadducees, the priestly class who were both rulers of the people after the Exile and, in principle, were in charge of the liturgical life of the people. They rejected Jesus, God's gospel and their long awaited Messiah, to the point of handing him over to be crucified. This history, too, is for our instruction.

In convoking the Second Vatican Council, John XXIII asked and desired that the windows and doors of the church be thrown wide open to let in fresh air. The general belief is that some forty years later, the windows have barely been opened (not to speak of the doors – Jesus is the door to the sheepfold, John 10,7), even then the shutters are not all drawn back and there are still barriers that prevent some from having a good view of what is going on inside the church[35]. For the Spirit to blow freely within the church, we will need to open wide not only the windows and shutters, but the doors as well so that we may see clearly by the searching, probing and transforming light of the Holy Spirit who "searches everything, even the depths of God" (1 Cor 2,10). We need to do this if we are to grow into fullness through the liberating "truth" who is Jesus, the head /source of the church and the only one who builds the church and sustains it alive (John 8,31-36; 15,1-6). Jesus promised that the sheep that belong to and follow him would have free access in and out of the sheepfold and find pasture and nourishment to enable and empower them

---

35. Cf. D.D. DODO, *The Clergy in Nigeria Today: A Layman's Perspective*, in *The Clergy in Nigeria Today* (n. 24), 31-48.

to live fully human lives as God had intended from the beginning. To make this happen concretely, he gave his life as food and drink for his sheep (John 10,7-10.17-18).

Theologically, the dialogue *ad intra* will move us to review how the Scholastic/Aristotelian philosophical and anthropological theology has over the centuries eroded crucial values of the Gospel and in many respects conditioned our being church till today. How this anthropology affected and continues to affect the church's attitude and stance towards women is yet to be seriously reckoned with. This needs to be done, not just by a few women scholars tagged feminist and dismissed, but also by the mainstream of the church, which sustains and has benefited over the centuries from this philosophical-anthropological theology at the expense of the gospel and women. The observation that for the first time we are on the road to becoming a truly universal church, not just a Hellenistic-Jewish and Greco-Roman church in European garb that has dominated and informed church structures and life until now needs to be taken seriously as part of the dialogue on ecclesiology. A handy indicator of this is the dominance of European languages, especially English, in the doing of theology, and in the translations of official church documents from the Latin. Even Latin itself is not such a neutral language since the conceptual frames of reference are still those of Europe. The Latin language borrowed much from Greek for its development, even as the English and most European languages borrowed from the Latin. To shy away from the negative influences of this Eurocentrism of our church and the yeast of its "pagan world" would be to resist the Spirit who wants to lead us into the complete truth and new way of being church. But we are too sensitive to the promptings of the Holy Spirit, our teacher, Counselor and co-witness to Christ in the world (John 14,15-17; 16,7-15.26) to allow this to happen.

What might also be difficult is for us to have that conversion which will free us to be church and to dialogue in spirit and in truth about the things that have prevented us in the past and those that can help us today to be this church. This, I believe, is what the Spirit urgently calls us to, as church at the dawn of this twenty-first century. The call of John Paul II, "launch into the deep" (*duc in altum*), the *leitmotif* of his *Novo millennio ineunte*, applies here. When we are authentically church according to God's gospel, Jesus Christ, we will have little or no problem dialoguing with the world or being present in the world and for the world as its servant.

Finally, we need to face and reject the genuine and deep-seated fear that the hierarchical leadership model of the Empire will crumble once the doors are thrown wide open and genuine partnership between the clergy and laity, men and women (who currently are at the very last rung of the ladder, even below little altar boys in some contexts) are brought to the top. For then the pyramidal structure will yield place to the circular with Christ/God at the centre. When this happens, and the top disappears, the church will attain the height of true greatness, according to Jesus' criteria. Then the church will truly become servant, woman, mother that it claims to be, one made in God's own image and likeness. For God (not only Jesus) is servant. God serves and has served humanity since creation. What a marvel! It is impossible for the changes required here to happen without the current hierarchical model crumbling to give birth to a church that is truly God's family where all members have different functions but where all, not just a privileged class, are given their full rights, dignity and status as God's first born in Christ (Heb 12,23).

XII. SIGNS OF HOPE

John Paul II is one sign of hope that the humble yet courageous and liberating review of our past advocated here is not impossible. He has given the church a sound leadership here both in his writings and by his example. He has asked everybody, outside the church and within (we believe), to help him understand through genuine dialogue how best to exercise his Petrine ministry today in a way that fulfils Jesus' mandate to strengthen the brethren (*Ut unum sint*, 96). A review of this leadership, if it is to be genuine, gospel and christologically based, will necessarily entail looking back and identifying those foreign accretions or anti-gospel values that crept into the church and took firm root over the centuries, what the Pope himself calls "deviations from the Gospel". And because they lasted for so long unchallenged, came to acquire the erroneous status of being God's express will. His leadership in breaking down age-old barriers between the churches, going to forbidden places is truly admirable.

One notices a marked difference in tone between his first encyclical *Redemptor hominis* and *Novo millennio ineunte* issued at the end of the Great Jubilee, some 22 years later. In the latter, the tone is more one of appeal, than of magisterial instruction, where he constantly addresses his dear "brothers and sisters" (not "dear sons and daughters"). Instead of declaring what is to be definitively done, he submits his own contribution on how we can launch into the deep in the new millennium (based on his reflection on what the Spirit had been saying to the churches during

the Jubilee Year), and asks others to bring forth their own reflective contributions (*NMI*, 3). The reference to Saints other than Popes or Fathers
of the Church (e.g., Saints Catherine of Siena, Thérèse of Lisieux and
Teresa of Avila [*NMI*, 27, 33], all of whom he declared Doctors of the
Church during his pontificate) shows that the Magisterium is not ashamed
to recognise and celebrate the contribution of women in the church. We
also recall his walking side by side with a woman evangelist leader of her
church in Assisi and other ecumenical gatherings. All this evidence shows
that he is genuinely listening and has listened to some of the issues raised
by women and some men in the church. One only wishes that he would
also walk side by side with women in the Catholic Church, up to the altar
of the Lord. But one should not expect him to do everything. God's time
is the best and growth takes time. If the rest of us in the church, especially
in the Roman Curia, were as open as John Paul II has been to the action
of the Spirit in the church and the world, we would have made incredible progress along the way of genuine dialogue on ecclesiology, both *ad
intra* and *ad extra*.

These efforts of the Pope and the call for dialogue within the church
are in keeping with the spirit of the Great Jubilee, which ushered us into
the new millennium and through the Pope's leadership, invited us to
"launch into the deep" (*duc in altum*). The biblical jubilee invites a return
to the people's roots and land, in our case, Jesus of the gospels. As our
founder and head/source, Jesus, can never be replaced in the church, his
body. This return is necessary if we are to remain true to our vocation of
being God's gathering and find the much needed energy, freedom from
fear and courage to joyfully (with jubilation, *TMA*, 16) cancel all the
debts we may have owed one another and return the lands (the Christian
heritage) we may have usurped from one another over the past two thousand years, under the influence of our illegal marriages with the Empire
and with Greek philosophical anthropology. We seek to identify the anti-
gospel influences from the Empire that occasioned our deviations from
the gospel, or that infiltrated and eroded our being church, but that subtly and progressively installed selves as our *modus operandi,* claiming
God's authority and justification for their existence. Luckily we have
Christ, the Way, the Truth and the Life (John 14,6) and his unchanging
gospel (Gal 1,6-10) to ensure that we are on track in this review of the
past, as we steer the right course in, with and through him on the road to
wholeness.

The second sign of hope, for me, is the refusal of women to be silenced
as they seek to claim their rightful place in the church. John XXIII who
saw the women's issue as a sign of the times, counselled that they who

know they have rights have the responsibility to claim their rights while others have the duty to respect them as they claim these rights (*PC*, 39-41). The women's struggle in the church and the resistance it meets is, I believe, part of God's plan to move us in spite of ourselves into a new church and a new humanity. Their staunchly resisted struggles may be seen as the pangs of giving birth to a new church, but there will be great joy for all when this new church comes to birth (cf. John 16,21). If there had been no staunch opposition, we might not have taken such pains to discover the real and true nature of the church and of Christ's priesthood. Ultimately, we are dealing with *his* priesthood, not that of men or women. What matters is what he intended to do "the night before he suffered", not how we have understood or misunderstood his action or co-opted his maleness into the system so that the system can remain challenged. But for the resistance from women and a few faithful men, including some in the hierarchy, we would not have made such efforts to understand Christ's priesthood as some of us are struggling to do. So I view both the prohibition by the hierarchy and the resistance from the women (the last rung of the ladder in the church) and their refusal to be silenced as an act of grace by which God wants to purify his church and move us all into the full maturity of Jesus. The birth pangs are great and protracted, because the child/church to be born will embrace all the nations (cf. Rev 12,1-12). We hold that the church is not a democracy; that is true, because the church is not a government of the people by the people for the people, even if the people in question are the clergy. The church is God's household and building. Ultimately we discover answers to our questions and solutions to our conflicts and disagreements through Jesus whom God has placed over his household to be our unfailing light, our liberating truth and our only way to God. We thank God for being present and active in the church, even where we least expect it or resist his actions.

XIII. Not a Conclusion

The church in the world, a dialogue in ecclesiology! We have shifted the focus of this discussion from that of a dialogue between the church and the world to that of a dialogue between and among us in the world who see ourselves as church, God's gathering in and through Christ. We have seen that we need to engage one another in dialogue on what it means to be church in our different locations, interacting with the rest of our brethren who do not share the same faith in Christ or in the Catholic Church, but who nevertheless are essentially God's gathering in and through Christ, "just as we are" (to borrow a perspective from Peter's words to the Jerusalem brethren when they squeezed him concerning his visit to Gentile Cornelius), but whom the Holy Spirit showed clearly that God makes no distinction between Gentile or Jew, or in our case, between Catholics and other Christians and between Christians and people of other faiths (Acts 11,1-17; esp. v. 17). The demands of dialogue on ecclesiology, understood as church existing in the world to be servant of the world, reposes on us who see ourselves as this church. This dialogue challenges us to seek to be church in the world as Christ was among his disciples and Jewish community. He came not to be served or to establish self, but to serve and, like a good mother of the family, to give his life for his little children and sheep (John 10). He became Eucharist, bread broken so that his disciples and all who believe may eat to their full satisfaction (cf. John 6,11b-12) and enjoy fullness of life, and, in turn, become Eucharist to one another and to the world (John 13,13-34; 15,12-13).

We who are church need to dialogue with one another (among ourselves) on how we can best have salt in ourselves, for otherwise we will be incapable of seasoning and preserving the world. To be light for the world to see, we first need to liberate ourselves from the cumulative darkness by which, over the centuries, we have placed ourselves by assimilating the anti-gospel values and ways of the world with its sinful cultures as norm for our ecclesial structures and self-understanding. Otherwise we will have no oil in our lamps to provide the light for the world to see, desire to come out of its darkness, its death dealing and dehumanising moral, religious, political and economic values and systems and join Christ the Bridegroom into the eternal wedding feast, to restore the integrity of all creation. The gospel is both salt and light. Light in particular has different ways of expressing itself, depending on the conditions in its location. Similarly cities differ in type, based also on conditions, such as where they are located and building materials available. What counts is that each be genuine and bloom where they are planted by God.

As church in the world, in its multi-cultural contexts, we will need to pay attention to the diverse ways by which we can be present in the world, drawing from the local materials (the cultures, mores and languages) which God places in any given place. We will need to cultivate the beauty of each culture and so enhance the beauty of God's creation. Beautiful people from beautiful places, cultures, creeds, faiths, will form the mosaic we use in expanding the church walls in the world so that this church, like the mustard seed (which started out as a narrow-minded structure and self conception) may grow and expand into a huge tree and provide *free* shelter for all the birds of heaven and itself find shelter in the world by finding itself expressed in all cultures, languages and customs and traditions of all the nations. The church will then embrace the world in faithfulness and love and gather all (or be the gathering [*ekklesia*] of all) into the embrace of God. This, I believe, is the road that we need to travel if we are to be effectively church in the world, for the world and in dialogue with the world.

Ecclesiology does not exist except as formulated and perceived by human beings. Sometimes this formulation with its attendant practices or programmes of action can actually conflict with the meaning of church as God's gathering of humanity. The idea that outside the church there is no salvation is a passing example of this. This applies not only in relation of the church to outsiders but also and even more so to members of the church in their different socio-cultural locations and "class" designations within the church. The divide between priest and laity is one such area for dialogue, so that we may not actually oppose God by our structures and classifications, and insistence on our laws and traditions. Treading on danger, we underscore the urgent need for the inclusion of women, real women, in this discourse. The need for our Roman Catholic Church to enter into serious dialogue with real women about their place in the church is self-evident and hardly needs to be emphasised, for "when we are personally concerned, we perceive reality differently"[36]. This dialogue *ad intra* is not only urgent but also long overdue[37]. Unless addressed with the urgency it requires, the Catholic Church will continue to diminish in strength, the strength of the gospel as well as the numerical strength of its "lay" faithful who migrate to those churches where they can claim and exercise their charism, gifts of the Holy Spirit for the building up of his body the church. When this continues to happen, the church may become the object of the world's pity, instead of being, in dialogue with the world, God's mercy and compassion to the world.

Ecclesiology is not limited to the Catholic church, but our focus has been the Catholic Church because we want to put our own house in order so that we may be better placed (or learn from our experience how) to help the world to put its own house in order. If when the world looks at us, a city on a hilltop, it sees only broken down fences, falling rafters, streets filled with potholes, dilapidated walls and pealing plasters, it will consider itself blessed for having nothing to do with us. On our part, we will have failed to live up to Christ's mandate and our own gospel

36. OKURE, *Contemporary Perspectives on Women* (n. 29), p. 4.
37. See L. ORSY, *The Papacy for an Ecumenical Age*, in *America* 183 (2000, October 21), 9-13.

identity. As city on the hill, people should look up and see that we, gathered from all nations under heaven, love one another across barriers of race, class and sex, colour and so forth, and are firmly committed to being good news to one another and to the world, because God in Christ is the mayor of our city. If they see God, not human beings, as the mayor of the city, they will be happy to become citizens of the city, for they will know that they too belong by their very nature, since they like us/church are God's work of art created in Christ Jesus (in the divine image and likeness) to live the good life as from the beginning God had intended us to live (Eph 2,10). The "beginning" here takes us back to Genesis where God saw all that he had made and found it very good. The mission of the church in the world is to be itself a witness to and an instrument for this perfect harmony in the world.

The church in the world, a dialogue in ecclesiology! We need to deconstruct our perception of the church-world relationship, and reconstruct it to include the awareness that the world in major instances has played and continues to play a prophetic role towards the church. We need to be humble enough to recognise and accept that God has spoken and continues to speak to us through the world in order to move us beyond our self-centeredness and pride towards a new humanity. God is and has never ceased being present and active in the world. It is God's world, not a man's or the church's world. This too is from God who is working in both the church and the world. We need to deconstruct our understanding of what it means to be church. Vatican Council II started the process by revising our conception of the church as the only boat (if not the only name), by which people could be saved. But we need to advance further to think of the church as God's gathering of humanity to the divine self in and through Christ, and ourselves, church, as those who are privileged to serve as God's servants in this ministry. We need to deconstruct the oppressive and marginalizing structures by which we govern ourselves, structures that tend to treat perpetually as "infants" a majority of God's children in the church, and, worse still, claim to do so in God's name.

We identify and put in operation new structures ("new wine, new skins") which will reveal and promote our true nature as members of God's family and household where Jesus is never replaced as our principle of unity, the only one who binds us to God and to one another as brothers and sisters, each with a different function, but each enjoying to the full their divine right, dignity and status as God's firstborn in Christ. We identify strategies of empowerment for all God's children *ad intra* and *ad extra* as a new way of being church, a church that transcends the barriers set by the major anthropological sins of racism, sexism and classism,

with their attendant "isms". We promote a church where each local community can use their God-given cultural blessings and graces to celebrate
the goodness of God in a process of sound inculturation. We undertake
a historical analysis of current structures and practices to sort out and
reject those foreign (to the gospel) influences which have hampered and
compromised our being Christ's church.

Above all, instead of fighting God in the name of our "traditions" (Mark
7,5.9 and par.), we align ourselves with God's action both in the margins
and (in some respects) in the topmost leadership of our church. We believe
that all Scripture is for our instruction (2 Tim 3,16). We need equally to
believe that all history is for our instruction. So we learn from the past in
all humility, as did our ancestors in the early church. Those who, like some
in the early church, are still inclined (with good intentions) to oppose what
the Spirit is doing in the world, the church and the churches, and to question Peter why he is making so many journeys and moves to break down
age-old barriers, need to recall the example of the early church. When it
became evident to the Jerusalem church, "the men from James" (have we
our own equivalents of these?) that they could no longer oppose the Holy
Spirit as She blew freely, turning their inherited theologies and self-perception (as *the* chosen people) upside down, bringing them and those they
once called Gentiles into a new creation and communion fellowship, they
decided to align themselves with Her and said, "It has seemed good to the
Holy Spirit and to us" not to burden you with the backlog of our human
traditions which even we ourselves found hard to bear.

May this openness to the Holy Spirit and Her exciting action in the
world and in the church in this era of a new Pentecost be our portion. May
we be open to the Spirit, the heart and principal agent of mission, as She
liberates us from our centuries old locked up Upper Room understanding of church and propels us with ever increasing joy and freedom into
the embrace of one another, of our sister churches and of all humanity and
ultimately into the embrace of God. The church in the world, a dialogue
on ecclesiology! The conversation continues with the keen awareness
that each of us is part and parcel of this church in the world. Therefore,
we the right and assume the responsibility to allow ourselves to be liberated by God's Spirit, and to rededicate ourselves to being truly God's
church in God's world. Come, O come. Come, Holy Spirit.

Catholic Institute of West Africa   Teresa OKURE, SHCJ
P.O. Box 499
Port Harcourt
Nigeria

MEDIATING THE GLOBAL AND THE LOCAL
IN CONVERSATION

CHALLENGES TO THE CHURCH IN THE TWENTY-FIRST CENTURY

I. INTRODUCTION

What does conversation look like as a theological principle when speaking and listening in a world such as ours today? We are aware of a multitude of voices around us: some so loud as to drown out the others, some so strident as to close off discussion, yet others suppressed into a silence which must eventually erupt into speech once again. We are likewise aware of the difficulty of listening, of being attuned to all these voices. Even when we are committed to engaging in this arduous task, we are confronted with the linking of what we hear to the contexts from which it has been spoken. Moreover, listening for the gaps in speech, where memory and identity may lie suppressed, makes the act of listening even a greater challenge. And when we in turn speak, reversing the roles of hearer and speaker in the act of conversation, we focus on what we wish to communicate, and seek ways to make that message most understandable to our hearers. This raises further questions about how we frame our message, how our hearers take in a message, and how we judge to what extent a message has been heard as we would want it to be received.

Communication is a complex act. It is complicated even further today because of all the boundaries of difference of which we have become so much more aware: boundaries in gender, class, and culture which, while not insuperable, pose challenges to our mode of speaking and listening.

"Theology and Conversation" is the theme of this symposium. The purpose of this presentation is to examine conversation as an act of communication and as a method in theology, especially as it relates to the complexities we experience within the Church, and the Church's role in conversation with and within the world. As Christians today, we experience the complexity of communication both within the community of faith, and between that community of faith and individuals, groups, and larger collectivities which make up our world. The nature of what is communicated is likewise varied: from communication of what might be discrete items of information, to the imparting of a world-view and way of acting in the world informed by revelation and faith. Needless to say, all the dimensions of such communicative action cannot be presented – let alone analysed – in a presentation of this short compass. What I would rather seek to do is to trace the broad lines which shape and direct the flow – and the disruption – of communication as conversation.

To do so, I will proceed through three steps. The first step will examine the matrix in which communication as conversation is occurring today, both within and beyond the Church. Understanding something of that matrix is important in order to account for how communication is or is not taking place. The features within this matrix are globalisation as a social force and postmodern experience. It should also be noted at the outset that, when I speak of the Church here, I will be referring especially to the Roman Catholic Church, although it is my hope that what I have to say will find resonance throughout the rest of Christianity. The Roman Catholic Church makes up about half of all Christians in the world today, and poses unique challenges for understanding both communication and conversation in its universal, global dimensions and in its local realizations. This is the case not only because of the territorial extension of the Roman Catholic Church, but also because of this Church's theological preoccupation with the nature of its unity. Thus, the issues are not only ones of communication strategy, but also of theology.

The second step in this presentation will look at two features pertinent to conversation which have arisen out of this matrix, namely, the global and the local dimensions of communication and conversation. What is of central interest here is the interaction between the global and the local, and how that ongoing interaction has pushed and pulled both the global and the local into new situations. The transitions which are taking place in both the global and the local will provide the central focus for this part of the presentation.

The third and final section looks to future directions. What does our current location in the interaction of the global and the local mean for ascertaining both where we want to go, and where we do not want to go, in the Church and in the interaction with the larger world? What challenges does this raise for a theological research program which has conversation as a central methodological principle? What does it mean for determining how we live together within the Church, and how this living together speaks to the larger world? While all the dimensions which will be suggested in this third part cannot be worked out here, it is hoped that what does emerge will contribute to that ongoing theological program we are trying to develop here.

II. THE MATRIX OF CONVERSATION TODAY: GLOBALISATION AND POSTMODERNITY

If one wished to give the broadest possible sketch of the matrix within which theological conversation takes place today, it would have to include two widespread phenomena: globalisation and postmodernity. Globalisation is no longer a new concept, either within the wider social and economic sphere, or in theology. As a social force, it bristles with energy and with contradictions. For those who benefit from globalisation, it is the harbinger of a sense of interconnectedness with a much larger world, carrying with it promises of ever greater prosperity. But for those who do not – and at this point in time, this constitutes the majority of the population of the world and the majority of Christians – globalisation means exclusion from these proposed benefits, and often an even worse state of life than was the case before the advent of globalisation.

We are now into the second decade of the current round of globalisation, and with that comes some perspectives on future steps. It is these which will be of central importance to us.

A second social feature of the environment in which we find ourselves today is postmodernity. This is a term which has come to mean many things. I will be using it here in a more restricted sense of the acknowledgment of the limits of modernity. That is to say, the postmodern will mean here not the rejection of the modern (I do not think that such a posture can be sustained for any length of time) but a recognition of the limits of modernity and a reshaping of the project of modernity accordingly.

It is the interaction of globalisation – now in its second decade – with postmodernity which will be of special interest here. The assumptions which drive globalisation are deeply modern ones, and our interpretation of the experience of the limits (and limitations) of modernity are bound up with postmodernity's stance regarding modernity. Postmodernity, then, provides a platform from which to view globalisation. This is important, since globalisation, as an economic and social force, has totalising pretensions, and as such seeks to brook no alternative to itself. The directions globalisation may take, and how it might even be directed, depend in some measure on our capacity to stand outside it and view it as a whole.

1. *Globalisation*

How might we think of globalisation as a social force? It is neither possible nor necessary to try to present a full picture of this phenomenon here. I would rather seek to concentrate on the dimensions of globalisation which are most pertinent to our discussion here of conversation as communication, and to the potential impact of the second decade of globalisation on conversation as a theological program. There are five points I wish to briefly make here.

First of all, globalisation is made possible by advances in communications technology. "Communication" is understood here both in terms of the conveying of information and of the transport of people and goods. The current globalisation depends upon the advances made in computer technology and telecommunications.

Researchers point to three periods in the last half millennium during which of globalisation have taken place[1]. The first was the European voyages of discovery beginning at the end of the fourteenth century. Advances in navigation and the building of ships allowed Europeans to wander further than they ever did before. The colonial empires which followed upon those discoveries represent one kind of globalisation, the effects of which continue down to the present time.

The second wave of globalization began with the invention of the steam engine in the late eighteenth century, which made the railroad train and the steamship possible. Added to this, in the nineteenth century, were inventions which speeded the flow of information: the telegraph and the telephone. The steam engine especially ushered in Europe's Industrial Revolution. New transportation and communication possibilities made greater empire expansion possible, one which began unravelling, beginning with the Great War of 1914, and continuing until the mid-twentieth century.

The third wave of globalisation has been fuelled especially by computer technology, as it has affected business and banking, and also in its more democratic forms through the personal computer and the Internet.

My focus here is on the current form of globalisation, where the capacity for communication, now shared by large numbers of people in the rich world and by the elites of the poor world, has been so greatly enhanced. When we speak of conversation or relation as a basis for theology, we must be as aware as possible of how these advances in communication affect the understanding of conversation itself. Take the World

---

1. This was first put forth in I. WALLERSTEIN, *The Modern World-System*, New York, 1974-1989, 3 vols. See also the discussion in D. HELD et al., *Global Transformations. Politics, Economics, Culture*, Oxford, 1999.

Wide Web and the Internet as the point of departure here. *Who* conversation partners can be is greatly expanded. Not only do they not need to be face-to-face with us, there may be no face-to-face relationship anywhere in the conversation network. Even though written communication is used in the form of e-mail, the reflection processes which had gone into letter-writing are becoming greatly curtailed. The conversation simulated by communication lacks significant elements, especially in gauging and regauging moments in the conversation due to the nonverbal reactions of the other. At the same time, the speed of the communication generally lowers the level of reflexivity which would go into a written response. Finally, the collectivities or groups of which we are part, or whom we engage as conversation partners, can be greatly altered by this technology. Because of the scattered character and even relative anonymity of the interlocutors, who the "we" is and how the collectivity views itself will be different.

The *qualities* which characterize good conversation for us may also change in light of this technology. The no-nonsense communication of an e-mail message and the sense of belongingness which may accompany participating in a chatroom can shape our idea of what constitutes a good conversation. Many of the specific cultural characteristics of conversation in different settings are erased here: the meaning of pauses or silence, the creating of context by gesture and tone of voice, and the experience of the accumulation of these contextual factors upon the conversation itself.

Following Clifford Geertz here, one might think of the impact of how the current communications technology provides both a *model of* and a *model for* conversation[2]. To what extent does technology determine what constitutes good conversation itself, what can be considered communicable, and how that communication can take place? In what ways does this technology open new possibilities for conversation and also set limits to it? We are already aware of how e-mail can be used to mobilize public opinion. We have also seen how undergraduate students will do all their research for essays on the Internet, and restrict their quest for knowledge to that medium. How much does the technology, therefore, shape our understanding of successful communication and of conversation, even if we are not aware of those forces?

Second, globalisation is, economically and socially, a totalising force. That is to say, it represents itself as the total, or potentially total,

---

2. Geertz introduced his terms *model of* (description) and *model for* (normativity) in his essay on religion in C. GEERTZ, *The Interpretation of Cultures*, New York, 1973. He and others have used it widely since.

realization of an economic and social order. We are all familiar with hearing about how neo-liberal capitalism is the only viable economic force. We hear too that the social order that is emerging from these same forces has meant death to utopian thinking, since such thinking can lead only to small-scale or short-lived action. Latin American writers such as Mo Jung and Hugo Assmann in Brazil and Franz Hinkelammert in Costa Rica have explored the legitimation of globalisation by means of a displaced Christian theology[3].

Totalising thought is not a feature unique to modernity, but it has taken on special force because of the powerful discourses of universality which were developed in Western philosophy from Descartes through Kant and Hegel. It has also spawned virulent ideologies in the twentieth century. I note here the importance of attending to the totalising features of globalisation because of the impact it has on free conversation. The strong forces toward homogenisation in the economic, social, and political sphere diminish if not rule out the flow of conversation as a quest for a point of view or for the truth. Jürgen Habermas and the proponents of discourse ethics have focused especially on creating the conditions for a free, undistorted communication in their work[4]. Whatever may be the cultural limitations of their work (in terms of culture-specific forms of representation and communication), they have contributed considerably to clearing the ground and creating communicative praxis within modern societies.

Third, globalisation bristles with contradictions. No doubt any social system suffers from the same thing, but globalisation's pretensions to totality require the suppression or the exclusion of all kinds of elements which do not fit into its pattern. Thus, its creation of new patterns of inclusion in its technology and economics has also meant exclusion for others. It offers a greater sense of participation (one thinks of the use of the Internet to heighten political participation, as was done in building support for the international treaty to ban landmines), but it also requires the surrender of much local autonomy about economics and even social arrangements to achieve its goals. The growing resistance in anti-globalisation movements derives much of its strength from its perception of these contradictions. And these contradictions run deep. Capitalism as an economic order has been characterized as a kind of bicycle: as long as

3. H. ASSMANN – F. HINKELAMMERT (eds.), *L'idolatrie du marché. Critique théologique de l'économie du marché* (Collection libération, 17), Paris, 1993; F. HINKELAMMERT, *The Ideological Weapons of Death: A Theological Critique of Capitalism*, Maryknoll, NY, 1986.

4. J. HABERMAS, *Theorie des kommunikativen Handelns*, Frankfurt, 1981, 2 vols.

the bicycle is moving, it moves us quickly and effortlessly. But a bicycle as a mode of movement can never stop, or its rider will topple off. The anti-globalisation protests are meant precisely to stop the bicycle, rather than offer an alternative.

Some of the struggle in theological conversation in the Church today can be attributed to being somewhat helpless in the face of the communicative contradictions which globalisation brings out: a greater articulation for some, but a suppression into silence for others; a strengthening of certain patterns of sameness or homogeneity, but at a price for those who are different or do not participate. The disrupted character of conversation, strategies to suppress conversation, and the silence which then ensues can be read in light of the contradictions which globalisation brings forward, but which it can neither resolve nor transcend.

Fourth, in its very attempts to erase difference, globalisation ends up heightening or strengthening it. The manifold ways in which difference manifests itself – as the decidedly local, as a form of resistance, as a reverse-mirror image, or as a separatist movement – depend in some way for its forms on the continuing press of the global. We have a heightened sense of difference through the migration of peoples which globalisation has fomented. The global media bring the distant and the different into our homes. The loss of local autonomy which globalisation often brings in its wake attenuates a sense of loss and difference. Why this is important for theology as conversation has to do with the emergence of the local as a theme in recent Roman Catholic theology, starting with the reaffirmation of the particular church in the Second Vatican Council, and continuing with discussions of inculturation, beginning in the 1970's. How we construe the local and the particular is formed partly by how we experience and construe the non-local and the non-particular.

Fifth and finally, globalisation – in its different impulses of totalisation, its inability to hide or deal with its own contradictions, and its rootedness in modernity – has brought about significant realignments of power. I think it becomes very important to delineate and analyse those realignments of power. Not to do so runs the risk of applying the wrong solutions to the problems we are trying to address, or granting ourselves the privilege of not having to rethink the issues now before us. Problems may seem very similar, and a certain historical continuity may lull us into thinking we are dealing with the same issue in only slightly different form. We may find ourselves, too, without the tools of analysis appropriate to engaging the problems we now face, and fall back on the tools with which we are already familiar. For example, simply to equate globalisation with colonialism is such an error in thought. While they bear many similarities and common historical roots, the political and even economic issues are not entirely the same. Power is present, and power is once again being misused. But to equate them can be a category mistake[5]. Nor should we reify relationships once identified, as other circumstances may have changed the actual nature of those relationships of power today. This has proven most difficult in moving from relationships of resistance when trying to overthrow very definable sites of oppression, to relationships of power which will make a just reconstruction of society possible. Elements in our conversations, therefore, must shift when we have to seek some partnership with one-time oppressors to guarantee the sustainability of society. Because of the nearly kaleidoscopic changes which relationships can take on in the processes of globalisation (speed is after all one of the characteristics of the new communications technology), attending not only to the changes themselves, but what they portend for shifts in the alignments of power – and their positive and negative impact on communication and conversation – must be kept constantly in sight.

2. Globalisation in Its Second Decade

I have tried to raise some of the salient characteristics of globalisation as they relate to communication, and especially to conversation as communication in a globalised world. Globalisation, even in different historical epochs and under different material conditions, exhibits a number of common characteristics. But globalisation, by definition, also continues to move, often at great speed. Such movement provokes new patterns within globalisation, and evokes reactions from those subject to its processes.

In this second decade of globalisation (taking 1989 as a point of departure), there are three features emerging in globalisation which have pertinence for our discussion of conversation.

First of all, patience with the promises of globalisation is running out. Protests in Seattle, Prague, and Genoa point to a growing convergence of anti-globalisation forces whose antipathy toward globalisation can turn into rage. In the vast and diverse world of Islam, much of the modernity (in its cultural, if not its structural form)[6] flaunted by globalisation has led

---

5. On this see J. NEDERVEEN PIETERSE, *Globalisation North and South. Representations of Uneven Development and the Interaction of Modernities*, in *Theory, Culture and Society* 17 (2000) 129-137.

6. The distinction between structural and cultural modernity is Bassam Tibi's. See B. TIBI, *The Challenge of Fundamentalism. Political Islam and the New World Disorder*, Berkeley, CA, 1998. Structural modernity, largely accepted in Islam, supports the empirical and experimental method in the natural sciences. Cultural modernity, found in the

to a fundamental rejection of that modernity – so important to globalisation. The events beginning with September 11, 2001 are a partial result of that. Even the most avid proponents of globalisation know that the current situation, as it now exists, cannot continue. For conversation as a form of communication, the possibility of such discourse becomes increasingly strained, as argument turns to silence and then to physical violence.

Second, the response to this situation has prompted a more concerted quest for a more humane form of globalisation – one which restores some measure of local autonomy, which does not require the acceptance of the totalising dimensions of global culture, and one which does not live by the cut-throat laws of an unbridled market. What social and political forms will need to be imagined to make a more humane form of interconnectedness possible? Conversation as communication will be needed to help establish the ground rules, and the social space, for a common quest for a more humane form of living together.

Third, while attenuated difference, often raw in its wounds, and a desperately sought base of commonality stand so clearly before us, how shall we develop a way of living in the world *which honors sameness and difference in a pluralistic framework, but also in a world which is becoming increasingly unstable*? This may be the greatest challenge ahead in the second decade of globalisation. We need some measure of sameness to ensure communication itself. We cannot dishonor difference. And we cannot collapse one of them into the other: hence a genuinely pluralist framework must be found. But the conditions under which all of this happens is being changed as the ground shifts beneath our feet. The events of September 11, 2001 may be a portent of that. What if identities come into overt physical conflict? How do conversations get restarted when they have been stopped? What if the globalisation juggernaut stops and collapses? Globalisation is not inevitable. We tend to see the times we ourselves live in as unique and without precedent. Historians, however, are trying to read current trends in globalisation against the background of the previous waves mentioned above. A reneging on the liberal assumptions of economic neo-liberalism (relatively free trade, open boundaries, a will to greater economic prosperity, the pursuit of individual liberty) could lead globalisation to a halt. And the halt will not be a peaceful one.

Conversation, in theology and the larger social sphere, becomes an alternative to a violence which will promise to be neither purgative nor

---

social sciences and the humanities, with their emphasis on the freedom of the individual and the emancipation from tradition, is rejected.

liberating. Conversation so understood here is more than mere talk: it is talk which leads to action.

3. *The Postmodern*

"Postmodern" first appeared as a term in art criticism in Europe in the 1920's. In the humanities and in religious studies, it has often taken its meaning from the report for the government of Québec prepared in 1979 by Jean Francois Lyotard[7]. Notable elements of that description of the postmodern important for this discussion here include the fragmentation of lifeworlds, the dissolution of the subject, and the disappearance of overarching master narratives (*les grands récits*). I am using the polyvalent term "postmodern" here to refer to those responses which show up the limitations of the modern. The elements of the modern which come into special consideration here include: a privileging of reason and consciousness over the authority of tradition, linear notions of history, an optimistic anthropology, the autonomy of the human subject, belief in the efficacy of human agency to bring about empancipation of individuals and groups, and a growing separation of the spheres of life.

Globalisation has been in its intents a thoroughgoing modernizing movement. As Roland Robertson, one of its most astute observers, has pointed out, it holds forth promises of progress, participation, and equality for those who submit to its requirements[8]. The postmodern position does not reject the modern; indeed, the postmodern is unintelligible without the modern. But from a position of experience of the limits of the modern, it raises questions about globalisation's confidence in progress, and its capacity to create participation (and therefore, inclusion) and equality. Postmodern thinking need not be against any of these ideas; it simply doubts modernity's capacity to achieve them.

What does this mean for the matrix in which theology as conversation is taking place? First of all, the postmodern questioning of progress creates a new relationship between the premodern, the modern, and the postmodern which is already the experience of people living in urban centers in many parts of the world. The premodern does not disappear into, nor is it superseded by, the modern. The premodern, the modern, and the postmodern live side by side, as *tiempos mixtos*, especially among the poor in the great urban centers. The struggle now taking shape

---

7. J.-F. LYOTARD, *The Postmodern Condition*, Manchester, 1984.
8. R. ROBERTSON, *Globalisation and Social Theory*, London, 1992.

between the secularised West and other forms of society we Westerners lump together as "traditional" will not be resolved by the traditional people giving up their ways and adopting the modern. Their protest is about fundamental flaws they see in the modern. We are living in a world that cannot be tracked by a unilinear philosophy (or theology) of history. The conditions of the premodern, the modern, and the postmodern are existing side by side, often in very uneasy relationship with one another.

Second, it must be remembered that protests against the modern are deeply shaped by the experience of the modern itself. So-called fundamentalisms are not a return to some premodern *status quo ante*. The selection of premodern elements as identity markers are meant to be a direct protest against the modern. Nor are modern means of communications eschewed to create networks of antimodern solidarity. So the critique of the modern and the global cannot be understood without reference to the modern. This must be kept in mind as we look at both the global and the local interlocutors in theological conversation.

III. MEDIATING THE GLOBAL AND THE LOCAL

Having tried to look at some of the prominent features of the globalisation process as it pertains to communication, we now turn to the second part, which looks at how global and local come together in conversation. The focus here will thus be on the global and the local within conversation, and particularly on conversation within and for the Church.

From what has been said in the previous section, it should be clear that the global and the local are highly attuned to each other in their construction, if not always in their interaction. One cannot understand the contours and the impulses of either without reference to the other. One has, therefore, in the interaction of the global and the local itself the elements of relation and conversation, albeit often deeply asymmetrical ones. Roland Robertson has called this interaction between the global and the local the "glocal".

Just as a distinction was made between the first and second decades of globalisation itself, one can speak of first and second generations of both the global and the local. By so doing, we are not exhausting the potential kinds of relationships between the global and the local, but only holding up certain relationships to illumine the current picture and to point to where the analysis might go.

1. *The Global*

Social developments are frequently hard to date exactly. Certain dates come to typify turning points, but they would not have had their impact if other things had not prepared the way for them. Periodization of history is a heuristic tool to help us organize our thinking.

A first period of the current wave of globalisation, rising more or less with the development of computer technology, exhibited a great deal of optimism about the possibilities which communication technologies would be able to provide. Much of the rhetoric of the 1980's was enthusiastic about the prospects of interconnectedness and coming together. Alvin Toffler's *Megatrends* and *The Next Great Wave* typify the thinking in this period.

This first wave of experience of the global was far from the same everywhere, and voices were already being heard against the onslaught of globalisation, often seeing it as another kind of colonial incursion. As theologies of liberation came under increasing ecclesiastical pressure, and the material and social circumstances which had first given them such powerful focus began to change, energies shifted to looking beyond national issues to the international ones posed by globalisation.

As has already been noted, a second decade of globalisation focuses much more on the inherent contradictions and paradoxes which underlie so much of globalisation. The first part of the current globalisation wave saw interconnectedness as creating a desirable homogeneity. The second decade, in pointing out the contradictions and paradoxes, underscores difference. Indeed, two strands can be detected. On the one hand, there is an ongoing deconstruction of the optimistic notions of globalisation itself. Anti-globalisation movements, with differing levels of refinement and analysis, continue to do this. On the other hand, efforts are being made to point a way through the contradictions to create a more humane world order. These deal especially with moving beyond formations of resistance to the problems of living with difference on a long-term basis, and bringing differences together in the reconstruction of societies[9].

Theology did not produce much response to globalisation as such in the 1980's. A more oblique response can be detected in the global discourses of emancipation which were developing in that time in theologies of liberation, in feminism, human rights thinking, and ecology[10]. It was only

---

9. See for example the discussions in C. GUNN, *Beyond Solidarity. Pragmatism and Difference in a Globalized World,* Chicago, IL, 2001.

10. I discuss these as "global flows" in *The New Catholicity. Theology between the Global and the Local,* Maryknoll, NY, 1997.

into that second decade, in the 1990's, when theology started relooking at the global with a critical eye. The experience of facing reconstruction in shattered societies helped theologians take cognisance of the larger forces shaping their societies. The time is especially ripe now for trying to re-imagine the whole. Attempts, for example, to look at Catholic Social Teaching in a changed world are examples of this[11].

2. *The Local*

The origins of the focus on the local as it relates to the global began in theology in the postcolonial period, and that postcolonial experience colored especially the first generation of contextual theologies. Contextual theologies, although first spoken of in Francophone Africa in the 1950's[12], received their special impulse in the 1970's. Their first preoccupation was attending to their own contexts as a viable and credible means of expressing Christian faith. Alongside these, theologies of liberation, too, wanted to break with Enlightenment models of theology which emphasized the universal and the transcendental over the immediate and the local.

The reassertion of the global on the local, starting from the mid-1980's onward, changed the nature of what constituted the local. The local was no longer able to seek out its own space on neutral or circumscribed ground, as it were. To be local now meant to experience the loss of autonomy over one's livelihood and the socialization of one's children. To be local meant to move into resistance against homogenizing forces which wished to erase the distinctive elements which were central to local identities.

These acts of resistance, and with them the strategies to reinstate local autonomy, carried dangers with them as well. The postmodern rejection of the modern found in fundamentalism would create the local as an alternative space marked off from the modern by specifically non-modern dimensions, such as the segregation and confinement of women, the rejection of modern moralities, and the adherence to beliefs not at all at home in the modern. A blending of cultural and religious identity could provide powerful identity markers which not only created new memories and histories for a group, but could be used as a means of subjugating or even eliminating neighboring groups[13]. Dangers of self-segregation, on the one

---

11. A recent attempt to do this is M. CAMDESSUS, *Church Social Teaching and Globalization*, in *America* (October 15, 2001), pp. 6-12.

12. A. ABBLE et al., *Des Prêtres noirs s'interrogent*, Paris, 1956.

13. Still one of the best descriptions of fundamentalism and modernity is B. LAWRENCE, *Defenders of God*, Durham, 1989.

hand, and of an ethnocentric aggression, on the other, now become potential outcomes of an extreme emphasis on the local. The upsurge of interest in religion itself as an identity marker in parts of the world, and the interreligious, interethnic strife which has emerged from this is testimony to a potential toxicity of the local.

3. *The Global and the Local Together*

One can see even in this rough sketch that speaking of either the global or the local in our current setting requires speaking of them both together. As dimensions of an interaction and a relation, they are constituting each other. Apart, they can be potentially destructive both of themselves and of the relationship. Together, too, they can create a spiralling violence. But there is also a potential for working together toward a mutual enhancement. Can we indeed engage sameness and difference, the global and the local, within a pluralistic framework, even as the matrix in which they find themselves may be becoming increasingly unstable? What role might faith and theology have in this? How can this take form within the Church?

IV. THE CHURCH AND THEOLOGICAL CONVERSATION BETWEEN THE GLOBAL AND THE LOCAL

Paradoxes, even contradictions, which can be found in the larger social setting of the encounter between the global and the local can also be seen within the Church itself. At this particular point in history, centralizing patterns in the Vatican seem to be pressing a kind of universal-global over against the local and the particular. There seems to be an underlying fear that the world is spinning out of control, and the only way to prevent the Church from being similarly fragmented and dissolved is to impose uniform expressions of faith, and to resist any suggestions from the side of modernity. The Church has a very long past, and it is from that past that it is reading the present. At the same time, statements on social issues and the continuing development of Catholic Social Teaching have permitted the Roman Catholic Church to address major issues of the day – including globalisation itself – in a way other parts of Christianity have not been able to achieve. Similarly, the Vatican has grasped the importance of the modern means of social communication, as the staging of papal visits to other countries clearly indicates, and a visit to the Vatican Website will confirm.

To call the Vatican response "fundamentalist" is too extreme. Its response might better be seen as a view caught in deep ambivalence about the current state of the world, an ambivalence shared in other quarters. The ambivalence accepts structural modernity, that is, the methods and the achievements of the natural sciences. Pope John Paul II has done much in his pontificate to move the Church beyond condemnations of modern science made in the past. Cultural modernity is the sticking point now, and a number of the papal encyclicals, beginning with *Redemptor hominis* on through *Centesimus annus*, have struggled to critique and offer some alternatives to cultural modernity. Maintaining tight discipline within the Church has been the most visible part of the strategy in an age of globalisation.

The purpose of this final section is not to engage in an extended analysis of the current reaction of the Church in its central government to the stresses of living in a globalised world. The lines are clear enough. What I think I am being called upon to do here is to provide some way which might be an alternative to these centripetal tendencies, especially as they relate to conversation as a theological mode.

Let me begin by saying that the interaction of the global and the local has both a social and a theological dimension for the Church. As a worldwide organization, embracing about eighteen percent of the world's population, the Roman Catholic Church has no choice but to experience the stresses and strains of globalisation. A great part, if not most of its membership, experiences exclusion in the face of globalisation. The tensions between the global and the local, part of the world's landscape, is also part of the Church's reality. This experience is one which touches more than the social sphere. It inevitably seeps also into religious understanding. From a social point of view, then, the Church must deal with the interaction of the global and the local, whether it wants to or not.

But there is also a theological basis for making a conversation between the global and the local more than a social problem to be confronted. The Second Vatican Council, in *Lumen gentium*, reaffirmed the theological concept of the particular or local church. The local church, gathered in prayer around its bishop, does represent the fullness of the body of Christ. However, that fullness only finds its completion in the local church's communion with all of the local churches, in communion with the church of Rome, with the successor of Peter as its head and symbol of unity. The reassertion of this ancient understanding of the Church creates the theological space for the conversation between the global and the local within the Church. The attempts to close that space, in the rhetoric shaping the extraordinary synods leading up to the Jubilee Year, and in some misuses of a theology of communion, do a grave disservice to the whole body of the Church. At a time when the Church needs this conversation between the global and the local most urgently, especially where religious belonging is being used to legitimate social and political violence, the closing of that space hampers the Church's mission in the world, and keeps it from being a genuine *sacramentum mundi*.

But the theological issue here is not just social expediency. It flows from deep christological sources, namely, how we understand that Logos has taken on flesh and dwelt among us (John 1,14). The Logos assumed not just a generic humanity, but assumed cultural particularity. This affirms the principle of how the fullness of the Church can be manifest in the local church, even if that manifestation is not complete without a concept of communion. Viewed in this way, a conversation between the global and the local is not only desirable or expedient, it is a theological necessity for the Church in order for the Church to be true to the doctrine of the Incarnation. The erasure of the local, and the failure to engage the difference which the local might present, seems to counter also an understanding of the *plenitudo* inherent in God's act of creation.

What would be the rules of communication in such a theological conversation between the global and the local? Those sketched out in *Gaudium et spes* in its meditation on culture in Chapter II provide a framework. The Gospel can find a home in every culture, yet is not beholden to any single culture. This dual principle means, it seems to me, that local manifestations of Christian faith can never be dismissed *a priori*. They must be taken into account, and must be taken seriously. At the same time, no culture – even so-called "Christian cultures" can claim to have become fully the ultimate bearers of the Christian message. Every culture carries sin with it as well. The local needs to be heard, and there are theological criteria to shape our listening for the presence of the Word in those settings.

Much of the writing on inculturation in the past two decades has focused upon legitimating the local as a theological interlocutor. In seeing theology as conversation, one must also look closely at global, universal manifestations of theology. It was noted above that globalisation has totalising pretensions. Perhaps that is an inevitable temptation of universalising systems. But it is also falling prey to a quest for power. Traditionally, the Hebrew Scriptures especially spoke to such totalising tendencies in the world of its time as idolatry. Latin American theologians have responded to globalisation using the same frame of analysis. But cannot theological expressions become totalising as well, by silencing voices of protest which challenge such totalisations, which do not have regard for the poor, which ignore or disregard even parts of Catholic Social Teaching so as to maintain control? The local is to be more than a tolerated conversation partner in theology. It provides voices which the global and the universal in theology needs to hear.

Perhaps this is most painfully clear today in the discussions around pluralism – theological and otherwise. What appears to be a consistent misreading of Asian theology, both in its intentions and its manifestations, a misreading both of bishops' conferences and of theologians, may provide the best test case of whether theology can truly become a conversation. Here the backgrounds of the interlocutors are so different that careful listening and probing becomes essential. Falling back on formulae created in different language families and in different eras will not help foster a necessary conversation. If one puts the faltering nature of this conversation alongside Vatican hopes for the evangelisation of Asia, one sees how much needs to be done.

Theologically, this theology of conversation comes together in the concept of catholicity. As I suggested some years ago, the necessity of communication and exchange needs to be added to the more traditional dimensions of catholicity as extension through the whole world and the rule of faith. That was not an original idea from me. But in the meantime, the importance of communication, especially in fundamental theology, has become evermore evident and is evermore affirmed[14]. Catholicity, it seems to me, forms the theological basis for a conversation between the global and the local. This is a conversation which cannot abstract itself from the larger social dynamics which mark the global and the local today, but also cannot forget the theological imperative and the theological basis for such conversation, rooted in the very meaning of the catholicity of the Church as both local and universal, and in the understanding of the Incarnation itself.

If the Church is able to engage in such a conversation, a conversation at once compassionate and critical, it can not only draw closer to its Incarnate and Risen Lord, it can address what I have suggested is the central question globalisation poses for the world today: how can sameness and difference come together in a pluralistic framework, even as the conditions under which this happens become more unstable. Here the Church has a chance of being a sacrament to the world, of being both a model of and a model for the human community. It is a tall challenge to face, and is one which conversation, as a theological principle and method, can make possible.

Catholic Theological Union   Robert J. SCHREITER
5401 South Cornell Ave
Chicago, IL 60615
U.S.A.

14. See most recently B. FRESACHER, *Kommunikation. Leitbegriff theologischer Theoriebildung. Fundamentaltheologische Anstösse*, in *ZKT* 123 (2001) 269-283.

CHRISTIANITY AND RELIGIONS

FROM CONFRONTATION TO ENCOUNTER

I. HISTORY AT A GLANCE

The topic of the theology of religions is a burning topic today, which will remain on the front-stage of theological reflection for a long time to come during this, our third millennium. The point is that interreligious dialogue which has become such a pressing need in the present pluralistic world must be based on a correct theological evaluation of the religious traditions.

Before moving to describe the new perspective adopted here, it may be useful to recall rapidly the different perspectives which through the centuries have marked the Christian theological evaluation of other religions. A first perspective, which lasted for more than ten centuries, consisted in asking whether salvation in Jesus Christ was possible for people who did not profess faith in him and were not members of the Church. To this question a negative answer was given through the axiom "Outside the Church no salvation", till such time as the discovery of the new world (1492) forced theologians to devise several theories according to which explicit faith in Jesus Christ and Church membership were no longer a *conditio sine qua non* for salvation. An "implicit faith", contained for instance in the sincere following of the personal conscience in the circumstances of each individual's life, could suffice. This partially positive answer to the question of the possibility of salvation for outsiders remained common doctrine till the decades that preceded the Second Vatican Council; it became part of the doctrine of the Council of Trent. Only shortly before the Second Vatican Council did some theologians adopt a second and more open perspective which, going beyond the purely individual consideration of the possibility of salvation for individual persons, spoke of positive values to be found not merely in the religious life of persons outside the Church but in the religious traditions to which those persons belonged. This, however, could be and was in fact understood in two vastly different ways. For some (J. Daniélou, H. de Lubac, H. Urs von Balthasar) such values were natural endowments of human nature which enabled people to reach a valid natural knowledge of God by itself incapable of leading to salvation; for others, on the contrary (K. Rahner is here the great protagonist) those values were in fact supernatural gifts of God, elements of "truth and of grace" inserted by God's gracious initiative into the various religious traditions of the world and conducive to human salvation. It is well known how the Second Vatican Council adopted various expressions used by the earliest Christian tradition with regard to Greek philosophy and Asian wisdom, and applied them to the religious traditions. The Council thus spoke of the "seeds of the Word" (*Ad gentes* 11), of a "ray of that Truth which enlightens all men" (*Nostra aetate* 2), found in the religions; but without stating explicitly which precise meaning it meant to attribute to these expressions. The Council in fact did not commit itself to stating that the other religions can be means or ways of salvation for their followers. Its open attitude notwithstanding, it left the question of the theological significance of the religions finally unanswered. The third perspective – into which a new book as well as its predecessor[1], mean to insert itself – is thus a recent post-conciliar development. Theologians today do no longer simply ask whether salvation is possible for individuals outside the Church; nor whether positive values, either natural or even supernatural, can be found in the religious traditions. They ask whether Christian and Catholic theology can affirm that the religious traditions have in the eternal plan of God for humankind a positive significance and are for their followers ways, means and channels of salvation willed and devised by God for their followers. This is the question of the meaning, in God's own mind, of the religious pluralism in which we find ourselves in the present world; religious pluralism, not only "de facto" but "in principle".

Let us note in passing that the Declaration *Dominus Iesus* of the Congregation of the Doctrine of the Faith, in its introduction (n. 4), fails to make an essential distinction. It rejects any theological theory of a religious pluralism in principle, which it considers theological relativism: "The Church's constant missionary proclamation is endangered today by relativistic theories which seek to justify religious pluralism, not only *de facto* but also *de iure (or in principle)*". Among other truths which, as the Document explains, are considered superseded by such theories, the Congregation mentions "the unicity and salvific universality of the mystery of Jesus Christ". The Declaration is, no doubt, right to reject any theory of religious pluralism in principle which would be founded on the

---

1. J. Dupuis, *Christianity and the Religions. From Confrontation to Dialogue*, London, Darton, Longman and Todd, 2002, [2]2003; Id., *Toward a Christian Theology of Religious Pluralism*, Maryknoll, NY, Orbis Books, 1997, [6]2002.

rejection of the "Unicity and salvific universality of the mystery of Jesus Christ". It would be wrong, however, where it seems to imply that any theological theory of religious pluralism in principle is based on the denial of what is in fact the very core of the Christian faith. I hope to show later that it is not so, and there is no lack of theologians today who seek to combine and to hold together, even if in a fruitful tension, their unimpaired faith in Jesus Christ universal Saviour of humankind, on the one hand, and, on the other, a positive, salvific significance of the other religious traditions of the world for their followers, in accordance to the eternal plan of God for humanity. This of course is the challenge with which the theology of religions is faced today, and represents the core of the third perspective recently opened after the Second Vatican Council.

Before entering into that new perspective, it may be useful to recall rapidly which are the main theological positions found in the present debate on the theology of religions. They largely correspond to the three successive perspectives which we have seen emerging in the course of the history of Christianity. A first "paradigm" – to express matters in the terminology currently in use in this debate – is called ecclesiocentrism, or equivalently exclusivism. It goes back to the perspective according to which explicit faith in Jesus Christ and Church membership are required for salvation. This was at the beginning of the last century the position of Karl Barth, which has been rejected by a document of the Holy Office under Pope Pius XII (1949) in connection with the famous Feeney case in U.S.A. That position is today virtually non existent among catholic theologians. A first change of paradigm consists therefore in passing from ecclesiocentrism to christocentrism, or equivalently from exclusivism to inclusivism.The vast majority of catholic theologians today follow that second paradigm according to which positive values are found operative in the religious traditions, whether these be understood as merely natural endowments of human nature or supernatural gifts of God conducive to salvation. This group corresponds to the second perspective which we have recalled in the historical unfolding of the Christian doctrine on the matter. However, a sizable number of theologians today advocate and promote a further paradigm shift from christocentrism to theocentrism or, in other words, from inclusivism to so-called "pluralism". According to these theologians, Christians, if they claim to be sincere in entering with others into interreligious dialogue, should first of all give up their traditional Christian faith in the uniqueness of Jesus Christ as universal Saviour. Jesus Christ is only one among other divine manifestations to peoples in the world, and nothing suggests – according to those "pluralists" – that a special claim of uniqueness ought to be maintained on his behalf.

All religions will then appear as different paths leading to a common goal which is "Absolute Reality", or whatever other term it may be called in the various religious traditions. The so-called "pluralist theologians" thus build up their own brand of "religious pluralism in principle" which, as should be clear, corresponds to the theory rejected by the Congregation for the Doctrine of the Faith in the Introduction to *Dominus Iesus*. But their theory of religious pluralism in principle is not the only one possible, and there is room, as I hope to show later, for a religious pluralism in principle in accordance with the Christian faith, and with the mystery of Jesus Christ as traditionally understood by the Church. This other kind of religious pluralism in principle would have to show how it is possible to combine an unimpaired faith in Jesus Christ with the positive salvific significance of the other religious traditions in God's plan for humankind. In my latest book I have suggested that, in the terminology currently used in the ongoing theological debate on the matter, my position could perhaps best be called an "inclusivist pluralism" or else a "pluralist inclusivism". The meaning of the expression should be self-explanatory.

II. SEARCHING FOR A MODEL

In my two books, I have proposed as a valid model for a religious pluralism in principle what I have called a "Trinitarian and Pneumatic Christology"[2]. What is meant by the expression is that the interpersonal relationships which exist in the mystery of God between the Son and the Father, on the one hand, and the Son and the Spirit, on the other, must be seen as intrinsic to the mystery of Jesus Christ. In other words, the christological mystery must always be related to the mystery of the divine Trinity from which it is inseparable. To take into account at every step of theological reflection the essential connection between both is an essential requirement if we want to avoid abstract christological considerations which fall short of and possibly distort the reality of the mystery of Jesus Christ. Christology has, in the past, often sinned by being impersonal. Its concern was the mystery of the "God-man" and the "hypostatic union" of the two natures in the God-man. The christology of which the New Testament speaks is not, however, a neutral, abstract christology of a God-man, but the concrete mystery of the Word-of-God-made-flesh in Jesus of Nazareth. In this mystery christology and the divine Trinity are

---

2. See the references in n. 1.

essentially united and inseparable. It is my conviction that to keep both closely united in our theological thinking is not without significance in view of a theology of religions which would combine the Church's christological faith with a salvific value and a positive significance in God's eyes of the religious traditions of the world. But this needs to be further explained.

The entire Christ-event, comprising the becoming man of the Word of God in Jesus, his entire life, his words and deeds, and finally the Paschal mystery of his death and resurrection must be seen, as God sees it, within the entire frame-work of God's gracious dealings with humankind through salvation history, that is, throughout the history of the world starting with creation. Throughout history, from the beginning, God has manifested himself to his human creatures in words and deeds, through his Word and his Spirit. This universal involvement of God with his creatures through history is marked by different covenants, of which St. Irenaeus in a celebrated text distinguished four as follows: "Four covenants were given to the human race: one, prior to the deluge, under Adam; the second, that after the deluge, under Noah; the third, the giving of the Law, under Moses; the fourth, that which renovates the human being, and sums up all things in itself by means of the Gospel, raising and bearing human beings upon its wings into the heavenly Kingdom" (*Adversus Haereses*, III,11,8).

The nature of the covenant with Noah must be correctly understood. There is no question here – as has too often been supposed – of a mere manifestation of God through the phenomena of nature and the constancy of their recurrence. The intimate relationship between God and Noah is stressed by the inspired text (Gen 9,1-17), as well as the universality of the "everlasting covenant" (Gen 9,16) struck by God with Noah and his descendants. These elements in the story symbolize a personal commitment of God toward the nations, that is, the universality of the divine intervention in the history of peoples, of which the religious traditions of humanity are the privileged testimonies. This true character of the Noah covenant has been well expressed by a recent author who wrote: "The covenant with Noah constitutes the lasting foundation for the salvation of every human person. Its true significance is falsified if one sees in it – as a long tradition in Catholic theology has done – nothing beyond the setting up of a "natural" religion having nothing to do yet with a supernatural revelation. The particular characteristics recorded in the Scripture concerning the Noah covenant make it clear that there is question here of a true event of salvation, marked by grace ... The entirety of the covenant with Noah appears as an outline of the covenants with Abrahan and Moses ... Israel and the nations have thus a common base:

they are in a state of covenantship with the true God and under the same salvific will of the one God"[3].

The covenant with Noah thus takes on a far-reaching significance for a theology of the religious traditions of peoples belonging to the "extra-biblical" tradition.They too are in a state of covenantship with God. They too are covenant peoples and deserve to be called "peoples of God". The one God is the God of all peoples.

Coming to the covenant with Moses, the question is asked whether it has been abolished in the advent of the "new covenant" established by God in Jesus Christ. In a discourse pronounced in Mainz (Germany), Pope John Paul II referred to "the people of God of the Old Covenant, which has never been revoked (cf. Rom 11,29)"[4]. How must the relationship between the Mosaic covenant and the Christic covenant be understood? More particularly: Is God's grace-filled relation today with persons belonging to the Jewish people to be assigned to an enduring efficacy of the Mosaic covenant *or* to the new covenant established in Jesus Christ? Does the latter simply substitute for the former, henceforth rendered inoperative? Israel and Christianity obviously represent a singular case, owing to the unique relationship existing between the two religions; however, it may furnish *mutatis mutandis* an emblematic model for the relationship between Christianity and the other religions.

The question has been asked anew in the context of the theological Hebrew-Christian dialogue. In a recent work bearing the title *The Covenant Never Revoked*, N. Lohfink has reexamined the biblical data in question[5]. Let it suffice to mention the results of the enquiry. The new covenant is no other than the first: it unveils the first by spreading abroad the splendour of the Lord which the first contained without revealing it fully. The fact is that in Jesus Christ the one covenant "has concentrated itself to eschatological radicalness" and so finds in him its "ultimate and most profound sense" (p. 81). And this leads the author to conclude: "I lean therefore to a "one covenant" theory which embraces Jews and Christians, whatever their differences in the one covenant, and that means Jews and Christians of today" (p. 84). But he adds: "From early Christian times Jews and Christians have been on two ways. Because the two ways run their course within the one covenant which makes God's salvation present in the world, I think that one must speak of a "twofold way of salvation" (p. 84).

---

3. B. STOECKLE, *Die ausserbiblische Menschheit und die Weltreligionen*, in J. FEINER – M. LÖHRER (eds.), *Mysterium Salutis*, 2, Einsiedeln, Benziger, 1967, pp. 1053-1054.

4. Text in *AAS* 73 (1981) 80.

5. N. LOHFINK, *The Covenant Never Revoked: Biblical Reflections on Christian-Jewish Dialogue*, New York, Paulist Press, 1991.

Independently from the formulation adopted, the divine plan of salvation has an organic unity, of which history marks the dynamic process. This unfolding process contains various steps, mutually related and complementary. For Christian faith the Christ-event does not exist without Israel or making abstraction from it; conversely, Israel never was chosen by God otherwise than as that people from which Jesus of Nazareth would issue forth. Israel and Christianity belong together in salvation history under the compass of the covenant. The covenant through which the Hebrew people obtained salvation in the past and continues to be saved even today is the same covenant through which Christians are called to salvation in Jesus Christ. There is no substitution of a "new" people of God to another, henceforth declared "ancient", but expansion to the boundaries of the world of one people of God, of which the election of Israel and the covenant with Moses were and remain the root and the source, the foundation and the promise.

The covenant with Moses endures, therefore, and is not abrogated by that in Jesus Christ. Let us note, moreover, that the case of the relationship between the Hebrew religion and Christianity can serve as an emblematic model for the relationship between Chrtistianity and the other religions. What is true in the first case is also valid, analogically, in the second case. The other religious traditions, symbolized by the covenant with Noah, keep also, *mutatis mutandis*, a permanent value. Just as the covenant with Moses has not been suppressed by the fact of having reached its perfection in Jesus Christ, in the same way the cosmic covenant established in Noah with the nations has not been cancelled either by the fact of having reached in the Christ-event the end to which it was destined by God. This means that the other religions too keep salvific value for their adherents, though not without being related to the Christ-event. A. Russo expresses the matter well where he writes:

> Thanks to the Mosaic covenant, ... we recognize a dignity and a permanent function of the Hebrew people in the plan of salvation. In an analogous manner, we should value the covenants which God has made with the other peoples of the earth, symbolically present in the story of Adam and more specifically in that of Noah. If the gifts of God are irrevocable, are not those granted to the other peoples equally irrevocable? If we use that principle to give credit to the religion of the Hebrews, why not apply it as well to the other covenants, of which the Scripture speaks, instead of considering them – and them alone – obsolete[6]?

---

6. A. RUSSO, *La funzione d'Israele e la legittimità delle altre religioni*, in *Rassegna di teologia* 40 (1999/1) 116.

The personal involvement of God with his creatures through history is everywhere marked with a Trinitarian rhythm. Yahweh (whom Jesus will call Father) reveals himself universally through his Word (the Wisdom of God) and through his Spirit. The Bible, the First Testament as well as the Christian Testament, testify to this Trinitarian structure. The Prologue of the Gospel according to John insists that God created all things through his Word, present with him from eternity (1,1-3); it adds that the Word of God has been throughout salvation history "the true light that, by coming into the world, enlightens all men" (1,9). The coming into the world of the Word of God does not here refer to the mystery of the Incarnation, but to the coming into the world of the Word as the Lady Wisdom of which the Sapiential literature of the First Testament spoke. Similarly, the Holy Spirit has been universally present and operative in God's personal dealings with humankind through history.

Among these divine manifestations of God through his Word and his Spirit, the Christ-event, made up of the entire human life, of the death and resurrection of Jesus Christ, marks undoubtedly the apex and the summit. God's self-revelation and self-gift to human beings in Jesus Christ is the centre of history and the key for interpreting the entire process of salvation. Jesus Christ is "constitutive" of universal salvation; he is truly the Saviour of the world. This is due to the fact that, by being raised from the dead by the Father, the human existence of Jesus, the Word incarnate, has become meta-historical or trans-historical, being no longer subject to conditioning by time and space. It is this real transformation of the human being of Jesus through his resurrection which confers upon his human existence, and in particular upon the paschal mystery of his death and resurrection, universal salvific value. Through it the Christ-event, which constitutes human salvation, is inclusively present and remains actual throughout time and space.

The unique significance of the event of Jesus Christ, as "constitutive" of universal salvation, must be clearly established on its true theological foundation. In the last analysis, it needs to be based on the personal identity of Jesus Christ as the Son of God. No other consideration would provide for it an adequate theological foundation. Through the mystery of the Incarnation the Word of God has inserted himself personally, once and for all, in the human reality and in the history of the world. In him God has established with the entire human race a bond of union which can never be broken. The Christ event is the sacrament of that decisive and everlasting covenant. The Incarnation represents in fact the deepest and most immanent possible manner of God's personal involvement with humankind in history. The Jesus Christ event occupies therefore a unique, irreplaceable place in the history of salvation. It is truly "constitutive" of the mystery of salvation for all humankind.

It remains, however, true that the historical event of Jesus Christ is necessarily particular and circumscribed by the limits imposed upon it by time and space. The human story of Jesus belongs to a precise point in space and in time. The mystery of the resurrection itself is an event inscribed punctually in human history, even though it introduces the human being of Jesus into a meta-historical condition. And, while it is true that in and through the glorified state of the Risen One, the historical event of salvation becomes present and remains actual for all times and places, it is equally true that even that event does not exhaust – and cannot exhaust – the revealing and saving power of the Word of God. While no separation can be admitted between the human being of Jesus and the person of the Word of God – as John Paul II has rightly insisted in his encyclical Letter *Redemptoris missio* (n. 6) – they cannot be identified, for the two natures of Jesus Christ remain distinct in their very personal union.

Undoubtedly the Word has been manifested in Jesus Christ in the deepest human way that may ever be conceived, and hence in the way best adapted to our human condition. But, paradoxically, this most human way of self-manifestation involves in itself and by its very nature its own limitations. The Word of God reaches beyond whatever the human being of Jesus, assumed by him personally, is capable of manifesting and revealing. Jesus Christ is, therefore, in his humanity the universal sacrament of the mystery of salvation offered by God to the whole of humankind through his Word (and his Spirit); but the God who saves through him remains beyond the human being of Jesus, even in his glorified state. Jesus Christ risen and glorified does not substitute for the Father; nor does his glorified human existence take the place of the Word himself, who could never be fully revealed through any historical manifestation.

I mentioned earlier, with reference to the Prologue of the Gospel according to John, that the Word of God, who exists eternally in the mystery of God's divine life, and through whom God created all things – and keeps them today in existence – was present and active throughout history *before* the Incarnation as "the true light that, coming into the world, enlightens all men" (1,9). It must be added that such a universal enlightening and saving activity of the Word as such perdures *after* the Incarnation of the Word and the resurrection of Jesus Christ. As X. Léon-Dufour puts it in his Commentary on the Gospel of John[7]: "If it is true

7. X. LÉON-DUFOUR, *Lecture de l'Évangile selon Saint Jean*, Vol. 1, Paris, Seuil, 1988, pp. 62-144.

that the *Logos* is God communicating himself, this communication has begun not with the Incarnation but since creation, and it has continued through the whole history of revelation" (p. 112). And, even while the Incarnation marks a "radical change" in the Word's mode of communication, involving the "concentration" in a man of the divine communication through the *Logos*, yet "this new stage does not supersede the previous one. The *Logos* continues to express himself thanks to creation of which he is the author and to the witness given to the light: many can receive him and become children of God" (p. 124).

It is possible, therefore, to speak of an enduring enlightening and saving activity of the Word of God as such, distinct from his saving activity through the risen human existence of Jesus. That, while becoming man, the "Word does not lose the glory which is his in equality with the Father", as St. Leo the Great remarked[8], must mean that he keeps exercising, in union with the Father, the actions which belong to him by reason of his specific character in the divine mystery: the mediation in creation (John 1,3), the universal enlightening action with regard to human beings (John 1,9), even the communication to them of the power to become children of God (John 1,12). In this sense, the Christ-event, however inclusively present, does not exhaust the power of the Word of God, who became flesh in Jesus Christ. The divine action of the Word cannot, by its nature, be reduced to the mode in which the Word expresses himself through the human actions of Jesus. The divine action of the Word is not "circumscribed" by, "exhausted" by, or "reduced" to its expression through the human being of Jesus. The saving action of the Incarnate Word through his glorified humanity does not exhaust the enligthening and life-giving power of the Word of God. This assertion, in fact, does nothing more than simply state that, while becoming man, the Word of God remains God. And, if the Word remains God, he too continues to act as God, beyond and over above his own human action. The action of the Word as such "exceeds" that of the Word incarnate in his glorified humanity.

We can thus affirm a diversity and a multiplicity of divine manifestations by the Word of God throughout human history, before and after the Christ-event. Not all those manifestations take place at the same depth or have the same value or significance. All of them are, however, "Logophanies" in the sense of being self-disclosures of God through his Word.

8. J. NEUNER – J. DUPUIS (eds.), *The Christian Faith in the Doctrinal Documents of the Catholic Church*, 7th rev. and enlarged ed., Staten Island, NY, Alba House, 2001, n. 612.

It is in this sense that the early Fathers of the Church could see the theophanies of the First Testament as manifestations of God through his Word, that is, "Logophanies". For Irenaeus the entire economy of salvation was made up of various divine manifestations through the Word; yet it remained true that the Incarnation of the Word in Jesus Christ – which he had been "rehearsing" through his previous involvements in history – brought "something entirely new" (*omnem novitatem attulit seipsum afferens*) (*Adv. Haer.* IV,34,1), because it marked the personal coming into the flesh of the Word of God.

That means that God's salvific action, which operates always within the framework of a unique design, is one, and at the same time has diverse facets. It never abstracts from the Christ-event, in which it finds its highest historical density. Yet the action of the Word of God is not necessarily bound by his becoming man historically in Jesus Christ. The mediation of the salvific grace of God to humankind takes on different dimensions which must be acknowledged, combined and integrated. Claude Geffré writes pointedly: "The very law of God's Incarnation through the mediation of history leads [us] to think that Jesus does not put an end to the story of God's manifestations. [...] In conformity with the traditional view of the Fathers of the Church, it is, therefore, possible to see the economy of the Word incarnate as the sacrament of a broader economy, that, namely, of the eternal Word of God which coincides with the religious history of humankind"[9].

The Christ-event, even while it is inclusively present and actual in all times and places through the glorified humanity of Jesus, does not exhaust the power of the Word of God who became flesh in Jesus Christ. The action of the Word reaches beyond the limits imposed on the operative presence of the humanity of Jesus, even in his glorified state, just as the person of the Word exceeds the human nature of Jesus Christ. One can understand then how "elements of truth and grace" (*Ad gentes* 9) can be found in the other religious traditions of the world, and how these serve, for their followers, as "paths" or "ways" to salvation. It is the Word of God who went sowing his seeds in the religious traditions. Nor must these seeds be understood as representing merely natural human endowments awaiting an eventual divine manifestation. They represent an actual divine self-manifestation and self-gift of God through his Word, however incomplete it may be.

---

9. C. GEFFRÉ, *La singularité du christianisme à l'âge du pluralisme religieux*, in J. DORÉ – C. THEOBALD (eds.), *Penser la foi: Recherches en théologie aujourd'hui*, Paris, Cerf, 1993, pp. 365-366.

The unlimited "enlightening" power of the divine Word has been unversally at work before its manifestation in the flesh, and remains at work throughout the history of salvation, even after the Jesus Christ event and beyond the confines of Christianity. As the first Christian apologists had already seen, individual persons could in fact be "en-light-ened" by the Word, who is the one source of divine light. It was not only individual persons – Socrates, Buddha and others – who received divine truth from the Word; but human designs and endeavours – Greek "philosophy" as well as Asian Wisdom – could be channels through which the divine light reached persons.

The religious traditions, which preserve the memory of experiences with divine truth made by the seers and prophets of various peoples, contain elements "of truth and grace" (*Ad gentes* 9), which the Word has sown in them, and through which his enlightening power remains operative. The Word of God continues even today to sow his seeds in the hearts of people and in their religious traditions. Revealed truth and salvific grace are present in them through his action.

Similar observations are called for where the Spirit of God is concerned. The universal presence of the Spirit has been progressively stressed by the recent Church magisterium – without, however, the implications of such a presence for the theology of religions being adequately brought out. The Holy Spirit is seen as present not only in persons but in cultures and religions. In his encyclical Letter *Redemptoris missio* John Paul II wrote: "The Spirit's presence and activity affect not only individuals but also society and history, peoples, cultures, and religions. Indeed, the Spirit is at the origin of the noble ideals and undertakings which benefit humanity on its journey through history" (n. 28). A pneumatic christology helps to see that the Spirit of God was and is universally present and active, before and after the Christ event. The Christ event results from the work of the Spirit in the world; it is in turn the source of the Spirit's action. Between the two aspects there exists a "relation of reciprocal conditioning", by virtue of which the Spirit can justly be called, throughout the history of salvation, the "Spirit of Christ"[10]. The divine salvific economy is only one, and the Christ event is at once its culminating point and universal sacrament; but the God who saves is tri-personal; each of the three is personally distinct and remains active in a distinctive manner. God saves "with two hands", the Word and the Spirit – Saint Irenaeus wrote in the second century (*Adv. Haer.* IV,7,4).

---

10. J.H. WONG, *Anonymous Christianity: Karl Rahner's Pneumato-Christocentrism and the East-West Dialogue*, in *Theological Studies* 55 (1994) 609-637.

The recent magisterium of the Church has insisted on the universal active presence of the Spirit. It may be asked, however, if after the Christ event the communication of the Spirit and his active presence in the world are realized exclusively through the glorified humanity of Jesus Christ, or if, on the contrary, they go beyond such limits. In other words, has the Spirit of God become to such an extent the "Spirit of Christ" that he can no longer be present and operative beyond the communication made of him by the risen Christ – with the result that his action be henceforth circumscribed by that of the risen Christ, and in this sense limited?

In the New Testament, and particularly in Paul, the Spirit is called either "Spirit of God" or "Spirit of Christ". The expression "Spirit of Christ" (Rom 8,9) seems to refer to the communication made of the Spirit by the risen Christ, which corresponds to the promise made by Jesus to the disciples in the Gospel of John (15,26; 16,5-15) and to its realization at Pentecost (Acts 2,1-4). It also means that the work of the Spirit establishes between human persons and the Lord Jesus Christ a personal relation by which they are incorporated into him: "Anyone who does not have the Spirit of Christ does not belong to him" (Rom 8,9). In that sense it has been noted that the Spirit is the "point of insertion" of God through Christ in the life of human beings, and that his work consists in making them children of the Father in the Son through the risen humanity of Jesus.

The fact remains, however, that the Spirit is more often called the "Spirit of God": "The Spirit of God dwells in you" (Rom 8,9); "If the Spirit of him who raised Jesus from the dead dwells in you, he who raised Christ Jesus from the dead will give life to your mortal bodies also through his Spirit that dwells in you" (Rom 8,11); "All who are led by the Spirit of God are sons of God" (Rom 8,14); cf. also 1 Cor 2,11; 2,14; 3,16; 6,11; 12,3; 2 Cor 3,3. The Spirit which is communicated to us is fundamentally the "Spirit of God". If, then, from the manifestation of God in history we ascend to the tripersonal communication which exists in the mystery of God himself, the Spirit is revealed to us as the person who "proceeds" primarily from the Father as "principle without a principle", through the Word or the Son. Taking into account the biblical and traditional data just recalled, one may ask whether after the Christ event there can be a salvific action of the Holy Spirit beyond that which takes place through the risen humanity of Jesus, just as before the historical event of the Incarnation the Spirit acted salvifically even though the humanity of Jesus did not yet exist.

The metaphor used by St. Irenaeus of the "two hands" of God may help to clarify the distinct activity of the Spirit arising from his distinct personal identity. In the background of that metaphor is probably the image of God as a potter (cf. Isa 64,6-7) who with two hands produces a single work – that is here, the one economy of salvation. The two hands of God, the Word and the Spirit – we may add – are conjoined hands. This means that, though being united and inseparable, they are also distinct and complementary. The work of each is distinct from that of the other; it is in fact the coincidence and the "synergy" of the two distinct works which produces the salvific effect of God. Neither one nor the other can be reduced to a mere "function" in relation to the other; on the contrary the two works converge to realize a unique economy of salvation. God acts with his two hands. In the light of this metaphor it becomes perhaps easier to conceive that the communication of the Spirit by the risen Christ does not necessarily exhaust the work of the Spirit after the Christ event.

It is well known that the Oriental and Orthodox tradition has often accused the Western tradition of holding and promoting a theological "Christomonism", in which the Holy Spirit is reduced to being a "function" of Christ. Y. Congar, though considering the accusation exaggerated, admitted that it is not altogether without foundation; it offers, in fact, to Western theology, the occasion to reflect on the inadequacy of its pneumatology[11]. While it is true that we may not build an "autonomous" economy of the Spirit, separated from that of the Son incarnate, it is also true that the Spirit may not be reduced to a "function" of the risen Christ, of which he would be so to speak the "vicar". The Spirit would then lose the fulness of his personal salvific action. V. Lossky accuses the Latin tradition, because of its concept of the procession of the Holy Spirit from the Father and the Son (filioque), of reducing on the one hand the personal identity of the Spirit within the intrinsic mystery of God, and on the other hand his salvific activity in the divine economy of salvation[12]. Reduced to the function of "bond" between the two persons of Father and Son, and unilaterally subordinated to the Son in his very existence, to the detriment of the authentic trinitarian perichoresis, the Spirit would lose, with his personal independent identity, the personal fulness of his action in the economy of salvation. This action is then conceived as a simple means placed at the service of the economy of the Word, on both the ecclesial and the individual plane.

Certainly no "subordination" of the Spirit in relation to the Son can be supposed in the intrinsic mystery of God, the "order" of the intra-trinitarian "processions" notwithstanding. The danger in the Latin tradition of reducing the salvific work of the Spirit in the divine economy is

---

11. Y. CONGAR, Pneumatologie ou "christomonisme" dans la tradition latine, in Ecclesia a Spiritu Sancto edocta. Mélanges théologiques, Gembloux, Duculot, 1970, pp. 41-63.

12. V. LOSSKY, Essai sur la théologie mystique de l'Orient, Paris, Aubier, 1944.

not, however, thereby overcome. A subtle form that such a reduction may take consists precisely in claiming that after the Incarnation the saving and vivifying action of the Spirit can take place only through the communication which the risen Lord makes to us of His Spirit.

Vatican II affirms very clearly (*Ad gentes* 4) and the recent Church magisterium repeats with insistence (cf. in particular the encyclical Letter *Dominum et vivificantem* 53) that the Spirit was already present and operative before the glorification of Christ, even before the Christ event, throughout the whole of history, from creation. It is understood that "This is the same Spirit who was at work in the Incarnation and in the life, death and resurrection of Jesus, and who is at work in the Church. He is therefore not an alternative to Christ, nor does he fill a sort of void which is sometimes suggested as existing between Christ and the Logos. Whatever the Spirit brings about in human hearts and in the history of peoples, in cultures and religions serves as a preparation for the Gospel and can only be understood in reference to Christ ...": so writes John Paul II in the encyclical *Redemptoris missio* (n. 29). This notwithstanding, one does not see why, while before the Christ event the Spirit was acting in the world and in history without being communicated through the risen humanity of Jesus – which did not yet exist – after the Christ event his action should be so bound to the risen humanity as to be limited by it. One must certainly hold that in both cases – before and after the historical event of the Incarnation – the outpouring of the Spirit is always related to the event in which the unfolding through history of the divine plan of salvation culminates. In that sense one may and must say that the gift of the Spirit before the Incarnation is made "in view of" the christological event. But this does not justify saying that an action of the Spirit as such is henceforth unconceivable after the event – though it needs to be seen as related to the event of the Incarnation. In the same way it has been possible, as we have seen, to affirm an action of the Word as such enduring after the Christ event. There are not two economies of salvation. But the two "hands" of God have and maintain in the one divine economy their own personal identity and action. The Word is that light "that enlightens every man" (John 1,9); as for the Spirit, he "blows where he wills" (John 3,8).

My intention in the two books mentioned here has been to show that a Trinitarian Pneumatic model of Christology can help us see how two apparently contradictory affirmations can be combined: on the one hand, the event Jesus Christ constitutes salvation for the whole of humanity; and, on the other hand, the "paths" proposed by the other religious traditions have authentic saving value for their followers. If these two affirmations can be held together, it also becomes possible to discover the meaning willed by God, within the framework of his unique plan of salvation for humankind, of the religious pluralism in which we are living. The solution I am proposing to solve the apparent dilemma between the two affirmations consists in uniting three complemetary and convergent aspects of the way in which, within the one divine plan for humankind, salvation reaches persons in the concrete circumstances of their life. The three elements to be combined are: 1. the lasting actuality and universal efficacy of the event Jesus Christ, notwithstanding its historical particularity; 2. the universal operative presence of the Word of God whose action is not restricted by the human existence assumed by him in the mystery of the Incarnation; 3. the equally universal action of the Spirit of God, which is neither limited nor exhausted by its communication through the risen and glorified Christ. Jesus Christ is universal Saviour; but the Word of God and the Spirit of God do not cease to infuse into the religious traditions of the world divine truth and grace conducive to the salvation of their followers.

Far from competing with each other, the different paths proposed by the different religious traditions make up, together with Christianity, the entire divine plan of salvation for humankind. One must, however, always remember that it is not in fact the religious traditions that save people, but God himself through his Word and his Spirit. The diverse "paths" are conducive to salvation because they have been traced by God himself in his search for people and peoples; and, even though not all have the same meaning or represent the same depth of divine involvement with people, yet all converge in the one plan designed by God eternally. The hidden manifestation of the Word of God through the seers of other religions and through the traditions which have found their origin in them, the inspiring breath of the Spirit on their prophets and their message, as well as the historical coming of the Word in the flesh in Jesus Christ and the outpouring of the Spirit through him at Pentecost to which the Christian community testifies: – all combine together in the overall ensemble of a unique divine plan.

III. CONCLUSION

Is it possible then to speak of a religious pluralism in principle, that is one intended and willed by God in his eternal design for humankind? It must be seen clearly that God has taken at every step of the history of salvation the initiative in coming to meet people and peoples. That is why one can and must say that the religious traditions of the world are "paths" or "ways" of salvation for their followers. They are such because they represent the paths traced by God himself in his search for people. Human beings were not the first to search for God through their history; God has been the first to search for them and in his search for them to trace the ways along which they could find him. If, as has been suggested by a recent author, the religions of the world are in themselves as many "gifts of God to the peoples of the world"[13], we need not seek further for the theological foundation of a religious pluralism in principle. The principle of the plurality of religions finds its foundation in the superabundant richness and variety of the automanifestations of God to humankind. Religious pluralism in principle is based on the immensity of a God who is Love and communication.

The two books, and perhaps the last one with greater vigour and intensity, suggest that a "qualitative leap" is required in the Christian and Catholic theology of religions if we wish to develop a deeper theological appreciation of the religious traditions and entertain with their followers more open and fruitful relations. In the conclusion to the most recent book I expressed my conviction that such a "qualitative leap" is necessary in order that the Christian message may retain its credibility in the pluri-cultural and pluri-religious world of today; or, better, in order that the credibility of the message may increase in the measure of its adaptation to the enlarged horizons of the present world. We must shun ways of "defending the faith" which turn out to be counter-productive, because they make it appear restrictive and narrow. I am convinced that a broader outlook and a more positive attitude, provided they be theologically well founded, will help Christians themselves to discover to their own surprise in the Christian message a new breath and a new depth.

Pontificia Università Gregoriana   Jacques DUPUIS, S.J.
4 Piazza della Pilotta
I-00187 Rome
Italy

13. G. ODASSO, *Bibbia e religioni. Prospettive bibliche per una teologia delle religioni*, Roma, Urbaniana University Press, 1998, p. 372.

INTERRELIGIOUS DIALOGUE
AS POLEMICAL CONVERSATION

Should Christians develop their theology in conversation with people of other religions? On the one hand, such a relational form of theology seems to be one of the generally accepted standards of modernity, since no religious tradition can afford to live in splendid isolation any longer. Moreover, since "no religion is an island", it cannot understand itself apart from its relation to other religions[1]. But, on the other hand, every religious tradition seeks to preserve its own identity, and therefore it engages in open dialogue with other traditions only under certain circumstances or with certain provisos. In this essay I want to investigate this hesitancy in the Christian tradition to engage in open conversation with other religious traditions. It is my objective to show that inter-religious communication has to be more open than the historically predominant forms of apologetics and polemics may suggest, but that it is not as soft as the modern concept of dialogue suggests either. Therefore, I speak about "inter-religious dialogue as polemical conversation"[2]. In the first section, I will discuss one of the questions posed by Thomas Aquinas in his *Summa theologiae*, viz. May we enter into communion (*communicari*) with unbelievers? After that, I will examine a second text by Aquinas, in which he discusses the characteristics of the companionship (the Latin word is *conversari*) between Christ and his disciples. In the third section, I will turn to the issue of inter-religious prayer, or *communicatio in sacris* as a special problem for Catholic theology. Subsequently, I will investigate the relation between conversation, identity and mission with reference to the text *Dominus Iesus*, published by the Congregation for the Doctrine of the Faith last year. Finally, I will return to the Dominicans in the thirteenth century in order to show how they tried to meet the requirements for a conversation with people of other religions by studying

1. See A.J. HESCHEL, *No Religion Is an Island*, in *Union Seminary Quarterly Review* 21 (1966) 117-133; reprinted in P.J. GRIFFITHS, *Christianity Through Non-Christian Eyes*, Maryknoll, NY, Orbis Books, 1990, 26-40. N. SMART elaborates on this idea in his *The World's Religions: Old Traditions and Modern Transformations*, Cambridge, Cambridge University Press, 1989.
2. The words "conversation" and "communication", although different in certain aspects, will be considered as roughly equivalent in this article.

the cultures and languages of those to whom their missionary effort would be directed. It goes without saying that the history of Christian mission has often been a history of atrocities. But at its best moments it has also been, and still intends to be, a history of taking seriously the religiously others.

I. THOMAS AQUINAS ON INTERRELIGIOUS COMMUNICATION

If one turns to a Medieval author like Thomas Aquinas in order to learn something about inter-religious communication, one has to be aware that one has to proceed carefully and with an "hermeneutics of suspicion", because of the differences between our modern questions and the worldview of a medieval theologian. One of the areas in which the difference between the world view of a Christian in the Middle Ages and a Christian in modern, pluralistic society is very much apparent, is precisely the assessment of people of other faiths[3]. In the Middle Ages, the general idea was that most of the people were Christians, and that those who did not follow the lead of the Church, did so out of stubbornness. It was generally assumed that practically everybody could know that they were to be saved by Christ.

Aquinas seems to share this mentality when he deals with disbelief as a vice contrary to the theological virtue of faith in his *Summa theologiae* II-II, qq. 10-16. For him, *infidelitas* is disbelief rather than unbelief: a rejection of what should be believed rather than a lack of assent[4]. For us, who are impressed by the multitude of cultures and religions as part of God's creation, the faith of those others would not be perceived primarily as a form of unbelief, let alone disbelief. But for Aquinas someone who does not believe willingly denies the truth of Christian faith, and thus commits a sin that excludes him or her from salvation. Even those who through no fault of their own have heard nothing about the faith, are condemned albeit because of other sins[5]. Disbelievers are not considered as different people believing different things, but as people who depart from the truth. There is no place for real difference here: the others are deviators, either because they resist the faith before it has been accepted

---

3. See O.H. PESCH, *Thomas von Aquin: Grenze und Grösse mittelalterlicher Theologie*, Mainz, Grünewald, 1988, pp. 52-65.

4. See the explanatory note in THOMAS AQUINAS, *Summa theologiae*, volume 32: *Consequences of Faith* (2a 2ae.8-16). Latin text, English translation, Introduction, Notes & Glossary T. GILBY, O.P., London, 1975, pp. 38-39.

5. AQUINAS, *Summa theologiae* II-II, q.10 a.1.

(such is the case of the pagans), or because they resist it after having accepted it either in the mode of a prefiguration (such is the case of the Jews), or in the mode of the truth itself (this is the case with the heretics)[6].

But what about inter-religious communication with people of other faiths? By now, one may expect Aquinas to be totally negative on this matter, but he is not. As regards *disputatio* or public debate with unbelievers, Aquinas thinks that this is useful and even to be praised if the debate is held in order to refute errors or for theological practice; but if someone debates without being certain of the faith, or if one tries to test it with arguments as if it were something about which one might doubt, then such a person is a sinner because he is a doubter in faith and an unbeliever[7]. But maybe it is possible to have another form of communication with unbelievers[8]? At this place, Aquinas uses the word *communicari*, which has in the Latin language a more pregnant meaning than the English verb "to communicate"[9]. *Communicari* is to have communion, to keep company, to associate with someone. It therefore includes living together or working together with someone. With reference to the communion of the faithful with unbelievers who have not received the Christian faith, Aquinas remarks that the Church cannot forbid this, because she has no right to pass spiritual judgement on such persons. But the Church forbids, under penalty of excommunication, any communication with heretics or apostates. As regards the persons who want to communicate with Jews or pagans, they may do so if they have a firm faith so that the communication will lead to the conversion of unbelievers rather than to the turning away from faith by the believers. If, however, one is not that firmly grounded in faith, communication with unbelievers should be forbidden, because the probability of downfall from faith is to be feared in such a case[10].

---

6. *ST* II-II, q.10 a.5.

7. *ST* II-II q.10 a.7: *utrum sit cum infidelibus publice disputandum*: "Si enim disputet tanquam de fide dubitans, et veritatem fidei pro certo non supponens, sed argumentis experiri intendens, procul dubio peccat, tanquam dubius in fide et infidelis".

8. *ST* II-II q.10 a.9: *utrum cum infidelibus possit communicari*.

9. In the next section, I hope to show that the same holds true for the word *conversari*. In both cases, the Latin word has a deeper and more existential connotation than the somewhat flat meaning of the (modern) English words "communication" and "conversation".

10. *ST* II-II q.10 a.9: "Si enim aliqui fuerint firmi in fide, ita quod ex communione eorum cum infidelibus conversio infidelium magis sperari possit quam fidelium a fide aversio; non sunt prohibendi infidelibus communicare qui fidem non susceperunt, scilicet paganis vel Iudaeis; et maxime si necessitas urgeat. Si autem sint simplices et infirmi in fide, de quorum subversione probabiliter timeri possit, prohibendi sunt ab infidelium communione; et praecipue ne magnam familiaritatem cum eis habeant, vel absque necessitate eis communicent".

The result of this first investigation seems to be rather disconcerting: Aquinas sees interreligious communication in terms of danger or chance for possible conversion. If the chances are that the unbelievers will be converted, this communication is permitted; this is especially the case with Christians who are sure of their ground and with theologians – at least in Aquinas' time. If, however, there is a chance that the Christian will become doubtful or even inclining to another faith, interreligious communication should be forbidden. Any form of intimacy with unbelievers has to be discouraged. Aquinas knows too well that communication with others is dangerous, since it does not only refer to theological discussions, but encompasses the practice of living together with people of other faiths. As we will see in the next section, the same holds true for the Latin word *conversari*.

II. AQUINAS ON CONVERSATION

In this section, I want to show that Aquinas uses the word "conversation" with the same connotation as "communication": these words do not primarily indicate a form of talking, but a form of living. Aquinas' Latin use has been stamped by some very important texts from the Vulgate, such as "thereupon Wisdom appeared on earth and lived among men (*conversatus est*)"[11]. This text, from Baruch 3,38 may be seen as a parallel text for the famous words from the Gospel according to John: "The Word was made flesh, and dwelt among us". But there is also a clear ethical connotation in texts such as "let your conduct (*conversamini*) be worthy of the Gospel of Christ, so that whether I come and see you for myself or hear about you from a distance, I may know that you are standing firm, one in spirit, one in mind, contending as one man for the gospel faith" (Phil 1,27), or again: "to let you know how men ought to conduct themselves (*oporteat te conversari*) in God's household" (1 Tim 3,15).

In his theology on Christ the Saviour in the *Summa theologiae*, Aquinas inserts a new series of questions concerning the life of Christ: his entrance in the world, his ongoing life in this world, his leaving from this world, and his exaltation after this life[12]. Right at the beginning of the second

11. My quotations from Scripture are taken from the *New English Bible with the Apocrypha*, Oxford – Cambridge, 1970.
12. See *ST* III q.27 intr.: "[...] primo considerabimus de his quae pertinent ad ingressum eius in mundum; secundo, de his quae pertinent ad processum vitae ipsius in hoc mundo; tertio, de exitu ipsius ab hoc mundo; quarto, de his quae pertinent ad exaltationem ipsius post hanc vitam".

part of these questions, relating to the ongoing life of Christ in this world, he investigates the way in which He "conversed" in this world. It may become clear what Aquinas meant by these words if we consider the articles of this question: Did Christ have to lead a solitary life, or did he have to keep company with human beings? Did he have to lead an austere life as concerns drinking, food and clothing, or did he have to behave like the others? Did he have to lead the life of an outcast, or did he have to be rich and famous? And finally: did he have to live according to the Law[13]?

This question about the *modus conversationis* of Christ relates to his way of life, his behaviour toward human beings. In his answer to the first sub-question, Aquinas says that the conversation of Christ had to be in harmony with the aim of his incarnation. Since He came into the world in order to show the truth, He had to live publicly among human beings; since He came to free human beings from their sins, He had to behave like a shepherd gathering his sheep. Since He came to give us access to God, He had to be on intimate terms with human beings. There is even a kind of familiarity in the behaviour of Christ, says Aquinas, because he wanted to be approached by human beings. As confirmation, he gives a quotation from Matthew 9,10: "When Jesus was at table in the house, many bad characters – tax-gatherers and others – were seated with him and his disciples"[14].

What strikes me in this text is that "conversation" suggests a notion of intimacy (*familiaritas*), and that this intimacy is characteristic of the manner in which God incarnate wants to have contact with human beings. Therefore, Aquinas quotes the text from Baruch as the main point of

---

13. *ST* III q.40 intr.: "considerandum restat de his quae pertinent ad progressum ipsius. Et primo considerandum est de modo conversationis ipsius; secundo, de tentatione eius; tertio, de doctrina; quarto, de miraculis. Circa primum quaeruntur quatuor. Primo, utrum Christus debuerit solitariam vitam ducere, an inter homines conversari; secundo, utrum debuerit austeram vitam ducere in cibo et potu et vestitu, an cum aliis communem. Tertio, utrum debuerit abiecte vivere in hoc mundo, an in divitiis et honore; quarto, utrum debuerit secundum legem vivere".

14. *ST* III q.40 a.1 resp.: "dicendum quod conversatio Christi talis debuit esse ut conveniret fini incarnationis, secundum quam venit in mundum. Venit autem in mundum, primo quidem, ad manifestandum veritatem ... secundo, venit ad hoc ut homines a peccato liberaret ... tertio, venit ut *per ipsum habeamus accessum ad Deum*, ut dicitur Rom. V,2. Et ideo, familiariter cum hominibus conversando, conveniens fuit ut hominibus fiduciam daret ad se accedendi. Unde dicitur Matth. IX,10: *Factum est, discumbente eo in domo, ecce, multi publicani et peccatores venientes discumbebant cum Iesu et discipulis eius*". Note the difference between the Latin text of Matthew 9,10 (publicans and sinners) and the English translation from the Greek (tax-gatherers and others).

departure for his theological reflections: "Wisdom appeared on earth and lived among men"[15].

When Aquinas talks about the way in which Christ wanted to manifest himself to his disciples after his resurrection, he underscores this connotation of familiarity once again: Christ had to keep company with his disciples in order to comfort them, and to make them suitable witnesses of his resurrection. But he could not be with them continuously, because in that case they would have thought that he lived a normal life just like before. So, he had to appear sometimes in order to manifest the truth of the resurrection; but he had to disappear in order to manifest the glory of the resurrection[16]. A companionship with the disciples suggests a kind of familiarity that is evaded by Christ after his resurrection, just as He avoided to be touched by Mary Magdalene. But, on the other hand, He had to meet with them a few times in order to comfort their faith.

This behaviour of Christ suggests that God wants to have a "conversation of life" with human beings. This way of life is not characterised by isolation but by communication, openness and an active presence among others. This offers the Church as the community of those who want to follow Christ a model of mission and dialogue[17]. In this model, however, not proclamation but presence is the major characteristic[18]. One wonders, therefore, how the Church could be so afraid of this openness if Christ, her model and teacher, wanted to keep company with publicans

---

15. *ST* III q.40 a.1 arg. s.c.: "Sed contra est quod dicitur Bar. III, 38: *post haec in terris visus est, et cum hominibus conversatus est*". For the function of quotations from Scripture in these arguments *sed contra*, compare W.G.B.M. VALKENBERG, *Words of the Living God: Place and Function of Holy Scripture in the Theology of St. Thomas Aquinas* (Publications of the Thomas Instituut te Utrecht, N.S., 6), Leuven, Peeters, 2000, p. 36.

16. *ST* III q.55 a.3 resp.: "circa resurrectionem Christi duo erant discipulis declaranda: scilicet ipsa veritas resurrectionis Christi, et gloria resurgentis. Ad veritatem autem resurrectionis manifestandam, sufficit quod pluries apparuit, et cum eis familiariter est locutus, et comedit, et bibit, et se eis palpandum praebuit. Ad gloriam autem resurrectionis manifestandam, noluit continue conversari cum eis, sicut prius fecerat, ne videretur ad talem vitam resurrexisse qualem prius habuerat". Aquinas gives the same reason in his commentary on John 20,26 (*super Evangelium s. Ioannis lectura*, ed. R. CAI, Taurini, Marietti, 1951, no. 2552).

17. In the document *Dialogue and Mission: The Attitude of the Church towards Followers of Other Religions*, issued by the SECRETARIAT FOR NON-CHRISTIANS (Rome, 1984), one can find an interesting parallel between five aspects of mission and four forms of dialogue. In both cases, the aspect of *conversatio* is mentioned first: mission is in the first instance constituted by the simple presence and living witness of the Christian life; dialogue is in the first instance a manner of acting and living in daily life.

18. It is this model of mission as presence that lies behind the movement of "urban mission". See, for instance, F. WIJSEN, *Geloven bij het leven: missionaire presentie in een volkswijk,* Baarn, Gooi & Sticht, 1997, p. 117. This model of mission has some older roots, for instance in St. Francis, see J. HOEBERICHTS, *Francisus en de Islam,* Assen, Van Gorcum, 1994.

and tax collectors? On the other hand, one can understand why the Church is sometimes hesitant to immerse itself into human affairs, since it is aware of having to preserve a treasure. This explains its rejection of *communicatio in sacris*, especially in interreligious services.

III. THE DANGER OF SHARING HOLY THINGS

If one reads the entry on *communicatio in sacris* in the previous edition of the famous *Lexikon für Theologie und Kirche*, one is struck by the negative tenor of this entry[19]. It is usually forbidden for a Catholic christian to participate actively in a religious ceremony of another Christian community; participation of a non-Catholic Christian in a sacrament can only be allowed in some special cases. This rather dissuasive line of reasoning does not come as a surprise to those who know about the problems that the Catholic church has to acknowledge other Christian churches as equals; if there is no full communion with these Christian communities, their members cannot be admitted to the sacraments of the Catholic church[20]. In this respect, the Congregation for the Doctrine of the Faith has, in its document *Dominus Iesus* (August 2000), once again underlined the difference between the Catholic church as instrument of salvation and the other ecclesial communities[21]. If there can be no access to the holy things of the Catholic church for those who are not in full communion with this Church, how can there be any sharing of these holy things with those who have another religion?

In this respect, there is an interesting tension between the official doctrine of the Catholic church and the practice of its highest representative. While the rituals and practices of other religions cannot be put on a par with the rituals of the Catholic Church, according to *Dominus Iesus*[22],

19. H. SCHAUF, *Communicatio in sacris*, in *LThK* 3 (^{2}1959) 24-26. The situation is not much better in G. HINTZEN – I. RIEDEL-SPANGENBERGER, *Communicatio in sacris*, in *LThK* 2 (^{3}1994) 1278-1280. In the latter, however, *communicatio in spiritualibus* is mentioned as a new encompassing term according to the *Ecumenical directory* issued in 1993.

20. For the Dutch situation, see R. HUYSMANS et al., *Intercommunie: het asymmetrische geloofsgesprek tussen protestanten en katholieken*, een publicatie van de sectie Geloofsvragen van de Raad van Kerken in Nederland, Zoetermeer, Boekencentrum, 1999. See also T. VAN EIJK, *Teken van aanwezigheid: een katholieke ecclesiologie in œcumenisch perspectief*, Zoetermeer, Meinema, 2000, pp. 254-257.

21. See *Dominus Iesus*, no. 17: "The ecclesial communities which have not preserved the valid Episcopate and the genuine and integral substance of the Eucharistic mystery, are not Churches in the proper sense; however, those who are baptized in these communities are, by Baptism, incorporated in Christ and thus are in a certain communion, albeit imperfect, with the Church".

22. *Dominus Iesus*, no. 21: "Certainly, the various religious traditions contain and offer religious elements which come from God, and which are part of what 'the Spirit brings

482   P. VALKENBERG

Pope John Paul II prays together with representatives of other faiths in a manner that seems to presuppose the idea that these religions are more or less equal. At least, this is the critique that has been levelled against the Pope because of his remarkable initiative, the World Day of Prayer for Peace in Assisi, now some 15 years ago[23]. This idea of equality between religions was one of the reasons for archbishop Marcel Lefebvre to leave the Church, and his followers go on criticizing the Assisi prayer gathering because of the same reason[24], while some conservative Dutch theologians have uttered the same complaint[25]. But the Pope was careful, of course, to avoid the idea of sharing prayer with other religions or of inter-religious services. He did not pray together with representatives of other religions, but he prayed in their presence, and they prayed in his presence. Since 1986, he has done so on several occasions, such as, for instance, his visit to the Umayyad mosque in Damascus in 2001 and his second World Day of Prayer in Assisi in 2002. While the difference between an interreligious prayer meeting and a prayer in the context of an interreligious meeting is theologically not without relevance, the main idea of such a meeting is to convey a sense of a common concern for peace that is shared by the different religious leaders. Therefore, one can say that the practice of the Pope legitimates a form of inter-religious communication, while the doctrines emphasised by influential parts of the Roman curia try to restrict this conversation as much as possible.

about in human hearts and in the history of peoples, in cultures, and religions'. Indeed, some prayers and rituals of the other religions may assume a role of preparation for the Gospel, in that they are occasions or pedagogical helps in which the human heart is prompted to be open to the action of God. One cannot attribute to these, however, a divine origin or an ex opere operato salvific efficacy, which is proper to the Christian sacraments. Furthermore, it cannot be overlooked that other rituals, insofar as they depend on superstitions or other errors (cf. 1 Cor 10,20-21), constitute an obstacle to salvation".

23. See *World Day of Prayer for Peace in Assisi* (27.10.1986), in *Bulletin Secretariatus pro non Christianis* 22 (1987) 11-160. A thorough investigation of this initiative has been given by G. RIEDL, *Modell Assisi. Christliches Gebet und interreligiöser Dialog in heilsgeschichtlichem Kontext*, Berlin – New York, Walter de Gruyter, 1998.

24. *Ibid.*, pp. 14-15 and 274-277.

25. "Men kan het betreuren dat dit samenzijn van vertegenwoordigers van verschillende religies op een schijnbaar gelijk niveau de indruk wekte dat alle godsdiensten min of meer van gelijke waarde zijn en dat het praktizeren van deze godsdiensten een normale zaak is. Men zou ook kunnen denken dat dit soort ontmoetingen nu belangrijker is dan het missiewerk. Tenslotte kan men zich ook afvragen wat deze niet-christenen met hun ceremonies in een katholiek kerkgebouw te zoeken hadden … Overigens is deze ontmoeting te Assisi een randgebeuren in de Kerk, dat misschien een soort profetisch gebaar is geweest dat op een wijze die alleen aan God bekend is, voor sommigen juist datgene betekende wat nodig was om hen dichter bij het heil in Christus te brengen": H.J.J.M. VAN STRAELEN – L. ELDERS, *De niet-christelijke Godsdiensten en het Christendom*, Brugge, Tabor, 1991, pp. 258-259.

In the next section of my contribution, I try to show that this double-faced attitude of the Roman Catholic Church toward inter-religious conversation has to do with a different idea of the identity of the Church and its mission. While the Pope carries forward a self-conscious idea of the Church and its mission, the Congregation for the Doctrine of the Faith bases its documents on a defensive idea of Church and mission. In a certain sense, this image of the Church is quite successful: it is rather cold and strict in its doctrinal assertions, but it is rather warm and "conversational" in the pastoral behaviour of its highest representative, who can afford to build bridges and offer relationships on the basis of a high self-awareness, or rather: an awareness of the unicity and salvific universality of Jesus Christ and the Church, as the subtitle of the document *Dominus Iesus* goes.

IV. Conversation, Identity, and Mission of the Church

The document *Dominus Iesus* is a good example of the way in which certain theological groups within the Catholic church consider interreligious dialogue as a threat. They propagate a fixed idea of Christian identity: the idea is that the Christian tradition has remained the same over the centuries, and therefore new questions may be answered by referring to these old traditions[26]. The authors of this declaration do need such a fixed identity for fear that some new influences from Asia might threaten their cherished missionary traditions. They cling to the ideal of a new missionary effort that would be able to win the six continents, particularly Asia, for Christ. But they are afraid of the consequences of a "theology of religious pluralism" that might lead people into confusion, as the *notificatio* by the Congregation for the Doctrine of the Faith on the book by Jacques Dupuis has it[27]. In my opinion, the real question that lies behind the conflicts between Father Dupuis and the Congregation is: will Rome still succeed in imposing its European idea of mission on Asia? Or will the reality of living together in India lead to an "inverted mission" from

---

26. *Dominus Iesus*, no. 3: "In the practice of dialogue between the Christian faith and other religious traditions ... new questions arise that need to be addressed through pursuing new paths of research ... In this task, the present Declaration seeks to recall to Bishops, theologians and all the Catholic faithful, certain indispensable elements of Christian doctrine".

27. J. DUPUIS, *Toward a Christian Theology of Religious Pluralism*, Maryknoll, NY, 1997. The *notificatio* on this book by the Congregation for the Doctrine of the Faith may be found through the internet: www.vatican.va.

Asia to Europe, guided by the idea that religious plurality is not only a matter of fact but an expression of God's will[28]?

This conflict of missionary tendencies reveals a different opinion on the relation between identity and conversation on both sides. If one has the idea that Christian identity can be attached to a determined set of propositions, a *depositum fidei*, conversation with people of other faiths must be perceived as a threat, since one runs the risk of losing this identity if one engages into dialogue too quickly without being properly educated in one's faith. This was the kind of identity presupposed by Thomas Aquinas, and it is still presupposed by the Congregation for the Doctrine of the Faith[29]. If, however, one conceives identity as a sense of self that is developed precisely in conversation with others, inter-religious dialogue is not a threat, but, on the contrary, a precondition of religious identity[30]. If one is of the latter opinion, one sees inter-religious dialogue as an opportunity for conversation in which both partners develop their own religious identity. If one is of the former opinion, one sees inter-religious dialogue as a threat or as a battlefield suitable for fighting out the question of truth. Again, we have two opinions on identity and two forms of mission. Since I think that there is truth in both opinions, I suggest that we talk about inter-religious dialogue as polemical conversation, since we have to wage our faith, including its truth claims, if there is to be any serious dialogue. But, turning it round, it is also true that we have to understand a stranger in order to be able to evangelize. And this brings us back to the Dominican friars of the thirteenth century.

V. How to Talk to Strangers

The Dominican friar Raymund of Peñafort (1180-1275), who is also connected with Thomas Aquinas and his so-called *Summa contra Gentiles*,

---

28. *Ibid.*, p. 11. This idea is expressly denied in *Dominus Iesus*: "The Church's constant missionary proclamation is endangered today by relativistic theories which seek to justify religious pluralisme, not only *de facto*, but also *de iure (or in principle)*" (no. 4).

29. In this respect, I must confess that I have connected too closely the idea of Christian identity and the person of Christ in my contribution *Christ and the Spirit: Towards a Bifocal Christian Theology of Religions* to the first LEST conference. See T. Merrigan – J. Haers (eds.), *The Myriad Christ: Plurality and the Quest for Unity in Contemporary Christology*, Leuven, Peeters, 2000, pp. 121-129.

30. In general, see the many contributions by Paul Ricœur (philosophical hermeneutics), Ninian Smart (comparative study of religions) and Ido Abram (Jewish intercultural education) in this respect. More specifically, I would like to refer to the third chapter in the thesis by C. Sterkens, *Interreligious Learning: The Problem of Interreligious Dialogue in Primary Education*, Leiden, Brill, 2001, pp. 75-124.

gives us an idea of this inter-religious dialogue as polemical conversation. His main objective as master general of the Dominicans and later as their leader in Spain was to promote the missionary movement to Jews and Muslims, but he was aware of the fact that one had to change the missionary methods in order to succeed[31]. Therefore, he established some language schools, so that the friars would be well versed in Hebrew and Arabic when they had to deal with Jews and Muslims; moreover, their training should include a basic knowledge of Islamic and Jewish doctrines, including the Talmud. His pupil Raymond Martin (c. 1220-1284) is a case in point with his famous polemical treatise *Pugio fidei adversus Mauros et Judaeos* (Dagger of Faith against Moors and Jews). As one of the first Dominicans of the *Studium Arabicum* in Tunis, and later of the *Studium Hebraicum* in Barcelona, he had an excellent knowledge of languages, Arabic philosophy and Jewish scriptures[32]. The same characteristics come to the fore in the life and works of another Spanish missionary among Muslims, Ramon Llull (1232-1316)[33]. One might say that the willingness to learn from the other, as a characteristic of conversation, is often greatest where the wish to define oneself over against another is greatest as well. That is why so many incipient dialogues in the Middle Ages turned to polemical defences of one's own faith. But, on the other hand, one can only posit one's identity if one knows about the identity of one's neighbour; if one has some real *conversatio* with one's neighbour. And therefore, every form of religious polemics requires a willingness to learn about the other. In short, dialogue requires polemics and conversation, since the formation of the self requires the presence of the others[34].

Faculteit der Theologie   Pim VALKENBERG
Radboud Universiteit Nijmegen
Postbus 9103
6500 HD Nijmegen
The Netherlands

31. See J. COHEN, *The Friars and the Jews; the Evolution of Medieval Anti-Judaism*, Ithaca, Cornell University Press, 1982; L. HAGEMANN, *Christentum contra Islam: eine Geschichte gescheiterter Beziehungen*, Darmstadt, Primus Verlag, 1999.

32. Cf. I. WILLI-PLEIN – T. WILLI, *Glaubensdolch und Messiasbeweis: die Begegnung von Judentum, Christentum und Islam im 13. Jahrhundert in Spanien* (Forschungen zum jüdisch-christlichen Dialog, 2), Neukirchen-Vluyn, Neukirchener Verlag, 1980; HAGEMANN, *Christentum contra Islam* (n. 31), pp. 59-63.

33. See R. ARNALDEZ, *À la croisée des trois monothéismes: une communauté de pensée au Moyen-Age*, Paris, Albin Michel, 1993, pp. 322-340; HAGEMANN, *Christentum contra Islam* (n. 31), pp. 63-67.

34. Some of the ideas in this last section will be published in a volume on *Religious Polemics in Context* by NOSTER, the Netherlands School for Advanced Studies in Theology and Religion.

LA DIVINA PASTORA FEAST OF TRINIDAD

CONVERSATION, POWER AND POSSIBILITIES

I. *LA DIVINA PASTORA*

The island of Trinidad is situated just above ten degrees latitude in the Caribbean Sea, about ten to fifteen kilometres from Venezuela. With an area of about 5,000 square kilometres, it is the southernmost island in the Caribbean. According to the 1994 annual statistical digest of Trinidad and Tobago the population is about 1.1 million persons, with the following denominational composition: 29.3% Roman Catholic, 23.6% Hindu, 10.9% Anglican, 7.4% Pentecostal, 6.8% Muslim, 3.7% Seventh Day Adventist, and 3.4% Presbyterian/Congregational. The remaining 14.9% consists of Baptists (2.9%), Jehovah Witnesses (1.3%), Methodists (1.2%), with 9.5% having none or no stated religion. Although this analysis shows that the island is predominantly Christian, there remains a large Hindu and Muslim community (30.4%), a fact that could be explained by the history of colonisation and its policies in the island. This also explains the wide ethnic cross section found within the Roman Catholic Church.

The inclusion of Trinidad into the Spanish Empire began with Columbus' arrival in 1498. This accounts for the establishment of the Roman Catholic religion whose denominational hold was threatened by the surrender of the island to the British in the 19th century. It was at this time that Anglicanism was introduced, along with Protestantism in general. Although Anglicanism became the official religion of the island for a few decades in the mid-19th century, it neither stemmed the influence of Roman Catholicism in the island nor brought about numerous conversions from Roman Catholicism to the Anglican Church. Within this wide Christian administrative umbrella there was, of course, the African slaves who constituted the bulk of the population and who, unofficially, made up the vast majority of the Christian population. Of greater interest to us here is the arrival of about 144,000 East Indian indentured labourers from 1845 to 1917. It is especially during these years that the island received the influx of French planters from the rest of the West Indies, especially Grenada and Guadeloupe, and of Chinese and Syrian merchants and shop owners who became adherents of the established Christian Churches of the island. Because of this ethnic and religious mixture, Trinidad finds itself in the unique position of being not only a melting pot of popular religiosity, but also of being the crucible of syncretistic amalgams that give expression to the religious impulses of its people.

With the established Churches generally upholding and furthering the aims and policies of the ruling colonising powers[1], the popular religious expressions of former slaves and indentured workers and their descendants were often suppressed and disdained as a "lower" religious form. But with the island claiming independence from the British Empire in 1962, and the institution of more indigenous leadership on both secular and religious levels, the popular religious expressions of the people gained greater force and asserted their right for a "respectable" inclusion in the lives of the people. It is in this context that the dreaded *Obeah*, as the dark side of powerful spirits, and the *Shango / Orisha* – the syncretistic merging of traditional Yoruba African religion and Christianity, especially regarding the veneration of ancestral spirits, the saints and the Virgin Mary – gained importance as religious practices. However, there is one popular religious festival, unique to the Trinidad situation, which shows how the religious impulse of a people cannot be stifled. This is the *Divina Pastora / Suparee Ke Mai* feast which is celebrated mainly by Roman Catholics and Hindus, and also by other Christians, Muslims, and persons of other religions. This does not imply that Roman Catholics and Hindus have generally agreed with regard to this feast. Over the years, an uneasy truce was held regarding the feast as a shared feast and not only a feast for Roman Catholics. Before discussing the feast, let us give a brief socio-economic and religious picture of the island, since social class and religion are fairly intertwined in Trinidad.

The island under colonial rule was chiefly a sugar economy, rather average in terms of its financial worth. In this system, Christians were the administrators, landowners, merchants, professionals, civil servants, etc., the people of "worth" in the island. Hindus, Muslims, and adherents of other religions generally fulfilled the menial tasks, especially work in the fields. To belong to the Christian Church was, thus, a sign of good class standing. To be a Roman Catholic was a sign of great economic and social achievement. This explains why the membership of the Presbyterian Church in Trinidad is mostly East Indian, since it was the only

---

1. For a collection of papers that echo this theme, see I. HAMID (ed.), *Out of the Depths*, San Fernando, Trinidad, St. Andrews Theological College, 1977.

Christian Church that accepted Hindu and Muslim converts as part of its missionary thrust. Later on, well-to-do East Indian families came to be accepted into the Roman Catholic Church.

With the oil boom of the 1970's the island achieved a measure of wealth that bolstered the image of those who were traditionally regarded as belonging to "lesser" churches. With the Black Power movement of the early 1970's, financial security engendered the need and the desire to give greater expression to indigenous religious practices. This encouraged not only the Christian Churches but also other religious communities, especially the East Indian group, to be more confident of their own indigenous religious expressions, and to present these fearlessly and with pride. Unfortunately, this optimism, as well as the financial security that bolstered it, is gone. It seems that the Churches in the island have not yet realized the religious and social visions of the 70's[2]. It is in this light that popular religiosity in Trinidad, indeed, in the Caribbean is seen as the new locus of attention and involvement, insofar as it is the expression of the vital and gut-level concerns of the people in the region. In this context, we shall now turn to the festival of *La Divina Pastora / Suparee Ke Mai*.

The feast of *La Divina Pastora* (the Holy Shepherdess) and *Suparee Ke Mai* (Mother Kali) are, respectively, the Christian and Hindu aspects of a celebration that is rooted in the cultural and religious values of the people of Trinidad. For a period of over a hundred years it has attracted Hindus, Muslims, as well as non-Catholic Christian groups, to a shrine dedicated to *La Divina Pastora* in Siparia, a village in the central southeastern part of the island. The Roman Catholic feast is itself celebrated on the second Sunday after Easter, but Hindu and Muslim devotees go on pilgrimage there on Holy Thursday and Good Friday.

The Catholic origin of the feast dates back to the early 18th century, in Andalusia, southern Spain, where it was believed that the Blessed Virgin Mary appeared to Isidore of Seville in the guise of an Andalusian shepherdess[3]. She told him that her role is to bring people into the sheepfold of her Divine Son. Isidore was a Capuchin monk, and his order brought the Holy Shepherdess devotion with them, as early as 1715, in their mission to the South American mainland, especially to what is now

---

2. This is one of the important points brought out in a congress on theological education in the Caribbean held in Jamaica from the 23rd to the 29th January, 1993. See H. GREGORY (ed.), *Caribbean Theology: Preparing for the Challenges Ahead*, Jamaica, Canoe Press UWI, 1995.

3. This information is taken from T. HARRICHARAN, O.S.B., *An Introduction to Novena Prayers*, Mt. St. Benedict, Trinidad, 1987.

known as Venezuela. Fleeing persecution by the Amerindians from the South American mainland, the Capuchin missionaries founded a mission in Siparia, Trinidad, in 1759. With them apparently came the statue that is now held in reverence in the shrine. The statue itself makes interesting comparison with other statues of Mary. It is short, with long black hair, copper-coloured skin, small cheeks, kindly eyes and a tiny nose. This statue is carried in solemn procession through the streets of Siparia while the rosary is recited and Marian hymns are sung. The popularity of the devotion is due to the many miracles and innumerable favours granted through the intercession of *La Divina Pastora*. At the time of the arrival of the Capuchins, Siparia was a centre for the Guaranon Indians, known as the *Warwarrhoons*, who carried out a lively trade in Trinidad in the 19th and early 20th centuries. The Guaranon Indians readily adopted this popular devotion, with its feasting, litany-praying, procession, and favour-seeking – elements similar to Amerindian religious practices.

On the part of the Roman Catholic Church, the feast was traditionally understood as an opportunity to shepherd all into the fold of Jesus Christ. It also provided an opportunity for evangelisation, which made many parish priests attempt, with little success, to convert non-Catholic devotees to *La Divina Pastora* to Roman Catholicism. Roman Catholics think of *La Divina Pastora* as "their feast", a Roman Catholic feast that has been distorted by other denominations. Like all other devotees, Roman Catholics see the Holy Shepherdess as a helper in time of need, granting favours and ensuring proper guidance and protection. As we shall see, this view is no different from other religious devotees' understanding of the Mother of Siparia.

On the part of the East Indians, devotion to *La Divina Pastora* grew out of events that occurred during their period of indentureship. From 1845 onwards, East Indians came on a labour contract that bound them, first for three, then for five years. The contract was extended to ten years with a guaranteed free return passage to India. Initially, the East Indian worker did not think of settling down in Trinidad. The chief aim was to finish one's contract in the sugarcane fields, to save as much money as possible, and then to return to India. Trinidad was an alien land to the East Indian, and their encounter with the Africans and the Christians was a strange and bewildering one. However, two events occurred in Trinidad that had consequences for linking the feast of *La Divina Pastora* to the East Indians.

In 1870 Governor Gordon decided to give, in return for free passage to India, a block of crown lands to East Indians who were desirous of settling in Trinidad. Many East Indians applied for lands. As a result of this positive response, many East Indian villages sprang up, mainly in the north-central, central, and south-central parts of the island.

The next event was the coming of the railway in the 1870's and its extension in the 1880's. This allowed easy access to the south of the island, and Siparia then became accessible to East Indians. It is not known exactly when they began to identify *La Divina Pastora* with *Suparee Ke Mai*, which really is an image of Mother Kali, one of the more popular Hindu goddesses. By 1890, the statue of *La Divina Pastora* was already attracting a large number of East Indians, Hindus as well as Muslims.

It is easy to understand their attraction to *La Divina Pastora*. Goddess Kali is the Goddess of famine, destruction, plagues, epidemics, illnesses, and other forms of disaster. Indentureship in Trinidad was a gruelling experience for the East Indians, virtually a form of slavery: they not only encountered a hostile environment but also had to endure harsh life in the sugar plantations. Their living conditions were subhuman and they contracted all kinds of illnesses. The workers got addicted to alcohol, started smoking *ganja*, and fell victim to crimes of passion. When they heard that favours were granted through the intercession of Mary, as represented by the statue, they came to her and saw her as Mother Kali. To her they poured out their woes, sorrows, and distress. Barren wives asked for children, and young children had their first long locks cut off as a sign of dedication and offering. The sick prayed for healing, young girls for proper husbands, and beggars for the alleviation of distress. As the East Indians were under the planter's control, the public holiday of Good Friday was chosen as the day to do homage to the Goddess Kali. They would travel by train, singing Hindu devotional hymns. These devotees would offer jewelry, gold and silver bracelets, chains and rings, candles, oil, and money, in supplication and in thanksgiving. For thanksgiving, Indian dances would be performed by colourfully clad dancers. Alms would be given to beggars and less fortunate members of society as an act of piety.

The East Indian understanding of the feast, though lacking an "evangelising" component, is not dissimilar to the Christian understanding, in that both devotions developed around the intercessory, restorative, placating, and generative powers of *La Divina Pastora / Suparee Ke Mai*. It is to be noted that the devotion to *La Divina Pastora / Suparee Ke Mai* has not significantly changed since the 19th century. Devotees still bring offerings to her, and young children still have their first haircut in her presence. The real problem with the feast of *La Divina Pastora / Suparee Ke Mai* deals not with its efficacy, but rather with ascertaining whose feast it really is. The Roman Catholic Church has always laid claim to it, to such an extent that, in the 1920's, attempts were made to prevent East

Indians from coming to the shrine. A decree of prohibition, in five languages, was posted. The police were even called in to implement the decree, but the attempt failed. Through the years, various parish priests have attempted different strategies – such as taking the statue out of the shrine, etc. – but the resulting upheaval, even among Catholics, has always seen the statue returned to the shrine.

In recent years the feasting aspect of the festival has gained such prominence that the days surrounding the feast are now known as *Siparia Fête*. In 1993 the community of Siparia argued with the parish priest over his decision to move the celebration of the feast by a week. They argued: "Siparia owns *La Divina* and *La Divina* owns Siparia"[4]. In other words, the feast really is a "community thing" and not only a "church thing", and the community could also derive some commercial profit from it. It seems that all expressions of popular religion eventually have to deal with this commercial aspect. Let us, nevertheless, attempt some clarification of the issues presented by the feast of *La Divina Pastora / Suparee Ke Mai* in Trinidad.

The feast has parallels in many other parts of the world. The veneration of a Black Virgin is not uncommon to this part of the world[5] and popular Marian devotion is marked by the same enthusiasm the world over. There was a time when such enthusiasm was discouraged in Roman Catholicism because it seemed to supersede the "official" liturgical celebration. Another popular Marian festival is hardly new. What is unique, however, in the Trinidad experience is the use of the statue of *La Divina Pastora* by Hindus who regarded it as a representation of Kali. Moreover, the tenacity of such a devotion to survive attempts to stamp it out as "superstition", and also to resist conversion, is a striking and instructive event in the religious life of a people. We must take this into account if we are to seriously and respectfully appreciate popular religiosity. Furthermore, the Trinidad experience discloses rich possibilities for interfaith dialogue.

Let us first say a word about popular devotion. Popular religious expressions arise out of the hopes and desires of peoples. This accounts for their enduring character. This also explains why popular religious expressions always find avenues of self-expression, surviving as forms of resistance rather than as formal theological structures with a clear metalanguage. Indeed, the Marian feast of *La Divina Pastora / Suparee Ke*

---

4. *Holy War Brews in Siparia*, in *Sunday Express*, May 9, 1993, p. 2.
5. See, for example, the popular devotion to Our Lady of Guadalupe in Latin America.

Mai continues to thrive, despite attempts of various parish priests to regulate and formalize the Siparia festivities. There is an important lesson here. In our desire to harness the vibrant and compelling impulse found in all popular religiosity, and in the Siparia devotions in particular, we have to be careful not to impose our own understanding of popular devotion and to allow indigenous religious expressions to develop in their own terms. The amazing thing about popular religiosity is that it instinctively resists such incorporation. Parish records in Siparia show that conversions do not necessarily occur simply because diverse peoples share a common reference or ground. On the contrary, the Hindus generally remained staunchly Hindu and other religious devotees maintained the belief structures they had when they came to pay homage to *La Divina Pastora / Suparee Ke Mai*.

While in Guyana in an Interfaith conference in early April 1993, a member of the Winty religion – a popular religion in Suriname similar to the *Shango / Orisha* in Trinidad, to *Pocomania* in Jamaica and *Voodoo* in Haiti – complained of how so-called "established" religions attempt to understand Winty so as to incorporate some of its elements in order to attract Winty followers. He was angry at the arrogance and lack of respect shown to Winty followers and also at the branding of their religion as "popular", thereby implying that it is not really a cohesive unit with a basic core of beliefs and a worldview. We must take this critique seriously and question our motives for wanting to understand popular religiosity: Is it to be able to exploit that which works well with peoples in order to use its devices to serve our proselytising ends?

Secondly, what is liberating about the *La Divina Pastora / Suparee Ke Mai* feast is not so much the symbolism involved, but the opportunity to invoke such symbolism in the lives of a people. It was in the midst of the hardship of indentureship in a foreign land that the East Indian finds a "home" not only in a physical but also in a religious sense. The *Suparee Ke Mai* feast allows for the worship of the Goddess Kali in very much the same manner as the local Caroni River takes the place of the Ganges River for the Hindu exiled in Trinidad. Wherever a people finds a sacred space that allows for the expression of their hopes and pains, there we will find the vibrancy that supports popular religiosity. This is a question that the "established" Churches need to consider: Where is the "space" that allows ordinary believers and worshippers to adequately express their hopes and pains?

Third, the discovery of this "sacred" space is only an initial step for the believer. Given the importance of resistance and survival for popular religiosity, we have to acknowledge that salvation is ultimately the most important goal for the genuine believer. Analyses of the need to resist exploitation and suffering tend to equate religious expression with the instinct to survive. Such analyses lose sight of the fact that salvation at times denies even the possibility of survival. Indeed, salvation demands at times death, the end of all possibilities. The equating of religious expression with survival, or with success, diminishes the important distinction to be made between survival and salvation. Thus understood, the theme of salvation can provide a critique of popular religiosity. Remember that the problem in Trinidad for the *Divina Pastora* celebrations is not only religious but also socio-economic in nature. The growing success of this devotion has expanded its social appeal, but, unfortunately, diminished its sacred space. Is this decline inevitable in all popular religiosity? Are the goals of resistance and survival in indigenous religious expressions achieved at the price of sacrificing the salvific content of religion? If this is happening in a significant manner in Siparia, then we are dealing not with authentic religiosity, but with ideological substitution, the replication of systems of domination dressed in local garb. Nothing more and nothing less. For any religion to retain its salvific qualities, there must be some sustained reflection and moral drive toward salvation that is built on, not replaced by, survival strategies. So far, popular religion has not manifested this quality.

Fourth, the *Divina Pastora* phenomenon points to an underlying issue that impedes meaningful conversation among religions: power. We would like to concentrate now on this fourth point since it impinges directly on the question of genuine conversation among religions, the primary concern of a relational theology. Why is it that, given the geographical and cultural proximity of Catholicism and Hinduism in Trinidad, adherents of these religions do not engage in any shared reflection on *La Divina Pastora*? Moreover, the adherents of each religion are careful to keep their devotion to the statue as culturally and religiously distinct from the other group. Indeed, more energy is spent in showing how their respective religious interpretations are incompatible. The reasons for this lack of conversation are complex and varied. We believe, though, that the root cause is the thorny issue of power – both "institutional" and "spiritual" – and of power sharing. While "institutional" power deals with institutional identity and the exercise of power, "spiritual" power deals with the salvific efficacy of sacramental and ritual practices. In our opinion, the lack of genuine conversation between Catholics and Hindus in the *Divina Pastora* experience is explained by the precarious relationship between conversation and power. We shall explore this topic in the next section.

II. CONVERSATION AND POWER

At the 2001 Annual Meeting of the Catholic Theological Society of America in the World Church Theology Group, Leo Kleden, SVD, presented a paper entitled "Missio Ad Gentes: An Asian Way of Mission Today". He spoke about how, in times past, European missionaries went to Asia from positions of political, cultural and religious superiority. Times have changed, however, for the Asian missionary of today. Allow us to quote here the section "Mission from the Position of Weakness" from Kleden's paper:

> In comparison to the former missionaries from Europe, the Asian missionaries today seem to be sent empty handed. This fact is their weakness and should be their strength as well.
> First of all, it is their weakness. Many of them come from a rural background with their cultural heritage in the pre-modern worldview. But very soon they enter into the modern world through education and schools. Now they are further confronted with the post-modern condition. They live in tensions between three worldviews which are not easy to harmonize. These missionaries need much more time than their predecessors not simply to learn another language and culture but also to orient themselves within the tensions and conflicts between those worldviews.
> And what can they concretely do in their mission? We know that former missionaries preached the Gospel, taught catechism, and baptized people; but they were also actively involved in education, health care, and in promoting social and economic development. All these were considered integral parts of their mission. Today many of these jobs have been taken over by the state or secular institutions. When new missionaries are sent from Asia to Europe or America they cannot get involved in these fields. Even in teaching catechism or preaching many local people can do better than they. From the religious perspective, former missionaries went to the countries where mythic-religious values were still predominant, whereas new missionaries are thrown into secularistic society. It is much more difficult to preach the Gospel in the post-Christian situation.
> On the other hand, this kind of weakness can and should be the strength of the new missionaries. Here is a golden opportunity to follow the example of the first disciples of Jesus who were sent empty handed but who were inspired by the Spirit of the Crucified and Risen Lord. The empty handed approach is therefore possible if their heart is full of faith, with the willingness to serve others as the Lord Jesus. Through the Spirit of the Lord human weakness (in socio-political sense) is transformed into evangelical kenosis. This approach becomes efficacious and fruitful on two preconditions. First, it presupposes that the missionaries believe in the people to whom they are sent. If you have nothing in your hand, and if you do not have any kind of superiority, then you have to rely on the people to whom you are sent. Missionaries are expected to work not simply for the people (from a position of superiority), but to work with the people. Above all, this

approach presupposes that missionaries believe in the One who calls and
sends them. "I am with you always to the end of time" (Matt 28,20)[6].

There are, however, problems that are not discussed in the above analysis. One is the problem of missionaries who are looking to clothe themselves in the "superiority" of the post-Christian countries to which they
are sent. Other factors are likewise at work apart from the missionary
impulse. Kleden, nonetheless, points out an aspect of power, and of weakness, that bears directly on our reflection. If mission is to be divested of
images of political, cultural, religious and economic dominance, it must be
taken up from the perspective of "weakness": one is forced to rely on and
to listen to the people to whom one is sent. This significantly shifts the tone
from "educating" the natives to "being educated" by them. The missionary needs to be attentive to the context in which he or she is sent.

This "empty handed" approach, as Kleden calls it, changes the understanding of power from one of an imposition – that already precludes and
determines the parameters of conversation – to one of service. Kleden
would speak even of the service of the missionary's contemplative presence. Kleden here echoes what Leonardo Boff wrote in his book *Church,
Charism and Power: Liberation Theology and the Institutional Church*
(1985). Boff advocates an understanding of the exercise of institutional
power in the church in terms of service[7]. He cites Mark 10,42-45 and
Luke 22,25-27 as examples of Christian service:

> You know how those who rule the nations exercise tyranny over them and
> they practice violence against them. This is not to be among you: on the con-
> trary, if one of you wishes to be great, he must be your servant; and he who
> desires to be first among you must serve all; because the Son of Man did
> not come to be served but to serve and to give his life for the redemption
> of many (Mark 10,42-45).

Boff favours *exousia* over *dynamis* as representing more adequately
how power and authority are to be exercised and, by implication, how we
should relate with each other. If one is to have genuine relationships it
must be rooted in an attitude of service that allows weakness to be one's
strength. But how is this to be understood? Perhaps Sobrino's reflection
on the presence and absence of God in the cross of Christ can be helpful here.

6. See L. KLEDEN, *Missio Ad Gentes: An Asian Way of Mission Today*, in the *Proceedings of the Fifty Second Annual Convention of the Catholic Theological Society of
America*, Milwaukee, WI, CTSA, pp. 197-198.
7. L. BOFF, *Church Charism and Power: Liberation Theology and the Institutional
Church*, London, SCM Press, 1985, p. 60.

In his *Christology at the Crossroads* Jon Sobrino reflects on the death of Jesus and the scandal of the cross. The cross is a scandal because it obliges us to raise questions about our image of God and about his relation to us: "The path to the cross is nothing else but a questioning search for the true God and for the true essence of power"[8]. For Sobrino, power is to be used in the service of the oppressed. But what sort of power makes God present in our midst? The cross of Jesus throws into serious doubt our notions of the power of God. The event of the cross shows God's power centered in suffering and love. Moreover, on the cross, "we see God submerged in the negative"[9]. Indeed, on the cross, God is against himself. God questions God. God "bifurcates" himself on the cross so that "transcendence is in conflict with history"[10].

> On the cross of Jesus God was present ... and at the same time absent ... Absent to the son, he was present for human beings. And in this dialectic of presence and absence is the way to express in human language the fact that God is love. The cross is the contradiction of humanity, but it is grounded on an ultimate solidarity with it[11].

In this abandonment of Jesus we have the theological ground for solidarity and relationship between the human and the divine: love born out of and in the midst of suffering. The "empty handed" approach of Kleden is to be understood in this light. It is precisely the giving up of institutional power – in the sense of *dynamis*, control, might – that allows for the presence of the true power of solidarity and love. Genuine power in this sense is always engendered in conditions in which one is forced to act with and on behalf of those one loves. True power is not a choice but a forced option. It is in this sense that it is necessary for genuine relationship and for meaningful conversation.

An authentic relational theology and interreligious conversation must therefore identify the context. The commitment to a people out of love demands an acknowledgment of the contours and shapes of their suffering and pain. Genuine conversation is possible only when power is exercised as engaging in the suffering of loved ones with a view to transform that void and pain into the presence of God's grace.

From this perspective, we see then that what is missing among Catholics and Hindus in the experience of *La Divina Pastora* is not opportunity, but love and solidarity born out of engagement with one

---

8. J. SOBRINO, *Christology at the Crossroads: A Latin American Approach*, Maryknoll, NY, Orbis Books, 1978, p. 204.
9. *Ibid.*, p. 221.
10. *Ibid.*
11. *Ibid.*, p. 225.

another. There seems to be disregard for the suffering undergone by all during slavery, indentureship, and colonization. This lack of conversation is not accounted for by mere misunderstanding or ill will. It is also explained by an inherited understanding of dominating power that prevents genuine conversation. What could be done then?

III. Power and Possibilities

Our understanding of identity should start with the relational structure as constitutive of one's personal identity. In other words, we are who we are because of the relationships we have with others. This relational perspective goes beyond the need to bridge the gap between the I and the Thou, and gives a more holistic perspective to identity. But it still equates identity with choice. In other words, if the understanding of identity in difference is to generate an understanding of relationality that is necessary, such relationality has to be understood not as a choice but as a forced condition. To my mind, this is the only means by which a relational theology can achieve genuine conversation.

We have presented this idea of doing theology in "forced" contexts over the years[12], and will continue to do so because we are convinced that this way of understanding theology today offers a direction that cuts through the rhetoric of choice and brings us face to face with the sufferings of those who live in these contexts. Keeping in mind the theme of this conference, allow us to delineate the characteristics of this "forced" context.

The first characteristic is precisely its "forced" nature: one does not have the luxury of "choices". The so-called availability of choices is but an illusion of self-determination that is provided by the dominant political and cultural economy. Such self-determining choice abrogates the necessity of relationship. Such self-determination merely replicates the ideology of the dominant structure(s) and is legitimated by it. Those subject to the illusion of self-determination are thus really forced into a particular stance and are bereft of choices that would liberate them from their condition of suffering. But, to acknowledge that one has no real choices but those offered by the structures of exploitation, one comes to realize that freedom is not dependent on will and personal choices.

---

12. See G. Boodoo, *Gospel and Culture in a Forced Theological Context*, in *Caribbean Journal of Religious Studies* 17 (1996) no. 2, 1-15; and *Paradigm Shift?*, in G. De Schrijver (ed.), *Liberation Theologies on Shifting Grounds: A Clash of Socio-Economic and Cultural Paradigms* (BETL, 135), Leuven, Peeters Press, pp. 351-364.

The genuine human act of the oppressed and the suffering is engendered neither by "reasonable choices" made by an exercise of free will, nor by the development of the individual's "character". Will and freedom are no longer issues of compatibility here. Indeed, freedom can be had irrespective of "self-determination", and that by the destruction of illusions created by such "willing". What we are advancing here is an understanding of the agency of the human that is based, not on the availability of choices, but on the lack thereof. We do theology because it must be done, and it must be done together if we are to further the Gospel of Life. Our actions are determined not by the numerous possibilities before us but by the urgency of our present condition. Our liberation from exploitation and suffering is, therefore, not dependent on new and alternative structures, but on our resisting the present condition of exploitation. The future can only promise an aggravation of the same situation for an exploited, suffering and forced people.

This brings us to the second characteristic: freedom is not to be understood in the light of hope, but in the light of despair. It is the condition of "being forced" that propels the human person to identify what is unliberating in their existing situation. It is true that the condition of "being forced" can generate a hope that gives one the illusion of "freedom" from the oppressive condition. This is seen in carnivalesque festivities that perpetuate the illusion of freedom by providing momentary release from the seriousness of oppression. This distracts from the need for a more lasting condition of freedom by suggesting that mimicry contains the dynamics for continued resistance that could bring about liberation. An example of this is *picong*, the Trinidad term for "banter": mimicking and cajoling someone until he admits defeat. It aims to exploit an already exploited person, and the "victor" unknowingly mimics the oppressor who exploits and vanquishes all who dare speak against him. The carnivalesque and the game of *picong* may be seen as attempts to navigate the terrain of the exploited, but they only serve to replicate the already existing condition of domination and do not offer any real solidarity with the condition of the forced and exploited human being. Indeed, in recent years, celebrations of the carnivalesque have been exploited by the dominant ideology and are being used to further the economic, political and cultural hegemony of those in power. The momentary sense of "freedom" offered by the carnivalesque is but an expression of the false hope based on mimicking real possibilities. Such hope is filled with hollow rhetoric and false ideology. It can only bring more oppression and renewed suffering. Can one really call this a "choice"? The "forced" context obliges us to reject the claims of false hope as a valid starting point of reflection. Freedom can only be had in the full recognition of the forced and despairing situation created by exploitation and suffering. This in turn propels us to confront such structures and to struggle for liberation. We have no choice but to liberate ourselves and those we love.

This leads to the third characteristic: the non-essentiality of the human condition. There is no essential human condition that can pre-determine the prescription for liberation. This should be clear when we understand identity as taking shape as a result of differentiation. In this case, a "common human experience" and "core" human values can sometimes be pseudo issues that distract from – in some cases, deliberately sidetrack – the movement toward solidarity. These appeals are based on the notion that there is some essential human condition towards which we strive and which is seen from our "common human experience". This commonality, however, is often a veiled attempt at further manipulation and exploitation. What allows us to understand humanity, love and solidarity is the stance of confronting actual situations of exploitation and evil with the incarnation of the kingdom of God in the face of such evil and suffering. Without this belief that the kingdom of God is immanent and liberating, the desire and goal of solidarity could become another "illusion" that replicates dominance and exploitation, another rhetorical device of misdirection. The non-essentiality of the human condition, therefore, obliges us to strive towards realizing a condition that allows us to be most fully human and most fully free. Freedom, from this perspective then, is the ability to confront empty concepts, false prophets, as well as the evil, suffering and exploitation they perpetuate in order to deny the kingdom of God.

A fourth characteristic of a "forced" context is found in its primary aim: not survival but liberation understood as salvation. Theology in "forced" contexts is not so much a theology of survival as it is a theology of salvation. Our equating religion with survival – or with success – has made us forget the distinction between survival and salvation. A religion of survival finds itself immersed in a rhetoric of historical liberation deprived of religion; as such, it finds itself as one alternative along with other liberation movements. In some ways, the religion of survival has become itself a-historical and interprets historical action and change from a paradigm of success.

IV. CONCLUSION

Despite their sharing the same geographical, historical, cultural, and religious space in *La Divina Pastora*, Catholics and Hindus in Trinidad have not acknowledged their relationship. As a result, they have not engaged in any meaningful conversation about the feast, nor about their relationship in the island. We have pointed out that the problem here is a result of the role of power in their relationship. Until the exercise of power is realized as an exercise of love and solidarity with and for all of those who suffer and are exploited, it will remain an exercise of might, manipulation and control. We claim further that the necessity of such love cannot be understood without clarifying the "forced" contexts of our theological reflection. Allow us to reiterate this conviction: we do not do theology because it is a nice enterprise of speculative stimulation, we do it because it must be done, because we opt for God against evil. In the end, a relational theology can only engender genuine conversation when it shows, out of its forced context, why we must opt for love in the face of evil.

Department of Theology   Gerald BOODOO
Xavier University of Louisiana
1 Drexel Drive
New Orleans, LA 70125
U.S.A.

THE *FIESTA DE MOROS Y CRISTIANOS*

A PARADIGM FOR A RELATIONAL THEOLOGY

I. AN HISTORICAL OVERVIEW

The *Fiesta de moros*[1] *y cristianos* is a social, economic and entertaining event that today takes place annually in many cities and towns in the Spanish Provinces of Murcia, Albacete, Alicante and Valencia. Its main elements consist of the "entrance" (*entradas*) or formal parading into the city or town of both the Moors and Christians, the "conquest" and subsequent "reconquest" of a castle, and the dramatization of the struggle by means of the respective groups attired in ornate and elaborate dress (*comparsas*), involving the various Moorish and Christian military units or bands.

The earliest reference to *moros y cristianos* occurs in the middle of the twelfth century, in the year 1150. During the wedding celebrations in

---

1. It is important to look at the term itself: *moro* (Moor), Titus Burckhardt gives the following perspective: "…it would be more accurate to refer to 'Arabic' culture in Spain, since its language was predominantly Arabic, or even 'Islamic' culture, since it actually belonged to the Islamic world. The word 'moorish' derives from the Spanish word, *moros*, that is 'Moors' or 'Mauretanians'. 'Moorish' culture in the literal sense does not exist any more than does 'Gothic' architecture. Yet the word 'Moorish' has become synonymous with 'Arab-Islamic'. The Moors were simply Maghrebins, inhabitants of the *maghreb*, the western part of the Islamic world, that extends from Spain to Tunisia, and represents a homogeneous cultural entity". T. BURCKHARDT, *Moorish Culture in Spain* [Original Title: *Die maurische Kultur in Spanien*], translated by A. JAFFA, München, 1972, p. 7. Nonetheless, a recent Spanish-language translation of this original German publication, has made the following point: "the original text constantly employs the term '*moro*', both in regard to its use as an adjective in reference to persons as well as to concepts or things. In the latter case this would be unacceptable in literary Spanish, and so 'Hispanic-Arabic' or simply 'Arabic' has been used [by this translator, Rosa Kuhne Brabant] instead". T. BURCKHARDT, *La civilización hispano-árabe*, Versión de ROSA KUHNE BRABANT, Madrid, 1999, p. 11, note by the translator [my translation]. Also, many would question whether one can speak of a "homogenous cultural entity" when referring to the people of the *maghreb*. It would be more accurate to speak of the heterogeneity that is hidden by the homogeneity of both language, Arabic, and religion, Islam. Burckhardt further sees a link between the term *moro* and the Berbers, who were located in North Africa primarily in the region of the Riff and central Atlas mountains: "The preponderance of Berbers [on the Iberian peninsula] can also be deduced from the fact that the Spaniards referred to all Muslims as '*moros*', which comes from the Latin, *mauri* or *maurusci*, the term used for all Atlas Berbers and can be traced back indirectly to the late Greek *mauroi*, 'black', or the Phoenician *mauharin*, 'Western'", p. 29.

Lleida honoring Queen Petronila's marriage with Don Ramón Berenguer de Barcelona, along with some two thousand "jugglers", there is noted *"un combate de moros y cristianos"*[2]. Clearly it is a dramatization but no more details are given.

The roots of this dramatization have been traced to *fiestas de alardo*. The term comes from the Arabic, "al-ard", and it is translated into Spanish as *alarde*. It was the review of the Arab-Islamic troops that was carried out to assure the preparedness of the local militia for the defense of the city[3]. This review of the troops was carried out at the end of the tenth century, for example, by Almanzor, in preparation for summer military campaigns.

It is in the sixteenth and seventeenth centuries that there is a shift in meaning and terminology. The military troop and weapons muster (*alarde*) gives birth to a new but very closely linked term: *alardo*. This new term carries with it the characteristics of a festival. It refers to the parading of the city or townspeople, dressed up as soldiers, going through the streets, firing weapons known for their noise (the use of gunpowder), and also imitating and adopting for themselves the titles of "captain" (*capitán*) and "lieutenant" (*alférez*)[4].

The *alardo* itself has two clear phases of evolution. There is at the beginning what could be described as the *alardo* in its simple form. A group of people of the city or town accompany the patron saint in the procession that takes place during the local festivities, without any other intention than the firing of loud weapons. But the second phase of development can describe the *alardo* as one that is more elegant, more "dressy" (*alardo compuesto*), Here there is not only the use of gunpowder, but there is also much more order and organization which includes music and a parade in military fashion. The role of the "captain" is key in the festivities, and the lieutenant (*alférez*) is often entrusted with the standard or the banner that is waved or "danced" in artistry at very places in the course of the parade[5].

---

2. M. GONZALEZ HERNANDEZ, *Moros y Cristianos. Del Alarde Medieval a las Fiestas Reales Barrocas (ss. XV-XVIII): Origines y evolución de la Fiesta*, Alicante, Ayuntamiento de Monforte del Cid, 1999, p. 25. With regard to scholarly discussion as to whether this is, indeed, the earliest reference, see M. HARRIS, *Aztecs, Moors, and Christians: Festivals of Reconquest in Mexico and Spain*, Austin, TX, 2000, pp. 32-36: "The evidence for the Lleida dance of Moors and Christians is therefore rather shaky ... This is not, however, quite the same as saying that the evidence has been proven false ... In the end, however, the Lleida *moros y cristianos* may be nothing more than legend. Unless we can locate and verify Teixidor's sources or some independent account of the Lleida performance, we must remain, at best, agnostic".

3. *Ibid.*, p. 265.
4. *Ibid.*, p. 266.
5. *Ibid.*, pp. 32-33.

The outcome of all this is that this festival of *alardo* is indeed a mixture on the one hand of the festival of the nobility and on the other of the popular festival organized and carried out by the Guilds and their members. It is that which gives birth to the *fiesta de moros y cristiano*[6].

On the Spanish peninsula itself, there is abundant documentation of the *fiesta de moros y cristianos* occurring in the coastal city of Alicante from at least 1599 to 1789[7]. The outline of the festivities begins with the disembarking of the Moorish troops at the port. There then follow subsequent street skirmishes, the 'conquest' followed by the 're-conquest' of a 'castle' [one made of wood] with appropriate 'delegations' playing their parts. It is clearly a festival organized and carried out by the Guilds and their members: with the role of the Moors normally being taken by those who are sailors and fishermen, and the role of the Christians often being filled by those who are carpenters[8].

There is a variation of the *fiesta de moros y cristianos* that takes place during the same time period in the city of Valencia. Here one finds a battle, described as a *naumaquia*, which takes place on the Turia River, followed by an assault staged at the river's bank, where there is a "festival" castle. These festivities are documented from as early as the year 1373, and continue up until 1769[9]. This variation of the festival may have some roots in the earlier Roman mock sea battles, that the Romans themselves inherited from the Greeks before them, where there is an explicit reference to this in the writings of the Roman author Suetonius[10].

During the nineteenth century, it was economic growth that was the principal factor in the expansion and growth of the *fiesta de moros y cristianos* in the two provinces of Alicante and Valencia. For example one finds the celebration in the interior city of Alcoy and in coastal town of Denia[11]. The structure of the festival also models itself on the structure of the earlier *fiestas reales*, or Royal Festivals, which lasted for three days: the first day consisted in the "entrances" or parades; the second day was dedicated to the city or town patron; and the third day saw the battles and eventual negotiations for peace by the various ambassadors. Over time the structure continued to develop into a more organized and complex one: more and more groups or *comparsas* were taking part, there was more music, greater variety with regard to the street routes for the

6. *Ibid.*, p. 33.
7. *Ibid.*, p. 155.
8. *Ibid.*, p. 35.
9. *Ibid.*, p. 34.
10. *Ibid.*, p. 25.
11. *Ibid.*, p. 238.

parading, and much more importance given to creating the "scenes" for the battle and the subsequent negotiations[12].

II. A SOCIOLOGICAL PERSPECTIVE

Gema Martín Muñoz, in an article entitled, "Lo real y lo irreal en la representación occidental del mundo musulmán", notes that in "Western societies the Muslim world is frequently perceived and interpreted in terms of a 'culturalist paradigm' in which the explanation of facts revolves around the principle of a *cultural difference* which recreates the East beyond its proper reality into what the West wants to see"[13]. This paradigm, she goes on to state, is rooted in an essentialist and comparative vision which corresponds above all else to the western need to constantly invent "the other", in this case, the Muslim, in order to complete the image of the one original, thus defining the boundaries of the supposed classical and universal subject of the Judeo-Christian tradition[14]. Furthermore, such an essentialist interpretation looks at these cultures as a closed universe, incapable of being modified, so that what results is a vision of the other culture as inferior or backward, the bearer of unchanging traditionalism, irrationality, and aggressiveness. In this way those values that are considered to be western are presented as the only valid

12. *Ibid.*, p. 270.
13. G. MARTÍN MUÑOZ, *Lo real y lo irreal en la representación del mundo musulmán*, in *Revista de Occidente* (2000) 106-122, esp. p. 106 [my translation].
14. The presence, the role and the relationship of the Jews on the Peninsula with both Christians and Muslims is itself a significant reality. For example, in BURCKHARDT, *Moorish Culture* (n. 1), he comments with regard to the "incredibly swift success of the Muslims" of its conquest of the Visigoths, dating from 711 and completed in less than three years, that one factor among many was "the assistance the Muslims received from the Jews, who had been oppressed by the Visigothic church", p. 24. And he goes on to add that "the greatest beneficiaries of Islamic rule were the Jews, for in Spain they enjoyed their finest intellectual flowering since their dispersal from Palestine to foreign lands". And he stresses that "guaranteeing peaceful co-existence between the three religious communities was not nearly so difficult as overcoming the tensions between the different races, and it was this that constituted the severest problem for the Arab rulers of Spain. Besides the indigenous mixed population consisting of Iberians and Romans, there was also the Germanic minority of Visigoths, who, as the former nobility, expected certain priorities even under Arab rule. The Jewish population was unusually large in Spain. Then there were the Arabs and the Berbers, not to mention all the different elements that had been introduced as a result of the slave trade", pp. 27-28. On this topic, see V. MANN – T. GLICK – J. DODDS (eds.), *Convivencia: Jews, Muslims, and Christians in Medieval Spain*, New York, 1992; N. ROTH, *Jews, Visigoths and Muslims in Medieval Spain: Cooperation and Conflict*, Leiden – New York, 1994; R. BURNS, *Muslims, Christians, and Jews in the Crusader Kingdom of Valencia: Societies in Symbiosis*, New York, 1984 and A. NOVINSKY – D. KUPERMAN, *Ibéria judaica: roteiros da memória*, Rio de Janeiro, 1996.

paradigm for humanity. All of this means that cultural diversity is not seen as a variety of options with equal importance, but in terms of an hierarchical scale of modernization versus backwardness. And this "ethnocentric cosmopolitanism", which lays claim exclusively to the paradigm of rationality and progress, tends to define the Muslim world as far from modernity. In fact this mental and social construct forms a part of the process of both the assimilation and the destruction of all those cultures which do not belong to the Western "nucleus", as well as the necessary invention of "the other" in order to achieve this process[15].

The view of "the other" that results is one that is fully univocal, that both idealizes (the exotic and the beautiful) and demonizes (the 'morisco' [the baptized Muslim], the "Turk", and the "terrorist"). This "culturalist paradigm" is one that is filled with both prejudice and stereotypes. It proceeds from a legacy of historical misunderstandings, the result of a relationship that has been interpreted primarily as one of confrontation for many centuries. And in our own day this "culturalist paradigm" has been promoted by focusing almost exclusively on this paradigm with regard to the development of Islamic movements[16].

John Esposito, writing from a religious context, points to the roots of concern and misunderstanding that have marked Islamic-Christian relations. Even though Christians and Muslims share many common beliefs

---

15. MARTÍN MUÑOZ, *Lo real y lo irreal* (n. 13), pp. 106-107. See, also, R. GONZALEZ-CASANOVAS, *Imperial Histories from Alfonso X to Inca Garcilasco: Revisionist Myths of Reconquest and Conquest* (Scripta Humanistica, 134), Potomac, MD, 1997. "The Reconquest of Iberia from the Moors and the Spanish Conquest of America present significant parallels as historical phenomena and subjects of historiography: They not only offer similar socio-political and ideological developments in eras of national formation but also give rise to hybrid types of historical writing in the vernacular", p. x. See, also, HARRIS, *Aztecs* (n. 2), concerning the specific question which is the focus of study for Max Harris: "In which direction did such folk dance traditions cross the Atlantic? We should not, because European ships first sailed westward, assume that subsequent cultural traffic always flowed in the same direction" (p. 169). And in agreement with Maria Soledad Carrasco Urgoiti, see, Mª.S. CARRASCO URGOITI, *Aspectos folclóricos y literarios de la fiesta de moros y cristianos en España*, in *El Moro Retador y El Moro Amigo (Estudios sobre fiestas y comedias de moros y cristianos)*, Granada, 1996, pp. 25-66, esp. p. 39. Harris notes that the "suggestion of mutual influence is one that few have considered, let alone pursued with any rigor" (p. 173), leading Harris to conclude that "traditional Spanish combat dances may have their roots not in Medieval Europe but in Native America" (p. 178).

16. MARTÍN MUÑOZ, *Lo real y lo irreal* (n. 13), p. 107. See, also, E. SAID, *Culture and Imperialism*, New York, 1993, p. 50, who stresses a very similar perspective: "Without significant exception the universalizing discourses of modern Europe and the United States assume the silence, willing or otherwise, of the non-European world. There is incorporation; there is inclusion; there is direct rule; there is coercion. But there is only infrequently an acknowledgment that the colonized people should be heard from, their ideas known".

and values, their relations with each other have been overshadowed by conflict. And he cites, as one example among many, the expulsion of the "Moors" from Spain. Tragically, "Islam's relationship with the West has often been marked less by understanding than by mutual ignorance and stereotyping, confrontation and conflict"[17].

Gerhard Böwering in a similar fashion notes that from the modern period, the West has seen itself in an even more emphatic way as the norm and standard. Through the Enlightenment, the West became almost obsessed with its own "knowledge, freedom and happiness", and this view of superiority was itself reinforced through the military colonial powers. The result was one that made the West "the standard of culture and induced the church to see no salvation beyond the confines of its own deposit of faith"[18]. Böwering notes, however, that this situation is no longer the same. He states that "in the changing world of today, the global religions are no longer confined within geographical borders. A great migration of people is in progress"[19]. This is certainly the case in Spain, and indeed in all of Europe itself. For in an ironic twist of fate, the lowering birth rates in Europe, and in Spain in a particularly pointed way, require the influx of approximately 250 million people over the next fifty years if the current level of economic and social well-being is to be maintained[20].

---

17. J. ESPOSITO, *The Threat of Islam: Myth or Reality?*, in H. KÜNG – J. MOLTMANN (eds.), *Islam: A Challenge for Christianity* (Concilium, 1994/3), 39-47, esp. pp. 39-40: "Ancient rivalries as well as modern-day conflicts have so accentuated differences as completely to obscure the shared monotheistic roots and vision of the Judaeo-Christian-Islamic tradition. Despite many common beliefs and values, throughout history, Muslim-Christian relations have often been overshadowed by conflict as the armies and missionaries of Islam and Christendom have been locked in struggle for power and for souls. This confrontation has ranged from the fall of the early Byzantine (eastern Roman) empire before the armies of Islam in the seventh century to the fierce battles and polemics of the Crusades, the expulsion of the 'Moors' from Spain and the Inquisition, the Ottoman threat to overrun Europe, European (Christian) colonial expansion and domination in the eighteenth and nineteenth centuries, the political and cultural challenge of the super-powers (American and the Soviet Union) in the latter half of the twentieth century, the creation of the state of Israel, the competition of Christian and Muslim missionaries for converts in Africa today and the challenge of the contemporary reassertion of Islam or 'Islamic fundamentalism'".

18. G. BÖWERING, *Christianity – Challenged by Islam*, in H. KÜNG – J. MOLTMANN (eds.), *Islam* (n. 17), 103-115, esp. pp. 103-104.

19. *Ibid.,* p. 104.

20. See the Press Release, 17 March 2000, from the United Nations Population Division of the Department of Economic and Social Affairs, "Replacement Migration: Is it a Solution to Declining and Ageing Populations?". The full report may be accessed on the internet site of the Population Division: http://www.un.org/esa/population/unpop.htm, as well as from the office of Mr. Joseph Chamie, Director, Population Division, United Nations, New York, NY, 10017, USA.

Today there are more than fifteen million Muslims living in Europe[21], with those in Spain numbering officially 500,000 (without counting those who are undocumented)[22]. Martín Muñoz outlines three different approaches as to how these individuals are seen relative to the larger society. The first approach is that of "assimilation", which is based on the acceptance of the Other through the denial of any difference. The Other is welcomed in as much as she or he renounces one's cultural personality in favour of the dominant culture of the country in which one is accepted. A second approach is that of "insertion", which stresses the importance of the community over that of the individual. In this approach, the minority group preserves its specific religious, familial and linguistic reality, but it does so at the risk of closing itself off from the dominant society, laying the basis for a ghetto mentality. The third approach is that of "integration", which is much more open and flexible. In this case one does not have to renounce one's culture of origin, but respects the fundamental laws of the country in which one is accepted. In the long run this promotes "mestizaje"[23].

But Martín Muñoz makes the point that one of the most important factors to bear in mind with regard to those who are Muslims living in Europe is that they have, in almost all cases, come from a country in which Islam is the official State religion – or at least is the majority religion – to countries in which one will now find oneself in a minority position. In fact in Spain the law has been in force only since 1980 guaranteeing the fundamental right of Muslim children to be taught Islam in the public schools[24].

In an effort to promote an integration approach that is built upon a true affirmation of the Other, Martín Muñoz looks to *al-Andalus*[25]. She argues

21. MARTÍN MUÑOZ, *Lo real y lo irreal* (n. 13), p. 114.

22. J. BEDOYA, *50,000 niños musulmanes que viven en España estudiarán islamismo en colegios públicos*, in *El Pais Digital*, Sociedad, Lunes 4 octubre 1999, No. 1249.

23. MARTÍN MUÑOZ, *Lo real y lo irreal* (n. 13), p. 114. On the topic of *mestizaje* in the Americas, see, especially, the writings of Virgilio Elizondo, who speaks of a "second" *mestizaje*: "In the pre-Colombian / Iberian-Catholic *mestizo* based culture of Mexico it is the one who can endure all the opposing tensions of life and not lose his or her interior harmony who appears to be the upright and righteous one" in contrast to the "secular based culture of the United States" where "it is the one who succeeds materially who appears to be the upright and righteous person" (V. ELIZONDO, *Popular Religion as Support of Identity: A Pastoral-Psychological Case-Study Based on the Mexican American Experience in the USA*, in N. GREINBACHER – N. METTE [eds.], *Popular Religion* [Concilium, 186], Edinburgh, 36-43, esp. p. 38). And see, also, the critical analysis by Roberto S. Goizueta of Mexican statesman-philosopher José Vasconcelos' development of the concept of *mestizaje*, R. GOIZUETA, *Caminemos con Jesús, Toward a Hispanic/Latino Theology of Accompaniment*, Maryknoll, NY, Orbis, 1995, esp. pp. 77-131.

24. J. BEDOYA, *50,000 niños* (n. 22).

25. The term itself, *al-Andalus*, has found many interpretations. These have been summarized by Pedro Chalmeta in the Introduction of his work, P. CHALMETA, *Invasión e*

that Arabic-Islamic culture must be seen as a constituent element of both the Hispanic and European personality[26]. This, in fact, is something that needs to be "recaptured" for the benefit today of both Spain and Europe. But the way in which *al-Andalus* is presented and taught in contemporary Spain constitutes, in her judgment, a clear example of the rejection of the Other. She points out how the terminology in both elementary and secondary school textbooks frequently refers to "the presence of Muslims in Spain", or that "the Muslims lived on the Peninsula for eight hundred years", marginalizing eight centuries of the history of Spain as provisional and not really "Spanish". Even the creation of the term, "Reconquista", represents the objective of seeking to de-legitimize the "Spanishness" of *al-Andalus*, and to present eight hundred years of Spanish history from the point of view of Christian continuity. The result is that eight hundred years of Arabic culture in Spain is viewed instead as an eight hundred year struggle of liberation. And this has produced an attitude, not of one that promotes cultural integration, but of one that unjustly demeans both the Arab and the Muslim[27].

III. Theological Analysis and Reflections

The Second Vatican Council's *Declaration on the Relationship of the Church to Non-Christian Religions*, officially promulgated October 28, 1965, voiced a fundamental change with regard to the relationship of Christians and Muslims. It stated:

islamización: La sumisión de Hispania y la formación de al-Andalus, Madrid, Mapfre, 1994, pp. 19-27, esp. pp. 22-26. In the end, Chalmeta argues that the only explanation that seems worthy of truth is that of Joaquín Vallvé: the North African Berber term has its roots in the Greek deity Atlas, from which is derived the term Atlantic. (The oldest inscription of the term *al-Andalus* is found on a coin, a *dinar*, minted in the year 916). But Chalmeta insists that it is important to recognize that the term *al-Andalus* is one that designates, primarily and essentially, a political-religious-cultural *community*, rather than a geographical territory. One always centers on the human person. In the Arabic context, one describes and identifies oneself in relation to one ancestors, one's belonging to a particular clan or tribe. Thus, the fundamental meaning of the term *al-Andalus*, must always be rooted in the human and not in the territory itself.

26. To cite one example, D. KING, *Astronomy in the Service of Islam*, Liverpool, Ashcroft Publishing, 1993. King is an historian of science at Johann Wolfgang Goethe University in Frankfurt. The 14 articles are reproduced from their original publication in various journals, 1982-91. See the article by D. OVERBYE, *How Islam Won, and Lost, the Lead in Science*, in *The New York Times (on the Web)*, October 30, 2001 [www.nytimes.com]: "From the 10th to the 13th century, Europeans, especially in Spain, were translating Arabic works into Hebrew and Latin 'as fast as they could', said Dr. King. The result was a rebirth of learning that ultimately transformed Western civilization".

27. MARTIN MUÑOZ, *Lo real y lo irreal* (n. 13), pp. 118-120.

Although in the course of the centuries many quarrels and hostilities have arisen between Christians and Muslims, this most sacred Synod urges all to forget the past and to strive sincerely for mutual understanding. On behalf of all humankind, let them make common cause of safeguarding and fostering social justice, moral values, peace, and freedom [§3][28]. More recently, in December, 1999, the Vatican International Theological Commission published a document entitled, *Memory and Reconciliation: The Church and the Faults of the Past*[29]. Here there is a call, *not* to "forget the past", but to face it, to acknowledge "what was done in contradiction to the Gospel"[30], and to strive for reconciliation. The task is not to eliminate these memories, but to "purify the memory of the past and generate a new one. The basis of this *new memory* cannot be other than mutual love or, better, the renewed commitment to live it"[31]. The document quotes the earlier words of Pope John Paul II himself: "Another sad chapter of history to which the sons and daughters of the Church must return with a spirit of repentance is that of the acquiescence given, especially in certain centuries, to intolerance and even the use of force in the service of truth". And it stresses the wrong that was committed by not respecting "the consciences of the persons to whom the

28. W. ABBOTT (ed.), *The Documents of Vatican II, Declaration on the Relationship of the Church to Non-Christian Religions*, New York, 1966, pp. 660-668, p. 663 [muslims and humankind, my modification]. The later ET, entitled Vatican Council II, *The Conciliar and Post Conciliar Documents*, ed. A. FLANNERY, Collegeville, MN, 1975, pp. 738-742, esp. 740 is substantially the same with regard to the above citation. However, in this same §three, there is a serious mistranslation of an earlier section on the part of the Flannery text, which states that "although not acknowledging him as God, they [Muslims] worship Jesus as a prophet". On the other hand, the Abbott text more accurately translates, "though they do not acknowledge Jesus as God, they revere him as a prophet" [my emphasis].

29. INTERNATIONAL THEOLOGICAL COMMISSION, *Memory and Reconciliation: The Church and the Faults of the Past*, [March] 2000, Vatican City. The "Preliminary Note" to the document provides its historical genesis: "The study of the topic 'The Church and the Faults of the Past' was proposed to the International Theological Commission by its President, Joseph Cardinal Ratzinger, in view of the celebration of the Jubilee Year 2000. A sub-commission was established to prepare this study; it was composed of Rev. Christopher Begg, Msgr. Bruno Forte (President), Rev. Sebastian Karotemprel, S.D.B., Msgr. Roland Minnerath, Rev. Thomas Norris, Rev. Rafael Salazar Cardenas, M.Sp.S., and Msgr. Anton Strukelj. The general discussion of this theme took place in numerous meetings of the sub-commission and during the plenary sessions of the International Theological Commission held in Rome from 1998 to 1999. The present text was approved in *forma specifica* by the International Theological Commission, by written vote, and was then submitted to the President, Cardinal Ratzinger, Prefect of the Congregation for the Doctrine of the Faith, who have his approval for its publication". The document was subsequently published March 7, 2000, and was available online at http://www.vatican.va/roman_curia.

30. *Ibid.*, §4.0 ["Historical Judgement and Theological Judgement"].

31. *Ibid.*, §5.2.

faith was presented, as well as all forms of force used in the repression and correction of errors"[32]. The document continues that acknowledging the faults of the past tend(s) toward the *purification of memory*, which – as noted above – is a process aimed at a new evaluation of the past, capable of having a considerable effect on the present, because past sins frequently make their weight felt and remain temptations in the present as well. Above all, if the causes of possible resentment for evils suffered and the negative influences stemming from what was done in the past can be removed as a result of dialogue and the patient search for mutual understanding with those who feel injured by words and deeds of the past, such a removal may help the community of the Church grow in holiness through reconciliation and peace in obedience to the Truth[33].

Kevin Lenehan has characterized the Pope's leadership for this *purification of memory*, as "an attempt at undoing the apocalyptic interpretation of history". The resulting outcome is that by "linking 'the structure of memorial with that of celebration', [one] opens up an alternative hermeneutical approach to history, one that is properly eschatological"[34].

A challenge that one encounters with regard to the *Fiesta de moros y cristianos* is interpreting this event not from the context of a closed and self-realizing worldview from which apocalyptic proceeds, but from the context of a worldview that is open to the remembrance of the suffering of the victims, from which the eschatological proceeds. All too often in the past, it is this apocalyptic trajectory that has emerged, using the language of conflict and conquest. But an eschatological perspective can and does emerge when "dialogue and the patient search for mutual understanding" come to the forefront. The *Fiesta de moros y cristianos* allows for a recognition of the mutuality of these two partners in dialogue[35].

---

32. *Ibid.*, §5.3. The citation is from JOHN PAUL II, *Apostolic Letter, Tertio Millennio Adveniente*, in *Origins* 24 (1994) 401-416, n. 35.

33. *Ibid.*, §6.1.

34. K. LENEHAN, *The Great Jubilee and the Purification of Memory*, in *Louvain Studies* 25 (2000) 291-311, p. 301. The citation is from JOHN PAUL II, *Apostolic Letter* (n. 32), n. 33. Lenehan argues that "the notions of time, history and human autonomy that characterize the modern era lead inevitably to the cultivation of a secularized apocalyptic hermeneutic" [299]. And that "when confronted with suffering, a worldview that is closed and self-realizing offers fertile soil for the cultivation of the apocalyptic imagination" p. 301.

35. See HARRIS, *Aztecs* (n. 2), where this same perspective and interpretation is unequivocally supported: "It seems to me that the nature of the Spanish folk festival of Moors and Christians is not to reenact history but to *embody* a vision of what might have been and what might yet be. The performers do not believe that historical battles between Moors and Christians ended with conversion and fraternity, but they may well wish that it had been so. And they may wish, too, that human relationships now could be less conflicted and more able to encompass difference without hostility. I am persuaded that Spain's

In Spain, in town after town, and city after city, the celebration of the *Fiesta de moros y cristianos* welcomes, honors and accepts – with an acknowledgment of the pain and suffering that was endured – those who have been instrumental in the reality that is Spain today, and with this honesty, provides hope toward a new future. This is the opposite of the type of forgetfulness promoted by the entertainment industry[36]. It is the face to face encounter of two Hispanic groups, of two Hispanic worlds, of two Hispanic religions which have interpenetrated one another[37].

festivals of Moors and Christians, by rewriting the country's most prolonged ethnic conflict so that it ends not in exile but in reconciliation, express that yearning ... The fiestas deliberately revise history, not to deny its pain or to conceal its guilt, but to envision a better outcome" (pp. 211-212). "Thus even though they entertained no hidden transcript of resistance, the medieval *moros y cristianos* were still about the dynamics of power. Insofar as they were also about those they named, the *moros y cristianos* offered a vision of *convivencia* rather than bloodshed. Moors do not get killed in these battles. They survive to be converted and to dance and feast with their former enemies. While such a resolution may require, as one modern scholar has put it, that the Moors lose 'their very identity', it still compares favorably with the harsh treatment afforded Spanish Moriscos in the sixteenth century and with the kind of ethnic cleansing we have seen in our own day. It is hard to imagine such a festive ending if Serbs were now to stage a mick battle between Christians and Muslims in the Balkans. Muslims, on the whole, are not demonized in the medieval festivals of the reconquest ... They are honored as worthy opponents and as welcome partners in feasting" (p. 62).

36. Lenehan cites Theodor Adorno's analysis of the category of *memory*. "He [Adorno] argues that the culture of mass capitalism sustains itself by insulating its consumers from the content of their own (alienated) experiences. Such experiences no longer arise freely and involuntarily in the memory, but are replaced by a culturally and socially induced content. The same capitalistic mechanism which produces alienation and suffering also produces an 'industry of oblivion,' the entertainment industry, to mask and conceal the suffering of its victims. Knowledge and reason are also marked by this socially engineered forgetfulness. [Quoting Adorno] "It is of the essence of domination to prevent recognition of the suffering it produces of itself". K. LENEHAN, *The Great Jubilee* (n. 34), pp. 295-296. Lenehan cites T. ADORNO, *Minima Moralia: Reflections from a Damaged Life*, London New Left Books, 1974, which itself is cited in A. MOREIRA, *The Dangerous Memory of Jesus Christ in a Post-Traditional Society*, in *Concilium* (1994) 39-48, p. 41.

37. María Soledad Carrasco Urgoiti notes the following: "In summary, the binomial '*moros y cristianos*' gives to the term '*moro*' a complex semantic content, in part passed on from the times in which the '*morisca*' minority maintained a certain level of connection to the Islamic world and was the object of a political ambivalence of being captured and of being rejected. This theatrical image is superficial art, and it encompasses the adversaries that are representative of the two laws, religions or cultures which dominated the Spanish Middle Age which had its evolution and its territorial and circumstantial fluctuations. Today, [the fiesta] comes to us altered, among other reasons because of the trace of romantic Medievalism. *But perhaps some day the lens of historical research will allow us to come to the point that connects the fiesta de 'moros y cristianos' with the conscious rejection of a plural identity*" [translation and emphasis mine], Mª.S. CARRASCO URGOITI, *La fiesta de moros y cristianos y la cuestión morisca en la España de los Austrias*, in *El Moro Retador y El Moro Amigo* (n. 15), pp. 67-90, esp. pp. 89-90. See, also, HARRIS, *Aztecs* (n. 2), where Harris points to the presence of *los moros* in the festival as representing "the temporary resurgence of all that is suppressed but cannot finally be expelled by church

Several months after the publication of *Memory and Reconciliation: The Church and the Faults of the Past,* the Declaration, *"Dominus Jesus"*, was published by the Vatican Congregation for the Doctrine of the Faith[38]. The Introduction of the Declaration provides the purpose of the document, namely "giving reasons for and supporting the evangelizing mission of the Church, above all in connection with the religious traditions of the world"[39]. It affirms the importance of "inter-religious dialogue", which "requires and attitude of understanding and a relationship of mutual knowledge and reciprocal enrichment"[40].

The sixth and final major section of the Declaration is entitled "The Church and the Other Religions in Relation to Salvation". Within this section it is stated that "if it is true that the followers of other religions can receive divine grace, it is also certain that *objectively speaking* they are in a gravely deficient situation in comparison with those who, in the Church, have the fullness of the means of salvation"[41]. The declaration immediately continues by quoting from the Vatican II Document, *Lumen gentium,* that "all the children of the Church should nevertheless remember that their exalted condition results, not from their own merits, but from the grace of Christ"[42]. While these two statements follow immediately upon each other in *"Dominus Jesus"*, they are really addressing two very different realities.

Karl Rahner employs the distinction between "offered grace" and "accepted grace"[43]. This double aspect of Offer-Acceptance recognizes the freedom of the human being as the addressee of God's self

and state. 'The Moors are not just a symbol', said one of my friends in Villena. 'They are something in us. Look at our faces. Many are Moorish'" (p. 221).

38. CONGREGATION FOR THE DOCTRINE OF THE FAITH, *Declaration "Dominus Jesus" on the Unicity and Salvific Universality of Jesus Christ and the Church,* published on August 6, 2000, and available online at http://www.vatican.va/roman_curia. The declaration is signed by Joseph Cardinal Ratzinger, with the concluding note that "the Sovereign Pontiff John Paul II, at the Audience of June 16, 2000, granted to the undersigned Cardinal Prefect of the Congregation for the Doctrine of the Faith, with sure knowledge and by his apostolic authority, ratified and confirmed this Declaration, adopted in Plenary Session and ordered its publication".

39. *Ibid.,* §2.

40. *Ibid.,* §2.

41. *Ibid.,* §22.

42. *Ibid.,* §22, citing in note 93, *Lumen gentium,* 14.

43. K. RAHNER, *The Trinity,* New York, 1974, pp. 92-93. This is a translation of K. RAHNER, *Der dreifaltige Gott als tranzendenter Urgrund der Heilsgeschichte,* in J. FEINER – H. LÖHRER (eds.), *Mysterium Salutis. Grundriss heilsgeschichtlicher Dogmatik.* Bd. II: *Die Heilsgeschichte vor Christus,* Einsiedeln, 1967, pp. 317-397 (to 401 with bibliography). For a study of this theme from an ecclesiological perspective, see my analysis in J. FARMER, *Ministry in Community. Karl Rahner's Vision of Ministry* (Louvain Theological & Pastoral Monographs, 13), Leuven, 1993.

communication. In an attempt to interpret how one ought to understand this statement in *"Dominus Jesus"*, I would argue that those in the Church who "have the fullness of the means of salvation" *have it* [my emphasis] with reference to offered grace. Rahner speaks of this offered grace as "a grace which always surrounds the human being, even the sinner and the unbeliever, as the inescapable setting of one's existence"[44]. One's "exalted condition" comes about in and through what the document *"Dominus Jesus"* calls the "grace of Christ", and which Rahner insists enables, but never forces, the acceptance of that grace. But one must also recognize that all who accept the one grace of Christ, both those in the Church as well as those from within other religious traditions and contexts, share in this "exalted condition"[45].

Rahner's distinction between "offered grace" and "accepted grace", is particularly significant. His distinction is rooted in the one self-communication of God, which he insists takes place in "two and only two manners": the modality of history and the modality of spirit[46]. Within this context, one identifies four double aspects of God's self-communication, one of which is that of Offer-Acceptance[47]. Rahner underscores the dimension of acceptance by affirming "that the very acceptance of a divine self-communication through the power and act of freedom is one more moment of the self-communication of God, who gives himself in such a way that his self-donation is accepted in freedom"[48]. The double aspect of Offer-Acceptance recognizes the freedom of the human being as the addressee of God's self-communication. Rahner goes on to stress that this aspect of acceptance must be brought about by the self-communicating

44. K. RAHNER, *Nature and Grace*, in *Theological Investigations*, Vol. 4, London, 1966, 165-188, p. 181. (It is the English translation of *Schriften zur Theologie*, Bd. IV, Einsiedeln, 1960, 209-236.)

45. Equally troubling in *"Dominus Jesus"* is the apparent deliberateness of the declaration to eliminate any reference to an important emphasis in the incomplete and therefore misleading citation of §2 of the Vatican II text, *Nostra aetate*. There one finds the following exhortation addressed to all Christians, which has been "edited out" of the *"Dominus Jesus"* declaration: "prudently and lovingly, through dialogue and collaboration with the followers of other religions, and in witness of Christian faith and life, acknowledge, preserve and promote the spiritual and moral goods found among these [men], as well as the values in their society and culture". CONGREGATION FOR THE DOCTRINE OF THE FAITH (n. 37), §22. See the Vatican II *Declaration on the Church to Non-Christian Religions [Nostra aetate]*, §2, in W. ABBOTT (ed.), *The Documents of Vatican II* (n. 28), pp. 662-663.

46. RAHNER, *The Trinity* (n. 42), p. 94.

47. *Ibid.*, p. 88. The other three double aspects are 1) Origin-Future; 2) History-Transcendence, and 3) Knowledge-Love; and this last pair actually follows that of Offer-Acceptance.

48. *Ibid.*, pp. 92-93.

God. If the acceptance were realized on the part of the human being, then the self-communication of God would be done away with. But God "creates the possibility of its acceptance and this acceptance itself", so that God's self-communication can take place[49].

To link this more explicitly to the reality of non-Christian religions, one finds a key perspective on the part of Rahner: the Christological aspect is seen to be Offer, and the pneumatological aspect, that is, relating to the Holy Spirit, is Acceptance. It is clear that through this concept Rahner is seeking to recognize more explicitly and more clearly the Trinitarian doctrine in both Christology and pneumatology[50]. For Rahner insists that between Jesus and the Spirit there is "both a unity and a difference, and a relationship of mutual conditioning"[51]. The Holy Spirit, the "universal self communication of God to the world", has an "intrinsic relation to Jesus Christ", because God's self-communication and its acceptance can never take place in "mere abstract transcendentality", but takes place in "historical mediation". And Jesus Christ is this historical mediation toward which the Spirit is directed from the very beginning[52].

49. *Ibid.*, pp. 97-98.
50. *Ibid.*, pp. 97-98. The Christological aspects are seen to be: Origin, History, Offer, and Knowledge. The pneumatological aspects, that is, those relating to the Holy Sprit, are: Future, Transcendence, Acceptance, and Love.
51. K. RAHNER, *Foundations of Christian Faith*, London, 1978 (English translation of *Grundkurs des Glaubens*, Freiberg im Breisgau, 1976), p. 334. This section in *Foundations of Christian Faith*, "Jesus Christ in Non-Christian Religions", pp. 311-321, corresponds substantially to K. RAHNER, *Jesus Christ in the Non-Christian Religions*, in *Theological Investigations*, Vol. 17, London, 1981, pp. 39-50 (English translation of *Schriften zur Theologie*, Bd. XII, Einsiedeln, 1975, pp. 370-383).
52. RAHNER, *Foundations of Christian Faith* (n. 51), pp. 317-318. Jesus is seen simultaneously as the "high point" of historical mediation, but also as the only point. Nevertheless, one must refer to Rahner's reflections on the "Anonymous Christian". For example, see K. RAHNER, *Observations on the Problem of the "Anonymous Christian"*, in *Theological Investigations*, Vol. 14, London, 1976, 280-294 (English translation of *Schriften zur Theologie*, Bd. X, Einsiedeln, 1972, pp. 226-251; this article was first presented as a lecture 22 January 1971). He states that his purpose is one attempt to explain "how true supernatural faith in revelation can be present in an individual without any contact with the explicit preaching of the gospel. For the fact that such a thing is possible is explicitly declared in the official doctrinal statements of the Church ..." (p. 291). He summarizes his view by saying: "There must be a Christian theory to account for the fact that every individual who does not in any absolute or ultimate sense act against one's own conscience can say and does say in faith, hope and love, Abba within one's own spirit, and is on these grounds in all truth a sister or brother to Christians in God's sight" (p. 294). See also, K. RAHNER, *Experience of the Holy Spirit*, in *Theological Investigations*, Vol. 18, London, 1983, 189-210 (English translation of *Schriften zur Theologie*, Bd. XIII, Einsiedeln, 1978, pp. 226-251), pp. 205-206: "The grace of God (which the history of the Crucified and Risen One made effective and irreversible in the history of humanity) is consequently the grace of Jesus Christ even when it is not explicitly and reflectively grasped and interpreted as such. This is not merely and opinion which a Christian may hold; it is

God's self-communication always takes place in and through histori-cal mediation. God's Spirit is clearly operative wherever there is, in the language of the Vatican document, *Memory and Reconciliation,* this "dia-logue and the patient search for mutual understanding".

The *fiesta de moros y cristianos* can be seen as a paradigm of God's self-communication. In the dramatization that takes place, neither the *moros* nor the *cristianos* are presented as "the Other". They are seen and celebrated as equal subjects. Indeed, one celebrates their mutual encounter. And it is proclaiming, in a powerful symbolic manner, that out of this encounter has emerged the reality that is Spain, and, to a cer-tain extent, the reality that is Europe itself[53].

To acknowledge the sins and weaknesses of the past, stresses the doc-ument, *Memory and Reconciliation: The Church and the Faults of the Past,* "is an act of honesty and courage. It opens a new tomorrow for everyone"[54]. This continuing encounter that takes place in Spain between *moros* and *cristianos* year after year can be seen as a paradigm of God's

part of his faith, which ... forbids him to hold the opinion that this salvific will of God in Jesus Christ effects a person's salvation only when the latter has explicitly become a Chris-tian".

53. See also M. HARRIS, *The Dialogical Theatre, Dramatizations of the Conquest of Mexico and the Question of the Other,* New York, 1993, where Harris refers to the foun-dational work of Martin Buber's 'dialogical principle': "that the other be recognized not only as an object of which we may speak or whom I may address as a Thou but also as a subject, an I who speaks about me within his or her own circle and who in turn addresses me as a Thou... This realization that the other is not merely an object of my discourse and my gaze, but that he or she is also a subject observing me, leads to the startling insight that the other has a point of view that is not my own and which is no more a defective version of mine than mine is a defective version of his or hers". Harris then goes on to further incorporate the perspective of Mikhail Bakhtin, for whom the other "was a source of joy... His 'other' signals the diversity of human experience, joyously challenging the totalitarian assumption that there can ever be a single point of view" (p. 157).

54. INTERNATIONAL THEOLOGICAL COMMISSION (n. 29), §6.4 ("Conclusion"). See, also, this repeated emphasis in the Apostolic Letter "at the close of the Great Jubilee of the Year 2000", JOHN PAUL II, *Novo millennio ineunte,* published on January 6, 2001, and avail-able online at http://www.vatican.va/holy_father. See in particular, the section entitled, "Dialogue and mission", §54-56: "In the years of preparation for the Great Jubilee the Church has sought to build, not least through a series of highly symbolic meetings, *a rela-tionship of openness and dialogue with the followers of other religions* [emphasis in text]. This dialogue must continue. In the climate of increased cultural and religious pluralism which is expected to make the society of the new millennium, it is obvious that this dia-logue will be especially important in establishing a sure basis for peace and warding off the dread spectre of those wars of religion which have so bloodied human history. The name of the one God must become increasingly what it is: *a name of peace and a sum-mons to peace"* [§55]. "We know in fact that, in the presence of the mystery of grace, infi-nitely full of possibilities and implications for human life and history, the Church herself will never cease putting questions, trusting in the help of the Paraclete, the Spirit of truth (cf. *Jn* 14:17), whose task it is to guide her 'into all the truth' (*Jn* 16:13)" [§56].

ongoing self-communication with humanity, deepening and developing the relational life that humanity is offered by God, and – even more remarkable – that life that God enables humans to accept.

Department of Theology   Jerry T. FARMER
Xavier University of Louisiana
1 Drexel Drive
P.O. Box 108
New Orleans, LA 70125
U.S.A.

THEOLOGY, CONVERSATION AND COMMUNITY

BAUMAN'S CRITIQUE OF COMMUNITY

I. INTRODUCTION

One of the pitfalls that theology has to avoid is the problem of talking "about" God. Since God is not an object open to positivist enquiry, knowledge of God must have an engaged, interactive character. Hermeneutical accounts of knowledge as understanding can supply part of such a requirement, and they inform much contemporary theology[1]. Theological understanding calls for a mutual engagement between the theological tradition, biblical witness and the worshipping Church community, which may be expressed in terms of reciprocal conversation. Edward Schillebeeckx presents a typical example of a model of the relation between theology and community using a hermeneutical approach. He grounds Christian experience in the shared human activity of specific, concrete Christian community, empowered by the Holy Spirit[2]. Human understanding of God is a dynamic process, involving repeated interplay of experiences and community reflection on those experiences[3]. Theology is here dependent on the existence of a worshipping community in touch with both its own past and the present world in which it is embedded[4]. Christian community described in this or similar manner is thus more than the aggregation of individuals in a group with common memories and values, and yet it presupposes such a grouping.

The context of community for conversation, as bearer of tradition, matrix of present understanding, and transmitter of future understanding, is essential to this kind of theological vision. Actual conversation has to

1. I have mainly in mind the philosophers Gadamer, Ricœur and McIntyre, and the theologians Schillebeeckx, Tracy and Pannenberg.
2. He observes: "Only if the living story of a particular religious tradition is told and put into practice in a specific community can men and women today have Christian experiences ...". E. SCHILLEBEECKX, *Church: The Human Story of God*, London, SCM, 1990, p. 25 and p. 158: "Faith in the Lord, in the risen Jesus – the origin and existence of the "church" – is the receiving of the Spirit".
3. *Ibid.*, p. 43.
4. For a convergent view of the relation between theology, church, Spirit and community, see the paper by Professor Schwöbel in this volume.

take place in groups, in communities and little detailed thought has been given to the nature of community and the interactions between community and conversation. Theological accounts of community may take in different perspectives on language in the construction of human relations. For instance, Dulles' well-known survey of models for church includes "mystical" models, which may depend more on actions and physical placement, and the repetitive or poetic use of language. It also includes "institutional" models, which depend on a rational-intentional use of language[5]. Conversation here can mean many things, but these differences are not often explored. The rational-intentional mode of discourse is commonly assumed; for example, Kirkpatrick's recent treatment of community seems to rest mainly on this view of language[6]. Schillebeeckx, on the other hand, discerns a recommendation for "pre-reflexive" conversation between Christians and the world in catholic ecclesiology as it emerges from the second half of the twentieth century[7]. More recently, Rowan Williams argues for a kind of language that is not propositional or goal directed, but which recognises and assumes the value of the conversation partner[8]. This kind of conversation is associated with social bondedness. He points to the need for (and loss of) what he calls "charitable space" in social relations. For Williams, charity refers to a social acknowledgement of the "other" which does not involve any transaction or manipulation. He is clear that charity is radically opposed to the prioritising of material gain in social relations[9]. If Williams is right, we come full circle; a conversation constitutive of "social glue" is necessary for the formation of community, which itself is necessary for the more complex conversation of understanding. Following insights from the Frankfurt School, there has been discussion of the imbalance of power relations between conversation partners[10], but this has not focussed directly on the role of community in conversation.

5. A. DULLES, *Models of the Church*, Dublin, Gill and Macmillan, 1988.

6. F.G. KIRKPATRICK, *The Ethics of Community*, Oxford, Blackwell, 2001.

7. See particularly *The Church as a Sacrament of Dialogue*, in E. SCHILLEBEECKX, *God the Future of Man*, New York, Sheed & Ward, 1968, 119-140, pp. 137-138.

8. R. WILLIAMS, *Lost Icons*, Edinburgh, T&T Clark, 2000, pp. 72-77. He draws on both Ursula Le Guin and Charles Taylor in this discussion.

9. *Ibid.*, p. 58: "Charity challenges any assumption that we are, as human beings, committed first and foremost to victory in the battle for material goods. There is such a thing as a social good (a social miracle), accessible only by the suspension of rivalry and the equalising of honour or status".

10. The debate between Gadamer and Habermas over this issue still stimulates developments e.g., Kögler's recent attempt to extend Gadamer's position by drawing on Foucault. See H.H. KÖGLER, *The Power of Dialogue: Critical Hermeneutics after Gadamer and Foucault*, Cambridge, MA, MIT Press, 1999.

In particular, community has too often been seen as uniformity, absence of diversity[11]. The relation between conversation (and therefore understanding) and community is of great significance.

And yet according to many disciplines, especially sociology, but also in general public discourse, all does not seem well with community. At least in Western Europe, increasing social isolation of marginal people, increasing violence, general disengagement from the political process, disintegration of social institutions: all point to some kind of crisis for contemporary understanding and practice of community in postmodernity[12]. This is often linked to the loss of so called "grand narratives" and the erosion of the concept of authority that follows the postmodern exposure of domination. Gillian Rose has explored the philosophical contours of this territory in difficult but brilliant works[13]. In this paper I wish to attempt a much simpler task in the analysis of community, theology and conversation. I intend only a preliminary examination of community as presented in the light of contemporary social theory. This turns out to be quite complex enough.

The Scriptural accounts of community are rich and varied. The First Testament speaks of God and humanity as a shepherd and his flock, as a king and his people, as the groom and bride, and so on. These are mostly images of faithfulness and covenant on God's part, and a response of justice and right action on the part of humanity. The Second Testament images are more complicated; they include the idea of temple, and the pervasive concept of the body of Christ. Second Testament practice, particularly of *koinonia*, has also been widely interpreted. For example, Schillebeeckx stresses the origins of the Second Testament Church in developing an understanding of community in his account of church for today[14]. These images and practices have been employed down the ages in the development of the many views of church – as society, as alternative, as monastic, and so on. Monastic orders and experiments such as those of the Shakers still provide a foundation for understanding community. Twentieth century experiments such as that of Bonhoeffer in

---

11. For instance, I have argued elsewhere that Pannenberg's understanding of community and culture is monolithic, and vulnerable to critique from social theorists. See J. STEWART, *Does Pannenberg's View of Culture and Social Theory have Ethical Implications?*, in *Studies in Christian Ethics* 13 (2000) 32-48.

12. Or late modernity; the argument about exactly how dead modernity is or is not does not efface its sickness, and I concur with Professor Schreiter's characterisation of it elsewhere in this volume.

13. G. ROSE, *The Broken Middle: Out of our Ancient Society*, Oxford, Blackwell, 1992; see also her *Diremption of Spirit*, in P. BERRY – A. WERNICK (eds.), *Shadow of Spirit*, London, Routledge, 1992, pp. 45-56.

14. SCHILLEBEECKX, *Church: The Human Story of God* (n. 2), chapter 3, section 4.

Finkenwalde or the Latin American Base Communities show the continuing significance of community for Christianity.

But these historical conceptions of community tend not to lend themselves to the modernist vision of an association of free agents with
equal, reciprocal and intentional relations expressed and negotiated
through rational language. The Enlightenment provided a critique of
abusive power and control, which depended on maintaining a fairly high
view of rationality, so that community today seems rather harder to
explain or understand[15]. And specifically Christian instantiations of
community in Western Europe also seem to have run into some difficulties in our postmodern age. The Religious Orders are in decline in
most denominations. Churches are also experiencing a widespread
decline in numbers attending worship, involved in other activities, giving financial support etc.[16]. Scandals involving sexual or financial mis-
conduct contribute to a loss of confidence in religious institutions and
accounts of negative experiences in specific contexts such as schools or
convents raise questions as to the basic ethics of community in a Christian context.

II. BAUMAN'S VIEW OF CONTEMPORARY "COMMUNITY"

If theology is to be seen as conversation in our present world, we have
to be able to give an account of the community contexts necessary for it.
And this is where I suggest some of our present difficulties lie, because
we appear to be entering an age of distorted community. The social theorist Zygmunt Bauman has recently contributed much relevant material
to discussions of the nature of community in postmodernity[17]. He is a
particularly interesting dialogue partner for the theologian, because his
analysis is extremely detailed and explicit, and because he stands in the
hermeneutic tradition in terms of his view of understanding and truth.

15. One of the most detailed theologies engaging with these issues is to be found
in D. BONHOEFFER, *Sanctorum Communio*, ed. C.J. GREEN, Minneapolis, MN, Fortress,
1998.
16. For example, see P. BRIERLEY, *The Tide is Running Out*, London, Christian
Research, 2000; S. BRUCE, *God is Dead*, Oxford, Blackwell, 2002; C.G. BROWN, *The
Death of Christian Britain*, London, Routledge, 2001.
17. See Z. BAUMAN, *Globalization; The Human Consequences*, Cambridge, Polity –
Blackwell, 1998; *In Search of Politics*, Cambridge, Polity – Blackwell, 1999; *Liquid
Modernity*, Cambridge, Polity – Blackwell, 2000; *Community: Seeking Safety in an Insecure World*, Cambridge, Polity – Blackwell, 2001.

He wishes to prevent the evacuation of moral value from sociological discussion[18].

Bauman argues that in present public language and conversation, the word "community" stands for something that feels good. It means "safe, supportive, reciprocal, forgiving". But it also represents a past Utopia, "Paradise Lost". The speakers in this conversation are not actually threatened by the absence of community (violence, break down), but by its subversion into an idealised "feel good" factor. Bauman claims that the present manifestation of community is actually in isolation, induced by the loss of autonomy resulting from the crucial balance between security and freedom. This balance is the key to the contemporary problems of community. The reality is a social structure that separates people and inhibits conversation, rather than enabling it.

The experience of community given to people in the long past is not available to modern and post modern humanity, because we are conscious of ourselves and each other precisely as community, something we can think about and investigate. The modern world is one of such mobility that community is no longer a given, an unseen matrix of life, but instead, "togetherness" has to be constructed. Hence the increasing importance of identity. It is not enough, therefore, to invoke the world of the Gospels and commend it as a model. That the disciples experienced and grew into community with Jesus, as he built it with them, is a starting point. But the post Easter construction of community in Christ is what is now in balance, in a world in which we are losing the ability to make basic contact with one another.

Bauman subscribes to Walter Benjamin's view of history as a flight into the future from the mistakes of the past, and he argues that the search for identity is a related endless quest. But if we want security from the horrors, some freedom must be sacrificed. The problem that Bauman identifies is that

> ... the security sacrificed in the name of freedom tends to be other people's security, and the freedom sacrificed in the name of security tends to be other people's freedom[19].

He develops his argument historically, citing Freud as a catalyst for concern about the tension between security and freedom in both sexual and wider social terms. The modern argument that the masses are

18. See ID., *Hermeneutics and Social Science: Approaches to Understanding*, London, Hutchinson, 1978; *Postmodern Ethics*, Oxford, Blackwell, 1993; *Postmodernity & Its Discontents*, Cambridge, Polity – Blackwell, 1997, pp. 107-108.

19. BAUMAN, *Community: Seeking Safety in an Insecure World* (n. 17), p. 20.

undisciplined in their passions, and so in need of social control, emerges partly from this. Hence in the Industrial Revolution, security for the few is bought by controlling the many[20]. This relation of control mutated into an unwilling marriage, with associated domestic strife, between employer and workers. Different models of supervision have been tried, but all regard management as necessary. Bauman concludes

> For the greater part of its history, modernity was an era of "social engineering" in which the spontaneous emergence and reproduction of order was not to be trusted[21].

By the time of the Second World War, managers had become the significant players; power lay not in ownership but in management control. This has mutated further in our own times, as deregulation, downsizing, and outsourcing become key terms. Bauman suggest that this is not only because the powerful do not want to be controlled, but because they want to rid themselves of the responsibility for the masses which was tied into the first moves to industrial social control. Domination is no longer achieved on a Panopticon model, but through uncertainty. The worker exists in state of permanent insecurity, since the ruled do not know what the rulers will do next. The physical manifestations of monolithic industry, the factories, canteens, and recreation facilities have vanished. The old social frame of work and livelihood is "falling apart". Bauman argues that this is paralleled by changes in the wider social world; corner shops replaced by supermarkets; the gasman by a call centre.

There may be parallels with community inside the churches. On the one hand, "management" has become a mantra in clergy training. Its consequences become visible as a concentration on buildings and infrastructure, with neglect of essential parts of the tradition, such as prayer and pastoral care. Within the churches, it is argued by some that present church leaders have abdicated responsibility; from the left, there are complaints that no clear political leads are given and from the right, the complaint that standards of personal morality have been abandoned. People do not know "where they stand".

Personal relations are also less stable; Bauman cites the newspaper comment that

> … embarking on matrimony in the 21st century appears to be as wise as taking to the sea on a raft made of blotting paper[22].

20. *Ibid.*, p. 26.
21. *Ibid.*, p. 37.
22. *Ibid.*, p. 47.

Bauman argues that this kind of uncertainty in a

> ... fluid, perpetually changing social environment ... does not unite suffer-
> ers: it splits them and sets them apart[23].

And in terms of process, this contains its own catalyst, leading to further fragmentation;

> ... the pains it causes to individuals do not add up, do not accumulate or con-
> dense into any kind of common cause[24].

so that there is no basis for common action against it. From a Christian perspective, concentrating on sexual and reproductive morality and
merely denouncing these evils is not likely to produce much change.
If theologians or any others are to have any effect on this situation, they
must first understand it. I would locate the "preferential option for the
poor" in this context.

The new elite that emerges as generators of this uncertainty lives
equally without community. They live separate, protected lives in insulated
and homogenous environments (the new electronically gated estates?) –
Bauman refers to the "secession of the successful"[25]. These individuals
do not want community, says Bauman, because community brings with it
obligations to share with others, regardless of their status. (Bauman's concept of community therefore has a moral dimension). But they do want
identity; the feeling of security that comes from belonging; "feel-good"
community. The shared values that feed identity require authority to legitimate them. Bauman argues that there are only two authorities left; one
is the authority of experts and the other is that of popular acclaim[26]. This
latter gives rise to the community of dreams; the aesthetic community; the
world of idols, pop or fashion, celebrities and so on. Bauman argues that
instability and transience exhibited by such idols are reassuring, and further, they "conjure up the joy of belonging without the discomfort of being
bound"[27]. This belonging feels real, although it does not display the

> ... toughness, resilience and immunity to individual desires which Durkheim
> believed marked reality[28].

These dream or aesthetic communities can be organised around
unpleasant as well as pleasant foci (such as recent British opposition to

23. *Ibid.*, p. 48.
24. *Ibid.*, p. 48.
25. *Ibid.*, p. 57.
26. *Ibid.*, p. 63.
27. *Ibid.*, p. 69.
28. *Ibid.*, pp. 69-70.

asylum seekers); they are short lived, and do not create either long term commitments or any ethical demands. They are clearly different from the kind of community based on egalitarian presuppositions, which requires a moral allegiance and concrete support. Bauman asserts that these two different kinds of community are being conflated in current discussion of these issues. Significantly, he argues that the problem should not be represented as one of epistemology but that the contradictions raised by the language of community should be "depicted as the products of genuine social conflicts that they really are"[29].

These social conflicts are being worked out in and between the parishes and groupings of churches across Britain today. People finding themselves in the fluid uncertainty of present structures, but not recognising the causes of their unease, struggle, not always successfully, with the apparent dissolution of both church and community. But they may not understand that the identification of "church" with both local and de-localised community, and with associated social groupings, is part of the problem.

The losses of social security, of faith in society, and the increase in "anxiety", have a visible outworking in the increasing premium being put on a defended physical location. Neighbourhood watch, burglar alarms, security patrols reflect this tendency. Further, it is a reaction driven by fear of the other as criminal. So in the attempt to keep the undesirable out of the safe place, another new notion of community is forming, which is based on sameness. The consequence, says Bauman, is that what emerges in the urge toward community as safety is a "bizarre mutant of a voluntary ghetto"[30]. This combines physical containment, social isolation, and homogeneity. These are voluntary ghettos;

> Real ghettos mean denial of freedom; Voluntary ghettos are meant to serve the cause of freedom[31].

And they grow on the backs of the real ghettos. As aggregations of dispossessed people are dumped on sink estates across Britain, so the "neighbourhood watch" signs multiply on their borders. And in the real ghetto, community has no more chance of development than in the voluntary one. Bauman says

> … ghetto experience dissolves solidarity and destroys mutual trust … A ghetto is not a greenhouse of community feelings. It is on the contrary a laboratory of social disintegration, atomization and anomie[32].

29. *Ibid.*, p. 73.
30. *Ibid.*, p. 116.
31. *Ibid.*, p. 117.
32. *Ibid.*, p. 122.

In fact, for Bauman, the existence of our ghettos reflects a policy of exclusion, which suits a society, committed to inequality, and which controls its members by fear. If we don't like the voluntary ghetto, there is always the real one.

These growing social inequalities are so blatant that they have been addressed, particularly by the Church of England, in initiatives from the report *Faith in the City,* which so displeased Margaret Thatcher, to the present Urban Fund for redistributing Anglican Church resources to poorer areas. But again, what is addressed are the results of the process Bauman describes, not the root cause. So temporary ameliorations can be effected, with this or that church project, but overall, the process is accelerating. This is surely one reason for the increasing sense of the political ineffectiveness of Christianity as an agent for social justice in Britain. The consequence of social fragmentation for communication, for conversation, is disastrous.

Just as uncertainty rules modernity in relationships and location, so it does in law and justice. Bauman argues that social justice as law and ethics has been replaced by human rights, as a flexible and ever open principle. However,

> ... it is in the nature of "human rights" that although they are meant to be enjoyed *separately* ... only collectively may they be granted[33].

The consequence in contemporary society, says Bauman, is recognition of difference without an egalitarian presupposition of equal worth, and thus, exclusivism. He wishes to reconnect the right to recognition with the right to redistribution. There can then be a chance of a "reconciliation to the prospect of perpetual coexistence" which is the ethical replacement of the now unattainable goal of a "conflict-free and suffering-free human condition"[34]. At the same time, human who struggle against oppression no longer look to a happier past for their standard; they look to currently available happiness and pleasure.

> "Injustice" changes its meaning: it now means being left behind in the universal movement towards a more pleasurable life[35].

But the conditions that Max Weber could describe for the emergence of communities of interest to act collectively against injustice no longer obtain, says Bauman. And he argues that fact that the collapse of such collective action is accompanied in our day with growing inequality is far from accidental. He says

33. *Ibid.,* p. 76.
34. *Ibid.,* p. 79.
35. *Ibid.,* p. 82.

... setting claims for recognition free of their redistributive content allows the ... anxiety and fear generated by the precariousness of "liquid modern" life to be channelled away from the political arena ... by blocking its social sources[36].

Bauman's deep concern with the apolitical and therefore amoral character of contemporary life extends to so-called "multiculturalism". Bauman argues that ethnic minorities are so designated not by themselves, or in their interest, but by "the promoters of the nation's unity". Ethnic minorities are an artifact of the modern concept of the state. They are those who the state has declared to be inassimilable. They are invariably disadvantaged, and the rhetoric about asylum seekers etc continues and strengthens this. Bauman is a fierce critic of the so-called multiculturalism that would seek to make this a matter of personal choice for those individuals. He asserts

The former blatantly arrogant habit of explaining inequalities by an inborn inferiority of races has been replaced by an apparently humane representation of starkly unequal human conditions as the inalienable right of every community to its own chosen form of life[37].

This is the result of the abandonment of any politics of change, and it ignores the previously noted tendency for divisions to promote and perpetuate yet further inequality.

Bauman's overall verdict on the consequences of these distortions of community is damning. He says of our postmodern societies that they suppress the question of right and wrong, truth and falsity.

One may say, using Heideggerian language, that the specifically postmodern form of "concealment" consists not so much in hiding the truth of Being behind the falsity of beings, but in blurring or washing away altogether the distinction between truth and falsity inside the beings themselves, and so making the issues ... of sense and of meaning senseless and meaningless[38].

Bauman's view of our contemporary situation is bleak. He sees the politics of disengagement and the pursuit of excess as its primary dynamics. We no longer have marching columns of workers, who were at least engaged; we have swarms of individuals with no cross linkage. Normative regulation is replaced by temptation and seduction. "Excess becomes a precept of reason"[39] and society is assumed to withdraw all claims to

---

36. *Ibid.*, p. 88.
37. *Ibid.*, p. 108.
38. BAUMAN, *Postmodernity and its Discontents* (n. 18), p. 125.
39. ID., *Community: Seeking Safety in an Insecure World* (n. 17), p. 132.

significance or value. He wishes to replace this relativist pluralism with a pluralism of engagement. He says

> ... recognition of cultural variety is the beginning, not the end, of the matter; it is a starting point for a ... *political process* [40].

His prescription for our ills depends on both human creativity and the rehabilitation of politics. Truth, he thinks, can still be revealed by creative art. Postmodern art is subversive (contra Habermas) because through precisely its deconstructive aspect, it displays the dependence of meaning on the processes of interpretation and critique. Bauman seems to think that contemporary fiction in particular, exposes the concealments of postmodernity, and makes the ethical again possible[41]. Bauman calls for a "republican society" in which individuals have both autonomy and individual rights. Such recognition doesn't dissolve the inevitable conflicts, but it provides a matrix in which they can be negotiated, rather than being suppressed or concealed. This is a curiously optimistic outlook, given his analysis, but I think is connected with the priority he gives the ethical, following Levinas. So it may be less a practical proposal than a call to recognise the essentially moral question of present society.

III. CONCLUSION

I think that Bauman has revealed a deeply worrying and challenging problem for Christian theology of community. Social anthropological studies in the UK, such as those of T. Jenkins, have confirmed the applicability of his analysis to British church communities[42]. These must be crucial issues for any Christian construction of community. Experience of the Spirit sent by Christ must be problematised in any so-called community that may be actually constituted to exclude and marginalise the less powerful, or to suppress the question of whether or not action is right. Communication and conversation cannot take place without affecting action. The basis of the message of Jesus is sacrificial love for the other; that is, in political terms, Christianity does imply that recognition is fundamentally linked to redistribution. Hence, no matter what model of the church is used, any ecclesiology for contemporary Western Christianity must take account of these new problems. A theological solution cannot

---

40. *Ibid.*, p. 136.
41. ID., *Postmodernity and its Discontents* (n. 18), pp. 107-108 and pp. 111-126.
42. T. JENKINS, *Religion in English Everyday Life*, New York, Berghahn, 1999.

depend on either assuming a premodern given sociality, as part of a theology of creation, or on accepting a modern intentional-rational free association of individuals. A Christian understanding of the growth of true community, of fellowship between humanity and God, must take into account non-volitional, pre-linguistic, non-conceptual and political factors. And it may be that a theology of community adequate to today's problems is not tied to ecclesiology as it has been in the past.

The corrosion of community described by Bauman and alluded to by many others is capable of destroying not only social well-being, political and educational institutions but also the institutions of Christianity in the Western world. Church is something that is always in need of renewal and reconstruction, always provisional. But we must enquire into the specific conditions this process requires today. Theology needs to engage with social theory. We need to ask what kind of communities our Western churches represent. What kind of communities are the churches that appear to flourish? We should note that social dominance is likely to render a church more, not less, vulnerable to the issues described by Bauman[43]. How can Christian community be formed in the midst of the disintegrative tendencies of today? Can social theory illuminate issues such as the role of the Holy Spirit in this? Can truth-revealing conversation take place among Christians in the West today? What new social forms may or should be generated for "Church"? C.G. Brown describes Britain as the first country in the world to experience the final failure of religious society[44]. He argues that this does not necessarily imply the death of churches as such. But a lot will have to be done, very quickly, if this is not also to be the outcome.

Departement of Theology and
Religious Studies
University of Leeds
Leeds LS2 9JT
UK

Jacqui A. STEWART

---

43. It is worth noting that in those parts of the world where Christianity is not in institutional decline, social growth and vitality is associated particularly with Pentecostal Churches. See D. MARTIN, *Pentecostalism: The World Their Parish*, Oxford, Blackwell, 2002.

44. BROWN, *The Death of Christian Britain* (n. 16).

COMMUNION ECCLESIOLOGY

FRIENDSHIP AS A MODEL OF CONVERSATION WITHIN THE CHURCH

I. INTRODUCTION

The title of the LEST III symposium is "Conversation and Theology". Currently, it is fair to say that the Catholic Church is experiencing a "crisis in conversation". This crisis is evident in several relationships within the church including relationships between pope and bishops, pope and theologians, bishops and theologians, the faithful and bishops, the faithful and pope, Roman curia and bishops, etc. The cause for this crisis can be traced, in part, to what might be called a dualistic *communio* ecclesiology. The majority of theologians note that there was a fundamental ecclesiological shift at Vatican II from a hierarchical to a *communio* or communion ecclesiology. In fact, the magisterium itself recognizes this shift. There are, however, fundamental theological disagreements regarding the interpretation of this ecclesiological model and the implications it has for conversation within the church. In this paper, we will describe the communion ecclesiological model, investigate two interpretations of this model as it applies to conversation between the universal and particular church, propose friendship as a model of conversation that bridges the dualistic communion ecclesiological gap, and point out some implications of this model for conversation between the universal and particular church.

II. COMMUNION ECCLESIOLOGY: THEOLOGICAL AND JURIDICAL

While the church generally recognizes the communion ecclesiology of Vatican II, especially as this was developed in *Lumen Gentium*, there is disagreement concerning the dimension(s) of the church to which the communion ecclesiology applies and how it is to be implemented.

The 1985 Synod of Bishops notes, "the ecclesiology of communion is the central and fundamental idea of the [Vatican II] documents". While recognizing the complexity of the meaning of the term "communion", it states that it is "a matter of communion with God through Jesus Christ in the sacraments"[1]. In addition, the Congregation for the Doctrine of the Faith (CDF) states "the concept of communion lies 'at the heart of the church's self-understanding', insofar as it is the mystery of the personal union of each human being with the divine Trinity and with the rest of mankind, initiated with the faith, and, having begun as a reality in the church on earth, is directed toward its eschatological fulfillment"[2]. The CDF further asserts that, while there is no univocal definition of the term communion and its ecclesiological implications, if it is to serve as a key concept for developing ecclesiology, it must be understood from the perspective of the Bible and the patristic tradition. From these sources, there are two essential dimensions to communion: "the vertical (communion with God) and the horizontal (communion with men)"[3]. The vertical or theological dimension is understood as God's gift to humanity, "as a fruit of God's initiative carried out in the paschal mystery". This dimension is communicated and experienced through the sacraments and has implications for the horizontal dimension as well. Horizontally, communion signifies the particular relationship between believers "which makes the faithful into members of one and the same body, the mystical body of Christ, an organically structured community, 'a people brought into one by the unity of the Father and of the Son and of the Holy Spirit', and endowed with suitable means for its visible and social union"[4].

In addition to the vertical and horizontal dimensions of communion, there are the invisible and visible dimensions as well. "As an invisible reality" ecclesial communion is "the communion of each human being with the Father through Christ in the Holy Spirit, and with the others who are fellow sharers in the divine nature, in the passion of Christ, in the same faith, in the same spirit"[5]. There is an intrinsic relationship between this invisible dimension and the visible dimension of the church on earth. The visible union is manifested in the apostle's teaching, sacraments, and hierarchical order[6]. Together, these dimensions, the vertical and horizontal, invisible and visible, make up communion and the church as a sacrament of salvation. In a communion ecclesiology, it is

1. Bishops' Synod, *Final Report*, in *Origins* 15 (1985) 444-450, p. 448.
2. Congregation for the Doctrine of the Faith, *Some Aspects of the Church Understood as Communion*, in *Origins* 22 (1992) 108-112, p. 108.
3. *Ibid.*
4. *Ibid.*
5. *Ibid.*
6. *Ibid.*

not a question of either/or, but both/and. As *Lumen Gentium* points out, "the society furnished with hierarchical agencies and the Mystical Body of Christ are not to be considered as two realities, nor are the visible assembly and the spiritual community, nor the earthly church and the church enriched with heavenly things. Rather they form one interlocked sacramental reality which is comprised of a divine and a human element"[7]. Whereas there is much agreement on the vertical and invisible dimensions of the communion model, ecclesiological debates frequently focus on the horizontal and visible dimensions, especially as these pertain to "an organically structured community", and a "visible and social union." The institutional and juridical structures within the church, and the exercise of power, authority, and the role and function of conversation within the horizontal and visible dimensions are key concerns in the church today. As Cardinal Danneels noted in his intervention at the 2001 Consistory of Cardinals, the need for participation and "the theme of collegiality in the church is, whether one wants it to be or not, at the top of the agenda in ecclesial public opinion and in the media"[8]. He suggests, "it is necessary to foster a true culture of debate in the church"[9]. This proposal is in stark contrast to the frequently favoured hierarchical and authoritarian approach of the universal church as exercised by the papacy that has predominated the second millennium of the church's existence and culminated with the declaration of infallibility in 1870. According to this approach, "reception" of church teaching is synonymous with obedience. In contrast, Vatican II's communion ecclesiology calls for genuine discernment through conversation among all the faithful, including the magisterium. A central aspect of this conference is to further reflect on the concern to which Cardinal Danneels and other cardinals and bishops make reference. Specifically, how are we to develop a credible model of conversation within the church that maintains the unity of the universal church while, at the same time, respecting the particular church and its unique issues, concerns, and culture? We will first explain two interpretations of this relationship and then investigate friendship as a model of conversation that respects both the vertical and horizontal dimensions of communion and provides a bridge between them.

7. *LG* 8. References to conciliar documents are from the edition by W.M. ABBOTT (ed.), *The Documents of Vatican II*, New York, The America Press, 1966.
8. Cardinal G. DANNEELS, *The Contemporary Person and the Church*, in *America* 185 (July 30-August 6, 2001) 6-9, p. 7.
9. *Ibid.*

III. THE RELATIONSHIP BETWEEN THE UNIVERSAL CHURCH AND PARTICULAR CHURCHES

Joseph Komonchak points out that *Lumen Gentium* clearly articulates the fundamental issue at stake in the relationship between the universal and particular church, but does not provide a systematic explanation of it. In the context of discussing the collegial union among bishops and their presiding over particular churches (i.e., dioceses) paragraph 23 states that the particular churches are "fashioned after the model of the universal Church" on the one hand; however, it is "in and from such individual churches there comes into being the one and only Catholic Church". In the first formulation, it appears that the universal church takes priority over the particular church. In the second formulation, it appears that the particular church takes priority over the universal church[10]. It is the priority given to each formulation, in part, that is at the root of fundamentally different interpretations of a communion ecclesiological model and the nature of the relationship between the universal and particular church.

The CDF takes up this issue. As Walter Kasper notes, one of the Congregation's concerns is "to oppose the thesis of the primacy of the [particular] church as proposed by some theologians"[11]. In so doing, the CDF articulates one interpretation of the nature of the relationship between the universal and particular church. A primary concern of the CDF is with the horizontal exercise of power and authority in the church and is expressed in Section II of *Some Aspects of the Church Understood as Communion* entitled: *Universal Church and Particular Churches*. It maintains that while the concept of communion can be applied analogously to the union that exists among particular churches, and the universal church can be seen as a communion of churches, there is a risk in such an assertion.

> Sometimes ... the idea of a "communion of particular churches" is presented in such a way as to weaken the concept of the unity of the church at *the visible and institutional level*. Thus it is asserted that every particular is a subject complete in itself, and that the universal church is the result of a reciprocal recognition on the part of the particular churches. This ecclesiological unilateralism, which impoverishes not only the concept of the universal church but also that of the particular church, betrays an insufficient

10. J.A. KOMONCHAK, *The Local Church*, in *Chicago Studies* 28 (1989) 320-335, p. 325.

11. W. KASPER, *On the Church. A Friendly Reply to Cardinal Ratzinger*, in *America* 184 (April 23-30, 2001) 8-14, pp. 11-12.

understanding of the concept of communion. As history shows, when a particular church has sought to become self-sufficient and has weakened its real communion with the universal church and with its *living and visible center*, its internal unity suffers too, and it finds itself in danger of losing its own freedom in the face of the various forces of enslavement and exploitation[12].

The CDF's concern seems to be that if the particular church claims too much autonomy, the unity of the church is threatened. History attests to the dangers of such autonomy (e.g., East/West schism and the reformation). The focus of the horizontal dimension of communion in the CDF's perspective seems to be the centralization of authority to preserve unity. While the unity of the church is a concern for all who propose a communion ecclesiology, Hermann-Josef Pottmeyer voices the danger of too much emphasis on unification through centralization in terms of one-way communication whereby there is no authentic conversation between the universal and particular church[13]. In this case, "reception" of teaching becomes obedience alone, without any genuine discernment of apostolicity.

The 1985 Synod of Bishops proposes an alternative view of the relationship between the universal and particular church that puts the horizontal dimension of communion in a different light. While many theologians were disappointed with the *Final Report* in that it did not draw out the full implications of Vatican II, especially with regard to the need for structural reforms within the church, Pottmeyer notes: "the significant and positive result of the Synod is that the institutional side of the Church, and its structures, are consistently and systematically related to the motif of 'communio'"[14]. Its *Final Report* addresses the concept of communion and the concerns with its implementation in the post-Vatican II church. Among its concerns is the relationship between the universal and particular church[15]. To understand the shortcoming of implementing the vision of Vatican II, the Synod observes that one of the primary internal causes

12. CONGREGATION FOR THE DOCTRINE OF THE FAITH, *Some Aspects* (n. 2), p. 109 (emphasis added).

13. See H.-J. POTTMEYER, *Dialogue as a Model for Communication in the Church*, in P. GRANFIELD (ed.), *The Church and Communication*, Kansas City, MO, Sheed and Ward, 1994, 97-103.

14. ID., *The Church as Mysterium and as Institution*, in *Concilium. International Journal for Theology* 188 (1986) 99-109, p. 108.

15. KOMONCHAK, *The Synod of 1985 and the Notion of the Church*, in *Chicago Studies* 26 (1987), 330-345, p. 330, notes that while it is the case that the *Final Report* indicated the implications of a communion ecclesiology for unity and pluriformity in the church, its statements "considerably tone down or even omit many of the appeals for structural change and for greater freedom which reports and speakers had associated with the notion of communion".

for the failure to implement many of the changes initiated by Vatican II is "a partial and selective reading of the council, as well as a superficial interpretation of its doctrine in one sense or another". Due to this partial reading, "a unilateral presentation of the church as a purely institutional structure devoid of her mystery has been made"[16]. This state of affairs is very unfortunate and is somewhat baffling, especially given the first chapter of *Lumen Gentium* that considers the church as Mystery. This focus on the institutional structure of the church, as compared to the church as mystery and sacrament, has affected the perception of the relationship between the universal and particular church. In a subsequent section of the *Final Report* the Synod clarifies how this partial reading has affected the institutional makeup of the church.

After explaining the meaning of communion and its central importance in the Vatican II documents, the Synod asserts that while "the ecclesiology of communion cannot be reduced to purely organizational questions or to problems which simply relate to powers", it is still "the foundation for order in the church and especially for a correct relationship between unity and pluriformity in the church". This unity exists in the faith, the sacraments, and the hierarchical unity, "especially with the center of unity given to us by Christ in the service of Peter, the church is that Messianic people …". However, true pluriformity, which is "true richness and carries with it fullness", is recognized in the particular churches through the one Eucharist. "For this reason, the unique and universal church is truly present in all the particular churches (*Christus Dominus*, 11), and these are formed in the image of the universal church in such a way that the one and unique Catholic Church exists in and through the particular churches (*Lumen Gentium*, 23)"[17]. Given these two dimensions of unity and pluriformity in the church, how does the Synod view the impact of these dimensions on the relationship between the pope and bishops? "The ecclesiology of communion provides the sacramental foundation of collegiality". As a result, "the collegial spirit is the soul of the collaboration between the bishops on the regional, national and international levels". In the strict sense, then, "collegial action … implies the activity of the whole college, together with its head, over the entire church". While affirming that this first collegiality understood in the strict sense fully affirms Vatican II's statement on the relationship between primacy and the College of Bishops, namely, that "a distinction cannot be made between the Roman pontiff and the bishops considered collectively, but

16. BISHOPS' SYNOD, *Final Report* (n. 1), p. 445.
17. *Ibid.*, p. 448.

between the Roman pontiff alone and the Roman pontiff together with the bishops", there is another way to interpret this relationship as well. The "diverse partial realizations" of collegiality are "authentically sign and instrument of the collegial spirit". These partial realizations are recognized both in the Episcopal conferences and Synod of Bishops as well as the pastoral journeys of the pope. The point to be emphasized in distinguishing between the collective actions of pope and bishops together and their partial realizations, either on the part of the bishops individually or the pope acting apart from the bishops, is that both are directed to the communion ecclesiology and service to the church.

The *Final Report* next highlights the importance of the collegial spirit, specifically in Episcopal Conferences. In these conferences, the Synod emphasizes its service to the unity and pluriformity of the church. "In their manner of proceeding, episcopal conferences must keep in mind the good of the church, that is, the service of unity and the inalienable responsibility of each bishop in relation to the universal church and the particular church". The implicit implications of the foregoing statements on the relationship between the universal and particular church seem to be emphasized in the following section that addresses the relationship within a diocese between the bishop, priests, deacons, religious, and laity, in particular women, entitled *Participation and Co-responsibility in the Church*. It notes, "Because the church is communion, there must be participation and co-responsibility at all of her levels". In the concluding statement for this section, part (c) recommends an investigation on the principle of subsidiarity and whether it "can be applied to the church and to what degree and in what sense such an application can and should be made". It seems clear from the Synod's *Final Report* that a major concern among the bishops is the spiritualization or vertical dimension of communion without recognizing its horizontal implications for the institutional and juridical structures within the church[18]. From these concerns and the proposal to investigate whether (and in what way) the principle of subsidiarity can be applied to the church, one could reasonably conclude with a minimalist interpretation that there was concern among some of the bishops over the exercise of primacy and the need for greater autonomy, self-responsibility, and diversity in the particular church[19]. Archbishop Lorscheider at the

18. In J. RATZINGER's response to W. KASPER regarding the relationship between the universal and local Church, we see a clear example of the spiritualization of the vertical dimension of the communion ecclesiological model without recognizing the horizontal implications for governance within the Church, see *The Local Church and the Universal Church: A Response to Walter Kasper*, in *America* 185 (2001) 7-11.

19. See KOMONCHAK, *Subsidiarity in the Church: The State of the Question*, in *The Jurist* 48 (1988) 298-349, p. 321.

Synod voices a stronger assertion of this concern. He notes, "thus it can be said that the universal church is not realized except through the communion of the particular churches and that any supradiocesan ecclesial structure cannot be at the service (subsidium affere) of the universal Church if it is not – at least in principle – at the service of the particular churches and their full realization as Church"[20].

From the above it is clear that there exists some tension with regard to the implementation of the horizontal dimension of the communion ecclesiological model. From the CDF's perspective, the universal church must maintain centrality and authority, seemingly reverting back to a pre-Vatican II ecclesiology on the horizontal level while embracing a communion ecclesiology model on the vertical level. A central virtue in its proposal seems to be obedience to authority, as is clear from some recent magisterial documents[21]. This one-way communication seems to violate the spirit and the letter of a communion ecclesiology. For the 1985 Synod of Bishops the communion model applies both to the vertical and horizontal dimensions for developing an authentic communion ecclesiological model. Authentic conversation between the universal and particular church that extends to all levels of church structure, is an essential component of this ecclesiology. The concept of friendship, as it has been developed in both Ancient Greek philosophy and throughout Christian tradition, has something to offer both the horizontal and vertical dimensions of communion and serves as the foundation for developing a model of conversation between the universal and particular church.

IV. ARISTOTLE: FRIENDSHIP AND THE HORIZONTAL COMMUNION DIMENSION

According to Aristotle, human beings are "*zoon politikon*", social animals, who are directed towards others in community. In and through the *polis* or community, human beings discover their humanity. A central theme in Aristotle's *Nichomachean Ethics* is the role and function of friendship in facilitating the realization of a just *polis*. For Aristotle, there is an intimate connection between friendship, justice, and equality.

---

20. G. CAPRILE, *Il Sinodo dei Vescovi: Seconda assemblea generale straordinaria (24 novembre-8 dicembre 1985)*, p. 299, cited in KOMONCHAK, *Subsidiarity* (n. 19), p. 322.

21. See, for example, *Veritatis splendor* in *Origins* 23 (1993) 297-334; and *Ordinatio Sacerdotalis (Apostolic Letter Reserving Priestly Ordination to Men Alone)*, in *Origins* 24 (1994) 49-52.

We will first define these terms and their relationship to one another, and then discuss their impact on social and political structures.

Aristotle distinguishes between three types of friendships depending on the reason for which friendship is sought. Friendship can be sought for the pleasant, the useful, or the good. Whereas the first two friendships are motivated by one's own pleasure or utility, "the perfect form of friendship is that between good men who are alike in excellence of virtue"[22]. This friendship, while reciprocal by its very nature, is other centered and seeks the good of the person for the person's own sake. In and through this reciprocity, friendship is pleasing to both people in the friendship. Since these friendships are grounded in and seek the good, they are permanent as long as each is committed to the good.

Whereas perfect friendships are rare, particular, and reciprocal, they can function as a basis for a just *polis* because such friendships shape one's perception of how to relate in all relationships. By way of analogy, just as a rock thrown into a pond creates concentric ripples that continue to expand, here the inner circles represent our perfect friendships. The virtues that constitute those relationships expand and shape the way we relate in our other relationships, including those that form and provide structure for the community. Horst Hutter, in his book *Politics as Friendship*, summarizes this idea. "Philia, which achieves its ideal end in perfect friendship, is imperfectly present in all civic and political relationships. It holds states together because it induces harmony and like-mindedness among the citizens. Where it prevails, discord and injustice disappear"[23].

Justice is closely linked to friendship for Aristotle. A friendship of usefulness or pleasure entails using the other as a means to an end. With perfect friendship, however, there is reciprocity whereby one suspends, at least in part, one's egocentricism and recognizes the other as other with his own identity, responsibilities, and needs. Friendship is dependent on justice, and vice-versa. Hutter summarizes the implications of friendship and justice on the socio-political structure. "Friendship as well as justice is dependent upon the capacity to form agreements and to share in a system of law, and every constitution involves friendship insofar as it involves justice. Friendship and justice are coextensive, therefore. They always occur together in every association of men that is a community of Self and Other ..."[24].

22. ARISTOTLE, *Nichomachean Ethics*, trans. M. OSTWALD, Indianapolis, IN, Bobbs-Merrill Educational Publishing, 1962, v. 1156b6 (hereinafter, *NE*).
23. H. HUTTER, *Politics as Friendship*, Waterloo, Ontario, Wilfrid Laurier University Press, 1978, p. 108.
24. *Ibid.* p. 111.

Equality is a key consideration in friendship and justice as well. Perfect friendship is established according to the absolute equality of virtue and merit. While both justice and friendship aim at equality, equality plays a unique role in relation to each. As Aristotle writes, "the term 'equal' apparently does not have the same meaning in friendship as it does in matters of justice. In matters of justice, the equal is primarily proportionate to merit, and its quantitative sense (i.e., strict equality) is secondary; in friendship, on the other hand, the quantitative meaning (of strict equality) is primary and the sense of equality proportionate to merit is secondary"[25]. In this sense, then, equality does not mean of equal status, power, or position, though too much of a disparity between these aspects certainly makes friendships more challenging. Rather, equality that is necessary for friendship is virtue; for only good people can be friends.

For Aristotle, *philia* is "the cement of all social and political relations"[26]. This focus on friendship in Aristotle's thought has parallels with the horizontal dimension of political and social structures and thus, has something profound to contribute to an overly juridical and authoritarian communion ecclesiology that will be explained below. While Aristotle did not draw out the logical conclusions of the impact of *philia* on unjust social structures (e.g., slavery) due to his own social/cultural context, therefore leaving those structures in place, a more nuanced perspective would certainly recognize the implications of friendship, virtue, equality and justice on the very structures themselves. Given the Christian tradition that emphasizes a fundamental equality in dignity of all Christians through baptism[27] and participation in the Eucharist[28], and Catholic social teaching and the principle of subsidiarity or participatory justice, the basis for this transition is evident. Not only does friendship have a crucial role to play in the horizontal communion dimension but also in the vertical communion dimension as well.

V. Aquinas: Friendship and the Vertical Communion Dimension

Aquinas' "Christianization" of Aristotle's *philia* transforms friendship from the horizontal dimension to the vertical dimension. Whereas

---

25. ARISTOTLE, *NE*, vv. 1158b29-33.
26. HUTTER, *Politics as Friendship* (n. 23), p. 110.
27. See J.A. CORIDEN – T.J. GREEN – D.E. HEINTSCHEL (eds.), *The Code of Canon Law: A Text and Commentary*, New York, Paulist Press, 1985, canon 208.
28. See *LG* 32-33.

friendship with the gods is impossible for Aristotle[29], Aquinas boldly states in the *Summa Theologica*, "charity signifies not only the love of God, but also a certain friendship with Him". Human beings' friendship with God "consists in a certain familiar colloquy with Him, is begun here, in this life, by grace, but will be perfected in the future life, by glory". Human beings' final *telos* or *summum bonum* is friendship with God. According to Aquinas, friendship consists of three aspects: benevolence, reciprocity, and communication[30]. Benevolence is not only wishing good for the other, but also actively working to bring about the other's well-being. The joy that friendship brings is not in seeking it for oneself, but through striving to bring joy and happiness to the other person. In and through this striving, a person's deepest self is fulfilled. In terms of our relationship with God, benevolence invites us to seek to do God's will that, inevitably, draws us to a fuller understanding of ourselves.

True friendship must be reciprocal. Reciprocity is dependent, first of all, on receptivity. It is God's very nature to offer his friendship to human beings. It is human beings choice first, to receive that friendship and second, to reciprocate that friendship in and through our loving response to God's invitation. As Aquinas explains, "good will alone is not enough for friendship for this requires a mutual loving; it is only with a friend that a friend is friendly. But such reciprocal good will is based on something in common". This something in common is the good. Without receptivity and reciprocity, charity may be agape, but not friendship[31].

Finally, friendship requires communication or conversation. As Aquinas writes:

> Accordingly, since there is a communication between man and God, inasmuch as He communicates His happiness to us, some kind of friendship must needs be based on this same communication, of which it is written (1 Cor. 1:9): "God is faithful: by Whom you are called unto the fellowship of His Son". The love which is based on this communication, is charity: wherefore it is evident that charity is the friendship of man for God[32].

---

29. ARISTOTLE, *NE* (n. 22), vv. 1158b32-35. See L.G. JONES, *Theological Transformation of Aristotelian Friendship in the Thought of St. Thomas Aquinas*, in *The New Scholasticism* 61 (1987) 373-399, p. 379.

30. AQUINAS, *S.T.*, II-II, q. 23, a. 1. See P.J. WADELL, *Friendship and the Moral Life*, Notre Dame, IN, University of Notre Dame Press, 1989, pp. 130ff.

31. See AELRED OF RIEVAULX who posits friendship as love, which encapsulates agape, but includes reciprocity and mutuality. He writes, "you can have love without friendship, but you cannot have friendship without love" (*Spiritual Friendship*, trans. M.E. LAKER, SSND, Kalamazoo, MI, Cistercian Publications, 1977, 3.2).

32. AQUINAS, *S.T.*, II-II, q. 23, a. 1.

As Paul Wadell writes, "the 'con-vivere' or life together of the friends is a 'conversation' in the good which joins them"[33]. It is conversation that introduces, establishes, and sustains friendship. While Aquinas "Christianizes" Aristotle's friendship, and thus focuses on the vertical dimension of communion, he also points out some implications for friendship and community on the horizontal level.

Through friendship humans can develop a society of friends or community who agree on the good they seek and develop a partnership in the good. Certainly, the church is such a community. A central concern of this paper is how to work out friendship as the foundation for a model of conversation in the relationship between the universal and particular church. To that concern we shall now turn.

VI. IMPLICATIONS OF FRIENDSHIP AS A MODEL OF CONVERSATION FOR THE UNIVERSAL AND PARTICULAR CHURCH

The vertical or theological dimension of communion within the episcopate is clear. Through episcopal ordination Bishops share a fundamental equality in the threefold ministry of the episcopate: as teachers, sanctifiers, and governors[34]. What remains to be worked out is a credible model of conversation between the episcopate on the horizontal or juridical level. Both Aristotle's and Aquinas' visions of friendship have profound implications for developing a model of conversation on this level. We will suggest three implications here, though two significant points must be noted. First, the implications of friendship as a model of conversation between the universal and particular church are far more extensive than we can do them justice in this short space and warrants further investigation. Secondly, since communion is an ecclesiological model that includes not only the episcopacy and papacy, but also more fundamentally, the entire "people of God", this model can be extended to all levels of conversation within the church.

First, friendship has implications for authority within the church. Aristotle, following Plato, makes a clear distinction between tyrannical authority and a just ruler[35]. As we have seen, justice is essential to friendship and governance[36]. What, then, are the implications of justice and friendship for authority within the church? Francis Sullivan describes authority

---

33. WADELL, *Friendship and the Moral Life* (n. 30), p. 136.
34. *LG* 20-21; and *The Code of Canon Law* (n. 27), canon 375, and commentary, pp. 319-20.
35. ARISTOTLE, *NE* (n. 22), vv. 1160a31-1161b10.
36. *Ibid.*, vv. 1161a10, 1161b7-8.

as "the quality of leadership which elicits and justifies the willingness of others to be led by it"[37]. In the case of authority within the church, we speak of "authorities that derive from the Word of God"[38]. Through their episcopal ordination, bishops are authorities within the church that are qualified to both judge and teach the faith. Archbishop John Quinn asserts, "it would be more in keeping with this truth of faith if bishops were seriously consulted, not only individually but also in episcopal conferences, before doctrinal declarations are issued or binding decisions are made of a disciplinary or liturgical nature. In this way there would be a true, active collegiality and not merely a passive collegiality"[39]. An environment that attempts to sway or intimidate bishops from voicing their opinions, such as the Roman Curia is sometimes prone to do[40], does not facilitate just authority and leadership within the church but more resembles tyrannical leadership and coercive power.

Francis Sullivan maintains that an ecclesiology of communion has implications not only for the relationships between the universal and particular church, but for all levels within the church. Such an ecclesiology "calls for an exercise of authority that encourages and promotes the participation of all its members in the life of the Church, according to the gifts and calling that each has received"[41]. He further maintains that "honest consultation" and "sincere dialogue"[42], or what might be referred to as a "dialogue of charity"[43], are essential to such participation.

For both Aristotle and Aquinas, conversation is an essential dimension of friendship. Two important questions regarding this dimension of friendship are the following. First, what is authentic conversation between friends? Second, how is authentic conversation to be implemented in the structures of conversation between the universal and particular church? Authentic conversation requires listening and speaking with a firm commitment to discerning the good and truth. By its very nature, such conversation can affirm one's perspective, but can also challenge one's views

---

37. F.A. SULLIVAN, *Authority in an Ecclesiology of Communion*, in *New Theology Review* 10 (1997) 18-30, p. 18.

38. INTERNATIONAL THEOLOGICAL COMMISSION, *Theses on the Relationship between Ecclesiastical Magisterium and Theology*. See the reference in SULLIVAN (n. 37), p. 19.

39. J.R. QUINN, *The Exercise of the Primacy and the Costly Call to Unity*, in P. ZAGANO – T. TILLEY (eds.), *The Exercise of the Primacy: Continuing the Dialogue*, New York, Crossroad Publishing Co., 1998, 1-28, p. 16. See also, SULLIVAN, *The Magisterium in the New Millenium*, in *America* 185 (August 27-September 3), 2001, pp. 12-16.

40. QUINN, *The Exercise of the Primacy* (n. 39), p. 18.

41. SULLIVAN, *Authority in an Ecclesiology of Communion* (n. 37), p. 29.

42. *Ibid.*

43. ID., *Ecumenism as Communication*, in P. GRANFIELD (ed.), *The Church and Communication* (n. 13), p. 114.

and even cause one to revise one's perspective in a spirit of fraternal correction. This process of conversation requires a firm commitment to the virtues surrounding friendship (e.g., patience, humility, honesty, prudence[44], good will, etc.) and pursuing the good in union with the friend.

In light of this definition of authentic conversation, one can reasonably ask whether or not it is currently exercised in conversation between the particular and universal church. Certainly, there are structures in place that may allow for, and facilitate, this type of conversation (e.g., bishops synods). Many within the church, however, are skeptical as to whether or not the full potential of these structures are being realized and if, perhaps, the structures themselves need to be reformed to facilitate this type of conversation. Archbishop Quinn comments, "Bishops around the world are dissatisfied with the treatment by Roman congregations of episcopal conferences"[45]. Quinn cites Cardinal Aloisio Lorscheider of Brazil who comments, "the decisions of Vatican Council II are not being applied, and we all suffer ... from a distant bureaucracy that is increasingly deaf"[46]. Entering into conversation both with individual bishops and the local bishop synods and taking a fervent interest in the concerns, ideas, and suggestions that they make are essential for authentic conversation.

Third, for both Aristotle and Aquinas, friendship must be reciprocal, i.e., friendship must not only be offered, but also, it must be received. This implies that receptivity is the flip side of reciprocity. If friendship is not received, it can never be realized. The concept of receptivity is an essential component of friendship and conversation and was an essential aspect of deliberation within the early church. As Hermann-Josef Pottmeyer notes,

> Structurally, the early Church was a communion of local churches (communio ecclesiarum) ... The relationship among the local churches and with Rome was not understood in the sense of jurisdictional superiority or subordination. Communication among the churches was achieved by mutual exchange of information concerning their respective traditions of faith and ecclesial customs and by mutual reception. In this way – whether through normal communal relations or at synods and councils – a consensus developed. It took place first among local churches and ultimately within the entire church[47].

On reception in the early church, Yves Congar provides the following definition: "The process by means of which a church (body) truly takes over as its own a resolution that it did not originate in regard to its self,

---

44. See QUINN, *The Exercise of the Primacy* (n. 39), pp. 15-16.
45. ID., *Synod 2001 and the Role of the Bishop*, in *America* 184 (July 30-August 6, 2001) 10-11, p. 11; see also *The Exercise of the Primacy* (n. 39), pp. 7-8.
46. ID., *Synod 2001 and the Role of the Bishop* (n. 45), p. 11.
47. POTTMEYER, *Dialogue as a Model* (n. 13), p. 100.

and acknowledges the measure it promulgates as a rule applicable to its own life"[48]. In his comments on ecumenical councils and their reception in the first millennium, Paul Hinschius asserts: "reception is not an action which brings about validity and constitutes it in principle; it merely declares that decisions have been valid since the beginning; non-reception, on the other hand, does not harm the perfection of validity (juridical validity, that is); instead, it affirms that decisions have been null since their making"[49]. In a communion ecclesiology, receptivity is the result of conversation and consensus. Congar, however, indicates that there are two means for arriving at unanimity within the church that correspond to the two ecclesiological communion models discussed at the beginning of this paper: obedience, and reception or consent. "The first is insisted upon if the Church is conceived as a society subject to a monarchical authority; the second comes into question when the universal Church is seen as a communion of churches. It is certain that this second conception was the one that prevailed effectively during the first thousand years of Christianity, whereas the other one dominated in the West between the eleventh-century reformation and Vatican II"[50]. With Vatican II, the communion ecclesiology on the horizontal level has attempted to reclaim this tradition of reception. According to Pottmeyer, the notion of reception and its attendant concepts of participation and responsibility is why canon law adopted the legal maxim of secular Rome: "'*Quod onmes tangit ab omnibus tractari et approbari debet*' ('What concerns all must be discussed and approved by all')"[51]. This concept of receptivity and friendship is summed up nicely by Hutter in his comments on Aristotle. "The truth, which is also the Good, can only be reached through the dialogue of friendship which must include the viewpoint of everyone concerned"[52].

VII. Conclusion

Friendship as a model of conversation for the horizontal communion ecclesiological model has profound implications for all relationships

48. Y. CONGAR, *Reception as an Ecclesiological Reality*, in G. ALBERIGO – A. WEILER (eds.), *Elections and Consensus in the Church*, New York, Herder and Herder, 1972, 43-68, p. 45.
49. P. HINSCHIUS, *Das Kirchenrecht der Katholiken und Protestanten in Deutschland*, Vol. *III/I*, Berlin, 1879, p. 349, cited in CONGAR, *Reception as an Ecclesiological Reality* (n. 48), p. 66.
50. CONGAR, *Reception as an Ecclesiological Reality* (n. 48), p. 62.
51. POTTMEYER, *Dialogue as a Model* (n. 13), p. 101.
52. HUTTER, *Politics as Friendship* (n. 23), p. 103.

within the church, especially the relationship between the universal and particular church. Some of its implications will entail more fully utilizing the structures that serve as a forum for conversation currently within the church; others will require a fundamental renewal or abandonment of current structures and an implementation of new ones in order to facilitate true conversation within the church. Walter Kasper sums up well some essential points within a communion ecclesiological model: "more collegiality, more say in things and more co-responsibility, greater permeability of information, and more transparency in the decision process than we have at present in our church"[53]. Friendship provides the theoretical, philosophical, and theological foundations for conversation in a communion ecclesiology for the church in the twenty-first century.

Theology Department   Todd A. SALZMAN
Creighton University
2500 California Plaza
68178 Omaha, NE
U.S.A.

---

53. W. KASPER, *Theology and Church*, New York, Crossroad, 1989, p. 161.

THE CHRISTOCENTRIC COMMUNITY

AN ESSAY TOWARD A RELATIONAL ECCLESIOLOGY

If there is any place where understanding theology as conversation can have a real impact, where building a relational, conversational theology has true ecumenical potential, it is in the area of ecclesiology. Most of us recognize, being the post- or late moderns that we are, that metaphysical and ontological types of understanding are easily totalized and so often end up in structures of oppression and domination. It has been contended that understanding the dynamics of conversation and a more relational ontology would ameliorate that danger, particularly as one keeps in mind the role of the preferential option for the poor[1].

Looking at ecclesiology historically, we see evidence for the kinds of things that relational theology and conversation are seeking to combat. We had Donatists arguing about purity with the Orthodox, Protestants fighting about hierarchy with Rome, and Modernists debating about change with Fundamentalists. In our more ecumenically sensitive time, few, I believe, do not see that there were at least some legitimate concerns on both sides of those conflicts, and fewer still would want to see these divisive clashes repeated. However, I would contend that as long as we define church by our understanding and our comprehension exclusively, such clashes are probably inevitable. Thus a more relational approach to theology might be of some assistance. A relational ecclesiology would address the various concerns of those who advocate for differing understandings of church by paying attention to the relational nature of those concerns.

In this paper, I will argue that approaching the church (I won't say understanding the church) relationally as a Christocentric community might provide a way to appropriately balance and constructively critique different ways of conceptualizing the church. By bringing to the fore the relational concerns at stake in talking about church, we can provide some measure of common ground between those who may have radically different understandings without necessarily having to resolve them into one.

---

1. Compare the article by J. Haers in this volume, pp. 1-40.

I will begin by explaining briefly what I mean by "relational theology". From there, I would like to take a relational look at the topic of ecclesiology to show how thinking "relationally" might contribute to a better approach to ecclesiology by discussing three facets of the church as a Christocentric community: its identity, its cohesion, and its boundaries. I will conclude with some brief implications.

I. RELATIONAL THEOLOGY

Ultimately, theology must be relational. This is because human life, in which theology is situated, is relational and because all of our human being, and thus our human speaking, and thus all areas of our human conceptualizing – including theology – spring, as it were, from this font. Relational theology attempts to make use of this phenomenological observation that all human speaking, including speaking about God, arises from human relating. We come to be in a network of relationships, a web of encounters, and Christians usually affirm that God himself is a part of this network in which we become – though of course they differ widely on how they understand this. In light of this, the task of a relational theology is to trace and elucidate the way theological language functions relationally, the shape of the relationships it would seek both to describe and to form. I believe that these relational concerns can be seen as upholding and critiquing conceptualizations of theology in much the same way as being a father would uphold and critique a rational conceptualization of fatherhood.

Relational theology is thus different from more deliberately conceptual theologies such as Process or Liberation. Relational theology could instead be thought of as a proto-theology, a tool for crafting better theological concepts by realizing and appreciating the relational underpinnings of those conceptualizations, underpinnings which are shared by otherwise disparate ways of conceptualizing the Christian faith. It provides a way to relativize the differences between various conceptual systems of doctrine without demeaning or glossing over such differences. We are relational creatures first and rational creatures second. Such a recognition does not make reason and conceptual structures unimportant – we could not do without them – but when such structures clash, it does make them easier to discuss. Disagreements can only be solved on the basis of relationships, and that makes relationships a more fundamental reality than the conceptual structures about which we disagree. Or, in the words of the 18th century Anglican evangelist and theologian John Wesley in his sermon on "The Catholic Spirit", "Though we cannot think alike, may we not love alike? May we not be of one heart, though we are not of one opinion ... If thine heart is as my heart ... give me thine hand"[2].

Aside from this inherent ecumenicity, relational theology has another benefit and that is keeping theology focused on its proper end. Relational theology is not just a theology for better understanding – it is a theology for better relating. It is *sapientia*, not *scientia*. To the extent it becomes a means of control, for com-prehension, grasping, it betrays its purpose. To the extent that it promotes relationships, openness, love, it fulfills the purpose, even though it should do so at the expense of what we normally call understanding. This is due to a peculiar dynamic in relationships and thus in relational theology.

Relationships live on mystery. It is what is yet hidden that enlivens relationship, not what is already known. People that you can figure out easily (or at least you think you can), you find boring and therefore difficult people with which to relate. Thus, in the broadest and most proper meaning of the term, relationships subsist in the "erotic", which is the word we use to discuss the dynamics of how the little-known invites the desire for the yet unknown and which dies when all is ultimately known. In this essay toward a relational ecclesiology, we will always seek to keep that in mind. Thus, it is not my purpose here to help the reader better to understand the church. For though the approach I am outlining does, I believe, give us better means of understanding, it is of the type of understanding that augments rather than detracts from mystery, that doesn't solve it but points more effectively toward it. For who we are relationally, for what love is, ultimately remains – thankfully – a mystery.

Thus, theology ought to pave the way to knowing God, not just knowing about God. This is what Karl Rahner talked about as the mystagogical function of theology[3]. Theology exists primarily to further our relationship with God, and only secondarily to describe God. Of course, relationships cannot exist without some objective knowledge. It would be very difficult, perhaps impossible, for us to get to know someone if we did not know anything about him or her. However, this knowledge is only useful insofar as it serves that more personal, relational idea of knowing, and one might critique any theology not just on the basis of the internal coherence or the external correspondence of its truth claims but

2. J. WESLEY, *The Catholic Spirit* (The Works of John Wesley, 5), Kansas City, MO, Beacon Hill Press, [3]1986.
3. K. RAHNER, *The Dynamic Element in the Church*, trans. W.J. O'HARA, Freiburg, Herder and Herder, 1964, p. 109.

also on the basis of the kind of relationships to God and others that it reflects and engenders.

II. THE IDENTITY OF A COMMUNITY

Turning now to the business of sketching some relational ecclesiological concerns, we begin with the question of identity. Who do we say that we are when we say, "We are the church"? A relational ecclesiology will assume, naturally enough, that this identity must be grounded in the relationships that the church embodies or represents just as it must be for any individual human identity. In our terminology, we point to the vertical dimension by the use of the word "Christocentric" and to the horizontal one with the word "community".

First of all, by addressing the question of the church's identity as a question of relationships, a relational ecclesiology is attempting to do justice to both the biblical witness concerning the church and to the tradition of the church's own reflection on its identity. All of the major biblical metaphors for understanding the church and the majority of "models" used throughout church history boil down to a question of relationships. When we say that the church is the "Bride of Christ", we seem ultimately to be concerned – not with some kind of ontological femininity that the church reflects – but with the shape of the relationship the church has with the One who called her into being. When Paul speaks of the church as the "Body of Christ", he is as concerned with how the members of the church relate to one another as he is with how the church as a whole relates to God. When we speak of the "People of God", we are affirming both what it means to be "a people" (and thus a set of horizontal relationships) and what it means to be a people "of God" (thus establishing the vertical dimension). Even the typically Free Church interpretation of the *ekklesia*, the group of "called-out ones", and the Tridentine Roman Catholic idea of the church as a perfect society were and are ideas that fundamentally rest on relational concerns, specifically whether we come together as a voluntary community or we are born into the group and must strive to make the natural relationships created thereby a reflection of divine reality.

In turning to the question of articulating the relational nature of the church, we have affirmed that the church is a Christocentric community. We will look briefly at each of those two words in turn, beginning with the latter. Fundamentally, the church is a community, a people, understood as a corporate whole composed of individual parts but also as a *gestalt* in which that whole is greater than the sum of those parts. There are other equally valid ways to talk about this kind of a network of mutual relationships, but community seems the broadest term, avoiding the connotations of blood relationship brought about by the word "family" or the connotation of ethnicity brought about by the word "people". The word evokes the ideas of mutual dependency and support, proximity, commonality on some level, and diversity in unity, all of which are important to maintain in any formal conceptualization of the church.

I believe these relational concerns are broadly recognized by Christians, and discussions about the church that explicitly acknowledge these concerns are liable to go further than those that do not. I hear Cardinal Ratzinger's concern for the priority of the community over the individual, but I wonder if his conception does not ultimately undercut the possibility of community[4]. I see us on the same side, with the same relational concerns, however much I may disagree with his particular conceptualization of those concerns.

But the mere idea of a community is insufficient to ground the identity of the church or to distinguish it from other communities. The identity of the church is grounded in the One who called the church into being – Jesus Christ. Thus, the church can be identified as that network of relationships that is centered on Jesus Christ, a Christocentric community.

Of course, what that means – conceptually speaking – is open to great debate[5]. But if the center of gravity is recognized to be Christ, if he is the reality around which the church revolves, and if our discussions of church seek to reflect and foster that mystery, then we can discuss each other's understandings of church in terms of their adequacy to that goal instead of claiming that we are "right" and accusing the other of being "wrong". If we agree that we must relate to God in Christ, then our discussions are over the "how" of that relationship and not over the "what". I can appreciate Karl Barth or Cardinal Ratzinger's radical focus on Christ and still express concern that their conceptualizations make the "gravity" of Christ so high that it threatens to ultimately merge the church into Christ. On the other side, I appreciate the freedom of movement and recognition of open possibilities implied by Process thinking, but there I am concerned that their conceptualization of Christ has insufficient gravity to keep

---

4. As seen, for example, in his work *Church, Ecumenism, and Politics: New Essays in Ecclesiology*, New York, Crossroads, 1988.

5. By the phrase "Christocentric", I do not mean to imply that Christ is the sole focus, but that he is the central one. One thing we learn by relating ourselves to Christ is that such a relationship cannot, by nature, be exclusive but always impels us toward other relationships – such as to the poor and marginalized.

the church from "spinning off into space", as it were. In both cases, agreed-upon relational concerns could guide the discussion of disagreed-upon conceptualizations.

III. The Cohesion of a Community

If the identity of the church as a Christocentric community ultimately flows out of relationships between members and to Christ, then the next question we might ask concerns the cohesion of the church, or how those relationships hold the church together. Traditional Roman Catholicism grounds this cohesion in an ontological view of the Eucharist. Reformed thinking articulated this cohesion in terms of God's will or election. Many strains of Liberal Christian thought find the cohesion of the church in common action or ethics. I have some sympathy with all of these conceptualizations, but I worry that any one of them could end up betraying the relational mystery of the church. I have visited Catholic services in which the members were so focused on the Mass that no one ever bothered to greet me as a visitor. If God's will and election constitutes the church independent of any human response, can we really call that a personal relationship, which in normal understanding always implies some degree of freedom? And if common action is all that binds us, could that not reduce our community to a play in which each member says their lines and performs their action without having to bother with "loving one another from the heart"?

A relational ecclesiology would consider that the cohesion in the Christocentric community comes from the love of the participants – both human and divine – in that community. Specifically, it is the facet of love that we point to in the idea of loyalty. Loyalty is that specific "vector" in love that points to the other-centered nature of our identity. To the extent that I "love" you, we have a relationship. To the extent that I am "loyal" to you, I understand that who you are constitutes a part of who I am and binds me to follow in the direction in which you are heading. In a Christocentric community, it is ultimately the mutual loyalties between Christ and church that bind the community together. We can then discuss to what degree the Holy Spirit is involved and whether Christ does not on some occasions follow the church rather than lead it, but those conceptualizations flow out of a distinctly relational dynamic.

This fundamental cohesion within a community allows us to approach the doctrine, practice and ritual of the church in terms of how they flow from and foster the loyalties discussed above and critique them where they do not. It also allows us to understand that we can be loyal to one another even when we conflict, that our unity comes from our mutual commitment more so than from our mutual agreement. We can serve as one another's "loyal opposition", as it were. These loyalties also serve normalize the relationship from the inside, which is how relational norms always function. Everyone knows that you cannot steal from a friend without someone having to legislate against such an action. Such a norm arises out of the very nature of the relationship we call friendship. Just so, there are actions and beliefs and practices that we want to be able to label unchristian, but the criteria for doing so flow out of what it means to relate to God and to others through Christ, and not out of conceptual referents to either internal coherence or external correspondence. Finally, there is a distinction between loyalties and their expressions. I can say the pledge of allegiance to the American Flag and still not be willing to die for my country. In the same way, to say that the church can only be those who ascribe to a certain list of fundamentals or those who submit themselves to the authority of a certain person is to mistake an expression of the cohesion of the community for the cohesion itself. Such expressions may be necessary but they can also be abused, and most of us would prefer a good loyalty badly expressed to a disloyalty properly expressed as a good one. If that is true for how we live our lives relationally, we need to let it be true of our theology as well.

IV. THE BOUNDARIES OF A COMMUNITY

Finally, we come to another sensitive issue in understanding the church; the understanding of boundary. A discussion of the identity of the church is meaningless unless there is some understanding that the church has boundaries. For something to have an identity "A", there must be the possibility of "not A". Loyalties must be in some measure exclusive. Both imply the idea of a boundary.

An ontological approach to ecclesiology usually understands boundaries to be of the kind that mathematicians call a Boolean variable – a condition that is either true or false. One is either in the church or out of it. A relational approach to the question of boundaries, however, raises a different dynamic. Relational boundaries are more fluid than institutional boundaries, and, moreover, they are boundaries of degree. Recognizing this allows us to maintain a true openness without dissolving all our discussions about church into a wishy-washy, blandly religious ecumenism.

Relational boundaries exist – there are people with whom I have no relationship – but they are rarely marked off in terms of external and fixed referents. We don't carry membership cards that say "Scott's Friend", and the act of taking off your wedding ring does not make you any less married. Real relational markers are internal and fluid, varying as the relationship varies and often only understandable to those sharing the relationship. To use a somewhat trite example, if two people strike up a conversation and decide to meet for dinner, one may say they are becoming friends, but that does not mean we can assume that one will buy the other dinner. On the other hand, should the two be friends who have not seen each other in a long time, one might be delighted to offer the other dinner so that they may have time to talk. So do friends buy dinner for other friends? That depends on the internal and variable referents of a particular friendship. Any relationship that would operate entirely by external and fixed referents, such as the childish, "I'll be your friend but only if you ...", by the very act of doing so obviates what we understand a personal relationship to be.

For the church as a Christocentric community our understanding of boundaries is tied much more to one's orientation toward (or against) the person at the center of the community and not to fixed boundary markers on the edges. Such things as church membership or willingness to recite the creed – or dare I say even something like Baptism – function to express and further our relationships to God and one another, but they cannot, by nature, constitute them. Such referents – such as Baptism – may be exceedingly important, but they derive their importance from their relational context, something that we often refer to by talking about "faith". Adolf Hitler was baptized and Simone Weil was not, but no one wants to judge their relationships to God simply in terms of that boundary marker. And if a non-Christian wants to start attending my church but tells me straight out that he will never believe in the doctrine of Trinity, I do not, on account of that, tell him that he is not welcome. Of course, we may understand Baptism and Trinitarian belief to be necessary and their proper conceptualization important, but only because they express and further a proper relationship to God.

And this brings us to the question of degrees in relationship. Relationships are never, by nature, Boolean variables; they are always matters of degree. Degrees, in this sense, are not just markers along a line (person A is a better friend than person Y) but show the possibility of movement and highlight the idea that relationships depend much more on their trajectories than on their fixed positions. A good friend is not one that has merely reached a certain "degree" of friendship but one with whom one's relationship continues to deepen. What constitutes a "good marriage" after one year may only constitute a poor one after five. The best of friendships are those that can grow deeper. Loving someone entails a desire to love him more.

So, too, is the church when viewed from this relational perspective. Being part of a Christocentric community means being drawn toward that One who is at the center of that community, and so also to others who are doing the same, much more than it means having crossed a certain boundary line. Both the one who takes the Eucharist as a kind of insurance against a God of wrath and the one who takes it because they just "can't get close enough to Jesus" may be said to be "a part of the church", but do we not mean something different thereby in each case? Is not *Unitates Redintegratio* of Vatican II, in opening up the possibility of dialogue with non-Catholic Christians (affirming that we are, indeed, Christian) while at the same time affirming the centrality of the Roman Catholic church, attempting to express just such a relational dynamic, an attention to a center of gravity and the possibility of movement and not to external boundary markers? When non-Christians become Christians, do they not tend to do so more often because they were gently "loved" into the community of faith by degrees than because they simply woke up one morning and "decided to join"? And in our ecumenical discussions, do we not progress further when we realize, "We are both heading in the same direction, so let's help each other get there" than when we say, "We can talk but only after you acknowledge this criteria or that doctrine"?

V. CONCLUSION

In this brief exploration of some of the concerns of relational ecclesiology, I have not attempted to propose anything like a systematic theology or even a better conceptual understanding of the church. I have only endeavored to point out that, if we move our approach to ecclesiology off of conceptual ground (either of the ontological or explicitly non-ontological type) and begin thinking about our conceptualizations in relational terms, then we stand a much better chance not only of getting along with each other but of furthering the very progress of those conceptual concerns. We would laugh at someone who, because she wanted to write the definitive philosophical work on the nature of community, deliberate shut herself up in a cave somewhere so that people would not distract her from her work. Have we not done the same when, in our conceptualizations of church, our agenda has been to protect our view of the church rather than to ever more deeply relate to God and others as the church? Certainly there are better or worse ways of understanding what it means to be a Christo-centric community. But the very nature of that understanding means that I cannot find it alone, and neither can you. We can only find it if we begin looking for it – and living it out – together.

Southern Nazarene University   Timothy J. CRUTCHER
6729 NW 39th Expressway
Bethany OK 73008
U.S.A.

THE CHURCH AS GOD'S FAMILY

PROSPECTS AND CHALLENGES OF THE FAMILY MODEL
FOR CHRISTIAN-MUSLIM RELATIONSHIP IN NIGERIA

INTRODUCTION

"Church as Family of God" is the ecclesiological vision proposed by the Special Assembly of the Synod of Bishops for Africa. In order to highlight its position as the organising metaphor of the Synod's reflection, the Symposium of the Episcopal Conferences of Africa and Madagascar (SECAM), compares it to the notion of *aggiornamento* of the Second Vatican Council[1].

A number of reasons are behind the choice of the family as the central model for the Church in Africa. These reasons converge on the fact that it highlights relationality and belongingness drawn from the experience of daily life in a family. As the Association of Member Episcopal Conferences of East Africa (AMECEA), puts it "the family is the place where the deep African value of life comes to be, is protected and nourished, a place of belonging where each one feels himself or herself to be truly at home"[2].

Beyond its resonance with the culture, family provides a vision for socio-economic and political transformation[3] through pastoral action[4].

---

1. SECAM, *The Church as Family of God*, Accra, SECAM Publications, n.d, p. 9.
2. AMECEA (ed.), *The African Synod Comes Home, a Simplified Text*, Balaka, Montfort, 1995, p. 20.
3. Conscious that the problems in Africa are partly due to the international system, the Synod hopes that a greater family feeling among humanity would move "our Christian brothers and sisters and all people of good will in the Northern hemisphere" to contribute to a "more just international economic order". *Message of the Synod*, in M. BROWNE (ed.), *The African Synod: Documents, Reflections and Perspectives*, Maryknoll, NY, Orbis, 1996, p. 81 (n° 40-41).
4. As Archbishop Monsengwo Pasinya of Kisangani, the Democratic Republic of the Congo (former Zaire) and a participant at the synod puts it, "the Church wants African families to become more and more Church themselves. This Church-Family should transform the society in which it finds itself, into the kind of family-society where there is more fellowship, more equality and more love". Monsengwo Pasinya, quoted in L. MAGESA, *End of Bishops' Assembly: Beginning and Future of African Synod*, in *AFER* 37 (1995) 2-14, p. 9.

Finally, the choice can also be seen as a pro-family stance addressed to the UN sponsored World Conference on Population and Development in Cairo later in the same year[5]. Thus, the family model, besides being rooted in the African experience aims also at addressing issues facing the Church, the African continent and humanity at large.

The family model can also be used to legitimise some negative elements. In his Post-synodal exhortation, *Ecclesia in Africa,* John Paul II identifies two of such possibilities – ethnocentrism and excessive particularism[6]. He does so after enumerating elements like care for others, solidarity, warmth in human relations, acceptance, dialogue and trust, that the model brings to focus. Aidan G. Msafiri speaks of the "negative ecumenical implication" of the model[7] and Cletus Umezinwa sees a link between ethnic politics and the prevalence of family as the root metaphor for political organisation in Africa[8]. However, the synod fathers chose the family model precisely in order to overcome these seeming weaknesses. Their choice seems to have been guided by the principle of homeopathy[9].

The Synod addresses itself to the economic and political elite in Africa. The call is for them to work for the good of all members of the family and to overcome the tendency to privatise their positions of power for personal, ethnic, or sectional interests or those of a narrow clientele. Against the tendency to draw the boundary lines of the family too narrowly, it challenges them to shift the boundaries in order to include *all members of God's family*. According to the Synod fathers, "at this time when so much fratricidal hate inspired by political interest is tearing our peoples apart, when the burden of the international debt and currency devaluation

5. The Synod warned Africans "not to allow the African family to be ridiculed on its own soil" and not to "allow the International Year of the Family to become the year of the destruction of the family". *Message of the Synod* (n. 3), p. 78 (n° 30).

6. JOHN PAUL II, *Post-Synodal Apostolic Exhortation, Ecclesia in Africa,* Vatican City, Libreria Editrice Vaticana, 1995, p. 65.

7. A.G. MSAFIRI, *The Church as Family Model, Its Strengths and Weaknesses,* in *AFER* 40 (1998) 302-319, p. 311.

8. C. UMEZINWA, *The Pre-eminence of Friendship over Justice in Aristotle's Philosophy,* Louvain-la-Neuve, unpublished doctoral dissertation, 2001. It seems to me unhelpful to contrast family and friendship as models. Both stress relationality. As political models, the friendship model can succumb as easily to "cliquism" as the family model to ethnocentrism.

9. Pope John Paul II seems to have been won over. In his speech to the Nigerian bishops on their *Ad limina* visit, he affirms that building up the Church as family would strengthen the foundation of harmony between different ethnic groups, contribute in the avoidance of ethnocentrism and encourage reconciliation, greater solidarity and a sharing of resources among people. JOHN PAUL II, *Address delivered to the Second Group of Bishops of the Nigerian Episcopal Conference,* Vatican City, April 30, 2002.

is crushing them, we, the Bishops of Africa ... want to say a word of hope and encouragement to you, the Family of God in Africa; to you, the Family of God all over the world: *Christ our Hope is alive, we shall live*"[10]. The family model is thus pastoral and political at the same time, local in its provenance but global in its implication.

In this essay, I will try to push beyond the frontiers of this model by exploring its possible contribution to the Christian-Muslim relations in the Nigerian context. Christian-Muslim dialogue occupied one short paragraph in the list of propositions sent to the Pope by the Synod Fathers although this aspect of the life of the Church in Africa hung over the deliberations[11]. In Proposition 41 to the Pope, the Synod fathers called for vigilance "in the face of dangers which come from certain forms of militant Islamic fundamentalism. We must become more vocal in exposing their unfair policies and practices, as well as their lack of reciprocity regarding freedom of worship". Indeed, events in Nigeria and in other African countries show that there is problem in the Christian-Muslim relationship. After the events of the September 11, it is also obvious that the problem is not confined to Africa. There has been a renewed discussion of Samuel Huntington's clash of civilisation paradigm.

A theological engagement with the Christian-Muslim relationship has, of necessity, to move beyond the imagery of a clash although there has been clashes. The paradigm of clash re-presents the two religious traditions as inevitably on a collision course. It is able to do this because of a prior essentialisation of these traditions. Consequently, these traditions appear as monolithic. But in reality, there are different strands of tradition in Christianity just as in Islam, although some of the strands have the weight of antiquity and general consensus behind them. A historical approach however highlights the processes that led to the ascendancy of particular tendencies and traditions. It also brings out the tension that still exists between the different strands Thus, inter-religious dialogue is as much a challenge as intra-religious dialogue. It is from this point that the vision of differentiated unity offered by the family model becomes helpful.

10. *Message of the Synod* (n. 3), p. 72 (n° 2). Let us remember that the synod was held when the news of the Rwandan genocide was emerging.

11. The synod started with the announcement of the absence of the Archbishop of Juba because the Sudanese authority did not allow him to attend. The Synod considered issuing a statement about the injustice done to Christians in Sudan but dropped the idea. Cardinal Otunga is reported as saying that "for so long, we have been the infidels". There are other accounts of the menace of Muslim integrism on the continent. See H. TEISSIER, *Christians and Moslems in Africa: Challenges and Chances for a Genuine Relationship*, in BROWN (ed.), *The African Synod* (n. 3), 152-159, p. 153.

I. CHRISTIAN-MUSLIM RELATIONS IN NIGERIA

The Christian-Muslim relationship in Nigeria has been a problematic one. The problem is presented as the consequence of the proselytising ambitions of both religions in comparison with African traditional religions[12]. In other words, the conflict between Christianity and Islam is inevitable because of their expansionist thrust. A variant of this position holds Islam solely responsible for the intolerance because of its legitimisation of militancy and its vision of theocratic Muslim socio-political and economic arrangement[13]. From a historical point of view, Yusufu Turaki traces the Christian-Muslim problem back to the colonial history of Nigeria. He claims that the policies of the Nigerian State towards Christianity and the Churches in Nigeria represent an extension of the colonial legacy in Northern Nigeria[14]. The conflict is put in a historical perspective. My attempt in this section is to show that the inevitability of the conflict is grounded in history. But there is need to draw attention to events before the colonial period.

Islam has a long history in present-day northern Nigeria[15]. However, 1804 marked a watershed in this history. That was the year of the *Jihad* of Shehu Othman Dan Fodio. As Lamin Sanneh explains, this *Jihad* is unrepresentative of the broad pattern of Islamisation in West Africa[16].

---

12. B. NWABUEZE, *Freedom of Religion, The Religious Neutrality of the State under the Constitution and the Sharia Controversy,* in *Bulletin of Ecumenical Theology* 13 (2001) 91-121, p. 94.

13. As Ibn Khaldun puts it, "If the power of wrathfulness were no longer to exist in (man), he would lose the ability to help the truth become victorious. There would no longer be holy war or glorification of the word of God". He also claims that Islam requires the power of the state in order to enjoin and protect the truth of the Islamic religion. IBN KHALDUN, *Al-Muqaddimah: An Introduction to History,* in L. SANNEH, *Piety & Power: Muslims and Christians in West Africa,* Maryknoll, NY, Orbis, 1996, p. 10.

14. Y. TURAKI, *The Social-Political Context of Christian-Muslim Encounter in Northern Nigeria,* in *Studies in World Christianity* 3 (1997) 121-137, p. 121.

15. As early as the 11th Century, there was already a hostel in Cairo for the students from the Kanem empire. Around late 14th Century, the Kanem rulers moved over to Borno in Nigeria. However, the *Mais,* that is, the leaders of the empire were nominal Muslims. It was during the reign of Mai Idris Aloma (1571-1603) that the majority of leading people of the empire got converted to Islam. See AECAWA, *Christianity and Islam in Dialogue: Proceedings of an AECAWA sponsored conference 22-26 October, 1986,* Ghana, AECAWA Publications, 1986, p. 30.

16. The Moslem scholar al-Bakri, writing in 1067/8 refers to the imposition of Islam in the kingdom of Takrur and the waging of a holy war against infidels. However, the rise of Islamic militancy is dated to the last quarter of the 17th Century (1675). This uprising led by Nasir al-Din failed but it was first in a series of other *jihad* movements. See, N. LEVTZION, *Islam in Sub-saharan Africa,* in M. ELIADE, *The Encyclopedia of Religion,* Vol. 7, New York, Macmillan, 1987, pp. 344-357. This notwithstanding, the position of Lamin Sanneh can be understood as drawing attention to the fact that Islam was carried across the Sahara

Sanneh contends that a pacifist and politically neutral Islamic tradition developed in West Africa from the contact between Islam and the African traditional religions. He draws attention to strong quietist clerical clans, such as the Serakhullé clerics, with a pacifist and politically neutral reputation and a long history of missionary endeavour. In other words, he strives to show that there is another Islamic tradition in West Africa that is not militant[17]. As evidence, he highlights the debate within Islam in West Africa about the appropriateness of theocracy and *jihad* for the spread of Islam. Mohammad al-Kanemi, the ruler of Kanem-Bornu (d. 1838) is said to have challenged Shehu Othman Dan Fodio with regard to the use of the sword for religious purposes. Al-Kanemi's argument as Sanneh presents it, is that religion is a matter of conscience and one cannot "find revealed truth in the blinding flames of fanaticism fed by short-fused *fatwas*"[18]. However, in spite of the debate, the *Jihad* took place and tilted the balance of Islamic tradition in the northern part of Nigeria towards militancy. The event also stands as a symbol of an interrupted programme of Islamisation and conquest stopped by the colonialism[19].

The *Jihad* marks the triumph of one tradition of Islam and the silencing of the counter-traditions that questioned the link between Islam and territoriality and the division of human beings into the *dar al-Islam* and *dar al-harb*. This tradition, Sanneh acknowledges, goes back to the Prophet's own legacy in Medina and Mecca, where he established a territorially defined community, the *dár al-Islám* that is both religious and political and in which the political was the handmaid for the religious. According to Sanneh, Ibn Taymiyya articulated this example of the prophet into a socio-political and religious principle in terms of "divine

by traders and scholars and not by the Arab conquerors. Islam spread through other means from the 8th/9th Century it crossed the desert before the emergence of the militancy.

17. Sanneh's effort here is in line with his belief that the encounter of Christianity and Islam with African traditional religions has endowed them with a tolerant absorptive capacity. "An atmosphere of hospitality has consequently been generated in which Christianity and Islam, along with older religious cultures, are made to share in an open, inclusive community without a repudiation of particularity". This seems like an expression of hope than the reality. See L. SANNEH, *West African Christianity, the Religious Impact*, Maryknoll, NY, Orbis, 1983, p. 87.

18. SANNEH, *Piety & Power* (n. 13), pp. 18, 122. It is also possible to interpret the difference between them not as theological but as political. The *Jihad* had a broad appeal because of the oppression and exploitation of the peasants by the ruling class. In this sense, the *Jihad* was not motivated only by religion. It was also a movement for social reform. See LEVTZION, *Islam in Sub-Saharan Africa* (n. 16), p. 349.

19. During the independence struggles, Sir Abubakar Tafawa Balewa who later became the first Prime Minister is quoted as warning the politicians from the South against provoking the North into continuing its "interrupted conquest to the sea". B.J. DUDLEY, *Parties and Politics in Northern Nigeria*, London, Cass, 1968, p. 22.

562   N.L. NWANKWO

government and prophetic vicegerency"[20]. This link between Islam and territoriality meant the introduction of the *Maliki* variety of the Islamic law. This variety seeks the application of the Islamic law, the *Shari'ah* to every sphere of life and thus beyond the law of personal status and family relations, as in other Muslim nations[21].

The second event of lasting significance is the colonial conquest and the policies it implemented. After the conquest of the emirate, the British replaced the emir and made the new one to swear "in the name of Allah and Mohammed his Prophet" that he would "serve well his Majesty King Edward VII and his representative the High Commissioner of Northern Nigeria" and that he would "obey the laws of the Protectorate and the lawful commands of the High Commissioner ... provided they are not contrary to my religion"[22]. This conquest has wide-ranging socio-political and psychological implications. According to Jibrin Ibrahim, "although the legitimacy of the Emirate aristocracies was derived from the Islamic *jihad* conducted by their forebears, they were constrained to obey a Christian ruler in order to protect their dynastic powers, albeit having negotiated a compromise whereby the Emirates would not be Christianised"[23].

Shielding the northern part of Nigeria from the influence of the Christian missionaries was of interest to both parties. For the Muslims, it preserved a vestige of Islamic theocracy and protected the authority structure of the ruling class. For the colonisers, it was a means of scaling down the influence of the Christian missionaries who, it was felt, failed in introducing Africans to the collective self-discipline but rather encouraged them to challenge traditional customs and authority. But beyond this, as Andrew E. Barnes shows, was a concern that the missionaries were compromising on the racial superiority of Europeans through close association with the "natives"[24].

20. SANNEH, *Piety & Power* (n. 13), p. 120.

21. Writing in 1959, J.N.D Anderson, a member of the panel of jurists appointed by the then Northern Nigerian Government to review the different systems of law in force in the region, named Saudi Arabia, Yemen and Afghanistan as the only Muslim countries that had not confined the *Shari'ah* to the law of personal status and family relations. See J.N.D. ANDERSON, *Conflict of Laws in Northern Nigeria: A New Start*, in *International and Comparative Law Quarterly* 8 (1959) 442-456, p. 443.

22. Quoted in J. IBRAHIM, *Religion and Political Turbulence in Nigeria*, in *Journal of Modern African Studies* 29 (1991) 115-136, p. 128.

23. *Ibid.*

24. A.E. BARNES, *"Evangelization Where It Is Not Wanted", Colonial Administrators and Missionaries in Northern Nigeria During the First Third of the Twentieth Century*, in *Journal of Religion in Africa* 25 (1995) 412-441. Consequently, the first efforts by missionaries from the Church Missionary Society (C.M.S.) in 1890-1892 and in 1900 to bring Christianity to what became the northern part of Nigeria ended in failure. Bishop H. Tugwell

The factors above are behind the particular history of Christian-Muslim relation in Nigeria. In a comparative case study of the Christian-Muslim relationship in Northern Nigeria and Tanzania, Lissi Rasmussen concludes that the two countries represent two contrasting tendencies. "In Tanzania, potentially divisive religious forces have been able to work for the good of the country as a whole, whereas Nigeria has been divided along religious lines"[25]. Religion is central in the articulation of identity and the politics of belonging. Christianity and Islam were both indicted by the Report of the 1987 Political Bureau for delaying national integration because of the competing social orders they create and their definition of community in a way that challenges the national community of Nigeria[26].

As early as 1917, a group of Protestant missions banded together in order to press for greater access to the Northern part of the country. Their argument was that the Colonial Office should follow the same principles of religious toleration in effect in other parts of the empire[27]. Three things are interesting about this demand. First, it remains the line of argument by Christians in their dealing with Muslims. In the debate over the *Shari'ah,* the argument has changed to a call for respect of the secular nature of the Nigerian state and its constitution. These are invoked almost in the same self-assured manner. The difference is that for the early missionaries, even if they anticipated the Universal Declarations of Human Rights, the formulated their demand in terms of the empire as guarantor of the value of tolerance. But, empire can no longer serve this purpose. The constitution has to be pushed up to do the job. The second point is that the embeddedness of the Constitution and the secular political arrangement in the history of Europe is very clear to the Muslims that oppose them. This is the point of the vitriolic polemic of the Muslim Students Society's Press Release during the 1977 *Shari'ah* debate. "We reject in absolute terms the elevation of the English Common Law over the *Shari'ah*. The English Law is relevant only to agents of imperialism and people who have neither culture nor way of life and who are

---

and Walter Miller were both expelled from Kano with the words from the emir, "we do not want you: you can go, I give you three days to prepare: a hundred donkeys to carry your loads back to Zaria, and we never wish to see you here again". W.R. MILLER, *Walter Miller: an Autobiography,* quoted in J. KENNY, *Christian-Muslim Relations in Nigeria,* in *Islamochristiana* 5 (1979) 171-192, p. 172.

25. L. RASMUSSEN, *Christian-Muslim Relations in Africa: The Cases of Northern Nigeria and Tanzania Compared,* London – New York, British Academic Press, 1993, p. 2.

26. FEDERAL REPUBLIC OF NIGERIA, *Report of the Political Bureau,* quoted in IBRAHIM, *Religion and Political Turbulence in Nigeria* (n. 22), p. 117.

27. BARNES, *"Evangelization Where It Is not Wanted"* (n. 24), p. 414.

therefore forced to submit to colonialists and imperialists ...[28]". The third point is that the history of the construction of the Nigerian State pushed religion to a state of prominence while shielding the religions from free interaction as was the case among the Yoruba[29]. The privileges extended to the North by the colonialists shunted the process of learning in mutual co-existence between the religions. There is therefore need for a re-negotiation of the basis of this co-existence.

In sum, we have seen that a combination of historical events has contributed to the particular nature of the Christian-Muslim relationship in Nigeria. This can also be said of the Christian-Muslim relations in other parts of Africa. As Henri Teissier reports, several interventions in the general assembly of the Synod of Bishops for Africa "did not fail to point out the disappearance of certain African Churches under pressure from Islam (North Africa, Nubia), or their dramatic reduction (Egypt), or again the ancient threat against the Christian identity of one people (Ethiopia). Finally there were also expressions of a more general resentment. As Cardinal Otunga said: "for so long, we have been the infidels"[30]. The bishops from different parts of Africa have stories about the difficulties in the relationship with Muslims and about the export of some militant forms of Islam, for example, from Nigeria to Niger Republic. On the Muslim side, there is equally the complain that Islam and Muslims are projected in the media as fundamenatlists, closed to reason, flawed in nature and motivated by hatred and rivalry of the secular west[31]. The result is the radicalisation of both communities towards greater militancy. The challenge then is for both communities to overcome these narratives of victimhood and re-engage themselves in the search for modes of peaceful co-existence and free witness to the truths of their religious traditions.

---

28. Press Release by the Muslim Students Society of Nigeria, Ahmadu Bello University Zaria. For the full text see, J. KENNY, *Christian-Muslim Relations in Nigeria* (n. 24), pp. 191-192.

29. See A.E. AKINADE, *The Enduring Legacy: Christian-Muslim Encounter in Yorubaland*, in *Studies in World Christianity* 3 (1997) 138-153.

30. TEISSIER, *Christians and Moslems* (n. 11), p. 153.

31. This is the argument of E. SAID, in his book, *Covering Islam: How the Media and the Experts Determine how we See the Rest of the World*, revised edition, London, Vintage, 1997. For such an explanation of Muslim fundamentalism as reaction to secular modernity see P. MAR GREGORIOS, *Liberalism and Fundamentalism in Islam and Christianity. How Two Traditions Have Handled Modernity*, in M. DARROL BRYANT – S.A. ALI (eds.), *Muslim-Christian Dialogue, Promise and Problems*, Saint Paul, MN, Paragon House, 1998, 3-13, p. 13.

II. Managing Difference:
The Challenge to Christians & Muslims

The antagonism between Christians and Muslims in Nigeria is often analysed in terms of the politicisation of religion. This theory presupposes that religious problems do not inhere from the religious beliefs and practices but from the wrong use by human beings. I can identify two forms of this politicisation theory. The first is the manipulation thesis. Yusuf B. Usman, from a socialist perspective, argues that the religious problems and riots are the result of the conscious amplification of religious differences and confessional conflicts by the "intermediary bourgeoisie" for political gains. They are results of the political manoeuvring of the elite who fan religious differences as cover-up for their exploitation of the masses.

A variant of this thesis is what I call the diversionary theory. Jibrin Ibrahim draws attention to factionalisation within the Christian and Muslim communities. Among Christians this is represented by the emergence of communities, the so-called "born-again" Christians who believe that Christians of other denominations are heading for damnation and that Muslims are already damned and need urgently to be saved for Christ. Likewise, despite the seemingly united front presented by the press release of Muslim students' Society, Muslims have internal divisions and the struggle between these groups is as bitter and violent as some of the riots directed against Christians. Jibrin Ibrahim gives the example of the struggle for control over the central mosque in Buru between the *Izala* movement and the *Darika* brotherhood. It became so intractable that the "solution" proposed by the Emirate Council was for the Central Mosque to be completely demolished[32]. Consequently, Jibrin Ibrahim argues that religious disturbances result from the diversionary tactics of the religious elite to "create its own political platform as a substitute for an ever-inclusive theology (sic) unity"[33]. In his view, the immediate purpose of heightening "confessional discord is to create unity within each religion as internal conflicts are subsumed in order to intensify the struggle against the 'external enemy'"[34]. Thus the conflicts between Christians and Muslims are strategic moves by religious elite to create common front and paper over the deep cleavages within their communities.

---

32. Ibrahim, *Religion and Politics in Nigeria* (n. 22), p. 123.
33. *Ibid.,* p. 122.
34. *Ibid.,* p. 130.

These approaches have their weaknesses. But they also, in my opinion, raise important points that are often overlooked. They highlight the oversight or over-generalisation involved in the perspectives that see Christianity and Islam as two monolithic blocks that are inevitably on a collision course. This is the simplified map of reality that Samuel Huntington's civilisational approach to international relations presents with dangerous consequences. For Huntington, "in the post-Cold War world, the most basic distinctions among peoples are not ideological, political, or economic. They are cultural". The central concern is with identity. Because identity is defined over and against an other, he immediately confounds otherness with enmity. He projects that "for people seeking identity and reinventing ethnicity, enemies are essential, and the potentially most dangerous enmities occur across the fault lines between the world's major civilisations"[35]. From this perspective, the problems that plague Christian-Muslim relation in Nigeria is the struggle for identity as well as a struggle between the Arabic civilisation and the colonial civilisation. The press release of the Muslim students echoes this view. But Bala Usman and Jibrin Ibrahim point out that the situation is more complex than that. They draw attention to the fact that neither Islam nor Christianity is monolithic nor are their canonical texts and traditions liable to one interpretation. One should rather speak of Islams and Christianities. One form of Islam can be at cross-purposes with another form of Islam, just as one form of Christianity often dares to pronounce on the eternal destiny of members of the other forms of Christianity. These can however disregard their differences and unite in order to fight a perceived enemy. In their view, the question that must be asked is who constructs this common enemy? How, for what purpose and under what circumstances are boundaries set up and dismantled? These are critical questions which broaden the view and the challenge the simple identification of otherness with enmity. It draws attention to the fact that although otherness is given, it is also constructed and thus liable to manipulation. More important for our argument is the fact that the traditions are in themselves heterogeneous. It is not a question of "we" versus "they". Rather, questions and choices have to be made with regard to the "we".

This brings us to a situation where there is need for choices. The question is what choice and commitments lie behind the reflections and what purpose they serve. A choice of peaceful co-existence would require collaborating with those of other traditions that share the same ideals in order

---

35. S. HUNTINGTON, *The Clash of Civilisations and the Remaking of World Order*, New York, Touchstone, 1996, pp. 19-21.

to develop and strengthen institutions and bring about contexts that would structure people's activity towards promoting the peace. The second and similar line of response is educational. It tries to illuminate and untie the narratives of superiority and victimisation, which have developed through time and shape people's perception and responses to each other. The third task is the articulation of a framework for relations, dialogue and collaboration which takes seriously the differences between their religious traditions while valorising their stress on witnessing to the truth of their religious traditions[36]. The family model especially in its extended form supplies this framework.

III. FAMILY: MODEL OF DIFFERENTIATED UNITY

In an ideal situation, family evokes homeliness, warmth, love, care, responsibility, community and solidarity. There is a human longing for these even if different cultures project a different vision of where these can be obtained. In a transferred sense, home is where one is made welcome. Family extends beyond blood relation, it is where there is love, acceptance, care and mutuality. Family is as much a biological given as it is a project. People are born into families and are challenged to make this human group a family.

The family is the basic unit of society but the society is not a family. However, metaphorically, one can look at society in the light of the family. It has to be kept in mind that such moves are meant to re-describe and change the way one looks at the society and to propose a vision to which people would commit themselves. Thus by speaking of the Church as a family or humanity as the family of God, the Synod is metaphorically mapping some values associated with the family on to the Church and to humanity as a whole in order to highlight aspects or projects both for the Church and for humanity at large. The aspects being highlighted are belongingness, mutuality, reciprocity, solidarity, warmth and affection.

There are different models of families. What is common to all is that a family has its boundary. Boundary implies otherness. Boundary delineates

---

36. Patrick Udoma warns against limiting the area of cooperation to the merely mundane concerns such as politics and economics. P. UDOMA, *Christian-Muslim Dialogue in the Twenty-First Century Nigeria*, in *Oracle* 1 (2001/2) 101. Put differently, Lamin Sanneh argues that dialogue and witness belong together. See SANNEH, *Piety & Power* (n. 13), p. 6. See also JOHN PAUL II, *Post-Synodal Apostolic Exhortation, Ecclesia in Africa* (n. 6), pp. 68-69.

and defines belongingness and identity. Boundary marks the distinction between insiders and outsiders. It raises the ethical question about relationship with the other. At the extremes of the broad spectrum of responses are assimilation or indifference. On the basis of a perceived similarity, the effort may be made to assimilate the "other" and make the "other" into an extension of the seemingly identical. Even here, the difference refuses to be obliterated. The process of assimilation presupposes that what is being assimilated is different. At the other extreme of the spectrum is a perception of difference, which turns into indifference or mindless exploitation. In the context of these two extremes, the challenge is to articulate a framework that avoids both – neither seeing otherness as a threat to be conquered nor as difference that leads to indifference, to recognise connection in and through difference.

One strategy for doing this is the recognition of the reversibility of the site of gaze. There is no privileged or absolute position or point of self-identity which reduces every other to the position of absolute otherness. Otherness is shifting and depends on the location of gaze. In line with the problematic of the Christian-Muslim relationship this means that Christians are outsiders as far as Muslims are concerned just as Muslims are outsiders to Christians. The intra-religious factionalisation show this very well. The fact that some Muslims and Christians place their fellow Muslims and Christians outside the Muslim and Christian fold should give pause for thought. It should lead to a reflection on the fact that people are reciprocally outsiders and others to one another.

On the other hand, in as much as the concept of family brings along the idea of boundaries, it offers an example of how boundaries can be transcended without being neutralised. Families are made up of individuals bounded off in space and time by the body. Each human face is distinct from the other. Yet, in the context of a family, individuality, difference, boundaries and diversity are the building blocks for harmony. They bring some difficulties, but the joy of the family lies in resolving these conflicts. Ideally, the family is the space for love, where people are acknowledged and accepted as they are, where "otherness" or individual differences are not threats to be overcome or problems to be solved but cause for celebration, for complementariety and solidarity. It is this possibility of the harmonisation of differences, the preservation of unity and identity in the midst of difference that gives cutting edge to the model of the family for reflecting on the Church and especially for Christian-Muslim relation.

The fact that some families fall short of the model does not detract from the dynamism that it embodies. This dynamism can be translated into the formula that had been used to express the vision of the ideal of African communitarian life: "I am because we are, and we are because I am". Here, the implication of the simultaneous affirmation of self and the community comes out clearly. The self is not a fully constituted autonomous entity that freely chooses to belong or to be connected with others. Rather, the self is constituted a self in and through the interconnection. The stress of the Synod on the model of family is thus a way of re-commending this vision of communitarian life characterised by reciprocal relationship between the self and the society. However, the Synod also transposes the principle of unity from the ancestors to God and consequently extends the scope of the interrelation and connectivity. It therefore calls for unity of humanity as members of God's family.

A reflection on the Igbo word for the family offers an insight into the relational scheme within which the family is embedded among this group in Southeastern Nigeria. For the Igbo, the family is "*ezinauno*"[37]. This is a compound word made up two terms – "*ezi*" (the outside, the road, the clan) and "*uno*" (the house, the home). Their combination shows a linguistic attempt to show the connectedness of each family group with the whole of the clan. "*Ezinauno*" evokes the inside and the outside, the home and the road that leads to and connects other homes. It is one of the points of intersection between the transcendent and the immanent and the gateway of the ancestors back to life. In this sense, it is very close to the imaginary of the crossroad as the "hotspot of diversity"[38]. Diversity and differentiation constitute the family. It begins with exogamous marriage. It spans over time and space to unit peoples by cementing a bond of relationship. This relation is not an addition to the family. It rather constitutes it. In other words, for the Igbo, *ezinauno* is the meeting point between inside and outside, the point constituted through the intersection of a network of relations that extends beyond the mundane and the material to include the ancestors and the spiritual.

The claim is neither that the Igbo are fully aware of this linguistic import of *ezinauno* nor that this pattern of thought is to be found in all African languages. The point is rather that this linguistic analysis offers a vision, a scheme of relations, and a way of dealing with boundaries, otherness and differences. However, the affective colouring of this relation

37. For a detailed development of this thinking see E. CHUKWU, *Ezinauno, The Extended Family of God, Towards an Ecological Theology of Creation*, Unpublished Doctoral Dissertation, Leuven, K.U. Leuven, 2002.
38. AKINADE, *The Enduring Legacy* (n. 29), p. 139. He alludes to the reflection of Chinua Achebe on the Crossroad, See C. ACHEBE, *The Crossroads in our Cultures*, in *The Sunday Time* (September 12, 1989) p. 18.

changes as one moves from the "*umunna*" – the kindred to the "*onuma*" – the clan. With the socio-political arrangement in villages, towns, local government areas, state and nation, this relations changes from solidarity to tolerance or worse to suspicion as one moves from the smaller to the larger group.

In sum, although the family offers the vision and possibility of integrating differences into harmony, the fact remains that in real life, human beings do not always exhibit that breadth of sensitivity and awareness of connectivity. While the connectivity may be acknowledged, it does not necessarily translate into moral commitment to solidarity especially with those who are at the periphery or outer margins of the nexus of relationship. Often, solidarity is limited to those manifestly sharing something in common. From this perspective, the family model proposed by the African Synod, is a call to a new form of consciousness and narrative memorialisation of belongingness and integration. This is the challenge that the model presents.

IV. FAMILY, POWER AND VIOLENCE

In spite of the longing for security, love, acceptance and belongingness and the co-ordination of these with the family, it is evident that the family is sometimes the site of much violence, physical as well as symbolic. The sustained feminist critique of the patriarchal system of social organisation and symbolic order has drawn attention to the legitimisation of the asymmetry of power and symbolic violence that takes place within the family system.

From the feminist perspective, family violence is not simply due to individual pathology. It is rather the product of the social structuring of gender relations. Nonetheless, it is like a profanation. It is the enactment of what is supposed not to obtain in the family. The fact that it takes place in the family shows the embeddedness of the family in the social context. Thus the campaign against family violence aims at not only legislatively making such acts sanctionable but also at changing the scheme, visions or categories that people draw from in their interrelationship. It aims at changing the symbolic order, that is, the system of meaning and symbols accumulated through history and transferred down the centuries which guide people as they negotiate reality. This task of changing the symbolic order is not only achieved through re-imagining the family, proposing visions and ideals for the family, but also through legislation and the commitment to enhancing the status of women in the society and protecting the rights of children.

The implication of the above for the conversation between Christians and Muslims is clear. This conversation has to take place on different levels. So far, we have explored one aspect of that conversation which is the articulation of a framework within which differences would cease to be perceived as threats, or in the worse case scenario, as enmity, but as a possibility for mutual and reciprocal enrichment. That is the aim of the reflection on the family model. But that reflection also highlights the need for socio-political and cultural engagement as part of the conversation. The inherited form of understanding of family and family relationship, what is designated as patriarchy by feminists, contributes among others to this violence. In like manner, the history of the relationship between Christians and Muslims shapes the way both groups respond to each other. Changing patriarchy is not achieved only through the proposal of a more inclusive vision but also through legislation and socio-political engagement. In like manner, Christian-Muslim relations require a partnership of Christians and Muslims of like mind to prevent their co-religionists of other persuasions from plunging the groups into destructive quest for power and domination. There is also need for joint effort to overcome the socio-economic and political situation that dispose people to violence.

V. CONCLUDING REFLECTION – CHRISTIANITY AND ISLAM: CLANS IN GOD'S FAMILY

The necessity of the Christian-Muslim dialogue is based on many factors. These range from the fact that all are created by God to the pragmatic necessity of finding negotiated solutions to common problems. Besides, there are many elements common to Islam and Christianity. But it is helpful to pay attention to the paradox pointed out by Lamin Sanneh who claims that Christianity and Islam are united perhaps less by things they have in common than by what divides them[39]. In a sense, the claim that both Christians and Muslims belong to clans in God's family is already a narrative of unity. However, it is an expression of what already is and what the communities are called to grow into.

This requires, as the African Synod puts it, collaborating with all Muslims of good will, reaching out to others even when this is not reciprocated and building bridges as the opportunity presents itself. There is also need to strengthen the social structures in order to make them able to contain the strain on it by groups. This has to be accompanied by dialogue

39. SANNEH, *Piety & Power* (n. 13), pp. 6-7.

and collaboration in order to know more about the different traditions, to overcome the mistrust and the mountain of prejudices that have built over the years. The guiding vision is surrender to the will of God in order to realise peace which is God's wish for all in God's clan.

Faculteit Godgeleerdheid   Nchekwube Lawrence NWANKWO
K.U. Leuven
St.-Michielsstraat 6
B-3000 Leuven
Belgium

"ABSENCE MAKES THE HEART GROW FONDER"

TOWARD A POSTMODERN THEOLOGY OF MARRIAGE IN AMERICA

I. INTRODUCTION

Postmodern theory has put contextuality and historicity at the center of its analysis of ideas, nature, truth and meaning. There is a deep appreciation of the relative composition and application of all human discourse and action. Since there is general acceptance among scholars and intellectuals across disciplines about the merits of such a claim, one may legitimately ask: is it ever possible to make any absolute, objectivist and essentialist claims about truth, meaning and significance that would be applicable always regardless of place, time and circumstance? This late twentieth-century philosophical concern is at the heart of the current American Catholic Church tension with the Vatican hierarchy over a number of doctrinal and praxis issues. But none is more heated and significant for the future complexion and vitality of American Catholicism than that over marriage and its associative behavior: the family is, after all, the "domestic church" and the most basic cell of society.

One fruitful way to abate some of the tension between American Catholic belief and praxis about marriage with the Vatican is to adopt a "conversational approach". The dialogue would be between the traditional vision of marriage and the stark realities of American family life: high divorce rates, many out of wedlock pregnancies and a general climate of distrust in relationships and society. It is clear that most Catholic Americans ignore the Church on marriage and sexual issues preferring to work out of what they perceive as a more "realistic" approach – one that deals with the concrete facts of the American experience as they encounter it in their own lives. It seems clear that such a situation will have a bleak future, barring some redirection, for the Catholic faith in the United States. An unbridgeable divide, at least in praxis, if not in theory, is the assured outcome between official church teaching and Catholic life. This result would be detrimental to the spiritual lives of American

Catholics because faith can never thrive without its grounding in tradition and community. Moreover, the reflection of the Magisterium will be a bloodless entity without the input from people's lived lives of faith. Therefore, it behoves American Catholic theology to attempt something of a rapprochement with the Church teaching on the sacrament of marriage. Thus, this investigation will attempt to make sense of that teaching (which has to undergo something of a renaissance itself) through a revaluation of it in light of interdisciplinary postmodern and American insights.

To approach such an ambitious enterprise with any hope of making a real contribution to appreciating a sacrament of marriage in America, it will be necessary to establish parameters for the consultation of data and the questions to be addressed. After all, it is a multi-dimensional phenomenon which could legitimately include numerous references to sociological, psychological and philosophical research as they relate to the faith-history nexus as expressed in intense personal relationships. Therefore, this essay will traverse only the four most salient questions about Catholics and their potential relationship to a sacramental theology of human relationships: first, a working theological method in the "conversation" tradition will be outlined so as to provide a heuristic tool for the analysis; second, a survey and analysis of the current state of marriage in general and the Catholic association in particular as understood from a social science perspective; third, a historical overview and contemporary summary of the sacramental theology of marriage from the New Testament origins to "personalist" approaches of the Vatican and Post-Second Vatican Council period; finally, a survey of the challenge of postmodern philosophy, an outline of the contemporary attempts at a postmodern theology of marriage and a postmodern conversation about the future of the sacramental theology of marriage as an encounter with God in the third millennium will be presented.

II. THE CONVERSATIONAL METHOD

One of the primary tasks of theology is to reflect on experience. Experience has always had a function within theology and the Christian life. As a matter of fact, the bringing together of human experience and the Christian story is the task of theology generally[1]. The magnificent success

---

1. E. LEONARD, *Experience as a Source for Theology*, in J.P. BOYLE – G. KILCOURSE (eds.), *The Sources of Theology* (Current Issues in Theology, 3), Macon, GA, 1988, pp. 44-45.

by patristic theology of blending biblical revelation and Greek philosophy to meet the pastoral and intellectual needs of early Christianity provides eloquent testimony to how successfully this can be done. Faith and
reason (experience) are understood as in a relationship of complemen-
tarity. The notion of double truth, one for faith and another for reason, is
rejected. However, the notion of experience as a viable part of the theological process eventually falls under suspicion because of perceived
unmanageability, unpredictability and propensity to err due to personal
finitude and sinfulness of the individual Christian. This aversion to experience seems especially pronounced in the post-Tridentine church and the
challenge of modernism. In experience's place, the church offered the
unchangeable and certain contents of revelation as found in the Bible and
reverently interpreted by the dogmatic, magisterial and papal traditions for
theological reflection with the assumption of universal applicability.

One of the outstanding events of Catholic theology in the 20th century
is the surmounting of Neo-scholasticism. Karl Rahner is one of the theologians who made this breakthrough possible[2]. Rahner's approach is a
reflection on the human consciousness of a transcendental orientation
toward mystery. The transcendental method investigates the conditions of
the possibility of knowing self, world and God. This is also known as the
"turn to the subject" or the "turn to experience" in theology. Rahner
taught the Catholic world to look for God in everyday life because the
God revealed in Jesus Christ has shown that human existence is already
with God because of humanity's transcendental orientation to the divine
mystery and the "supernatural existential". This theological approach has
been interpreted as being more "existentially attuned" to the totality of
faith and the totality of being human. Rahner says, "kerygma will be more
worthy of belief through the overt connection of doctrine with human
experience"[3].

The return of experience to theology fits well with the Catholic doctrine
of the "sense of the faithful" or *sensus fidelium*. The "sense of the faithful" is the teaching that the entire church is animated by the Holy Spirit
which guides the clergy and laity into the truths of salvation. The church,
as a whole, is preserved, in infallibility, when a given belief is generally
accepted by all. The People of God, as such, in its faith in Christ and
its preaching of him are infallible[4]. The "sense of the individual" or *sensus*

2. W. KASPER, *Theology and Church*, New York, 1989, p. 1.
3. K. RAHNER, *Theology and Anthropology*, in *Theological Investigations* 9 (1977)
p. 83.
4. M. SCHMAUS, *Dogma. IV. The Church. Its Origin and Structure*, London, 1989,
p. 202.

fidelis is a related notion in the experiential search for the truth of the faith but is grounded in its ecclesial dimension. One learns to interpret the event of revelation and salvation in one's own life through the narration of the ecclesial body and the individual members about the same events. This *sensus fidei* is the imaginative capacity that enables the believers' attempts to make sense of the God reaching out to them through Christ and the Spirit in daily life and to be truly shaped by these new experiences to such an extent that the received tradition in turn is corrected by new insights and makes available new and enriching possibilities[5]. This "sense of the divine" sensitizes the imagination of the believer to pay attention to all things because anything has the potential (like a man tortured on a cross) to mediate symbolically the divine[6]. What this means for believers when they attempt to articulate personal faith is that they do have real teaching authority which comes from the dignity of being recipients of God's revelation[7].

The assumption behind Rahner's transcendental or anthropological approach and the analysis of the individual believer's "sense of the divine" is that, at the heart of the theological enterprise is a dialogue between the formal contents of the faith and its connection with the lived life of faith. There is a process of correlation or conversation between life and religion in which a common point of reference and idiom must be found. Theology must be attentive to the "contemporary plausibility structures" to avoid appearing anachronistic and irrelevant[8]. Plausibility gives the dialogical model the potential to reach people in language and life terms that can make the faith real for believers and credible for consideration; however, it can also lead to theology being corrected by experience or the results of the secular investigations, particularly the social sciences[9]. As David Tracy has said, the conversation approach for religion must allow for genuine dialogue on the meaning and truth of their classics and the applicability or nonapplicability of their strategies for resistance in the particular life situation[10]. Theology, for today, must keep the "conversation going" if it is to have any hope of changing the

5. O. RUSH, *Sensus Fidei. Faith "Making Sense" of Revelation*, in *TS* 62 (2001) 231-261, pp. 236-239.
6. *Ibid.*, p. 247.
7. *Ibid.*, p. 261.
8. J. COLEMAN, *Every Theology Implies a Sociology and Vice Versa*, in M.H. BARNES (ed.), *Theology and the Social Sciences*, Maryknoll, NY, 2001, p. 22.
9. BARNES, *Introduction*, in ID. (ed.), *Theology and the Social Sciences* (n. 8), p. xiv.
10. D. TRACY, *Plurality and Ambiguity. Hermeneutics, Religion, Hope*, Chicago, IL, 1987, p. 84.

thinking and living of people in the real world and, consequently, presumes no definitive resting point.

One of the most pervasive and influential experiences of human existence is family life in general and married life in particular. Pope John Paul II notes the role of the "sense of the faith" in discerning how marriage and the family are to be preserved and realized[11]. The laity has the specific role of interpreting the history of the world in the light of Christ insofar as they are called to illuminate and organize temporal realities according to the plan of God and Christ[12]. These experiences must be part of any serious analysis of existence and its possible connection with the divine. Each person is so deeply influenced by these social networks in how he or she views the self, the world and others that they will, in their own way, provide valuable sources of information for theological reflection on God, relationships, love, hate, commitment and abandonment. It seems fitting to look at the American cultural situation of marriage from the perspective of the social sciences first to try to listen carefully and respectfully to what the "other" has to say before bringing it into "conversation" with the tradition and seeing what it gives rise to.

III. AMERICAN AND CATHOLIC FAMILIES

Francis Fukuyama, a social scientist at George Mason University, has said that the cultural shift in the developed world that has happened between the early 1960s and the mid-1990s should be recognized as on par with the two previous epochal changes in human history: hunter-gatherer to agricultural society and agricultural to an industrialized society. This "third wave" happened quickly and is regarded as the technological or information age where the values of freedom and equality achieve new found expression. This cultural shift has seriously undermined the modern norms that governed social and family life and has required America to embark on a radical re-norming for the functioning of society, politics and family/sexuality. The changes have been so extreme that Fukuyama has characterized them as forming the "Great Disruption" in life in the developed world[13].

11. Pope JOHN PAUL II, *The Role of the Christian Family in the Modern World. Familiaris Consortio*, Boston, 1982, p. 15.
12. *Ibid.*, pp. 15-16.
13. F. FUKUYAMA, *The Great Disruption. Human Nature and the Reconstitution of Social Order*, in *The Atlantic Monthly*, May, 1999, p. 55.

The Great Disruption has manifested itself in the deterioration of foundational cultural conditions. The numbers from the United States Census Bureau are telling: the divorce rate today is twice what it was in 1960; the number of cohabiting couples has risen 800% since 1970; the number of households with a child has gone from 50% in 1960 to 34% in 1998; the percentage of children living in a traditional nuclear family went from 88% in 1960 to 68% in 1998 and the number of births to unmarried women went from around 5% in 1960 to nearly 33% in 1998[14]. Part of all these shifts, according to Fukuyama, is a movement toward less permanent involvement with people and a preference for smaller groups. He describes this as the advent of "moral individualism" and the "miniaturization of community"[15]. This disruption means the end of the modern age with its social bonds and common values that kept freedom in check and protected people (especially women and children from abandonment) from harm through social pressure and chastisement for transgression to a reorientation based on individual choice and personal taste with much less regard for the wider social impact of one's actions. Government, bureaucracies, corporations, trade unions and religion have their authority significantly displaced by the authority of the self. This type of self-organization is guided by internal rules and informal norms[16]. As a result, there is a continual tension in this age between the social nature of the human being to be part of community but wanting at the same time to have ample room for personal autonomy.

There are no easy causes to point to when trying to ascertain just what exactly are the driving forces behind this social change of course. One could probably list many possible contributors in light of American religious tradition, law, history, economics, political experience, geography, climate and the social impact of generations of immigrants. Yet, the greatest contributors to the revaluation of marriage and the family seem to be limitable to six. First, there is a changing conception of work. Work has drifted away from being a physical endeavor that produces goods to an intellectual undertaking with an orientation toward services. One of the major outcomes of this change has been the entrance of women in large numbers into the workplace to fill not only clerical positions but professional and managerial ones as well. Second, there is the economic reality that a single income can no longer support a married couple and their

14. D. POPENOE – B. DAFOE WHITEHEAD (eds.), *The State of Our Unions 2000. The Social Health of Marriage in America* (The National Marriage Project), New Brunswick, NJ, Rutgers – The State University of New Jersey, 2000, pp. 1-36.

15. FUKUYAMA, *The Great Disruption* (n. 13), p. 72.

16. *Ibid.*, p. 56.

children. Men's salaries, in other words, have not kept pace with inflation. This has created the need for women to work outside the home to supplement the family's income and to achieve the required level of education to do the job. Third, the opportunity and need for women to enter the workplace has gained a further boost from the feminist movement and its clarion call for equal rights as citizens, both at home and at work. This has had a freeing effect on women in that they are no longer total dependents on their husbands and so have more choices. Women's entrance into the workplace and universities is considered, by many, as a contributing factor in the increase in divorce. Fourth, advances in medicine have contributed to the changes in the technological age. The invention of reliable birth control and the increases in human longevity have changed the marriage/sex relationship drastically. With regard to the former, it has meant the possible disconnecting of sex from marriage and childbirth; with regard to the latter, it has meant the reconsideration of a marital vow that could now mean a union of sixty years in duration. Fifth, the government has had a role in this reorientation of marriage as well. Its expansion of welfare support has meant that family and social support for a struggling family is no longer crucial. In its own inadvertent way, it may have rewarded illegitimacy and encouraged complacency for many. Also, it probably did a disservice to marriage by legalizing "no fault divorce" and severing the decision to end a marriage from its social aspects. Sixth, and really part of the preceding five, is America's deep love of rugged individualism. This individualism, today, as opposed to the past, has come to question all forms of authority, which has enfeebled the bonds that hold families, neighbourhoods and nations together over long and difficult challenges[17]. This effect has produced what some have called a "low commitment culture". A mating culture, such as this, readily accepts cohabitation and unwed pregnancy as viable options to embrace along with marriage: "sex without strings, relationships without rings"[18]. Often, the media is charged with contributing unrealistic notions of love and glamorizing independence to an extent detrimental to others and so valorizing non-commitment.

Gallagher and Waite have described this form of egoism as "psychological gentrification". It is a form of individualism that is focused on self-fulfilment and perceives the values of autonomy, independence, growth and creativity as of the greatest worth for human flourishing. These convictions have given rise among many to the idea that marriage

17. *Ibid.*
18. POPENOE – DAFOE WHITEHEAD, *The State of Our Unions 2000* (n. 14), p. 2.

may be a trap because it reduces options[19]. Thus, for those deciding to enter marriage under these individualistic terms, its main purpose and benefit is emotional gratification (romance and support) and is reckoned as a private matter that will tolerate no outside intervention[20]. Warmth and intimacy are what is valued most in the relationship (which has brought newfound expectations, tensions and risks)[21]. In such a configuration, the need and role of children is downplayed. Nearly seventy percent of Americans polled believed that marriage is about something other than children[22]. Marriage is no longer "child-centered". This focus on feelings has provided the opportunity for serious discussions about the legitimacy of gay marriages. In short, all of these forces impact American life, but religion in particular.

American Catholicism is a religion that esteems tradition and its venerable past but lives in a society that oftentimes values the present over the past in many of the same ways just discussed above[23]. Sometimes, it is difficult to distinguish a Roman Catholic from a contemporary non-Catholic, which would not have been very difficult thirty years ago when Catholicism was still living in insular ghettos and had its distinctiveness well in tact[24]. Divorce, as just one example, happens just as often in Catholic marriages as others[25]. There is a segment in today's Catholic America that is reluctant to adhere to authority, especially Roman, and that finds traditional Catholicism very unappealing[26]. Furthermore, the wider Catholic community is indecisive about its Catholic identity as well. Many church-going Catholics disagree with official church teaching on premarital sex, homosexuality, the mediation of the priest for reconciliation, birth control, the role of women in the church, capital punishment and nuclear arms[27]. The dissent is even more severe among what are called "cultural Catholics" who do not attend church regularly but consider themselves Catholic because of their baptism and family roots in the faith. While there are Catholics who do give unswerving loyalty to

19. L.J. WAITE – M. GALLAGHER, *The Case for Marriage. Why Married People Are Happier, Healthier, and Better Off Financially*, New York, 2000, p. 1.

20. *Ibid.*, p. 176.

21. *Ibid.*, p. 17.

22. POPENOE – DAFOE WHITEHEAD, *The State of Our Unions 2000* (n. 14), p. 30.

23. C. GILLIS, *Roman Catholicism in America*, New York, 1999, pp. 6-7.

24. J. CAPUTO, *Philosophy and Prophetic Postmodernism. Toward a Catholic Postmodernity*, in *American Catholic Philosophical Quarterly* 74 (2000) 549-567, p. 551.

25. GILLIS, *Roman Catholicism in America* (n. 23), p. 164.

26. T.P. RAUSCH, *Reconciling Faith and Reason. Apologists, Evangelists, and Theologians in a Divided Church*, Collegeville, MN, 2000, p. viii.

27. GILLIS, *Roman Catholicism in America* (n. 23), pp. 1-2.

the pope and do try to live the counter-cultural lifestyle of Catholicism (such as those advocated by Mother Angelica and her EWTN television network and the conservative Catholic journal *First Things*), they are really in the minority. Many Catholics, reflecting their American culture, use a combination of personal beliefs and experiences as norms to justify practices, moral positions and theological interpretations that are at odds with Rome but seem reasonable to them[28]. Moreover, this situation among Catholics seems to confirm the findings of Paul Heelas about the general New Age movement's influence on American religion (and Western Europe): there is a shift toward detraditionalization, individualized, eclectic spiritualities in service of personal enhancement, outside and inside of conventional religious institutions and continuous with contemporary consumerist life industries[29]. As American Catholics continue their embrace of individuality, it really makes it impossible to give a definitive portrayal of the Catholic faith that will hold for all of them. Pluralism has definitely found a home in the American Catholic experience.

IV. THE CHALLENGE OF POSTMODERNISM

Kenan Osborne begins his book on a theology for the third millennium by stating that there is no doubt that postmodern philosophy has already reshaped the thinking of many people in the West and will play a major role in the 21st century. America is certainly no exception. If Christian theologians, he continues, do not avert to this and do not seek a bridge between postmodernity and sacramental theology, it would be profoundly shortsighted[30]. While nearly all scholars agree that America and Europe have entered the postmodern period in intellectual and cultural history, there is hardly unanimous agreement as to what the term means. However, some working idea of the phenomenon will have to be chanced for analysis. Therefore, postmodernism could be understood as a critique of foundationalism, such as rationalism, universalism, objectivism and certitude about truth and knowledge in the Enlightenment mindset. It is a radical questioning of all established beliefs and ideas. The postmodern consciousness constitutes a radical break with the assumptions of

28. *Ibid.*, p. 128.
29. R. LITTLEJOHN, *Comparative Moral Philosophy. Learning Ethics Through Other Cultures*, in *The Council of Societies for the Study of Religion Bulletin* 30 (2001), p. 12.
30. K.B. OSBORNE, *Christian Sacraments in a Postmodern World*, New York, 1999, p. 1.

previous generations[31]. Particularly, it is critical of the tendency of modernism to claim an Archimedean point upon which to judge, as if beyond space and time, all things. The positivism and empiricism that have dominated much of scientific theory and method is the driving force of this modernistic thinking[32].

Postmodern thought has made its presence known not just in academic and scholarly analyses but also in the wider realm of culture. Postmodernism is said to describe the emergence of a social order in which the importance and power of the mass media means that they govern and shape all other forms of social relationships[33]. The idea is that popular cultural signs and media images increasingly dominate an individual's sense of reality and the way that one defines oneself and the world. Individuals consume images and signs for their own sake rather than for their usefulness or for the deeper values which they may symbolize. Popular culture is transfixed by surface and style and, oftentimes, at the expense of content, substance and meaning[34]. It is the advent of the age of "virtual reality". There is an avoidance of realism. Truth claims are contingent and probabilistic. There is also a mixing of styles and genres to create new sub- and pan-cultural identities in postmodern culture which is sometimes referred to as *bricolage*: the defiance of the traditional attempt to coordinate individual pieces of clothing into a unified look. Moreover, this media saturation of American culture is inherently connected to consumerism. As capitalism moves from production to consumption in its advanced stages, there is increased affluence, hedonism and style[35]. Fictitious capital and credit are the currency of the day. There is an erosion of secure collective identities, increasing fragmentation of personal identities and a gradual disappearance of traditional sources of identity: social class, family, local communities, religion, trade unions and the nation state. This is the natural outgrowth of the move to the consumerist individual who is able to function only according to the dictates of personal taste. With nothing really emerging to take their place, that is, no new institutions, consumerism is, by nature, seen to foster a self-centered individualism which disrupts the possibilities for solid and stable identities[36].

31. S.J. GRENZ, *A Primer on Postmodernism*, Grand Rapids, MI, 1996, p. 13.
32. T. GUARINO, *Postmodernity and Five Fundamental Theological Issues*, in *TS* 57 (1996) 654-689, p. 654.
33. D. STRINATI, *An Introduction to Theories of Popular Culture*, London, 1995, pp. 223-224.
34. *Ibid.*, p. 225.
35. *Ibid.*, p. 236.
36. *Ibid.*, p. 239.

Many of the aspects of the postmodern movement can be found quite readily in contemporary American society and academic life. America, surely, has come to accept, as a matter of course, individualism, reduction of the role of community, consumerism, immersion in mass media, pluralism, relativity and the proclivity to hide from what is unpleasant. These kinds of thoughts have influenced all aspects of American life. Marriage and family are included. Taking one example of how modern institutions have given way, one can take a look at the postmodern version of marriage. While the modern family was traditional in form with the husband working outside of the home and the wife specializing in domestic duties and the raising of the children, the postmodern version of marriage has both parents working outside of the home, working 80 hours or more a week and sharing the domestic duties more evenly. Children see much less of their parents and their raising falls less into the hands of other family members than to daycare centers. Moreover, in terms of cultural phenomena, it has given rise to what some have called a "serial monogamy": where one has several people with whom he or she has had an exclusive, marital relationship over different segments of one's life. Monogamous marriage is replaced by "monogamous relationships" instead[37]. In either case, the fundamental ideas of marriage and commitment are being redefined and understood in new terms.

V. POSTMODERN THEOLOGICAL APPROACHES TO MARRIAGE

The kinds of changes in American marriage that have been discussed in this article have generated some pessimism and sarcasm about the future of the institution. An American newspaper, *The Boston Globe,* ran a piece that wondered whether America was drifting to a "postmarital" culture where marriage would become a "tacky" arrangement only practiced by a few[38]. The concern over whether venerable values and institutions are becoming antiquated and ineffective has been expressed by the church as well. Walter Kasper has observed how a "gap is emerging and steadily increasing between the norms promulgated in Rome for the universal church and the needs and practices of the local church"[39].

37. D. HARVEY, *The Condition of Postmodernity,* Oxford, 1989, p. 9.

38. F. SCHÜSSLER FIORENZA, *Marriage,* in F. SCHÜSSLER FIORENZA – J.P. GALVIN (eds.), *Systematic Theology: Roman Catholic Perspectives,* vol. 2, Minneapolis, MN, 1991, 305-346, p. 308.

39. W. KASPER, *On the Church. A Friendly Reply to Cardinal Ratzinger,* in *America,* April 23-30 (2001) 8-14, p. 8.

The specific doctrine of marriage has been affected by the general post-modern quest to step back from absolute, universal doctrinal claims that require adherence by all people regardless of the particulars of time and place. Some theologians have even wondered how much longer the Magisterium can require strict adherence for Catholics all around the globe to a view of the sacrament of marriage that is only the product of the historically-recent past and is insensitive to multiculturalism[40]. To better appreciate the issues that divide the traditional notion of the sacrament of marriage and its postmodern theological critics, it seems fitting to provide a brief history of the sacrament, take a quick look at its refurbishment in the catechism and survey contemporary approaches at modernizing marriage to meet the new demands of the twenty-first century.

In ancient Israel, marriage was a family affair that was arranged privately and did not involve any public religious ritual. The relationship of union in one mind and body was grounded in the commandment from Genesis for men and women to be "fruitful and multiply". The unique contribution of the religion of Israel to the notion of marriage came from the prophets. They proposed the faithful love between one husband and one wife as the ideal intended by God[41]. The flow of meaning, as in Hosea, is not from human marriage to divine covenant, but from divine covenant to human marriage. The experience of God's steadfast love and care creates the possibility of believing that fidelity in marriage is an achievable goal, which, then, begins to function as a prophetic symbol of the covenant[42]. For the Hebrews, divorce was allowed, though regretted. Jesus, the Jewish rabbi, did not say very much about marriage, but he did speak about divorce on occasion. There are texts where he denounced divorce and remarriage and boldly reiterated the permanence of marriage, which was a radical departure from Hebrew tradition: "What God has united, man must not divide" (Mark 10,1-12). Some scholars may disagree as to whether Jesus had "exemptive clauses" or not, but it seems clear that some early Christian communities allowed divorce for certain reasons at the time that the gospels were written[43]. Paul, too, stressed the ideal of marital fidelity but allowed divorce in certain situations. The so-called "Pauline Privilege" states that, if a Christian was married to an

40. M.G. LAWLER, *Becoming Married in the Catholic Church. A Traditional Post-Modern Proposal*, in *International Academy for Marital Spirituality Review* 7 (2001) 37-55, p. 37.

41. J. MARTOS, *Doors to the Sacred. A Historical Introduction to the Sacraments in the Catholic Church*, Tarrytown, NY, 1991, p. 346.

42. LAWLER, *Secular Marriage, Christian Sacrament,* Mystic, CT, 1992, p. 11.

43. MARTOS, *Doors* (n. 41), pp. 347-349.

unbeliever who wanted a divorce, the unbeliever could separate; it could be granted and the Christian would be free to marry again. This exception allowed Paul to hold Jesus' absolute prohibition in principle and yet have room for certain allowances[44]. However, the main teaching of Paul and the New Testament is found in Eph 5,21-33. Here the relationship between Christ and his church is offered as a model for marriage, though a "great mystery", in terms of sacrificial love, commitment and obedience. In this mutual gift of self and personal unity, the spouses live only for the good of the other person. Mutual giving way, mutual subordination, mutual obedience are nothing other than total availability and responsiveness to one another so that both spouses can become one body[45]. According to Michael Lawler, "for Christian spouses their married life is where they are to encounter Christ daily, and thereby come to holiness"[46]. The covenantal symbol from the Hebrew tradition between Yahweh and Israel is carried forward to the covenantal relationship between Christ and his church and, consequently, to marriage.

These basic scriptural insights inspired the rest of the Christian tradition about marriage but gave no direction to any ritual formulation. Generally, the Eastern and Western Fathers believed that marriage was created by God and was primarily for procreation. Basically, it was a family affair. The most influential father to write on marriage was Augustine. He taught that sexuality and marriage were created good by God and cannot lose their intrinsic goodness. The goods of marriage are threefold: fidelity, offspring (and for companionship, friendship, mutual support) and sacrament (indissolubility)[47]. During the time of the Fathers, divorce was, often times, allowed in the case of adultery. Late in the 4th century, it became customary, in some Eastern places, for a priest or bishop to bless a newly married couple either during the wedding feast or even on the day before. By the 8th century, liturgical weddings had become quite common and they were, usually, performed in a church rather than in the home as before[48]. However, it was not until the 11th century that an obligatory church ceremony was connected to marriage. In order to ensure that marriages took place legally and in front of witnesses, all weddings had to be solemnly blessed by a priest. This led to wedding ceremonies being performed at the church door, followed by a nuptial mass inside during which the marriage was blessed. Peter Lombard declared, in the 12th century,

---

44. H. Vorgrimler, *Sacramental Theology*, Collegeville, MN, 1992, p. 289.
45. Lawler, *Secular Marriage* (n. 42), p. 13.
46. *Ibid.*, p. 19.
47. *Ibid.*, pp. 31-32.
48. Martos, *Doors* (n. 41), p. 355.

that marriage is a sacrament[49]. Additionally, by the 12th century, various parts of Europe had established a wedding ceremony that followed a basic pattern with many aspects being taken over from local marriage customs. In short, by this point, there was agreement that marriage was a sacrament: a relationship of grace, a natural context of friendship and support with potential to overcome sexual temptation[50].

The Council of Florence, in 1439, summarizes the tradition to this point and provides canonical sanction. Yet, it was really left to the Council of Trent for matters to get finalized for the next five hundred years. The Council proclaimed the sacramentality of marriage and the church's right to regulate it. It states that marriage is unbreakable, instituted by Christ and gives grace. The greatest threat to marriage was the fairly common European practice of "secret marriages". To combat this, Trent mandated in *Tametsi* that no Christian marriage would be valid and sacramental that was not contracted in the presence of a priest and two witnesses. That such indissoluble marriages, of Christ and the church, would simply cease to be at someone's unsubstantiated whim was intolerable to the church[51]. The wedding was to be publicly announced three weeks in advance and entered into the parish record afterwards[52]. However, this decree applied only to baptized Catholics. Catholic theology of marriage remained relatively simple. Marriage was a sacrament instituted by Christ in which two legally competent persons became permanently united as husband and wife. The primary purpose of marriage was the procreation of children; its secondary purpose was the spiritual perfection of the spouses by means of the grace of the sacrament, the mutual support they gave each other and the morally permissible satisfaction of their sexual needs. Thus, the official Catholic attitude toward marriage was to emphasize legal rights and social responsibilities[53]. Trent emphasized the indissolubility of marriage that even makes adultery false grounds for divorce (the inseparability of the contract and the sacrament)[54]. The wake of Trent's decrees inspired the search for the "juridical essence" of marriage by canon lawyers. The *Code of Canon Law* of 1917 taught that

49. K.B. OSBORNE, *Sacramental Theology. A General Introduction*, New York, 1988, p. 6.
50. B. COOKE, *Historical Reflections on the Meaning of Marriage as Christian Sacrament*, in ID. (ed.), *Alternative Futures for Worship*. Vol. 5: *Christian Marriage*, Collegeville, MN, 1987, 33-46, pp. 44-45.
51. LAWLER, *Secular Marriage* (n. 42), p. 40.
52. MARTOS, *Doors* (n. 41), pp. 375-376.
53. *Ibid.*, p. 379.
54. VORGRIMLER, *Sacramental Theology* (n. 44), p. 300.

marriage is a contract, the formal object of that contract was the permanent and exclusive right of the spouses to each other's bodies for sexual intercourse and the primacy of procreation over the other ends of marriage. These notions, says Michael Lawler, controlled the Roman Catholic approach until Vatican II[55].

Vatican II and Pope John Paul II move from contract to covenant. This does not ignore the traditional procreation aspect but recontextualizes it within a phenomenology of the person and flow of history. Now, marriage is viewed more as a union of life and love reflecting Christ and his church and the Trinity. Gone are the discussions of the primary and secondary ends and the impression that marriage is only about children[56]. Many theologians, however, do not think this theological personalism goes far enough in redressing the problems of the dominance of procreation, the excessive contract focus, the significance of multiculturalism, the plurality of relationship forms and the rampant inequality for women in marriage of so much of the tradition[57]. Moreover, there is a truncated notion of the body in marital spirituality and theological anthropology[58]. However, it still seems an advance over previous formulations of marriage because of the entrance of the personal (unique) dimensions of each marriage and a notion of love that has to be seen in less essentialistic categories, and so, a corrective to modern, legalistic notion of marriage. Pope John Paul II has inspired some scholars to develop theologies of marriage based on his foundational work[59]. Pope John Paul II is not postmodern per se, but he does exemplify someone who is thinking through the deficiencies of the enlightenment idea of truth to some degree and its static sense of reality. Many of the social changes listed in earlier sections of the paper that marked the postmodern culture could be listed as reasons why many theologians do not think Pope John Paul II has gone far enough in his reassessment of marriage. However, it seems that the phenomena of cohabitation, divorce and inequality in so many Catholic marriages are the main reasons. In response to these challenges, postmodern theologies of marriage make seven proposals needing to be added to

55. LAWLER, *Secular Marriage* (n. 42), p. 44.
56. M.D. PLACE, *Familiaris Consortio. A Review of Its Theology*, in C.E. CURRAN – R.A. McCORMICK (eds.), *John Paul II and Moral Theology* (Readings in Moral Theology, 10), New York, 1998, pp. 184-210, esp. 191.
57. See L. SOWLE CAHILL, *Marriage*, in M.J. WALSH (ed.), *Commentary on the Catechism of the Catholic Church*, Collegeville, MN, 1994, pp. 318-329.
58. See L.T. JOHNSON, *A Disembodied "Theology of the Body. John Paul II on Love, Sex & Pleasure*, in *Commonweal*, January 26 (2001) 11-17.
59. See M. SHIVANANDAN, *Crossing the Threshold of Love. A New Vision of Marriage in Light of John Paul II's Anthropology*, Washington, DC, 1999.

the conversation. While no one has really attempted anything like a comprehensive analysis, they offer trajectories to be followed.

First, marriage is recognized as an "evolving" institution and sacrament. Given the fact that marriage has been interpreted in different ways throughout history and has had ample expressions from different cultures, marriage cannot be understood statically or essentially. It is an "event" in its context and so there is always the potential for pluralistic expressions. Thus, the Catholic understanding of marriage has changed in the past and there is no reason why it cannot change again[60].

Second, marriage is not an instantaneous moment during the wedding ceremony but a "process". The Catholic tradition has already implicitly affirmed this with its acceptance of a valid marriage involving the two stages of consent and sexual consummation. However, postmodern theologians add that the process notion has a relationship to cohabitation in the ancient practice of betrothal. Before the council of Trent, Christian couples officially pledged themselves, to one another, with the intention to marry and began living together and having full intimacy. Later, the actual ceremony would ratify this relationship fully with a church ritual[61]. Moreover, the process dimension is raised, in postmodern theology, in terms of developmental psychology, with the recognition that the spouses are developing and the marital union is dialogical in nature. In other words, marriage changes with the stages of life[62]. Some theologians see the couple's initial interview with a priest for marriage as a possible encounter with the gospel and an opportunity to begin a lifelong reflection on the sacramentality of their relationship[63].

Third, the role of community is highlighted, not so much to correct the Christian tradition but more to abate the excessive individualism of so many understandings of marriage. Marriage is a social reality that goes beyond just the couple and their romantic bond. It includes children, families, a church community and society[64].

Fourth, justice is brought into all postmodern discussions of marriage. There is a reinvigoration and application of "love thy neighbor" among

60. LAWLER, Becoming Married (n. 40), p. 45.

61. A. THATCHER, Marriage After Modernity. Christian Marriage in Postmodern Times, Washington Square, NY, 1999, pp. 103-131.

62. S. ROSS, God's Embodiment and Women: Sacraments, in C. MOWRY LACUGNA (ed.), Freeing Theology. The Essentials of Theology in Feminist Perspective, New York, 1993, pp. 185-209, esp. 202.

63. L.-M. CHAUVET, The Sacraments: The Word of God at the Mercy of the Body, Collegeville, MN, 2001, pp. 173-200, esp. 198.

64. R. GALATZER-LEVY – B. COHLER, The Essential Other. A Developmental Psychology of the Self, New York, 1993, pp. 254-255.

these thinkers. Marriage needs to become a place where justice reigns. The traditional understanding as a symbol of Christ's relationship to his church has led to strict gender roles and excessive demands on women and a dwarfing of their personal development. These unions were usually asymmetrical in form and many times led to abuse and violence against women. Some have advocated in place of the Christ-Church symbol, the church as "sacrament of the Spirit". The Church is a post-Easter phenomenon in which the apostles are brought together into a community by the Spirit of God and Christ. The distinction between Christ and the church and the proposed symbol of the Spirit is that the latter allows marriage to be reconceived as a union of two individuals to form a new community as equal partners under the impact of the Spirit[65]. Additionally, when justice begins to make a real presence in marriage, it will inculcate a love that is oriented toward a "preferential option for the poor". This option will take the love and justice experienced in the family and use it as an instrument of social change[66].

Fifth, an ethics of "common decency" is offered as a way of fulfilling the command to love thy neighbor. Scholars who advocate this ethic step away from the historic focus of marriage in terms of procreation and validity. Instead of using heterosexual marriage as the guiding norm for permanent relationships, the notions of responsibility, justice and the quality of the union become the driving forces. What really matters in relationships is the commitment to promote one another's common decency and to honor the human need for intimacy and affection: honest, caring, respectful, intimate and equal. The quality/ substance is what counts in relationships, the actualization of mutuality and not the form[67].

Sixth, there is a reaffirmation of the "contractual" dimension of marriage to go along with the covenantal. Feminist theorists have emphasized the protective quality for women and children that a binding and obligatory oath can provide. The contract aspect of marriage has the capacity to combat the individualism of the day and be a force against the "absent father" syndrome.

Seventh, each of the approaches wants a more realistic grounding in experience for understandings of marriage. The facts of divorce, cohabitation, premarital sex and birth control need to be taken into consideration

---

65. SCHÜSSLER FIORENZA, *Marriage* (n. 38), p. 332.
66. L. SOWLE CAHILL, *Family. A Christian Social Perspective*, Minneapolis, MN, p. 136.
67. M.M. ELLISON, *Common Decency. A New Christian Sexual Ethics*, in P.T. JERSILD, *et. al.* (eds.), *Moral Issues and Christian Response*, New York, 1998, pp. 62-66.

when formulating any sacramental theology of marriage. They are not extrinsic to the institution. Nothing can substitute for lived experience[68].

In short, these trajectories in postmodern theologies of marriage attempt to improve appreciation of what should be part of any sacramental understanding of marriage without actually defining one. Additionally, it includes admitting that artificial contraception, cohabitation, divorce, weakening of gender roles and the recognition of gay and lesbian people can only be assessed after admitting the possibility that some of these may be prompted by the Spirit of God[69].

VI. A POSTMODERN CONVERSATION ABOUT THE THEOLOGY OF MARRIAGE: TOWARD A CONCLUSION

This essay, thus far, has been an attempt to show that the American experience and understanding of marriage does not fit with the traditional definition put forward by the Vatican. While continuing to seek marriage as a personal goal, the experience of many American Catholic couples is touched in some way by the fracturing of the traditional marriage values of life-long commitment and the reservation of sex for the sacramentally united. While many of these Catholics still feel they are part of the church, they have empowered themselves to decide as a couple what is best in such matters given the particulars of their marriage. Few in postmodern America are of the opinion that a general, singular definition can be promulgated from Rome that will be applicable and binding on all[70]. As the foregoing has shown, there is actually some latitude in the Catholic tradition on marriage if viewed historically. The early Christians and Church Fathers were not averse to making exceptions to the absolute prohibition of Jesus against divorce if adultery had taken place or if a non-Christian spouse wanted to separate. Also, recognition of grounds for annulment for marriage has long since

---

68. J.P. SOTO, *The Church and Marriage. Looking for a New Ethic*, in *Witness* 78 (1995) 16-19.

69. THATCHER, *Marriage After Modernity* (n. 61), p. 30.

70. One could piece this single vision together from different paragraphs in the *Catechism of the Catholic Church*, Mahwah, NJ, 1994: Marriage is a covenant and partnership between a man and woman for the whole of life and it is ordered to the good of the spouses and the procreation and education of offspring (1601). It is indissoluble (2364). Artificial birth control is prohibited (2364/2399). Divorce and polygamy are against the natural moral law (2384/2387). Premarital sex and cohabitation, even for the engaged, is illegitimate (2390-2391).

been on the books, if true consent or sexual consummation was missing. Moreover, cohabitation, with full sexual access before the nuptial rite, has precedents in the tradition for the engaged to be married. Finally, the fact that marriage has changed over the centuries in the eyes of the church and in light of cultural conditions enable it to be seen as a dynamic union that can change again if not in structure then in substance. However, what does remain the same is the central constellation of symbols that provide sacramental coherence to the configuration of marriage in the Christian tradition. Symbols give rise to thought and thought must return to symbols. Thus, if a community of believers is part of a hermeneutical circle of interpretation, the present should not proceed without a grounding in the past, but the past will need to be opened to the light of the present day and its experiences. This approach could be configured around the individual and social poles of the sacrament of marriage.

There is a widespread practice in the Catholic world, explains Kenan Osborne, of speaking and defining sacraments and their validity or invalidity with great "hermeneutical ease". Church leaders and theologians assume they know the essential nature of each of the sacraments and are able to make judgments about such events in abstraction from the particulars[71]. In the postmodern context, this easy hermeneutics meets with great suspicion. Sacraments only really exist in the "doing" and one must "unpack" the actual liturgical experience itself to understand sacramental life[72]. This is so because each sacramental event is disparate and not homogeneous. For example, what is meant by marriage is that multiple events are similar but not episodic replication[73]. Osborne says that a sacrament is an existential event, an existential action. It is an *Ereignis* or individualized, historically concrete, temporally unrepeatable moment of a particular community and the temporal-historical presence of an active God. There exists an interplay of many subjectivities and an interfacing of comminglized intentionalities. The individuality of each sacramental act is not peripheral to what makes a marriage. There is no essence but only existence to marriage. The personal, physical, temporal and spatial coordinates for the actual moment of marriage will never occur again and could never be anticipated in advance. Therefore, any theology of marriage is only about marriage, descriptive and not prescriptive[74].

71. OSBORNE, *Christian Sacraments in a Postmodern World* (n. 49), p. 57.
72. *Ibid.*, p. 12.
73. *Ibid.*, p. 16-17.
74. *Ibid.*, pp. 58-61.

This postmodern insight about uniqueness/*Haecceitas* does have some resonance in the Catholic tradition. For instance, the *New Rite of Marriage* shows the sensitivity to the personal dimension of each union. It offers a rich variety of biblical readings, prayers and blessings to try to capture the particular couple's hopes for the future[75]. The homily is to be directed to the particular circumstances of the couple and there are allowances made for the adaptation of individual celebrations into the nuptial liturgy in accord with regional or ethnic variations[76]. The incipient insight here could be understood as the affirmation that each couple builds its own version of marriage in relation to the individual spouses and their context. An approach such as this relates to the postmodern notion of a fundamental heterogeneity for narrative (ritual being a form). Narratives are only plausible in their specific context and one can never abstract from one's own narrative. The multiplicity of narratives relativizes any absolute claims to universal truth. Heterogeneity cannot be made simply present, but rather an "absent presence". God is revealed anew in such moments of heterogeneity[77]. It makes sacramental time an interruptive, apocalyptic, now moment. According to Boeve, the sacramental event opens up the particular and contingent through the in-breaking of the divine while preserving the particularity[78]. Moreover, since the sanctioned sacramental practice should never be treated in an arbitrary manner, it is helpful to a postmodern rendering that such insights about "particularity" already exist to some extent in the tradition. Every marriage rite, then, is a unique opportunity to encounter God in a way tailored to the story of the specific couple.

Louis-Marie Chauvet has taught that the symbolic, as opposed to symbol, avoids fixing the gaze on the symbols and reorients to the One who approaches humanity through the symbolic[79]. Sacraments are bearers of the joy of the "already" and the distress of the "not yet". They are witnesses of a God who is never finished with coming, of a God who is not here except by a mode of passage and of the passage the sacraments are the trace[80]. It is within the web of sacrament that this divine presence as other is manifest as it is also in sacrament that the church is configured to Christ's Pasch. In each of the sacraments the "dangerous memory" of

75. J.M. CHAMPLIN, *Liturgy of Marriage*, in P. FINK (ed.), *The New Dictionary of Sacramental Worship*, Collegeville, MN, 1990, pp. 796-801, esp. 797.

76. *Ibid.*, p. 801.

77. L. BOEVE, *Postmodern Sacramento-Theology: Retelling the Christian Story*, in *Ephemerides Theologicae Lovanienses* 74 (1998) 326-343, p. 340.

78. *Ibid.*, p. 342.

79. CHAUVET, *The Sacraments* (n. 63), pp. 83-89.

80. CHAUVET, *Symbol and Sacrament. A Sacramental Reinterpretation of Christian Existence*, Collegeville, MN, 1995, p. 555.

Christ is commemorated and each of the sacraments are related fundamentally to the Eucharist. The Catechism is correct, then, when it states that "it is fitting that the spouses should seal their consent to give themselves to each other through the offering of Christ for his Church made present in the Eucharistic sacrifice, and by receiving the Eucharist so that, communicating in the same Body and the same Blood of Christ, they may form but 'one body' in Christ"[81]. Sacramental theology must have an intrinsic connection with liturgical praxis; otherwise, it is an academic study. If this is so, in the case of marriage, the primary symbol for the sacrament remains the relationship between Christ and his Church as a "great mystery" in terms of sacrificial love, commitment and obedience. In this mutual gift of self and personal unity, the spouses live only for the good of the other person. Mutual giving way, mutual subordination, and mutual obedience are nothing other than total availability and responsiveness to one another so that both spouses can become one body. According to Michael Lawler, "for Christian spouses their married life is where they are to encounter Christ daily, and thereby come to holiness"[82]. When marriage is understood this way, it means that it is a process that develops over time and is enriched and reinvigorated as the relationship matures and is more and more configured to the "dangerous memory of Christ" through participating in the Eucharist and living an ethical life. Sacraments reach their plentitude, in love of the neighbor, by recognizing the dignity of all through just treatment, with the spouse being the primary locus[83]. In this sense, God is historicized or incarnated today.

The contemporary experience of marriage is, often times, an experience of "absence" more so than loving and faithful presence (interpersonal). The experience of absence is usually understood either neutrally to refer to the fact that couples have little actual time together and even less "quality time" in the postmodern age, or it is in association with the negative absence that comes from emotional withdrawal, separation or divorce. However, absence is not a peripheral experience to marriage that only the overly wrought or relationally troubled have to confront. Actually, it permeates all relationships, even the one with the individual self. Postmodernism has sensitized individual appreciation to the role of absence in understanding and experience. It has brought out more fully that the self is constituted by the relation to the "Other". For example,

81. *Catechism of the Catholic Church*, § 1621.
82. LAWLER, *Secular Marriage* (n. 42), p. 19.
83. CHAUVET, *The Sacraments* (n. 63), p. 63.

the "arch-symbol" of the body illustrates the inescapability of symbolic mediation in human knowledge and experience. It is the only access that a person has to other subjects and the only way other subjects can have access to the person. But, the embodied person is not made immediately present by physical or even emotional presence. The presence of another mediated by his or her body is always accompanied by an absence. The Other is forever beyond the individual's grasp. The making present is always accompanied by an unbridgeable absence. This *brèche* or difference is the space of the symbolic action[84]. The abyss within symbolic mediation is the space of the self and its life. Postmodern sacramental theology tries to think within the abyss between representation and reality[85]. This presence is not amenable to possession since symbolic mediation is a "gift of grace" embodied in this dialectic. The presence that is mediated is a "presence of absence". The apophatic moment or the difference is what gives life, as the Eucharist mediates salvation by making present the absence of Christ. What bridges the distance is only the divine initiative where God's self-giving in agapic love (an excess that surpasses any conceptualization) arrives and heals the wounded divide. Chauvet says the relation of reciprocal gifts between lovers is an apt analogy for the grace in the sacraments[86]. One could add that it is responsive to the romantic dimension of marriage and avoids any mechanistic understandings of how God acts in the sacraments in general and marriage in particular. The sacrament is an occasion to receive a "gift" and in marriage this gift comes principally through the human face of the Other. It is the place of the revelation of the transcendence of the Other where one, especially, appreciates that love can never be forced but only thankfully received. So, the Other forever evades the individual's grasp in the symbolic mediation of the spouse but one does detect a real trace of its presence within the space/distance of love with one's beloved. The Other's joy and particularly his or her suffering breaks into the person's world and obliges one to action, which can be a salvific moment as one breaks out of egocentrism and finds one's God-intended self[87].

One can conclude, from this study, that marriage is a sacramental process that mediates traces of God through the couple in certain

---

84. V.J. MILLER, *An Abyss at the Heart of Mediation. Louis-Marie Chauvet's Fundamental Theology of Sacramentality*, in *Horizons* 24 (1997) 230-247, p. 233.

85. *Ibid.*, p. 234.

86. D. POWER – R. DUFFY – K. IRWIN, *Sacramental Theology: A Review of Literature*, in *TS* 55 (1994) 657-705, p. 657.

87. MILLER, *An Abyss at the Heart of Mediation* (n. 84), p. 245; *Catechism of the Catholic Church*, § 1609.

contextual moments during dating, engagement, in the marriage rite and throughout life. These are kairotic moments in the in-breaking of the not-yet God of the Apocalypse within the already life of grace in the faith life of the married couple. For all encounters with God to be realized, the divine gift of God self must be recognized and freely accepted no matter the form it may come in. However, the individual spouses can choose to thwart or even kill the possible offer by emptying the symbol of such meaning. So, over the course of a marriage, there could be moments of superabundant giftedness that can only be met with praise and an undeserving thanks as well as moments of emptiness and total absence of any real grace. There will be times when the couple successfully symbolizes Christ's love for the church to each other, their children and the world, and others times will not. This sporadic flow means that one cannot really seriously talk about revelation as a constant event in sacramentality and be able, at the same time, to protect its gift character. Furthermore, one has to make allowances for times when God's offer is rejected. Any understanding of salvation history must be tutored by the insights of postmodernism about the role of absence. In certain cases, the structural "presence of absence" can become just an "absence". Just as the "presence of absence" is the symbolic space for interpretation and understanding, so "absence" that is part of all sacramental marriages can be opportunities to love as God has loved in Christ. This distance allows for perspective and generates longing for more of what one desires: the presence of the Other. In other words, absence can make the heart grow fonder! In short, the sacrament of marriage can fail, like all symbols, if it loses its meaning for the couple or the communal context. The only real hope is for God to graciously act to bridge the divide of absence by opening up the symbols to new variations. However, such a hope must be tempered by history, which has taught continuously that God's presence is often "interrupted" by exile (divorce in interpersonal relationships). These kinds of reflections could help with the church's understanding of the role and function of marriage as well as that of the couple.

Finally, one would be remiss not to mention the corrective capacity inherent in the Catholic sacrament of marriage for the postmodern dance with absence, plurality and individuality. There is a turn to the social, familial and religious in the sacrament that necessarily grounds the couple's relationship within a complex of interconnections with other people who have the right to ask or even to demand that the couple do everything possible to maintain the union: children, extended family, friends, neighbors, co-workers, society and the ecclesial community. Many times, the call of the Other is heard from these others. Therefore, as each couple builds its own unique version of a sacramental marriage, they must be cognizant that the union is symbolically and existentially greater than themselves and that the necessary moments of absence are only ultimately capable of being overcome by the gracious presence of God encountered in the absence. The "perfect marriage" is as elusive as the sacramental yearning for the absolute presence of God.

Division of Humanities   Craig A. BARON
St. John's University
8000 Utopia Parkway
Jamaica, NY 11439
U.S.A.

LAY CHURCH AND WORLD

Practice as Conversation
A Prolegomenon to a Total Ecclesiology

I. Introduction

Yves Congar argued that a total ecclesiology, "a whole ecclesiological synthesis wherein the mystery of the Church has been given in all its dimensions" must be one that incorporates a full exposition of the "ecclesial reality of laity"[1]. This ecclesiology must consider "the principles on which a 'laicology' really depends". To this end, ecclesiology's subject will be conceived in regard to two basic dispositions: the Church in herself and the Church as she is on mission, as she is in her relationship to the world[2].

To date, that total ecclesiology has yet to be written. For some reason, theologians – certainly U.S. theologians – have been little interested in explicating the lay experience of being church in all its variety, complexity and richness. Little has been done to develop the Council's insights concerning laity, and study of the postconciliar experience of lay Catholics – whether in terms of their extensive participation in the ecclesial ministries or their active involvement in the local church's social action and outreach programs – seems to be of greater interest to social scientists than to theologians.

This is curious given that the Council's teaching served to underscore that one cannot really grasp what the Church is unless one gives an accounting of lay ecclesial experience. But while studies in ecclesiology continue to be written, many reflect clerical interests and concerns, focusing primarily on *ad intra* matters[3]. In example, I would cite *A Theology of the Church: A Bibliography* prepared by Frs. Dulles and Granfield[4].

---

1. Y. CONGAR, *Lay People in the Church*, Westminster, MD, 1985, pp. xv-xvi.
2. R. PELLITERO, *Congar's Developing Understanding of the Laity and Their Mission,* in *The Thomist* 65 (2002) 327-359, p. 333.
3. That for centuries theology has been the endeavor mainly of clerics and religious helps explain the types of questions and themes that have come to shape the discipline.
4. A. DULLES – P. GRANFIELD, *The Theology of the Church. A Bibliography*, Mahwah, NJ, 1999.

Not only are the type and number of bibliographical references indicative of their fifty-three category entries, it is not until Section 46 that the subject of laity is even introduced. Likewise, "The Church in the World: the Social Mission of the Church" is not mentioned until Section 49!

Even ecclesiologies of communion which are so popular today either ignore the Church's life in the concrete or else reduce it to an abstraction. While considerable has been written about the inner Trinitarian dynamic, the divine *communio*, that generates the Church, very little attention is given to the visible historical forms, the structures in and through which this communion must be mediated. But as J.M.R. Tillard once warned, to concentrate on communion at the expense of mission gives rise to the false assumption that communion is an "already" achievement of the Church rather than the "not yet to come" it actually is[5]. In turn, Orthodox theologian John Zizioulas claims that the weakness of Orthodox ecclesiology has been an emphasis on the eucharist that "risks undermining mission and involvement in history and being satisfied with a beautiful liturgy without bothering to draw its social and ethical implications"[6]. On Congar's terms, what is wanting from such interpretations is consideration of the Church's pneumatological element. For Congar, the Church's engagement with history is also definitional for it is here that the economy of the Spirit unfolds[7]. And, it is also here that the lay church moves to the foreground.

What would an integral ecclesiology look like? How would ecclesiology differ if it reflected the fact that 99% of church members are lay? One way to begin is to try and identify the principles on which, as Congar suggests, an account of lay Catholic reality rests. Part I of this paper will examine four areas of Council teaching that attempt to delineate theologically the ecclesial reality of Catholic laity. We shall see that the Council directs attention to the fact that lay ecclesial reality becomes most visible when the Church is considered in the mode of its everyday existence. When not gathered for worship, the Church is actualized primarily in and through the operations of the ordinary baptized as they go about infusing Catholic meanings and values in the socio-cultural contexts they inhabit. I believe that this lay agency can best be understood when construed as a form of dialogue, as conversation.

In Part II, I propose that because key elements of lay ecclesial reality converge on this quotidian activity of the ordinary baptized, categories

5. J.M.R. TILLARD, *Church of Churches. The Ecclesiology of Communion*, Collegeville, MN, 1992, p. 32.

6. In P. McPARTLAN, *The Eucharist Makes the Church. Henri de Lubac and John Zizoulas in Dialogue,* Edinburgh, 1999, p.299.

7. D.M. DOYLE, *Communion Ecclesiology*, Maryknoll, NY, 2000, pp. 48-50.

developed by Michel de Certeau in *The Practice of Everyday Life*[8] are useful for theorizing what can be described as a continuing dialogue that transpires among the laity, local church, and world. In and through this conversation, integral to the Church's mystery because it is the domain of the Spirit's action, the divine *communio* is embodied in history. I argue elsewhere that the lay theologian has an indispensable role to play in developing this theology of the laity[9].

II. VATICAN II ON LAY ECCLESIAL REALITY

1. *Laity*

For purposes here, *Lumen gentium* makes three essential points about Catholic laity[10]. First of all, laity are presented not just as being *in* the Church; they are understood here to actually *constitute* the Church. In this, Vatican II effected what Johannes Metz calls "a transition from a Church of dependents to a Church of agents"[11]. In baptism, laity are incorporated into the Body of Christ and receive a share in Christ's three-fold office of priest, prophet and king. As such, lay people no less than clergy and religious bear responsibility for the Church and its mission. Such responsibility may be discharged by participation in *ad intra* ministries like catechesis or spiritual direction or by some other service that facilitates the evangelizing witness of church members. But in the main, lay ecclesial activity is in *ad extra* outreach, whether this takes the form of hands-on works of charity or public advocacy for social justice. The point is, laity are ecclesial subjects whom baptism calls to witness to their faith in and through the acts and decisions of their everyday living. Says Metz, "The Council emphasizes the active role of the faithful in articulating and developing the authentic witness of the gospel"[12]. Only in and through their efforts does the Church acquire a viable, lasting historical presence.

A second point: While not wanting to offer a formal definition, *LG* 31 does ascribe a secular character to laity. As interpreted by Congar and others, the term "secular" indicates that certain members of the Church (the majority of them, in fact!) have been called to ecclesial service in

8. M. DE CERTEAU, *The Practise of Everyday Life*, Berkeley, CA, 1988.
9. G.M. KEIGHTLEY, *The Lay Perspective on* Theology, unpublished ms.
10. We will refer to the documents of the Second Vatican Council from the following edition: W. ABBOTT (ed.), *The Documents of Vatican II*, New York, 1966.
11. J.B. METZ, *Theology Today. New Crises and New Visions*, in *CTSA Proceedings* 40 (1985) 1-14, p. 5.
12. *Ibid.*

the world; indeed, they have been commissioned sacramentally to do this[13]. As *AA* 7 confirms, the laity's secular character is intrinsic to church mission and has as its aim evangelization, witness and Christian presence. But Council documents emphasize that laity have also been called to the life of the world in order to renew it. It is "the 'laity' with all the fullness of the gifts, charisms, and ministries with which the Spirit enriches it" that is mainly responsible for carrying out this practical and creative task[14]. G. Magnani observes, however, that there has been an unfortunate tendency to reduce lay participation in Christ's royal function to Christian service to others[15]. In doing so theologians overlook "the christic dimension of all created things and the cosmic dimension of Christ taking up the whole of creation again into himself"; in this way lay participation in Christ's work of recapitulation goes undervalued[16].

A third point pertains to the nature of the witness that lay Catholics give. *LG* 12 attributes to laity, under the guidance of the Spirit, a certain unerring capacity to judge what is the Christian thing to do in their everyday choices. In so saying, the Council intimates that this daily witness has significant truth value. On the one hand, the lay effort to translate the gospel into a spirituality is a means by which Christ's teaching is enfleshed; however, it is also a means by which this teaching is advanced and fulfilled. At the same time, because guided by the Holy Spirit, this concrete witness has a certain inerrant quality. For both reasons then, this living testimony of lay Catholics is an indispensable instrument of the Church's evangelizing activity.

2. *Local Church*

In the course of its reflections, Vatican II made two important assertions about the local church. As a first, the Council acknowledged the presence of the universal Church in the local church. "The universal Church exists 'in and from' the local church and the local churches exist 'in and from' the universal Church"[17]. This means that since all the

---

13. While the sacraments of initiation underlie all Christian activity, some theologians as well as some official church documents tend to view marriage as being the sacrament of secularity *par excellence*.

14. G. MAGNANI, *Does the So-Called Theology of the Laity Possess a Theological Status?*, in R. LATOURELLE (ed.), *Vatican II. Assessment and Perspectives, Twenty-five Years After (1962-1987)*, Vol. I, Mahwah, NJ, 1988, pp. 568-633, esp. 623.

15. *Ibid.*, p. 600.

16. *Ibid.*, p. 623.

17. K. McDONNELL, *The Ratzinger/Kasper Debate. The Universal Church and Local Churches*, in *Theological Studies* 63 (2002) 227-250, p. 247.

elements that constitute the Church are present to each local community, to understand what the Church is in its essentials, one need only look here[18]. And when one does look to the local church as it exists concretely, what one sees is the parish community, a group of laity gathered around a pastor and intent on doing ecclesial things.

A second of the Council's points: To say that the Church is local directs attention to its situatedness in the world. In truth, it is context – the Church's insertion into a particular geographic, temporal circumstance – that makes a church local. But to speak of the Church as local also implicates the Church's catholicity. Tillard describes catholicity as a result of that process whereby the Spirit directs the Christian community "toward the checkered multitude of human milieux in order to bring also to them the gospel of God, but in their language, their culture, their ways of thinking, their being, so that it would becomes *theirs* in the full sense of the word and not something borrowed"[19].

For Tillard, "catholicity is actualized when salvation is incarnated in a new human place where faith, *koinonia*, the Eucharist, solidarity, the mission of all the churches of God are found"[20]. While catholicity is not something usually considered in respect to laity, Tillard's remarks suggest that it does pertain in two important ways. First, one may describe the laity as being the local church in all its socio-cultural particularity. That is, catholicity is manifested in the distinct lay gifts and charisms present to each local Christian community at any given time. Secondly, catholicity also has to do with the way laity actualize the gospel according to the unique social and cultural exigencies of their lives.

Most attempts to understand exactly how the Church becomes local, how it becomes "catholic" Church in a place, tend to focus on institutional structures, on what Joseph Komonchak calls "the objective representations of Christian meaning and value"[21]. But these objective representations must be vitalized by faith, otherwise a religion is no more than

18. J. KOMONCHAK, *Ministry and the Local*, in *CTSA Proceedings* 37 (1981) 56-82, p. 58: "The universal, catholic church arises, if you will, from below, because in every local church the full reality of what is called 'the Church' is realized: the communion of believers in the holy things won for us by Christ". Here Komonchak describes the constitutive principles of the church as being "the call of God, the grace of the Holy Spirit, the preaching of the gospel, the celebration of the Eucharist, the fellowship of love, and the apostolic ministry".

19. TILLARD, *The Local Church within Catholicity*, in *The Jurist* 52 (1992) 448-454, p. 452.

20. *Ibid.*, p. 449.

21. KOMONCHAK, *Ministry* (n. 18), p. 70.

sociologically functional[22]. Just as important a feature of enculturation, then, is the faith-filled manner in which laity go about creating an authentic Catholic identity, a genuine Catholic spirituality in and out of the elements of the various milieu in which they find themselves. In the lives of laity, ecclesiology is translated into spirituality. The local church takes on flesh and bones in concrete women and men; it takes its existence from the way they shape their lives in the networks and cultural systems within which they live. If at the outset clergy are instrumental in planting the Church, the lay members are the ones who from then on enact it locally and perpetuate it in existence.

3. *Church Mission*

In contrast to past treatments of mission as something the Church does, Vatican II asserted that mission is the very essence of what the Church is. According to *Ad gentes 8,* the Church's missionary activity is rooted in the Trinitarian economy, it is an "epiphany of God", of God's desire to be with humanity. As indicated above, the responsibility for this witness in all its forms is a charge given to laity as well as to clergy.

For centuries, mission tended to be regarded as just another church activity. It was equated with the establishment of new churches in foreign lands and this was held to be the rightful endeavor of religious and clergy. But developing positions taken in *Lumen gentium, Ad gentes* began to examine the task of mission in terms of the local church. While certainly clergy are indispensable to establishing the Church in new places, to become self-sustaining a local church must engage in such basic ecclesial activities as proclamation, catechesis, liturgical praise and thanksgiving, public witness, and fellowship on a regular basis.

Thus the Council, in recognizing the gifts and charisms given at baptism, called laity to participate in the various ecclesial ministries so necessary to supporting and strengthening local church life. *Ad gentes* cites specifically the importance of catechists, lay associations and those groups dedicated to apostolic works (*AG* 15). Thanks to the Council, laity today not only participate in the liturgical ministries, they have become the mainstay of a multitude of other parish ministries – catechetical, pastoral, and social justice. Increasingly, in most areas the health of the local church is directly related to the strength of the ministerial activity of laity. And across the world Church, and in the future as the shortage of clergy

---

22. C. STARKLOFF, *Inculturation and Cultural Systems (Part II),* in *Theological Studies* 55 (1994) 274-294, p. 282.

grows, local churches will literally be kept alive only in and through the work of dedicated lay ministers.

The point I would make is that when speaking about inculturation, it is important not to overlook these indispensable *ad intra* activities by which the laity too contribute to building the local church and fostering its missionary outreach. Also of interest to the ecclesiologist will be the manner in which these local ecclesial ministries are created/defined in and out of the symbols and structures of the laity's cultural milieu.

4. *World*

In defining the Church, Vatican II reflected deeply on the Church's relationship to the world. And while the Council did not offer a formal definition of the world *per se*, it did specify the nature of the Church's relationship with it. According to *Gaudium et spes,* the Church is in dialogue with the world, its posture is that of speaking and listening[23]. But this dialogue is by no means to be understood as being some new endeavor for the Church; to the contrary, such interaction is seen as fundamental to its mission (and so to the very essence of what it means to be Church).

According to Bryan Hehir, a decisive contribution of Vatican II was "to provide a description of the Church's role in the world which was properly theological and ecclesial in tone and substance"[24]. Following Rahner, Hehir asserts that this relationship is seen by the Council as rooted in the Church's very nature as mission as opposed to being something it chooses to do or is something forced upon it by external circumstances[25]. Also influencing the Council's understanding of the world was its rediscovery of eschatology. As Gustavo Gutierrez argues in *A Theology of Liberation*, "If human history is above all else an opening to the future, then it is a task, a political occupation ... Faith in a God who loves us and calls us to the gift of full communion with God and fellowship with others not only is not foreign to the transformation of the world; it leads necessarily to the building up of that fellowship and communion in history. We need to recognize the work and importance of concrete behavior, of deeds, of action, of praxis in the Christian life"[26].

---

23. *GS* 3: "This Council can provide no more eloquent proof of its solidarity with the entire human family ... than by engaging with it in conversation".

24. J.B. HEHIR, *Church-State and Church-World. The Ecclesiological Implications*, in *CTSA Proceedings* 41 (1986) 54-74, p. 56.

25. *Ibid.*

26. G. GUTIERREZ, *A Theology of Liberation*, Maryknoll, NY, 1988, p. 8.

Gaudium et spes described the Church's mission to the world as *diakonia*, but one could say that this is simply the mode of the Church's participation in dialogue. This sort of engagement with the world is necessary in that Christ is the goal of history, and to that end, the Church is called to assist humanity in building a community life that has human dignity and well-being as its object. As noted above, the Council emphasized that because of their expertise, both theoretical and practical in the areas of politics, business, education, technology and science, etc., lay Catholics play a critical part in renewing the temporal order. Indeed, this sort of outreach has its germ in the laity's secular character.

But the practical question is: Where and how does this dialogue take place? At one level – and as post-conciliar history shows – the conversation between Church and world occurs in the teaching and formal statements of pope, bishops and synods. Following the recommendations of *Gaudium et spes*, on these occasions the hierarchy proceeds inductively, reading the "signs of the times" and prescinding from the language of theology, speaks in the world's own idiom to address the pressing human questions and social issues of the day[27].

But it is also the case that a much more extensive and intimate, but little noticed, conversation between Church and world transpires in the lives of ordinary laity as they go about their daily affairs. This is a conversation that pertains not just to the immediate demands of practical witness to the gospel; it also is a part of the more comprehensive ecclesial task of christic recapitulation. Everyday situations posit questions of meaning and value to which laity, informed by a Christian conscience and their faith commitment, respond by what they say and do. In the course of this informal dialogue, the local church becomes ever more "catholic" as its life is shaped in and out of this everyday encounter between personal faith and local culture. But likewise, so does the world become ever more ecclesial and Catholic in this exchange!

A related question pertains to the Church's response of *diakonia* to dialogue: How and in what ways does the Church carry out its service to

---

27. J. HAMER, *Gaudium et Spes. Preparation, Significance and Importance in the Context of Vatican II*, in *Laity Today* 39 (1995) 32-43, p. 37. Increasingly today, however, conflict has arisen within the Church about the hierarchy's right to be the exclusive public voice of the Church, especially on issues where laity are acknowledged to have greater expertise. An example here is the lay letter prepared by Catholic business executives and academics critiquing positions taken by the U.S. bishops in their 1985 pastoral letter on U.S. economic life.

the world? At a formal level, the institutional church, through its organizations and agencies provides for a whole host of social needs: schools, hospitals, soup kitchens, homeless shelters, legal aid societies, social justice committees, all of which represent an identifiable ecclesial embrace of the world. But the world is no less served in and through the smaller operations of laity, as gospel meanings and values motivate their decisions and acts as parents, business people, citizens. It is by means of a complexus of daily personal mediations that faith becomes embedded in a culture; it is in and through the committed Christian activity of laity transforming social networks and structures that the Word is served, the world renewed. The theologian's challenge is to bring these quotidian operations of the lay church to the foreground for reflection and study.

The fact is, as the Church becomes incarnate, it manifests itself for what it is – a mission of service. This happens not in the abstract, and neither is it limited to celebration of the liturgy. Rather, the Church takes its vitality and life in the individual choices and actions of everyday. To quote Chenu, in and out of this dialogue that is both quotidian and local, "the Church defines its own mystery through and in the movement of the world ... By seeking the world, the Church comes out of itself in order to be itself"[28]. But again, the most significant interaction between *ecclesia* and world is found in the quiet conversation and Christian permeation of culture that occurs in the everyday operations of Catholic lay people. And it is for this reason that such activity becomes a critical *locus theologicus* for ecclesiology.

5. *Summary*

This examination of points of teaching of the Second Vatican Council has identified some basic elements of lay ecclesial reality.

First, according to *Lumen gentium*, to be lay is to be thoroughly and fully ecclesial. One is made so by baptism. Secondly, the term "lay" refers to a historically and socially situated, culturally determined status. Practically speaking, one is never born into the universal Church; instead, one is baptized and received into the fellowship of some local community. Likewise, one's life of Christian witness and service is usually carried out in conjunction with that of a particular eucharistic community. Third, as we have seen, in baptism, laity are given responsibility for carrying out the Church's mission on behalf of the gospel. But this too is

28. M.-D. CHENU, *A Council for All Peoples*, in A. STACPOOLE (ed.), *Vatican II. By Those Who Were There*, London, 1986, pp. 19-23, esp. 20.

always directed toward some concrete, historically situated work of service. For example, the spiritual gifts and charisms one receives at baptism are always called forth by and put to work on behalf of the parish community to which one belongs. Similarly, the secular character that the Council identified with laity is also socially and culturally bound. That is, the individual Catholic is called to perform some special service, to respond in a gospel way to some local, determinate need. The point to be made here is that one's personal skills, professional expertise, education and spiritual gifts are also unique to one's time and place, as are the needs of the situation; all are local and catholic.

Most important, this review of conciliar teaching shows that lay ecclesial reality converges on and thus presses the question concerning the Church's everyday existence. Yet absent from most ecclesiologies is an accounting for this lay enactment of the Church. Missing has been a studied exploration of the living – and lived – Church, an examination of personal faith as it is witnessed to in the exigencies of the quotidian, a faith that is local, catholic, evangelizing, that is an ecclesial becoming in and on behalf of the world. In Part II of this paper, I want to suggest a way these minuscule operations of the everyday can be captured for theological analysis.

III. Everyday Lay Practice
Explicating the Lay Church's Dialogue with the World

The challenge for the theologian is to give an adequate account of this lay ecclesial reality that is necessary for composing Congar's total ecclesiology. The question is how to conceptualize the Church as it exists in a missionary mode, as it is in its daily engagement with what is not church?

In describing the Church's relation to the world as taking the form of a conversation, *Gaudium et spes* provides an apt starting point for thinking about the agency of the lay church. This, for the reason that conversation is a common mode of human interaction; it implies a back and forth movement, as well as the need to be open and tolerant of difference. Conversation too, in this acceptance of plurality and ambiguity, is "an exploration of possibilities in the search for the truth"[29]. As David Tracy

---

29. D. Tracy, *Plurality and Ambiguity. Hermeneutics, Religion, Hope*, Chicago, IL, 1987, p. 20.

observes, the structure of human life itself is essentially dialogic[30]. We come to know, understand self, others, the world only in and through the continual interaction and exchange with them that takes place through the medium of language shaped by culture and history

But conversation – dialogue – is also requisite to the functioning of communities. Kathryn Tanner's summary of the postmodern critique of classic construals of Christian experience indicates how this is so[31]. Unlike prior conceptions that held that there exists a readily identifiable body of beliefs and practices that are exclusively Christian, a postmodern reading of culture sees Christianity as being but one subculture extant in a world of many subcultures. More specifically, it is a way of life, a set of beliefs and practices that is dependent on and even formed in and out of its interaction with these other cultural ways of being and doing[32]. In other words, Christians are obliged to shape a gospel discipleship not just in dialogue with but by actually borrowing and working over the practices of others[33]. A review of Christian history substantiates Tanner's claim; such shows the extent to which what originate as the peculiar beliefs and practices of outsiders, over time come to be transformed into religiously meaningful ones for Christians.

Tanner also shows that while Catholics presume that they hold many beliefs and values in common, the truth is otherwise. Certainly members of the Catholic community do agree *in principle* on a set of core ideas/values; for instance, the beliefs that God speaks through scripture, that Christ has redeemed all, that Christ is present in the eucharist would be among them. However, Tanner argues that among Catholics there is disagreement about the exact meaning of these claims and such agreement as is ever achieved is the outcome of serious discussion and often fractious debate[34]. What Tanner wants to emphasize is that it is this continuing conversation about the content of Christian belief and practice that actually helps keep Christians together. "What makes for Christian identity is the fact that such *investigation* is viewed as critical, not *agreement* on its outcomes"[35].

---

30. *Ibid.*, p. 28.
31. K. TANNER, *Theories of Culture. A New Agenda for Theology*, Minneapolis, MN, 1997.
32. *Ibid.*, p. 152.
33. Michel de Certeau, for one, argues that in its origins Christianity was a form of social practice rather than an institution.
34. TANNER, *Theories* (n. 31), p. 124. The Catholic Common Ground Initiative, a regularly scheduled gathering of liberal and conservative Catholics organized by Cardinal Joseph Bernardin in1996, presents a good case in point.
35. *Ibid.*, p. 125.

Seen in this light, Catholic Christians may properly be described as constituting a community of conversation[36]. Continuity in fellowship comes, on the one hand, from believers' willingness to learn from, admonish and be corrected by others who share their desire to practice an authentic Christian discipleship. But uniting them, too, is a common commitment to try to figure out, by talking together, the sort of everyday practices the following of Christ requires of church members. From Tanner's standpoint, it can be argued that conversation is a key practice by which the Christian community not only clarifies its beliefs and values; it is also an activity that knits them together ever more tightly as the Body of Christ.

The Practice of Everyday Life

Michel de Certeau builds on language theory and its account of how language functions to explore the micro operations that are everyday practise. His analysis helps to detail the specific moves of the lay Catholic conversation with the world that contribute to giving the Church an effective historical presence. We begin with his examination of what he calls "the scriptural economy"[37].

De Certeau argues that writing is a basic form of modern social power; more to the point, it is a significant act of production[38]. The real is generated by writing; the real is what has a place and an identity within the discourses of the individual disciplines. Writing is a series of mental and linguistic operations through which the ambiguities of experience are classified, systematized and brought under human control.

a) Tactics

The question de Certeau poses in *The Practice of Every Life* is this: Given the totalizing thrust of the discourse of the capitalist economy – which is increasingly abetted by technological discourse – can there be any freedom of action left to the individual? For this determination, one has to look beyond the usual objects of analysis, i.e., the productions of a society and its modes of behavior, to examine "the everyday practices, the ways of operating, the ways of doing things which compose a culture". In short, one must "bring to light these models of action characteristic of users whose status as the dominated element in society is concealed by the euphemistic term 'consumers'"[39]. De Certeau argues that

36. *Ibid.*, p.154.
37. See DE CERTEAU, *Practice* (n. 8), Ch. 10.
38. *Ibid.*, p. 135.
39. *Ibid.*, pp. xi-xii.

the mere presence or circulation of things tells us nothing about the actual use people make of the cultural products that are produced, disseminated and imposed upon them by society's elites. And so, while weighty theological tomes are intended for reading and reflection, some students find a better use for them as doorstops!

It is then this use of the products of culture and the specific operations this usage involves that is the subject of de Certeau's investigation. He shows that not only are consumers free to utilize culture and its objects in ways other than intended, but by and in such elementary maneuvers users actually re-appropriate the social order to their own purposes. Furthermore, these "tricks", "ruses" to which consumers resort must be seen for what they are – meaningful exercises of power by those subjects presumed to have none[40].

De Certeau describes these everyday practises as being instinctive, creative acts of *poesis*, as actions having their own special logic. Above all, he wants to emphasize that human beings are not just passive consumers of culture, that in fact because practice involves movement, activity, and agency, all of us become cultural innovators and creators. He likens the practices of everyday to the movement of trajectories:

"In the technocratically constructed, written and functionalized space in which the consumers move about, their trajectories form unforeseeable sentences, partly unreadable paths across a space. Although they are composed with the vocabularies of established languages (those of television, newspapers, supermarkets, or museum sequences) and although they remain subordinated to the prescribed syntactical forms (temporal modes of schedules, paradigmatic orders of spaces, etc.) the trajectories trace out the ruses of other interests and desires that are neither determined nor captured by the systems in which they develop"[41].

De Certeau describes practises as being tactical in character in that their reality is time, not space. That is, they are temporary actions that come into play only when the right circumstances present themselves; to become operational, tactics must be inserted into the already existing, predetermined "space" of an established discourse. And unlike strategies, tactical operations do not involve long-term planning. They are mainly operations of the moment; they leave scarcely a trace, certainly not enough of one to be captured by statistics. Further, tactics constantly manipulate events seeking to turn them into opportunities for action.

40. *Ibid.*, p. xix.
41. *Ibid.*, p. xviii.

To illustrate his thesis about uses and tactics, de Certeau cites two everyday activities – walking and reading. While city planners intend that walkers use sidewalks to reach their destinations, in the interest of time some walkers innovate and create their own path by such tactical operations as jaywalking or cutting across in the middle of a street. Additionally, as they go along walkers may also impose meaning on and/or create emotional links to the neighborhoods, streets, buildings they pass. In this way, says de Certeau, the simple act of walking becomes a practice whereby individuals rewrite the abstract discourse of city space and create a place that is both more habitable, more their own. Similarly a book's reader may find that a particular passage conjures up such strong personal memories that these intrude themselves on her appropriation of the text's meaning. The point is, in this instance too, a pre-existing order supplies the framework that becomes the site for the innumerable creative, productive acts of meaning[42].

All that de Certeau says about tactics applies to the activity of lay Catholics. The following of Christ requires that Catholic beliefs and values be written into today's cultural spaces to which they are not native. Let us use as our example the dilemma of a Catholic business woman who unintentionally intercepts a phone call that potentially gives her an unfair advantage over a co-worker. According to the rules governing a competitive market economy, taking advantage of the situation is simply good business practise. In contrast, the gospel value of justice calls one to put other over self and allow him to rightly profit through the opportunity. By adopting the ethical norms of the gospel instead of those of the market, the Catholic succeeds in overwriting the modern capitalist discourse and in this way overturns standard patterns of relating. And while such an action may seem an insignificant gesture, as de Certeau's thesis would have it, it is the cumulative effect of such small practises that the reign of God is effectively inscribed in contemporary cultural spaces.

b) Story

De Certeau's notions about discourse, consumer uses of existing practices, and tactics establish the context for his more detailed look at the minute operations of the everyday and the critical role of story and memory therein.

In de Certeau's terms, Christianity is a discourse of stories that has its proper social location in the ecclesial body. According to de Certeau,

42. *Ibid.*, p. xxi.

story is a narrative activity whose primary function is to open up a theatre for practical activity; above all, story "creates a field that authorizes dangerous and contingent social actions"[43]. The gospel stories present alternate ways of being and doing in the world, and, like games, these narratives present a menu of tactics for use in responding to everyday situations. Stories of Jesus recount, convey the ruses, the very moves that effectively transform an already culturally demarcated place into a free space, i.e., a place where new things can happen. For example, the gospel stories describe Jesus' own everyday practises: He listens, he comforts, he affirms, he heals, he loves.

But besides presenting models of action, stories also set boundaries, limits, and determine rights[44]. And so the parables recount other elements of his practice: Avoid greed, get priorities straight, don't avoid the leper, the stranger. The point is, Jesus' own tactics aim at undoing the relational patterns, the social interaction prescribed by the controlling socio-cultural milieu. As de Certeau observes, religious stories create a fictional space, a utopia that stands outside, alongside the ruling order. Such stories are not only a source of hope to their hearers; they are so because they model the actions necessary to instituting a new state of affairs[45].

Based on de Certeau's theory, the Christian stories have greatest impact and create their strongest, most lasting consequence when the members of the Church gather in their local parish communities to celebrate the eucharistic liturgy. At such times and by all that they see, hear and do, parishioners are literally formed in; they learn how to appropriate the gospel way of living. Here the Word is proclaimed, heard and responded to; here the stories of faith are narrated and "tried on" for size. Here in and through the various actions of the liturgy – e.g., the greetings of welcome and hospitality, the bodily moves that express forgiveness and reconciliation, the emphatic proclamation of the prophetic call to justice, the physical offering of money that bespeaks concern for the poor, all those actions that manifest the solidarity existing among those who participate in the eucharistic meal – in all these ways, day after day, week after week, the gospel word itself is duly practiced.

Contemporary ritual theory supports the thesis that by means of the liturgy, Christians reiterate in their own physical movement the everyday tactics of Jesus. Theory explains how in and through ritual, the practices of Jesus come to be inscribed on the bodies of individual Christians and

43. *Ibid.*, p. 125.
44. *Ibid.*, p. 122.
45. *Ibid.*, p. 16.

thus are committed to physical memory[46]. De Certeau suggests that it is
only by means of this actual entering, literally, moving into and with the
Christian stories, that believers are able to appropriate their fullest, deepest meaning[47]. In this way he implies that before Christian practices can
be embedded in the social structures and the schemas within which we
live, these practises must first be inscribed in and borne in/by human bodies, both individual and collective. And the place where this happens is
the local church. It is here through the proclamation of the Word and the
performance of ritual that lay Catholics continue to be instructed and
formed in the tactics of Christian practice.

c) The Operations of Practice

Since his analysis aims at explicating what takes place at the most
concrete level of existence, de Certeau proceeds to a closer examination
of the operations that practices are. He asks, "What occurs that leads to
the practice of practices?" and concludes that it is "practice's own
logic"; it is the sudden activation of an innate intelligence that discerns
the appropriate time to act and by a subsequent act of judgement, proceeds to do so[48].

Individual practices come into play at those moments of everyday
experience, which de Certeau calls "the occasion"[49]. These are discrete
events resulting from the unique conjuncture of historical circumstance
into which memory intervenes to disrupt the controlling social order[50].
According to de Certeau memory suddenly introduces other possible ways
of responding to the occasion[51]. It brings to the fore past knowledges and
experiences but it also incorporates these antecedent particularities creating out of them imaginative future scenarios. For our interests, what de
Certeau calls "the occasion" is the point at which Christian memories of
Jesus intervene and present to consciousness 1) the menu of tactics presented in the gospel stories; 2) the practises ritually inscribed on the body;

---

46. See for example, T.W. JENNINGS, JR., *On Ritual Knowledge*, in R.L. GRIMES (ed.),
Readings in Ritual Studies, Upper Saddle River, NJ, 1996, pp. 324-334.

47. DE CERTEAU, *Practice* (n. 8), p. 80.

48. De Certeau suggests that these instinctual responses are ancient, perhaps going
back "to the age-old ruses of fishes and insects that disguise or transform themselves in
order to survive and which has, in any case, been concealed by the form of rationality currently dominant in Western culture". *Ibid.*, p. xi.

49. *Ibid.*, p. 83.

50. *Ibid.*

51. *Ibid.*, p. 82.

and 3) other relevant memories of personal, practised discipleship of the past. In this way, memory illuminates the occasion.

But the interjection of memory is also a challenge to act and at this point, the faculty of judgement is called into play[52]. Following Kant, de Certeau describes judgement as "a logical tact" which "bears on the relation of a great number of elements, and which exists only in the act of concretely creating a new set by putting one more element into a convenient connection with this relation"[53].

An autonomous faculty, judgement involves "a subjective equilibrium of imagining and understanding". Everyday practises then depend on just this sort of artful rearrangement of what is given in the occasion, what is introduced to it by memory, and the ability to decide between the various scenarios. This discerning "know what to do" of practical judgement is a fundamental requirement of daily living; de Certeau describes it as an art, one that is acquired only by a practice of doing, by putting oneself in connection with the very things on which action is to be exercised and in exercising it oneself[54].

This combination of occasion, memory and judgement constitutes the basic operation of everyday practice. De Certeau finds it similar to the Greek notion of *"metis"*, but the terms he uses to describe it – "a form of intelligence ... which combines flair, sagacity, foresight, intellectual flexibility, resourcefulness, vigilant watchfulness, a sense for opportunities, diverse sorts of cleverness, and a great deal of acquired experience"[55] – could just as well be used to describe the operation of the *sensus fidei*. This too is a type of practical judgement, the art of Christian discernment that is honed in the space of liturgical ritual and by the experience of everyday living.

IV. CONCLUSION

It is then in and through this same series of moves that individual Christians embody their faith via the language, thought forms and patterns of culture as they meet the situations, whether challenging or mundane, presented by the everyday. Through a Christian tactics, they become agents of the Church's building up in each time and place. And like the parables of growth, while this activity appears minuscule, ambiguous,

52. See the discussion, *ibid.*, pp. 72-76.
53. *Ibid.*, p. 73.
54. *Ibid.*
55. *Ibid.*, p. 81.

even goes unnoticed, it actually constitutes the very "salt" and "light" of which the gospels speak. It is an activity having rich eschatological consequences and whose future is like to that of the mustard seed.

And, as I have attempted to outline here, the metaphor of conversation represents a most appropriate category for interpreting lay ecclesial reality and for finally bringing to word the total ecclesiology that Congar called for so many years ago.

The St. Anselm Institute   Georgia MASTERS KEIGHTLEY
for Lay Theology
P.O. Box 125
Crawford, NE 69339
U.S.A.

NEGOTIATING GUILT

GOD AND MAN AS PARTNERS IN FORGIVENESS AND RECONCILIATION

I. FORMULATING THE QUESTION

A new optional course was introduced in the Law Department at Tilburg University in September, 2001: Negotiation and Mediation[1]. It deals with a new way of settling disputes. Instead of appearing before a judge and having a verdict handed down, there is arbitration by a mediator who assists both parties in finding a solution to a legal dispute. There are three reasons for the success of this new approach to conflict management in the Netherlands[2]. The first is that it provides a solution to the increasing shortage of competent judges and the frustration of those seeking legal redress. Those who have participated are extremely satisfied with the results. Following a satisfactory mediation outcome, 90% indicate they would opt for mediation again in another conflict; 70% of those whose cases could not be resolved by mediation would once more attempt to resolve future disputes through mediation. A second reason is that resolving legal conflicts through consensus by means of a mediator fits extremely well into the Dutch "polder model", in which things are arranged through thorough discussion. The third reason is that negotiating guilt, although it mainly occurs in administrative law and not in criminal law, very adequately reflects the degree to which notions of guilt have changed over the past decades. One can observe an increasing tendency toward greater flexibility in the rigid norms that have surrounded guilt and punishment, for a long time.

Changes in ideas about guilt and punishment in the public sphere have certainly had an effect on the sense that believers have of the gravity of their guilt and on how they deal with their feelings of guilt toward God.

---

1. M. DE JONG, *Mediation als alternatief voor gang naar de rechter*, in *Univers* (September 13, 2001), p. 9.
2. See also P. PLESMAN, *De grote verzoening*, in *Aaneen* 21 (2001) 18-19; A. GROTENHUIS, *Bemiddeling op het belastingkantoor. Nieuw initiatief om fiscaal geschil te lijf te gaan*, in *NRC Handelsblad* (October 6), 2001.

In the case of the average church member, there is also hesitancy to attribute sin, guilt, and punishment, which does not differ very much from the trend in society. Such hesitancy chiefly involves the question as to what can be regarded as sin and guilt. The certainty of past formulations is gone. Ample space for negotiation and mediation also seems to have arisen within the concept of sin, just as it has in the concept of guilt in general.

Thus we have the outline of the subject of this paper. The problem that has arisen through the developments I have sketched above is the following: is it possible to consider the sin and guilt which people feel in relation to God as the object of argument, dispute, and negotiation? What argues for such a view, apart from the changed views of the law, judicial process, and allocation of guilt? What argues against it considering the significance of sin, forgiveness, and reconciliation in the relation between God and human beings? In the first section, I will deal with changes in the sense and consciousness of guilt and sin. In the second section, based on a communicative understanding of the relation between God and man, I will discuss the question as to what extent the determination of guilt, sin and punishment can be the object of negotiation and mediation. In the third section, I will deal with new images people have of God in the present. Can He or She still be conceived as a person rather than as a force or all-inclusive entity, transcendent or not? Does this completely change the discussion with God about guilt, sin, forgiveness, and reconciliation? Finally, I will summarise the main ideas in the conclusion.

II. Changed Concept of Guilt and Sin

After the 1960s, the compartmentalised society of the Netherlands with its fixed confessional traditions has changed into an open marketplace for opinions and values. Most people who have lived through this process as conscious participants have the clear impression that a lot has also changed in the experience of guilt. This, however, is not easy to substantiate. It is true that the study of guilt and pastoral care, for which Hans Strijards was awarded his doctorate a few years ago by the Theology Department at Tilburg University, is based on empirical research[3]. However, the empirical material is limited to the development experienced

---

3. H. STRIJARDS, *Schuld en pastoraat. Een poimenische studie over schuld als thema voor het pastorale groepsgesprek*, Kampen, Kok, 1997.

by participants in group pastoral counselling. Through what is called "self-confrontational investigation"[4] some participants seem to have evolved from traditional views of guilt (the displacement and self-punishment models) to the more open, communication model. There is no research into shifts in society, but social shifts are presupposed in the construction of the models. In doing so there is a clear preference for the latter model, focused on open communication, over the traditional model, in which God is either seen as the Saviour who has already dealt with sin (displacement) or as an infinitely exalted being who leaves punishment for sin to sinful mankind itself (the self-punishment model). The communication model corresponds to an image of God in which God is close, inwardly perceptible as solidarity, but transcendent and distant at the same time[5]. There is much to be said for this model as the ideal understanding of guilt in relation to God, toward which thinking about guilt and punishment is evolving. There are some developments to corroborate the preference for communication over imposition, such as the gradual replacement of guilt by shame, the loss of the readiness to accept guilt, and, finally, the changing conscience.

Guilt and shame have been discussed together in recent American studies[6]. This is not the old discussion of the differences between the Western guilt culture and the Eastern shame culture. That myth has by now been successfully deflated[7]. New studies focus on something different, which is appearing to an increasing degree in the individualised West. When people feel shame for their acts, they no longer gauge their conduct according to standards of good and evil – or at least that is no longer the first standard they use – but according to how they look in the eyes of others. This attitude is designated by the somewhat exaggerated adjective "narcissistic"[8]; in fact, it reflects the increased

---

4. A method developed by H.J.M. Hermans at Nijmegen. Cf. H.J.M. HERMANS – D. VERSTRAETEN, *Zelfonderzoek. Waarderingen van mensen in diverse toepassingsvelden*, Deventer, 1980; HERMANS, *Persoonlijkheid en waardering*, Lisse, 1984.

5. STRIJARDS, *Schuld* (n. 3), p. 108.

6. M. LEWIS, *Shame. The Exposed Self*, New York, 1992; D. CAPPS, *The Depleted Self. Sin in a Narcissistic Age*, Minneapolis, MN, Augsburg Fortress, 1993; cf. L. DERCKX, *Zonde en narcisme. De invloed van narcistische kwetsbaarheid op de hedendaagse religieuze communicatie*, in K. SONNBERGER (ed.), *Redden pastores het? Religieus leiderschap aan het begin van de eenentwintigste eeuw*, Budel, 2001, pp. 114-130.

7. J.-C. WOLF, *Stellvertretende Verantwortung und der moralische Begriff der Scham*, in *Evangelische Theologie* 53 (1993) 549-565.

8. C. LASCH, *De cultuur van het narcisme. Leven in een tijd van afnemende verwachtingen*, Amsterdam, Uitgeverij de Arbeiderspers, 1980; A. ULEIJN, *Helpen als identiteit. Het Echo-syndroom in de hulpverlening*, in R. NAUTA (ed.), *Helpen. Zin en onzin. Over de zin en de betekenis van helpen*, Kampen, Kok, 1993, pp. 73-90.

individualisation and privatisation of religious and philosophical questions. In this context, there is a natural tendency to reject guilt. It is true that shame is a negative evaluation of conduct displayed, but in many cases it is linked to absolving one's own responsibility to the other through whose gaze the shamefulness of the conduct is exposed. What is not seen cannot give rise to shame, and even less to the feeling of being guilty.

If shame arises instead of guilt as a reaction to deviant behaviour, then the reality of guilt disappears. Guilt then becomes something entirely different from a feeling that makes a person passive, silent, and ready to accept the burden of guilt and punishment. The conduct that is considered guilty according to the standards of tradition is open to re-evaluation when the traditions are no longer binding. Of course, the verdict of guilt can still be pronounced, but the attribution of guilt is no longer self-evident. Guilt is no longer objective: an act does not have to be what it appears to be. The premise of each legal system that someone is innocent until proven guilty is not just a formal premise that can coexist well with the consciousness of really being thoroughly guilty. In many cases, the premise serves as the point of departure for a long process of rebutting the bad sides of the conduct, of whitewashing and freeing oneself from a consciousness of guilt. Being guilty has become the main issue in argument and dispute. People no longer allow themselves to be convinced of guilt from outside themselves, by tradition or custom. Guilt has become the subject of negotiation.

One can rightly point to conscience as the faculty that makes people aware of the wrongness of their conduct. Conscience does indeed indicate to people real guilt deep in their hearts, even if the voice of conscience is repressed or drowned. However, the claim on conscience cannot prevent guilt from becoming more open to discussion, for conscience is also to a large extent determined by the context in which it is formed. That context is undeniably one of increasing liberality. Ad Verbrugge points out that what began in the 1960s as a process of emancipation, of accentuating autonomy, has now disintegrated into the denial of guilt and evil by both foreigners and native-borns[9].

---

9. A. VERBRUGGE, "Zinloos" geweld, in E. BRUGMANS (ed.), Rechtvaardiging en verzoening. Over de fundamenten van de moraal in een tijd van geweld, Budel, Damon, 2000, pp. 30-65, esp. 51-54.

III. Mutual Communication: Bargaining about Guilt

The culture of negotiation appears to go together with the new way of dealing with guilt, with the illusion of one's own innocence[10]. At first glance, the specifically religious understanding of guilt would seem to have a different structure: the exaltation and holiness of God are at the centre, and the acknowledgement of guilt and sinfulness on the part of man, therefore, follows as a matter of course. The recent pronouncement on the doctrine of justification, which was drawn up by the Lutheran World Council and the central institutions of the Roman Catholic Church and signed on October 31, 1999[11], is absolutely clear about the sinful state in which people, left to their own devices, constantly find themselves or actively enter. No resistance is possible against that. In ecclesiastical traditions, contrite acknowledgement and confession of sin and guilt have always been presented as the only adequate response. It is, therefore, all the more remarkable that the picture is different when the traditional dogmatic concepts are put aside and the sources themselves are examined.

The God of the Old Testament is often held up as a jealous and vengeful God. This is not entirely without reason, if you read how He presents himself in Exod 20,5: "I the LORD your God am a jealous God, visiting the iniquity of the fathers upon the children unto the third and fourth generation". This image is confirmed in many other places in the Bible. Yet, the God of the Bible is not an exalted God who will not tolerate argument. Israel's God establishes a community through His words and deeds, and His words invite response. The confession of God as the creator, an insight which was committed to words only rather late in the history of Israel, is the acknowledgement of God as the One who speaks the first, the creative word. Goethe altered the first line of the Bible and spoke of "In the beginning was the deed", in order to provide a foundation for his activistic vitalism. John the evangelist is apparently a more congenial interpreter of the creative power of Israel's God with His fascinating "In the beginning was the Word". The Word, the appeal, the prophetic call better characterise the God of the Old Covenant than the image of an implacable nemesis to wrongdoers.

---

10. Cf. the beginning of "Unsere Hoffnung", a text approved at the Synod of German Bishops at Würzburg (1971-1975). It speaks of the "heimliche Unschuldwahn". It is generally assumed that this text was written by the famous German defender of "political theology" J.B. Metz.

11. The text of the *Gemeinsame Erklärung über die Rechtfertigungslehre* which was ultimately signed at Augsburg on October 31, 1999, was available previous to this, among other sources in *Herder Korrespondenz* 50 (1997) 191-197.

Let me present some examples to support this. The story of Abraham negotiating with God about the gravity of the guilt of Sodom and Gomorrah is familiar. Is the guilt so heavy, if 50, 40, yes even 10 innocent men are enough to avert punishment? This classic example of a negotiating tactic, not without risk and fought out on the cutting edge, has to be contrasted with the scene in which the same Abraham obeys the order to sacrifice his own son, without argument and without objection. Other impressive examples are the plea of Moses for the preservation of the disobedient company he had led out of Egypt, as the object of God's covenant love (Exod 32,31-32), and the complaint of Elijah under the broom tree on His flight into the wilderness (I Kings 19). Moses had given himself over completely to the service of the Voice that revealed Itself from the burning bush as the One who would be for the people whose cry had reached Him and to which He had given His ear (Exod 3,1-14). He is bold enough to remind God of His first love, and he succeeds in convincing Him, that the guilt of the Israelites is not grave enough to destroy them. Elijah, in his turn, is granted an answer to His complaint. After his cry of despondency and rebelliousness, he is strengthened for the encounter with God on Mount Horeb (I Kings 19,4-8). The leader of the people and the prophet both quarrel with God in a context of guilt. They challenge God's right to react to guilt with punishment. But they do so in response to God's call. Their dealings with God have the nature of a response. They answer God, who is the first to speak.

One might object that these examples of negotiation are restricted to a very limited number of people who occupy a position near to God. They are the exception, just as forgiveness is restricted to those who are in power[12]. This type of conversation of humans with God is not accessible to ordinary people. However, there is another example, of a different nature, of the interactive character of the human relationship with God that includes more participants. It deals directly with the interpretation of law and punishment. Adrian Schenker and Bernd Janowski have investigated the origin and history of the charged word *kofèr*[13]. They concluded

12. Cf. C. HOUTMAN, *"Wie kan zonden vergeven dan God alleen?"* Over menselijke vergeving in het Oude Testament, in ID., et al. (eds.), *Ruimte voor vergeving,* Kampen, Kok, 1998, pp. 31-44.
13. A. SCHENKER, *Versöhnung und Widerstand. Bibeltheologische Untersuchung zum Strafen Gottes und der Menschen, besonders im Lichte von Exodus 21-22,* Stuttgart, Verlag Katholisches Bibelwerk, 1990; ID., *Sühne statt Strafe und Strafe statt Sühne! Zum biblischen Sühnebegriff,* in J. BLANK – J. WERBICK (eds.), *Sühne und Versöhnung,* Düsseldorf, Patmos Verlag, 1986, pp. 10-20; ID., *Versöhnung und Sühne. Wege gewaltfreier Konfliktlösung im Alten Testament. Mit einem Ausblick auf das Neue Testament,* Freiburg, 1981; B. JANOWSKI, *Sühne als Heilsgeschehen,* Neukirchen-Vluyn, Neukirchener Verlag, 1982;

that, in some cases, punishment for violating the law could be bought off. In that case, *kofèr* is the compensation that must be paid to the injured party in order to avoid the consequences – generally the death penalty – of the guilt incurred. The amicable settlement that comes instead of punishment is only valid if the offence has been committed without premeditation. In our view, this may not really be a negotiation about the degree of guilt and punishment. In such cases, we would not speak of guilt at all. However, for the parties involved, which include all ranks of the Israelite people, guilt was obvious and the way out acceptable.

These situations were negotiated in the presence of representatives of the law and brought the injured party in touch with the offender. Janowski demonstrates that the *kofèr*, or ransom, was later also employed to literally buy off guilt and punishment with God[14]. Here it appears that bargaining about the consequences of a violation of the law often involved offerings. Specifically it is the *placatio* aspect, the attempt to bring the deity to a favourable disposition again with the aid of the offering, which made sacrifices popular with ordinary people[15]. Remarkably enough, the common practice of sacrificing, which is an institutionalised form of negotiating guilt and reconciliation, is met with suspicion and theological objections[16]. It is often Christians from strong Reformation traditions who have problems with sacrifice. They do not doubt that God addresses man and can be addressed in turn. They are the first to speak of the Voice and the Word when they want to denote God. But they believe there is no room for God to have a negotiating partner[17]. The human partner is the one who is addressed, and he or she is not an equal partner in a dialogue, and certainly not someone who is in the position to extract something from the relationship. God is not to be drawn into the earthly matter of human failures. Even the suspicion that the principle of "do ut des" might be involved, is enough to reject all kinds of initiatives taken by humans to plead with God over guilt and sin.

ID., *Auslösung des verwirkten Lebens. Zur Geschichte und Struktur der biblischen Lösegeldvorstellung*, in *Zeitschrift für Theologie und Kirche* 79 (1982) 25-59.

14. JANOWSKI, *Auslösung des verwirkten Lebens* (n. 13), p. 45.

15. Cf. E.P. SANDERS, *Judaism. Practice & Belief 63 BCE – 66 CE*, London, SCM Press, 1992, pp. 103-118 ("Sacrifices").

16. Cf. N. SCHREURS, *A Non-sacrificial Interpretation of Christian Redemption?*, in T. MERRIGAN – J. HAERS (eds.), *The Myriad Christ. Plurality and the Quest for Unity in Contemporary Christology*, Leuven, Peeters, 2000, 551-565.

17. Cf. I.U DALFERTH, *Die soteriologische Relevanz der Kategorie des Opfers. Dogmatische Erwägungen im Anschluß an die gegenwärtige exegetische Diskussion*, in *Jahrbuch für Bibl. Theol.* 6 (1991) 173-194.

Taken to an extreme, several biblical scholars have wanted to keep God entirely out of the conflict over guilt and punishment. In this view, God does not dirty His hands with people who do not wish to follow Him and His law. Wrongdoers, idolaters, and all who think they can manage without God, who resist His guidance or persist in doing their own will rather than that of God, will discover that they have got themselves into a corner from which there is no way out, and the evil of their deeds redounds upon them. No punishing God needs to act. Evil punishes itself[18].

I shall return to this view presently. It postulates a division between God and human kind that is similar to the distinct roles of God and autonomous person in today's secularised society. First, I will return to the conception of the response of God and people to evil and sin that I find more representative of the Bible as a whole, including the books in what we have come to call the New Testament. Although the ancestral God with the unutterable name YHWH loses much of His directness and appetite for intervention in the course of Israel's History, He (or She) remains involved with humankind, and people remain in dialogue with God. Sometimes the dialogue takes the character of bitter reproaches or deep self-pity, as in some psalms[19]. Sometimes it becomes an outright war of words with God, as when Job challenges God to come and justify the suffering that he, Job, has been forced to undergo (Job 30-32). Sometimes a prophet fights against the voice and the call that emanates from God and that seriously thwarts the life and plans of the prophet (Jonah 4,2-3). Jesus adds himself to the list of Jewish believers who argue with God about His policy and who feel unjustly dealt with, calling upon the words of Psalm 22: "My God, My God, why have You forsaken me?" (Mark 15,34; Matt 27,46). In Luke and John this complaint is transformed into a loud cry of surrender, to soften the offence that the versions of Mark and Matthew still allowed to stand. Luke, however, tolerates this same disunity between the Father and the Son when he reports how Jesus prays for His enemies, "Father, forgive them, for they know not what they do" (Luke 23,24). Here, Jesus is in the tradition of the outspoken, faithful Jew who argues against a justified punishment and pleads for forgiveness.

---

18. K. KOCH, *Gibt es ein Vergeltungsdogma im Alten Testament?*, in *Zeitschrift für Theologie und Kirche* 52 (1955) 1-42. Cf. B. JANOWSKI, *Die Tat kehrt zum Täter zurück. Offene Fragen im Umkreis des "Tun-Ergehen-Zusammenhangs"*, in *Zeitschrift für Theologie und Kirche* 91 (1994) 247-271.

19. Cf. U. BERGES, *Zwijgen is zilver – klagen is goud: Pleidooi voor een herontdekking van het bijbelse klagen*, in *Tijdschrift voor Theologie* 41 (2001) 231-252.

These examples are insufficient to reflect the whole wealth of the relation between God and man that is encompassed in the stories in Scripture, but they do remind us of a dominant tradition that opposes the concept of an authoritarian, unapproachable God who instantly and personally punishes everyone guilty of violating His law and of sin. The examples present an image of a God who speaks to humankind and lets Himself be addressed. God is approachable, responsive to prayer, and enters into dialogue and even disputes. Mutual relations and their restoration are part of the deepest core of God, although that may be hidden from the eye by bellicose language that announces the destruction of Israel's enemies (or Israel itself), or by patriarchal relations that are only focused on the powerful and, for instance, exclude women. The ideal of a good mutual relationship is expressed more clearly in the inviting, provocative, summoning and engaged Word than in the stories of a God who shapes and acts in history. Is the theology of the history of salvation, for decades the pet of leftist liberation theology and progressive political theology, to be cast off in favour of the theology of the Word? Things are not that simple. But the theology of God's mighty acts has certainly more difficulty making itself credible than a theology of the relation between God and humanity, initiated by God's address in the Word and continued by the response of humankind, assenting or praising the words of God's wisdom, but also, as the case may be, disputing them. A theology or theory of God's acts posits a God with an intention and an end goal, or, as the American theologian Gordon Kaufman once expressed it, a master-plan. Within such a plan, the terrorist attack on the World Trade Center, for instance, must also have a place and objectively make sense. A theology of the word, however, with relations and communication between God and man, calls upon people to give their own response.

However, one factor from the legacy of modern times comes into play and threatens to also undermine this theology of communication and relation. What happens if this communication turns out to be a dialogue with a God who does not listen and does not react, a God who is, so to speak, a deaf-mute? That seems to be the general direction in which our concept of God is moving. This is true not only for all sorts of vague, new religious movements, from New Age to Zen meditation groups, but for traditional denominations and churches as well that cannot entirely escape this way of seeing God[20]. Does God still play a role in relation to guilt, punishment, forgiveness, and reconciliation, or must we, as in the above

---

20. A. VAN HARSKAMP, *Het nieuw-religieuze verlangen*, Kampen, Kok, 2000.

mentioned view of evil, which is its own punishment, leave God out of this, or, at most, retain God but only as an impersonal force behind human freedom and autonomy?

IV. DIALOGUE WITH A DEAF-MUTE?

The image is crude: God as a deaf-mute in conversation. Yet, that is the implication of the appearance of pantheism that surrounds many contemporary concepts of God. Pantheism itself, the identification of the whole of reality with God, is seldom openly avowed, because pantheism is too much a philosophical position and too little a profession of faith with an ecclesiastical or confessional following. Increasing numbers of people have difficulty imagining God as a person with clear intentions and plans who intervenes to punish sinners or avenge violations of His law. But if God is no longer credible as an acting person, then the communication we are accustomed to engage in with a speaking person who promises forgiveness is also hard to imagine. The critique of religion by the "masters of suspicion", Feuerbach, Marx, Nietzsche, and Freud, suggested that images of God are the result of projection. In a recent book, Kuitert has very expressively characterised this as follows: God is an enlargement of man[21].

Until recently, pantheism was no more a serious theological option than were atheism and agnosticism. The concept often functioned as a "no trespassing" sign: unacceptable conceptions of God were combated by pointing to pantheism as their ultimate consequence. It was precisely at those moments in history in which radical revolutions in religious life and theology were taking place that the tactic was most used. The period around 1800 was such a time of transition. Attempts to see belief and God from other vantage points quickly fell into a suspicion of pantheism. Friedrich Schleiermacher, who moved in the salons of Berlin where free and enlightened thinking had gained currency, wrote an apology in 1799 for the rightness and reasonableness of religion and Christianity, which made a considerable impression on early Romantic circles[22]. In these circles – unlike in the heyday of Enlightenment rationalism – people had again become quite sensitive to religion and welcomed

---

21. H.M. KUITERT, *Over religie. Aan de liefhebbers onder haar beoefenaars,* Baarn, Ten Have, 2000, pp. 44-46.
22. F.D.E. SCHLEIERMACHER, *Über die Religion. Reden an die Gebildeten unter ihren Verächtern,* Berlin, 1799.

Schleiermacher's argument. The label of pantheism, which was attached to the book in orthodox Christian quarters, has long continued to plague it, however[23]. Evidently we find ourselves once again in such a transitional period. The "God-is-dead" days are now behind us. There is a renewed interest in religion and discussion of God and religion is once more uninhibited. There is one important difference with the period of confessionalism and "columniation". People refuse to accept the anthropomorphic images prescribed or implied in church doctrine. Empirical research among students at the Catholic University at Nijmegen indicates that the classic image of a God as a person who intervenes in individual lives and in the cosmos (theism) comes in last place among them. Panentheism and pantheism, on the other hand, come in first and second place[24]. Research in theodicy also indicates that there is a preference for models that do not proceed from a God who intervenes, who is out for revenge, but rather from a God of compassion, proceeding from immanent fulfilment and proximity[25].

Does the preference for a pantheistic concept of God mean the denial of all personal characteristics? In general, people do not go that far. In fact, what they espouse is panentheism, the concept that God is present in everything, rather than pantheism, which in a strict sense equates reality with God. Despite his rejection of God as an enlargement of the human person and his warning that everything that is said to come from above in fact comes from below, i.e., from the human imagination, Kuitert also appears to continue to consider God as a discreet, independent reality. In his eyes, God is the Creator, who has power to make and break people, and who addresses them. Religion is feeling and knowing that one is being approached by the Word of a speaking God[26]. The glimmer of pantheism that Van der Ven detects with those he interviewed appears to be reconcilable with celebrating liturgy and prayer[27]. Michael Levine, an Australian theologian who has devoted himself to the in-depth study of

23. J. LAMM, *The Living God: Schleiermacher's Theological Appropriation of Spinoza*, University Park Pennsylvania, State University Press, 1996.

24. J.A. VAN DER VEN, *God in Nijmegen. Een theologisch perspectief*, in *Tijdschrift voor Theologie* 32 (1992) 225-249.

25. E. VOSSEN, *Religieuze zingeving een troost voor het lijden?*, in B. VEDDER, et al. (eds.), *Zin tussen vraag en aanbod. Theologische en wijsgerige beschouwingen over zin*, Tilburg, TUP, 1992, pp. 301-319. The data for this research came from five Catholic parishes in Ottawa Canada, and was gathered in 1990.

26. KUITERT, *Over religie* (n. 21), pp. 119-120; pp. 171-191.

27. J.A. VAN DER VEN, *De structuur van het religieuze bewustzijn. Verkenning van de spanning tussen religiositeit en kerkelijkheid*, in *Tijdschrift voor Theologie* 36 (1996) 39-60, esp. p. 59.

pantheism, takes great pains to arrive at adequate definitions and clear distinctions of his concepts. It is too simple to view pantheism and a personal God as opposites, or mutually exclusive concepts[28].

This last observation is a good place to begin theological investigation. Dealing with guilt, punishment, forgiveness, and reconciliation are topics of great weight in a world that is subject to influences from cultures and religions from around the globe. If the biblical and Christian tradition also continues to play a role in a convincing manner, then the obvious biblical concept of God as a person committed to mankind must be able to be reconciled with the contemporary reservations with regard to viewing God as a person. It is not an acceptable answer to theologically resign oneself to proceeding from the impossibility of knowing but little of God or God's intentions. Agnosticism or its non-philosophical variant, dubiety, simply leave the riddles of existence untouched. Although mysteries will remain that will never yield up their profoundest depths, there are enough possibilities for speaking about the roles of God and man in guilt, the acknowledgement of guilt and the discharge of guilt in an intelligible manner. The concept of a God prepared to communicate and enter into relationships is perhaps as anthropomorphic as that of an intervening God. But the word that God is the first to speak invites endorsement from humankind, without coercion and with full respect for human freedom. The Voice that proposes relationship and the restoration of relationship is personal and not just a voice in someone's head or an anonymous message from the cosmos. That does not mean that God is a person in a literal sense. Being a person involves limitation, individuality and indivisibility[29]. The modern concept of the "subject" (God as the acting subject or forgiving subject) is too much a product of the Cartesian distinction between consciousness and the world of objects. Adhering to the concept that God, despite everything, is still a person follows from the (religious) conviction that God has made Himself known as a personal factor in the experience of Israel, the prophets, the writers of the biblical texts, and the witnesses in the history of Christianity and the Church. Conceiving God as a person remains a metaphor, and in that sense a construction to aid human discourse. God is not a person in the strictly human sense. God is more than a person. However, God is conceived as if He or She were in a certain sense a person, namely to the extent that God is able to enter into relationships and

28. M. LEVINE, *Pantheism. A Non-theistic Concept of Deity*, London – New York, 1994.

29. Boethius famously defined it in the words "persona est individua substantia rationalis naturae".

communicate, and to speak words of forgiveness and reconciliation. It must always be borne in mind that the differences with the human sense of being a person are always much greater than the similarities[30].

When we are conscious that metaphors are approaches that touch upon the core, the images in which God's solution to sin and guilt are expressed all have their own value. There is the image of the victorious warrior on the battlefield, in combat with the Devil and evil, of the judge and the accused before the court, and of the priest and the sacrifice on the altar[31]. All express the sovereignty of God with respect to evil, sin, and guilt. The emphasis lies very strongly on the evidence of human wrong and the inescapable sinfulness of humankind. However, there is also an element of conflict and opposition in all. Human responsibility depends upon the acknowledgement of our failures out of our own free will. Responsibility also implies the answer, our own input, and the consideration of the response to the appeal. That presupposes a relation, as between two partners. The openness derived from that is founded precisely in the belief in God's offer of open communication. Enough indications of this can be found in Scripture and tradition, as Dorothea Sattler demonstrates in her book on relationship thinking in soteriology[32].

A final deepening of the proposition that guilt and sin are not to be settled without dispute or negotiation can be found in the very abstract sounding but far-reaching proposal by Edward Schillebeeckx to attribute mediated immediacy to God[33]. The saving closeness of God is effected in God's way: directly, without the intervention of anyone or anything. That argues for the divine sovereignty of the grace of forgiveness and reconciliation, and obedient acceptance by man. However, the immediacy only takes into account the perfect reality of God. If that reality wishes to reach mankind, then mediation is necessary. Mediators are necessary, such as Abraham and Moses, who plead for others, who ask God to look at sin and guilt once more, in a different way. The immediacy

---

30. Cf. the famous pronouncement of the Fourth Lateran Council (1215): "... inter creatorem et creaturam non potest tanta similitudo notari, quin inter eos maior sit dissimilitudo notanda" (DH 806).

31. C. GUNTON, *The Actuality of Atonement. A Study of Metaphor, Rationality and the Christian Tradition*, Edinburgh, T&T Clark, 1988.

32. D. SATTLER, *Beziehungsdenken in der Erlösungslehre. Bedeutung und Grenzen*, Freiburg – Basel – Vienna, Herder, 1997, pp. 330-426 ("Tiefenschärfe: Biblische Bilder für Gottes erlösende Beziehungssuche").

33. E. SCHILLEBEECKX, *Gerechtigheid en liefde, genade en bevrijding*, Bloemendaal, Nelissen, 1977, pp. 752-755 ("Bemiddelde onmiddellijkheid: biddende omgang met God").

demands mediation. Otherwise God remains the Absent One, as is often the case in our time, with its largely silted up sense of the sacred and transcendent. Mediation has always been necessary, either in the metaphors of word, the act of creation and restoration of relationship, or in covenant or partnership. The most far-reaching mediation is the union of God with the mediation itself, the incarnation or coming down of God Himself, the self-emptying of God in a man, Jesus of Nazareth. Jesus is the mediator between free, autonomous people and God. He is the one who fills the place of people with God, speaking for them as an intermediary. Dorothee Sölle turns this proposition of faith around and suggests that Jesus also represents the absent, elusive God presenting himself in immediacy, making God' presence with humanity felt[34]. He passes God's liberating readiness for reconciliation on to humankind. With God, he is like the person "who we would want to be": a free person, conscious of His human dignity. He is the mediator who negotiates between parties. To stay with the metaphor of negotiation, he determines the compensation to be paid. To use another metaphor: he explores the relationships and deems blessed those who deserve it and summons to repentance, in order to "stand upright before God"[35].

V. Conclusion
Dialogic/Relational Interaction with God and Forgiveness

I will now briefly summarise the argument and results. The verdict of guilt and the infliction of punishment are not a sovereign act or word from God coming from on high, poured out over sinful people, and received passively by them. God is indeed the first to make the offer of restoration of communication and relationship. In this sense God's attitude regarding humankind is that of a person: compassionate, opening communication and inviting response. The consequence of the divine appeal is the establishment (or re-establishment) of people as free covenant partners. Negotiating guilt seems to be going too far in the relation between Creator and creation. But the mediation that is necessary in order to make the immediacy of God's relation to humankind perceptible and understandable, in fact, leads to the representation of the

---

34. D. SÖLLE, *Stellvertretung. Ein Kapitel Theologie nach dem Tode Gottes*, Stuttgart, Kreuz Verlag, 1965.

35. The quotations in the final sentences are taken from Huub Oosterhuis. His poetic, liturgical language points toward the reality which is difficult to catch in everyday language other than in abstracta, as in the case of "mediated immediacy".

transcendent God among us, and in particular, to Jesus of Nazareth. The way in which Jesus deals with guilt – He, one of us, a human being in His role as mediator between God and humanity – has been called *commercium admirabile*. It is the ultimate result of God's offer of communication and relation, of transcendence and immanence. In the spirit of that communication, it can be proposed that the questions surrounding guilt and punishment, forgiveness and reconciliation are settled at the level of open exchange between free partners – or, expressed metaphorically, with indictment and rejoinder.

Theologische Faculteit Tilburg   Nico SCHREURS
Universiteit van Tilburg
Academielaan 9
NL-5037 ET Tilburg
The Netherlands

CATHOLIC SOCIAL THOUGHT AND THE GLOBAL
COMMON GOOD

AN EMERGING TRADITION

I

Roman Catholic social ethics has traditionally been grounded in moral objectivity, in common moral goods, and in progressive social reform. These values are at the root of the traditional just war theory, but they are challenged by contemporary critical philosophies, by confessional as well as communitarian religious ethics, by cultural pluralism, and by sanctioned violence. Increasingly, ethno-political conflict makes intercultural discourse about socio-political change both urgent and simultaneously problematic. The real dilemma of social ethics is whether, as well as how, it can extend the community's sphere of solidarity to its historical victims.

Given potential nuclear destruction and the apparently increasing need for humanitarian intervention Catholic social theorists are more reticent now about justifying violence, since aggression seems to precipitate more destruction. The premise of the just war theory, now increasingly dubious, was that human life would be improved by carefully calibrated violence. Ethicists are now more interested in strategies of reconciliation and the reconstruction of societies after civil conflict. Practice-based theories of reconciliation have to be grounded on an understanding of moral objectivity that can be developed historically and inductively from experience so that the yield will be a common good. In brief, the central concern of an authentic Christian ethics is not to be a merely unique conception of the human good, based on tradition, but has to be the development of a "common good" that will lead to the expansion of moral solidarity toward the oppressed and the antagonist.

It seems clear that religion has had a major role in perpetrating ethnic violence[1]. In the former Yugoslavia, for example, religion has motivated

---

1. R.S. APPLEBY, *The Ambivalence of the Sacred: Religion, Violence, and Reconciliation*, New York, Rowman and Littlefield, 2000; M. VOLF, *Exclusion and Embrace: A Theological Exploration of Identity, Otherness, and Reconciliation*, Nashville, TN, Abingdon Press, 1996.

or legitimated hatred and killing in the name of God by building group identity and linking it to a transcendent absolute. Tragically and sinfully, religious identity is often a tool in defining the "human" sphere in exclusivist terms. Faith is used as a weapon against outsiders as well as the actual motivation behind killing. Christian ideals of forgiveness and peacemaking have to begin playing a guiding role in what finally must be a public, ecumenical process of recreating a humane common life. In very practical terms, the "word of God" has to drive men and women to build a society in which nutrition, employment, health, education, and a share of happiness are no longer luxuries for a small elite group. Human rights are not the exclusive property of a few, but rather are possessed by all God's images.

II

For Catholic ethicists, this reappropriation of Aquinas' "communal context" also makes it necessary to show the continuity of new perceptions with this earlier tradition and to defend the consistency as well as the objectivity of ethics against the possibility that historical contextualization signals absolute relativity. David Hollenbach, for example, argues that the current Catholic ideal of human rights demands a reinterpretation of the individualist presupposition of liberalism in light of a more communitarian perspective on the social order. He also refutes the historical and social constructionist objections to natural law theory, which have been proposed by MacIntyre, Rorty, and Rawls. Their positions seem to undermine transcommunal bonds of solidarity. If rights are granted and weighted by their recognition in community, then the relevant community of human rights is "the community of all human beings as such[2]". Similarly, David Tracy takes for granted that moral appeals must be rooted in particular traditions, yet endeavors to show "why an appeal to particular traditions needs not be merely particularist or private". Although he "fully endorses the turn to inner-Christian resources ... in contemporary Catholic social thought", he does so without giving up

2. D. HOLLENBACH, *A Communitarian Reconstruction of Human Rights: Contributions from Catholic Tradition*, in R. DOUGLAS – D. HOLLENBACH (eds.), *Catholicism and Liberalism: Contributions to American Public Philosophy*, Cambridge, Cambridge University Press, 1994, pp. 127-150; A. MACINTYRE, *Whose Justice? Which Rationality?*, Notre Dame, IN, University of Notre Dame Press, 1988, Chapter XVIII; R. RORTY, *Postmodernist Bourgeois Liberalism*, in R. HOLLINGER (ed.), *Hermeneutics and Praxis,* Notre Dame, IN, University of Notre Dame Press, 1985, pp. 219-220; J. RAWLS, *The Idea of an Overlapping Consensus*, in *Oxford Journal of Legal Studies* 7 (1987/1) 1-25, p. 4.

appeals to reason and even to a type of objectivism in discussing "the good life" within a pluralistic society. Hollenbach more recently has proposed a "dialogical universalism", in which reason is embedded in history and nurtured by tradition, yet also committed to appropriating a "transcultural ethic for an interdependent world". Respect for human rights requires an ongoing dynamic between universal standards of justice in an inclusive community and the particularist self-understandings of diverse local communities. "Dialogue – the active engagement of listening and speaking with others whose beliefs and traditions are different – is the key to such dynamism[3]".

To develop a theory that addresses the importance of solidarity with victims, the first step is to show that Catholic social thought can nourish an understanding of the global common good. This millennium confronts all religious communities with a challenge: how can they relate their distinctive vision of the good human life to the notion that all persons are linked together in a web of a global awareness. This interdependent world is increasingly aware of a religious and cultural pluralism that means that there is no agreement about the meaning of the good life. In addition, the complexity of emerging world realities is leading many communities to seek reaffirmation of the distinctive traditions that have historically set them apart from others. Paradoxically, attaining a vision of the global common good is increasingly problematic at the very historical moment when the need for such a vision is growing[4].

Roman Catholic social thought has sought to address this paradox. Since Vatican II, Catholic social thought has been more sensitive to the distinctive biblical and religious faith of the Catholic church, while it has also tried to contribute through discourse, ecumenical understanding and interreligious dialogue to the common moral vision needed in an interdependent world. The Catholic community has been only partially successful in these efforts to be faithful to its own beliefs while making a contribution to the global common good since the era of Vatican II. Prior to Vatican II, the main lines of Catholic social teaching were derived from the conviction that human reason is capable of discerning the basic

---

3. D. TRACY, *Catholic Classics in American Liberal Culture*, in DOUGLAS – HOLLENBACH, *Catholicism and Liberalism* (n. 2), pp. 197-199; D. HOLLENBACH, *The Distinctiveness of Catholic Social Thought and the Global Common Good*, in J. CALWEG – A. KRASIKOV (eds.), *Church and Society: A Dialogue*, Paris, Cerf, 2001.

4. L. MILLER, *Global Order: Values and Power in International Politics*, 4th ed., Boulder, CO, Westview Press, 1998; J. MOORE (ed.), *Hard Choices: Moral Dilemmas in Humanitarian Intervention*, New York, Rowman and Littlefield, 1998.

outlines of the human good. From Leo XIII's *Rerum Novarum* (1891) to John XXIII's *Pacem in Terris* (1963), Catholic contributions to social morality appealed to human reason to uncover the moral demands of human nature created by God[5].

Human rights as articulated in *Pacem in Terris* are founded on a dignity manifested in rationality and freedom. Such rights are discernible by all reasonable people and so not restricted to Christians. Although the encyclical asserted that human rights will be esteemed more highly when considered in the light of revelation and grace[6], it is clear that the Pope proposed an ethical standard that can be known by those who are not Christian and to which all people can be held accountable independent of their religious or cultural traditions. Christian faith serves to reinforce a sense of human worth through its belief in God's redemptive love.

This natural law ethic of human rights was seen as universal, transcultural, and suited to the promotion of the common good in a religiously pluralistic world. Such a natural law-based, universalist ethic has deep roots in the Roman Catholic tradition beginning in Paul's letter to the Romans and reinforced by Thomas Aquinas. This desire to find a common moral ground between Christians and non-Christians is also a deep impulse in the Catholic tradition because of its belief that one God has created the whole of humanity and that all human beings share a common origin, destiny and nature.

Because Vatican II was the first gathering of bishops as a World Church[7], it heightened awareness that the cultural and religious pluralism of the world has an effect on what people see as the reasonable demands of social morality. Because of the growing sense of the unity of the human family along with the increased exchange of ideas across cultural and religious boundaries, "the very words by which key concepts are expressed take on quite different meanings"[8]. This expansion of the church's self-consciousness at Vatican II questioned whether universal norms of social morality are, indeed, readily evident to all reasonable people. There emerged a suspicion of universalism, but certainly not an

5. JOHN XXIII, *Pacem in Terris*, 9-10. See for a translation D. O'BRIEN – T. SHANNON (eds.), *Catholic Social Thought: The Documentary Heritage*, Maryknoll, NY, Orbis Books, p. 199.
6. K. RAHNER, *Toward a Fundamental Theological Interpretation of Vatican II*, in *TS* 40 (1979) 716-727.
7. References to all the remaining Vatican II documents are from W. ABBOTT – J. GALLAGHER (eds.), *The Documents of Vatican II*, New York, American Press, 1966.
8. *Gaudium et Spes*, 4.

abandonment"[9] of traditional Roman Catholic social thought. How to root theology in universalism and pluralism became the issue.

Vatican II highlighted the tensions that have confronted Catholic social theorists. *Gaudium et Spes*[10] challenged the rationalist bent that Christian ethical reflection can rely exclusively on philosophical reason and natural law. The church's social mission is a religious one that flows from the heart of the Christian faith. In essence, the Council and subsequently John Paul II through his encyclicals *Veritatis Splendor* and *Evangelium Vitae* have sought to sustain this tense balance in moral reflection. They have reaffirmed that a universal ethic or common morality is normative in all cultures and for all religious communities. They have also affirmed a distinctively Christian ontological foundation for this ethic as well as an epistemology based on revelation through which this ethic can be known. Is such a position coherent?

Several interpretations of the relationship between universalist and particularist sources that could help explain the dualism have been offered. First, one could affirm that universal moral standards are theoretically knowable by all persons, but that in practice revelation is required because of the distortions created by the human mind because of sin. In the concreteness of existence, for most people, revelation and grace are needed to know and live by the natural law. The problem, of course, is that this approach ignores the presence of sin in the Christian community itself. Second, like John Paul II, one could assert that the authoritative teaching office of the church guarantees that the magesterium is capable of teaching the universally normative natural law in ways that are preserved by the Holy Spirit. But such a response would not be appreciated by a pluralistic world. A third approach, i.e., dialogic universalism, conceived of reason as embedded in history and less abstract than that propagated by the Enlightenment. Neither the questions addressed by rational discourse nor the thought patterns available to address these questions are the products of an ahistorical pure reason. Urgent questions, for example, arise from the anomalies that become apparent within an ongoing tradition of inquiry[11].

Several Catholic theologians[12] have tried to combine fidelity to the particularistic, Catholic based social thought with a commitment to the

---

9. *Optatam Totius*, 16.

10. *Gaudium et Spes*, 22.

11. P. LAUREN, *The Evolution of International Human Rights: Vision Seen*, Philadelphia, PA, University of Pennsylvania Press, 1998.

12. J.F. KEENAN, *Moral Theology and History*, in *TS* 62 (2001) 86-104; J. PORTER, *The Search for a Global Ethic*, in *TS* 62 (2002) 105-121.

common morality needed in a pluralistic, historically interdependent world. This awareness of historical, cultural, and religious pluralism has been forcefully re-introduced into Catholic thought with force since Vatican II. Such sensitivity has raised new questions about the possibility of the transcultural ethic sought by a natural law theory that is based upon transhistorical human reasoning. Doubts about such powerful claims for pure reason led this historically conscious Council to reemphasize the distinctively religious basis of Catholic social thought. The recognition of pluralism simultaneously also led to a heightened awareness of the need for a transcultural ethic for an independent world.

The Council began to respond to this paradox by stressing dialogue and mutual inquiry among the diverse communities of the world. For the Catholic church this meant pursuing a common morality from the vantage point of its own theological convictions. It also has meant bringing these convictions into an active encounter with other religious communities. Such a method of dialogue does not necessarily mean relativism, but rather seems to acknowledge that there is a truth about human good that must be pursued and that makes a claim on the minds and hearts of all persons[13].

III

When the Council stressed the particularity of its theological understanding of human dignity, this did not lead it to deny the universality of morality rooted in this theology. Such universalism, however, was conceived as the outcome of inquiry and dialogue, not one already in full possession by the church, simply to be proposed to or imposed upon others. *Gaudium et Spes* urged dialogue with other traditions as potential sources for an ethic that would be more adequate theologically and would be normatively human. The council also stressed inter-Christian ecumenical dialogue and conversations with the other great world religions[14].

This commitment to dialogue was demanded by Christian faith and required by reasonableness. Christian faith entails the respect for the dignity of all persons and means listening to their interpretations of the common good. Christians have also called for the construction of bonds of solidarity to connect all persons. Such an approach would seem to require efforts to understand those who are different, to learn from them, and to

13. *Gaudium et Spes*, 40, 44; *Unitatis Redintegratio* and *Nostra Aetate*.
14. *Dignitatis Humanae*, 2.

develop an understanding of the good life. A reasonableness that avoids the rationalist dismissal of historical traditions and communal particularities would have to take seriously the diversity of the traditions and cultures of the world as well as both listen carefully to them and to respond with respect. For Christians, such dialogue embodies the dynamic interaction between the biblical faith handed on to them through the centuries of the Christian tradition and the attribute of reason that manifests the *imago Dei* in all human beings.

Such dialogue and the dynamic linkage of faith and reason impacts on such substantive questions of social morality as the delineation of a political and economic ethic of human rights. The social nature of human beings and their intrinsic dignity means "the goal of all social institutions is and must be the human person"[15]. The implementation of this commitment to human rights in an ethic of dialogue has important implications for the way these rights play out. A dialogic ethic means that any engagement must be conducted with deep respect for those who hold differing beliefs. Thus, the faithful should "at all times refrain from any manner of action which might seem to carry a hint of coercion"[16]. Persuasion through reasonable discourse is the proper mode of public participation by religious believers, who seek to influence law or public policy.

More broadly, such a dialogical understanding has implications for how to address the meaning of the full range of human rights. The West, for example, has generally conceived of human rights in individualistic terms by giving priority to the civil and political rights inherent in free speech, due process of law, and political participation. Nations in Eastern Europe and developing nations have adopted Marxist inspired ideologies that stress such social and economic rights as adequate food, work, and housing. A dialogical ethic would suggest that these two traditions ought to learn from the strengths of one another and would insist that the opposition between individual freedoms and mutual solidarity in society is a false dichotomy. Dignity and a community of freedom go together. Both personal initiative and social solidarity have to be valued. The linkage of personal initiative and social solidarity has material dimensions and will emerge only when persons have both economic and political space for action as well as the institutional and material bases for communal life that make such action possible. As an agenda both sets of rights as human rights should be respected in all societies. Despite the challenging nature of such an agenda, it can guide social, political, and

15. *Gaudium et Spes*, 25, 41.
16. *Dignitatis Humanae*, 4.

economic institutions in a way that a one-sided emphasis on the interpretation of human rights would fail to provide[17].

A dialogical approach to the interpretation of human rights is needed in a religiously diverse world, since human rights are moral norms proposed as protections for all persons. Western Enlightenment thought interpreted such universality to mean that human rights are moral standards independent of all traditions, cultures and religions. The contemporary awareness of the historical embeddedness of rationality, however, seems to dispute this claim to transcend history and communal traditions. This has led such theorists as Richard Rorty to reject the very notion of human rights as an Enlightenment illusion[18]. Mainstream Catholic social thought, however, still affirms the reality of normative human rights. Such a continuing defense seems crucial, since threats to human dignity continue today on a massive scale. Any such defense must take into account, however, the ways that "normative human rights" and the interpretation of their concrete implications would vary from one philosophical, ideological, or religious tradition to another.

Judaism, Christianity, and Islam as religious traditions, for example, influence the way human rights are understood by the adherents of these faiths. The central place of communal identity and of the meaning of Israel in Judaism leads to human rights that emphasize the right of the Jewish people to national self-determination. Western Christians stress the political rights of individual persons. The radical monotheism of Islam leads many Muslims to argue that universal human rights will only be secured in a society submissive in some fashion to Allah. The religious beliefs of each community shape the intellectual and affective horizons that structure the human rights conversation. Thus, both the theoretical and practical defense of human rights must take into account the influence of these religious traditions. Pursuing respect for human rights requires an ongoing dialogue about how universal standards relate to the distinctive, particularist self-understandings of the religious communities of the world. Such a perspective would seem to mean that commitment to ecumenical and interreligious dialogue is at least one prerequisite for a global human rights ethic today[19].

17. D. HOLLENBACH, *A Communitarian Reconstruction of Human Rights* and *Afterward: A Community of Freedom*, in DOUGLAS – HOLLENBACH (eds.), *Catholicism and Liberalism* (n. 2), pp. 127-150 and pp. 323-343.

18. RORTY, *Postmodernist Bourgeois Liberalism* (n. 2), pp. 219-220.

19. H. KÜNG – K.J. KUSCHEL (eds.), *A Global Ethic: The Declaration of the Parliament of the World's Religions*, trans. J. BOWDEN, New York, Continuum, 1993; H. KÜNG (ed.), *Yes to a Global Ethic*, trans. J. BOWDEN, New York, Continuum, 1993; KEENAN,

IV

The challenge of today's pluralistic and interdependent world leads to a new way of conceiving the ancient question of the relationship between faith and reason in the context of the development of an ethic that can guide the church's social role. This new relationship has to be the product of the interaction between fidelity to the distinctive traditions of Christianity and to the pursuit of an inclusive, universal community. Dialogue as the active engagement of listening and speaking with others, who do not share identical beliefs and traditions, is the key to such a dynamic. Vatican II launched the Roman Catholic community on this path of dialogue.

A consciousness of history seems to suggest that moral theology must not only develop, but also be alert to the foundational impulse that norms need to be consonant with human motives and needs. Historical investigation has served as a corrective to theory regarding the immutability of moral truth. Christianity itself has developed through its practices, which continuously identify the fundamental moral concerns of the faithful. The very successes of pragmatic negotiation, for example, seem to suggest that there are significant commonalities in human existence that make cross cultural moral consensus a real possibility. Such a consensus is not a given, bestowed on us by universal norms; but that does not mean that we have to despair of attaining the transcultural. The best way to achieve consensus that is sensitive to varied religions and cultural traditions as well as to the contemporary political, social, and economic realities impacting on men and women today is to engage in authentic dialogue. In this model faith can engage culture.

Catholic social ethics can meet the moral challenge mounted by ethnic violence only by providing a moral paradigm that can honestly confront human evil, while offering us a common human nature that urges us toward greater solidarity as we embrace the contribution of differing cultures. Whether Catholicism can also help create real communities, in which these ideals become practical norms, remains to be seen. Through

Moral Theology and History (n. 11), pp. 93, 103; PORTER, *The Search for a Global Ethic* (n. 11), p. 120; B. HINZE, *Ecclesial Repentence and the Demands of Dialogue*, in *TS* 61 (2000) 207-238, p. 219; C. SHRAG, *The Self After Modernity*, New Haven, CT, Yale University Press, 1997, pp. 128-138; W. STEGMAIER, *Heimsuchung: Das Dialogische in der Philosophie des 20. Jahrhunderts*, in G. FÜRST (ed.), *Dialog als Selbstvollzug der Kirche?* (Quaestiones disputatae, 166), Freiburg, Herder, 1997, pp. 9-29; J. DEAN, *Solidarity of Strangers: Feminism after Identity Politics*, Berkeley, CA, University of California Press, 1996; T.J. MARTIN, *Living Words: Studies in Dialogue about Religion*, Atlanta, GA, Scholars Press, 1998.

a dialogical model, moral theology will be taking a real risk by entering the world of marching soldiers.

Department of Theology   Donald DIETRICH
Boston College
140 Commonwealth Ave.
Chestnut Hill, MA 02467
U.S.A.

FROM A PRIVATE TO A PUBLIC CONVERSATION IN THE CHURCH

THE CASE OF THE CATHOLIC CHURCH IN SLOVENIA

This article reflects on the situation of the Catholic Church in Slovenia, within which the existing relationship between clergy and laypeople is becoming increasingly unsupportive of its mission. In the first part I present the circumstances at the local level and then turn to some insights about political communities as analysed by Hannah Arendt, Claude Lefort and Pierre Manent. These insights could, *mutatis mutandis*, help us reconsider relationships within the Church. Part three, as there is not enough space for a theological and ecclesiological analysis, tentatively states that an attempt at reshaping of relationships within the Church is not necessarily fashionable conformism[1].

I. THE CATHOLIC CHURCH IN SLOVENIA

After the fall of communism in Slovenia, it seemed that everything was possible and that a new era would begin both for the society and the Catholic Church within it. The end of the communist era, moreover, coincided with the founding of the independent state of Slovenia, which was carried out mainly by the forces of the so-called "democratic spring", among which there were many active Catholics. However, hope waned soon after the international recognition of Slovenia as the old forces returned to their dominant position and have remained there until today. Their communist ideology was traded for extreme liberalism in the sphere of economy, retaining as its prevalent political ideology the old anti-Catholic discourse now enriched with individualism and libertinism. This anti-Catholicism reveals itself as extreme secularism and laicism that push the Church out of the public domain, where it managed to place itself towards the end of the communist regime, back to strict privacy. The ruling elite controls all the influential public media except the Catholic

---

1. Translated from the Slovene original by Urška Sešek.

weekly *Družina* and two opposition weeklies. These influential media portray the Church in the same way the old totalitarian regime did: the Church's actions are treated with hostility or ridiculed, and, as a result, her members are becoming disheartened and passive and are withdrawing from public life.

Because of these political and media pressures, many Christian laypeople lament the passing of the "good old" communist times, when the Church was the only institution of civil society which was not under direct control of the Communist Party and therefore respected even by the non-believers who rejected communism, regardless of their religious affiliations. However, this general negative attitude of the society towards the Church, which some consider a form of *Kulturkampf,* was not the only cause of dissatisfaction among believers – it had as much to do with the relationships within the Church herself, which were shaped by her experiences of surviving in a totalitarian society.

As the possibilities of Church activities were strongly limited (almost reduced to the cult alone), the Church became extraordinarily clerical. The burden of responsibility, initiatives and decision-making lay upon the shoulders of the clergy. As authorities were suspicious of laypeople for even regular participation in the cult, Church members gladly let the priest take on all the activities and decisions necessary for the preservation of the Church community. With the dawn of a new social order, however, such a relationship between clergy and God's people, which was the only type possible in the conditions of survival, seems more and more inadequate as a means of developing the life and mission of the Church community. As neither clergy nor believers have any other experience or patterns of behaviour except those which they adopted during the time of communism, the new circumstances have brought about discontent on both sides.

It is becoming clear that the main cohesive forces in the Church community in the past were outside pressures and the resulting solidarity and familiarity among the repressed. These are now gone; people have many and varied possibilities of communication and participation in the institutions of the emerging civil society. Even within the Church herself numerous spiritual and cultural movements have been initiated as well as numerous charitable and professional associations. The clergy feels that it is losing control of all these activities, that it is not capable of handling this branching out. This is partly due to lack of staff, which is both dwindling and aging. The clergy as the institution which considers itself responsible for all the Church is increasingly facing the fact that people do things their own way and are not as obedient as they were in communist times. On the one hand, the clergy welcomes initiatives from laity, but on the other hand, it is worried by the loss of control. The laity is also undergoing these double processes. On the one hand, they still expect the clergy to be present everywhere, to do everything and decide about everything, but on the other hand, they refuse this and want to take over responsibilities, initiatives and decision-making.

The Church community is thus facing a double problem. On the one hand, normal cooperation between the Church institution and the state, as per European standards, cannot be established, but on the other hand, the Church community herself is divided by the different expectations of a dissatisfied clergy and an equally dissatisfied laity. As a consequence, the image of the Church as an institution is deteriorating in the public and among laypeople. Although the laity rejects tensions between the Church and the state, they abandon the Church community because of the feeling that they cannot contribute much to her and that their talents and abilities are not needed and appreciated.

All this shows that troubles and confrontations in the Church community are arising mostly because of unsuitable patterns of relationships between clergy and laity, or, to be precise, because of concentration of power, responsibility and decision-making in the hands of clergy. This is becoming more and more unacceptable for the laypeople, especially in the light of new experiences and needs fostered by the emerging democratic culture and society in which they now live. Of course ecclesial structures cannot change with each slight wave of social and cultural changes, but the demands of inculturation must not be neglected. If the faithful want to avoid the reproach of conformism, theological and ecclesiological reasons must be taken into account when changing the structures and establishing new relations in the Church. Before we look at these, let us consider the complex and inadequate relations between laity and clergy in the light of some insights from modern political thought.

II. COMMUNITY IN A TIME OF INDIVIDUALISM

Political philosopher Hannah Arendt distinguishes two spheres of existence: the private and the public. The private sphere is the basic one because it protects humans from nature and is the place where vital needs are satisfied (e.g. nutrition, procreation). It is about preservation of life. If biological survival is not possible without this environment, in modern society, one cannot reach full self-realization without leaving it. This is possible only in a common world, i.e. in the public sphere. Here, individuals are liberated from family bonds and connect with others, thus transcending the sphere of the mere satisfying of needs and being elevated to the world of meaning. Through public expression and action people appropriate the world into which they are born, and participate in its shaping as they make it meaningful and human and appear in its pluralism as equal and different at the same time. Since humans are living beings, they need the private sphere to survive, but no less do they need the public sphere to realize their uniqueness in plurality. It is understood, of course, that they can only appear in public as free subjects, or, in other words, that the public sphere is a stage where liberty is shown and attested. In the human world, adherence to this commonality which requires common consensus to order it, to act in it, to shape it into existence, merges the private with the public, domestic with political.

In ancient Greece the word *ekklesia* meant a public institution, and based on that we might assume that the Church is a public institution. But Arendt's division, no matter how schematic it may seem, has its validity and clearly implies that Church life with all its dynamics and imagery is subject to the logic of the private sphere[2]. The priest in Slovenia is referred to either as Sir or Father, and, in relationship to him, the believers are either his subjects or his children. The clergy expects all to play their predetermined roles in this "family" framework. When this is not the case, the cleric as *pater familias* feels threatened and betrayed, perceives the world as decadent and decomposing. An attempt was made at the recent Slovenian synod to address this issue by accentuating a greater responsibility to laypeople for the life, work and mission of the Church. Unfortunately, these guidelines cannot easily be translated into practice as there is no proper institutional and organizational framework for actual change of relations between clergy and laity, which largely continue to follow the set familial patterns.

---

2. Historian A. Paul says the following about the "social body" which was created around Jesus of Nazareth: "This body has a name which could have been first used by the founder and which the founder learned from some member of his group who was well-acquainted with Greek culture. The name is *ekklesia*, literally meaning 'community', and this word later evolved into 'Church'. This is a political term! Since the 5th century B.C. onwards it has denoted a people's forum of equal and fully competent citizens. (...) *Ekklesia* was a vital institution for the town in which it existed. Its legislative and decision-making role was central to the establishment and maintenance of democracy. It is no coincidence that this word was used at a very early time to denote a Christian community in its social dimension. Such a community had rules which were in sharp contrast to the rules of the Qumran community". A. PAUL, *Jésus Christ, la rupture. Essai sur la naissance du christianisme*, Paris, 2001, pp. 172-173.

The logic of the public sphere considers all people equal before law, mature and responsible, and in this transcends the private sphere and the relations of dependence and subordination. This is precisely what makes the public sphere the place of full human self-realization. It is the only domain where freedom of every individual is acknowledged, where his/her uniqueness is respected and where responsibility is personal. These characteristics – freedom, uniqueness and responsibility – are revealed in the political field. None of them is attainable without institutions which operate not according to familial but according to political logic. Only such institutions enable plurality in conjunction with solidarity, public debate and engagement. This implies that any community, including the Church, is responsible for allowing, cultivating and promoting the public sphere if individuals are to make the transition from the sphere of mere survival into the personal, free, responsible, common and active world. However, not every model of sociality enables this transition from the private to the political.

Claude Lefort shows that two models of sociality emerged with the rise of modern individualism: the democratic and the totalitarian. The democratic model is based on acknowledging every individual and his/her freedom, and is shaped so as to enable the respect and freedom of each individual. This makes the democratic society "a society in which radical lack of definition tests the law, the power, and the knowledge; the society becomes a stage of an adventure that is out of control. In this adventure what seems institutionalized is never quite defined, the known is constantly undermined by the unknown, and one cannot name the present (...); an adventure in which search for identity does not abolish the experience of being divided. It is a historic society *par excellence*"[3]. An attempt to control this democratic amorphity leads to totalitarianism. "The imaginary whole, the 'One-body', which is abolished with the acknowledgement of individual, is re-established, and the regime becomes one with 'the People'. Totalitarianism, feeding from a democratic source, incarnates the idea of the 'One-body' or 'One-people', the idea of society as such, which fully knows itself and is transparent to itself, homogeneous, the idea of a mass opinion, confidently normative, the idea of a patronizing State. The body is thus born from democracy and against it"[4].

3. C. LEFORT, *L'invention démocratique, Les limites de la domination totalitaire*, Paris, 1981, p. 174.
4. *Ibid.*, p. 174.

The totalitarian body is not a reproduction of a monarchical model of society, which was also formed on the idea of a body. This body, however, was not a social body, but the body of Christ. In this way the monarchical society fostered internal divisions, which is seen even in its ruler figure. A ruler "contained within him the principle of power, the principle of law, and the principle of knowledge, but was always *assumed* to be obedient to a higher power; at the same time he was not considered bound by any law but the one that made him father and son of righteousness; he possessed wisdom, but was subject to reason. According to the medieval formula, the ruler was *major et minor se ipso*, above and beneath himself"[5]. This is the main difference between a monarch and an Egocrat, a totalitarian ruler[6]. "The Egocrat coincides with himself as society is assumed to coincide with itself. This is projected as a kind of impossible suction drawing the body into the head and the head into the body"[7]. The closed and unified space of totalitarianism, the unified social body, is in stark contrast both with the monarchic society and with the body of Christ as open and pluralistic spheres of democracy which are no longer defined by an image of any kind of body.

As the monarchic and democratic systems foster divisions, the former very cautiously and the latter to the point of social collapse, they exclude violence to the greatest possible extent. For Arendt, violence and the political are mutually exclusive; the political transcends violence and tyranny through conversation and common action. In *Truth and Politics* she shows that politics transcends partial interests, is a place of a common realisation, yet is limited. "Therefore, we should not remain unaware of the actual content of political life – of the joy and the gratification that arise out of being in company with our peers, out of acting together and appearing in public, out of inserting ourselves into the world by word and deed, thus acquiring and sustaining our personal identity and beginning something entirely new. However, what I meant to show here is that this whole sphere, its greatness notwithstanding, is limited – that it does not encompass the whole of man's and the world's existence. It is limited by those things which men cannot change at will. And it is only by respecting its

---

5. *Ibid.*, p. 175.
6. "It is I myself the State!", is an almost liberal exclamation if we compare it with the reality of Stalin's totalitarian regime. Louis XIV equated himself with the State only; Roman Popes equated themselves with the State and the Church at the same time, but only while they were heads of State. The totalitarian state, however, goes far beyond caesaro-papism in consuming the entire functioning of the country. Compared to Louis XIV, Stalin is justified in saying "It is I myself the society"! L. TROCKI, *Staline*, t. 2, Paris, 1979, p. 338.
7. LEFORT, *Invention démocratique* (n. 3), p. 175.

own borders that this realm, where we are free to act and to change, can remain intact, preserving its integrity and keeping its promises"[8].

Power and political community are linked: there is not one without the other. Each member of a community habilitates the ones in power to guide and order the community in his/her name. Power, then, is an expression of this assent. In a similar way, the community is an expression of free engagement, action and will of its members. From this common assent, power structures derive their legitimacy and fulfil their only task: the preservation and development of political, public space. In a public, political sphere, conceived in such a way, there is no room for divisions typical of the private sphere: superiority/subordination, power/obedience, elite/folk, clergy/laity. In the public sphere relationships are based on shared responsibility, cooperation and shared decision-making. Inasmuch as responsibility is transferred to individual representatives, they receive assignments to fulfil and are authorized to make decisions, but they remain responsible to the whole community.

There is another dimension of modern political community which is relevant to our rethinking of relationships within the Church: the question of authority. What or who is the carrier of authority in the eyes of modern citizens of democratic countries? This question is answered by Pierre Manent in his *Cours familier de philosophie politique*: "We acknowledge the authority of *science* in the field of theory, and *liberty* in the field of activity"[9]. But the relationship between science and liberty is complex. Science, namely, has its logic which excludes liberty, and with it the values which we may choose as guiding principles in the development of science, although they are neither scientific nor necessary. A system symbiosis of science and liberty in a democratic society causes tensions, "so that sometimes science intimidates liberty and forces it to withdraw, and other times liberty takes its turn and tells science to stand back. Because of this we could say: just as the people of the Middle Ages had to find their way in a world which was organized and disorganized at the same time because of the coinciding of two great authorities (the Pope and the King), we citizens of modern democracies have to find our way in a world which is organized and disorganized at the same time because of battles between the two great authorities of science and liberty"[10].

8. H. ARENDT, *Truth and Politics*, in her *Between Past and Future, Eight Exercises in Political Thought*, New York, 1993, pp. 263-264.
9. P. MANENT, *Cours familier de philosophie politique*, Paris, 2001, pp. 9-10.
10. *Ibid.*, p. 15.

III. Theological and Ecclesiological Arguments
for the Public Sphere as a Suitable Model
for Relationships within the Church

I am aware of the fact that political models cannot be directly applied to the Church community. However, achievements of political thought can support a rethinking of the Church community, the structural and organizational relationships between its members, of jobs, professions and the sacrament of holy orders, of the mediation and testing of God's will, of the assistance of the Holy Spirit in the government of the Church and the explication of its faith.

Inasmuch as the Church in Slovenia is ready to open and to submit herself to the logic of the public sphere, the current controversies will be overcome and the quiet withdrawals of her members, let me hope, will be prevented. It is, however, also true that this would require a thorough change of the basic structure of the relations within the community and of the whole community itself, and with the new practices even the image of God, the human being, the Church, the world and the relations among all these would be subject to change. According to the old scholastic principle *Gratia suponit naturam*, these changes should not present a major difficulty.

Adapting the principles of political analysis of the modern democratic society to the needs of a specific community is one of the tasks of modern theology, particularly ecclesiology. Unfortunately there is no room in this context for a thorough theological and ecclesiological analysis, so I would like to turn to two "shepherds" whose testimonies from amidst the practicalities of life call for new relationships within the Church.

The Brazilian Cardinal Lorscheider reconsidered his role when he found himself in new circumstances. "I became Bishop on May 20th, 1962 (...). When in August 1973 I came to Fortaleza (Ceara), I gradually began to see my service as a bishop in a different light. I think that back in the south I acted more as someone who knows and who teaches, without particular interest in the everyday problems of people. (...) I brought faith to people like a recipe, without paying attention to its meaning in the social, political, economic, cultural and religious context of the people. I was more like a professor and performer of ceremonies than an actual evangelist in the reality in which the people lived. In Nordeste (Ceara-Fortaleza), in contact with a different type of congregations, which were not formed on the basis of the requirements of the cult but out of the need of people to find Christian answers to life's questions, my service as a bishop was being reshaped. (...) Gradually I realized that I was going to go about my work in a different way. I was supposed to be a part of the community, carrying my responsibility without considering myself or being considered the head of the community, a superior (...) I was no longer so much a professor, a teacher, but more of an animator of animators. I was to become a disciple before I was allowed to think I was a master. I no longer have the ambition of becoming a master, as there is only one Master"[11].

Another shepherd, Cardinal Winning, expressed the wish before he died for the new century to be a time when "Christians will take seriously the priesthood of all the baptised; the universal call to holiness and the need to read the signs of their times. (...) Today the need is for witness in the market place – where the action is ... The laity are called to witness in temporal society, to reach places others cannot reach"[12]. Thus, leadership will need to come as much from lay men and women as from the clergy. The Cardinal summed up his image of the Church of the new century:

> *Living.* Challenging people with "a coherent and vibrant message" that demands a response of love, compassion, solidarity and faith.
> *Free.* The Church has never been as free from temporal shackles before, and so is able to make her voice heard loud and clear at all times.
> *Courageous.* The Church will need to be a sign of contradiction, even to the point of "literal or metaphorical" martyrdom.
> *Involved.* Because "the Church purified will be at the heart of the world – involved in the day to day struggles of all peoples, especially the marginalised, those without a voice and those who are excluded".

This is the Church of the future that I can begin to see emerging – "a purified Church, a renewed Church, a brave Church, a humble Church"[13].

From a theological point of view Christianity conceives of this world as contingent, transient. In this kind of world the Church can realize herself in following Christ by being continuously engaged in building the kingdom of God in a given society. In this respect it is difficult not to see a certain familiarity with the logic of democracy, which renounces any fixed point of power, law and knowledge[14]. It is this very potential that was perceived by the great Christian layman of the early 20th century, Charles Péguy: "M. Bergson ... reintroduces us to the Christian situation and stance, the only Christian situation and stance, he literally makes us

---

11. See A. LORSCHEIDER, *The Re-defined Role of the Bishop in a Poor, Religious People*, in *Concilium* 176 (1984) 47-49.
12. Cited in *Cultures and Faith* 3 (2001), p. 246.
13. *Ibid.*
14. Cf. C. LEFORT, *La question de la démocratie,* in his *Essais sur le politique XIXe – XXe siècles*, Paris, 1986, pp. 18-32.

find a Christian vantage point, the point of life and the main point of Christianity. He has returned us to the insecurity, transitivity and the nakedness that define the human condition"[15]. A similar point is made by the Polish philosopher Leszek Kolakowski: "Christianity said: 'The philosopher's stone, the elixir of immortality, these are superstitions of alchemists; nor is there a recipe for a society without evil, without sin or conflict; such ideals are the aberrations of a mind convinced of its omnipotence, they are the fruits of pride'. But to admit all this is not to give way to despair. The choice between total perfection and total self-destruction is not ours; cares without end, incompleteness without end, these are our lot"[16].

The difficulties facing the Church in Slovenia as regards her environment and the relations between her members are definitely not insurmountable. We believe that in trying to overcome them a model of relationships between laity and clergy plays an important role: a transition from the logic of private conversation to the logic of public conversation. The more this takes into account the democratic culture and human dignity, liberty and responsibility, the better our chances for a truly full life of the Church community and a successful participation of all her members in solving shared social problems. It would be worthwhile for the faithful to consider what benefit can be gained in trying to reshape relations within the Church from a philosophical analysis of the functioning of modern societies. The logic of faith far from excludes a certain unpower, un-archy, and un-knowledge. All that leads us to search for the God of Jesus Christ in everyday engagement with and for the people.

Theological Faculty   Drago Karl OČVIRK
University of Ljubljana
Poljanska 4
1000 Ljubljana
Slovenia

15. C. PÉGUY, Note conjointe sur M. Descartes et la philosophie cartésienne, in his œuvres en prose 1909-1914, Paris, 1961, p. 1520.
16. L. KOLAKOWSKI, Looking for the Barbarians. The Illusion of Cultural Universalism, in his Modernity on Endless Trial, Chicago, IL, 1990, pp. 30-31.

CONVERSATION IN HISTORY

The Case of the *Vota Antepraeparatoria* of the Benelux Bishops and of the Faculties of Theology of Leuven and Nijmegen

I. Announcement and Preparation

January 25, 1959, at the end of the International Week of Prayer for the Unity of the Churches, Pope John XXIII made a spectacular announcement. First he mentioned his intention to gather a local synod in Rome to discuss future pastoral care in the Eternal City. Then he expressed the wish to hold a general ecumenical Council as well[1]. Soon after the first commotion had subsided, on May 17, 1959 a commission was founded to prepare for and to implement the first major step to be taken: a worldwide consultation of bishops, heads of religious orders and congregations, as well as of Catholic faculties of theology and canon

---

1. For general surveys of the Council's history, see K. Buchberger – J. Höfer – K. Rahner (eds.), *Das Zweite Vatikanische Konzil: Konstitutionen, Dekrete und Erklärungen, LTK*, Freiburg, Herder, 1966-1968, 3 vols.; G. Caprile, *Il Concilio Vaticano II: Cronache del Concilio Vaticano II edite La Civiltà Cattolica*, Rome, Civiltà Cattolica, 1965-1969, 5 parts in 6 vols.; G. Alberigo – J.A. Komonchak, *History of Vatican II, Volume I, Announcing and Preparing Vatican Council II, toward a New Era in Catholicism*, Leuven, Peeters, 1995. All of the *vota*, as well as the *acta* of Pope John XXIII regarding the coming Council and the *Commissio Antepraeparatoria* were gathered, ordered and edited: *Acta et Documenta Concilio Oecumenico Vaticano II apparando, series I: antepraeparatoria*. The following volumes have been used: *Volumen I* (acta of John XXIII, further abbreviated as AD I, acta), *volumen II (partes I & II)* (*vota* of European bishops, abbreviated as AD I, II-1 or AD I, II-2), and *volumen IV, pars II: universitates et facultates extra urbem* (*vota* of faculties of theology and canon law of Catholic universities, abbreviated as AD I, IV-2). Some more specific works on the preparatory period: *Le deuxième concile du Vatican (1959-1965)* (Collection de l'École Française de Rome, 113), Rome, École Française de Rome, 1989; Cl. Soetens – M. Lamberigts, *À la veille du Concile Vatican II: vota et réactions en Europe et dans le Catholicisme oriental* (Instrumenta Theologica, 9), Leuven, Bibliotheek van de faculteit Godgeleerdheid, 1992; J. Grootaers, *Actes et acteurs à Vatican II* (BETL, 139), Leuven, Peeters, 1998.

On the announcement, see: AD I, Acta, 3-6, esp. 5: "Pronunciamo innanzi a voi, certo tremando un poco di commozione, ma insieme con umile risolutezza di proposito, il nome e la proposta della celebrazione: di un Sinodo Diocesano per l'Urbe, e di un Concilio Ecumenico per la Chiesa Universale".

law[2]. This *commissio antepraeparatoria* or "pre-preparing commission" was composed of the different Roman Congregations' *assessores* and was presided over by Domenico Cardinal Tardini, then Secretary of State of the Vatican. *Assessor* to the commission was Bishop Pericles Felici, who later became secretary to the *Commissio Praeparatoria* and to the Council itself[3]. The Commission received a clearly stated task. First, it had to consult all the bishops of the world including heads of religious orders and congregations, in order to receive advice and propositions for the coming council. Second, it had to gather propositions and suggestions made by members of the Roman Curia, and third, it should consult the opinion(s) of faculties of theology and canon law of Catholic universities. The consultation's results would be used to draw the first general outlines of subjects to be treated in the council. Subsequently, the members of the *Commissio praeparatoria*, would have to prepare the actual texts to be discussed during the Council, based on these outlines.

Nearly a month after the commission had started its activities, on June 18, 1959, a letter was sent to all the bishops in the world asking for *consilia et vota*. A month later, July 18, a similar missive went to the Catholic faculties. In total 2812 letters were sent. About a year later, June 5, 1960, when the *commissio antepraeparatoria* ended its activities, 2150 answers had been received, representing almost seventy-seven percent of the addressees[4].

A worldwide consultation as performed by the *commissio* was an almost unparalleled feat in the history of the councils. While preparing for the First Vatican Council, Pius IX consulted his entourage as well, several cardinals were secretly asked to give advice on the feasibility of gathering a council and a carefully selected group of bishops was asked to fill out a questionnaire on the matter (1867)[5]. But this consultation was to be general, open and more or less free. It had taken therefore a direct

2. AD I, Acta, 22-23: *Constitutio Commissionis Antepraeparatoria*.

3. See G. NICOLINI, *Il Cardinale Domenico Tardini*, Padua, 1980, pp. 306-315. On Bishop Felici, see: *In memoriam*, in *Apollinaris* 55 (1982) 241-244; J. GROOTAERS, *Pericles Felici: Le "patron" du Concile*, in ID., *Actes et acteurs* (n. 1), pp. 301-313.

4. Besides those not answering at all, some of the respondents did not reply with usefull answers in the light of the Commission's purpose. For example, the answers returned by two retired Belgian missionary bishops. Bishop Lagae (o.p.) and Bishop Stappers (o.f.m.) were only to let the Commission know they had no *consilia* or *vota* for the coming council. See AD I, II-1, 131-132. Bishop Stappers referred to his health condition and to the fact that he had been out of active duty too long to give usefull insights. For Lagae, see AD I, II-1, 156: "... non habeo consilia aut vota quae utiliter proponere possim".

5. ALBERIGO – KOMONCHAK, *History* (n. 1), pp. 63-65; F.-C. UGINET, *Les projets de concile général sous Pie XI et XII*, in *Deuxième* (n. 1), pp. 65-78.

and personal intervention by Pope John XXIII to avoid the addition of a questionnaire to Tardini's letter. This questionnaire would have steered the answers in a certain direction some members of the *Commissio* would have liked[6]. The only "restriction" the bishops had been given now was that they were asked to answer in Latin and to keep the best intentions for the Church in mind[7].

Since a great deal of the addressees sent back a variety of answers, these *vota* are at least an interesting source for the history of Church and theology, for in fact they reveal information on the theological and pastoral situation throughout the world at the end of the 1950s. Nevertheless, they have to be read in connection with contextual data.

Therefore the question is raised here whether the *vota* from the Benelux area (both by the bishops and the universities) form the result of conversation between the pastoral and theological context and their authors. In order to formulate an answer, first the pastoral situation in the Benelux in 1959 will be described, second, the theological input made by three so-called "theological movements" will be investigated, and third the *vota* of the bishops and both the faculties of theology and canon law of Leuven and Nijmegen will be presented. Finally, some conclusions will be drawn.

II. THE SITUATION IN THE BENELUX-DIOCESES

At the time when Tardini's commission consulted the world episcopate, thirty-nine bishops were residing in Belgium, The Netherlands and Luxemburg. Their number covered a remarkable mixture of ordinaries

---

6. Some of the members of the *Commissio* had already been part of a preparatory commission established by Pius XII in 1948. This secret commission had to study the possibiliy of gathering a general council in Rome, and to define some of the themes that could be discussed. The comittee conceived a plan to perform a consultation among a selected group of cardinals and bishops, to which purpose it had prepared a number of thematicaly organised questions. In the end, the Holy Office delayed the consultation and Pius XII cancelled all plans for a Second Vatican Council. John XXIII was informed about the initiative taken by his predecessor only after having announced the coming Council. Three members of the former commission became member of the "new" commission: Fr. Coussa (basilian), Fr. Philippe, the general of the Dominicans, and Bishop Parente. Cardinal Ottaviani and Fr. Tromp S.J. became involved in the central *commissio praeparatoria*. ALBERIGO – KOMONCHAK, *History* (n. 1), pp. 64-65; G. CAPRILE, *Pius XII. und das Zweite Vatikanische Konzil*, in H. SCHAMBECK (ed.), *Pius XII. zum Gedächtnis*, Berlin, Duncker & Humblot, 1977, pp. 649-691.

7. The language request would not bother several bishops in any way. For instance Bishop Moors and Charue, who replied in French. See AD I, II-2, 492-498 (complete text in French) and AD I, II-1, 115-117 (two added *vota*).

and their auxiliaries, two papal nuncios, retired missionary bishops, and even two Russian bishops -one from a uniate church- living in exile in Brussels[8]. Out of twenty-six Belgian bishops twenty-two would send back an answer, nine Dutch bishops out of twelve and Bishop Lommel from Luxemburg would also do so.

1. *The Benelux-dioceses: Some Facts and Figures*

In 1959 Belgium counted six dioceses, an equal number of ordinaries and five auxiliaries[9]. The Belgian bishops, unlike their Dutch and Luxemburg colleagues, had received academic training either in Leuven or in Rome, generally in theology and often at the highest level possible[10]. After their respective studies and ordination, almost all had been sent to work in pastoral care *in casu* education[11]. In a later stage, all of them had

8. Actually, the number of active Dutch and Belgian bishops at the time was higher, especially since a large number of them lived and worked in missionary territories, Central Africa for the Belgians, Indonesia and West-Africa for the Dutch. There was also a significant presence of especially Belgian bishops in Rome, superiors of different orders and congregations (e.g. Fr. Janssen S.J., general of the Jesuit order), or being professor at one of the Pontifical Universities (e.g. Fr. Van den Eynde O.F.M., *rector magnificus* of the Antonianum). The Russian bishops were Bishop Boleslao Sloskans (Russian-Orthodox) and Bishop Paul Meletjew (Uniate). The papal diplomats were Bishop Beltrami (internuncio residing in The Hague, but since he was appointed only a year before the Council's announcement, he was not well acquainted with the situation of Dutch Catholicism), and Bishop Forni, nuncio for Belgium and Luxemburg. Forni, a career diplomate, had resided in Brussels since 1953. Beltrami did not reply to Tardini's request.

9. The dioceses are named in alphabetical order and between brackets the name(s) of their respective residentiary and auxiliary bishop(s): Bruges (De Smedt), Gent (Calewaert and auxiliary Joliet), Liège (Kerkhofs, but his auxiliary Van Zuylen *de facto* governed the diocese), archdiocese of Malines (cardinal Van Roey and auxiliaries Schoenmaeckers and Suenens), Namur (Charue and auxiliary Musty) and Tournai (Himmer). In fact the *rector magnificus* of Leuven, Van Waeyenbergh also was an auxiliary bishop of cardinal Van Roey. Van Waeyenbergh replied together with the Leuven faculties of theology and canon law.

10. Bishop Charue was a Leuven *magister theologiae* (1929), as was cardinal Van Roey (1903). Schoenmaeckers (1940, bachelor of arts) and Calewaert (1924, licenciate in theology, 1955, honorary doctorate) were also alumni of the same *Alma Mater*. Bishop De Smedt held a Roman doctorate (1934, philosophy) and licentiate (1934, theology), as did Joliet (1901, doctorate in philosophy, 1905, theology, 1907, canon law), Kerkhofs (1897, doctorate in philosophy, 1900, theology), Van Zuylen (1929, doctorate in philosophy, 1931, baccalaureate in canon law, 1933, licentiate in theology, 1935, licentiate in church history), Suenens (1924, doctorate in philosophy, 1927, baccalaureate in canon law, 1929, doctorate in theology) and Himmer (1923, doctorate in philosophy, 1927, theology), all alumni of the Gregoriana. Bishop Charue also was an alumnus of the Roman *Biblicum* (1927), and Bishop Joliet had been president of the Belgian Pontifical College in Rome from 1927 till 1945. See also J. ICKX, *De alumni van het Belgisch Pauselijk College te Rome 1844-1994*, Rome, 1994, 759 p.

11. Bishop De Smedt had been teacher at the Malines minor seminary of Saint Joseph (1933-1945), Joliet taught at the minor seminary of St.-Niklaas (1907-1919), as did

been teaching at the major seminaries of their dioceses. Besides Cardinal Van Roey, who had been archbishop of Malines since 1926 and Bishop Kerkhofs, bishop of Liège since 1927, all of them were relatively "new on the job", being designated to the episcopate in the (late) forties, early fifties[12].

At the time, an average of about ninety-five percent of the country's population called itself Roman Catholic. Fairly high numbers of parishes, church buildings, seminarians, neophytes, as well as of participants in Catholic action, in *Caritas* and in education, confirm the general impression of a "Catholic" Belgium. However, in some ways, prospects did not look quite so good. Illustrative are the numbers of seminarians and neophytes in the Belgian dioceses. When compared over the years 1945-1959, from the mid-fifties on their numbers decreased slowly and a movement towards an even much greater decline can be noticed[13]. This also had to do with conditions in the different dioceses regarding pastoral care and participation of the faithful in everyday Church life. A situation that clearly had changed after the Second World War. Except maybe for Namur, all of the Belgian dioceses incorporated within their geographical borders different contexts regarding pastoral care. In the archdiocese for example, there were at least two major cities surrounded by strongly industrialised zones (Brussels, Antwerp), large rural territories in the north and to the east and several small provincial towns like Malines itself and Louvain. This situation created different pastoral challenges and necessitated a variety of approaches adapted to the situation. These challenges

Kerkhofs at the minor seminary of St.-Truiden (1900-1917). Bishop Himmer was named chaplain in Beauraing (1927-1929) and taught at the minor seminary of Floreffe (1929-1949), in the meantime he became the diocesan chaplain for the A.C.J.B. (Catholic action for youth). Schoenmaeckers taught both at Saint Peter's College (Leuven) and at the Malines minor seminary (1940-1948), as did Bishop Suenens, after having taught in Schaarbeek (1929-1930).

12. De Smedt (1952), Calewaert (1948), Joliet (1948), Kerkhofs (1927), Van Zuylen (1951), Van Roey (archbishop 1926, cardinal 1927), Schoenmaeckers (1952), Suenens (1945), Charue (1942), Musty (1957), Himmer (1949).

13. Numbers of seminarians (and between brackets of ordinations) are given in *Annuario Pontificio*, 1944, 1949, 1954 and 1959:
   Bruges: 1944 > 339 (44), 1949 > 273 (50), 1954 > 219 (38) and 1959 > 224 (24).
   Ghent: 1944 > 283 (31), 1949 > 195 (41), 1954 > 194 (40) and 1959 > 184 (17).
   Liège: 1944 > 310 (45), 1949 > 281 (44), 1954 > 245 (35) and 1959 > 250 (44).
   Malines: 1944 > 623 (71), 1949 > 553 (88), 1954 > 531 (72) and 1959 > 454 (68).
   Namur: 1946 > 197 (21), 1949 > 198 (30), 1954 > 185 (25) and 1959 > 134 (22).
   Tournai: 1944 > 221 (30), 1949 > 192 (31), 1954 > 181 (28) and 1959 > 132 (38).

   For the diocese of Namur there are no figures for the years 1944-1945. Although numbers might show strong fluctuations within the different dioceses, from the mid-fifties a general downward tendency becomes notable.

were not always met properly. At the same time as the numbers of seminarians and neophytes decreased, the number of parishes and churches gradually increased, as well as the number of inhabitants, faster than the accompanying parish structures, especially in industrialised regions. According to a then accepted pastoral standard, each priest should be able to take care of two thousand parishioners. About three quarters of all parishes more or less met this standard. But about a quarter did not, and their parish structures were completely unfit to cope with the often rapidly changing situation in pastoral care, even in spite of some minor adaptations the ecclesiastical authorities had made[14]. Several bishops judged the evolution critical and made this clear in their *vota*.

In 1959 the Grand-Duchy of Luxemburg was a diocese under direct control of the Holy See. It faced similar problems: declining numbers of ecclesiastical personal and pastoral structures hardly adapted to the rapidly changing needs, especially industrialised areas.

The overall situation in The Netherlands on the other hand was somewhat different. In 1959, The Netherlands counted seven dioceses, an equal number of ordinaries and one auxiliary bishop[15]. Compared to their Belgian colleagues, the Dutch bishops had a rather different background. Besides Van Dodewaard and Alfrink, alumni of the *Biblicum* in Rome, none of them had received academic training, but all were versed in pastoral practice. Directly after their ordination, they had been named assistant parish-priests, most often in a large parish of major importance. After several years, they became either dean of a major deanery like Amsterdam, Leiden or Groningen, or, secretary to their bishop. Only four of them had been given teaching assignments at their respective major Seminaries[16]. Like their Belgian colleagues however, and with the exception of Huibers, who was appointed bishop in 1936, most of them were also relatively new to the job, assigned to their episcopal sees in the late forties and fifties[17].

14. For a sharp analysis of this problem in Belgium, see J. KERKHOFS – J. VAN HOUTTE, *De Kerk in Vlaanderen*, Tielt, Lannoo, 1962, 24-56. Problems arose especially in urban parishes, as well as in parishes in newly industrialised areas.

15. The dioceses are named in alphabetical order, between brackets the name(s) of their respective residentiary and auxiliary bishop(s): Breda (Baeten), Groningen (Nierman), Haarlem (Huibers and his auxiliary Van Dodewaard), 's Hertogenbosch (Mutsaerts), Roermond (Moors), Rotterdam (Jansen), Utrecht (archbishop Alfrink).

16. These four were: Alfrink (who also had been professor of Old Testament at the Catholic University of Nijmegen, from 1945 until 1951), Van Dodewaard, Moors and Jansen (the latter only for a short period of time).

17. Baeten (1951), Nierman (1956), Huibers (1936), Van Dodewaard (1958), Moors (1959), Jansen (1956), Mutsaerts (1943), Alfrink (coadiutor 1951, archbishop 1955). Alfrink was created cardinal March 28, 1960.

Only the southern dioceses Breda, 's Hertogenbosch and Roermond had a substantially high number of Catholic inhabitants, up to ninety percent of the population. For the rest of the country the percentages were much lower. For example, only ten percent of the population in the diocese of Groningen was Roman Catholic.

When compared to its Belgian and Luxemburg counterparts, Dutch Catholicism was of a more "ghetto-like" nature. In spite of some openness towards other denominations and towards developments outside the Church, it remained focused *ad intra*. An important reason for this closeness had been the fact that the Dutch Catholic hierarchy (and thus the ecclesiastical organisation in dioceses) was restored to its pre-Counter Reformation organisation only in 1853. Before, for about three centuries the officially protestant Netherlands had been missionary territory under direct control of Rome. On celebrating the first centennial of the restoration in 1954, Dutch bishops showed their intransigence by writing a pastoral letter dated May 1, 1954. They forbade their flock to become members of protestant and socialist cultural organisations and political parties[18]. Earlier in 1951, in light of the pastoral situation, Rome had begun a procedure to create new dioceses by dividing up the existing ones. Only by the end of 1955 a "compromise" was reached between the strongly opposing Dutch bishops and the Vatican: two new dioceses were created, Groningen and Rotterdam, and some diocesan borders were redrawn[19]. By 1959 however, most of the bishops had been replaced by younger bishops with other, relatively more open views on how to govern the Dutch Catholic Church.

The pastoral challenges the Dutch bishops were facing, were the same as those of their colleagues. Slowly declining numbers of seminarians for instance, which would lead eventually to a shortage of priests[20], while fast-growing industrialisation and urbanisation of parts of Holland would be the instigator of a growing secularisation. The most striking difference

18. The letter, also known as *het mandement*, forbade Catholics to become member of the PvdA (social-democratic party) and the VARA, socialist radiostation. For the text of the *mandement* and comments, see *Katholiek Archief* 9 (1954) col. 489-520, 621-638, 792-793, 933-940.

19. On Pius' letter of December 23, 1955, creating the new dioceses, see *Katholiek Archief*, 10 (1955), col. 1221-1226. In reaction to the news, Bishop Baeten of Breda published a short note in which he shows to be dissatisfied with the Roman decision. See *Katholiek Archief* 10 (1955) col. 1228. The news was first published in the *Osservatore Romano* of October 8, 1955.

20. In 1958, the average rate for the Dutch dioceses was two priests per parish, with an average of 2700 members per parish. Most of the dioceses however did not meet the average. Compare the figures as given in *Annuario Pontificio*, and in the KASKI-report, in *Katholiek Archief* 13 (1958) col. 1137-1152.

was no doubt the fact that The Netherlands was a protestant country, especially in its western and northern parts. This made the debate of an ecumenically open versus ghetto-like Catholicism a more urgent one compared to Belgium and Luxemburg, where a vast majority of the population was Catholic.

In general, by 1959, the Benelux region had become subject to growing secularisation as manifested in lack of interest and unease with everyday Catholic life, and in the decrease in numbers of ecclesiastical personnel, though not yet dramatically. It was however clear that this would become a serious problem in the (near) future. Also a growing diversification in pastoral needs emerged, unfortunately this only instigated a rather slow adaptation of pastoral structures and care by the ecclesiastical authorities.

2. *The* Vota *and their Theological Context*

Late November 1961, a conference was held in Genoa on the coming council. One of the main speakers was Cardinal Frings of Cologne (Germany), member of the Central Preparatory Committee. He presented an important paper on "the relation between Church and modern thought"[21]. In his closing remarks, Frings described the existence within the Church of two influential, mainstream, so-called "theological and charismatic movements", centred around liturgy on the one hand and around the Virgin Mary on the other[22]. These two "movements" were not the only ones at the time. It lies however far beyond the scope of this paper to present a complete survey of the theological situation within the Catholica in 1959, but it is worthwhile to have a look at the input made by three of these so-called "theological movements" on the eve of the Council.

2.1. The liturgical movement

By the end of the 1950s the liturgical movement already had won its battles. It began in the early twentieth century at the Benedictine abbey of Mount Cesar in Louvain, when a young Benedictine, Dom Lambert Beauduin, presented a pastoral program to improve active participation of the faithful in Sunday mass[23]. Study and concrete action spread the

21. J. FRINGS, *Le Concile et la pensée moderne*, in *Documentation Catholique* 44 (1962) 255-268.
22. FRINGS, *Le Concile* (n. 21), p. 262.
23. See: R. LOONBEEK – J. MORTIAU, *Un pionnier Dom Lambert Beauduin (1873-1960). Liturgie et Unité des Chrétiens* (Recueil de travaux d'histoire et de philologie, 7e série, 12-13), Louvain-la-Neuve, Éditions de Chevetogne, 2001; A. HAQUIN, *Dom Lambert Beauduin et le renouveau liturgique* (Recherches et synthèses, section d'histoire, 1), Gembloux, 1970, pp. 92-103.

movement's program through other Benedictine monasteries like Maria Laach in Germany. It was rather well received in the Catholic world[24]. The movement's main purpose had been the restoration of Sunday liturgy as the central focus of everyday Catholic life by enhancing active participation of the faithful to nurture their spiritual life and to re-centre communal life around the Eucharist. This was to be achieved by acting against out-dated ritualism as well as the perception of the Sunday liturgy as a private and devotional matter. In 1959, its most important success thus far had been the encyclical *Mediator Dei* from November 1947, which officially embraced the movement's agenda[25], the yearly International Liturgical Congresses, and the foundation of centres for the study of liturgy (Paris, Trier).

After the Second World War the debate within the movement shifted towards the use of the vernacular in liturgy. This was believed to be the best way to enhance active participation. The idea however was dissuaded by Roman authorities as long as possible, arguing that the use of Latin expressed the Church's unity, and that the use of the vernacular would open doors to confusion and even heresy among the faithful. Eventually, it would be up to the Council to make decisions regarding liturgical renewal and the use of the vernacular in liturgy.

2.2. The ecumenical movement

At the time the Council was announced, the ecumenical movement could hardly be ignored. In spite of repeated Roman prohibitions during the past century against contacts with other denominations[26], a shift had taken place from a so-called ecumenism-of-return to an open view focused on dialogue. The former was characterised by an apologetic position. Other denominations were urged to return to the One, Holy and Catholic Church, the only and visible Church of Christ on earth, which

---

24. Not everyone was pleased with the attention the movement officially received as becomes clear in a *votum* by Bishop Mutsaerts of 's Hertogenbosch, who warned against the harmful influence this "abbey-liturgy of the sacred *triduum*" might have on the personal devotions of the faithful. See: AD I, II-2, 508: "… ut habeatur maior distinctio inter liturgiam populi et liturgiam manochorum. Licet addere exemplum: Ut nihil gravatur monachi ampliore et diuturniore sollemnitate paschali … ita in liturgia populi praecavendum erit, ne nimia prolixitate devotioni plebis noceatur".

25. See *AAS* 39 (1947) 521-595.

26. Like in the encyclical *Mortalium animos* (January 6, 1928) (see *AAS* 20 [1928] 5-16), putting an end to the so-called *Mechelse gesprekken*, discussions between representatives of the Anglican and the Catholic Church as organised in Malines, under the protection first of Cardinal Mercier and later of his successor Cardinal Van Roey.

had to be seen as a *societas perfecta* and was not to blame for the defections that had taken place in the past. In case of refusal to return, missionary activities leading to conversion were to be displayed. This spirit of hostility slowly faded under the influence of contacts with and the study of other denominations. Again it was the Benedictine order that played a leading role. On the request of Pope Pius XI, the order began studying the theology and liturgy of Oriental Churches[27]. In Belgium this would eventually lead to the foundation of the priories of Amay and Schotenhof, ultimately relocated to the monastery of mixed rites at Chevetogne (1938). In The Netherlands, after the Second World War, the Catholic Society of Saint Willibrord emerged as a result of contacts between Protestants and Catholics. This society was led by Father Willebrands, once a participant in the so-called *Larense gespreksgroep* (a discussion group from the Dutch town Laren). Later Willebrands became head of the Secretariat for Christian Unity[28]. Initiatives taken in the protestant world to cooperate, first in the field of missionary activities, later on the level of doctrine (in the commission *Faith and Order*), eventually leading to the foundation of the World Council of Churches (Amsterdam, 1948), and the initiative taken by the French priest Couturier (International Prayer Week) would considerably enhance the objectives of the movement[29]. By 1959 it was clear there was great need for more dialogue. On the theological level it also had become clear that stressing particular subjects of (Catholic) theology in opposition with other denominations, had led to a devaluation of important elements of that same Catholic theology. For instance in ecclesiology, where the emphasis put on the supreme pontiff and his infallibility had set the development and theological debate on collegiality aside. Scripture received less attention in reaction against the protestant *sola scriptura*, and developments in liturgy and ecclesiology moreover made clear that the ecclesiological *societas perfecta*-model was questionable, at least from an historical point

27. March 21, 1924, Pope Pius XI in his brief *Equidem Verba*, asked the Benedictine order to concentrate on unity with Eastern (i.c. Orthodox) churches through study of their liturgy, language, history and theology. To this purpose special monasteries were to be founded in each province of the order. For the text of the brief (in translation), see *Irénikon* 22 (1949) 189-190. Instigators in Belgium were Benedictines like dom Beauduin, dom Bosschaerts and dom de Wyels, also active in the liturgical movement.

28. J. JACOBS, *Een beweging in verandering. De inzet van de Belgische en Nederlandse Katholieken voor de eenheid der Kerken*, in *Trajecta* 1 (1992) 67-91.

29. For the World Council of Churches, see P. CHENAUX, *Le conseil oecuménique des Églises*, in LAMBERIGTS – SOETENS, *À la veille* (n. 1), pp. 200-213. For the activities of Fr. Couturier, see for instance É. FOUILLOUX, *"Mouvements" théologico-spirituels et Concile*, in LAMBERIGTS – SOETENS, *À la veille* (n. 1), pp. 185-199, esp. 196-199 (on ecumenism).

of view. Although ecclesiocentric in a way, the theology of the *vestigia ecclesiae* or *vestigia veritatis* outside the Church gained foothold as well. But in spite of the progress made, ecumenism still met resistance, especially from higher Roman authorities, as would become clear during the conciliar debate on religious freedom[30].

2.3. Theology of the episcopate

Since the unforeseen ending of the First Vatican Council, due to the outbreak of the Franco-Prussian War in 1870, the request for an elaborated theology of the episcopate never disappeared from the realm of theological debate. This was no different in 1959. Ecclesiological studies focussing on the bishop all referred to Vatican I. Both the liturgical and the ecumenical movement had added some specific elements to the question. Study of ancient liturgy had led to the rediscovery of the specific role played by (local) bishops[31] as did the study of Protestant and Orthodox ecclesiastical structures. It became clear that in different ecclesiological models bishops played a more important role by almost independently governing local churches, instead of being local annexes of a central Roman apparatus. Both movements stressed one element in particular: that of collegiality in the threefold episcopal task of administering, sanctifying and teaching. This would lead to the discussion on the precise relationship between Rome and the local churches, and to the debate on the powers granted to local churches, especially to their (often national) episcopal conferences. Until the Council, bishops were more or less tied to their dioceses while Rome had plenty of possibilities to interfere with local administration, often with a lethargic effect on local pastoral praxis[32]. Several bishops like Cardinal Van Roey, De Smedt and Charue, had already been studying the subject, *albeit* in different contexts[33].

---

30. See for instance M. LAMBERIGTS, *Mgr. Emiel Jozef De Smedt, bisschop van Brugge, en het Tweede Vaticaans Concilie*, in *Collationes* 28 (1998) 281-326.

31. For instance the edition of Hippolytus of Rome's *traditio apostolica*, by dom B. BOTTE, *La tradition apostolique* (Sources Chrétiennes, 11), Paris, Cerf, 1946.

32. As became clear in the position held by regular houses of pontifical law, as well as the possibilities for direct appeal, the so-called *recursus* to Roman instances when disagreeing over local episcopal decisions.

33. Cardinal Van Roey in the context of the *Mechelse Gesprekken* (see A. DENAUX – J.A. DICK, *From Malines to ARCIC: The Malines Conversations Commemorated* [BETL, 130], Leuven, Universitaire Pers – Peeters, 1997, esp. pp. 1-93). De Smedt started with the idea of *fidei donum*-priests (European priests sent to especially Latin America to help the Catholic Church) as a concrete expression of collegiality, and Charue devoted several articles to the subject (e.g., A.-M. CHARUE, *L'évêque dans l'Église*, in *Revue diocésane de Namur* 11 [1957] 1, 1-13).

By 1959, it had become clear this was to be a subject of great importance in the *vota* as well as for the future Council.

III. THE *VOTA* BY THE BISHOPS FROM THE BENELUX REGION

Upon receiving Cardinal Tardini's letter most of the bishops gave a personal answer. Only the Dutch bishops at first decided to present a collective answer. They gathered in the autumn of 1959 but eventually did not succeed in editing a text everyone could approve. Given the urgency of the Roman request, it was decided to submit answers separately and keep each other informed on the contents of their respective *vota*. However, in writing their answers several bishops used the existing editing-scheme, as the bishops of Roermond (Moors) and Rotterdam (Jansen) deliberately did by way of protest against the fact that at first they were not allowed to send in personal answers[34].

In general, the Benelux *vota* clearly focused on three points of particular interest: the ecclesiological debate on the power and position of local bishops, subjects related to the ecumenical and liturgical movement, and elements of canon law.

1. Vota *on Canon Law*

Contributions on canon law make a large part of the Benelux *vota*, both in quantity and in number of bishops sending them. There is a twofold explanation for this fact. In 1959, none of the bishops could estimate which direction the Council was going to take. Although Pope John XXIII had used the word *aggiornamento* while announcing the Council, the phrase had a more or less different *ad intra* denotation compared to the meaning it would have six years later, stressing the relations of the Church *ad extra*. Canon law, on the other hand, limited and restricted exercise of power by local bishops, especially in their relationships with religious and with the ecclesiastical authorities in Rome. While most of the bishops wanted an *aggiornamento* in handling specific pastoral needs and concerns, the most appropriate way to do so was to extend canonical powers at the local level.

The main topic in the Benelux *vota* on Canon Law therefore focused on administrative powers granted to local bishops. In order to gain more scope on the administration of their dioceses, and especially in the light

---

34. ALBERIGO – KOMONCHAK, *History* (n. 1), 103-104. See also J. JACOBS, in LAMBERIGTS – SOETENS, *À la veille* (n. 1), pp. 98-110, esp. 101-102.

of the changing pastoral context, most of the bishops asked for an extension of their rights over religious orders[35] and for an improvement of their judicial position. The latter had to be accomplished by receiving more executive rights directly from Rome[36], by diminishing their subject's possibilities of direct appeal to Rome, and by extending the bishops' rights in ecclesiastical procedural law, in granting dispensations, and in administrative and financial matters.

Several *vota* concern the *Index* of prohibited and restricted books. None of the bishops asked for its abolition. Instead the *Index* had to be adapted to modern times[37] and its procedures changed in order to improve and guarantee the defendant's rights[38].

Vota on canon law also incorporated requests to change fasting regulations: these had to be simplified and made uniform. The number of dispensations had to be diminished as well, exemptions only eroded the basic principles of fasting and made it more difficult to have the regulations accepted by the faithful[39].

None of the bishops wanted the law of clerical celibacy to be abolished, but in extreme psychopathological cases, dispensation should be granted more easily[40]. Only Bishop Lommel (Luxemburg) would have

35. Especially those orders and congregations active in pastoral care (caritas and education) which had the right to appeal directly to the Holy See. Compare the *vota* by Bishop Suenens: AD I, II-1, 141: "Quae exemptio spectat vitam religiosam 'ad intra' nec potest religiosos subtrahere iurisdictioni episcopi in omnibus quae sunt 'ad extra'"; De Smedt: AD I, II-1, 103: "Religiosi iuris diocesani ... considerentur tamquam adiutores directi ordinarii loci ..."; Moors: AD I, II-2, 495: "... il est nécessaire qu'on formule plus clairement et plus conséquemment le principe de l'exemption; que cette exemption perde sa valeur au moment où il est question de la cure d'âmes des religieux à l'égard des diocésains ..." and Bishop Lommel: AD I, II-2, 566-567: "Amplificetur potestas episcoporum visitandi et dirigendi congregationis religiosis ...".

36. For instance in the quinquiannal rights, a "limited package" of special rights reserved for a period of five years, which had to be obtained from Roman authorities time after time and could be refused. See: R. NAZ, *Facultés Apostoliques*, in *DDC* 5 (1980) col. 802-807.

37. Incorporating also other media. Bishop De Smedt in his *votum* in AD I, II-1, 104: "Invigilantiae Ecclesiae in libros hodiernis circumstantiis adaptetur et extendatur ad periodica, diaria, libellos necnon ad emissiones radiophoniae et televisionis".

38. Compare Bishop Suenens asking that the *Index* not only would be an institution for repression, see AD I, II-1, 147-148: "Nova institutuatur procedura in prohibitione librorum relinquendo scilicet auctori libri ... facultatem instituendi defensionem suam ...".

39. See for instance AD I, II-1, 147 (Bishop Suenens): "Norma sit simplex et facile observanda ...".

40. For instance the *vota* by Bishop Jansen, AD I, II-2, 502: "Nonne possibilitas dispensationis super coelibatu, in casu clare psycho-pathologicis, considerari possit?" and AD I, II-2, 512 (archbishop Alfrink): "... an fieri possit ut salvo bono communi sacerdotes nonnulli saecularisati a coelibatus onere liberentur ... unus vel alter propter difficultates psychicas coelibatum observare non valet".

liked to see matters on canon law treated by a commission acting separately from the Council itself[41].

2. Vota *concerning Ecclesiology*

Vota on ecclesiological subjects constitute the major part of the
Benelux contributions.

A central issue was the question of the position and role of bishops in
the Church. Their judicial powers had to be extended and Vatican I had to
be brought to an end by the coming Council. Therefore the episcopacy's
nature *vis à vis* the nature of priesthood had to be determined. Another
issue to be discerned was the exact relation between Pope, bishops and
priests. The Belgian *Vota* generally showed two opposing opinions on this
matter. One wanted to add the episcopal consecration to the list of sacraments, while the other did not see episcopal consecration as a sacrament as
such, but as the completion of the sacrament of the priesthood. According
to *vota* adhering to the latter opinion, it should be made clear in what way
and to what extent priests take part in this completion[42]. Most of the Dutch
bishops in their turn, also urged the Council to complete the ecclesiological thought of Vatican I by further explaining the Church model as stated
in the encyclical *Mystici Corporis Christi*, using more biblical terminology
as opposed to juridical language: the Church as Christ's bride instead of
the *societas perfecta* model. Consequently this should lead to a clarification of the role and the place of the bishops in the Church, in relationship
to Pope and council, to their clergy, the religious and the laity. In practice
this should mean a direct extension of episcopal powers. The *votum* of
Bishop Lommel of Luxemburg concurred with this point of view[43].

On the practical level both the Belgian and Dutch bishops requested
that local episcopal conferences should be granted a more important role

41. AD I, II-2, 567 (Bishop Lommel): "Attamen Concilio Oecumenico de hac re agen-
dum non esset, sed potius speciali commissioni episcoporum et peritorum ex universo
mundo constitutae".

42. See the following *vota:* AD I, II-1, 113 (Bishop Charue): "Affirmetur episcopatu
esse veri nominis sacramentum"; AD I, II-1, 104 (Bishop De Smedt): "Consecratio epis-
copalis est sacramentum veri nominis". On the second opinion, see the *votum* by Bishop
Himmer: AD I, II-1, 118: "Perscrutari notionem 'plenitudinis sacerdotii' quam Traditio
episcopatui tribuit et modum quo sacerdos secundi ordinis sacerdotii episcopi particeps
fiat".

43. For example the *votum* of Bishop Nierman: AD I, II-2, 485: "Imprimis et in genere
optarem ut ... profundius etiam quam Encyclica 'Mystici Corporis Christi' concilium
elucubraret ac definiret – terminis non iuridicis sed biblicis – naturam, structuram inti-
mam et finem Ecclesiae Catholicae ...". The position of Bishop Lommel can be found at
AD I, II-2, 565-566.

in the administration of the Church[44], while the central Roman administration should be reformed by decentralising and internationalising the
offices, meaning employing less Italian administrators, more non-Roman
experts and allowing more influence from young churches and missionary territories. Archbishop Alfrink of Utrecht, who had returned the most
extensive *votum* on ecclesiology, also asked the Council to install permanent episcopal councils acting as the executive power in the Church.
This Church Senate should be a concrete expression of collegiality.
Alfrink also wanted a clear definition of nuncios' powers regarding the
local episcopate[45].

Concerning the priesthood, only some of the Belgian *vota* focused on
the need to add specific pastoral training in the theological preparation
offered in major seminaries. Theological study should be re-adapted to
specific pastoral needs and should point candidates towards a genuine
priest- or diocesan-centred-spiritualityas opposed to a more monastic form
of spirituality[46]. The Dutch bishops added more general and practical *vota*
on the priesthood[47].

Another important *votum* presented by most of the Belgian bishops, is
the request to restore the ancient institution of the permanent diaconate.
The reason why the Council should do this differs according to the bishops adding the *votum* [48]. In general the bishops proposed that the Council should decide over three elements. First, permanent deacons would not

---

44. See for instance the *votum* by Bishop Geeraerts, AD I, II-1, 150: "Ut conferentiae
Ordinariorum in variis regionibus et nationibus magis efficaces reddantur ... Ut iisdem con-
ferentiis episcoporum intersint etiam superiores maiores religiosorum ..." (in order to
enhance cooperation between religious and episcopate).

45. AD I, II-2, 510-511 (archbishop Alfrink): "Optandum denique est, ut relatio, quae
intercedit inter S. Sedis Nuntios atque hierarchiam localem, clarius circumscribatur".

46. AD I, II-1, 142 (Bishop Suenens): "Institutiones in seminariis theologicis reex-
aminentur ut exigentiis apostolatus hodierni melius conformentur. Sacerdotes fere omnes
dolent formationem in seminario receptam fuisse nimis abstractam et mere theoreticam,
sine respectu ad vitam apostolicam futuram ... per ipsos annos formationis in seminario
in hunc finem (= specific training in the light of pastoral praxis) adhibenda".

47. For instance the *votum* of Bishop Moors, AD I, II-2: "Qu'on crée la possibilité de
la concélébration à certaines occasions ...".

48. Following arguments occur: to compensate for lack of priests (see *votum* by Bishop
Forni, AD I, II-1, 124: "Attentis penuria sacerdotum ... utilis fortasse erit haec modifi-
catio actualis disciplinae"), especially in missionary territories (i.e. Bishop Geeraerts, AD
I, II-1, 149), to relief pastoral needs (i.e. *votum* by archbishop Morel, AD I, II-1, 135-136:
"... scio missionarios sacerdotes saepe cruis temporalibus distrahi ... Nonne opportunum
esset quaestionem de 'diaconatu' secundum mentem primitivae Ecclesiae considerare?"),
as a specific sign of cooperation by lay people in the Church (Suenens, AD I, II-1, 143-
144: "Eadem Ecclesiae traditio semper intimae cooperationi laicos inter et sacerdotes
favere solebat: quae per institutionem diaconatus huius generis supremam acciperet con-
secrationem") and in the light of the "ecumenical" question (i.e. Bishop Paulissen, AD I,

be obliged to live in celibacy. Second, they should act both as a help in catechesis, or perform other practical tasks in parishes, and third, they should give shape to the framework of organisations of lay apostolate and/or Catholic action as well. Bishop Calewaert of Ghent disagreed over the obligation for celibacy. In case of shortage of priests, which was the argument most used, he found it more likely to grant lay people the possibility to perform certain tasks in parishes[49]. Only a few among the Dutch bishops asked the Council to consider re-installing the permanent deaconate, a *votum* presented in the light of a requested reformation of the lower ordinations[50]. Among the Belgian *vota*, there was a peculiar one from Bishop Suenens. He also added a *votum* on the temporary diaconate as a step towards the priesthood. He suggested prolonging its temporary nature by raising the age for ordination to the priesthood from twenty-five to thirty years. The period of time between ordination and the end of the theological training could then be used for an extensive introduction to the area of pastoral care.

Almost all Benelux bishops added *vota* on the role of religious in the Church, mainly asking to adapt both training and functioning in their respective apostolates to modern times.

Concerning the role played by laity in the Church, most of the *vota* stress the need for the Church to have lay people cooperating in order to perform its tasks as assigned by Christ. The bishops differ however on the specific place lay people should have within the ordering of the Church: from labourers under supervision of the higher clergy to equal co-workers performing a specific task[51]. The same can be established in the Dutch *vota* on this subject, though most of them base these *vota* on the assumption of the general priesthood of the baptised[52]. Bishop Suenens even added a *votum* asking that future priests not only should be taught methods and means for lay apostolate, they also should learn how

---

II-2, 517: "Ita (= restoration of the permanent deaconate) difficultas magna pro conversione removeretur, inprimis pro iis ex Ecclesia Anglicana").

49. AD I, II-1, 106 (Bishop Calewaert): "Ne admittantur diaconi uxorati ... Si in quibusdam regionibus desit copia sacerdotum melius est tribuere laicis facultatem ... quam permittere ut diaconi uxorem ducant".

50. AD I, II-2, 497 (Bishop Moors): "Les quatre ordres mineurs devraient être révisés ou peut-être même réduits à un ordre. Ne pourrait-on faire de la fonction du diaconat une fonction indépendante...".

51. *Votum* by Bishop Charue (AD I, II-1, 113: "Hortentur fideles ut in organismus Actionis Catholicae partem habeant: sint adiutores cleri in apostolicis oneribus"). For the opposite point of view, see AD I, II-1, 142 (Bishop Suenens): compare n. 46, at the end.

52. See for instance AD I, II-2, 487 (Bishop Nierman): "Optarem ut profundius Concilium conferret studium ad naturam 'sacerdotii laicorum' in Ecclesia ...".

to cooperate with the laity[53]. In this respect it is quite strange to find only few *vota* in which the Council is asked to investigate what role women can play in Church life, and this as a parallel with the discussion in civil society[54].

Bishop Lommel (Luxemburg) also asked for an extension of episcopal judicial powers. He further stated the importance of elaborating the ecclesiological body of Vatican I by using and extending the theology of *Mystici Corporis Christi*, and by defining the role of and the relationships (theologically) between bishop, clergy, religious and laity[55].

3. Vota *Related to "Theological Movements": Liturgy and Ecumenical Theology*

Achievements made by the ecumenical and liturgical movement clearly influenced the *vota* of the Benelux bishops, *albeit* more on the level of practical reforms than on that of theoretical questions posed.

A majority of the bishops wanted to extend the use of the vernacular in liturgical contexts in order to improve active participation of the faithful. Moreover, liturgy had to be simplified, less devotional, and more attention had to be paid to Scripture. The bulk of saints' feasts overshadowing the Proper in liturgy had to be diminished as well[56]. Few bishops added a request for the specific possibility of concelebration and receiving communion under both species on special occasions like the celebration of a marriage[57].

Concerning the ecumenical question it is clear that the Benelux bishops hardly could ignore the results booked by the ecumenical movement in the preceding decades, also because of the fact the movement had been very active in its apostolate both in Belgium and in the Netherlands. On the other hand this was a more urgent problem for the Netherlands than it was in Belgium and Luxemburg. It is therefore quite surprising to find

---

53. See AD I, II-1, 142 (Bishop Suenens), compare notes 46 and 52.

54. See *votum* by Bishop Geeraerts, AD I, II-1, 149: "Quaenam pars mulieribus, quae nostra aetate in re civili ubique optimum laborem praestant, tribui possit in re ecclesiastica?".

55. See *votum* by Bishop Lommel, AD I, II-2, 565-566.

56. AD I, II-2, 567 (Bishop Lommel): "Kalendarium clarificetur in dispositione et simplificetur in numero festorum"; AD I, II-1, 114 (Bishop Charue): "Proponatur participatio activa fidelium ad sacram liturgiam: ... definiatur usus linguae vernaculae in sacra liturgia"; AD I, II-1, 127 (Bishop Schoenmaeckers): "Lectiones sumantur e Sacra Scriptura quibus modo authentico lineamenta operis Salutis dilucidentur ...".

57. See *votum* by Bishop Moors, AD I, II-2, 497: "Qu'on envisage la possibilité de recevoir la Sainte Communion sous deux espèces à certaines occasions comme à l'occasion de l'ordination, du marriage et d'autres occasions spéciales".

only few *vota* – if compared to the *vota* on the episcopate for instance – on the question, again only few of them introducing the theoretical debate.

Most of the bishops asked the Council not to proclaim new dogmatic definitions, especially in the field of Mariology[58]. They also requested permission to engage in a more open dialogue, therefore the coming Council should lift the ban on participating in meetings and debates with other denominations. The Council also should give up negative language when speaking of other denominations, and discuss the question whether the Catholic Church bore any guilt on the schisms that had taken place in the past[59]. On the level of theological debate, several bishops invited the Council to investigate and to determine the meaning of the saying *extra ecclesiam nulla salus* and of the *vestigia ecclesiae* -theology[60].

It is however striking to observe no reference was made to the idea of the Church as a *communio* on its way to the unity of the celestial Jerusalem, or to a more ecclesiological foundation of ecumenical theology. In spite of some openness and the will to enter the dialogue, most of the *vota* represented a more ecclesiocentric point of view, not uncommon among the Catholic hierarchy of that day.

IV. THE *VOTA* OF THE FACULTIES OF THEOLOGY OF LEUVEN AND NIJMEGEN

Although the *vota* and opinions of the Roman pontifical faculties seemed to have been of more importance for the *Commissio Antepraeparatoria*, nevertheless the answers of the faculties were gathered and added to the collection of the *vota*.

---

58. For instance AD I, II-1, 154 (Bishop Catry): "Opportunitatis causa melius nobis videtur quaestionem de mediatione B.M.V. non tractare in Concilio Oecumenico, ne maior scissio fiat inter Ecclesiam Catholicam et ecclesias dissidentes"; and AD I, II-2, 507 (Bishop Mutsaerts): "Si evenerit, ut disseratur de Maria magnopere intererit ea evitari vocabula, quae a sacra Scriptura et a theologica Catholica non solide probantur".

59. Compare the *votum* by Bishop Charue, AD I, II-1, 115: "... ne dedignetur fateri ambiguitates deflendas et errores, saltem psychologicos, a nobis contractos", and by Bishop Nierman, AD I, II-2, 486: "Edicat demum publico et officiali quodam modo et quantum veritas ac veracitas exigit et sinit, communitatem Catholicorum et quoad originem schismatum et quoad modos agendi, loquendi, opinandi erga schismaticos et errantes multoties peccasse defectu amoris et humilitatis, lenitatis et patientiae".

60. See the *votum* by Bishop Himmer, AD I, II-1, 118: "Quomodo hoc assertum 'extra Ecclesiam nullam esse salutem' rite est intelligendum?", and by Bishop Moors, AD I, II-2, 493: "La doctrine des 'vestigia Ecclesiae' hors de l'Église ne devrait-elle pas être examinée en ce sens qu'on admette la possibilité que des éléments de la vérité aient également pu vivre et se développer hors de l'église ...".

It took most of the faculties a long time to respond. Leuven and Nijmegen, receiving the letter of Tardini around July 18, 1959, answered respectively March 7 and April 19, 1960. Nijmegen's *vota* were brief, only four pages in the *Acta et Documenta*, and to the point, the *vota* from Leuven were more elaborate, showing the same spirit[61].

The Nijmegen *vota* are divided into four major parts: ecclesiology, the relation between Church and world, pastoral theology and canon law[62]. The first *votum* concerning ecclesiology asks for a completion of Vatican I and to define all relationships between Pope, bishops (also *in collegio*), priests and laity. The Nijmegen *vota* also plea for the re-installation of the permanent diaconate and ask that the position of the laity and of women in the Church should be investigated and clarified more specific in relation to ministry. In the light of ecumenical developments, the Nijmegen *vota* ask to describe more accurately the notion of *membrum ecclesiae*. Concerning liturgy the vernacular is proposed as a liturgical language since it would enhance active participation of the faithful. Also the possibilities of concelebration and receiving communion in kinds are considered. *Vota* are added on the training of seminarians with special attention for the missions and for the oriental churches. The canon law *vota* mention adaptation of the *index* and an improvement of the defendants' position in ecclesiastical courts. In general the Nijmegen *vota* do not differ much from the *desiderata* sent back by the Dutch bishops.

The Leuven *vota* are more extended and more "theologically elaborated" than their Dutch counterparts[63]. They are divided into two main parts. The first part containing *vota* on ecclesiology, the second *vota* on practical matters. Following an old Leuven tradition, these are formulated in theses[64]. The ecclesiological part is structured around the main features of the Church: It is one, apostolic, holy and Catholic. In the light of unity it is asked not to proclaim new dogma but to show the reason why the Church is *vere et authentice*. The apostolic character should be

61. AD I, IV-2, 221-238 (Leuven), and AD I, IV-2, 476-480 (Nijmegen).
62. Apparently the Nijmegen *vota* were discussed and eventually returned by the university board, the *senate*. It is however not clear whether only the faculties of theology and canon law wrote the text of the *vota* or that the complete senate discussed the matter and edited the text.
63. Both the faculties of canon law and theology discussed Tardini's request on their joint monthly faculty board, from October 1959 till March 1960. A first draft was presented on the December meeting; the final text was approved on March 7, 1960, signed by the *rector magnificus*, Bishop Van Waeyenbergh, and sent to Rome and to the Belgian bishops. For the *vota* in general, see M. LAMBERIGTS, *The Vota of Louvain and Lovanium (Zaïre)*, in SOETENS – LAMBERIGTS, *À la veille* (n. 1), pp. 169-184, esp. 169-175.
64. Candidates for the doctorate had to present and defend theses added to their doctoral thesis. These "added" theses were published by the faculty.

demonstrated not only by explaining the Christian truth in an infallible way, also by elaborating the theology of the episcopacy. Defining the holiness of the Church asks for another view on the world itself, stressing its goodness, and the Church's Catholicity should become clear in its universal outlook and its attention towards all people.

The added theses treat subjects like judicial power of bishops, tasks and authority of theologians, study of the Bible (with a request for a new edition of the Vulgate), liturgy (at least partial implementation of the vernacular, more attention to the Proper, less saints' feasts and revision of liturgical books), moral theology and canon law (i.e. questions on fasting regulations, the *Index*).

V. CONVERSATION IN HISTORY?

After having sketched both the theological and pastoral context and the contents of the Benelux *vota* and by way of conclusion we return to the main question of this paper: has there been some form of "conversation" between the authors of the Benelux and university *vota* on the one hand and the pastoral and theological context of 1959 as represented in pastoral context, theological movements and figures concerning praxis, on the other hand?

In his analysis of the totality of the *vota*, Étienne Fouilloux, in a chapter on the activities of the *Commissio Antepraeparatoria* in 1959-1960[65], assessed three types of *vota*. The major part being practical *vota*, focusing on extending the power of local bishops[66], second, a minority of strictly theological *vota*, and third, a rather large group of undetermined *vota*, not belonging to one or another category[67]. Looking at the *vota* from the Benelux region, it has to be concluded that they are not as impressive as one might expect them to be. Excepting perhaps some *vota* on ecclesiology, most of the answers to Cardinal Tardini's request were more practical than fundamental-theological in nature. The average Benelux *votum* therefore seems to belong to the main (first) category as sketched by Fouilloux.

Since bishops, academic theologians and canon lawyers had to cope with a Roman administration pressing their boundaries and checking their

65. É. FOUILLOUX, *The Responses: Three Sets of Attitudes*, in ALBERIGO – KOMON-CHAK, *History* (n. 1), pp. 109-132.
66. *Ibid.*, 109: "… the great mass of vota, which were content to make diciplinary demands that would turn each bishop into a Pope in his own diocese".
67. A remarkable example in this category is the reply by the Brazilian bishop Proenca Sigaud, fulminating against Jews, communism and free-masonery. Even today, the text is being used by certain intransigent movements as an example of "what the Council should have done".

authority[68], it is quite understandable the *vota* might leave a dim impression because of the, at first, wait-and-see attitude towards the coming Council. Also most of the addressees of Tardini's letter expected the Council to focus on church-life *ad intra*, thus explaining the general lack of *vota* addressing problems of the world and the attitude of the Church towards it.

Clearly the bishops did not know exactly what to expect from the coming Council, but they did think that some adaptations were to be made concerning the pastoral context. In order to do so they turned to what might be called "the safest way": changing canon law in order to extend local bishop's authority, which would allow them to change praxis in order to face the challenge of secularisation on short notice. In the meantime, some theological debate on ecclesiology could be held, but the main differences and changes to be made were found in the adaptation of the episcopal judicial position and power, in the exact definition of the bishop's relation with his clergy, the other bishops, the Pope, and the laity. Other important proposals therefore treated problems in pastoral theology.

However, this does not imply the Benelux bishops were not aware of the latest developments in, for instance, liturgy or ecumenism: apart from a few, most of them elaborated, even cautiously, the main themes of these movements in their *vota*[69]. Comparable observations apply to the *vota* from both faculties of theology. Although having the space, time and knowledge (which accounted for most of the bishops as well) to focus on strictly theological themes, they also offer *vota* concerning pastoral care. They were, likewise, unaware of the direction the Council was going to take, and similarly they inserted themes as presented by theological movements. So it is quite clear there has been, to some extent even considerable, conversation between context, theology and bishops or theologians.

It also became quite clear that in spite of the bishops' awareness of growing secularisation, they still underestimated its rapid advance and impact on everyday Church life. The consequences of the problem would become clearer during the Council itself, hence the more fundamental discussions on Church *ad extra* then.

---

68. Although not the main reason (both bishops and theologians proved to be loyal towards Rome), it does explain in a way the wait-and-see attitude towards the coming Council.

69. Most of the bishops supported the ecumenical movement's aspiration for more dialogue with and openness towards other denominations with a more or less realistic and even ecclesiocentric motivation. Therefore only practical *vota* were given, asking for ecclesiological debate and some practical adaptations to liturgy and the administration of sacraments. Practically all of the bishops were more or less inclined to endorse the liturgical movement's aims, as they saw in it a means to enhance not only the spiritual life of their flock, but also to turn the tide in pastoral praxis.

During the Council several of the themes proposed in the Benelux *vota* would lead to much discussion and some fierce debating. As an example the debate on the episcopate can be named, in which the Leuven professor of canon law, Willy Onclin, had to compete against an Italian and curial group who severely disliked the idea of collegiality[70].

Finally, the commissio antepraeparatoria's work has been described as "one big ecclesiastical examination of conscience"[71]. The fact that the consultation had been carried out worldwide, together with the high number of responses, make the *vota* an interesting source for the history of Church and theology, for in fact they reveal information on the theological and pastoral situation throughout the world at the end of the 1950s.

However, some remarks have to be made. In spite of the fact that bishops were completely free in answering, a considerable number among them gave answers they expected the Vatican wanted to receive and answered in rather general terms. Those who did offer *vota* based on the situation in their respective dioceses and on the theological and pastoral challenges they had to meet, left us with a valuable source on Church life for the year 1959, on condition these *vota* are read in connection with contextual data.

And the *vota* are clearly not the only source concerning the preparatory period. As Fouilloux has stated[72], bishops (and university faculties) had other means to prepare for the Council as well, and eventually several among them would use these means. This preparation however, mostly took place in the space of time between the final redaction of the *vota* and the opening of the Council[73], showing another form of interaction or conversation between the historical context and the Council.

Faculteit Godgeleerdheid   Dirk CLAES
K.U. Leuven
St.-Michielsstraat 6
B-3000 Leuven
Belgium

---

70. GROOTAERS, *Actes et acteurs* (n. 1), 420-456, esp. pp. 423-443.

71. Quote taken from unpublished course notes of J. VANDEKERKHOVE, *Twintig jaar na het Tweede Vaticaans Concilie*, course taught at the former *Centrum voor Kerkelijke Studies* (centralised theological training for religious orders and congregations) in Leuven, 1985.

72. FOUILLOUX, *The Responses* (n. 65), p. 109.

73. Compare for instance the talks Suenens had in 1960 with the journalist Maria Rosseels on marital moral theology and on the place and role of religious in Church life. See R. BOUDENS, *De Kerk in Vlaanderen. Momentopnamen*, Averbode, 1994, pp. 406-412, esp. 409-410. Journals like *De Maand* also excerted a certain influence on the Belgian and Dutch bishops.

III

REFLECTING ON THEOLOGY AND SPIRITUALITY

CONVERSATION AS A PARADIGM FOR THEOLOGY

LA SÉPARATION ENTRE THÉOLOGIE ET SPIRITUALITÉ

ORIGINE, CONSÉQUENCES ET DÉPASSEMENT DE CE DIVORCE

Vous savez tous que les divines Écritures ne mentionnent nulle part un divorce possible entre théologie et spiritualité. Elles ne décrivent que le divorce entre la foi et l'incrédulité. De même, les écrits patristiques ignorent tout divorce entre la connaissance et la pratique de la foi. Les écrits du premier millénaire chrétien ne connaissent pas nos distinctions entre dogmatique et vie sacramentelle, entre morale et droit canonique, entre ascèse et mystique. Les sermons de saint Augustin et du pape Grégoire le Grand abordent tous les niveaux de la foi et de la vie ecclésiale.

Pourtant de nos jours on constate un vrai divorce entre la réflexion théologique et la vie spirituelle dans l'Église latine. Ce divorce est sans doute moins évident dans les Églises orthodoxes, quoique même ces vénérables Églises, tellement attentives à leurs traditions ancestrales, ne semblent pas insensibles aux sirènes d'un certain rationalisme ambiant. Mais restreignons-nous à l'histoire de la théologie dans l'Église latine.

Il faut d'abord réfléchir sur l'origine de ce divorce, à la fois regrettable et inéluctable dans une culture comme la nôtre, tellement imprégnée de rationalisme. Certains auteurs pensent que ce divorce a été provoqué surtout par la mentalité juridique du Concile de Trente. Mais des historiens plus perspicaces se rendent compte qu'il existait déjà du temps de la scolastique naissante, disons au début du treizième siècle. Les Sommes scolastiques se proposent de présenter une science structurée et bien organisée des vérités de la foi. Elles n'effleurent qu'occasionellement des questions de vie spirituelle. Pour cette raison j'ose vous proposer l'hypothèse que la théologie et la spiritualité se trouvaient, pour la dernière fois, harmonieusement réunies chez les auteurs monastiques du douzième siècle (surtout dans les œuvres de Bernard de Clairvaux et de Guillaume de Saint-Thierry et dans les écrits de Hugues et de Richard de Saint-Victor). En plus, on pourrait trouver la vraie origine du divorce dans le conflit qui a opposé les cisterciens Bernard et Guillaume au premier maître de la dialectique, Pierre Abélard.

I. L'ORIGINE DU DIVORCE

De nos jours il est extrêmement dangereux de critiquer maître Abélard, car on touche alors à un sujet très sensible pour pratiquement tous les théologiens. Précisons donc notre point de vue. Nous n'avons nulle intention de juger la doctrine ni les mérites de maître Pierre; nous n'avons aucune compétence pour le faire. Nous essayons seulement de comprendre les raisons qui ont incité Guillaume et Bernard à réfuter plusieurs de ses doctrines et à refuser de suivre les nouvelles voies que proposait Pierre Abélard à ses étudiants.

Il n'y a pas de doute que le signal d'alarme ait été donné par Guillaume. On peut s'en rendre compte en lisant la lettre incendiaire qu'il a envoyée, pendant le carême de 1140, à son ami Bernard et à Godefroid de Chartres, légat du pape pour la France:

> Aux révérends Seigneurs et Pères dans le Christ, à Godefroid, évêque de Chartres, et à Bernard, abbé de Clairvaux.
> Je suis confus, moi, le dernier des hommes, d'être contraint de vous interpeller. Votre devoir est de parler et vous gardez le silence sur une affaire des plus graves, qui intéresse le bien commun des fidèles! Puis-je me taire à la vue du danger que court la foi de notre commune espérance? Cette foi que Jésus-Christ a scellée de son sang, pour la défense de laquelle les apôtres et les martyrs ont versé le leur, que les veillées et les travaux des docteurs ont transmise pure et sans tache au siècle malheureux que nous vivons[1].

Où et comment Guillaume s'est-il rendu compte que la foi était en danger? Il nous le confie dans l'introduction de sa *Lettre d'or*. Nous y apprenons qu'au monastère de Signy il a fait la connaissance de deux novices qui avaient suivi les cours d'Abélard et qui portaient dans leur bagage le traité *Theologia Summi Boni*. Ce traité excita la curiosité de Guillaume qui s'empressa de parcourir l'ouvrage, passant d'un sujet d'étonnement à un autre. Guillaume se sentit appelé à dénoncer et à combattre les erreurs qu'Abélard enseignait à ses étudiants.

> Ne vous imaginez pas qu'il soit question de bagatelles. C'est la foi en la sainte Trinité, la personne du Médiateur, celle du Saint-Esprit, la grâce de Dieu et le sacrement de notre rédemption qui sont en cause. Pierre Abélard (déjà condamné à Soissons en 1120) se remet à enseigner et à écrire des nouveautés. Ses livres passent les mers: ils vont au-delà des Alpes[2].

On connaît la suite des événements. Bernard ne se fit pas prier longtemps. Il proposa à Abélard un dialogue public à Sens. Abélard accepta,

1. GUILLAUME DE SAINT-THIERRY, *Lettre à Bernard* (PL, 182), Paris, Migne, 1860, pp. 531-533.
2. *Ibid.*

mais dut s'apercevoir à la dernière minute que le dialogue proposé prit la forme d'un concile jugeant l'orthodoxie de ses écrits. Il le récusa et fit appel à la cour papale. Innocent II ne tarda pas à condamner Abélard et à le réduire au silence.

Reprenons notre question initiale à propos de cette affaire. Pour quelles raisons Guillaume et Bernard se sont-ils opposés à la théologie d'Abélard? Nous pensons à deux motifs de caractère différent.

D'abord la méthode dialectique de son enseignement. Guillaume résume cette objection en cette phrase: «Il traite les divines Écritures comme il a l'habitude de traiter la dialectique». Abélard était avant tout un dialecticien. Il espérait rendre compréhensibles les vérités de la foi à l'aide de la logique. «En effet, disait-il, que signifient pour le laïc croyant des dogmes dont il ne comprend rien?» Guillaume et Bernard affirmaient qu'Abélard soumettait toutes les données de la foi à la critique de la raison. Dans son système, la raison avait le premier mot et aussi le dernier! C'est pourquoi ils pensaient que l'essence même de la révélation chrétienne était en danger.

Il y avait un second motif qui expliqua la méfiance de Guillaume et de Bernard vis-à-vis de ce maître tellement populaire: sa vie privée faisait circuler beaucoup de bruits. Tout le monde se souvenait de son «affaire» amoureuse avec Héloïse. On savait que le chanoine Fulbert s'était vengé en le faisant émasculer. On savait qu'Abélard avait semé la division et la discorde dans tous les monastères où il était passé. Bernard résume:

> Au-dehors il se présente comme un moine, mais au dedans il est un hérétique. Sa vie, sa conduite et ses livres prouvent qu'il est un persécuteur de la foi catholique et un ennemi de la croix du Christ[3].

Au fond, Guillaume et Bernard se méfiaient de ce professeur célèbre parce que sa vie ne s'harmonisait guère avec son enseignement. Avant l'entrée en scène d'Abélard, il était admis par tous que la science du mystère divin ne pouvait être obtenue que dans les monastères ou dans les Écoles collégiales. Tout enseignement de la théologie était soumis à l'autorité de la hiérarchie et supposait une conduite conforme. Abélard voulait libérer la théologie de ce corset ecclésiastique et la considérait comme une science rationnelle, sans lien avec la vie privée. On peut en voir l'expression symbolique dans le conflit qui l'opposa, déjà en 1110, à Guillaume de Champeaux, archidiacre de Paris. Ce dernier avait interdit à Abélard de continuer son enseignement à l'École Notre-Dame. Abélard emporta sa chaire de professeur et alla s'installer un peu en dehors

---

3. BERNARD, *Lettre* 331, in J. LECLERCQ – H. ROCHAIS (eds.), *Epistolae* (Sancti Bernardi opera, 8), Roma, Ed. Cistercienses, 1977, p. 269, 9-11.

des murs de la ville, auprès de l'église Sainte-Geneviève (l'actuel Panthéon). C'est avec raison que l'on considère ce geste symbolique comme la première fondation d'une université totalement libre. C'est en effet au même endroit, le Quartier latin, que la Sorbonne s'établira plus tard.

Abélard et sa théologie furent clairement condamnés par le pape Innocent II. On n'a pas le droit de faire d'Abélard un hérétique, puisqu'il se soumit à la décision de l'Église. Mais il mourut comme un homme brisé. La suite de l'histoire de la théologie a fini par lui donner raison. Ce novateur condamné fut de plus en plus considéré comme le précurseur de la théologie scolastique. Celle-ci fut un phénomène exclusivement universitaire. Pierre Lombard convertit la théologie en une discipline d'université. Ceci signifia la fin de la théologie monastique. Vers l'année 1250, l'abbé de Clairvaux, Etienne de Lexington, fonda à Paris le Collège Saint-Bernard, à côté des grandes Écoles, pour y faire étudier les moines les plus doués. De la sorte, à peu près un siècle après sa mort, Abélard obtint gain de cause. Les cisterciens eux-mêmes n'étudieraient que la théologie scolastique.

Guillaume et Bernard eurent le pressentiment du danger et ils essayèrent de renverser le cours des choses. Du point de vue de l'histoire, leurs efforts furent vains. Ils discernèrent cependant un problème tout à fait réel: le divorce imminent entre la théologie et la spiritualité. La théologie allait devenir une science purement rationnelle, et la spiritualité finirait par être reléguée aux marges de l'ascèse et de la mystique (ou plus grave encore: vers la zone irrationnelle de la sensibilité). Au treizième siècle, un Thomas d'Aquin saura réconcilier la raison avec la foi. Mais la raison et l'amour de Dieu n'ont cessé depuis de s'éloigner l'un de l'autre.

Guillaume et Bernard n'ont pas voulu négliger l'aspect cognitif de la vie spirituelle. Ils étaient très attentifs au rôle de la raison. Le spirituel doit acquérir une vraie science de la foi. Mais cette science qui maîtrise et organise, doit être accompagnée de la sagesse qui goûte et savoure dans l'affectivité.

> Le rôle tenu dans l'activité par la science et la raison, la sagesse le joue dans l'affectivité. La science amasse (les informations) mais pas pour elle-même. Comme les abeilles elle fabrique du miel, mais pour un autre. Ces provisions, on lui en permet bien quelque usage extérieur, mais leur saveur intime, on la réserve à un autre. L'étude de la science requiert la discipline de la vie de société. La perfection de la sagesse, au contraire, exige la solitude et le secret, un coeur solitaire, même au milieu des foules[4].

---

4. GUILLAUME DE SAINT-THIERRY, *Commentaire du Cantique* 28 (Sources Chrétiennes, 82), pp. 108-109.

Marie, Mère de la sagesse (*sedes sapientiae*), est la patronne de plusieurs universités. Mais on peut se demander où cette sagesse s'est réfugiée au cours du second millénaire.

II. LES CONSÉQUENCES DU DIVORCE

Plusieurs siècles durant, la scolastique occupait tout le terrain de la théologie. La spiritualité était pratiquement exclue des programmes d'école, au grand dam aussi bien de la théologie que de la spiritualité. Cette dernière a trouvé un refuge dans les écrits des moniales et des béguines au cours du treizième siècle et dans les œuvres de quelques auteurs mystiques du quatorzième siècle. En général, les représentants de ces domaines séparés se sont royalement ignorés. Des contacts sporadiques font preuve de malentendus réciproques et souvent de condamnations mutuelles. Les critiques formulées par Jean Gerson contre certains écrits de saint Bernard et de Ruusbroec sont très instructives à cet égard. Gerson rejette en bloc tout le troisième livre des *Noces spirituelles*. Surtout parce que Ruusbroec ne fait aucune mention de la «lumière de gloire» (*lumen gloriae*) que saint Thomas juge nécessaire pour que l'homme créé puisse contempler la lumière incréée. C'est donc le sommet de la vie spirituelle, la rencontre amoureuse entre Dieu et l'âme humaine, qui est en cause. Ruusbroec a été défendu par son confrère Jean de Schoonhoven, mais également par un chartreux anonyme d'Erfurt qui était parfaitement au courant de la polémique entre l'éminent auteur mystique et le grand chancelier de l'université de Paris. Le chartreux d'Erfurt remarque très judicieusement que Gerson avait les sens de la vue et de l'ouïe très développés (*acutissimus in duplici sensu visus et auditus*), mais que les trois autres sens, notamment l'odorat, le goût et le toucher, étaient parfaitement émoussés et faibles. Par contre, il y a des personnes moins instruites, qui sont aveugles et sourdes pour comprendre les maximes de la philosophie scolastique, mais qui ont les sens très développés pour respirer, goûter et toucher les réalités spirituelles.

O excellent maître docteur Gerson, je vais me servir de vos propres mots. Je les trouve écrits dans votre traité sur la théologie mystique, dans son avant-dernier chapitre. Vous y traitez de la difficulté qu'ont les savants et les doctes de bien connaître la théologie mystique. Vous procédez ainsi: «Mettons devant les yeux de notre entendement deux personnes, dont l'une a la vue et l'ouïe extrêmement développées, tandis que les trois autres sens (l'odorat, le goût et le toucher) restent très faibles et obtus. L'autre personne est aveugle et sourde, mais ses trois autres sens (l'odorat, le goût et le toucher) sont alertes et pénétrants. Il est certain que cette seconde personne pourra éprouver des jouissances sensuelles plus intenses que la première». A la lumière de cette comparaison, nous pouvons présumer que les savants philosophes et théologiens sont forts quant à la vue et l'ouïe spirituelles. Mais il s'avère que beaucoup d'entre eux sont privés des trois autres sens, ou que ces sens restent obscurs et obtus. Par contre en ce qui concerne les gens simples et sans instruction, on peut dire qu'ils restent aveugles et sourds quant à la compréhension de la philosophie scolastique, mais que leurs autres sens sont très développés quand il s'agit de l'odorat, du goût et du toucher spirituels.

O excellent maître Jean, docteur réputé, vous avez écrit et dit vouloir accorder la théologie mystique avec la scolastique. Il est clair que vous êtes très fort quant à la vue et l'ouïe spirituelles, mais que vous restez bien borné quant à l'odorat, le goût et le toucher. Parce que vous n'êtes pas encore parvenu à la sagesse de la théologie qu'il faut apprendre par l'ignorance, par des chemins non rationnels, par l'aliénation et la (sainte) folie. Pourtant on peut lire dans la lettre que vous avez écrite au chartreux Bartholomé, là où vous rejetez le troisième livre du traité de Ruusbroec nommé *Noces spirituelles*: «Les deux premiers livres, à mon avis, sont assez utiles. Je n'y trouve rien qui soit contraire à la foi ou aux bonnes moeurs, quoiqu'ils demandent souvent beaucoup d'un lecteur modeste ou d'un lecteur n'ayant que peu d'expérience des affections que l'on trouve évoquées dans le second livre»[5].

Après la période scolastique, la réforme a focalisé l'attention sur les divergences doctrinales de part et d'autre. La spiritualité se cantonne dans quelques mouvements piétistes, qui se trouvent en marge des Églises. Les oeuvres musicales de Jean-Sébastien Bach sont plus spirituelles que les cours de théologie des universités allemandes.

Et pourtant, dès le quinzième siècle des voix s'élèvent contre la dichotomie entre la réflexion théologique et la vie pratique des fidèles. Ces voix se font entendre dans deux mouvements distincts mais souvent alliés: l'humanisme et la dévotion moderne. Qu'il me soit permis d'évoquer ici la grande figure d'Érasme (1469-1536). En 1503 il a décrit son programme de théologie dans le *Manuel du soldat chrétien*:

En fouillant les sens cachés (de l'Écriture) il ne faut pas t'attacher aux conjectures de ton esprit, mais connaître une méthode et pour ainsi dire une sorte d'art qu'enseigne un nommé Denys dans son livre *Des Noms divins* et saint Augustin dans son ouvrage *Sur l'Enseignement chrétien*. C'est l'apôtre Paul qui, après le Christ, a ouvert certaines sources d'allégories. À sa suite Origène obtient facilement la première place dans cette partie de la théologie.

---

5. WEIMAR H.A.A.B., Qu 51, *Ex Carthusia Erfordis – saeculi* XV, 242r°, traduction par P. Verdeyen. Pour le texte originel, voir l'annexe.

Mais nos théologiens dédaignent l'allégorie ou bien la traitent d'une manière tout à fait frigide. Dans la manière subtile de faire des distinctions, ils sont égaux aux Anciens, voire supérieurs, mais quand ils touchent à ce mode d'exégèse, on ne peut même pas les comparer aux Anciens. Et cela principalement pour deux raisons je suppose. L'une que l'exégèse allégorique doit nécessairement rester glacée quand elle n'est pas assaisonnée par la force de l'éloquence ou par un style gracieux. Les Anciens y ont excellés, nous ne nous en approchons même pas. L'autre raison: on se satisfait du seul Aristote et on bannit de l'école les Platoniciens et les Pythagoriciens. Il n'est donc pas étonnant que les anciens Pères aient traité plus commodément les allégories théologiques, eux qui pouvaient par leur abondance oratoire enrichir et habiller n'mporte quel sujet même sec et frigide, et qui, d'autre part, connaissant très bien toute l'antiquité, avaient jadis exercé dans les poètes et les livres des Platoniciens la manière d'interpréter qu'il fallait appliquer aux mystères divins. Je préfère donc que tu lises leurs commentaires, puisque j'ai le souci de te former non aux disputes scolastiques, mais au progrès moral[6].

Léon Halkin a résumé ce programme dans son excellent livre *Érasme parmi nous* (1987). Érasme prêche l'humilité aux théologiens, parce que la théologie a pour objet le mystère par excellence. Puisque ce mystère est inscrit dans la révélation, la théologie est d'abord *biblique*; elle est *patristique*, car elle est histoire et tradition, conscience de l'Église en marche. Enfin, elle est *mystique*, parce qu'elle doit s'élever jusqu'au sens spirituel de l'Écriture, pour la goûter par le coeur autant que par l'esprit.

Ce programme, Érasme ne l'a pas seulement proposé dans ses écrits. Il en a fait le programme de sa vie. Il a édité le texte grec du Nouveau Testament. Il a étudié et édité plusieurs Pères de l'Église, des Pères grecs, tout comme plusieurs Pères latins. C'est dans cette ville de Louvain qu'il a fondé, avec l'argent légué par son ami Jérôme Busleyden, le *Collegium trilingue*, pour assurer l'enseignement des trois langues bibliques: le grec, le latin et l'hébreu. Au cours des années 1517 à 1521 il s'occupait intensément de cette fondation qui voulait assumer la subsistance de trois professeurs et huit étudiants. Les facultés des lettres et de théologie ont pris peur de ce collège indépendant. On le considérait comme un cheval de Troie, dont les guerriers pourraient attaquer le bastion de la théologie.

On peut faire la remarque qu'Érasme n'a pas écrit un cours de spiritualité ni même une histoire de la spiritualité. Il aurait répondu que les circonstances ne le lui ont pas permis. Il fallait d'abord préparer le terrain, c'est-à-dire éditer des textes fiables, aussi bien du Nouveau Testament que des grands Pères de l'Église. C'est cette tâche dont Érasme

---

6. D. ÉRASME, *Œuvres choisis*, trad. J. CHOMARAT, Paris, Librairie générale française, 1991, pp. 81-82.

s'est chargé. Et l'on peut dire que beaucoup de théologiens belges lui ont
emboîté le pas. Je mentionne l'entreprise des bollandistes, la bibliothèque
des textes syriaques, les études du Père de Ghellinck, la revue *Scripto-
rium*, le *Corpus Christianorum* (latin et grec), etc. Il est impossible de
nommer ici tous les grands travaux de théologie positive qui préparent le
terrain et rendent accessibles les trésors spirituels du passé.

Quels que soient les mérites d'Érasme et de ses disciples, il faut
admettre que la situation actuelle a besoin d'autres initiatives. Il me
semble que les facultés théologiques (et les séminaires) doivent chercher
d'autres structures. Il faut également reprendre la question de la nature
exacte de la connaissance théologique. Précisons notre idée à propos de
ces deux sujets.

III. Le dépassement du divorce

On se souvient de la parole de Malraux: «Le vingt-et-unième siècle
sera spirituel ou il ne sera pas». Étant donné que les facultés de théologie ne sont point préparées pour cette nouvelle tâche, on cherche des
structures plus adaptées. Les facultés universitaires créent un département
de spiritualité qui multiplie les cours d'histoire de la spiritualité chrétienne et organise des «workshops» sur des thèmes précis de la vie spirituelle. Il s'agit là d'un progrès remarquable, quand on se souvient de la
situation du siècle passé. Seulement, la multiplication des instituts et des
cours ne garantit d'aucune façon que la recherche théologique globale
suivra des chemins plus spirituels. La spécialisation est sans doute inévi-
table mais elle pose aussi de nouveaux problèmes. Qu'on pense aux relations entre l'exégèse et la dogmatique, entre le droit ecclésiastique et la
morale évangélique. La nouvelle attention donnée à la spiritualité ne la
sortira pas forcément de l'isolement et du cloisonnement actuels.

Les nouvelles structures doivent aller de pair avec une nouvelle
réflexion sur le caractère propre de la connaissance théologique. Posons
comme axiome que la théologie chrétienne cherche une connaissance
approfondie de la foi chrétienne. Nous savons, bien sûr, que l'on pourrait parler d'une théologie agnostique. Nous savons que la Bible et le
Coran appartiennent au patrimoine universel de l'humanité entière. Tou-
tefois il faut concéder à chaque Église le droit de formuler et d'élucider
le contenu de son propre message.

Très tôt la foi chrétienne a dû chercher ses propres lumières au milieu
d'une civilisation pluriforme, mais foncièrement rationnelle. Le message
évangélique a dû s'inculturer dans la civilisation hellénistique qui,

quoique moins scientifique que la nôtre, était très attentive aux possibilités de la raison humaine. Par tous les chemins les Alexandrins cherchaient la «gnose» ou la connaissance de l'ultime vérité. Il ne faut pas hésiter de parler d'une gnose typiquement chrétienne. On la trouve évoquée aussi bien dans les écrits de saint Paul que dans ceux de saint Jean. Comment définir le sens de cette «gnose chrétienne»? Reprenons la description que Karl Rahner en a faite dans plusieurs de ses écrits. Il s'agit d'une connaissance qui est le fruit de la charité plutôt que des raisonnements et qui, selon saint Paul, appartient aux hommes spirituels. Cette connaissance fait connaître à l'âme spirituelle l'amour incompréhensible de Dieu, qui s'est révélé surtout par la croix du Christ. Grâce à cette compréhension, le fidèle se laisse saisir de plus en plus par cet amour ultime. Il est évident que cette connaissance est un élément de la foi et se développe à l'intérieur de la foi (sans jamais la dépasser).

On trouve la même intelligence de la foi dans le traité de Guillaume de Saint-Thierry intitulé *Le miroir de la foi*. L'auteur distingue dans la foi, en tant que science, trois degrés:

> Le premier consiste à ne pas refuser, pour ainsi dire, la grâce de l'hospitalité à ces vérités venues du dehors … et à leur donner simplement sa foi, par obéissance à celui qui commande. Le deuxième degré consiste à se familiariser, par la bonne volonté, avec ces mêmes vérités et … à les recevoir à la participation au même pain et à la même coupe (que les vérités purement humaines)[7].

L'esprit alors se met en devoir de méditer, d'approfondir ce qui lui parvient du dehors. C'est l'activité de l'examinateur spirituel. Tôt ou tard sa persévérance et son zèle ardent lui méritent la lumière d'en-haut, l'intervention de l'Esprit. La grâce illuminante le transporte au dernier degré de la connaissance de la foi. Ce dernier degré se réalise par le sens de l'amour illuminé. C'est à ce propos que Guillaume peut écrire: «*Amor ipse intellectus est*». «L'amour est lui-même connaissance». Disons le plus explicitement encore: l'amour est la seule source de toute vraie connaissance de Dieu.

Cette conception de la vie spirituelle est présentée de façon plus dynamique dans la *Lettre d'or*, qui distingue trois niveaux de la vie spirituelle: l'homme animal, l'homme rationnel et l'homme spirituel. Tout auditeur attentif comprend facilement que la doctrine de Guillaume se rapproche beaucoup de la gnose alexandrine, ce qui n'est pas étonnant quand on se

---

7. GUILLAUME DE SAINT-THIERRY, *Le miroir de la foi* (Sources Chrétiennes, 301), Paris, 1982, p. 151.

souvient que Guillaume était un lecteur assidu d'Origène. Seulement la gnose alexandrine situe l'intelligence de la foi au sein des conceptions de la philosophie grecque. Pensons par exemple au *Contra Celsum* d'Origène. Guillaume situe l'intelligence de la foi au sein d'un nouveau mouvement dialectique de son temps, en s'opposant au rationalisme de la scolastique naissante. Il me semble que la mission de la spiritualité actuelle est de situer la vie chrétienne dans ses rapports avec la vision à la fois scientifique, sociologique et psychologique de nos contemporains.

Précisons encore la pensée de Guillaume. L'intelligence de l'amour est une vraie intelligence. Il faut se garder du schéma traditionnel: l'intelligence est affaire de raison, l'amour est affaire de volonté. Grande erreur! L'amour n'est pas l'affaire de la volonté seule. Il concerne tout l'être humain et rénove l'activité de toutes les facultés humaines. Pour cette raison même les cinq sens corporels sont changés par l'amour et se comportent réellement comme des sens spirituels. L'anthropologie origénienne est à la base de l'anthropologie de Guillaume.

Quant à l'influence de la théologie alexandrine, il faut se prémunir contre un malentendu possible. Guillaume n'a pas voulu reprendre ni actualiser la doctrine d'Origène. Il n'est pas un «*laudator temporis acti*», il ne veut pas idéaliser le passé. L'évolution de sa pensée n'a pas été déterminée par des études historiques. Il a par contre été interpellé par les questions de son temps. Il a surtout été attentif aux affirmations du Pseudo-Denys et de la théologie négative: «Jamais la raison humaine ne parviendra à comprendre le mystère divin». «La meilleure connaissance de Dieu, possible en ce monde, c'est de comprendre que Dieu est inconnaissable»[8]. Progressivement Guillaume a remarqué que cette approche négative du mystère divin menait à une sorte d'agnosticisme. Il a été sauvé des ténèbres dionysiennes par le verset de Matthieu 11,27: «Nul ne connaît le Fils si ce n'est le Père, et nul ne connaît le Père si ce n'est le Fils, et celui à qui le Fils veut bien le révéler». C'est la révélation biblique qui ouvre le chemin vers une connaissance positive de Dieu.

On peut suivre la progression de Guillaume vers cette connaissance positive dans ses *Oraisons méditatives*:

> Où es-tu, Seigneur, où es-tu? Et où n'es-tu pas? Je suis certain qu'ici maintenant tu es avec moi. Mais puisque tu es avec moi, pourquoi moi aussi ne suis-je pas avec toi? Mon âme a l'impression de ne pas t'aimer tout à fait si elle ne jouit pas de toi. Mais jouir de toi, elle ne le pourra pas, si elle ne te voit et ne te comprend[9].

8. Voir DENYS L'ARÉOPAGITE, *La hiérarchie céleste* (Sources Chrétiennes, 58), Paris, 1958, *passim*.
9. GUILLAUME DE SAINT-THIERRY, *Oraisons méditatives* III,4 (Sources Chrétiennes, 324), Paris, 1986, p. 66.

Résumons: L'âme qui aime Dieu, veut jouir de lui. Mais cette jouissance suppose la présence de Dieu de même que sa connaissance. L'intelligence de Dieu est un élément essentiel de l'expérience spirituelle.
On trouve le même cheminement en lisant plus loin:

> Dis à mon âme qu'est-ce donc qu'elle désire quand elle désire ta face. Elle est
> à ce point aveugle ... qu'à la fois elle se consume de désir et pourtant ignore
> ce qu'elle désire. Est-ce qu'elle veut te voir tel que tu es? ... Voir cela est
> au-dessus de nous, parce que voir ce que tu es, c'est être ce que tu es.
> Or «personne ne voit le Père sinon le Fils, et le Fils, sinon le Père ...»
> Mais il poursuit et dit: «et celui à qui le Fils veut le révéler» ... Donc, par
> l'Esprit-Saint, la Trinité Dieu se révèle elle-même à tel ami de Dieu qu'elle
> veut particulièrement honorer[10].

Guillaume se rendait parfaitement compte que cette connaissance de la
foi n'est pas celle de la raison raisonnante. Il le dit expressément dans son
Commentaire sur l'Epître aux Romains par une longue citation emprun-
tée à saint Augustin:

> Tout ce qui vient au devant de sa pensée, il le rejette, le méprise, le désap-
> prouve. Il sait parfaitement que ce n'est pas cela qu'il cherche, bien qu'il
> ne sache pas encore ce qu'il cherche. Il y a donc en lui une sorte de docte
> ignorance, enseignée par l'Esprit de Dieu qui vient en aide à notre fai-
> blesse, humiliant l'homme par l'épreuve. Jusqu'à ce que cet homme soit
> renouvelé à l'image de celui qui l'a créé, et commence à être fils par unité
> de ressemblance[11].

C'est dans son chef d'œuvre, le *Commentaire sur le Cantique*, que
Guillaume décrira cette connaissance révélée comme intelligence de
l'amour (*intellectus amoris*). Rappelons que cet amour n'est pas une activité de la volonté humaine, mais une activité du Saint-Esprit, avec lequel
cet amour est identifié.

> Le premier mouvement de connaissance entre l'Époux et l'épouse fut don
> de la divine sagesse. Le premier élan de dilection fut gratuite effusion du
> Saint-Esprit. Mais dans la relation de l'épouse à l'Époux, connaître et aimer
> c'est tout comme un (*idem est*), car l'amour est lui-même intelligence[12].

Guillaume écrira plus loin:

> Quand l'épouse se souvenait de l'Époux, quand elle pensait à lui pour le
> comprendre, elle le tenait pour absent aussi longtemps que sa connaissance
> ne tournait pas en amour ... Sans aucun doute l'amour de Dieu s'identifie
> avec sa connaissance: on ne le connaît qu'aimé; on ne l'aime que connu.

10. *Ibid.*, pp. 69-71.
11. ID., *Expositio super epistolam ad Romanos* (CCCM, 86), Turnhout, 1989, p. 124;
AUGUSTIN, *Lettre* 130, 27-28, in *Epistulae* (CSEL, 44), Wien, 1904, p. 72,10-14.
12. GUILLAUME DE SAINT-THIERRY, *Commentaire sur le Cantique* (n. 4), p. 153.

Oui, à son égard, la connaissance mesure l'amour et l'amour mesure la connaissance[13].

Là encore la raison formelle de la connaissance d'amour est la présence de l'aimé: une présence active et passive à la fois, car il s'agit vraiment d'une connaissance relationnelle. Il faudrait montrer ici de quelle façon Guillaume compare cette connaissance amoureuse à la connaissance réciproque des Personnes divines. Mais en suivant ce chemin on se trouverait du même coup dans les vastes champs de la mystique chrétienne. Ce n'est pas le sujet de ce colloque.

Citons par contre le texte qui exprime la complémentarité de la raison et de l'amour, deux chemins parallèles qui mènent à la contemplation de Dieu:

> La contemplation a deux yeux, la raison et l'amour; selon le mot du prophète Isaïe: «Sagesse et science, voilà les richesses du salut». L'un de ces yeux scrute, en appliquant les règles de la science, les choses humaines; l'autre les choses divines, en appliquant les règles de la sagesse. Quand ils sont illuminés par la grâce, ils se prêtent un mutuel et sérieux appui: l'amour vivifie la raison et la raison clarifie l'amour. Leur regard devient un regard de colombe: simple pour contempler, prudent pour se garder[14].

Ce texte reprend une intuition de jeunesse que Guillaume a exprimée dans son traité *De la nature et de la dignité de l'amour*. Tout au long des années de l'âge adulte, il a mieux apprécié le rôle de la raison, qu'il a toujours considérée comme irremplaçable dans l'évolution de la vie spirituelle. Guillaume n'est jamais irrationnel ni anti-intellectuel.

Essayons, en guise de conclusion, de donner quelques caractéristiques de la connaissance amoureuse:

1. La connaissance amoureuse fait partie de l'expérience spirituelle. Vers 1130 saint Bernard et Guillaume ont découvert ensemble, dans l'infirmerie de Clairvaux, l'importance de l'expérience personnelle du mystère divin. Depuis lors ils ont essayé de décrire cette expérience dans le langage et avec les symboles du *Cantique des cantiques*.
2. La connaissance amoureuse est passive plutôt qu'active. Guillaume dit à cet égard:

> L'objet que l'âme pénètre par l'intelligence naturelle, elle le saisit; mais pour l'intelligence spirituelle, elle saisit moins qu'elle n'est saisie (*non tam capit quam capitur*). L'objet qu'elle saisit par l'intelligence naturelle, elle en discerne les éléments intelligibles par son opération rationnelle;

---

13. *Ibid.*, p. 189.
14. *Ibid.*, p. 213.

mais un objet que son regard ne peut percer, elle n'y peut pas faire des distinctions[15].

3. La connaissance amoureuse est fruitive. Elle n'éclaire pas seulement la raison, mais touche à la fois les cinq sens de l'être humain et surtout les sens affectifs, à savoir: le goût, le toucher et l'odorat. L'âme humaine n'a pas l'impression d'aimer parfaitement, tant qu'elle ne jouit pas de la présence du Bien-aimé.

4. La connaissance amoureuse suppose qu'on conforme sa vie aux exigences de la personne recherchée et aimée. Saint Bernard et Guillaume ont pensé que la vie monastique était la seule école possible de la charité chrétienne. A ce sujet ils ont été, sans aucun doute, trop exclusifs. Mais ils ont très bien compris les multiples invitations de la Bible à une foi sincère et sans ambiguïtés. Ils suivent l'adage bien connu que le texte inspiré doit être lu et compris selon l'esprit dans lequel il a été conçu.

5. La connaissance amoureuse enrichit tous les domaines de l'intelligence humaine. «L'amour vivifie la raison et la raison clarifie l'amour». En se rappelant l'harmonie qui est nécessaire entre la science et la sagesse, Guillaume est devenu un précurseur de l'humanisme typiquement chrétien. N'est-ce pas un tel humanisme qui nous a rassemblés en ce colloque pour le développement d'une théologie vraiment relationnelle?

ANNEXE

WEIMAR, H.A.A.B., Qu 51., *Ex Carthusia Erfordis – saeculi* XV, 242r°:

242/R (-9) O egregie domine doctor Gerson, verbis tuis modo utor, verba que scripsisti in tractatu de elucidacione mistice theologie in penultima consideracione. Ubi scripsisti de difficultate cognoscendi theologiam misticam a litteratis et doctis et ita dicens:

> Constituamus duos homines coram oculis nostre considerationis, quorum unus sit acutissimus in duplici sensu visus et audibus, sed habeat hebetatos penitus et oltusos tres alios sensus (241/V) qui sunt olfactus, gustus et tactus. Constituatur alius qui cecus sit et surdus, sed habeat expeditos alios et vivaces sensus, scilicet olfactum, gustum et tactum. Constat quod iste secundus poterit maiores experiri delectationes sensuales quam primus.

---

15. *Ibid.*, p. 195.

Coniecturemus ex ista similitudine quod philosophi vel theologi litterati vigent in visu et auditu spiritualibus, sed advenit multis quod tribus aliis careant sensibus vel impeditos vel obtusos prorsus habeant. Advenit contra de simplicibus illiteratis quod velut ceci et surdi sunt ad philosophie scolastice perceptionem, qui ceteris sensibus vigent in spiritualium olfactu, gustu et tactu.

O egregie domine Johannes, doctor eximie, scripsisti, dixisti te velle concordare misticam theologiam cum scolastica. Perspicuum est quod viges in visu et auditu in spiritualibus, sed omnino in olfactu, gustu et tactu obtusus es, quia nondum pervenisti ad practicam huius sapientie, huius theologie quae per ignoranciam, per irracionabilitatem et per amentiam et stulticiam addiscitur. Scripsisti tamen in epistola ad patrem Bartholomeum carthusiensem, in qua repudias tertiam partem libri *De spiritualibus nupciis* a Ruysbroeck compositi. Ibi inter cetera scribis ita:

> Sunt, ut meum interim est iudicium, due partes priores satis utiles, in quibus nichil deprehendi quod non posset salva fide et morum probitate salvari, quamquam modestum lectorem in multis efflagitent, et talem qui non sit penitus expers earum quae secunda pars loquitur affectionum.

(l'auteur désire remercier sincèrement Dr. K. Schepers, qui lui a communiqué le texte de Weimar).

Graanmarkt 9-11   Paul VERDEYEN
B-2000 Antwerpen
Belgium

ATHEISM, APOPHATICISM AND "DIFFÉRANCE"

"Tout autre est tout autre"[1], says Jacques Derrida, with characteristically unanalysed ambiguity; and, surprisingly, too many critics and commentators have let him get away with it. "Every other is wholly other": which could mean, I suppose, that every case of otherness – of this rather than that – is a case of complete otherness, so that there are no differences within the logic of difference, no kinds of difference, whatever values one substitutes for the variables "this" and "that" – which is manifestly false; or it could mean the opposite, namely, that there *are* kinds of otherness, but that all "othernesses" are of completely different kinds from one another; which is also false, and as manifestly so: and for the same reason, namely that either way complete "otherness" is an unintelligible notion, as we shall see in due course. In the meantime, if Derrida is right, that everything in his account of deconstruction follows from every "other" being "wholly other", then it would be worthwhile considering how this principle generates those consequences, at any rate two of them; first, the consequence of how "deconstruction" stands in relation to classical forms of negative theology; second, of how, for our part, a negative theology so retrieved from within deconstruction stands in relation to contemporary accounts of spirituality.

I

Hierarchy is understood ineradicably from the classical formulations of negative theology. In the fourth and fifth chapters of his *Mystical Theology* the pseudo-Denys describes a hierarchy of differentiated denials, denials, that is, of all the names of God. Those names, to use a later, medieval, metaphor, form a ladder, ascending from the lowest "perceptual" names – "God is a rock, is immense, is light, is darkness ..." – derived as metaphors from material objects – to the very highest, "proper" or "conceptual" names of God – "God is wise and wisdom, good and goodness, beautiful and beauty, exists and existence" – and all

---

1. J. DERRIDA, *Tout autre est tout autre*, in J.-M. RABATÉ – M. WETZEL (eds.), *Donner la mort. L'éthique du don: Jacques Derrida et la pensée du don*, Paris, Métaillié-Transition, 1992, pp. 79-107.

these names the pseudo-Denys negates one by one as he progresses up the scale of language until at the end of the work the last word is that all words are left behind in the silence of the apophatic. This ascending hierarchy of negations is, however, systematic, it is governed by a general theological principle and is regulated by a mechanism.

As to the general theological principle, the pseudo-Denys has already said earlier in *Mystical Theology*[2] what he had emphasised in *Divine Names*[3], that all these descriptions denied are legitimate names of God, they yield the possibilities of true and of false statements about God. Hence, these fourth and fifth chapters of his *Mystical Theology* are, in the first instance, expositions of an intrinsically hierarchical affirmative theology. For his being the cause of all is what *justifies* God's being described by the names of all the things he has caused, even if what they *mean* as thus predicated of God must fall infinitely short of what God is; nor is there any sign, anywhere in the *corpus dionysiacum*, that Denys anticipates a problem of consistency between an epistemologically realist affirmative theology and a thoroughgoing apophaticism. Indeed, it is probably one of the chief arguments of *Divine Names* that if we are not to be misled in our theological language, we not only may but *must* use as many different ways of describing God as possible[4]: as he himself says, if we gain something in how we think of God by describing him as a "king in majesty", then we ought to remember that she can appear to behave towards us in a manner so irritable and arbitrary that we may as appropriately describe him, in the manner of the Psalmist, as like a soldier with a hangover (Ps 78,65)[5]. Theological language, for the pseudo-Denys, consists not in a restraint, but in a clamour of metaphor and description, for negative theology is, essentially, a *surplus*, not a *deficit*, of description, you talk your way into silence by way of an *excessus*, embarrassed at its increasing emptiness; hence, if we must also deny all that we affirm, this does not, for the pseudo-Denys, imply any privileging of the negative description or metaphor over the affirmative. For we must remember that those denials and negations are themselves forms of speech; hence, if the divine reality transcends all our speech, then, as he says in the concluding words of *Mystical Theology*, "the cause of all ... is both beyond every assertion *and beyond every denial*"[6]. The point of

---

2. DIONYSIUS AREOPAGITA, *Mystical Theology,* in *The Complete Works*, trans. C. LUIB-HEID, New York, Paulist, 1987, p. 139.
3. DIONYSIUS AREOPAGITA, *Divine Names*, 593C-D, in *The Complete Works* (n. 2), p. 54.
4. *Ibid.*
5. *Ibid.,* p. 141.
6. ID., *Mystical Theology* (n. 2), p. 141.

the serial negations of the last two chapters of that work, therefore, is not to demonstrate that negative language is somehow superior to affirmative in the mind's ascent to God; rather it is to demonstrate that our language leads us to the reality of God when, by a process simultaneously of affirming and denying all things of God, by, as it were in one breath, both affirming what God is and denying, as he puts it, "that there is any kind of thing that God is"[7], we step off the very boundary of language itself, beyond every assertion and every denial, into the "negation of the negation" and the "brilliant darkness"[8] of God.

So much for the theological principle of his apophaticism – which is necessarily at the same time the general principle of his cataphaticism. As for the mechanism which governs this stepwise ascent of affirmation and denial, we may observe how that mechanism is itself a paradoxical conjunction of opposites: the ascent is, as I have said, an ordered hierarchical progression from denials of the lower to denials of the higher names, and yet at every stage on this ascent we encounter the same phenomenon of language slipping and sliding unstably, as the signifying name first appears to get a purchase on and then loses grip of the signified it designates. We may say legitimately, because the Bible says it, that "God is a rock" and as we say the words they appear to offer a stable hold on the signified, God: we have said, Denys supposes, something true of God, albeit by metaphor, and something of the divine reliability is thereby disclosed. But just as we have let some weight hang from the grip of this word "rock" on the being of God, the grip slips: God is not, of course, "lifeless", as rocks are, and we also have to say, since the Bible tells us we must, that God is love and must be possessed of intellect and will, and so enjoys the highest form of life that we know of. Hence, in order to retain its grip on the signified, the signifier has to shift a step up the ladder of ascent there itself to be further destabilised. For God is not "intelligence" or "will" either, and the signified again wriggles away from the hook of the signifier and shifts and slides away, never, as we know, to be impaled finally on any descriptive hook we can devise, even that of existence: in affirming "God exists", what we say of God differs infinitely more from what we affirm when we say that "Peter exists" than does "Peter exists" from "Peter does not exist". For the difference between Peter's existing and Peter's not existing is a created difference, and so finite. Whereas the difference between God's existing and Peter's existing is between an uncreated and a created existence, and so is infinite. Hence, any understanding we have of the distinction between

7. *Ibid.*, p. 98.
8. *Ibid.*, p. 135.

existence and non-existence fails of God, which is why the pseudo-Denys can say "It falls neither within the predicate of nonbeing nor of being"[9]. Mysteriously, the pseudo-Denys insists that we must deny of God that she is "divinity"[10]; more mysteriously still the signified eludes the hold even, as he puts it, of "similarity and difference"[11]; mysteriously, that is, until we remember that God cannot be different from, nor therefore similar to, anything at all, at any rate in any of the ways in which we can conceive of similarity and difference: or else God would be just another, different, thing. Just so, for the pseudo-Denys: for "there is no kind of thing", he says, "which God is"[12]. Therefore, there is nothing we can say which describes what God is, and, which is more to the point; there can be no language of similarity and difference left with which to describe God's difference. In short, for the pseudo-Denys, only God's otherness is "totally" other, and that otherness of God is, perforce, indescribable.

For the pseudo-Denys, then, we are justified in making true affirmative statements about God, because if God is the creator of all things, all things must in some way reveal, in what they are, the nature of their origin. But creatures do not all reveal the same things about God, or in the same way, or to the same extent. For this reason, it is correct to say that, for the pseudo-Denys, there is a "grammar" of talk about God, which governs equally its cataphatic and the apophatic "phases": for even if we do not have a proper "concept" of God (there being no kind of thing which God is for there to be a concept of), we have a *use* for the name "God", a use which is governed by determinable rules of correct and incorrect speech. In fact, it is clear that, for the pseudo-Denys, that grammar is complex and differentiated, governing, that is to say, different logics of grounding in truth, different logics of consistency, and above all, different logics of negation, negation being the foundation of all logic.

These "logics" are determined by the order of creation insofar as creation is an order and scale of revelation, an hierarchy, for as some things are "nearer" to God in their natures, and others "further" from God, so their likeness to God is more or less "similar". Of course, all the names of God fall short of what God is: you can even say that God is equally "other" than all these names, though they are not equally "other" than God[13].

---

9. *Ibid.*, p. 141.
10. *Ibid.*
11. *Ibid.*
12. *Ibid.*, p. 98.
13. See *Divine Names*, 680B. This paradox is not entirely incoherent. All numbers fall short of infinity infinitely. On the other hand, 4 is larger than 2, and 5 than 4. Created differences are not eliminated by their all falling infinitely short of their uncreated cause.

But because there is an hierarchy of affirmations, there is a corresponding hierarchy of denials. A *negative metaphor* negates an affirmative, such as "some men are islands", but is for all its negativity, still a metaphor, as is "no man is an island"; but the *negation of a metaphor* negates quite otherwise than does a negative metaphor, for the negation of metaphor simply consists in a recognition of its literal falsehood: "It is not the case that God is a rock". But then again, the negation of a literal affirmation will in one way entail its literal contradictory, for, as Aristotle used to say, *eadem est scientia oppositorum*[14] – you cannot understand an affirmation without knowing its contradictory; but in another way functions as the "negation of the negation", the "negation by transcendence", as in: "he falls neither within the predicate of nonbeing or of being". Here, then, there is an hierarchical differentiation and structure within negativity, and so within "otherness", an hierarchy which is intrinsic to the statement of his apophaticism.

If we are to understand the theology of the pseudo-Denys we have to admit this; and such an admission will not be so readily conceded in some quarters today; for it is commonly supposed that if we are today to gain profit from the theology of the pseudo-Denys for our own spiritual purposes, it will have to be at the cost of his clearly "pre-modern" hierarchicalism, for which (it is thought) any contemporary ontology can find no place. For no contemporary ontology concedes the pseudo-Denys' scale of being, descending, as I put it elsewhere[15], like a lava flow from the pure fire of its origin down through the slopes of the volcano, hardening and cooling as it flows away from its source. We have no conceptions today which correspond with the pseudo-Denys's platonic notion of "degrees of reality" such that some things "realise more" of what it is to exist than other things do, still less of the Christianised platonic notion that the existence which creatures "more or less" realise consists in their degree of participation in the divine existence. Hence, Christian theologies today, even those claiming much influence from the antique and medieval traditions of negative theology, feel that they know what they can and what they cannot take from that source: negative theology they will embrace, on condition of its detachment from a hierarchical platonic ontology[16].

They are sustained in their hopes for such selectivity by the fact that the theology of the pseudo-Denys is governed by a double movement of

---

14. Or rather, as Aquinas used to quote Aristotle's remark in *Peri Hermeneias*, 17a 31-33.
15. D. TURNER, *The Darkness of God. Negativity in Christian Mysticism*, Cambridge, Cambridge University Press, 1995, ²1998, p. 29.
16. See *ibid.*, pp. 26-33 for a fuller account of the role of hierarchy in the thought of the pseudo-Denys.

thought, the one rooted in an antique hierarchical ontology, the other, corrective of the first, in the directly Christian teaching of the creation of all things "out of nothing". If from the first point of view, a theological language of greater and lesser distance from God is legitimised; from the second point of view this hierarchicalism is radically qualified: all things are also in a certain sense equidistant from the God whose action sustains them equally in existence as opposed to the nothingness "from which" they are created. For there is no such kind of thing as the kind of thing which exists; there is no kind of being, therefore, which prior to or beyond its character as pure gift, has any claim on existence because of the kind of being that it is. Hence, from this point of view, an angel has no better claim on existence than a worm has. The "aristocratic" theological language of the angelic hierarchy cannot be justified except in its dialectical tension with, and ultimate subordination to, the "democratic" ontology of creation *ex nihilo*.

Nonetheless, those hopes are vain which are sustained by a prospect of a Dionysian apophaticism rooted in the democratic negativity of *creatio ex nihilo* but detached from an hierarchical affirmativity, at least because of the distortions thus visited upon the pseudo-Denys' theological project. For a theological apophasis whose denials are disengaged from the hierarchy of affirmations will have to abandon, along with the hierarchy of affirmations, also the pseudo-Denys's careful distinctions within the hierarchy of denials themselves – or, to put it in other terms, within the hierarchy of difference.

Hence, it is not so easy as it might be thought to disengage an apophatic theology from those hierarchical conceptions that, in antique and medieval traditions, underpinned an affirmative theology. For at work within the pseudo-Denys' articulation of theological language is the Aristotelian principle, *eadem est scientia oppositorum* – affirmations and their corresponding negations are one and the same knowledge. In *general*, therefore, "otherness" and negation are inconceivable except in terms of sameness and affirmation; hence, what it is to deny something – what kind of "otherness" you thereby affirm – depends on what it is to affirm it. It further follows that if the logic of affirmation is hierarchically differentiated, then we have to say that the logic of negation and otherness is differentiated. And it follows finally that if "otherness" is differentiated, then the differences between one kind of otherness and others are themselves intelligible only against the background of sameness. The conception of an "otherness" being "*tout* autre" is, therefore, unintelligible. Just so, says the pseudo-Denys: to the "*tout* autre" we would have to give the name "God", for it is here alone that logic breaks down, and the principle *eadem est scientia oppositorum* itself fails, as it must, since God "is beyond [not only] every assertion ... [but also] beyond every denial". As it were, to reverse Nietzsche s famous formulation: we can get God *only* at that point where we have got rid of grammar.

Hence to dislodge any one element in this complex structure of differentiated difference is to cause the whole edifice to collapse. What, of course, it collapses into if we remove from it that articulation of differentiated differences is precisely what we get in Derrida: a univocity of difference for which every difference is reduced to but one logical type, a type which is, moreover, logically impossible: *total* difference. What the pseudo-Denys recognises is that no two "anythings" can be "totally different", for that is why he concludes that God, being totally different from all creatures, could not be any kind of thing. As between God and creatures there is, of course, all the difference, but, being beyond description, it cannot be a difference of any *kind*; but the thought that that, precisely, is how God is different from creation – more "other" than any creature than any two creatures could be – is one which gets its full development in later Dionysian theologies, in particular those of Meister Eckhart and Thomas Aquinas, to whom we must now turn.

II

With Meister Eckhart, however, hierarchy – whether in the form of an ontology of degrees of being, or in that of the outflow of descending illuminations – plays little or no part in the formulation of his theology. If difference is central to that theology and spirituality, the carefully structured hierarchical gradations of the pseudo-Denys collapse into one central distinction which entirely eclipses all others: the distinction, on the one hand, between those created distinctions which obtain between one creature and another –between each *hoc aliquid* as an *unum distinctum* – and, on the other, that distinction which obtains between every *esse hoc et hoc* and the *unum indistinctum* of the divine *esse*.

I must compress. An individual is an instantiation of a kind, a *hoc et hoc*, enumerable on condition of falling under a description. I can count the number of people in this room if I know what counts as a person, the number of desks if I know what counts as a desk. But I cannot count the number of *things* in this room, because "thing" is not a definite description such that enumerable instances fall under it. Likewise, I can distinguish kinds from one another against the background of more general descriptions: I can tell horses from sheep because they differ *as animals*, or chalk from cheese because they differ in chemical composition, or taste or texture. But note here an apparent paradox: the less things differ, the easier it is describe how they differ. It is easy to say how a cat and a mouse differ, because we can readily describe what they differ *as*, they belong, we might say, to a readily identifiable community of difference. But how does this piece of Camembert cheese differ from 11.30 in the morning? Here, the community of difference is too diffuse, too indeterminate, for this difference, obviously bigger as it is, to be so easily described. In general we can say that the bigger the difference, the harder, not easier, it is to describe the manner of its difference.

Of course, the logic of difference thus described does not require of us any very particularly deterministic account of types or species, for this logic entails no particular ontological commitments as such. As it stands, however, this logic already has consequences for the question: how may we describe the difference between God and creation? It follows that we cannot describe it at all, for there is no kind of difference as that between God and creatures; or, if we are to say anything about this distinction it is what Eckhart says about it, namely that God is distinct from any creature in this alone, that if the creature is necessarily a distinct being, an *hoc aliquid*, God is not; a creature is, as he puts it, an *unum distinctum*, distinct by means of its difference in respect of some sameness, whereas God is an *unum indistinctum*, that is to say, is distinct from any creature whatsoever in this, that, unlike any creature, God is not distinct in a describable way from anything created at all. Therefore, God is distinct because God alone is not distinct. "Indistinction", as he puts it, "belongs to God, distinction to creatures"[17].

But if God is not distinct in a describable way from anything, God cannot be an individual, and so cannot be counted at all. Suppose you were to count up all the things in the world on some lunatic system of enumeration, all the things that there are, have been and will be, and suppose they come to the number n. Then I say, "Hold on, I am a theist and there is one being you haven't yet counted, and that is the being who created them all, God"; would I be right to say that now the sum total of things is n+1? Emphatically no. I do not need to reconstruct Eckhart here, for he says for himself in his *Commentary on Exodus*: "God is one in all ways and according to every respect so that he cannot find any multiplicity in himself ... Anyone who beholds the number two or who beholds

---

17. MEISTER ECKHART, *Commentary on Exodus*, 20.104, in B. McGINN (ed.), *Meister Eckhart, Teacher and Preacher*, New York, Paulist, 1986, p. 79.

distinction does not behold God, for God is one, outside and beyond number, and is not counted with anything"[18]. So how can God be one – *unum* – if not countable in any series, if not in any way another individual, one more something, not a *hoc aliquid*; how an *unum* if *indistinctum*? And if God is not an individual, is God therefore many? That neither, for the argument which shows that God is not one more individual must also show that God is not many more individuals. Neither one nor many: so neither an individual distinct from everything else, nor many, identical with everything else; hence "one", but not an individual; "distinct" from everything, but not as anything; hence, an *unum indistinctum*. And we should note that what holds for the divine oneness holds also for the Trinity itself. If there are in any sense "three" in God, there is nothing of which there are three instantiations in God, anymore than there is any "one" instance of anything, called "God" in which there are "three". The same principle of apophaticism holds of the divine Trinity – not three instances of anything – as of the divine essence – there is nothing of which God is one instance.

Now I said that *eadem est scientia oppositorum*. Hence, if God is beyond difference, then God is beyond sameness. If what Jacques Derrida means by saying that "every other is completely other" is that there is no ultimate sameness of such nature that it stands in no possible relation of "otherness", then of course he is right, for of course every "sameness" is resolvable into its differences from something else. But then it follows *also* that there can be no ultimacy to "*différance*" either. For "sameness" and "difference" have the same apophatic destination, as it were, in that they can only ultimately disappear into that same vortex which is beyond both. Just as you could not have a sameness that establishes itself beyond all possible difference, so you could not have a difference that is, without qualification, beyond similarity alone.

To which Derrida may be construed as replying: I affirm this rule of *différance* not in order to affirm some new ultimacy, only now a purely negative one, but in order to affirm only a *pen*ultimacy – which is not, by the way, to *insist* upon anything, but rather to *desist* from all possible forms of ultimacy, from every "destination", even an ultimacy of the negative. To declare the ultimacy of "*différance*" is precisely not to propose, but on the contrary to deny, some new ontology of difference, according to which *there is an ultimate difference*, which is what he accuses the negative theologians of affirming when they insist upon their "ontological distinction". For it is precisely in that insistence of negative

18. *Ibid.*, p. 63.

theology, in that surreptitious, last-minute, retrieval of the existential quantifier "there is an ..." attached to their ultimate difference, that an ontotheological sleight of hand is revealed, thus to regain for their apophaticisms a divine "destination", their postponements and deferrals notwithstanding- a given, superessential presence of an absolute absence, generative of all lesser, postponable, essential difference. For Derrida, this *khora*, this "place" of "otherness", cannot possess the name of the God of the negative theologians because it cannot be, as God is, "a giver of good gifts"[19], could not therefore be the creator.

In any case, this tactic of the negative theologians contains, he thinks, an impossibility, a contradiction. For the theologians' "there is an ..." must itself either be cancelled as affirmative utterance by their negative theology of ultimate difference; and, after all, they do concede this erasure, for how can theologians allow an ordinary, un-deconstructed existential utterance as a foundation for their apophaticism, and do they not insist that their God is "being beyond being"[20] and "within the predicate neither of nonbeing nor of being"? On the other hand, if not thus cancelled, must not this "there is an ..." remain in place as an existential quantifier, which therefore ontotheologically and idolatrously cancels the apophaticism. Hence, negative theology collapses either into the ceaseless penultimacy of an atheistic deconstruction or else into an idolatrous ontotheology. As a project, therefore, negative theology is impossible.

To which, in turn, it may be replied: the negative theology of the pseudo-Denys and an Eckhart does not affirm, as if at the last minute to hypostatise, *a* difference as ultimate any more than it affirms the ultimacy of some sameness and presence, of some given identity. For both recognise that *a* difference, *any* difference, is determinable. But what is "beyond similarity and difference" is not in some measurable, calculable degree of difference from creation, even if different beings in the created order *are* in determinably different degrees of difference from God. Nor is "the ontological distinction" in any *knowable* sense or degree "beyond" anything knowable; for our language of "difference", that is to say, our language *as such*, falls short of God to a degree which is itself absolutely beyond description: it could not be the case that we could *say* how different God is. This ontological distinction is "beyond" precisely

19. J. DERRIDA, *How to Avoid Speaking: Denials*, in H. COWARD – T. FOSHAY (eds.), *Derrida and Negative Theology*, Albany, NY, State University of New York Press, 1992, 73-142, pp. 106-108.

20. MEISTER ECKHART, *Renovamini Spiritu*, in E. COLLEDGE – B. MCGINN (eds.), *Meister Eckhart: The Essential Sermons, Commentaries, Treatises and Defense*, New York, Paulist, 1981, p. 206.

by reason of its unknowability and indetermination, so that it inhabits neither some place of absolute presence, nor of absolute absence; hence, we might just as well say, as Nicholas of Cusa in fact does say, that God is *ly non-Aliud* as say that he is in *any* way "*aliud*" – which, after all, is the same logic as Meister Eckhart's "distinct by virtue of indistinction".

It is such things which you have to say if you are to speak intelligibly of an "otherness" which is "totally other". No such otherness could be a finitely knowable, determinable, otherness, which is why Derrida's principle, "every other is completely other", is a straightforward logical absurdity, and a Nietzschean one at that. For it leaves all negation and otherness without "grammar" just as it takes leave of God[21]; Derrida can have no God precisely because he collapses all the differentiations of difference into a monolithic, univocity of absolute difference. And insofar as his abandonment of the antique differentiations of difference and negation and otherness requires his rejection of negative theology, Derrida's polemic makes one thing clear about the antique and medieval traditions of apophaticism: the links between that hierarchy and the apophaticism are logically unbreakable.

III

In turning next to Thomas Aquinas, we turn to a negative theologian who has fallen under the suspicion, in some Christian theological circles, of the heresy, as it is supposed to be in our post-Heideggerian times, of "ontotheology" – this, on account of his "natural theology"; and in other Christian circles, equally under the influence of a Heideggerian motivation, it is denied that Thomas offers a natural theology, lest he should be accused of this egregious heresy. A Marion and a Milbank share this much in common, at least: that were Thomas to be read as proposing a theological "foundationalism" in a *pre-required* rational proof of the existence of God, then his theology would have to be read as an "ontotheology". What neither entertains is a third possible reading: that, for Thomas, the possibility of a rational demonstration of the existence of God might be *entailed by* his theology, by his understanding of what is implied by theology's rootedness in what he calls *sacra doctrina*, rather than being *presupposed to* that theology as its "foundation". In any case, what *is* clear enough in Thomas' argument is that he thinks *both* that the existence of God is rationally demonstrable, *and* that

21. Nietzsche describes this, for example, in *The Twilight of the Gods*.

what you have thus proved the existence of is not the *instantiation* of any concept whatsoever, whether of "being" or of "goodness" or "oneness", or of anything else.

In fact it might seem curious that Thomas sets about demonstrating the existence of God *without* giving even preliminary thought to the definition of God. Stranger still to those who suspect in Thomas an ontotheology, the reader will be at a loss to find *any* "definition" of God anywhere at all, even were he to read right through to the end of the *Summa*. All Thomas appears to say on this matter, at any point, is immediately at the end of each of the five ways, when he says (to the dissatisfaction of most readers today) that the prime mover, the first efficient cause and the necessary being and the rest, are "what all people call God"[22]. And even when, immediately after his discussion of whether God exists, Thomas does appear to set about the more formal discussion of what it is that he might have proved the existence of, he tells us flatly that there is no definition to be had, for *there can be no answer to the question of what God is*, but only of what God is not. "Once you know whether something exists", he says,

> it remains to consider how it exists, so that we may know of it what it is. But since we cannot know of God what he is, but [only] what he is not, we cannot inquire into the how of God ['s existence], but only into how he is not. So, first we must consider this "how God is not", secondly, how she is known by us, thirdly, how he is spoken of[23].

That said, the reader will be further puzzled by the fact that, nonetheless, Thomas then proceeds for a further nine questions to discuss what, on most accounts, will be considered classical attributes of God – his simplicity, perfection, goodness, infinity, ubiquity, immutability and unity – as if thereby ignoring what he has just said and supplying us with what to many is an account of God's multiple "whatnesses", apparently quite untroubled by apophatic scruple. Something is badly wrong here: either, on this way of reading what Thomas' theological method is, he is plainly muddled, or, if consistent, then some other way of reading his method will have to be found.

It is charitable at least to *try* for a consistent Thomas. Nor is it difficult. Nothing is easier, to begin with, than to see that, in his discussion of the divine simplicity in question three, what is demonstrated is not some comprehensible divine attribute, some *affirmation* which marks out God from everything else, but some marker of what constitutes the divine

22. *Summa Theologiae*, 1a q2 a3, corp.
23. *Ibid.*, 1a q3 prol.

*in*comprehensibility, as distinct from the incomprehensibility of every-thing else. For what Thomas recognises to be in need of determination about God's distinctness is the precise nature of *God's* incomprehensi-bility, lest it be mistaken for that more diffused and general sense of the mysteriousness with which we are in any case confronted within and by our own created universe – for there is puzzlement enough in creatures. "You do not know the nature of God", he seems to say. "All you can know is the divine unknowability". But all the same, there is a job to be done of determining that the "unknowability" you may have got to from your contemplation of the world is in truth the *divine* unknowability – as distinct, for example, from simply throwing in one's hand at some lesser point of ultimacy.

For *penultimate* unknowability is always idolatrous. "Giving up" at the point of penultimate unknowability is exactly what Bertrand Russell once recommended when, confronted by Frederick Copleston with the question "Why is there something rather than nothing?" he urged us to be content with no answer at all, to be satisfied that the world is "just there", and to deny that the question can make sense[24]. For Thomas, on the contrary, in the very form of that question, "Why is there something rather than nothing?", we are confronted not with a mere passive igno-rance of a dull fact, but with a divine causality so powerfully creative that it *must* be incomprehensible to us – as the thought of creation "out of nothing" must be. The question "Why is there something rather than nothing?" is after all, intelligible enough to us, for we can *ask* it out of the native resources of our finite cognitive capacity: the question is plainly causal. And, as Geach points out, "cause of ..." has an earthly sense, comprehensible to us; so does "... every mutable thing". But the question which conjoins them: "What is the cause of every mutable thing?", though thus far arising from within what is intelligible to us must bear an answer which, demonstrably, is incomprehensible to us: we know that we *could not know* the nature of what it refers to[25]. For the only senses of "cause" available to us are those that causally link particular, or particular kinds of, mutable things and cannot, as Kant famously proved, in any *such* sense, have application to *every*thing. So what the five ways prove is *simultaneously* the existence of, and the unknowability of, God: God is shown to exist, but what is also shown is that, in *that* case, we have lost almost all our grip on the meaning of "... exists" as pred-icated of God. But only such demonstrated unknowability deserves

24. See J. HICK (ed.), *The Existence of God*, London, Macmillan, 1964, p. 175.
25. P.T. GEACH, *God and the Soul*, London, Routledge, 1969, p. 81.

the name "God"; which is why Thomas says that what is thus shown is what all people call by that name[26].

Now the argument for the divine simplicity in *Prima pars*, question three, is designed to demonstrate the ultimacy of that divine "otherness" so that we could not confuse that divine otherness with any lesser, created form of otherness. In fact, of course, in thus demonstrating God's otherness to be ultimate – hence the source of that *divine* unknowability which surpasses all other unknowability – he thereby demonstrates that otherness itself to be finally incomprehensible to us: not only can we not know the how of God, so other is it; *so* "other" is God, that even the concept of otherness has, in respect of God, itself lost its threads of straight-forward continuity with any conception of created otherness which we do know the how of. Once again: we know how "other" chalk and cheese are. We do not know how "other" God is: which is why Thomas is at one with the pseudo-Denys and the later Meister Eckhart, when he says that, at the climax of ascending scales of God's differences from all else, God must be thought of as off *every* scale of sameness and difference and thus to be beyond "every assertion ... beyond every denial"[27].

So, now: if you want to know what the "distinctness" of God is, that standpoint from which your speech about God is marked out as properly *theological*, then the answer is: you know you are talking about God when all your theological talk – whether it is *materially* about the Christian doctrines of the Trinity, or the Incarnation, or the presence of Christ within Church or sacrament, or about grace, or the Spirit in history, or the manner of our redemption – is demonstrably ultimate, when, through the grace of revelation, we are led *deeper* than we otherwise might be, into the unknowability of the Godhead. We might find it surprising that grace and revelation make things *worse*, epistemologically speaking, than they are for reason. Christians today might be scandalised by so extreme a view: they might more readily say, as many late medieval opponents of Thomas clearly did, that *reason* fails to reach God at all, and that a philosophical apophaticism claiming access to the divine incomprehensibility is a pretentious pagan, Neoplatonic, merely rationalist thing; but they will say that the more readily because they assume that they, in their Christian

26. Incidentally, "*et hoc omnes dicunt Deum*" is probably best translated as "and this is what all people refer to by the name 'God'" – which does not necessarily entail, still less does it necessarily mean, "this is *how* all people refer to God". So it is rather beside the point to observe that hardly anyone ever refers to God by the names "prime mover", "necessary being" and so forth. It is perfectly obvious that Thomas knew *that*.

27. DIONYSIUS AREOPAGITA, *Mysical Theology*, 1048A, in *The Complete Works* (n. 2), p. 141.

faith, are better informed than the natural philosophers are about God, for Christians have been given the revelation of the Trinity in the visibility of Jesus Christ. But not so, either way, for Thomas: he firmly rejects that dualism of the apophatic and the cataphatic according to which it is God's essence which is unknowable, his relations knowable. Indeed, there is a sense in which Christians *do* have a better knowledge by grace and revelation, but only because by faith they are inserted by way of participation into a darkness of God that is deeper than it could possibly be for "unaided reason". For unaided reason can only *think* this unknowability, as it were, from outside it and cannot be drawn into its nature as unknowable love, so as to share it in friendship with God. It is a darkness, therefore, which for the Christian is deepened, not relieved by the Trinity, intensified by the Incarnation, not dispelled. For which reason, Thomas says:

> ... in this life we do not know what God is [*even*] *through the revelation of grace*, and so [by grace and revelation] we are made one with him as to something unknown[28].

IV

What prospects are there today of retrieving from within the medieval traditions of negative theology resources for a contemporary spirituality? The outlook is unpromising, though there are those who, through a re-reading of those traditions, seek hope in a mystical outflanking of atheistic deconstruction, while yielding to the anti-metaphysical impulses of postmodernity.

It seems to such that it is possible to read Meister Eckhart in those terms – though he himself could not possibly have conceded them – as set an apophatic spirituality in opposition to a theological metaphysics, so as to defend him against suspicions of an "ontotheology". On what terms of apophaticism can one read today Eckhart's answer to the question, "Then how should I love God?" He answers:

> You should love God unspiritually, that is, your soul should be unspiritual and stripped of all spirituality, for so long as your soul has a spirit's form, it has images, and so long as it has images, it has a medium, and so long as it has a medium, it is not unity or simplicity. Therefore your soul must be unspiritual, free of all spirit, and must remain spiritless; for if you love God as he is God, as he is spirit, as he is person and as he is image – all this must go! "Then how should I love him?" You should love him as he is nonGod,

28. "... per revelationem gratiae in hac vita non cognoscamus de Deo quid est, et sic ei quasi ignoto coniungamur ..." *ST*, 1a q12 a13 ad1.

a nonspirit, a nonperson, a nonimage, but as he is pure, unmixed, bright "One", separated from all duality; and in that One we should eternally sink down, out of "something" into "nothing"[29].

And if we think we can read this Dominican's words in apophatically anti-metaphysical terms – anti-metaphysical *because* of its apophaticism – then at least we will need some response at the ready to the challenge of his Franciscan contemporary, Duns Scotus, who contested: *Negationes etiam non summe amamus* – also, it is not negations which we love in the highest degree[30].

Not for one moment do I suppose that, on any informed reading of his theology, Eckhart could be construed as dissenting from Scotus' strictures, or as colluding in a contemporary fashion for an anti-metaphysical reading of his apophaticism. That it was probably not at Eckhart that Scotus directed his criticism is not to the point; but it is to the point that under the pressure of our contemporary deconstructions there are theologians today who are tempted to read Eckhart in such wise, and to any such, Scotus' has reason to say: no one can love a negation. But what is there in Eckhart, which no one to my knowledge has thought to find in Thomas Aquinas, which might lay him open to so mistaken (as I think it to be) a reading?

Perhaps the answer lies in the most palpable difference there is between Eckhart and Thomas, which we could very well put down simply to a difference of *style and imagery*, if it were not for the fact that that difference of style and imagery derives from a difference of another kind, much more fundamental than the first, which indicates what is very nearly – or perhaps it is – a conflict of theological truth-claims.

At any rate, the difference of style and imagery is obvious: years ago Oliver Davies pointed to the significance of rhetorical features of Eckhart's theology, features which are, of course, more prominent in the vernacular sermons – naturally enough, since they *are* sermons, but by no means absent from his more technical, Latin treatises. As Davies says, Eckhart's theology is a sort of "poetic metaphysics", in which, as in all poetry, there is a certain "foregrounding" of the language itself, of the signifier[31]; and, one might add, this "poeticisation" of theological discourse goes along with a certain rhetorical "performativeness", or, as one might say, a quasi-sacramental character. For it is a characteristic of

29. MEISTER ECKHART, *Renovamini Spiritu* (n. 20), p. 208.

30. DUNS SCOTUS, *Ordinatio*, I d3 q2, in P. CAROLUS BALIC (ed.), *Doctoris subtilis et mariani Duns Scoti Opera Omnia III*, Vatican City, Typis Polyglottis Vaticanis, 1954, p. 5.

31. O. DAVIES, *Meister Eckhart, Mystical Theologian*, London, SPCK, 1991, p. 180.

Eckhart's language that it does not merely *say* something: it is intended to *do* something by means of *saying,* and on the classical medieval account, that is the nature of a sacrament: it is "a sacred sign which effects what it signifies".

When, therefore, we note the obvious, but otherwise incidental[32], fact of the extreme negativity of Eckhart's theological language – saturated as it is with images of nothingnesses and abysses, by the featurelessness of deserts and ground, and by nakedness and emptiness – we can begin to see what is going on. The negativity of his theology is a living, organ-ising feature of the language itself and intrinsic to its compositional style: it is as if Eckhart was trying to get the paradoxical nature of his theology (it is at once a *language*, but, as Michael Sells has so aptly put it, "a lan-guage *of unsaying*") into the language itself, so that it both directly says and as directly unsays in the one act of saying: he "foregrounds" the sig-nifier only immediately to disrupt its signification, block it, divert it, post-pone it. Thereby the language *performs rhetorically* what it says techni-cally. And this rhetorical device, as it were of forcing into the sensuous, material sign the character of its own self-subversion as signifier, is what accounts for that most characteristic feature of Eckhart's language: its strained and strenuous, hyperactively paradoxical extravagance. The language, naturally, bursts at the seams under the pressure of the excessive forces it is being made to contain.

The superficial, stylistic contrast with the sobriety of Aquinas' theo-logical discourse could not be more marked. If Thomas can understate the case, he will seize the opportunity to do so. If a thought can be got, as it were, to speak for itself he will do as little as necessary to supplement it. But this economy of speech accompanies, and probably derives from, a fundamental confidence in theological speech, a trust that our ordinary ways of talking about creation are fundamentally *in order* as ways of talking about God, needing only to be subordinated to a governing

---

32. I say "incidental" because so often the negativity of Eckhart's imagery is taken to be in itself indicative of his apophaticism. Perhaps Eckhart thought it was. But if so, to that extent he departs from the Dionysian understanding of the apophatic. It cannot be emphasised enough that negative imagery is, for all its negativity, still imagery; negative language is still language; and if the "apophatic" is to be understood as that which sur-passes all language, then, as the pseudo-Denys says, it lies beyond *both* "affirmation" *and* "denial": for *eadem est scientia oppositorum,* what is sauce for the affirmative goose is sauce for the negative gander. Connected with this fundamental failure to understand medieval forms of apophaticism is all sorts of nonsense, still unfortunately to be heard and read these days, about apophatic *language,* and worse, of an apophatic language which "transcends Aristotelian logic": insofar as it is language which is in question, theology can-not transcend Aristotelian logic; insofar as the "apophatic" is in question, it is not lan-guage, but the *failure* of language, to which we refer.

apophaticism, expressed as an epistemological principle: theological affirmation is both necessary and deficient. We must say of God anything true of what he has created, because that is all there is to say, and because we know that whatever we say is in any case inadequate. Once we know that everything we say about God all fails anyway, we can freely indulge the materiality of those metaphors, the carnality of that imagery, calmly exploit all those possibilities of formal inference and logic, which appear so to unnerve the anxious Eckhart. Eckhart shares something spiritually with Derrida here, his *fear of the* sign: he seems perpetually afflicted with a theological neurosis lest he get God wrong, so he watches his theological language with a vigilance so anxious as to arouse our suspicions: that he writes as if imagining what he knows to be impossible, that there is some superior ideal theological syntax reserved for addressing God correctly, which his rhetoric strains, deficiently, to attain to – or as Derrida puts it, Eckhart's language strains for an impossible *hyperessentiality*. Christoph Schwöbel said the other day that it was a mark of our philosophical sinfulness that we make the pattern of our existence to be the pattern of the divine – as if there were some, even notional, alternative state of affairs, some other, *pre*-lapsarian possibilities of language about God from which we have fallen away[33]. This sounds pretty Origenistic to me, and in any case, I wonder what Christoph can possibly be imagining, which makes him so *worried* about our fallen speech? What else could speech be but that which, before God, fails? Thomas, knowing that you will never get God right anyway seems less anxious, and that applies to anything you say: hence, a demotic ordinariness of speech is all as right, one way or another, as it will ever be, for there is no other, higher, language by which its deficiency can be measured. Why this difference in theological temperament and style?

I think for this reason. Eckhart, as I have said, wants to constrain all the paradoxical tensions of the theological project into each and every theological speech-act. It is *the language itself* that is the bearer of these contrary forces of saying and unsaying, of affirmativeness and negativity, and so his discourse must be got endlessly to destabilise itself. And Eckhart must in this way compel the rhetorical dimension of his discourse to do all the work of theology, he must bend, and twist and stretch theological language, because he wants theology to be grammatically *special*, because he resents its failure even as he asserts the inevitability of

---

33. See in this volume C. SCHWÖBEL, *God as Conversation. Reflections on a Theological Ontology of Communicative Relations*, section IV, *Disrupting the Conversation: Sin*, pp. 53-55.

it, a sort of "Macbeth-like" tragedy of theological language, compelled by ambition to "o'er-leap itself" in a hyperactive negativity. And I think, in the end he differs from Thomas because he cannot trust *creatures* to proclaim God and so mistrusts the ordinariness, the demotic character, of theological speech as Thomas conceives of it. In that linguistic ordinariness, from which there is *no* escape, we can, for Thomas, speak confidently of God, because that same theological act by which our carnal speech is shown to be *justified as theology*, also shows that the God thus demonstrated lies, in unutterable otherness, beyond the reach of anything we can say. So, unlike Eckhart, there is no need to try especially hard to say it.

It is not difficult to see, given this, why theologians of a postmodern mentality should be so tempted to enlist Meister Eckhart in support of a project of theological deconstruction, and should experience no such temptations in Thomas Aquinas, even if Eckhart himself could have had little sympathy for the anti-metaphysical implications of such a reading. But if it is possible to be misled about his purposes, as not only some of his contemporaries were, into suspecting a certain, paradoxical, "hypostatisation" of the negative, a certain reduction of theology to a rhetoric of postponement, indeed into suspecting, God help us, a sort of post-modern spirituality or "mysticism", it is at least partly his own fault. Whether or not this is a fault, and whether or not it is one of Eckhart's, it is precisely on that anti-metaphysical reading of him that he reflects the image most appealing to the anti-metaphysical instinct of our contemporary deconstructions. Thomas, by contrast, sits ill to our contemporary debates, since he is a theological metaphysician, but not one as offering an ontotheology; he is a theist who knows nothing of "deism", an apophaticist whose negativity is rooted in rational foundations, and a rationalist whose conception of reason is as distanced from that of the Enlightenment as it is possible to be. As such, perhaps his position has some capacity to loosen the grip of those antinomies of rationalism and irrationalism, modernity and postmodernity, foundationalism and anti-foundationalism, perhaps even of theism and atheism, which so constrain the philosophies and theologies of our day. All this is by way of "perhaps". But what can be said is that if you want to be an Eckhartian, and say, as he does, that "you should love God as he is nonGod", then you had better be a Thomist first, if you do not want to hear it being said in response, as Scotus with justice responded to others: *negationes ... non summe amamus*.

But therein lies our problem about "spirituality": or rather, therein lies *my* problem with what today gets called by that name. A recycling today of the classical, late antique and medieval *vocabularies* of the apophatic, but uprooted from their soil in a metaphysics, leaves that vocabulary suspended in a vacuum of *rhetorics*, a displaced, residually Christian semiotics, retaining the illusion of a force from the metaphysics it has abandoned as no longer possible – even if, for sure, half-remembered traces of what it was once able to signify preserve the illusion of life, as a wrung chicken struggles and kicks for a while after death. To that extent, at least, Derrida does us a service: if you insist in following fashion down that anti-metaphysical line from Nietzsche through Heidegger to French deconstruction, you had with better consistency concede to Derrida his atheistic conclusion. On the other hand, believing as I do that what passes today for a "foundationless", anti-metaphysical Christianity and spirituality is but the writhing of a dead theological chicken, my question is: who is there today who can restate the case for a theological metaphysics?

Faculty of Divinity   Denys TURNER
University of Cambridge
West Road
Cambridge
CB3 9BS
U.K.

THE DREAMS OF THEOLOGY AND
THE REALITIES OF CHRISTIANITY

When I was invited to give a public lecture in the context of the "Leuven Encounters in Systematic Theology", I was pleased as well as a bit suprised[1]. Since I am not a theologian (let alone a systematic theologian) but a practitioner of the historical and systematic study of religion, and since I have no reason to doubt that the organizers were aware of that fact, I could only assume that in their view the "conversation" mentioned in the title of the congress should include a conversation between theology and the study of religion. I decided that if I could make a modest contribution in that regard, I would be happy to do so. It should be clear, however, that the perspective from which I will approach my subject is quite different from any theological one, and that it entails a quite profound criticism, not of the discipline of systematic theology as such, but of a set of assumptions by which it tends to be guided.

I. CHRISTIANITY VERSUS CHRISTIAN THEOLOGY

Perhaps the most fundamental of these assumptions is that theologians, including systematic theologians, are the appropriate public and intellectual representatives or spokespersons of Christianity. Most people believe that if you want to know what Christianity is all about, you should ask a theologian. This fundamental assumption, obvious though it might seem at first sight, is a fundamental mistake. In reality, if you ask a theologian what Christianity is all about, he or she is rather likely to tell you what Christian *theology* is all about. Implicitly or explicitly, however, his or her statement is likely to deny or minimize the very existence of a distinction between Christianity and Christian theology[2].

---

1. I am grateful to Roelof van den Broek, Olav Hammer, Joke Spaans and Mirjam Westbroek for reading and commenting upon earlier versions of this paper.

2. As a result of the traditional dominance of theology over the study of religions in academic contexts, the study of Christianity from the latter perspective is still underdeveloped, so that the incorrect idea of Christianity as largely coinciding with Christian theology, is allowed to continue relatively unchallenged. As succinctly formulated by Monika Neugebauer-Wölk, "die Arbeitsteilung zwischen den Theologien und der Religionswissenschaft

Academic theology is the product of an intellectual and social elite within Christianity. That such an elite claims for itself the role of public representative of a given religion, and the authority to define the nature of that religion according to its own preferences, is of course neither a new phenomenon nor one that is restricted to Christianity[3]. In Christianity as in other religious traditions, the bottom line of such hegemonic claims is never doctrine as such, but conditions of social, political or economic power. Put concretely: Christian theology has been able to present itself as encapsulating what Christianity was all about, only as long as Christian institutions were powerful enough to by and large monopolize the perception and self-perception of Christianity as a religion. As we all know, processes of modernization and secularization since the 18th century have eroded that monopoly and created an entirely new situation in which Christianity, at least in western democratic societies, has become merely one competitor within a highly pluralistic market. Moreover, the same processes of modernization and secularization stimulate an increasing plurality *within* Christianity itself: since doctrinal conformity can no longer be enforced, average Christians enjoy an unprecedented amount of

ist ja traditionell dadurch bestimmt, dass die Religionsgeschichte des christlichen Abendlandes theologisch bearbeitet wird, nur aussereuropäische Kulturräume religionswissenschaftlich erforscht werden". M. NEUGEBAUER-WOLK, *Esoterik in der frühen Neuzeit. Zum Paradigma der Religionsgeschichte zwischen Mittelalter und Moderne*, in *Zeitschrift für historische Forschung* 27 (2000) 321-364, p. 323. Some readers will object that many academics working in a "theological" context actually apply the same criteria of critical data verification/falsification as scholars of religions, and are in no way guided by confessional agendas. This is correct; however, in itself this is not enough to make them into *Religionswissenschaftler*. The difference between a "theological" and a "study of religions" perspective does not only have to do with whether or not one adheres to methodological agnosticism, critical methods of dealing with sources, and so on. As will become evident from my argument in this article, it also has to do with how one approaches the relation between religious doctrine and religious practice. The tendency to discuss doctrine as relatively autonomous with respect to practice, and to see the history of a religion as largely synonymous with the history of its official beliefs, with little attention to its social conditioning, runs against the grain of a study of religions approach.

3. See e.g. G. SAMUEL, *Civilized Shamans. Buddhism in Tibetan Societies*, Washington – London, 1993, about the difference between "Clerical Buddhism" and "Shamanic Buddhism" in the Tibetan context. Samuel argues that scholars have tended to concentrate on the "Bodhi orientation" focused on the attainment of individual salvation and on the "Karma orientation" focused on morality and socially correct behaviour, while underestimating the importance in Tibetan Buddhism of the "Shamanic orientation" focused on this-worldly goals such as health and prosperity. The first two orientations by and large represent the "official" face of Buddhism and are linked to social and intellectual elites, but Buddhism as it is actually lived and experienced by the Tibetan people is pervaded by the Shamanic orientation and may be quite unconcerned with many of the beliefs and aspirations that are officially considered central to Buddhism. In short: from the perspective of Buddhist theology, much of Tibetan Buddhism is not "really" Buddhist. On Buddhist practice, cf. also e.g. D. LOPEZ, *Buddhism in Practice*, Princeton, NJ, 1995.

freedom to experiment with various originally non-Christian ideas and to attempt the creation of new doctrinal syntheses[4]. Predictably, they take full advantage of that freedom. Thus, for example, the time is already long past that one had to be a self-professed "New Ager" to believe in reincarnation; this belief is now shared by great numbers of people who otherwise consider themselves average Protestant or Catholic churchgoers[5].

Nothing I have written above is particularly new or original. The facts are widely known; by and large, theologians have been slow to draw the consequences. The point I hope to make is considerably more radical, however: contemporary theologians should realize that their traditional status as official representatives of what Christianity is all about *has never been* justified by any actual conformity or identity between Christianity as a religion and Christian theology. Rather, this status is merely the lingering legacy of a time when the official representatives of Christianity had the power to uphold the *illusion* of such conformity or identity. Contrary to widespread assumptions, the widely-perceived gap between theology and what nowadays tends to be referred to as "Christian spirituality" – alluded to by various keynote speakers at this congress – is not at all something new, and has not been caused by modernization and secularization. I will argue that the gap between Christian theology and lived Christianity (in Dutch: *geloofd Christendom* and *geleefd Christendom*) is as old as Christian theology itself; processes of modernization and secularization have merely created a new social context which causes the gap to become blatantly visible.

Below I will develop this thesis in greater detail. It implies that theologians faced with the challenges of the 21st century are not justified in claiming that they can speak with authority about the nature of the Christian tradition. They can speak with authority only about the nature of Christian *theology* and its traditions[6]. To the extent that theologians will

---

4. A classic analysis is P. BERGER, *The Heretical Imperative: Contemporary Possibilities of Religious Affirmation*, Garden City, NY, 1979.

5. See e.g. G. DEKKER – J. DE HART – J. PETERS, *God in Nederland 1966-1996*, Amsterdam, 1997.

6. Unless, of course, they thoroughly train themselves in new approaches and perspectives derived from the study of religions. The main objection to my lecture at the LEST conference 2001 was that I might have underestimated the extent to which theologians have actually been moving, during the 1980s and 1990s, into the direction pointed out by me. There could be a core of truth to that objection: I do not claim to be thoroughly familiar with the full scope of new departures in international theology. Still, the very program of the LEST congress itself abundantly confirms that I am not attacking straw men: among the many titles and abstracts, valuable and interesting though they may certainly be in and for themselves, I have found almost nothing that pointed into the direction I will be suggesting here. Granted, then, that I might somewhat underestimate the amount of

(consciously or unconsciously) continue to ignore, deny, or minimize this distinction, they will condemn themselves to increasing irrelevance. Christianity will keep developing, as it has always done, into new directions involving various syncretisms with originally non-Christian elements, and this will happen whether theologians like it or not. At the same time, unless it makes a radical new beginning, Christian theology will increasingly become an insulated and elitist pursuit interesting only to academic specialists: a conversation of theologians among themselves, with little relevance to Christian realities[7].

Systematic theologians, and theologians generally, will only be able to avoid this bleak perspective of increasing irrelevance and isolation if they radically redefine the very project of systematic theology in such a way that it becomes relevant to the actual realities of Christianity as a lived religion. In order to do so, they need the modern study of religions – not as an addition to their discipline, but as its foundation.

innovative activity on the international theological scene, theologians for their part tend to underestimate the extent to which they are still wedded to traditional theological paradigms.

7. The irony is that theologians traditionally tend to criticize the study of religion for being an academic pursuit interesting merely to specialists, but irrelevant to real life and out of touch with the concerns of religious believers. My argument is that theology is increasingly losing what is left of its potential for being relevant to Christians; as for the study of religion, in spite of its doctrinal neutrality (and partly *because* of it) it does have that potential, but far too often fails to capitalize on it (cf. R.T. McCutcheon, *Critics not Caretakers. Redescribing the Public Study of Religion*, Albany, NY, 2001, ch. 8). To some extent this is because too many scholars of religion restrict themselves exclusively to specialized historical or philological studies and make no effort to address questions of a more general nature, thus failing to demonstrate the broader relevance of the study of religion; these scholars are actually historians of religions rather than scholars of religion in the full sense of the word (W.J. Hanegraaff, *Defining Religion in Spite of History*, in J.G. Platvoet – A.L. Molendijk [eds.], *The Pragmatics of Defining Religion. Contexts, Concepts & Contests*, Leiden – Boston – Keulen, 1999, 337-378). And to a large extent, the unsatisfactory situation results from longstanding traditions in the academic institutionalization of the disciplines of theology and the study of religion: to put it very bluntly, the study of religion tends to be marginalized because too much of the financial budget still goes to theology (quite frequently, to make matters considerably worse, masquerading as "study of religion"). The result is a vicious circle: due to the lack of structural positions for study of religion in the full sense of the word, and prevailing misperceptions about its relation to theology, not enough students graduate in this discipline; hence there is a scarcity of high quality candidates if a new position becomes available; hence there is an increased likelihood that such a position will be filled by a theologian or crypto-theologian rather than a scholar of religion; and hence an increased likelihood that theological agendas will keep dominating appointment committees for positions in the study of religion.

II. History of Christianity versus Church History

The fundamental distinction between Christianity and Christian theology cannot be discussed in isolation from another distinction: the one between Christianity and the Christian churches. Most traditional textbooks of church history are at pains to draw that distinction in their introductions. Thus, for example, J.N. Bakhuizen van den Brink opened his 4-volume *Handboek der kerkgeschiedenis* of 1965 as follows:

> The term *Church History* ... seems to imply a restriction in comparison with the appellation *History of Christianity* ... The broader appellation hangs together with the first flourishing of the general history of religions in the 19th century, and intended to autonomize the practice of the history of the Christian religion ... with respect to the Church or the Churches. Theoretically there is no objection against this. After all, it is absolutely clear that the significance of Christianity in all domains of human life, culture in general, political and social life, and the arts, can by no means always be defined in church terms[8].

After these promising beginnings, unfortunately Bakhuizen van den Brink engaged in a fatal attempt to eat his cake and have it too. He first suggested that it was nevertheless possible to define the concept of "church" in such a way that it would coincide with Christianity, namely, by focusing on "the church of the Credo, the Body of Christ ... His life in the community of the faithful and in the world, and the presence and activity of the [Holy] Spirit in the life of humanity and in history"[9]. He admitted that the church understood in this sense is a non-historical entity; history, he writes, can only discuss the ways in which the true Church of Christ manifests itself historically in the actual churches known to us. While thus openly admitting the gap between a theological concept of the *true* church and the historical concept of the *actual* churches, he then proceeded to nevertheless suggest that the former provided the basis for the latter, while conveniently ignoring the more fundamental distinction with which he had opened his discussion, that is, between Christianity and the Christian churches. In other words, Bakhuizen van den Brink's textbook is based upon a double reduction: Christianity is reduced to the churches, and the churches are reduced only to those Christian institutions believed by the author to be manifestations of the Body of Christ. The construct is as shaky as it could possibly be, but at least Bakhuizen van den Brink is honest enough to admit what he is doing:

8. J.N. Bakhuizen van den Brink, *Handboek der kerkgeschiedenis*, Vol. I, The Hague, 1965-1968, p. 1. All translations are mine.
9. *Ibid.*

The difference between church history and all forms of profane historiography, including a general history of culture, consists in its attempt to do justice to the Christian faith as an objective power that emerges from the Gospel only. In this sense, church history is history of religion[10].

The last sentence is a quite open reflection of a position known as *religionism*[11]: it means that the history of religions should focus on the history of "true religion". But while Bakhuizen van den Brink so much as admits that "truth" is not a historical category, he refuses to draw the implications. Clearly he has no intention to study the reality of Christianity as a lived religion, and he finishes by writing that church history is indeed "a truly theological subject"[12]. Exactly the same kinds of disclaimer with respect to the difference between church history and history of Christianity are to be found in the introductions to all the traditional church histories that I have consulted, such as the 9-volume *Geschiedenis van de kerk* edited by Itterzon & Nauta and published in 1963-1967, the 5-volume *Nouvelle histoire de l'église* edited by Rogier, Aubert & Knowles and published from 1963-1975 (also published in German,

10. *Ibid.*, I, p. 2.
11. This approach to the study of religions is nowadays particularly influential in the United States (for a good introduction, see J.G. PLATVOET, *Het religionisme beleden en bestreden. Recente ontwikkelingen in de angelsaksische godsdienstwetenschap*, in *Nederlands Theologisch Tijdschrift* 48 (1994) 22-38. It is inspired by influential authors such as Rudolf Otto and Mircea Eliade, by traditional phenomenology of religion (e.g. G. van der Leeuw), and by the "spiritual" perspective of the famous Eranos meetings that took place in Switzerland since 1933 (see H.T. HAKL, *Der Verborgene Geist von Eranos. Unbekannte Begegnungen von Wissenschaft und Esoterik. Ein alternative Geistesgeschichte des 20. Jahrhunderts*, Bretten, 2001; W.J. HANEGRAAFF, *Beyond the Yates Paradigm. The Study of Western Esotericism between Counterculture and New Complexity*, in *Aries* 1 (2001) 5-37. Religionists believe that religion is a *sui generis* phenomenon which cannot be grasped by reducing it to its social and historical manifestations; in the end, in order to understand religion one needs to have recourse to an intuitive understanding of its essence, i.e. "religious experience" in this sense is necessary in order to understand religion. Particularly under the influence of the "Chicago school" inspired by Mircea Eliade, religionism has become a paradigm which allows various theological approaches to present themselves as "history of religions"; the result is a type of "religious studies" that is actually crypto-theological. It has come under frequent attack by defenders of a consistently secular study of religions, some of whom run the risk of emphasizing a social-science perspective to the extent of ignoring historical perspectives (for discussion of this debate see e.g. C. ALLEN, *Is nothing Sacred? Casting out the Gods from Religious Studies*, in *Lingua Franca* 6 (1996) 30-40; W.J. HANEGRAAFF, *Empirical Method in the Study of Esotericism*, in *Method and Theory in the Study of Religion* 7 (1995) 99-129; McCUTCHEON, *Critics* (n. 7). In the European context the influence of religionism is nowadays minor as far as the academic context is concerned, but books about religion from a religionist perspective are highly popular among the general public; see for example the bestselling books by Karen Armstrong, which reach sales figures that no secular study of religion can even approach.
12. BAKHUIZEN VAN DEN BRINK, *Handboek der kerkgeschiedenis*, Vol. I (n. 8), p. 2.

Dutch, Italian, Spanish and Portuguese, in several cases simultaneously with the French edition), and the 10-volume *Handbuch der Kirchengeschichte* edited by Hubert Jedin and published from 1962-1979.

From the perspective of an historian of religions, this is a melancholy, if not to say a dramatic sight. Generations of theologians, up to very recent times, have been raised with a picture of the history of Christianity that subtly indoctrinates them into reductive and historically misleading ideas about the nature and history of their own religious traditions. Of course I do not mean to suggest for a moment that the information in these authoritative and extremely erudite church histories is factually incorrect as far as it goes. I would not dare even for a second to question the fact that the authors knew their business. The important thing is what these histories do *not* contain, and their criteria for selecting what is relevant and what is not[13].

III. CHRISTIANITY AS LIVED RELIGION

How, then, might Christianity look from the perspective of the history of religions? First of all, I would suggest, it would be presented as a religion that is lived and practiced in the daily life of its adherents, rather than as a set of doctrines adhered to by believers. I certainly do not intend to deny the great importance of beliefs and doctrines to the history of Christianity, least of all taking into consideration the great – or rather, enormous – influence that theologians have traditionally wielded over it. However, my thesis is that due to the decline of such influence in late modernity, the underlying and more fundamental stratum of Christianity as a religion that is lived rather than believed is once again claiming its rights. It is this stratum – Christianity as religion rather than Christianity as adherence to beliefs – which contemporary systematic theologians will have to come to terms with; and for this reason we have to understand its essential nature as well as the nature of its relation to theology.

---

13. A different and much more promising approach can be perceived in some very recent histories of Christianity, such as notably D. CHIDESTER, *Christianity: A Global History*, San Francisco, CA, 2000. An earlier example is N. SMART, *The Phenomenon of Christianity*, London, 1979. Although it is now inevitably somewhat dated in terms of the type of study of religions it represents, Smart's book remains a refreshingly original and thoroughly enjoyable pioneering work. Significantly (although its author was one of best known historians of religion of his generation), I have yet to meet the first church historian who has heard of it, let alone read it. In any case, both Smart's and Chidester's contributions are single-volume works which cannot be compared in scope and wealth of detail with the traditional church histories I mentioned.

As a starting point, I propose to take a look at how Christianity functioned for common practitioners in the context of the Middle Ages. The first thing to notice is quite obvious, i.e. the fact that theology was not, and could not possibly be, essential to the way he or she experienced his or her religion. The simple reason is, of course, that most Christians were unlettered and theological discussions in Latin were inaccessible to them. The contents of the Bible were inaccessible as well, except in mediated form. These mediations took essentially two forms, as they do in all religions: mythological and symbolical. The mythical dimension of his religion was represented for the common medieval Christian by the essential biblical stories, reduced to their basic outlines. Most important of these was the story of the birth, life, death, resurrection and ascension of Jesus Christ: this story was told to the believers in simplified form, and expressed by potent pictorial images accessible particularly in church buildings. When I refer to this story as Christian mythology, debates about the relation between "myth and history" are irrelevant: I am not claiming that Christians did not believe that the events of the life and death of Jesus Christ had really happened, I am claiming that the story functioned (to quote a popular contemporary author) as a "myth to live by"[14]. It provided Christians with a basic model of the ideal life, which made sense to them emotionally because it resonated with their own everyday experience. We are born in a world full of evil, in which we are beset by dangers and are bound to suffer, but there is a way through suffering and death to eternal life. The Son of God himself has shared our own human experience of life, suffering and death; but since he overcame death, we may hope for the same. No complex theology was needed to understand this simple but extremely potent story, or to get the point of how naturally it resonated with other basic biblical stories, such as the liberation of the chosen people from their exile in the land of Egypt, their exodus through the desert, and their final arrival in the promised land.

Christians lived by basic myths, in a daily context that was charged with potent carriers of symbolic meaning. Everywhere – particularly in churches, but outside them as well – they found themselves surrounded by such symbols. Perhaps no symbol was more potent than the sign of the cross, since it encapsulated the very essence of the basic Christian myth. But of course there were others: the bread and wine used in mass,

---

14. J. CAMPBELL, *Myths to Live by*, New York, 1972. If I quote Campbell, this does not mean I subscribe to his Jungian-religionist perspective. His many writings on mythology are thoroughly enjoyable and often inspiring, but problematic from the perspective of the modern academic study of myth.

the very building of the church (not to mention cathedrals), images of saints or of the mother of Christ, opposed to images of tempting demons, the smell of incense, even such small things as burning candles, all were heavy with symbolic significance. And symbolic meaning could easily be encountered in the natural world as well, as seen for example in the medieval concept of the "two books", the book of holy scripture and the book of nature, which mirror and amplify each other because the whole creation carries the fingerprints of God[15].

Perhaps most important to Christianity, finally, was the ritual dimension. Ritual cannot be simply reduced to a symbolic enactment of underlying myths, but has an autonomous and largely irreducible reality. We do not practice ritual "because" we believe in an underlying myth, so that the ritual would be merely a secondary offshoot or translation of a basic mythology. Rather, human beings have a natural tendency to perform rituals, regardless of whether these can be brought into conformity with basic myths – religious or otherwise. But of course such conformity was in fact present in rituals such as the Roman Catholic mass. The common Christian was an essentially passive witness of the central mystery of his religion: he beheld the priest celebrating the incarnation of God himself, whose son took on our very own bodily reality of flesh and blood. The American historian of religions J.Z. Smith has suggested that what he calls the "bare facts of ritual" have a primary and irreducible reality with respect to any particular theological and even mythical "explanation"[16]. Ritual behaviour is based upon the very basic recognition that human realities fall short of ideal realities. Whenever inexplicable evil or suffering befalls us, reminding us of our vulnerability and the fact that we are not "in control", we perform rituals: for in the controlled space of ritual, at least, we are able to "get it right". This happens when innocent children become the victims of senseless violence or when airplanes crash into skyscrapers: we participate in silent marches, we flock to church, and we celebrate rituals to honour the victims. Likewise with the medieval Christian: he knew that he was not able to lead his life in such a way that God was continually present in it on a day-to-day basis, so it was all the more important for the ritual to celebrate that presence[17].

Was my common medieval Christian a true Christian? Of course he was. Did he understand theology, or would he need to, in order to be a

---

15. E.R. CURTIUS, *Europäische Literatur und lateinisches Mittelalter*, Bern – München, 1948, pp. 323-329.

16. J.Z. SMITH, *The Bare Facts of Ritual*, in ID., *Imagining Religion. From Babylon to Jonestown*, Chicago, IL – London, 1982, pp. 53-65.

17. And ritual did more: it created and confirmed close relations, very much like family ties, between the divine and the human, God and mankind, saints and sinners, and

Christian? Certainly not. But could he have been a Christian without symbol, myth and ritual? We do not see how he possibly could. The point is that the common Christian I have tried to evoke here *was not a believer*. One does not believe in ritual: one practices it. One does not believe in myths: one lives by them. One does not believe in symbols: one uses them. This is what the great majority of Christians have in fact been doing throughout the history of Christianity, and what they are still doing today.

IV. THE VARIETIES OF CHRISTIANITY

If one looks at Christianity from this perspective, there are a number of far-reaching implications to be drawn. Most important: obviously it is out of the question to define or demarcate "Christianity" on the basis of doctrine. One can only define and demarcate it according to the nature of its basic myths and symbols. "Religion" in general, I would suggest, can be technically defined as "any symbolic system which influences human action by providing possibilities for ritually maintaining contact between the everyday world and a more general meta-empirical framework of meaning"[18].

Religion in this sense can manifest itself in two ways. If the symbolic system in question is embodied in a social institution, religion has taken the form of *a* religion. In other words, religion can take the form of specific religions. However, religion can also manifest itself in the form of

---

between individual Christians. See e.g. J. BOSSY, *Christianity in the West 1400-1700*, Oxford, 1985.

18. HANEGRAAFF, *Defining Religion* (n. 7), p. 371. As explained in this article, my definition is a variation on the famous definition by Clifford Geertz (C. GEERTZ, *Religion as a Cultural System*, in M. BANTON [ed.] *Anthropological Approaches to the Study of Religion*, London, 1966, pp. 1-46). A separate article would be required to flesh out the implications to my definition of Talal Asad's highly important criticism of Geertz (T. ASAD, *The Construction of Religion as an Anthropological Category*, in ID., *Genealogies of Religion: Discipline and Reasons of Power in Christianity and Islam*, Baltimore, MD – London, 1993, pp. 27-54). Suffice it to say here that in most respects I find myself in enthusiastic agreement with Asad's perspective, but that, whether or not Asad is correct in perceiving Geertz's definition as reflecting an essentialist *sui generis* view of religion, I regard my own definition strictly as a nominalist construct (cf. Asad's reference to "simple nominalism", *Ibid.*, p. 29). The present context does not allow me to investigate whether – assuming that it is accepted as being consistently nominalist – my definition would (1) nevertheless remain vulnerable to Asad's charge against Geertz's definition, i.e. that it is a product of the very thing it claims to analyze (i.e., the history of Christianity) and therefore leads to tautological reasoning, and (2) imply a denial or marginalization of how power and discipline constitute religion. With respect to this last point, I only remark that the importance of social, political and economic power to understanding Christianity should be obvious from my discussion in this article, but that an operational definition does not need to refer to all aspects of religion in order to define and demarcate it.

what I refer to as "spiritualities" (and please note that I do not speak of "spirituality" in the singular: this term I find too vague to be meaningful or useful). I would define as a specific spirituality: "any human practice which maintains contact between the everyday world and a more general meta-empirical framework of meaning by way of the individual manipulation of symbolic systems"[19].

Now if we apply this threefold definition to Christianity, we get some surprising results. I will discuss them under six headings.

1. Christianity as a Symbolic System

Christian religion is defined by the nature of its basic symbolic system, rather than by any doctrinal beliefs. The symbolic system – consisting of myths and symbols per se – is basic to the particular forms taken by the ritual behaviour which, as in any other religion, makes it possible for Christians to maintain contact with the meta-empirical framework of meaning that they happen to postulate. Of course I do not deny that Christians "believe"[20] in that meta-empirical framework: surely they believe in the existence of God, Christ, life after death, and so on, as essential parts of a general framework that remains essentially invisible except by mediations such as symbol and ritual, and in terms of which the ordeals of human life are given a deeper and lasting meaning. But the precise doctrinal form given to these beliefs, while highly important to the theologian, is of minor importance to the common practitioner.

2. Christianities as Symbolic Systems

The concept of "Christian religion" is much wider than the concept of *a* Christian religion, based upon the social institutionalization of a symbolic system. Where we have social institutions, we are dealing with power, and theologians have traditionally been extremely influential in the institutionalization of Christianity. Theological doctrines have heavily

19. *Ibid.*, p. 372.
20. However, in a recent article Benson Saler rightly addresses the neglected question of "what does it mean to say that anyone believes anything". The relevance of the question is well illustrated by Saler's own opening example: according to well-known polling organizations, more than half of the American population believes that at least some unidentified flying objects are really space vehicles from other civilizations, and one quarter of the population believes that intelligent beings from outer space have been in contact with humans. While representatives of the UFO community have concluded triumphantly that therefore there are twice as many UFO believers as there are Roman Catholics and five time as many as there are fundamentalist Christians, Saler rightly points out that such data force us to problematize naïve notions of what constitutes religious "belief".

influenced the development of Christian symbolic systems within specific Christian institutional contexts[21]. One obvious example would be the symbolic system of Dutch Calvinism compared with that of medieval Roman Catholicism. I select this example because I suspect that some readers will have been thinking by themselves that my earlier example of medieval Christianity was too conveniently chosen, and that even if my argument works for that context, it does not work for a form of Christianity which is squarely based upon the authority of the Word of God. I would contest that. Calvinism as a religious innovation may have been largely created by theologians, but from the practitioners' perspective it still functions in the same way that Roman Catholicism did. For example, the dramatic story of the Reformers' battle against Roman Catholicism, with its "pagan" and "magical" practices, its idolatrous statues and its corrupt priesthood, has become highly important to Calvinist mythology and has added new dimensions to the system of myths that was already present. The conspicuous *absence* in Calvinist churches of images and statues of the saints, combined with the prominent presence – on a pulpit located in the center of an austere and unadorned church building – of the open Bible, the Word of God, is an extremely powerful symbolic statement. The symbolic system of Calvinism is every bit as powerful as its Roman Catholic counterpart – it just conveys a different message. Finally, the emphasis on the word and on doctrinal content has become heavily ritualized in Calvinism. The singing of hymns, the listening to long sermons, and communal prayer (like even the collection of financial donations), are essential parts of Calvinist ritual, and still perform the basic ritual function: the celebration of ideal acts within controlled ritual space, as a counterpart to the much more messy realities of everyday life.

3. Heretical Movements as Symbolic Systems

If Christian religions are based upon the social institutionalization of a Christian symbolic system, we have no choice but to accept a variety of so-called heretical movements as legitimate expressions of Christianity, on a par with the churches whose theology is considered "orthodox". Since distinctions between orthodoxy and heresy are of a doctrinal nature, they are very important for understanding the differences between specific Christian symbolic systems, but quite irrelevant to the question of what does and does not count as "Christian" from a historical point of

---

21. Obviously Asad's emphasis on "discursive discipline" is highly relevant in this context. ASAD, *Construction* (n. 18).

view. Therefore the history of Christianity as a lived religion includes not just the mainline churches, but also for example the many medieval heresies, including movements such as the Cathars, as well as many currents that hardly show up at all in any traditional church history, such as the Mormon Church, the Swedenborgian Church, or the Jehovah's Witnesses. These and many similar movements are characterized by overwhelmingly Christian symbolic systems, and therefore have to be recognized as forms of Christian religion. It is not a question of adding extra chapters or footnotes to some central core narrative of Christianity, admitting (whether grudgingly or not) that these folks are "also Christians". Rather, it is a question of perceiving Christianity in its entirety as a complex phenomenon displaying may shades of doctrine, none of which can be used as yardstick for evaluating any other or for suggesting an implicit hierarchy between "core" and "periphery"[22].

4. *Folk Magic as Christian Religion*

In case the reader might find the resulting relativist picture of "Christianity" difficult to accept, I beg him to bear with me, for it gets worse. My distinction between Christian religion as such and Christian *religions* (social institutions, or churches) implies what was already admitted by Bakhuizen van den Brink: that the Christian churches, and even the Christian heresies, by no means exhaust the richness of Christianity as a phenomenon in western culture. Even if we leave aside important aspects of Christian culture such as art and literature, there is no way we can ignore that Christian religion finds a highly important non-institutional manifestation in the interrelated domains associated with folklore, magic and so-called superstition.

I will not try to enter here into the extremely complex problems of terminology and methodology related to this domain[23]. The important thing

---

22. Of course this does not mean we should ignore the fact that Christians themselves have always set up such hierarchies and have evaluated other Christians' beliefs as superior or inferior: obviously one cannot hope to understand the history of Christianity without analysing those processes. My point is just that the historian of Christianity cannot afford to adopt such a normative stance. Although many contemporary theologians will readily agree if the point is formulated that way, I am convinced that many of them will nevertheless flinch at the relativist picture that actually results from applying it radically and consistently. See for example my remarks in note 41: the theologies of e.g. the Mormon church or the Swedenborgians, and countless others, would have to be taken as seriously as those of the mainstream churches. Studying Christianity "from the point of view of one's own tradition" is incompatible with the approach I am advocating here; rather, what is required is continuous vigilance with respect to how one's personal biases may lead to a distorted perception of Christianity.

23. From the abundant theoretical literature on magic, see e.g. S.J. TAMBIAH, *Magic, Science, Religion, and the Scope of Rationality*, Cambridge, 1990; A. GLUCKLICH, *The*

to note is that they do not show up in traditional church histories but are of great importance to understanding the ways in which Christianity has actually functioned for common practitioners throughout its history. If we wish to understand the realities of Christianity as lived religion, including the ways it is developing in our contemporary society, we have to try to understand on a profound level the nature of extremely common, traditional practices such as Marian devotion and pilgrimages to the sites of apparitions of the Virgin; veneration of holy relics such as bones of the martyrs or splinters of the true cross; prayers for healing that may look more like magical spells or business interactions between humans and saints, Jesus Christ and even God himself; folk rituals surrounding important moments of transition such as delivery and death; and even seemingly non-religious phenomena such as magical spells directed at the saints, angels or demons for such mundane purposes as getting money, sex, or revenge on one's enemies[24].

The importance to Christian culture as well as to contemporary practice of these and related phenomena has come to be recognized increasingly during the last decades, also among theologians. But how seriously has this really affected the way "Christianity" is understood? Even if it is granted that these kinds of practices do make up part of the history of Christianity as lived religion, many theologians will feel that they do not represent what Christianity is really about; and furthermore, such

End of Magic, New York – Oxford, 1997; and especially the Ph.D. (forthcoming as a monograph) by R.G. STYERS, *Magical Theories: Magic, Religion and Science in Modernity*, unpubl. Ph.D. dissertation, Duke University, 1997. On superstition, see esp. D. HARMENING, *Superstitio. Überlieferungs- und theoriegeschichtliche Untersuchungen zur kirchlich-theologischen Aberglaubensliteratur des Mittelalters*, Berlin, 1979. See, about the concept of "magic", also the last part of my *The Study of Western Esotericism: New Approaches to Christian and Secular Culture*, in P. ANTES – A.W GEERTZ – R. WARNE (eds.), *New Approaches to the Study of Religion*, Berlin – New York, 2004 (forthcoming). My argument about this concept is essentially the same as Asad's about "religion"; but I would add to his recommendations that any analysis of Christian "authorizing processes" or "regimes of truth" should discuss the two concepts of "religion" and "magic" as inextricably linked.

24. Cf. ASAD, *Construction* (n. 18), pp. 37-38. There is inevitably something arbitrary about any selection from the wealth of modern studies in this domain, but a few relevant titles are the classic K. THOMAS, *Religion and the Decline of Magic*, Harmondsworth, 1971; R. BROOKE – C. BROOKE, *Popular Religion in the Middle Ages: Western Europe 1000-1300*, London, 1984; E. MUIR, *Ritual in Early Modern Europe*, Cambridge, 1997; M.P. CARROLL, *The Cult of the Virgin Mary. Psychological Origins*, Princeton, NJ, 1986; D. MORGAN, *Visual Piety. A History and Theory of Popular Religious Images*, Berkeley, CA – Los Angeles – London, 1989; KIECKHEFER, *Magic in the Middle Ages*, Cambridge, 1989; C. FANGER, *Conjuring Spirits: Texts and Traditions of Medieval Ritual Magic*, Sutton, 1998. On any of the domains mentioned in the text, the number of titles can easily be multiplied.

practices are widely perceived as pagan relics that already came under heavy criticism by the Protestant Reformation centuries ago and even more so under the influence of the Enlightenment and the disenchantment of the world. But any claim about "real" Christianity is in fact a claim about one's own preferred type of Christianity, and as such does not belong in any scholarly study of it.

It would seem beyond doubt that for a common Christian whose children are ill, the power of Maria or the saints to heal and protect will be very much part of what Christianity is and should be all about. And more importantly, we should not allow ourselves to be sidetracked by the specific forms that such practices take in a given cultural situation, but try to understand their essential structure and religious function. If we do so, we find not only that all the practices I mentioned are still very much alive in their classic forms, but more importantly that new practices have been invented which may look outwardly different but have the same structure and perform the same functions. What they have in common is their pragmatic orientation: religion has relevance not only for salvation after death, but should also have its uses in this life[25]. Practically-oriented forms of religion, including Christian religion, have not died out under the impact of the Reformation and the disenchantment of the world – they have survived in their classical forms, and in addition they have taken on new forms congenial to contemporary life. To convince ourselves of this, we merely need to take a look at the enormous market for a variety of "alternative" or New Age therapies, all of which are characterized by a religious dimension (although practitioners mostly prefer to call that dimension "spiritual")[26]. Some of these therapies are based upon symbolic systems with little relation to Christianity, in others we find Christian and non-Christian mixtures, and yet others are thoroughly Christian. Furthermore, the boundary between healing practices in the "New Age" context and in the modern Christian evangelical and charismatic context is far more fluid than one might think[27]. Again, we find here what I have already pointed out at other examples: the boundaries are drawn on doctrinal-theological grounds, resulting in relatively different symbolic

25. I refer again to SAMUEL, *Civilized Shamans* (n. 3).
26. W.J. HANEGRAAFF, *New Age Religion and Secularization*, in *Numen* 47 (2000) 5-37; ID., *New Age Religion and Western Culture: Esotericism in the Mirror of Secular Thought* (Studies in the History of Religions: Numen Book Series, 72), Leiden, Brill, 1996; M.F. BROWN, *The Channeling Zone. American Spirituality in an Anxious Age*, Cambridge, MA – London, 1997.
27. See e.g. P.C. LUCAS, *The New Age Movement and the Pentecostal/Charismatic Revival. Distinct yet Parallel Phases of a Fourth Great Awakening?*, in J. LEWIS – J.G. MELTON (eds.), *Perspectives on the New Age*, Albany, NY, 1992, pp. 189-211.

systems, but the nature of the rituals and practices is often similar if not identical. My point in calling attention to all these kinds of practices is that the pragmatic goal-oriented dimension has always been highly important to lived Christianity and, moreover, that its importance relative to doctrinal faith is steadily increasing in contemporary western society. This phenomenon has nothing to do with a decline of religion or of Christianity, but merely with a decline in power and influence of Christian theology.

5. Syncretic Christian Spiritualities

The persistence of the pragmatic orientation I have just discussed is a highly important example indeed of the fact that Christian institutions, even including organized heretical movements, each with their own theologies, do not exhaust the phenomenon of Christianity. Heretical movements as well as pragmatic forms of Christianity have their origin in the fact that any form of religion, including Christianity, inevitably *generates* spiritualities. I repeat that I am using a precise definition of "spiritualities": they are based upon what I called the individual manipulation of available symbolic systems. People may manipulate such a system in order to make it useful for the attainment of practical goals, as we have just seen. The manipulation may also take the form of a theological innovation; and if the innovator attracts enough followers, his spirituality may become institutionalized into a new religious movement (usually a heresy) within Christianity, and thus evolve into a "Christian religion". But heretical movements and Christian magic or folk practice still do not by any means exhaust the possibilities of how Christianity may – and actually does – manifest beyond the domains of the established churches and normative theologies. Christian spiritualities may also take shapes that are neither folk magic nor heretical theology, but somehow in between. I propose to call them syncretic spiritualities.

From the perspectives of traditional theology and church history, "syncretism" used to be a term loaded with pejorative connotations. From the perspective of the study of religions it is a neutral term referring to one of the most important factors of creative innovation in religion: the process of cross-fertilization between the symbolic system of a given religion, Christianity in our case, and another symbolic system – religious or otherwise[28]. I would suggest that the emergence and development of syncretic spiritualities in the context of Christian culture has been neglected

28. Cf. HANEGRAAFF, *New Age Religion* (n. 26), pp. 396-397, n. 55.

perhaps even more seriously than any other of its dimensions, and yet is of great importance to understanding the dynamics of Christianity in past and present. I would like to demonstrate this with a few examples.

In the second half of the 15th century, in the context of the Italian Renaissance, interest was revived in a variety of late-antique paganisms. One example was neoplatonism, understood by Renaissance thinkers not just as a philosophy in the modern academic sense, but as a religious system that included a kind of religious magic known as theurgy. Another example was the so-called hermetic philosophy, the fundamental writings of which (known as the *Corpus Hermeticum*) had just been rediscovered and translated into Latin, and which preached a mystical religion focused on true knowledge of God, the world, and the self. Yet another example was the theurgy of another recently rediscovered corpus, the *Chaldaean Oracles*, incorrectly attributed to Zarathustra. Highly influential Christian theologians and philosophers such as Marsilio Ficino and Giovanni Pico della Mirandola believed these sources to be in essential accord with the Christian revelation: ancient sources such as the *Corpus Hermeticum* and the *Chaldaean Oracles* demonstrated, according to them, that the essential verities of Christian theology had already been revealed by God to the heathens in very ancient times. Nowadays we know that these sources in fact date from the early centuries CE, and are products of hellenistic culture; but during the 15th and 16th centuries almost nobody doubted their enormous antiquity, and the authority that came with it. The Christian reception and accomodation of these non-Christian sources produced a new syncretic spirituality, often referred to as Renaissance hermetism, which has exerted an enormous and often underestimated influence over the culture of the period and beyond[29].

Closely connected to this new type of "hermetic" Christianity was another syncretic spirituality, this time based upon the cross-fertilization of Jewish and Christian traditions. Certain strands of Jewish mysticism, or kabbalah, as well as generally Jewish currents incorrectly interpreted as kabbalistic[30], came to be adopted into Christianity in the same period.

---

29. The classic study of Renaissance hermetism is F.A. YATES, *Giordano Bruno and the Hermetic Tradition*, London – Chicago, IL, 1964 (but to be read with caution; for the critical debate on her perspectives, cf. HANEGRAAFF, *Beyond the Yates Paradigm* [n. 11]). For the syncretic process in this context, see S.A. FARMER, *Syncretism in the West: Pico's 900 Theses (1486). The Evolution of Traditional Religious and Philosophical Systems*, Tempe, 1989. On the Renaissance reception of the Chaldaean Oracles, see M. STAUSBERG, *Faszination Zarathushtra. Zoroaster und die Europäische Religionsgeschichte der frühen Neuzeit*, Berlin – New York, 1998, pp. 44-92.

30. On this point, see J. DAN, *The Christian Kabbalah. Jewish Mystical Books and their Christian Interpreters*, Cambridge, MA, 1997.

The result is known as Christian kabbalah[31]. Together with Christian hermetism it became basic to Renaissance projects of a purified Christian
magic, or *philosophia occulta*[32], in the context of which Christian symbolic systems came to be enriched with new elements derived from astrol-
ogy, natural magic, and alchemy.

An explanation in further detail of how these and similar traditions
have continued to play a significant role in the history of Christianity
would amount to a summary of my own field of specialization, the history of hermetic philosophy and related currents, also known as western
esotericism[33]. My point here is merely that these traditions keep being
edited out of the history of Christianity because they do not fit any of the
standard categories. They do not belong to the domains of Christian orthodoxy, Christian heresies, or Christian folk magic. Yet if we ignore them,
we are overlooking an important dimension of the reality of Christianity.
This fact is relevant not only from a strictly historical point of view; it
is also important because many aspects of contemporary "alternative religiosity", inside or outside a Christian context, happen to have their historical origins precisely in these "esoteric" Christian traditions[34].

6. *Syncretic Post-Christian Spiritualities*

All the varieties of Christianity that I have been discussing so far have
at least one thing in common: they are thoroughly grounded in a Christian symbolic system. Finally, I come to a phenomenon particularly relevant to the contemporary situation: the emergence of Christian spiritualities which, paradoxical though this may sound, are *not* grounded in a
Christian symbolic system.

I repeat that spiritualities, as defined earlier, are based upon the individual manipulation of existing symbolic systems. In a case such as the
Christian hermetism of Renaissance culture, we saw Christians manipulating their basic symbolic system of Roman Catholicism so as to make

---

31. The classic study is F. SECRET, *Les kabbalistes chrétiens de la Renaissance*, Milan
– Neuilly-sur-Seine, 1964 (repr., 1985). See also DAN, *The Christian Kabbalah* (n. 30).

32. The classic Renaissance treatise is C. AGRIPPA, *De occulta philosophia libri tres*,
ed. V. COMPAGNI, Leiden – New York – Cologne; for an excellent discussion of the embeddedness of the occult philosophy in a Christian context, see e.g. M. VAN DER POEL, *Cornelius Agrippa. The Humanist Theologian and his Declamations*, Leiden – New York –
Cologne, 1997.

33. For an introduction and synthesis, see W.J. HANEGRAAFF, *Some Remarks on the
Study of Western Esotericism*, in *Theosophical History* 7 (1999) 223-232; and ID., *The
Study of Western Esotericism* (n. 23). See also www.amsterdamhermetica.com.

34. As I demonstrated in *New Age Religion* (n. 26), part III.

it accomodate pagan sources. The result was a new creative syncretism. Likewise, for example, young theologians in early 17th century Tübingen manipulated their Lutheran symbolic system so as to make it accomodate novel aspects such as alchemy and the teachings of Paracelsus; the result is known as Rosicrucianism[35]. Many more examples could be given of Christians for whom their own Christian symbolic system was the normative basis, but who gave a new creative twist to it by adding elements from other sources. Now, such syncretic Christian spiritualities are qualitatively different from what I propose to call syncretic *post*-Christian spiritualities, which may use Christian language to various extents but are not grounded in a Christian symbolic system.

One convenient example among many would be the case of Anthroposophy. This new religious movement was created by the Austrian philosopher Rudolf Steiner in the early decades of the 20th century, and has become one of the more successful forms of modern alternative religion[36]. Steiner's early intellectual sources and backgrounds are complex and do not need to be discussed here in detail; but there can be no doubt about the formative influence on his mature thought of the metaphysics of modern Theosophy. The theosophical system, created during the later decades of the 19th century by an eccentric Russian woman, Helena P. Blavatsky, is most definitely not based upon a Christian symbolic system[37]. Nor, by the way, is it based upon oriental religions such as Buddhism, as many theosophists would like to believe[38]. Theosophy is a textbook case of 19th-century occultist metaphysics, deliberately and explicitly put in opposition against the Christianity of the churches and orthodox theologies as well as to the materialism and positivism of contemporary science, but actually strongly influenced by the latter. The complex question of Blavatsky's sources need not detain us here. The interesting thing, for us, is that Rudolf Steiner took the basic

35. See e.g. R. EDIGHOFFER, *Rose-Croix et société idéale selon Johann Valentin Andraea*, 2 Vols., Neuilly-sur-Seine, 1981/1987.
36. Unfortunately the critical literature on Anthroposophy is still scanty. The only available study from a non-anthroposophical perspective is G. AHERN, *Sun at Midnight. The Rudolf Steiner Movement and the Western Esoteric Tradition*, Wellingborough, 1984; but we are awaiting the forthcoming monograph by H. Zander.
37. The situation of scholarly research on Theosophy is somewhat better than that related to Anthroposophy. For a historical introduction see B.F. CAMPBELL, *Ancient Wisdom Revived. A History of the Theosophical Movement*, Berkeley, CA – Los Angeles – London, 1980; for a synthesis of Theosophical doctrine, see R. ELLWOOD, *Theosophy. A Modern Expression of the Wisdom of the Ages*, Wheaton, IL – Madras – London, 1986. The standard work on the entire occultist milieu in which Theosophy played a central role is J. GODWIN, *The Theosophical Enlightenment*, Albany, NY, 1994.
38. HANEGRAAFF, *New Age Religion* (n. 26), pp. 443-455, 470-482.

symbolic system of modern Theosophy, but changed it in such a way that its center came to repose in what he called "the mystery of Golgotha". In other words: he manipulated the theosophical symbolic system so as to make it accomodate elements taken from Christian theology. The resulting Anthroposophical system is explicitly presented as "esoteric Christianity", and is closely affiliated to a new church, the *Christengemeinschaft* (Community of Christians). Accordingly, there is no lack of attempts by modern Anthroposophists of initiating a "dialogue" with the traditional Christian churches, and some Christian theologians have responded positively to the challenge.

The point I would like to emphasize, however, is that this type of "Christianity" is structurally different from any of the forms of Christianity I discussed above. Anthroposophy was created by integrating Christian ideas into a non-Christian system of symbols (including a complex mythology). It is not the other way around. If one would remove all Christian references from Anthroposophy, one would be left with a Theosophical system that would still be perfectly capable of functioning as the foundation of a lived religion. It is impossible, conversely, to even imagine Anthroposophy as retaining its christology but without its Theosophical underpinnings.

The fact that Anthroposophy is a self-professed "Christian" religion nevertheless based upon a non-Christian symbolic system makes it into an example of a syncretic post-Christian spirituality; and as such, it belongs to an analytical category entirely different from the Christian esotericisms discussed earlier. I would suggest that this category is of the greatest importance for understanding the nature of many forms of religion in contemporary western democracies. Spiritualities I defined as based upon the individual manipulation of available symbolic systems. In traditional Christian contexts, the basic available system was Christian, and spiritualities were developed in order to "fine-tune" the system to the individual needs of specific Christians. In contemporary western society, by contrast, individuals find themselves in a highly pluralistic market of symbolic systems, some of which are socially more powerful than others, but none of which dominates society as a whole to the extent that the Christian symbolic system used to do. As a result, frequently the spiritualities developed by contemporary individuals are no longer grounded in an already-existing religious symbolic system: many of them are free-floating spiritualities, so to speak. They can no longer be seen as attempts to "fine-tune" *any* underlying symbolic system to individual needs: instead, they are wholly individual and essentially independent mixtures, consisting of disparate fragments taken from a variety of available symbolic systems – religious or non-religious. This phenomenon of spiritualities entirely detaching themselves from any basic religious symbolic system, and becoming free-floating units based upon a process of picking and choosing among the symbolic commodities available at the pluralistic market, is a characteristically modern (post-18th-century) phenomenon without historical precedent[39]. I suggest that any attempt at a systematic dialogue between Christian theology and such syncretic post-Christian spiritualities should start with recognizing their structural difference with respect to all traditional kinds of Christianity. The fact that this has not been done is perhaps the main reason for the doubtful intellectual quality of most attempts at a dialogue between "Christianity and New Age"[40].

V. MANY CHRISTIANITIES, BUT TWO TYPES

Let me summarize the central part of my argument so far. Firstly, I have argued that Christianity as lived religion cannot be understood as based upon doctrinal content, but can very well be understood as based upon a foundational symbolic system. Secondly, I have argued that just as religion can manifest itself in many specific religions, Christian religion can manifest itself in many specific Christian religions. Such Christian religions are religious institutions that have mostly come into existence as a result of theological differences of opinion; but in the way they are actually *practiced*, each one of them manifests itself as a new type of Christian symbolic system. I used Dutch Calvinism as an example of such a new symbolic system, different from that of Roman Catholicism, but quite as potent. Thirdly, I argued that if Christian religions are based upon the social institutionalization of a Christian symbolic system, and if we cannot define "Christianity" on the basis of doctrinal content, we have no choice but to accept the full variety of so-called heretical movements as legitimate expressions of Christianity, on a par with the "orthodox" churches. This goes as far as having to include, on a basis of strict equality, movements such as the Mormons or the Jehovah's witnesses, including their theologies[41]. Fourthly, I argued that lived

---

39. See W.J. HANEGRAAFF, *New Age Spiritualities as Secular Religion. A Historian's Perspective,* in *Social Compass* 46 (1999) 145-160. See also ID., *New Age Religion* (n. 26).

40. W.J. HANEGRAAFF, *Christelijke Spiritualiteit en New Age* (Utrechtse Theologische Reeks, 39), Utrecht, 1997.

41. Obviously my recommendations for a new-style theology imply that the theologies of such groups need to be taken as seriously as those of any other Christian tradition. A pioneering effort in that direction was M.F. BEDNAROWSKI, *New Religions and the*

Christianity takes forms that are not captured by the categories of social organizations (whether church or heresy), but cannot for that reason be disregarded: here, we are dealing to a large extent with the domain of "folklore magic", in its traditional as well as in its modern forms. Characteristic of this type of religion is its pragmatic, goal-oriented approach. Fifthly, I called attention to the neglected domain of syncretic Christian spiritualities, which result when an existing Christian symbolic system is manipulated so as to accomodate elements from non-Christian symbolic systems (religious or otherwise). This domain largely coincides with that of hermetic philosophy and related currents, also known as western esotericism. All the categories mentioned so far – Christian religion, Christian religions, Christian heresies, Christian folklore magic, and Christian esotericisms – are grounded in Christian symbolic systems and cannot possibly be understood without them. In this regard, all of them should be distinguished sharply from a sixth and final category, that of syncretic post-Christian spiritualities, which are based upon modern post-Christian symbolic systems of various provenance, manipulated so as to make them accomodate certain elements taken from Christianity.

In other words, the "realities of Christianity" take two forms. On the one hand, we have Christianity as an extremely diverse religious phenomenon, all manifestations of which have in common that they are grounded in Christian symbolic systems. I suggest that the richness of Christianity in this sense should be the point of departure of any kind of theology that has the ambition of being representative of Christianity as a historical phenomenon. The inevitable question is then the following: what would a theology look like, which understood itself not as systematic reflection on Christian doctrine considered to be true, but as systematic reflection on actual lived Christianity considered to be true? The normative focus on religious truth would distinguish such a type of systematic theology from a systematic philosophy of religion; but the very notion of a systematic reflection on *truth and falsity in religious life*, rather than in religious doctrine, would obviously imply a dramatic shift of emphasis, entailing a whole range of theoretical and methodological problems. I am convinced it would amount to a Copernican revolution in theology, because it fundamentally changes the very rules of the game.

Theological Imagination in America, Bloomington, IN, 1989; in the Foreword, Catherine L. Albanese remarks that "it is virtually impossible to overstate the prevailing disdain these new religious movements receive in contemporary theological circles", and rightly criticizes "the academy's unwillingness to consider the religious ponderings of a non-elite, non-professional group of writers and thinkers who have not been trained at a seminary or in a university".

On the other hand, we have a variety of modern and contemporary phenomena that call and consider themselves "Christian" but are not actually grounded in a Christian symbolic system. I used Anthroposophy as an example, but we could also think for example of the phenomenon known in the Netherlands as *nieuwe tijdsdenken* and which has its equivalents in other countries. "Nieuwe tijdsdenkers" attempt to introduce New Age thinking into the churches, and usually claim that this is the way for the churches to find the way back to the true essence of Christianity[42]. Actually, however, their perspectives are to various extents grounded in modern occultist or quasi-occultist symbolic systems (frequently with a Theosophical orientation). With respect to this second type, based upon syncretic post-Christian spiritualities, I suggest that theologians might take either one of two perspectives. It might of course be argued that Christian theologians need not consider it their business to engage in systematic reflection on the practices and beliefs of a type of religion based upon an alien symbolic system. It could also be argued, however, that such an attitude assumes too easily that contemporary theologians are still securely located "on the other side" of the divide, i.e. that they are the representatives of a perspective still grounded unproblematically in a Christian symbolic system.

It is extremely doubtful whether they are. I have been claiming throughout this article that there has traditionally existed a gap between lived Christianity and Christian theology; but I would not doubt for a second that, in spite of this gap, theology has been securely grounded in Christian symbolic systems during most of its history. I would suggest, however, that much of contemporary theology has come to be grounded in *secular* symbolic systems to a much larger extent than one might perhaps think or would like to admit. In other words, traditional theological narratives tend to be adapted to the requirements of modernity, rather than that a Christian symbolic system defines the parameters within which modern secular influences can be accepted[43]. If this is correct, important parts at least of contemporary theology will find themselves, probably to their own surprise, in the same modernist or secular camp as the post-Christian syncretic spiritualities of an occultist or New Age type. In addition to the traditional gap between theology and lived Christianity, then, there is a second gap of another kind: traditional and modern theologians

---

42. See HANEGRAAFF, *Christelijke spiritualiteit* (n. 40), pp. 20-23.
43. Such an approach is typical of the so-called "Traditionalist" school. For a good example of Christian (Roman Catholic) traditionalism, see J. BORELLA, *The Sense of the Supernatural*, Edinburgh, 1998.

no longer share the same symbolic system, just like traditional esoteric Christians and modern occultists no longer share it[44]. Like their occultist or New Age counterparts, many Christian theologians have actually developed post-Christian syncretic spiritualities of their own.

It seems to me that the depth of the divide between pre-secular and secular types of religion is seldom recognized by practitioners and believers. Contemporary "nieuwe tijdsdenkers" in the churches like to assume a continuity between their perspectives and what they call the real "spiritual Christianity" of all periods[45]; likewise, most Christian theologians would like to believe that their modernist/secular basic assumptions do not keep them from participating in the great continuity of the Christian faith. I believe that both are mistaken. Surely the old-fashioned secularization theory, which predicted a decline or disappearance of religion, has long been discredited, and rightly so; but the arrival of secular modernity did indeed herald a momentous change in the history of religions[46]. Never before in recorded human history has there been a human society, the fundamental and collectively-shared symbolic system of which was not religious, that is to say (in terms of my definition), did not provide human beings with the possibility of ritually maintaining contact with a meta-empirical framework of meaning. The implications are far-reaching but, as far as I can see, remain underestimated.

VI. CONCLUSION

I would like to express my appreciation to the organizers of LEST III for inviting me, as an outsider, to express in this context my opinion about the challenge that faces Christian theology in the 21st century. I have been extremely critical of the way theology looks at Christianity, but if it is any comfort, let me add that I am hardly less critical about the way my own discipline looks at it – or perhaps more correctly, about the way it tends to look the other way. None of the world's great religions is ignored by the study of religions as painfully as Christianity – apparently on the indefensible assumption that, after all, "it is already being covered by theology and church history". While we are flooded every day by new academic publications on all kinds of subjects, I'm not aware of a single

---

44. Cf. HANEGRAAFF, *How Magic Survived the Disenchantment of the World*, in *Religion* 33 (2003) 357-380.

45. A good example is the Dutch success author Jacob Slavenburg.

46. This is strongly emphasized by ASAD, *Construction* (n. 18) and HANEGRAAFF, *Defining Religion* (n. 7), pp. 368-369.

authoritative study that writes the history of Christianity as lived religion more or less along the lines I suggested, and that could be considered serious competition for those good old multi-volume church histories I have criticized. So if I have spent most of my time criticizing theology, let me end by addressing my own discipline. It may be true that the study of religion has accomplished the Copernican revolution; oddly enough though, its practitioners seem to believe that one particular continent on the globe – that of Christianity – need not turn around the sun quite as badly as the others do ... The same point could be made by paraphrasing one of the inimitable one-liners of George W. Bush, who during his 2000 election campaign is supposed to have exclaimed that "it's time for humanity to enter the universe". Against the influence of Karl Barth and his school (whose thesis that "religion is unbelief" cannot but make any adequate understanding of Christianity impossible), I would suggest it is high time for Christianity to finally become religion.

Faculteit der Geesteswetenschappen   Wouter J. HANEGRAAFF
Universiteit van Amsterdam
Oude Turfmarkt 147
NL-1012 GC, Amsterdam
The Netherlands

"YOU WILL THINK MORE FRUITFULLY
AS YOU THINK MORE PIOUSLY"

AUGUSTINE AND SPINOZA ON FAITH AND REASON

"[U]nde tanto fructuosius cogitabis, quanto magis pie cogitaueris" (*Epistula* 140) writes Augustine in a letter to Honorius in 411 or 412 AD. Together with his often quoted *vetus latina* translation of Isaias 7,9 ("nisi credideritis, non intellegetis" cf. e.g. *De libero arbitrio* II, 2 and *Epistula* 120), this statement reflects most accurately Augustine's struggle with the relationship between faith and reason while simultaneously providing a point of access to his spirituality. One could attribute many kinds of spirituality to Augustine (e.g. his spirituality for priests, religious and bishops), but perhaps one of the most extraordinary is the spirituality that can be derived from his epistemology, a ladder of intellectual ascent to God (*sentire Deum*). The human effort to understand God could be a source of mystical encounter with God because – as *imago Dei* – man's rational apparatus is structured analogously to the Trinity and because love is involved in every act of knowing. God is love, and in order to know Him, one must love Him and for our loving Him, one should turn inwardly in order to purify one's heart by loving one's neighbour: "Diligo ergo proximum, et intuere in te unde diligis proximum; ibi videbis, ut poteris, Deum" (*In Iohannis euangelium tractatus* XVII, 8). In this essay we will investigate the concept of love of truth (*amor ueritatis*) in Augustine's spirituality. Love has to be verified by means of truth and, as a consequence, love and knowledge walk hand in hand in Augustine's spirituality[1].

---

1. We prefer the vague terminology of spirituality because we will not claim that all the different spiritualities which Augustine developed (for lay people, or priests, or several other professions) were still popular in the seventeenth century. In this essay, we use "spirituality" in a broad sense. On Augustine's long lasting spiritual heritage: W.J. HANKEY, *Augustine and Theology in the Modern World. The Future of Augustinian Spirituality*, in J.E. ROTELLE (ed.), *Augustinian Spirituality and the Charism of the Order of St. Augustine*, Villanova, 1995, 32-45: "His [=Augustine] spirituality was the crucial bond between the Catholic tradition and Modern thought. For various reasons these efforts were condemned in the nineteenth century. Augustinian ways of thinking were replaced by a revived Thomism explicitly closed to those features of Augustine which opened Catholicism to Modernity".

We will thoroughly discuss Augustine's biblical spirituality, since it has long influenced the West. To prove this influence, we compare his notion of *amor ueritatis* or *amor sapientiae* with Spinoza's *amor Dei intellectualis*. This shows that, at the end of the seventeenth century, Augustinian thought was still widely accepted and consequently, the gap between faith and reason developed only much later[2]. The fact that this gap emerged very late (eighteenth century) has to do with the fact that since Antiquity, science (in all its forms) had never been free of spirituality (*infra*). Love and knowledge, which are both fundamental elements of Augustine's spirituality, go together, and this view has its roots in Western (Judeo-Christian and Greek Hellenistic) thought. We will now further discuss these aspects.

I. Augustine's Spirituality

Augustine describes his own spiritual evolution extensively in the *Confessiones*, a work that is generally accepted to be autobiographical to a great extent. It is sure that Augustine follows a different spiritual path than some of his contemporaries, be they Manicheans, Neo-Platonists, or fellow Christians. In general, he rejects rather than appreciates the strictly ascetical practices of, among others, the Desert Fathers, an aspect that Augustine will assimilate into his monastic rule. The purpose of that rule is, indirectly, to educate the monks[3], but still we cannot suspect Augustine of intellectualism[4]. Key terms for Augustine are *knowledge* and *love*.

---

2. Spinoza is but one example, but there are several others, e.g. Montaigne and Descartes.

3. Van Bavel finds proof in the *Regula: Praeceptum* V, 10. Cf. T.J. VAN BAVEL, *Augustinus van Hippo: regel voor de gemeenschap*, Averbode, 1982, pp. 86-87.

4. The question remains highly disputed whether the experiences of Milan and Ostia should be interpreted as a *mystische Vision* or as a *Höchstleistung der aktiven Vernunfttätigkeit*: J. KREUZER, *Pulchritudo: vom Erkennen Gottes bei Augustin. Bemerkungen zu den Büchern IX, X und XI der Confessiones*, München, 1995, p. 256 n. 115. See also G. BONNER, *The Spirituality of St. Augustine and its Influence on Western Mysticism*, in *Sobornost (New Series)* 4 (1982) 143-162. Mandouze, who agrees with Gilson, gives a nice summary: "Quand nous parlons d'un mysticisme à tendance intellectualiste, c'est cette participation de l'intelligence à l'ascension vers Dieu, plutôt que sa prédominance, que nous voulons marquer puisqu'il arrive un moment où il devient impossible de distinguer les deux éléments". See A. MANDOUZE, *Les maîtres et les modèles. Saint Augustin et son Dieu: Les sens de la perception mystique*, in *La vie spirituelle, ascétique et mystique* 21 (1939) 44-60, p. 51. Some authors try to turn Augustine into an apophatic theologian, but therefore they have to exaggerate hermeneutically some of his assertions: D. CARABINE, *The Unknown God. Negative Theology in the Platonic Tradition: Plato to Eriugena* (Louvain Theological & Pastoral Monographs, 19), Leuven, 1995. According to us, Augustine should not be interpreted too soon as if he where an apophatic theologian. Some of his "apophatic" claims are nothing else than critical remarks on the use of language.

The importance of Augustine is that he does bifurcate spirituality and theology, or faith and reason. Both are partners in dialogue, a dialogue with God.

Augustine attaches most importance to certain knowledge, based on the principle of non-contradiction and the eternity of truth[5]. These truths are largely derived from mathematics and logic. Long before Descartes, Augustine had thought that the subject – specifically the consciousness of an ego that is spiritually active and that uses thought as a starting point to end up with certain knowledge – can end up at certain knowledge[6]. Even doubt puts one on the path toward truth, because he who knows that he doubts is thus aware of truth[7]. If one observes reality one must make subtle distinctions regarding optimism vis à vis certainty. When can one say for certain that one is certain? When does one know that one is wrong? Why does one at times refuse to accept the truth?

The will (*uoluntas*) is a key element in Augustine's epistemology, contra Aristotle. This is due to his conviction that the mind (*mens*) cannot reach the truth without the moral qualities of the heart[8]. As Socrates said, God can only be known by a purified *mens*[9]. Divine Providence makes a genuine confession possible, only for those who are looking for it *pie, caste ac diligenter*[10]. If philosophers do not want to reconcile themselves to the proofs of faith, this is not because they are epistemologically unable, but because they insist on their pride and envy[11]. Knowledge of the truth is the result and not the cause of their virtue[12]. Religious truths are not detached propositions which can be studied; rather, they must be

---

He discovers the boundaries of our language without developing a systematic negative theology. Carabine is obliged to ease off on pp. 272-276.

5. AUGUSTINE, *Contra Academicos* III, 10, 23 and ID., *De libero arbitrio* II, 8, 21. See E. PORTALIÉ, *Saint Augustin*, in *Dictionnaire de théologie catholique*, Paris, 1905, dl. 2, 2268-2472.

6. AUGUSTINE, *Contra Academicos* III, 11, 25-26.

7. ID., *De uera religione* 39, 73.

8. On the meaning of *uoluntas*: J. RIST, *Faith and Reason*, in E. STUMP – N. KRETZMANN (eds.), *The Cambridge Companion to Augustine*, Cambridge, 2001, 26-39, esp. pp. 33-38.

9. AUGUSTINE, *De ciuitate Dei* VIII, 3 and ID., *De Trinitate* I, 2, 4. The Augustinian *mens* is the immaterial part of reason which is an image of the trinitarian God and which is able to know God (*Confessiones* VII, 1, 2; *De Trinitate* I, 1, 1; II, 18, 54; III, 1, 1; X, 10, 15-16). *Mens* is a common characteristic of God and man.

10. AUGUSTINE, *De quantitate animae* 14, 24 and also ID., *De uera religione* 10, 20; ID., *De ordine* II, 19, 61; ID., *De moribus ecclesiae Catholicae et de moribus Manichaeorum* I, 1, 1 and also the title of this essay, a quotation from *Epistula* 140.

11. ID., *De uera religione* 4, 7.

12. ID., *Contra Faustum Manichaeum* XXII, 52 and ID., *De utilitate credendi* 16, 34.

contemplated. The truths of faith are embraced by the soul and provide the rulebook for a virtuous life.

Love is not only the motive behind the search for truth, it also reveals truth: "Deus caritas est"[13]. Augustine randomly and interchangeably employs three terms for love (*amor, caritas* and *dilectio*), because all three can in fact mean the opposite (*cupiditas, concupiscentia*), depending upon the object of love[14]. Science and knowledge are indeed important factors, but they cannot cause a human being to be good and, more importantly, they do not bring salvation[15]. The link between knowledge and virtue has been discussed above. However in this case, love is necessary, because love (*caritas*, 1 Cor 13) encapsulates all other virtues: moderation is love that maintains its integrity; strength is love that can endure much hardship out of a commitment to the beloved one; justice is love that does not egoistically hoard good things but shares them[16].

With respect to religious pedagogy, Augustine's spiritual bond between knowledge and love requires a special approach, namely, a mystagogical approach (*disciplina arcani*)[17]. Augustine is aware that faith cannot be communicated by words alone – they often have an allegorical meaning and thus, in such cases literal interpretation alone cannot suffice[18].

But as far as all those things which we "understand," it is not the outward sound of the speaker's words that we consult, but the truth which presides over the mind itself from within, though we may have been led to consult it because of the words. Now He who is consulted and who is said to "dwell in the inner man" [2 Cor 4, 16], He it is who teaches us, namely, Christ, that is to say, "the Unchangeable Power of God and everlasting wisdom"[19].

Catechumens can say that they believe in the truths of the faith, but this does not mean that faith lives in them: "Look, they already believed in Jesus and Jesus himself did not trust himself to them. Why? Because

---

13. ID., *De moribus ecclesiae Catholicae et de moribus Manichaeorum* I, 17, 31 and II, 2, 4. Based on 1 John 3, 1; 4, 7 and so on.

14. T.J. VAN BAVEL, *Love*, in A.D. FITZGERALD (ed.), *Augustine through the Ages. An Encyclopedia*, Cambridge, 1999, 509-516, p. 509.

15. AUGUSTINE, *Contra duas epistulas Pelagianorum* 4, 5, 11 and *In epistulam Iohannis ad Parthos tractatus* 2, 8 quoted by VAN BAVEL, *Love* (n. 14), p. 509.

16. AUGUSTINE, *De moribus ecclesiae Catholicae et de moribus Manichaeorum* I, 15, 25 quoted by VAN BAVEL, *Love* (n. 14), pp. 509-510.

17. T. VAN DEN BERK, *Mystagogie. Inwijding in het symbolisch bewustzijn*, Zoetermeer, 1999, pp. 96-99.

18. AUGUSTINE, *De catechizandis rudibus*, 13.

19. AUGUSTINE, *De magistro* II, 38, transl. R.P. RUSSELL in the series *The Fathers of the Church*, Vol. 59, Washington, DC, 1968, p. 51.

they were not yet born again of water and the Spirit [John 3, 5]"[20]. The catechumens are called *audientes* because they hear, but they do not necessarily understand[21]. A person's faith has to come from inside, because faith is an interior gift.

Augustine views the world and sensory perception in a positive light, because of his biblical sources, the absence of strong ascesis, and his conflicts with Manicheism. The ultimate spiritual goal is for the soul to ascend (*ascensio*) towards God *per visibilia ad invisibilia*. In this manner, humans receive the *visio beatifica*. One cannot find this expression in the work of Augustine, who always speaks of *acies mentis* or *animae*, *acies cordis* or *intellectus*. Some people can have a direct, unmediated contact with God through the *acies mentis*. From the year 393 AD[22], Augustine no longer admitted that humans on earth can reach the *visio beatifica* and from that time onward, he restricted it to the blessed in heaven[23]. Nevertheless, on earth everything remains eventually limited to *une perpétuelle dialogue* with God[24].

These ideas are related to Augustine's ideas on the Fall. In approximately the year 415 AD, Augustine is confronted with a controversy about death, sin, the purpose of baptism and related problems and a debate takes place between the Pelagians and himself. In *De Genesi ad litteram* (401/415 AD) Augustine delivers a literal hermeneutic on the Fall which results in his well-known though often exaggerated pessimism. All people suffer from the consequences of Adam and Eve's seduction: the loss of immortality, the revolt of body against soul and of the soul against itself, sin, all wrong desires and above all the damage to *memoria*, our deepest *esse*. The Fall does not only prevent our luck, but it also affects our cognitive power[25].

---

20. AUGUSTINE, *In Iohannis euangelium tractatus*, 12, 3, trans. J.W. RETTIG (The Fathers of the Church, 79), Washington, DC, 1988, p. 30.

21. AUGUSTINE, *Sermo* 122, 1.

22. F. VAN FLETEREN, *Acies mentis*, in FITZGERALD, *Augustine through the Ages* (n. 14), pp. 5-6, esp. 6.

23. Compare F.J. THONNARD, *Traité de vie spirituelle à l'école de Saint Augustin*, Paris, 1959, p. 787: "C'est cette amour de Dieu pour nous que jaillit, après le péché, le divin remède de l'Incarnation du Verbe et de la Rédemption par le sacrifice de la croix. Désormais, c'est par le moyen de la grâce du Christ que nous remontons, par le rude chemin de la purification, vers la possession de Dieu dans la charité, vers cette 'vie bienheureuse' commencé ici-bas dans la vie contemplative, consommé au ciel dans la vision béatifique, lorsque notre *amour* deviendra *jouissance*".

24. The terminology is from MANDOUZE, *Les maîtres et les modèles* (n. 4), p. 49. Mandouze bases his statement on two claims of Augustine in the *Confessiones* (I, 5, 5 and X, 2, 2).

25. On the consequences of the Fall: M. LAMBERIGTS, *Augustine, Julian of Aeclanum and E. Pagels' Adam, Eve, and the Serpent*, in *Augustiniana* 39 (1989) 393-435 and also

II. AUGUSTINE: *AMOR UERITATIS / AMOR SAPIENTIAE*

At this point it is necessary to delve deeper into the terminology that relates love to knowledge. The term *amor ueritatis* does not appear very often in Augustine's work; in fact it is irrregularly spread throughout his entire work, occuring mostly before the year 400 AD [26]. A similar situation obtains for the term *amor sapientiae*, especially as a synonym for philosophy. It is plausible that this imbalance is related to the fact that Augustine's attention throughout the years changed from philosophy as searching for the truth to *philosophia christiana*, the only truth. True philosophy identifies itself with true religion in the religious science that – with a *terminus technicus* – had been called "theology" since Abelard[27].

Amor ueritatis / amor sapientiae consists of an objective and a subjective element. *Amor ueritatis* brings about understanding – e.g. in the dogma of the solely spiritual nature of the spirit, which was a tricky problem then (Augustine remained agnostic on this topic till the end of his life)[28] – and creates openness towards God[29]. *Amor ueritatis* is aroused through many causes, e.g. the enigmatic nature of many biblical stories. The secret, symbolical meaning of those biblical texts serves to arouse our love for the truth and to increase our aversion to ignorance[30]. Most

J. LÖSSL, *Intellectus gratiae: Die Erkenntnistheoretische und hermeneutische Dimension der Gnadenlehre Augustins von Hippo* (Supplements to Vigiliae Christianae, 38), Leiden – New York – Cologne, 1997.

26. On that concept: G. MADEC, *Petites études Augustiniennes* (Collection des Études Augustiniennes. Série Antiquité, 142), Paris, 1994, pp. 163-177.

27. On the concept of "theology" in the works of Augustine: G. MADEC, *Theologia*, in ID., *Petites études* (n. 26), pp. 261-270. Augustine often writes *amor sapientiae* as synonymous with *philosophia* (*Contra Academicos* II, 3; *De ordine* I, 11; *Contra Iulianum* IV and so forth). Sometimes *amor ueritatis* and *amor sapientiae* are synonymous to the extent that they both indicate the *philosophia christiana*, the only true philosophy. Only neoplatonists deserve the title *philosophi* in Augustine's later works (*De ciuitate Dei* VIII, 1).

28. AUGUSTINE, *De quantitate animae* XIV, 24: "Quod facilius contingit iis, qui aut bene eruditi ad haec accedunt, non studio inanis gloriae, sed diuino amore ueritatis accensi; aut qui iam in his quaerendis uersantur, quamuis minus eruditi ad inuestiganda ea uenerint, si patienter bonis se dociles praebent, atque ab omni corporum consuetudine, quantum in hac uita permittitur, semet auersunt".

29. ID., *De ciuitate Dei* X, 29: "Scio me frustra loqui mortuo, sed quantum ad te adtinet; quantum autem ad eos, qui te magnipendunt et te uel qualicumque amore sapientiae uel curiositate artium, quas non debuisti discere, diligunt, quos potius in tua compellatione alloquor, fortasse non frustra".

30. ID., *De catechizandis rudibus* IX, 13: "[...] deque ipsa utilitate secreti, unde - mysteria uocantur, quid ualeant aenigmatum latebrae ad amorem ueritatis acuendum, decutiendumque fastidii torporem, ipsa experientia probandum est talibus, cum aliquid eis quod in promptu positum non ita mouebat, enodatione allegoriae alicuius eruitur".

important is that our love for the truth leads us to God, because God is the truth[31]. When seen from the human perspective, God's authority is heteronomous and thus ensures our love for the truth[32]. The last aspect of objectivity manifests itself in that the *amor ueritatis* is not an intrinsic motivator; more efficient in this respect is fear of damnation[33]. Augustine proves that love exceeds the purely objective, by mentioning that one can even die for it[34]. To reach the Truth, we have to ascend (*ascensio*) out of the body and tend to the eternal essence of love for the truth, which is the subjective component. Thus we get round the limitations of our reason, caused by the Fall. The Fall does not hinder our love for the truth[35]. The heart can only be purified by undivided and sincere attention for eternal life and by pure love for wisdom[36]. It is thus predictable that Augustine relates the notion of "conversion" to *amor sapientiae*: on the one hand pagans and heretics shun the love for the truth[37] (*i.e.* the love towards God) which is the most important in the way to their conversion, on the other hand the love for the truth leads to a conversion as a preliminary path[38].

III. SPINOZA: *AMOR DEI INTELLECTUALIS*

In the seventeenth century, the biblical vision of Augustine is still influential. In order to demonstrate that the antagonism between faith and reason is of a later date than is generally acknowledged, we compare

31. ID., *De musica*: "[...] atque uni Deo et Domino rerum omnium, qui humanis mentibus nulla natura interposita praesidet incommutabilis ueritatis amore adhaerescerent". The *amor sapientiae* is there where God is. In the here-after *amor sapientiae* will be complete and so we do not have to worry any more about earthly desires and concerns (*De continentia* VIII, 20).
32. ID., *De ciuitate Dei* XVIII, 41: "[...] quid agit aut quo uel qua, ut ad beatitudinem perueniatur, humana se porrigit infelicitas, si diuina non ducit auctoritas?".
33. *De dono perseuerantiae*: "[...] quod ipse Pelagius, non quidem amore ueritatis Dei, sed tamen suae damnationis timore damnauit".
34. ID., *De diuersis quaestionibus octoginta tribus* LXXXII, 1: "[...] ita compensarent, ut spe futurae uitae iucundius et laetius prae amore ueritatis torquerentur, quam luxuriosi prae cupiditate ebrietatis epulentur".
35. ID., *De uera religione* XVI, 30: "Ita [corpus hominis] enim nobis suadetur a corporis uoluptatibus, ad aeternam essentiam ueritatis amorem nostrum oportere conuerti".
36. ID., *De sermone Domini in monte* II, 11: "[...] quod non mundat nisi una et simplex intentio in aeternam uitam solo et puro amore sapientiae". In other words: "[...] nullo modo nos posse securo otio simul in amore sapientiae uiuere [...]" (*Confessiones* VI, 12).
37. ID., *De Genesi contra Manichaeos* II: "[...] et cauent flagrantissimo amore ueritatis [...]".
38. ID., *Quaestiones euangeliorum* II, 33.

the spirit of Spinoza – and more particularly the concept of *amor Dei intellectualis* – to Augustine's concept of *amor ueritatis*. The application of the concept *amor Dei intellectualis* to Augustine would be an anachronism; however, our intention in the article is to demonstrate the extent to which Augustine and Spinoza coincide.

Concerning his spirituality, Augustine emphasises love as well as intellect, both elements that could be discovered in Spinoza's definition of *amor Dei intellectualis*. In translation the Spinozian proposition reads as follows: "The intellectual love of the mind for God is the love by which God loves himself; not in so far as he is infinite, but in so far as he can be explained through the essence of the human mind, considered under a species of eternity; that is, the love of the mind for God is a part of the infinite intellectual love with which God loves himself"[39]. At the moment of the aforementioned "privileged moment", intuitive and discursive knowledge are no longer opposed because at this precise moment intuition becomes immediate knowledge of the terms of a deduction. This is comparable to Cartesian *clara et distincta*. Spinoza's "originality" however lies in the idea that rationalism can be combined with religious salvation and absolute love. The origin of highest knowledge (being the original desire in which natural love for truth becomes true love) is located in the nature of the mind itself and not in the transcendent. *Amor Dei intellectualis* would be impossible if the activities of the mind (*intellectus*) were passive; otherwise stated, if beatitude would not be analytically comprised of the knowledge of one truth or another. We can only experience joy and delight if they correspond with the truth[40].

Spinoza and Augustine concur in their treatment of the above mentioned themes in that they share nearly identical anthropological presuppositions. They share the same aspects of Aristotelian teleology, i.e. every being attempts to correspond to its essence – in the case of humans, this means rationality – for Spinoza, acting according to the virtues and reaching the perfection of our nature; for Augustine, corresponding to the *imago Dei*. Apart from this teleological anthropology, Spinoza shares Augustine's voluntarism and interiorism. At first sight, both thinkers seem

---

39. B. DE SPINOZA, *Ethica* V, 36: "Mentis Amor intellectualis erga Deum est ipse Dei Amor, quo Deus se ipsum amat, non quatenus infinitus est, sed quatenus per essentiam humanae Mentis, sub specie aeternitatis consideratam, explicari potest, hoc est, Mentis erga Deum Amor intellectualis pars est infiniti amoris, quo Deus se ipsum amat". Quotation from SPINOZA, *Ethics* (Oxford Philosophical Texts), transl. G.H.R. PARKINSON, Oxford, 2000, p. 310.

40. J.-M. BAI, *Amour*, in S. AUROUX (ed.) *Encyclopédie philosophique universelle. Les notions philosophiques*, Paris, 1990, II, 74-76, p. 75.

to differ regarding voluntarism. Spinoza holds that if one is disconnected from one's essence, this is not due to one's mistakes or to perversion of the will, but rather to intellectual impotence. For Augustine reason remains not independent from the intellectual consequences of original sin. Indeed, reason is affected by the Fall, but not answering to one's essence is due to corrupt use of the will[41].

The above mentioned options coincide in the interiorism of both authors. The Spinozian essence as well as the Augustinian *imago Dei* can be achieved by means of the *via interior*. If a human being cannot fully express the state of being human, then, according to Spinoza, this lack is due to inadequate self-knowledge as well as from faulty knowledge of the will. According to Augustine as well, this lack stems from inadequate self-knowledge and love, because the *imago Dei* is to be found within our most intimate self, more precisely in the mind. Epistemologically both authors attribute positive meaning to the concrete and to the subjective, because according to both authors, human beings reach a type of self knowledge that is free from superfluous and abstract concepts which cannot be reduced to objectivity. In the case of both thinkers, the precondition for that type of knowledge is a change in mentality that could be characterized as a "conversion" which finds its origin in Divine Grace according to Augustine, and in the contemplation of the necessary order of nature according to Spinoza[42]. One meets a comparable Spinozian necessity (cosmic rationality) in the works of the Church Father in the form of Divine Providence[43]. For Augustine, fatalism is the consequence of thinking in terms of the aforementioned necessity, whereas for Spinoza the consequence is determinism. Spinoza is more Epicurean than Augustine in the sense that knowledge of universal necessity liberates us from being torn between hope and anxiety. Furthermore, proof of this distinction lies in his belief that knowledge of the process of putting one's desires into perfect equilibrium guarantees perfect serenity. According to the bishop of Hippo, self knowledge leads to a similar outcome; one desires none but the necessary (God) and this fills man with delight in a manner very similar to Spinozian insight which likewise fills man with

41. Augustine's late view on this matter: M. LAMBERIGTS, *Julian of Aeclanum: A Plea for a Good Creator*, in *Augustiniana* 38 (1988) 5-24.

42. To the extent that the soul understands that everything that happens, happens necessarily, it has power over the events and it will be less enticed by them: "Quatenus Mens res omnes, ut necessarias intelligit, eatenus majorem in affectûs potentiam habet, seu minùs ab iisdem patitur". Cf. SPINOZA, *Ethica* V, 6.

43. It is Augustine's later view that everything that God foresees, must happen necessarily, but not in a necessary way which hinders human freedom. Cf. AUGUSTINE, *De libero arbitrio* III, 1-3.

delight. According to Augustine, self knowledge leads to a similar result; one desires only the necessary (God) and that fills one with delight (*delectatio*), just as Spinozian insight fills one with delight (*acquiescentia in seipso*)[44].

A similar ambiguity arises concerning the relation between faith and reason. Spinoza was often accused of exhibiting elitist tendencies in his work because his path was considered to be exclusively reserved for savants, i.e. a limited elite audience of *sapientes*. Spinoza's idea can be derived from his attitude towards the Bible. In certain traditional readings of the Bible, God is depicted as a legislator and a judge. Spinoza recognises that such an approach is necessary for two reasons. One is the control of the profligacy of the *ignari*, but more importantly that salvation through faith would be made accessible to the largest possible number of people. In the Bible, God is depicted as such, simply for the purpose of making Him accessible to the masses. For the sage, biblical promises and threats are naught but superficial, because the wise person behaves according to reason, which by definition presupposes knowledge of God[45]. Similar features appear in the work of Augustine, but a very sharp distinction exists between Spinoza's disparaging attitude toward faith as contrasted with Augustine's placement of faith at the highest level in the hierarchy of knowledge of God. According to Augustine, the highest level of religious experience consists in the transition from mere belief to reasoned belief, taking into account that faith always remains a "gift"[46]. Because the path to reasoned belief is not always available to the masses, the path of faith may alternatively be achieved via Scriptures and authority. Unlike Spinoza, Augustine does not deprecate the path of faith. Quite the contrary, the bishop steadfastly adheres to the idea that the path of faith precedes the path of reasoned belief [47].

Notwithstanding the great many similarities between Spinoza and Augustine which have been pointed out above, and, while one may observe a certain conceptual continuity between the two thinkers, one must nevertheless recognise several major dissimilarities between them[48].

44. The *acquiescentia in seipso* is defined in the *explicatio* of *affectuum generalis definitio*, completely at the end of *Ethica* III. See also SPINOZA, *Ethica* III, 53 and IV, 52.
45. SPINOZA, *Ethica* V, 42 (especially the *scholium*).
46. AUGUSTINE, *Contra litteras Petiliani*, 1, 6-8 and ID., *Ad Cresconium grammaticum partis Donati*, 3, 6-7, 22-23.
47. That statement could easily be discovered in early as well as in later works of Augustine: *Soliloquia* I, 6, 13-I, 7, 14; *De libero arbitrio* II, 2, 5-6; *De doctrina christiana* II, 12, 17; *De Trinitate* VIII, 5, 8; XII, 15, 25 and XIV, 1, 3.
48. Nothing has been published yet which proves that Spinoza is directly dependent of Augustine, but indirect dependence is not excluded.

The greatest difference between Spinoza and Augustine lies in their definition of the ultimate goal of knowledge, i.e. how each of them conceptualises God. For Augustine, self knowledge is essential in order to reach the ultimate goal of knowledge (God). For Spinoza, insight into the necessary order of nature – which is synonymous with God, *deus sive natura* – is sufficient in order to attain knowledge of God. Thus their goals are identical (God) but their understanding of God differs appreciably. Augustine could never declare himself in agreement with Spinoza's panentheism; it would have been impossible for him to reconcile himself with Spinoza's extreme determinism which manifests itself as staunch apathy toward misfortune and total indifference to the whims of fate, a state reached by intellectual activity[49]. Augustine would continue his critique, emphasising that Spinoza reduces his purified religion to a salvation based ethic, this being a totally unacceptable notion to Augustine for whom grace alone is salvific. Once again, it is clear that on crucial points where Spinoza identifies with some Stoic ideas, he differs from Augustine[50]. Another important difference between the two is the manner in which they reach their goal. For Spinoza, insight into the chain of causality suffices to liberate us from obsessive passion[51], while for Augustine divine grace remains essential[52]. For Spinoza, the human person can autonomously attain insight as far as epistemological and moral maxims (which inspire religious conversion) are concerned.

At this point, it appears relevant to elaborate further on the issue of spiritual conversion. According to Spinoza, man must steer his passions (i.e. bodily drives) in order to prevent disturbing his equilibrium. Passions are ordered by imagination (*imaginatio*) and according to rules worked out by the mind[53]. This process involves absolutely no decision making at the level of the will, nor any intervention of the will, but rather

---

49. SPINOZA, *Ethica* IV, appendix to chapter 32: "Attamen ea, quæ nobis eveniunt contra id, quod nostræ utilitatis ratio postulat, æquo animo feremus, si conscii simus nos functos nostro officio fuisse, et potentiam, quam habemus, non potuisse se eò usque extendere, ut eadem vitare possemus, nosque partem totius naturæ esse, cujus ordinem sequimur".

50. This is even more clear in the case where both authors disagree on moral matters and where Spinoza opts for a Stoic approach.

51. SPINOZA, *Ethica* V, 9: "Affectus, qui ad plures, et diversas causas refertur, quas Mens cum ipso affectu simul contemplatur, minùs noxius est, et minùs per ipsum patimur, et erga unamquamque causam minùs afficimur, quàm alius æquè magnus affectus, qui ad unam solam, vel pauciores causas refertur".

52. AUGUSTINE, *De Genesi ad litteram* I, 2, 5 and VII, 9, 12.

53. SPINOZA, *Ethica* V, 10: "Erga rem futuram, quàm citò affuturam imaginamur, intensiùs afficimur, quàm si ejus existendi tempus longiùs à præsenti distare imaginaremur; et memoriâ rei, quam non diu præteriisse imaginamur, intensiùs etiam afficimur, quàm si eandem diu præteriisse imaginaremur".

a progression of rational knowledge to which each and every individual is inclined. One has to make certain that those aforementioned general maxims provide true rational knowledge concerning the nature of our passions (*affectus*). Translated into practical life and concrete terms, this means that one should not direct one's passions to vain and empty things, but rather only toward values which will enable one to lead a life based on reason. In this manner, passions are transformed into rational desires, which can be identified with *honestas* and *pietas*[54]. Augustine's writings are repleat with similar notions; he defines passions only in a positive way as long as one directs these passions to God[55].

With respect to the concept of conversion, for both thinkers the process begins with objective knowledge of one's passions, which shows us that as long as one's desires are ruled by one's imagination, then one is subjected to external distractions and temptations, and consequently one does not act in accordance with one's own authentic will, nor in accordance with the desire of one's rational nature. The moment that one discovers that rational autonomy – i.e., the intellectual faculty which is illuminated through perfect knowledge and which finds its origin in the inborn *imago Dei* – is the point of the soul's true fulfilment, then one no longer is obstructed by a faculty of fantasy and can freely act, delivered from all fear[56]. For Augustine, conversion takes a totally different path. Conversion is preceded by inner turmoil and conflict. The soul has turned away from God, and, if God does not convert us, conversion will never occur, because conversion – as all things – is in the hands of God[57]. A conversion is the total about-face of the soul toward God; it results in a life totally devoted to the service of God. In contrast to Spinoza's increasing autonomy-based way of thinking, Augustine emphasises the heteronomous aspect of conversion[58]. According to him, conversion is not brought about through philosophical reasoning, but through the God-induced humility of the *imitatio Christi*[59].

54. ID., *Ethica* IV, 37, *scholium* and *Ethica* V, 4, *scholium*.

55. Cf. *Confessiones* X, 42-51, concerning Augustine's attitude towards the five senses.

56. SPINOZA, *Ethica* IV, 63 and also *Ethica* V, 41, *scholium*: "Qui Metu ducitur, et bonum, ut malum vitet, agit, is ratione non ducitur".

57. AUGUSTINE, *Enarrationes in Psalmos* 79, 4: "Auersi enim sumus a te, et nisi tu conuertas, non conuertemur".

58. God's activity is always stressed in the *Confessiones*. For example *Confessiones* VII, 10, 16: "Et inde admonitus redire ad memet ipsum intraui in intima mea duce te et potui, quoniam factus es adiutor meus".

59. AUGUSTINE, *De ciuitate Dei* X, 32. This does not mean that Augustine is fideistic. Just like Spinoza, Augustine thinks that the existence of God can be reasonably demonstrated. Cf. *De libero arbitrio* II, 3, 7 – II, 15, 39.

It is God who intervenes so that the soul may liberate itself from itself as well as from evil inclinations. This process occurs in three stages: the state of chaos, the intermediate period of crisis, and the ultimate state of order and unity in the soul[60]. The result is not Spinozian *honestas* or *pietas*, but rather a *gratia delectans*, the experience of God's presence[61].

Despite similar features, increasing autonomy versus heteronomy is the fundamental difference between Augustine and Spinoza. This opposition is explicitly demonstrated in their epistemological presuppositions. For the African church father, knowledge begins with the senses and the imagination, which can only retard uncertain knowledge due to their changeability and unreliability. Such truth remains uncertain because the senses are so easily deceived. Therefore, one is inclined to think that truth has to emanate from the soul where one discovers truth that cannot be found in things external, for truth is immutable. However, since the soul is mutable as well, one must search for the truth beyond one's soul, namely in the light of the intelligible sun, that is God himself. God is the *magister interior*[62]. This heteronomous supposition is absent from Spinoza's philosophy. He distinguishes among three immanent levels of knowledge. In the first place he considers sensible or imaginative knowledge to distinguish similarities, dissimilarities, and discrepancies within sensible ideas[63]. Spinoza then speaks of rational knowledge which reduces all external objects to determinations of extension, whereby all phenomena are made comprehensible by means of geometrical principles, being clear and distinct[64]. The final stage is intuitive science that is rational (it provides one with objective certainty about the laws of nature, because it shows them under the aspect of eternity – *sub quâdam æternitatis specie* – so typical of mathematical objects) because it grasps the essence (the individuality and the foundation in God) of singular things[65].

---

60. ID., *Confessiones* IX, 1, 1 describes the beginning of the crisis: "Et hoc erat totum nolle, quod uolebam, et uelle, quod uolebas".

61. ID., *Enarrationes in Psalmos* (n. 57) 57, 4; 71, 7; ID., *De ciuitate Dei* XIII, 5; ID., *De doctrina Christiana* IV, 14 and so on.

62. This is the issue of *De magistro*, an early work of Augustine, but *De Trinitate* XII, 15, 24 demonstrates that – on this topic – Augustine sticks to his original ideas till the end of his life.

63. SPINOZA, *Ethica* II, 29, *scholium*.

64. ID., *Ethica* II, 40, *scholium* 2.

65. SPINOZA, *Ethica* II, 44, corollarium II + *demonstratio*.

IV. THE END OF THE DIALOGUE BETWEEN
FAITH AND REASON IN SPINOZA?

In his *Ethica*, Spinoza examines how man can purify his mind in order to attain true freedom. In the *Tractatus Theologico-politicus* he examines how social life must be organised to attain the goals of the *Ethics*. To recapitulate: because living in freedom through the way of philosophical reasoning is not possible for all, there is the non-philosophical way of religion. The early Augustine holds similar views in, e.g., *De dono perseverantiae*. Because not everybody is talented enough to reach God through reason, there is the way of faith, which is much faster and generally accessible. Undoubtedly, reasoned faith is Augustine's preferred path, whereas it is not entirely clear which path is preferred by Spinoza. Opinions on this matter differ to a significant extent[66].

For example, two recent studies, authored by Angela Roothaan and Wim Klever, shed light on the theme of the dialogue between faith and reason – theology and philosophy – in Spinoza's *Tractatus Theologico-Politicus*[67]. Angela Roothaan states that Spinoza makes a radical distinction between theology and philosophy (or more correctly: between faith and reason) in chapters 14 and 15 of the *Tractatus*: "Spinoza's movement toward identifying theology and faith is based upon restricting theology to the interpretation of the traditional religious texts on the level of their most concise sense, namely the prescribing of God's moral laws regarding love of neighbour and righteousness. According to Spinoza, in this process of interpretation, theology ought to restrict itself to the sacred texts alone and to keeping that practice separate from the assistance of philosophy, while demonstrating their consistency and reasonableness. Regarding it, he noted: "[...] that which I have just proven, is in fact the most important goal with this tractatus [...]"[68]. Klever agrees with Roothaan: "Theology is primarily concerned with obtaining clarity with respect to prophetic revelation, namely an exhortation to virtue, most especially righteousness and love of neighbour and its ongoing elucidation by means of appropriately symbolic imagery as the only way leading to true happiness, as the only religious requirement that will be rewarded. According to Spinoza's formulation, theology stripped from

---

66. A. ROOTHAAN, *Vroomheid, vrede en vrijheid. Een interpretatie van Spinoza's Tractatus Theologico-Politicus*, Assen, 1996, p. 4.

67. For this debate, see A. ROOTHAAN, *Vroomheid* (n. 66). The other study agrees with Roothaan: W. KLEVER, *Definitie van het christendom. Spinoza: Tractatus Theologico-Politicus opnieuw vertaald en toegelicht*, Delft, 1999.

68. A. ROOTHAAN, *Vroomheid* (n. 66), pp. 47-48 (translation: Jonathan Yates).

all philosophical and speculative components"[69]. In this respect, both authors disagree with older authorities such as Mönnich, Zac and Malet, who believe that Spinoza could not maintain the dichotomy between theology and philosophy[70]. In my view, it is the presupposition of the author which has determined his analysis.

The question remains whether the God of Spinoza still has some affinity with the God of Christianity. One is inclined to answer this question in the negative. In Klever's opinion, Spinoza presents an alternative theology, one opposed to the classical one: "The central theological concepts of revelation, creation, sin, grace, redemption, and liberation are addressed. However, these concepts receive a meaning which does not coincide with the conventionally assigned contents they receive in most ecclesiastical contexts. Spinoza's alternative theology is a philosophical theology, a fact which makes a substantial difference for some particular types of Christianity, such as its Western variants"[71]. Spinoza is well aware of the shift in emphasis which he introduced, but it was never his intention to forge a split between faith and reason. On the contrary, his ultimate aim was to demonstrate that belief is rational and that God is the supporting foundation of this rationality. Essentially, Augustine and Spinoza do not disagree on all fundamental issues, they differ in their priorities. According to Spinoza, God is encapsulated in a rational system, whereas for Augustine, God created the rational system. Spinoza does not question religion itself, however he deviates from the Jewish-Christian image of God that predominantly ruled at the time and was drawn from Scripture.

It would be premature to speak of the end of the dialogue between faith and reason as having occurred as early as the end of the seventeenth century. Therefore, authors like Mönnich, Zac and Malet are correct. The data will not allow a conclusion beyond the fact that Spinoza correctly envisioned the approaching split but did not attempt to reinforce the splitting factions. He took interest in a new type of dialogue. At this time, it was accepted practice in theological circles to defend the reasonableness of faith with so-called rational arguments and natural theology (ontological, cosmological, and teleological proofs of the existence of God), and, according to Spinoza, that was no longer sustainable. Instead of

---

69. KLEVER, *Definitie* (n. 67), p. 26. Between quotation marks he cites Roothaan (*ibid.*, p. 47) (translation: Jonathan Yates).

70. C. MÖNNICH, *De verhouding van theologie en wijsbegeerte in het Tractatus Theologico-Politicus*, Leiden, 1966; S. ZAC, *Spinoza et le problème de l'interprétation de l'Écriture*, Paris, 1965; A. MALET, *Le "Traité Theologico-Politique" de Spinoza et la pensée biblique*, Paris, 1971.

71. KLEVER, *Definitie* (n. 67), p. 43 (translation: Jonathan Yates).

considering reason to be an enemy of faith, Spinoza attempts to establish the right of theology to exist with its own paradigms, which define its own autonomous position. He writes in the *Principia Philosophiae Renati des Cartes*, which predates the *Tractatus* by seven years: "Although in theology it is said that God does things at his own good pleasure and with the purpose of displaying his power to men, nevertheless, because those things that depend merely on his good pleasure are known by no other means than divine revelation, to prevent philosophy from being confused with theology, they are not to be admitted in philosophy, where enquiry is restricted to what reason tells us"[72]. In the fifteenth chapter of the *Tractatus*, it is said that subordinating faith to reason would allow for criticism of the Scriptures and that subordinating reason to faith would be fatal to scientific reasoning. Consequently, faith and reason must be kept separate and allowed to function autonomously. He adds that the so-called testimony of the Holy Spirit can be nothing but the voice of reason[73]. Roothaan subtly nuances this point when she writes: "When we assume that Spinoza possessed an accurate insight in the developmental tendencies of the scientific disciplines. We can even formulate the idea somewhat differently: he attempted to preserve theologies" time-honored prerogatives in a world in which the sciences, and also philosophy, were in the process of assuming their own autonomous positions"[74].

Roothaan and Klever correctly assert that Spinoza has a different understanding of theology than was prevalent in his era. In 13/3, a central paragraph of the *Tractatus Theologico-Politicus*, Spinoza clearly maintains that obedience to God consists only in love of neighbour and that, in Scripture, it is only the superstitious who are obsessed with the mysterious and the supernatural. When a rational, true believer is confronted with new scientific insights – which contradict his religious conviction – he can no longer maintain his superstitious beliefs; he is forced to integrate these new positions into his former framework. Herein lies the major difference with Augustine, according to whom faith and reason are never mutually contradictory, and if this ever be the case, reason must be in the wrong. For Spinoza, reason outweighs all, and faith must accompany reason, even if a reinterpretation of dogma is required[75].

---

72. SPINOZA, *Principia Philosophiae Renati des Cartes*, part 2, proposition 13, *scholium*, quoted by KLEVER, *Definitie* (n. 67), pp. 45-46. For the English translation see *Baruch Spinoza: The Principles of Cartesian Philosophy and Metaphysical Thoughts*, transl. S. SHIRLEY, Indianapolis, IN – Cambridge, 1998, p. 63.

73. We use the translation of KLEVER, *Definitie* (n. 67), pp. 260, 265 and 268.

74. ROOTHAAN, *Vroomheid* (n. 66), p. 40 (translation: Jonathan Yates).

75. H. DE DIJN, *De uitgelezen Spinoza*, Tielt-Amsterdam, 1999, p. 200.

V. Cultural Context

Neither in Augustine nor in Spinoza, does a gap exist between faith and reason (though the gap is growing in Spinoza's work). In Antiquity, science and spirituality were happily married. This was true for both the Jewish and the Greek wisdom traditions[76]. The Jewish intellectuals developed a fundamental attitude of reverence (*jira'*) as the source of all wisdom related to the human person and the world. That fundamental attitude was developed by practising virtues, through which one receives contemplative insight in the surrounding world, a clear understanding (*bina*) of all existing things. In ancient Israel, that experience of reality was closely linked to the experience of God.

Similarly, the link is preserved by the Greeks, without therefore being direct heirs of the Hebrews. Greek philosophy shows three important interfaces with what today is often termed spirituality. Firstly, at the attitudinal level, the search for truth is supported by the fundamental attitude of reverence (*eusebeia*). A precise translation of this term is problematic, yet it contains elements such as awe, amazement, and serious attention. Secondly, on the level of praxis several codes of conduct (*askèsis*) arise in the different schools to liberate thinking from passions and desire. The spiritual leaders of those schools therefore developed practices such as fasting, examination of one's conscience, exercises for purification of body and soul in order to lead a virtuous life. Finally, on the level of the ultimate goal, reverence and ascesis are the conditions for reaching *theoria* (contemplation as the ultimate goal of thinking and of the human condition in general).

Contrary to the East, in the West the gap between philosophy and the sciences on the one hand, and spirituality on the other, progressively increased until the eighteenth century. The serene dialogue between philosophy/sciences and theology which had been going on for centuries, received its first debilitating critique by the development of the *via moderna* in the late Middle Ages and later, when ancient cosmology was shaken by Copernicus. The direct provocation was the one-sided interpretation of Aristotle by the nominalists, who paid attention only to the concept of *epistèmè* and its associated logic. All sciences, theology included, were reduced to conceptual constructions of a particular reality.

---

76. These three paragraphs are based on Waaijman's concise summary on the relation between spirituality and philosophy/sciences: K. WAAIJMAN, *Wijsgerige verstandigheid en onderscheiding der geesten*, in G. GROENEWOUD – W. DE HAAS – J.F. VAN OS – B. VOORSLUIS (eds.), *Tegenwoordigheid van Geest. Opstellen over spiritualiteit en mensbeschouwing*, Zoetermeer, 2001, pp. 135-152, esp. 135-136.

This approach reached its culmination in the modern concept of ratio-nality.

We have demonstrated that in the seventeenth century, and particu-larly in the works of Spinoza, faith was never questioned, but under the influence of the Modern worldview, the relation between faith and rea-son, or between theology and philosophy/sciences became increasingly problematic[77]. For example, a thinker such as Descartes believed, as did Augustine, that faith necessarily precedes knowledge. Had he not been convinced of this certainty, he would never have begun his experiment of doubt. Descartes' problematic has to be situated elsewhere. New insights into the sciences could no longer be combined with the Aris-totelian and scholastic worldview and thus, it was better to explain the world by scientific than by theological arguments ...[78].

VI. CONCLUSION

Contrary to present day values in which spirituality can operate in a vague atmosphere of religiosity, at the time of Augustine, spirituality was firmly embedded in the legacy of the Bible and the Christian tradi-tion on the one hand, and in Greek philosophy on the other. Though nowadays reason is often considered to be a danger to the autonomous experience of spirituality – which explains why there is more a conflict than a dialogue between faith and reason – at the time of the African church father no such dichotomy existed. Augustine was no exception, since he consciously associated himself with a long standing philosoph-ical/theological tradition. Our examination of Spinozian thinking sug-gests that this link still existed at the end of the seventeenth century. The-ology and philosophy had not yet become enemies, but with the passage of time, philosophy increasingly rebelled against its role of *ancilla the-ologiae*.

Despite more than a millenium which separates their work, Augustine and Spinoza were chosen for this study as the main exponents of classi-cal views on faith and reason. Moreover, it was our aim to demonstrate that Spinoza was motivated like Augustine to engage in science, namely the search for salvation by means of reason/reasonable faith. Moreover,

---

77. This is the main subject of M. WILDIERS, *The Theologian and His Universe. The-ology and Cosmology from the Middle Ages to the Present*, San Francisco, CA, 1984.
78. P. WILLEMSEN, *Cartesiaans geloven. Een verhandeling over het cogito ergo sum*, Leende, 2000, pp. 14-16.

we have shown many other "Augustinian" concepts and relations in Spinoza's thinking: the relation between religion and ethics, our inborn knowledge of God, love as a virtue which transcends emotion and so forth. Their solutions are based on being liberated from wrong desires and on placing created objects into proper perspective. Spinoza seems to be one of the later variants of this classical model of which Augustine was a major representative. As previously stated, Spinoza's thinking stands in a tradition, in which philosophy and theology are both forms of spirituality and of which Augustine was one of the exponents. Consequently, Spinoza's writings were too often considered Enlightenment treatises, with all the dangers inherent to such an interpretation, since there a dialogue between faith and reason is no longer possible[79].

Thus, the use of the term "Modernity" as such is problematic. When it is used to discuss the gulf between faith and reason, thinkers like Spinoza, Descartes, Locke and Hume are often accused of something that they simply did not completely cause. These authors share many ideas and presuppositions with Augustine. In short, early Modernity did not instigate the paradigm shift which separated faith and raison. In fact, it is late Modernity, and particularly the thinkers of the (especially French[80]) Enlightenment, are responsible for a real gap. Perhaps, the deeper reason for the dichotomy should be sought inside, rather than outside theology, i.e. in the inner logic of the theological evolution which had its genesis in the high Scholasticism of the Late Middle Ages.

Faculteit Godgeleerdheid   Hans GEYBELS
K.U. Leuven
St.-Michielsstraat 6
B-3000 Leuven
Belgium

---

79. Quotation of A. Malet in ROOTHAAN, *Vroomheid* (n. 66), p. 53.
80. Still an interesting study on this subject is P. HAZARD, *La crise de la conscience Européenne (1680-1715)*, Paris, 1935.

THE CONVERSATION OF LOVE AS
UNFULFILLING UNION

It is common experience as well as a long-standing truism that friends desire to converse with one another. Thomas Aquinas even claims, "this appears to be the most characteristic mark of friendship"[1]. He emphasizes this by remarking, "we even take more delight in conversing with a friend than in conversing with ourselves"[2]. A closer analysis of love reveals that it consists in a reciprocal encounter revolving around different kinds of union. The thesis that my paper is to support maintains that the essential union of love is not the fulfillment of the longing for union with the beloved, but the union of longing itself with the beloved.

Human love is commonly understood as the fulfillment of the desire for union with another person. The classic defender of this position is Aristophanes in Plato's *Symposium*. Perhaps the best-known defender of it today is Erich Fromm in his famous book *The Art of Loving*[3]. My strongest witness for my own opposing thesis is Thomas Aquinas, who has taken the standpoint that love, rather than consisting in fulfillment, is itself a desire for union arising out of the essence of love, namely, the union of desire itself [*unio affectus*]. The differentiated perspective that he presents should result in some light being shed on the nature of the conversation of love.

Fromm speaks often of "the experience of union" and describes love itself as "active penetration of the other person, in which my desire to know is stilled by union"[4]. He describes the essence of "love as the overcoming of human separateness, as the fulfillment of the longing for union"[5]. Knowledge is for him an integral component of love: "I know [...] by experience of union not by any knowledge our thought can give.

---

1. In Aquinas, *In III Sent.*, dist. 29, a. 5, ad 6.
2. Id., *Summa contra gentiles*, IV, cap. 22, n. 2: "Hoc videtur esse amicitiae maxime proprium, simul conversari ad amicum". Cf. also *In III Sent.*, dist. 29, q. 1; *In Ethic.*, IX, lect. 13, n. 12.
3. E. Fromm, *The Art of Loving*, New York, Harper & Row, 1974; originally published in 1956.
4. *Ibid.*, p. 25.
5. *Ibid.*, p. 27.

[...] The only way of full knowledge lies in the act of love: this act transcends thought, it transcends words. It is the daring plunge into the experience of union"[6]. And such fulfilled union with the beloved is commonly taken to be the ideal of happiness. In reality, what love can achieve is not the realization of this goal, but the discovery of the ideal of such union. Human love is in other words more a revelation of fulfillment than the fulfillment itself. Its ultimate meaning lies precisely in being unfulfilling union.

Self-Reflection lies at the core of the problem of human love, for it is on the one hand a pre-requisite for fulfillment and on the other hand an ineluctable deterrent. Fundamental is that happiness must be conscious, if it is to be happiness at all. There is nothing that we value more highly than consciousness. Human love is specifically conscious love. It is precisely *I*, or *we*, who love. The human is able to view whatever is good *qua* good[7]. Aquinas teaches, furthermore, that humans, as opposed to animals, are able to view sensual beauty as beautiful[8]. Whereas, according to Aristotle and Thomas, animals experience pleasure, humans additionally take pleasure in the beauty of sensible things[9]. The spirit enhances the sensual.

The most important aspect of love is the awareness of the existence of the other. Self-reflection is nothing else but the apprehension of existence. As Aristotle expressed it: what we desire most in regard to ourselves is the apprehension of our existence. Hence, since the friend is a second self, what we desire most of him is his existence. Aristotle gives the following explanation: "As then lovers find their greatest delight in

6. *Ibid.*, p. 26.
7. AQUINAS, *Summa theologiae*, I, q. 59, a. 1c: "Quaedam vero inclinantur ad bonum cum cognitione qua cognoscunt ipsam boni rationem, quod est proprium intellectus. Et haec perfectissime inclinantur in bonum; non quidem quasi ab alio solummodo directa in bonum, sicut ea quae cognitione carent; neque in bonum particulare tantum, sicut ea in quibus est sola sensitiva cognitio; sed quasi inclinata in ipsum universale bonum; et haec inclinatio dicitur voluntas. Unde cum angeli per intellectum cognoscant ipsam universalem rationem boni, manifestum est quod in eis sit voluntas". Cf. ID., *De veritate*, q. 23, a. 1c.
8. ID., *Summa theologiae*, I, q. 91, a. 3, ad 3: "Sensus sunt dati homini non solum ad vitae necessaria procuranda, sicut aliis animalibus; sed etiam ad cognoscendum. Unde, cum cetera animalia non delectentur in sensibilibus nisi per ordinem ad cibos et venerea, solus homo delectatur in ipsa pulchritudine sensibilium secundum seipsam".
9. ID., *Summa theologiae*, II-II, q. 141, a. 4, ad 3: "Delectationes aliorum sensuum aliter se habent in hominibus, et aliter in aliis animalibus. In aliis enim animalibus ex aliis sensibus non causantur delectationes nisi in ordine ad sensibilia tactus, sicut leo delectatur videns cervum vel audiens vocem eius, propter cibum. Homo autem delectatur secundum alios sensus non solum propter hoc, sed etiam propter convenientiam sensibilium. [...] Inquantum autem sensibilia aliorum sensuum sunt delectabilia propter sui convenientiam, sicut cum delectatur homo in sono bene harmonizato, ista delectatio non pertinet ad conservationem naturae".

seeing those they love, and prefer the gratification of the sense of sight to that of all the other senses, that sense being the chief seat and source of love, so likewise for friends (may we not say?) the society of each other is the most desirable thing there is. Firstly, friendship is essentially a partnership. Secondly, a man stands in the same relation to a friend as to himself, but the consciousness of his own existence is a good; so also therefore is the consciousness of his friend's existence. This consciousness, however, is actualized in intercourse; hence, friends naturally desire each other's society. Thirdly, whatever pursuit it is that constitutes existence for a man or that makes his life worth living, he desires to share that pursuit with his friends. Hence, some friends drink or throw dice together, others practise athletic sports and hunt, and still others study philosophy in each other's company. Each sort spends their time together in the occupation that they love best of everything in life, for wishing to live in their friends' society, they pursue and take part with them in these occupations as best they can"[10].

Here the typical irony of the basic human situation comes into play: self-reflection means both self-possession and self-alienation. For conscious living implies observing oneself, which in turn involves a gap between oneself as subject and as object. Even in the word "I", which appears to attain complete identity, there is still a dualism of the observer and the observed. "I" thus involves a certain self-alienation. Living in reality implies an asymptotic hiatus. Justice cannot assuage this ontological suffering. Human experience remains *per se* conscious experience. A statement like, "I love you", is disappointingly complex for the union it is trying to express with its three distinct words. The complete union with the other can be achieved only with a being whose essence and existence are identical.

We conceive of complete happiness as comprising the perfect identity of the apprehension of the presence of the loved-one together with one's consciousness of this. Ecstasy is thus imagined to imply the extinguishment of self-consciousness, self-forgetfulness, on the one hand, and, on the other hand, the total and immediate presence in the other. However, the realization of this dream shatters the dream, cracks it open. Complete union with the other with full awareness would indeed overcome the dualism of the experience and the experienced. The gap would in fact be eliminated between being both one with oneself and one with the other. Intentionality would indeed attain fulfillment: it would actually disappear.

---

10. ARISTOTLE, *Nicomachean Ethics*, transl. H. RACKHAM, Cambridge, MA, Harvard University Press; London, William Heinemann Ltd, 1934, p. 12 (Book IX, 1171b29–1172a3). Cf. *ibid.*, p. 9 (1170b10–19).

If truth were to obtain complete objectivity, according to the argument of
Thomas Aquinas, it would not be truth at all, since truth always involves
two factors, namely, the object and subject, and the subject must contribute something of its own [*aliquid proprium*], otherwise, Aquinas
explains, one could not speak of an *adaequatio*, as in the traditional definition of truth[11]. Not having the problem of intentionality, an animal can
be subsumed into its object uninhibitedly. A dog eating is one with its
food. Not having intentionality, that is, being completely one with itself,
it is devoid of an awareness of distance from its object. Separateness from
oneself and separateness from one's object have the same source. Truth
is the conscious presence of an object together with the active awareness
of this presence. Without this duality, this separation, there cannot be that
phenomenon which we call truth.

Happiness for us must be true, i.e., conscious, happiness. I have to be
aware that I am happy in order really to be happy. I have to observe
myself being happy. But this self-observation per force undermines happiness. Ecstasy is pure happiness only in our memory or in our hope.
As it occurs in actual reality, happiness is accompanied by a dimension
of disappointment.

The Union that Is Love Is the Union of Longing Itself

Precisely speaking, love consists in the desiring of the existence of the
beloved. It is located in the affect. It is a force, a striving, a willing.
No doubt, the essence of love lies not in praxis, not in doing, but in the
will. Helping is not love itself, but an expression of love.

Thomas Aquinas clearly distinguishes three kinds, or stages, of union
related to love: (1) the union that gives rise to love, (2) the union that
love desires and (3) the union of desiring love itself[12]. It belongs to the

11. *De veritate*, q. 1, a. 3c.
12. *Summa theologiae*, I–II, q. 28, a. 1, ad 2: "Unio tripliciter se habet ad amorem.
Quaedam enim unio est (1) causa amoris. Et haec quidem est (a) unio substantialis, quantum ad amorem quo quis amat seipsum, quantum vero ad amorem quo quis amat alia, est
(b) unio similitudinis, ut dictum est. Quaedam vero unio est (2) essentialiter ipse amor.
Et haec est unio secundum coaptationem affectus. Quae quidem assimilatur unioni sub-
stantiali, inquantum amans se habet ad amatum, in amore quidem amicitiae, ut ad seipsum;
in amore autem concupiscentiae, ut ad aliquid sui. Quaedam vero unio est (3) effectus
amoris. Et haec est unio realis, quam amans quaerit de re amata. Et haec quidem unio est
secundum convenientiam amoris, ut enim philosophus refert, II Politic., Aristophanes dixit
quod amantes desiderarent ex ambobus fieri unum, sed quia ex hoc accideret aut ambos
aut alterum corrumpi, quaerunt unionem quae convenit et decet; ut scilicet simul con-
versentur, et simul colloquantur, et in aliis huiusmodi coniungantur".

essence of love between friends, desiring mutual conversation, that this desire remains essentially unfulfilled. This is owing primarily to reflective consciousness. Reflection renders love in the present human condition unfulfillable. The more love becomes self-conscious, the greater the cleft between desire and its fulfillment. Thomas explains that the first kind of union consists in knowledge of the beloved, who thus becomes attractive for the will. The second kind "is caused by love effectively, since it moves the lover to desire and see the presence of the beloved as fitting and pertaining to himself". The third kind, finally, is caused by love "formally, since love itself is such a union or connection". Thomas then quotes Augustine's remark in Book VIII of the *De trinitate* that "love is a kind of life, joining two, or desiring to join them, i.e., the lover and the beloved". Thomas interprets Augustine's statement as meaning that the joining itself pertains precisely to a union of the affect [*unionem affectus*], without which there is no love at all, whereas the desiring of union pertains to the physical union [*unionem realem*][13].

The union, therefore, which love is in its essence takes place in the affect [*unio affectus* or *unio affectiva*]. There occurs a mutual presence: "The beloved is contained in the lover insofar as he or she is impressed upon his or her affect by a kind of participative complacency [*per quandam complacentiam*]"[14]. "And, conversely, the lover is also truly contained in the beloved insofar as the lover pursues in a certain manner what is intimate in the beloved"[15].

Aristotle does not go deeply enough, when he defines love as benevolence. According to Thomas Aquinas, benevolence follows upon love. The essential union is not the union of the object desired, or for whom it is desired, but rather, as Aquinas inceptively puts it: "Love precedes desire"[16]. "The affective union [...] precedes the movement of desire"[17].

---

13. Cf. *Summa theologiae*, I–II, q. 25, a. 1c.

14. *Summa theologiae*, I–II, q. 28, a. 2, ad 1: "Amatum continetur in amante, inquantum est impressum in affectu eius per quandam complacentiam".

15. *Summa theologiae*, I–II, q. 28, a. 2, ad 1: "E converso vero amans continetur in amato, inquantum amans sequitur aliquo modo illud quod est intimum amati. Nihil enim prohibet diverso modo esse aliquid continens et contentum, sicut genus continetur in specie et e converso".

16. *Summa theologiae*, I–II, q. 25, a. 2c: "Amor praecedit desiderium".

17. *Summa theologiae*, I–II, q. 25, a. 2, ad 2: "Unio affectiva [...] praecedit motum desiderii".

THE STRIVING FOR UNION WITH THE BELOVED
IS THE STRIVING FOR UNION WITH THE BELOVED IN GOD

Human love opens the religious dimension, for God brings the difference between being and its knowability to a union of identity. In God, essence and existence are identical. "This sublime truth", as Thomas Aquinas calls it[18], lies at the final ground of all reality, love being no exception.

There is logic, then, in Erich Fromm's definition of love and his understanding of God, i.e., what he calls his non-theism. "The problem of knowing man", he states, "is parallel to the religious problem of knowing God"[19]. Hence, love of God is analogous to our love of humans. "The basis for our need to love lies in the experience of separateness and the resulting need to overcome the anxiety of separateness by the experience of union. The religious form of love, that which is called the love of God, is, psychologically speaking, not different. It springs from the need to overcome separateness and to achieve union"[20]. "To love God [...] would mean, then, to long for the attainment of the full capacity to love, for the realization of that which 'God' stands for in oneself"[21]. All forms of atheism result ultimately in an abbreviation of everything that is absolutely important. It truncates reality by insisting on limiting everything to immanence within the horizon of the world.

In other words, the union demanded by love requires divine being, which alone has the necessary ontological structure to bring about a union in which union and its reflection attain the desired fulfillment. Thus, in the present human condition love is opened to a kind of union that can be attained only in the mode of eschatological hope. It awakens a vision that animates hope. This dimension is necessarily eschatological. The fact that the experience of love awakens a vision in us that can find no satisfying fulfillment in this life is purposeful. We dream of finding someone who is completely one with us. Neither is the dream fulfilled nor is it in vain.

Katholisch-Theologische Fakultät   William J. HOYE
Westfälische Wilhelms-Universität Münster
Hüfferstr. 27
D-48149 Münster
Germany

18. *Summa contra gentiles,* I, p. 22: "Hanc autem sublimem veritatem". Aquinas considers this to be the divine revelation to Moses.

19. *Ibid.,* pp. 26-27.

20. *Ibid.,* p. 53.

21. *Ibid.,* p. 60.

THE COMMUNICATIVE THEOLOGY OF
WILLIAM OF OCKHAM

A CONTEMPORARY INTERPRETATION

Many believe that the loss of Christian understanding of life and Christian culture starts with Ockham (1280-1350). He is regarded as an anti-metaphysicist and an epistemological relativist. Since he supposedly undermined the ontological basis for the *adequatio rei et intellectus*, he gave room to modern epistemological scepticism that resulted in the loss of meaning and belief in God[1]. Moreover Ockham has obtained a stereotypical place in controversy literature. It is supposed that he has prepared the way for the "nominalistisch-protestantische Dogma, daß schlechthin unbedingtes Sein sich nicht in bedingtem, geschichtlichen Sein wirklich erkennen lasse und nichts in der Sinnenwelt Gottes Handeln wirklich zu vermitteln vermöge"[2].
In the opinion of Louis Dupré, Ockham obstructs "an integral and all integrating Christian humanism"[3]. Who follows his lead, can impossibly

---

1. W. BEINERT calls him the "Hauptvertreter des Nominalismus, der den thomanischen Zusammenhang von Glaube und Verstand auflöst und damit das neuzeitliche Denken einläutet" in his *Das Christentum. Atem der Freiheit*, Freiburg, Herder, 2000, p. 48. G. LARCHER speaks of "das Ende des Ideals des 'intellectus fidei' ... Dementsprechend zieht Ockham eine scharfe Trennungslinie zwischen Offenbarung und Vernunft, Glauben und Wissen ... Der Glaube hat keine Unterstützung mehr in der 'natürlichen Vernunft'" in his *Modelle fundamentaltheologischer Problematik im Mittelalter*, in W. KERN – H.J. POTTMEIER – M. SECKLER (eds.), *Handbuch der Fundamentaltheologie* 4, Freiburg, Herder, 1988, p. 345. B. STUBENRACH writes: "Der Voluntarismus Wilhelms verfälschte die Freiheit Gottes dermaßen zur Willkür, daß Bindung in Gott gar nicht mehr denkbar schien" in his *Dialogisches Dogma. Der christliche Auftrag zur interreligiösen Begegnung*, Freiburg, Herder, 1995, p. 195.
2. W. SCHÖPSDAU, *Offenbarung zwischen Sinnforderung und unmöglicher Möglichkeit*, in *Materialdienst des Konfessionskundlichen Instituts Bensheim* 52 (2001) 10-13, p. 11.
3. *De andere dimensie. Geestelijk leven in een seculiere samenleving*, in L. DUPRÉ – F. MAAS (eds.), *De andere dimensie. Intellectuele cultuur en religie*, Vught, Radboudstichting, 1998, 7-20, p. 13. Dupré admits: "Much of what earlier generations considered to be a truth as solid as a rock has indeed turned out to be very shaky" (p. 16). Great theologians have been more careful. Thus in the eyes of Augustine the present shape of the world, also of the church, is full of ambiguity; present time is the stage between lost ideal beginning and ideal end. It becomes dangerous, however, if the fear to let creation participate in God gets linked to Plato's thesis of fall on the one hand and Aristotle's idea that God has to do with the world from a distance as causa efficiens only on the other hand. Thomas is able to cause the tide to turn by speaking of participation based on Scripture.

attain a society and a culture that are permeated with God's grace. With
Ockham "the passage to modernity" starts. From this point on "the sacred
canopy" disappears, "the rumours of angels" fall silent, God withdraws
and all that remains in the end is a universe without ultimate meaning.
Ockham "no longer takes such a built-in-harmony between mind and
nature for granted, which subjects God's ways of creation to human
norms. Even the assumption that in knowledge the mind shares a universal form with the real, however deeply entrenched in the tradition, is abandoned. Ockham does not question the need for universals in the process
of human cognition. But they exist neither in an independent realm outside the mind as Plato was believed to have held, nor even inside the singular reality as Aristotle had taught. Our only access to reality consists in
an intuition normally conveyed through the senses. To know by means of
a contact with physical reality, however, is essentially a process of efficient causality, wherein no form is transferred from that reality to
the mind. Indeed, God may directly infuse an intuition without sense

This unstable model however goes wrong if either participation or infinite distance gets
emphasized unilaterally. The former occurs in the pantheism of Spinoza and in Marsilio
Ficino and other Florentine Platonists before him (cf. J. ASSMANN, *Moses the Egyptian.
The Memory of Egypt in Western Monotheism*, Cambridge, MA, Harvard University Press,
1997). There is also a different German version: *Moses der Ägypter. Entzifferung einer
Gedächtnisspur*, Darmstadt, Wissenschaftliche Buchgesellschaft, 1998). The latter occurs
when nominalists regard grace as "a matter of divine decree unmeasured by human standards and randomly dispensed to an unprepared human nature" (L. DUPRÉ, *The Dissolution of the Union of Nature and Grace at the Down of the Modern Age*, in C.E. BRAATEN
– P. CLAYTON [eds.], *The Theology of Wolfhart Pannenberg*, Minneapolis, MN, Augsburg
Publishing House, 1988, 95-121, p. 102). Following this nominalistic tendency God and
worldly reality will be pulled apart more and more in later days. "The delicate balance
between transcendence and immanence would soon be broken in favour of an ever-increas-
ing immanentism" (p. 109). Dupré himself follows Nicholas of Cusa. "Unitas alteritatem
praecedit. The creature's *Being* is not another, but God's own Being in a contracted mode
(cuius esse est ab-esse). The absolutely *one* tolerates no total otherness; it must include
all otherness in itself. Hence what appears most other to the finite is, in fact, what is most
identical. But if God remains so intimately present to creation, then that creation must,
despite its unlikeness, in some way also reflect the hidden presence – not as a likeness but
as a cipher. To detect God's reflection in what is 'unlike' God requires the intellectual powers of the human being, the only creature made into 'the image and likeness' of God" (p.
118). "Though the created cosmos is indeed distinct from the divine unity, God's immanence in it continues to secure the cosmos's unity. Only insofar as created being coincides
with uncreated Being does it attain the unity that conveys its self-identity. The same term,
which most adequately describes God's being, also defines the creature's innermost reality" (L. DUPRÉ, *Passage to Modernity. An Essay in the Hermeneutics of Nature and Culture*, New Haven, CT, Yale University Press, 1993, p. 187). I do not rule out that Nicholas
of Cusa might be able to help us rediscover the evangelical shape of Christianity. In this
article I remind you of Ockham's warning to never consider the immanence of God as a
possession that has already been decided once and for all in the culture of church and world.

impression"[4]. From the nature or structure of reality nothing can be gathered about the nature of God according to Ockham, says Dupré. We only know God, when he speaks through a prophet (sola scriptura) or places intuitive insights directly into the heart. In the nature or structure of the world no trace of God is present. "It now fell upon the human mind to interpret a cosmos, the structure of which had ceased to be given as intelligible" (3). Humans live in a world that knows neither a natural law nor teleology. "The argument implied that no predictable order ruled the world and hence that only empirical observation could establish the nature of that order. The new voluntarism even affected the intellect's own activity. Truth was not simply given with insight; it required an assent of the will. The knower assumed full responsibility for what he or she affirmed... Freedom henceforth became a self-choice, more than a choice that selects among given alternatives. It refused to be restricted by the given" (129).

I. IN THE GRASP OF ARISTOTELIANISM

It is, however, also possible to associate the desolate feeling of modern man with the circumstance that since medieval aristotelianism we have been saddled with a longing for fixed structures, a wish to make everything fit, plug all the holes and answer all the questions, indeed the idea of necessity. We have been unable to live with holes and questions without them leading to despair and agnosticism ever since. The realization of contingency caused by aristotelism implies that "dass sich mir die Ereignisse als in dem Sinne zufällig darstellen, dass ich sie nicht einordnen kann, dass ich ihnen keinen Sinn beimessen und daher weder gedanklich noch handelnd mit ihnen umgehen kann, sie machen mich orientierungslos"[5]. The longing for the obscure to become clear and for the uncertain to become certain, runs through scholastic theology from the 17th century onwards like a continuous thread. It colours all kinds of utopic expectancies and culminates in fundamentalist tendencies. Not biblical trust, but certainty based on unquestionable facts and insights is the ideal. The self-evidence that existed before the discovery of the personal nature of the world is longed for. This discovery implies that "Personen sind auf der Suche nach Personen, und so kann auch nur die

---

4. DUPRÉ, *Passage to Modernity* (n. 3), p. 39. Page numbering in this paragraph refers to this book.

5. H. DÖRING – F.-X. KAUFMANN, *Kontingenz und Sinnerfahrung*, in F. BÖCKLE – F.-X. KAUFMANN – K. RAHNER – B. WELTE (eds.), *Christlicher Glaube in Moderner Gesellschaft*, 9, Freiburg, Herder, 1981, 8-67, p. 12.

absolute Person mit absoluter und vollendeter Freiheit dem Menschen die letzte Antwort auf seine Fragen bedeuten ... Was ersehnt wird, ist jene personale Macht, die aus Liebe zum Menschen in Beziehung tritt und ihn so zur eigenen Freiheit befreit"[6]. Was not Ockham out to maintain this personalism?

When by means of Islamic scholars a number of new texts by Aristotle end up on the desks of Christian theologians, notions known from time immemorial like causality, principles, necessity, and nature get a new meaning. They try to confront the ideas of Aristotle with Christian thinking and to reconcile them. Thomas, Duns Scotus and William of Ockham struggle fiercely with this problem. In a broader sense this is also about *anagkè, ma'at, karma*, fate, coincidence on the one hand and grace and freedom on the other. The Christian worldview is traditionally permeated with personalism. It is concerned with relationships between subjects who communicate with each other in freedom. Our world is neither a matter of arbitrariness nor of fixed necessity. It is a space in which God's freedom counts for a great deal but human freedom as well. How does communication work here? Of which nature are the patterns of relationships in this order? What type of order is relevant here? How does life run its course here? Of what nature is the freedom of God? And what does this freedom imply for our view of (the stability of) the worldorder, society, state and church? What does it mean if God imparts his freedom and creativity to us? In what sense does God mean to direct our contingent and mortal existence? God and man each posses a specific potentia, specific possibilities. They are beings that can do things. People, however, are contingent; they do not find the ground and the space of their possibilities entirely within themselves. This is different for God. Different in what way? Does God necessarily act this way or that according to his nature? Or should we not talk like this? As said, God is indeed a space of freedom. At what level, in what measure, in which sense can we distil God's nature from his acts? Which "ratio"(nality) do God's deeds possess? How should we regard them and deal with them?

Certainly, God is not arbitrariness. Acts of God will possess reason. The reason (lex divina) of affection and care, originating from an infinite and inexhaustible creativity. How can we bring up this reason for discussion? What is its truth? How adequate is it? Adequate with respect to who or what? What is the "*recta ratio*" here? God seeks communication with people. He wants to be understood or heard. What understanding and hearing is involved here? The Scripture is a series of fragments

---

6. *Ibid.*, p. 51 and p. 57.

that indicate what kind of understanding or hearing appear on the scene here. Truth and reliability are introduced. Is truth the same as reliability? Which kind of truth is concerned in the contact between free subjects? After all, free subjects have more possibilities than the ones they give concrete form to in their actions. "Von jetzt an muss du mich wieder anderswo erwarten!", is the way Buber and Rosenzweig translate the Name or JHWH. Therefore the deeds of God cannot be grasped in a system of biblical theology. We have to be prepared for surprising turns. We cannot peg God down. He is a God of promise. This promise promises no-thing that we can get a grip on. "Stop holding on to me" (John 20,17). Nevertheless something other than chaotic plurality comes into existence. An order takes shape. Of what nature is it? Augustine thinks in "de civitate Dei", that this order is not the reality of our world yet. Even in the church we do not find it as a fact. We are heading for it. Tracks have been made that we have to follow. What do we call them and how do we regard them? Which evidence, which truth is present in them?

How much influence Aristotelian necessitarianism has had, is evident from the fact that in modernity many consider the contingent nature of reality an indication that God does not exist. Apparently one cannot think God in other ways than the realm of an all-permeating necessity. On the other hand the contingent nature of reality is indeed in keeping with the Christian view that God calls free beings to life out of abundance and without necessity. What does this statement mean for our life and experience? Upon this subject Ockham has reflected in his own special way.

II. THE CONCERN OF OCKHAM

The final years of Ockham's life are dominated by his struggle with John XXII, who had condemned the thesis that a church with possessions cannot be the true church of Christ. In a good Franciscan manner Ockham emphasizes "daß Christus und seine Apostel in ihrem Erdenleben keinerlei Güter im Sinne eines Eigentums oder eines Besitzes hatten, weder als Einzelpersonen noch als Gruppe"[7]. Poverty is the basis of the right relation to everything and everyone. Only that way can we let each other be. The viewpoint of John, however, breathes the spirituality of almighty

---

7. J. MIETHKE, Nachwort, in WILHELM VON OCKHAM, Dialogus. Auszüge zur Politischen Theorie, ausgewählt, übersetzt und mit einem Nachwort versehen von J. MIETHKE, Darmstadt, Wissenschaftliche Buchgesellschaft, 1994, p. 213.

power; he makes the order-founding impulse of God into a massive worldview. Ockham writes: "Johannes XXII lehrt und beweist, daß alles aus Notwendigkeit geschieht, denn alles ist von Gott vorherbestimmt; eine Bestimmung Gottes aber läßt sich nicht behindern. Daher meint er in seiner Bulle *Quia vir reprobus* ausdrücklich, daß Christus gemäß seiner Menschheit auf zeitliche Königsherrschaft und auf die allgemeine Bestimmung über die Dinge dieser Welt nicht Verzicht leisten konnte, da er damit gegen die Anordnung des Vaters verstoßen hätte. Aus diesem Grund bekämpft er auch die Unterscheidung der Theologen von Gottes absoluter und ordentlicher Macht. Aus diesem Grunde sagt er auch, daß Gott den Erwählten mit Notwendigkeit das ewige Leben bestimmt hat und keineswegs kontingent. Somit glaubt er offensichtlich, daß alles mit Notwendigkeit geschieht"[8].

According to Jan Beckmann[9] the orthodoxy trial against Ockham in Avignon "in der Sache" had nothing to do "mit der Auseinandersetzung um die päpstliche Jurisdiktion" in the controversy on poverty, in which Ockham, together with other Franciscans defends that Christ and the apostles neither together nor separately owned anything and that this should be the case for the church as well. I wonder if Beckmann is right. I recognize in the linguistic and logical work of the young Ockham the same intuition and concern. The importance that he attaches to the virtue of poverty in later years, explains what he had in mind all along. The principle of poverty accords with his theory of communication and philosophy of science. In a letter to his confrères, he states that his opposition against John XXII has to do with "dem Glauben, den guten Sitten, der natürlichen Vernunft, der sicheren Erfahrung und der brüderlichen Liebe"[10], and, therefore, with the reasonable way of communicating as well. Ockham wants to speak about God carefully and not just identify God with something else. That was also the concern of Duns Scotus before him. According to Scotus, God is the destination that man is living towards rather than already present in man with a presence that has only to be discovered, if necessary with supernatural help. The participation in the divine nature has to be born and realized in a life-long process in confrontation with the Word. In the course of our life we do not unfold a nature given in advance, but engage in communication with others and the Other, respectful of each other's freedom. Ockham radicalises this point of view. He sharpens the

---

8. OCKHAM, *Dialogus* (n. 7), p. 22.
9. J.P. BECKMANN, *Wilhelm von Ockham*, München, Beck, 1995, p. 23.
10. *Ibid.*, p. 25.

distance between one and the other, between perceiver and the perceived, between origin and final destination, between man and God
– not to cause defeatism, but in order to highlight the exciting adventure that life is in general and the God-man-relationship in particular.
He emphasizes the distance between "Ich und Du" to make the
encounter all the more exciting. Nevertheless he increases the demands
of "it is necessarily this way and not that" in justification of the epistemic and ethical relationship towards the other in order not to forget
that this relationship is not self-evident and not-necessary, but is based
on freedom and respect.

From the desire to communicate with the world around us and with others we cannot derive the nature of what surrounds us and of others.
We are always heading for it, while a distance remains. The other remains
the other and God is infinite. We pick up signals from them and attempt
to put these into words as clearly as possible and to comprehend. But this
does not completely bridge the gap. We can decrease the distance, but
with this nearness the respect for the freedom of others grows at the same
time. Therefore the appeal not to rule over others remains necessary.
That calls for a spirituality of poverty, of letting be. As soon as we are
given an inch, we often take a mile and do not allow others to be themselves. This *"incurvatio in seipsum"* renders all possession into a precarious undertaking. That is what the controversy on poverty in the Franciscan movement is about. Within the scope of this Franciscan spirituality,
Ockham studies the range of our terms and concepts. In his early work,
it is true, he does not make this link explicitly, but he also questions the
way that we deal with reality and experience it. He considers the groping nature of words and concepts characteristic for our situation.

III. The Process of Cognition

Confronted with something, someone, a concept, an affect, an expectation or an idea, I have an intuitive link with this singular matter.
To Ockham intuitive cognition means that I truly make contact with others in their singularity and that I am able to communicate with them, but
not that I fathom them from within. "Il en résulte que le terme "idée"
n'est pas un nom absolu, mais un nom connotatif, plus précisement un
nom relatif"[11]. This cognitive intuition shows a certain analogy to the act

---

11. J. BIARD, *Guillaume d'Ockham et la Théologie*, Paris, Cerf, 1999, p. 77.

in which God creates the singular, namely not as an application of eternal ideas, but exactly as the singular[12].

The first act in my encounter with the other is: "he, she, it exists, is there". Therefore the statement "this is" does not concern something universal, but this concrete singular thing. The is-statement wants to point out the being-there of this particular thing in its concreteness; the is-statement is not meant to connect the singular with something universal that's supposed to be higher in value or meaning[13].

When I come to a judgement about the who and the what of the other, not only the intellect but also the will and thus the ethical responsibility are involved according to Ockham. Thanks to the Spirit of God I thereby have this ability and I possess the cognitive power; in this way God creates me in his own image and likeness; of this Jesus Christ is the acme. I abstract[14] to come closer to this concrete singular being, not to classify it under something universal. In this act of abstracting, I do not confront

---

12. K. BANNACH thinks that Ockham "die franziskanische Schöpfungstheologie zu ihrem Ende führt: Alle Dinge sind je für sich von Gott geschaffen. Deswegen können sie nur als einzelne existieren" in his *Relationen. Ihre Theorie in der spätmittelalterlichen Theologie und bei Luther*, in *FZPT* 47 (2000) 101-125, p. 106. "Das bedeutet, dass Schöpfung nicht mehr beinhaltet, ein Geschöpf innerhalb eines ganzen Seinszusammenhanges hervorzubringen, sondern *unmittelbar*, im blossen Gegenüber von Schöpfer und Geschöpf. In aller Konsequenz ist der Gedanke, dass von Geschöpf nur im Zusammenhang mit einer Schöpfung gesprochen werden kann, eliminiert. Alle Geschöpfe werden ekstatisch. Sie sind, was sie als Geschöpfe sind, nur in ihrer Beziehung zu Gott. Sie stehen untereinander nicht in einem Verbund oder gar in einem Netzwerk" (112). As long as one does not draw the conclusion from this that no relation is possible between one creature and another. That would be very un-franciscan indeed.

13. "Wir stossen hier auf ein Grundprinzip der Ockamschen Metaphysik: Sein heisst verschieden sein ... Die Allgemeinbegriffe verdanken sich ausschliesslich der Tätigkeit des Verstandes. Es sind die Begriffe in Form von Denkintentionen, mit deren Hilfe der Intellekt sich der Wirklichkeit zu vergewissen versucht", BECKMANN, *Wilhelm von Ockham* (n. 9), p. 93 and p. 98.

14. "Abstrahieren heisst zum einen, vom situativen, individuellen, raum-zeitlichen Gegebensein von Einzelfällen absehen, und es heisst zum anderen eine Mehrheit von Einzelfällen unter einem ihnen gemeinsamen Aspekt zusammenfassen", BECKMANN, *Wilhelm von Ockham* (n. 9) p. 69. R. IMBACH stresses this even more radically: "Viel eher bedeutet dies, dass die Begegnung mit der Dingwelt die begiffsbildende Tätigkeit des Geistes provoziert ... Diese Interpretation des Begriffs als Zeichen der Wirklichkeit ist deshalb von entscheidender Wichtigkeit, weil sie eine klare Absage an der *Abbildtheorie* des Erkennens enthält ... Das Konzept ist ein Zeichen, mittels dem wir uns auf die extramentale Wirklichkeit beziehen" in his *Wilhelm von Ockham*, O. HÖFFE (ed.), *Klassiker der Philosophie*, 1, München, Beck, 1981, p. 236. Eucharist is not an example of general semiotics, but concerns the concrete sign in which Christ comes to me. Categorising it under something general would be at the expense of the concrete sign of Christ. That is the reason that the Eucharist without the liturgy of the Word is dangerous. Ockham assumes that (the intuition of) the transubstantiation theory can correct the aristotelian way of thinking about the nature of the sign.

the concrete being with "species intelligibiles"[15] present in the mind, as if I had prior knowledge of this or that reality (for example, based on my participation and theirs in the uncreated being). Ockham thus rejects the existence of such universals. "The universalia are not substance and do not belong to the substance of the singular, rather they only declare the substance of things as signs"[16]. "Semantisch bedeutet dies, dass Allgemeinbegriffe als Zeichen zwar etwas allgemein bezeichnen (nämlich eine mehr oder weniger grosse Anzahl von Einzeldingen), aber nichts Allgemeines benennen (weil es in den Einzeldingen nichts gibt, was allgemein wäre)"[16a].

I will explain once more by way of an is-sentence the terms that I use. In this premise, I put my first groping determination of the singular (John is a human being) in relation to the experience that human beings are able to communicate. Based on this I call attention to a certain aspect of John's being (human), without it immediately being obvious how and what John is communicating. This conclusion does not finish my looking at John but starts it again. I have caught sight of what John is and does in his uniqueness and attempt to map this out more clearly by way of new reasoning. I am not allowed to stop thinking due to insolent laziness, pleased with my own intelligence.

Ockham speaks of science if the steps towards the eventual judgement or proposition about this or that are indicated and taken in an orderly fashion. In science it is up for discussion if statements and/or judgements about this or that are brought about in the right way and can be verified step by step. "Solae propositiones sciuntur". I have to put remarks and feelings into propositions or is-sentences; only then do I leave my spontaneous sentiments in an orderly fashion and does it become possible to judge my knowledge. Constantly the awareness remains in this process that *I* am speaking and asserting; thus ill-considered self-evidences can be cleared out of the way. Theology and other scientific disciplines want to "préciser la signification des termes employés, évaluer la vérité des jugements, préciser le statut (variable) des conclusions établies"[17].

Continuously, Ockham is concerned with alertness and carefulness in dealing with myself, with the world around me and with God. He fears

15. According to M. GRABMANN no less than 18 explanations were current regarding the aristotelian theory about the intellect *agens* and the intellect *possibilis*. Cf. his *Thomas von Aquin*, München, Kösel, 1949, p. 143.

16. W. VON OCKHAM, *Opera Theologica* II, Saint Bonaventura NY, St. Bonaventura Press, 1970, p. 254.

16a. BECKMANN, *Wilhelm von Ockham* (n. 9), p. 123.

17. BIARD, *Ockham et la Théologie* (n. 11), p. 16-17.

rash self-evidence. He is afraid that I will rule over life with no respect. In that case I am in fact possessed and behave as one possessed, scared to lose my grip on life, scared to lose power. That I become lonely because of it, I hardly realize. I try to drive out demons only by the power of Beelzebub, by attempting to get control. But that is more of the same. Respectless behaviour towards others and lack of self-knowledge only increase as a result. Does the aniconic tradition not relate to this tendency to get a grip on everything, to mould and get a handhold? Doesn't the aniconic tradition turn against any form of absolutism that does not respect the other in his uniqueness?

Every statement about someone else has to result in my expressing honour and respect and acknowledging his or her freedom. Speaking and acting thus become a precarious affair. It might even make me scrupulous! But I have to address myself and others; I have to relate to others and myself. Because life presents itself, looks for communication, asks for acknowledgement and invites me to walk along for a while. Respectfully relating to others and other things asks the utmost of my freedom, implies radical obedience and at the same time appeals to my creativity. Behaving responsibly almost requires the humanly impossible. It can only be accomplished in a spirituality of poverty.

Ockham does not want the me-you-relationship to be blocked by something we put between ourselves as some sort of higher reality. That starts with the relationship between things and animals and culminates in the relationship with people and with God. I have to prevent my is-sentences from coming between me and others. They are propositions, "proposed" literally. They are always open to improvement and have to be appropriated with wisdom and deliberation. I have to keep trying to speak of others with respect for their being and freedom. Only if language and other forms of expression serve this communication in freedom and respect, they are aesthetically sound. That's where the standard for aesthetics lies. This standard cannot be determined in a purely aesthetical way, that is to say without appreciating the being of others and the respect they deserve. Beauty asks for good company. Ockham does not rule out my ability to truly know the reality of myself and others. However, that succeeds only when communication is established in freedom and respect.

That is also true for my own nature and being. I cannot account for it by something outside myself. I am free and not the prisoner of my surroundings. When I act, I act; I have to accept that responsibility. I do not act in the name of paternity or nationality but I am a father or a Dutchman on the basis of my own possibilities and responsibilities. Ockham agrees with the opposition against the saying "The fathers ate unripe grapes, and the children's teeth are set on edge". He makes much of everyone's personal responsibility. I may not underestimate the being and acting of myself and others.

IV. CULTURE AS OFFER

All this does not make Ockham a Philistine. He doesn't want to banish all language, science, technology, art and tradition (devotion, liturgy) for fear of them coming between me and the reality of myself and others and preventing communication. He does, however, turn against the tendency to give culture an indisputable position, to consider its authority self-evident and put it on an unquestionable pedestal. A civilized culture is characterized by the strength to prevent its own idolization. It should not claim to be the ultimate reflection of pure external ideas of "rationes intelligibiles" that subsequently start regulating and ruling life with so-called logical or rationalistic relentlessness[18].

Thus, communication in freedom and respect does not stay limited to the immediate relationship of one individual with another. The entire culture takes part in it, sometimes positively sometimes negatively. That depends on the degree of freedom and respect that a certain culture breathes. The world is not full of God's presence just like that. No one can take it for granted. This has consequences for those institutions and authorities that speak of God. They do not participate directly in God. Thus they should be transparent and not claim a special position or grace; if they do, they will soon start behaving as owners or rulers over God as well other people. Shrinking from this resembles the attitude of Dante (1265-1321), Eckhart (1260-1327) and Nicholas of Cusa (1401-1464). Each of them downplays in his own way the sacramental-hierarchical view of Christianity and church. Sacraments and authorities are not

---

18. In this sentence I oppose so-called logical reasoning from standpoints that do not allow questioning. Ockham shows how careful logic really is. "Der stark disputative Charakter mittelalterlichen Philosophierens bringt es mit sich, dass sich die Logik intensiv auch mit den sprachlichen und semantischen Voraussetzungen und Weiterungen der in den Wissenschaften verwendeten Argumentationen beschäftigt ... Immer stärker gesellt sich zur Logik die Theorie der Sprache, der Zeichen und ihrer Bedeutung, so dass sich ab etwa der Mitte des 13. Jahrhunderts in der Sache Logik und Semantik kaum noch sinnvoll voneinander trennen lassen", BECKMANN, *Wilhelm von Ockham* (n. 9), pp. 64-65. To what degree logic had degenerated in modern scholastics, became obvious when theologians educated with this logic could not deal with rediscoveries in the philosophy of language.

static incarnations of God. Ockham does however come to the realisation following the transubstantiation theory that large transformations can take place in created reality. The transformation of bread and wine during the Eucharist is analogous to the radical way in which the humanity of Christ subsists in the Word of God. It is possible to efface oneself radically for the sake of others. Culture can participate in this. But cultural heritage may never be viewed and experienced as incontrovertible authority.

It is true that I am helped by Scripture and other authorities, but the standard for my actions is what I should do according to my own insight and judgement. I cannot shift this responsibility onto them. An authority that takes over or eliminates my responsibility does not show respect. Politicians and other leaders make their largest mistake when keeping or bringing others in a state of dependence. When this happens, authorities in church and state become accomplices of the devil. They do not let be. Jesus is a true leader from a Christian viewpoint. He is called the Word and the Wisdom, because he brings others to insight, creativity and responsibility. He is not a leader, a prophet, a wise man or rabbi without respect for others. On the contrary, he liberates others.

V. OCKHAM AS A METAPHYSICIST

If metaphysics is not put on a par with the idea that reality is supported by eternally immutable ideas, one cannot deny Ockham a certain metaphysical sensibility. Therefore caution is needed, as Kurt Flasch puts it: "Was die Welt an metaphysischen Glanz verlor, gewann das Denken an Radikalität und das Handeln an Spielraum zurück"[19]. He is neither an empiricist for whom life consists of facts and figures, nor spokesman for a one-dimensional positivism. He regards reality as a space in which communication in freedom and respect really matters. Empirical observations do not get around to that. The transcendental nature of humans is nothing other (and nothing less) than the possibility to communicate with all that is, in a conscious, free and responsible way. Metaphysics is concerned with that possibility; it differs immensely from sciences that only observe and describe facts. This communication reaches into the nature of God, even though I can only fathom God's works (*potentia ordinata Dei*) and not penetrate the Secret of God (*potentia absoluta*

19. K. FLASCH, *Das philosophische Denken im Mittelalter von Augustin zu Machiavelli*, Stuttgart, Reclam, 1987, p. 451.

Dei)[20]. Thus the goal is not to fathom the O/other, but to meet and to cherish in a way that differs radically from the mentality of possessing, using, dominating, ignoring. Put differently, "Keine Bemühung um ein theoretisch in sich geschlossenes Weltbild, kein ideales Menschenbild, auf das hin der Mensch über sich selbst hinaus geführt werden soll, keine wissenschaftliche Systembildung, viel eher eine spürbare Zurückhaltung gegenüber übergreifenden Erklärungsversuchen; demgegenüber ein unabgeschlossener und auch unabschließbarer Dialog über Welt und Menschen auf Grund eines Wissens um die Ambivalenz der wahrgenommenen Phänomene, Vorrang des (u.U. kontingenten) Geschehens vor jedem 'Logos' usw. Aber sind das nur Negativa? Stand nicht hinter dem allem ein grundlegendes Wissen, das Israel im Bereich der ihm gegebenen Möglichkeiten und auch der ihm gesetzten Grenzen praktizierte? Daß sich nämlich die Wahrheit über die Welt und den Menschen nicht zum Gegenstand unseres theoretischen Erkennens hergibt; daß ein verläßliches Wissen nur im vertrauendem Umgang mit den Dingen zu gewinnen ist; daß es eine große Weisheit ist, von dem Versuch abzustehen, ihrer begrifflich Herr zu werden, daß es vielmehr weise ist, den Dingen ihr zuletzt doch immer rätselhaftes Wesen zu lassen, und das hieße, ihnen Raum zu geben, selbst aktiv zu werden, um durch ihre Sprache den Menschen zurechtzubringen"[21].

Even more emphatically than Pannenberg, Ockham would say: "Die Bindung metaphysischer Reflexion und Rekonstruktion an die Endlichkeit und Geschichtlichkeit der Erfahrungssituation, von der sie ihren Ausgang nimmt, lässt sich nicht überholen, sondern nur aufklären"[22]. By no means

20. For Ockham "potentia absoluta Dei" indicates God's mystery of which we may never attempt to take possession. We have to put our trust in what God (in Scripture, in the history of salvation) has done and said, without wanting to penetrate God's ultimate secrets. Against this thinking in terms of necessity of some medieval aristotelians "potentia absoluta Dei" wants to guarantee God's freedom. Contrary to assertions of H. BLUMENBERG, *Die Legitimität der Neuzeit*, Frankfurt, Suhrkamp, 1996 (erneuerte Ausgabe), it has nothing to do with a God of despotic arbitrariness and unreliability (cf. J. GOLDSTEIN, *Nominalismus und Moderne. Zur Konstitution neuzeitlicher Subjektivität bei Hans Blumenberg und Wilhelm von Ockham*, Freiburg – München, Alber, 1998). "Potentia ordinata Dei" refers to the divine ordinance in which we live. God is near to us with a number of "leges ordinatae et institutae" to protect us from foolishness. The most important ordinatio or cue is the poor Jesus. In our human wisdom we have to remain hearer of this Word. Revelation is not Selbstoffenbarung; even though God's word is reliable and without contradiction.

21. G. VON RAD, *Weisheit in Israel*, Neukirchen-Vluyn, Neukirchener Verlag, 1970, pp. 404-405.

22. W. PANNENBERG, *Metaphysik und Gottesgedanke*, Göttingen, Vandenhoeck & Ruprecht, 1988, p. 19.

the contingent worldly reality may be looked upon with contempt. Therefore I should not become detached, since God reveals Himself in it and stands up for it. As a result I should not react by speculating but by reasoning, in thankful doxological praise for God as the "gründende Grund des Seienden im Ganzen"[23]. But with caution, since terms like "Grund" and "Ganze" easily divert attention from the concrete or the singular.

Confirmation of God's omnipotence is nothing other than respectfully submitting to the fact that God's works excel in communication in freedom and respect. God can communicate in an ever-creative manner. The language of faith expresses this explicitly by crediting God with mercy, compassion, forgiveness and encouragement; the Whit Sunday hymn "*Veni Sancte Spiritu*" attributes this to the Holy Spirit. This space of compassion and mercy is also evoked at the beginning of mass in the hopeful Kyrie and the grateful Gloria. In theology these doxological or evocative terms are converted into propositions. In these propositions or is-sentences the horizon of doxology becomes subject of dialogue, in order to encourage new creativity to burst out and erupt. Then questions arise like: what exactly is said or meant here? What does this imply for concrete situations? That is expressed in many ways in Scripture and Tradition or in the "*communio sanctorum*" (holy matters, holy people). Those who listen well to them leave self-evidence behind and come to new reflection and communication. Not in order to create something new at any price, as if new automatically means better. We are often impressed by the wealth of old comprehension and expression and therefore like to keep them. That, however, is not necessarily the starting point of reflection.

VI. FAITH AND EVIDENCE

Ockham has no problems with what the church professes doxologically about God. His question is: how can we translate doxology in a scientific way? Can we clarify in an orderly fashion what we profess as believers about the nature and the horizon of life and God? That is not a new question, but it is posed more fiercely than ever in the academic environment to which Ockham belongs. First he states that God is free in an absolute sense and that we may not conceive him in terms of necessity. We have to allow for this realisation in language and understanding.

---

23. *Ibid.*, p. 11.

Thus we have to keep away from any type of necessitarism and acknowledge that there are limits to our rational explanations of the meaning and the wherefore of the world. Theological knowledge is not based upon necessities and does not concern an incontrovertible state of affairs, but concerns a contingency that is connected with freedom. The only necessity that is defended by theology is that we participate gratuitously in the freedom of God and offer others room to live from there. In following God we have to creatively surround the world with freedom and respect and thus establish shalom.

Who believes, concerns himself with the ways of God who acts in complete freedom and after his own good will. That is why Ockham hesitates at Anselm's phrase: "*credo ut intelligam*". To him it suffices that God's acting in freedom is without contradiction and not necessarily impossible; I do not have to fathom it from within or have to be able to explain it. Thus he wants to prevent "dass die vom Menschen betriebene Wissenschaft mit ihrer Forderung nach Notwendigkeit und Allgemeinheit in Gott irgendwelche Notwendigkeiten hineinträgt und so Gottes absolute Freiheit fehlinterpretiert ... Eine Theologie, welche sich zu einer Dogmatik verfestigt, die Gottes Freiheit einschränkt, verliert den Anspruch, wissenschaftlich ausweisbare Rede von Gott zu sein"[24]. That God acts without contradiction we can see. However we cannot design how God should act from our notions of non-contradiction, order and disorder. In retrospect we speak of non-contradiction and order, in gratitude.

What is called God's humanity in the language of faith, Ockham translates with the scientific term "*potestas ordinata*". With this he indicates among others that charity is without contradiction. It is possible therefore to relate to God and each other in an orderly fashion, respecting the singular being and freedom of others. As a creature of God every singular being is in principle good and precious; it deserves respect in advance. Experience teaches that we have trouble bringing ourselves to do this; we become tyrannical, trespass and attempt to subject others. We should, however, not shout ourselves down and not indulge in this type of behaviour but know when to stop. We have to take ourselves and others seriously. In this respect Ockham asks especially about myself: Who am I? How do I think? How do I act?" Not to strengthen my egocentrism, but to come to insight about the way we deal with one another.

What I say about God has to be in keeping with the way God speaks to me. I have to keep examining my insights. How are they brought about? Can they be justified? Do they do justice to the way that God

24. BECKMANN, *Wilhelm von Ockham* (n. 9), p. 148.

speaks? In God's Word I discover a trace of God. Don't I run off with it? Don't I jump to conclusions that are too fast and too far-reaching? Do I draw the right conclusion, such as the importance of freedom and respect? Ockham has great respect for traditions or dogmas of the church, precisely because they have arisen from praying and imploring. To him they are not merely hypotheses. But neither are they dogmas in the modern sense. They cause us to reflect because of the spiritual poverty in which they were conceived. That gives rise to gratitude. But they are human words, notions, and language. They continue to evoke thought on the condition that the thinker displays the same spiritual intensity.

This determines the status of hope doubly. First we hope that our insight in God's humanity is correct. Subsequently we approach the future with it "until he comes". We imagine what God's future will bring without absolute insight into the nature of God's charity. The terms, expressions and images of hope that live within us we have to surround with reserve, without obstructing the trusting surrender to God. This reserve should not end up in speculations about predestination that are pushed too far. Ockham puts his trust in God's humanity and does not limit God's mercy, without calculating.

This approach fits in with the emphasis on the viatorical nature of human existence. Our world is not founded in an order that encloses all singularities. A communication process is in progress, in which we should participate together and individually in freedom and respect. Revelation does not plug all the holes in our understanding but wants to help us to live in communication. It comes to us through people who are radically poor, who know how to become the servant of others and guard the tendency to rule in the name of subservience. Through them God hands us wise insights and challenging examples, that we may not expand to a worldview in which everything has been filled in and determined. God's word leaves room for free will and creativity. Everybody has to search for his own destination, inspired by the freedom that God offers and that Jesus found in his receptiveness characterized by a spirituality of poverty. God's will does not stand in the way of autonomy, as long as it listens to the commandment to "love God (God's Word) and neighbour as myself". Life is not determined by necessities. We have to reflect critically and be open to what is and happens around us.

This point of view contradicts a culture that demands absolute certainties and guarantees. It is at odds with the way in which revelation has been understood and theology has developed during past centuries. That order in the world is not based on immutable structures and positivist regulations, but is the beginning and the end of the acts of God and the standard for the relations in creation. It does not concern an arbitrary God (as Blumenberg states), but a God who opts for communication in freedom and respect. The desire for all-encompassing totalitarian systems is diametrically opposed to the notion of a cloud of not-knowing. To keep that notion alive, Ockham deems a spirituality (and practice) of poverty necessary. The church should resist the tendency to reason in an apodictic way. In the church our words and actions are surrounded by silence, in order to let the wise word of God sound and his hiddenness be respected. That fails if the views of John XXII on poverty and possession gain ground. In continuation of this Ockham raises protest against theologians who strive for an absolute knowledge and inconvertible conclusions. Theological research about the content and the meaning of God's word and our experience thereof (put differently, attempting an orderly theology) may not result in a system of necessities. We have to realise that our talking about God originates from the free initiative of God, in which not all of God's godness is revealed. Put in a Jewish way, we only know the aleph, the first letter of ani – I (am). Theology therefore is not scientia in the sense of Aristotle. That is: the word of God does not offer us the principle with which we can reason logically. God refuses flatly to be God in the way that we (sometimes, often) long for a God. In this sense Ockham seems rather a Jewish than a heathen-Christian[25].

Communication in freedom is "mehr als notwendig", but not arbitrary. The law of the Spirit "that is perfect and free" (Jas 1,25) can only be found if we take the risk allegorically, ethically and anagogically. In the kingdom of God not everything is definite, but laws are meant to serve freedom and respect. The kingdom of God is violated, as long as structures and individuals do not leave others room to live. In Auschwitz the negation of the singular cried to heaven. "Der gedanklichen Suprematie des Allgemeinen gegenüber dem Besonderen" ruled; there was no room for "kontingenzempfindliche Rationalität"[26]. Ockham stimulates the "intelligible Macht der Erinnerung" (152). As Adorno puts it: "Leiden beredt werden zu lassen, ist Bedingung aller Wahrheit" (153). In the communication with each other we should be led by "die Autorität der Leidenden" (156). Their authority should not evaporate in favour of a "höhere Allgemeinheit" (157) or a theological idealism (147). This way I understand the opinion of Nicholas of Cusa that truth calls in all streets

---

25. W. LOGISTER, *Een dramatische breuk. De plaats van Israël in de eerste eeuwen van het christendom*, Kampen, Kok, 1997, pp. 77-83.

26. J.B. METZ, *Gott und Zeit. Theologie und Metaphysik an den Grenzen der Moderne*, in *Stimmen der Zeit* 125 (2000) 147-159, p. 149. References in this paragraph refer to this article.

and alleys and that its voice should be heard before one starts practicing philosophy.

VII. CHRISTIAN EXISTENCE

The worldview of Ockham makes a sober impression. He does not fill reality with ideas or ideal worlds that would explain what I, you, and we are and do. Thus he wants to keep us from not taking ourselves and others sufficiently seriously. I am able to perceive myself, the world around me and God the way we are (truth), to respect our positive possibilities (goodness), to prevent conflicts (unity) and let everything shine in its own right (beauty). Transcendentalia are not well-defined domains. In the communication between me and others truth, goodness, unity and beauty have to be realised time and again, possibly with words and images, rituals and standards from the past. Provided that I appropriate them consciously and attentively and take responsibility for them, critically reflecting whether they are not carriers of "verzerrte Kommunikation" (Habermas). What the transcendentalia imply today and tomorrow I do not learn by staring at the heavens, but by looking at myself and others in a spirit of poverty and acting subsequently. In this I can learn much from those before me who have occupied themselves with truth, goodness, peace and beauty. However, I am and I remain responsible for what I say and do. The same is also true for Jesus. He is not the incarnation of a pre-existent Wisdom or Logos, but judges truly, acts justly, makes peace and makes everything find its own lustre. Ockham refuses to substantialise Wisdom, Logos etc. He does acknowledge an "ordre d'origine" between Father and Son, "mais aucunement entre l'essence divine (qui serait ici posée comme première) et sa sagesse"[27].

During the Eucharist Christ comes present again as witness of God's humanity for the entire world. In radical poverty Christ meets God and people without hybrid claims. Thus as the Son he shares the nature of the Father and of us (homoousios) and is the image of who God wants to be for us and how we may be and become human beings. He is this without laying claim to possession. In the way he communicates, lustre arises that lifts others up and encourages them. Any place where the name of Christ is celebrated, true communion and communication arise and the kingdom of freedom, that is the kingdom of God breaks through in all areas of life. In that kingdom one allows the singular

27. BIARD, *Ockham et la Théologie* (n. 11), p. 71.

nature of the other to blossom and institutions no longer arise for the sake of those institutions nor for the sake of its servants. In his explanation of transubstantiation, Ockham says that bread and wine are fully determined by Christ who holds them without him behaving like the owner. The ability to be determined by another that characterises the *being* of bread and wine and even more freely the *being* of Christ, should also determine the person who becomes one with Christ during Holy Communion.

The power of Christ shows its nature in the fact that he lets others be, that he frees from fixation on certainty (that eventually results in fixation on chance and fate) and stimulates to look around in open creativity. He opposes a plurality that stands in the way of unity or shalom, but his ideal of unity is also at right angles to eurocentrism, imperialism and totalitarianism. Nevertheless it is not a perspective that evaporates constantly. The appeal to devote to God with all the heart, all the soul and all the mind has a tenor with respect to content: equality of all people, respect for each other, offering each other space. It supposes kenosis. This kenosis is *"id quo magis cogitari nequit"* or the absolute moment; which is not negotiable; which cannot be relativated. Kenotic existence should become the breadth and length and height and depth of life (Eph 3,18). It is the ground, the foundation, the rock that enables nations, cultures and religions to relate without imperialism. In that sense I read Vaticanum II: "But whatever truth and grace are to be found among the nations, as a sort of secret presence of God, this activity frees from all taint of evil and restores to Christ its maker, who overthrows the devil's domain and wards off the manifold malice of vice" (*Ad Gentes* 9). The deeds and words of Jesus are the exemplary form of this kenosis.

In the Christian divine ordinance freedom goes hand in hand with poverty, i.e. with not ruling over each other, not trapping each other in necessities. Jesus shows how people may offer each other room and thus become children of God. His radical openness is not without structure; it has a law, a line, and dynamics: letting be. This law should be the yeast in every dimension of life. In the name and the space of God this becomes possible. The qualities or characteristics that we attribute to God, relate to this offering of space. They indicate that God's creative possibilities are directed at what they intend. Believing is stepping into the space of all those possibilities, even though at first sight an abyss or the loss of all certainty threatens. What happens to me, if I depend upon the grace and the mercy of others? Christian truth unfolds from the promise that this threat does not have the last word. Who enters the space of grace and mercy and of communication that arises there, gains life.

The Christian vision of reality and life gets sidelined, if I put myself forward in order to win a position and establish my Ego. This "*incurvatio in seipsum*" is diametrically opposed to the shalom that Jesus wants to establish in the name of God. That Ego demands clarity, because otherwise it feels threatened. Clarity is a basis for ruling and exercising power. Because others cause a break in that desire, they become a threat. Biblical faith emerges in another space and has a different perspective. The horizon of my destination changes. Listening to the O/other and letting him be, become fundamental. In that communication dawns what truth is and how it enters life. Kenosis, poverty, letting be, not clinging to imperialistic ideas about God and truth belong to the core of Christian divine ordinance. Any claim to truth should relate to this. It is the heart of the "*hierarchia veritatum*" and the "*articulus stantis et cadentis ecclesiae*". We exist thanks to a potentia that lets us be. Claims of truth that are contradictory to this, are untrue, false, heretical. Contingent beings, however, easily yield to the temptation to start thinking and acting imperialistically. The claims to truth that they propose thus become – theologically speaking – perilous.

VIII. THE CHALLENGE OF OCKHAM

Ockham stresses the frailness of culture and tradition, also in church. All too easily they are taken for granted as foundation and become something like "potentia absoluta". In Ockham's opinion, one not only makes oneself all too comfortable that way, but also gets trapped in rigidity. Communication in freedom and respect has to be realised again and again. Tradition can assist in this, but Ockham recognizes in much of tradition and in living the tradition, the possessive mentality of John XXII. He cannot protest too much against it.

Many Catholics regard this criticism and actualism of Ockham as a step towards the Reformation. According to them, the theology of Ockham is at the expense of the real presence of God (and Christ) in creation, in the Eucharist and in ecclesiastical structures. This assessment is linked in my opinion with the difficulty mentioned above that one demands a certainty in the line of aristotelianism, that differs from the experience of God's presence in the first millennium. That demand is diametrically opposed to the old Christian conviction that the letter is only correctly experienced as Word of God, if the person who hears, is set in motion spiritually, allegorically, morally and anagogically. In that sense God's Word wants to challenge life in one great, hopeful and patient encounter in freedom and respect.

Ockham wants to prevent the Word and everything that the Word creatively calls to life from being deformed into a motionless substance in which God is within reach. The word is more lively, free and communicative. It is the word of a God who cherishes this liveliness, freedom and communication and that creates human beings in a exceptional way in order to hear the word and fulfill it. The person and the life of Jesus Christ are permeated with that. That should also be the horizon of expectation, when Christians gather around him to break the bread. However, the knowledge, the insight and the life that well up from it, only remain authentic in a setting of radical spirituality of poverty. This insight of St. Francis has been defended by Ockham against John XXII. Karl Rahner once said that the Christian of the future has to be a mystic. Ockham pictures the Christian as poor. Poverty is the core of his mysticism and of his view of Christianity with a future.

Theologische Faculteit Tilburg   Wiel LOGISTER
Universiteit van Tilburg
Academielaan 9
NL-5037 ET Tilburg
The Netherlands

DIVINE TRANSCENDENCE AND
THE "LANGUAGES OF PERSONAL RESONANCE"

THE WORK OF CHARLES TAYLOR AS A RESOURCE
FOR SPIRITUALITY IN AN ERA OF POST-MODERNITY

The focal text for this essay is the final chapter of Charles Taylor's *Sources of the Self: The Making of the Modern Identity*, which he has titled "The Conflicts of Modernity" (Chapter 25). I shall argue that this chapter, in ways that are at once provocative and richly allusive – yet also fragmentary and frustratingly elusive – has embedded within it resources for a spirituality appropriate to a culture standing on the cusp between modernity and post-modernity.

The confines of this essay do not allow rehearsing the full scope of the arguments constructed throughout *Sources of the Self* by which Taylor reaches the most encompassing of the conclusions about "the making of the modern identity" enunciated in this chapter. I thus simply take as a given starting point the reliability of the account he offers of "the modern self" and of the polarities that emerged in the long historical process of its construction – polarities that have more recently been named, dissected and dismantled by various forms of post-modernism. These polarities arise within and across the elements of the modern "sense of self" that Taylor takes to be "defined by the powers of disengaged reason as well as of the creative imagination, in the characteristically modern understandings of freedom and dignity and rights, in the ideals of self-fulfilment and expression and in the demands of universal benevolence and justice"[1]. These polarities, moreover, pose in concert a serious challenge to the very possibility of construing the spiritual as a constitutive element of the deepest part of our reality as human and thereby rule out spirituality as an intelligible form of human activity.

In order to uncover the resources that Taylor's work provides for spirituality in a post-modern age, it will be useful to start with an examination of the strategy he proposes for addressing the most intractable of the

---

1. C. TAYLOR, *Sources of the Self: The Making of the Modern Identity*, Cambridge, Cambridge University Press, 1989, p. 503.

polarities he diagnoses in the dynamics of the modern self. He formulates this polarity as "the general truth that the highest spiritual ideals and aspirations also threaten to lay the most crushing burdens on humankind" and then observes that "[t]he great spiritual visions of human history have also been poisoned chalices, the causes of untold misery and even savagery"[2]. Behind his remarks is an earlier discussion (Chapter 3) of "hypergoods" i.e., "goods which not only are incomparably more important than others but provide the standpoint from which these [other goods] must be weighed, judged, decided about"[3]. Taylor argues that the naturalist tendencies of modern moral theory – which rule hypergoods out of their explicit accounts of moral justification – have thereby occluded the "qualitative difference" so "central to much of our moral life, [namely] that something incomparably important is involved" in our moral conduct[4]. Although Taylor is well aware that many factors have played a role in such discrediting of hypergoods and the qualitative differences they indicate, he is most interested in bringing to the foreground the moral concerns that, even as they have fueled the engine of this naturalist critique, have themselves become opaque in consequence of that critique. The most prominent of these moral concerns cluster around the perception that, however noble the ideals that hypergoods inspire, they also have enormous power to distort, dominate and crush. Taking cognizance of more recent manifestations of that concern, such as Foucault's insight into "the ways in which high ethical and spiritual ideas are often interwoven with exclusions and relations of domination" and the feminist critique "that certain conceptions of the life of the spirit exclude women, accord them a lesser place, or assume their subordination", Taylor then observes: "The sense that in this and other ways hypergoods can stifle or oppress us has been one of the motives for the naturalist revolt against traditional morality and religion"[5].

As Taylor sees it, this revolt has not been without its own price – especially in view of the fact that the twentieth century has shown that religion has no monopoly on the destructive power of hypergoods: "The Kharkov famine and the Killing Fields were perpetrated by atheists in an attempt to realize the most lofty ideals of human perfection"[6]. In the face of such destruction, a "sober, scientific minded secular humanism" takes the polarity embedded within hypergoods as a dilemma that

2. *Ibid.*, p. 519.
3. *Ibid.*, p. 63.
4. *Ibid.*, p. 87.
5. *Ibid.*, pp. 518-519.
6. *Ibid.*, p. 519.

is inescapable. It therefore advises the "prudent strategy" of managing the dilemma "by stifling the response in us to some of the deeper and most powerful spiritual aspirations that human beings have conceived"[7]. It is a strategy of self-induced amnesia of the spiritual in the name of getting on with life[8]. Although Taylor acknowledges that this strategy may very well be "a good way to live with the dilemma", he also quite cuttingly characterizes the choice it presents us with as one "between various kinds of spiritual lobotomy and self-inflicted wounds"[9].

This strategy simply will not do because Taylor does not consider the dilemma that "a stripped down secular outlook" perceives within moral perspectives framed by hypergoods to be an *inescapable* one. He does not take it to be the case that "that the highest spiritual aspirations must lead to mutilation or destruction"[10]. Even in the aftermath of modernity, he contends, we can rightly and coherently affirm our human possibilities in terms of such aspirations – but only to the extent we can legitimately articulate them by reference to a hope of the kind that is instanced (though not exclusively) in "Judeo-Christian theism and in its central promise of a divine affirmation of the human, more total than humans can ever attain unaided"[11]. In this chapter Taylor thus connects his earlier analyses of the "inarticulacy" of moral life lived in accord with the ideals and demands of modernity to the claims he now sketches that the moral sources empowering the highest human spiritual aspirations can be articulated most adequately from "a certain theistic perspective"[12]. These connections could be rendered, I believe, into a intriguing variant of a "moral argument" for God – but as challenging as that line of inquiry would be, it is not my focus here.

I am more concerned, instead, with exploring and understanding the proposal he sketches for removing our "selective blindness" about the goods that would fully empower the human spirit, and thereby restoring our articulacy about them – as well as our articulacy about our humanity as itself spiritual in its constitutive reality. This proposal instances the intent with which he has shaped the trajectory of *Sources of the Self* to be a work that is not mere diagnosis but also an aid to "liberation"

---

7. *Ibid.*, p. 519.
8. For a more extensive treatment of this, see P. Rossi, *The Leveling of Meaning: Christian Ethics in the Face of a Culture of Unconcern*, in J. Runzo – N. Martin (eds.), *Ethics in the World Religions*, Oxford, Oneworld Publications, 2001, pp. 161-174.
9. Taylor, *Sources* (n. 1), p. 520.
10. *Ibid.*, p. 520-521.
11. *Ibid.*, p. 521
12. *Ibid.*, p. 518.

from ways that "we tend in our culture to stifle the spirit"[13]. The path that he charts to such liberation lies through the devising of "new languages of personal resonance to make crucial human goods alive for us again"[14]. This kind of language is needed, he claims, "because we are now in an age in which a publicly accessible order of cosmic meanings is an impossibility. The only way we can explore the order in which we are set with an aim to defining moral sources is through this part of personal resonance"[15].

The phrase "new languages of personal resonance" is certainly apt rhetorically in that it indicates the need for a new form of articulacy about matters of the [human] spirit that "have been read out of our official story". Yet, to the extent that it also suggests that such new articulacy issues primarily from the very kind of "inwardness" of the self that has been deconstructed in post-modernist critiques, it seems also problematic with respect to the central issues it is supposed to address. The proximate origin of this notion of "languages of personal resonance" lies in what Taylor terms the "expressivist" strand of 19th and 20th century art and literature. He is well aware that a crucial issue with respect to such "languages" – and, a fortiori to his proposal that they are important to the recovery of the spiritual in human life – is that they are vulnerable to the same charges of subjectivism that he would himself acknowledge are often legitimately leveled against the expressivist movements that first articulated them. Put in terms of our conference theme of "Theology and Conversation", the issue is whether such "languages" must remain trapped by origins that stamp them in some indelible fashion with a monological character – or can they, instead, function as modes of genuine conversation engaging selves with other selves who stand in a social wholeness that is itself referred to a transcendent divine Other. While Taylor implies that "languages of personal resonance" can function conversationally, he does not mount a full scale argument to show this – and so is my hope that the rest of this essay can provide at least an initial sketch of three of the important elements that are needed to mount such an argument.

The first important element needed to move these suggestive claims about the languages of personal resonance to a more clearly delineated

---

13. *Ibid.*, p. 520. "The intention of this work was one of retrieval, an attempt to recover buried goods through rearticulation – and thereby to make those sources again empower, to bring the air back again into the half collapsed lungs of the spirit".

14. *Ibid.*, p. 513.

15. *Ibid.*, p. 512.

argument justifying their role in liberating us from the self-stifling of the spirit is, at best, only partially given in *Sources of the Self*. Moreover, because it is given quite early on (Chapter 2), it is quite easy to overlook as an operative element in the claims set forth in the concluding chapter. This element is one that Taylor terms "the transcendental condition of interlocution"[16]. It inescapably links a self's identity – of which a fundamental function for Taylor is a self-interpretation that operates in a "space" of meaning and value – to "a defining community" in terms of "webs of interlocution"[17]. Taylor puts this conversational locus for a self's identity in forceful terms:

> ... My self definition is understood as an answer to the question Who am I. And this question finds its original sense in the interchange of speakers. I define who I am by defining where I speak from, in the family tree, in social space, in the geography of social statuses and functions, in my intimate relations to the ones I love, and also crucially *in the space of moral and spiritual orientation within which my most important defining relations are lived out.*
> *This obviously cannot be a contingent matter. There is no way we could be inducted into personhood except by being initiated into a language.* We first learn our languages of moral and spiritual discernment by being brought into an ongoing conversation by those who bring us up[18]. (Emphasis added)

"Languages of personal resonance" thus need to be understood to stand *within* this transcendental condition of interlocution, not as an exception to it. Placed within this condition, their origin from the "inwardness" of particular human individuals does not render them ineluctably monological; on the contrary, it orders them to the conversational.

Taylor's placement of these languages under the condition of "interlocution", however, may seem to many to be an *obiter dicta* that stands in tension with what is often taken to be the trajectory of the history from which "expressivist" understandings of the human person have emerged. According to this version of that history, the strands of science, literature, art and philosophy that weave into modern notions of

---

16. *Ibid.*, p. 39. Taylor's frames this understanding of the self in terms of self-interpretation – and the related categories of meaning and strong evaluation – to be a programmatic counterweight to naturalist accounts of the human i.e., those that model the study of the human on the natural sciences. He gives an overview of this program in the introductions to *Human Agency and Language: Philosophical Papers I*, Cambridge, Cambridge University Press, 1985 and *Philosophy & the Human Sciences: Philosophical Papers II*, Cambridge, Cambridge University Press, 1985, a collection of essays published prior to *Sources of the Self*.

17. *Ibid.*, p. 36.

18. *Ibid.*, p. 35.

the self have made it possible to deny that selves stand under the necessity of the condition of interlocution. Taylor describes this view quite pointedly:

> Modern culture has developed conceptions of individualism which picture the human person as, at least potentially, finding his or her own bearings within, declaring independence from the web of interlocution which have originally formed him/her, or at least neutralizing them. It's as though the dimension of interlocution were of significance only for the genesis of individuality, like the training wheels of nursery school, to be left behind and to play no part in the finished person[19].

Not surprisingly, Taylor views such a monological rendering of the self's identity to be incoherent – as well as dangerous. At the same time, however, he is very much aware that "there is a common picture of the self, as (at least potentially and ideally) drawing its purposes, goals and life-plans out of itself, seeking 'relationships' only insofar as they are 'fulfilling'", and that this picture manifests the "hold of certain deeply entrenched modes of thought in modern culture"[20]. When understood as part of this picture, languages of personal resonance would indeed seem to be nothing but monological; but this conclusion goes counter to a key aspect of the "liberation" envisioned in *Sources of the Self* to be effected – at least in part – through languages of personal resonance, viz., loosening the hold this very picture of the monological self has upon the thought and imagination of modern culture. On Taylor's account, the monological self neither historically nor conceptually arises primarily in consequence of expressivist understandings of the human person; rather, those understandings have themselves been swept up into a monological trajectory that seeks to strip them away from any condition of interlocution.

Accounting for the grip that such a monological view has had upon modern thought is thus essential to the liberation Taylor hopes to effect in *Sources of the Self*. The account he gives, moreover, indicates that opposition to monological theories of language was itself fundamental to the historical origins of expressivism. As noted at the outset, retelling that account in all its complex historical and conceptual detail is not within the purview of this essay. I shall only attempt here to identify two elements in that account that I believe – in addition to his claim about the transcendental condition of interlocution – are needed to construct an argument on behalf of the conversational function of languages of personal resonance for "bring[ing] air back again into the half-collapsed

19. *Ibid.*, p. 36.
20. *Ibid.*, pp. 38-39.

lungs of the spirit"[21]. The remainder of this essay will thus bring these two elements into focus and indicate their importance for that argument.

One element arises from Taylor's analysis of the problematic character of designative accounts of language and meaning that he sees arising in connection with the seventeenth century scientific revolution. These accounts played a key role in "[t]he philosophies of the seventeenth century [that] remade our conceptions of man, thought and knowledge to fit the new [scientific] dispensation"[22]. He alludes to this in his discussion of the transcendental condition of interlocution when he notes that "the early modern theories of language, from Hobbes through Locke to Condillac, presented it as an instrument potentially inventable by individuals"[23]. He does not, however, elaborate any further on this in *Sources of the Self*; he instead makes reference to an earlier essay, "Language and Human Nature", in which he analyses and criticizes those theories in the light of an alternate account, originating with Herder, according to which "language is not just a set of words which designate things; it is the vehicle of this kind of reflective awareness. This reflection is a capacity which we only realize in speech"[24]. He then expands this remark along the following lines:

> What, then does language come to be on this view? A pattern of activity by which we express/realize a certain way of being in the world, that of reflective awareness but a pattern which can only be deployed only against a background we can never fully dominate; yet a background that we are never fully dominated by, since we are constantly reshaping it. Reshaping it without dominating it, or being able to oversee it, means that we never fully know what we are doing to it ...
> ... If language serves to express/realize a new kind of awareness; then it may not only make possible a new awareness of things, an ability to describe them; but also new ways of feeling, of responding to things. If in expressing our thoughts about things we can come to new thoughts, then in expressing our feelings we can come to have transformed feelings[25].

Taylor sees Herder's expressivist understanding of language helping to launch a trajectory for understandings of the self that, even as they value

21. *Ibid.*, p. 520.
22. TAYLOR, *Language and Human Nature*, in ID., *Human Agency* (n. 16), p. 224.
23. ID., *Sources* (n. 1), p. 38.
24. ID., *Language* (n. 22), pp. 228-229. Also relevant are his essays, *Theories of Meaning*, in TAYLOR, *Human Agency* (n. 16), pp. 248-292 and *The Importance of Herder*, in TAYLOR, *Philosophical Arguments*, Cambridge, Harvard University Press, 1995, pp. 79-99. In the latter he notes (p. 92) that for Herder "expression *constitutes* the linguistic dimension" and "language comes about as a new *reflective* stance toward things" (emphases added).
25. TAYLOR, *Language* (n. 22), pp. 232-233; he reiterates this in *The Importance of Herder* (n. 24), p. 97.

"inwardness", move in directions quite counter to a monological subjective individualism. These expressivist understandings are anti-subjectivist inasmuch as their "inwardness" provides a route of access for locating the self within a web of meaning that is larger than the self. In "the epiphanies of modernism", which Taylor references to writers such as Rilke, Joyce, Mann, and Wallace Stevens, he finds a "multilevelled consciousness [that] is thus frequently 'decentered'; aware of living on a transpersonal rhythm which is mutually irreducible to the personal"[26].

Taylor thus finds that these forms of expressivist understanding hold forth possibilities for an "interweaving of the subjective and the transcendent"[27]. Such interweaving can then provide a basis on which to shape a spirituality appropriate to the human circumstances that Taylor describes as facing us in consequence of the polarities of modernity. This possibility – and the spirituality it can engender – may appear quite surprising if the origins of expressivist accounts of language and meaning are seen, as they most often are, in terms of a history of the inexorable progress of the forces of secularization. Taylor, however, vigorously contests this telling of history in *Sources of the Self* and suggests, in its stead, that we read the development of expressivist understandings of language, meaning, and self against the background of the Christian doctrines of creation and of grace. The link that Taylor makes between an expressivist account of language and the Christian doctrines of creation and transfiguring grace is the third element that I think needs to enter into the construction of an argument showing how "languages of personal resonance" can function conversationally to "bring air back again into the half-collapsed lungs of the spirit".

Taylor finds this link in the history he recounts of the modern preoccupation with language. Behind designative theories of meaning lies the medieval nominalisms that rejected an ontology that had an expressivist theory of meaning embedded in it: this, however, was not a theory of human but of the divine language:

> ... Just as our thought is clothed externally in our words, so is the thought of God, the *Logos* – the *Verbum* for Augustine – deployed externally in the creation. This is, as it were, God's speech ...
> ... the paradigm and model of our deploying signs is God's creation. But now God's creation is to be understood expressively. His creatures manifest his *logos* in embodying it; and they manifest the *logos* as fully as it can be manifest in the creaturely medium ...[28].

26. ID., *Sources* (n. 1), p. 481.
27. *Ibid.*, p. 493.
28. TAYLOR, *Language* (n. 22), p. 223.

Human language thus is secondary in this account, and Taylor acknowledges that the nominalist rejection of this "discourse-thought model of the real" gave human language a far more central role. That role, however, is one of

> ... an instrument of control in the assemblage of ideas which is thought or mental discourse. It is an instrument of control in gaining knowledge of the world as objective process. And so it must itself be perfectly transparent; it cannot itself be the locus of mystery, that is of anything which might be irreducible to objectivity ...
> ... the alternative is to lose control, to slip into a kind of slavery; where it is no longer I who make my lexicon, by definitional fiat, but rather it takes shape independently and in doing shapes my thought. It is an alienation of my freedom as well as the great source of illusion; and this is why the men of this age combated the cosmos of meaningful order with such determination[29].

In this context, Herder's challenge to a designative account continued to see human language as central but offered a strikingly different understanding of its role: "language is not just a set of words which designate things; it is the vehicle of ... reflective awareness"[30].

Herder thus reinstates the earlier expressivist theory, but as a theory of language, rather than of the cosmos. According to Taylor, Herder and other expressivist theorists "transposed what belongs to God on this older theory on to man. For man like God embodies his ideas and makes them manifest. But unlike God, man needs his expression to make his ideas manifest ... his ideas do not properly exist before their expression in language or some other of the media men deploy"[31]. Taylor is aware, of course, that this transposition of expressive power from the creative activity of God to the articulations of meaning in human language has taken trajectories along which lie the displacement of God – be it terms of an explicit atheistic denial of God or a pantheistic collapse of the difference between God and the world. While the credibility of the latter – at least in the form that Taylor terms the "too indulgent pantheism" of Romanticism – has receded, Taylor does not think that we must inevitably be drawn along the atheistic trajectory. There is a choice:

> Is the expression which makes us human essentially a self-expression, in that we are mainly responding to our way of feeling/responding the world, and bringing this to expression? Or are we responding to the reality in which we are set, in which we are included, of course, but which is not reducible to our experience of it[32]?

29. *Ibid.*, p. 226.
30. *Ibid.*, pp. 228-229.
31. *Ibid.*, p. 229.
32. *Ibid.*, p. 239.

Using language he will later echo in *Sources of the Self* when describing moral sources as "something the love of which empowers us to be and do good"[33], Taylor sides with a choice for the latter:

> Some contemporaries would argue that the most expressive creations, hence those where we are closest to deploying our expressive power at the fullest, are not self expressions; that they rather have the power to move us because they manifest our expressive power itself and its relation to the world. In this kind of expression we are responding to the way things are, rather than just exteriorizing our feelings[34].

There is a further connection Taylor makes between a Christian understanding of creation and this capacity of such expressive power to move us to be and to do good that has a bearing upon the function of "languages of personal resonance". He makes this connection in terms of the affirmation of the goodness of creation.

Taylor claims that "a stark rejection of any spiritual dimension may easily engender a sense that the affirmation [of the goodness of nature] is insufficiently based, that there isn't much to affirm at all"[35]. In such a context, Taylor thinks it is necessary, even for those within a Christian theological "tradition [of] affirming the goodness of nature ... to find new languages to say what they wanted to say"[36] in this affirmation. He finds resources for such a new languages in the expressivist tradition, particularly as it understands such affirmation to involve "a transfiguration of our own vision, rather than simply ... a recognition of some objective order of goodness ... it may have to take the form of a transformation of our stance toward the world and self, rather than simply the registering of external reality"[37]. In his account of such transformation, moreover, Taylor portrays it in terms of a link between creation and grace:

> What we have in this new issue of affirming the goodness of things is the development of a human analogue to God's seeing things as good: a seeing which also helps effect what it sees. This can mean, of course, that the self-attribution of this power is a resolutely atheist doctrine, the arrogation to man of powers formerly confined to God. This will be so with Nietzsche ... But this doesn't have to be so. One of the most insightful thinkers to explore this power is Dostoyevsky, who sees it in a Christian perspective. In fact the notion of a transformation of our stance towards the world whereby our vision is changed has traditionally been connected with the notion of grace. Augustine holds that in relation to God, love has to precede

33. TAYLOR, *Sources* (n. 1), p. 93.
34. ID., *Language* (n. 22), p. 239.
35. ID., *Sources* (n. 1), p. 448.
36. *Ibid.*, p. 446.
37. *Ibid.*, p. 448.

knowledge. With the right direction of love, things become evident which are hidden otherwise. What is new is the modern sense of the place and power of the creative imagination. This is now an integral part of the goodness of things, and hence the transformation of our stance and thus our outlook helps bring about the truth it reveals[38].

The mention of Augustine is not a mere passing remark, inasmuch as Taylor had earlier characterized "the expressivist revolution" as "a prodigious development of modern post-Augustinian inwardness in its self-exploratory branch"[39]. That development, however, has been one in which a fundamental Augustinian trajectory has been rendered problematic. In an age of post-modernity it cannot be taken for granted that exploration of "inner" will take a path by which we are also – be it by a Platonic attraction to the good or by the irresistibility of grace – drawn to the "higher". At the same time, Taylor claims that, in circumstances in which "a publicly accessible order of cosmic meanings is an impossibility", such an exploration of inwardness is needed to make it possible for us to have access to very goods that have been occluded by modernity.

In consequence, in order to make "languages of personal resonance" a fundamental resource for spirituality, ways must be found to restore credibility to the Augustinian trajectory that draws us to the higher along the path of the inner. How might this be done? I believe that Taylor provides at least two clues for this: the first is in his identification of the kinds of goods to which he thinks we have access primarily "through personal sensibility ... for instance, why it matters and what it means to have a more resonant human environment, and even more, to have affiliations with some depth in time and commitment"[40]; the second is in a remark he makes about Dostoyevsky, who "brings together a central idea of the Christian tradition, especially evident in the Gospel of John, that people are transformed through being loved by God, a love that they mediate to each other, on one hand, with the modern notion of a subject who can help to bring on transfiguration by the stance he takes to himself and the world, on the other"[41]. As I read these remarks – particularly in the light of the important connections that I see them affirming between creation and grace – they suggest a spirituality in which "personal resonance" is attuned with and to "a demand that our natural surrounding

38. *Ibid.*, p. 449.
39. *Ibid.*, p. 389.
40. *Ibid.*, p. 513.
41. *Ibid.*, p. 452.

and wilderness make on us"[42] and also with and to the most abiding affiliative relationship to which we have been granted graced access – the trinitarian dynamic of God's own life. As a Jesuit, I cannot help but thinking that what Taylor allusively suggests can be placed in continuity with the spirituality of the *Spiritual Exercises* with its attentiveness to the inner movement of God's grace in the individual and its deep rooting in the theology of Creation and the Trinity – but that is work for another essay.

Department of Theology   Philip ROSSI, S.J.
Marquette University
100 Coughlin Hall
P.O. Box 1881
Milwaukee, WI 53201-1881
U.S.A.

---

42. *Ibid.*, p. 513.

PRAYER AS UTOPIAN MEMORY

I. INTRODUCTION

In this paper I would like to present some results of my current research[1], which can be situated within the wider theme of theology and conversation. I shall confine my presentation to two items. First I shall consider a specific form of theological communication, or, in other words, I shall say something about theology *on* communication. Here, I am referring to prayer as communication between God and humans. Second, I shall try to illustrate by means of an example how such a theology can communicate. In other words: I would like to offer some reflections about theology *as* communication, especially as communication with other disciplines.

In the first part of my paper, I shall base my thoughts mainly on the theology of Karl Barth, more specifically "Paragraph" 76 of his *Church Dogmatic*, entitled "Der Vater und seine Kinder" (The Father and His Children). This paragraph is to be found in the unfinished Part Four of his doctrine of reconciliation, and is thus part of the ethics of reconciliation[2]. There, Barth structures his ethical approach so as to correspond to the petitions of the Lord's Prayer, and in "Paragraph" 76 he concentrates especially on the first part of the first petition, the "Anrufung", or invocation of God as a Father in heaven[3].

---

1. See also S. HENNECKE, *Zu dritt, oder: Das Gebet als eine utopische Erinnerung*, in M. DE HAARDT – A.-M. KORTE (eds.), *Common Bodies. Everyday Practices, Gender and Religion* (Theologische Frauenforschung in Europa, 6), Münster, LIT, 2002, pp. 157-176.
2. See K. BARTH, *Das christliche Leben*, in *Die Kirchliche Dogmatik* IV/4: *Fragmente aus dem Nachlaß und Vorlesungen 1959-1961*, Zürich, 1999.
3. Other important thoughts about the prayer in the theology of Barth are to be found in KD II.1, pp. 574 ff., KD III.3, pp. 299 ff., KD III.4, pp. 95 ff., KD IV.1, pp. 643 ff., KD IV.2., pp. 797 ff., KD IV.4. (Das christliche Leben), §77-78, Das Vaterunser, pp. 19-39. For a more general review of the thoughts of Barth concerning prayer see O. HERLYN, *Religion oder Gebet. Karl Barths Bedeutung für ein religionsloses Christentum*, Neukirchen-Vluyn, 1979. For more recent research about the meaning of the Lord's Prayer as it is presented by Barth see H. RUDDIES, *Anrufung Gottes. Das Gebet als Grundgedanke des christlichen Lebens bei Karl Barth*, in *Zeitschrift für dialektische Theologie* 17 (2001) 8-24; G. NEVEN, *Schlichter Verantwortlichkeit: Über das christliche Leben im Kontext der Versöhnung*, in *Zeitschrift für dialektische Theologie* 17 (2001) 37-49.

In the second part, I consider more how theology itself can communicate and shall introduce some thoughts of the French feminist philosopher and psychoanalyst Luce Irigaray[4]. My specific interest here is to initiate a dialogue between Barth and Irigaray. My aim is thus to facilitate a conversation between the theology of Barth on the one hand, and the more secular, feminist ideas of a French philosopher on the other[5]. My final question, then, is: How do I challenge the dialectical theology of Barth from the vantage point of a feminist philosophy of difference? Is it possible to articulate this theology in terms of difference?

Limited by the extent of this paper I can, of course, do no more than present some highlights from the work of these two thinkers, and I shall not get beyond an initial encounter between Barth and Irigaray on the subject of prayer. As a first step, however, it seems useful for me to explore the possibility of articulating Barth's theology in terms of difference.

II. THEOLOGY ON COMMUNICATION

I start with my first point, i.e. prayer as communication between God and humans as it is presented in the theology of Karl Barth. According to Barth, the Word of God constitutes a double relationship: that of God to humanity, and (vice versa) of humanity to God. Prayer can be seen as the concrete practice of this double relationship. Prayer, as the concrete practice of the double relationship and like the theological ethic more generally, is thus not to be seen as separate from dogma, but rather as included in dogmatic thinking.

When we attend to the literary structure of paragraph 76, we see that Barth treats the subject of prayer in three sections.

In the first section, he discusses the subject of God the Father, who is to be addressed. Following the first petition of the Lord's Prayer, Barth stresses, among other things, that God the Father must be regarded as an "original vocative". That is to say, God is a speaking and acting Person

---

4. For an introduction of Irigaray's work see A. HALSEMA, *Dialectiek van de seksuele differentie. De filosofie van Luce Irigaray*, Amsterdam, 1998; A.-C. MULDER, *Divine Flesh, Embodied Word. Incarnation as a Hermeneutical Key to a Feminist Theologian's Reading of Luce Irigaray's Work* (unpublished dissertation), Amsterdam, 2000; M. WHITFORD, *Luce Irigaray. Philosophy in the Feminine*, London – New York, 1991.

5. An earlier project to initiate an encounter between the theology of Barth and the philosophy of Irigaray, especially on the subject of the Creed, can be found in S. HENNECKE, *Der vergessene Schleier. Ein theologisches Gespräch zwischen Luce Irigaray und Karl Barth*, Gütersloh, 2001.

with whom one must speak in an interpersonal way. It excludes, for example, the possibility of speaking in an objective way. It means speaking *with*, rather than *about*. According to Barth the truth and reality of God the Father are not explicit subjects for the praying person. Here, Christians are merely following a directive that has already been established by Jesus Christ. Prayer is an imitation of the decision of Christ; it is following him, discipleship.

In the second section, Barth discusses the subject of humanity, who has to address God. Here he inquires how the relationship between God and humanity can really be a possibility from the human point of view. On the one hand, a relationship with God implies great intimacy between humans and God. On the other hand, this supposition is contradicted by another important notion in the theology of Barth, namely the well-known supposition of an infinite qualitative difference between God and humanity, the great distance between the two, the impossibility of any contact. In Barth's view, the possibility of this impossibility is realised by thinking these two suppositions together. If we think both aspects, the intimacy and the distance, together, then we can speak of an impossible possibility. What is thus made possible is not grounded ontologically, but rather theologically: The possibility of this intimacy is given only through the free grace of God, which became concrete in the history of Jesus Christ.

Thus, we may conclude that, in the first two sections on prayer, Barth looks forward to something concrete beyond both God's self and faithful human beings in themselves. This event beyond God and humanity is Jesus Christ. According to Barth, this event liberates humans from any doubtful questions about the truth and reality of God's self. God's reality and truth is not an open question to Christians, because here they have only to follow what Jesus Christ has already decided in the place of humanity. This event also makes it clear and tangible that the essence of God is divine grace. God's grace constitutes human subjects as *always already* related to God. In this way, Jesus Christ liberates human beings from all pious duties.

Last but not least, let me turn to the third section of the paragraph, entitled "Die Anrufung", the invocation. This section is the most important in the whole "Paragraph". Barth discusses the double relationship between God and humanity as such. This exchange consists in the answer of the children to the word and the work of the Father. In other words, this exchange is the practice of prayer, seen as a movement of the children towards God. As Barth sees it, then, prayer is a constellation that is structured by not only two, but three factors: first, the Father, second, the children, and third, the practice of praying as such – the invocation, which is to be seen as the place of exchange between the first and the second factor. Let us now look at this last theme a bit more closely.

Considering the structure of the exchange as such, one thing is very clear for Barth: The relationship between God and humans should always be seen as an asymmetrical one. God is the gracious, giving Father; we are the grateful, receiving children. Therefore, if we look for the specific content and wish to know more about the specific sense of the invocation, it is important to keep in mind that its structure is asymmetrical. Barth distinguishes three points concerning the specific sense of the invocation as such: memory, anticipation and transformation. Let me explain briefly the meaning of these three expressions in the ethical context of the Christian practice of prayer:

First, by practising prayer, humans are reminded of the asymmetrical structure of the relationship between God and themselves, and therefore the fundamental difference between the gracious, giving God and receiving humans crying out for grace. What actually transpires in this double movement – that of the giving God towards humanity and, vice versa, of humans crying out towards God – is a confrontation with the Holy Spirit. The Holy Spirit is understood as the bond, in God, between the Son and the Father. Just as Jesus Christ is the possibility to think together intimacy and distance between God and humankind, so the Holy Spirit functions in the vital exchange between God and humans as a *vinculum pacis,* a bond of peace between them[6].

Secondly, it is important to Barth that this confrontation with the Holy Spirit, this third moment in the practice of prayer, must have public, political, social and cosmic implications. The praying practice of the Christian minority anticipates a universal human practice, and thus the community of all people. What seems important to me here, is not merely the universal meaning of prayer, but also its guiding towards the future, what Barth calls the prophetic dimension of praying.

The third important aspect of the practice of prayer is transformation. Just as memory is useful to people for remembering the asymmetrical structure of the relationship as such, the transformation for its part ensures the asymmetrical structure of the relationship from the point of view of God. The problem here is that, on the one hand, prayer can only

6. The *vinculum pacis* in the theology of Barth can be seen as a correction of the christological concentration in the Church Dogmatic. See D.L. MIGLIORE, *Vinculum pacis – Karl Barths Theologie des Heiligen Geistes,* in *Evangelische Theologie* 2 (2000) 131-152. Migliore also mentions that the introduction of a Trinitarian analogy could be a possibility to revise the well-known hierarchy of sexual difference given in the theology of Barth.

make sense if it is answered, while on the other, the necessity of answering the children, may not contradict the sovereignty and freedom of God. The solution is transformation, because in the transformation of human prayer, God can answer the cry of his children in another, unexpected way, better than that which the children could initially expect. Because the answer of God is not congruent, the relationship retains its asymmetrical structure.

Thus it becomes clear that, in the double movement of the relationship as such, there are again not only two, but three factors, namely the transforming movement of God, the remembering movement of humans, and the confrontation with the Holy Spirit, who binds together. In my opinion, this connective confrontation can be seen as the heart of invocation. It is ordered in a prophetic way, as Barth would say, or, as I would say in more secular terms, as "utopian memory".

This means that Christians live towards a universal communication, not only between God and humankind, but also between humans. Barth thinks that, in the first instance, this future universal conversation will involve communication between Christians and non-Christians.

III. THEOLOGY AS COMMUNICATION

In this part, I would like to focus in some more detail on the concrete possibility of such prophetic or utopian communication. As I announced at the beginning, I would now like to reflect further on theology *as* communication. If Systematic Theology is to take this project seriously, then the need for assistance from the other disciplines is evident. In my opinion, Systematic Theology needs to follow Barth beyond Barth. It has to make contact with other disciplines, like communication theories and political theory, as well as other theological disciplines, such as ecumenical and feminist theology. To give a concrete example of the possibility of such a theology *as* conversation, let me now present some thoughts of the French feminist philosopher Luce Irigaray.

One of Irigaray's starting-points is the critique of religion from a feminist perspective. Thus, she provides an interesting opportunity to reflect on the meaning of religion in a modern or post-modern context. It is my hope that her thoughts may assist theology in continuing to speak theologically in a more or less agnostic culture.

According to Irigaray, religious phenomena have to be unmasked, so that the forgotten material base of these phenomena can be discovered. In her work, the term "material" functions in a very specific sense, namely as something concerning the mother, or in more general terms, the feminine. What actually happens in religion, is that she forgets her material base. Another starting-point of Irigaray's is her attempt to construct a new kind of religion, namely a feminist one. In this feminist variety of religion, the mother and, more generally, the feminine, will not be forgotten. This new religious production turns on one central term, namely "difference", and more specifically sexual difference. According to Irigaray, difference means a relationship, structured by not only two, but three instances. In sexual difference, then, we have not only the two human subjects, especially the man and the woman, but also a room between them, a space where the relationship between the sexes can take place. So, if Irigaray uses the term "difference", she means difference in this very specific, threefold way[7].

As will be obvious by now, it is precisely this use of the term "difference" that encourages me to initiate an encounter between the philosophy of Irigaray and the theology of Barth on the subject of prayer. In both cases, we observe an interest in a type of relationship, which is structured by not only two, but three factors. Moreover, in both cases, the exchange between two subjects *as such* gets a place of its own.

According to Irigaray, this specific threefold form of difference is closely related to the feminine, or at least to the bodies of women. To make this clear, she evokes several magnificent images of difference in her work[8]. One of the most impressive, which is also of interest to the subject of prayer, is the image of the prenatal situation in the womb of the mother[9]. In my opinion, this image can be seen as a re-imaging of prayer. More specifically: The image of the situation in the womb of the mother can be seen as a re-imaging of invocation as such. Let me explain this by giving a brief description of the prenatal situation in the mother's womb. In Irigaray's research on the prenatal condition, at least three important elements play a role. First, there is the gracious, giving mother, who, through her nourishment, constitutes the child as a subject. Secondly, there is the needy and receiving child. It is evident here that mother and child do not exist in an equal relation, but in a hierarchical one. Thirdly, there is the placenta, which, in Irigaray's opinion, should not

7. See L. IRIGARAY, *Ethik der sexuellen Differenz*, Frankfurt am Main, 1991, especially pp. 11-20.

8. The most well known image of difference created by Irigaray is that of the two lips who are speaking together.

9. This image is worked out by Irigaray in L. IRIGARAY, *Over de moederlijke orde*, in ID., *Ik jij wij: voor een cultuur van het onderscheid*, trans. A. VINCENOT – D. VERBERK, Kampen, 1990, pp. 43-50.

merely be seen as part of the child. Rather, the placenta is to be regarded as a regulating instance between mother and child. The placenta is thus an instance where the hierarchical exchange of mother and child gets a place of its own. It is important to Irigaray that the prenatal exchange is neither a symbiotic one, as is often supposed in psychoanalytic theory, nor an aggressive one. According to Irigaray, such an exchange would be structured by either too much intimacy, or too much distance.

The image of the relationship in the womb of the mother is thus both hierarchical and threefold. It implicates a re-imaging of the utopian aspect of invocation as well, because it is an image that bears the promise of birth. Thus it is an image that guides towards the future. Therefore, in my opinion, the image of the prenatal relationship can be seen as a more feminine re-imaging of the relationship given in prayer.

This image could, furthermore, be helpful in arriving at a re-interpretation of prayer in more secular terms. It could be an inspiration to challenge the theology of Barth. In my opinion, such a reinterpretation of prayer would offer distinct advantages.

First, it offers an alternative to both patriarchal and matriarchal fixations of the direction of the prayer. Although Irigaray chooses an image related to the body of a woman, she does more than merely speak of God in feminine terms. Stressing the threefold structure of relationship, she avoids a simple substitution of the Father by a godlike Mother. Thus, she inspires me to think less about problems concerning God's self, such as the question of God's gender, which is an important subject in feminist theology[10]. Rather, she encourages me to think more about the structure and the possibility of the relationship between God and human beings as such.

Secondly, the image of the child, connected with the mother by means of the placenta, is helpful in arriving at a reinterpretation of the utopian aspect of invocation as well. As I have noted already, it is an image that bears the promise of birth. Thus, in my opinion, this image can be seen as an anticipation of a future form of communication. In the logic of Irigaray, this future communication would also be a communication in terms of difference – that is to say, a threefold form of communication. In Irigaray's work, this utopian communication is worked out, first of all, as communication or relationship between the two sexes, man and woman. This communication, in a utopian sense, will also be threefold. Man and woman will both have a room or a place of their own. More importantly,

---

10. As important examples I want to mention S. McFague, *Modellen voor God. Nieuwe theologie in een bedreigde wereld*, Zoetermeer, 1990; K. Biezeveld, *Spreken over God als vader. Hoe kan het anders?*, Baarn, 1996.

in this utopian communication there will also be a memory of the placenta, the regulating factor of exchange and communication as such. This third factor, which also plays a role in sexual difference, is thus the space for both distance and intimacy, situated between the sexes. It is true that this utopian form of sexual difference differs somewhat from its original form, regulated by the placenta in the womb of the mother. It is, after all, not hierarchical, but based on equality. Thus it is clear that, in Irigaray's opinion, difference is itself a "differing" project. Difference itself always bears little differences[11].

Thus, in my opinion, the philosophy of sexual difference, as Luce Irigaray presents it, can be regarded as a more secular articulation of prophetic prayer. It inspires me to think about the prophetic prayer of Barth, not only as a universal communication between Christians and non-Christians, but also more concretely, as communication between men and women. At the same time, it offers a more comprehensive theory with which to interpret the traces of a more relational theology that are already to be found in the theology of Barth. Last but not least, both Barth and Irigaray challenge me to think more about theology *as* communication, a theology that increasingly communicates with other disciplines in a "different" way.

Faculteit Godgeleerdheid   Susanne HENNECKE
Universiteit Utrecht
Vrouwjuttenstraat 20
NL-3512 PS Utrecht
The Netherlands

---

11. Irigaray's project is based on what I want to call here a theory of mimetical shifting. Concepts like that of mimesis, difference and deconstruction, as well as the connection between this different concepts are not worked out in a theoretical way by Irigaray self. In my opinion a good example of the working of mimetically shifting, especially what concerns religious productions, can be observed in L. IRIGARAY, *Der Glaube selbst*, in ID., *Genealogie der Geschlechter*, Freiburg i.Br., 1989, pp. 47-52. For an analysis of this text and its mimetical shiftings see HENNECKE, *Der vergessene Schleier* (n. 5). A first attempt to analyze her concept of mimesis in general and to compare it with that of deconstruction can be found in RINA VAN DER HAEGEN, *In het spoor van seksuele differentie*, Nijmegen, 1989. Another attempt to work out theoretically the mimetical strategy of Irigaray can be found in HALSEMA, *Dialectiek van de sexuele differentie* (n. 4), pp. 95-116.

RELIGIÖSE (NICHT-)IDENTITÄT

REFLEXIONEN MIT JACQUES DERRIDA

I

Jacques Derrida, 1930 im algerischen El-Biar geboren, ist Jude[1]. Derrida betreibt keine Religionsphilosophie. Mehrfach jedoch hat er sich zu seiner jüdischen »Identität« geäußert. Dabei ist der Gebrauch des Begriffs »Identität« mit »Mahnungen zur Vorsicht«[2] (gemeinhin An- und Abführungszeichen genannt) zu umstellen, denn Derridas Verständnis von »Identität« ist konstitutiv ein Moment der »Nicht-Identität« eingeschrieben. Derrida sagt:

> ... so wäre einer um so jüdischer, je mehr die Selbstidentität aufgelöst würde, je mehr er also sagte, »meine Identität besteht darin, nicht mit mir selbst identisch zu sein, fremd zu sein, nicht mit mir übereinzustimmen« (...) Jeder wird dann das beste Beispiel der Identität (als Nicht-Identität mit sich selbst) und folglich ein exemplarischer Jude sein[3].

Ich lese Derridas Arbeit *Circonfession* (deutsch: *Zirkumfession*)[4]. Dieser autobiographische Text Derridas findet sich parallel montiert zu Geoffrey Benningtons Text *Derridabase* über Derrida[5]. Als ergiebig erweist sich die Relecture von *Circonfession* für ein jüdisch-christliches *Conversation Project*, insofern Derrida in seinem Text jüdische und christliche Kategorien verknüpft: das Kunstwort »Circonfession« kombiniert die französischen Begriffe für Beschneidung (= Circoncision) und Bekenntnis (= Confession). Mit einander verbunden, gar verschmolzen werden also der jüdische Initiationsritus wie auch das Bekenntnis, das in seiner

---

1. Zum Judentum Derridas vgl. J. VALENTIN, *Jacques Derrida – Judentum als Unmöglichkeit des Zu-sich-Kommens*, in ID. – S. WENDEL (eds.), *Jüdische Traditionen in der Philosophie des 20. Jahrhunderts*, Darmstadt, 2000, pp. 279-295.
2. J. DERRIDA, *Wie nicht sprechen. Verneinungen* (Edition Passagen, 29), Wien, 1989, p. 122.
3. J. DERRIDA, *Zeugnis, Gabe*, in E. WEBER (ed.), *Jüdisches Denken in Frankreich. Gespräche mit Jacques Derrida, Emmanuel Levinas u.a.*, Frankfurt/M., 1994, pp. 63-90, esp. 65.
4. J. DERRIDA, *Zirkumfession*, in G. BENNINGTON – J. DERRIDA, *Jacques Derrida. Ein Portrait*, Frankfurt/M., 1994, pp. 9-323 (im folgenden zit. mit Nr. und Seitenangabe).
5. G. BENNINGTON, *Derridabase*, in ID. – DERRIDA, *Jacques Derrida. Ein Portrait* (n. 4), pp. 9-323.

genuin christlichen Ausprägung mit den *Confessiones* des Augustinus die neuzeitliche Tradition der Autobiographie begründet[6]. Beide Institute, Initiation wie Autobiographie, suchen »Identität« zu konstituieren – ursprünglich religiös konnotiert, später in säkular abgewandelter Form.

Hier wie in seinem gesamten Werk (zu denken ist an Derridas Auseinandersetzung mit Emmanuel Levinas, Edmond Jabès und Paul Celan sowie mit Texten der talmudischen und kabbalistischen Tradition auf der einen – jüdischen – Seite und beispielsweise mit seinem »Landsmann«[7] Augustinus oder mit Meister Eckhart auf der anderen – christlichen – Seite) bewegt sich Derrida an der Grenze zwischen Judentum und (hellenistisch geprägtem) Christentum und führt genau diese Grenze wieder in die Mitte des abendländischen Denkens ein. Von dieser die Grenze markierenden Differenz her denkt Derrida (Nicht-)Identität.

II

Mit dem Essener Literaturhistoriker *Manfred Schneider* verstehe ich die Autobiographie als »Ausdruck neuzeitlichen Bewußseins und Speicher des ausgearbeiteten Wissens, das das Leben über sich selbst hervorbringt«[8]. Damit konstruiert die Autobiographie Selbstbewusstsein. Mehr noch: »Der autobiographische Text ist das (Selbst)Bewußtsein«[9]. Eine solche bewusste und selbstbewusste Autobiographie *er-/schreibt* sich das eigene Leben als Wahrheit. Diese Wahrheit *grenzt sich ab:* gegen nicht akzeptierte fremde Herrschaftsansprüche etwa. Und sie *grenzt aus:* alle, die ohne Bewusstsein sind oder als »bewusst-los« gelten, Kinder, Ungebildete, Wahnsinnige und Wilde; sie alle besitzen keine Autobiographie – noch nicht oder sind ihr verlustig gegangen.

Wichtig im vorliegenden Zusammenhang ist das Moment der *Verschriftlichung*. Um seine Autobiographie niederzuschreiben, bedarf der Autor, der als Biograph in eigener Sache zum Mnemotechniker seiner

---

6. Zur Geschichte der Autobiographie, speziell zu Augustinus vgl. F. BRUNHÖLZL, Art. *Autobiographie II. Mittellateinische Literatur*, in *Lexikon des Mittelalters* 1 (1980) 1262-1263 (Lit.!). Brunhölzl gewichtet die *Confessiones* des Augustinus von Hippo im Vergleich zu Derrida geringer.

7. DERRIDA, *Zirkumfession* (n. 4), Nr. 9, p. 57.

8. M. SCHNEIDER, *Das Geschenk der Lebensgeschichte: Die Norm. Der autobiographische Text / Test um Neunzehnhundert*, in M. WETZEL – J.-M. RABATÉ (eds.), *Ethik der Gabe. Denken nach Jacques Derrida* (Acta humaniora), Berlin, 1993, pp. 249-265, esp. 252.

9. *Ibid.*, p. 252.

selbst wird, eines Schreibgerätes. Mit Hilfe dieses technischen Instruments materialisiert der Autor das lebendige Wort und wandelt es in »tote Buchstaben«. Allerdings erschöpft sich der Gebrauch des Schreibwerkzeugs nicht in der Vernichtung, in der Negierung, insofern mit Griffel, Stift oder Computertastatur Gedächtniszeichen (z.b. Buchstaben) produziert werden können, die gemäß einem festgelegten Verfahren zeitunabhängig intersubjektiv reproduzierbar sind und auf diese Weise »das Begehren nach einem *anderen, nicht gegenwärtigen* Leben«[10] wach halten bzw. erwachen lassen. Erst also der negierende Zug, welcher der Verschriftlichung inhärent ist, bezeugt ein *surplus* des Lebens. »Die Gravuren oder Markierungen, welche die Schreibinstrumente hinterlassen, erinnern daran, dass das Leben über die Präsenz seiner Gegenwart hinaus 'bedeutet'«[11]. Die Spuren der Verneinung, der Negation, der Durchkreuzung und der Abwesenheit markieren also nicht bloß ein Nichts, sondern sie verweisen auch auf ein »Anderswo«!

Derridas Kritik an der autobiographischen Konstruktion von Identität setzt an bei den Kategorien wahr/falsch, die dem Bekenntnis immanent sind. Insofern der Biograph seiner selbst danach trachtet, sich das eigene Leben als Wahrheit zu erschreiben, eignet seinem Unternehmen ein aufklärerischer Impetus: Er sucht sein eigenes Unbewusstes zu entschleiern, will das Unter- und Unbewusste ans Licht holen, es *schwarz auf weiß* besitzen. Diesen Gestus des In-Besitz-nehmen-Wollens entlarvt Derrida als das typische Paradigma der Psychoanalyse, insofern diese meint, auch letzte Wahrheiten ent- und aufdecken zu können[12]. Vehement bestreitet Derrida, dass es dem Menschen möglich sei, sich die volle Wahrheit des eigenen Unbewussten aneignen zu können. Denn das Unbewusste, so Derrida, das die Psychoanalyse aufzudecken sucht, ist der Unterscheidung zwischen Realität und Fiktion, der Differenz zwischen Wahrheit und Falschheit nicht zugänglich. (Ähnliches gilt nach Aristoteles übrigens auch für das Gebet![13]) Genau diese Unterscheidung aber zwischen *real* und *fiktiv* bzw. *wahr* und *falsch* ist der westlichen Tradition nach

---

10. J. Hoff, *Spiritualität und Sprachverlust. Theologie nach Foucault und Derrida*, Paderborn, 1999, p. 144.
11. *Ibid.*, p. 144.
12. Hier wendet sich Derrida gegen den französischen Psychoanalytiker Jacques Lacan (1901-1981), der die letzte Wahrheit im Signifikanten des Signifikanten, dem Phallus, erkennt und von dort zu entziffern gewillt ist. Vgl. J. Lacan, *Die Bedeutung des Phallus*, in Id., *Schriften II. Ausgewählt, übersetzt und hrsg. von Norbert Haas*, Weinheim – Berlin, Quadriga, 1991, pp. 119-132.
13. Vgl. Aristoteles, *De interpretatione*, 17a: Organon. Neu übersetzt und mit erklärenden Anmerkungen versehen von E. Rolfes, Bd. 2: Peri hermeneias oder Lehre vom Satz (des Organon zweiter Teil), Hamburg, 1974.

806   U. ENGEL

notwendige Voraussetzung für jedwedes wahrhaftige Sprechen, für alles autobiographisch wahre Schreiben.

In diesem Zusammenhang kommt Derrida zu dem Schluss, dass das Unbewusste eine dem Bewusstein resp. der Vernunft wie auch der Sprache *vorgängige* Instanz ist. Joachim Valentin fasst zusammen: »Im Unbewussten, sofern es *vor* der Sprache, *vor* der Trennung (in Wahr und Falsch) situiert wird, fände sich folglich so etwas wie die 'eigentliche' Realität«[14]. Wo also Sprechen und Schreiben beginnen, verschleiert sich das Voraus. Die im Voraus liegende Wahrheit kann nicht ausgesagt oder erschrieben werden, ist nicht erreichbar, kann nicht in Besitz genommen werden. Jedes Bemühen, sich dem Geheimnisse dieser vorgängigen Wahrheit dennoch bemächtigen zu wollen, denunziert Derrida als unlauteres Streben nach unerreichbarem Eigentum.

Gerade diese Einsicht in eine der Sprache *vorgängige* Wahrheit mag den engen Konnex des autobiographischen Bekenntnisses zum *Gebet* erklären. Verdeutlicht werden kann das im Blick auf die geschichtlichen Anfängen der Autobiographie. Diese stehen – wie oben schon kurz erwähnt – in engstem Zusammenhang zu den *Confessiones* des Hl. Augustinus, auf dessen Leben sich Derrida in *Circonfession* übrigens durchgängig bezieht. Zu Zeiten Augustins verband sich das autobiographische Bekenntnis eng mit der literarischen Gattung des *Gebetes*. Entsprechend heben auch die Augustinischen Bekenntnisse mit einem Gebet an: »Groß bist du Herr, und hohen Preises würdig überaus ...«[15]. Bei diesem Zusammentreffen zwischen autobiographischem Bekenntnis und Gebet handelt es sich nach Derrida nun keinesfalls bloß um einen Zufall, sondern – philosophisch betrachtet – um eine Notwendigkeit: »... man *muß* mit den Gebeten beginnen«[16], bemerkt Derrida an anderer Stelle, Dionysios Areopagita zitierend[17]. Demnach ist die Autobiographie (in ihrer ursprünglichen Form zumindest) als ein verschriftlichter Gebets- und Bekenntnistext zu verstehen, mit dem der Mensch vor Gott Rechenschaft ablegt.

Das im autobiographisch verfassten Bekenntnis sich konstituierende »Ich« ist also aufgrund des der *Confessio* eng verbundenen Gebetes auf

14. J. VALENTIN, *Atheismus in der Spur Gottes. Theologie nach Jacques Derrida*. Mit einem Vorwort von Hansjürgen Verweyen, Mainz, 1997, p. 77.
15. AUGUSTINUS, *Confessiones*. I,i,1: *Bekenntnisse / Gottesstaat*, hrsg. von J. BERNHART, Stuttgart, ⁵1951, p. 63.
16. DERRIDA, *Wie nicht sprechen* (n. 2), p. 78.
17. DIONYSIOS AREOPAGITA, *De mystica theologia*, 680d, in K. ALAND – W. SCHNEEMELCHER (eds.) *De coelesti hierarchia; De ecclesiastica hierarchia; De mystica theologia; Epistulae* (Patristische Texte und Studien, 36), Berlin, 1991.

ein dem Selbst außerhalb liegendes Anderes bezogen. Derrida sagt: »Es müßte in jedem Gebet eine Adresse an den anderen als anderen geben und ich möchte sagen, auf die Gefahr hin zu schockieren: *Gott zum Beispiel*«[18]. An den Anderen – religiös gesprochen: an Gott, »den ganz anderen«, wendet sich der Bekenner in seinem Gebet; von ihm erhofft er sich ob seiner autobiographisch verschriftlichten Rechenschaftslegung Entlastung.

Vor diesem Hintergrund betrachtet kann im Bekenntnis konstruierte religiöse Identität niemals selbstreferentiell funktionieren. Vielmehr ist sie relational, denn nur in Bezug auf das ihr *Andere* kann sich Identität, einschließlich der religiösen, konstituieren.

III

Wie das Bekenntnis ab- und ausgrenzt, so separiert auch der Ritus der Beschneidung, und zwar in zweifacher Hinsicht: (1) insofern die Beschneidung als geburtlicher Initiationsritus seit jeher den Abstand des Juden zu seiner nichtjüdischen Umgebung offen legt, und (2) indem die Beschneidung (zumindest im jüdischen Raum) wesentlich die Differenz zwischen Mann und Frau markiert.

Derrida verbindet nun das Motiv der Beschneidung mit dem der Kastration und knüpft damit an eine alte, von Philo von Alexandrien bis hin zur Psychoanalyse reichende gedankliche Verbindung an. In Auseinandersetzung mit Hegel nennt Derrida die Beschneidung eine »castration symbolique«[19], insofern die Nacktheit des Phallus die männliche Kastrationsangst ansichtig und offenkundig macht. Damit behauptet die *Offenlegung* dieser Angst im Akt der Beschneidung ein alternatives Modell zum gängigen *Kompensation* der Angst im Streben nach Eigentum. Dieses Streben nach (unerreichbarem) Eigentum aber – so wurde weiter oben ausgeführt – ist nichts anderes als der unlautere, von Derrida denunzierte Versuch, sich des Geheimnisses einer im unzugänglichen Voraus liegenden Wahrheit bemächtigen zu wollen.

18. DERRIDA, *Wie nicht sprechen* (n. 2), p. 76. Vgl. hierzu auch H.J. LUIBL, *Beten begreifen. Über die seltsame Lust der Philosophie am Gebet*, in E. SALMANN – J. HAKE (eds.), *Die Vernunft ins Gebet nehmen. Philosophisch-theologische Betrachtungen*, Stuttgart – Berlin – Köln, 2000, pp. 31-59, esp. 48-53.
19. J. DERRIDA, *Glas*, Paris, [16]1995, p. 51.

Was im Zusammenhang mit dem autobiographisch verschriftlichten Bekenntnis über die Bedeutung der Schreibwerkzeuge gesagt wurde, gilt hinsichtlich der Beschneidung auch für die Werkzeuge des Mohels (= Beschneider)[20]. Auch hier *verneint* der Einsatz der technischen Instrumente, insofern das Messer die körperlich-leibliche Integrität des Sohnes zerstört. Allerdings erschöpft sich der Gebrauch der Beschneidungswerkzeuge nicht bloß in negierender Destruktion. Gemäß einem im Kontext des Judentums intersubjektiv reproduzierbaren *Verfahren* produziert das Messer des Beschneiders ein Narbenzeichen, das den Körper des Beschnittenen und damit diesen als Individuum markiert: »als dem jüdischen Glauben zugehörig, also als jemanden, der den Namen Gottes nicht aussprechen darf, obwohl er ihn aussprechen kann[,] und zieht damit eine Grenzlinie zwischen – natürlichem – Vermögen und – göttlichem – Gesetz. Identität, wie sie in der Beschneidung konstituiert wird, ist nicht Identität durch Eigenschaft oder Eigentum, sondern Identität durch das gemeinsame Stehen unter einem Gesetz, das beschneidet und unterscheidet«[21]. Derrida interpretiert die Beschneidung entsprechend als Narbe gewordenen Verweis auf eine Wahrheit, die als unaussprechliches Geheimnis vor jeder sprachlichen Äußerung liegt[22]. Diese kann sich der Mensch nicht im Sinne des Besitzen-Wollens aneignen.

Im Anschluss an und in Auseinandersetzung mit Hegels Interpretation der Beschneidung formuliert Derrida schon 1974 in seiner Arbeit *Glas*: »La circoncision est une coupure déterminante«[23] (»Die Beschneidung ist eine determinierende Verwundung«). Im selben Text verortet er die Beschneidung u.a. in dem Gegensatzpaar *Beheimatung* und *Exil*[24]. Und genau dort, im Grenzland zwischen Heimat und Unbehaustsein, Zugehörigkeit und Ausgrenzung siedelt sich Derrida persönlich an. Dabei kann er auch sein eigenes Jude-Sein nur im Sinne einer negativ formulierten Identität behaupten. Diese Selbstverortung zwischen Identität und Zerstreuung, zwischen Schnitt und Geschlossenheit gründet sicher nicht unwesentlich in seiner Biographie: herkünftig aus dem akkulturierten algerischen Judentum und am 3. Oktober 1941 als Jude »von der Schule und aus dem Franzosentum«[25] verwiesen. Die Ausweisung identifiziert

20. Vgl. dazu die Abb. in BENNINGTON – DERRIDA, *Jacques Derrida* (n. 4), p. 76.
21. VALENTIN, *Jacques Derrida* (n. 1), p. 290.
22. VALENTIN, *Atheismus in der Spur Gottes* (n. 14), p. 78.
23. DERRIDA, *Glas* (n. 19), p. 51.
24. Vgl. *ibid.*, p. 51.
25. DERRIDA, *Zirkumfession* (n. 4), Nr. 47, p. 258.

ihn als Opfer. Sie hat bei ihm ein lebenslängliches Misstrauen gegenüber jeder Logik des Eigentums und der Zugehörigkeit zur Folge. Derrida ist Jude und als solcher beschnitten. In seinem Subtext zu Benningtons *Derridabase* hat er eine Autobiographie vorgelegt, in der er sich auch zu auch seiner jüdischen »Identität« äußert (und damit bin ich wieder bei der *Confessio* angelangt):

> Ich »gehöre, wenn ich denn eine Art Marran[26] der katholischen französischen Kultur bin, und ich habe auch meinen christlichen, in einer mehr oder weniger verschlungenen Linie von SA [= Sankt Augustin; U.E.] ererbten Körper, *condiebar eius sale* [(Ich wurde gezeichnet mit dem Zeichen seines Kreuzes und) *gesalzen mit seinem Salz* (...) – Conf. I, xi, 17; Einschub U.E.], zu jenen Marranen, die sich selbst im Geheimnis ihres Herzens nicht Juden nennen – nicht, weil sie auf beiden Seiten der öffentlichen Grenze authentifizierte Marranen sein wollen, sondern weil sie an allem zweifeln, niemals die Beichte ablegen und die Aufklärung nicht preisgeben, koste es, was es wolle, bereit, sich verbrennen zu lassen, beinahe, in dem einen und einzigen Augenblick des Schreibens unter dem monströsen Gesetz des unmöglichen Von-Angesicht-zu-Angesicht (...)«[27].

Autobiographie und Bekenntnis greifen hier ineinander, werden eins: »Autobiographie ist Bekenntnis, Bekenntnis ist Autobiographie. Dabei aber ist Derridas Bekenntnis nicht eindeutig. Er bekennt sich nicht zu Gott, sondern zum Marranentum, zum Nicht-Eindeutigen, zum Wechsel zwischen der jüdischen und der christlichen Seite. Er bekennt keine Wahrheit, sondern zweifelt an der Möglichkeit von 'reiner' Wahrheit«[28]. Derridas Bekenntnis zum Judentum ist im Anschluss an *Circonfession* als ein »beschnittenes« zu verstehen: als eines an der Grenze zwischen Judentum und Christentum, aber auch als eines, mit dem Derrida sich zu seinem Jude-Sein nur beschnitten im Sinne von *unvollständig* bekennt.

Bekenntnis (im autobiographischen Text aufbewahrt) und Beschneidung funktionieren hier in relationaler Hinsicht als »trennende Verbindung«[29]. Diese »trennende Verbindung« ist Einschnitt, bleibt Narbe und markiert als solche eine Schwelle. Entsprechend versteht Derrida Bekenntnis wie Beschneidung als Des-Identifizierung.

---

26. Marranen = eine im 15. Jahrhundert aufgekommene abfällige Bezeichnung für die unter Druck der Inquisition christlich getauften Juden.
27. DERRIDA, *Zirkumfession* (n. 4), Nr. 33, p. 182.
28. VALENTIN, *Atheismus in der Spur Gottes* (n. 14), p. 84.
29. *Ibid.*, p. 80. Vgl. dazu auch den Hinweis zum Terminus »Hymen«, der sowohl die Jungfernhaut als auch die diese verletzende und zerstörende Hochzeit bezeichnet; ebd. Anm. 46.

IV

In systematisch-theologischer Hinsicht schließt sich hier die Frage an, inwieweit auch jedes christliche Glaubensbekenntnis, das seine jüdischen Wurzeln ernst nimmt, konstitutiv unvollkommen ist bzw. sein muss. Meine These lautet: Nur im Bezug auf das dem gläubigen Bekenntnis *Andere*, auf das, was dem Identität stiftenden Bekenntnis *außerhalb, jenseits* und *konträr* ist – was dem Bekannten das *Nicht-Bekannte* ist, dem Zugegebenen das *Verleugnete*, dem Akzeptierten das *Verdrängte*, dem Orthodoxen das *Heterodoxe* –, kann religiöse Identität im Sinne Derridas als (Nicht-)Identität gedacht werden.

Was das Grunddatum der göttlichen Selbstoffenbarung betrifft, wie es in Ex 3,14 überliefert ist: »Ich bin der Ich-bin!«, so hat die jüdische Sprachpragmatik angesichts des nicht-nennbaren Gottesnamens eine »Sondersemantik«[30] der »Benennung« entwickelt, die das Tetragramm JHWH im Sinne eines Platzhalters an die Stelle des Nicht-Namens setzt, um so die göttliche Andersheit zu retten. Um der Alterität willen, die die »Identität« Gottes ausmacht, wird – hier auf die Sprachebene bezogen – der Name negiert, und zwar gerade in der Nennung seines Platzhalters.

Christlicherseits kommt die *memoria passionis et resurrectionis Jesu Christi* in den Blick. Symboltheologische Orte dieses Gottgedenkens sind die platzhalterisch funktionierenden Signifikanten von Kreuz und leerem Grab. Im Zeichen der durchkreuzten Balken erweist sich die Abwesenheit Gottes als Bestreitung der göttlichen Identität des Sohnes: »Eli, Eli, lema sabachtani? – Mein Gott, mein Gott, warum hast du mich verlassen?« (Mt 27,46) Und im Zeichen der Leere des Grabes erweist sich der abwesende Tote in seiner Identität als Gottes Sohn.

Im Sinne Derridas können beide Platzhalter – Tetragramm wie Kreuz / leeres Grab – in ihrer Verortung zwischen Affirmation und Bestreitung als theologisch legitime Formeln des (Nicht-)Identischen interpretiert werden. Was daraus folgt, ist eine Neudefinition dessen, was Orthodoxie (als Ausdruck des Identischen) und Häresie (als Ausdruck des Nichtidentischen) bedeuten. In Anknüpfung an Karl Rahner[31] (und zugleich gegen seine theologisch-dogmatische Intention gewendet...[32]) ist das

---

30. E. NORDHOFEN, *Der Fromme hat kein Bild. Ikonoklasmus und Negative Theologie*, Stuttgart, 1990, p. 16.

31. Vgl. K. RAHNER, *Was ist Häresie?*, in ID., *Schriften zur Theologie V*, Einsiedeln – Zürich – Köln, 1962, pp. 527-576, esp. p. 560.

32. Das gilt insofern Rahner die »Wahrheit Gottes gegen den (ausdrücklichen oder latenten) häretischen Irrtum der 'Welt'« (*Ibid.*, p. 565) in Stellung bringt und die kryptogame Häresie als »Gefahr in der Kirche« (*Ibid*, p. 565) wertet.

Glaubensmoment exakt *zwischen* Affirmation und Bestreitung zu situieren – und zwar begriffen als eine *legitime* Form gläubiger (Nicht-)Identität, einer christlich-religiösen (Nicht-)Identität, deren identifizierendem Glaubensbekenntnis unabdingbar das des-identifizierende Moment des Heterodoxen innewohnt. »Man könnte (...) sagen, daß es immer Häresie geben 'muß' (in einem heilsgeschichtlichen 'Muß', das es unbeschadet dessen gibt, daß es so etwas nicht geben 'soll'), und zwar als eine Möglichkeit, die nicht so von der Kirche von vornherein abgesetzt sein kann, daß der kirchliche Christ als solcher von ihr gar nicht ernsthaft bedroht sein kann«[33]. Das hier formulierte »Muß« markiert theologisch die Differenz/Différ()nce[34] – in den Worten Rahners: »die Zweideutigkeit der Glaubensexistenz jedes Menschen«[35]. Wo Rahner auf die *»Möglichkeit, unthematisch ein Ungläubiger zu sein«*[36], verweist, behaupte ich im Ausgang von Jacques Derrida das im Glaubensakt strukturell angelegte und somit unumgängliche *Erfordernis* der Heterodoxie. Dabei tendierte der so orthodox-heterodoxe verfasste Gläubige dazu, seine »häretische Grundhaltung sowohl zu objektivieren als auch zu verbergen«[37].

Meinem Gedankengang entsprechend wohnt jedem orthodox-christlichen Bekenntnis *notwendig(!)* eine kryptogame Häresie inne. Diese ist allerdings nicht (mehr) als »Gefahr«[38] für Glauben und Kirchengemeinschaft zu werten, sondern als unerlässliche Bedingung für jedweden (sich seiner jüdischen Wurzeln bewussten) christlichen Glaubensakt zwischen »Doxa und Praxis«[39], mithin: als Bedingung der Möglichkeit für die Konstruktion christlich-religiöser (Nicht-)Identität überhaupt.

Institut M.-Dominique Chenu   Ulrich ENGEL
Schwedter Straße 23
D-10119 Berlin
Germany

---

33. *Ibid.*, p. 561.
34. Vgl. U. ENGEL, *Wer B(eth) sagt, muss auch A(leph) sagen. Philosophisch-theologische Spekulationen zur klanglosen »différ()nce« (Derrida)*, in *Wort und Antwort* 42 (2001) 9-14.
35. RAHNER, *Häresie?* (n. 31), p. 562.
36. *Ibid.*, p. 562.
37. *Ibid.*, p. 565.
38. *Ibid.*, p. 565.
39. T.R. PETERS, *Orthodoxie in der Dialektik von Doxa und Praxis*, in *Concilium* (D) 23 (1987) 312-318, p. 312.

TASTES OF INCARNATION AND CARNIVAL

CRITICAL CONVERSATIONS IN THEOAESTHETICS FROM THE PERSPECTIVE OF MIKHAIL BAKHTIN

> *Aesthetics is born as a dis-course of the body.*
>
> Terry Eagleton

A good number of theoaesthetic literature explicate the collaboration between religion (or theology) and arts within the *classic* purview of taste by extolling form over function, manner over matter, technique over theme, product over process in the appraisal of Beauty itself[1]. For them, taste remains to be an indubitable marker of distinction for what would be considered aesthetic proper. Foremost consideration in this arbitration is the maintenance of an *aesthetic distance* that isolates an artwork in order to cause maximal focus of attention upon itself – unpurposively and disinterestedly. This distantiating technique can also be termed as *foregrounding*. It is the claim of this paper, taking cue from a Russian social thinker, Mikhail Bakhtin[2], that the arbitration of taste is a privileged claim; hence, far from a disinterested posture.

---

1. Among many, see F. BURCH BROWN, *Religious Aesthetics: A Theological Study of Making and Meaning*, Princeton, NJ, Princeton University Press, 1989; J.A. MARTIN, JR., *Beauty and Holiness: The Dialogue between Aesthetics and Religion*, Princeton, NJ, Princeton University Press, 1990; P. SHERRY, *Spirit and Beauty: An Introduction to Theological Aesthetics*, Oxford, Clarendon, 1992; R.VILADESAU, *Theological Aesthetics: God in Imagination, Beauty and Art*, New York, Oxford University Press, 1999; ID., *Theology and the Arts: Encountering God through Music, Art and Rhetoric*, New York, Paulist Press, 2000; J. BEGBIE, *Voicing Creation's Praise: Towards A Theology of the Arts*, Edinburgh, T&T Clark, 1991; ID., *Theology, Music and Time*, New York, Cambridge University Press, 2000.

2. Among his most important works are M. BAKHTIN, *The Dialogic Imagination*, ed. M. HOLQUIST, trans. C. EMERSON – M. HOLQUIST, Austin, TX, University of Texas Press, 1998 [1981]; ID., *Speech Genres & Other Late Essays*, ed. C. EMERSON – M. HOLQUIST, trans. V. MCGEE, Austin, TX, University of Texas Press, 1996 [1986]; ID., *Art and Answerability: Early Philosophical Essays*, ed. M. HOLQUIST – V. LIAPUNOV, trans. V. LIAPUNOV, Austin, TX, University of Texas Press, 1990; M.M. BAKHTIN – P.N. MEDVEDEV, *The Formal Method in Literary Scholarship*, trans. A. WEHRLE, Cambridge, MA, Harvard University Press, 1985. For some works on Bakhtin, see T. TODOROV, *Mikhail Bakhtin: The Dialogical Principle*, Minneapolis, MN, University of Minnesota Press, 1984; M. HOLQUIST, *Dialogism: Bakhtin and His World*, London, Routledge, 1990; A. MIHAILOVIC,

I. Askesis: A Manner of Taste

García-Rivera's *The Community of the Beautiful: A Theological Aesthetics* (1999) employs Mukarovský's *foregrounding* as the basis for his proposal for a "community of the beautiful"[3]. Foregrounding or deautomatization is a literary technique, a de-schematizing tool to violate "that which is normal". As for the formalists, the use of "braked" words attracts attention to itself – beached, as it were, in the shores of poetic waters. In this case, Beauty/beauty shows itself in the violation of the norm and elevating the creaturely background; thus, endowing it with aesthetic value. Its contrast from the background accentuates some elements that highlight its own distantiated posture. Also, foregrounding for García-Rivera becomes an analogue of the Incarnation (of the Word) because of its redeeming quality to salvage the aesthetic work from "automatized" existence by "embodying" it with a new, resurrected meaning. What García-Rivera, in fact, intends to do is to "deautomatize" the norm, a way of "making it strange" in order to accentuate his theological aesthetics with the touch of Kantian purity and disinterestedness.

An illustration of García-Rivera's foregrounded application is his "mosaic method" in his essay, *San Martin de Porres: Criatura de Dios*: "[t]he mosaic method sees the violent and unequal encounter of cultures as creating a combination of "tiles," each one carrying a meaning and capable of combining with other "tiles" to form a larger and meaningful "mosaic""[4]. In a carnivalesque imagery, he gives an ecological example of dogs, cats and mice eating from the same bowl at the feet of their mulatto friend Martín de Porres, and recommends a mosaic of creatureliness that crosses asymmetric boundaries and propounds cosmic dialogue, en route to the creation of the "community of the beautiful". Indeed, by way of transposition, the varied instantiations in a mosaic are but repetitions whose individual particularities and differences are accidental relative to the all-encompassing harmony or homology[5].

Corporeal Words: Mikhail Bakhtin's Theology of Discourse, Evanston, IL, Northwestern University Press, 1997; R. COATES, *Christianity in Bakhtin: God and the Exiled Author*, Cambridge, Cambridge University Press, 1998; S. FELCH – P. CONTINO (eds.), *Bakhtin and Religion: A Feeling for Faith*, Evanston, IL, Northwestern University Press, 2001.

3. A. GARCIA-RIVERA, *The Community of the Beautiful: A Theological Aesthetics*, Collegeville, MN, The Liturgical Press, 1999. See also J. MUKAROVSKÝ, *Aesthetic Function, Norm and Value as Social Facts*, Ann Arbor, MI, University of Michigan, 1970 [1936], p. 21.

4. GARCÍA-RIVERA, *San Martín de Porres: Criatura de Dios*, in *Journal of Hispanic Latino Theology* 2 (1994) 26-54, p. 30.

5. This is consistent with García-Rivera's Mukarovskían influence on foregrounding. Mukarovský may be similar to Bakhtin in understanding language as a social datum that

For Bakhtin, foregrounding or deautomatization "is primarily understood as abstraction from semantic context", employed in poetics. Rather
than discover new meanings, it is bent on subtracting meaning in the
word's meaningful sound. Foregrounding's originary definition, far from
emphasizing the enrichment of the word with new and positive constructive meaning, simply *emphasizes the negation of the old meaning.* If for
Mukarovský and García-Rivera language resolves into an abstract, unitary
discourse; for Bakhtin, it is multi-accentual and perpetually negotiated.
Language is a "marketplace", in which competing ideologies and interests collide within a cultural flux. Against the "managed" type of communication common in pacifist discourses, Bakhtin's carnival aesthetic
creates the space for marginal voices to be heard and exposes systems
that valorize their own interests in well-hidden hegemonic mechanisms.
As caution to Garcia-Rivera's dog-cat-mice pacifism, Lindsey cites
Clodovis Boff, who states: "when wolf meets sheep, no one must be
deceived as to the ideological value of calls for 'cooperation' or 'dialogue' or 'pluralism'". In Boff's reflection, "carnival is not about the
meeting of the wolf and the sheep in a 'free', [genial] discourse. It is
about the freedom of the sheep to speak in systems that pretend the wolf
and sheep are equal"[6].

In a different context, Bourdieu in his book, *Distinction: A Social
Critique of the Judgment of Taste,* echoes a similar protestation against
the "virginal status" accorded to the Kantian "pure" taste and the aesthetics which offers its theorization. He cites the value of the Kantian
deferment of time: "This capacity for facing up in the present to the

---

dialogically interacts with value-laden contexts. But how this insistence on such link between
text and context can resort to foregrounding finds explication in Kurt Konrad's, maybe one-
sided, but not entirely unfounded, criticism of Mukarovský "false" totality. For Konrad, the
"false" totality in the abstract Hegelian sense, "leads structuralism to consider the influence
of non-literary elements on literature merely as an "outside influence", not as the living
soil, the medium in which the life of the literary fact originates". Cf. K. KONRAD, *Der Streit
um Inhalt und Form. Marxistische Bemerkungen zum neuen Formalismus,* p. 141, cited in
P. ZIMA, *Text and Context: The Socio-Linguistic Nexus,* in *Semiotics and Dialectics: Ideology and the Text,* Amsterdam, John Benjamins, 1981, p. 112. There is no wonder that,
while Mukarovský talks of a consensual view of society (that is, a relatively homogenous,
albeit ever-altering, totality), he does not take into account the conflictual social interests
and modes of domination within the society, for the crucial "influence" of values is not
inherent, only *juxtapositional,* towards the formation of the whole. This may not be far
from García-Rivera's structuralist framework that "stitches" various thoughts together in
a reversible, predictable patchwork. For instance, its employment of the "lifting up of the
lowly" begs for the concrete faces of the liberated and the oppressed.
    6. C. BOFF, *Theology and Praxis,* trans. R. BARR, Maryknoll, NY, Orbis, 1987, p. 48,
cited in W. LINDSEY, *The Problem of Great Time: A Bakhtinian Ethics of Discourse,*
in *Journal of Religion* 73 (1993) 311-328, p. 323.

often very distant future, instead of being wholly absorbed by the enjoyment of the present, is the most decisive mark of the human's advantage" in the assessment of the aesthetic[7]. The whole aesthetic language
distantiates itself from the immediacy of the "facile", "undemanding",
"shallow" and "visceral" as over-proximate in their acquisition of raw
pleasure, preventing the contemplative deferment of the future[8]. Such
immediacy deposes the Kantian epistemic subject into a *desiring* subject captive to the nitty-gritty involvement with the world. What this
implies is the collapse of distance which is supposed to accord the aesthetic object a status of "finality with no other end than itself"[9]. Hence,
"pure" taste is the language of repugnance against the violent dissolution of the subject into the object. It opposes itself against the "taste
of nature" in order to assert an attitude of *disinterestedness*, preserving the objectivity of the aesthetic work. The polarities are demarcated:
the virtuous soul of culture in its "virginal state" versus the vicious
embodiment of nature that needs to be subdued, cultivated and
redeemed.

Yet, this schema has an ethical impact given the fact that the yardstick
of virtue is always measured by the subjugation of vices – the test of
"pure" taste, being its tenacity to withstand the vulgar and the pleasur-
able. In fact, in Bourdieu's reading of Kant, the "control of passion"
reined in anticipation of the (eschatological?) future mutates into a "cultured" pleasure enjoyed for its own sake. "Thus the 'purest' form of the
aesthete's pleasure, aisthesis purified, sublimated and denied, may, paradoxically, consist in an asceticism, *askesis*, a trained, sustained tension,
which is the very opposite of primitive, [grounded] aisthesis"[10]. This
ascetic pleasure embodies the attitude of the religious and the aesthete,
hailed for their moral ascendancy by mortifying crass ludicness to achieve
a renunciated type of pleasure. The aesthetic work becomes a gauge of
distinction to define genuine personhood on the basis of one's "capacity
for sublimation". Indeed, an imposition happens: "that is, the transmutation of an arbitrary way of living into the *legitimate way of life* which
casts every other way of living into arbitrariness". Bourdieu clarifies that
what is crucial in this transmutation of values and "the attempted imposition of a definition of the genuinely human, is nothing less than the
monopoly of humanity ... [that is], art is called upon to mark the

7. P. BOURDIEU, *Distinction: A Social Critique of the Judgment of Taste*, trans. R. NICE,
Cambridge, MA, Harvard University Press, 1998 [1984], p. 598, n. 10.
  8. *Ibid.*, p. 498.
  9. *Ibid.*, p. 488.
  10. *Ibid.*, p. 490.

difference between humans and non-humans"[11]. Here again, the category of taste becomes an indisputable marker of "class". He writes:

> The opposition between the tastes of nature and the tastes of freedom introduces a relationship which is that of the body to the soul, between those who are "only natural" and those whose capacity to dominate their own biological nature affirms their legitimate claim to dominate social nature[12].

This categorization produces the "*homo aestheticus*" whose ethos of distilled pleasure and detached subjectivity constitutes the warrant of becoming *the* arbiter of tastes – "the universal subject of aesthetic experience"[13] – although not without the hidden violence of sublimating opposing dispositions of, say, the popular and the vernacular. From Bakhtin's lens (as from Bourdieu's), the process is clear: dominant institutions produce an official aesthetics, which takes into account the variant expressions involved in the field but arranges them in a hierarchy, so that the "low-key" appears dissonant, cheap, but most often, negligible in relation to the encompassing clout of the official *askesis/aisthesis*. Bakhtin refers to the valued, aesthetic discourse as *poetics*[14] (or at times, epic) and the strategic maintenance of asymmetric arrangement in language as *monologism* because it tends to stifle the natural dynamics of dialogical discourse.

II. AGORA: A MATTER OF DISTASTE

Bakhtin puts forward his "primary philosophy" – dialogism[15]. For him, language is not a formalist system of static grammatical elements which point to an "outside" referent; instead, language is dialogic, invested with prior meanings and future enunciations. Bakhtin notes:

> any concrete discourse (utterance) finds the object at which it was directed already as it were overlain with qualifications, open to dispute, charged with value, already enveloped in an obscuring mist – or, on the contrary, by the

11. *Ibid.*, p. 491 [emphasis his].
12. *Ibid.*
13. *Ibid.*, p. 493.
14. For instance, "Aristotelian poetics, the poetics of Augustine, the poetics of the medieval church, of 'the one language of truth' ... – all these, whatever their differences in nuance, give expression to the same centripetal forces in socio-linguistic and ideological life; they serve one and the same project of centralizing and unifying the European languages". BAKHTIN, *The Dialogic Imagination* (n. 2), p. 271.
15. BAKHTIN, *The Dialogic Imagination* (n. 2), pp. 191-192, 271, 279, 288; ID., *Speech Genres & Other Late Essays* (n. 2), pp. 69, 71, 88-89, 91-94, 120-127, 162; ID., *Art and Answerability* (n. 2), pp. xxii-xxiii, xxv; BAKHTIN – MEDVEDEV, *The Formal Method in Literary Scholarship* (n. 2), p. xix.

"light" of alien words that have already been spoken about it. It is entangled, shot through with shared thoughts, points of view, alien value judgments and accents[16].

In this sense, art and its expressions (as forms of discourse) cannot be "innocently" divorced from the "dialogically agitated and tension-filled" milieu as they perpetually negotiate a web of interrelationships with other accents and values, which may result in the flexible contour of any aesthetic piece – with shards of semantic intentionality lodged onto its layers, hence, affecting the entire stylistic profile altogether. In this sense, meaning is never stable or unitary since each artistic expression is densely inhabited with *other* values. It may be said that aesthetes do not extract "appropriate" expressions from a system of normative forms but "appropriate" them, refracting meanings and evaluations from previous contexts to fit their own contexts. Given this fundamental supposition, Bakhtin eschews the language of *disinterestedness* by stating a proviso: "there are no 'neutral' words or forms – words and forms that can belong to 'no one'; language has been completely taken over, shot through with intentions and accents ... [In this way,] each word *tastes* of contexts and context in which it has lived its socially charged life"[17].

Dialogism goes beyond the ken of a simple linguistic barter between persons in two senses. First, it recognizes the polyvalence of voices in the aesthetic field without conflating their radical exteriority or heterogeneity into the unitary language of an author(ity). Secondly, it creates a democratic space that depicts the anatomy of the carnival. This space upturns the sociodicy of classic aesthetics by affirming the ordinary over (and despite) the elite – not in the sense of putting the "low" on top, but of bringing the monologic "high" to touch base and dialogue with the "low" as equal interlocutor in the social discourse; hence the possibility of *co-agencies*. Both instances are located in the practices of people largely inferiorized by their distance from the aesthetic-ascetic core, and their practices are ones that do not divide life from art.

1. *The Novelistic Text*

Underneath the panegyric of "foregrounded" poetics lurks the "grounded" prosaics in the open spaces of the marketplaces, streets and border villages. These "open spaces" find aesthetic expression in the

16. BAKHTIN, *The Dialogic Imagination* (n. 2), p. 276.
17. *Ibid.*, p. 293 [italics mine].

novel which takes the quotidian as its social discursive *locus*, transgressing the transcendent *epic*ness of official discourses. In contrast to the elite taste of "braked" constructs – climax and denouement, a bang or a whimper, *adagio* or *allegro*, burning passion or jilted love, rhythm and metre, catastrophic events and historic catapults – stands the ordinariness and spirituality of popular distaste, situated on the stages of local fairs and at buffoon spectacles, the heteroglossia of the clown sounded forth, ridiculing all "languages" and dialects; there developed the literature of the *fabliaux* and *Schwänke* of street songs, folksayings, anecdotes ... where no [one] language could claim to be the authentic and incontestable [norm][18].

The distinct character of the novelistic genre is the "collision of accents" in a triadic constellation, namely: the self, the other and the "thirdness" in the relation[19]. According to Gardiner[20], the novel (in contrast to the epics) shows some distinct characteristics, namely: it demolishes the authorial pretension to omnipotence by postulating authorship as *co*-authorship, equal to the "hero/ine" or the reader in the active understanding of the text; it dialogues with different voices and multifarious points of view, putting to question the unitary, absolute claims of "official" discourse; it embraces elements of humor, play, parody, irony to serve as corrective to "all one-sidedness, dogmatic seriousness (both in life and thought) and all one-sided pathos"; it decanonizes the hegemony of "epic" time (used to legitimize the ascendancy of pure taste) by pointing to the utopic potential of a "still-ahead-and-always-will-be" moment; it is receptive to self-critique; and it ostensibly connects itself to the festive-folk culture of the *hoi polloi*. Here, the site of the novel becomes a dynamic, multiaccentual *agora*, whose real value is its unfinalizability – a critical stance against the fetishizing currents of the official culture – that commits to truly tensive (albeit meaningful) dialogue rather than mere transposition of values in the hierarchic order.

In *Art and Answerability*, Bakhtin expounds his "surplus of vision"[21]: the axiom that we cannot truly see ourselves as others see us, and vice

18. BAKHTIN, *The Dialogic Imagination* (n. 2), p. 273.

19. HOLQUIST, *Dialogism* (n. 2), p. 38: "In so far as my 'I' is dialogic, it ensures that my existence is not a lonely event but a part of a larger whole. The thirdness of dialogue frees my existence from the very circumscribed meaning it has in the limited configuration of self/other relations available in the immediate time and particular place of my life".

20. M. GARDINER, *The Dialogics of Critique: M.M. Bakhtin and the Theory of Ideology*, New York, Routledge, 1992, p. 175.

21. This is the belief that there is no way for us to exhaust the knowledge of ourselves (as others see us), as there will always be a deficit of knowing in the process of any

versa. It is the mutual yet, non-coinciding exchange between the unique
position of the self in existence and the unique places of other selves in
existence. The exchange from both polar ends does not annul each other
in *aporia*. Rather, deeper meaning and understanding are gained by the
exchange of "surplus". The subjects (I's) in both interactive positions
yield to the "consciousness of the fact that I, in my most fundamental
aspect of myself, still am not. I live in an 'absolute future'"[22]. The self
must embark on a "project" of achieving oneself. It is a surplus that is
at once, a "loophole" that serves to protect the self or other's transgre-
dient potentials from being sublated into the unitary consciousness of the
*author*ity. This propitious "loophole" bespeaks the "non-alibi in existence" as one's radical rootedness in embodied existence which is, at
once, unrepeatable, unique and "once-occurrent", and becomes the gateway for greater creativity and unfinalizability.

Lindsey claims that the lived-relation between the self and the other
is simultaneously ethical and aesthetic[23]. On the one hand, it is ethical
because it is only through this I-Thou dialectic (*plus* its excessive "thirdness") that one is able to respond to the deepest need of the other's lack
(or even reckon the other's "lack" as a hidden potential). The responsibility toward alterity comes in rescue of the fact that one exists fully
only in relation to the other. On the other hand, its aesthetic value
emerges in the constant re-fashioning of the task to bring the self, the
other and the perspective of the "third" into a viscerally-sensed open-
completion, like the relationship of the artist, artifact and art mutually
shaping each other. Thus, our unfinalized conditions are stamped with the
vocation of responsibility and answerability towards our own selves and
others. It is in this sense that Lindsey strikes a crucial critique to the
dominant Western aesthetics: instead of art mirroring life, it is life that
reflects art[24].

---

self-objectification. The position of the person in relation to the other is one of "surplus"
for there is an excess of elements given to that person which is not accessible to the latter's own othering, hence, a "loophole" as well. Correlative with the "surplus" is a certain "loophole", "a certain deficiency, for precisely that which only I see in the other is
seen in myself, likewise, only by the other". This "loophole" is not only an affirmation
of the "surplus" the other gives but also a guarantee of "unfinalizability" in the dialogic
relations between the self, the other and the "thirdness" in the relation. Cf. BAKHTIN, *Art
and Answerability* (n. 2), pp. 12, 22-27, 166.

22. M.M. BAKHTIN, *Èstetika slovesnogo tvorchestva*, Moscow, 1979, p. 112, cited in
K. CLARK – M. HOLQUIST, *Mikhail Bakhtin*, Cambridge, MA, Harvard University Press,
1984, p. 72.

23. LINDSEY, *The Problem of Great Time* (n. 6), p. 318.

24. *Ibid.*

2. The Carnival as Context

The carnival is the novel in context. It is meant to interrupt the canonized horizon of history embodied in epics. Carnivalistic discourse suggests a new awareness of historical, and cultural plurality and a mediated recovery of cultural practices that are perpetually subjected by "institutional forgetting" into a kind of social limbo. As it seems, the damage done to many minority cultures is precisely because of the "control of memory" and the "arrest of senses/sensibilities" by the institutions who arrogate upon themselves the power to arbitrate taste and morals. In the carnival context, Bakhtin upturns (not simply inverts) the hierarchy of an official sociodicy by countering the aesthetics of sublimation with the carnivalesque strategies of degradation and grotesque realism. In his book *Rabelais and His World*, he complements eschatology with scatology, empty space-time with chronotopic sense[25], "pure" pleasure with crass enjoyment, monologue with heteroglossia[26], and so on. In the site of the carnival, the border between stage and street collapses; in it people live – not watch or act – by recognizing an equally "official" voice: the "unofficial". What this ludic carnivalization may attempt to evince, or even subvert, is the hegemonic power of poetic universalization endemic in "high" aesthetics: the propensity for some cultural formations "to position everything else in a negative relationship to it"[26a]. Mikhail Bakhtin's theory of the prosaics presents a *different* vision of aesthetics as comprising various carnivalizing forces and plural systems that confront a centralizing canon. The disavowal of universalization does not follow the patterns of high/low or central/margin polarity: "The low is thus no longer the mirror-image subject of the high, waiting in the wings to substitute it ... but another related but different figure". For, as Hall hastens to add, "in Bakhtin's carnival, it is precisely the purity of this binary distinction which is transgressed. The low invades the high, blurring the hierarchical imposition of order; creating, not simply the triumph of one aesthetic over another, but those impure and hybrid forms of the grotesque"[27].

---

25. "Chronotope is the specific form-shaping ideology for understanding the nature of events and actions". It is the matrix of lived time-space which shapes experience itself. G.S. Morson – C. Emerson, *Mikhail Bakhtin: Creation of a Prosaics*, Stanford, CA, Stanford University Press, 1990, p. 367.
    26. Simply put, heteroglossia refers to poly-speechness or multivoicedness with its ongoing and unfinalized character. *Ibid.*, pp. 139-149.
    26a. N. Armstrong – L. Tennenhouse (eds.), *The Violence of Representation: Literature and the History of Violence*, London, Routledge, 1989, p. 15.
    27. S. Hall, *For Allon White: Metaphors of Transformation*, in *Carnival, Hysteria and Writing: Collected Essays and Autobiography by Allon White*, Oxford, Clarendon Press, 1993, pp. 1-25, 8.

Basic to the Rabelaisian notion of the carnival is grotesque realism – the emphasis on the "collective, ancestral body of the people"[28]. It poses itself as a "counter-discourse" that highlights bodily debasement as a grounded requisite for a festive rebirth. Against anti-body classicism, Bakhtin stresses the anatomical openness of bodiliness to give due importance to the posture of *becoming* rather than finality, the latter of which can be observed in the rounded completion of classic artworks. One aspect of grotesque realism is its bodily emphasis on festivities. Here, the fiesta is seen not as a form of negative escapism but a creative alternative to relatively closed and historical protocols that aristocratic ideologies dictate to the fluidity of time. It is not a ritual of frenzied licentiousness ending in bulimic agitation; rather, it draws a physical proximity that "generate[s] in each member of the crowd a profoundly visceral sense of *communitas* ... where life patterns are reconstructed in a manner independent of official norms"[29]. Another aspect of grotesque realism is degradation. For the arbiters of taste and decorum degradation spells distaste and disreputation, but for the carnival symbolic it represents something deeper and more profound.

> To degrade is to bury, to sow, and to kill simultaneously, in order to bring forth something more and better. To degrade also means to concern oneself with the lower stratum of the body, the life of the belly and the reproductive organs ... Degradation digs a bodily grave for a new birth; it has not only a destructive, negative aspect, but also a regenerating one[30].

Here, we might add, the ruler is enthroned into the chamberpot as revaluation of the "throne" where all men and women are considered equal. The debunking is by way of revivification. In all, carnival provides an exit from the over-seriousness of life as well as an opening to launch a festive raid on immutable cosmologies and intolerant fixities that "subdue the populace and dampen [their] critical consciousness ... legitimate the existing hierarchy and the systems of taboos and prohibitions which reinforce it"[31].

28. BAKHTIN, *Rabelais and His World*, trans. H. ISWOLSKY, Bloomington, IN, Indiana University Press, 1984 [1968], p. 19.

29. R. CUNLIFFE, *Charmed Snakes and Little Oedipuses: The Architectonics of Carnival and Drama in Bakhtin, Artaud and Brecht*, in *Bakhtin: Carnival and Other Subjects, Critical Studies*, Vol. 3/4, ed. D. SHEPHERD, Amsterdam, Rodopi, 1993, p. 50 [italics his].

30. BAKHTIN, *Rabelais and His World* (n. 28), p. 21.

31. GARDINER, *The Dialogics of Critique* (n. 20), p. 51.

III. INCARNATION AS GROUNDED AESTH-ETHICS

The following section will show that: first, Bakhtin understands Incarnation as the "carnivalization of God" rather than the "elevation of humanity" projected in elite aestheticism. Secondly, that the aesthetic of Incarnation allows the reemergence of hidden voices and subtexts, which effectuates responsibility toward the other. Thirdly, the Incarnation in Bakhtin's reflection paves the way towards the *eschaton* of great time, and not a dehistoricized timelessness of a contemplative "community of the beautiful".

1. *Carnival and Incarnation*

Perhaps the central argument around the paradigms of taste revolves around the status and value of matter. For high theoaesthetics perpetuate the dichotomies between matter/spirit, body/mind, time/eternity, etc. For Bakhtin's grounded aesthetics, these dichotomies are invalidated by the Incarnation, by the action of the Logos who did not enter flesh, or choose to situate itself within flesh, but became flesh. As a destroyer of boundaries Incarnation then echoes the paradox: there is nothing elevated that has not been debased, nothing eternal that has not entered time, nothing divine that has not become human. Where for high aesthetics Incarnation's proximity to matter constitutes a spiritual anarchy shamefully unworthy of the divine, Bakhtin sees matter as anticipatedly divine to the extent that "even the excremental can be sacramental"[32]. In his reflection, the mediation of carnival intimates a kind of low-key Incarnation whereby all matter is ordained with a redemptive worth. Something like this was hinted at by García-Rivera in his "exaltation of God by abasement". The embodiment and the upturning that happen in the carnival are precisely the materials upon which the Word-made-flesh founds Itself. After all, earthiness is both carnival's and Incarnation's axial meeting point. The border that sets apart (holiness) is the one that connects (wholeness). Ward affirms that, indeed, this transgression of margins is best illustrated in the "degraded" life of Christ himself[33].

In Coates' reflection, the renunciation of the transcendent Word into the realm of the material instantiates Bakhtin's reflection of the Incarnation as the "ahistorical, metaphysical truths enter[ing] into the realm of

---

32. C. LOCK, *Carnival and Incarnation: Bakhtin and Orthodox Theology*, in *Journal of Literature and Theology* 5 (1991) 68-82, pp. 72-73.

33. F. WARD, *Writing the Body of Christ*, in *Theology* 11 (1997) 163-169.

the chronotopic (spatial and temporal) limitation and possibility and are thereby divested of their power to distance and terrify the believers"[34]. The Matthean "Immanuel, God-with-us" (1,23) signifies the positive valuation of the bodily and highlights the cessation of an abstract understanding of the Word. Indeed, Bakhtin finds solution to the structuralist *problematique* concerning the divorce between formal linguistic and the material body. For him, the "Word made Flesh" (John 1,14) is the supreme witness that in Christ language and body are reconciled in an act of divine debasement. Bakhtin's project, we might recall in our critique of Mukarovský's foregrounding, has always been to recuperate both "a language and a meaning to the body"[35], rather than to the system of linguistic signification. After all, context is not that which enables text to be manifest, but that which is integral to text if text is to avoid the abuses of system and monologue. And the principle of heteroglossia extends Bakhtin's "theological materialism" to language. There can be no privileging of discourses, nor among discourses: all words are potentially Word, and the Word lurks in words. And embedded in the seeming *car-*nal (root term for both Incarnation and carnival) superficiality is a profound aesthetics of responsibility for the concrete other.

2. *Exotopy and Responsibility*

The popular space propounds Bakhtin's mindfulness of the other as emergent voices from the margins seeking equal hearing from those occupying the privileged center. Known as exotopy, this language of othering becomes no longer a task of objectification but identification of selves ("I"s) as simultaneous subjects[36]. To elaborate, Bakhtin's revisionist writings rethink the traditional philosophy of the *individuum* as an independent unit whose identity is defined by its demarcation from the other – "a closed circle of a single consciousness [that leaves out]

34. COATES, *Christianity in Bakhtin* (n. 2), p. 133.
35. BAKHTIN, *The Dialogic Imagination* (n. 2), p. 171.
36. Exotopy is also known as outsideness and extralocality, it refers to the event of othering "whose essential and constitutive element is the relation of a consciousness to *another* consciousness, precisely because it is *other*", cited in TODOROV, *Mikhail Bakhtin* (n. 2), p. 100. "Othering" is an active noun that accentuates its departure from "static" other/ness. It bespeaks an "open" alterity in dynamic, dialogic, unfinished relationship with those outside it. One's "own othering" here means I-for-others or the self as it appears to those external to it. There are also two other moments: I-for-myself (how my self looks and feels my own consciousness) and Other-for-me (how outsiders appear to the self). These triadic relations debunk the classic subject-object configuration, saying that "there neither exists a stable self nor a 'given' outside world to which it might be opposed". MORSON – EMERSON, *Mikhail Bakhtin* (n. 25), p. 180.

the axiological category of the other"[37]. For Bakhtin, the myth of individuation perpetuates an aesthetics of autonomy that, quite perilously, excludes the other *as* other and mutes heteroglossia. And it is against this backdrop of solipsistic closedness that unjust structures are likely to emerge. From Bakhtin's view, this Kantian construct needs a new Cartesian revolution that must start to understand the axiological embodiment of the self as only possible in relation to the other – without sublating the "loopholes" into a dialectical mosaic. For instance, it may well be the case that the gain of "cat-dog-mice" democracies (García-Rivera) is the recognition of the *different* voices from the social fringes; its loss is the non-cognition of the fringed voices as the *difference* in a democratic society. The latter depicts what Bakhtin calls "theoretism": the archetypal synchronizing of diachrony or the abstract generalization of "humanity" that divests the person of one's compelling relations with the world[38]. Our critique of idealist aesthetics (as in the case of García-Rivera) is precisely against its *habitus* of ideological abstractions.

Therefore, carnival is a dissent against unitary authorial dispensation. Like the novelistic form in context, carnivalization confers the space for alterity to have a voice. Hence, heteroglossia is not so much a semantic tool than it is an ethical reserve: it denounces the dogmatism of a closed linguistic circuit understandable only to the *insiders*. It retraces the true meaning of language to its *other* relations. In Bakhtin's estimation, the self and the other are two *equal* interlocutors, two subjects in dialogue – the "I" and the other "I". Both realize their "non-alibi in existence" as they immediately become grounded and implicated in the production of value-laden meanings, which give shape to the events in the world. Democracy only *creates* the opportunities for change. It is ethical responsibility towards alterity that *empowers* oneself to commit to the task.

Indeed, carnival is not just about party time, but also about democracy. Such is the case of EDSA[39], an empowered, democratic space

37. BAKHTIN, *Art and Answerability* (n. 2), p. 80.
38. MIHAILOVIC, *Corporeal Words* (n. 2), p. 160.
39. EDSA refers to the chain of ludic People Power events in the Philippines (ca. 1986-2001) that symbolically converged in Epifanio de los Santos Avenue (EDSA, for short), Manila to seek the ouster of perceived corruption in governance. Elsewhere in the different islands in the Philippines, there were similar, simultaneous uprisings. EDSA is a paradox of a revolution. It has a semblance of war because of the presence of military, psy-war tactics and armored tanks; a semblance of carnival because of an overflow of potlatch, community singing, performances and street dancing; a semblance of liturgy and festive faith with sacred icons, pop devotions, BECs on the street, rosary rallies, bible sharing; a semblance of protest with placards, "nude" marches, water canons and hunger strikes.

intent on collapsing the charade affixed upon the "faceless masses" or "noisy mobs" – those sociological calculi that tend to translate people's marginality into invisibility or view their impoverished conditions as the normal landscape in the portrait of life's existence. Under such value-judgments (by mandarins of Power), the "ordinary" (which constitutes the population of majority), remain voiceless and demystified in an "aesthetic of indifference". But in EDSA, the "Great Unwashed" regain their voices and their potentials. It became incumbent upon participants (of the playful Revolutions) to bring healing to the social cancer infesting their own national community. For instance, the people's invocation of the "right not to understand, the right to incomprehension" brings the world to see the extreme condition that sets itself as the norm, not by way of aesthetic "defamiliarization" but of engaged *aesthethics*[40]. Social advocacies result in the form of enacted spiritualities: that is, prayer and praxis that bred the historic toppling of regimes, the halting of national plunder and the setting up of open platforms that would hopefully bring societal transformation. This, again, is a far cry from Garcia-Rivera's beautiful community whose "social act" seems to eschew dealing with the concrete faces of want and poverty. For him, "[s]uffering Christians in the Latin church of the Americas ... [need only] to be consoled by the wisdom of Sophia [reason] in order to be lifted up towards the higher vision of Beatrice [faith]. As such, consolation and ecstasy constitute the "social" act, a discernment of signs which begins in consolation and ends in praise"[41]. Here is a holist view that sets the parameters of social act within a non-conflictual, harmonic utopia. What is obviously amiss, in Gutierrez's view, is a critical look into the questioning spirituality born in the midst of the struggles of the Latin American *anawim*[42]. For his part, Bakhtin's social responsibility is highly *kenotic* in that it is patterned after the exemplary gesture of self-emptying done for the other – "only by becoming other to myself ... can I become for-the-other"[43].

Contexted in institutional corruption, domestic poverty and fluctuating currencies, EDSA then is an offspring of crisis-moments in a nation's history. The carnival allegories in EDSA is not meant to defamiliarize the ordinary, but to waken the ordinary to such unjust, demystifying processes, as political or aesthetic "defamiliarization".

40. MORSON – EMERSON, *Mikhail Bakhtin* (n. 25), p. 402.

41. GARCIA-RIVERA, *The Community of the Beautiful* (n. 3), p. 195.

42. G. GUTIÉRREZ, *A Theology of Liberation*, Maryknoll, NY, Orbis Books, 1973, pp. 203-208. See also ID., *We Drink From Our Own Wells*, Maryknoll, NY, Orbis Books, 1984.

43. BAKHTIN, *Toward a Philosophy of the Act*, trans. and notes by V. LIAPUNOV, ed. V. LIAPUNOV – M. HOLQUIST, Austin, TX, University of Texas Press, 1995, pp. 38-39.

For Bakhtin, Christ is the paragon of *respons-ability* for in him we have a deep concurrence between "ethical solipsism and ethical-aesthetic kindness". This means that, in the first instance, Christ has truly and solipsistically deepened his own personality by shaping "an immaculately pure relationship to oneself" and in the second instance, he is authentically other-oriented. As Bakhtin ponders, God is set to reveal in the incarnation the possibility of *simultaneous* other-centeredness and self-gaining. Bakhtin writes: "For the first time, there appeared an infinitely deepened *I-for-myself* – not a cold *I-for-myself*, but one of boundless kindness toward the other; an I-for-myself that renders full justice to the other as such, disclosing and affirming the other's axiological distinctiveness in all its fullness … In all of Christ's norms the *I* and the *other* are contraposed: for myself – absolute sacrifice; for the other – loving mercy"[44]. Christ's aesthetics, for Bakhtin, beholds not only the rapture of God's glory (as in the case of García-Rivera) but moreso, the rupture of human consciousness; that is, "the [unsettling] consciousness of the self's relation to the other"[45]. Christ becomes the foundation for the understanding of all human consciousness, making him the incarnate key for unlocking the complexities of being human and being human for others.

Lindsey observes this Bakhtinian kenotic turn as decisive in "remov[ing] extrinsicality from the imperative to love one's neighbor"[46]. For him, it swerves away from simply external fulfillment of ethical norms (which is paramount in Western theology) to a dialogic understanding of the self and the other whereby the two are so intimately and paradoxically linked: "one cannot love oneself without loving the other [*as* other]"[47]. After Incarnation, *love thy neighbor* is no longer an exterior command because in Christ God has shown the fundamental mission of all humanity – "to fulfill themselves in dialectic relation to [the strangeness and alterity of] the other"[48]. This is consistent with what Bakhtin professes as a personal credo: "What I must be for the other, God is for me"[49]. Indeed, his "religiosity of responsibility" affirms that God's other is the human person[50]. Nothing could be truer here than Christ's paradoxical gospel of "the least": "Just as you did it to one of the least

---

44. BAKHTIN, *Art and Answerability* (n. 2), p. 56.
45. CLARK – HOLQUIST, *Mikhail Bakhtin* (n. 22), p. 86.
46. LINDSEY, *The Problem of Great Time* (n. 6), p. 326.
47. *Ibid.*
48. *Ibid.*
49. BAKHTIN, *Art and Answerability* (n. 2), p. 56.
50. D. PATTERSON, *Bakhtin on Word and Spirit: The Religiosity of Responsibility*, in *Cross Currents* 41 (1991) 33-51, p. 40.

of these who are members of my family, you did it to me" (Matt 25,40).
If there is one thing in EDSA that outshines any *other* carnivalia it is the
emergence of "the least" from the fringes, whose *difference* becomes for
all the responsibility for *non-indifference*.

3. *Chronotope and the Ethics of "Great Time"*

Another factor to be critiqued in monologic idealist aesthetics is connected to the "problematique of seriousness": the type that congeals into
the template of dogmatic authoritarianism that extirpates itself from the
"culture of redemptive laughter". Seriousness is not a problem in itself;
but its recourse to dreary self-centeredness and monologism is.
Hirschkop explains that the false type of seriousness often "makes the
individual more than merely individual – it wants to help the individual
transcend its earthly limits, whilst retaining the essential changeless
attributes of the singular person"[51]. Its warrant lies not in "transformation, but immortality, in the form of ascension into heaven for the many,
and an eternal presence on earth, embodied in memory and monuments,
for the powerful few"[52]. Here, the ideology of art, according to Bourdieu,
shows its full force: the language of immortality creates a cleavage for
the legitimation of "social difference". Only a "gifted minority" is able
to appreciate the genuinely aesthetic while the mediocre majority is con-
signed to the greyness of events. Hence, the clamor for an unaltered tradition rendered timeless by certificated myths and books, statues and
monuments.

For Bourdieu, timelessness is an important analogue for "pure" taste.
For instance, the difference of the comic magazines found in the night
shops of Leuven and the comic strips mounted onto an expensive frame
in the National Gallery marks the distinction that produces "a sort of
ontological promotion akin to a transubstantiation"[53]. Here, the surrounding dispositions must secure the measure of temporality that supports the legitimations of its own social differences. The epic's eternal tradition defines itself against the time-bound historicalness of the multitude,
which is characteristic of the novelistic prosaics. Among the requisite for
epicness is the annulment of time from its present ideological life. Its dis-
tantiation from the everydayness of life becomes one's "alibi in existence", which invokes the epic past as the source of durable norms. These

---

51. K. HIRSCHKOP, *Mikhail Bakhtin: An Aesthetic for Democracy*, Oxford, Oxford
University Press, 2000, p. 277.
52. *Ibid.*
53. See BOURDIEU, *Distinction* (n. 7), p. 6.

norms draw people into decisions of obedience and loyalty without having to (re)shape history at all. The passion for immortality is therefore the prolongation of the status quo in the manner that translates history as *merely* continuation rather than potential becoming. Contrary to abstract time, carnival teems with historical time – a time spent under the sun in the public square with real people and actual events. In this popular aesthetics, "time, as it were, thickens, takes on flesh, becomes artistically visible; likewise, space becomes charged and responsive to the movement of time ... and history"[54].

Lindsey seems to suggest that finding a history and a voice for the silent/silenced majority brings us to Bakhtin's notion of "great time"[55]. Simply put, *every* time is replete with the heterogeneity of everyday events, whose meanings congeal over long periods of a particular culture's development. Great time then, is about the "attentiveness to the ordinary [viewed from] the perspectives of centuries"[56], rather than the appraisal of precious legacies by the judgments of taste. Great time is the belief in the *un*-closedness of events whose *other* possibilities are latently waiting for their time of (re)birth. It is the eschatological horizon that announces the verdict of un-finality to the uneven arrangements of status quo. Even this monumental *loophole* will have its own time, (although we wonder whether this could not be invoked as a license to passivity as well). Anyhow, great time is never ready-made "[f]or in later times, and in other places, there will always be other configurations of [self/other] relations, and in conjunction with *that* other, my self will be differently understood ... Poets who feel misunderstood in their lifetimes, martyrs for lost political causes, quite ordinary people caught in lives of quiet desperation – all have been correct to hope that outside the tyranny of the present there is a possible addressee who will understand them"[57]. In time, the cosmic arrangement set by tradition will be shattered by the historicizing discovery of the loopholes' worth. Great time then, is the time of carnival where

> [t]here is neither a first nor a last word and there are no limits to the dialogic context (it extends into the boundless past and the boundless future). Even past meanings, that is, those born in the dialogue of past centuries, can

---

54. BAKHTIN, *Dialogic Imagination* (n. 2), p. 84. See also B. SANDYWELL, *The Shock of the Old: Mikhail Bakhtin's Contributions to the Theory of Time and Alterity*, in *Bakhtin and the Human Sciences*, ed. M. BELL – M. GARDINER, London, Sage, 1998, pp. 197-213.

55. LINDSEY, *The Problem of Great Time* (n. 6), pp. 323-326.

56. MORSON – EMERSON, *Mikhail Bakhtin* (n. 25), p. 35. See also BAKHTIN, *Response to a Question from the* Novy Mir *Editorial Staff*, in *Speech Genres & Other Late Essays*, (n. 2), p. 5.

57. HOLQUIST, *Dialogism* (n. 2), p. 38.

never be stable (finalized, ended once and for all) – they will always change (be renewed) in the process of subsequent, future development of the dialogue. At any moment in the development of the dialogue there are immense, boundless masses of forgotten contextual meanings, but at certain moments of the dialogue's subsequent development along the way they are recalled and invigorated in renewed form (in a new context). Nothing is absolutely dead: every meaning will have its homecoming festival. The problem of *great time*[58].

Still, Bakhtin's philosophy stands trial to a number of criticisms[59], among which is the need to develop, say, with Bourdieu, *open frameworks of praxes* that will further fortify the social role of agency in societal transformation. Suffice it to say, Bakhtin thrives in the "loopholes" of his own philosophy. It is from there that dialogism, and not a *fixed* body of truths, proceeds.

IV. POSTSCRIPT: THEOLOGY OF A DIFFERENT TASTE?

We have argued so far for the emergence of a grounded theoaesthetics. It is a kind of *theoludics* that is folk and popular, whose carnivaludic and "distasteful" elements contain a subversion against, and an advance from, the unitary understanding of what theoaesthetics should be. It is a playful theology capable of initiating revolutionizing "socioreligious projects" (EDSAs) by empowering new agencies. It satisfies Gutiérrez's prescription: "the project of crafting a new and different society includes the creation of new human persons as well, who must be progressively liberated from whatever enslaves them"[60]. Somewhat akin to it is Kathryn Tanner's "theologies of the popular", embodied in the concrete religious and social practices of a people largely distanced from

58. BAKHTIN, *Toward a Methodology for the Human Sciences*, in *Speech Genres and Other Late Essays* (n. 2), p. 170.

59. Two pervasive criticisms against Bakhtin's carnival themes are: (a) the cooptation of carnival as a "safety valve" or an officially sanctioned transgression of the social order, hence, domesticate the inherent unpredictability and liberatory content of the dissent itself. and (b) its failure to submit to a *sustained* analysis of the hegemonic forces that perpetuate society's stratal unevenness. These critiques are a persistent "loophole" that commits Bakhtin to dialogue with *other* disciplines. For more criticisms, see R. BERRONG, *Rabelais and Bakhtin: Popular Culture in "Gargantua and Pantagruel"*, Lincoln, University of Nebraska Press, 1986; K. HIRSCHKOP, *Introduction: Bakhtin and Cultural Theory*, in *Bakhtin and Cultural Theory*, ed. K. HIRSCHKOP – D. SHEPHERD, Manchester, Manchester University Press, 1989; P. STALLYBRASS – A. WHITE, *The Politics and Poetics of Transgression*, New York, Cornell University Press, 1986, among others.

60. GUTIÉRREZ, *The Power of the Poor in History*, Maryknoll, NY, Orbis Books, 1983, p. 192.

the societal center by reason of their educational training, social status, economic capital and/or political posture[61]. They are homegrown theologies – practical, hospitably inclusive, selective in appropriating forms, situationally responsive and unconflatable into one canon – hatched in the outskirts of official ecclesial orbits. Their theological production may not be in consonance with the aesthetics of formal theorizing, hypostatic prescriptions and clear methodologies; yet, their practice of theology is no less inferior.

It is possible then, to "produce" theology in the "low" public square where sacral elements mix with profane matters. Without regard to rubrics or *anathemas*, the people celebrate with the plenitude of their bodies. Far from García-Rivera's view of Incarnation as the "elevation of humanity" in the transcendental experience of Beauty carnival, in the manner of Bakhtin, conceives of it as the "degradation of God" that confirms the materiality of the Word-made-flesh. From henceforth, bodiliness is not only something distasteful and uneasthetic, but redemptive. Carnival upturning is affirmed as liberative corrective. Apart from García-Rivera's "timeless" transcendentals, a profound theology effuses from Bakhtin's *eschaton* of the "great time" as a this-worldly horizon of hope that breaks open the sealed-off, monologic reading of the future by those who, because of position and status, have the vantage to *say* what the future must be. Above all, this theology from below intimates a kind of *aesthethics* that dispels the art-life divide (which haunts the epistemology of "high" aesthetics), and gives a concrete shape to the face of embodied alterity. From henceforth, loving our neighbor is no longer just a question of exterior ethics which we can do away with, but a self-realizing vocation which we cannot do without.

Faculteit Godgeleerdheid   Lope Florente A. LESIGUES
K.U. Leuven
St.-Michielsstraat 6
B-3000 Leuven
Belgium

---

61. K. TANNER, *Theology and Popular Culture*, in *Changing Conversations: Religious Reflection and Cultural Analysis*, eds. D. HOPKINS – S. GREEVE DAVANEY, New York, Routledge, 1996, pp. 101, 103.

A POETICS OF PLACE AND
AN ENTANGLEMENT WITH PEOPLE

A RELATIONAL READING OF BONHOEFFER'S THEOLOGY

> *They sentenced me to twenty years of boredom*
> *for trying to change the system from within.*
> *I'm coming now*
> *I'm coming to reward them.*
> *First we take Manhattan then we take Berlin.*
>
> Leonard Cohen

[Author's note: This article is a summary of a forthcoming book treating the development of Dietrich Bonhoeffer's theology within its relational contexts of the people and places important to him. It is titled, *First We Take Manhattan, Then We Take Berlin: Bonhoeffer's New York.* Portions of this work have been published in *Cross Currents* journal and is used here with permission.]

By 1930 Dietrich Bonhoeffer had completed his doctorate at the University of Berlin, Schleiermacher's University. However, by then, many had grown suspicious of Schleiermacher's *Gefühl,* that deep, romantic religious feeling that so characterized cultured, nineteenth century theological thought. Even Bonhoeffer had his doubts, not because he lacked religious feeling, but because a certain melancholia drew his gaze again and again to that ugly ditch another nineteenth century thinker called, "the infinite qualitative difference between the human and the divine".

Bonhoeffer was the son of a liberal, humanistic, yet aristocratic German home. This home was also well aquatinted with sorrow. Young Dietrich had been deeply saddened by the death of his eldest brother Walter in the First World War. Dietrich was given Walter's autographed Bible at his confirmation. Another brother, Karl-Friedrich, had come home from the Western Front wounded, cursing militarism and the motherland, questioning God, and reading aloud to the family large passages from Feuerbach. As Dietrich Bonhoeffer began his theological studies he learned of what theologian Karl Barth called a "black day" in early August 1914 when ninety-three German professors, some of them prominent theologians, announced their support of the war policy of Wilhelm II. It seemed to Barth and his circle that theology had become little more than a mirror of nineteenth century German culture[1].

It is therefore not surprising that Bonhoeffer found himself desiring something other, something different, something more. As he pondered the ugly ditch of European history, it is not surprising that early in his academic career he was drawn to Karl Barth's dialectical construction of God: a God who is Wholly Other, *Ganz Anders*. Like Barth, Bonhoeffer hoped that the vast distance between the human and the divine could be measured although never shortened through thick tomes of dogmatic theology. Yet even Barth knew that the angels would one day laugh at such a theology.

At the time Bonhoeffer thought the ugly ditch of history that so tormented his soul was the emblem of the infinite qualitative difference between the human and the divine. Only later would he see that he was looking deep into what Cornel West has called the gorge caused by the tragedies and terrors of this ghastly century. Only later would he understand that the Other has a human face. Only later would he turn from normative ethics to aesthetics; only later would he move from metaphysics, morality and a dogmatics underwritten by a positivism of revelation to a theopoetics. But that is later.

The University of Berlin was also the university of Karl Bonhoeffer, Dietrich's father, the distinguished professor of psychiatry and neurology and the most prominent psychiatrist in the city. Karl was very disappointed by Dietrich's decision to become a Lutheran pastor-theologian. Why would his gifted son choose a churchly vocation that would likely promise an uneventful life? Bonhoeffer's dear friend and biographer, Eberhard Bethge, answers the question this way: "Dietrich became a theologian because he was lonely"[2].

The lonely theologian chose for his dissertation topic, *Sanctorum Communio – The Communion of Saints*. Bonhoeffer became an earnest churchman and he believed in the communion of saints. His curiosity, and his consciousness that the communion of saints was large, much larger than the civil religion of German Christendom, led him to catch a steamer

---

1. The Bonhoeffer-Barth relationship has often been discussed and debated in the theological guild. The most comprehensive treatment may be found in the new book by A. PANGRITZ, *Karl Barth in the Theology of Dietrich Bonhoeffer*, Grand Rapids, MI, 2000.

2. Eberhard Bethge's classic biography of Bonhoeffer has recently been expanded by the author and released in a newly revised edition. E. BETHGE, *Dietrich Bonhoeffer: A Biography*, Minneapolis, MN, Fortress Press, 2000. Bethge's full statement on the lonely theologian is as follows: "With some exaggeration, it might be said that because he was lonely he became a theologian, and because he became a theologian he was lonely" (p. 37).

named the Columbus, bound for America. After the Columbus docked in New York, Bonhoeffer soon found his way up Broadway to 121st Street and entered the gate of Union Theological Seminary, an institution that had a reputation of being somewhat avant-garde, if theology can ever be avant-garde!

Bonhoeffer came to Union as a post-doctoral student and teaching fellow for the 1930-1931 academic year. He came to do serious theology. He didn't understand at the time that it would be *a poetics of place and an entanglement with people* that would produce this serious theology. He didn't know then that the best theology is often that which comes before the text and in front of the text. Walter Benjamin, Jewish literary critic and philosopher, lived across town from the Bonhoeffers in Berlin. Dietrich and Walter never met. If they had, Benjamin would have likely told Bonhoeffer, "In the fields with which we are concerned, knowledge exists only in lightening flashes. The text is the thunder rolling along afterward"[3]. Like Benjamin, Bonhoeffer would later see that it was the literary fragment – the letter, the paper, the poem, the story, not the systematic manuscript – that best reflected traces of the lightening flash.

As a pastor-theologian, Bonhoeffer was eager to take a course from the Detroit socialist preacher who had come to Union only two years earlier. As a public intellectual and prophet to politicians, the socialist preacher, Reinhold Niebuhr, taught "Applied Theology". Bonhoeffer was prepared for Niebuhr's political theology and American pragmatism but he was nevertheless surprised by the syllabus Niebuhr distributed to the students. The course was titled, "Ethical Viewpoints in Modern Literature". For Bonhoeffer, it was the beginning of an ethics instructed by aesthetics. Bonhoeffer did theology in conversation with James Weldon Johnson's *Autobiography of an Ex-Colored Man,* W.E.D. DuBois' *The Souls of Black Folks* and the collected poetry of Langston Hughes and Countee Cullen, poets of the Harlem Renaissance. With an emerging analogical imagination, Bonhoeffer entered the creative space between heaven and earth, nature and grace, saint and sinner, self and other as he began to consider Niebuhr's experiment of viewing theology and ethics as a

---

3. Benjamin as cited in W. WHITSON FLOYD, JR., *Style and the Critique of Metaphysics: The Letter as Form in Bonhoeffer and Adorno,* in W. WHITSON – C. MARSH (eds.), *Theology and the Practice of Responsibility: Essays on Dietrich Bonhoeffer,* Valley Forge, PA, Trinity Press International, 1994, pp. 239-251. Stanley Cavell has recently commented on the philosophical or aesthetic importance of Walter Benjamin in his refusal (or inability) to become a systematic thinker. See S. CAVELL, *Remains to be Seen: On* The Arcades Project, in *Art Forum* (April 2000) 31-35.

kind of writing. This was perhaps the first class in an American seminary to turn to literature as a source for doing applied theology.

Not only did Bonhoeffer learn of another America through reading the writers of the Harlem Renaissance, he began to ponder what the New York black evangelist Tom Skinner was fond of calling "the blackness of the Gospel". Countee Cullen's collection *Copper Sun* was on the Union class syllabus and in the poem, "Colors", Bonhoeffer read: "The play is done, the crowds depart; and see/ That twisted tortured thing hung from a tree,/ Swart victim of a newer Calvary./ Yea, he who helped Christ up Golgotha's track,/ That Simon who did not deny, was black"[4]. Reflecting years later on the poetry of Cullen, Bonhoeffer commented on "the black Christ" being led into the field against "a white Christ" by a young Negro poet revealing to us the deep cleft in the church of Jesus Christ[5]. Indeed, Cullen's narrative poem, "The Black Christ", has a rather astonishing conclusion. As the story of a racist lynching develops, the subject position of a black man who is lynched by whites for his love of sensuality, the spring, and a white woman is assumed, in the end, by Christ[6].

As at least part of his quest for the communion of saints Bonhoeffer formed several close friendships at Union. Here I can only mention two of his good friends: Jean Lasserre, a French Reformed pastor, and Franklin Fisher, an African-American divinity student. Jean Lasserre was French Reformed yet almost Tolstoyan in his religious and ethical vision. In terms of H. Richard Niebuhr's classic typology of Christian religion, he fit the "Christ against culture" paradigm.

He was an unapologetic Christian pacifist who identified the essence of the faith as ethical and embodied concretely in discipleship, community and peace. His book, *War and the Gospel,* was published by the Mennonite Publishing House and its style and substance is reflected in Bonhoeffer's work, *The Cost of Discipleship*: "When Jesus calls a man he bids him to come and die". There is no cheap grace here, and little tolerance for the plurality and ambiguity of human nature beyond the revelation of God in Jesus Christ. *Discipleship* calls the true believer to crucify the flesh and inhabit the strange new world of Jesus' Sermon on the Mount.

Bonhoeffer was very drawn to Lasserre's ethical zeal. He had found a true saint in Jean Lasserre. This unqualified call to the costly grace and

4. C. CULLEN, *Copper Sun*, in G. EARLY (ed.), *My Soul's High Song: The Collected Writings of Countee Cullen*, New York, Anchor Books, 1991, p. 145.
5. D. BONHOEFFER, *No Rusty Swords: Letters, Lectures and Notes, 1928-1936*, New York, Harper and Row, 1965, p. 112.
6. C. CULLEN, *The Black Christ and Other Poems*, New York, Harper and Brothers, 1929.

radical discipleship was for Bonhoeffer totally other, and he liked it. Lasserre took Dietrich to see the film *All Quiet on the Western Front* and it greatly disturbed him. He left the New York theater shaken and more deeply committed to the path of Christian pacifism[7]. Soon, Bonhoeffer made a trip across America with Lasserre in an old Buick that ended at an ecumenical peace conference in Mexico. There the Frenchman and the German spoke together on discipleship and peace. Dietrich would never forget Jean.

When Dietrich's father learned of their planned trip across the United States he warned them not to stay in the City of New Orleans. He knew of malaria on the Gulf Coast yet perhaps as a psychiatrist he also knew what Tennessee Williams later would teach us. In the City of New Orleans, there is a place where the line of the streetcar named Desire intersects with the line of the streetcar named Cemeteries. To understand this is to understand a great deal. Dietrich and Jean didn't go to New Orleans but later, much later, Dietrich would encounter the meeting of eros and thanatos, desire and death, and it would do important things to his theology.

Franklin Fisher grew up in Birmingham, Alabama. He was the son of a Black Baptist minister who was also dean of the theology department of Alabama's Selma University. Franklin, or Frank, as his friends called him, did his B.A. at Howard College, now Howard University. There he became interested in the Harlem Renaissance. He came to New York to study theology, but also to explore Harlem, and he took his new German friend Dietrich along with him. Bonhoeffer became a regular attender of Harlem's Abysinnian Baptist Church and for six months taught the boys Sunday school class and helped with various youth clubs there. Once, Pastor Adam Clayton Powell, Sr. yielded his pulpit to this young, German Lutheran pastor.

At Abysinnian, Bonhoeffer sat under the ministry of Powell almost weekly for over six months. Powell's culturally engaged sermons blended the artful rhetoric and congregational, noncreedal style of the black Baptist church with the best of American social pragmatism. Powell had leaned to appreciate John Dewey through their work together at the NAACP. We have recently learned through the research of Ralph Garlin Clingan that some of Bonhoeffer's theological vocabulary was borrowed

---

7. The best study of Bonhoeffer's movement to Christian pacifism is F. BURTON NELSON's *The Relationship of Jean Lasserre to Dietrich Bonhoeffer's Peace Concerns in the Struggle of Church and Culture*, in *Union Seminary Quarterly Review* 8 (1985) 71-84. Another important treatment of Bonhoeffer's struggle around peace and pacifism is Union Professor L. RASMUSSEN's, *Dietrich Bonhoeffer: Reality and Resistance*, Nashville, TN, Abingdon Press, 1972.

from the pulpit work Pastor Adam Clayton Powell, Sr. For example, Powell complained that the problem of the Euro-American church was "cheap grace"[8]. The problem of cheap grace – grace without the price of following after Jesus – of course, became a central focus of Bonhoeffer's *Discipleship*. The phrase, "world come of age", a familiar and frequently debated concept in Bonhoeffer's prison letters was used by Powell in his preaching: "The world come of age asks only one question: What can you do to make the world happy? What can you do to uplift humanity?"[9].

Frank Fisher introduced Bonhoeffer to both sacred and secular Harlem, not that the two could always be easily pried apart. As a pastor, Bonhoeffer spoke of the Black church with uncharacteristic feeling. As a classical pianist, Bonhoeffer was very interested in the music. He found it strange and other yet he was fascinated by it. At Harlem, it seems, Bonhoeffer began to learn about the improvisation of jazz, the contingency of the blues, and the liberation of black spirituals. Much later in his intellectual and spiritual development he applied a musical rather than a biblical or ethical metaphor to the task of theology: polyphony. Theology, Bonhoeffer suggested, is not a neat harmony neither is it a mere symphony, but it is a polyphony. A polyphony in this context is musical piece in which two or more different melodies come together in a satisfying way. According to Bonhoeffer, the church's *cantus firmus*, its fixed traditional melody, must remain in place yet invite the addition and innovation of other voices into the flow of the music. The introduction of this metaphor into his theology marked a movement in his thought from the imitation motif of *The Cost of Discipleship* or *Nachfolge* to the more improvisational style of his later works, such as *Ethics* and *Letters and Papers from Prison*[10].

Bonhoeffer was intrigued by the music and culture of New York but he hated its racism. He became a smart and sensitive critic of American racism and this attention to racism seemed to deepen his critiques of German anti-Semitism. He discussed this problem freely with his brother

8. R.G. CLINGAN, *Against Cheap Grace in a World Come of Age: A Study in the Hermeneutics of Adam Clayton Powell, 1865-1953, in His Intellectual Context*, a Drew University Ph.D. dissertation, UMI Microfilm 9732791, Ann Arbor, MI, 1997.

9. A. CLAYTON POWELL, *Palestine and Saints in Caesar's Household*, New York, Richard and Smith, 1939, p. 187.

10. Bonhoeffer discusses his application of polyphony to theology, ethics, and indeed life with great enthusiasm in his correspondence with Bethge. See BONHOEFFER, *Letters and Papers from Prison*, enlarged edition, New York, Macmillan, 1971, pp. 302-312. The theme of improvisation (and polyphony) in music and how this musical method and metaphor can inform other disciplines is explored in an important special issue of *The Journal of Aesthetics and Art Criticism* 58:2 (Spring 2000).

Karl-Friedrich, who had studied at Harvard on a physics fellowship. Karl-Friedrich concluded that the problem of racism in the United States was so terrible that he could never imagine raising a family in America. Hitler had of course not yet ascended to power in Germany. Racism was *the* American problem for any person of conscience Dietrich's older brother concluded. Dietrich seemed to agree. It was in New York that this German Lutheran theologian first began to truly understand the issues of racism and nationalism as serious theological problems.

Josiah Ulysses Young III has recently published the first book length study of Bonhoeffer and the problem of racism. *No Difference in the Fare* brings Bonhoeffer's theology into very creative conversation with African-American theology and culture. Young shows how the attention to alterity, otherness or difference in Bonhoeffer's theological work contributed to a profound social understanding of the relationship of the self to the other that fostered respect in spite of radical difference[11]. The other, Bonhoeffer suggests, in the I-Thou relationship, presents us with the same problem of cognition as does God. The Thou of the other – the neighbor, the friend, the stranger – is analogous to the divine Thou. Thus, one must resist projecting an easy sameness or harmony upon the other and encounter or receive him or her as a "Thou", outside of any centered or self-present conception of the "I". This I-Thou or I-You encounter becomes crucial not only for understanding the other but also for understanding the self. Authentic relationality must be grounded in the recognition of uniqueness and separateness, Bonhoeffer argues. He then asserts, "The individual becomes a person ever and again through the other, in the moment"[12]. Bonhoeffer's experience in Harlem helped him translate the heavenly categories of transcendence into relational expressions of worldly holiness.

At the end of 1931 it was time for Bonhoeffer to return to his old intellectual center: Berlin. So he packed up his books and Paul Robeson records and returned home. For the next couple of years he was a lecturer

---

11. J. ULYSSES YOUNG III, *No Difference in the Fare: Dietrich Bonhoeffer and the Problem of Racism*, Grand Rapids, MI, Eerdmans, 1998. Bonhoeffer began the development of his theology and sociology of the social category of the I-Thou relationship in his dissertation.

12. D. BONHOEFFER, *Sanctorum Communio: The Theological Study of the Sociology of the Church*, Minneapolis, MN, Fortress Press, 1998, pp. 55-56. This is the first volume in the newly translated works of Bonhoeffer, Wayne Whitson Floyd, Jr., General Editor. This philosophy of self and other of course makes one think of Martin Buber's *I and Thou*. Those familiar with the philosophy of Emmanuel Levinas will note possible correlations. See especially E. LEVINAS, *Alterity and Transcendence*, New York, Columbia University Press, 1999.

at Berlin as well as a chaplain and pastor. In 1933 Adolph Hitler became Reich Chancellor of Germany with the support of many German Christians. While other pastors were writing sermons and other theologians were occupied with classical Christological questions, Bonhoeffer went on the air and strongly criticized the rise of Fascism in a radio address that was cut-off by the authorities before it was completed. He was the first pastor to offer such a public protest. This was only the beginning of Bonhoeffer's troubles with the Reich and thus he found the invitation to leave Berlin to pastor the German Lutheran congregations in London from 1933-1935 too inviting to decline. He continued his resistance work in ecumenical circles there while remaining in close contact with his colleagues and family in Berlin.

By 1935 in Germany it was necessary for the Confessing Church opposing Hitler to establish a seminaries in exile. Bonhoeffer was called from London by the Confessing Church to return to Germany and head the resisting seminary at Finkenwalde. His book *Life Together* recalls this experiment of viewing the church as an alternative, counter-cultural community at a time when the German church and society were marching to the music of the Nazism. Bonhoeffer's students at Finkenwalde found his spirituality and theology challenging yet wondered about his strange musical tastes as they listened to the unfamiliar voice of Paul Robeson on the Victrola lament, plead, and prophesy: "Go down. Go down Moses! Way down in Egypt's land. Tell old, Pharoah, Let my people go!"[13].

In April 1938, Bonhoeffer fell into deep despair when the majority of Confessing Church pastors – his students, friends and colleagues – fearing for their lives and the lives of their families, took the oath of allegiance to the Fuhrer. Within two months there was *Kristallnacht*, the night of broken glass, and all Jewish businesses were liquidated by January. Hitler's totalitarianism now threatened all dissenters with punishment or death. In the Spring of 1939 Bonhoeffer caught a steamer back to New York, to the safety of Manhattan.

As he revisited New York, his Babylon, his Jerusalem, the world came of age and in his words, he "gathered up the past". He spent time with old friends and met new ones, including the poet W.H. Auden. He spoke with them about the fate of the German Jews. He spoke with them about the fate of all German people under Fascism, his people. We have no

---

13. Bonhoeffer wrote of his love of the Negro spirituals in *No Rusty Swords*, p. 109. Then he observes in dismay, "Negro singers can sing those songs before packed concert audiences of whites, to tumultuous applause, while at the same time these same men and women are still denied access to the white community through social discrimination".

record of his conversations with Auden but several years later Auden wrote a poem dedicated to Bonhoeffer entitled, "Friday's Child"[14]. We do know this was the year that Auden was questioning his own politics and pacifism in face of the evolving European totalitarianism. He was keeping a notebook of aphorisms and reflections after his meditations on William Blake's *The Marriage of Heaven and Hell*[15]. Their conversation likely turned to models of resistance and to pacifism. One must wonder if Auden didn't raise the Blakean question of "fearful symmetry" with Bonhoeffer: "Did he who made the Lamb make thee [the Tyger]?"[16]. Indeed, there was little tiger in the Jesus of Bonhoeffer's Christology (and therefore neither in his theological anthropology) and there was much of the obedient, sacrificial lamb. As the poet and the pastor talked, one must wonder if Auden didn't confess to Bonhoeffer privately what he said in public over a year later, "I have absolutely no patience with Pacifism as a political movement, as if one could do all the things in one's personal life that create wars and then pretend that to refuse to fight is a sacrifice and not a luxury"[17].

Friends at Union worked to secure Bonhoeffer teaching positions at American colleges or seminaries so that he could remain in the United States even as he pondered what has now become the classic question of his life and witness, "Will the church merely gather up those whom the wheel has crushed or will it prevent the wheel from crushing them?". During the hot and humid July of 1939, his room at Union cluttered with cigarette butts and mounds of spent papers from too many unsuccessful writing attempts, Bonhoeffer decided to return to Berlin to join the active resistance to Hitler and the Third Reich. "Only he who cries out for the Jews may sing Gregorian chants!"[18], he would declare. He concluded that he would have no right to take part in the restoration of Germany after the war unless he shared with the people in the trials of the country's most horrible time in history.

He would later write these words to Eberhard Bethge describing his decision to enter fully and responsibly into the dramas of history on behalf of the other:

14. See E. MENDELSON, *Later Auden*, New York, Farrar, Straus and Giroux, 1999, pp. 425-427.
15. This "notebook" was later published as W.H. AUDEN, *The Prolific and the Devourer*, Hopewell, NJ, The Ecco Press, 1976.
16. W. BLAKE, *The Complete Poetry and Prose*, Newly revised edition edited by D.V. ERDMAN and commentary by H. BLOOM, Berkeley, CA, The University of California Press, 1982, pp. 24-25.
17. W.H. AUDEN, *The Prolific and the Devourer* (n. 15), p. x.
18. E. BETHGE, *Bonhoeffer* (n. 2), p. 607.

There remains an experience of incomparable value. We have for once learnt
to see the great events of history from below, from the perspective of the
outcast, the suspects, the maltreated, the powerless, the oppressed, the reviled
– in short from the perspective of those who suffer. ... This perspective
from below must not become the particular possession of those who are
eternally dissatisfied; rather, we must do justice to life in all its dimensions
from a higher satisfaction, whose foundation is beyond any talk of, "from
below" or "from above". This is the way in which we may affirm it[19].

This movement in Bonhoeffer's thought, I would suggest, signals the
possibility of a transcendence without either classical metaphysics or an
orthodox positivism of revelation; it is at once both a worldly and a spiritual transcendence. It is a naming of oneself and a rendering of God in
history "as another" in an improvisational ethics called forth by the aesthetic encounter with the face of the other. Paul Ricœur's Gifford Lectures are quite helpful in unpacking this point about alterity. Like Bonhoeffer, Ricœur resists a Romantic notion of self-consciousness or
God-consciousness. Ricœur, who was himself a French prisoner of war
from 1940 to 1945, contends that the shortest path of the self to itself lies
in the speech of the other. Self-understanding therefore involves a
long detour through narratives and encounters with others, with self-
consciousness as the final destination, not the starting point[20].

One can discern a movement in Bonhoeffer's religious and intellectual
formation from the mimesis of discipleship to a more innovative poetics
of obligation. In this worldly holiness Jesus truly becomes "the man for
others". There has been much debate on precisely what Bonhoeffer really
meant by his famous celebration of the advent of "religionless Christianity"[21], but there is little disagreement that there was an aesthetic turn in his
life and work[22]. This can be seen in the texts of Bonhoeffer written between
1939 and 1945: the fragments of his incomplete *Ethics* which explore
human desire along side of Christian duty, his drama and fiction from
prison, his love letters, and his many moving letters, papers, and poems
from prison. Defining aesthetics as the artful, sensuous perception of reality, this turn is indeed striking and satisfying in Bonhoeffer's final works[23].

19. BONHOEFFER, *Letters and Papers from Prison* (n. 10), p. 17.

20. P. RICŒUR, *Oneself as Another*, Chicago, IL, University of Chicago Press, 1992.

21. The most recent study of this theme is R.K. WUSTENBERG, *A Theology of Life:
Dietrich Bonhoeffer's Religionless Christianity*, Grand Rapids, MI, Eerdmans, 1998.

22. The most interesting piece I have seen on this aesthetic turn is C.M. JONES, *Dietrich Bonhoeffer's Letters and Papers From Prison: Rethinking the Relation of Theology
and the Arts, Literature and Religion*, in *Literature and Theology* 9 (1995) 243-259.

23. Within the past year new translations of both Bonhoeffer's poetry and fiction from
prison have been published. See E. ROBERTSON (ed. & trans.), *Voices in the Night:*

This aesthetic turn opened him to a faith that was polyphonic and multi-dimensional. Bonhoeffer celebrated its multiplicity in a letter to Bethge:

> Christianity puts us into many different dimensions of life at the same time; we make room in ourselves, to some extent, for God and the whole world ... [Life] is kept multi-dimensional and polyphonous. What a deliverance it is to be able to *think*, and thereby remain multi-dimensional[24].

This kind of artful thinking led Bonhoeffer's theological reflections beyond the sacred text into the world of material culture. As the Greek term *aisthesis* implies, aesthetics takes one into the whole embodied realm of sensation and perception[25]. Aesthetics signals the body's long rebellion against the tyranny of static systems and totalitarian ideologies, even any attempted totality of theology and ethics. I love this expression of Bonhoeffer's incarnational desire from the *Letters*:

> I should like to be tired by the sun, instead of by books and thoughts. I should like to have it awaken my animal existence – not the kind that degrades a man, but the kind that delivers him from the stuffiness and artificiality of a purely intellectual existence and makes him purer and happier. I should like, not just to see the sun and sip at it a little, but to experience it bodily[26].

By 1943 Dietrich Bonhoeffer had been arrested and imprisoned for his part in a plan to kill Hitler. He wrote one of the most important theological fragments of the twentieth century in a lengthy letter from Tegel Prison dated 21 July 1944. He confesses that in the past year he has come to know and understand the "profound this-worldliness of Christianity". He writes that the Christian is not a *homo religiosus*, but simply a man, as Jesus was a man – in contrast to John the Baptist. He then makes another startling contrast. He contrasts himself with his old friend Jean Lasserre:

> I remember a conversation I had in America thirteen years ago with a young French pastor. We were asking ourselves quite simply what we wanted to do with our lives. He said he would like to become a saint (and I think it's

---

The Prison Poems of Dietrich Bonhoeffer, Grand Rapids, MI, Zondervan, 1999, and C.J. GREEN (ed.), *Dietrich Bonhoeffer: Fiction from Prison*, Minneapolis, MN, Fortress, 2000, in the new series, *Dietrich Bonhoeffer Collected Works, Volume 7*. Also see R.-A. VON BISMARCK – U. KABITZ (eds.), *Love Letters From Cell 92: The Correspondence Between Dietrich Bonhoeffer and Maria Von Wedemyer*, Nashville, TN, Abingdon, 1992.
    24. BONHOEFFER, *Letters and Papers from Prison* (n. 10), pp. 310-311.
    25. A good discussion of the evolution of the term aesthetics and its use in philosophy and theology can be found in R. VILADESAU's new work, *Theological Aesthetics: God in Imagination, Beauty and Art*, New York, Oxford University Press, 1999.
    26. BONHOEFFER, *Letters and Papers From Prison* (n. 10), pp. 339-340.

quite likely that he did become one). At the time I was very impressed but I disagreed with, and said, in effect, that I should like to learn to have faith. For a long time I did not realize the depth of that contrast. I thought I could acquire faith by trying to live a holy life, or something like it. I suppose I wrote *The Cost of Discipleship* as an end of that path. Today I can see the dangers of that book, though I still stand by what I wrote ... I discovered later, and I'm still discovering right up to this moment, that it is only by living completely in this world that one learns to have faith.

When Bonhoeffer was arrested and imprisoned for his part in an active plot to assassinate Hitler he had acted with the sense that he was transgressing normative Christian morality on behalf of something other. Participation in an act of violent resistance was far from the biblical ethics of Christian pacifism that he and Lasserre had preached in Mexico. Bonhoeffer came to understand that to love the neighbor is to accept some responsibility for the neighbor's history. He insisted that he accepted this responsibility as a man, not as a saint, a priest, a righteous individual, or even a churchman. He accepted it in face of historical ambiguity and infinite mystery. He accepted it as one living and loving and thinking completely in this blessed fallen world. He acted in a faith beyond ethical correctness or dogmatic certitude.

Let me conclude this essay with one of his final poems. Art, like its closest analogue religion, must be both world confirming and world disconfirming. It must seek meaning and understanding by means of the exception and not merely by means of the rule. It must confront one as "other" yet also touch deeply some analogy of seeing, hearing, feeling or thinking because human consciousness requires the art of connecting. It must probe both the dialectical imagination and the analogical imagination. In Bonhoeffer's life art possessed the sacramental power to turn theology into theopoetics:

WHO AM I?

Who am I? The often tell me
I would step from my cell's confinement
Calmly, cheerfully, firmly,
Like a squire from his country-house.

Who am I? The often tell me
I would talk to my warders
freely and friendly and clearly,
as though it were mine to command.

Who am I? They also tell me
I would bear the days of misfortune
Equably, smilingly, proudly,
Like one accustomed to win.

Am I then really all that which men tell of?
Or am I only what I know of myself,
Restless and longing and sick like a bird in a cage,
Struggling for breath, as though hands were compressing my throat,

Yearning for colours, for flowers, for the voices of birds,
Thirsting for words of kindness, for neighborliness,
Trembling with anger at despotisms and petty humiliation,
Tossing in expectation of great events,
Powerlessly trembling for friends at an infinite distance,
Weary and empty at praying, at thinking, at making
Faint, and ready to say farewell to it all?

Who am I? This or the other?
Am I one person today, and tomorrow another?
Am I both at once? A hypocrite before others,
And before myself a contemptibly woebegone weakling?
Or is something within me still like a beaten army,
Fleeing in disorder from victory already achieved?

Who am I? They mock me, these lonely questions of mine.
Whoever I am, thou knowest, O God, I am thine[27].

On the 9th of April, 1945 Dietrich Bonhoeffer was executed at Flossen-
burg Concentration Camp only days before its liberation. He was hanged
by the Nazis. He was 39 years old. I would like to think that in the end
there was no great chasm to cross. I would like to think that in the end,
in the dark beauty of worldly holiness, for Bonhoeffer, *the Infinite and
the intimate became one*[28].

Bethany Theological   Scott HOLLAND
Seminary & Earlham School
of Religion
615 National Road West
Richmond, IN 47374
U.S.A.

---

27. *Ibid.*, pp. 347-348.
28. Special thanks is due here to my friend and editorial colleague Catherine Madsen
for insight into this graceful or theopoetic moment in which "the Infinite and the intimate
become one".

CONVERSATION PEACE

AUTOBIOGRAPHY AND THE HEALING OF MEMORIES*

I. INTRODUCTION

Autobiographies, biographies and diaries are a perennial source of human curiosity and interest. Perhaps because everyone loves a good story and we often find renewed inspiration and hope from the example and experience of another's life. Take for instance the study and devotion that the diaries and letters of Etty Hillesum have enjoyed since their publication after the second world war. Etty's memoirs represent more than just the moving story of a twenty-nine-year-old whose life ended in a concentration camp.

Rather, she charts in autobiographical notes, a spiritual journey which engages in profound conversations with her deepest self, on love and hate, revenge and forgiveness, despair and hope. In a sense, she is paradigmatic for our time, torn as it is, between forgetting and remembering history; between forgiveness and revenge. Etty Hillesum desired to encounter God even in the camps as expressed in her declaration to be "... the thinking heart of the barracks"[1] (Diary entry 15th September, 1942).

The telling of stories against the background of horror and tragedy is a ritual which still goes on today. In Northern Ireland, narratives are now emerging in the form of personal accounts of living through almost thirty-two years of violent conflict. Exemplary among them is the unique *Bear in Mind-Stories of the Troubles*, which is a collection of the personal accounts of ordinary people whose lives have been shaped and some-times shattered by conflict[2]. The originality of this collection lies in its inclusiveness: there are largely unedited, firsthand testimonies from all

---

* This title is inspired by a *Stevie Wonder* peace song of the same name: "There's no way we'll reach our greatest heights unless we heed the call. There's no chance of world salvation unless the conversation's peace". Universal Music for the World, 1995. www.universalmusicworld.com.

1. E. HILLESUM, *An Interrupted Life and Letters from Westerbork*, New York, 1996, p. 199.

2. An Crann-The Tree (ed.), *Bear in Mind – Stories of Troubles*, Belfast, 2000. Founded in 1994, An Crann-The Tree is an arts-based, charitable organization dedicated to providing a space in which people can tell and hear personal narratives of "the troubles", a popular local term used to describe the thirty year conflict in Northern Ireland. *Bear in Mind* is a significant narrative contribution to understanding and healing as the peace process evolves.

848 M. DUFFY

sides of the community including members of the police, the emergency services, the military, even children, in the belief that everyone's perspective, whether it be that of an ex-terrorist, a soldier or a community worker or the survivor of trauma, has a place of value in building a more respectful and tolerant society. Though often conflicting, contradictory and fragmented, the editors hoped that these stories could be respected through being heard and help to stimulate an intensive dialogue on healing and the conversion of prejudices and sectarianism.

These moving testimonials from two contrasting eras and cultures, bear witness to the dynamic voice of narrative, which in conversation with theology, can positively influence fundamental social issues, such as how we deal with the past and suffering, and how we can rebuild society and facilitate sustainable peace in an ongoing process of reconciliation.

This paper reflects on the contribution which narrative, still an impoverished discourse in theology, can contribute to the search for peace and reconciliation by challenging the way in which society deals with wounded memory so that conflict itself can be a source of healing rather than the sustenance of division. To the extent that autobiography helps to facilitate this narrative goal, it is transformed beyond the personal and particular into a gestalt of socio-biography which helps shape a new self-image, belief and identity in torn communities. In other words, the sharing of personal experience has a value in the context of suffering and violence because stories can powerfully evoke or awaken the civic spirit to an "ethical imagination". Not the kind which perpetuates hate or the seeking of revenge, but another kind of revolution of the *heart,* that consists of learning to see and to love instead of being disgusted by, "imperfect human beings"[3]. Insofar as narrative points divided communities in this direction, it gestures to the transcendent[4].

Why Narrative?

First, it is necessary to ask why narrative and narrative forms such as autobiography are important for this task? Principally because narrative is the genre of *story* and telling stories is basic to human beings.

It was Aristotle who first worked philosophically with the principle of *mythos* or story and who developed the notion that "the art of storytelling – defined as the dramatic imitating and plotting of human action – is what gives us a *shareable* world". It is only when haphazard happenings are transformed into a story, and thus made memorable over time, that we

3. M. NUSSBAUM, *Love's Knowledge. Essay's on Philosophy and Literature,* New York, 1990, p. 200.
4. R. KEARNEY, *The Poetics of Modernity,* Atlantic Heights, NJ, 1992, p. 106.

become full agents of our history[5]. Another modern thinker, Hannah Arendt, claims: "The chief characteristic of the specifically human life … is that it is always full of events which ultimately can be told as a story. It is of this life, *bios* (fully human), as distinguished from mere *zoe* (biological life), which led Aristotle to conclude that story is also a kind of action *(praxis)*".

This suggests, as Kearney has argued, that storytelling *humanizes* time by transforming it from "an impersonal passing", into a plot, a pattern, a mythos. Therefore, in both personal and cultural contexts, the narrative paradigm is indispensable to bestowing meaning and identity in life and essential to creating relationship.

Inevitably the reality of evil inflicted, of lives extinguished before their time, brings any conversation about story, spirituality and theologizing to an uneasy silence. Holocaust literature or the stories arising out a people's lived experience of "the troubles" in Ireland, ask us to choose either to fill the silence with revenge and violence or forgiveness and justice and to seek more imaginative paths to peace.

Autobiography can be a source and a means of creating new spiritual spaces for difficult conversations to take place in strife-torn societies by helping to re-construct the fragile human story and to build up personal lives. Personal stories that arise out of violence and conflict, whether the Holocaust of Europe, the apartheid regime of South Africa, terrorism in Northern Ireland or elsewhere, help to reclaim the personal in the midst of deeply inhuman circumstances.

For example, Etty Hillesum's, *"An Interrupted Life and Letters from Westerbork"*, constructs for us a particular human story in a particular phase of history. This young woman claims her story against the "big story". She *personalizes* the struggle between love and hate, forgiveness and revenge and *experienced* a moral duty to tell her story for future generations and to interpret her moment in history, for others. Amidst an increasingly inhuman regime, she nurtured the fragile flower of human dignity, even displaying a kind of spiritual ambition to seek the transcendent despite her miserable circumstances. Remarkably, Etty managed to find the world both "beautiful and good, despite everything human beings were doing to one another". (Diary entry 15th September, 1942).

Similar counter-narratives are emerging in our times, as the search for reconciliation and the building of a more just and tolerant society continues. We can become deeply engaged with stories which describe what

---

5. R. KEARNEY, *On Stories*, London, 2002, p. 4.

it is like to be on the receiving end of persecution, suffering and violence, whether its source is Auschwitz, Belfast, or elsewhere. Stories
wrought from radical *hamartia*, that is, missing the mark of what it is to
be human together, can call forth conversion or *metanoia* to right ways
of living with diversity and difference in the quest for lasting peace. Indirectly, personal testimony can move us to change attitudes and behaviour
by demonstrating that ignorance, bigotry, ethnic cleansing and sectarian
hatred are ultimately futile. Simply put, this means that the lessons learned
in one spot on the globe can save lives elsewhere.

To the extent that autobiographical aesthetic can act as an impetus for
this breakthrough, then narrative crosses the threshold of the particular to
a more socially founded conversation about what we share in common as
distinct from what divides us.

II. AUTOBIOGRAPHY AND THE DUTY TO REMEMBER

What might the spiritual or social value of personal anthologies of pain
be, apart perhaps from their therapeutic worth in exorcising suffering?
Perhaps they make the profound suggestion that communities have a duty
to remember. For example, it is in recognition of the "hurt" memory of
those who have sadly died in the troubles of Northern Ireland, that the
words of the Ulster poet, James Hewitt, are borrowed for the title of the
narrative anthology, *Bear in Mind*.

> Bear in mind these dead
> I can find no plainer words ...
> They propose no more
> Than thoughtful response.

The Irish have a culture and tradition of storytelling, for having long
memories and for ritualizing the past. However, there is now a growing
recognition of the need for liberation from "old stories" in order to re-
create new narratives, in the belief that this will open up a better future[6].
One of the lessons which emerges out of *Bear in Mind* is that Ireland is
a country which has many *conflicting* stories about itself, its past and
therefore its identity. In light of this complicated history, it is hoped that
these fragmentary and indeed conflicting stories of "the troubles" can be
respected by being heard, and that others will be encouraged to talk, to

---

6. *Imagination, Testimony and Trust – An Interview with Paul Ricœur*, in R. KEARNEY
– M. DOOLEY (eds.), *Questioning Ethics. Contemporary Debates in Philosophy*, London,
1999, p. 12.

share their stories, as a result, in the hope of evolving a culture of "just memory"[7].

The philosopher, Paul Ricœur, suggests that the problem of finding a common narrative calls for an *ethics of discussion* or conversation. It is part of life that there are conflicts but the challenge is to bring conflicts to the level of discourse and not let them degenerate into violence. The collection of autobiographical material in *"Bear in Mind"* serves to illustrate Ricœur's point that histories can compete in a fierce conversation or "competition of discourse"[8]. Yet, it is precisely this competition between historical narratives that makes for historical education. We can therefore interpret the autobiographical data of *Bear in Mind* and similar material from conflict elsewhere, as a form of discourse ethics in which diverse and competing interests are brought together in the hope that they will engage each other in rigorous conversation with a view to resolving conflict.

Competing narratives, in Irish culture as elsewhere, only serve to illustrate the permanent tension that exists between what Ricœur refers to as the "space of experience and the horizon of expectation"[9] which the Northern Irish poet, Seamus Heaney, expresses in verse as a yearning for the rhyme of hope and history:

> History says, don't hope
> On this side of the grave
> But then, once in a lifetime
> The longed for tidal wave
> Of justice can rise up
> And hope and history rhyme'
> *(The Cure at Troy)*

A critical exchange between memory and expectation is fundamental to any hope or prayer for the rhyming of hope and history. Autobiographies point us to the "truth claim" of memory. In the words of Paul Ricœur: "what really happened must concern us"[10]. Autobiography suggests that it is ethical to remember history as it really happened. We are to an extent summoned by what was beyond the loss of what is no longer. In the face of dealing with opposing claims about the past as real or unreal, we must never eliminate the "truth claim" of what actually *has* been[11].

---

7. P. RICŒUR, *Memory and Forgetting*, in *Questioning Ethics* (n. 6), p. 11.
8. *Ibid.*, pp. 14-15.
9. *Ibid.*, pp. 13-14.
10. *Ibid.*, p. 15.
11. RICŒUR, *Imagination* (n. 6), p. 9. He suggests that a "duty to remember" (*devoir de mémoire*), has an ethico-political dimension also, because it concerns not only the past but the transmission of the meaning of past events to the next generation.

The young Etty Hillesum was acutely aware of the need to record the history of her time from her own experience, declaring her intention to

> wield my slender fountain pen as if it were a hammer
> and my words will have to be so many hammer
> strokes with which to beat out the story of our fate
> and of a piece of history as it never was before.
> A few people must survive, if only to be the chroniclers of this age.
> I would very much like to be one of their number.
> *(Diary entry Friday 10th August, 1942).*

Her sentiments are acknowledged by Ricœur who has argued that "it is good that the wounds of humanity remain open to thought. Those who have shared their story of suffering and victimization have trusted in language as a weapon against violence"[12]. Autobiography has moreover the potential to act as a kind of "*hermeneutic of suspicion*" by critiquing power systems or the mechanisms of regimes which have a vested interest in preventing a confrontation between competing arguments at the level of genuine discourse. Personal testimony attempts to correct the "big story" by engaging us in subversive conversations about what has happened from the viewpoint of history's victims.

III. AUTOBIOGRAPHY AND RECONCILIATION

Autobiography suggests that if we remember history honestly and recognize the viewpoint of those who have suffered, then this of itself, is an act of reconciliation with the past.

The diaries of Etty Hillesum and the experiences shared in the "stories of the troubles" test our taste for forgiveness and reconciliation. It was important to Etty that she share her story to make sure that future generations would know what hers and the fate of many others was, and that in dire circumstances, she struggled not to hate. In the Sermon on the Mount she discovered a meaningful root metaphor for living: to love her enemies and do good in a cataclysmic situation (Diary entry 22nd September, 1942). Similarly, the objective of the *An Crann The Tree* organization in publishing memoirs of "the troubles" is simply to put the stories into wider circulation in an attempt to find new ways of talking about the past and its experience, from the viewpoint of those who suffered[13].

---

12. *Ibid.*, p. 16.
13. MCKIMM, *Bear In Mind* (n. 2), p. xi.

Such first-hand accounts verify what Ricœur describes as "the indispensable issue" of *testimony*[14] which is the ultimate link between memory and imagination because the witness says, "I was part of the story. I was there".

The sensitive cherishing of memory, especially of suffering, through the means of autobiography, is a way of telling a story *otherwise*, as Ricœur would have it, over against the general tendency of history to celebrate the victors[15]. While recognizing that narrative memory is never entirely innocent, or on the side of angels, and that it risks distortion and is always likely to be a conflictual discourse, to quote Richard Kearney, nonetheless, in the recollecting we are compelled to remember atrocities which "might otherwise be forgotten and, by being forgotten, repeat themselves"[16]. In the case of Etty Hillesum and others like her, who have told their story, such as Holocaust survivor Elie Wiesel, the reason for the telling and re-telling is, "to give victims the voice that was denied them by history". By acting as a channel of remembrance, witness, testimony and experience, the autobiographical project can serve a community in the process of forgiveness by liberating people from "the debilitating impasse of hurt and the desire to hurt in return"[17]. Thus a narrative process of remembering can help to move us from separation to community, from mutual suspicion to trust.

IV. Autobiography and Theology

Autobiography gains part of its "compelling" quality by claiming to be "true to life" according to Michael Goldberg[18]. Personal stories "ring true" to some common ground of human experience and by being true to the facts of the individual lives of which they speak. If narrative helps us to encounter the lived experience of people then the genre, as a combination of history, witness and testimony, is an important theological source of research into questions of identity, meaning and the link between culture and faith. Therefore, in their role as social institutions, the Church and the religions can be very effective partners in the shared conversation about how best to help a broken humanity to live in dignity

---

14. Ricœur, *Imagination*, in *Questioning Ethics* (n. 6), p. 16.
15. Ricœur, *Memory* (n. 6), p. 10.
16. R. Kearney, *Narrative and the Ethics of Remembrance*, in *Questioning Ethics* (n. 6), p. 28.
17. G. Mueller-Fahrenholz, *The Art of Forgiveness*, Geneva, 1997, pp. 86-87.
18. M. Goldberg, *Theology and Narrative. A Critical Introduction*, Eugene, OR, 2001.

with the burdens of the past and to secure greater justice and sustainable peace.

Furthermore, the delicate process of healing and reconciliation demands that theologians develop a fine-tuned sensitivity or "*insiders feel*" to the lived-experiences of the people[19]. Autobiographical material, such as that which this paper has presented, helps to foster that "*insiders feel*". Through the device of story, memory and imagination, we are presented with the face of the dispossessed and the voices of those who have died too soon. In other words theology finds itself as a partner in a fragile dialogue which happens in a space of "un-assured, existential life-schooling"[20].

To the extent that theology can intensify its commitment to being an aesthetic of resistance, then it has something real and convincing to say about the *meaning* of life in its extremities of brutality and failure[21]. Theologian Enda McDonagh, has suggested, from the Irish experience of conflict, that any deepening or opening up of a sense of life-meaning which theology might bestow, hinges precisely on the relationship between theology and life experience. The importance of autobiography for theology is also noted by Sally McFague: "Autobiographies give practical wisdom because they are the story of the engagement of a personality in a task, not just the task alone". Hence the truth claim of autobiography comes from another feature as well: "the truthfulness of the self who writes the story of the self who is", to quote Michael Goldberg.

V. In Conclusion

Autobiography is not merely a matter of memory; it is also the art of recollection, of transforming *chronos* (linear time) into *kairos* (a moment of change)[22]. If undertaken with integrity, as the stories explored in this paper bear witness, then autobiography can open up to us a life ethic, a paradigm through which to see and live life truthfully. At the deepest level of our engagement with them, we might discover a "life-option" for our own story.

19. E. McDonagh, *Doing the Truth. The Quest for Moral Theology*, Dublin, 1979, p. 3: "The methodological significance of 'insider' analysis lays fresh emphasis on the autobiographical quality of effective theological work".

20. K.-J. Kuschel, *Literature as Challenge to Catholic Theology in the 20th Century: Balthasar, Guardini and the Tasks of Today*, in *Ethical Perspectives* 7 (2000) 257-268, p. 267.

21. *Ibid.*

22. Goldberg, *Theology* (n. 17), p. 98.

Thus, the narrative path becomes an adventure through the extremities of being human together. We may glimpse a ray of light even in history's dark moments, as can be discerned in the themes of the memoirs shared here. The insights and conversations which these autobiographies courageously open up for individuals, communities, for theology and faith, may well lead us to conclude, with the poet, T.S. Eliot:

> At the end of all our exploring
> Will be to arrive where we started
> And know the place for the first time...
> And all shall be well and
> All manner of thing shall be well.
> *(Little Gidding, Part V)*

Faculteit Godgeleerdheid   Maria DUFFY
K.U. Leuven
St.-Michielsstraat 6
B-3000 Leuven
Belgium

TOWARDS A THEOLOGICAL AESTHETICS

KARL RAHNER'S CONTRIBUTION

Karl Rahner did not emerge as one of the great theologians of the twentieth century due to his contribution to a theological aesthetics, or, to a theology of art. His contemporary, Hans Urs von Balthasar, or, in a rather different vein, Paul Tillich, will far more likely be mentioned in the context of theological aesthetics. Nevertheless, it is true that Rahner wrote a few significant and relevant essays on the topic, which hitherto have received comparatively little attention.

Rahner emphasises that fundamentally theology must not, and cannot be, reduced to verbal theology[1]. Given that only relatively few theologians have *explicitly* or extensively discussed the fact that our theological ideas and concepts must include the non-verbal, this simple statement indeed deserves attention.

Theology, as Rahner reiterates, is basically to be understood as the total self-expression of the human being, insofar as this self-expression arises out of God's self-communication to us, i.e. through the grace of divine self-revelation. In taking this concept also as his point of departure in the context of theology and the arts, he points out that theology therefore cannot be regarded as complete until it includes the arts as "an integral moment of itself and its own life, until the arts become an intrinsic moment of theology"[2]. This integration he considers essential since art is a deep, authentic expression of the human being, and because both, theology and art, are located in the transcendental nature of the human being. This, Rahner holds, not only applies to verbal art, i.e. literature, but to all the arts. *All* arts are forms of human self-expression. He writes: "If theology is simply and arbitrarily defined as being identical with verbal theology ... we would have to ask whether such a reduction of theology to verbal theology does justice to the value and uniqueness

---

1. K. RAHNER, *Theology and the Arts*, in *Thought – A Review of Culture and the Arts* 57 (1982) 17-29, p. 25.
2. *Ibid.*, p. 24.

of these arts, and whether it does not unjustifiably limit the capacity of these arts to be used by God in his revelation"[3]. Hence for him the idea of art being a source of theology essentially arises from a theology of revelation. He emphasises that art due to its revealing dimension is *not* to be understood merely as an *ancilla theologiae*, as an aid or an illustration of a religious truth[4], but it can in itself become a source of theology, a *locus theologicus*. Rahner reflects thereby the modern idea of imagination, i.e. the stress on the creative power of the human being, and thus of originality in a work of art[5]. For him the imagination and the image do not have a mimetic, subordinate function, located somewhere between sense and intellect as in medieval theology from John of Damascus, Richard of St Victor, Bonaventure to Aquinas. Rahner's view implies that the imagination has an important, original, innovative function and the work of art a positive and autonomous position. As such and precisely in that power and with this status the work of art becomes a relevant source in and of theology.

Further, in the context of the interpretation of art, he rightly adds that one ought to be aware always, that non-verbal art can never be fully captured in words. If one was to try such a translation, the unique and autonomous aspect of the non-verbal arts would, of course, loose its whole raison d'être. Yet, Rahner is aware that despite the autonomy and uniqueness of visual art, interpretation of works of art, especially those with Christian subject matter, are necessary in order to bring out more clearly the Christian message contained in the works. In this way then the visual and the verbal can complement each other.

I. SENSORY-SPIRITUAL EXPERIENCE OF TRANSCENDENCE IN ART

In line with what has just been said about Rahner's insistence of the arts being intrinsic to theology he points out furthermore that a work of art, in order to be experienced as spiritual, must not necessarily contain religious subject matter. Today this view no longer surprises or seems particularly remarkable. Paul Tillich already developed this insight in his

---

3. *Ibid.*, p. 25.
4. K. RAHNER, *Zur Theologie der religiösen Bedeutung des Bildes*, in *Schriften zur Theologie* 16, Zürich – Einsiedeln – Köln, Benziger Verlag, 1984, pp. 348-363, esp. 356.
5. For an extensive analysis of the role of the imagination and its perception through history see R. KEARNEY, *The Wake of Imagination*, London, Routledge, 1994 (1988).

numerous essays on theology and the arts in the sixties[6]. Indeed, Tillich was the first among theologians who made this momentous observation in his analysis of expressionist and abstract art and thereby recognised modern art without explicit Christian iconography as a relevant source for theology. This presented a milestone in the dialogue between theology, the church, spirituality and art[7]. Naturally, this idea was to be particularly relevant in the context of engaging with abstract art and a corresponding apophatic theology.

According to Rahner then, what matters, is the fact that *both* in hearing *and* in seeing we can have a sensory experience of transcendence and that this experience may become a genuine religious experience, an experience of God, of divine self-communication. One has to be aware that it is always the *whole* person who is involved in a religious or in another type of experience, it always concerns body, mind and soul. Here Rahner rightly states that it would be theologically naïve to think, that "only explicitly religious acts" will be conducive to a salutary relationship with the divine. He argues that a painting or a symphony may be "so inspired and borne by divine revelation, by grace and God's self-communication" that they convey something about the human being in the light of the divine[8]. When a work of art reaches, and is revelatory of, the depths of human existence, it reaches the realm where true religious experience takes place. Pious, well-intended, but third-rate works of art with explicit religious subject matter often fail to achieve this. As he notes: "When I paint the crib with Jesus, Mary and Joseph, where through their halos it is immediately clear what is depicted, then in an objective sense this is a religious picture. But perhaps it is actually not at all that religious, because it fails to stimulate any genuine or radical religious processes in the viewer. Thus we also have religious kitsch. On the other hand, a work by Rembrandt, for example, – even if it does not contain any specific religious theme – may nevertheless confront the whole human being, indeed in such a way, that she or he is faced with the total meaning of existence.

6. See the first chapter of my book *Theology and Modern Irish Art*, Dublin, Columba Press, 1999, which deals extensively with Tillich's theology of art. Cf. also P. TILLICH, *Art and Ultimate Reality* (1960), in ID., *Writings in the Philosophy of Culture/Kulturphilosophische Schriften*, ed. M. PALMER (Main Works/Hauptwerke, 2), Berlin – New York, De Gruyter, 1990, pp. 317-332.

7. Whether Rahner was aware of Tillich's writings on art and appropriated them in his own writings cannot be ascertained. It may well have been the case that he read Tillich's articles. However, there are no direct references to Tillich in his articles on theology and the arts.

8. K. RAHNER, *Die Kunst im Horizont von Theologie und Frömmigkeit*, in *Schriften zur Theologie* 16, Zürich – Einsiedeln – Köln, Benziger Verlag, 1984, p. 365 (Translation here, and of the following quotations, by the author).

That is, in fact, in a most fundamental sense, a religious image"[9]. This statement is not only important concerning art, i.e. great art, but it hints at how religious or spiritual experience happens through the work of art, with or without Christian iconography. This issue is, in fact, at the very centre of the dialogue between theology and the arts.

Yet, Rahner observes that in Christianity and in our personal-spiritual life we also need specifically religious images that are easily understood by all. These help us to grasp the message of the Bible, and they remind us of the Gospel stories. They thereby also have a didactic role. Ultimately, he concludes, word and image should be seen as complementing one another in our religious acts, knowledge and spiritual life. Images have an aesthetic, epistemological, mediative and meditative function, not only in the more secular spheres of life but also with regard to the Christian message. They therefore are not to be undervalued. In this context he reminds us once more of Christian anthropology's claim of the unity between sense knowledge and spiritual-conceptual knowledge[10]. Sense, intuition, emotion always ought to form a fundamental unity in our understanding and knowledge. It is in this way that the arts, with their strongly aesthetic-sensory dimension, must have a place in the work of academic theology.

II. SUBJECTIVITY IN THEOLOGY AND IN ART

Theology, Rahner repeatedly pointed out, must be subjective, it begins with subjective experience. (I will not discuss here the criticism of Rahner by Metz and others on Rahner's emphasis on subjectivity and on the individual, and lacking in concern for the social, but rather consider his stress on the subjective in relation to the dialogue between theology and the arts)[11]. Rahner notes: "Christian theology must be subjective, insofar as it must speak of faith, hope and charity, of our personal relationship with God"[12]. Art, he then acknowledges, is also essentially subjective and particular. "Everything that is expressly manifested in art, are individual processes of that transcendentality of the human being, through

9. *Ibid.*, pp. 369-370.
10. *Ibid.*, p. 371. See also ID., *Theology and the Arts* (n. 1), pp. 26-27 and ID., *Zur Theologie der religiösen Bedeutung des Bildes* (n. 4), pp. 349-350.
11. For a critical analysis of this issue see D. MARMION, *A Spirituality of Everyday Faith, A Theological Investigation of the Notion of Spirituality in Karl Rahner* (Louvain Theological & Pastoral Monographs, 23), Louvain, Peeters Press; Grand Rapids, MI, Eerdmans, 1998, pp. 296-305.
12. RAHNER, *Die Kunst im Horizont von Theologie und Frömmigkeit* (n. 8), p. 368.

which he [or she], as an individual of spirit, intellect and freedom, is connected with the whole of reality. Only because the human being is *a priori* a being of transcendence, only because the human being is faced always already with the unfathomable mystery ... can art and theology really exist"[13]. Real theology and real art happen where the subject's experience plays its role. However, that is certainly not to say that anything goes. Bernard Lonergan speaks of "authentic subjectivity" as opposed to subjectivism, and it is such subjectivity which Rahner appears to have in mind. Theology, like art, cannot simply be developed through abstract concepts, but it must be mystagogical, Rahner insists. He emphasises that people must be encouraged to genuinely experience what is implied in such concepts[14]. In this context Rahner refers to von Balthasar's comment that in modern times we lack a kneeling theology (*knieende Theologie*), and adds that we might also need a poetic theology (*dichtende Theologie*), which should be understood as mystagogical theology, i.e. a theology that arises from the experience of the mystery of God.

It is in a work of art then – whether verbal, visual or musical – that the Spirit, human and divine, may find expression. As the human being – and therefore the artist or the theologian – is a transcendental, spiritual being, the artist can point us through her or his art to the transcendent other. One concludes that it is precisely in and through the particular, subjective, immanent and historical, that a glimpse of the universal, objective, transcendent and eternal can be expressed. In a genuine work of art the artist's particularity and the revelation of a glimpse of the universal divine can merge – even if only for a moment – and become one. Naturally however, the fact that God is and always remains the totally other of whom we can never have *any* image and in the light of whom all our words fail, is as clear to Rahner[15] as to anyone else engaged in theology. At the same time it is only our limited human language, our symbols, images and metaphors that allow us to speak, sing or paint of God.

Rahner's affirmation that theology *must* be subjective because it speaks of our personal relationship with God thus parallels his views on subjectivity in art and in the artist. It is, however, important to remember always,

---

13. *Ibid.*, pp. 368-369.
14. *Ibid.*, p. 367.
15. Cf. Rahner's comments on the analogical nature of our talk about God in the last paper he delivered before his death in 1984. *Experiences of a Catholic Theologian*, in *Theological Studies* 61 (2000) 3-15; trans. D. MARMION – G. THIESSEN from the German original: *Erfahrungen eines katholischen Theologen*, in A. RAFFELT (ed.), *Karl Rahner in Erinnerung*, Düsseldorf, Patmos, 1994, pp. 134-148.

862 G.E. THIESSEN

that it must be truthful, authentic subjectiv*ity* rather than subjectiv*ism* that ought to inform both the theologian's and the artist's work.

III. POETRY AS AN AUTHENTIC EXPRESSION OF TRANSCENDENTALITY

In *The Word of Poetry and the Christian*, an article from 1964 on the relationship between poetry, theology and Christian living, Rahner asks whether, despite the decline of Christian themes in literature (and in art) in modern times, this decline, on a more fundamental level, has, in fact, taken place. Perhaps it is simply through new and renewed symbols, forms and images that something of the spiritual and/or religious is expressed[16]. Poetry, especially great poetry, he feels, is important, because "it happens where the human being radically faces who he [or she] is"[17]. Great poetry – as also great art and music – and great, i.e. authentic, Christian living have therefore an "inner affinity"[18]. In Christian existence, as also in composing and listening to music or through writing and reading great poetry, the individual is lead into heights and depths, into hope, doubts and even moments of despair and has to render her or himself and confront these[19].

Both, the poetic word and the theological word can reach the human heart, which in turn may encourage and enable the person to open up to the divine mystery. In this context Rahner mentions four preconditions which need to be fulfilled in order to hear especially the *word* of the Christian message. Firstly, the human being must open her or his ear, to hear *that* word, which speaks of "the silent mystery as the ground of our being". Secondly, we must develop the ability, to hear words, which hit the centre, namely, the human heart[20]. The third, and especially important, precondition is the ability to hear the words that *unite*. Normally words are used to distinguish, to isolate. The ultimate words, however, Rahner emphasises, are those *that unite, reconcile and liberate*. The

16. See also in this context, RAHNER, *The Spirituality of the Church of the Future*, in *Theological Investigations* 20, London, Darton, Longman & Todd, 1981, pp. 143-153.
17. ID., *Das Wort der Dichtung und der Christ*, in *Schriften zur Theologie* 4, Zürich – Einsiedeln – Köln, Benziger Verlag, 1964, pp. 441-454, esp. 451.
18. *Ibid.*
19. *Ibid.*, p. 452: "Je tiefer große Dichtung den Menschen in die gründenden Abgründe seines Daseins hineinführt, um so mehr zwingt sie ihn doch vor menschliche Selbstvollzüge, die dunkel und geheimnisvoll sind, sich verbergen in jene Zweideutigkeit, in der der Mensch grundsätzlich nicht sicher sagen kann, ob er der Begnadete oder der Verlorene ist. Es ist nicht von ungefähr, sondern im Wesen der Sache begründet, daß große menschliche Dichtung dunkel ist und meist uns mit der unbeantworteten Frage entläßt, ob in ihr nun das Mysterium der Gnade oder der Verlorenheit geschehen und geschildert ist".
20. *Ibid.*, p. 444.

ultimate words unite, as they speak of the *one* thing of the Christian message, indeed, of love, which is "not some kind of feeling, but the true substance of reality, that desires to become manifest everywhere"[21]. The final precondition is "to perceive in the individual word the unutterable mystery, the ability to hear the incarnational and incarnate incomprehensibility, indeed, to hear the word which became flesh"[22]. For this reason, Rahner concludes, we must become open to the word, to the word made flesh, as through and in this word the human word is filled with truth and grace.

In this way then, to perceive the poetic word becomes a pre-condition of hearing the word of God[23]. The individual does not thereby necessarily have to be particularly gifted, musically, artistically or poetically. We need only to become receptive and learn to hear those words that are able to hint at what is deepest and unutterable, the words which convey something of the silent, eternal mystery of the divine[24]. And in this way, he concludes, the question of how we, as Christians, deal with poetry, becomes a "very serious and truly Christian question".

IV. CONCLUSION

By way of conclusion it must be said that for Rahner then potentially *all* art – literature, theatre, film, music, architecture, painting, sculpture, etc. – can speak, paint, show or sound of what concerns us profoundly in our human existence, of what brings great happiness or deepest sadness into our lives, of what makes us ecstatic, calm, empathetic or even apathetic. Art is therefore existential and part of what it means to become truly human. It is precisely in that way that art can point us to meaning and it can reveal glimpses of the mystery of the unfathomable divine. It can provide for us moments of genuine seeing, hearing, tasting and feeling, and thus understanding. In this way the arts further knowledge through a unity of sensuous-spiritual-intellectual perception.

Human existence and transcendentality, and God's self-communication through the Cross and the hope for redemption can be revealed and expressed in both art and theology. Hence art becomes a source of and for theology. In more concrete terms and in the words of Rahner: "[W]hen

---

21. *Ibid.*, p. 446.
22. *Ibid.*
23. *Ibid.*, pp. 448-449: "Das Dichterische ist in seinem letzten Wesen Voraussetzung für das Christentum".
24. *Ibid.*, p. 448.

we listen to a Bach oratorio, why might we not have the impression that not only through its text but also through its music, we are in a rather special way brought into relationship with divine revelation about the human being. Why should one not believe that this, too, is theology?"[25].

Milltown Institute of   Gesa Elsbeth THIESSEN
Theology and Philosophy
Milltown Park
Dublin 6
Ireland

25. ID., *Die Kunst im Horizont von Theologie und Frömmigkeit* (n. 8), p. 365.

THE COMPOSER AS INTERPRETER OF
THE EASTER CREED

THE MUSIC AND TEXTS OF BACH, BRAHMS, AND BRITTEN

In this paper, a theologian and a musicologist will discuss the Requiem, an important genre in sacred music. No doubt, an excellent performance of Mozart's Requiem will be able to move an audience, but from a theological viewpoint that composition is less interesting, for the composer did not dare to change the traditional text. For that reason we have selected three other compositions in which several texts have been combined: *Gottes Zeit ist die allerbeste Zeit* (BWV 106), an early *Trauerkantate* by Johann Sebastian Bach, also known as *Actus tragicus*; *Ein Deutsches Requiem* (op. 45) by Johannes Brahms, and the *War Requiem* (op. 66) by Benjamin Britten. The composers' selection of texts shows their personal spiritual struggle to give meaning to Christian belief in the resurrection. We can see how believers try to solve the tension between death and the Christian narrative of hope, or how they at least try to make it bearable. It will also become clear that the composers' sense of hope is in no case identical.

I. JOHANN SEBASTIAN BACH (1685-1750):
ACTUS TRAGICUS (BWV 106)

1. *Musicological Background*

The *Actus tragicus* (BWV 106) is one of many cantatas by Johann Sebastian Bach. The work was written in 1707 when the young Bach, at that time aged 22, lived in the German town Mühlhausen[1]. Although the exact occasion for which this so-called *Trauerkantate* was composed is still unclear, it was presumably written as a funeral ode for his uncle Tobias Lämmerhirt[2]. The nickname of this cantata, *Actus tragicus*, was

---

1. C. WOLFF (ed.), *The World of the Bach Cantatas. Johann Sebastian Bach's Early Sacred Music*, New York – London, Norton, 1997, p. 109.

2. The hypothesis in H. SCHMALFUß, *Johann Sebastian Bachs "Actus tragicus" (BWV 106). Ein Beitrag zu seiner Entstehungsgeschichte*, in *Bach-Jahrbuch* 56 (1970) 36-43,

found in a manuscript in Leipzig that goes back to 1768 and was thus compiled after Bach's death. It is uncertain if the title was given by the master himself, but in any case it perfectly evocates the atmosphere of the work[3]. Furthermore, Bach prescribed an extremely small number of intimate and silent instruments (two recorders, two viola da gambas and continuo) that reflect that atmosphere as well; in line with the limited number of instruments, he probably had a rather small group of singers in mind.

As in all of his cantatas, Bach combined texts of different origin in his *Actus tragicus*: fragments from the Old and New Testament are woven together with contemporary poems by Luther and Vulpius. Such a compilation of texts originated in the Protestant funeral service, where a reflection on biblical passages about death and resurrection was alternated with the singing of strophic hymns[4]. Secondly, recent research has shown that, specifically in the case of the cantata BWV 106, Bach seems to have based the precise order of his texts on a source entitled *Christliche Bet-Schule*. This prayer book was written in 1668 by Johann Olearius, and is part of a long tradition of books on the spirituality of dying[5]. In the chapter "Tägliche Seuffzer und Gebet üm ein seliges Ende" one can find most of the texts Bach used in his *Actus tragicus*[6].

Let us now take a look at the structure of cantata BWV 106 (see appendix 1). To simplify things, one could say that the parts differ in scoring, tempo and time signature: the work contains passages for both soloists and chorus, slow and fast tempi, as well as double and triple time

---

according to whom Bach wrote this piece at the occasion of Dorothea Susanna Tilesius' death on 1 June 1708, is now generally rejected.

3. The reception of BWV 106 during and after Bach's life is being discussed in C. DAHLHAUS, *Analyse und Werturteil* (Musikpädagogik, 8), Mainz, Schott, 1970, pp. 69-72, and F. KRUMMACHER, *Bachs frühe Kantaten im Kontext der Tradition*, in *Die Musikforschung* 44 (1991) 9-32.

4. A. NOWAK, *Trauermusik und Trauerrede. Zur musikalischen Werkgestalt in der Exequien-Tradition*, in H. DANUSER – H. DE LA MOTTE-HABER – S. LEOPOLD – N. MILLER (eds.), *Das musikalische Kunstwerk. Geschichte – Ästhetik – Theorie. Festschrift Carl Dahlhaus zum 60. Geburtstag*, Laaber, Laaber-Verlag, 1988, pp. 373-383.

5. J. PELIKAN, *Bach Among the Theologians*, Philadelphia, PA, Fortress Press, 1986, pp. 56-71 (*Pietism, Piety, and Devotion in Bach's Cantatas*).

6. Cf. R. STEIGER, *J. S. Bachs Gebetbuch? Ein Fund am Rande einer Ausstellung*, in *Musik und Kirche* 55 (1985) 231-234 and *Actus tragicus und ars moriendi. Bachs Textvorlage für die Kantate "Gottes Zeit ist die allerbeste Zeit" (BWV 106)*, in *Musik und Kirche* 59 (1989) 11-23. OLEARIUS wrote two other books that treat a similar topic, namely the *Christliche Sterbe-Schule*, Leipzig, 1669, as well as the *Christliche Geduldt-Schule*, Halle, 1661.

signature. If we now link this observation with the seven movements the piece contains, an ingenious symmetrical construction appears. More specifically, the central fourth part – which forms the climax of the cantata on both musical and textual level – can be considered the axis around which the other movements are organised. This central part is flanked by two passages for vocal soloists, and those two parts are again surrounded by choruses. The first chorus is preceded by an instrumental sonatina, while the final chorus concludes with a monumental fugue in which the Holy Trinity is praised[7].

How do the different texts Bach selected fit into this musical structure? The central theme of our paper, "death and resurrection" serves as the guideline for our interpretation. In the first three movements, which precede the central section, a typically Old Testament vision on death prevails. Death is interpreted under the old covenant, which says that death is inevitable, the end without hope. This idea constitutes the leitmotiv between Ps 90,12 ("So teach us to count our days that we may gain a wise heart") and Isa 38,1 ("Set your house in order, for you shall die"). The message is most threatening in the central part of the cantata: "for the decree from of old is, 'You must die!'" (Sir 14,17).

Precisely in this central part, the Old Testament message is linked to a "new sound", namely the new law of the Gospel. This law says that Jesus died on the cross for us, and that death does not mean the end, but rather union with Christ. This is most clearly expressed in the last verse of Revelation: "Amen. Come, Lord Jesus!" (Rev 22,20). After confronting the Old Testament law with that of the New Testament in this central movement, Bach unmistakably continues the message of hope and bliss in the second part of the *Actus tragicus*. Biblical texts such as "Into your hand I commit my spirit" (Ps 31,5) and "Truly I tell you, today you will be with me in Paradise" (Luke 23,43), as well as Luther's chorale *Mit Fried und Freud ich fahr dahin* invariably stress the hopeful aspect of the redemptive death of Christ.

---

7. According to M. WESSEL, *Der schöne Tod. Trauerkantaten von Bach und Telemann im Vergleich*, in *Musik und Bildung* 19 (1987) 827-830, the narrator's perspective equally follows a symmetrical pattern. At the beginning and the end of the cantata, the we-perspective prevails, whereas the parts in between stress the I-perspective. NOWAK, *Trauermusik* (n. 4), pp. 377-378 argues that the cantata is conceived as a rhetorical speech: *exordium* (instrumental sonatina and chorus), *narratio* (tenor solo and bassus solo), *argumentatio* (central part), *confirmatio* (altus solo and bassus solo) and *peroratio* (concluding choir).

Bach tried to express the contrast between the Old and the New Testament by effective musical means[8]. The severe words of Jesus Sirach "Es ist der alte Bund, Mensch, du mußt sterben" are sung by the three lower voices in an equally rigorous fugue: the rigid character of the laws of counterpoint perfectly mirrors the inevitable threat of the Old Testament law. The soprano enters some bars later singing the final verse of the Book of Revelation "Ja komm, Herr Jesu, komm!". Bach translates this positive and liberating exclamation into music by giving this voice a melody that almost sounds like an improvisation, thus creating a sharp contrast with the fugue we can hear in the lower voices. Moreover, he adds a third element to those two semantic layers. While the fugue of the lower voices and the soprano's line resound, the instruments are playing the melody of a sixteenth-century chorale, namely the hymn *Ich hab mein Sach Gott heimgestellt* by Vulpius[9].

We could thus say that a far-reaching interaction between different layers takes place not only on the level of music, but also on the level of text and content. The theme of "death and resurrection" clearly functions as common denominator. Bach treats this topic from no less than three different angles, namely from the perspectives of the Old and New Testament and from that of contemporary poetry.

2. Theological Observations

It is interesting that Bach – or his librettist – always focuses attention on the theological essence, which is to him the different view on death in the Old and in the New Testament. It strikes us that Bach looked in the book of Jesus Sirach for the central theological notion "for the decree from of old is, 'You must die!'" (Sir 14,17b). The profane implications of that idea are not interesting for the composer or librettist, or are not shared by them. "Give, and take, and indulge yourself, because in Hades one cannot look for luxury. All living beings become old like a garment" (Sir 14,16-17a). Brahms will do exactly the opposite. He dwells on a New Testament text in which Christ declares that the sadness of the disciples will make place for joy, not because Christ's second coming is

8. An analysis of this central part can be found in A. GERSTMEIER, *Der "Actus Tragicus". Bemerkungen zur Darstellung des Todes in der Musik Johann Sebastian Bachs*, in H. BECKER – B. EINIG – P.-O. ULLRICH (eds.), *Im Angesicht des Todes. Ein interdisziplinäres Kompendium* (Pietas liturgica, 3), St. Ottilien, Eos-Verlag, 1987, pp. 421-452; A. DÜRR, *Johann Sebastian Bach. Die Kantaten*, Kassel etc., Bärenreiter, [8]2000, pp. 832-839.

9. DÜRR, *Johann Sebastian Bach* (n. 8), pp. 837-838 convincingly demonstrates that the content of Vulpius' chorale *Ich hab mein Sach Gott heimgestellt* and Bach's cantata BWV 106 show some striking parallels.

clearly announced in that text, but because it contains a profane comparison to the ambivalent feelings during childbirth.

In this composition there is a direct confrontation between Old and New Testament, Adam and Christ, death and life, which shows Bach's dependence on Lutheran theology, which is strongly influenced by the letter to the Romans. These contrasts, however, do not imply that Christians as a result of their baptism have been totally freed from the stranglehold of the Old Testament, of their Adamite habits and of death. On the contrary, in Luther's opinion Christians have the permanent task of turning towards Christ. Despite the grace of baptism, Christians easily fall into earlier Adamite habits. However, in most cases, the call of eternal life will make a more profound impression than the temptations of the Old Testament. Bach translated this into music by giving the last word to the soprano soloist.

The contrast between the messages of the Old and the New Testament is not the only aspect we will discuss. This cantata also reveals that Bach had to take a certain position in the seventeenth-century debate between two theological movements that claimed to be the heirs of Luther's theological intuitions, namely Lutheran orthodoxy and pietism. The exclamation "Come, Lord Jesus!" sounds of course completely different if expressed by an orthodox theologian than by a pietist. Luther's prophetic protest against a church that had lost its evangelical inspiration had itself become a rigid dogmatic system in Bach's time. To orthodox Lutherans, the expectation of Christ's second coming still remained a part of Christian dogmatics, but it no longer made their lives restless. They lived by the conviction that those who had become members of the Protestant church by baptism would forever be justified by faith.

Pietism was a devotional movement that invited Protestants to place an emphasis on the inner experience of faith. The content of faith was considered less important than the personal experience of being reborn. The pietist longing for the final encounter with Jesus does not refer to his return on the Last Day, but to the mystical union with Jesus in death. Death is no longer experienced as a threat, but as a happy event that preferably should happen as soon as possible. It is certain that Bach was partly influenced by this spiritual movement. We can gather this, for example, from another cantata by Bach on an eschatological subject, *Komm du süsse Todesstunde*, which as a matter of fact contains a similar plea as his quote from the Book of Revelation in *Gottes Zeit*: "O Jesu, komm nur bald!" [Jesus, come soon!]. However, we have to be careful of labelling Bach as a pure pietist on the basis of such quotes. Luther also regularly speaks in his work about the loving relationship between bride and bridegroom. In other cantatas Bach puts the longing for death into perspective by mentioning the opinion of Luther that eternity already starts in this life[10]. Pietists also tended to forsake the world, which Bach did not. If Bach had been a true pietist, he would have had other ideas about the musical ornamentation of church services. Moreover, there exist biographical records that Bach did not want to be identified with the pietist movement. In the conflict between a pietist and an orthodox pastor in Mülhausen, he chose the side of the faithful Lutheran and he refused the position of organ player in the pietist bastion Halle.

In my opinion it is not impossible that Bach, being confronted with orthodox Lutheranism and sectarian pietism, deliberately chose to place Luther's genius in the forefront[11]. Moreover, theorists about Luther's theology of music are convinced that it would be against the spirit of Luther, who considered music as the "optima ars", to see church music as merely functional[12]. Referring to Josquin, Luther once affirmed that "God proclaimed the Gospel also through music"[13]. In a similar way Bach wrote in the margin of his Bible, commenting on 2 Chron 5,13: "in liturgical music God is always present with his grace"[14]. In the opening lines of the *Actus tragicus*, the only ones which he did not borrow from another source, Bach expresses his religious conviction that every moment in life, from the moment of our birth to the moment of our death, is a divine gift

---

10. See the following passage from the cantata *O Ewigkeit, du Donnerwort* (BWV 20):

Die Zeit so niemand zählen kann,	[The time which none could ever count
fängt jeden Augenblick	Each moment starts again,
Zu deiner Seelen ewgem Ungelück	To this thy soul's eternal grief and woe,
Sich stets von neuem an.	Forevermore anew.]

11. Attention is given to Bach's relation to Lutheran orthodoxy and pietism in the following works: J.D. KRAEGE, *La théologie de Jean-Sébastien Bach*, in *Études théologiques et religieuses* 60 (1985) 553-572; R.A. LEAVER, *Bach and Pietism: Similarities Today*, in *Concordia Theological Quarterly* 55 (1991) 5-22; PELIKAN, *Bach Among the Theologians* (n. 5); G. STILLER, *Glaube und Frömmigkeit des Luthertums im Leben und Werk Johann Sebastian Bachs*, in *Ökumenische Rundschau* 35 (1986) 53-70.

12. F. KRUMMACHER, *Luthers Musikbegriff und die Kirchenmusik Bachs*, in *Luther* 56 (1985) 136-153; M. PETZOLDT, *Zur Musiktheologie Martin Luthers und ihrer Auswirkung auf Johann Sebastian Bach*, in *Lutherische Kirche in der Welt. Jahrbuch des Martin-Luther-Bundes* 45 (2000) 51-60.

13. M. LUTHER, *Tischreden* (Weimarer Ausgabe), II 1258, p. 11f: "So hat Gott das Evangelium auch durch die Musik verkundet", as quoted in KRUMMACHER, *Luthers Musikbegriff* (n. 12), p. 138.

14. *Die Heilige Bibel ... verfasset von D. Abraham Calovio*, Band 1, Wittenberg, 1681, col. 2088 in Bachs copy, which has been preserved in Concordia Seminary Library, St. Louis, USA. Bach literally wrote: "NB. Bey einer andächtigen Musique ist allezeit Gott mit seiner Gnaden=Gegenwart". The quote is borrowed from PETZOLDT, *Zur Muziktheologie* (n. 12), p. 59.

(*Gottes Zeit*). Throughout his life Bach, as a good Lutheran, endeavored to articulate his belief in God's presence in his church music[15].

II. JOHANNES BRAHMS (1833-1897): *EIN DEUTSCHES REQUIEM* (OP. 45)

1. *Musicological Background*

Johannes Brahms wrote his monumental *Ein Deutsches Requiem* approximately 150 years after Bach's *Actus tragicus*[16]. Despite the wide span of time between the two works, we can still notice some similarities, as well as some obvious differences. For example, we cannot say with certainty for which occasion Bach wrote his cantata, but we do know the origin of Brahms' work. The death of several loved ones seemed to have been an important impetus for writing his magnum opus: his friend, the composer Robert Schumann died in 1856, Brahms' mother in 1865. In the fifth movement of *Ein Deutsches Requiem*, that will be discussed below, the mother figure is prominent.

The text of this work, which consists of seven movements, was drawn from various sections of the Bible (see appendix 2)[17]. However, whereas the structure of Bach's *Actus tragicus* was influenced by Protestant funeral services on the one hand and Johann Olearius' prayer book on the other, the texts of the German Requiem were entirely chosen by Brahms. Contrary to what the title might suggest, the composer did not make use of the traditional Latin requiem text – something that Benjamin Britten will do in his *War Requiem*[18]. Rather, he bases his work on the Bible,

---

15. See also M. WALTHER, *Musik-Sprache des Glaubens. Zum geistlichen Vokalwerk Johann Sebastian Bachs*, Frankfurt am Main, Knecht Verlag, 1994, esp. chapter 1 ("Theologische Bachforschung") and 5 ("Gotteserfahrung in der Musik? Aspekte der Musik-Sprache des Glaubens in 'Actus Tragicus'").

16. For a general introduction to this work, cf. M. MUSGRAVE, *Brahms: A German Requiem*, Cambridge, Cambridge University Press, 1996. D. BELLER-MCKENNA, *How deutsch a Requiem? Absolute Music, Universality, and the Reception of Brahms's Ein deutsches Requiem, op. 45*, in *19th Century Music* 22 (1998) 3-19 offers a profound, somewhat unexpected analysis of the meaning of the title.

17. Three texts from Brahms' *Ein Deutsches Requiem* had already been set to music by HEINRICH SCHÜTZ: "Die mit Tränen säen" (part I) in *Psalmen Davids* (Dresden, 1619) and *Geistliche Chormusik* (Dresden, 1648); "Wie lieblich sind deine Wohnungen" (part IV) in *Psalmen Davids* and *Symphoniae Sacrae* (Dresden, 1650); "Selig sind die Toten" (part VII) in *Geistliche Chormusik*.

18. A. NOWAK, *"Ein deutsches Requiem" im Traditionszusammenhang*, in F. KRUMMACHER – W. STEINBECK (eds.), *Brahms-Analysen* (Kieler Schriften zur Musikwissenschaft, 28), Kassel-Basel, Bärenreiter, 1984, pp. 201-209 points to the numerous correspondences between the Latin requiem and Brahms' texts: e.g. "die mit Tränen säen" (part I) and

which he rather admires as profound poetry, independent from any liturgical praxis. Some other notorious contemporaries share Brahms' reception of the Bible that is unrelated to the church, e.g. the philosopher Arthur Schopenhauer, the poet Heinrich Heine and the composer Richard Wagner[19].

Precisely because of this free selection of texts, Brahms was able to communicate a very personal vision of "death and resurrection"[20]. In fact, we could say that the first movement of the German Requiem presents Brahms' central message in a nutshell. He incorporates both a verse from the Eight Beatitudes as well as a psalm verse, both of which contain several contrasting images: "Blessed are those who mourn, for they will be comforted" (Matt 5,4); "May those who sow in tears reap with shouts of joy. Those who go out weeping, bearing the seed for sowing, shall come home with shouts of joy, carrying their sheaves" (Ps 126,5-6). On the one hand, death provokes feelings of sorrow, crying and passing away, but on the other it implies the promise of comfort, joy and return[21]. It is at this point that Brahms' Requiem already deviates from its traditional Latin pendant. For example, a passage such as *Dies irae*, that describes Judgement Day and the horrible threats that go with it, is far removed from the message of hope in Brahms' texts[22]. This does not mean that the

---

"qui seminant in lacrymis"; "gen Zion kommen mit Jauchzen" (part II) and "te decet hymnus in Sion".

19. Nowak, *"Ein deutsches Requiem"* (n. 18), p. 204 and W. Döbertin, *Johannes Brahms'* Deutsches Requiem *als religiöses Kunstwerk*, in K. and R. Hofmann (eds.), *Brahms-Studien*, Tutzing, Schneider, 1990, pp. 9-30.

20. There are different opinions concerning the way Brahms conceived the structure of his *Deutsches Requiem*. C. Rostand, *Brahms*, Paris, Fayard, 1978, p. 427 sees a dichotomy between the parts I-III (stressing the transitoriness and miseries of the earthly life) and IV-VII (stressing the bliss and promise of eternal life). W. Abercrombie, *What's in a Label? Structure and Emotion in Brahms's Requiem, Movement Six, Finale*, in *Choral Journal* 38 (1997) 17-21 notices an evolution from more or less traditional, comforting texts towards visionary, apocalyptic ones. Different authors plea for a symmetrical construction, with part IV functioning as the axis around which the other movements are organised. Most musicologists, however, argue against any rigorous interpretation. E. Horn, *Johannes Brahms – Ein Deutsches Requiem*, in *Musica Sacra* 103 (1983) 215-226, 303-314, 343-399 offers a survey of these hypotheses.

21. Cf. the chapter *A German Requiem. Johannes Brahms*, in P.S. Minear, *Death Set to Music. Masterworks by Bach, Brahms, Penderecki, Bernstein*, Atlanta, GA, John Knox Press, 1987, pp. 67-69.

22. Rostand, *Brahms* (n. 20), p. 426: "[…] Brahms, en choisissant ses textes, s'est efforcé d'une part de poétiser son sujet, d'autre part de l'universaliser, de l'élargir. Il n'insiste pas, ainsi qu'on le fait dans l'office romain, sur le jour de colère qui, s'il annonce une éternelle félicité grâce à l'intercession des Saints et aux prières de ceux qui survivent, est cependant lourd de menaces. Il n'évoque les trompettes du Jugement que d'une façon très fugitive, et nullement terrifiante, mais au contraire comme l'heureux et glorieux signal d'une vie nouvelle où les corps des justes ressuscités seront réunis au ciel".

composer is blind to the finiteness of human existence and the inevitability of death. It does mean, however, that to him the aspect of bliss and reunion with people who have departed from this life is more essential and important.

Brahms added the fifth movement of *Ein Deutsches Requiem* in 1868, some years after his mother's death. And though it is always dangerous to consider extra-musical elements as an "explanation" of the musical content, the theme of the mother figure undeniably prevails in the fifth movement[23]. What immediately strikes us as different from Bach's *Actus tragicus*, is the big, romantic orchestration: besides strings Brahms also used flutes, hoboes, clarinets, bassoons and horns. This evokes a rich tone colour, which clearly contrasts with the intimate atmosphere that was created by the instruments of the cantata BWV 106. An important similarity with Bach's work is the aspect of conversation. Here a dialogue takes place between the chorus and the soprano soloist.

The soprano starts with a verse from the Gospel of John: "So you have pain now; but I will see you again, and your hearts will rejoice, and no one will take your joy from you" (John 16,22), that is followed by a verse from Jesus Sirach: "See with your own eyes that I have labored but little and found for myself much serenity" (Ecclus/Sir 51,27). "Pain" is thus opposed to "seeing again", and "labour" to "serenity". Brahms translates this contrast into music as follows: "Ihr habt nun Traurigkeit" is written in a slow tempo with a descending, mainly chromatic melody, while "ich will euch wieder sehen" uses a fast tempo and ascending, diatonically constructed lines[24].

Then the chorus begins a dialogue with the soprano, singing a verse from the book of Isaiah: "As a mother comforts her child, so I will comfort you" (Isa 66,13). Through the constant interaction with the soloist – whether on a simultaneous or successive level – the chorus functions like an ostinato[25]. At the very end of the fifth movement the part of the soprano

23. A musical analysis of the fifth part can be found in H.E. BACH, *Johannes Brahms: Ein Deutsches Requiem*, in S. HELMS – R. SCHNEIDER (eds.), *Werkanalyse in Beispielen. Große Chorwerke*, Kassel, Bosse, 1994, pp. 98-124, and MUSGRAVE, *Brahms* (n. 16), pp. 47-50.

24. In the opening section of his *Actus tragicus*, Bach makes use of similar stylistic elements. The contrast between the words "in ihm leben, weben und sind wir, solange er will" and "in ihm sterben wir zur rechten Zeit, wenn er will" is equally expressed by opposing quick and slow tempi, diatonic and chromatic writing, as well as ascending and descending melodies.

25. A beautiful effect is thus created in bars 62-66, where the choir sings the same melody as the soprano, although in a rhythmic value that is twice as slow.

symbolically coincides with the chorus: the promise "I will see you again" from the Gospel of John is combined with Isaiah's "I will comfort you".

Comparing the fifth part of Brahms' *Ein Deutsches Requiem* with the central movement of Bach's *Actus tragicus*, we can say that in the former there is no contrast between the two performing groups. They are, instead, parallel. Bach's chorus proclaims the Old Testament view on death, whereas the soprano soloist sings the New Testament view. Brahms' conversation partners have evolved into a complementary duo, because they both proclaim one and the same message of hope and comfort from another perspective.

2. *Theological Observations*

Is it legitimate to consider Brahms' *Deutsches Requiem* "sacred music"[26]? In my opinion, arguing that the text of the composition consists of a number of biblical texts is not sufficient as a proof. Undoubtedly, there is a personal existential experience of the finiteness of human life at the basis of this composition. It is, however, striking that the name "Christ" never occurs in this Requiem. After the first performance Brahms was asked why he had made no reference to the theme of Christ's redemptive death. Brahms answered that he had deliberately avoided certain biblical passages and mentioned John 3,16 as an example. "For God so loved the world that he gave his only Son, so that everyone who believes in him may not perish but may have eternal life". To make the performance of his Requiem acceptable to a religious environment, the famous aria "I know that my Redeemer liveth" from Händel's *Messiah* used to be inserted in the middle of the Requiem.

In his *"German" Requiem* Brahms speaks about a universal human being, who restores the ties with its Creator during experiences of contrast, and is thus practising "religion". The biblical texts that appealed to him most insure that sorrow is passing and will be followed by comfort and a renewed zest for life. Praying for the eternal rest of the deceased is central to the Latin Requiem, whereas Brahms focuses instead on the survivor. That person must be sustained in his or her loss in order to be able to take up life again. We have already emphasised the introductory quote that serves as a motto. "Blessed are those who mourn, for they will

26. In this paragraph apart from personal reflections also thoughts are used from: S. BREDEN, *Brahms on Death and Destiny: Philosophical, Theological and Musical Implications*, in *Choral Journal* 38 (1997/5) 9-14; DÖBERTIN, *Brahms' Deutsches Requiem* (n. 19), pp. 9-30; B.C. LATEGAN, *Ein Deutsches Requiem: Notes on Brahms' Selection of Biblical Texts*, in *Scriptura* 1 (1980) 29-41 and MINEAR, *Death Set to Music* (n. 21), pp. 65-83.

be comforted" (Matt 5,4). Likewise, biblical quotes in the fifth movement are interpreted in a profane way. Was Brahms' selection of biblical texts determined either by the original context of the verses or by the existential situation of the loss of his mother? First, I will discuss the only quote from the New Testament: "So you have pain now; but I will see you again, and your hearts will rejoice, and no one will take your joy from you" (John 16,22).

In the context of the farewell speech it is clear that the I-person is the resurrected Lord who will make the Johannine community happy with his presence. This community was confronted with increasing aggression from official Judaism[27] after the destruction of the Jewish temple in 70 A.D. and it was worried because Christ's return[28] had failed to happen. Both in the farewell speech and in the whole Gospel of John, the early Christian community gets a double answer. It already experiences the positive consequences of praying to the Father in Jesus' name[29], and at the same time it keeps looking out for the Second Coming of Christ at the end of time, when the community and Christ will meet again[30].

John 16,22 probably charmed Brahms, because in the preceding verse John compares the regained joy of the disciples with the switch from terrible pain to immense joy during a successful delivery. "When a woman is in labor, she has pain, because her hour has come. But when her child is born, she no longer remembers the anguish because of the joy of having brought a human being into the world" (John 16,21). Because he entrusted this musical line to a soprano soloist, the composer seems to be longing more for the comforting reunion with his mother than for the *parousia*. To him comfort is not any longer a common human experience but something individual.

---

27. "They will put you out of the synagogues. Indeed, an hour is coming when those who kill you will think that by doing so they are offering worship to God" (John 16,2). See also v. 20: "Very truly, I tell you, you will weep and mourn, but the world will rejoice" and v. 33b: "In the world you face persecution".

28. "Then some of his disciples said to one another, 'What does he mean by saying to us, 'A little while, and you will no longer see me, and again a little while, and you will see me'" (John 16,17).

29. "Very truly, I tell you, if you ask anything of the Father in my name, he will give it to you". (...) "On that day you will ask in my name" (John 16,23.26).

30. "... and you will see me" (John 16,16) and "I will see you again" (John 16, 22). The final text of the Gospel of John contains the traces of present and future eschatology, which is defended with verve in the monumental study by J. FREY, *Die johanneische Eschatologie. I. Ihre Probleme im Spiegel der Forschung seit Reimarus*; II. *Das johanneische Zeitverständnis*; III. *Die eschatologische Verkündigung in den johanneischen Texten* (WUNT, 96, 110, 117), Tübingen, Mohr, 1997, 1998, 2000. The pericope John 16,16-33 is discussed in the last volume, pp. 204-222.

In his search for biblical texts about the mother-child relationship Brahms also decided to integrate Isa 66,13 in his composition. In that chapter it is described how the small group of Jewish believers experienced rejection and contempt in post–exilic Israel[31]. The prophet Isaiah announces the eschatological rebirth of God's people and, as John would repeat several centuries later, he uses the metaphor of delivery. "Before she was in labor she gave birth; before her pain came upon her she delivered a son" (Isa 66,7). And in the verse quoted by Brahms: "As a mother comforts her child, so I will comfort you" (Isa 66,13a). God's mercifulness towards the small Jewish community after the exile is compared to the comforting attitude of a mother. It might be gathered that Brahms was not interested in the content of the original dialogue between God and his people from the fact that he omitted the last part of this verse "you shall be comforted in Jerusalem (Isa 66,13b). To the composer it was apparently sufficient that the biblical verse aroused personal memories.

Brahms also added a quote from the final chapter of Jesus Sirach. This quote, however, got a different sense in Brahms' composition. Sirach calls the ignorant from Jerusalem to be taught by him: "See with your own eyes that I have labored but little and found for myself much serenity" (Sir 51,27). Is Brahms here alluding to the deserved rest his mother has found after a laborious life rather than the internal rest one gets after acquiring God's wisdom?

Moreover all biographers and commentators try to find an explanation for Brahms' quote that he has never believed in an afterlife. Some take this statement literally, while others think that Brahms only rejected the orthodox conception. It is striking that, in the seventh and last movement, death is represented as a period of permanent rest. "Blessed are the dead who from now on die in the Lord. Yes, says the Spirit, they will rest from their labors, for their deeds follow them" (Rev 14,13). However, in the sixth movement the composer used some verses from 1 Cor, in which Paul offers a concrete description of the Last Judgement. "Listen, I will tell you a mystery! We will not all die, but we will all be changed, in a moment, in the twinkling of an eye, at the last trumpet. For the trumpet will sound, and the dead will be raised imperishable, and we will be changed. Then the saying that is written will be fulfilled: Death has been swallowed up in victory. Where, O death, is your victory? Where, O death, is your sting?" (1 Cor 15, 51-52, 54b-55). Certainly, "a complete reversal has taken place, compared

---

31. "Your own people who hate you and reject you for my name's sake have said, 'Let the Lord be glorified, so that we may see your joy'" (Isa 66,5b).

to the beginning of the Requiem: From the transitoriness of life to the imperishableness of the resurrected man, from the relentless finality of death to the complete destruction of its power"[32]. In my opinion, however, it is striking that the answer to this last question is no longer quoted, because it was probably too christological for the composer. "The sting of death is sin, and the power of sin is the law. But thanks be to God, who gives us the victory through our Lord Jesus Christ" (vv. 56-57).

Let us now return to our initial question. In Brahms' *Deutsches Requiem* a personal confrontation with the biblical tradition takes place. I am convinced, however, that it was the main goal of the composer to make the listeners cherish life again. He wanted to invite them to a religious experience as part of natural religion, but his interest was not necessarily to communicate the integral story of hope as narrated in the Scriptures.

III. BENJAMIN BRITTEN (1913-1976): WAR REQUIEM (OP. 66)

1. Musicological Background

The *War Requiem* by the English composer Benjamin Britten premiered in 1962, approximately 100 years after Brahms' *Ein Deutsches Requiem*[33]. The title of the work leaves no doubt as to which occasion Britten wrote this masterpiece. As a matter of fact, his *War Requiem* was commissioned for the re-consecration of St. Michael's Cathedral in Coventry. When the centuries-old cathedral was destroyed in 1940, the British architect Basil Spence was asked to conceive a new design to be built beside the ruins of the eleventh-century structure. It is here that the piece was performed for the first time.

Britten dedicated his *War Requiem* to four soldier friends. Three of them had died in the Second World War, and the fourth had committed suicide. Their names figure, as an ultimate mark of honour, on the title

---

32. LATEGAN, *Ein Deutsches Requiem* (n. 26), p. 39.

33. For a thorough discussion of this piece, see E.J. LUNDERGAN, *Benjamin Britten's "War Requiem": Stylistic and Technical Sources*, Ph.D. dissertation The University of Texas at Austin, 1991, and M. COOKE, *Britten: War Requiem*, Cambridge, Cambridge University Press, 1996. The article of A. ROBERTSON, *Britten's War Requiem*, in *The Musical Times* 103 (1962) 308-310 is interesting as it was written shortly before the premiere of the *War Requiem*. Britten's music moreover served as the point of departure for a film from Derek Jarman (1988).

page of the score[34]. Britten, however, not only wanted to commemorate the evils of the Second World War, but the atrocities of the First World War and, indeed, of all wars. This purpose clearly appears from the texts he selected for his work (see appendix 3)[35]. As I have briefly indicated in my discussion of Brahms' *Ein Deutsches Requiem*, Britten uses the traditional Latin Requiem, and he combines this text with the war poetry of the English poet Wilfred Owen (1893-1918)[36]. Owen, who was a soldier during the First World War, was killed at the age of 25, ironically enough some days before the Armistice. Britten incorporates his highly emotional poetry as a kind of medieval tropes that comment upon the Latin Requiem and interact with it excessively. The result of that interaction is often quite ironic and sometimes absolutely shocking, as we will demonstrate in our discussion of the offertory.

The composer's use of two different kinds of texts determined the scoring of his *War Requiem* in a fundamental way. The Latin Requiem with its rather detached character on the one hand, and Owen's extremely individual poems on the other are distributed among three distinct ensembles, which were placed on different spots in St. Michael's cathedral. At the first level we can find the tenor and baritone soloists, who are accompanied by a small chamber orchestra. They perform Owen's poems and could be said to represent the war victims. Because the experience of death is expressed here in the most direct way, Britten places this group close to the audience by way of direct confrontation. The soprano soloist, the large orchestra and chorus constitute the second group of performers. They sing the text of the Latin Requiem. Britten translates the distant and less personal character of their texts into music by placing this group of performers somewhat further away from the audience. The last group, a chorus of boys with organ accompaniment is the furthest removed from the audience. They too sing parts of the Latin Requiem text, and their angelic innocence stands for humankind's eternal hope.

It is important to note that Britten did not choose Owen's most brutal and shocking poems, where he describes the horror of war in a very explicit way[37]. Rather he preferred to reveal the meditative and almost

34. Roger Burney (Sub-Lieutenant, Royal Naval Volunteer Reserve), Piers Dunkerley (Captain, Royal Marines), David Gill (Ordinary Seaman, Royal Navy) en Michael Halliday (Lieutenant, Royal New Zealand Volunteer Reserve).

35. Cf. R. SHAW, *The Texts of Britten's* War Requiem, in G. PAINE (ed.), *Five Centuries of Choral Music. Essays in Honor of Howard Swan* (Festschrift Series, 6), Stuyvesant – New York, Pendragon Press, 1988, pp. 357-383.

36. LUNDERGAN, *Benjamin Britten's "War Requiem"* (n. 33), p. 13 discusses the tradition in British music of connecting Latin mass texts with poetry.

37. *Ibid.*, p. 106.

religious side of his poems by selecting those texts that not only examine the cause of the mass deaths, but that also enable a far-reaching interaction with the Latin Requiem. The composer convincingly reveals this dimension of Owen's poetry in the offertory of the *War Requiem*, where the text of the Latin offertory and Owen's poem *The Parable of the Old Man and the Young* are interwoven[38]. This poem is a bitter parody of Gen 22, where the story of Abraham and Isaac is told. Since the name Abraham also occurs in the Latin offertory, this theme forms an ideal occasion to link both texts and to let them interact.

Britten's musical vocabulary is again totally different from that of Bach and Brahms. The composition as a whole often sounds atonal and is sometimes spiced with lively dissonances. Still, at the start of the offertory Britten tries to fit in with the centuries-old tradition of Gregorian music[39]. The boys pivot around two central tones (d and c sharp), which gives their singing the character of a trance-evoking litany.

Then the chorus starts with the phrase "sed signifer sanctus Michael repraesentet eas in lucem sanctam". When they arrive at the crucial words "quam olim Abrahae promisisti et semini ejus", the chorus bursts into an overwhelming fugue. I briefly want to refer here to the fugue in the central part of Bach's *Actus tragicus*, on the words "Es ist der alte Bund". It is striking that Britten equally writes a fugue on words that recall an age-old promise. Moreover, this fugue is a quotation from an earlier work, namely his *Canticle II: Abraham and Isaac* (op. 51, 1952)[40].

After this follows a long passage for the tenor and baritone soloists, who sing Owen's *Parable of the Old Man and the Young*. At the point where the old Abraham is preparing to kill Isaac, the dramatic nature not only reach a highpoint, but we hear references to earlier passages of the *War Requiem*. The central theme of Owen's poem, i.e. the fact that Abraham's atrocity stands in for the slaughtering of half the European continent lingers on, even when the boys have already started their endless praise of the Lord, "Hostias et preces tibi Domine laudis offerimus". Because of the

---

38. A musical analysis of the offertory can be found in P. EVANS, *The Music of Benjamin Britten*, Minneapolis, MN, University of Minnesota Press, 1979, pp. 460-461, and COOKE, *Britten* (n. 33), pp. 67-70.

39. LUNDERGAN, *Benjamin Britten's "War Requiem"* (n. 33), p. 27 remarks that the linguistic distinction between the Latin requiem and Owen's poetry also has important musical consequences. A similar stylistic difference is made in a song from Britten's *Ceremony of Carols*: "In 'There is no Rose' the English text is set in three-part harmony under a wide-ranging melodic line, while the Latin text, a series of declamations of wonder at the miracle described in the English, is chanted on a unison C".

40. E. ROSEBERRY, *Abraham and Isaac Revisited: Reflections on a Theme and Its Inversion*, in Ph. REED (ed.), *On Mahler and Britten. Essays in Honour of Donald Mitchell on His Seventieth Birthday*, Woodbridge, Boydell Press, 1995, pp. 252-266.

constant confrontation with the motto "half the seed of Europe one by one" the boys' innocent praise sounds extremely bitter and ironic.

The chorus eventually returns, singing the fugue "quam olim Abrahae promisisti" once more. But on the musical level apparent changes have taken place. First, the melody has been turned upside down completely. Instead of the ascending lines we originally heard, the melody is now descending; instead of tenor and bass, soprano and alto are now striking up; and finally, the loud overwhelming volume made room for extremely quiet singing. At the very end the music fades away into pure silence. It may be clear that Britten loaded his music with highly symbolic significance and wanted to make an unmistakable and unforgettable statement.

2. *Theological Observations*

In my commentary on Britten's *War Requiem* I want to point to the theological sparks that spring from the interaction between the Gregorian offertory and Owen's parable. Where needed I will briefly refer to other movements of the Requiem.

The offertory consists of two parts. First, the people – expressed by the voice of boys – are praying to him who has already been glorified by His Father after His grievous passing: *Domine Jesu Christe, Rex gloriae*. The exalted one is no longer invoked by his first name only, but with a whole range of christological titles. Britten repeats this invocation three times, which is not the case in the original version. He who has already made the transition from life to death is begged[41] to liberate the souls of the deceased from the gates of hell and from purgatory. The archangel Michael, who is also the patron saint of Coventry Cathedral, will lead them on their way toward the eternal light on the Day of Judgement.

Why would the Lord comply with their demands? Because, according to the text, this had been promised to "Abraham and his descendants". (Quam olim Abrahae promisisti, et semini ejus). This verse – a free

---

41. The imperative verb form often returns in the ordinarium of the funeral liturgy: "Requiem aeternam dona eis, Domine"; "Libera me, Domine, de morte aeterna". Cf. SHAW, *The Texts of Britten's* War Requiem (n. 35), p. 382: "It is interesting, it seems to me, to note that in terms of text alone the Missa is entirely a petition: 'Make them, O Lord, to pass from death unto life...', 'Deliver me, O Lord, from death eternal...', 'In paradise may the angels lead thee...', 'Let eternal light shine on them. May they rest in peace'. Some, undoubtedly, could recite this in full confidence that it already had been assured. With others, even of similar religious tradition, it might be murmured 'bowed and kneeling' with 'heart contrite as ashes', and uncertain – not quite sure. For still others it must suffice that after all, there is still in man's being – an unearthly being – a mystery into which none of the statistical forms of man's intelligence can carry him. That it involves a life beyond the present, most men have hoped and few gainsaid".

adaptation of Luke 1,55: "according to the promise he made to our ancestors, to Abraham and to his descendants forever" – functions as a refrain
that will be repeated after the verse. The repetition, that Britten has
respected, indicates that the verse contains an important message.

According to Genesis, Abraham had received a promise several times.
"I will make of you a great nation" promised God to Abraham, when he
asked him to leave his country. (Gen 12,2). When it seems that his wish
would remain unfulfilled, God again assured Abraham: "Look toward
heaven and count the stars, if you are able to count them. So shall your
descendants be" (Gen 15,5). And after the story of Isaac's sacrifice, this
promise is repeated again. "I will indeed bless you, and I will make your
offspring as numerous as the stars of heaven and as the sand that is on
the seashore. And your offspring shall possess the gate of their enemies,
and by your offspring shall all the nations of the earth gain blessing for
themselves, because you have obeyed my voice" (Gen 22,17-18).

The Requiem interprets the promise to Abraham probably from the
perspective of the Easter creed. According to the summary of the story
of Abraham's sacrifice in the letter to the Hebrews, the patriarch could
only obey God because he had received the promise of eternal life.

> By faith Abraham, when put to the test, offered up Isaac. He who had
> received the promises was ready to offer up his only son. (...) He consid-
> ered the fact that God is able even to raise somebody from the dead – and
> figuratively speaking, he did receive him back.

The reference to Abraham's promise in the Requiem reminded Britten
of the story of Isaac's sacrifice and, therefore, he decided to incorporate
Owen's version of that story. Owen presents no literal translation of Genesis 22. The poet makes a connection between Isaac's sacrifice and all the
people in history who died pointlessly. He already announces this by having Abraham build "parapets and trenches", instead of an altar. As in
Genesis, an angel mediates God's opposition to any human sacrifice,
whether it concerns Isaac, his Son, or innocent soldiers.

> An angel called him out of heaven, Lay not thy hand upon the lad, Neither
> do anything to him. Behold, A ram caught in a thicket by his horns; Offer
> the Ram of Pride instead of him.

It is human beings, not God who are responsible for the countless crosses
in history, but man. In Owen's unexpected rereading of the story of Isaac's
sacrifice – "But the old man would not so, and slew his son, and half the seed
of Europe, one by one" –, Abram precedes all later commanders, though his
son called him "my father" three times, in line with the invocation at the start
of the offertory. In the poem he is called Abram, the name he carried before

his first encounter with God. Though Abraham's seed has produced numerous offspring, half of it was lost in the most gruesome war ever. It is remarkable, however, that even during the part about Abraham's disobedience we still hear the melody of *Quam olim Abrahae* echoing on occasion.

The hard truth that the sacrifice of Isaac was followed by that of many other soldiers in history is spoken, and now the Gregorian offertory continues. However it now sounds particularly cynical. While the tenor and baritone soloists sing on about real child sacrifices, children's voices bring "sacrifices of prayer and love to God" (*Hostias et preces tibi Domine laudis offerimus*) with death bells ringing in the background. The prayer is again about the transition from death to life of the people who are remembered in the funeral liturgy. From the repetition of the chorus we can gather that this hope is based on the promise to Abraham.

Eventually the listener has to judge, what prevails in Britten's personal arrangement of the Requiem: either the horror of the sacrifice of Europe's offspring or the hope that sound from the promise to Abraham and his offspring. Abraham's living seed is having the last word, instead of Europe's perished seed. I have the impression that Britten deliberately chose to let the hope of God's promise of eternal life prevail, albeit in the sourdine, after having deplored the evil caused by his fellow beings, whether it concerns the sacrifice of Christ or that of victims in history. It is not only in the *Agnus Dei*, but also during the *In Paradisum* that the theme of *Quam olim Abrahae* is repeated instrumentally, by means of a *cantus firmus* that enforces the soldier's wish of finally being granted rest. In an unforgettable way Britten realised his task of writing an ode to Coventry cathedral about the superiority of life to death, though death seems to be omnipotent and omnipresent. But after all, the cathedral itself had eventually risen out of its ashes[42].

Actually it is striking that in the remaining movements of the *War Requiem* text and counter-text grow towards one another. The *Sanctus*, the part that follows the offertory, still contains the greatest contrast. On the day that the risen Lord will return, according to the tradition "heaven and earth are filled with God's glory". In this joyful central part, the sadness of the funeral liturgy is broken. However it is exactly in this part that the poet dares to question the resurrection of the dead: "Shall life renew these bodies?". Earth answers that her old scars will not be glorified.

---

42. Still, J.D. HERBERT, *Bad Faith at Coventry: Spence's Cathedral and Britten's War Requiem*, in *Critical Inquiry* 25 (1999) 535-565, p. 543 notices with reason: "Where Spencer's plan had a cathedral rise out of the ashes of war, Britten's requiem allowed the ashes of war to issue out again from the new cathedral".

And when I hearken to the Earth, she saith:
"My fiery heart shrinks, aching. It is death.
Mine ancient scars shall not be glorified.
Nor my titanic tears, the sea, be dried".

"All death will He annul, all tears assuage" is a truth that does not seem to hold true to Owen and Britten, at least for the moment.

Shall life renew these bodies? Of a truth
All death will He annul, all tears assuage?

The final parts tells us that "the truth" is "the pity of war, the pity war distilled"[43]. Towards the end of the work there is of course no total fusion of both registers, but still the messages are gradually becoming similar. The poem that Britten chose as a commentary on the *Agnus Dei* describes how soldiers experience the crucified Nazarene as a companion when they were accidentally confronted with a mutilated crucifix. These soldiers do not sneer at him.

One ever hangs where shelled roads part.
In this war He too lost a limb.
But His disciples hide apart.
And now the soldiers bear with Him.

This is the only occasion in the work where a soloist who normally performs Owen's poetry, now takes over the traditional language. After the third resume of the *Agnus Dei* by the chorus, Britten personalises the "Dona eis requiem sempiternam" from the funeral liturgy to "Dona nobis pacem", grant us peace.

In the final part Britten incorporates an unfinished poem by Owen in which a British soldier is having a "strange meeting"[44] at the end of a dark tunnel with the soul of a German soldier he has killed. His former enemy seems to bless him and also he speaks to him that there is no longer any reason for hostility. Both will find comfort in the sleep of the dying, as the funeral ritual traditionally ends with the "Requiescant in pace"[45].

---

43. Compare also the extract from one of Owen's letters, that was put as motto on the score of the War Requiem. "My subject is War, and the pity of War. The Poetry is in the pity. Yet these elegies are to this generation in no sense consolatory. They may be to the next. All a poet can do today is warn. That is why the true Poets must be truthful".

44. Owen's title.

45. Compare the commentary of HERBERT, *Bad Faith at Coventry* (n. 42), p. 560: "Here, then, is the closest the War Requiem can approach the higher platform of a reconciliation between the blessings of heaven and the ravages of war; a suspension, held in waiting, of the difference between life and death, between killer and killed; a suspension in sleep (for Christ it lasted three days; for the rest of us...). As limited as it may be, perhaps we can entrust our faith in this tentative accord".

By confronting the different parts of the Latin Requiem with *capita selecta* from Owen's war poetry, Benjamin Britten indicates that belief in the resurrection of the dead is never self-evident. He fears that the traditional texts, on their own, could become the opium of the people of God. By only hearing the proclamation of the story of Christ's victory over death, Christians run the risk of closing their eyes to the reality of suffering. Still I do not think that the Christian story of hope in Britten's eyes has been falsified by Owen's war story. In the offertory, which we have analysed in detail, the promise to Abraham and his offspring remained.

Wilfred Owen's struggle with the Gospel went probably even more pronounced than Britten's. Because he was faced with the sorrow of the war, he could only assent to pieces of the Christian story, for example that Christ shared the fate of those killed in action. He rewrites the biblical representations he thinks are unacceptable. This has obviously occurred in his parable about Abraham and Isaac. A parable is meant to shock people, and make them face the facts. It protests against the soldiers' lack of freedom, because they are driven into death by their generals. The means of this protest is a rereading of the biblical story of Isaac's sacrifice, in which Abram neglects the solution that was provided by God and offers up his son anyway.

Owen, who belongs to the Protestant wing of the Anglican church and who used to work for some years as a pastoral worker was certainly familiar with the bible, but was not a theologian. The reinterpretation of the story of Genesis was probably the tormented poet's own idea. He probably did not realize that in some old Jewish Midrash commentaries on Genesis Isaac had already been sacrificed. The same interpretation reoccurs in post-Holocaust literature[46]. As a martyr Isaac became a prototype for the many other innocent Jewish victims in history[47].

---

46. We can find many examples in W. ZUIDEMA – E. VAN VOOLEN – A. SOETENDORP – C. DEN HEYER, *Isaak wordt weer geofferd: de verwerking van de holocaust door jodendom en christendom*, Baarn, Ten Have, 1980.

47. A first example comes from a Jewish commentary on the *aqeda* or binding of Isaac, written in the period of the crusades: "When he slaughtered with the knife his hands didn't tremble. (...) Take into account, O Lord, the many *Aquedot*, faithful men and women who were killed because of you" (pp. 49-50). The poet Jacob Gladstein (1896-1970) makes the link between Isaac's sacrifice and the flames of Auschwitz: "It was no good angel that came flying by. The fire burns, the flames rise. (...) Isaac, old, was not deceived as when he was that boy from Genesis; He knew no lamb would appear. When he was tied and put on the slaughter table, and he could smell it burn, the horrible stench, he said with resignation: I know, God will not stop the slaughtering now. He cried with a tired voice: 'Here I am, prepared to be your ram!'" (p. 90).

IV. CONCLUSION

In this paper we have discussed the interpretation of the Easter creed in the works of Bach, Brahms and Britten. In their compositions, they have integrated their faith, or at least some crucial aspects of it, in a very personal way. For these composers sacred music has become a means of religious experience. Their interpretation of the Easter creed, however, is profoundly different.

Bach is confidently looking towards the end of his life, because it is God who decides what is best for humans: "Gottes Zeit ist die allerbeste Zeit". His faith assured him that Christ's incarnation and his death on the cross constituted the end of the tyranny of death under the old covenant. Christians can hopefully long for Christ's second coming. It is significant that the interaction between the Old and the New Testament view on death takes place precisely in the middle of his cantata. Bach's message seems to be clear: Christians cannot live on clouds permanently; they have to take serious the moral demands of life in view of God's judgment. It was Luther who taught him that the Christian remains both a person who sins and a person who has been justified.

Brahms is also reckoning with a future realm where people who are separated by death will be reunited. In line with his universalizing intentions, he detaches his message from any christological subtleties. Moreover, he also pays attention to those who remain behind and are in need of comfort. The fifth movement of *Ein Deutsches Requiem* contains a most personal interpretation of the theme of death and resurrection. Brahms selected those biblical texts that assure him that his beloved mother has found eternal peace.

Owen and Britten proclaim a biblically-inspired pacifist spirituality. Christians may continue to pray the text of the Latin Requiem. Their longing for God's promise of eternal life, however, must not make them blind for the reality of the victims, whose suffering is never to be regarded as God's will.

Faculteit Godgeleerdheid   Peter DE MEY
K.U. Leuven
Sint-Michielsstraat 6
B-3000 Leuven
Belgium

Faculteit Letteren   Katelijne SCHILTZ
K.U. Leuven
Blijde-Inkomststraat 21
B-3000 Leuven
Belgium

APPENDIX 1: JOHANN SEBASTIAN BACH, *ACTUS TRAGICUS* (BWV 106)

Part	Performers	Texts and sources	Translation
I.	Instr. sonatina		
	Chorus:	*Acts 17,28*	
		Gottes Zeit ist die allerbeste Zeit.	The time of God is the best of all times.
		In ihm leben, weben und sind wir, solange er will.	In him we live and move and have our being, as long as he wills. In him we will die at
		In ihm sterben wir zur rechten Zeit, wenn er will.	the appropriate time, when he wills.
II.	Tenor solo:	*Ps 90,12*	
		Ach, Herr, lehre uns bedenken, daß wir sterben müssen, auf daß wir klug werden.	So teach us to count our days that we may gain a wise heart.
III.	Bassus solo:	*Isa 38,1*	
		Bestelle dein Haus, denn du wirst sterben und nicht lebendig bleiben!	Set your house in order, for you shall die; you shall not recover.
IV.	Chorus:	*Ecclus 14,17*	
		Es ist der alte Bund: Mensch, du mußt sterben!	For the decree from of old is, You must die!
	Soprano solo:	*Rev 22,20*	
		Ja, komm, Herr Jesu, komm!	Amen. Come, Lord Jesus!
	Instruments:	Chorale (*Vulpius*)	
		"Ich hab mein Sach Gott heimgestellt"	"I have entrusted my case to God"
V.	Altus solo:	*Ps 31,5*	
		In deine Hände befehl ich meinen Geist; du hast mich erlöset, Herr, du getreuer Gott.	Into your hand I commit my spirit; you have redeemed me, O Lord, faithful God.

VI.	Bassus solo:	*Luke 23,43*	Truly I tell you, today you will be with me in Paradise.
		Heute wirst du mit mir im Paradies sein	
	Altus (chorus):	*Chorale (Luther)*	
		Mit Fried und Freud ich fahr dahin in Gottes	With peace and joy I move to there, for this is
		Willen, Getrost ist mir mein Herz und Sinn,	God's will. My heart and feelings are comforted,
		sanft und stille, Wie Gott mir verheißen hat:	calm and quiet. As God has promised me:
		der Tod ist mein Schlaf worden.	death has become sleeping to me.
VII.	Chorus:	Glorie, Lob, Ehr und Herrlichkeit	Honor, praise, adoration and glory
		Sei dir Gott, Vater und Sohn bereit,	Be prepared to you, o God, who have been named
		Dem heilgen Geist mit Namen!	Father, Son and Holy Spirit.
		Die göttlich' Kraft	The divine power
		Macht uns sieghaft	Makes us victorious
		Durch Jesum Christum,	Through Jesus Christ,
	Fugue (chorus):	Amen.	Amen.

APPENDIX 2: JOHANNES BRAHMS, *EIN DEUTSCHES REQUIEM* (OP. 45)

Part	Texts and sources	Translation
I.	*Matt 5,4* Selig sind, die da Leid tragen, denn sie sollen getröstet werden.	Blessed are those who mourn, for they will be comforted.
	Ps 126, 5-6 Die mit Tränen säen, werden mit Freuden ernten. Sie gehen hin und weinen und tragen edlen Samen, und kommen mit Freuden und bringen ihre Garben.	May those who sow in tears reap with shouts of joy. Those who go out weeping, bearing the seed for sowing, shall come home with shouts of joy, carrying their sheaves.
II.	*1 Pet 1.24* Denn alles Fleisch ist wie Grass und alle Herrlichkeit des Menschen wie des Grases Blumen. Das Gras ist verdorret und die Blume abgefallen.	For all flesh is like grass and all its glory like the flower of grass. The grass withers, and the flower falls.
	Jas 5,7 So seid nun geduldig, lieben Brüder, bis auf die Zukunft des Herrn. Siehe, ein Ackermann wartet auf die köstliche Frucht der Erde und ist geduldig darüber, bis er empfahe den Morgenregen und Abendregen.	Be patient, therefore, beloved, until the coming of the Lord. The farmer waits for the precious crop from the earth, being patient with it until it receives the early and the late rains.
	1 Pet 1.25 Aber des Herrn Wort bleibet in Ewigkeit.	But the word of the Lord endures forever.
	Isa 35.10 Die Erlöseten des Herrn werden wieder kommen, und gen Zion kommen mit Jauchzen; ewige Freude wird über ihrem Haupt sein; Freude und Wonne werden sie ergreifen und Schmerz und Seufzen wird weg müssen.	And the ransomed of the Lord shall return, and come to Zion with singing; everlasting joy shall be upon their heads; they shall obtain joy and gladness, and sorrow and sighing shall flee away.

III.

Ps 39,4-8

Herr, lehre doch mich, daß ein Ende mit mir haben muß, und mein Leben ein Ziel hat, und ich davon muß. Siehe, meine Tage sind einer Hand breit vor dir, und mein Leben ist wie nichts vor dir. Ach wie gar nichts sind alle Menschen, die doch so sicher leben. Sie gehen daher wie ein Schemen, und machen ihnen viel vergebliche Unruhe; sie sammeln und wissen nicht wer es kriegen wird. Nun Herr, wess soll ich mich trösten? Ich hoffe auf dich.

Lord, let me know my end, and what is the measure of my days; let me know how fleeting my life is. You have made my days a few handbreadths, and my lifetime is as nothing in your sight. Surely everyone stands as a mere breath. Surely everyone goes about like a shadow. Surely for nothing they are in turmoil; they heap up, and do not know who will gather. And now, O Lord, what do I wait for? My hope is in you.

Wis 3,1

Der Gerechten Seele sind in Gottes Hand und keine Qual rühret sie an.

But the souls of the righteous are in the hand of God, and no torment will ever touch them.

IV.

Ps 84,1-2-5

Wie lieblich sind dein Wohnungen, Herr Zebaoth! Meine Seele verlanget und sehnet sich nach den Vorhöfen des Herrn; mein Leib und Seele freuen sich in dem lebendigen Gott. Wohl denen, die in deinem Hause wohnen, die loben dich immerdar.

How lovely is your dwelling place, O Lord of hosts! My soul longs, indeed it faints for the courts of the Lord; my heart and my flesh sing for joy to the living God. Happy are those who live in your house, ever singing your praise.

V.

John 16,22

Ihr habt nun Traurigkeit; aber ich will euch wieder sehen und euer Herz soll sich freuen und eure Freude soll niemand von euch nehmen.

So you have pain now; but I will see you again, and your hearts will rejoice, and no one will take your joy from you.

Ecclus 51,27

Sehet mich an: Ich habe eine kleine Zeit Mühe und Arbeit gehabt und habe großen Trost funden.

See with your own eyes that I have labored but little and found for myself much serenity.

Isa 66,13
Ich will euch trösten, wie einen seine Mutter tröstet.

As a mother comforts her child, so I will comfort you.

VI.

Heb 13,14
Denn wir haben hie keine bleibende Stadt, sondern die zukünftige suchen wir.

For here we have no lasting city, but we are looking for the city that is to come.

1 Cor 15,51-52.55
Siehe, ich sage euch ein Geheimnis: Wir werden nicht alle entschlafen, wir werden aber alle verwandelt werden; und dasselbige plötzlich, in einem Augenblick, zu der Zeit der letzten Posaune. Denn es wird die Posaune schallen, und die Toten werden auferstehen unverweslich, und wir werden verwandelt werden. Dann wird erfüllet werden das Wort, das geschrieben steht: Der Tod ist verschlungen in den Sieg. Tod, wo ist dein Stachel? Hölle, wo ist dein Sieg?

Listen, I will tell you a mystery! We will not all die, but we will all be changed, in a moment, in the twinkling of an eye, at the last trumpet. For the trumpet will sound, and the dead will be raised imperishable, and we will be changed. Then the saying that is written will be fulfilled: Death has been swallowed up in victory. Where, O death is your victory? Where, O death, is your sting?

Rev 4,11
Herr, du bist würdig zu nehmen Preis und Ehre und Kraft, denn du hast alle Dinge geschaffen, und durch deinen Willen haben sie das Wesen und sind geschaffen.

You are worthy, our Lord and God, to receive glory and honor and power, for you created all things, and by your will they existed and were created.

VII.

Rev 14,13
Selig sind die Toten, die in dem Herrn sterben, von nun an. Ja der Geist spricht, daß sie ruhen von ihrer Arbeit; denn ihre Werke folgen ihnen nach.

Blessed are the dead who from now on die in the Lord. Yes, says the Spirit, they will rest from their labors, for their deeds follow them.

APPENDIX 3: BENJAMIN BRITTEN, OFFERTORY FROM THE WAR REQUIEM (OP. 66)

Boys:

Domine Jesu Christe, Rex gloriae,
Libera animas omnium fidelium defunctorum
De poenis inferni et de profundo lacu:
Libera eas de ore leonis,
Ne absorbeat eas tartarus, ne cadant in obscurum.

Chorus:

Sed signifer sanctus Michael repraesentet eas
In lucem sanctam:
Quam olim Abrahae promisisti et semini ejus.

Tenor and Baritone:

So Abram rose, and clave the wood, and went,
And took the fire with him, and a knife.
And as they sojourned both of them together,
Isaac the first-born spoke and said, My father, behold the preparations,
Fire and iron, but where the lamb for this burnt-offering?
Then Abram bound the youth with belts and straps,
And builded parapets and tranches there,
And stretched forth the knife to slay his son.
When lo! An angel called him out of heaven, saying,
Lay not thy hand upon the lad, neither do anything to him.
Behold, a ram, caught in a thicket by its horns;
Offer the ram of pride instead of him.

Lord Jesus Christ, king of glory,
Deliver the souls of the faithful
Departed from the pains of hell, and the bottomless pit:
Deliver them from the jaw of the lion,
Lest hell engulf them, lest they be plunged into darkness.

But let the holy standard-bearer Michael
Lead them into the holy light,
As thou didst promise Abraham and his seed.

But the old man would not so, but slew his son,
And half the seed of Europe one by one.

Boys:
Hostias et preces tibi Domine laudis offerimus;
Tu suscipe pro animabus illis,
Quarum hodie memoriam facimus:
Fac eas, Domine, de morte transire ad vitam.
Quam olim Abrahae promisisti et semini ejus.
Chorus:
Quam olim Abrahae promisisti et semini ejus.

Lord, in praise we offer to Thee sacrifices and prayers;
Do Thou receive them for the souls
Of those whom we remember this day:
Lord, make them pass from death to life.
As Thou didst promise Abraham and his seed.

As Thou didst promise Abraham and his seed.

CARDINAL RATZINGER AND ROCK MUSIC

Is Conversation Impossible?

I. Introduction

The recent renewal of theological interest in the way in which popular music serves as a source of meaning for young people has placed the relation between popular culture and Christian theology on the agenda of contemporary theology. Many contemporary studies in the field of theology deal with the question of how theology should enter into dialogue with the all-pervasiveness of popular music[1]. Several possible ways of closely relating Christian theology to popular music have been explored, documented and proposed. These theological attempts, however, contrast sharply with Cardinal Ratzinger's recent condemnation of the possibility of there being any link between the Christian tradition and popular music.

In his book *The Spirit of the Liturgy*[2], Cardinal Joseph Ratzinger clearly dissociates himself from pop as well as from rock music. He describes pop music as follows: "It is aimed at the phenomenon of the masses, is industrially produced, and ultimately has to be described as a cult of the banal". In addition, he describes rock music as "the expression of elemental passions, and at rock festivals it assumes a cultic character, a form

---

1. To mention but a few: P. Bubmann – R. Tischer (eds.), *Pop – Religion. Auf dem Weg zu einer neuen Volksfrömmigkeit?*, Stuttgart, 1992; J. Koenot, *Voorbij de woorden. Essay over rock, cultuur en religie*, Averbode, 1996 (translated as J. Koenot, *Hungry for Heaven, Rockmusik, Kultur und Religion*, Düsseldorf, 1997); H. Treml, *Spiritualität und Rockmusik. Spurensuche nach einer Spiritualität der Subjekte. Anregungen für die Religionspädagogik aus dem Bereich der Rockmusik* (Glaubenskommunikation Reihe Zeitzeichen, 3), Ostfildern, 1997; B. Schwarze, *Die Religion der Rock- und Popmusik. Analysen und Interpretationen* (Praktische Theologie heute, 28), Stuttgart – Berlin – Köln, 1997; U. Böhm – G. Buschmann, *Popmusik – Religion – Unterricht. Modelle und Materialien zur Didaktik von Popularkultur* (Symbol – Mythos – Medien, 5), Münster, ²2002; G. Fermor, *Ekstasis. Das religiöse Erbe in der Popmusik als Herausforderung an die Kirche* (Praktische Theologie heute, 46), Stuttgart – Berlin – Köln, 1999.
For an extensive bibliography on the relation between rock music and theology: see Fermor, *Ekstasis*, pp. 245-301 and also Böhm – Buschmann, *Popmusik – Religion – Unterricht*, pp. 275-293.
2. J. Kardinal Ratzinger, *Der Geist der Liturgie. Eine Einführung*, Freiburg-Basel-Wien, 2000. In this article, we use the English translation: Ratzinger, *The Spirit of the Liturgy*, trans. John Saward, San Francisco, CA, 2000.

of worship, in fact, in opposition to Christian worship"[3]. Ratzinger's conclusion is predictable: no conversation is possible between rock music and Christian theology. This view is well known and generally considered as the severe judgment of a conservative and restorative thinker.

The marked manner in which Ratzinger's interpretation differs from that of recent studies raises the question of the proper methodology: precisely how should Christian theology relate itself to this relative new phenomenon of popular music?

Another problem is that the authors who examine and defend a close relation between popular culture and Christian theology, although being well informed about the judgment of Ratzinger, actually devote very little attention to the Cardinal's statement. The few studies that actually deal with Ratzinger's opinion tend to gloss over this confrontation by labeling his position a misinterpretation of what is going on in popular music today. The response of two theologians, Hubert Treml and Peter Wirtz, is an example of such a reaction. Both authors evaluate the Cardinal's view as a "misunderstanding of popular music"[4].

The question at hand in this contribution is to what extent we can dismiss Ratzinger's judgment by denouncing it as a misunderstanding of popular culture. To what extent does the argumentation of both Treml and Wirtz really address Ratzinger's statement? On the basis of this investigation, I will try to answer our main question: the search for the proper methodological approach to today's popular culture. Finally, I will attempt to draw up the methodological conditions necessary for bringing rock music and theology into conversation with each other.

Ratzinger only mentions the problem of popular culture in passing within the context of an examination of Christian liturgy. I shall therefore situate the motivation to focus on this topic. First, the statement of Ratzinger about popular culture is not as accidental as it seems. In fact, it illustrates very well his view of contemporary culture as a whole. Examining Ratzinger's view of popular culture is therefore an excellent starting point for examining the soundness of his cultural theology as a whole. Secondly, to the extent that Ratzinger's reservations about popular culture are symptomatic of a more widespread reservation among theologians toward popular culture in general and popular music in particular, the question at hand is central to a broader fundamental theological discussion.

---

3. RATZINGER, *The Spirit of the Liturgy* (n. 2), p. 148.
4. TREML, *Spiritualität und Rockmusik* (n. 1), p. 212 and P. WIRTZ, *Nicht nur mit Engelschören. Zum Verhältnis von Christentum und Rock-Musik*, in *Entschluß* 44/6 (1989) 10-15, p. 10.

In the first section, I sketch the insights of Cardinal Ratzinger and the particular arguments in which he both evaluates and condemns popular music as a whole. In the second section, I look at the few theological studies that deal with Ratzinger's thesis. Finally, in section three, I will reflect upon the appropriate methodology necessary for theology and rock music to enter into a fruitful conversation in our current, post-modern context.

II. Cardinal Ratzinger on Popular Music

In presenting Ratzinger's statement, I will refer to two documents in which the Cardinal explicitly mentions pop as well as rock music[5]. These two documents do not discuss popular music at length, but consider its phenomenon as emblematic of the current state of affairs in today's culture.

In both texts, Ratzinger examines the phenomenon in the broader framework of Christian liturgy. While ostensibly investigating the liturgical applicability of pop and rock music, Ratzinger in fact examines its real Christian applicability since he considers the Christian liturgy as the core of Christian life. This consideration has already been justified in the first chapter of his book, *The Spirit of the Liturgy*, where Ratzinger looks for the essential character of Christian liturgy. This essence, according to Ratzinger, is not to be found in the ritual act itself but rather in the way in which Christian liturgy, defined as the worship of God[6], prescribes the essential characteristics of Christian life. In this sense, Christian liturgy should be seen as the "canon in the canon"[7] on which the whole of Christian life should be grounded. Liturgy is defined as worshipping God, in the way God himself desires: "Cult, liturgy in the proper sense, is part of this worship, but so too is life according to the will of God; such a life is an indispensable part of true worship"[8]. Christian liturgy, since it is an act dictated by God himself, guarantees the proper relationship between God and men and women, which, according to Ratzinger, is the condition for the proper relationship between human beings, other human

5. RATZINGER, *The Spirit of the Liturgy* (n. 2), pp. 136-156 and ID., *Liturgie und Kirchenmusik. Vortrag zur Eröffnung des VIII. Internationalen Kongresses für Kirchenmusik in Rom im Europäischen Jahr der Musik am 17. November 1985*, Hamburg, 1987. The Cardinal takes up this text in his book: *Ein neues Lied für den Herrn. Christusglaube und Liturgie in der Gegenwart*, Freiburg – Basel – Wien, 1995, pp. 145-164.
6. RATZINGER, *The Spirit of the Liturgy* (n. 2), pp. 13-23.
7. *Ibid.*, p. 20.
8. *Ibid.*, pp. 17-18.

beings and the rest of creation. In this way liturgy not only "transcends" the act of liturgy itself but also our own understanding of the way in which liturgy should be conceived. Our own conceptions, when not interrupted and instructed by the way in which God revealed himself, remains a self-made construction, "a festival of self-affirmation" resulting in a "feeling of emptiness"[9].

Ratzinger develops the same argument in his speech opening the "VIII. Internationaler Kongress für Kirchenmusik" in Rome[10]. In the context of a reflection on liturgical renewal after Vatican II, Ratzinger searches for the essential definition of liturgy. This definition goes clearly beyond the definition of a certain rite or cult: the Christian liturgy distinguishes itself by establishing a unique idea of freedom, which exceeds the pure autonomous understanding of it. The question of whether or not a liturgical renewal is applicable does not depend on its creative or revived character but exclusively on the way in which it corresponds with the Christian concept of freedom. This understanding of freedom contrasts with that of pure autonomy and emancipation, but is grounded in an attitude of receptiveness, understood as the constitutive attitude that identifies a human being as human. Only such receptiveness is able to recognize the truth of Christianity, as fundamentally based upon the incarnation of God and exclusively experienced in the Christian liturgy.

This is the basic background to Ratzinger's evaluation of popular music. Thinking about popular music is, according to Ratzinger, looking for its resemblance with Christian notions of freedom, incarnation and redemption. He comes to the conclusion that the grounds on which popular music is based fundamentally contradict those of Christianity.

This general view, elaborated in the first chapter of Part One of *The Spirit of the Liturgy*, is further developed in the second chapter of the third part, entitled "Art and Liturgy". This part examines the possible role music can play in the Christian liturgy. Since Christian liturgy is not limited to the spoken word, music serves as a necessary addition: liturgy and music need each other. "When man comes into contact with God, mere speech is not enough. Areas of his existence are awakened that spontaneously turn into song"[11]. In transcending purely rational and verbal language, music allows other ways of the expression of bearing witness to one's worship of God. While recognizing the undeniable importance of this musical language, Ratzinger remains on his guard: only if

9. *Ibid.*, p. 23.
10. This conference took place on 17 November 1985.
11. RATZINGER, *The Spirit of the Liturgy* (n. 2), p. 136.

the musical expression remains within the boundaries of the essence of the Christian liturgy can it be considered as a worthwhile aspect of the worship of God. Liturgical singing is not based on artistic freedom or on any human standard: it has its own theological basis[12]. If this basis is not respected music becomes a product of overconfidence, following fleeting artistic rules, leading into a self-made fantasy world and deluding people with a false image of freedom. For Ratzinger, the twentieth-century phenomena of both pop and rock music are examples of this overconfidence. The problem of popular music for Ratzinger is just another version of an old and repeatedly recurring temptation during the history of mankind: the temptation of over-emphasizing self-emancipating subjectivity at the cost of an open and constitutive attitude towards otherness. For this reason Ratzinger places popular music along the same lines as "the Gnostic temptation, the crisis at the end of the Middle Ages and the beginning of modernity and the crisis at the beginning of the twentieth century"[13]. Pop music should be questioned because of its industrial production, which, according to Ratzinger, necessarily serves as a "cult of the banal". Rock music, in addition, should be rejected because of the self-centred and conceited mentality on which rock music seems to be based. "People are, so to speak, released from themselves by the experience of being part of a crowd and by the emotional shock of rhythm, noise, and special lighting effects. However, in the ecstasy of having all their defenses torn down, the participants sink, as it were, beneath the elemental force of the universe"[14].

At first sight, this escapism seems to interrupt the self-centeredness of the modern autonomous subject. For Ratzinger, however, this kind of escapism is nevertheless completely in line with the tendency towards autonomy and self-determination. It is still built upon humanity's intention to self-determine limits. Pop as well as rock music still remain, according to Ratzinger, within the same self-centered circle of the autonomous subject.

As mentioned earlier, Ratzinger uses the same argument in the opening lecture above cited. In arguing against a false interpretation of the liturgical renewal, he warns against autonomous reactions based upon a false interpretation of freedom. Creativity founded solely upon autonomy and emancipation should be banned and condemned, since it necessarily

---

12. *Ibid.*, p. 143: "Thus, in the musical sphere, biblical faith created its own form of culture, an expression appropriate to its inward essence, one that provides a standard for all later forms of inculturation".

13. *Ibid.*, p. 147.

14. *Ibid.*, p. 148.

results in arbitrariness and artificiality[15]. Ratzinger calls such kind of self-deception "Gruppenliturgie". This "Gruppenliturgie" is:

> Flucht aus der *conditio humana* und darum Unwahrheit. Dies ist der Grund, weshalb dort Kulturzerfall einsetzt, wo mit dem Verlust des Glaubens an Gott auch eine vorgegebene Vernunft des Seins bestritten werden muß[16].

Although music should be a substantial part of the worship of God, this contribution is bound to a certain concept of freedom. Therefore Ratzinger concludes:

> Richtig ist aber, daß die Musik, die der Anbetung "in Geist und Wahrheit" dient, nicht rhythmische Ekstase, nicht sinnliche Suggestion oder Betäubung, nicht subjektive Gefühlsseligkeit, nicht oberflächliche Unterhaltung sein kann, sondern einer Botschaft zugeordnet ist, einer umfassenden geistigen und im höchsten Sinn vernünftigen Aussage[17].

Pop as well as rock music, considered as an example of such a "Gruppenliturgie", does not witness to the Christian message and should therefore be classified as contrary to Christian anthropology.

> Weil Rock-Musik Erlösung auf dem Weg der Befreiung von der Personalität und von ihrer Verantwortung sucht, ordnet sie sich einerseits sehr genau in die anarchischen Freiheitsideen ein […] sie ist aber gerade darum der christlichen Vorstellung von Erlösung und von Freiheit von Grund auf entgegengesetzt, ihr eigentlicher Widerspruch[18].

The criterion by which Ratzinger judges popular music is that of "sober inebriation"[19]. This criterion determines any possible relation between music and liturgy. Sober inebriation, as a characteristic of true art, is able

---

15. RATZINGER, *Liturgie und Kirchenmusik* (n. 5), p. 12: "Ihre Kennzeichnen sind die Willkür als notwendige Form der Absage an jede vorgegebene Form oder Norm; die Unwiederholbarkeit, weil ja im Nachvollzug bereits Abhängigkeit läge; die Künstlichkeit, weil es sich ja um reine Erschaffung des Menschen handeln muß".

16. *Ibid.*, p. 13.

17. *Ibid.*, p. 14.

18. *Ibid.*, pp. 16-17. To guard his own position against possible popular reproaches, Ratzinger continues: "Nicht aus ästhetischen Gründen, nicht aus restaurativer Verbohrtheit, nicht aus historistischer Unbeweglichkeit, sondern vom Grund her muß daher Musik dieses Typs aus der Kirche ausgeschlossen werden".

19. RATZINGER, *The Spirit of the Liturgy* (n. 2), p. 140: "It is the true glossolalia, the new tongue that comes from the Holy Spirit. It is above all in Church music that the 'sober inebriation' of faith takes place – an inebriation surpassing all the possibilities of mere rationality. But the intoxication remains sober, because Christ and the Holy Spirit belong together, because this drunken speech stays totally within the discipline of the Logos, in a new rationality that, beyond all words, serves the primordial Word, the ground of all reason".

to express an authentic freedom and counts as a true answer to "our vocation as human beings"[20]. For Ratzinger, however, this vocation is true so
long as it is in line with the way in which it is formed by the Christian
notion of incarnation and resurrection. Therefore, Ratzinger's argument
is a christological one, since he specifies this sober inebriation as one
from the Holy Spirit, which for Ratzinger is identical with the Spirit of
Christ[21]. Since our vocation is constituted by the Christian message, our
answer should be formed in the same way. Ratzinger's evaluation of popular music stems from a theological argumentation in which it is the christological norm that determines whether or not music should be welcomed.

III. AGAINST RATZINGER'S "MISSVERSTÄNDNIS"

The two theological reactions that I will now focus upon evaluate
Ratzinger's thoughts on popular music as a "Mißverstandnis" of pop as
well as rock music.

1. *Peter Wirtz*[22]

In his article "Nicht nur mit Engelschören", Wirtz tries to develop a
possible dialogue between rock music and Christianity. His essential argument is the history out of which popular music was born. The different
traditions out of which popular music has grown all stem from a religious origin. It is exactly this origin that Wirtz uses as an argument
against Ratzinger and as the basis for his attempt to combine popular
music and Christian theology.

> Vom Blues übernahm sie [die Pop/Rock-Musik] im wesentlichen das Takt-
> schema und das Notensystem, vom Country die Rhythmik und vom Gospel
> die Exaltiertheit des Gesanges. Gerade jenes Element also, das Kardinal
> Ratzinger als unvereinbar mit katholischem Musikverständnis bezeichnete,
> entstammt dem Erbe religiöser Musik der Farbigen Amerikaner. Dieses
> Mißverständsnis wirft ein deutliches Licht auf das Verhältnis von Pop/Rock-
> Musik und Religion/Kirche[23].

---

20. *Ibid.*, p. 156.
21. *Ibid.*, p. 148 and p. 151: "If we want to know whom we are dealing with, the Holy
Spirit or the unholy spirit, we have to remember that it is the Holy Spirit who moves us
to say, 'Jesus is Lord' (1 Cor 12:3)".
22. Besides the already cited article, I also refer to P. WIRTZ, *Mauern aus Klang und
Rythmus*, in *Jugend & Kirche* 24/4 (1990/91) 2-5, and *Tod als Thema der Rock- und Popmusik*, in *Diakonia* 27 (1996) 184-190.
23. WIRTZ, *Nicht nur mit Engelschören* (n. 4), p. 10.

On the basis of this historical argument, Wirtz develops four common fields in which the relationship between popular music and Christian theology can be developed in a concrete way. He defends a relation with regard to the cultural, emotional, moral and religious fields.

Firstly, popular music is deeply rooted in a post-Christian culture. Although the Christian message has lost its self-evidence as well as its reserved character, Wirtz suggests that the symbols and the vocabulary of the Christian tradition are still well known. They are freely available and actually used by musicians. For Wirtz, this fact creates a first common field that allows the bridge between popular music and Christian theology to take place. A second bridge can be found in the emotional field. In its symbolic setting, pop music dreams of a better world in disapproving injustice and hoping for a foundational ground of life. By placing this restlessness in relation to the restlessness of which Saint Augustine spoke in his famous statement in the *Confessiones*, Wirtz defends the possibility of an intrinsic dialogue[24]. This possibility is confirmed by the same ethical objective for which both popular music and Christianity stands. This same ethical objective constitutes a third field. In fighting against "apartheid" or hunger and in appealing for sustainable peace, pop as well as rock music encounter Christian moral wisdom. A last field bridging Christian theology and popular music is the way in which pop and rock music express its Christian connection. Wirtz distinguishes between a song of Praise (e.g. Bruce Cockburn, "Lord of the Starfields"), a song of confession (e.g. Bob Dylan, "Precious Angel"), a song of critique (e.g. U2, Sunday Bloody Sunday) and the personal song in which the singer/the group expresses his/her/their own religious feelings (e.g. Bob Dylan, Every Grain of Sand)[25].

According to Wirtz, Ratzinger misunderstands the essence of popular music because he neglects the religious inheritance on which popular music is based. This religious basis is a sufficient ground for combining it with Christian spirituality.

2. *Hubert Treml*[26]

In his book "Spiritualität und Rockmusik", Hubert Treml looks for a "Spurensuche nach einer Spiritualität der Subjekte". According to this

---

24. See AUGUSTINE, *Confessiones* 1, 1, 1. This argument recurs in O. SIGURDSON, *Songs of Desire: On Pop-Music and the Question of God*, in *Concilium* 2001/1, 34-41. See also B. SCHWARZE, *"Everybody's Got a Hungry Heart ..." Rockmusik und Theologie*, in BUBMANN – TISCHER (eds.), *Pop Religion* (n. 1), pp. 187-201.

25. These are Wirtz' own examples: cf. WIRTZ, *Nicht nur mit Engelschören* (n. 4), pp. 11-14.

26. In addition to his book cited earlier, his most important publications are: TREML, *Aktuelle Trends religiöser Ausdrucksformen Jugendlicher im Medium Musik*,

practical theologian, the worldview of youth should be taken more seriously by contemporary theology.

For Treml, the question of the spirituality of rock music is in fact a question of the spirituality of the subject. He is clear about his presuppositions: for him, there is a common human religiosity present in every human being. Christian faith should be seen as building upon this common religiosity. "Christlicher Glaube ist eher als eine Ausformung der dem Menschen eigenen Religiosität zu verstehen"[27].

Thus, the question for Treml is to what extent popular music bears witness to this common religiosity. He enquires after the "spiritual potential" within rock music. In order to recognize this "potential", Treml searches for different aspects which constitute the religious identity to which rock music is able to contribute: analogies between rock music and religion.

First, there is a historical analogy: as growing out of the Afro-American context, rock music was originally allied to religious aspects[28]. Spirituals, just as Gospel, are an outcome of the missionary work among the slaves and count for a combination of both European ecclesiastical chorales and Afro-American style. Blues as well as Rhythm & Blues are offshoots of this tradition and became symbols of black identity. Both styles empowered the black people in order to resist – spiritually – their oppression. Ecstasy was therefore one of the most important tools. Treml bases ecstasy on musical elements such as Rhythm, Improvisation, "Call and Response", and Blue-notes[29]. In addition to this aspect of ecstasy, rock music was also "music of the body". Its corporal as well as creative character are constitutive elements in building up a (religious) identity. The second analogy comes from the religious themes to which singers and songwriters refer explicitly (the way in which the text explicitly refers to religious and symbolic traditions) and implicitly (the way in which the text deals with existential and moral questions). Thirdly, there are various external elements that enable Treml to define rock music as a functional equivalent of religion. Treml attaches great importance to the

in H. HOBELSBERGER (ed.), *Engagement und Religion im Leben von Jugendlichen* (Kath. Akademie für Jugendfragen), Odenthal, 1998, pp. 69-93, and *Anklänge. Von der Nähe der popularmusikalischen Szene zur Religion und vom theologischen Umgang mit beiden*, in G. FERMOR – H.-M. GUTMANN – H. SCHROETER (eds.), *Theophonie. Grenzgänge zwischen Musik und Theologie*, Rheinbach, 2000, pp. 180-203.

27. TREML, *Spiritualität und Rockmusik* (n. 1), p. 96.

28. *Ibid.*, pp. 171-174.

29. These Afro-American roots are an integral and decisive element in the thought of G. Fermor on ecstasy. Cf. FERMOR, *Ekstasis* (n. 1), pp. 121-152. The argument developed by Fermor is part of the critical research I am currently engaged in.

cult-character within rock: the way in which concerts serve as "Ersatz-religion"[30] and the analogy between the singer and a liturgical minister are decisive characteristics of this cult-character. For Treml, this functional equivalence proves rock music's power to transcend: "Was also zunächts als äußerlich funktionales religiöses Phänomen gedeutet wird, könnte durchaus einen unbewußten Transzendenzvollzug zur Kontaktnahme mit dem Lebensgeheimnis darstellen"[31].

Because of the power to constitute one's identity as well as the power to transcend, Treml denotes rock music as able to exceed the triviality of the commonplace. By doing so, Treml does not establish a systematic way to combine rock music and religion but only founds the conditions of a possible connection between the two.

In the context of this search for a possible dialogue, Treml mentions the position of Cardinal Ratzinger. Like Wirtz, Treml considers the Cardinal's position as a misunderstanding of what is really at stake in popular music[32]. Treml critiques Ratzinger's view by referring to the process of identity building in which popular music has an indispensable function for the current generation[33]. The manner in which rock music can stand for a dynamic experience of life legitimates the fact that rock music can hold an authentic spiritual identity too.

> Zwar versuchen Jugendliche mit Hilfe der Rockmusik ihrem Alltag immer wieder zu entfliehen, sie wollen sich dadurch aber nicht einer Verantwortung entledigen, sondern wieder neue Kraft schöpfen für die Dinge, die ihre konkrete Lebenssituation ihnen abverlangt. Rockmusik ist weniger Flucht als Hilfe bzw. Begleitung zur Ausbildung einer Identität, in der ja das Ich, die eigene Person, gerade nicht verloren gehen, sondern aufgehoben sein soll[34].

---

30. TREML, *Spiritualität und Rockmusik* (n. 1), p. 221.

31. *Ibid.*, p. 232.

32. *Ibid.*, p. 212: "Im Anschluß an die bisherigen Ausführungen zur Rockmusik kann deutlich werden, wie sehr die Interpretation Ratzingers – und vieler ähnlicher Stimmen – auf einem Mißverständnis beruht".

33. Treml's statement is repeated by Schäfers in his book *Jugend – Religion – Musik*. He mentions the position of Ratzinger (p. 10) as merely an example of a theological disagreement on popular culture. He does not actually elaborate the position of Ratzinger but in the context of his introduction it is clear that Schäfers would argue against Ratzinger along the same lines as Treml. Citing Ratzinger, Schäfers states: "Ob mit Hilfe der Rockmusik eine illusorische Befreiung vom Ich stattfindet, oder ob die Rockmusik nicht gerade dadurch, daß sie den Alltag vergessen läßt, vielen Jugendlichen die Möglichkeit bietet, wieder zu sich selbst zu kommen und damit Identitätsbildung unterstützend begleitet, wird im 4. Kapitel noch zu diskutieren sein". Chapter 4 answers this (rhetorical) question in favour of the second possibility (pp. 119-147). See M. SCHÄFERS, *Jugend – Religion – Musik. Zur religiösen Dimension der Popularmusik und ihrer Bedeutung für die Jugendlichen heute* (Theologie und Praxis Abteilung B, 1), Münster, 1999.

34. TREML, *Spiritualität und Rockmusik* (n. 1), p. 212.

According to Treml, Ratzinger misinterprets the culture of popular music because he overlooks the fact that rock music can build up a (religious) identity. Ratzinger understands this identity as the loss of the real (Christian) identity. The culture of rock music, being for Ratzinger an offshoot of a runaway autonomous culture, only mirrors the view of an ominous emancipating subject and therefore blocks the process of a responsible and earthly spirituality. For Treml, however, the feasibility to exceed the superficiality of the commonplace is the crucial argument for defending the potential of an authentic spirituality within rock music. "Die sogenannte Flucht ist dann in Wirklichkeit eine Konfrontation, eine Auseinandersetzung mit den Anfragen des Lebens"[35].

IV. EVALUATION AND METHODOLOGICAL REFLECTIONS

For Ratzinger, any dialogue between Christian theology and popular culture is out of the question from the outset. On the basis of the Christian message about freedom and redemption, Ratzinger scrutinizes the manner in which popular culture tries to cope with the human condition. A dialogue with music or art is only possible in cases where the musician or the artist speaks from out of the same Christian background. In such a scenario, Ratzinger would welcome the language of music for it interrupts an exclusive tongue of rationality and speech[36].

The question can be asked to what extent Ratzinger really enters into dialogue with popular culture. His severe verdict on popular culture seems to be determined by a christological presupposition – a clear criterion on the basis of which he clearly distinguishes between true and untrue. Due to this clear distinction, Ratzinger is not able to consider the phenomenon

---

35. *Ibid.*, p. 192. Treml's thought is inspired by the thought of Spengler: P. SPENGLER, *Rockmusik und Jugend. Bedeutung und Funktion einer Musikkultur für die Identitätssuche im Jugendalter*, Frankfurt a. M., 1987.

36. In an interview with Peter Seewald – published as *Salz der Erde* – Ratzinger testifies to the power of Mozart's music which he admires: "Die Kunst is schon elementar. Die Vernunft allein, wie sie sich in den Wissenschaften ausdrückt, kann nicht die volle Antwort des Menschen auf die Wirklichkeit sein und nicht alles ausdrücken, was der Mensch ausdrücken kann, will und auch muß. Ich denke, das hat Gott in den Menschen hineingelegt. Kunst ist mit der Wissenschaft die höchste Gabe, die er Ihm gegeben hat". J. RATZINGER, *Salz der Erde. Christentum und katholische Kirche an der Jahrtausendwende. Ein Gespräch mit Peter Seewald*, Stuttgart, [9]1997, p. 50. For a comprehensive analysis of the thought of Ratzinger on the relation between culture and theology, see L. BOEVE, *Kerk, theologie en heilswaarheid. De klare visie van Joseph Ratzinger*, in *TvT* 33 (1993) 139-165.

of today's popular culture and therefore risks overlooking possible links between rock music and Christian theology.

On the basis of the search for these links, Wirtz and Treml incorporate Ratzinger's statement. They do so by pointing to the similarities between the way in which popular music frames itself and the way Christian theology frames itself. Both authors stress the religious context out of which popular music has grown, the way in which musicians allow themselves to be inspired by the Christian tradition and the way in which they implicitly or explicitly deal with religious questions. In addition to these aspects, Treml stresses the cultic character on which popular music is styled and uses it as the fundament to argue for a possible dialogue between the two.

Anthropological similarities between popular culture and Christian theology are indeed easily conceivable: for instance, concerts can rightly be considered on the basis of their cultic and liturgical characteristics. Without denying these similarities or the force within popular culture to build up a certain (religious) identity, I wish to ask whether the argument based on these similarities really tackles the problem brought to the fore by the statement of the Cardinal. Ratzinger's argument that the entire culture of popular music instills a kind of self-deception is not diminished in any way by highlighting that pop culture can build up an identity or by pointing to the extent to which singers and song writers implicitly or explicitly refer to religious traditions. That is to say, simply stating the opposite does not undermine Ratzinger's point. The real question that the statement of Ratzinger poses to contemporary theology is one of criteria.

The argument that popular music is one of the unavoidable aspects of the identity of youth today is correct but does not answer the question whether this identity is deceptive or not. The same can be said of the conceivable anthropological similarities between popular music and religion. These similarities are recognizable and point undoubtedly to possible links between the two, but they do not address the question of the appropriateness of such parallels. Although it was one of their objectives, Wirtz and Treml do not actually succeed in taking the edge off Ratzinger's argument.

What is problematic in Ratzinger's thought is not so much his severe assessment of rock 'n roll's spirituality: namely, that the search for authenticity within the whole range of popular culture is in need of a critical reflection and a responsible criteriology. Rather, the difficulty of Ratzinger's judgment lies in his presupposed christological argument that condemns popular music as a whole. As indicated above, music for Ratzinger is only true if it comes out of the "true spirit", which is defined by Ratzinger as "the Holy Spirit who moves us to say, "Jesus is Lord"

(1 Cor 12,3)"[37]. By this definition Ratzinger evidently condemns the whole of popular culture as an act of human overconfidence and thus contradicting the core of the Christian message. Ratzinger's assessment on popular culture should therefore be questioned first and foremost with regard to his christological presupposition. In a second move, a balanced distinction regarding the whole range of popular culture could then be a possible further scope of research.

The argumentation of Wirtz and Treml seems to be built upon a sociological conclusion to (religious) identity. This identity as the basis on which they defend the dialogue between popular culture and Christian theology relies upon the history of rock 'n roll, the corporality of popular music and the function it plays in the identity of youth today. This is their counter-argument to Ratzinger's severe and blanket judgment. In their discussion with Ratzinger, however, neither Wirtz nor Treml examine the question of criteria. Yet, a careful analysis of Ratzinger's argumentation shows that it is only an examination based upon the search for the proper criteriology that can seriously address Ratzinger's christological argumentation.

V. CONCLUSION

We have set out to show that the argumentation on the basis of identity, anthropological similarities, and implicit and explicit references to the Christian tradition fail to enter into dialogue with Ratzinger's condemnation of popular music as self-deceptive and false. Therefore, a proper response to the Cardinal's statement cannot merely be reduced to the issue of whether Ratzinger rightly interpreted popular music. Wirtz and Treml's contention that popular music need not necessarily result in self-deception should proceed from a discussion that first treats the christological presuppositions underlying Ratzinger's misinterpretation or indeed any other possible interpretation. It is therefore regrettable that Treml's book, although extensive and detailed in its search for a spirituality of the subject, does not go on to make use of this elaborate thought to enter into any real detailed discussion with Ratzinger.

To conclude, then, if theology is looking for a bridge with popular culture, this search should go beyond the question of whether or not popular music creates a (religious) identity for young people. Research should

37. See n. 21.

not be limited to the search for eventual religious references within the texts (whether implicit or explicit) or even within the whole of popular culture (e.g. ecstasy). In order to treat the question posed by Ratzinger's statement seriously, one needs to go beyond merely searching for similarities between popular music and Christian theology.

Searching then for other tools that bring popular culture and Christian theology together, I therefore plead for an alternative criteriology. In moving beyond a focus upon the similarities between popular music and Christian theology, this criteriology must be able to judge the whole range of popular music in a fair and balanced manner.

While an extensive discussion into such a criteriology falls naturally outside the scope of this article[38], it has been the purpose of this article to show that a more balanced evaluation is needed when discussing the apparent barrier that Cardinal Ratzinger's thought seems to present to the notion of there being a bridge between Christian theology and popular music.

Faculteit Godgeleerdheid   Johan ARDUI
K.U. Leuven
Sint-Michielsstraat 6
B-3000 Leuven
Belgium

---

38. The project I am currently engaged in is aimed at the search for such a criteriology. The project incorporates a critical investigation of the thought of Adorno, a study of his ideal of art and an exploration of its applicability to the phenomenon of popular culture. In addition to this, current theological studies that explicitly deal with popular culture will also be analysed. The main purpose of the project is to develop a defensible dialogue between popular music and theology.

INDEX OF AUTHORS

BIBLIOTHECA EPHEMERIDUM THEOLOGICARUM
LOVANIENSIUM

SERIES I

* = Out of print

29. M. Didier (ed.), *L'évangile selon Matthieu. Rédaction et théologie*, 1972. 432 p.   25 €
*30. J. Kempeneers, *Le Cardinal van Roey en son temps*, 1971.

Series II

31. F. Neirynck, *Duality in Mark. Contributions to the Study of the Markan Redaction*, 1972. Revised edition with Supplementary Notes, 1988. 252 p.
30 €
32. F. Neirynck (ed.), *L'évangile de Luc. Problèmes littéraires et théologiques*, 1973. *L'évangile de Luc – The Gospel of Luke*. Revised and enlarged edition, 1989. x-590 p.   55 €
33. C. Brekelmans (ed.), *Questions disputées d'Ancien Testament. Méthode et théologie*, 1974. *Continuing Questions in Old Testament Method and Theology*. Revised and enlarged edition by M. Vervenne, 1989. 245 p.
30 €
34. M. Sabbe (ed.), *L'évangile selon Marc. Tradition et rédaction*, 1974. Nouvelle édition augmentée, 1988. 601 p.   60 €
35. B. Willaert (ed.), *Philosophie de la religion – Godsdienstfilosofie. Miscellanea Albert Dondeyne*, 1974. Nouvelle édition, 1987. 458 p.   60 €
36. G. Philips, *L'union personnelle avec le Dieu vivant. Essai sur l'origine et le sens de la grâce créée*, 1974. Édition révisée, 1989. 299 p.   25 €
37. F. Neirynck, in collaboration with T. Hansen and F. Van Segbroeck, *The Minor Agreements of Matthew and Luke against Mark with a Cumulative List*, 1974. 330 p.   23 €
38. J. Coppens, *Le messianisme et sa relève prophétique. Les anticipations vétérotestamentaires. Leur accomplissement en Jésus*, 1974. Édition révisée, 1989. xiii-265 p.   25 €
39. D. Senior, *The Passion Narrative according to Matthew. A Redactional Study*, 1975. New impression, 1982. 440 p.   25 €
40. J. Dupont (ed.), *Jésus aux origines de la christologie*, 1975. Nouvelle édition augmentée, 1989. 458 p.   38 €
41. J. Coppens (ed.), *La notion biblique de Dieu*, 1976. Réimpression, 1985. 519 p.   40 €
42. J. Lindemans & H. Demeester (ed.), *Liber Amicorum Monseigneur W. Onclin*, 1976. xxii-396 p.   25 €
43. R.E. Hoeckman (ed.), *Pluralisme et œcuménisme en recherches théologiques. Mélanges offerts au R.P. Dockx, O.P.*, 1976. 316 p.   25 €
44. M. de Jonge (ed.), *L'évangile de Jean. Sources, rédaction, théologie*, 1977. Réimpression, 1987. 416 p.   38 €
45. E.J.M. van Eijl (ed.), *Facultas S. Theologiae Lovaniensis 1432-1797. Bijdragen tot haar geschiedenis. Contributions to its History. Contributions à son histoire*, 1977. 570 p.   43 €
46. M. Delcor (ed.), *Qumrân. Sa piété, sa théologie et son milieu*, 1978. 432 p.   43 €
47. M. Caudron (ed.), *Faith and Society. Foi et société. Geloof en maatschappij. Acta Congressus Internationalis Theologici Lovaniensis 1976*, 1978. 304 p.   29 €

*48. J. KREMER (ed.), *Les Actes des Apôtres. Traditions, rédaction, théologie*, 1979. 590 p.

49. F. NEIRYNCK, avec la collaboration de J. DELOBEL, T. SNOY, G. VAN BELLE, F. VAN SEGBROECK, *Jean et les Synoptiques. Examen critique de l'exégèse de M.-É. Boismard*, 1979. XII-428 p.   25 €

50. J. COPPENS, *La relève apocalyptique du messianisme royal. I. La royauté – Le règne – Le royaume de Dieu. Cadre de la relève apocalyptique*, 1979. 325 p.   25 €

51. M. GILBERT (ed.), *La Sagesse de l'Ancien Testament*, 1979. Nouvelle édition mise à jour, 1990. 455 p.   38 €

52. B. DEHANDSCHUTTER, *Martyrium Polycarpi. Een literair-kritische studie*, 1979. 296 p.   25 €

53. J. LAMBRECHT (ed.), *L'Apocalypse johannique et l'Apocalyptique dans le Nouveau Testament*, 1980. 458 p.   35 €

54. P.-M. BOGAERT (ed.), *Le livre de Jérémie. Le prophète et son milieu. Les oracles et leur transmission*, 1981. Nouvelle édition mise à jour, 1997. 448 p.   45 €

55. J. COPPENS, *La relève apocalyptique du messianisme royal. III. Le Fils de l'homme néotestamentaire*. Édition posthume par F. NEIRYNCK, 1981. XIV-192 p.   20 €

56. J. VAN BAVEL & M. SCHRAMA (ed.), *Jansénius et le Jansénisme dans les Pays-Bas. Mélanges Lucien Ceyssens*, 1982. 247 p.   25 €

57. J.H. WALGRAVE, *Selected Writings – Thematische geschriften. Thomas Aquinas, J.H. Newman, Theologia Fundamentalis*. Edited by G. DE SCHRIJVER & J.J. KELLY, 1982. XLIII-425 p.   25 €

58. F. NEIRYNCK & F. VAN SEGBROECK, avec la collaboration de E. MANNING, *Ephemerides Theologicae Lovanienses 1924-1981. Tables générales. (Bibliotheca Ephemeridum Theologicarum Lovaniensium 1947-1981)*, 1982. 400 p.   40 €

59. J. DELOBEL (ed.), *Logia. Les paroles de Jésus – The Sayings of Jesus. Mémorial Joseph Coppens*, 1982. 647 p.   50 €

60. F. NEIRYNCK, *Evangelica. Gospel Studies – Études d'évangile. Collected Essays*. Edited by F. VAN SEGBROECK, 1982. XIX-1036 p.   50 €

61. J. COPPENS, *La relève apocalyptique du messianisme royal. II. Le Fils d'homme vétéro- et intertestamentaire*. Édition posthume par J. LUST, 1983. XVII-272 p.   25 €

62. J.J. KELLY, *Baron Friedrich von Hügel's Philosophy of Religion*, 1983. 232 p.   38 €

63. G. DE SCHRIJVER, *Le merveilleux accord de l'homme et de Dieu. Étude de l'analogie de l'être chez Hans Urs von Balthasar*, 1983. 344 p.   38 €

64. J. GROOTAERS & J.A. SELLING, *The 1980 Synod of Bishops: «On the Role of the Family». An Exposition of the Event and an Analysis of its Texts*. Preface by Prof. emeritus L. JANSSENS, 1983. 375 p.   38 €

65. F. NEIRYNCK & F. VAN SEGBROECK, *New Testament Vocabulary. A Companion Volume to the Concordance*, 1984. XVI-494 p.   50 €

66. R.F. COLLINS, *Studies on the First Letter to the Thessalonians*, 1984. XI-415 p.   38 €

67. A. PLUMMER, *Conversations with Dr. Döllinger 1870-1890*. Edited with Introduction and Notes by R. BOUDENS, with the collaboration of L. KENIS, 1985. LIV-360 p.   45 €

68. N. LOHFINK (ed.), *Das Deuteronomium. Entstehung, Gestalt und Botschaft / Deuteronomy: Origin, Form and Message*, 1985. XI-382 p.   50 €
69. P.F. FRANSEN, *Hermeneutics of the Councils and Other Studies*. Collected by H.E. MERTENS & F. DE GRAEVE, 1985. 543 p.   45 €
70. J. DUPONT, *Études sur les Évangiles synoptiques*. Présentées par F. NEIRYNCK, 1985. 2 tomes, XXI-IX-1210 p.   70 €
71. *Recueil Lucien Cerfaux*, t. III, 1962. Nouvelle édition revue et complétée, 1985. LXXX-458 p.   40 €
72. J. GROOTAERS, *Primauté et collégialité. Le dossier de Gérard Philips sur la Nota Explicativa Praevia (Lumen gentium, Chap. III)*. Présenté avec introduction historique, annotations et annexes. Préface de G. THILS, 1986. 222 p.   25 €
73. A. VANHOYE (ed.), *L'apôtre Paul. Personnalité, style et conception du ministère*, 1986. XIII-470 p.   65 €
74. J. LUST (ed.), *Ezekiel and His Book. Textual and Literary Criticism and their Interrelation*, 1986. X-387 p.   68 €
75. É. MASSAUX, *Influence de l'Évangile de saint Matthieu sur la littérature chrétienne avant saint Irénée*. Réimpression anastatique présentée par F. NEIRYNCK. Supplément: *Bibliographie 1950-1985*, par B. DEHANDSCHUTTER, 1986. XXVII-850 p.   63 €
76. L. CEYSSENS & J.A.G. TANS, *Autour de l'Unigenitus. Recherches sur la genèse de la Constitution*, 1987. XXVI-845 p.   63 €
77. A. DESCAMPS, *Jésus et l'Église. Études d'exégèse et de théologie*. Préface de Mgr A. HOUSSIAU, 1987. XLV-641 p.   63 €
78. J. DUPLACY, *Études de critique textuelle du Nouveau Testament*. Présentées par J. DELOBEL, 1987. XXVII-431 p.   45 €
79. E.J.M. VAN EIJL (ed.), *L'image de C. Jansénius jusqu'à la fin du XVIIIe siècle*, 1987. 258 p.   32 €
80. E. BRITO, *La Création selon Schelling. Universum*, 1987. XXXV-646 p.   75 €
81. J. VERMEYLEN (ed.), *The Book of Isaiah – Le livre d'Isaïe. Les oracles et leurs relectures. Unité et complexité de l'ouvrage*, 1989. X-472 p.   68 €
82. G. VAN BELLE, *Johannine Bibliography 1966-1985. A Cumulative Bibliography on the Fourth Gospel*, 1988. XVII-563 p.   68 €
83. J.A. SELLING (ed.), *Personalist Morals. Essays in Honor of Professor Louis Janssens*, 1988. VIII-344 p.   30 €
84. M.-É. BOISMARD, *Moïse ou Jésus. Essai de christologie johannique*, 1988. XVI-241 p.   25 €
84A. M.-É. BOISMARD, *Moses or Jesus: An Essay in Johannine Christology*. Translated by B.T. VIVIANO, 1993, XVI-144 p.   25 €
85. J.A. DICK, *The Malines Conversations Revisited*, 1989. 278 p.   38 €
86. J.-M. SEVRIN (ed.), *The New Testament in Early Christianity – La réception des écrits néotestamentaires dans le christianisme primitif*, 1989. XVI-406 p.   63 €
87. R.F. COLLINS (ed.), *The Thessalonian Correspondence*, 1990. XV-546 p.   75 €
88. F. VAN SEGBROECK, *The Gospel of Luke. A Cumulative Bibliography 1973-1988*, 1989. 241 p.   30 €

89. G. THILS, *Primauté et infaillibilité du Pontife Romain à Vatican I et autres études d'ecclésiologie,* 1989. XI-422 p. 47 €
90. A. VERGOTE, *Explorations de l'espace théologique. Études de théologie et de philosophie de la religion,* 1990. XVI-709 p. 50 €
*91. J.C. DE MOOR, *The Rise of Yahwism: The Roots of Israelite Monotheism,* 1990. *Revised and Enlarged Edition,* 1997. XV-445 p.
92. B. BRUNING, M. LAMBERIGTS & J. VAN HOUTEM (eds.), *Collectanea Augustiniana. Mélanges T.J. van Bavel,* 1990. 2 tomes, XXXVIII-VIII-1074 p. 75 €
93. A. DE HALLEUX, *Patrologie et œcuménisme. Recueil d'études,* 1990. XVI-887 p. 75 €
94. C. BREKELMANS & J. LUST (eds.), *Pentateuchal and Deuteronomistic Studies: Papers Read at the XIIIth IOSOT Congress Leuven 1989,* 1990. 307 p. 38 €
95. D.L. DUNGAN (ed.), *The Interrelations of the Gospels. A Symposium Led by M.-É. Boismard – W.R. Farmer – F. Neirynck, Jerusalem 1984,* 1990. XXXI-672 p. 75 €
96. G.D. KILPATRICK, *The Principles and Practice of New Testament Textual Criticism. Collected Essays.* Edited by J.K. ELLIOTT, 1990. XXXVIII-489 p. 75 €
97. G. ALBERIGO (ed.), *Christian Unity. The Council of Ferrara-Florence: 1438/39 – 1989,* 1991. X-681 p. 75 €
98. M. SABBE, *Studia Neotestamentica. Collected Essays,* 1991. XVI-573 p. 50 €
99. F. NEIRYNCK, *Evangelica II: 1982-1991. Collected Essays.* Edited by F. VAN SEGBROECK, 1991. XIX-874 p. 70 €
100. F. VAN SEGBROECK, C.M. TUCKETT, G. VAN BELLE & J. VERHEYDEN (eds.), *The Four Gospels 1992. Festschrift Frans Neirynck,* 1992. 3 volumes, XVII-X-X-2668 p. 125 €

SERIES III

101. A. DENAUX (ed.), *John and the Synoptics,* 1992. XXII-696 p. 75 €
102. F. NEIRYNCK, J. VERHEYDEN, F. VAN SEGBROECK, G. VAN OYEN & R. CORSTJENS, *The Gospel of Mark. A Cumulative Bibliography: 1950-1990,* 1992. XII-717 p. 68 €
103. M. SIMON, *Un catéchisme universel pour l'Église catholique. Du Concile de Trente à nos jours,* 1992. XIV-461 p. 55 €
104. L. CEYSSENS, *Le sort de la bulle Unigenitus. Recueil d'études offert à Lucien Ceyssens à l'occasion de son 90e anniversaire.* Présenté par M. LAMBERIGTS, 1992. XXVI-641 p. 50 €
105. R.J. DALY (ed.), *Origeniana Quinta. Papers of the 5th International Origen Congress, Boston College, 14-18 August 1989,* 1992. XVII-635 p. 68 €
106. A.S. VAN DER WOUDE (ed.), *The Book of Daniel in the Light of New Findings,* 1993. XVIII-574 p. 75 €
107. J. FAMERÉE, *L'ecclésiologie d'Yves Congar avant Vatican II: Histoire et Église. Analyse et reprise critique,* 1992. 497 p. 65 €

108. C. BEGG, *Josephus' Account of the Early Divided Monarchy (AJ 8, 212-420). Rewriting the Bible*, 1993. IX-377 p.   60 €
109. J. BULCKENS & H. LOMBAERTS (eds.), *L'enseignement de la religion catholique à l'école secondaire. Enjeux pour la nouvelle Europe*, 1993. XII-264 p.   32 €
110. C. FOCANT (ed.), *The Synoptic Gospels. Source Criticism and the New Literary Criticism*, 1993. XXXIX-670 p.   75 €
111. M. LAMBERIGTS (ed.), avec la collaboration de L. KENIS, *L'augustinisme à l'ancienne Faculté de théologie de Louvain*, 1994. VII-455 p.   60 €
112. R. BIERINGER & J. LAMBRECHT, *Studies on 2 Corinthians*, 1994. XX-632 p.   75 €
113. E. BRITO, *La pneumatologie de Schleiermacher*, 1994. XII-649 p. 75 €
114. W.A.M. BEUKEN (ed.), *The Book of Job*, 1994. X-462 p.   60 €
115. J. LAMBRECHT, *Pauline Studies: Collected Essays*, 1994. XIV-465 p.   63 €
116. G. VAN BELLE, *The Signs Source in the Fourth Gospel: Historical Survey and Critical Evaluation of the Semeia Hypothesis*, 1994. XIV-503 p.   63 €
117. M. LAMBERIGTS & P. VAN DEUN (eds.), *Martyrium in Multidisciplinary Perspective. Memorial L. Reekmans*, 1995. X-435 p.   75 €
118. G. DORIVAL & A. LE BOULLUEC (eds.), *Origeniana Sexta. Origène et la Bible/Origen and the Bible. Actes du Colloquium Origenianum Sextum, Chantilly, 30 août – 3 septembre 1993*, 1995. XII-865 p.   98 €
119. É. GAZIAUX, *Morale de la foi et morale autonome. Confrontation entre P. Delhaye et J. Fuchs*, 1995. XXII-545 p.   68 €
120. T.A. SALZMAN, *Deontology and Teleology: An Investigation of the Normative Debate in Roman Catholic Moral Theology*, 1995. XVII-555 p.   68 €.
121. G.R. EVANS & M. GOURGUES (eds.), *Communion et Réunion. Mélanges Jean-Marie Roger Tillard*, 1995. XI-431 p.   60 €
122. H.T. FLEDDERMANN, *Mark and Q: A Study of the Overlap Texts*. With an Assessment by F. NEIRYNCK, 1995. XI-307 p.   45 €
123. R. BOUDENS, *Two Cardinals: John Henry Newman, Désiré-Joseph Mercier*. Edited by L. GEVERS with the collaboration of B. DOYLE, 1995. 362 p.   45 €
124. A. THOMASSET, *Paul Ricœur. Une poétique de la morale. Aux fondements d'une éthique herméneutique et narrative dans une perspective chrétienne*, 1996. XVI-706 p.   75 €
125. R. BIERINGER (ed.), *The Corinthian Correspondence*, 1996. XXVII-793 p.   60 €
126. M. VERVENNE (ed.), *Studies in the Book of Exodus: Redaction – Reception – Interpretation*, 1996. XI-660 p.   60 €
127. A. VANNESTE, *Nature et grâce dans la théologie occidentale. Dialogue avec H. de Lubac*, 1996. 312 p.   45 €
128. A. CURTIS & T. RÖMER (eds.), *The Book of Jeremiah and its Reception – Le livre de Jérémie et sa réception*, 1997. 331 p.   60 €
129. E. LANNE, *Tradition et Communion des Églises. Recueil d'études*, 1997. XXV-703 p.   75 €

130. A. DENAUX & J.A. DICK (eds.), *From Malines to ARCIC. The Malines Conversations Commemorated*, 1997. IX-317 p. 45 €
131. C.M. TUCKETT (ed.), *The Scriptures in the Gospels*, 1997. XXIV-721 p. 60 €
132. J. VAN RUITEN & M. VERVENNE (eds.), *Studies in the Book of Isaiah. Festschrift Willem A.M. Beuken*, 1997. XX-540 p. 75 €
133. M. VERVENNE & J. LUST (eds.), *Deuteronomy and Deuteronomic Literature. Festschrift C.H.W. Brekelmans*, 1997. XI-637 p. 75 €
134. G. VAN BELLE (ed.), *Index Generalis ETL / BETL 1982-1997*, 1999. IX-337 p. 40 €
135. G. DE SCHRIJVER, *Liberation Theologies on Shifting Grounds. A Clash of Socio-Economic and Cultural Paradigms*, 1998. XI-453 p. 53 €
136. A. SCHOORS (ed.), *Qohelet in the Context of Wisdom*, 1998. XI-528 p. 60 €
137. W.A. BIENERT & U. KÜHNEWEG (eds.), *Origeniana Septima. Origenes in den Auseinandersetzungen des 4. Jahrhunderts*, 1999. XXV-848 p. 95 €
138. É. GAZIAUX, *L'autonomie en morale: au croisement de la philosophie et de la théologie*, 1998. XVI-760 p. 75 €
139. J. GROOTAERS, *Actes et acteurs à Vatican II*, 1998. XXIV-602 p. 75 €
140. F. NEIRYNCK, J. VERHEYDEN & R. CORSTJENS, *The Gospel of Matthew and the Sayings Source Q: A Cumulative Bibliography 1950-1995*, 1998. 2 vols., VII-1000-420* p. 95 €
141. E. BRITO, *Heidegger et l'hymne du sacré*, 1999. XV-800 p. 90 €
142. J. VERHEYDEN (ed.), *The Unity of Luke-Acts*, 1999. XXV-828 p. 60 €
143. N. CALDUCH-BENAGES & J. VERMEYLEN (eds.), *Treasures of Wisdom. Studies in Ben Sira and the Book of Wisdom. Festschrift M. Gilbert*, 1999. XXVII-463 p. 75 €
144. J.-M. AUWERS & A. WÉNIN (eds.), *Lectures et relectures de la Bible. Festschrift P.-M. Bogaert*, 1999. XLII-482 p. 75 €
145. C. BEGG, *Josephus' Story of the Later Monarchy (AJ 9,1–10,185)*, 2000. X-650 p. 75 €
146. J.M. ASGEIRSSON, K. DE TROYER & M.W. MEYER (eds.), *From Quest to Q. Festschrift James M. Robinson*, 2000. XLIV-346 p. 60 €
147. T. RÖMER (ed.), *The Future of the Deuteronomistic History*, 2000. XII-265 p. 75 €
148. F.D. VANSINA, *Paul Ricœur: Bibliographie primaire et secondaire - Primary and Secondary Bibliography 1935-2000*, 2000. XXVI-544 p. 75 €
149. G.J. BROOKE & J.D. KAESTLI (eds.), *Narrativity in Biblical and Related Texts*, 2000. XXI-307 p. 75 €
150. F. NEIRYNCK, *Evangelica III: 1992-2000. Collected Essays*, 2001. XVII-666 p. 60 €
151. B. DOYLE, *The Apocalypse of Isaiah Metaphorically Speaking. A Study of the Use, Function and Significance of Metaphors in Isaiah 24-27*, 2000. XII-453 p. 75 €
152. T. MERRIGAN & J. HAERS (eds.), *The Myriad Christ. Plurality and the Quest for Unity in Contemporary Christology*, 2000. XIV-593 p. 75 €
153. M. SIMON, *Le catéchisme de Jean-Paul II. Genèse et évaluation de son commentaire du Symbole des apôtres*, 2000. XVI-688 p. 75 €

154. J. VERMEYLEN, *La loi du plus fort. Histoire de la rédaction des récits davidiques de 1 Samuel 8 à 1 Rois 2*, 2000. XIII-746 p.   80 €
155. A. WÉNIN (ed.), *Studies in the Book of Genesis. Literature, Redaction and History*, 2001. XXX-643 p.   60 €
156. F. LEDEGANG, *Mysterium Ecclesiae. Images of the Church and its Members in Origen*, 2001. XVII-848 p.   84 €
157. J.S. BOSWELL, F.P. MCHUGH & J. VERSTRAETEN (eds.), *Catholic Social Thought: Twilight of Renaissance*, 2000. XXII-307 p.   60 €
158. A. LINDEMANN (ed.), *The Sayings Source Q and the Historical Jesus*, 2001. XXII-776 p.   60 €
159. C. HEMPEL, A. LANGE & H. LICHTENBERGER (eds.), *The Wisdom Texts from Qumran and the Development of Sapiential Thought*, 2002. XII-502 p.
80 €
160. L. BOEVE & L. LEIJSSEN (eds.), *Sacramental Presence in a Postmodern Context*, 2001. XVI-382 p.   60 €
161. A. DENAUX (ed.), *New Testament Textual Criticism and Exegesis. Festschrift J. Delobel*, 2002. XVIII-391 p.   60 €
162. U. BUSSE, *Das Johannesevangelium. Bildlichkeit, Diskurs und Ritual. Mit einer Bibliographie über den Zeitraum 1986-1998*, 2002. XIII-572 p.
70 €
163. J.-M. AUWERS & H.J. DE JONGE (eds.), *The Biblical Canons*, 2003. LXXXVIII-718 p.   60 €
164. L. PERRONE (ed.), *Origeniana Octava. Origen and the Alexandrian Tradition*, 2003. XXV-X-1406 p.
165. R. BIERINGER, V. KOPERSKI & B. LATAIRE (eds.), *Resurrection in the New Testament. Festschrift J. Lambrecht*, 2002. XXXI-551 p.   70 €
166. M. LAMBERIGTS & L. KENIS (eds.), *Vatican II and Its Legacy*, 2002. XII-512 p.   65 €
167. P. DIEUDONNÉ, *La Paix clémentine. Défaite et victoire du premier jansénisme français sous le pontificat de Clément IX (1667-1669)*, 2003. XXXIX-302 p.   70 €
168. F. GARCÍA MARTÍNEZ, *Wisdom and Apocalypticism in the Dead Sea Scrolls and in the Biblical Tradition*, 2003. XXXIV-491 p.   60 €
169. D. OGLIARI, *Gratia et Certamen: The Relationship between Grace and Free Will in the Discussion of Augustine with the So-Called Semipelagians*, 2003. LVII-468 p.   75 €
170. G. COOMAN, M. VAN STIPHOUT & B. WAUTERS (eds.), *Zeger-Bernard Van Espen at the Crossroads of Canon Law, History, Theology and Church-State Relations*, 2003. XX-530 p.   80 €
171. B. BOURGINE, *L'herméneutique théologique de Karl Barth. Exégèse et dogmatique dans le quatrième volume de la Kirchliche Dogmatik*, 2003. XXII-548 p.   75 €
172. P. DE MEY & J. HAERS (eds.), *Theology and Conversation: Developing a Relational Theology*, 2003. XIII-920 p.   90 €
173. M.J.J. MENKEN, *Matthew's Bible: The Old Testament Text of the Evangelist*, 2004. XII-336 p.   60 €

PRINTED ON PERMANENT PAPER • IMPRIMÉ SUR PAPIER PERMANENT • GEDRUKT OP DUURZAAM PAPIER - ISO 9706
N.V. PEETERS S.A., WAROTSTRAAT 50, B-3020 HERENT